TAKE US ALONG.

We're a good friend to have in Europe.

There's no better guidebook for budget travel abroad than *Let's Go: Europe*.

Each summer Harvard students comb Europe, seeking out the best bargains and the most exciting places for you to see. We cover the big cities, and we also cover the countryside, where the prices are lower and the people are friendlier. And we tell you how to get off the beaten track altogether—to the Scottish highlands, the Middle East, North Africa, and Eastern Europe.

Since you may not get a chance to go back every summer, we do it for you—so that when you take *Let's Go,* you're guaranteed the most up-to-date information possible. We're not satisfied to just change prices from year to year like most other guidebooks do; we go back to the places. Every year. If a nice little hotel has become a noisy ripoff since last year, we'll tell you about it. If a new resort has quietly opened in the French countryside, our researcher will find it for you.

We've been around. You can't afford not to take us along.

LET'S GO:

The Budget Guide to Europe

Eric D. Goldstein, Editor

1979-80

Written by Harvard Student Agencies
A Sunrise Book/E. P. Dutton

Published simultaneously in Canada
by Clarke, Irwin & Company Limited, Toronto and Vancouver

ISBN: 0-87690-301-4
LCC: 63-36598

Publishing Manager: Robbin L. Feibus

Editor: Eric D. Goldstein

Assistant to the Editor: Elena Cohen

Advertising Manager: Carol Lynn Dornbrand

Staff Assistants: Nancy Tentindo, Sarah G. Boxer, Ann Luppi, Seth Sicroff, Sara Stopek, Diana Koricke

Proofreaders: C. Howard Buford, Adela Cepeda, Lis Clemens, Erik Dahl, Martha Davis, Wendy L. Farrow, Mary Holland, Helen Ingerson, Eleni Istavridis, Stephen Morillo, Kim Patton, Patricia Anne Rogers, Ralph Zito

Researcher/Writers

David Apgar: *Czechoslovakia, France (Alsace), East Germany, West Germany*

Christopher Baker: *Bulgaria, Hungary, Poland, Romania*

William R. Brubaker: *Belgium, Denmark, Finland, Norway, Sweden*

Jonathan Finegold: *Ireland*

Jay Golan: *Italy, Yugoslavia*

Louise C. Healey: *Great Britain (London, Midlands, Southern England)*

Joanne Hochberg: *France (Alps, Brittany, Corsica, Côte d'Azur, Provence, Southwestern France)*

Thomas Hogan: *Greece, Israel, Turkey*

Susan Pollak: *Austria, France (Champagne), Luxembourg, Netherlands, Switzerland*

Keith Brian Russell: *Great Britain (East Anglia, North England, West Country, Wales), Iceland*

Carey Sassower: *France (Paris, Burgundy, Loire Valley, Normandy)*

Seth Sicroff: *France (Bordeaux), Morocco, Portugal, Spain*

Frank Tracy: *USSR*

James B. Witkin: *Great Britain (Scotland)*

Maps: Chris Nolan

Index: Sarah G. Boxer

Legal Counsel: Harold Rosenwald

Let's Go: Europe is written annually by Harvard Student Agencies Inc., 4 Holyoke Street, Cambridge, Massachusetts 02138. A Sunrise Book published by E.P. Dutton, a division of Sequoia-Elsevier Publishing Company, Inc., New York.

ACKNOWLEDGEMENTS

My deepest gratitude goes to Elena Cohen for the countless hours and painstaking care she invested in *Let's Go: Europe*—the book is much the better for it. Robbin Feibus gave constant advice and support toward making the guide the balanced work it should be. The suggestions and encouragement of Dan DelVecchio and Jeff Brown are much appreciated, as are the helpful comments and late nights contributed by Nancy Tentindo. The confidence, friendship, and good judgment of P. Quinn Moss increased both the quality and the enjoyment of the job. Finally, many thanks are in order to the hundreds of readers who took the time to criticize us and share their discoveries.

E.D.G.

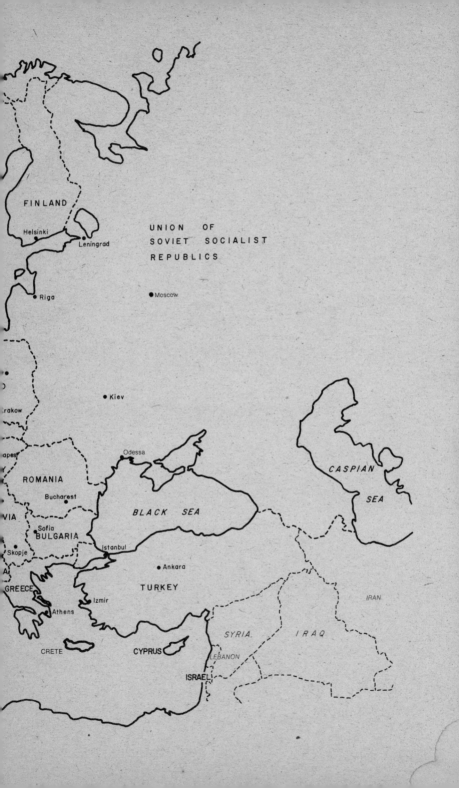

CONTENTS

**PLANNING EUROPEAN
TRAVEL** 17
Cutting Costs 18
A Note on Prices 21
Women 21
Off-Season Travel 22
Organizations to Help You 24
Getting There 25
Transportation in Europe 28
Accommodations 45
Packing 51
Documents and Formalities 53
Money 58
Work in Europe 61
Study in Europe 62
Drugs 63

AUSTRIA 65
Vienna 67
Southern Austria 78

Graz 79
Salzburg 81
The Salzkammergut ....
Innsbruck ....
The Vorarlberg 90

BELGIUM 91
Brussels................... 93
Antwerp 97
Ghent 101
Brugge 103
Namur and the Southeast 105

BULGARIA 107
Sofia 109
The Mountains 112
Plovdiv 113
Veliko Turnovo 114
Black Sea Coast 115
    Nesebăr 116

CZECHOSLOVAKIA 117
Prague 120
Bohemia 126
Moravia................... 127
Slovakia 127
  The Spišské Towns 127
  Bratislava 128

DENMARK 130
Copenhagen 132
Aarhus................... 142
Fyn 144
The Southern Islands 145

FINLAND 147
Helsinki.................. 149
Turku 155
Savonlinna 156
Northern Finland 158

FRANCE 159
Paris 161
Champagne 184
  Reims 185
Loire 186
  Chartres................ 187
  Bourges 188
  Beaugency, Chambord,
    and Blois.............. 189
  Chaumont, Amboise,
    and Chenonceaux 190
  Tours.................. 191
  Villandry, Langeais, Ussé,
    Azay-le-Rideau,
    and Chinon 192
  Fontevrault and Saumur 193
Normandy 193
  Rouen 194
  The Normandy Coast 195
  Bayeux and
    Mont-St.-Michel 196
Brittany 197

Alsace 200
  Strasbourg 200
Burgundy 202
  Dijon 202
  Beaune 204
  Vézelay and Cluny 204
The Alps 205
  Annecy 206
  Chamonix 207
Côte d'Azur 210
  Monaco 211
  Nice 212
  Cannes 215
  St. Tropez 216
Corsica 217
  Ajaccio 218
Provence: The Southern
    Rhone 220
  Aix-en-Provence 220
  Arles 221
  Avignon 222
  Nîmes 223
Southwestern France 224
  Carcassonne, Albi, and
    Castres 224
  Périgord and Auvergne 225
  Bordeaux............... 227

WEST GERMANY 229
Munich 233
The Romantic Road 239
  Würzburg 240
  Rothenburg-ob-der-
    Tauber 241
  Dinkelsbühl............. 242
  Nördlingen 243
Black Forest 244
Freiburg 245
Heidelberg and Tübingen 247
Frankfurt................. 248
Rhine and Moselle
    Valleys 250

Trier 251
Moselle Towns 254
Bonn-Bad Godesberg 255
Cologne..................257
North Germany.............257
Hamburg 257
Celle 258
Lübeck 259
West Berlin..............260

EAST GERMANY 267
East Berlin 269
Potsdam 274
Dresden.................. 275
Weimar 277
Erfurt...................... 278

GREAT BRITAIN 279
London 281
Southeast of London 300
Dover and Folkestone 300
Canterbury 300
The Southern Counties....... 301
Salisbury and
Stonehenge 301
Isle of Wight 302
Other Turrets and
Spires in the South 303
The West Country............304
Bath.................... 304
Mendip Country 307
West Country Moors:
Exmoor and Dartmoor 310
Devon 311
Cornwall 312
The Midlands 313
Oxford................... 313
Stratford-upon-Avon 316
East Anglia 317
Cambridge 318
North England 321
York 322

North York Moors,
Yorkshire Dales,
Pennines 325
Lake District..............326
WALES 328
South Wales 329
Mid-Wales 332
North Wales 333
SCOTLAND 335
Edinburgh 335
Inverness................340
The Highlands 340
Torridon Region 344
The Far North............345
The Inner Hebrides:
The Isle of Skye 347
The Outer Hebrides:
Lewis and Harris
Island 347
The Orkney Islands 348

GREECE 351
Athens....................355
The Peloponnese 362
Northern Greece 363
The Islands 364
Argo-Saronic Islands 365
Cyclades 365
Sporades 367
Islands in the Northeast
Aegean 367
Dodecanese 368
Crete 369
Corfu and the
Ionian Islands 371

HUNGARY 373
Budapest 376
Danube Bend 381
Eger......................382
Western Transdanubia 383

ICELAND 384
Rekjavík 386
Vestmann Islands 391
The Western Fjords 392
Akureyri and the Mývatn
    District 392

IRELAND 394
Dublin 397
Southeast 404
   County Wicklow 404
   County Wexford 404
   County Kilkenny and
     County Tipperary 405
Southwest 406
   County Cork 406
   Galway 408
Northwest 410

ISRAEL 413
Jerusalem 418
The West Bank 424
Tel Aviv 425
Haifa 428
Galillee, the North,
    and the Golan 430
Negev Desert 432
Eilat 433
Sinai Desert 435

ITALY 437
Northern Italy 441
   Milan 441
   Verona 444
   Mantua 445
   Padua 446
   Venice 447
   Dolomites 452
Latium 453
   Rome 453
Umbria 461
   Perugia 462

Spoleto 463
Assisi 463
Tuscany 464
   Florence 464
   Siena and San Gimignano . . . 470
   Pisa 471
Emilia Romagna 472
   Bologna 472
   Ravenna 473
   Ferrara 474
Southern Italy 474
   Naples 474
   South of Naples 477
   Sicily 478
   Sardinia 481

LUXEMBOURG 485

MOROCCO 489
Tangier 493
Tetuan 493
Meknes 495
Fez 497
Azrou 499
Marrakesh 500
Essaouira 503
Rabat 504

NETHERLANDS 507
Amsterdam 508
The Hague 519
Delft 521
Utrecht 521
Arnhem and the
    Zuid-Veluwe 523
Friesland and the
    Westfriese Islands 524

NORWAY 525
Oslo 526
Oslo-Bergen Railway
    and the Sognefjord 531

Bergen 532
Trondheim 535
Bodø 536
Narvik 538
Finnmark 539

POLAND 541
Warsaw 544
Gdańsk 549
Lublin and the
    Swietokrzyskie Hills 552
Kraków 553
The Southeast 555

PORTUGAL 557
Lisbon 559
Northern and Central
    Portugal 566
    Viana do Castelo 566
    Costa de Prata 567
    Coimbra 568
Evora 570
The Algarve 571

ROMANIA 575
Bucharest 578
Transylvania 581
    Braşov 581
    Sighisoara 582
Moldavia 583
    Suceava 584
Danube Delta and the
    Black Sea Coast 584

SPAIN 587
Pais Vasco 591
    San Sebastián 592
    Santander 594
Galicia 596
    Santiago de Compostela 596
    La Coruña 598

Central Spain 599
    Madrid 599
    Salamanca 607
    Segovia 610
    Toledo 610
Andalucía 612
    Seville 612
    Costa de la Luz 616
    Córdoba 617
    Granada 619
    Costa del Sol 623
The Mediterranean Coast 625
    Barcelona 625
The Balearic Islands 629
    Majorca 630
    Ibiza and Minorca 633

SWEDEN 635
Lund 637
Stockholm 638
Uppsala 646
Gothenberg 647
Swedish Lapland 648
    Kiruna 651

SWITZERLAND 653
Zurich 655
Lucerne 659
Bern 662
Interlaken 665
Grindelwald and
    Lauterbrunnen 666
Zermatt and Saas Fee 668
Geneva 669
Lausanne-Ouchy 675
St. Moritz and the Engadin 677
Ticino 679
    Lugano 679
    Locarno 679

TURKEY 681
Istanbul 684

Central Anatolia: Ankara,
Kayseri, Cappadocia,
and Konya 692
Mediterranean Coast 694
Aegean Coast 695

USSR 697
Moscow 705
Leningrad 709

YUGOSLAVIA 715
Slovenia 718
Ljubljana 718
Serbia 720
Belgrade 721
Bosnia-Hercegovina 725
Sarajevo 726
Croatia 727

Zagreb 728
Croatian Coast: Istria
and Dalmatia 730
The Coast North from
Split 731
Split 732
Dubrovnik 733
The Islands 736
Montenegro and Macedonia ... 737
The Coast South of
Dubrovnik: The
Montenegran Riviera 737
Inland 737
Skopje 739
Lake Ohrid 740

INDEX 741

PLANNING EUROPEAN TRAVEL

Let's Go is designed to help you meet two challenges: fighting high prices and making your European trip special by taking you away from the beaten tourist track. Inflation has wracked the Continent, and the dollar has shrunk considerably, but within expensive countries there are enclaves of low prices, and there are bargains in the most outrageously-priced cities—if you know where to look. In the following pages, we list places to stay, places to eat, and places to see that are cheap enough to let you get by for under $10 a day, if you want to.

Secondly, we emphasize some lesser-known sights in the great cities and many areas of the countryside because you'll undoubtedly want to begin to experience Europe on its own terms. In the cities, get out into the streets and wander for a day. And don't just hop from one capital to the next. Pause and spend a few days in small towns or hiking in the countryside. Every country in Europe has wondrous natural scenery, and if you take the time to enjoy it, your trip won't seem merely a whirlwind express of train rides and museum corridors. Trips like that are the ultimate irony—because, taken at its own pace, European life is slower, more subtle and more attentive to the senses than life in the States. After all, getting away from the places everyone sees doesn't mean you won't go to the Louvre or St. Peter's—but the discoveries you make on your own will mean much more to you than the treasures emblazoned on every postcard.

The most important decision to make before you go is what kind of trip you want. If you're willing to camp, you've picked the cheapest way to go, but you may have to make an initial outlay for equipment, and you'll need to do some research on European campgrounds and terrain. Are you a hosteler? For those who don't mind curfews and sex-segregated dormitories, hosteling is a great way to meet European students and to get out into the countryside. Do you want to get completely into the spirit of a particular country? Maybe a few months spent studying at a European university or living with a family is what you're looking for. Or are you ready for the Grand Tour—the capitals-sights-and-museums route? If you're concentrating on the cities, expect to take time—both before you go and during your trip—to search out the best deals in hotels and restaurants. Do you intend to get around by train, car, bike, or thumb? Before you leave, check into the variety of railpasses, car and bike purchase plans, and reports on hitching conditions in the countries you want to visit.

Whatever style of travel you choose, we can help. *Let's Go* is rewritten every summer by students traveling on a student budget, who are familiar with the countries they're covering. To focus your trip, *Let's Go* provides general introductions to each country and to regions, cities and towns within. Read and let your imagination wander—but please don't follow it everywhere. Don't try to do too much; keep yourself open and flexible. Don't go through a country in a week or London in three days. Nobody ever called that "seeing Europe."

If you find the size of the book inconvenient, you can carefully tear out entire chapters and leave the remainder of the book intact. Then you should be able to keep a chapter in one piece throughout your stay in that country.

Cutting Costs

The golden age of cheap travel is long dead and buried by rising prices, the weakened dollar, and government regulations. Cutting costs is an art, and it's one that you will need to master early—long before you leave home you should start thinking about where you'll have to scrimp and where you can afford to splurge.

How much you spend in Europe will depend on two things: where you are and how you choose to live. You can travel cheaply anywhere, but you'll have to try a lot harder in some areas than in others. Seven dollars in the Spanish countryside will get you a night in a hotel and three good restaurant meals; to get by on that amount in Stockholm you'll have to live in a tent and do your dining on store-bought groceries—and even then you'll have trouble. Here's a country-by-country breakdown:

Sweden, Denmark, Switzerland, Norway, and Iceland are impossible—the most expensive countries in Europe—with **West Germany** not far behind. **Austria, Belgium,** the **Netherlands,** and **Finland** are a bit less expensive, although not much. Paris and London are both very expensive, particularly for accommodations, but the countryside and smaller cities of **France** and **Great Britain** are still manageable. **Italy** lies somewhere in between her prosperous northern neighbors and other Mediterranean countries—prices are rising, but the exchange rate has been favorable to tourists in the last few years. **Spain** and **Portugal** are slightly cheaper than **Italy. Greece, Morocco,** and **Turkey** can all be dirt cheap, especially if you accept them on native terms.

Eastern Europe is inexpensive per se, but minimum-currency conversion rules put a floor under your budget in **Poland, Czechoslovakia,** and **Romania. Poland** and **Bulgaria** offer some of the lowest price levels in Europe, while **Hungary,** Czechoslovakia and Romania can be considerably less cheap. **Yugoslavia** is a truly mixed situation: its mountainous inland areas are still rock-bottom, its heavily touristed coast more in line with Western Europe.

It's clear, given the huge price discrepancies between, say, Sweden and Greece, that you can make your trip last weeks longer if you cut down your stay in Northern Europe in favor of the south. To help you do that, we've added a good deal of practical information on some of the less Americanized countries—Morocco, Turkey, Greece, and Eastern Europe—which might

help you get more out of the time you have there. But if you work it right, it is still possible to spend time in France, Germany, or even Scandinavia without throwing your budget to the wind. Camping and hostels are cheap everywhere; and preparing your own food will tack extra days onto your trip. Search out bakeries and open-air markets, watch the natives shop, and ask their advice on local specialties.

Your biggest temptation will probably be food and drink—crêpes on the streets of Paris, smorgasbord in Scandinavia, beer in Germany—and we urge you to give in some of the time, not least because eating is so much a part of the European experience. And even if you can't afford to feast, don't scrimp so much that you're literally tightening your belt. Nothing is more insidious than the depression you get from not eating. It is worse than all the peeling-wallpaper, smelly-bed depressions you can get from saving on accommodations—it is physical, and you can get quite neurotic attributing your lethargy to unfriendly natives, loneliness, or inconvenience. The world will look much better to you as you sit digesting even the simplest three-course *prix fixe* meal.

Then there's the lure of nights in real hotels, freeing you to stay out until all hours without getting locked out of your room (as you would in a hostel). Again, we feel that you should eschew hostels in favor of a pension or other curfew-free form of accommodation while you're in lively cities like Amsterdam or Paris. Leafing through the sections on these cities will convince you that there are alternatives almost as cheap as official youth hostels, where you can save money without shackling yourself to the hosteler's schedule.

Depending on what part of Europe you're in, expect to spend between $8 and $15 a day, adding a little extra for mistakes, especially if it's your first trip. Going to Europe for the first time is both a more exciting and more hassling experience than a return trip, but there is one rule of thumb that works pretty much for everyone—don't try to do too much. Don't go to too many cities (even if Plovdiv *is* only eight hours away and you've always wanted to see it), and don't go to too many sights in the course of a single day. The only way to enjoy traveling in Europe is to assume—no matter what the chances seem to be at the moment—that you'll be returning.

The key to an inexpensive trip is to adopt the lifestyle of a permanent resident wherever possible. Buy food in grocery stores; get out into the areas of town where people really *live,* instead of where they keep house for tourists. But if you don't have the time to get to know a city well enough to live like a native, you can cut down on your costs by planning enough of your trip in advance so that you can write ahead for reservations in the big cities. London, and Paris, among others, are stuffed to the gills in the summer, and finding a cheap room will be tough and time-consuming. In order to avoid the temptation to settle for a room a bit more expensive than you'd planned on (rooms like that are *always* available), you might consider sacrificing some of your spontaneity and writing in advance. If you want to feel totally free, fine; but you'll probably wind up paying for the privilege in time and money.

Finally, bring more money than you actually intend to spend. If you're staying in hotels, figure $18 a day for the most expensive countries, though with skill and care you can stay below that limit. For the less expensive countries, figure on $3-6 dollars less per day. Add your plane and train fares, and then some extra for irresistible bargains and/or emergencies. If you need more money, you can send home for more, as explained in the Money section, but it will mean delays, costs, and often incredible tangles of red tape. The alternative is to bring all you've got and stay till you run out. Just make sure that you save enough time and money to get back to the city from which your plane home departs. And if you don't have a reservation, keep some money to hold you for a few days, in case you have to wait for a flight.

If you're planning to do any major shopping in Europe, there is one way of recouping some of your expenses. Many non-essential items, in Western European countries carry a special "Value Added Tax" (V.A.T. or T.V.A.). As a foreigner, you are often entitled to have the tax reimbursed. It's not worth the trouble for everyday items, but for things like musical instruments, cars, electronic equipment, and other expensive items, you should inquire at the time of purchase. In some countries, the tax will simply be deducted from the purchase price, after the inevitable forms are filled out. In others, you'll have to present receipts to customs officials on your way out, for reimbursement by mail.

We've tried to include plenty of sections on small towns and rural areas, and we hope you'll sample them. Besides the financial gain, you'll get a chance to see Europe at its most European, free from the urban sprawl that looks the same everywhere. With luck, you may get invited to dinner at a farmhouse, run across a village wedding, or hear some *real* folk music. And while you're in the country, we urge you to hike, boat, and ramble instead of driving and hitching all day. You'll cover less ground, but you'll see and remember more.

A NOTE ON PRICES

The prices in this book were researched during the summer of 1978. Given the current rates of inflation in Europe, *Let's Go* cannot be responsible for their accuracy in the summer of 1979. You should pretty much expect increases of anywhere from 10–30% over the prices we quote. Please do not accuse the proprietors of an establishment of trying to cheat you; instead, send us a note with the new prices.

Each year, hundreds of readers send us suggestions and corrections, each of which is carefully considered and replied to. Whenever possible, our research staff checks them out in Europe, and quite often incorporates them into the next edition. If you have discoveries you would like to share with other readers, or criticisms of any part of the book, please use the tear-out postcard and send them to us by no later than August 31, 1979. (We can best insure use of your information if your card or letter reaches us before May 15.)

WOMEN

Women traveling in Europe run up against attitudes and experiences that are more difficult to deal with than those their male counterparts face. Europeans tend to differentiate sex roles and mores to a greater degree than you are probably used to. While feminism is actively discussed in France, Sweden and England, its influence is miniscule in Mediterranean countries such as Spain, Greece, and Morocco.

Europe is safer than much of America for a single woman. However, a big city has the same problems everywhere—certain flophouses can be more of a risk than a savings; and hitching, even in places like Wales, is just not safe for a woman alone. The unfortunate result is that you will not be able to hitchhike and stay in rock-bottom hotels with the ease of a man on a shoestring budget: expect to spend 25% more on accommodations and transport than he would. Minimal precautions taken, two women traveling together are absolutely safe anywhere (except in Muslim countries, where they are simply doubling the trouble). And it is always cheaper and less hassle to travel with a guy.

There are some countries where you are going to be hassled, pretty much regardless of what you do. Particularly in areas of Southern Europe and North Africa, American women are assumed to be easy targets. We offer a few tips, but you should play it by ear in the cultures you visit. In some areas, women wearing cut-offs, T-shirts, halter tops, or not wearing bras can expect problems. You may want to watch local women and learn from their dress and behavior how to avoid these as much as possible. Especially in Muslim countries, you should dress as comfort and your own activities will allow, not only for your own protection, but out of respect for their culture. The habit Southern European women have of strolling arm in arm, although foreign to Americans, may help make it clear that you are not on the prowl. And some women we know claim that wearing a wedding ring often humbles even the most macho of street Romeos.

In general, you should try to be sensitive to the culture you are visiting. Regardless of how you feel about the local attitudes towards women, your short visit is going to do little to change the situation. The best strategy is usually to completely ignore propositions and hoots, since any kind of response is regarded as a come-on. If the situation becomes more annoying or threatening, you should not hesitate to be rude. A harsh scolding (in any language), especially in the presence of onlookers, should cool the pursuit. In real emergencies, of course, you may have to scream for help. We list emergency, police, and consulate phone numbers in every large city.

One more problem—your purse. Standard tourist practice is to put your passport, travelers checks (and numbers), all your money, valuables, and documents in a shoulder bag which is slung behind you on a long strap. Carry everything together like this and you're just asking to be left destitute. If you don't leave the thing behind somewhere, you can be relieved of it on an overnight train or just in the street. Remember that saying about eggs and baskets, and don't carry *anything* valuable in a shoulder bag. We recommend either carrying money and valuables around your neck, or in a money pouch or belt at your waist.

Although many European men may be sexists, they are brought up with the habit of flattering every female they meet. Try not to let it get to you— and remember that a damsel in a bit of well-timed distress stands a surprisingly good chance of finding a room in a full town, getting a ticket to a sold-out event, or getting into a closed museum.

Those interested in women's issues or just tired of being hassled may want to visit some of the women's centers in many large cities. At these, you may find out a lot about local attitudes and issues affecting women. If *Let's Go* doesn't list one, contact the local tourist office for the address and telephone number.

OFF-SEASON TRAVEL

Anyone who has the option should seriously consider making his European trip sometime between September and May. You'll have to compete

Introducing the half ounce, vest-pocket tent.

The weight of tents keeps dropping, ounces at a time. But even with the progress seen in the last decade, American Youth Hostels (AYH) still offers the lightest, smallest, and most convenient key to inexpensive overnight shelter. An AYH membership card opens the door to more than 4,500 youth hostels around the world. AYH, a nonprofit service organization, has been helping travelers on shoestring budgets since 1934. An AYH membership card, tucked away in your handlebar bag, knapsack, or wallet, is always ready to provide shelter—in rural Vermont, the New Zealand high country, or central Paris. It's a piece of outdoor equipment you can't afford to be without. For more information about the "world's lightest tent," write to us at our national headquarters, or to one of our 27 local AYH councils listed below.

ARIZONA STATE COUNCIL
14049 N. 38th Place
Phoenix, AZ 85032

GREATER BOSTON COUNCIL
251 Harvard St.
Brookline, MA 02146

METRO. CHICAGO COUNCIL
3712 North Clark St.
Chicago, IL 60613

COLUMBUS COUNCIL
125 Amazon Pl.
Columbus, OH 43214

DELAWARE VALLEY COUNCIL
4717 Old York Rd.
Philadelphia, PA 19141

METRO. DETROIT COUNCIL
3024 Coolidge
Berkley, MI 48072

ERIE-ANA COUNCIL
304 N. Church St.
Bowling Green, OH 43402

GOLDEN GATE COUNCIL
625 Polk St.
Mezzanine
San Francisco, CA 94102

HARTFORD AREA COUNCIL
P.O. Box 10392
Elmwood, CT 06110

LIMA COUNCIL
P.O. Box 173
Lima, OH 45802

LOS ANGELES COUNCIL
1502 Palos Verdes Dr., North
Harbor City, CA 90710

MINNESOTA COUNCIL
475 Cedar St.
St. Paul, MN 55101

METRO. NEW YORK COUNCIL
132 Spring St.
New York, NY 10012

NEBRASKALAND COUNCIL
333 N. 14th St.
Lincoln, NE 68508

NORTHWEST INDIANA COUNCIL
5908 W. 41st St.
Gary, IN 46408

NORTHEAST IOWA COUNCIL
P.O. Box 10
Postville, IA 52162

OZARK AREA COUNCIL
5400 A Southwest
St. Louis, MO 63139

PITTSBURGH COUNCIL
6300 Fifth Ave.
Pittsburgh, PA 15232

POTOMAC AREA COUNCIL
1520 16th St., N.W.
Washington, D.C. 20036

ROCKY MOUNTAIN COUNCIL
1107 12th St.
P.O. Box 2370
Boulder, CO 80306

SAN DIEGO COUNCIL
1031 India St.
San Diego, CA 92101

SYRACUSE COUNCIL
P.O. Box 6135
Teall Station
Syracuse, NY 13217

TOLEDO AREA COUNCIL
3440 Lawrin Dr.
Toledo, OH 43623

TRI-STATE COUNCIL
5400 Lanius Ln.
Cincinnati, OH 45224

WESTERN MICHIGAN COUNCIL
Box 6241, Station C
Grand Rapids, MI 49505

WESTERN WASHINGTON COUNCIL
1431 Minor Ave.
Seattle, WA 98101

WISCONSIN COUNCIL
7218 West North Ave.
Wauwatosa, WI 52313

American Youth Hostels • National Office, Dept. H • Delaplane, Virginia 22025

with only a fraction of the tourists that crowd hotels, sights, and streets in the summer, driving up prices and local tempers. You'll feel less a part of an invading horde, and find that the local residents take more interest in you.

On the other hand, while European winters are mild by northern U.S. standards, camping will be less appealing when possible at all, and the rain and overcast days can get to you after a while. Many hotels close for long Christmas vacations, museums and tourist offices keep shorter hours, and the streets are more subdued. But there are so many things to go for that are missed by summer travelers, like the fall wine harvests and festivals, the Alps in the winter, and Paris in the springtime. People who travel in Europe in the low season frequently find their journey a more personal, relaxed experience.

ORGANIZATIONS TO HELP YOU

Student Travel Agencies. Almost every country in Europe has at least one national organization specializing in the needs of student travelers: discounted transportation, accommodations and sightseeing, ID cards, meeting other students, etc. They are usually good places to get general advice, too, even if you are not a student.

Two such organizations in the United States are the **Council on International Educational Exchange** (CIEE) and the **United States Student Travel Service** (USSTS). Their services are mentioned throughout this section of the book. Here are the addresses: CIEE, 777 U.N. Plaza, New York, NY 10017 and 236 North Santa Cruz #314, Los Gatos, CA 95030; USSTS,

801 2nd Ave., New York, NY 10017. Write for their free catalogues (include $.50 for postage and handling for the CIEE one). In New England, visit **Harvard Student Agencies,** at 8 Holyoke St., Cambridge, MA 02138. In Canada, contact **Canadian Universities Travel Service, Ltd.,** 44 St. George St., Toronto, Ont. M5S 2E4. For each country in Europe, we list one or more student travel offices.

National Tourist Offices. These vary in helpfulness and friendliness from country to country, but are usually valuable sources of information before you go and once you're there. Their American branches will send you free brochures and help plan your itinerary. In European cities, they'll provide you with the same services, as well as give you city maps free of charge or at a nominal cost, which we urge you to get as soon as you arrive in a city. For each country, we describe the services of their national tourist office.

Embassies and Consulates. An embassy is the main office of a country's diplomatic mission in a foreign country, and is located in its capital. A consulate is a representative in lesser cities, performing the same functions as the embassy. Like the tourist offices, the services and cooperativeness differ from country to country. In case of a dire emergency (such as an arrest, hospitalization, or stolen passport), you should, of course, contact your local consulate. For lesser emergencies (such as homesickness or leaving messages for a friend), you'd do better to look elsewhere. But in countries where North Americans are rarer and more likely to get into trouble, such as the Eastern Europe, the embassies are more receptive. In Prague, for example, they will hold mail for you.

Getting There

BY AIR

Once again, the transatlantic air fare situation is in flux as we go to press. A couple of general rules still apply, however. Chances are that you will have to do a lot of calculation and planning ahead this year to find the best combination of economy and convenience. You will probably find that the lower the cost, the greater the restrictions on booking, destinations, and itinerary. Find a good travel agent—one able to keep up with the airfare chaos—and do some research yourself.

All of the bargain fares available in 1978 will most likely be sold again this year: these are standby, APEX, charters, and budget. In addition, **Icelandic Airlines** is initiating a very low regular fare on its scheduled flights from New York to Luxembourg (with a stop in Iceland). This means that you can book a confirmed seat anytime up to the moment of departure for $149.50 one way, or $299 round trip. This offer may change after March 31, 1979, so contact Icelandic or your travel agent.

The **budget** fare was quite a success last year, and its availability may be increased. Budget works as follows: at least three weeks before the week in which you want to leave, you specify to the airline or your travel agent the week in which you want to depart. Then, 7-10 days before the start of the week you requested, you are told the exact date and flight on which they have assigned you a *confirmed* seat. The same procedure applies for your return from Europe. Budget fares are available from all U.S. gateway cities, and to many European destinations. From New York, approximate one-way budget fares are: to Amsterdam, $148 low season, $170 high; Belgrade,

$209 low, $225 high; Berlin, $162 low, $186 high; London, $146 low, $169 high; Rome, $199 low, $221 high; and Warsaw, $199 low, $221 high.

The Advanced Purchase Excursion Fare (**APEX**) is the most flexible of the reduced fares, as far as points of departure and destination go. You can fly APEX from most U.S. cities to most European ones. The savings are especially high if you fly from a city in which no other forms of cheap transatlantic fares are available; or if you are flying to a city other varieties of cheap flights don't reach. So, from New York to London, there are many attractive alternatives to the $429 peak season APEX roundtrip ticket to London; but there may be no cheaper way to go from St. Louis to Lisbon than the APEX roundtrip cost of $574. Another great feature of APEX packages is the possibility of returning from a different city from the one you flew into (the so-called "open-jaw APEX"). Now for APEX's drawbacks: 1) you must fly back within a specified period of time, usually either 7–60 or 22–45 days after leaving; 2) tickets must be paid for three to five weeks in advance; and 3) APEX fares are considerably higher in peak season. Depending on your travel plans, however, these may not be disadvantages at all. Also look for a somewhat cheaper "Super-APEX" fare available to some cities, which works in much the same way. A stiff cancellation fee applies for both APEX and super-APEX.

The **charter** scene is rapidly changing. The big news this year are the "public charters." Unlike advanced booking charters (ABC), which were previously the most popular type of charter in operation—but whose fate is now in question—public charters have no advance booking requirement. They can be bought one way, or with a return ticket for a specified date. It is not yet clear to which countries they will fly, since some European governments may not approve them. But at this time, it looks like they will serve several U.S. cities and several European ones, at prices at least competitive with any currently available, charter or otherwise (they may be substantially lower). Once again, in most cases there is a big penalty for cancellation or for changing the date. One exception worth noting is CIEE's charters: if you wish to change your return date, you can do so for a $25 fee by contacting their Paris office.

There has been a lot of misunderstanding about **standby** fares. The mob scenes and near riots in London airports last August were in part the result of this. Although you can purchase standby tickets in advance of departure (except on Laker Airways—see below), the airline has no obligation to fly you until a vacant seat is available on one of its flights. Availability becomes known only on the day of departure, so you can get your seat confirmed only on that day. Most airlines, however, will be able to predict your chances of success on any given day. Because of regulations governing standby, there are no waiting lists for standby customers (although impromptu lists are often formed), so your body must be there in line. Obviously, getting a standby seat out of the States is least dependable from mid-June to early July, and out of Europe at the end of August. Standby fares, when available, are very close to budget fares on the same route.

Laker Airways, which gets credit for starting the airfare turmoil, has settled down to a routine. They take no reservations; all their U.S.-London business is standby. Tickets are sold only on the day of departure, and unlike all the other fares discussed in this section, can be purchased only from the airline's offices. The year-round "Skytrain" fare is $135 New York-London and $124 (£59) London-New York, or $259 round trip. From Los Angeles, the cost is $220 in low season, $248 June through August; from London, the respective fares are $176 (£84) and $201 (£96). Round trip is simply the sum of whatever one-way fares you purchase. In New York, Laker tickets are sold at the Laker Travel Center, 95–25 Queens Blvd., in Queens, and at two Manhattan locations. In the former, tickets go on sale at 4am, while the branch offices open two hours later and are closed weekends. During the busy weeks, you may have to go to the Queens office, since tickets sell out right away. It is open twenty-four hours and is quite comfortable, in case you want to come early to assure a place. Laker has a recorded phone message, updated hourly, informing you how many seats remain for that day's flights, or the hour they sold out: in New York, it's (212) 459-7323. During the off-season, if you've just flown into New York from another city and have a ticket to prove it, you can purchase a Laker ticket at their Kennedy Airport terminal. If you do try for a Laker flight, make sure you bring enough money to handle a day or two in New York or Los Angeles in case you have to wait; and don't forget to bring food for the flight, or money to pay for meals.

If you fly standby to Europe and are worried about being caught in the mobs of standby passengers trying to get back, consider purchasing in advance a one-way charter, budget, or Icelandic ticket for the trip home.

Air fares are strictly regulated—any ticket sold for less than the published price is illegal. If you have any questions about this, or about the reputability of a charter outfit (and you should look into this), contact the **Civil Aeronautics Board** (CAB) at one of their regional offices, or care of the Bureau of Consumer Protection at 1825 Connecticut Ave., N.W., Wash., D.C. 20428.

Besides going to the U.S. to fly, Canadians have only two budget airfare options: ABC charters and the Charter Class Fare. But, as with the American fare structure, things can always change, so contact a travel agent and watch the newspapers for developments.

BY SEA

If you find the thought of spending large sums of money for an eight-hour flight across the Atlantic unbearable, you might consider going in style on the **Cunard Line's** *Queen Elizabeth II*. Passengers between the ages of 12 and 26 are eligible for youth rates, about $370–420 one way, New York to Cherbourg or Southampton. The crossing takes five days and you get room and board, but no frills. Youth rates are available on a standby basis only. Register your name through a travel agent or Cunard up to two months before departure. Cunard will give you confirmation about two weeks before sailing date. You might have trouble getting space. Their main office is at 555 Fifth Ave., New York, NY 10017. The **Russian Baltic Shipping Co.** offers transatlantic crossings on the *Mikhail Lermontov* from New York and on the *Alexandr Pushkin* from Montreal. For students (with ID) between eighteen and thirty inclusive, the one-way fares in U.S. dollars from either city are: to Le Havre $310, London $325. Bremerhaven $340, Leningrad $390. Details are available from **March Shipping,** One World Trade Center, Suite 5257, New York, NY 10048; or 400 St. Antoine Street W., Montreal, Quebec H2Y 1K1. **Polish Ocean Lines** lowers prices on crossings from Montreal for students under 25 on the *Ts/S Stefan Batory:* to Rotterdam $344, London $328 one way. There are about eight crossings between April and December; non-summer trips cost less. For information, contact Mc-Lean Kennedy, Ltd., 410 St. Nicholas St., Montreal, Quebec H2Y 2P5.

Freighter crossings are possible, but freighters seldom carry more than twelve passengers, so reservations must be made at least six (if not twelve) months in advance. Fares are either comparable to or higher than the rates on the ships listed above. Food and service are usually excellent, but you must be prepared for delays in embarkation, and changes in schedule to suit the vagaries of the cargo. **Gdynia American Line** has weekly freighter crossings from the East Coast, and monthly ones from the Gulf of Mexico area. Depending on the point of embarkation, one-way fares start at $330 to Rotterdam; $340 to Bremerhaven; and $350 to Gdynia, Poland. From the Gulf of Mexico, fares are $30 higher. Write the line at One World Trade Center, Room 3557, New York, NY 10048. For information on other freighters, contact the lines directly, your travel agent, or **Air and Marine Travel Service** at 501 Madison Ave., New York, NY 10022. An annual booklet called *Travel Routes Around the World* ($2 postpaid) lists scores of freighter routes, but only a handful are between North America and Europe. Available from Harian Publications, 1 Vernon Ave., Floral Park, NY 11001.

Transportation in Europe

TRAINS

Trains can take you almost anywhere you want to go in Europe, often retaining the romance and convenience that American trains lack. They can sweep you across the Continent and, at the least, give you a glancing impression of the countryside. Therein lies the hazard—the train can only too easily and comfortably move you from city to city, and without realizing it, you'll zoom through the countryside which holds so much of the personal discoveries and lesser-known delights that can make your European trip special.

PICK UP A CAR
WITH A EUROPEAN ACCENT
IN EUROPE.
THEN SEND IT HOME TO
MEET YOUR FAMILY.

It's easier than you think. We do all the work.
All you do is pay for your Fiat here and pick it up in Europe.
(It's a lot cheaper than renting a car in Europe.)
Write us and we'll tell you how very little you have to do.

To: Overseas Delivery Department
    Fiat Motors of North America, Inc.
    155 Chestnut Ridge Road, Montvale, NJ 07645

NAME_____

ADDRESS_____

CITY_____STATE_____ZIP_____ LGE

SEEMS THE MORE YOU DRIVE IT, THE BETTER IT GETS.

On board, you will find the trains better for meeting people than any other means of transportation. You're far more likely to meet young people and non-wealthy Europeans in second class. Bring food on board, and be prepared to feed and be fed. You can save on accommodations by taking an overnight train; but for your body's sake, don't do this often, especially in crowded second-class cars.

Several kinds of rail passes are available, allowing you virtually unlimited rail travel in one or several countries. The various **Eurailpasses** are valid in all Western European countries, including Greece, but not Great Britain or Ireland. They entitle you to free travel on all trains, with a few exceptions, such as those in Corsica and on most privately-run railroads in Switzerland. In some countries, you will also have to pay the fee for seat reservations, usually around a dollar or less. On the other hand, the pass gives you reduced rates on many bike rentals, buses, and ferries, including free passage between Brindisi (Italy) and Greece, Denmark and Sweden, and Sweden and Finland. If you are 26 or over, you must purchase the Eurailpass, good for first-class travel. It costs $190 for 15 days, $230 for 21 days, $280 for one month, $390 for two months, and $460 for three months. Those under 26 have the option of buying the **Eurail Youthpass** instead, good for second-class travel, available for two-month periods only, at $260. Eurailpass holders will have to pay supplements on a few express trains which only have first-class cars, such as the elegant Trans-Europ Express. These can always be avoided, with some inconvenience.

Eurailpasses are supposedly available only in North America, although some large stations in West Germany or Luxembourg may sell you a pass with proof of North American residency. (A passport isn't enough—you've got to show a return plane ticket as well.) Don't count on being able to buy one, though, after leaving home. For more information, contact a travel agent, CIEE, USSTS, Harvard Student Agencies, or one of the following: **German Federal Railroad,** 630 Fifth Ave., Suite 1418, New York, NY 10020 or 45 Richmond St., Suite 706, Toronto, Ont. M5H 1C2; **French National Railroads,** 610 Fifth Ave., New York, NY 10020 or 1500 Stanley St., Rm. 436, Montreal, Quebec; **Italian State Railroad,** 500 Fifth Ave., New York, NY 10036 or 2055 Peel St., Montreal, Que.; or **Swiss Federal Railways,** 608 Fifth Ave., New York, NY 10020 or Box 215, Commerce Court, Postal Station, Toronto, Ont. M5L 1E8. We have generally found the German Railroad the most helpful in dealing with specific problems or requests.

An excellent alternative for those under 23—depending on what countries are on your itinerary—is the **InterRail pass,** good for one month of unlimited second-class travel (with exceptions similar to those of the Eurailpass). InterRail is valid in all countries covered by the Eurailpass plus Great Britain, Ireland, Morocco, Yugoslavia, Romania, and Hungary. The catch is that it gives you only a 50% reduction in the country you buy it in. So get yours either in Luxembourg or on your way out of the first country you visit. InterRail is sold in major rail stations throughout Europe for about $170. When the first month's pass expires, you can buy your next at any main station (same rules apply). We've heard stories about people having to prove European residency when buying it, but this is rare, and inconsistent even within some countries. Give the address of a European friend or fake an address, if you have to.

If you will be spending long periods in individual countries, you should look into national railpasses, such as the **Britrail** pass or those offered by West Germany, Finland, Austria, Switzerland, Belgium, Poland, Italy, and others. New in 1979 is the Scandinavian Railpass, valid for travel in Denmark, Finland, Norway and Sweden. These cost less than the international passes. For information, write to the country's national rail office, or care of their tourist bureau in New York.

If a rail pass seems expensive, go to a travel agent and consult the current *Eurailtariff Manual*. Estimate the number of trains you plan to use and add up the fares. If the sum comes close to the price of the pass, the convenience of the pass is probably worth the difference. One word of warning: the passes can be very useful, but also easily overused, especially by the first-time traveler. Try not to be obsessed with making the pass pay for itself, or you may return with little but blurred memories of train stations and corridors.

If you don't think you will use trains enough to make a pass worthwhile, youth discounts are available on many train trips. The **Transalpino/BIGE** agency offers reduced-fare tickets mainly on international trips to anyone under 26. They have offices in fifteen large Western European cities, as well as hundreds of selling agents (usually local student travel organizations). The savings are 20–50% off regular second-class fares. Transalpino/BIGE tickets are valid for two months, except those to Istanbul, which are good for three months. You can, with some formalities, make stop-offs wherever you want, except in Belgium. For example, you can get from London to Istanbul for $110, stopping off in half a dozen countries along the way. You will also save on shorter trips, such as between Copenhagen and Paris ($45 instead of $73 second class).

Transalpino offices are given in the city listings in this book. For information, write their office at 71-75 Buckingham Palace Road, London SW1W 0QL, England. This branch sells tickets between Great Britain and other countries, as well as between points on the Continent.

Unlimited travel in 15 European countries.
Without a hitch.

Beat the hike in prices, the hassles of hitching. Hook up with one of our incredible rail bargains.

If you're under 26, a Eurail Youthpass gives you unlimited travel for less then $5 a day. Pay a bit more and go first class with a Eurailpass. Or tour Germany with a money-saving Germanrail Tourist Card.

But send now before you go—you can only get them here. Just complete and mail the postcard opposite.

And put an entire railroad system right in your pocket.

DB GERMAN RAIL

630 Fifth Avenue, New York, N.Y. 10020 • (212) 977-9300.

SEND US A POSTCARD

We'd like to hear your reaction.

Did you make any discoveries?

Did we steer you wrong?

Let us know.

Please send me information on ☐ Eurail Youthpass/Eurailpass
☐ GermanRail Tourist Card

Enclosed is a certified check or money order for the following:

☐ 2 month Eurail
Youthpass @ $260
☐ 15 day Eurailpass @ $190
☐ 21 day Eurailpass @ $230

☐ 1 month Eurailpass @ $280
☐ 2 month Eurailpass @ $390
☐ 3 month Eurailpass @ $460

GermanRail Tourist Card
☐ 9 days, First Class @ $135
☐ 16 days, First Class @ $180

☐ 9 days, Coach @ $95
☐ 16 days, Coach @ $135

Date of birth (Eurail Youthpass only):_____
                                              Day/Month/Year
Passport No. (all orders)_____
Name_____
Address_____
City_____ State_____ Zip_____

Note: If placing an order, enclose this post card with check or
money order in envelope. If ordering more than one rail pass or rail
card, list name, address, passport number and birthdate (if appli-
cable) of each additional purchaser on a separate sheet of paper.

FOREMOST EURO-CAR

5430 Van Nuys Boulevard
Van Nuys, California 91401

Phones: (213) 872-2226
(213) 786-1960
Call toll free 800-423-3111 USA
California 800-272-3299

**EUROPE
HAWAII & MEXICO**

"LET'S GO" DISCOUNTS

Please send materials for:
☐ RENTAL
☐ YOUTH PASS
☐ LEASE NEW CARS
☐ EURAILPASS
☐ PURCHASE
☐ TRAIN TICKET

Car make desired_____ Model_____

Departure date _____ Length of stay _____

Delivery city _____ Delivery date _____

Drop off city _____ Drop off date _____

Countries I'll visit _____

Name _____ Phone (   ) _____

Address _____ No. of people in car _____

City _____ Zip _____

Free Travel Kit with order application upon request.   Deposit $ _____

Yes! I want to smile and save like Mr. Diddle. Send me:

☐ An International Student ID Card $ 3.00

    I am a ☐ High School Student   I am a ☐ College Student

☐ A Eurail Pass   15 day - $190; 21 day - $230;
   1 month - $280; 2 month - $390; 3 month - $460 $_____

☐ A Eurail youth pass (through age 25)
   2 months - $260 $_____

                Certified mail $_____.80

                Total $_____

For 72-hour processing, send certified check or money order made payable to
The Educational Cooperative Processing Center, and mail to us at,
176 W. Adams Street, Chicago, Illinois 60603.

        Be sure you fill out the reverse of the card completely.

              Give this card to a friend.

Yes! I want to smile and save like Mr. Diddle. Send me:

☐ An International Student ID Card $ 3.00

    I am a ☐ High School Student   I am a ☐ College Student

☐ A Eurail Pass   15 day - $190; 21 day - $230;
   1 month - $280; 2 month - $390; 3 month - $460 $_____

☐ A Eurail youth pass (through age 25)
   2 months - $260 $_____

                Certified mail $_____.80

                Total $_____

For 72-hour processing, send certified check or money order made payable to
The Educational Cooperative Processing Center, and mail to us at,
176 W. Adams Street, Chicago, Illinois 60603.

        Be sure you fill out the reverse of the card completely.

It is extremely important that you follow these instructions carefully.
Incomplete applications will be returned.

Application for International Student Identity Card Enclose: 1) Dated proof
of current student status. The proof should be from a registered educational
establishment and CLEARLY show that you are a currently-enrolled full-
time student. This will be kept on file and not returned; 2) Small picture
(1½ x 1½, signed on reverse side).

Application for Rail Pass Passport number_____.

Use block capital letters only; one box for each letter. Don't use more space
than is provided and use abbreviations if necessary.

Last Name [| | | | | | | | | | | | | | | | | | | |]

First Name [| | | | | | | | | | | |]   Sex [|]

Street [| | | | | | | | | | | | | | | | | | | |]

City [| | | | | | | | | | | | | | | | | | | |]

State [| | | |]   Zip [| | | | | |]

Date of departure from the U.S. _____
(month/day/year)

Year in School   Fr ☐ A So ☐ B Jr ☐ C Sr ☐ D Grad ☐ E HS ☐ F

Date of Birth [| | | | | |]   Citizenship [| | | | | |]
Month Day Year

School/College [| | | | | | | | | | | | | | | | | | |]

It is extremely important that you follow these instructions carefully.
Incomplete applications will be returned.

Application for International Student Identity Card Enclose: 1) Dated proof
of current student status. The proof should be from a registered educational
establishment and CLEARLY show that you are a currently-enrolled full-
time student. This will be kept on file and not returned; 2) Small picture
(1½ x 1½, signed on reverse side).

Application for Rail Pass Passport number_____.

Use block capital letters only; one box for each letter. Don't use more space
than is provided and use abbreviations if necessary.

Last Name [| | | | | | | | | | | | | | | | | | | |]

First Name [| | | | | | | | | | | |]   Sex [|]

Street [| | | | | | | | | | | | | | | | | | | |]

City [| | | | | | | | | | | | | | | | | | | |]

State [| | | |]   Zip [| | | | | |]

Date of departure from the U.S. _____
(month/day/year)

Year in School   Fr ☐ A So ☐ B Jr ☐ C Sr ☐ D Grad ☐ E HS ☐ F

Date of Birth [| | | | | |]   Citizenship [| | | | | |]
Month Day Year

School/College [| | | | | | | | | | | | | | | | | | |]

We made
Mr. Diddle
smile.

We saved him a bag full on his daughters' trip to Europe.

We'll make you smile too.

The International Student ID Card and Eurail/Youth Rail Passes will save you money on your trip to Europe - ask anyone who's gone. Mr. Diddle's daughters know. The Educational Cooperative makes it easy for you to get these two money-savers ... in one place and fast.

Order your ID card and a pass and we'll send you a **$4.95 Rand McNally map of Europe FREE.**

Just fill out the facing application,* mail it along with payment, and you'll get your card and/or pass in a flash!

The Educational Cooperative

*Card gone? Write to us for an application.
176 W. Adams, Chicago, IL 60603

A few countries, such as Turkey and Israel, offer regular reductions for students on their trains. On international rail travel within Eastern Europe, holders of the IUS card get 25% off (see Student Identification section later in this chapter).

Before you leave, you may wish to consult the *Thomas Cook International Timetable*. Published monthly, it contains a complete schedule of all European trains and ferry routes, as well as the main routes everywhere else in the world. In Great Britain, the *Timetable* can be purchased at Cook's offices for £2.50. In the U.S., you can order the current or pre-order future editions for $11.50 from the Travel Library, P.O. Box 2975, 9154 West 57th St., Shawnee Mission, KA 66201. They also sell slightly out-of-date editions, which are fine for a general overview of the networks and the frequency of service, at $8.50. Many travel agents have the *Timetable* in their offices. An abridged timetable called *The Best Trains in Europe* (80 pages, valid from late May to the end of September) is available free from travel agents and railroad offices selling the Eurailpass.

BUSES

Bus service varies considerably from country to country; but with the excellent train networks, most countries in Europe are less dependent on buses as a means of long-distance ground transportation than is the United States. Israel, Morocco, Turkey, and Greece are notable exceptions. In most countries, buses go to towns or sights in the countryside that are not on the train routes.

When you arrive in a country, ask about discount programs for bus travel. Israel and Great Britain, among others, offer bus passes; Israel also offers a student discount on inter-city fares. In some Western European countries such as Germany and France, most inter-city buses are operated by the national railroads. Eurail and InterRail passes are valid on many routes.

There are private bus lines which offer long-distance jaunts across Europe and even as far as India. **Magic Bus** is one of the most established lines. Though these buses concentrate on London-Istanbul or Paris-Athens length routes, they can also be used for shorter connections. You may find the atmosphere and camaraderie which develops among the riders well worth the trouble of occasional breakdowns and less-than-rigid itineraries. For addresses and prices, see our Amsterdam section. Athens and Istanbul are other centers for cheap long-distance buses.

There are also many companies offering overland bus trips to India and Nepal of varying degrees of regimentation. One offering a good deal of independence along the way is **The Road to Katmandu, Inc.** A thirty-day trip from London or Frankfurt to Delhi costs $320, accommodations (mostly camping) included. A 63-day trip costs $950. For details, contact them at 4 Jones St., New York, NY 10014.

CARS

In some respects, the most convenient and rewarding way to see Europe is by car. You can go wherever you want, whenever you want, thus making more territory accessible in a limited amount of time. Some of the disadvantages: the high cost of gasoline almost everywhere on the Continent; the mountains of red tape in the event of auto theft or collision; parking problems in congested cities; and unfamiliar driving habits and laws in each country.

Hiring a car in Europe can nonetheless easily justify the money and trouble invested, especially if shared by three or more people. For periods of three weeks or under, the only option is to **rent**; if you want the car for 22 days or more, **leasing** is the most economical method. For example, a Citroen CV6 (the "deux chevaux" model) can be leased for two months in France for $629 ($585 for students) including unlimited mileage and comprehensive insurance. Most firms lease to 18-year-olds, while rentals have an age minimum of 21 and up, depending on the country.

For some reason, rental and leasing costs vary radically from country to country, with taxes of up to 18% tacked on in some places. France seems to have the best deals on leasing, while Great Britain and Spain are among the countries offering specials on rentals for as low as $80–90 a week for a compact, with unlimited mileage.

If you're planning ahead, several U.S. firms offer renting-leasing plans throughout Europe at competitive prices. Send away for their catalogues and compare; if you qualify, ask about special student-faculty discounts. Among the major firms are: **Auto Europe,** 770 Lexington Ave., New York, NY 10021 and 1722 East Olive Way, Seattle, WA 98102; **Europe by Car,** 45 Rockefeller Plaza, New York, NY 10020 and 9000 Sunset Blvd., Los Angeles, CA 90069; **European Car Plan,** 420 Lexington Ave., New York, NY 10017; **Eurorent,** 801 Newport St., Ann Arbor, MI 48103; **Foremost Euro-Car,** 5430 Van Nuys Blvd., Van Nuys, CA 91401; **Intercontinental Travel System,** Inc., 630 Fifth Ave., New York, NY 10020; **Kemwel**

It's so easy to See Europe and Save in a...

NEW RENAULT TAX FREE

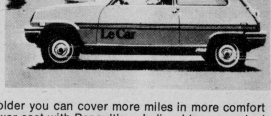

If you're 18 or older you can cover more miles in more comfort and at much lower cost with Renault's unbelievably economical and all-inclusive Financed Purchase-Repurchase Plan (commonly called LEASE). You may keep the car for 3 weeks to 1 year. Many TAX-FREE Renault models to choose from.

THE LOW, LOW COST INCLUDES:

- NEW, FACTORY FRESH RENAULT
- COMPREHENSIVE AND COLLISION INSURANCE (NON-DEDUCTIBLE)
- UNLIMITED MILEAGE
- CONVENIENT PICK-UP AND RETURN LOCATIONS

AND IT'S SO EASY! *Renault* USA takes care of all the paperwork before you leave.

If you prefer to purchase a new Renault to be either kept in Europe or shipped back to the USA, Renault's Outright Purchase Plan brings you substantial savings on taxes and transportation in Europe.

For full details of Renault's lease plan, purchase plan, or both phone:

(201) 461-6000

or write:

RENAULT USA, INC.
Overseas Delivery Department
100 Sylvan Ave., Englewood Cliffs, N.J. 07632

Please send information on Renault's

☐ Financed Purchase Repurchase Plan (lease)   ☐ Outright Purchase Plan (Overseas Delivery of U.S. specification and European models)

Name ....

Address ....City....................

State ....Zip..........Phone....................

Group, Inc., 247 West 12th St., New York, NY 10014; and **Kinney Europe,** 170 Broadway, New York, NY 10038. Some manufacturers offer rental or leasing of their make cars in Europe. Contact their American headquarters for details. CIEE, USSTS, and Harvard Student Agencies have discounted leasing plans for students and faculty.

If you wait until you're in Europe to rent or lease, you may lose time making the arrangements, especially in the peak season. At other times, or when business is slow, you may land a bargain if you shop around and haggle a little.

Car **purchase** by Americans in Europe has declined now that transatlantic shipping costs and other factors have in most cases eliminated the savings on the price of a European car purchased on the Continent. Still, if you plan to use the car extensively while in Europe, you will save the hundreds of dollars you would otherwise pay to lease. When sending your auto home, expect to pay $350–500 for shipping costs to the East Coast plus 3% customs duty on the vehicle's *assessed* value. How much you save depends on what car you buy, where you buy it, and where you ship it. Almost all the firms listed above have car purchase plans. Another one to try is **Nemet Auto International,** 153-03 Hillside Avenue, Jamaica, NY 11432. The agency catalogues give full information on prices and shipping rates. Saab of Sweden is one of the few manufacturers that still offer free transatlantic shipment of its cars. In general, you save more on expensive makes when buying in Europe.

It's best to order your car in advance from the U.S. if you're bringing it back with you, to ensure that it meets American specifications (seatbelts, anti-pollution devices, etc.). Many of the U.S. firms listed above offer car purchase plans. In Europe, one of the best known of the "Don't bother to wrap it, I'll just drive it away" car-purchase shops is **ShipSide Tax Free World on Wheels** right in Schiphol Airport, Amsterdam; they can have a car waiting for you if you let them know ahead of time through P.O. Box 7568, Schiphol Airport C. Many of the European car manufacturers have their own overseas delivery plans; contact their American headquarters. You can also order through your local car dealer. Make sure he is familiar with the red tape. If you order through him, you are likely to get better service on the car when you return; in Europe, however, the European dealer will be less inclined to correct any mistakes that were made when filling the order.

If you are brave and know what you're doing, buying a used car in Europe and selling it before leaving can give you the cheapest wheels on the Continent. West Germany is reputed to be the best country for buying used cars, while sellers are advised to try other countries.

Another alternative is what are called **motor caravans.** Caravan is British for trailer, and "motor-caravaning" encompasses car-and-trailer, car-and-tent, and outfitted-bus arrangements. In other words, you bring your accommodation with you, thus saving the cost and hassle of room-finding, and freeing more of each day for travel. It is possible to purchase used (and sometimes completely outfitted) VW buses in major western European cities, but once again, know what you're buying. Amsterdam and Munich are centers for unofficial dealers who retrieve vans from scrap yards and patch them up into running condition. The cost of some of these vehicles is low, but they're often badly rusted from the inside out. Police in many cities make spot inspections and often haul rusted vehicles off the road.

It is also possible to rent or buy caravans from established firms. For two people, the cost is perhaps too high for *Let's Go* readers, except for some of the small-car-and-tent arrangements, which run $105 per week and up, unlimited mileage. Larger groups can economically rent outfitted minibuses which sleep four for as low as $350 for two weeks, unlimited mileage, in the off-season. Even with the high cost of gas, that still comes out to only $10 a day for accommodations and transportation—and freedom. Add to that the money you'll save if you use the van's built-in cooking facilities. Prices vary drastically from season to season, and from country to country. Contact the American firms listed above for catalogues. The prices of British companies are low by European standards, but if you're crossing the channel with the vehicle, don't forget to add the cost of the ferry. On the Continent, try **Car Camping in Europe, Share-a-Car, Inc.**, 61 Studiestraede, DK 1554, Copenhagen, Denmark. All companies rent optional tenting equipment along with the vehicles.

If you're caravaning or camping out often, we recommend that you purchase the latest edition of *Europa Camping and Caravaning,* an encyclopedia of about 5000 campgrounds throughout Europe. For initial trip planning, the AAA maps, listing only primary roads, are useful. But for minute detail, purchase of maps in each country is recommended. You might also consider getting the Michelin series of maps (cheaper in Europe than here) or the Shell or Rand McNally Road Atlases.

Whatever arrangements you make, be sure you know exactly what legal documents are involved in your transaction, and what to do in case of accident or breakdown. Car insurance in the form of the standard **International Insurance Certificate,** or "green card," is a prerequisite for driving in Europe. Most rental agencies include this coverage in their prices. If you buy or lease a car, you can obtain a green card through the dealer, from an office of the AAA or CAA, or from some travel agents. As for license

*This advertiser is listed on the Reader Service Card.

requirements, the **International Drivers Permit,** available for $3 from the AAA and many travel agents, will suffice anywhere. A few countries will accept your state license as valid, while others require a certified translation of it before allowing you to drive. Before you get on the road, check out each country's laws, especially concerning the right of way, accidents, and liability.

Many European countries issue **gas coupons** which entitle tourists to purchase gasoline at a reduced rate. Regulations and eligibility vary greatly from country to country, so check with the national tourist office of the country concerned for details. Remember that in some countries you can only buy these coupons at the border when you enter with your car. If this is the case, be sure to purchase enough coupons to last your entire stay.

MOPEDS

Mopeds are a good compromise between the high cost of car travel and the limited range of bicycles. Similar to motor scooters, mopeds are far more popular in Europe than in North America. They can cruise at about 35 mph and get outstanding mileage. They are easily put on trains and ferries for longer hops. The drawbacks are that they don't handle well in rain, the spark plugs need frequent attention, they can't carry much luggage, and long journeys are tiresome. Still, mopeds can take you through the countryside and give you maneuverability in the city at a total cost of under $500 for the summer. Mopeds can be bought or rented for a day or more in almost every country. Try car and bicycle shops.

BICYCLES

Cycling is extremely popular in Europe, and though it can be harrowing in the big cities, it's one of the best ways to see the countryside and endear yourself to the natives. There are limitations: for long-term cycling you can carry very little baggage, you must be in excellent shape, and your mileage is, of course, low compared to other means of transport. It is often possible, though, to put your bike in the baggage car of a European train for a small fee, and we're even told that hitching with a bike is feasible in Britain and Ireland. So long-distance hops aren't out of the question.

Long-range touring does offer the opportunity to truly experience the people and pleasures of the countryside. It can bring rewards like no other means of transportation. The **German Cyclists' Association** (Bund Deutscher Radfahrer), Otto Fleck Schneise 4, 6000 Frankfurt N71, West Germany, will provide you with any information you might need for bicycle travel in that country. The **Cyclist Touring Club,** Cottrell House, 69 Meadrow, Godalming, Surrey GU7 3HS, England, can provide similar information about England. A variety of bicycle tours are sponsored by **American Youth Hostels** (AYH), Delaplane, VA 22025.

Bringing a bike across the Atlantic by plane can be a hassle, as almost every airline has its own regulations. Some carriers will include the bike as part of your baggage allowance, but will only consider bikes of a certain size (usually under 62 inches) as baggage. Others charge a flat fee of $35-90 for bikes, while still others have different rates for different destinations. The amount of disassembling and crating you have to do also varies from airline to airline. Check with your airline before you leave.

European manufacturers make slightly different models for their Continental and American markets. Bike shops in major U.S. cities carry parts for both American and European models. If there is a bike shop near where you live that carries European parts, then it is a good idea to buy a European model in Europe, since the shops on the Continent won't have the parts to repair American models. If you want an American model, you must order it in advance. If you want to buy an American model on the spot while you're in Europe, your best bet is in Great Britain, since American and British parts are the same.

Long and short-term bike rentals are available all over Europe, and we've listed rental agencies in many towns. In addition, the national railroads of many countries offer relatively inexpensive bike rental plans at certain stations. Check for details at stations, particularly in France, Germany, the Netherlands, Switzerland, and Belgium.

HITCHHIKING

There is no cheaper means of travel in Europe than by thumb. Unfortunately, there is also no means more uncertain for getting you from one place to another.

A single woman makes the best time on the road, and takes the greatest risk. Nowhere in Europe will you be truly safe, even in the British Isles, Scandinavia, and the northern half of Eastern Europe. A couple can hitch quite swiftly and with much less danger. The red carpet is unrolled less often for single men, but those who travel light will discover that some cars will prefer them to a couple with baggage. Two men will do far worse; three is a white elephant.

The lighter you travel, the better your luck will be. Stack baggage carefully in a tight pile so that the total amount appears quite small. Once the driver halts, you can hope to find enough space—many vehicles will whip by if your baggage seems excessive. A pack may discourage a few drivers, but on the other hand, it makes you look "legitimate."

The only sign we recommend is a destination sign. It may help you get longer rides, and avoid the ten-minute lifts. In places where there's no long-distance traffic, though, a sign can be a handicap. Feel out the traffic, and use your own judgment.

Where and how you stand is important. Pick a place where the driver can stop easily, get back on the road safely, and has as much time as possible to look you over as he approaches. Never hitch on hills, curves, or superhighways. You'll often have to hitch on freeway entrances, in company with others—try to put a good distance between yourself and the next hitcher. Standing makes you and your thumb more visible than does sitting. Walking while you hitch is not a good idea: your back faces the driver, and he doesn't get the benefit of your dazzling smile.

Getting out of town can be time-consuming. In the Orientation sections of many cities, we list the tram or bus lines that will take you to strategic points for hitching out of town. If you're passing through, ask advice from your driver, and try to get dropped off in a convenient spot. Don't be fooled by your road map into trying to walk across a big town—ask the driver if it's feasible.

Dress as clean-cut as possible—shorts and T-shirts or clean pants (it may help not to wear blue jeans). Women often do better wearing a skirt, and not pulling their hair back, chauvinistic as that seems. Fancy duds—heels, three-piece suits, etc.—are impractical and don't help, since Europeans, like

Americans, are suspicious of hitchhikers who look *too* well-off and respectable. In less-touristed areas, a U.S. flag sewn on your backpack may win over some intrigued motorists. But be familiar with the prevalent attitudes locally, lest the Stars and Stripes achieve the opposite effect.

Should you take every ride? Trucks are slower than cars, we grant, but truck drivers often make the inconvenience worthwhile. Some of our most interesting rides have been with lorry drivers in England and Scotland, who can tell you the complete life story of the load of Scotch whiskey they're carrying, and then pull over so you can hop out and see a little-known monument to Bonnie Prince Charlie. In most countries, where both cars and trucks stop for you, we think you should sample both.

Beware, though, of those situations where any ride less than a through ride is a disaster. Those hitching, for example, from the Romanian border to Budapest should invest a half-day wait before getting in any car whose final destination is short of Budapest. Between Oradea (on the Romanian border) and Budapest, the long distance traffic outnumbers the local.

The German *autobahn* entrances may test your manners. In high season scads of dour hitchhikers stand at major entrances. Usually, but not always, there is some sort of line. European kids, however, often reverse the North American procedure of making the latest arrival stand furthest down the road from the oncoming cars; instead, the most recent arrivals go to the head of the queue. All you can do is size up the local rules and the strength of your competitors. Once in the car, exchanging cigarettes, not falling asleep, and agreeing with your driver's politics are polite tactics. In a few countries, such as Poland, Romania, and eastern Turkey, you may often be expected to pay the driver a small amount.

How do you handle crises—speedballs, drunk drivers, passes? There's not

much you can do about a reckless driver, short of getting out of the car as fast as possible. Wandering hands, however, can often be anticipated. In Southern Europe and especially in Yugoslavia, couples will avoid hassles by letting the woman sit next to the door, and by refusing lifts from burly—and boozed up—truck drivers. Another good rule of thumb is not to allow your baggage to be put in the trunk of the car or the back of the truck if you suspect there may be trouble.

Finland, Ireland, Great Britain, and Poland are probably the easiest countries to hitch in. Spain, France, Switzerland, Belgium, and Yugoslavia are reputed to be the worst; but even here, women will have no trouble, and not looking like a hippie helps somewhat. The other countries fall somewhere in between—your luck will depend on traffic, weather, volume of baggage, how you look, and the concentration of other thumbers on the road. In general, morning and evening rush hours are the best time to hitch; Sundays, lunchtime, and night are the slowest.

If you prefer not to stand on the road, it is frequently possible to join up with drivers when in cities. Check message boards for rides in student travel offices or in student hangouts. (For example, the Lale Pudding Shop in Istanbul is a good place to score a ride east to India.) In a few other cities, there are agencies that bring together drivers and passengers. Riders are charged a fee, and are expected to share driving expenses. Still, the cost comes to only half the train fare, on the average. Check our listings in Munich, Frankfurt, and Paris.

CHEAP FLIGHTS WITHIN EUROPE

There are basically two types of reduced-rate flight possibilities in Europe: special student flights, and youth fares on regular scheduled flights.

The student flights, organized by the **Student Air Travel Association (SATA),** are basically student charters leaving on specific dates. They are very reliable; if one is canceled, you will be placed on another with very little delay. Since there are a limited number of student flights, it is wise to purchase seats in advance. Any of the student travel agencies listed in this chapter will book these flights. They will be able to give you a schedule of SATA flights as well as a directory of SATA offices overseas. Many of these are listed in the appropriate sections of *Let's Go*.

To qualify, you must be a full-time student no older than 30 with a valid ISIC card, or an accompanying spouse or child of an eligible person.

The cost of the SATA flights has risen lately, but they still come to only a fraction of the cost of regular fares. For example, one way Athens-Tel Aviv costs $60; London-Madrid $70; Paris-Copenhagen $65. Very often taking a cut-rate flight from America to, say, London and then continuing with a student flight to a city in southern Europe, Asia, or Africa is cheaper than a direct flight from the United States.

Many European airlines also have youth and student fares, both on domestic flights and on service between different European countries. Age limits on these vary, but the maximum is usually 26 or 30. Savings are usually 10-25%. They sometimes go as high as 75%, however, depending on the airline and route, making them competitive with the SATA flights—and much easier to get seats on or change flight dates on short notice. Until now, the American offices of these airlines were not allowed to give out information about these reductions, but as *Let's Go* went to press, regulations were changing in the direction of permitting them to do so. If the American offices won't give you the information you need, contact the European offices.

Accommodations

YOUTH HOSTELS

For the low-budget traveler, there are no institutions in Europe more frequented than the youth hostels run by the **International Youth Hostel Federation (IYHF)**. The prices are almost always the next best thing to camping: between $1 and $5.50, usually $2.50 to $3, depending on the country and quality of the hostel. But other than the low prices, it is difficult to generalize about hostels. Some are strikingly well situated—one near Tiberias, Israel, boasts tame peacocks and a private beach—while others are in run-down barracks on the outskirts of cities. In general, hostels in Southern Europe are less rule-conscious and more easygoing than their northern counterparts, and rural hostels are more appealing than the ones in big cities.

Whatever the conditions in the hostel you're staying in, you're likely to meet youths from all over the world. This is what makes hosteling so fun. In the hostel dormitories and dining rooms, you'll find bunkmates a very outgoing and varied bunch. Hostels are great places to swap travel tips and meet up with travel partners. Also, they often serve the cheapest (if blandest) meals in town. Many even have kitchens for the use of members.

And now the disadvantages: most hostels have early curfews—not too compatible with your plans for nights-on-the-town in Paris or Copenhagen. (But OK if you're rising at six in the morning to climb a mountain.) Conditions are spartan, often cramped; there's little privacy. Rooms are segregated by sex; drinking and smoking in the rooms are usually forbidden. In most countries, there is a lock-out from the morning to the early afternoon, which means that you can't hang around all day or return for a siesta, if you feel like resting. In a few hostels, all these restrictions create a prisoner-of-war-camp atmosphere. In most cases, however, they will prove only minor inconveniences; in some, they are all but ignored, and a spirit more like a college frat prevails.

Hostels are open to people of all ages, with the exception of some German hostels, which give priority to people under 27 when crowded. The majority of hostelers are between 17 and 28. *Let's Go* warns you about idiosyncratic hostels, such as those that cater to hordes of school kids, or seedy ones (where you should watch your belongings with particular care). Most hostels charge extra for sheets, if you don't have a sleeping bag. A few forbid sleeping bags, requiring you to have your own sheet sleeping sacks (a folded sheet sewn shut on two sides), if you don't want to pay for sheets.

In most countries, hostels require that you be an IYHF member to use the facilities. Others, like those in Israel and Sweden do not, but charge non-members higher rates. In Greece and a couple of other countries, hostels let anyone stay who wants to. Unless you'll only be visiting countries in the latter category, a hostel card will more than pay for itself in no time. Annual membership costs $11 for those 18 and over ($12 in Canada), $5 if you're younger ($6 in Canada). Write to American Youth Hostels, Delaplane, VA 22025; or the Canadian Youth Hostels Association, Place Vanier, Tower A, 333 River Road, Vanier City, Ottawa, Ont. K1L 8B9. You can also get IYHF cards abroad (sometimes for less, if you can produce a local address) at offices of the national IYHF chapter and at some hostels.

For most countries, we tell you where the card is required. IYHF hostels are designated as such in our listings to distinguish them from student hotels and private hostels.

STUDENTS HOTELS AND PRIVATE HOSTELS

These include a diverse array of inexpensive accommodations, ranging from privately owned pensions catering to students, to university dorms which rent rooms to tourists in the summer, to run-down flea bags that try to pass themselves off as official hostels. They have some advantages over the IYHF hostels: no membership is required; there is seldom a curfew or day-time lock-out. Still, facilities vary tremendously, and careful selection is required.

The **International Student Travel Conference (ISTC)** runs a loose net-work of student hotels in major cities. Write CIEE for the *Hostel List and Handbook for the Young Traveller* ($1.00).

ISTC's **Check-In** hotel plan allows you to book in advance accommoda-tions in any of about forty European hotels, mostly in the $7-15 range. Your local student travel bureau will, upon payment, issue a voucher for presenta-tion at the hotel. You could usually find a place for less, but the convenience may be worth it for your first couple of days abroad, or if you're in an especially crowded city.

HOTELS AND PENSIONS

If hostels or student hotels are unavailable (or too austere for your tastes), you can turn to regular hotels and pensions. For those oppressed by dreary old hotels, the pensions (guest houses) are usually more personal and friendly. The owners of these establishments are used to dealing with student

travelers and will often help you make the most of the town or the countryside.

If you wish to make advance reservations, enclosing two International Postal Reply Coupons, available at any Post Office, will ensure a prompt reply. If, on the other hand, you choose the more fancy-free method of arriving in town without a room on reserve, train stations in the major cities usually house room-finding services. In most cities, cheap hotels cluster around train stations, but try not to fall victim to the track-side hotel syndrome. These hotels can get depressing after a while; vary the types of neighborhoods you stay in during your trip.

"HOST-TRAVELERS" ORGANIZATIONS

Servas and **Travelers' Directory** are two organizations whose members are willing to put up affiliated travelers in their own homes. Travelers' Directory requires that you be equally willing to host other members in your home. Servas does not, but has a screening procedure for its traveler members. With membership in either, you get a current directory of members worldwide, with short self-descriptions of those listed.

Member travelers are asked to contact hosts in advance of their desired stay and to comply with any preferences specified by the host in the directory or in person. You may be asked to help in household chores; and, as a general rule, you should stay no more than two nights unless invited to do so. Obviously, these organizaitons are in no way for freeloaders.

Host-traveler organizations bring you together with people of various cultures who are interested in meeting foreigners, and, very often, in giving them an insider's view of a city or region.

Servas asks each traveler to contribute $25 and a refundable $15 fee. It has host members in about seventy countries. The smaller Travelers' Directory requires a minimum donation of $10 for annual membership. Their host membership is growing abroad, but is still overwhelmingly North American. For information write Servas at 11 John St., Room 406, New York, NY 10038; or Travelers' Directory at 6224 Baynton St., Philadelphia, PA 19144.

CAMPING

In their own travels Europeans have long favored the tent, the sleeping bag, and the camping-gas stove as the best combination of economy, convenience, and personal freedom. In almost all European cities, there are low-key, organized campsites. And while some cities will allow you to sleep in the parks, most have restricted sleeping to specific areas and developed campsites. Rave reports do come in from sun-bleached islands and abandoned castles, scenes of lonely campfires, and refreshing nude swims, but these are more the exception than the rule. Nonetheless, a tent frees you from hostel regulations, the drabness of cheap hotels, and the limitations of advance reservations.

On any given evening there are always at least two roads leading to ground space for the night. You can follow the colorful hieroglyphic signs (look for either a large white C encircling a tent on a green background, or for a black tent in a white square on a blue background) leading to one of the thousands of organized campsites. Or you can head out of town, judiciously taking the smaller of the two roads at every fork until that perfect spot appears. The former is the practical method to be used in urban centers; the latter is for the idyllic wanderer with no schedule and rural countryside at hand. If you do camp *au sauvage*, make sure it's not on the property of a farmer who may object, or on a beach where you may get ripped off.

Which ever approach you choose, it is also wise to have one of the camping guides listing locations and available facilities. The encyclopedic, if bulky, *Europa Camping and Caravaning* is the best such guide. It's available in many book stores, or for about $7 through Recreational Equipment, Inc., P.O. Box C-88125 Seattle, WA 98188. If you're going to be camping, you may want to purchase an **International Camping Carnet.** The carnet acts as a membership card in European camping associations, and entitles you to certain privileges in some private campgrounds. The few campgrounds that require it, however, usually sell the carnet (or a temporary version of it) at the site. The carnet is available through the National Campers and Hikers Association, Inc., 7172 Transit Rd., Buffalo, NY 14221, and costs $14, including mandatory membership in the association. Contact them directly for further details. Tourist centers at border crossings and in most towns dispense local camping information, and national tourist offices often have a complete catalogue of campsites within the country. Two other places to seek help (and sometimes a wash or shave, as well) are local train stations and gas stations.

A typical campsite will provide a grassy area on which to pitch your tent, parking facilities, showers, bathrooms, and a small restaurant or store for the purchase of food and other incidentals. Some areas will also have facilities for swimming, washing clothes, tennis, riding, and getting together in the evenings. Be forewarned that some urban sites are badly situated, poorly kept up, choked with middle-aged Europeans, and reminiscent of American trailer parks and the style of life they engender. On the other hand, first-rate facilities appear in great concentrations near the more scenic rivers, beaches and mountains. Prices vary from about $.50 to $2 per tent, plus that much per person per night. Sometimes a 50% reduction is granted for a student ID. Hot showers, when available, usually cost $.40 to $.60 extra.

EQUIPMENT

In camping your way across Europe you are literally carrying your home on your back, so take care in selecting your equipment. *The New Complete Walker*, by Colin Fletcher, Knopf Publishing, $12.50 hardbound, is an excellent text on backpacking and outfitting for the novice or the seasoned veteran. Though geared to the solitary traveler who treks for days without ever seeing a soul, the book is loaded with useful information, and is a joy to read.

Tent. Those traveling by car face a selection of sizes and weights, but the backpacker will be best off with a light, waterproof, synthetic-fiber tent. Cotton tents, although cheaper, tend to be heavy, poorly ventilated, and hot. A good two-man tent, preferably one with a fly-sheet to keep the water out and let the humidity escape from within, goes for $65 and up. It should weigh four to seven pounds. *The New Complete Walker* lists some of the better mail-order houses, but you may want to visit a camping goods store and compare tents.

Sleeping bags. Unless you're doing serious backpacking in cold weather, it is not necessary to spend the extra money to purchase a down-filled bag. Models containing a quality synthetic filling, such as Polarguard, cost less

Ireland

Land of youth

Where you'll discover a wealth of activities for little cost.

One of the most attractive air fares to Europe lands you in Ireland. Low cost connections are easily available by plane or by ferry to the continent. ■ Once in Ireland you'll find excellent value for your dollars. Stay in youth hostels, farmhouses and guesthouses. Wherever you stay, the Irish have a way of making you feel welcome. ■ Cycle down country roads that wend through the magnificent Irish countryside. ■ Cruise down the Shannon River on a barge. ■ Discover the miles and miles of uncluttered beaches where you can walk, swim, ride. ■ Sail in the many sheltered bays and coves. ■ Study the great literature and heritage of Ireland in her universities. ■ Or take a summer course in anything from music to crafts. ■ And you can always attend one of the many festivals which take place throughout the year. ■ Need some more reasons to come to Ireland? We'll send you lots of them in a special youth travel packet of information and ideas. Just mail the coupon to:

($45 and up for a good one), dry faster, and keep their shape, even if they are slightly heavier. If you're camping in cold weather, you can always purchase a liner for the bag. Couples can find matching bags that zip together. When traveling, carry your sleeping bag in a waterproof bag, or in a plain plastic bag. An air mattress or a foam pad cushions your rest and provides insulation against the cold ground.

Backpack. It is definitely advisable to purchase your pack before you leave. American packs are generally more durable and comfortable than European ones, and better values. Go to a good camping store and try out several models—as with shoes, not every style pack fits everyone. Make sure to fill the pack with weights at least as heavy as what you plan to carry on your back when traveling. Have the salesman adjust the straps for you, and see if you feel comfortable walking with it.

Backpacks come with either an exterior frame or an interior 'X' or 'A' frame. If your load is not extraordinarily heavy and you plan to use the pack mainly as a suitcase, an interior-frame model is preferable. It will be less cumbersome and bulky, which is especially important if you'll be hitching or traveling on crowded trains.

The main advantage of the exterior-frame pack is that it distributes the weight more evenly, but this is only crucial if you plan to carry a heavy load, say more than forty pounds. Even so, the top-quality interior frame models being made today do as good a job in spreading the weight, but you'll be paying for it.

Which ever model you choose, invest in one with a good frame: the cheap ones are often mangled by the airlines or rough handling. Also, look for a sturdy material, one that won't rip and is reasonably waterproof. Most packs these days are made of nylon. Make sure the shoulder straps won't rip or fray with all the strain and adjusting you'll give them. Also important is a padded belt; it's unbelievably more comfortable to have all the weight riding on your hips, so you don't want a belt that wears away the skin around your midsection. Most packs have outer pouches that give you access to small items without having to untie the main compartments—these are extremely convenient, but they are also more vulnerable to thieves, so don't store valuables in them. A good pack, with all the above features, should cost you at least $55.

Hiking boots. It is still possible to save money by buying European boots on the Continent, but you should carefully weigh against this the inconvenience of having to break them in for a couple of weeks before using them for heavy-duty hiking. Germany, Switzerland, and Austria offer you hardly any savings these days; your best buys are probably Italian makes.

Cooking. Even if you have never cooked before, camp cooking can provide decent meals at a fraction of the cost of meals in even inexpensive restaurants. We highly recommend the purchase of a small camp stove. European models are cheaper and available everywhere. The **Camping-gaz super Bluet** runs on inexpensive, prepackaged gas (refills cost about $3 and last for eight hours). A small model, weighing one and a half pounds, including two small pots, costs $25 in the U.S. **Primus Stoves,** which run on white gasoline, are more efficient, but the fuel is unavailable in some countries, such as Spain, Italy, and parts of France. Great Britain is OK. Check in camping and hardware stores, and even gas stations. The Primus stoves start at about $24 for the simplest model.

If you need some equipment while in Europe, shop around and compare. Unlike the U.S., specialty stores in Europe often have the best gear at the lowest prices. London and Stockholm are good cities for locating equipment.

Packing

A tried and true method is to set out the items and clothes you think you'll need for your trip. Then cut the amount down by half and pack the bare minimum. Remember you'll want to buy shoes, sweaters, and gifts in Europe, so leave some space.

We feel that the most efficient way for budget travelers to tour Europe is with a backpack. If you must carry luggage, get something with a shoulder strap; carrying a suitcase in your hand can be unbelievably tiresome. With your weight on your back, you will find yourself more mobile and comfortable, your hands being free to handle maps and tickets. See the section on Equipment for advice on what to look for. Buy your pack well in advance and then break it and yourself in by wearing it with increasing weights.

Whatever you carry your belongings in, make sure you label every piece of baggage with your full name and address. Be especially careful when you fly. That sleeping bag tied to your pack may be forever separated from it during handling by the airline.

Choose inconspicuous clothes with darker colors which will not show the beating you will be giving them. If you maintain a neat and sober appearance when hitching, you'll go a lot farther. Since laundry service in Europe is expensive, take perma-press or wrinkle-free clothes that you can wash in a sink or a laundromat. You might take a mild soap in a small plastic bottle and use it for everything from laundry and dishes to your own bathing.

Footwear is the crucial item on your packing list; walking shoes are a must. Don't rely on just your sandals or sneakers to support you and your pack for eight hours a day. A pair of sturdy rubber-soled, lace-up shoes or lightweight hiking boots are advisable. Break them in before you leave. A double pair of socks, light absorbent cotton inside, and rag wool outside, will cushion your feet, help avoid blisters, and keep your feet dry. A pair of sandals or light shoes, which can double for dress shoes, may be worth their weight to give a refreshing change when you are in transit.

Two very handy items to bring are a rain poncho and a day pack. It is worth paying a little more for a lightweight poncho that unbuttons to form a ground cloth. These are useful for beach picnics and for sleeping on, if you're camping out. Make sure the poncho will cover your pack when it's on your back. A small rucksack is useful for your daily excursions. It will hold maps, canteen, and shopping, and will keep your hands free.

You should also have some sort of pouch or money belt to hold your money, passport, and articles you'll want with you at all times. The necklace pouches which go underneath your shirt are probably the most theftproof, but are also somewhat inaccessible. The best combination of convenience and invulnerability we know of is a nylon, zippered pouch with slits on the back that you loop your belt through (about $4). It sits over your front pocket, where you can keep an eye on it and reach what you need with ease. One essential item you can keep in such a pouch is a small notebook to write down addresses, phrases, directions, or whatever else you discover or need during your day's perambulations.

Here's a checklist of sundry items you should consider taking: a jackknife (a must!), mess kit, flashlight, first-aid kit, needle and thread, string, plastic bags, canteen or water bottle, and traveler's alarm clock. You need not pack a summer's worth of toiletries such as aspirin, razor blades, or tampons, as familar American brand names are in evidence throughout Western Europe. You may have trouble getting some items, though, particularly tampons, in Eastern Europe.

In most European countries, electricity is 220 volts AC, which is enough to blow out any of your appliances. (North American electricity is 110 volts AC.) An **adaptor** only changes the shape of the plug—it's not enough if you want to use your appliances overseas. You can purchase small **converters** for this purpose for about $12. They'll enable you to plug your shaver or hair dryer into most European sockets with no damage. But remember that you can only use these converters in areas with AC current. They will not work in certain areas of Germany, Greece, Morocco, Portugal, and Sweden which use **DC.** Check with the national tourist office of the country concerned for further details, or contact the **Franzus Company,** 352 Park Ave. S., New York, NY 10010.

If you're undecided about whether to take a camera or not, consider whether you want the bother of the extra weight and another valuable to watch out for. If you do take cameras and equipment abroad with you, be sure to register everything with customs at the airport before departure. Otherwise, you may have some trouble bringing it all back into the country. You can protect your film from airport x-rays by buying a special lead-lined plastic bag at any photo shop. North American x-ray equipment allegedly won't do any harm, but some airport equipment overseas may fog up your carefully planned memories. Please note that you should carry your film with you in your *hand* luggage, especially if you're using these lead-lined bags. Otherwise, you're liable to delay your flight while security teams check out that mysterious opaque blob in your x-rayed suitcase. If you don't mind the extra bulk, you should consider buying all of the film you'll need ahead of time—it's much more expensive in Western Europe, and not readily available in some countries in Eastern Europe, so stock up before departure.

If you have some room left and want to take along some gifts for European friends you'll make, colored, printed T-shirts make the most all-purpose, lightweight, and popular presents. They are the rage these days, and cost as much as $15-20 on the Continent. Everyone, from Parisian left-bankers to Greek shepherd boys, seems to crave shirts proclaiming Ohio State or Bob's Auto Repair.

Documents and Formalities

PASSPORTS

A valid passport is necessary for entering any European country and for reentering the U.S. or Canada. You can obtain a U.S. passport, valid for five years, at any Passport Agency. To locate the nearest agency, check your local telephone book under U.S. Government, Department of State, or call your local post office. You must apply in person, and present evidence of U.S. citizenship (birth certificate or naturalization papers), two recent photographs meeting specifications (2 inches square with a plain white background), identification and $13. Under some circumstances, you may apply by mail. Check with the passport office for details. Processing usually takes at least two to three weeks. Renewals are no longer possible, so after five years you must reapply for a new passport.

If you lose your passport abroad, notify the local consulate and police

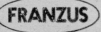

immediately. The U.S. consulates can now issue you a new five-year passport for $13, but usually with some delay and inconvenience. In emergencies where time or money are short, temporary passports can be issued immediately.

Canadian passports are available by mail from the Passport Office, Department of External Affairs, Ottawa, Ont., K1A OG3, or in person at the regional passport offices in Vancouver, Edmonton, Winnipeg, Toronto, Montreal, and Halifax. You'll need a completed application, evidence of Canadian citizenship, two photographs, and $12 cash or certified check. Canadian passports are also valid for five years only.

Visas

Western European countries do not require Americans or Canadians to obtain visas for stays of less than three months, and the same applies to Israel, Morocco, and Turkey. For longer periods, contact the Immigration Officer of the country in which you are residing.

Czechoslovakia, Poland, and the USSR do require visas procured in advance; while Yugoslavia, Bulgaria, and Romania will usually issue visas at their frontiers. East Germany will issue a visa on arrival in East Berlin, but travel arrangements themselves must be made ahead of time. A visa for a day visit to East Berlin will be issued when you arrive at the border. Hungary will issue visas on arrival in certain circumstances, but you're better off getting it in advance. It's usually much quicker and easier to get Eastern European visas in Europe—especially Austria—than in North America.

Details on the procedures for each country are contained in their introductory sections.

STUDENT IDENTIFICATION

There is no single piece of identification so generally respected and so widely honored for procuring discounts and services as the **ISIC (International Student Identity Card).** Such a card is a necessity for those desiring to make use of the student flights, trains, and clubs mentioned earlier, as well as for sailing student fare on commercial ship lines. It also gives discounts on museum admission, theater tickets, local transport, and more. If you follow no other piece of advice in this book, get an ISIC. For the $3 involved and the time spent in applying, the rewards are considerable.

All the student travel offices listed earlier in this chapter issue the ISIC, as do many student offices in universities. No application form is needed but all of the following information must be supplied, whether you apply in person or by mail: 1) current *dated* proof of your student status (a photocopy of your school ID showing this year's date, a letter on school stationery signed and sealed by the registrar, or a photocopied grade report). 2) a vending-machine-size photo with your name printed on the back. 3) your birthdate and nationality. The card is good until the end of the calendar year in which you bought it. Unfortunately for people taking a year off from school, a new one cannot be purchased in January unless you were in school during the fall semester. If you have just graduated, you may still obtain an ISIC during the year in which you graduated.

The **International Union of Students (IUS)** card is the ISIC's Eastern European counterpart. This card is usually (though not always) recognized as proof of student status, and should entitle you to discounts of 25% on international trains within Eastern Europe. You are supposed to be able to obtain an IUS card by presenting an ISIC card in any student travel office in Eastern Europe, along with a fee of about $1. However, we can only verify that it's available at **ARTU** in *West* Berlin, **CKM** in Prague, **ALMATUR** in Warsaw, and possibly in Vienna. Anywhere else, take your chances.

With the increase of phony ISIC cards and improperly issued ones, many airlines and some other services require double proof of student identity. Therefore, we strongly recommend that you take with you to Europe a signed letter with the school seal from the registrar of your school testifying to your student status.

If you don't qualify for the ISIC and are under 26 years of age, do not hesitate to ask about youth discounts wherever you go. Your passport is the best proof of your age, but the **FIYTO Youth Card** available from USSTS may be more convenient to use. For $2, one vending-machine-size photograph, and proof of age (a photostat copy of your birth certificate or driver's license), they will send you the card and a brochure listing FIYTO member organizations in thirty countries and the concessions available to card holders.

INTERNATIONAL DRIVING PERMIT

This is a necessity in order to drive legally in many countries. If you have a valid American license, you can obtain the IDP from the **American Automobile Association,** 8111 Gatehouse Road, Falls Church, VA 22042, or more quickly from your local AAA or Motor League office. They require a completed application form, two photographs, and $3. This can be handled by mail or by one person on another's behalf.

INSURANCE

Before you head for Europe, you should give some thought to what will happen if you're stranded—by accident, illness, or loss of your baggage, for example. Check your insurance policy (or your parents' if it includes you) to find out whether it covers medical care abroad, baggage loss, and more grisly possibilities like death and disability. If it doesn't, you may want to look into a short-term policy to cover your trip. One inexpensive plan has options that cover medical treatment and hospitalization, accidents, lost baggage, and even loss of charter flight due to illness. For a brochure, write to CIEE, 777 United Nations Plaza, New York, NY 10017, or your local student travel office. If you are covered by a plan at the school you are attending, check if it includes summer travel—many do.

Car insurance in the form of a standard *International Insurance Certificate* or "green card," is a prerequisite for driving in Europe. Most rental agencies include this coverage in their prices. If you buy or lease a car, you can obtain a green card through the dealer, or from an office of the AAA or CAA.

The health insurance plans of most of the Canadian provinces will cover you while you're abroad, but the details vary from province to province. Check with the provincial Ministry of Health or the health plan head office for details.

MEDICAL PRECAUTIONS

An International Vaccination Certificate is no longer necessary in order to travel in or return from Western Europe. If you're going to Eastern Europe, the Middle East, or North Africa, however, you should check with the local Department of Public Health to make sure you've complied with their current requirements. Sometimes the health situation (e.g. the 1973 cholera epidemic in Naples) makes shots advisable even when they *aren't* required. No matter where you're going, you'll probably want to be sure that your tetanus-diphtheria and typhoid-paratyphoid inoculations are up to date. If you're a student, the health services at your university may advise you on and administer vaccinations.

The most thorough booklet on the subject is *How to Stay Healthy While Traveling,* by Dr. Bob Young. It deals with immunizations, what to bring, what afflictions you're likely to get, and what to eat. Send $2.50 postpaid to Bob Young, M.D., P.O. Box 567, Department of Health, Santa Barbara, CA 93102.

Medical care is one area where you should not try to cut costs while traveling. In many countries, though, you may receive low-cost or even free medical care if you need it. We've listed first-aid centers and hospitals in major cities. It is essential that you deal with a physician who speaks English. A correct diagnosis and treatment may depend on his understanding of your medical history and symptoms. To obtain the names of English-speaking doctors, try the American, Canadian, or British embassies or consulates; American Express or Cook's offices; or the police.

CUSTOMS

Upon re-entering the U.S., you must declare all articles acquired abroad. The new liberalized duty regulations allow you to bring in $300 worth of goods duty-free; you pay a flat 10% duty on the next $600 worth. The duty-free allowance must be for your personal or household use, and cannot include more than 100 cigars or one quart of liquor (you must be 18 to bring liquor into New York, 21 elsewhere.) All items included must accompany you; you cannot have them shipped separately. There is no duty, however, on unsolicited gifts mailed from Europe, so long as they are under $10 in value, and you can also ship home personal goods of U.S. origin duty-free if you mark them "American goods returned."

According to the U.S. customs service's brochure, "Certain articles considered injurious or detrimental to the general welfare of the United States are prohibited by law." Among these are narcotics, drugs containing narcotics, obscene publications, lottery tickets, liquor-filled candies, and switch-blade knives.

Canadian customs regulations are somewhat different. Once every calendar quarter you can bring in goods to the value of $50. Once every calendar year, you're allowed $150. However, these two allowances can't both be claimed on the same trip. Anything above the duty-free allowance is taxed at 25% on the first $150, and at varying rates afterwards.

Whether you're American or Canadian, you have to declare any items which you bought at duty-free shops abroad with your other purchases, and you may have to pay duty on them if they exceed your allowance. Remember that "duty-free" only means that you didn't pay local taxes in the country of purchase. Also remember to watch the prices in the duty-free shops: some capitalize on their image to capitalize on you.

In Europe customs inspections are usually less thorough than at home, but you will be subjected to at least perfunctory searches at many borders. In Southern and Eastern Europe, customs checks can be harrowing if you've got what they're looking for, and that usually means either drugs or large amounts of Eastern European currency. A separate section on drugs will be found later in this chapter.

MAIL

Sending mail home across the Atlantic can take as little as three days, but you'd better count on more. Between major Western European cities and the East Coast, air mail averages four to six days. From Southern Europe, count on seven to ten days; from Eastern Europe, eight to twelve days (and much more for East Germany). Air mail is fairly dependable, although the postal services seem to be more careless with postcards, which often wander in a month after they were sent. To speed things up, send your mail from the largest post office near you. Surface mail is much cheaper, but takes one to three months to arrive, and is more risky. It is adequate for getting rid of books or clothing you no longer need in your travels.

As for receiving mail in Europe, there are two alternatives, if you'll have no fixed address. **American Express** and **Cook's** will receive and hold mail for their customers, but their definition of "customers" varies from office to office. Most American Express offices will hold mail for you free of charge if you have their travelers checks, but some require that you be an American Express card holder. If you don't have what they want, you may be charged a couple of dollars to pick up the mail that they have been holding for you. If you have the travelers checks or the cards, this is the best place to have mail sent to you if you don't have the address of where you'll be staying. American Express offices return mail to the sender if it is not claimed after thirty days. For $3, you can arrange to have them forward mail. Cook's offers shorter lines than American Express, but they have fewer locations and only hold mail for two weeks, with no forwarding arrangements.

A free booklet, *Services and Offices,* contains the addresses of American Express offices everywhere, and can be obtained from any American Express branch or from the American Express International Headquarters, 65 Broadway, New York, NY 10006. A list of Cook's offices is available from Thomas Cook and Son, 587 Fifth Avenue, New York, NY 10017.

Alternatively, have your mail sent to you c/o *Poste Restante* (General Delivery) in any European city or town, and the central post office will hold it for you. This is your only alternative in towns with no American Express or Cooks branches. In major cities, the post office handling *Poste Restante* is efficient and open long hours, seven days a week. Some post offices charge you a minimal fee ($.10-.40) per item that you pick up. In parts of Southern and Eastern Europe, *Poste Restante* is less reliable. Have the people who write you address the envelope as neatly as possible and underline your last name. If the clerk insists that there's nothing for you, ask him to check under your first name. If that doesn't work, ask if you can look through the pile of mail yourself. For Eastern Europe, have people put a "1" after the city name to make sure it goes to the main post office (i.e. Bratislava 1, Dresden 1, etc.).

American and Canadian embassies in Eastern Europe will hold your mail for you, but they don't like to advertise it. This is usually more reliable than *Poste Restante.*

MONEY

Nothing is likely to cause more headaches than money—even when you have it. Carrying large amounts of cash, even for those with money belts, is just too risky. Travelers checks are the safest and least troublesome means of carrying your funds. These are sold by several agencies and major banks, usually at the rate of 1% over the value of the checks you are buying. Some of these have sales in May; **Barclay's,** an international Britain-based bank, always issues their own checks free of charge. They have a branch in the British Airways terminal at Kennedy Airport. For locations of other branches in North America and abroad, write to Barclay's Bank of New York, 200 Park Ave., New York, NY 10022. If you buy Barclay's checks at banks or agencies other than Barclay's branches, you may have to pay a service charge.

Should you buy checks in dollars or in foreign currencies? There are advantages to both. If you buy them in a foreign currency in North America, you will pay slightly more than you would pay for that currency in Europe. (This is due to brokerage fees and bank commissions.) On the other hand, if you have checks in, say French francs, you can use them to pay for hotels and purchases in France, just as you can use dollar travelers checks as payment here. Also, in many countries, hotels, stores and even banks, charge a commission to cash foreign travelers checks. Italy is especially bad about this. You can always avoid this by cashing American Express checks at A.E. offices, or Barclay's checks at their branches, etc., but this may be inconvenient at times. One last thing: if the dollar continues to drop, your checks in marks, Swiss francs, or pounds sterling will prove a better investment. To repeat, the main advantage to checks in dollars is the better exchange rate you'll get abroad.

If you buy checks in dollars, we recommend that you purchase some of your supply in small denominations, such as $10 and $20. That way, if you're stuck in some situation where you need cash quickly and the exchange rate is lousy or you're only spending a couple of days in a country, you won't have to change more than you need at the moment.

Be sure to keep the receipts for the checks in a safe place separate from the checks. If you do need replacement checks, this will speed up things dramatically. Be warned, however, that full replacement is not as instantaneous as the various companies promise; expect a fair helping of red tape in most cases.

Credit cards are generally useless for the budget traveler as far as purchases go—the cheap places just don't honor them. But they are useful in case of financial emergency. If you don't have a round-trip ticket, you can charge your flight back. American Express will allow you to cash a personal check drawn on a North American bank if you have an American Express card—the money then comes directly out of your account at home. The only restrictions are that you can't cash more than $500 in checks in any 21-day period, and most of the amount is payable only in travelers checks, and not cash. With other credit cards, such as Visa or Master Charge, you can get an instant cash advance, essentially a loan on which interest is charged, up to your credit limit.

Overall, we feel that the American Express card is the most versatile and convenient. They have hundreds of branch offices around the world. If you are a student or your income level is low, you will of course have difficulty acquiring your own international credit cards. But if someone in your family already has a card, it is often easy for him or her to get additional, joint-account cards for other members of the family.

In many countries hungry for hard currency, U.S. dollars are accepted as payment by almost everyone. (Canadian money is less widely taken.) In some countries, the exchange rate is fixed by the government; except where there's a black market, banks and American Express offices usually offer the best rates. Always inquire whether there's a commission for the exchange; there's usually a way to avoid these in each country.

Some people like to have a supply of foreign currency before they arrive in Europe. This saves waiting on line when you arrive at the airport, but you pay for this convenience in the slightly lower exchange rate you'll get here. If you want to purchase a small amount of currency before leaving, contact a local bank that does international banking; if there is none around, most banks will order foreign currencies for you.

There are a few ways of having money transferred to you in Europe. The fastest way is by cable transfer. If you think you might need to do this, visit your bank before you leave, ask them for a list of their correspondent banks in the cities you plan to visit, and let them know who is authorized to initiate cable transfers for you. If you then need money when you're in Europe, telegram or call your bank at home and give the name of the bank you want the money sent to. Within 48 hours, if you're in a major city (longer if you're in a less central location), you should have the cash in dollars or local currency, whichever you specify. You'll have to pay the cabling charges both ways, in addition to a commission charged by your American bank. If you're somewhere in Europe, this should add up to $15-20 for amounts of $1000 and under.

A cheaper, but slower method of receiving money is by bank drafts. Again, find out the European banks which your bank does business with; have the draft made out in your name and give the name of the branch of the correspondent European bank where you will cash the draft. The only service charges are the $3-5 commission on the draft, plus the cost of sending it air mail (preferably registered). You can have a friend at home buy the draft and send it to you, or you can write directly to the bank; or, even before you leave, arrange with it to process drafts from your account and send them when and where you want them.

You can have someone at home cable you up to $500 through American Express for a fee of $25. The entire amount can only be paid out in travelers checks. This will take one to three days, depending where you are. If the person sending the money is an American Express card holder, he can pay for the amount by personal check; otherwise, cash is required.

Finally, if you are stranded in Europe with no recourse at all, a consulate will wire home for you and deduct the cost from the money you receive. They are often less than gracious about performing this service, however, so you should turn to them only in desperation.

To avoid all this, it may be wisest to simply carry a credit card, or a separate stash of $50 to $100 on your person at all times (preferably in travelers checks). You should plan not to spend this money, but rather save it for emergencies and for display to local border authorities who may otherwise find an excuse to hassle you on charges of vagrancy.

You can exchange foreign bills when you leave a country, but the only thing you can do with coins is to save them for your next trip. Strong currencies are exchangeable everywhere; weaker currencies, when taken, usually bring an unreasonably low rate outside of their homeland. It is a good idea to bring a few dollar bills to oil ,some palms, where appropriate.

We list the rates of exchange *within* each country that are valid as we go to press. East Germany, Poland, Czechoslovakia, and Romania maintain an official rate of exchange and require a minimum conversion per diem, not reconvertible at the end of your trip. In many cases the exchange rates available on the black markets of Eastern Europe are considerably (up to 300%) better than those we quote. Whether or not you should consider risking such transactions is discussed in the individual country chapters. The rates we give may have changed since we went to press. *The New York Times* and some other papers list daily fluctuations, in a small box tucked away in the back of the financial pages.

Work in Europe

You won't get rich working in Europe, and you may get an ulcer trying to get a work permit, but there is no better way to really get the feel of a country than by working in it. And if the red tape snarls, don't despair. Probably half the American students working in Europe get their jobs illegally, without work permits. We do recommend that you plan in advance, though, especially if you are unskilled. If it comes to looking for a job without a permit, prepare yourself for menial work and poor conditions, similar to what most illegal aliens in the U.S. have to content themselves with. Look in employment offices and local newspapers, or ask at hotels, bars, restaurants, and farms. The persistent usually succeed.

There are many agencies here that place Americans in jobs abroad. Many of these are dishonest, so before you hand over any fee, check out the firm carefully.

For $40, USSTS will obtain a permit and summer job for you in Austria, Finland, or West Germany. The positions are on farms, at hotels and resorts, or as mother's helpers, and will cover your living expenses, but little more. You usually work 40-48 hours a week, as much as 60 in some jobs. To qualify for work in Austria or Germany, you must demonstrate fluency in German. CIEE will obtain a work permit for you in Britain (up to six months, $35), Ireland (up to four months, $20), or France (summer only, $35), but locating a job is up to you. Write to CIEE for their booklet on *Student Work in Europe*. It also includes details on a job placement service in West Germany, the Zentralstelle für Arbeitsvermittlung (ZAV), 6 Frankfurt am Main 1, Feuerbachstrasse 42, West Germany. If you're in Great Britain, France, or West Germany without a permit, and want to obtain one and meet the requirements, you can get one there. In France, contact CIEE's Paris office; in Germany, contact ZAV at the above address; in Great Britain, contact the Department of Employment, or have your prospective employer obtain the papers for you.

There are several good books for job-hunting, each revised annually. The *Directory of Overseas Summer Jobs* ($6.95) lists 50,000 vacancies worldwide, volunteer and paid, at firms that asked to be listed in the book. *Summer Jobs in Britain* ($5.95) and *Emplois d'été en France* ($4.95, in French) each list hundreds of possibilities in their respective countries (mostly hotels and resorts, but some others). All of the above are available from CIEE (include $.50 for handling). CIEE's annual *Whole World Handbook* ($3.95) is another excellent source for leads, but does not list individual openings. It's a compendium of everything they've been able to find out in all their years of helping students work, study, and travel all over the world. Any question you can't answer by looking in the book, they'll be happy to help you with if you write them.

For all jobs, the longer you're willing to work, the better your chances are. Some employers require you to stay a minimum of one or two months. If you're writing to an employer in Europe, send a cover letter, resumé, and an international reply coupon so he can get back to you. Great Britain is the easiest country to locate work in, with Germany and France a little behind. The easiest jobs to find are generally *au pair* positions, where you get room and board with a family in exchange for household chores and babysitting. There are also seasonal opportunities for work, such as helping with the autumn wine harvest in France (when you'll have no problem finding employment. See the *Directory of Overseas Summer Jobs* or the Bordeaux section of *Let's Go*.).

Volunteer jobs are also readily available almost everywhere; in some countries, such as most Eastern European nations, they're about your only hope. You are sometimes provided with room and board in exchange for your labor. Volunteer opportunities include kibbutz work in Israel, archaeological digs, and work-camp projects, such as building facilities in underdeveloped areas. You might not make money, but the work can be fascinating, and you're likely to meet European students.

A number of programs offer positions for people with particular skills or qualifications. **AIESEC-U.S.,** 622 Third Ave., New York, NY 10017, operates a business student exchange program by placing members in meaningful job positions throughout the world. All positions pay a minimum stipend to cover living expenses. Participation is limited to students at schools with AIESEC chapters. **IAESTE,** American City Building, Suite 217, Columbia, MD 21044, performs a similar service for students in engineering, architecture, mathematics, and the sciences. You must apply by December 15 for summer placement, six months in advance for long-term or non-summer placement. $50 non-refundable application fee.

Positions as group leaders are available from **American Youth Hostels** and from the **Experiment in International Living (EIL),** Brattleboro, VT 05301. For both, the minimum age is 21. AYH gives you a week-long leadership course ($85), and requires you to lead one trip in America before leading one in Europe. EIL requires fluency in language for French-German- and Spanish-speaking countries, established leadership ability, and in-depth overseas experience.

Study in Europe

Studying at a school in Europe guarantees nothing. You can find yourself in a program set up for Americans and not meet a single native of the country or learn a word of its language. Still, you may have a grand time. Or you can immerse yourself as a full-time full-fledged student of a European university, and never feel as if you fit in. Before you go, find out as much as you can about the options you're considering. Start by sending for the excellent brochure, *How to Read Study Abroad Literature,* available from CIEE (include $.25 for postage).

Most Americans who study abroad enroll in programs sponsored by one or more of the several hundred North American universities. These vary tremendously in academic quality, living conditions, degree of contact with the local students, and exposure to the local culture. When you send for information, ask for the names of students who have recently participated in the program, and try to contact them to get a feel for whether the program suits you.

Enrolling directly into a European university is a braver, more chancy, but potentially more rewarding choice. You'll have to be fluent in the language and be able to adjust rapidly to a quite different academic system and atmosphere. Before you go, make sure that your American university will accept the credits you earn in Europe.

The third possibility is to enroll at one of the two European universities which are actually American-run and fully accredited by the American College Accreditation Service: American College in Paris (write to: U.S. Executive Board, American College in Paris, Box 133, Demarest, NJ 07627; or Admissions, American College in Paris, 31 avenue Bosquet, Paris, France 75007) and Schiller College, (write to: 429 N.W. 48th St., Oklahoma City, OK 73118; or Friedrich-Ebert-Anlage 4, 6900 Heidelberg, Germany).

The Institute of International Education (IIE) publishes several books on study abroad. At their headquarters at 809 U.N. Plaza, New York, NY 10017, they provide information and advice on higher education in the U.S. and abroad, and maintain a reference library, which includes catalogues of schools abroad, and works on educational systems. Smaller facilities are available in Chicago, Atlanta, Denver, Houston, Los Angeles, San Francisco, and Washington, D.C. For more information, write IIE. Some of their more helpful publications are:

Handbook on International Study for US Nationals: Study in Europe (Vol. I), available from IIE for $6.95 in paperbound edition. This book describes the higher education systems of all European nations, identifying nearly 200 fields of study and the degree program offered for each by all universities and selected post-secondary schools in 28 European countries. The book includes information on scholarship and fellowship programs; describes sponsored study-abroad programs and volunteer, employment, and trainee opportunities abroad for U.S. citizens and gives a summary of pertinent government regulations.

U.S. College-Sponsored Programs Abroad: Academic Year ($5) describes almost 800 study-abroad programs on the undergraduate and graduate level run by U.S. colleges and universities. The book gives information on courses, credits, housing, scholarships, language of institution and suggestions on choosing a program. Published annually in March.

Summer Study Abroad ($5) covers over 800 summer study-abroad programs sponsored by U.S. colleges and those sponsored by foreign and private institutions. Included is information on courses, costs, scholarships, and accommodations. Published annually in February.

For a general background to the higher education systems of various Western European countries, the brand new *Higher Education Reform: Implications for Foreign Students* is excellent, if expensive at $12. CIEE's *Whole World Handbook* (see the preceding section on work in Europe) lists many study programs abroad and gives some basic pointers. In addition, national tourist offices frequently have information about the educational programs available in their countries.

Drugs

The horror stories about drug busts in Europe are scary and unfortunately grounded in solid fact. Every year, hundreds of young travelers are arrested in foreign countries for illegal possession, use, or trafficking in drugs. Some countries—Turkey, Morocco, East Germany—are stricter and more severe in their treatment of those arrested on drug-related charges, but even reputedly liberal countries—i.e. the Netherlands and Denmark—contribute to the sorry statistics. Remember that you are subject to the laws of the country you are visiting.

Unfortunately, even where drugs are apparently freely available, the openness can be an illusion. In Turkey, North Africa and Israel, for example, dealers often work hand-in-hand with the police. Typically, a drug dealer sells to a foreign visitor, heads straight for the police, describes the buyer in detail, collects a fee for his information, and gets his goods back when the student is arrested. Accordingly, the best advice is to stay away from drugs in Europe, and *under no circumstances* to try and bring anything into or out of a country. (Don't let those international-seeming express trains fool you, by the way. You're liable to be searched right on a train, entering a country that you'll be leaving a half hour later—and you will be arrested right off the train, too, if you let the dream of Pan-European unity blur your sense of what a national border is.)

The assistance available from the US consulates to anyone arrested is minimal. Consular officers can visit the prisoner, provide him with a list of attorneys, and inform his family and friends. However, as a State Department bulletin dourly states, "US officials cannot ask for or obtain different treatment for American citizens than that given to others under the laws of the country concerned. You're virtually 'on your own' if you become involved, *however innocently,* in illegal drug trafficking."

The Canadian Department of External Affairs adds these cheery warnings. "The legal codes of some countries provide for *guilt by association* under which someone may be charged simply for being in the company of a person suspected or found guilty of a crime (e.g. trafficking or possessing drugs . . .) . . . Because drug offences are particularly distasteful to some countries, the suspected drug offender, regardless of nationality, may be last to be brought to trial!" Like American officials, the Canadian consular staff "*cannot provide you with legal advice* or interfere with the course of local justice."

AUSTRIA

$1U.S.=14.9 Austrian Schillings (AS)   **1AS=$.067**

A land that for centuries marched to strains of *The Emperor*—having been dominated by a series of conquerers and diplomats since the establishment of the Holy Roman Empire—Austria is now orchestrated more along the lines of *The Pastoral*. Her cities remain somehow incurably romantic, despite the country's modern political and economic structure. And her mountain paths beckon to those who love to hike and wander amidst striking natural beauty.

In her days of power, Austria benefited from the cultures she conquered: Italian, French, German. Baroque architecture, brought over the Alps from Rome by the archbishops of **Salzburg,** caught on instantly; its elaborate flourishes complemented imperial dreams. Baroque now characterizes the country to such an extent that the government is removing additions from that period from churches that were originally Gothic or Renaissance in style. The French taught the Austrians how to build palaces; the **Hofburg** and the **Schönbrunn** in **Vienna** show how the Austrians altered the style to suit their taste and aspirations.

Today, folk customs and regional issues are much more alive than the Hapsburgs and their pomp. For every street named after an emperor, there are ten named for Andreas Hofer, the popular hero who organized the Tyrolese uprising against Napoleon. But much of the old way of life seems happily incorporated with the new—women wear *dirndl* skirts one day, jeans the next.

Set off like precious stones against an unspoiled countryside, Austria's cities keep an old-fashioned charm. In the northeast, Vienna, the crown jewel, rests in calm elegance. **Innsbruck** lies cradled in the Alps, a marvelous location for skiing and hiking in winter and summer, but not so enviable in the spring, when the *Föhn*, the hot dry breeze from the south, causes avalanches, fire hazards, and general tension. (The *Föhn* is used as an excuse by criminals and failing students.) Salzburg, set on the Salzach River among steep ridges crowned by castles, is the fairy-tale capital of a province of lakes and mountain ranges. **Graz,** the capital of Styria and a university town, lies among gentler slopes.

Rail travel in Austria is expensive unless you have a railpass, but there are a couple of discount plans. Tourists can purchase an **Austria Ticket** valid on all trains and on certain inter-city buses. Second-class passes cost $85 for nine days and $117 for sixteen days, but those under 23 pay half of these rates. It doesn't take a lot of travel to make these passes pay for themselves. They're available anywhere in Austria or from Austrian Airlines, 608 Fifth Ave., New York, NY 10020. You can rent a bike at any of 36 rail stations and drop it off at another station.

Driving costs a fortune. Gasoline costs almost $2 per U.S. gallon. And watch out for some of the toll roads in the Alps—one 40-mile stretch will cost you $12. Be prepared for the mountain conditions and remember that the car going up a hill has the right of way. Buses are not as efficient as the rail and road networks, but if you're not in a hurry, they provide a scenic and cheaper alternative. Hitching is slow, although relatively safe. All Austrian cities have excellent tram and/or bus systems; tickets are bought on board.

Stores in Austria are closed Saturday afternoons and Sundays, while museums and monuments close on Mondays. Aside from the outstanding concerts and theater, nightlife in Austria is rather sedate. A quiet evening in a *Weinstube* (wine tavern) may prove an enjoyable change from rat-race pleasures. Make sure you give a general greeting when you enter (*Grüss Gott*), and a general goodbye when you leave (*Auf Wiederschauen*). The same applies in stores, and will win you a certain amount of consideration.

The Alps

The mountains and foothills of the eastern Alps cover about 70% of Austria. When going up into the mountains, even if only for a stroll near one of 350-or-so upper stations of the Austrian cable cars and chair lifts, be sure to have the proper clothing. Sturdy mountain boots are a must, and be sure they're broken in before attempting a long hike. You should also have some waterproof clothing.

Check the information offices in each village (*Verkehrsbüro* or *Verkehrsverein*) for local conditions, or ask for the advice of people at a pension or *Gasthof* (inn). Respect their opinions. Most of the higher peaks and ranges are extremely dangerous even when most of the snow is gone in July and August. Should you get into trouble, assistance is summoned by giving the Alpine Distress Signal. This is done either by visual or audible means at the rate of six signals per minute spaced evenly, followed by a break of one minute before repetition.

There are presently more than 700 mountain refuges or huts run by various Alpine associations, most of which are kept open under proper supervision from spring until autumn, some throughout the year. They have a total of 10,000 beds as well as room to accommodate another 10,000 on "shakedown" beds. Prices for an overnight stay vary between 50AS and 150AS. Members of Alpine societies enjoy as much as 50% reductions in hut refuges, and non-Austrians are entitled to become members of Austria's Alpine clubs and societies. Before commencing a tour, ask at the local Alpine club or society or at the nearest valley village about refuges along the route you contemplate. Each of the following Alpine clubs offers numerous refuges and has reciprocal agreements with other clubs:

Osterreichischer Alpenverein (AV): Headquarters at Wilhelm-Greillstrasse 15, A-6020 Innsbruck, Tyrol, Austria.

Deutscher Alpenverein (AV): Praterinsel 5, Munich 22, Germany.

Osterreichischer Touristenklub (OTK): Headquarters Baeckerstrasse 16, A-1010 Vienna, Austria.

Vienna (Wien)

Vienna has rightly been called a head without a body—a huge, gray city without any empire left to rule. The halls and ballrooms of its Baroque palaces are now silent, save for the footsteps of tourists and the typing in offices. Vienna retains the grace of bygone years, though, with its gilded angels and menacing gargoyles, its manicured gardens and elaborate fountains. But with half the city's population over 60—Vienna has been nicknamed "the city of pensioners"—sadness lingers behind the façade, from the memory of an empire vanquished and a city devastated.

The citizens of Vienna are in large part the product of an intermingling of many peoples, and differ from their fellow countrymen as much as from the rest of the world. Serbian, Czech, and Hungarian influences are not simply exotic accessories, but basic parts of the city's character. As Metternich said, "Asia begins at the Landstrasse"; the East starts making its moods known in the streets of Vienna, and onion domes begin competing with spires in the skyline.

Though the downtown area is the most interesting part of the city, you should make an attempt to get beyond the **Ring.** Take a walk along the **Donau Kanal,** from which you will perhaps get a better impression of the size of the city. Upstream, among the hills visible from Franz-Josefs-Kai, lies **Klosterneuberg,** horse country by the Vienna woods. If you don't want to go that far (and Vienna does extend that far), visit **Türkenschanz Park** in the eighteenth district, where you can join the Viennese for their Sunday afternoon stroll, complete with *Dackels* (dachshunds) on the leash and peacocks on the well-tended lawns. Or visit the districts beyond the **Gürtel,** the outer belt, where the buildings are gray and plain, but markets are still held in small squares.

Orientation

Vienna's charm and beauty carry a price tag, but restaurants and accommodations get a little cheaper as you get away from the Ring.

The city is divided into 23 districts, arranged in two concentric circles about the inner city, at the heart of which is **St. Stephen's Cathedral.** The

Ring and **Danube Canal** enclose district 1; the **Gürtel** encloses districts 3-9. Addresses give the district first, then the street, then the number. The **Opera** is the real center of the town for visitors. At the information booth in the Opera underpass for pedestrians, pick up a free map of the city which covers the streetcar network adequately, and a weekly program of Vienna's cultural events. You will also find a branch of Vienna's room-finding service here.

The streetcar network is thorough and efficient, but it closes down for the night between 11:30pm and 1am. You can change trams with your 10AS ticket so long as you make a direct connection and do not change your direction of travel. Buy your tickets at any **Tabak Trafik.** A book of five is 36AS. These are good on the **Stadtbahn** (subway), and on the **Schnellbahn** (express tram), within city limits. If you're staying longer, invest in a weekly ticket (Mon.-Fri. 58AS; Mon.-Sat. 68AS; Mon.-Sun. 79AS). You can also buy a 24-hour ticket for 36AS which is valid for one day from the hour of validation. A regular bus service links the airport and the air terminal building near the Bahnhof-Wien-Mitte. Fare is 35AS.

The currency exchange at the Westbahnhof stays open daily until 10pm. Big hotels will also change money at odd hours or on holidays at a somewhat lesser rate. Eastern European currencies can be bought in Vienna at rates much better than the official rates in those countries, but in most cases you'll have to smuggle them past their customs officials when you enter. (Check the regulations for each country.)

For bicycle rental try **Radfahrverein Prater,** 2, Bocklinstrasse 2 (tel. 24 85 38). They have the best rates around—20AS an hour, 100AS a day, and 400AS a week. When you cross streets, don't cross against the light, and always use the underpass. Policemen ruthlessly enforce 50AS fines. Traveling on the tram system without a valid ticket can cost you 100-3000AS. Honking of car horns is strictly forbidden inside the city limits, except when a life is in danger. You can park in a *Kurzparkzone* for thirty minutes if you buy a special ticket from a Tabak (2AS). Be sure to put the ticket in your window. Viennese police, however, seldom ticket cars with foreign plates.

Addresses and Telephone Numbers

Information Service: Opernpassage (tel. 43 16 08), open daily 9am-7pm. Also at the Westbahnhof, open 6:15am-11pm and the Sudbahnhof, open 6am-9:30pm. They'll also find you a room for a fee of about 20AS.

The Austrian Student Travel Service (ASTS): Reichsstrasse 13 (tels. 52 66 63 and 64; at night 42 63 74). Student flights and accommodations. They run three student hotels in the city and know of others. Open 9am-4pm, July 1-September 30.

ÖKISTA: Türkenstrasse 4 (tel. 34 75 26) Rooms 314 and 315. They will help with all information needs on Austria and Vienna, and will book student flights, trains, tours, and get you tickets and rooms. They also publish a student guide to Austria (free).

American Express: Kärtnerstrasse 21-23 (tel. 52 05 44).

Mitfahrzentrale Wien, Neustiftgasse 5 (behind the Kunsthistorisches and Technisches Museum; tel. 93 62 79 or 32 34 80). Brings drivers and riders

Vienna

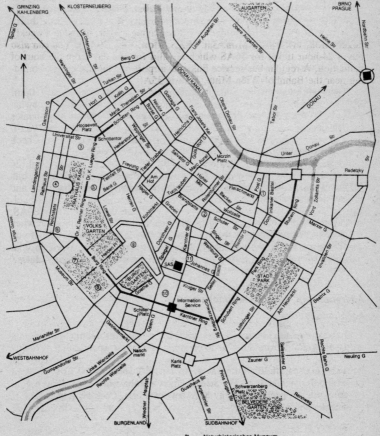

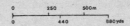

1	Post	7	Naturhistorisches Museum
2	Stephansdom	8	Kunsthistorisches Museum
3	University	9	Hofburg
4	Neues Rathaus	10	Staatsoper (Opera)
5	Burgtheater	11	American Express
6	Parliament	12	Schloss Belvedere

together for inter-city trips—see West Germany introduction.

Main Post Office: 1, Fleischmarkt 19 (tel. 52 76 81). Open 24 hours.

Central Telegraph Office: Börseplatz 1 (tel. 63 16 31). Open 24 hours.

Cook's Travel: Kärtnerring 2 (tel. 65 76 31).

Police Emergency: tel. 133. **Headquarters:** *Fremdenpolizei*, Bäckerstrasse 13 (tel. 63 06 71).

Medical Emergency: tel. 144.

U.S. Embassy: Boltzmanngasse 16 (tel. 34 66 11).

Canadian Embassy: Dr. Karl-Lueger-Ring 10 (tel. 63 66 26).

Lost Property Office: Bräunerstrasse 5 (tel. 52 46 17). Open Mon.-Fri. 8am-3pm.

English Bookstore: Corner of Dorotheergasse and Plankengasse.

For written information on Vienna and Austria: **Fremdenverkehrsverband für Wien,** 9, Kinderspitalgasse 5; and the **Fremdenverkehrswerburg,** 1, Hohenstaufengasse 3-5.

Automatic laundromats travel under the alias *Wäscherei,* and are scattered inconspicuously throughout the city. Most centrally located of these is the one at Krugerstrasse 8; so bring your laundry when you go to see the Vienna Boys Choir, or drop in after picking up your mail at AmEx. Most are open 7am-8pm.

Accommodations

In the summer accommodations will pose a major problem. Many hotels are booked solid from June to September, and most of the student hotels don't open until July. If you arrive in June, your best bet is either a private home or a pension. If you want to stay in the heart of the city, make a reservation. If you don't have a reservation, phone from the station before tramping all over town. If you really get stuck, most hostels have attics or basements where they sometimes allow you to sleep on the floor at a reduced rate. If they tell you they are booked, be persistent, but polite.

STUDENT ACCOMMODATIONS

The ASTS and especially ÖKISTA are helpful as room finders. Vienna's **Jugendgästehäuser** (IYHF hostels) are very pleasant, but located in the suburbs, far from the center of the city. IYHF card required.

Hütteldorf-Hacking (IYHF), 8, Schlossbergasse 8 (tel. 82 15 01). Take W Stadtbahn to endstop Hutteldorf. Open all year. First night 52AS, 47AS after that. Breakfast included. 10:30pm curfew, which is sometimes ignored; check with the management first, though.

Pötzleinsdorf (IYHF), 17, Geymüllergasse 1 (tel. 47 13 12). Large bunk-bed rooms, free showers. 52AS the first night, 47AS each night after. Near several outdoor wine cellars and a park. Lenient about the 10pm curfew. Take tram #41 to endstop. Open April-October.

Hostel Ruthensteiner, 15, Robert Hammerlinggasse 24 (tel. 83 46 93). Located near the Westbahnhof and a short ride from the Ring with tram #52 or 58. Open all year, with a small patio in the back. Singles 107AS, doubles and triples 82AS per person. Dorm rooms 52AS. Breakfast included.

International Studenthaus, 1, Seilerstätte 30 (tel. 52 84 63). A student dorm in the center of the city; modern, clean rooms with showers on every floor. Singles 150AS, doubles and triples 125AS per person. Kitchen available. Open July-September.

Gästehaus der Musikhochschule, 1, Johannesgasse 8 (tel. 52 05 05). Also in the center of the city, and you pay for the location. Singles 210AS, doubles 170AS, triples 140AS. Breakfast included. The rooms are large and clean, music abounds, and the location is worth the extra money. Open June 30-September 30.

Asylverein der Wiener Universität, 9, Porzellangasse 30, (tel. 34 72 82). A student dormitory with old rooms, a small courtyard, and kitchens. Open July 1-September 30. 195 beds, free showers. Only 60AS a night. D trolley from the Opera.

Boltzmannheim, 9, Bolzmanngasse 10, near the U.S. Embassy (tel. 34 44 64), is a large student dorm with typical dorm rooms. Singles, doubles, triples 150AS per person, including breakfast. Open July-September. Take tram E2 and walk.

Hotel Auge Gottes, 9, Nussdorferstrasse 75 (tel. 34 25 85). Open July-September. Take tram G2. Clean, modern, and simple rooms, colorfully decorated. Singles, doubles, and triples 100AS per person. Bar stays open until 5am.

Pfeilheim, 8, Pfeilgasse 6 (tel. 43 84 762). One of the better places in town. Free hot showers, and one-, two-, and three-bed rooms. 100AS per person. Take tram J to Strozzigasse, or tram #5 to Albertgasse.

Haus Korotan, 8, Albertgasse 48 (tel. 43 41 93). Less antiseptic than most. 90 single rooms; 150AS, breakfast included. Take trolley J from the Opera to Albertgasse. Open July and August.

Turmherberge "Don Bosco," 3, Lechnerstrasse 12 (tel. 73 14 94). Limited to men only, but the price may compensate for the loss—only 30AS (no breakfast). Take tram J from the Opera.

HOTELS AND PENSIONS

If you arrive late in the day or without a reservation, try the **Zimmernachweise** and **Informationstellen,** located at all train stations, the Opera underpass, the Danube Steamer Station, the airport, and the south and west Autobahn exits. Although you may face a long line, they will place you in a hotel, pension, or a private home within your specified price range.

The agencies charge a 20AS booking fee, so call on your own first (most proprietors speak English). Private homes are not much costlier than hostels, but you must stay a minimum of three nights. They range from 100-200AS.

Pension Pertschy, 1, Habsburgergasse 5 (tel. 52 38 67). Superb location minutes from the Spanish Riding School. The building once housed a count, and is now a historical landmark, with a courtyard and flowers in the window boxes. Herr Pertschy is a gracious and friendly host. Prices run high, 200AS for a single, 340-360AS for a double. Breakfast included. Also the owner of the new **Pension Christina,** Hafnersteig 7 (tel. 63 29 61), which is furnished in elegant, old Viennese style, but more expensive.

Pension Astra, 9, Alserstrasse 32 (tel. 42 43 54). Large, clean, and quiet rooms, singles 150AS, doubles 230-240AS. Showers and breakfast extra. One of the best buys in town—the woman who runs the pension is extremely friendly and helpful. Take tram #42, 43, or H2 from Schottentor.

Pension Vera, 9, Alserstrasse 18 (tel. 43 25 95), on the same street, is also a good deal. The rooms are unadorned, but clean and not cramped. Singles 165AS, doubles 280-320AS. Breakfast included.

Pension Columbia, 9, Kochgasse 9 (tel. 42 67 57) is located right off Alserstrasse. The rooms are large and sunny and there is a lovely crystal chandelier in the dining room. Doubles only 350AS, shower and breakfast included.

Pension Nossek, Graben 17 (tel. 52 45 91) is the place to go if location, not budget, is your top priority. The rooms are large and elegantly furnished, and it is right in the heart of the city. As always, you pay for charm and location. Few singles, and doubles start at 350AS.

Pension Wild, Langegasse 10 (tel. 43 51 74) is one of Vienna's better buys. Showers are free, and every room has hot plates so you can cook your own food. Singles 180AS, doubles 270AS. The rooms are what you might call "basic," but Frau Wild's hospitality makes up for any lack of decor. Take tram #46. Reservations strongly suggested. There are other places on the same street, if you hit Vienna at a poor time. Try pension **Edelweiss,** Langegasse 61 (tel. 42 23 06) which has singles for 200AS, doubles 380AS, or **Pension Zipser,** Langegasse 49, (tel. 42 02 28) with rooms that overlook a small garden. Singles 190AS, doubles 215AS.

Hotel Thüringerhof, 18, Jörgerstrasse 6-8 (tel. 42 81 98). Out of the way, but quiet and clean with cold cuts or eggs instead of the usual two hard rolls for breakfast. Singles 170-200AS, doubles 280-320AS, showers 20AS. Take tram H2 or 43.

CAMPING

Wien West, Hüttelbergstrasse 80 (tel. 94 23 14). 6 km from the center of town. Take streetcar #49 to end stop. Open April-October. 22AS per person, 25AS parking.

Wien Süd, Strandbad Rodaun (tel. 86 01 34). Open all year. Take the subway to Hietzind, change to streetcar #60.

Food

Viennese cooking is simple, good, and filling. Step into almost any small **Gasthaus** and try the local specialties: *Leberknödelsuppe* (soup with liver dumplings), *Wienerschnitzel,* and boiled beef. Even *bachendl* (fried chicken) can be a great delicacy on a warm evening with a little Strauss in the background. Most of Vienna's restaurants add a 20% service charge to menu prices, while places with music may tack on 5-10AS as well. And keep in mind that dinner rolls, even on the table, are not included in the price. For dessert try *Apfelstrudel* or *Sacher Torte,* a rich chocolate cake filled with apricot pureé and glazed with chocolate.

There is an outdoor market in the fifth district, **Naschmarkt,** only five minutes from the Opera House. For those who really stick to a tight budget, dark bread, *Bauernbrot,* is government subsidized and is cheaper than rolls or white bread (higher in vitamins, too).

Gösser Bierklinik, Steindlgasse 4 (behind Graben). This restaurant is alleged to be the site of an ancient Roman camp. The atmosphere on the street floor is warm and cozy, with dark wood and hand-painted stained-glass windows. The upstairs is more refined, with linen cloths and paintings. The food is great on either level, and the waiters are helpful in deciphering the menu. A full meal runs about 70AS.

Leupold, Schottengasse 7. A favorite among university students. Filling food, reasonably priced. The soups are meals in themselves (16AS); inexpensive sandwiches too. Open Sundays.

Vegetarian Restaurant, Währingerstrasse 57. In a country tough on vegetarians, this is one place with filling and balanced veggie meals. A good buy.

Stadtbeisl Hubertus Stube, Naglergasse 21. Sidewalk café; more rustic decor downstairs, complete with deer antlers. If your German is good enough, ask the waiter about the story of Hubertus and the deer. The food is nearly as good as the atmosphere, and the prices are reasonable. Closed Sundays.

Diogenes, Landesgerichtsstrasse 18, is located near the University. Filling Greek cuisine for 30-50AS. Try it for lunch or dinner. The stuffed eggplant is especially good. Closed Saturdays and Sundays.

The **Mensa,** in the Neues Institutesgebäude, Universitätstrasse 7 (sixth and seventh floors). Has an impressive view from the terrace. The cheap, greasy food is less breathtaking. 20-40AS. Open 11:30am-2pm and 4:30-7pm. Open Saturdays for lunch only. Closed Sundays.

W.Ö.K.'s. At these municipal-run temperance restaurants, the food is a little above the mensa in quality and the prices are the same. They are scattered around the city; try the one at Schottengasse 1 or Mariahilferstrasse 85. Open for lunch only.

Trzesniewski, Dorotheergasse 1, is a famous stand-up sandwich restaurant. They have been serving their open-face delicacies for over 75 years. Go in, wait in line, and point. Sandwiches (the size of tea sandwiches) average 4AS. Try the chopped egg and mushroom. **Pic Pic,** Bräunerstrasse 4, has a wider variety, but prices run slightly higher than its competitor. Come here for the fish sandwiches (the ones with mussels and caviar are specialties).

Cafés and Konditoreis

The café, a Viennese institution that is an integral part of the city's unhurried charm, is giving way to the "Café Espresso," or five-second coffee bar. Austrians who aren't in quite so much of a hurry spend hours here, studying, reading newspapers (which the cafés supply), conversing, or just passing the time. Order a *Mocca* (black), *Brauner* (brown), or *Melange* (light) cup of coffee and a piece of pastry. The ones listed below haven't given up the cherished *Gemütlichkeit* (warmth and coziness).

There are also plenty of outdoor cafés, and you are sure to find your favorites. The ones along Kärtnerstrasse are the best for people-watching, but prices run high. Some of the most interesting places are located in the side streets near St. Stephens.

Sperl, 6, Gumpendorferstrasse 11, hasn't been altered since the days when the Vienna art nouveau circle gathered here; marble tables, mahogany chairs, velvet-covered booths, mirrors, and chandeliers. A very cozy place to pass the evening in old Viennese style.

Alte Backstube, Langegasse 34, is both a café and a museum of baking. Go there in the evening and sit by candlelight over coffee and pastry.

The Café Hawelka, Dorotheergasse 6, just off the Graben. A long-time hang-out for artists, intellectuals, and radicals. Trotsky was a regular here. After 10pm ask for the warm *Büchteln*, sweet rolls filled with preserves. Open daily til 2am, except Tues.

Demel, Kohlmarkt 14, is the most famous bakery in Austria. With gilded mirrors, marble tables, and deeply polished wood. Snotty, expensive, and delicious.

Brezel Gwölb, on Ledererhof, off Am Hof, is an indoor cellar as well as an outdoor café. You will often hear the strains of local musicians on violin or cello. Mixed crowd, including gays.

Sights

The center court of the **Hofburg,** the huge residential complex of the Hapsburgs, is called *In der Burg*—"In the City"—a name which reveals the extent to which the dynasty dominated Vienna. The palace set the architectural style for buildings within the Ring—a precedent later made law. The Hofburg grew in blocks and curves from the **Schweitzer-hof** (Swiss Court) whose Renaissance portal is the most harmonious part of the whole palace. One side of the Schweitzer-hof now contains the **Schatzkammer,** the imperial treasury, a glittering collection of royal accessories. (Open Mon.-Sat. 8:30am-4:30pm, Sun. 8:30am-1pm. Entrance 15AS.) The Hofburg also contains the **National Bibliothek,** one of Fischer von Ehrlach's more elaborate structures. Ehrlach's influence marks all Austrian Baroque buildings. In the summer, the Bibliothek houses special exhibits. (Open 10am-4pm Mon.-Fri., admission to exhibits 5AS with student ID.)

The most famous possessions of the Hapsburgs are now the Hofburg's greatest attraction—the **Lipizzaner** horses of the Spanish Riding School, founded in the seventeenth century. Despite being saved by Patton and immortalized by Walt Disney, the horses maintain the grace and dignity of their tradition. Fischer von Ehrlach's ring, complete with chandeliers, makes the perfect dance floor. Tickets to the shows (March through June and mid-October through mid-December, Sun. at 10:45am and Wed. at 7am) are always sold out, but you can tour the stalls or see a morning rehearsal

(10am-noon Tues.-Fri.) Line up early; 30AS, 10AS with student ID. You may be disappointed with the rehearsal though, unless you are a real horse lover.

The **Church of the Augustinians,** where Hapsburg marriages took place, owes the purity of its Gothic interior to restoration. If you like pickled hearts, there are 54 of the imperial family in urns in the Chapel of St. George, off to the right of the nave. Back in the good old days, the Emperor's family used to move every summer to **Schloss Schönbrunn,** a small Versailles on the outskirts of the old town. The surprisingly interesting required tour provides all the gossip on the private lives of Maria Theresa, Franz Josef, the young Marie Antoinette, and Napoleon's son, confined here until his death. Tours run about every 45 minutes. You can escape Baroque finery at the **Gloriette Monument** or the **Zoo,** both located in the elegant gardens.

The **Belvedere** is a much lovelier and more graceful palace than Schönbrunn. Designed by Lukas von Hildebrandt, it is considered one of the world's finest Baroque buildings. The lower Belvedere houses a spectacular collection of Austrian medieval art. The upper Belvedere has a fine collection of the Jugendstil, with works by Klimt, Schiele and Kokoschka. (Open Tues.-Thurs. and Sat. 10am-4pm, Fri. 10am-1pm, Sun. 9am-noon. 15AS with ID, 25AS without). Don't leave without seeing **Belvedere Palace Park,** the most beautiful and elegantly-designed of Vienna's gardens. The best way to see the entire grounds is to enter through Rennweg and walk up. Besides the superb view and the Sphinxes, there are vast botanical gardens with an exhibit of alpine plants that can grow at sea level. 4AS admission to the alpine garden. The man at the ticket booth has an encyclopedic knowledge which he gladly shares. Belvedere is especially nice for a Sunday morning walk when the Viennese come for their strolls. For a less formal atmosphere try **Volksgarten,** where people sit around playing guitars and socializing. The rose garden is exquisite, with hundreds of varieties all carefully labeled.

In the heart of the Ring rises Gothic **Stephansdom (St. Stephen's Cathedral),** which is covered inside and out with first-rate medieval sculpture. You can go down to the catacombs, or up to the towers, from which there is a fine view of the city (3AS with ID). St. Stephen's has free organ concerts on Wednesdays at 7pm. Other churches worth seeing include **Maria Am Gestade,** a Gothic jewel, and **St. Charles,** a stately Baroque structure.

The famous **Kunsthistorisches Museum,** Maria-Theresien Platz, is Vienna's main fine arts museum and the fourth largest gallery in the world. Be sure to see the entire room dedicated to Breughel (especially *The Hunter's Return*), Vermeer's *Allegory of Painting* and Rembrandt's portraits of his son Titus and the apostle Paul. There are also some fine works by Dürer, Van Eyck, and Velasquez. For many, this is the prime attraction in Vienna. (Open Tues.-Fri. 10am-3pm, Sat.-Sun. 9am-1pm, Tues. and Fri. 7-9pm. Admission free with student ID.)

Down the street from the Belvedere is the **Museum des 20 Jahrhunderts** (in the Schweizergarten across from the Südbahnhof). This is a fine modern art museum with a permanent collection of German expressionists, the Blue Rider school, and the Jugendstil. The building was Austria's pavilion at the 1958 World's Fair in Brussels and was brought back to Vienna. (Open Mon., Thurs., Fri., Sat. 10am-4pm, Wed. 2pm-7pm, Sun. 10am-1pm. Admission 1AS with student ID.)

The **Albertina Museum,** Augustin Eistrasse 1, offers a welcome change from endless walls of paintings. Representative works in the development of the graphic arts since the fourteenth century (alas, facsimiles of their closely-guarded masterpieces) are available for scrutiny, including examples of Dürer, Michelangelo, Rembrandt and Rubens. If you want to see a specific work, they will personally bring it for you to examine. (Open Mon.,

Tues., Thurs. 10am-4pm; Wed. 10am-6pm, Fri. 10am-2pm, Sat.-Sun. 10am-1pm. Closed Sundays during July and August.) The building houses a film museum which shows old classics, on the ground floor; and the Music Library, where you can see Beethoven's scores or use the listening room (open Mon., Wed., Fri., 9am-1pm., Tues. and Thurs. noon-3:45pm). Free concerts and talks are also given here, periodically.

In 1971 Vienna finally recognized one of its famous native sons, **Sigmund Freud,** by establishing a museum in his former house, at Berggasse 19. Open Mon.-Fri. 10am-1pm and weekends 10am-4pm.

For entertainment of a less serious nature, the **Prater** offers the world's grandest ferris wheel ride, but is otherwise old and a bit seedy. You may also want to visit the **Watch Museum,** Schulhof 2, which is a charming old museum. Fascinating, even if you don't particularly like watches.

For swimming try the Danube. Take streetcar #25 or 26, get off at Erzherzog or Karlstrasse, and walk along the beach on the right-hand side. It is a five-minute walk with a meadow and steps to the water. You can also rent boats for rowing, sailing, or wind surfing.

Evenings

MUSIC AND THEATER

The **Wiener Sängerknaben** (Vienna Boys Choir) sing at 9:25am mass at the **Burgkapell** (Royal Chapel) in the Hofburg every Sunday except during July, August, and the first half of September, when the boys go on vacation. Tickets are hard to come by; try the box office at 5pm Fridays. Standing room is free, and if you get there around 8:30am, you may be able to enter the church, otherwise you will stand in a room with a closed-circuit TV. It is worth the trouble. People in the front often leave, so by the end you may even have a seat.

At the **Staatsoper** you can buy standing-room tickets for 15-20AS; the price for regular tickets soars to 350AS and nearly all seats sell out. Plan to get in line early (around 4:30pm) to insure a ticket. Wear comfortable shoes as the performance doesn't let out until late (10-11pm).

The **Burgtheater, Akademietheater, Staatsoper,** and **Volksoper** are closed from July 1 to August 31, but music is always flourishing. If you speak German, you might enjoy a theatrical performance at the **Volkstheater** or the theater in **der Josefstadt.** The **Theater an der Wien** opens with light opera during the second week in July. **Arkadenkonzerte** are a series of outdoor concerts given in the courtyard of the **Rathaus** by top Viennese orchestras, Tuesdays and Thursdays at 8pm during the summer. The setting is theatrical, and the prices low—40AS admission. A cut above these are the concerts in the grand hall of the **Musikverein,** where the tickets begin at 50AS. There are also good vocal and instrumental recitals, ensembles, and choirs at the **Wiener Palais** from July to the middle of September, every Monday, Wednesday, and Thursday at 8pm.

For all the above, including the Opera, it is standard practice to slip the guard about 20AS if standing room is "sold out." A well-worded plea about how you have traveled from America just for the glories of Austrian music will help get you through if there is any trouble.

There is lots of free music in Vienna, too. **St. Stephen's** makes a grand setting for the Wednesday evening organ concerts (7pm all year). Strauss is played in the Stadtpark every afternoon from 3:30-5:30 and in the evenings as well when the Viennese get up to waltz. Every Monday at 5pm in July and August there is classical music in the **Upper Belvedere Palace Gardens** and on Tuesdays at 5pm the same orchestra plays jazz in front of the Rathaus. Something is always being played at 5:30 in the parks—check posters or newspapers.

Finally there is Vienna's **English Theatre,** the only professional English-language theater on the Continent. It is located on Josefgasse 12; take streetcar H2, E2, or G2.

WINE CELLARS AND WINE GARDENS

There are vineyards all over Austria, but some of the best grapes ripen on the hills overlooking Vienna. *Keller,* downtown wine cellars, and *Heurigen,* outdoor-indoor wine gardens, provide the chance to see the Viennese at their most carefree. Violin, accordion, and spontaneous song and dance often accompany the nightly festivities. White wine tends to be better than red around Vienna.

Zwölf Apostel Keller, Sonnenfelsgasse 3. It has many levels—the lowest is the liveliest. One of the best of the Viennese cellars, great atmosphere, and lots of locals. Open Sundays.

Esterhazykeller, Haarhof 1 (Off Naglergasse). Empress Maria Theresa granted the concession for this cellar on the condition that it close at 10:30pm. It has remained faithful to tradition, but the atmosphere is pleasant and unpretentious. Prices are good for a tight budget. Outdoor café in good weather.

Melkerkeller, Schottengasse 3, is run by Benedictine Monks. The wine is excellent; try the house specialty—*stelze,* roasted pig's thigh. For the less adventurous, a good choice is roast veal (70AS).

Hofburgkeller, Schauflergasse 1, is the home of the emperor's wine cellar. Expensive and snooty, but the food is superb. Zither music instead of the usual accordion or violin.

Austrians tend to avoid **Grinzing,** the largest *Heurige* area; the atmosphere and the wine is better in **Sievering, Nussdorf,** or **Salmannsdorf.** One of the best *Heurigen* is in Beethoven's home in **Heiligenstadt.** Take tram G2 to the end stop. Walk down the street and through the park. Take a right, then your first left on Pfarr Platz. Here you will find some fantastic outdoor *Heurigen.* The one in Beethoven's house is the largest, and has a small orchestra and an excellent buffet with cheeses, chicken, meat, and vegetables. There are other *Heurigen* on the same street, less popular and smaller, but with better prices. Be sure to explore. A great way to spend the evening. Things get liveliest after 10pm.

Near Vienna

The southern and western sides of Vienna are bordered by the famous **Wienerwald** (Vienna woods). Take trolley #38 to Grinzing (end stop) and continue by bus #385 to **Kahlenberg** (16AS) where you have a lookoutpoint over the entire city. Wander off into the woods on well-marked trails. It is a pleasant (but long) walk back to Grinzing or Nussdorf, via Leopoldsberg, where you can take the D tram to the Opera. Come in the late afternoon or early evening so that you can stop in at one of the many *Heurigen* on your way back.

Try to include a trip on a Danube steamer in your Austrian travels. You can sail from **Passau** (on the German-Austrian border) to Vienna for 358AS; upriver from Vienna to Passau costs 288AS. With a Eurailpass there is no charge; the trip takes two days, however. If you want a shorter ride, take the boat from **Linz** to Vienna (258AS) or Vienna to Linz (208AS). Eurail also valid. You can book passage through ÖKISTA, the student travel bureau, at Türkenstrasse 4 (tel. 34 75 26) or at their office at Reichsratstrasse 13. You can also book directly through the agencies themselves. Contact **DDSG-Reisedienst,** 2, Mexikoplatz 8 (tel. 26 25 91) or **Schiffsstation** (Reichsbrücke), Mexikoplatz 8 (tel. 24 34 20). In Passau, check at the **DDSG-Schiffsstation,** Im Ort 14a, Dreiflusseck, (tel. 3 30 35).

You can also check with ÖKISTA about excursions to the nearby Danube cities, **Budapest** (Hungary) and **Bratislava** (Czechoslovakia). There are also inexpensive trips to **Prague.** The three-day student tour to Budapest or Prague costs 950AS, food, accommodations, and visa included. A one-day tour to Bratislava costs 320AS, boat and lunch included.

Shorter excursions include **Burg Kreuzenstein,** a medieval castle complete with moat, weapon rooms, armor, and tower. About a half-hour drive up Bundesstrasse 2 from Vienna, or a ride of comparable length on the Schnellbahn, direction Stockerau. Catch the train at Praterstern or Wien Mitter, two blocks from the Ring. **Kloster-Neuberg** is a well-preserved medieval monastery with a fantastic gold altarpiece from 1181. Open 9am-6pm. Take the train from the Franz-Josef Bahnhof or hitch out Heiligenstädterstrasse. (Mark Twain said that some German words have geographical perspective.)

If Vienna begins to weary you, head to **Baden,** which has a public swimming pool and a sulphur bath cure, as well as parks and woods. Beethoven lived here, and in the nineteenth century Baden was the resort for Austria's aristocracy. Also to the south is **Heiligenkreuz,** one of Austria's most beautiful monasteries. Sample the fresh trout at one of the restaurants along the main road to the monastery.

If you are heading west (toward Salzburg), you may want to consider visiting **Mariazell,** a tiny village unknown to most Americans, but the most important religious pilgrimage site in Austria. The town is a delight and offers hills to climb as well as a spectacular view from the cable car. From the West-Bahnhof go to **St. Pölten** for the train to Mariazell.

Southern Austria

Innsbruck, Salzburg, and Vienna do not constitute the whole of Austria. Anyone headed south to Yugoslavia and Italy will probably pass through one or more of the three provinces of southern Austria. **Kärnten** (Carinthia) varies the rugged Alpine aspect of the country with smaller, more rolling mountains. The town of **Villach** hosts the "Carinthian Summer" music festival in July and August. Tickets are relatively inexpensive (around 80AS), but Villach fills up quickly during those weeks. Reservations are definitely advisable. **Klagenfurt,** the provincial capital, lies at one end of the **Wörthersee,** the largest of a series of lakes in the area. There is **camping** on the lake (and another camping ground to the south which is less expensive and less crowded) and an IYHF Youth Hostel on Kumpfgasse in the center of town. The area is a naturalist's paradise: the **Naturpark Kreuzbergl,** overlooking Klagenfurt and the lake, offers trails, lakes, and a way to see the glories of the Austrian hills without too much effort. The province of **Steiermark** (Styria) occupies much of the southeastern corner of the country from Salzburg to the Hungarian border. **Graz,** the capital of Styria and the second largest city in Austria, sponsors the excellent *Festival of Styria,* which features orchestras, dance, and opera from Austria and abroad. South of Graz, along the Yugoslav border, the **Weinstrasse** (Wine Road) stretches for kilometers through well-tended vineyards. **Burgenland,** a narrow province bordering on Hungary, is famous for its wines as well. You may also want to visit **Eisenstadt**, capital of Burgenland, with its rennants of the Jewish ghetto. The **Wine Week** in Eisenstadt at the end of August offers an excuse to try all the different varieties, and to partake in what is for Austria a rather wild festival.

Nearby is **Lake Neusiedl,** which borders on the Hungarian Plains. Surrounded by wildlife reserves and small villages, this is a favorite excursion for the Viennese.

If you only have time for one stop, go to **Rust,** whose chimneys are famous for the storks that return each year to nest on them. Check at the restaurant by the waterfront to see if there is a boatman willing to take you out to see the birds. The ride leaves at 5am, lasts about three hours, and will cost around 200AS. Rust is also a wine-making center. There is an **Information Center** in the main square, which will find you a room, or direct you to the IYHF Youth Hostel if you decide to spend the night.

Graz

Graz rests content with the knowledge that the right people know of its existence. Tourism is not a major business, but the city has much to offer. The **Alte Universität** (University), housed in some stately seventeenth-century buildings, has in recent times turned out four Nobel Prize winners. The **Graz Center** sponsors international summer study of the economics, politics, and culture of Eastern Europe. The Graz **Oper** is a breeding and proving ground for singers who go on to international fame through the Vienna Opera. From a historical point of view, Graz served as a fortress and refuge for early Christians (the word *graz* means fortress). The town played a crucial role in the resistance of the West to Turkish incursions from 1453 to 1700. The **Landeszeughaus** became a commemorative museum in 1749, and contains the armor and weapons for 30,000 soldiers, equipment made specifically for the battle against the hordes who twice fought their way to the gates of Vienna.

The Allies bombed Graz a number of times from 1943 to 1945, and much of the city is new, consisting of high-rise apartments and a disproportionate number of gas station-car wash complexes. The inner city, divided by the River Mur, preserves a quiet and stately air. The buildings, both secular and religious, are largely late Gothic, Renaissance, or early Baroque. Italian architects did much of the work, such as the **Landhaus,** the most beautiful Renaissance building in the south of Austria. It was built in the mid-sixteenth century as a governing seat for Styria.

The **Bemaltes Haus,** a ducal palace until the mid-fifteenth century, presents a beautiful painted façade, which hides the remains of an equally lavish job inside by an earlier Italian painter (unfortunately, entrance is not permitted).

Graz has quite an array of churches. Be sure to see the **Stadtpfarrkirche,** which houses Tintoretto's *Ascension of Mary,* surrounded by an ornately carved and gold-leafed altarpiece. The tiny **Minoriten Church,** Mariahilferstrasse 3, has an exquisite gold and silver altarpiece, and delicate crystal chandeliers. Concerts are held in the small courtyard in the summer. The **Mausoleum** of Emperor Ferdinand II has Baroque interior decorations by Fischer Von Erlach, Graz's native son. These were done in an early, comparatively simple style. The **Dom** (Cathedral) also merits a visit—it combines a simple exterior with an elaborate late Baroque interior.

Either walk or take the lift (6AS) from Frans Joseph Kai to **Schlossberg,** the mountain ridge which rises over the inner city. On the ridge stands the Uhrturm, the clock tower, emblem of Graz. Further up, you will find the remains of the fort which resisted Napoleon and 10,000 men for a month (until a peace treaty did it in). The ridge, once barren rock, is now clad by rich vegetation, and etched with steep paths.

Orientation

Graz spreads out over a large plain, and is surrounded by forests—the part of town visitors will find of interest is the area from the train station in the west, to the center-city on both sides of the Mur, and to the Stadtpark in the east. The main information bureau at Kaiserfeldgasse 25 (tel. 765-91/92/93) is open from 8am to 6pm Mon.-Fri. and 9am-noon on Saturday. For information about the province of Styria. go to the **Steiermarkisches Landesreisebüro,** Hauptplatz 14. **ÖKISTA,** the student travel service, is located at Glacisstrasse 5A (tel. 23482).

The surplus of gas stations may be due to Graz's location on major routes into Yugoslavia and Italy. Hitchers headed for Ljubljana or Zagreb via Maribor should go out Lazarettgürtel, either on foot or the bus to Certus, which leaves from the Andreas Hoferplatz Station. Those going to Klagenfurt should take the local bus down Kärntnerstrasse. Those headed to Vienna can take streetcars #4 and 5 north. **Jakominiplatz,** two blocks from the Information Center and just south of the *Schlossberg,* is the crossing point for all these lines. Bus tickets cost 8AS.

The **Verkehrsamt,** Kaiserfeldgasse 25, will find you a room free of charge. Prices are reasonable in Graz, so you can get a decent room for 100-120AS. There is no room-finding service at the Train Station, but the Money Exchange at the Station will give you a hotel list and map. Or, try one of the following:

Jugendherberge (IYHF), Idlhofgasse 74 (tel. 91 48 76). Nice new building, rooms are spacious and clean. 58AS a night (with breakfast). Closed 9am-5pm, with 10pm curfew.

Gasthof Zu den 5 Lärchen, Griesplatz 6-7 (tel. 91 24 06). Located by the River Mur, this hotel offers a wide range of rooms, starting at 90AS per person, without breakfast. Showers 20AS.

Hotel Strasser, Eggenbergergürtel 11 (tel. 91 39 77). Just down the street from the Station, with a very pleasant owner. Spacious rooms begin at 95AS for a single, 180AS for a double, with breakfast and showers included.

Camping: Camping Central, located off Kärntnerstrasse, southwest of the city. Open April-October. **Camping Zur Weinlaube,** accessible by bus from the station, open May-Sept. **Graz-Ost,** bus from Jakominiplatz, open all year. In addition, there are sites in Graz-Eggenberg and Graz-Mantscha, prettier but accessible only by car.

Food

Sporgasse, one of the most picturesque streets in Graz, offers many restaurants. For the best value and ambiance, try the **Goldene Pastete,** at #28, or the **Weinstube Turkenloch** at #8. The **Winterbierhaus,** Bindergasse 1, offers great food at mensa prices. (Open Sundays; try the lasagna).

The **Student-Mensa,** at Schubertstrasse 2-4, has about the cheapest meals in town, though it's not much above institutional slop.

Evenings

Pick up the monthly schedule of concerts and theater at the Verkehrsbüro or in a restaurant. The **Opera** is hard to get into but worth it: performances start at 7:30pm. Get there an hour early and try for standing room tickets, or bribe the ushers. There is lots of free music—organ concerts in the churches and in the parks and the Hauptplatz in the evenings. The concerts at Schloss Eggenberg are worth it not so much for the music as for the setting. Local wine cellars abound. If you're in the neighborhood, try **Klosterkeller,** Mariahilferstrasse 15; **Weinstube,** Burggasse 10; or **Acabona,** Sackstrasse 40.

Near Graz

Schloss Eggenberg is a most unusual castle within city limits. It has some fine Baroque rooms with frescoed ceilings, and houses a hunting museum as well (be sure to see the "freak room"). The Palace is set in a large park, complete with peacocks and herds of wild deer. The building is open 9am-noon and 2-5pm daily. Admission 10AS, free with student ID. Take street-car #1 to Eggenberg, and get off at Schloss Strasse. **Schöckel,** the highest mountain near Graz, and a lovely spot to picnic, can be reached by cable railway starting from **Rodegund.**

Piber, some 45 kilometers west of Graz on Route 70, is the site of the Lipizzaner stud farm. Go on your own, or check with the Verkehrsamt for tours. The Weinstrasse, mentioned in the introduction, stretches from Ehrenhausen to Elbiswald. Take E93 south from Graz (also the road to Maribor). Finally, those interested in Austrian folk culture should pay a visit to the open-air museum at **Stübing.** Run by the Austrian government, the museum is a collection of houses from different parts of Austria, furnished according to the custom of the region. The museum is set in the forests northwest of Graz. Head out Route E93 north, or check with the Verkehrsamt for Post-autobus schedules to Stübing.

Salzburg

Salzburg, city of Mozart, has turned its native son into a major tourist industry. Along with concerts, you will find Mozart key chains and candies (with his face on the wrapper). The purist may be offended, but when the sun shines, all is forgotten. Baroque churches with bronze domes, castles on hill tops, palaces, and formal gardens are framed by the surrounding Alps. The churches were built by various archbishops who wanted to make Salzburg another Eternal City. The program began in the seventeenth century with the **Dom,** which was intended to rival St. Peter's in Rome. Salzburg's own **St. Peter's,** with the lovely Margaret Chapel in its cemetery, is worth a visit for the unusual colors of the interior. On the other side of town, the **Church of the Holy Trinity** is the prototype of Baroque architect Fischer von Ehrlach's style (done in his early and comparatively simple period). The **Residenz,** the archbishops' ornately-furnished palace, epitomizes their aspirations for Salzburg. It is now a museum with an eclectic collection of European art. Be sure to see Rembrandt's portrait of his mother in prayer, as well as secessionist artist Gustav Klimt's painting *At the Attersee.*

For all the effort, Mozart did more than the church could to immortalize

Salzburg. The house at Getreidegasse 9, where he was born, is painted a golden yellow so no tourist will miss it. The house is now a museum with letters, pictures, and models of stage sets for the operas. Mozart buffs will be enthralled, others may be bored. Open daily 9am-2pm. Admission 20AS, 10AS with student ID. Mozart is the glory of the **Salzburg Summer Festival,** Europe's most important summer music festival, (July 25-August 30) when every room in Salzburg is full; try to reserve a bed in advance if you come then. Unfortunately the festival can be more grief than bliss, packed as it is, with tickets scarce and accommodations scarcer. The more popular performances are sold out long in advance, and though you may be able to get tickets for the minor ones, you may find yourself snoozing on the streets or under the church-towers during your stay.

Castle lovers will find three in Salzburg. **Schloss Mirabell,** just off Makartplatz, offers fountains, gardens, and marvelous statuary. (Be sure to see the unicorns and the dwarfs.) Concerts are often given beside the fountain in the evening. Be sure to go inside Mirabell Palace, which was rebuilt and simplified after a fire, by Lukas von Hildebrandt (responsible for Belvedere in Vienna). The marble "Angel Staircase" is lined with golden cherubs. **Schloss Hellbrunn** is less frequented, but more fun. It includes a castle, a world-famous Alpine zoo, a large park and trick fountains which do things you never thought possible. With a student ID you can see everything for 14AS, 25AS otherwise. Take bus K to the Schloss; it's about a fifteen-minute ride. Another castle, **Festung Hohensalzburg** can be reached by funicular and offers armor, swords, and instruments of torture by day, and beer by night. The funicular will cost 14AS, a guided tour 10AS with student ID.

For a magnificient view of the city, walk up the **Kapuzinerburg** to the **Hettwei Bastei,** and look out over all the Mozartiana and the churches, past the fortress, to the Alps beyond.

Orientation

The official **City Tourist Service,** Auerspergstrasse 7 (tel. 7 15 11), opposite the Kurhaus, offers useful tourist information and can find you a hotel room. Be sure to pick up one of their beautiful posters, too. There are branches at the Train Station, the Airport, on all main arteries leading into Salzburg, and in the old town at Mozartplatz 5 (next to American Express). In July and August most are open weekdays from 8am-7pm, though the office at the Station stays open until 9:30pm daily. The Mozartplatz 5 branch (tel. 4 75 68) can give you information about excursions to mountain and lake areas. There is also a "Youth Info" service which will give you tips on student reductions, free concerts, and an excellent brochure, *Salzburg für die Jugend,* which has excellent listings of accommodations, sites, and restaurants (in English).

The **Salzach River** divides the city into the old and the new towns. In the new town, where the train station is, orient yourself by Makartplatz. The labyrinth of narrow streets which comprises the old town is best negotiated on foot, since certain of these streets are one-way or closed to traffic. Public transportation is cheap and efficient (8AS) but stops at 11pm. To hitch out of Salzburg toward either Innsbruck or Vienna, take bus #2 from the Train Station, get off at Mirabell Platz, cross the street, and ride bus #4 as far as the Autobahn entrance. Bus #4 can also be picked up at various points in town and should be taken direction Liefering. Hitching can be frustratingly slow.

Addresses and Telephone Numbers

American Express: 5 Mozartplatz (tel. 4 25 01). Weekdays 9am-5:30pm, Sat. 9am-noon.

Post Office: Residenzplatz 9 (tel. 4 41 21). Open until 7pm; the one in the Train Station open 24 hours.

Music Ticket Offices: Neubaur, Getreidegasse 14 and Griesgasse 15; Polzer, Bergstrasse 22.

Money Change: at the Station until 9:30pm **(Bankhaus Carl Spangler & Co.)**

Police Emergency: tel. 133; **Headquarters:** Churfürstenstrasse 1 (tel. 4 45 51).

Medical Emergency: (tels. 144 and 7 35 25).

Public Baths: Andrä, Hubert-Sattlergasse 4 (tel. 71 97 93); **Gnigl,** Minnescheimstrasse (tel. 78 93 35); A bath costs 15AS, a shower 7.50AS. Check poster at Verkehrsamt.

Sauna: People come to "take the cure" here, and saunas abound. They run about 50AS. Try **Sauna Im Kurmittelhaus,** Auerspergstrasse 2, or **Volksgarten Sauna,** Ignaz-Rieder-Kai 1a (tel. 2 33 54).

Laundromat: corner of Paris-Lodron-Strasse and Wolf-Dietrich-Strasse; also **Constructa,** Kaiserschötzen Strasse 10; **Top Express,** Neutor Strasse 43.

Accommodations

The **Verkehrsamt** and its many branches will find you a room for a fee of about 10AS. Private rooms, with breakfast and some sort of bathing arrangement, are usually available for about 100AS. Prices in Salzburg continue to rise, and the accommodation situation is tight. An early morning arrival (or a reservation) pays off. The city map is rather misleading; places are a bit further from the old part of town than they appear.

Naturfreundehaus, Mönchsberg 19 (tel. 41729). Small, clean dorm rooms with a breathtaking view. 35 beds. Only 45AS, breakfast 25AS. A small outdoor café too. Open May-September. A wonderful motherly owner. Take the lift on Gstättengasse (8AS round trip), then follow the signs. Walk right, then under the bridge, and take a sharp left. Take bus #1 from the Station.

Jugendherberge (IYHF), Josef-Preis-Allee (tel. 42670). 58AS bed and breakfast. 400 beds. 10:30pm curfew, but for 5AS you can stay out til midnight. Inefficiently run: you may find yourself changing beds every night. Check-in at 5pm but they let you come in during the day. Take bus #3 or 5 to Justizgebäude.

Jugendherberge (IYHF), Glockengasse 8 (tel. 76241), off Linzergasse. 54AS. 200 beds, 10:30pm curfew, but for 5AS you can stay out on the town till midnight. Open April-September. Closed till 6pm. Take bus #1, 2 or 3 to the center, then change to bus #4, which stops about a block away. If they are full, ask for the attic (it's cheaper too).

International Youth Hotel, Paracelsusstrasse 9 (tel. 79649). Just a few blocks from the Station. Open June 20-August 13. During the year it's a private school. Sparkling clean with a piano in the lounge and fluffy eiderdown quilts on the beds. 50AS per person, breakfast 15AS, sheets (if you need them) 10AS. Singles, doubles and dorm rooms. A good value.

Gasthof Hollbrau, Judengasse 15 (tel. 42132). Right in the center of the old city, with huge rooms. Singles from 180AS, doubles 260-310AS with breakfast. There is a 15AS reduction with student ID, and 10AS after three nights. Extra beds in a room 43AS. No showers, but great location.

Gasthof Zum Jungen Fuchs, Linzergasse 54 (tel. 51496). An old building, but centrally located. Singles 90AS, doubles 140-160AS, triples 200-240AS. No breakfast, showers 10AS.

Camping: Stadt-Camping, Bayerhammerstrasse 14a (tel. 71169). Open May 15-Oct. 15. Salzburg-Ost, Gnigl, Parscher Strasse 2 (tel. 702744). Open April 15-Oct. 15. Salzburg-West, ASK Flughafen, Karolingerstrasse 4 (tel. 85602), April-Oct.

Food

When you're not preparing meals yourself, we suggest saving money at the two student mensas and then splurging at one of the many wine cellars that feature lavish buffets.

Salzburg's best open-air market is held on Thursdays by **St. Andrews Church.** On any weekday, try **Franz-Josef Strasse.**

Salzburg has three outstanding coffeehouses: **Tomaselli,** on the Alter Markt; **Glockenspiel,** on Mozartplatz; and **Bazar,** on Schwarzstrasse, by the Staatsbrücke. The ambiance of these is enchanting, but you are certain to be brought gently to earth again by the 20AS price of a cup of coffee.

Mensa (Frau Schöppel): Sigmund-Haffner-Gasse 20 (44511); (Kapellhaus): (tel. 42638). Conveniently located opposite the Franziskammerkirche. Full of students. The food is surprisingly good for a mensa. Open 11:30am-1:30pm for lunch. 21AS. Call to check on breakfast and dinner.

Wolf-Dietrich Heim, Wolf-Dietrich Strasse 16 (tel. 71691), is the more pleasant of the two mensas, and serves larger portions. Open for lunch only (11:30am-1:30pm). 21AS. Closed weekends.

Zwettler-Stiftskeller, Kaigasse 3 in Mozartplatz. Serves excellent and filling three-course Austrian meals at 40AS. One of the best buys in town.

K & K, Am Waagplatz, is a good place to try for dinner. Go downstairs where there is a cellar with candlelight and rough-hewn tables. Try the buffet, especially the salads, since the menu is expensive. Superb desserts. Warm and cozy atmosphere.

Beer Gardens

Stieglkeller, Festungsgasse 10. Incredible view. Be sure to sit on the top level. Also open for lunch. Meals average 50AS, beer 12AS. A buffet as well. On

Wednesday and Saturday nights there is the Alpina Show, admission 70AS: This Austrian version of Lawrence Welk, minus the bubbles but with yodels included, is a real tourist rip-off.

Mülln Beer Garden, Augustinergasse 4-6. A huge former monastery; the atmosphere is now like a fraternity house. Buy your food at one of the small stores and delicatessens in the building. Half a liter of beer only 9.50AS.

Sog, Erzabt-Klotzstrasse 21, is less popular with Americans but a good, relaxed place to drink and meet European students.

Evenings

The world-famous annual summer festival runs from late July to the end of August. Performances generally begin at 8 or 8:30pm. Detailed programs in English are available in February from Direktion der Salzburger Festspiele, Festspielhaus, Salzburg. You would do well,to buy your tickets far in advance from the Austrian National Tourist Office, 545 Fifth Avenue, New York, NY 10017. Sales start in January. The few tickets still available in the summer are sold at the Festspielhaus box office. Travel agencies in Salzburg should be a last resort, since a 20% service charge is added to the ticket price. Opera seats go for 300 to 1500AS, concert seats for 200 to 750AS.

The **Salzburger Marionetten Theater,** on Schwarzstrasse near Makartplatz, features Salzburg's famous handmade puppets in performances of Mozart's operas. The background music comes from recordings of select festival performances. It is expensive, though. You probably won't get seats for under 120AS; they go up to 300AS. Sitting up front makes all the difference; buy the cheapest ticket possible and attempt to move up to the always-empty front rows. If you can, go backstage after the performance and watch the family pack up the marionettes with their elaborate costumes, and the simple stage set materials that are used to produce such remarkable effects.

In summer there are good, nightly chamber music concerts at the Mirabell Palace and the Residenz. Student tickets can be purchased for 50AS at the box office before the concert. Other tickets start at 100AS. There are also daily concerts in Mozart's **Wohnhaus,** Makartplatz 8 at 5pm and 7:30pm except Sundays and holidays. It's 50AS, 25AS with student ID. Open July and August. Organ concerts in the various churches of Salzburg run about 20AS with a student ID. Free music includes concerts in Mirabell Gardens at 8pm on Wednesdays and at the **Mozarteum,** Schwarzstrasse 26, Wednesdays at 6pm. Check with the **Tourist Office** on special concerts of the week or look at the posters plastered all over town. For jazz or Indian classical music, check on the concerts held at **Salzburger Universität.** There are many others as well—there is music everywhere in Salzburg.

Near Salzburg

The area around Salzburg has much to offer—mountains to climb, salt mines and ice caves to explore, and churches and castles to visit. There is skiing in summer, too, if you go up high enough. The **Gaisbergspitz** (4219ft.) is fifteen kilometers by mountain highway from the center of town. The bus from Mirabellplatz takes an hour, costs 60AS, and leaves at 9am, 11am, and 2pm, June 15-September 15. From this peak you will have a spectacular view of Salzburg, the surrounding mountain ranges, and the deep blue lakes. Twenty kilometers from Salzburg, near Hallein, are the **Dürnberg** salt mines. Although the ride up the cable railway to the mine entrance is worth the 45AS roundtrip fare just for the view, the mines themselves at 70AS are costly.

The mines in **Berchtesgaden,** across the German border in Bavaria cost only 6.50 German marks. Take a train from Salzburg and then a bus to the mines from the station (you can use the Eurailpass). The mines are fun—you put on funny costumes and slide down the mine shafts. There are lakes and some good climbing in this area. Also Hitler had his "Eagle's Nest" retreat here. There is a direct train, except on Sundays when you have to change. (Get on the train to Freilassing, change at the first stop after the border.)

The **Eisriesenwelt** (ice caves) near **Werfen** are fifty kilometers from Salzburg. There are trains and buses from the Station. The tours run about two hours and begin hourly in July and August; less frequently during the rest of the year. The caves are expensive, but contain spectacular ice sculptures. Dress warmly and wear sturdy shoes.

From Salzburg there is a bus that will take you to the monastery of **Kremsmünster.** Founded in 877, it is one of the oldest and most exquisite abbies in Austria. The buildings are full of frescoes and paintings and there is a pond surrounded by arches and Renaissance statuary. Well worth the trip. The monastery is famous for its white wine—ask to sample some.

If you're contemplating driving to Italy, you should go via the **Grossglockner Strasse,** one of Austria's most scenic Alpine roads. It takes you close to the peak of the Grossglockner, which, at over 12,000 feet, is the highest mountain in Austria. The 200AS toll is a poor bargain if you go earlier than June (when the road may be closed on account of snow), or at any time when the visibility is poor.

For those hitching or driving to Innsbruck, take the Alpine **Gerlosstrasse,** so you can see the **Krimmler Waterfalls** and the Tyrol's **Ziller Valley.** And if you're going to Vienna, there's a more pleasant way to do it than by train. Get off at Linz and continue by *Donaudampfschiff* (steamer) which leaves for Vienna at 10am. Your Eurailpass is valid. You'll pass through **Wachau,** a beautiful part of the Danube Valley with castles, vineyards, and high, jutting ridges.

The Salzkammergut

The Salzkammergut is one of those "undiscovered" regions so beautiful that guidebooks hesitate to include them. It lies in the heart of Austria, just south of the main railway line between Salzburg and Linz. The area features lakes, low mountains, historic towns, old churches with artistic treasures, and castles dating from medieval times to the eighteenth century.

Lodging and food are inexpensive. Transportation, however, is often a problem as service is infrequent and hitching is poor. From Salzburg or Vienna take the train to Attnang Puchheim where you change to a smaller line that will take you through the little villages (direction Stainach). The train runs through **Gmunden, Ebensee, Bad Ischl, Hallstatt,** and **Obertraun;** there is also a small line that takes you to the **Attersee.**

Gmunden is situated at the northern end of the **Traunsee,** the largest lake of the Salzkammergut. The town also has the largest concentration of tourists, so you might want to stay elsewhere. By the lake, however, it is lovely. The town has been a center of porcelain production for centuries. Check with the **Kurverwaltung** (Information) in the center of town at Am Graben 2 (tel. 4305) about pottery workshops to visit. If you want to stay in Gmunden, try the **Brünner's Home** on Schiffslände. It is run by a friendly and charming woman who will help you find a place if hers is full. The

Kurverwaltung will also find you a room for around 90AS. It is a good walk from the Bahnhof to the center; take the tram instead (8AS).

Ferries leave from Gmunden's pier (the Landungsteg, in the center of town) regularly for rides to Altmunster, Ebensee, and other towns around the lake (50AS round trip). Get off at **Traunkirchen** and see the elaborate gold "fisherman's pulpit" in a church right on the lake. Stop at one of the many lakeside cafés and enjoy the surroundings.

To the south (direction Stainach on the train) **Bad Ischl** offers fashionable sulphur baths, a splendid imperial villa, and a **music festival** in July and August. Continue south towards **Hallstatt,** where you take a small ferry (10AS) over the aqua lake to the tiny village. It is an absolute jewel, surrounded by high mountains, with a tranquil lake and friendly people. This is the place to go for solitude amidst the splendid scenery. You can stay at the IYHF **Youth Hostel** on the main street (30AS a night) or at one of the small pensions overlooking the water (look for a *zimmer frei* sign). There isn't much to do here, but you can visit the salt mines (the oldest ones on earth), see the church, with its gold altarpiece, and the museum, with its collection of prehistoric artifacts. Concerts are often given at lakeside. You can also rent a small boat and explore on your own.

Continue on to **Obertraun** (either by train or ferry) and take the cable car (70AS) up to the **Dachstein ice caves.** Admission is 30AS. The caves here are smaller than the ones near Salzburg, but more beautiful, especially the "ice chapel," which really looks like a carved chapel. From here you can explore more of the region on your own, hiking from town to town. The **Youth Hostel** (IYHF) in Obertraun at Winkl 26 (tel. 4831) is modern and is a good place to spend the night.

Innsbruck

Innsbruck, capital of the Tyrol, is the center of Austria's winter activities. More than 150 cable cars and chairlifts, over 1250 miles of mountain paths, and 250 mountain huts serve as extensions of this city, site of the 1964 and 1976 Winter Olympics. During the summer, patches of snow on the heights, open ski shops and cars with skis in racks, as well as an evening chill in the air, remind the visitor of the city's major occupation.

For all that, a summer visit to Innsbruck will be as cosmopolitan an event as you could wish. Scandinavians, Germans, French, British and Americans pass through the city by the thousands to enjoy a few days in the Tyrol. Despite the numbers, Innsbruck asserts itself. Stroll along the prosperous **Maria-Theresien Strasse,** with its striking view of the **Nordkette** (Northern mountain range). In the **Altstadt,** don't miss the **Goldenes Dachl,** the emblem of Innsbruck, which served as a vantage point for spectators during medieval tournaments, in the square below. The **Dom Zu St. Jakob,** also in the old city, has an altar with Lukas Cranach's *Virgin and Child,* and beautiful *trompe d'oeil* ceilings (they look domed, but they're flat). In the same vein, you might find the **Basilika Wilten,** in the western part of the city, of interest. Considered the most beautiful Rococo church in Tyrol, it contains a well-known statue of the Virgin (fourteenth century).

The natural setting of Innsbruck should get a fair share of your attention. At **Hafelekar,** you can enjoy the panoramas of the **Inn Valley,** the city beneath, and the somber mountain chains of the Tyrolean Alps surrounded by their giant glacial peaks. By cable car go first to **Seegrube,** the midway station (6200ft above sea level, terrace hotel), and then to the mountain station Hafelekar (7300ft), which is only a few minutes from the summit

(7700ft). **Hungerburg** offers another splendid view of the city below. You can walk up by way of **Buchsenhausen Castle** and Weiherburg or take tram #1 to the base of the cog railway.

Orientation

Innsbruck lies in a bend of the **Inn River.** The city is concentrated enough to make any excursion walkable. Public transportation is efficient, though (9AS). You can buy a series of three tickets for 22AS, or five for 33AS.

Train connections are frequent, to Switzerland and France in the west, to Salzburg, Vienna and Italy in the east and south. The **Brenner Autobahn** comes up from the south, just below the city, makes a sharp bend eastward, and becomes the **Inntal Autobahn** to Salzburg. Hitchers headed toward **Italy** should walk out Leopoldstrasse to Brennerstrasse (don't bother to walk as far as the Autobahn entrance). Hitchers headed east can either do the same, or cross the Olympia Brücke (across the railroad tracks just south of the Station) and walk out Burgenlandstrasse and Amraser-See-Strasse (or take streetcar #3, direction Amras, from the stop at the north end of the Station).

Addresses and Telephone Numbers

Verkehrsverein: Burggraben 3, 8am-noon and 2-5:30pm Mon.-Fri., 8am-noon Sat. Closed Sun. Ask about day hikes in the surrounding hills.

Student Travel: Josef-Hirnstrasse 7/2 (tels. 28997 and 05222).

American Express: Brixnerstrasse 3 (tels. 22491 and 27386).

Post Office: Maximilianstrasse, one block down from the Triumphpforte.

Thomas Cook's: Brixnerstrasse 2 (tel. 23789).

Police Emergency: tel. 133. **Headquarters:** Kaiserjägerstrasse 8 (tel. 26721).

Medical Emergency: tel. 144.

Alpine Information (Alpenverein): Wilhelm-Greillstrasse 15 (tel. 23171).

Accommodations

Innsbruck has one of the most helpful student agencies in Austria. Their office at the Train Station gives out youth hostel information and the pamphlet *Innsbruck—for Young People.* If you want a room in a private home, the **Zimmernachweis** will find one for 8AS. The Verkehrsverein books rooms, too. A private room will run 80-120AS per night. Innsbruck has good student accommodations, so you might try one of the hostels first.

Innsbruck Hostel (IYHF), Reichenauerstrasse 147 (tel. 46179). One of the fanciest hostels—electric doors, sunken living room with plants. 69AS includes breakfast, sheets, and strong, hot showers. Opens at 5pm and strict about 10pm curfew. Take Bus R or O to Campingplatz.

St. Pauls, Reichenauerstrasse 72, near Pauluskirche (tel. 44291). Open mid-June through mid-August. Not nearly as classy as the above (on the dismal side, in fact). But it is cheaper, and the management is friendlier and more easygoing. Only 30AS; 15AS for breakfast. Bus R or O.

Jungendherberge "Torsten-Arneus" (IYHF), Rennweg 17b (tel. 25814). On the Inn River. Serves meals at 35AS. Open July and August. Rooms for 35AS. Take Bus C to Handelsakademie. Open at 5pm.

OH-Student Center, Josef-Hirn-Strasse 5 (tels. 237080 and 35184). Open early July through mid-September. Singles 150AS, doubles 130AS per person, with breakfast and free showers. No curfew.

Jugendherberge Sigmund-Kripp-Haus (IYHF), Sillgasse 8a (tel. 31311). Only five minutes from the Station, with pool and ping pong. But the place is dirty and serves as a sort of "Y"—you may hear people running track when you want to sleep. No card required. 35AS.

Pension Paula, Weiherburggasse 15 (tel. 37795). Pretty, chalet-style pension, well-situated, a little way up the mountains that overlook the Innsbrucker Altstadt from across the river; yet close enough to reach the city by a fifteen-minute walk. Tram #1 will take you within easy reach. 120AS singles, 200AS doubles, without breakfast.

Camping: Reichenau, Reichenauerstrasse (tel. 51164), bus R or O; Innsbruck-west, Kranebitten (tel. 34170) Bus LK.

Food

Near the University, try either **Gasthaus Innrain,** or **Gasthaus Gruber.** Both are filled with students and serve good Austrian food at reasonable prices. The former has an outdoor terrace. Meals average 50AS at both places.

The **Mensa** is housed in the **OH-Student Center,** Josef-Hirnstrasse, off Innrain. Breakfast, lunch, and dinner served. Meals will run 20-50AS. The portions are generous, but not very good.

The **St. Nikolaus Kellerei,** on the corner of Innstrasse and St. Nikolaus, is an untouristy wine cellar.

Evenings

During July and August, Innsbruck sponsors musical performances at **Ambraser Schloss,** concerts in the churches, and occasionally, outdoor jazz festivals. Check with the Verkehrsamt on times and prices. Special buses leave from in front of the Station for the concerts at the Schloss. The bus is free, but concert tickets run 50-70AS.

Near Innsbruck

Igls is a small, resort village, right outside of Innsbruck. It is sure to fit your picture of what Austria is "supposed to look like:" picturesque chalets with hand-carved hearts on the shutters. It is also a good base for hikes. Take Bus J from Innsbruck Station (18AS). From the Station take tram #6 (which leaves hourly) to **Schloss Ambras** (11AS). The tram ride is a delight, and passes by forests and numerous hiking trails. The Schloss is the palace of the Archduke Ferdinand, a part-Baroque, part-medieval structure filled with armor and furniture (closed Tues.). Entrance free with student card. The grounds of the castle have waterfalls and woods with many trails to climb.

Undoubtedly one of the most rewarding daytrips from Innsbruck is to the tiny mountain village of **Fulpmes.** You can get here either by train or bus, but take the little red mountain train, which lets you stand outside and look at the scenery. The trip takes about an hour, costs 35AS each way, and is worth it. It passes mountain villages and little wooden huts where hay is stored, with the snow-covered Alps always in view. Take tram #1 to Stubaitalbahn, where the little mountain trains depart. Take hiking boots.

The Vorarlberg

The summertime Alps of the Vorarlberg are storybook Alps: brilliant sunlight, gushing streams, green meadows covered with mountain flowers and bell-clanging, tranquil cattle. This region of Austria stretches east from Liechtenstein and the **Bodensee** (Lake Constance) as far as the **Arlberg Tunnel** and the **Valluga,** at 2811 meters one of the higher peaks in the Austrian Alps.

The **Bregenz Festspiele** (Festival) from mid-July to mid-August offers concerts, ballet, and opera on a floating stage in the middle of the lake—an impressive sight when illuminated at night. Tickets start around 100AS and are available from the Bregenz Festival Booking Office, Kornmarktstrasse 6, (tel. 22458). The town, which is touristy to begin with, gets packed during the festival. The **Information Office,** to the left of the Station, near the lake, will find you a room in a home for about 90AS. You can also try the IYHF **Jugendherberge,** Belruptstrasse 16a (tel. 22867) near the bottom of the Pfanderbahn and a short walk from the Station. Take the **Pfänder Railway** up to the top, where you can see the whole of Lake Constance and the Alpine peaks (48AS round trip). Boats go to Germany (Mainau, Konstanz) and to Switzerland (Rheineck, Rorschach). The **Landesmuseum,** on Kornmarktplatz, has a good collection of medieval primitive art and some fine religious statues. Food prices run high, but the fresh fish from Lake Constance is more reasonably priced.

Bregenz is by no means the best of the Vorarlberg. The train will take you to **Feldkirch,** where you can walk among Gothic balconies and stone towers, sit by the fountains, or take off for dayhikes. There is a wine-tasting festival the second week in July. From the charming old town of **Dornbirn** you can take the road over the mountains to **Schwarzenberg,** whose dark seventeenth-century houses stand in striking contrast to the light church. With a car, you can continue along the Hochtannberg road; the higher you go in the mountains, the more untouched and picturesque the towns become.

South of Bludenz (on the train line to Innsbruck), the **Silvrettastrasse** runs through the lush, fertile Montafon valley. The most beautiful part is beyond the end of the railway line, around **St. Gallenkirch** and **Partenen;** if you don't have a car, try hitching.

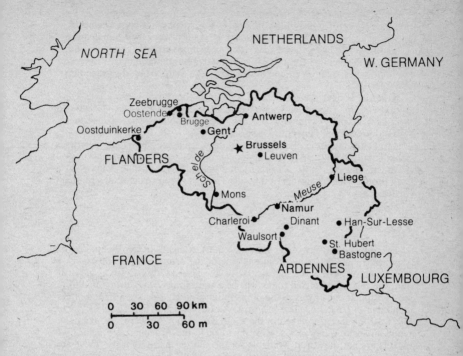

BELGIUM

$1 U.S. = 30 Francs (F)   **1F = $0.033**

Don't hurry Belgium. Its allure is quiet, and its soul takes time to know. Flemish Belgium, in the north and west, has tenaciously preserved the old piety and quaintness, while the less-visited Walloon country to the south and east—except for the Ardennes Mountains—is industrial and relatively no-nonsense. Together, with their blemishes and splendors, they comprise a country rich in confused history, steady ethnic emnity, and superb art.

Brussels, the capital and center of Europe's Common Market, is a modern, somewhat bland city, except for a few stunning monuments of its past. **Antwerp,** Belgium's second city, combines the toughness of docks and diamonds with the art of its excellent museums. **Liège** is unexpectedly gracious—the most lightheartedly French city in the country. And **Brugge** and **Ghent** make up the Flemish heartland, the former an intact medieval city full of Gothic churches, guild houses, and winding canals.

The Flemish coast is like a more modest and slightly chillier version of the Riviera. The Belgians claim over forty miles of beaches and provide good campgrounds and accommodations, sometimes quite reasonably, in little rooms over cafés. **Oostende** is the Nice of this coast—a large center, with casino and yacht harbor. **Nieuwpoort** is a historical town turned resort. **Oostduinkerke** offers peace and a large beach. **Westende** claims to be the "pearl of the Belgian coast," while **Zeebrugge** is a quiet family resort with an important fishing fleet, and the advantage of being near the attractions of Brugge.

The low-budget traveler who is willing to rough it might well seek out rural Belgium. The **Ardennes,** in the Walloon country, offer lush forests and excellent hiking, swimming and camping, as well as spectacular underground grottoes at **Han-Sur-Lesse.**

From time to time, Belgium's language squabbles upset the country's usual amity. Southern Walloons speak French while Northerners speak Flemish, and it is only in Brussels that both sides peaceably coexist. You will probably be better received by the Flemish if you speak English instead of French.

PRACTICAL INFORMATION

Belgium's train network is one of the most extensive in Europe and one of the most reliable. Getting from one side of the country to the other takes a maximum of three and a half hours. If you have a railpass, this is great. If not, the prices of Belgian trains will be a rude surprise. One way of cutting costs is to use one city as a base of operations for daytrips: each station offers a number of *Un beau jour à* . . . trips. An *Un beau jour* ticket entitles you to 50% off the fare if you return the same day. From Antwerp, for example, you can spend a day at a seaside resort or in the Ardennes. *Un beau jour* tickets are not, however, available for the shorter inter-city trips. There are also passes for the national train system, available at any station. They cost 850F for five days, 1180F for ten days, and 1520F for fifteen days. At these prices you'd have to do laps around Belgium to get your money's worth.

For international trips, student travel offices sell **Transalpino/BIGE** tickets, which give anyone under 26 a discount of 20-50% off the regular train fare to foreign cities, with a few exceptions. A BIGE ticket to London from anywhere in Belgium costs 690F, so you don't have to wait for Oostende to get it. You can rent a one-speed bike at any of 22 stations (in Brussels go to the suburban Groenendaal Station) and drop it off at any of one hundred (125F per day, 100F per day for three or more days). If you show a Belgian train ticket or railpass, you get a discount: 95F per day, or 80F per day for three days or more. Hitching in Belgium is mediocre—at least inter-city distances are short.

Youth information offices called **Infor-Jeunes** (in Flemish, **Info-Jeugd**) are found in most of the larger towns. Services vary from town to town, but you'll almost always find friendly people to help with medical or legal problems, work or study in Belgium, and short- or long-term accommodations.

Hotels in Belgium are expensive, with the rock-bottom price about $8 for a single with breakfast, doubles slightly less than twice that. The country's Youth Hostels are spread out and generally in good condition. The managers are usually strict about IYHF cards. Also look for unofficial hostels and student hotels. There are some in every large city (eight in Brussels!) and their atmosphere and regulations are often preferable to that of the IYHF Hostels. In all hotels, pensions, and hostels, unwed couples over 21 will encounter little trouble getting a room together, but if you are younger, don't argue if hotel managers refuse to let you share a room. The strict Belgian laws can imprison them for three years if caught.

Belgian cuisine has pretty much surrendered to the cooking of its French neighbors to the south. You should still try to seek out these regional specialties: *carbonnades flamandes* (beef stewed in beer), *boudins Liège* (sausage), *waterzooi* (chicken and vegetables stewed in a mustard sauce), and chocolate truffles. Eels, mussels, rabbit, and pigeon are cooked in dozens of ways. Don't be afraid of *filet Américain,* which is raw ground meat, often served on toast.

If the national cuisine leaves you unimpressed, you should at least respect the Belgian claim to being neck to neck, or rather belly to belly, with the Germans as far as per capita beer guzzling goes. There is a saloon on nearly every city block, and the average one serves 30-45 different types of beer. *Guvel* is the strongest.

All banks, by mutual agreement, take a fat 89F commission on every travelers check when you change money. Usually, the only way to get around this is to go to the local train station, where a change office keeps long hours and doesn't take a commission. But you should only use them for changing small amounts, since their rates are about 10% lower than the official rate. The best place to convert your dollars are the American Express offices in Brussels and Antwerp where you get the highest rate and avoid all commissions.

Brussels (Bruxelles)

It's difficult to believe that Brussels is an important center of world trade and politics, much less a several-centuries-old capital. You expect a Common Market capital to have something going for it—important museums or an exciting nightlife, if not beauty and charm. Not Brussels. Aside from the magnificent **Grand'Place** and one or two museums, Belgium's capital offers little except waffles, precious lace doilies, and the prospect of eating mussels 37 different ways. What is there to say about a town whose trademark, the **Mannekin-Pis,** is a statue of a small boy urinating?

Orientation

The center of Brussels is a compact area which can easily be seen on foot, but most accommodations lie in the outer sections of the city and are best reached by using the excellent tram, metro, and bus system. A free map of the public transportation network is available at the Tourist Office and at information desks in some of the stations. Service stops around midnight.

Brussels has three train stations. The **Gare du Nord** is near many hostels, but has no orientation services; you can get a city map at **American Express,** three blocks away. The **Gare Centrale** is indeed central—near the Grand'Place and Tourist Office—but there are no inexpensive accommodations in the area. The **Gare du Midi** houses the most helpful information bureau (see below), and there are some hostels and cheap hotels in the neighborhood.

The city revolves around the Grand'Place and the nearby **Place de la Bourse.** Between them and the boulevard du Jardin Botanique lie the major department stores; while the **Place Rogier,** the Gare du Nord, the red light district and some major construction work lie just north of the boulevard. In the opposite direction and further out from the Grand'Place are the elegant **Porte Louise** section (to the south) and the older, less expensive **Gare du Midi** student quarter (to the southwest). All public transportation costs 20F, but transfers are free if you request a *transit* when you buy your ticket. For

100F, you can buy a two-day pass; a ticket good for five trips costs 75F.

Hitchhikers for Luxembourg should take the subway #1 to the end. Tram #92 stops near the road to Antwerp and Amsterdam; the Diamant Station on the tram #90 route is near the Liège-Germany road. For Oostende, take bus #62 or 85.

Infor-J sells for 20F an excellent off-beat guide to Brussels called *See Brussels and Die (Laughing)*. In addition to a map and a list of hostels and cheap restaurants, it describes several interesting, untouristy things to do in town. We highly recommend this booklet, which can be purchased at the Gare du Midi and at many hostels.

Addresses and Telephone Numbers

Tourist Office: rue Marché aux Herbes 61 (tel. 513 90 90), near the Grand-'Place. Information on the city, the province, and the country. Open daily 9am-7pm, summer weekdays until 9pm.

Welcome to Brussels—Centre d'Acceuil: Gare du Midi (tel. 522 58 66). A very friendly information center, staffed by young volunteers. Open *en principe* 9am-10pm daily, shorter hours on Sundays. Will reserve you a hotel room, direct you to a hostel, and supply you with city and transit maps, all without charge. If the office is closed, look for the information vending machines in the Station.

Infor-J: rue Marché aux Herbes 27 (tel. 512 32 74), near the Grand'Place. Open Mon.-Sat. 10am-7pm. A friendly, student-run organization that helps with rooms, jobs, legal problems, etc., all for free.

Acotra: rue de la Montagne 38 (tel. 512 55 40) is another youth organization that has a free room-finding service. Open in summer Mon.-Fri. 9am-6pm. Desk at the Airport open daily 7am-10pm all year. They also sell reduced-price train tickets to foreign destinations as well as student/youth plane tickets.

TEJ Belgian Student Travel Office: rue de la Sablonnière 20 (tel. 219 02 43), affiliated with CIEE. Charter flights to everywhere, package tours for students, BIGE train tickets. Open Mon.-Fri. 9am-6pm, Sat. 10am-4pm. Affiliated with nearby C.H.A.B. which offers 15% off the guided tours of Brussels. The C.H.A.B. Hostel sells BIGE tickets until 1am and on weekends, but phone ahead.

American Express: Place Rogier 24 (tel. 219 01 90), near the Gare du Nord. Open weekdays 9am-5pm, Sat. 9am-noon. No mail pick-up noon-2pm.

Central Post Office: in the tall building at Place de la Monnaie. Open Mon.-Sat. 9am-10pm.

Police Emergency: tel. 906.

Red Cross Emergency: tel. 900.

SOS-Jeunes: rue de la Blanchisserie 27 (tel. 736 36 36). Psychological help, friendly assistance for any kind of crisis. 24-hour telephone service.

U.S. Embassy: blvd. du Régent 27 (tel. 513 38 30).

Canadian Embassy: rue de Loxum 6 (tel. 513 79 40).

Accommodations

Reservations are recommended, especially for summer weekends, but the **Centre d'Accueil** or **Acotra** will always find somewhere for you to sleep. Hotels are invariably expensive. Cheaper are all of the city's eleven Youth Hostels and student hotels. Most have single and double rooms in addition to dormitories. All hostel prices include breakfast.

Sleep-Well, rue de la Blanchisserie 27 (tel. 218 13 13), the most centrally located of the hostels (a block from Place Rogier), the friendliest, and one of the cheapest. Could be cleaner, though. Dorm beds 100F for men (available in summer only), 120F for women (in a smaller room). Nice doubles 150F (bunk beds), singles 220F. All prices without sheets. Showers free, meager breakfasts. Pleasant bar downstairs serves forty different natural beers.

Youth Hostel (IYHF), rue Verte 124 (tel. 217 45 59). Only two blocks from the Gare du Nord. Dorm beds 130F. Dirty and overcrowded; but a young, relaxed manager is trying to turn the place around. Mediocre breakfast. IYHF card required. Closes at 11:45pm.

Youth Hostel (IYHF), rue de la Poste 91 (tel. 217 86 55) is clean, but the neighborhood isn't very nice. 120F to sleep in 10- to 20-bed dorms; good breakfast. IYHF card required. Strict management, rooms closed 9am-5pm, 11:45pm curfew. Ten minutes from the Gare du Nord. No atmosphere.

C.H.A.B., rue Traversière 6 (tel. 219 47 50). One of the nicest hostels but slightly expensive. Singles 350F, doubles 500F, triples and quads 220F per person, dormitory 140F. Free showers, sheets included, except in dorm rooms. 1am curfew. There's a student travel bureau in the reception office. Ten minutes by foot from the Gare du Nord.

Hôtel des Jeunes, rue des Etudiants 14 (tel. 539 07 25), has a large number of singles (240F for IYHF members, 290F for nonmembers) and 2- to 4-bed rooms (200F per person, 250F for nonmembers). Sheets and showers included; closes at midnight.

Centre International des Etudiants, 26 rue de Parme (tel. 537 89 61). A fifteen-minute walk from the Gare du Midi, uphill on a quiet street. Singles and doubles 200F per person, just 120F per person per day if you stay six days or more. Dorm for men with 8 beds, 150F, just 100F per day for six days or more (available in summer only). Sheets and showers included. Rooms are clean, open 24 hours.

HOTELS

Résidence Berckmans, 12 rue Berckmans (tel. 537 89 48). Singles 280-420F, mansard 140F, mansard double 250F. Other doubles 420-560F, triples 620-750F. Showers 35F.

Le Rosario, 4 blvd. du Jardin Botanique (tel. 218 17 99). A small hotel with large, nicely furnished rooms. Singles 400F, doubles 500F, baths a whopping 60F extra. Breakfast not included, but owners run a restaurant downstairs where you can get a hearty breakfast for 60F.

Food

Chez Léon, 18 rue des Bouchers, is a well-known Brussels mussels emporium. In the heart of the *bistro* district, but with a bustling, open atmosphere that is a welcome contrast to the strained intimacy of the surrounding restaurants. 90F for a plate of *moules parquées* (raw), 165F for a big bowl (and a refill) of *moules marinières* and chips.

L'école Buissoniere, 13 rue Traversière, is a recently-opened restaurant run on a non-profit basis by C.H.A.B., the same group that runs the nearby Hostel. *Plat du jour 130F, menu du jour* 160F includes soup and dessert. Open only weekdays 11:30am-2pm and 6-10pm.

Brussels Snack, rue de la Colline 2, is the cheapest place in the Grand'Place area to get a sandwich: 30-40F. Platters also available 70-90F. Eat in or take out.

La Grande Porte, 9 rue Notre Seigneur. A very pleasant atmosphere; classical music played. Open Tues.-Thurs. 6pm-2am, Fri.-Sat. 6pm-4am, closed Mon. Big, steaming bowl of onion soup 75F, omelettes 100-140F, meat dishes 200-250F.

Le Breton, 59 rue des Drapiers (near Place Louise). *Menu du jour* at 140F, *service* included. In a modest setting, but with a lively, youthful ambiance. Open weekdays noon-2pm and 6-9:30pm., Sat. 12:30-2:30pm and 7-9:30pm.

The cheapest place in town to get a prepared meal is at the University campus. The cafeteria of the **Faculté de Médecine de l'Université de Bruxelles,** 2 rue Evers serves lunch all year round. The rest of the University is out in the suburbs, a 20 minute train ride on #32 or 94. The **Restaurant Universitaire** ave. Paul Heger 22, serves lunch and dinner. A good place to meet Belgian students. Check with the *Centre d' Accueil* about hours and prices.

Sights

"The most beautiful square in the world," wrote Victor Hugo—not without justification—of the **Grand'Place.** This magnificent collection of guildhalls and public buildings teems with visitors day and night, and is perhaps the only "must" on any tourist's visit to Brussels. With its flower market in the morning and its illuminated buildings after dark, it is the *sine qua non* of the city.

Brussels does boast some fine museums, including the **Musée d'Art Ancien,** 3 rue de la Régence; it has a huge collection of early Flemish masters as well as many Rubens and Breughels. (Open 10am-5pm daily except Mondays; admission 5F.) Next door, the new **Musée d'Art Moderne** is still under construction, but check out the temporary exhibits in the old building.

If you've never seen a flea market with real junk before, spend a morning wading through the piles of it in the **Place du Jeu de Balle.** This square is in the **Marolles,** a lower-class area of narrow streets and old houses. This district may be the last hold-out of old Brussels. If you are intent on absorbing every drop of life in this city take an off-the-beaten-track tour called *The Alternative Brussels* (in French only). Contact **Aran Agency** (tel. 219 07 99); 200F, 150F if you're under 25. **St. Michael's Cathedral** is the city's most impressive Gothic edifice. The **Royal Arms Museum of Porte de Hal** features a large collection of arms from the Middle Ages to the eighteenth century. If that whets your appetite for blood, take the #5 bus to **Waterloo,** the celebrated battlefield.

Evenings

The Grand'Place with its adjacent streets is the center of the city's nightlife. Except for this area, and a few isolated pockets of resistance, Brussels is dead by 9pm. There are several movie theaters near Place Louise. A few blocks away, the **Styx,** a twin-cinema at 72 rue de L'Arbre Benit (tel. 512 21 02) features revival films in the evening and off-beat fare every midnight. The real temple of celluloid in Brussels, however, is the **Musée du Cinéma,** at rue Baron Horta (tel. 513 41 55), which features three film classics daily (mostly real oldies) for 30F each in addition to a permanent display on film history. Open every day 5-11 pm; first showing at 6:15pm. The famous marionette theater **Chez Toone,** on the petite rue des Bouchers (tel. 511 71 37) performs classical drama in French with a Bruxellian accent and humor. Shows at 8:30pm daily except Sundays. Seats 125F and up, but it pays to reserve in advance. Warning: you must speak French to follow the plot, and be a Bruxellian to get all the jokes.

Antwerp (Flemish: Antwerpen, French: Anvers)

Antwerp is at once Belgium's most workaday city and its most unworldly. Its appeal comes from the truly bizarre agglomeration of styles you find here: there's the no-nonsense part of town, the office buildings that house the diamond and shipping companies that have provided the city's wealth for the past four centuries; then there's the art and culture all that wealth has bought. Antwerp's favorite son, Pieter Paul Rubens, ambassador as well as artist, is well represented in the excellent local museums, as are most of the other Flemish Old Masters. The architecture of the older parts of the city is predominantly Renaissance and Baroque, and even the younger buildings of Antwerp, though decidedly urban and functional, are more decorous than those in other Belgian cities.

Orientation

There are two train stations in Antwerp: **Berchem** and **Central Station.** International trains stop only at Berchem: otherwise get off at Central. The helpful **Information Pavilion** directly in front of it (open weekdays 8:30am-8pm, Sat. 10am-8pm, Sun. 9am-5pm) will supply you with brochures and a map (5F, but indispensable), and will help you find a room (no service charge). You can buy two pamphlets here detailing excellent self-guided walking tours of the old city, which will lead you to places you may have otherwise missed. Watch out for Mondays, when three-fourths of Antwerp's museums are closed.

The old part of town, where most of the sights are concentrated, is a twenty-minute walk toward the **Schelde River** (or take a tram to Melkmarkt or Groenplaats). Just to the north, near the beginning of the immense port, is the quarter of drunken sailors, tattoo parlors, and Mediterranean immigrants.

All hitchers except those heading to Brussels or points south, should take bus #20 from the Train Station to the big interchange outside of town. Have a sign with your destination on it: traffic to Holland, Germany, and Ghent passes by here. For Brussels, take tram #2 to the intersection of Jan Devoslei and Jan Van Rijswijklaan. The autoroute south starts here.

Trams and buses cost 16F, 19F with transfer; pick up the rather confusing transport map at the Information Pavilion. A seven-ride ticket costs 66F if you buy it in the Train Station, otherwise 85F. The Information Pavilion sells a tourist card for unlimited tram and bus travel for two days (80F).

Addresses and Telephone Numbers

City Tourist Office: Suikerrui 19 (tel. 32 01 03). Open weekdays 8:30am-6pm, Sat. 10am-6pm, Sun. 9am-5pm. Same services as the Information Pavilion.

Student Travel Office: JEST, Pieter Van Hobokenstraat 20. General and travel information.

American Express: Meir 87 (tel. 32 59 20).

Police: Emergency tel. 906, headquarters, Oudaan 5 (tel. 31 68 80).

Medical Aid: ambulance, 24 hours, tel. 900. Clinic at St. Elizabeth Hospital (tel. 31 48 80).

U.S. Consulate: Frankrijklei 64-68 (tel. 32 18 00).

Laundromat: Geuzenstraat 24 (near the International Youth and Student Home).

Public Bathhouse: on Zakstraat (tel. 32 20 53). Shower 5F, bath 10F.

Accommodations

Beware of the cafés around the Train Station that advertise "rooms for tourists": there are rooms, but they are for the local prostitutes. Antwerp is not on every tourist's itinerary so you can usually find a room at one of the student hotels or hostels.

International Youth and Student Home, Volkstraat 58 (tel. 38 47 82), half a block from the Royal Gallery of Fine Arts. Once a rambling bourgeois townhouse, now has rooms with 6-8 beds and one large dormitory. The multilingual father-son management is very helpful. If you are down and out, they'll let you stay free for two hours work but you must be really broke, not just hoping to save money. 145F with breakfast, 25F for sheets. Some doubles for 300F. Showers 25F. No curfew. Substantial midday (125F) and evening (100F) meals are served if you order them the day before. Tram #12 or 24, or bus #23 from the Station. An affiliated hostel at Bolivarplaats 1 (tel. 37 59 27) has doubles for 375F, if the main hostel is full; showers included but not breakfast.

Youth Hostel "Opsinjoorke" (IYHF), Eric Sasselaan St. (tel. 38 02 73). At 120F per night with shower and breakfast, it's cheaper than the IY&SH above, but has the drawbacks of a poor location (20 minutes from downtown on the #27 bus or #2 tram), an 11pm curfew, and a less relaxed atmosphere. Very good dinner served, though, for 90F; and the clean, modern building is located near the excellent Wezenberg indoor swimming pool.

Florida, De Keyserlei 59 (tel. 32 14 43), right in front of Central Station. Rooms are clean and spacious. Singles 450F, doubles 580F, triples 850F. Showers and an American breakfast are included.

Miro, Pelikaanstraat 34 (tel. 33 11 22), also directly across from Central Station. 345F for a single, 455F for a one-bed double. Rooms are large and clean; all have sinks. Continental breakfast included; shower 40F extra.

Residence Rubens, Amerikalei 115 (tel. 38 30 31). With its ornate Baroque marble and ersatz gold-leaf lobby, you might think that the master himself had done the interior decoration. Large, clean, almost luxurious doubles for 450F; smaller, more modest singles cost 270F. Showers 5F extra; 75F for a substantial breakfast. Good value. Take tram #12 or 24 from the Station.

Camping, Jan Van Rijswijklaan St. (tel. 38 57 17). 20F per person, 20F per tent. Hot showers on the grounds. Near the IYHF Youth Hostel; follow same directions. Unbeatable price, but inconvenient location.

Food

The area around the Central Station is full of restaurants, snack bars, sandwich shops, and *friteries*. To save money, picnic on the benches in Groenplaats; stock up on cold cuts and salads at **Klein Beenhouwerke,** Hoogstraat 53 (closed most of July); on cooked or pickled fish at the shop on Hoogstraat near Suikerrui; or on kosher deli fare at **Fruchter's** near Central Station at Simonstraat 10 (closed in August). If you want to get bar mitzvahed or married in Antwerp, they'll cater the reception for you.

University restaurant: the only one open in the summer is in Middleheim, way outside town. You can get there on bus #32, but unless you're going to see the open air sculpture exhibit there it's too far out of the way. During the school year the restaurant in **St. Ignatius' University,** Prinsstraat, is open for three meals a day.

Lien, Kammenstraat 64, is a small and sober but very nice Indonesian restaurant run by a middle-aged Indonesian couple. You can make a filling meal out of the *rijsttafel*—which includes meat and vegetables (120F), or the delicious chicken soup (100F) with rice (20F, and you get all you want if you're a student). Service included in prices, and students get free tea with their meals. Open daily except Wednesday 11am-2pm, and every day 5-10pm.

Brabo, Korte Winkelstraat 4, has a steak-*frites*-salad dinner for 155F (less with a student card). Omelettes 65-85F. Open 11am-11pm, closed Sun.

Viskeuken, at the corner of Melkmarkt and Koepoortstraat, is the cheapest place to get a good seafood meal. Fish is expensive, so you won't get out for under 240F, but the dishes are fresh and carefully prepared, and if you sit at the counter the service is free. Grilled sardines 160F, various cold seafood salads 100-150F, *anguilles au vert* (eels) 320F. Highly recommended for a modest splurge. Wine served.

Sights

There is more to see and do in Antwerp than in any other Belgian city. It will take at least three days to explore the streets of the old town and to visit those of the city's 21 museums that are worth seeing, with the evenings devoted to relaxing in the inviting bars or in the crowded discotheques. A good starting point for your sightseeing is **Our Lady's Cathedral,** a spectacular, airy Gothic structure (the largest in Belgium), built between the fourteenth and sixteenth centuries. There are three famous Rubens paintings inside (10F admission). To get to the Church just look for its tower—it's 123 meters high. The nearby **Grote Markt** is bordered by restored guild houses; the **Brabo Fountain** in the center is one of the few you'll see in Europe without a catch-basin underneath. Down by the river is the **Castle Steen,** a beautiful story-book fortress first used in the tenth century that is now a maritime museum, open 10am-5pm daily, free. **Saint Charles Borromeo's Church,** on Hendrik Conscienceplein, is Antwerp's most impressive Baroque edifice. Rubens had a hand in the design of the façade.

The museums in Antwerp would be an attraction even if an art thief cleaned them out; museum curators from all over the world should be forced to come here to learn how to display their wares. The **Royal Gallery of Fine Arts** (Leopold de Waelplaats, open 10am-5pm daily except closed Monday; admission free) has a great collection of Flemish Old Masters, displayed in large, naturally-lit rooms, and the collection of modern Belgian art downstairs is worth seeing as well. **Rubens House,** Wapper 9-11, is proof that not all artists starve—Rubens lived and worked for thirty years in this sumptuous house, now a repository for many of his paintings and other memorabilia. The **Plantin-Moretus Museum,** Vrijdagmarkt 22, has various gadgets from the infancy of printing trade, as well as early manuscripts and books produced in the area and, sure enough, more paintings by Rubens. The restoration of the house of Rubens' friend **Nicolaas Rockox** at Keizerstraat 10, has recently been completed. The layout of this house museum is one of the most tasteful anywhere. The Baroque paintings are plentiful—but more unique is the collection of antique furniture and tapestries.

If you have Rubens, the Renaissance, and the Baroque coming out of your ears, visit the open-air museum of modern sculpture at **Middleheim,** an estate about half an hour from the city. Open 10am-dusk. Free except during the special biennial exhibitions held during odd-numbered years, when admission is 25F per person, 15F under 25. Bus #17, 26, 27 or 32 from Central Station or the #7 tram from Groenplaats.

A site which few tourists know about but which is not to be missed, is **Cogels Osylei**, a wide avenue in the southeastern part of Antwerp which is an uninterrupted procession of Art Nouveau mansions, each one outdoing the one before it in architectural fantasy. There are a few more dazzlers on the adjacent streets, especially **Transvaalstraat** (don't miss #59). The #11 tram from Nieuwstraat at Melkmarkt will let you off at the beginning of Cogels Osylei. Highest recommendation.

Evenings

As in Brussels, most of the nightlife in Antwerp is in the vicinity of the old town square, the **Grote Markt.** Most of the youth hangouts are between the Square and Saint Charles Borromeo's Church. Try a bar called **De Muze** on Melkmarkt at Nieuwstraat. A little further away, at Keizerstraat 38 is the **King Kong Café,** run by a student club; it offers movies and other activities during the school year. There is a three-day **music festival** here in mid-August (student tickets 120F). The **Ciné Monty** (tel. 38 29 41), at Montignystraat 3-5, is a revival moviehouse with several different double features each week. The streets near the Central Train Station are also lively (plenty of cinemas), if somewhat greasy, but nothing should be sniffed at after the nightlife famine in Brussels.

Ghent (Flemish: Gent, French: Gand)

Ghent is a largest city which, if it lacks the well-defined character and unity of Brugge, is still well worth a visit. Like its sister city, Ghent's appeal lies in its old buildings, winding canals, and art treasures. It's a long walk from St. Pieters Station to the center, so it's best to take tram #4 to the Koornmarkt. Here, you are near all sights in the old city. On the Koornmarkt is the thirteenth century **St. Niklaaskerk.** Behind the square, on the canal, you'll find the **Graslei,** lined with guild houses from the fifteenth to seventeenth centuries. The anomalous building among them is a twelfth-century warehouse. Crossing a canal north of Koornmarkt, you come to the forbidding **Castle of the Counts of Flanders.** This grim fortress, restored extensively in the last century, is the kind of place where you can imagine evil barons throwing miserable peasants into the dungeons (of which there are several). There is also a grisly collection of instruments of torture and execution from the eighteenth and nineteenth centuries, when the castle served as a prison. Open 9am-5:15pm, 10F.

Taking the Limburgstraat from the Koornmarkt, you pass the handsome medieval **cloth hall** and **Belfry.** Take a detour to see the **Botermarkt,** with the Gothic and Renaissance **Stadhuis** (Town Hall), and return to **St. Baafs Kathedral,** a fine edifice dating from the fourteenth to sixteenth centuries. It houses the famous Van Eyck painting of *The Adoration of the Mystic Lamb* and Rubens' *St. Bavo's Entry into the Monastery.* The splendid Baroque interior decorations will remind you that Belgium was once an Austrian province. The *Mystic Lamb* is on view Mon.-Sat. 9:30am-noon and 2-6pm, Sun. 1-6pm; admission 15F. Also worth a visit are the **Museum Voor Schone Kunsten** and the **Museum van Oudheden.** The former (open every day 9am-noon and 2-5pm, entry free), located in the Citadel park, has a good Flemish collection and an outstanding exhibit of modern works by Belgian artists. The latter (open 10am-noon and 1:30-4:30pm every day, free), occupies the **Van de Bijloke Abbey,** and has a fine collection of local social history, and beautiful rooms from monasteries and guild halls. If you have time, there are several other museums, churches, castles, and abbeys in town. The Tourist Office has a good brochure available free.

Orientation and Accommodations

If you're coming by train from Antwerp for a day visit and have no luggage to store, you can get off at **Dampoort Station,** a fifteen-minute walk from the center. Otherwise continue to **St. Pieters Station** (the only stop for all other trains). The **Tourist Office,** across the square from the Station, at Koningen Maria-Hendrikan Plein 27 (tel. 22 16 37), will supply free of charge a city map, walking tour brochure, and a list of hotels and restaurants (including prices); it's open weekdays only 8:30am-noon and 1:30-5:30 pm. The downtown office at Borluulstraat 9 (tel. 25 36 41) provides the same services and is open 9am-noon and 2-7pm, Sunday 9am-noon. Tram and bus tickets cost 15F (16F with transfer); if you'll be taking more than three rides you should buy a six-ride ticket (50F in the Train Station, 65F on the tram). Routes are marked on a city map. For help with hassles or student- and youth-oriented information, contact the **Foreign Student Service** at St. Pietersniewstraat 45 (tel. 23 55 82), or **Info-Jeugd** at Geldmunt 24 (tel. 25 24 23); both are open weekdays only.

There are several small pensions along **Prins. Clementinalaan** near St. Pieters Station. The **Azalea,** #147 (tel. 22 50 67), is the cheapest and has a friendly manager; the rooms are clean if unaesthetic. 275F for a single, 220F per person for 2- to 4-bed rooms, breakfast included. Bath 30F. **Lanterne,** #118 (tel. 22 39 96) has large, comfortable, very nice doubles (one bed) for 420F; breakfast 70F, showers 30F.

Between July 15 and September 15 there are over a thousand modern singles at the **University of Ghent** that are available to tourists; bed-and-breakfast 300F, 250F for students and young people (the line is imprecisely drawn). Free showers and use of very nice kitchen. Try first the **Home Vermeylen** (tel. 22 09 11), which has over 400 rooms; located off Overpoortstraat at Stalhofstraat 6. Bus #9 from the Train Station.

> **Youth Hostel "De Draeke"** (IYHF), St. Pietersplein 12 (tel. 22 50 67) is strikingly situated in the abbey of a Baroque church. Unfortunately, the discipline of the clerics who used to reside here lives on in the hotel: 11pm curfew, ice-cold showers, and strict eviction time in the morning. The uptight little *aubergiste* who runs things here is right out of a Balzac novel. There's always space though (200 beds), and it's the cheapest place in town: 120F for bed-and-breakfast. 45F extra for sheets. IYHF card required. Dinner costs 90F. Half way between the Train Station and the center. Take the #9 bus.

> **Café du Progrès,** (tel. 25 17 16) is right in the middle of things at Koornmarkt 9. 15 rooms: 275F for a single, 350-400F for a double, without breakfast. Watch out, though: the manager does not like Americans.

Food and Evenings

The cheapest place to eat is the modern **university restaurant** on Overpoortstraat near Citadellaan. In the summer it is only open for weekday lunches; a full meal costs 70F. During the school year there is another **university restaurant** at St. Pieters Niewstraat 45. **De Paddestol** at Guinardstraat 9 is a simple, macrobiotic restaurant where a full meal costs 80-100F. Open daily except Sunday 11:30am-2pm. Mon.-Thurs. also open 6-7:30pm; open for lunch only from mid-July to mid-August. Guinardstraat (not marked on most maps) runs south from Bagattenstraat, not far from the Youth Hostel. There is an excellent seafood delicatessen on the square next to the Castle of the Counts. You can buy bread at a bakery across the street and picnic a few blocks away on Koornlei, across the street from the guild houses on Granslei.

Nightlife is better during the off-season when Ghent University, the second largest in the country, is in session. Try the cafés and discos near the university restaurant on Overpoortstraat. **Info-Jeugd,** a youth organization, runs a pleasant café at Geldmunt 24 (open every day 10am-1am, but may close on weekends and earlier on weekdays in summer). Every year in August and September, the **Flanders Festival** brings important orchestras and performers to Ghent and other Flemish cities. Information at the Tourist Office.

Brugge (French: Bruges)

You will find something of the old Flanders of burghers and Breughels in Brugge. In the Middle Ages, Brugge and its cousin town of Ghent were the heart of Flemish industry, piety and wealth; and Brugge has changed relatively little since its commercial heyday. A leisurely two-day visit will allow the city to surround you with mementos of its glory: tinted glass windows, Van Eyck faces and medieval turrets. Buy flowers, listen to the carillon and the clock towers, and discover swans in the backyards of old houses of flax merchants.

From the Train Station, either walk or take any local bus to the **Markt,** the heart of old Brugge. The **Tourist Office** here (open 9am-8pm weekdays; 9:30am-12:30pm and 2-8pm on Saturdays and Sundays) has free maps, a reduced-price pass to the city's four major museums for 60F, and a currency exchange office that is open on Saturday afternoons and Sundays (same hours as the Tourist Office).

A climb up the tower of the **Belfry** next door (10F), built in the thirteenth to fifteenth centuries, will give you an uninterrupted view of what is perhaps the purest medieval town in Northern Europe. Starting from its right side, the square you see just a block away is the **Burg;** the first building is the **Basilica of the Holy Blood,** whose relic is still actively venerated. Next door, the **Town Hall,** one of the oldest Gothic civic buildings in the low countries (1376) sports a vigorous façade and fine Gothic hall, with its sumptuous carved roof. To the left, the **Palace of Justice** contains a fantastically ornate chimney piece dedicated to Charles V (admission 5F).

Two of Brugge's best museums are right next to each other on the Dyver: the **Groeninge** (open 9:30am-noon and 2-6pm; closed Tuesdays in the winter) and the **Gruuthuse,** with the same hours. The former (20F) contains three Van Eycks, including the *Virgin of the Canon Van der Paele.* The latter (20F), housed in a fifteenth century mansion, is devoted to applied arts, including weapons and musical instruments. The **Church of Our Lady** is joined to the Gruuthuse by a chapel. Inside this church, which was begun in the thirteenth century, there is a *Madonna and Child* by Michelangelo that puts all the sculpture near it to shame. Crossing Katelijnestraat you come to

Brugge's other great museum, the **Memling** (20F), containing several paintings by the city's favorite son, Hans Memling (1435-1493). The building itself was built as a hospital in the thirteenth century and part of the building still serves as a medical clinic.

On weekend afternoons, the canal bank in front of the museums becomes a crowded flea market. For lace, go to the **Kantcentrum** on Balstraat, a lace workshop with an impressive exhibit of the craft; open 2-6pm, Wed. and Sat. 2-4pm, Sunday closed; admission 10F. Around the **Walplaats** you can see women (some of them in their eighties) making lace by hand, and of course, numerous shops where you can buy their wares.

As in Venice, pollution once made a mixed blessing of the canals of Brugge. They have been pretty much cleaned up now, and a restful half-hour boat ride (65F) will afford you another perspective on the delightful town.

Brussels-bound thumbers should take bus #5 or 7 to St. Michael, or pick up the highway behind the Railroad Station.

Bike Rentals: at the Train Station (tel. 33 24 06) or in town, at the **Cactus Café** (tel. 33 20 14), St. Amandstraat 13. The Cactus charges 60F for four hours, 90F for one day, 80F per day for longer periods.

Laundromat: Belfort, Ezelstraat 51, next to the Snuffel Sleep-In.

Swimming: Take the train to the beach at Zeebrugge (14 km). Indoor pool: **Zwembad Jan Guilini,** Lauwerstraat 15 (tel. 31 35 54). Take bus #3. Open daily 7am-1pm and 3-7pm except Sunday. 30F admission.

Accommodations

Snuffel Sleep-In, Ezelstraat 49 (tel. 33 31 33). The reputation of this recently opened hostel has spread quickly. Cheap (120F including breakfast but not sheets), centrally located, 2am curfew, and a very friendly atmosphere. A nice bar with delicious spaghetti (80F) and a great selection of classical and jazz music. No hostel card required. Showers are free. There should be a sleep-in like this in every European city. Come early, since there are only 38 beds. Rooms are cramped, though, and there could be more toilets and showers. Open all year.

Europa-Jeugdherberg (IYHF), Baron Ruzettlelaan 143 (tel. 35 26 79). A decent hostel, but once again on the edge of town and with an 11pm curfew. 120F for bed and good breakfast; sheets are 45F extra for the first night. It's large (208 beds) and rarely full. Free showers. IYHF card required. Take the #2 bus to Steenbrugge. Closed 10am-5pm and most of October and November.

Achiel Van Acker, Barrierestraat 11, St. Michaels (tel. 31 35 83). A large suburban house about five minutes behind the Train Station with doubles, triples, and multibedded rooms. For the night: 195F per person for bed-and-breakfast, 155F thereafter. Showers 20F; 11pm curfew (midnight on weekends). Pleasant and quiet. Open all year.

Spermalie, Snaggaardstraat 11 (tel. 33 52 19). A hotel school in winter that rents its 450 clean, modern rooms (mostly singles) to tourists from the beginning of July until mid-August. 240F for bed (with sheets), breakfast, and, in August, great music: Flanders Festival orchestras often stay here and practice in the building. 340F includes dinner too; full pension 400F. Showers 30F, midnight curfew. Garden, bar, and nice dining room.

Hotel Cosmopolite, Kuiperstraat 18 (tel. 33 20 96). This very comfortable hotel is a couple blocks from the Markt. Singles 300F, doubles 600F, quads 1120F, breakfast included. Baths 50F extra.

Camping St. Michael, Tillegemstraat 29, St. Michaels (tel. 31 38 19). 40F per person, 50F per tent. Hot showers, 5km from town. Bus #7 from the Markt or the Train Station.

Food

The **Ganzespel,** Ganzestraat 37, is a pleasant coffeehouse-restaurant frequented by young people, with a very reasonable *menu du jour:* 140F for soup, meat, and two vegetables, tax and *service* included. Wine served. Open Wed.-Fri. noon-2:30pm and 6-10pm, closed Mon.-Tues. **Des Brasseurs,** at Zuidzandstraat 43, has a daily soup-meat-*frites* lunch combination at 140F, everything included. There is a seafood delicatessen at Langestraat 15; good shrimp salad for 39F. The best *charcuterie* in town is **Frank** at Steenstraat 72.

There are innumerable late-night cafés around the old town. Among the most interesting are **Vlissinge,** Blekerstraat, which claims to be the oldest in Europe, and **Spaans Heester** (Pottenmakerstraat) of nearly the same vintage and perhaps more authentic in atmosphere. **Stokerhuis,** Langestraat 7, is popular with local students. So are the **Cactus,** St. Amandstraat 13, and the café at the **Snuffel Sleep-In,** which features cheap beer and good stereo. There are carillon concerts three evenings a week in the summer at 8:30pm.

Namur and the Southeast

Castles, caves, and kayaks greet those who flee the cities to spend a few days in the province of Namur. Of course, a car is best for exploring, but trains link up the larger towns and buses cover the rest. Check schedules in advance, as service to some places is infrequent. There are a few IYHF Youth Hostels and many campgrounds in the region. If you wish to camp out in the provinces of Liège and Luxembourg, east and south of Namur, get a list of farmers who let campers stay on their property and use their facilities for about 75F per tent plus 15F per person. Though the program isn't in effect in Namur, many farmers are cooperative about letting you camp on their land.

At the confluence of the **Sambre** and **Meuse** Rivers is the city of Namur, capital of the province and the best base for explorations. Climb up to the city's immense **Citadel** for a magnificent view. The **Musée Archéologique** (open daily 12:30-5:30pm except Tuesday; admission 15F) is worth a visit, as is the italianate **Cathedral.** Between the two is the most interesting part of town to explore on foot. In the medieval **Belfry** you'll find **Infor-Jeunes** (tel. 71 47 40), open weekdays 9am-5pm. Here you can get touring information and help with hassles, or rent a bicycle for 50F per day. The **City**

Tourist Office is in the pavilion near the Rail Station, but you'll get more information on the region at the **Fédération Provinçale de Tourisme,** rue Notre Dame 3 (tel. 22 29 98), open weekdays 8am-noon and 1-5pm.

You'll feel instantly at home at the IYHF **Youth Hostel,** 8 ave. F. Rops (tel. 22 36 88, take bus #1 or 4 from the Train Station). Facilities are ordinary, but thanks to the energy and warmth of Jacques Thibaut, the Hostel has acquired a reputation as one of Europe's finest. Bed 90F. Relaxed atmosphere: the huge breakfast (40F) is served until noon; you can hang around the Hostel all day if you like; delicious dinner (100F) served at 8pm. If you're traveling over Christmas or New Year's, don't miss the chance to celebrate with Jacques. Open all year and always has room; 30F supplement if you don't have a Hostel card. There is another extraordinary IYHF **Youth Hostel** in St. Gérard, to the southwest, situated in the **Abbaye de Brogne** (tel. 79 91 35). The Abbey is also a cultural center, where you can participate in crafts workshops. Bus from Namur, or about 20 kilometers by bicycle from Namur or Dinant.

From Namur good rail and bus connections facilitate several excellent daytrips. Check current prices and opening hours in the pamphlet *Province de Namur: Attractions,* available at any tourist office. The most spectacular grottoes in the region are at **Han-sur-Lesse** (150F). Train to Jemelle, then hitch or take a short bus ride. There is an IYHF **Youth Hostel** here at 8 rue de Gîte d'Étape (tel. 37 74 41). At **Floreffe,** the Abbey, which has a thirteenth-century *moulin-brasserie,* serves visitors cheese, bread, and homemade beer.

The region's most striking architectural perspective is found at **Dinant;** the bizarre bulb atop a late Gothic church is outlined against a cliff and the severe citadel above. Dinant is also the most touristed town in the region, and has no particularly cheap places to stay. While in Dinant, try a *couque,* a hard, molded gingerbread specialty available in any *pàtisserie.*

There are several castles in the vicinity of Dinant. Bicycles can be rented at the Dinant Train Station. The ride to Namur is very pleasant: the main road along the left bank is flat, but the smaller road on the other side is more interesting despite a couple of big hills. There are also frequent trains between Namur and Dinant, and hitching is easy.

The descent of the **Lesse River** by kayak from **Houyet** to **Anseremme** makes a good daytrip. You must reserve a boat (two-person kayak 550F, single 500F) in advance at one of the offices in Anseremme and arrive in Houyet before 11am (take the early train from Namur). Call **Ansiaux** (tel. 082/22 23 25), **Libert** (tel. 082/22 24 86), or **Lesse Kayaks** (tel. 082/22 43 97) for information and reservations. For a more unusual daytrip, take the train from Namur or Dinant to **Givet,** just across the French border. Hike through the fields and quiet towns, which have an atmosphere different from their Belgian neighbors.

BULGARIA

$1U.S.=0.94 leva   **1 leva=$1.06**

Historically, visitors to Bulgaria have not come as tourists. The Turks came and stayed for four hundred years, until they were thrown out in 1877 by Bulgarian Nationalists and Russian Imperial armies. In spite of Turkish rule, the Bulgarian people retained both the strong nationalism of their forebears under King Assen, and the ethnic unity which took root when St. Cyril and St. Methodius worked from Bulgaria to bring the gospel to the Russian principalities. Nowadays this "Slavism" is strongly encouraged by the Soviet neighbor, and slogans proclaiming Soviet-Bulgarian friendship drape monuments to the Russian and Bulgarian soldiers of 1877. Today, the feared hordes are the masses of vacationers from the Soviet Union and other Eastern European countries, who flock to the **Black Sea Riviera.** The few Western tourists who have ventured into Bulgaria have been pleasantly surprised by what they have found in the mountainous hinterlands: monasteries nestled in narrow, wooded valleys, alpine peaks towering to more than 8000 feet. What's more, the Bulgarian people are overwhelmingly hospitable.

107

PRACTICAL INFORMATION

Regardless of what tourist offices say, get your Bulgarian visa before you get to the border, and you will save both time and money. Write to the Bulgarian Embassy (at 2100 16th St., NW, Washington, D.C. 20009 or 325 Steward St., Ottawa, Canada), or stop in at any of the embassies in Europe, where a couple hours' wait and $14 will get you a thirty-day tourist visa. If you get your visa at the border, the price will probably be at least $25. Make sure you receive a thirty- and not a four-day visa.

Fortunately, Bulgaria recently abolished its enforced minimum currency exchange, so you spend only what you wish to. You can change money at train stations, **Balkantourist** offices, and large hotels. Keep the receipt—it is the only proof that you have changed money legally, and the only thing which will enable you to change levas back to dollars when you leave Bulgaria.

In Bulgaria, you will have to deal with two organizations for arranging accommodations. The most important is Balkantourist. You may want to contact their New York office for information and reservations (50 East 42nd St., New York, NY 10017; tel. (212) 661-5733). In Bulgaria, Balkantourist runs a chain of expensive hotels and a service for finding rooms in private homes. The second organization is **Orbita,** the youth travel bureau. It is staffed mainly by young people, and runs hostels and camps in numerous locations. It's best to book in advance at their Sofia office, either by mail or upon arrival in Sofia. In most cases, two or three days' warning will be sufficient, but the Black Sea village of Primorsko, Orbita's pride, must be booked months before.

For accommodations, Balkantourist only reluctantly directs you to hotels which are not their own, so you must check the telephone directory or tourist brochure for the town. Private homes are often the least expensive and most comfortable solution. You can arrange them either through Balkantourist or on your own. If you do it yourself, you are supposed to register with the police, about which your host may be uncomfortable. However, if you have already slept in a hotel and have a stamp or two on the back of the "statistical card" which you received at the border, then you can get away without registering. Camping is officially allowed only in campgrounds where a place for your tent will cost 1 leva, or a two-person bungalow will cost about 3-5 leva. However, in the mountains, you may pick your site as long as you are discreet.

Public transportation in Bulgaria is expensive, crowded and slow—you will often find yourself waiting two or three hours at intermediate stations, and you should always recheck schedules to avoid getting stuck halfway to somewhere with no train or bus to take you the remaining distance. Buses are usually for distances less than 100 kilometers, and the longer distance buses are infrequent and generally leave very early in the morning. Both buses and trains are always crowded; especially at large cities, arrive about an hour before departure to brave the ticket lines and try for a seat. If possible, buy both train and bus tickets the day before you travel; buses in particular get sold out in advance. Along the coast, hydrofoils are a good alternative. They are fast, reasonably priced, and guarantee a seat for each ticket holder.

Bulgarian hitchhiking is slow. Few Bulgarians own cars, and most vehicles are full. But thumb everything that moves—taxis, army trucks, hospital delivery trucks, motorcyclists. Women hitchers should have a male companion.

The easiest way to travel is by car. Car rental plans are good possibilities for daytrips if you can get a deal for unlimited mileage. Gas coupons have been discontinued, but gas is still relatively cheap, and most roads are good.

Bulgaria is a country of monoglots. Russian is the only really useful foreign language; German and French are spoken much less often, and English almost never. We strongly recommend learning the Cyrillic alphabet, as signs for almost everything essential will otherwise be incomprehensible to you. If you know that you will be visiting Bulgaria, pick up a Bulgarian phrase book or Bulgarian-English dictionary before you leave home. These books do exist in Bulgaria, but they are virtually impossible to find.

FOOD

Food is cheap everywhere, but restaurant cooking is so inexpensive and tasty that doing your own shopping is pointless. *Kebabches* resemble fat Wimpy burgers; Bulgarians consume an enormous number of them, not only at restaurants, but at special and ultracheap *kebabche* bars, where they are served with a huge splat of mustard. *Kisselo mleko,* Bulgarian yogurt, is a pleasant mixture of sweet and sour. Bulgarians consume it by the gallon. Try *tarator* as well—a cold soup made with yogurt, cucumber, and garlic.

Bulgarians work wonders with vegetables. *Chopska salada* is available in almost all restaurants, and is an addictive salad of tomatoes, peppers, and cucumbers covered with *siren,* grated white goat cheese. *Appetit* is a hot pepper salad. *Kiopolou* and *imam bayalda* are vegetable dishes based on eggplant); a *guvetch* is a mixed vegetable stew with onion, eggplant, peppers, beans and peas.

Main dishes usually consist of grilled meat, skewered Turkish style, and pork and lamb are the most common (along with *kiflete*—meatballs). Variations are *popska iakhnia* (veal cooked with onions), *sarmi* (chopped meat with onion, tomato, and pepper), and *haiduchki kebab* (lamb grilled with onion, white wine, and pepper).

A Bulgarian meal should always be introduced by a glass of *Slivova,* a plum *eau de vie.* The *Trojanskaia Slivova,* from the Trojanskii Monastery, is one of the best.

Sofia

Today, placid and soporific Sofia retains a small-town atmosphere, despite its efforts to impress the world as an elegant socialist capital. Wide streets, mammoth squares, and elephantine white marble government buildings imitate the openness of Paris and the monumentality of Moscow—but in Sofia they seem out of place, simply widening the distance you have to walk to get from A to B. More appealing than the main streets are the parks, including gigantic **Park na Svobodata,** and the back streets with their coffee shops and nineteenth-century houses.

Orientation

There is a **Balkantourist** office at the Railway Station but all they will do is change money. The main office of Balkantourist is at Dondukov Ulica 37, down the street from the Balkan Hotel (take tram #1, 7, or 9 from Railway Station to center). Here you can get a sketchy map of the city—try to talk them into selling you one of their more detailed ones, or go to a book store.

A map which shows tram and bus routes is especially helpful, but hard to come by. The international book store, at 6 Boulevard Rousski, can sell you English guidebooks and maps not in Cyrillic. The office for rooms in private homes is at the **Balkantourist** Office on Dondukov. **Orbita,** Anton Ivanov Blvd. 76 (tel. 65 29 52), Bulgaria's youth travel bureau, will try (often unsuccessfully) to find you a room in a student hostel and arrange excursions outside Sofia. Make reservations here if you plan to use Orbita facilities in the rest of the country.

Trams in Sofia are indispensable and very cheap (6 stotinki). Buy your tickets at kiosks near the stops and punch them yourself when you board. There is a stiff fine if you're caught not punching your ticket and officials don't accept ignorance as an excuse.

Addresses and Telephone Numbers

Poste Restante: Gurko Ul. 2.

Rila: International Railway Bureau (for *all* international tickets), Gurko Ul.5 (tel. 87 07 77).

Police: (tel. 87 77 77).

Medical Emergency: tel. 150.

U.S. Embassy: Stamboliyski Blvd. 1 (tel. 88 48 01). Open 8am-1pm and 2-5:30pm, except closed Wed. afternoon, Sat., and Sun.

Accommodations

You may be approached on the street by private citizens who will offer to rent a room in their home, especially if you look Western or wait in front of a deluxe hotel. Prices for a double room should run around 10 leva (half if you pay in dollars). Balkantourist on Dondukov Ulica can also place you in a private home and they ask 10-12 leva per double. So unless you want to pay in dollars (which is illegal) you might as well use Balkantourist. There is one student hotel run by Orbita, but it is quite expensive. Look for **Turistica Spalna** (tourist dorms) where beds are available for about 2 leva.

Turistica Spalna Zdravetz, Klokotnitza Ul. 4 (tel. 31 60 32). Barracks-like, no showers, but clean. Beds about 2 leva with IYHF card, 4 leva without. Take tram #2 or 9 down Georgi Dmitrov Avenue and ask a fellow passenger when to get off—go right on Klokotnitza for three blocks. Call first, it's often full.

Student Hotel Orbita, Anton Ivanov 6 (tel. 65 29 52). ID required. Beds about 5 leva, doubles starting at 10 leva. The hotel is Orbita's official student lodging. Tram #6 away from the center city about 6 km. Call in advance.

Hotel Preclav, Triadiza Ul. 5 (tel. 87 65 86). An old hotel in the center of the city. Singles from 9 leva, doubles from 15 leva, with breakfast.

The following hotels are not supposed to give you a room without a voucher from Balkantourist. But if you show up on your own and they have space, they may accommodate you.

Pliska, Lenin Blvd. 87 (tel. 72 37 21), has singles starting at 10 leva. Clean and comfortable.

Sendika, Levski Mon. (tel. 44 34 11). Same idea as Pliska.

Food

Dining well costs little; even at the best restaurant in the city, atop the **Hotel Sofia,** it is difficult to spend more than 10 leva per person. Considerably less expensive, but quite good, are the **Krim** at Ulica Slavianska 17, the **Opera** at Ulica Rakovski 116, and the **Budapest** at Ulica Rakovski 145. Taverns decorated in Bulgarian style—like **Mekhana Strandzhata** in Lenin Square or **Koprivshitsa,** Vitosha Blvd. 3—serve Bulgarian specialties for about 2.50-5 leva. Cheapest of all are the self-services. There is a good one on **Stamboliyski Boulevard** in Lenin Square and another on **Graf Ignatiev Ul.,** near the main Post Office. Here you can eat a full meal for about 1.50 leva.

There is a large open-air market on **Georgi Kirkov Ul.** (not very far from Railway Station) where vegetables, fruits and cheeses are sold at very low prices.

Sights

Sofia has several famous churches; the two oldest are **Sveti Gyorgi,** a Roman church from the fourth century, and the later **Sveti Sofia.** Far more wonderful than these is the tiny **Boyanska Church** (Boyánska Tserkva) in the hillside suburb of Boyana, a twenty-minute ride on bus #63 (20 stotinki, leaves from Vazrazdane Square, at the intersection of Stamboliyski and Hristo Botev Boulevards). The church, open 10:30am-12:30pm and 1:30-5:30pm, is decorated inside with thirteenth-century frescoes that represent the height of Bulgarian religious painting. The unusual neo-Byzantine **Alexander Nevsky Church** should be seen for its shock value, but don't just gasp and leave—go to the **Crypt,** which is a museum of exquisite painted icons from all over Bulgaria dating from the twelfth to nineteenth centuries.

Of the three large mosques, one houses the **Archaeological Museum** (2 Boulevard Stamboliyski, open Tuesday, Wednesday, Thursday, Friday and Sunday from 10am to 12:30pm and 2:30 to 6pm, Saturdays 10am to 1:30pm), an interesting mishmash of relics from the Thracian, Greek, Roman, and Turkish settlements in Bulgaria, as well as religious articles from the Bulgarian kingdom. The **Georgi Dmitrov Mausoleum** contains the plasticized, cold-storage remains of the chubby little man with a moustache you've seen on all the posters. People are allowed to file past his serenely smiling visage on Wed., Fri., and Sun. from 3-6pm. Each Bulgarian town has its **Museum of the Revolutionary Movement in Bulgaria;** Sofia has the biggest and best at Rousski Boulevard 14 (open noon-7pm; Fridays 8am-1pm). Here you can see the personal effects of almost every dead party member in Bulgaria. Included are shaving soap, toothbrushes, and underwear, as well as your more run-of-the-mill machine guns, secret radios, and printing presses.

Near Sofia

Eight kilometers from Sofia is the **Vitosha Mountains National Park,** often referred to as the "lungs of Sofia." The mountain air attracts walkers from the city and hikes are quite demanding. The **Zlatniy Mosty** is a glacial moraine of boulders several yards in diameter, upon which you can scramble or sun yourself. Buses run to restaurants and hotels throughout the area. Inquire at Balkantourist or the Bus Station.

The Mountains

In Bulgaria, there are four main mountain ranges. The **Stara Planina** bisects the country horizontally, from Sofia to Varna. The **Rila** and **Pirin** Mountains are south of Sofia, and the less interesting **Rhodopi** Mountains center around the resort of **Pamporovo** south of Plovdiv.

Unfortunately, crowds of East Germans have begun to occupy the Bulgarian summits; but by Swiss and Austrian standards, the trails are un-crowded. There are many scenic resort towns, but old costumes, buildings, and traditions have survived best in the mountain valleys and are preserved as a way of life rather than as a tourist attraction.

Because the Bulgarian mountains have not been developed as tourist cen-ters, hotels are scarce and transportation indirect. Trains take you to the hills, and buses to the foot of most mountains; but from there you must hike and camp. Check, though, with **Orbita** and **Balkantourist** in Sofia for informa-tion about hostels and *hizhi* (huts), but go prepared to spend the night in a tent.

Stara Planina Range

The Stara Planina was a natural barrier between the Russians and the Turks; in 1877, some of the heaviest fighting occurred in these mountains. Near **Shipka** is the site of a decisive victory by the Russians and the Bulgar-ians, commemorated by Alexander III's church, whose golden onion-shaped cupolas remind one of Mother Russia. The **Shipka Pass,** however, is more than a geographic monument to the "eternal bond of friendship," which unites the Bulgarian Socialist Republic and the Soviet Union. Shipka is one of the best hiking areas of the Stara Planina. Nearby is the village of **Buz-ludza,** from which trails take off towards the summits. There is an IYHF **Hostel** at the Pass, Shipchenski Prohod, but it is usually quite crowded. Beds start at 3 leva.

Another fine center for hiking and resting is the **Trojanskii Monastery,** home of the famous *Trojanskaia Slivova.* The Monastery also serves as a hotel, and although the monks beat the cimandra and ring the bells at 3am when they begin their morning service, the general atmosphere is one of peace and quiet. Beds in the monastery start at 3 leva. Write for reservations to Trojanskii Monastery, postal code 5629, Bulgaria. If the monastery hotel is full, cross the street to the hay barn. If someone asks you what you are doing in the hay, explain (or pantomime) that the monk with the beard who was dressed in black said you could spend the night there.

Hiking in the area is rewarding, as the summits are not too high, the slopes not too steep, and yet the views reach as far as the eye can see. Pleasant villages nestle in unexpected valleys, and shepherds walk their flocks up into the mountains every day. Tradition here is barely touched by the mechaniza-tion called for by the government "Plans"; grass is still scythed and hand-stacked.

The Rila Range

The Rila mountains are certainly the most crowded of the Bulgarian ranges, since they are close to Sofia and the hiking is excellent. Explore the trails between the village of **Maljovica** (hotels, huts, and camping) and **Rila Monastery,** seven hours away. The Monastery, founded by the hermit Ivan Rilski in the tenth century, was enlarged and fortified between 1335 and 1342 by the feudal overlord of the district, Chreljo, whose despotic rule finally caused his neighbors to incarcerate him in the monastery and have him strangled. During the centuries of Turkish rule, Rila kept alive the arts of icon-painting and manuscript-copying. It was destroyed by fire in the nineteenth century, and the present fairy-tale wooden structure is the result of rebuilding by three local architects. The inner walls of the galleries are decorated with murals meant as a ''poor man's Bible,'' and the museum houses marvelous medieval icons and possessions of the monastery.

There are **campgrounds** near the monastery and a **Tourist Hotel** right next door, where dorm beds cost less than 2 leva.

The Pirin Range

The Pirin Mountains are the most interesting and the least crowded of all. The highest peaks are there, as are the most desolate villages, accessible only on foot or by mule ride through the secluded valleys. Try hiking around Bansko, up to the camp of Vihren at the foot of **Mt. Vihren.** On clear days, you can see the Adriatic from the summit. Near the once-beautiful village of Melnik, close to the Greek border, is some of the most unspoiled hiking in Europe. Head for the **Rozenski Monastery** along the untraveled dirt track; and if you arrive as a pilgrim rather than a tourist, you will be offered bed and board. Further along the same road is the village of Pirin—a couple dozen poor, wooden homes clustered at the meeting of two dust tracks. Try the natives' hospitality, since the nearest hotel is twenty miles away. From Pirin to Goce-Delcev there is nothing but mountain, so head off on your own and you will be rewarded by magnificent vistas and ancient, gloomy forests. The road which is indicated on some maps is unpaved and rarely traveled, so the area is ideal for hiking.

Plovdiv

Don't allow your first impressions of Plovdiv to cause you to judge the city too harshly. Modern, drab apartment complexes, huge parks, and sterile government buildings might lure you into thinking that Plovidiv is simply a provincial version of Sofia. Hold your disappointment in check, however, until you have wandered up Plovdiv's Three Hills into the rambling stairway-streets of the Old Town. Here ''Bulgarian Baroque'' houses hang their beamed, protruding upper stories over the cobblestones, windows stare down into alleyways at impossible angles, churches and mosques hide in secluded corners.

Start your touring at the main square, **Ploshtad Tsentralen,** which can be reached from the **Train Station** by tram #2 (tickets 6 stotinki at the kiosk). The main office of **Balkantourist** (tel. 3 25 69) is on Ul. Vassili Kolarov, just off Ploshtad Tsentralen, around the corner from Hotel Bulgaria. Balkantourist is open daily 8:30am-noon and 1-5pm. Here you can get a map of Plovdiv and a couple of brochures. The Balkantourist Offices at the desks of the main hotels (**Bulgaria, Trimontium, Novotel**) and the one on Blvd. Moskva 34 (tel. 5 28 07) will find a private room costing 3.50-7 leva. The **Orbita Office** on Ul. Ivan Vasov 23 will find a room for you in their hostel (doubles 8 leva). Try these first:

Hotel Rhodopi, Ul. 11 August (tel. 2 43 32). Dorm beds for 1 leva, normally only for Bulgarians. Singles 2.30 leva, doubles 3.40 leva, triples 3.90 leva, quads 4.80 leva. Bathrooms and showers in the halls, no breakfast.

Hotel Republica, Vassili Kolarov 39 (tel. 2 30 69), right next door to the hard-currency store (good place for black-market transactions). Clean, central, and the restaurant is excellent. Doubles for 7.50 leva.

Motel Camping Maritza, 9 km from Plovdiv on the road towards Sofia. Tent space 1 leva; and 1 leva per person. No good if you don't have a car.

Sights

Wander up the hill from the main square to find a steep, narrow, cobbled street where "Bulgarian Baroque" houses hang over the street. At the top of the hill is the best and most expensive restaurant in town, **Poldin.** Walk in and let the beautiful setting convince you to spend the 8 leva necessary for a full meal. Around a couple of corners—on Ul. Mouravenov, in the amazing nineteenth-century home of the merchant Kujumjioglu—is the well-presented local **Ethnographical Museum,** interesting for the evidence of Turkish and Armenian influences.

Twenty-nine kilometers from Plovdiv (take the bus going to Pavelsko) is the **Backovski Manastir** (Backovo Monastery). Founded in 1083 by the Georgian nobleman Gregorios Pakurianos, it has always been overshadowed by the Rila Monastery, but it contains some of the best eleventh- and twelfth-century Byzantine frescoes in existence. If you go on a Sunday, you'll see peasants wearing local costumes to the church.

Veliko Turnovo

Veliko Turnovo is possibly the most beautiful town in Bulgaria, and certainly among the most unspoiled. It was once the capital of the powerful Second Bulgarian Kingdom, an empire that defied Rome and Constantinople, and extended from the Black Sea to the Adriatic. During the twelfth-century reign of Ivan Assen II, the now-ruined **Fortress of Tsarevitz** contained palaces and splendorous Byzantine churches, and was the country's administrative seat. Now Veliko Turnovo is a quiet, provincial town, dramatic only in its magnificent and improbable setting on the steep banks of the Jantra River Canyon. The old town's eighteenth- and nineteenth-century wooden houses still cling to the slopes and stare down onto the red-tiled roofs below, while the uncrowded street and alleys wind their way from church to church. The town and its environs are a treasure trove of ruins and monuments from almost every period of civilization in Bulgaria.

Orientation and Accommodations

The **Balkantourist Information** desk at the Jantra (Veltschova-Savera Ploshtad, tel. 2 17 13), and the **Etar Hotels** (Ivailo Ul. 2, tel. 2 71 95) will give you a map of the town. The office on Tolbuchin 6 (tel. 2 16 17), next door to the "Club for Battle against Fascism and Capitalism," will find you a room in a private home for 3-5 leva, which is probably the best solution. A good alternative if you have a car are the **campgrounds** at the Sveta Gora and Boljarski Stan. Both are on the road to Varna and two-bed bungalows go for 6 leva. If neither of these suit you, Veliko Turnovo has several hotels.

Hotel Stadiona, (tel. 2 03 24), in the sports park down the main street. Doubles for 9 leva. Clean, but a fifteen-minute walk from the center.

Hotel Orbita, (tel. 2 20 41), near the Hotel Etar. Best if you can make reservations at Sofia or by mail. Doubles 7-12 leva.

Hotel Jantra, Veltschova Savera Ploshtad (tel. 2 03 91). Balkantourist's pride, all rooms with bath and breakfast. Beds starting at 12 leva.

Food

Balyar Izba, on Blvd. Blagoev, opposite #26. Go down the stairs to the right of the door for a table overlooking the Jantra. Bulgarian specialties and fine wine (try the *Melnik* red) at moderate prices: meals 2-4 leva.

Mexana, on the upper right corner of the small square off the main street, open evenings. Go early and try the *guvetch* (2.50-4 leva).

Sights

The ruins of the fortress, **Tsarevetz,** occupy the top of an entire over-grown hill (open 7am to 10pm, entrance 10 stotinki). You can climb around among the old walls, picking out the ruins of the Royal Palace and cathedral, and stand on the rock from which traitors were hurled to their death. In much better condition are the old churches: **St. Dmitri,** where in 1185 the insurrection leading to the Second Bulgarian Kingdom was planned; the **Church of the Forty Holy Martyrs** *(40 Macenizi),* constructed in the thirteenth century by Czar Ivan Assen II to commemorate his victory at Klokotnitza; the **Church of St. Peter and Paul** *(Petr i Pavel)* with fourteenth-century frescoes.

The **Archaeological Museum** (open 7am till 6:30pm; closed Mondays) is well-organized and contains wonderful Thracian pottery, a fine collection of medieval crafts from the Turnovo ruins, and copies or originals of the most famous frescoes in Bulgarian medieval churches.

The environs of Turnovo offer settlements from three far-separated periods: the old Roman town of **Nikopolis ad Istrum** 20 kilometers north, founded by Emperor Trajan; the medieval **Preobrazhenski Monastery,** with frescoes by the two greatest painters of the nineteenth-century renaissance, Zographe and Dosperski; and the village of **Arbanassi,** full of seventeenth- and eighteenth-century merchants' houses and churches.

The Black Sea Coast

In the summer, the Black Sea Coast is just as Balkantourist wants it: crowded. All the new white hotels are full, the campgrounds are tent-to-tent, and the beaches are paved with oily bodies.

Some spots, however, have escaped this plague, in particular the areas

south of Burgas and north of Varna. In the south, the student village of
Primorsko blends a beautiful site with an atmosphere unknown to Westerners: that of a happy socialist playground. Make reservations through Orbita
in Sofia to get a place in one of Primorsko's hotels, mini-hotels, bungalows,
or chalets which nestle at the foot of the wooded hills along a fine sand
beach. To the north is the isolated spot of **Rusalka,** discovered by the French
Club Méditerranée. But there is nothing but the Club's ultra-modern complex and public campground on a torn cliff coastline.

Unfortunately, transportation along the coast is far from ideal. In the
crowded areas buses run quite often, but to reach the more desirable, secluded beaches further north and south, you must use the local bus service.
The **Kometa** line runs hydrofoil service between Varna, Nesebăr, Burgas,
Sozopol, Primorsko, and Michurin. The service is frequent, fast, and not
much more expensive than the bus; tickets go on sale about forty minutes
before each sailing, but you should arrive earlier because lines are long.
Traffic along the roads is quite heavy, so hitching works a little better here
than in the rest of Bulgaria. Be sure that you are recognizable as an exotic
foreigner—not just another hot and salty Soviet—and you should travel
quickly.

Nesebăr

Nesebăr is an old merchant town, built on a peninsula, that has conserved
much of its eighteenth-century charm. Four hundred years of Turkish rule
failed to destroy the early buildings and churches like **St. Ivan Aliturgetos,**
the **Pantokrator,** and the **Church of Archangel Michael and Gabriel** (all
thirteenth and fourteenth-century) still retain their unique tile-and-brick decorations. Another church, **St. Ivan Krastitel** (tenth century) houses the town
Archaeological Museum. The **Balkantourist Office** in Nesebăr, Ul. Yana
Liskova 18 (open 7am-10pm), can arrange rooms in private homes at about 3
leva per person. If they have nothing, ask about third-class rooms. Technically, these are only for Bulgarians. But if you smile and look down-and-out,
they'll eventually find you something. **Hotel Messambria,** Ul. Ribarska
(tel. 3 255) is the only hotel in Nesebăr. Rooms are small but comfortable,
with one to four beds, from 4 to 8 leva per bed. Snack bars serve fresh fish
and all the Balkantourist restaurants are excellent, so eating in Nesebăr is no
problem.

Nesebăr has the additional advantage of being within a ten-minute bus ride
from the huge, sterile resort of **Slancev-Brjag,** where over one hundred new
hotels line a wonderful sand beach. Here you will be able to sample a couple
hours of what is for many Eastern Europeans the dream summer. You can
book a room around the clock at **Balkantourist** (tel. 2152), or they will try
to find something for you on the spot if you want.

CZECHOSLOVAKIA

$1U.S.=10 koruna (Kčs)   **1Kčs=$.10**

Czechs sometimes compare their country with Israel. "You have to be very clever," they say, "to survive in the middle of Europe." There are no more open protests in the squares of Prague. "Prague Spring" is now an annual music festival. Yet somehow, the new toleration of socialism seems only skin deep, just as the four-hundred-year acceptance of Austrian Hapsburg rule vanished quickly before ardent Czechoslovak nationalism in 1918.

Czechoslovakia is a union of two nations, the Czech and the Slovak. **Slovakia,** closest to Russia, shows the combined influence of its neighbors in the Slavic customs and folklore of the countryside, and in the Austro-Hungarian polish of the provincial capital **Bratislava** (formerly Pressburg). The Czech nation comprises **Moravia,** still quaint but rapidly industrializing; and rich **Bohemia** in the west, land of the Moldau River, **Prague,** and the medieval legacy of Charles IV. The Bohemians have made as much of a tradition of rebellion as of excellent beer, defenestrations dotting their history. But Dubček was born in Slovakia.

PRACTICAL INFORMATION

The current policy is to bolster an already booming economy with foreign tourism, and although advance visas are required, they are issued automatically for $8 and two photos. At home the forms are available at **Cedok,** 10 E. 40th St., New York, NY 10016, or at the **Czechoslovak Embassy,** 3900 Linnean Avenue, NW, Washington, D.C. Complete the forms, include a certified check or money order for $8 and return this with a stamped, self-addressed envelope enclosed. Visas are normally granted within 48 hours of application. In Europe call at any Czech embassy. The one in Vienna, Renzingerstr. 11, gives out visas by the hundreds. You should get yours the very day you apply. If you get your visa in an East European embassy, you will have to pay in Western *cash*—either U.S. dollars or West German marks. If you should decide to prolong your stay in Czechoslovakia your visa can be extended at the local Police Station for 60 Kčs (in Prague, Bartolomějská 14). Open Monday, Tuesday, Wednesday and Friday 7:30am-3pm and Thursday 12:30-3pm. The wait is between half an hour and an hour. Remember when in the country to have your visa form stamped every place you spend the night. If staying in private homes, register *daily* or for the entire stay in one place at the local police. You must have stamps for each day in Czechoslovakia. At the border when you enter, you will have to change $10 per day for your entire stay into Czech koruna on the spot. Your visa isn't valid until you exchange this money, so make sure you get those ubiquitous all-important stamps on the slip. If you prolong your stay, you'll have to change more money at that time.

It's a good idea to carry your currency slip with your passport; you need it to change money and buy international train tickets. Otherwise, money could be less of a problem in Czechoslovakia than virtually anywhere else. Outside of Prague the $10 per day should be more than enough to live comfortably. Food is tasty, filling and inexpensive. 16 Kčs buys you a decent meal; 32Kčs brings a feast. East European countries consider "black market activities" a crime against the state and punish the guilty severely, so save changing money for trusted friends only. Don't accept any offers of less than 20-25Kčs per dollar.

Czech and Slovak are closely related; Russian is every student's mandatory second language, and German is the most common third. Older people speak German throughout Bohemia, in most of Moravia, and parts of Slovakia. Unfortunately, English, which was popular in the sixties, is fading, since it is virtually useless for most Czechs. Nevertheless, we recommend that you address people in English, and then if necessary, let them know if you speak German or Russian. In the largest cities, English should get you by.

If you are flying to Czechoslovakia from within Europe the **Czechoslovak National Airlines** (CSA) offers a 25% reduction to students under 25. Remember also that if you are traveling to Czechoslovakia by train to or from any other Eastern European country you can get discounts of 25% with an IUS (the East European student organization) ID card. Inside the country, the **CSAD** buses provide the fastest connections; look for the terminal under **Autobusové Nádraží.** Many longer and more popular routes require reservations, so buy the tickets in advance.

Trains are slower by as much as 100%, but on major routes they are more frequent. Tickets are issued according to the kind of train—*osobný* or *rýchlik*, the latter also good on *ekspresný*—so check beforehand which kind you want. The faster ones *(ekspresný* and *rýchlik)* normally require a seat reservation *(záznam),* but these can usually be bought the same day at the station, except on international trains, which are booked well in advance.

City bus and tram lines require tickets bought in advance at *tabaks* or magazine stands. They must be canceled on board. There is an honors system, but trams are checked regularly, with a 50Kčs fine imposed on the dishonorable.

Almost everyone, young and old, hitches in Czechoslovakia. Unfortunately, the only people who seem to get picked up are single women and the elderly. It's worth a try though, if you can make yourself interesting (flag? slogan? dress?). The Czechs begin the work day very early, and best hitching hours are 6-8am. If you're out after 9am, leaving most cities will be difficult. The signal for hitching in Czechoslovakia is a simple downward wave of the forearm with fingers extended and palm facing the traffic.

ACCOMMODATIONS

There are two national travel agencies to deal with. **Čedok** handles almost everything—international tickets, hotels, area tours, local information—but be insistent with them or they will milk you for your last dollar. **CKM** is the student travel bureau. They issue the IYHF card and the IUS card, mentioned above. In July and August, CKM converts student dormitories in all the major university towns into youth hostels *(juniorstřediska),* with very comfortable two- to four-bedded rooms costing 25Kčs per person with a hostel card, 39Kčs without. These usually have space, although they may be hard to find (outside of Prague the addresses change yearly). CKM is run by and for students. It can be a prime source of information and help, although in Prague it is large, fragmented, and despairingly bureaucratic.

Hotels, like everything else, are governmentally grouped into categories of price and quality, from A to C. Except in the countryside, however, the government has been rapidly closing the class C hotels. Class B singles cost 86-125Kčs and doubles 126-186Kčs. Camping is available everywhere—check bookstores and tourist offices for the several directories—and it's dirt cheap if you have your own tent. Otherwise it is usually possible to stay in bungalows or four-person huts at 25Kčs per bed, but you have to pay for every space in a private hut, whether or not it's filled.

FOOD

Even in the private area of gastronomic pleasure, the Czech government controls prices and categorizes. Prices are scaled from I to IV (top to bottom), and the class *(skupina)* is always listed on the menu. These seem to depend more on service and decor than quality of food—even low price eateries can serve fantastic home cooking. The cheapest food is to be found at a stand-up *bufet,* also called *samoobsluha* (self-service). A *hostinec* is also inexpensive, but caters more to a steady clientele of local beer drinkers, and is one of the best places to meet people. A *pivnice* is a beer hall, but can range from raucous to refined, and *vinárna* is a wine bar, usually specializing in fine Slovak wines. *Kavárny* and *cukrárny* serve exquisite pastry, such as *závin* (strudel), *kobliha* (raised donut), *koláč* (a sort of cheesecake) and *dorty* (tortes). The noon meal customarily begins with a soup *(polévka).* Some of the best are *bramboračká* (potato soup with mushrooms), *zeleninová* (a creamy and delicate vegetable soup) and *hovězí vývar* (consommé). Pork *(veprová)* is the most popular meat, especially *žebírko* (rib). For a splurge, try *svíčková pečené na zelenině*—sirloin steak served with vegetables and sour cream. *Knedlíky* are the fluffy bread dumplings that accompany everything; *kyselé zelí* (sauerkraut) is also often served. There is no question what to drink—Czech beer is probably the world's best. The most famous are **Pilsner Urquell** *(plženský Prazdroj)* and **Budvar** (the original Budweiser). At 2-4Kčs per half liter, it is the best bargain around.

Prague (Praha)

Prague blossomed early and never faded. No other European capital so combines the vast monuments of its kings and bishops with such a rich array of works of the private citizenry. A thriving community of medieval craftsmen was protected by Charles IV, the enlightened monarch who made Prague the glorious fourteenth-century capital of the Holy Roman Empire. After him the Hapsburgs ruled for four hundred years, and added a gracious Baroque front to the Gothic town. The municipal tradition culminated in the *Jugendstil,* which dressed all the squares in geometric designs and left monuments such as the expansive statue to *Jan Hus* on Staroměstské náměstí. Since then soot may have blackened much of the town, but a massive clean-up is underway, and the bright façades of Prague's hundred spires and thousands of houses are beginning to shine once again.

Orientation

From Prague's **Ruzyně Airport,** take tram #11 to the center of town (a twelve-mile trip). From the main Train Station (**Praha-hlavní nádraží),** or the nearby Station **Praha-střed,** it is a short walk on Hybernská to the center of town (if your ticket just specifies "Prague," it will be good for an inter-city rail connection to the center).

The busiest street downtown, Na příkopě, forms an extension of Hybernská. **Čedok,** the Czech travel agency, lives here at #18. These accommodating people speak all languages, exchange money, arrange rail and plane tickets, and operate a room-finding service around the corner at Panská 5. You can also exchange money at the bank on the corner where Na příkopě becomes Hybernská. The **Prague Information Service** (PIS) at Na příkopě 20 offers maps and programs for Prague, and usually has someone on hand who speaks English. This office is bound to be less crowded than Čedok.

Prague straddles the Moldau (also called the **Vltava**) right where the river makes a ninety-degree bend. The Old Town (**Staré Město)** nestles just inside the bend, encircled by some of Prague's busiest commercial streets. Just south of the Old Town on the same side of the Moldau, is the New Town (**Nové Město),** established in 1348 by Charles IV to divert the bustle of the growing community from his fledgling University. The New Town engulfs Wenceslas Square (Václavské náměstí), Prague's widest boulevard, which leads away from the Old Town, starting at the west end of Na příkopě.

The **Pražký Hrad** (Prague Castle) lies across the river from these districts. Most of the architectural monuments are concentrated around the Castle and in the Old Town. Prague's characteristic beer halls *(pivnice)* are everywhere.

To hitch to the east, take tram #9 or 21 to the end. To hitch south, take the metro (1Kčs) to Pražského povstáni. From this metro stop, cross a green area (náměstí Hrdinů) to 5 Května, the access road to the highway. You will want the side on náměstí Hrdinů.

We recommend the *Prague Guide* to architecture buffs—it is somewhat heavy and expensive (42Kčs), but effectively covers most historical buildings in the city. Good maps are available at book stores and magazine stands for 8Kčs. They are necessary to figure out the transit system, which, until Prague finishes its metro, will remain a confusing tangle of tram and bus lines.

Addresses and Telephone Numbers

Čedok: Prague 1, Na příkopě 18 (tel. 22 42 51). Open Mon.-Fri. 8:30am-4pm, Sat. 8:30am-noon. Accommodations service at Panská 5 (tels. 11 70 04 and 22 56 57). Open Mon.-Fri. 8am-10pm, Sat. 8am-8pm, Sun. 8am-5pm.

Pragotur: An accommodations service at Prague 1, U Obecního domu 2 (tels. 616 51, 616 52, and 616 53). Open Mon.-Fri. 8am-10pm, Sat. 8am-8pm, Sun. 8am-5pm. Located on a side street off náměstí Republicky one block north of the old Powder Tower. No police registration services here on Saturdays and Sundays.

CKM: Main office in Prague 2, Junior Hotel Praha, Žitná 12 (tel. 29 85 87); information and tickets also available in Prague 1 at Jindríšská 28 (tel. 26 85 07). Both open 8am-3pm Mon.-Fri.

Prague Information Service: Tour guides hired at Panská 4 (tel. 22 43 11). Information and theater and concert listings at Na příkopě 20 (tel. 54 44 44).

Post Office: Jindřišská 14 (tel. 26 48 41). 24-hour service.

Train Stations: There are three, but the only two you will use are a 10-minute walk apart. **Praha-střed** on Hybernská and **Praha-hlavní nádraží**. Vitěznéhó února. The latter handles more local traffic, but international trains leave from both, so check beforehand.

Bus Stations (Autobusovè hádraží): CSAD has four terminals in town; the central one is **Florenc,** at metro Sokolovská behind the Praha-střed railway station.

Police: Bartolomějská 14 (tel. 2149).

Emergency First Aid: (tel. 155); or Jungmannova 14 (tel. 24 77 71).

Ambulance: tel. 333.

All Night Pharmacy: Na příkopě 7 (tel. 22 00 81).

U.S. Embassy: Prague 1, Malá Strana, Tržiště 15 (tel. 53 66 41). Will hold mail for you.

Canadian Embassy: Prague 6, Hradčany, Mickiewiczova 6 (tel. 32 69 41). Will hold mail for you.

Accommodations

Prague is full of tourists, so rooms are hard to find and reservations should if possible be made through Čedok in the States. In Prague, Čedok and **Pragotur** have room-finding offices: Čedok at Panská 5 (tel. 22 70 04, 22 60 17, and 22 56 57), and Pragotur, U Obecního domu 2 (tel. 616 51/52/53). Pragotur is less crowded and perhaps better for cheaper lodging, but neither office lists class C hotels. Both are open weekdays 8am-10pm, Saturday 8am-8pm and Sunday 8am-5pm. Theoretically Pragotur also lists the city's seven **campgrounds,** but they may automatically tell you there's no space. Ask at either place for the brochure *Praha Camping* and call the campgrounds yourself—both English and German are spoken. The service charge for the booking offices is 5Kčs per person per night.

One of the nicest alternatives is staying in a private home. Both Pragotur and Čedok do have a list of private apartments, but they may not readily admit it since the government is discouraging the practice. Be stubborn but polite. The cost per night is 55Kčs for a single, 85Kčs for a double, plus the 5Kčs booking fee.

If nothing else works and you want to search on your own, check the booklet *The Month in Prague,* available free from the information services and in hotel lobbies, for a complete list of hotels.

There seems to be no way of registering with the police on a weekend, since the Police Office and registration sections of the room-finding services are all closed. You have 48 hours before you must register, however, and you run little risk of problems on this count.

HOSTELS (STUDENTSKÁ KOLEJ)

There are many hostels open each July and August in Czechoslovakia, but it is never clear who is running them—whether CKM, Čedok, or someone else. CKM Prague will book only large groups of foreigners, so your best bet is to go to the hostels in person, or to phone (but automatic "no's" are sometimes given over the phone). The standard Čedok price for a double room per night is 55Kčs. Couples may stay together.

Hotel Jarov, in Prague 3 at Koněvova 196 next to the Economics Institute (tel. 82 46 41), is the most attractive alternative to a hotel. Somewhat barren, this hostel (capacity 300 beds) is a student dormitory during the school year. Doubles, triples, and quads. Hot showers. Reservation recommended. Open July 1 to August 31. Tram #9 or 21.

Kolej 5. Kvetna, in Prague 3, Slavíkova 22 (tel. 27 88 01/02/03) is somewhat smaller, but just as nice. Bus #120 from Karlovo nám. or tram #11, 20 or 29 to náměstí Jiřího z Poděbrad, then backtrack to Slavíkova.

Strahov, Spartakiádní Stadión, is the least desirable accommodations. Huge and barren, some buildings with no hot water, it makes you wonder how the Czech students can stand it. Open July 1-August 30. Bus #176 from Karlovo nám., bus #132 or 143 from Obráncu míru, or tram #2, 8 or 22 stop at the bottom of the hill (a long walk up).

Suchdol, in Prague 6, in the suburb of the same name (tel. 34 41 10), is modern, comfortable and near some gorgeous scenery, but also very far.

Almost always has space. Take tram #23 from Národní to the end at Podbaba, and then bus #107 or 147 to the Vysoká škola zemědělská—ask the driver. The building is unmarked, but it's behind a soccer field.

Junior Hotel Praha, in Prague 2, Žitná 12 (tel. 29 99 41) has mostly doubles and quads, but also some singles, and is open throughout the year. Excellent location, good company, all amenities, but always full, so make a reservation. Beds 63Kčs in a single, 42Kčs in shared accommodations. Take any bus or tram to Karlovo nám.

Větrník-Petriny, on Větrník Hill (tel. 35 52 51), is normally the luxury student dormitory, which Cedok converts into a hotel for July and August. Doubles only at 105Kčs. Tram #1 gets you there. Tends to have space, but is large and impersonal.

C HOTELS

Prices begin at 63Kčs for a single, 84Kčs for a double, 18Kčs for a private bath.

Stará Zbrojnice (the old armory), Prague 1, Všehrdova 16 (tel. 53 28 15). Across 1 Máje Bridge from Národní. Good location.

Hotel Balkan, Prague 5, Svornosti 28 (tel. 54 07 77). Large rooms make this a solid bet. The pub on the first floor is an excellent place to eat, if you can get a seat. Take tram #14 or 15 to the first stop across Palackého.

Národní dům, Prague 3, Bořivojova 53 (tel. 27 53 65). Take tram #7 or 26 to Sladkovského náměstí, walk south one block. 4- and 5-bed rooms, which cost 35-40Kčs per person. Open all year. Go in person; you will be turned down on the phone. Recommended.

Food

Cheap *pivnice* (beer halls) and *vinárny* (wine cellars) are all over town, usually with very good local specialties, and always with posted menus. The *cukrárny* and *kavárny* offer pastries, coffee, and sometimes homemade ice cream. You won't have any trouble finding quality food, but nonetheless we recommend:

U Prince is one of the best inexpensive restaurants in the Staroměstské nám (old Town Square). Opposite the Old Town Hall, it offers fine food in attractive surroundings. Open 9am-10 pm.

Kosher Restaurant Maislova, inside the Jewish Town Hall, (tel. 62541), serves a fine meal consisting of roast beef, chicken soup, boiled cabbage and potatoes for only 8Kčs. One of the best places to go in the Jewish neighborhood. Open noon-1pm only.

U Supa (The Vulture), Celetná 22 near Staroměstské náměstí, has a historic wine cellar and an excellent atmosphere. Duck and goulash for 15Kčs. Open 11am-9pm, Sat. 11am-5pm.

The following class II restaurants are more expensive, but you can still gorge yourself for 40Kčs.

Vikárka, Vikářská 6, is located in the small alleyway next to St. Vitus Cathedral. Food is better than average at standard prices. Packed at lunch, so be prepared to wait. Open 11am-9pm.

Klášterní Vinárna, Národní 8. An excellent restaurant in an old monastery, one block east of the National Theater. Beef specialties 14-20Kčs. Open 11am-midnight.

Sights

Prague grew up as five independent towns with separate characters, first united by central administration in 1784. **Staré Město** was the first and most important, but the Jewish village, **Josefov,** was not far behind, winning its own banner and government in 1358. **Hradčany** was the royal city, crowned by the sprawling Gothic **Castle** *(hrad),* and beneath it **Malá Strana** arose on the seventeenth-century ambitions of the local gentry. **Nové Město** was once the Hussite stronghold, but it was repeatedly destroyed in the religious wars, and now it forms the commercial center, with rich nineteenth-century fronts and spacious squares.

The heart is **Václavské náměstí,** a favorite meeting place of Czech and foreign students in the days of the liberalization. In the grimmer months of 1968 and 1969, it was the site of mass protests and demonstrations, but now it's a hole in the ground due to metro construction.

Staroměstské náměstí is the city's most famous square, dominated by the **Old Town Hall,** which grew from the original fourteenth-century tower to include several neighboring buildings. Townspeople as well as tourists gather on the hour to see the famous clock with twelve Apostles and a bell-ringing skeleton. The square was the site of May Day demonstrations, protest rallies and sit-ins, and the statue of the Protestant heretic **Jan Hus** occupies an appropriate position in its center. Across from the Town Hall is the **Tyn Church,** once a center of the Hussite movement. The difference between the two towers is intentional: one represents Adam, the other Eve. A short detour down Jilska will bring you to the **Bethlehem Chapel,** where Jan Hus preached to his loyal congregation from 1402 until just before his death at the stake in Constance.

The second area to be settled was the **Jewish Quarter,** around Parižská and U St. Hrbitova. The fascinating underground **Staranová** (old new) synagogue is the oldest in Europe—parts date back to 1270. You can attend services here on Saturdays, and daily at dawn and dusk. While the Jewish culture has mostly died out, the area is well maintained, and is on the main tourist route. There is no attempt here at all to minimize the significance of the old ghetto, as is the case elsewhere in Eastern Europe. The nearby Jewish cemetery crowds 12,000 tombstones within its walls.

The center of Renaissance social life was **Karluv Most,** the bridge connecting the Old Town with **Malá Strana,** a sixteenth- and seventeenth-century noblemen's suburb. If renovation of the Gothic defense tower is completed, climb it for a fantastic view of the city; otherwise simply enjoy the thirty Baroque statue groups that line the bridge. From here climb through **Malostranské náměstí,** past the greatest of Jesuit Baroque, **St. Nicholas' Church,** up to the **Pražský Hrad** (castle). The **Katedrála Sv.**

Víta is probably the most intricate Gothic structure in Central Europe. The tombstones inside are extraordinary: there are 21 carved portraits from the fourteenth century, an immense Renaissance mausoleum in white marble, and to the right of the High Altar a twelve foot baroque bonanza of glistening silver. A few steps away is the **National Gallery,** strong on Bohemian painting and sculpture from the thirteenth to the sixteenth century—a must for those who thought the Renaissance was really Italian. Next door the **Royal Palace** offers a whole array of Gothic designs. Higher up there is a tiny street carved into the fortified wall, **Zlatá Ulička** (the Golden Lane), where the court alchemists are supposed to have worked. The tiny bookstore at #22 was Kafka's home for a time in 1917.

MUSEUMS

State Jewish Museum (Zidovské), located at Jáchymova 3 in the Old City. Includes six synagogues, an ancient cemetery and an extensive collection of Jewish artifacts from Bohemia and Moravia. Most of the exhibits were collected during World War II under Hitler's direction so that a museum of "decadent" Jewish culture could be founded in Prague after the war. Most of the museums are open 9am-5pm, closed Saturday. A ticket purchased at one site (3Kčs for students) is good for all of the exhibits in the ghetto area.

National Gallery (Národni Galerie), located inside the castle at Hradčanské nám. 15. An excellent collection of woodcuts and paintings, including works by Dürer and Breughel. Open daily (except Mon.) 10am-6pm.

The Lenin Museum, Hybernská 7, and the **Klement Gottwald Museum,** Rytířská 29, are the two Communist Party and general ideology centers. It's worth visiting at least one of them. Both open daily except Mon. 9am-5pm.

Evenings

Most of Prague's nightlife occurs behind closed doors—among friends, in the beer halls, or in the excellent theaters. Every year from May 12 to June 4, the **Prague Spring Festival** draws musicians from all over the world, and in the summer there are outdoor concerts in the courtyards all over the city. Remember that all plays and operas are in Czech. Tickets are cheap, even though there are no student discounts, and can be bought at **Sluna,** at Panská 4, Cerná růže Arcade (tel. 22 12 06), open July and August Mon.-Fri. 8am-6pm. The same goes for the office at Václavské nam. 28 (Alfa Arcade, tel. 26 16 02). Pick up a monthly calendar of events here, or at **PIS,** Na příkopě 20. The star tourist attraction is the **Laterna Magika,** Národní 40. You shouldn't leave Prague without seeing this review of cleverly integrated films, live drama, and ballet which has drawn large international audiences. Performances nightly at 8pm, Fridays and Saturdays at 5 and 8pm. 35Kčs.

Loutka, the central puppet theater, is at nám. M. Gorkého 28 (tel. 22 51 41). There's lots of cinema in Prague, listed in the daily papers. The two houses specializing in classics are **Illusion,** Vinohradská 48 (tel. 25 02 60) and **Ponrepo,** Letohradská 2 (tel. 37 29 93).

But the best way to enjoy Prague at night is to head to a *pivnice* (beer hall) or a *vinárna* (wine cellar) and meet East European students. If you speak German, you will probably meet East German students rather quickly, who

are just as baffled by Czech as you are. Some Czech students speak English,
however, and are almost always receptive and extraordinarily friendly. We
recommend:

U fleků, Křemencova 11, Prague's answer to the German beer house, but with
weekend cabaret and occasional dancing. They serve their own beer.

U Malvaze, 10 Karlova, open 2-10pm, except Wed. and Thurs. Serves a
mysterious, dark brew guaranteed to make you honest. 2.40Kčs for a half liter.

Ve staré radnice, Loretánská, corner of Hradčanské náměstí, open 9am-8pm.
In a delightful old building.

U Zelené Žáby (the green frog), U Radnice 8, is a dark and intimate *vinárna*
in a building from the 1400's. The music can be a bit loud, but the wine is
excellent. Open 3-11pm; closed Fri. and Sat.

Bohemia

While we usually don't recommend packaged tours, especially packaged
socialist tours, Čedok has a few one-day tours through parts of Bohemia and
Moravia which are relatively inexpensive and generally informative. Ask
them for their booklet *One Day with Cedok,* which gives complete information. Rather interesting is the tour to **Karlovy Vary** (Karlsbad) where everybody in nineteenth century literature used to go to be cured—Goethe, Schiller, Gogol, Turgenev, even Marx. It costs $15 and includes lunch and
dinner. You can do it more cheaply, if less conveniently, on your own.
Buses leave the CSAD bus station Florenc about every hour (reserve the day
before), and there are agonizingly slow trains from the **Hlavní nádraží.** Bus
costs 39Kčs, train 44.60Kčs—no discounts. Try to book return space in
advance or you risk getting stranded.

Southern Bohemia is the country that inspired Smetana's *My Fatherland.*
České Budějovice, home of the original Budweiser beer, has a Renaissance
square, dominated by the ancient **Black Tower.** From here it is a short bus
ride to **Ceský Krumlov,** a beautiful Gothic town lying under a Renaissance
castle. Even closer is **Hluboká,** a neo-Gothic castle that looks disturbingly
like a residential college at Yale.

Between České Budějovice and Prague lies **Tábor,** the Hussite town.
Like most South Bohemian towns, it prospered around 1500, and straddles
the border between medieval and Renaissance styles. Try to get a guide
through the underground tunnels, accessible from the Town Hall. An hour's
drive west of Tábor is **Zvíkov,** a medieval castle that earned a place in
Smetana's piece for its location above the confluence of the Vltava and
Otava rivers.

A half-hour train ride (8Kčs) from Station Praha-smíchov brings you to
Bohemia's greatest castle, **Karlštejn,** a fourteenth-century walled and turreted fortress with a neo-Gothic interior. Just before the Moldau reaches
Prague, it passes Czechoslovakia's most revered landmark—**Vyšehrad,** the
seat of the legendary Princess Libuše, who supposedly prophesied the
dominion of the city. There remain on the mount a Neo-Gothic church, a
Romanesque rotunda, and the Vyšehrad Cemetery, all one half-hour's walk
south of the New Town.

Moravia

From the Austrian provincial town of Brünn, **Brno** has expanded into the bustling and industrial Moravian capital. The old town is still pleasantly Baroque, and the Austrian spirit lingers in the numerous *pivnice*. The **Dóm sv. Petra a Pavla** rises on Petrov Hill. Across town on a separate hill looms the **Spilberk Castle,** a medieval fortification that served as state prison until the mid-nineteenth century, and again in the last war.

The location of the CKM *středisko* (25Kčs with IYHF card, 39Kčs without) changes yearly, so check with the central CKM office, Česká 11 (tel. 23641-3). The probable locations are: Kounicovy Koleje, Králova 45 (tel. 43051; tram 4 from station to end, then walk downhill on Brezinova); Leninova 88 (tel. 57166; tram 12 or 13 from station to door); or Purkynova 93 (tel. 41341; tram 13 to end or 12). This last is a rather posh class C hotel even when CKM isn't around, with doubles for 84Kčs and triples for 126Kčs. Otherwise, the cheapest hotel in town is **Tatran,** Kopecná 16-20, a ten-minute walk from the station, with singles 63Kčs, doubles 84Kčs. **Čedok** lives by the Rail Station at Tatranská 2a. They can help you plan daytrips to places like **Pernštejn,** the unconquerable castle; Moravian **Karst,** with its underground river and drip formations; or **Slavkov** (formerly Austerlitz), where Napoleon won the battle of the Three Emperors.

Olomouc, formerly seat of an Archbishopric and a flourishing bourgeoisie, has preserved monuments from both traditions. In the center of the town is the Gothic-Renaissance **Town Hall,** featuring an astronomical clock and *Glockenspiel,* with social-realist figures. Just north of the **náměstí Míru** (Central Square) is the **Church of St. Morice,** retaining a fabulous Romanesque tower. To the east of these buildings extends the precinct of the former archbishop's residence, including a Baroque palace and the Gothic **Cathedral of St. Wenceslas.**

There is a large **Youth Hostel** at Třída 17 listopadu #54. Take tram #1, 2, 3, 4, or 5 two stops from the Station. (Get off and turn left from the direction of travel—hostel will be on the left.) Or try the **Kolej B.Václavka** (tel. 23841), a large hostel with doubles for 52Kčs. Look for the twin towers behind the first hostel.

Slovakia

Slovakia is the point where all the expanding empires since Rome ran into the Carpathian Mountains and stopped. Until 1945, there were settlements of every nearby ethnic group—the ruling Hungarians and Poles, colonizing Germans, peasant Ukrainians, Jews, and the ubiquitous gypsies. Southern Slovakia is now a major mining center and not very exciting, but the northern rim is crowned by several dramatic mountain ranges—the **Vysoké Tatry, Slovenský Raj,** and **Velká Fatra.** The region is called **Spiš,** meaning Saxon, in reference to the local German population, invited by Hungarian King Béla IV to resettle the province after the Tatar invasions in 1247.

The Spišské Towns

Poprad is the major jumping-off point for mountain excursions towards

Tatranská Lomnica and **Strbské Pleso.** An industrial town, Poprad is rather ugly except for the suburban **Spišská Sobota,** a medieval German-Hungarian settlement. **Kežmarok** is quietly German Baroque, skirted by a medieval castle and the **Trinity Church,** a wooden Lutheran monument from 1717.

Another architectural gem is the town of **Levoča,** still surrounded by its medieval wall. The **Kostol sv. Jakuba** is an exceptionally rich and purely Gothic church, with a sixty-foot altar. Every niche holds a work of Gothic carving in lindenwood, and the fourteenth-century frescoes have been perfectly preserved. The Renaissance **Radnice** (town hall) is next door, but the backstreet **Spišské Muzeum** has a more interesting exhibition—lovely bric-a-brac and a room explaining what Europe's royal machinations meant in local ethnic, geographic and political terms.

There is a quaint governmental atmosphere in **Spišská Nová Ves** and a good Gothic church, for it was capital of the thirteen Spiš towns that Poland ruled until 1772. This is the central starting point for hiking into the **Slovenský Raj** (Slovak Paradise). The ride east through the green fields of the glaciated **Hornád Valley** is beautiful, and among older women, folk costume is still the rule: a broad, colorful pleated skirt with a dark apron, head-scarf, and intricate embroidery. The next major city is **Prešov,** a prototypical provincial outpost. **Košice** is the governmental seat of Eastern Slovakia, but other than its famous Cathedral, it offers only steel mills. Košice is the only town with a CKM hotel, but camping is widespread, with tentsites for 6Kčs and often four-person huts for 105Kčs. Smaller towns often have class C hotels. Otherwise it may be best to approach a waiter or hotel night clerk and ask where you can sleep for a few dollars.

Bratislava

After the Ottoman conquest of Buda in the sixteenth century, Bratislava became the Hungarian capital. The town is appropriately dominated by **Bratislavský Hrad,** formerly a Roman fortification that was continuously remodeled and expanded and has now been restored to its Baroque form. At its base is the **Dóm sv. Martina,** the early Gothic coronation cathedral of ten Hungarian kings and eight queens. **Námestie Hviezdoslavovo** is surrounded by some of the city's best architecture, including the **Slovak National Theater** and the fifteenth-century **University Building** (now the Music Academy) on ul. Jiráskova. The best preserved section of the town wall is the **Michalská Veža,** a tower embellished in a Baroque style and now full of ornamental weapons. The Franciscan church at Diebrovo nám. 1 is an amazing hybrid of Gothic, Renaissance, and Baroque styles.

Boat trips down the Danube (10Kčs) leave hourly from the foot of ul. Mostová, and there is daily hydrofoil service to Budapest costing 70Kčs. Trains and buses each leave twice daily to Vienna; the bus takes half as long (two to two and a half hours), leaves at 7am and 6pm, and costs about $3. Remember, international tickets are available *only* at Čedok. Some trains from the north (Žilina or Berlin) leave and arrive at the suburban station Nové Mesto. From there take tram #6 to the center of town.

To hitch to Vienna, cross the new Danube bridge and walk down Viedenská Cesta. The same road will take you to Hungary via Györ, but the hitching is more difficult. Trying to get north towards Brno or Prague is virtually impossible because of autoroute construction. Don't waste your time trying.

Addresses and Telephone Numbers

CKM: Hviezdoslavovo nám 16 (tel. 33 16 07), open Mon.-Fri. 1-4pm. In the Old Town, near the Danube *(Dunaj)*.

Čedok: 13 Štúrova (tel. 52142), open 9am-6pm weekdays, 9am-noon Sat. Travel department open 9am-3pm weekdays (tel. 55279). You must buy international tickets here. They offer all Čedok services, including money exchange.

CSAD Bus Terminal: "Avion," located diplomatically between Americké nám and Sovetské nám. Tram #2, 3 or 8 from the Train Station.

Accommodations

All the class C hotels in Bratislava appear to have been closed. Try the **CKM Hostel** (25Kčs per person), but the address changes yearly, and even switches from July to August, so check with the CKM office. The most recent locations have been **Mlynská Dolina**, ul. Osmolovova (tel 33 88 75); at the end of bus line 39 from Hurdanovo nám.), and **Horský Park** (tel. 44183). Some years it has also been housed at ul. Bernolákova 1 (tel. 44228; tram #3 from station to Belojanisova.

Next try the **Motel Zlaté Piesky**, ul. Vajnorská in suburban Trnávka (tel. 67264), which has a campground with bungalows; tram #2 or 4, or bus #32.

Food

Dining well is inevitable in Bratislava. Grilled meats of various kinds and Slovak wine are the local staples. You will be able to find good places for yourself just by wandering through the Old Town. Don't neglect the city's countless *cukráreni*, with sumptuous Viennese-style pastry at 2-4Kčs, and often homemade ice cream *(zmrzlina)*.

Vinaren pod Baštou, ulicá Baštova, just off Sedlaska near Michael's gate. Reasonable meals for about 12-15Kčs, specialties from 17Kčs. Open 11am-midnight except Sunday.

Slovanské Reštaurácia, Štúrova 3, in the arcade. Open weekdays 11:30am-3pm and 6-10pm, Sat. 11am-4pm. Try this one for a splurge (at 15-25Kčs per person, or one of the heaping Slovakian platters for two at 40Kčs). Fine service, good food, and menus in English.

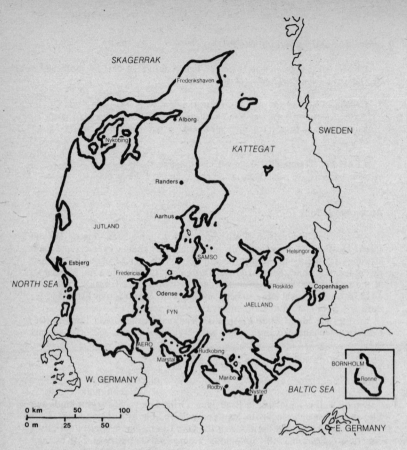

DENMARK

$1 U.S.=4.8 kroner (kr)   **1 kr=$.21**

Denmark's charms are modest. You won't discover here the natural grandeur of Norway, nor will you be overwhelmed, as in Italy, by the splendors of its cities. Denmark's buildings and social institutions, like its land, are shaped on a small, very human scale. But small is indeed beautiful in Denmark. From crowded Copenhagen to the remotest fishing or farming hamlet, you'll find gentle, rich countryside; simple, perfectly proportioned buildings; and unpretentious, vigorous people.

Yet Denmark is no quaint relic of the past. Like its Scandinavian neighbors, it is fully industrialized, modern, sophisticated, and very wealthy, with a reputation for sexual freedom, high taxes, and comprehensive social services. But no single theme predominates: the entire country seems as carefully balanced as a piece of the famous Danish furniture.

Transportation and Practical Information

The quiet, rolling countryside makes Denmark a cyclist's paradise. Bicycles can be rented through the tourist offices of most towns for about 15kr per day. Several train stations, including those in **Aarhus** and **Helsingor** now rent bicycles; this arrangement allows you to return the bicycle to a different station for a small fee. Ask at the station or tourist office for the pamphlet *Go by Train—Rent a Bike*.

For faster travel, an efficient network of trains and buses covers most of Denmark. The *Koreplan*—the schedule of trains, buses, and ferries for the entire country—costs 12kr; tourist offices and train stations will give you free schedules for individual routes. Hitching is fairly difficult.

Efficient tourist offices, maps and information. Many will find you a room in a private home. These rooms are less expensive than hotel rooms (about 40kr for a single) and often nicer; also you will usually have access to a kitchen. Tourist offices will also book you into a hotel for a small fee. In several towns (but not in Copenhagen), they run a **Meet the Danes** program: you spend an evening with a Danish family that shares your interests at no cost.

There are youth hostels scattered throughout Denmark; they generally include rooms for families, and are well run and pleasant. Outside of Copenhagen, all are official IYHF hostels, charging 15-18kr per night, and requiring hostel cards and sheets or sheet sleeping sacks (no sleeping bags). Charges for sheets run 8-12kr. You usually have to register before 9pm; curfew (outside of Copenhagen) is 11pm. Many of the smaller hostels are open only during the summer; all are closed for a couple of weeks at Christmas. Pick up a free brochure listing all hostels and many camping sites from a tourist office.

Camping is permitted only in authorized places, butere are so many of these that you'll seldom have a problem finding a place (though you won't be alone). Pick up a copy of *Campingpladser i Danmark* (18kr) for a full list, or ask at the local tourist office. The overnight charge is usually 8-11kr per person. Camping carnets are required; you can purchase temporary ones, good for four weeks, at the sites for 8kr.

Danish food is world famous. The pastry can be sampled in a *konditori* or *bageri*. Standard, inexpensive dishes include *biksemad*, chopped meat and potatoes, fried with onion and topped with a fried egg; *hakkebof*, chopped beef or hamburger steak; and *fiskefilet*, simply fish fillet.

For lunch, Danes eat *smorrebrod*, literally "butter and bread," but in fact an open-faced sandwich made from all sorts of meat, smoked or pickled fish, cheeses, eggs, and vegetables. Specially-trained women, known as *smorrebrodsjomfruer*, prepare these sandwiches as much for the eye as for the stomach. You may grow fond of the Danish *polse* (hot dog), which is better than the American variety. Specify *med brod* if you don't want a *polse* wrapped in a piece of wax paper. Danish blue cheese and *havarti* are internationally famous so you might want to sample the local favorites: *danbo*, *maribo*, or *skole*.

Telephones are either fully automatic (dial six digits) or, if the number begins with letters, operator-controlled (dial the two letters and then give the operator the remaining numbers). In pay phones, insert .50kr and then dial. Your money will not return if a connection is not made, but you can go on dialing for three minutes.

There are town festivals at different times of year all over Denmark. Of particular interest is the **Roskilde Festival,** a three-day music festival (mostly rock music) held in late June or early July. Ask the Tourist Office for detailed information on festivals.

Finally, a warning to winter travelers. Hostels, campsites, and tourist offices in smaller towns are often open only during the summer. Also in both Copenhagen and the countryside, you should expect the hours kept by tourist-oriented places to be shorter than the summer hours listed here.

Copenhagen (København)

A vigorous egalitarian spirit pervades Copenhagen. Both six- and sixty-year-olds clamber around in clunky clogs and patched jeans; old and young, men and women bicycle unfazed through heavy traffic. Despite its elegant pastries and expensive, delicate porcelain, Copenhagen is a relaxed city. More than fifteen pedestrian streets and many lush parks make Copenhagen ideal for wandering and picnicking before the night's excitement begins. Watch for the spontaneous concerts, carnivals, swaggering sailors, and non-stop sex shows, set in cobbled streets of centuries-old churches and houses. Copenhagen is more raucous than quaint, and certainly the liveliest center in Scandinavia. You'll find Copenhagen worth the high price of your visit.

Orientation

Compact central Copenhagen is easily explored on foot. The central city is bounded on the southeast by the harbor **(Inderhavnen)** and on the north and west by the broken semicircular ring of park which extends from the **Kastellet** (Citadel) to Tivoli. These parks once comprised the city's fortification: today's gentle slopes and ponds were ramparts and moats. Across the harbor is the district of **Christianshavn,** known for its canals and its commune, **Christiania.**

Rail travelers arrive at the **Central Station.** Here, a post office and grocery store keep late hours every day. A currency exchange is open 7am-10pm daily, but charges 8kr to cash a travelers check. **American Express,** only two blocks from the station, at 12 H.C. Andersens Blvd., will cash any brand of travelers check for 5kr. Bags may be stored in the station's lockers for 3kr, but **Use-It** (see below) provides the same service for free. **Kiosk P,** also in the Central Station, is a room-finding service (see Accommodations section).

Travelers arriving by air at **Kastrup Airport** may take bus #32 to Rådhuspladsen (Town Hall Square). Here you are only two blocks from the Central Station (follow Vesterbrogade). Those arriving by boat from Malmö can reach the Rådhuspladsen or the Central Station by bus #41.

Just outside the main entrance to the Central Rail Station is the **Danmarks Turistraad** (Tourist Information Center). Ask for a map and for the booklet *Copenhagen This Week,* which has useful general information and complete listings of prices and hours of museums and other sights.

Although the Tourist Office is generally quite helpful, you are likely to benefit more from the remarkable range of free services offered by **Use-It,** a city-sponsored information center for young travelers. Here you may store your stuff for free (10kr deposit for lock). Be sure to get Use-It's own city map and a copy of *Playtime Magazine,* Use-It's disarmingly relaxed city guide, full of information about survival and good times in Copenhagen. Look for Use-It's "Info-Papers" on special subjects (hostels, entertainment, work in Denmark, etc.). There are ride boards and message boards; they will hold mail, c/o: Poste Restante. Use-It, Magstraede 14, DK-1204 Copenhagen K. Best of all, the young, friendly, and knowledgeable staff will help you, in person or over the phone, with any problem—from finding a bed in a hostel to handling a lost-passport crisis. Use-It is located on the first floor of the **Huset** (House) for Copenhagen Youth, at 14 Magstraede, a short walk from the Central Station; open daily 10am-8pm in summer (tel. 15 65 18), open in the off-season Mon.-Fri. 10am-5pm, till 7pm Tues. and Thurs. The Huset also contains a jazz club *(Vognporten)*, restaurant *(Spisehuset)*, a movie theater, and a rock/folk club *(Musikcafen)*.

Copenhagen boasts an excellent bus system. Routes are indicated on city maps; most lines pass through the Rådhuspladsen. Buses run at frequent intervals until 12:30am; night buses (designated by letters instead of numbers) continue service on selected routes until 2:30am. An individual ticket costs 2kr, but eight tokens *(poletter)* may be purchased from the driver for 12kr. Tickets are valid for transfers within one hour of purchase.

For more rapid transportation, Copenhagen offers electric S-trains, or S-*tog*. Trains run at twenty-minute intervals between 5am and 1am (closing at midnight on Sunday); avoid using them during the rush hours, 8-9am and 4-5pm. An individual ticket costs 2kr; four tickets may be purchased for 6kr. Supplementary fares are charged for journeys outside the central zone. S-*tog* tickets, like bus tickets, are valid for transfers within one hour of purchase. All S-*tog* rides are free with Eurail or InterRail passes.

Perhaps the best way to explore greater Copenhagen is by bicycle. The **Cykelbørsen**, at 157 Gothersgade (tel. 14 07 17), is open weekdays 9am-5:30pm, and Saturdays 9am-2pm. Bicycles may be rented here for 12kr per day, 20kr for the weekend, or 30kr for three days; a 50kr deposit is required. Drivers are used to cyclists, and many of the main streets have separate cycle lanes. If, however, you do not thrive on big-city traffic, you should rent a bicycle for a weekend, when traffic is not bad at all.

GETTING OUT OF COPENHAGEN

Use-It can help your hitching: they supply materials for making destination signs. The best hitchhiking routes out of Copenhagen may be reached in the following ways. For Helsingor and Sweden, take bus #6, 24, or 84 to Hans Knudsens Plads or the S-*tog* to Ryparken. For the Continent, take bus #16 to Gammel Koge Landevej or the S-*tog* to Ellebjerg Station. Then hitch west on Folehaven (Ring II). For Funen and Jutland, take the S-*tog* to Taastrup Station and go to Roskildevej.

There are two principal ferry crossings between the Copenhagen area and Sweden. **Oresundsselskabet** operates ferry service (12.05kr; free with Eurail or InterRail pass) and hydrofoil service (25kr, 15kr with rail pass) between downtown Copenhagen and Malmö. Departures from Havnegade can be reached by bus #41. The shortest ferry crossing leaves from Helsingor, an hour north of Copenhagen, to Sweden's Helsingborg (5.80kr; free with either rail pass). This is the best crossing to take if you are continuing to Stockholm by rail or thumb.

Addresses and Telephone Numbers

Danmarks Turistraad (Tourist Information Center): outside main entrance to

Copenhagen

1 Amalienborg Palace
2 Frihedmuseet
3 Langelinie/Little Mermaid
4 Von Freisers Kirke
5 Stock Exchange
6 Christianborg Palace
7 Thorvaldsen Sculpture Museum
8 Nationalmuseet
9 Raadhuset
10 American Express
11 Mekanisk Musik Museum
12 Post Office
13 Carlsberg Brewery

the Central Train Station (tel. 11 14 15). May-September office hours: Open daily 9am-7pm (till 9pm July and August) and Sun. 9am-1pm. Winter hours: Mon.-Fri. 9am-5pm, Sat. 9am-noon.

Use-It: Magstraede 14, (tel. 15 65 18). Open daily in summer 10am-8pm. Off-season hours: Mon.-Fri. 10am-5pm, till 7pm Tues. and Thurs.

Danish International Student Committee (DIS): 28 Skindergade, three blocks from Rådhuspladsen (tel. 11 00 44). Helps with trains, flights, and group tours. Open Mon.-Fri. 9:30am-5pm.

Transalpino: 106 Vester Voldgade (tel. 14 46 33). Gives reduced international train fares for anyone under 26.

Spies Rejse Bureau: 42 Nyropsgade, near Vesterport S-*tog* station (tel. 12 35 00). Offers terrific air travel bargains in the off-season.

American Express: 12 H.C. Andersens Blvd. (tel. 12 30 01). Open Mon.-Fri. 9am-5pm, and Sat. 9am-noon.

Post Office: The Main Post Office, at 37 Tietgensgade (behind the Central Station) keeps *poste restante* letters and is open Mon.-Fri. 9am-7pm, Sat. 9am-1pm. The branch in the Central Station is open daily 8am-11pm, Sun. 8am-9pm. Public telephones and telex boxes are open 7am-midnight every day at the Post Office at 33 Kobmagergade.

Police: Stations and cars marked *Politi,* tel. 000 in an emergency.

Medical Aid: Free medical help in emergency cases is available day and night at the casualty wards of most hospitals. Try the Kommunehospitalet, 5 Oster Farimagsgade (tel. 15 85 00), accessible by bus #14, 40, or 43. Medical treatment for accidents and ailments developed inside the country is generally free. You can get a doctor to come to you in an emergency by dialing 0041; this will cost 100-300kr.

24-hour Pharmacies: Steno Apotek, Vesterbrogade 6C (tel. 14 82 66); and Sonderbro Apotek, Amagerbrogade 158 (tel. 58 01 40). A surcharge of 1-2kr is added for late-night customers.

Psychological help-line: Nikolajtjenesten, in the basement of the Nikolaj Kirke (which is no longer a church, but an exhibition hall; (tel. 12 14 00). Accessible by bus #28, 29, or 41. Open Mon.-Fri. 9am-3am, and Sat.-Sun. 1pm-3am.

U.S. Embassy: 24 Dag Hammarskjoldsalle (tel. 12 31 44).

Canadian Embassy: Princess Mariesalle 2 (tel. 31 33 06).

Laundromat: Nyvaskrens, 2 Teglgaardstraede, near Strogert (the pedestrian street). Use only the soap you buy there. Laundromats are expensive: figure 12-15kr to wash and dry a load.

Accommodations

There are three ways to beat Copenhagen's high hotel prices, which start at over $10 per night. First, the city offers hostels, where bed and breakfast costs between 20 and 38kr per night. Second, rented rooms in private homes cost about 40kr. Camping, as usual, is the cheapest of all at 11kr per person in one of the city's seven campgrounds.

HOSTELS

Be warned: the hostel scene changes very rapidly. Last year three hostels closed and one changed location. Also many hostels fill up fast in the summer. Avoid long and fruitless treks: call the hostel or visit Use-It before you go hostel-hunting. Use-It will give you complete information on hostels (after hours, this information is posted outside their office). They will even call the hostel to make sure that there is room for you.

The first three hostels listed below require IYHF cards. These may be purchased for 60kr at **Dansk Vandre Laug,** Kultorvet 7 (open Mon.-Fri. 9:30am-5pm); or from the **Danish Youth Hostel Office** at Vesterbrogade 35 (a couple blocks from the Central Station), open Mon.-Fri. 9am-4pm. You may also be able to buy a card at the hostel; call to find out.

Bellahoj Vandrehjem, on Herbergvejen (tel. 28 97 15), is set on a park and small lake in the quiet Bronshoj section of the city, twenty minutes by bus or bicycle from Rådhuspladsen. Costs 17kr if you have your own sheets; an additional one-time charge of 12.50kr is made for sheets. Breakfast (11kr) and dinner (18kr) are available. Reception open noon-1pm and 3-10:45pm. If you can, avoid the large basement dormitories; the 8-bed rooms on the upper floors are more pleasant. The 344 beds fill up fast; women especially should register early. 1:30am curfew. Open all year except Christmas vacation. Take bus #2 (direction Bronshoj) to Fuglesang Alle, or night bus *(natbus)* B. Get the 1 am bus from Rådhuspladsen if you don't want to be locked out.

Lyngby Vandrehjem is located 7½ miles north of the city at 1 Rådvad (tel. (02) 80 30 74). 94 beds at 17kr each; lunch and dinner for 20kr each. Reception open 8am-1pm and 4pm-9pm. 11pm curfew plus long commute might dampen your night life. Open all year. Take the S-*tog* to Lyngby, then bus #187 to Radvad.

The **Copenhagen Hostel** reopens this year after being dismantled, moved to its current location near the new Bella Center (an exhibition hall), and reassembled. Take bus #46 to Bella Center. Check with Use-It to see if it's open before going out yourself. About 500 beds.

Vesterbro Ungdomsgaard, 8 Absalonsgade (tel. 31 20 70), is well located several blocks down Vesterbrogade from Tivoli, next to an attractive municipal park. This most expensive of hostels charges 38kr for bed and breakfast, plus an additional 9kr once if you need the required sheets. It's a little gritty, but there are advantages: no curfew, reception open 24 hours, pleasant garden for picnics, laundromat around the corner, bar (the **Kobenhavner Stuen**) open till 1am across the street. Open May 5-September 1. Accessible by bus #6, 28, or 41.

Active University, 40 Olfert Fischers Gade (tel. 11 91 91). Stay away from here unless you don't have an IYHF card, are in Copenhagen in the off-season, and have a high tolerance for filth and stuffiness. 20kr for bed and breakfast; use your sleeping bag, or pay 5kr once for sheets and blanket. 2am curfew, 5kr fine if you're late. Closed 12:30-5pm. Open all year. Take bus #1 or 6 to Fredericiagade, then walk four blocks.

Sleep-In. The city will probably run a Sleep-In from mid-June to late August. Bed and breakfast is about 20kr. Use your own sleeping bag. Coed dorms and no curfew. Inquire at Use-It.

PRIVATE HOMES AND HOTELS

Kiosk P, located in the Central Station, is open every day in the summer from 9am-midnight. For a fee of 7kr for a single or 14kr for a double, the staff will find you a room in a private home or hotel. Specify your price range on a preference sheet, and Kiosk P does the rest. We recommend staying in a private home. Many of the people who offer rented rooms are well off and take in visitors mainly out of curiosity or kindness. Most homes are in pleasant residential neighborhoods fifteen to twenty minutes by bus from the center. Singles with a family usually cost 40kr, doubles 65kr. Breakfast is not included, but kitchen facilities may be available. Use-It also might be able to find you a room in a private home. They have fewer rooms available, but the rooms are somewhat cheaper, and there is no finding fee.

Copenhagen's "inexpensive" hotels are generally quite adequate: pleasant managers, clean rooms, and good breakfasts. All prices quoted are for rooms without baths (though in all cases, there are toilets and showers on each floor.) The hotels on Colbjornsensgade and Helgolandsgade, behind the Central Station, are in one of the city's sleaziest areas: be careful at night.

Hotel West, 11 Westend (tel. 24 27 61) has the cheapest rooms downtown in a 51-bed hotel run by a pleasant married couple. Singles 60kr, doubles 90-120kr, triples 130-150kr. No breakfast served, but good atmosphere and very clean.

Somandshjemmet Bethel, 22 Nyhavn (tel. 13 03 70), is a seaman's hotel, located across the canal from the rowdy side of Nyhavn. Facilities are adequate and extremely clean; popular with seamen and students. Singles 63kr, doubles 120kr, breakfast 15kr.

Saga Hotel, Colbjornsensgade 20 (tel. 24 99 67). Friendly manager who keeps the place spotless. Singles 80-95kr, doubles 140-170kr, including breakfast; a little cheaper through the end of June.

Hotel Absalon, 19 Helgolandsgade (tel. 24 22 11), has 150 modern and well-furnished rooms which cost 100kr for a single, 160kr for a double, and 210kr for a triple (price includes breakfast). Under the same pleasant, efficient management, and charging the same prices, a door away is the **Selandia Hotel** (12 Helgolandsgade).

CAMPING

Copenhagen provides extensive camping facilities in and around the city. You can pitch a tent at any one of the seven campgrounds for 11kr per person per night. If you don't have the required International Camping Carnet, you can purchase the temporary carnet at any campground for 8kr. Get Use-It's complete list of Copenhagen campgrounds, or call the campground before you go to make sure that it's open.

The only site open all year is **Absalon Camping,** 132 Korsdalsvej (tel. 41 06 00). Take S-*tog* to Brøndbyøster, then walk for five minutes. Closer to the center (about three miles out) it **Bellahøj Camping,** a 600-tent site on Hvidkildevej (tel. 10 11 50), a short walk from the Bellahøj Youth Hostel. Open June 24-August 27. Take bus #8 from Rådhuspladsen. **Sundbyvester Camping,** 54 Kongelundsvej (tel. 58 10 06), has 316 sites and is about as far from the center as is Bellahøj, but in the opposite direction. Open April 28-September 3. Take bus #31 from Kongens Nytorv to Kongelundsvej.

If you're broke but have a sleeping bag, you might try to sleep out in one of the parks. Since the police do not encourage this practice, get out to the outskirts, find a park that doesn't look too well tended, and camouflage yourself.

FOR LONGER STAYS

Use-It can help you find a room in a pension for about 200kr (single) or 300kr (double) per week. In the summer, economical stays of a month or more are possible, since many students sublet rooms (with kitchen privileges) for about 500kr per month.

Food

Copenhagen can furnish you with the finest cuisine in Northern Europe, but you must pay dearly for it. With a little forethought and occasional picnics, however, you needn't starve nor confine yourself to mediocre cafeteria fare. You can often save by ordering the daily special *(Dagens Ret),* usually priced a few kroner below other dishes. Note: all prices include tax and service, but none of the prices quoted for meals include drinks. A beer with your meal will set you back an additional 7-8kroner.

Rundepoppen Mensa (University Cafeteria), 52 Kobmagergade, next to the Round Tower, offers the most filling portions of any place—stuff yourself for 12-15kr. Acceptable (institutional) food, and excellent salads. Student ID is required, but they usually don't check for it.

Skodsborg Helserestaurant, 14 Linnesgade, is a pleasant vegetarian cafeteria, run by Seventh Day Adventists, offering great daily specials for 21.50kr. Try a large bowl of delicious homemade soup, served with fresh, home-baked bread, for only 7.50kr. Wonderful omelettes. Open 11am-8pm Sun.-Thurs., closed two hours before sunset on Fri. (never later than 6pm), closed Sat. There's a health-food store underneath. Use-It can refer you to other vegetarian restaurants.

Hand I Hanke, 20 Griffenfeldsgade (across Peblinge Lake from the central city), is a friendly native hangout for generous, inexpensive meals (15-20kr), and good folk music. Kitchen open weeknights 3-9pm, weekends 1-9pm. Music Thurs.-Sun. 9pm-1am (admission 10kr).

Skindbusken, 4 Lille Kongensgade, serves wonderful 24kr specials during lunch. The place is small and smoky, and fills up fast. Try to arrive at 11am, when it opens. Open till 8:30pm.

Rådhuskroen, 21 Longangstraede (near Use-It), is a comfortable pub with a rustic interior and candlelight for late-night dining. Filling portions of schnitzel or stroganoff cost 18.75kr; the daily special goes for 16.75kr. Food is average, but you can get hot meals from 10am-4:30am every day.

Vista Self Service, 40 Vesterbrogade, offers substantial (though not especially distinctive) meals at very low prices. Daily specials, including soup or dessert, as well as the main course, are from 13.50kr. Open 9am-8pm.

Spisehuset, 14 Magstraede (part of Huset), serves fine meals at moderate prices. Try their all-you-can-eat lunch buffet—which features many varieties of herring, chicken, meat, casseroles, cold cuts, cheese, salad, and homemade bread. Offered daily noon-3:30pm for 24kr. In the evening, the Spisehuset splits into a pub (where cheese and salads may be ordered along with drinks) and a dining room (where complete 20-45kr meals may be ordered from 5-11pm). The Spisehuset's rustic decor, relaxed atmosphere, and high-quality food make it equally well suited for a single beer or a complete dinner.

J. Knygberg, 18 Kattesundet, near the Rådhus, is a smorrebrod shop as tempting to the eye as any pastry shop in Europe. It is possible, of course, to get smorrebrod in a restaurant; but at a street shop like J. Knygberg, you can have twice as much fun for half the cost. Window shop first, while watching the Danes line up for their lunch packets. Prices range from 3-10kr. Shop opens at 7am; get there before noon, or you'll see only skeletal remains.

Grocery Stores: Shops marked "Brugsen-DB" are run cooperatively, and should have high-quality goods. Try the one at Nørrevoldgade 15 (by the Norreport S-*tog* station). There are other grocery stores along Vesterbrogade, towards the suburbs (within a ten-minute walk from the Central Station).

Sights

An excellent way to get to know Copenhagen is to take one of the guided walking tours. The city's 800-year history is explained through its architectural styles and boundary changes. 5kr for those under 26. Specifics available at Use-It and Tourist Offices—ask for the brochure *Copenhagen on Foot.* The tours are offered from mid-June through September.

Tivoli, Copenhagen's happy amusement park, stands between the Central Station and the Rådhuspladsen, and draws Danes as well as tourists to its gardens, gambling rooms, restaurants, pantomime shows, ballets, concerts, comedy-acrobat routines, and midnight fireworks. Tivoli has two faces. Most tourists go in the evening when the grounds are romantically illuminated; concerts and shows (most free) are in full swing; and there are closing fireworks on Wednesday, Saturday, and Sunday. In the morning and early afternoon, however, the crowd is primarily Danish: people taking lunch in the park, women squeezed around a roulette wheel, kids on the famous (but overrated) roller coaster. Tivoli is open May 1-September 17, 10am-midnight. Admission is 5kr before 1pm, otherwise 7kr. Two warnings: don't gamble all your money away; and eat before entering, or the roller coaster won't be the only thing that takes you for a ride.

Copenhagen's **Zoologiske Have** on Roskildevej, is one of the most charming and progressive zoos in the world. Flamingoes come and go as they please; lions are not caged or fenced in (but rest easy: they're surrounded by a moat—only appearances have changed). Open all year, 9am-6pm daily, admission 18kr. Work up a thirst watching the gorilla artfully wrangle munchies from the crowd. Then head for the **Carlsberg Brewery** for a fascinating view of what happens between barley and bottle. The chief attraction of the brewery visit, for some, follows the tour: free beer. Carlsburg tours start at 9am, 11am, and 2:30pm weekdays. They start at Ny Carlsburg Vej, a ten-minute walk from the zoo (or take bus #6 from the center). **Tuborg,** on the other side of town at Strandvejen 54 (bus #1), offers equally good tours and equally good beer; their tours run continuously from 8:30am-2:30pm weekdays. Tours at both breweries are free.

Everyone makes a pilgrimage to **Langelinie,** where Hans Christian Andersen's Little Mermaid *(den lille Havfrue)* sits atop a rock overlooking the harbor. You might want to avoid the company of clicking cameras on the special "mermaid bus" (#50), which leaves across the street from American Express on H.C. Andersens Blvd (2kr round trip). You can also take bus #1, 6, or 9 to Esplanaden, and walk five minutes.

Harbor and **canal tours** leave every half hour from the head of the Nyhavn canal (16kr with guide, 12kr without) and from Gammel Strand (guided tours only, 16kr). The cool, hour-long cruise under low bridges and around the harbor is worth it for those staying only a short while. You'll go through **Christianshavn,** a district worth exploring on foot. Apart from the quaint canals and houses, you'll see the commune **Christiania,** a former military district occupied in 1971 by young people, on Prinsessegade (if it's still there: the Danish Supreme Court ordered in 1978 that Christiania be cleared.)

The **National Museum, Glyptotek Museum,** and most other art collections in Copenhagen are good, but not outstanding. Exceptions are the **Mechanical Music Museum,** 150 Vesterbrogade (open daily 10am-5pm), featuring mechanical orchestras (highly recommended, worth the 8kr for admission and guided tour); **Thorvaldsen's Museum** for sculpture (next to Christiansborg Palace), open 10am-4pm, admission 2kr (free on Wednesdays, Fridays, and Sundays); and **Louisiana,** Denmark's famous ultramodern museum of contemporary art, located on the coast at Humlebaek, 45 minutes north of Copenhagen by S-*tog*. A combined train-and-museum ticket is available for 24kr.

The **Frilandsmuseet** is a huge open-air museum featuring old Danish farmhouses from all parts of the country. S-*tog* to Sorgengri, then a fifteen-minute walk. Admission 2kr. The **Frihedsmuseum** in Churchill Park is a documentary collection of photos and sabotage equipment complete with tapes in English discussing the articles' significance in World War II. Admission free.

Daytrips

A trip to **Roskilde,** only half an hour from Copenhagen by train, makes a rewarding day excursion. In late June or early July, you might synchronize your visit with the three-day **Roskilde Festival** (mostly rock music). Get the exact dates from the Tourist Office. **Roskilde Cathedral** was built by Bishop Absalon, founder of Copenhagen, in 1170, and houses the tombs of most of Denmark's kings and queens since the fourteenth century. The **Viking Ship Museum** houses five nine-hundred-year-old ships, and exhibits on the process of restoration as well as on Viking culture. Ask at the Tourist Office about boat sailing on the fjords of Roskilde. West of Roskilde, at **Lejre Oldtidsbyen,** a prehistoric village has been reconstructed. People from all over the world spend the summer here, practising ancient methods of weaving, agriculture, pottery and dye-making, and you can walk around and talk to them about what they are doing. There is a **Youth Hostel, Horgaarden,** at Horhusvejen (tel. (03) 35 21 84).

Numerous daytrips are possible combining North Zealand attractions. Distances are short, and frequent train and bus service connects major points. If you visit Louisiana, it is only slightly further north to **Helsingor** (Elsinore in English), site of **Kronborg Castle** of Hamlet fame (castle open daily from 10am-5pm, admission 4kr). There's a fine sandy beach near the Kronborg. For an even better beach, complete with dunes, continue to **Hornbaek** (half an hour further by train). It is also possible to turn inland from Helsingor and travel by train to the castles at **Fredensborg** (the Royal spring and fall residence) or **Hillerod** (stately Frederiksborg Castle).

Shopping

Denmark is world-renowned for its tasteful and practical design, notably in furniture and kitchenware. Before doing any serious shopping, take the tour of the **Royal Copenhagen Porcelain Factory** (free, Tues. and Fri. at 10am); take bus #1 or 14 to 45 Smallegade. Or, visit **Den Permanente,** the permanent exhibition of Danish arts and crafts at Vesterport, Vesterbrogade 8. The prices are a bit higher than in other stores, but you are guaranteed the finest. There are commune shops in Peder Huitfeldtsstraede and Klosterpassagen for clothes and ceramics. Wooden shoes are perhaps the one very Scandinavian item you ought to be able to find cheap. Definitely take advantage of the delivery service of most Danish arts-and-crafts stores: everything sent out of country avoids the whopping tax. There's a fine English bookstore right off the Radhuspladsen at the beginning of Frederiksberggade.

Evenings

Nighttime in Copenhagen offers the visitor a broad spectrum of bars, discotheques, and folk or jazz clubs. Ask Use-It for their current list of discos and private clubs which admit non members.

Nyhavn, Copenhagen's sailor district (at the east end of Gothersgade), is lined with bars, tattoo parlors, and sailors' shops. The houses bordering the canal are attractive, but unescorted women should steer clear. Nyhavn #17 is the most famous and authentic bar and shop.

Huset, 14 Magstraede, is Copenhagen's city-sponsored youth center. Jazz on the ground floor 9pm-1am; admission 10-15kr. Pub on the first floor, open 5-11pm. Movies in the original languages are shown every night (on the second floor) for 20-22kr. On the third floor, rock or folk bands play 9:30pm-1:30am, admission 10-25kr.

Café Rosa Luxembourg, also a part of Huset, is located around the corner at 13 Radhusstrade. A bit cozier than Huset, and more costly, too.

Jazzhus Montmartre, 41 Norregade (tel. 12 34 94), is considered the best of the jazz clubs. Entry 20-40kr. Open Tues.-Thurs. 10pm-2am, Fri.-Sat. 10pm-5am. Call to see who is playing.

Pilegarden, 44 Pilestraede, has good folk/blues playing on Thursdays and on an occasional Sunday. Admission is free; on weekdays, you can enjoy dinner (20-30kr) while you listen. Open Mon.-Fri. 3pm-2am, Sat. and Sun. 7pm-2am.

De Tre Musketerer, 25 Nikolaj Plads, offers great live jazz bands every night, with the best saved for the weekends when the cost is 10kr; otherwise free. Open 8pm-2am, closed Sunday.

The Students' Club (Studenterforeningen) at 26c Kobmagergade (tel. 12 81 02). Lectures and discussion groups on issues from "Home Rule for Greenland" to "Hans Christian Andersen's Tales." Also, a bar, music and dancing. Free Tues. and Thurs. (7:30pm-1am). Fri. and Sat, open 9pm-3am.

Aarhus

Sidewalk shows, jazz concerts, fairs, and fishing contests proliferate during **Aarhus Festival Week** in the start of September. Otherwise, it's best to use Aarhus, a busy port and university city, as a base for daytrips into the east Jutland countryside.

A fine open-air museum, **Den Gamle By** (The Old Town), consists of about fifty old marketplace houses, instead of the usual farmhouses. The buildings and craft shops close at 5pm (each, fully furnished, is a miniature museum; 2kr to visit one, five houses for 6kr). The streets of the reconstructed town, however, remain open, ideal for an evening stroll; the **Botanisk Have** (Botanical Gardens), right behind, is a good place for a picnic. There are two interesting medieval churches in the center of town: the **Cathedral** and the **Vor Frue Kirke** (Church of Our Lady).

Tagskaegget is Aarhus' world-famous jazz house, where Duke Ellington and a host of other great musicians have played. It features consistently excellent jazz, and is located at 2 Klostergade (tel. 12 96 44), five blocks north of the Rail Station. Admission is 15-20kr; the Tourist Office will give you a pass for a 5kr discount. Open daily 9am-5pm; music starts about 10pm.

Aarhus' friendly **Tourist Office,** staffed chiefly by students, is open daily in summer from 9am-9pm (tel. 12 16 00); they're located in the Town Hall, a block from the Rail Station. Pick up a map of the city, and a road map of Central Jutland (essential if you'll be doing any bicycle touring). The **International Student Center,** 84 Niels Juelsgade (bus #1, 2, or 7 to Trojborgvej), sponsors frequent activities (talks, meals, bicycle trips) for students; pick up their program at the Tourist Office. **DIS,** the student travel agency, on Nordre Ringgade next to the University administration building (tel. 12 89 44), sells discount air and rail tickets; they're open Mon.-Fri. 10am-3pm.

Accommodations and Food

The **Youth Hostel "Pavillonen,"** Ostre Skovej (tel. 16 72 98), is well situated on the edge of a forest, near the beaches. Reception closed 1-4pm and 9-10:45pm; the enforced 11pm curfew makes it impossible to hear the jazz at Taskaegget. Hostel charges 17kr per night; good breakfast for 12kr. Take bus #1 or 2 to Marienlund. The Tourist Office will find you a room in a private home for 40kr (37kr for stays longer than one night). The **Hotel Aarhus Somandshjem,** 20 Havnegade (tels. 12 15 99 and 12 10 36) is directly across from the port area, and offers beautiful, modern (although smallish) rooms at 70kr for singles, 95kr doubles. **Camping** is very good at **Blommehaven** (tel. 27 02 07), right near the beach and woods, and about 7 km from town center. Take bus #19 (summer only) from the Train Station.

For lunch, soup (1.65kr), sandwiches (from 1.50kr), and hot dishes (from 3kr) are served at the **Matematiske Fag** at the University (just off Langelandsgade); open Mon.-Fri. 8am-4pm. For more natural fare, eat at the **Huset,** 15 Vesteralle. 17kr for very generous portions of the daily special; vegetarian daily special for 15kr. Open weekdays 11am-midnight, Sun. noon-8pm, closed Sat. Huset, a city-sponsored youth center, also offers free concerts and plays in the same building. The communist student organization also serves meals at **Fronthuset,** 53 Mejlgade (near the harbor, the restaurant is well hidden in an inner courtyard). Vegetarian meals 12kr, other meals 14kr, served from noon-2pm, and 6-8pm. Get there early, or they may be out of food. Closed Sun.; pub open 10am-midnight every day. Check with the Tourist Office to make sure they're still open.

Excursions

An excellent day excursion combines the superb **Prehistoric Museum** at **Moresgaard,** south of Aarhus, and the nearby beach. Take bus #6 from the Train Station to the end of the line, at the museum. Entrance is 4kr (2kr for students). Features include the 1600-year-old body of the Grauballe Man, extensive collections of Iron Age artifacts, and Viking art. Before leaving, buy the 3kr pamphlet and take the **Prehistoric Walk,** lined with ancient burial chambers, past dolmens and barrows. When you're finished, the sea lies only about a half-hour away by foot. Bus #19 will return you to Aarhus from the coast every half hour.

The bus to **Ebeltoft** follows a beautiful route around two bays; it costs 35kr round trip and takes an hour and a half (the Aarhus Bus Station *(rutebilstationen),* is a few blocks from the Train Station). The streets of Ebeltoft are lined with half-timbered houses—but they are also overrun by tourists. Still, take half an hour to explore the town. In the process you can pick up maps of the town and surrounding area at the **Tourist Office,** Torvet 9 (tel. 34 14 00; open in the summer Mon.-Sat. 9am-6pm, Sun. 10am-1pm). Bicycles are rented for 12kr per day at Norrebakke 8. There are excellent, uncrowded beaches at Boeslum and Draby, each about 3km from Ebeltoft. The **Youth Hostel** in Ebeltoft is at 43 Sondergade (tel. 34 20 53); 17kr per night.

Silkeborg, in the heart of Jutland's lake district, is an hour and a quarter from Aarhus by bus (30.50kr round trip). The **Tourist Office,** located right at the Bus Station (tel. 82 19 11, open Mon.-Fri. 9am-6pm, Sat. 9am-1pm and 4-6pm, and Sun. 10am-noon), can suggest touring routes and tell you where to rent boats and bicycles. Ask for detailed information on the forty-mile landscape path (for cyclists and hikers) from Silkeborg to Horsens. The **Youth Hostel** in Silkeborg at 55 Ahavevej (tel. 82 36 42) charges 17kr per night and is open all year.

Fyn (Funen) and the Archipelago

Fyn is called Denmark's garden island. It comes close to the stereotyped image of Denmark as a series of meticulously well-kept small villages, manor houses, and farms; a colorful flowerbed graces nearly every house. Even **Odense,** one of Denmark's main industrial towns, is hardly an ugly duckling. The home of Hans Christian Andersen, Odense holds an annual festival for the author who immortalized her in fairytales. During the celebration weeks (the last two in July and the first in August), Hans Christian Andersen plays are performed on the open-air stage of **Funen Village.** Odense sits on the main railway line between Copenhagen and Jutland, and merits a short visit. The **Tourist Office** (tel. 12 75 20) in the Town Hall, a few blocks south of the Station, is open in the summer from 9am-8pm daily; 10am-noon and 6-8pm Sun. They'll change your money when the banks are closed, and arrange for you to spend an evening with a Danish family. Bicycles can be rented for 15kr a day at 34 Klaregade, a few blocks from the Tourist Office. For 17kr, you can stay at Odense's **Youth Hostel,** 121 Kragsbjergvej (tel. 13 04 25); 300 beds. Reached by bus #6.

Don't bother going inside Andersen's one-room childhood home. Instead, visit the house of his birth, Hans Jensenstraede 39-43, converted into an excellent museum where you can listen to recordings of fairy tales. Open every day 9am-7pm; admission 5kr, but only 1kr with hostel card. The streets around the museum are lined with beautifully restored houses.

Svendborg is the best base for longer stays on Fyn and for bicycle trips to the islands of the **South Funen Archipelago.** Svendborg is only an hour south by train from Odense.

The **Youth Hostel Soro** in Svendborg is situated on Svendborg Sound, and run with a friendly touch by Bertha Lind Petersen, who serves delicious family-style dinners every evening for 18kr, and hearty breakfasts for 12kr. The Hostel is at 3 Bellevuevej (tel. 21 26 16) and costs 17kr per night; open March through October. It is best reached by a fascinating 25-minute walk: follow the busy harbor's edge to the left as you face the water, past the Kellog's plant, then continue on the path along the sound where the forest begins.

On the islands, youth hostels are small and often full; if you don't have a reservation, try to call in the morning the day you plan to arrive.

The **Tourist Office,** at 20 Mollergade (tel. 21 09 80) just up the hill from the Rail Station is open Mon.-Sat. 9am-6pm, Sun. 10am-noon in summer. They'll find you a room in a private home for 35kr per person, plus a 3kr fee. Their general brochure on Svendborg lists the prices of hotels in town and on the islands. The **Hotel Aero,** by the harbor at 1 Brogade, has the cheapest rooms in town—singles 50kr, doubles 100kr—but it's usually full. Camping sites are plentiful in the area; on some of the smaller islands you can camp for free.

Fyntour, located above the Svendborg Tourist Office, offers bicycle-trip packages which arrange accommodations and meals in advance and outline routes in detail. Week-long tours cost 650-750kr. Fyntour gives excellent, detailed route plans to those who purchase a complete bicycle-trip package; others must pay 25kr. If you'll be cycling for several days, the map and route description are probably worth it: directions are precise and accurate, and the suggested roads are always quiet, often deserted.

Bicycles are available at the Svendborg Tourist Office (15kr per day), at 29 Norrebro in Rudkobing on the island of Langeland; and from the Tourist Office at 25 Kirkestraede in Marstal on Aero. While cycling is definitely the most rewarding way to tour the islands, bus and ferry service is surprisingly good between major points; get information on routes and schedules from the Tourist Office.

Taasinge, Langeland, and **Aero** are the three largest islands, all easily accessible from Svendborg. All have constantly changing vistas of field and sea, and villages with white-walled churches and half-timbered houses. The most varied countryside is found on Taasinge. Langeland has the finest (but most crowded) beach at **Ristinge;** it's probably the least interesting of the three for cyclists.

Aero is perhaps the most delightful, because it has the most interesting towns: **Marstal** and **Aeroskobing.** The ferry from Rudkobing, in Langeland, to Marstal costs 23kr, but you should buy the round-trip ticket for 33kr, which is also valid for the trip from Aeroskobing to Svendborg, or Soby to Faaborg. Bicycles are 6.50kr extra, or 9kr round trip. Marstal was a thriving shipping center in the nineteenth century; today the interesting harbor is primarily a haven for pleasure sailors. The town has many attractive old streets, though not as much has been preserved here as in Aeroskobing. Sailing buffs will enjoy the large collection of model ships in Marstal's **Maritime Museum;** it's open every day from 9:30-5pm, admission 5kr. The **Youth Hostel** is located right by the harbor at 29 Faergestraede, to your left down Havnegade when you get off the ferry (tel. 53 10 64); it's open May through August. Beds are 17kr, and the friendly management serves a good breakfast for 12kr. There's camping (tel. 53 15 20) just beyond the Hostel. The **Tourist Office,** at 25 Kirkestrade (tel. 53 19 60), open Mon.-Sat. 10am-noon and 2-5pm, has bicycles and maps of Marstal and Aero.

Aeroskobing is a gem. The centuries-old town plan has not been altered, and nearly all of the houses (some from the seventeenth century) have been perfectly preserved. There is a collection of bottle ships on Smedegade. You can camp for 8kr per person near a rocky but pleasant beach, on Sygehusvejen, northwest of town (tel. 52 18 54); tiny cabins for four people cost 40kr. The **Tourist Office,** located near the church on Torvet, the main square, is open Mon.-Fri. 9am-noon and from 2-5pm, Sat. 10am-1pm (tel. 53 13 00).

Several smaller islands are ideal for daytrips—you won't even need a bicycle to get around. Remote **Lyo,** with its village ponds, good beaches, and ancient burial mound at **Klokkestenen,** is the most charming of the smaller islands. Make sure you have ferry schedules before venturing to the smaller islands.

The Southern Islands

Three large islands south of Zealand, all easily accessible from Copenhagen, offer more fine beaches, fishing villages, and quiet countryside for bicycle trips. **Lolland** and **Falster** are on the principle railway route between Germany and Copenhagen; the best beaches, near **Marielyst** on Falster, are very crowded. **Mon,** the most interesting island, is also the least touristy; its eastern coast is fortified by spectacular, towering chalk cliffs.

LOLLAND AND FALSTER

The attractions of **Maribo,** in the center of Lolland, are its lakeside location, a fifteenth-century church, and (you guessed it) an open-air museum. There is a **camping site** right on the lake at **Mindsten/Bangs Have,** at the end of Bangshavevej (tel. 88 00 71). The **Youth Hostel** is located at 2 Ostre Landevej (tel. 88 12 96); it's only open from June 25 to August 20. The **Tourist Office** is at 8 Jernbanegade (tel. 88 04 96), down the street from the Train Station; inquire about bicycle rentals.

MON

Stege, the only sizeable town on Mon, is reached by bus from Vordingborg, which is an hour and a half by train from Copenhagen. It has well-preserved ramparts and a medieval town gate. But the eerie, strangely beautiful chalk cliffs, which seem out of place in small-scale Denmark, are Mon's chief attraction.

The small, friendly **Youth Hostel** near **Somarke,** at 18-19 Stendyssevej (tel. 81 21 42), is beautifully situated in the middle of open fields. The hostel is open from Easter until September 15; 16kr for a bed; free kitchen. Getting to the hostel and the cliffs may be difficult. A bus runs infrequently from Stege towards the cliffs; the stop at Somarkesvinget is 2 km from the hostel. Bus schedules are available at the Vordingborg Train Station. **Store Klint** is the most popular access point to the cliffs; the hostel is only 2 km from the park and cliffs at **Liselund.** From here it is 5 km along the beach—a spectacular hike to Store Klint.

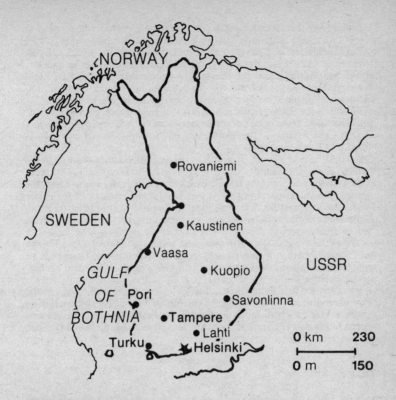

FINLAND

$1U.S.=4.1markka (mk)   **1mk=$.24**

(Note: There is a map of Northern Scandinavia in the Sweden chapter.)

Living where darkness never comes in summer, where winter skies are only twilight and night, the Finns cultivate balancing extremities: 200° steaming saunas are followed by plunges into icy waters, and salty pickled herring is served with bland boiled potatoes. Finland takes painful pride in being the least industrialized, least Westernized and least wealthy of the Scandinavian nations.

The Finns exult in their land of slender pine forests and unpolluted air and lakes; there is a Finnish style which reflects this enthusiasm. It is evident in architecture and textile design: Alvar Aalto and Marimekko are world famous for their stress on comfort, simplicity, and bold primary colors. It is evident in the market displays of fresh fruits and vegetables: the colors are clearer and brighter, the arrangements cleaner and simpler than in other countries. It is evident even in the cool, clean lines of Helsinki's neoclassical center.

You will see this style in Finnish cities, but you'll probably be tempted to seek out its source. Hike over village dirt roads and undulating hills spotted by red farmhouses, and navigate the archipelagoes and the world's largest labyrinth of lakes. For water lovers, the principal attraction lies in the east, around **Savonlinna,** with the heaviest concentration of Finland's 62,000 lakes. You can cruise all the way to **Kuopio,** a distance of about 350 kilometers. Kuopio's outdoor revolving theater is the scene of a ten-day music and dance festival in the second week of June. This region of Finland, called **Karelia,** is the center of the country's forest industry. When passing through **Lapienranta** or **Parikkala,** you might stop to watch how pine is turned into planks and pulp.

Much of Finland's small (five million) population huddles together in the southern part of the country, but the vestiges of civilization reach as far north as the country's borders. At **Rovaniemi,** the largest center in the north, the railroad ends and Lapland begins. Only a few kilometers south of the Arctic Circle, Rovaniemi is the hub of an extensive bus network serving the small communities of the northern regions and continuing on into Norway. Here, four countries meet at Europe's last frontier—a gently rolling land with occasional lakes, crystal-clear rapids, and less occasional villages. Though most Lapps have now settled into permanent residence, thousands of reindeer-herding nomadic Lapps still roam with a general disregard for borders and eternal nights.

The short Finnish summers are filled with music festivals; some of the more interesting are in the smaller, more remote towns. For information on the **Pori Jazz Festival,** the **Kaustinen Folk Festival,** or the **Savonlinna Opera Festival,** write Finland Festivals, Simonkatu 12B, SF 00100 Helsinki 10.

TRANSPORTATION

If you're indifferent to the comforts of a cabin, then deck passage for the twelve hours or so from Stockholm to Turku or Helsinki is a reasonable alternative. The cruise is beautiful, day or night. Sailing to Turku, all but a couple hours of the trip are spent navigating the two splendid archipelagoes. If you travel at night you can spread your sleeping bag in the lounge. Turku lies only three hours by train from Helsinki and is a good introduction to the country. If you travel at the cheapest hours on the **Silja Line,** the cost one way to Turku is $17 and to Helsinki about $21. Eurailpass holders can make the trip for free; InterRail gets you a 50% discount. The less fancy competitor, the **Viking Line,** charges slightly more: $18 to Turku and $22 to Helsinki. Ignore the costly cafeterias; both ships serve marvelous smorgasbords.

If you plan to do a lot of rail travel in Finland and don't have a railpass, you may consider buying a **Finnrail Pass**—eight days of second-class travel for 180mk, or fifteen days for 240mk. You can buy the pass in Finland at major rail stations. **Finnair** gives a 25% student discount, which sometimes makes domestic flights very little more than the bus fare.

Hitchhikers will delight in Finland. The people are friendly, the roads are good and the crime rates very low. Distances are never great between good campsites, clean youth hostels, and saunas (there are over 800,000 in Finland). Sometimes all three will be on the same acre. Pick up a copy of *Campsites in Finland* at the **Finland Travel Bureau,** Kaivokatu 10 in Helsinki.

FOOD

Besides the staples of salty Baltic herring and *ruisleipa* (a hard rye bread), you should experiment with salmon soup, *kaalipiirakka* (cabbage pie), *maksalaatikko* (liver pudding), *kaalikääryleet* (ground beef wrapped in cabbage leaves) and *kalakukko* (specialty of East Finland, a meat and fish pie). More costly are delicacies like *poronliha* (reindeer meat) or even *karhunliha* (bear meat). Various fresh berry soups and thin pancakes stuffed with strawberries or cloudberries are sweet and healthy desserts.

In late July and August you have a chance to participate in a *rapukesti*, a crayfish orgy in which everyone gorges on the large, meaty crustaceans. It is not unusual to eat twenty at a sitting, with ritualized gulps of vodka in between. It is worth adjusting your itinerary to participate, especially if you can indulge with a seaside village group.

Helsinki (Helsingin)

Helsinki knows two moods: she is both the shining Daughter of the Baltic and the stern neighbor of Russia. If you arrive by boat on a sunny day, the city will strike you as clean, bright, and airy, for Helsinki greets sea travelers with the lively colors and odors of the harborside market and the visual harmonies of **Senate Square**. In this mood, Helsinki is one of Europe's most beautiful cities, even though virtually no buildings date from before 1800. But the city also has a cold and forbidding side, expressed in the less imaginative modern architecture and in the public statues, with their unsmiling, almost defiant, emphasis on strength.

Like the rest of Finland, Helsinki is sparsely settled despite her half million inhabitants. Yet the winters bustle with theater, political institutes, and 20,000 university students. Even after many residents evacuate for the summer, you still should come. Join in on one of the two huge June celebrations: **Helsinki Day,** June 12, commemorates an edict of 1550 which obliged people to move to the newly-founded town; while on **Midsummer's Eve** the Finns—with folkdancing, bonfires and boozing—mimic the sun by staying up all night. Or come during the two-week **Helsinki Festival** for fine arts in late August.

Orientation

If you arrive by air, take the city bus (4.20mk) which goes to the **Central Railway Station,** a half hour away in the center of town. The Finnair bus costs more and will leave you in a less central location. At the Central Station (one of the world's few architecturally notable rail stations, designed by Eliel Saarinen) there are several different banks of luggage lockers. Don't bother going to the information office upstairs. Downstairs at **Hotellikeskus** you can get a transit map and a complete list of IYHF Youth Hostels in Finland. Also pick up the very useful *Helsinki This Week*, which includes a map with a street index as well as current information on prices and opening hours. A currency exchange in the Station is open until 8pm weekdays and until 7pm Sun.

If you come by boat to Helsinki, a half-mile walk will bring you to **Market Square,** which bustles with food stalls until 2pm (those arriving by Silya Line can also take tram 3T). **American Express,** just a block south, is the best place to change money, but they will cash only American Express checks. Just west of the market is the **City Tourist Office,** Pohjoisesplanadi 19 (tel. 1693 757); open weekdays 8:30am-6pm, Sat. until 1pm, closed Sun. You can get your orientation material here. Be sure to pick up the four excellent self-guided walking tour brochures (free). You can use a free telephone here to call for accommodations.

Trams and buses crisscross the city. Individual tickets cost 3mk, but are not valid for transfers. The **tourist ticket** (12mk) gives you unlimited use of trams, buses, and some ferries, for 24 hours from the time you first use it. Another good alternative, for those staying several days, is the ten-trip ticket (24mk) which entitles you, each time you use it, to unlimited free transfers within an hour. When you begin a ride, get your ticket stamped and pick up a "control slip"; when you transfer, show the control slip and your stamped ticket. Times of service are indicated on the transit map. A good way to get your bearings in Helsinki is to take a round trip (about 45 minutes) on tram 3T (you can get on near the Rail Station or at Market Square). A loudspeaker commentary points out the chief sights (weekdays in summer 10am-3pm and 6-8pm, weekends 9am-8pm).

Bicycles can be hired at the Olympic Stadium Youth Hostel for 10mk per day. Telephones are very easy to use: insert 50p or 1mk; coin drops down if there is an answer.

Addresses and Telephone Numbers

Finnish Tourist Board: Kluuvikatu 8 (tel. 650 155). General travel information for the entire country. Open only weekdays: 8am-3:15pm.

Hotellikesus: downstairs in the Central Station (tel. 171 133). Primarily a room-finding service (10mk fee for a single or double), but also has brochures. Very friendly staff. Open in the summer 9am-9pm weekdays, 9am-7pm Sat., noon-7pm Sun. Rest of the year open Mon.-Fri. only 9am-6pm.

American Express: Travek, Eteleranta 16 (tel. 171 900). Open 8am-4:30pm; closed Sat.

Main Post Office: Mannerheimintie 11, open weekdays, 9am- 10pm Sun. Long-distance phone calls must be placed at the Telegraph Office in the same building. Open 24 hours, but after 11pm ring the bell for entrance. The Railway Station branch has stamps only, but is open until 9pm every day.

Police: Central Station, Aleksanterinkatu 22-24 (tel. 002 and 003).

Medical Emergency: First-aid station at Töölö Hospital, Töölönkatu 40 (tel. 499 610) or the Hakaniemen Poliklinikka Siltasaarenkatu 18C (tel. 737 400). **Ambulance:** tel. 0066. **Doctor:** tel. 008 at any time.

24-hour Pharmacy: Yliopiston Apteekki, Mannerheimintie 5 (tel. 415 778).

U.S. Embassy: Itainen Puistotie 14A (tel. 171 931).

Canadian Embassy: Pohjoisesplanadi 25 (tel. 171 141).

Festival Office: Unioninkatu 28 (tel. 659 688). Open 9am-3:15pm weekdays only

News in English: tel. 018.

English Bookstore: Academic Bookstore, Keskuskatu 1, is Finland's largest. Open 9am-6pm weekdays, Mon. until 8pm, Sat. until 2pm.

Accommodations

Helsinki's hotels are modern, immaculate, and expensive; in July and August you will have trouble finding a room without a reservation. **Hotellikeskus** will find you a room for a 10mk fee (single or double) or give you current information on IYHF Youth Hostels. Besides the Hostels, the only inexpensive accommodations (though these are still not cheap) are the student residences that serve as summer hotels. As Finnish students live very well, the gain in economy is not a loss in luxury. The rooms are all modern and very clean. See the first four listings below.

Tent owners, however, get the real bargain, taking advantage of the never-darker-than-dusk nights for a mere 10mk (per night for one) or 20mk (per night with a tent, no matter how many people sleep under it). After May 15, try **Rastila** (tel. 316551), a well-protected campsite with showers, telephones, and easy access to stores. Only twelve minutes east of Helsinki via bus 96v or 98 from Central Station. Also offers two- and four-person cottages, saunas and, unfortunately, mosquitoes. No reservations necessary

Hotel Dipoli, Espoo (tel. 460 211), is an absolutely great student-run summer hotel, designed by Alvar Aalto, and beautifully situated between trees and sea. Spacious, quiet rooms from 50mk for singles, 70mk for doubles, rooms with showers costing a whopping 35mk more. In the immediate vicinity are a student center with a discotheque and restaurants; and a swimming pool, where you can swim and sauna for 6mk. Within walking distance is **Tapiola Garden City,** a famous planned community. Reservations are advisable in June and August, when the hotel is crowded with conventions. Just twenty minutes out of town by bus #102 or 192 from platform 51 at the Bus Station. Open June 1-August 31.

Ylioppilaskoti, Vironkatu 7C (tel. 665 078), has a central location on a quiet side street, and large, nicely furnished rooms. Singles 50mk, doubles 70mk, larger groups an additional 25mk per bed. Open 24 hours. Inexpensive laundry facilities available. From the Rail Station, take the scenic route via Hallituskatu; turn left beyond the Cathedral, and walk up park-like Snellmaninkatu to Vironkatu. If the large steel doors are shut, ring the tiny bell to the far right and cross the courtyard to "C" doorway, then to the second floor. Open May 20-September 10.

HKTY, Kalevankatu 21A (tel. 603 931), is a very small student house run by the Helsinki Christian Workers Association. Rooms are good sized, but rather antiseptic and sparsely furnished. Free use of a very nice kitchen. Singles 50mk, doubles 65mk, one triple for 80mk. Students, though, get Helsinki's best bargain: just 10mk per day for a single, without sheets. The major drawback is limited reception hours: Mon.-Fri. 9am-noon and 6-9pm; Sat. 9am-noon; Sun. noon-3pm. Excellent central location, just ten minutes' walk from the Train Station. Open June 1-August 31.

Satakuntatalo, Lapinrinne 1 (tel. 647 311), has singles for 70mk, doubles

95mk, triples 120mk, quads 145mk, all prices including breakfast. Free use of laundry room. Reception open 24 hours, but you're charged 1mk to be let in after midnight. Open June 1-September 8, though some rooms are available in late May. Located a bit west of the center, about a fifteen-minute walk from the Rail Station.

Retkeilymaja Stadion (IYHF), Pohjoinen Stadiontie 3B (tel. 496 071), is friendly, but rather grim. Sparsely-furnished singles 28mk, doubles 22mk per person, triples or quads 18mk per person, dorm bed 15mk, all 2mk less with IYHF card. Required sheets 6mk extra if you don't have your own. Small café is open for breakfast. Closed 10am-3pm; 1.50mk charged if you come in after 11:30pm, and you won't be let in after 2am. Often full in summer. Located in the Olympic Stadium complex; take tram 3T from Mannerheimintie (to your right as you leave the Rail Station) to Auroran Sairaala. Open all year.

Kalliola Youth Hostel, Sturenkatu 11 (tel. 753 2004). 12mk for clean but ascetic dormitory accommodations. Free showers, only in the morning. Closed 10am-4pm, reception open until 2am, but 3mk fee if you come in after 11pm. Almost always has room. Tram 3B or 3T north to Kalliola (the end of the line). Open May 1-August 31.

Food

Low-priced meals and refreshments are served at cafeterias called *baari*. Numerous kiosks sell good-sized *lihapiirakkas* (meat pies, usually more pie than meat) for 3-4mk, but in summer, the best place to buy food (fresh fish and vegetables) or grab a healthy snack is the **Kauppatori** (open Market Square) near the harbor. (There is another open market at **Hakaniementon,** but that one has not been dignified by such visitors as Nikita Khrushchev and Henry Kissinger.) The fruit is cheap and delicious, and the hot doughnuts and meat pies are the best in town. Wander a while soaking up the sounds and smells, looking at the old fishermen and flower women working next to the college girls in T-shirts. Best after 11am when some prices drop even further. After 2pm—Beggars' Banquet. Most of Helsinki's drunks (the only visible social problem in the city) arrive punctually to share with the seagulls the citrus left behind for their hangovers. Half a block away on **Etelaranta** is an indoor market whose beautifully arranged merchandise is in contrast to the bustling anarchy of Market Square. Between these two markets, peddlers of potatoes and onions balance their boxes on the sterns of fishing boats.

There is a big supermarket in the **A.B. Stockman** department store, and another, **Valintatalo,** at the corner of Lönnortinkatu and Annankatu (the latter is open until 8pm Mon.-Fri., until 3pm Sat.). The one under Central Station is open until 10pm every day.

Corso, Vuorimiehenkatu 3, just north of lovely Kaivopuisto Park, is a small indoor-outdoor café serving large portions of very good food for 8-15mk. Open Mon.-Fri. until 5:30pm, closed weekends.

Pizzeria Rivoli, Albertinkatu 38, has the best pizza in Helsinki at reasonable prices (10-20mk). Try the *Päivän,* with sardines, for 12mk. Popular with young people. Open weekdays 10am-1am, weekends noon-1am.

Kellari Krouvi, Pohjoinen Makasiinikatu 6, just south of the Esplanadi, Helsinki's most popular promenade, is a comfortable cellar restaurant. Fancy buffet lunch with beautifully-prepared fish dishes (25mk) served Mon.-Fri. 11am-3pm, Sun. noon-5pm.

Vanhan Kellari, set back from the street at Mannerheimintie 3, is located in the busiest part of town and is popular with young people. The self-service section is a good place for a beer or for large portions of inexpensive food (spaghetti 8mk). Open until 1am every day.

Tervasaaren Aitta, on Tervasaari, the island-peninsula off the northern harbor at the end of Liisankatu. Try *Isoisän eväs* (grandfather's knapsack), made from Karelian *pirakka* (pastry), egg butter, and smoked reindeer meat (14.50mk). It's a rather slim snack for the price, but worth it for the atmosphere and Finnish crowd. In nice weather, have a beer on the patio outside. Open 10am-midnight every day.

Helsinki has several excellent Russian restaurants. If you can't arrange to take the no-visa cruise to Leningrad (see below), splurge at small, dark, romantic **Troikka,** Caloniuksenkatu 3. Lunch special for 15mk, served weekdays 11:30am-2pm. Dinner will run 25-40mk. Open 11:30am-midnight every day.

Sights

Helsinki will delight architecture enthusiasts. The handsome neoclassical center (the area around **Senate Square**) was designed almost singlehandedly by the German architect Carl Ludwig Engel in the early nineteenth century, just after Helsinki had replaced Turku as Finland's capital. And the bold, simple buildings of the city's twentieth-century architects—notably Saarinen and Alvar Aalto—harmonize well with the clean neoclassical lines. The self-guided walking tours, available at the Tourist Office, make the best introduction to Helsinki's architecture. The most interesting are the **Kruununhaka** tour and the **Kaivopuisto-Eira** tour.

Three islands surrounding Helsinki are excellent for day visits. A 4mk motorboat ride or a 5mk ferry ride takes you to **Suomenlinna,** nicknamed Gibraltar of the North when it withstood an Anglo-French attack during the Crimean War in 1855. Suomenlinna's **Armfelt and Ehrensvärd Museums** are open daily 11am-5pm. The island is superb for picnicking with the goodies you can purchase at Market Square before boarding the boat. The island zoo, **Korkessaari,** only seven minutes by ferry from the North Harbor (at the end of Aleksanterinkatu) includes 1000-plus animals, featuring dozens of European bison and Alpine goats. The zoo is open every day in summer 10am-8pm, admission 5mk. Helsinki's 24-hour Transit Pass is valid for the ferry; otherwise you pay 9mk total for a round trip on the ferry and entrance to the zoo. There are also direct boat connections between Korkesaari and Suomenlinna. Clear waters, sandy beaches, and smooth rocks for sunbathing make **Pihlajasaari,** the most attractive of the islands, a popular recreational spot for Helsinki residents. Boat service (3mk one way) runs from Merisatama, the city's southern harbor.

In the early nineteenth century, there was a popular spa in **Kaivopuisto Park,** frequented by Russian nobility. East of the park is an elegant residential neighborhood where many embassies are located.

At the intersection of Helsinki's two busiest streets (long Mannerheimintie and Aleksanterinkatu) is the **Kolmeseppa,** a sculpture of three blacksmiths poised to strike blows on the anvil. Legend has it that every time a virgin passes by, they hit. From here, walk (or take tram 3T, 4S, or 4N) to the **Kansallismuseo** (the National Museum), Mannerheimintie 34, for wonderful displays of Finnish culture, from Gypsy and Lapp costumes to *ryijy* rugs (woven as far back as the Middle Ages for boats and sledges). Open Mon.-Sat. 11am-3pm (Tues. also 6-9pm), Sun. 11am-4pm; admission 1mk, free Tues. The **City Museum,** across the street at Karamzininkatu 2, has fascinating exhibits on the history of Helsinki (open Sun.-Fri. noon-4pm, Thurs. to 8pm; admission 1mk, students 0.50mk; free on Thurs.).

The art of having fun is practiced at **Linnanmaki,** Helsinki's Tivoli (open Tues.-Fri. 6-11pm, Sat. 3-11pm, Sun. 1-10pm, closed Mon.). Admission is 2mk, 3mk Sun. All other arts, from opera and sculpture to motion pictures and avant garde mixed-media materials, are represented during the **Helsinki Festival** in late August and early September.

The Finnish mastery of graphic and industrial design makes shopping in Helsinki a pleasure. Look for **Marimekko** fabrics and dresses at the main shop, Pohjoisesplanadi 31; for a 30% discount on "damaged" items, go to the branch at Tunturikatu 1. "Damaged" is almost meaningless: the damage is practically invisible. For superb ceramics and glassware, try **Wartsila,** Pohjoisesplanadi 25, the makers of Arabia ware. Check the shipping costs—they are extremely high. Finnish hand-crafted jewelry is both excellent and very expensive. To get a good idea of the range of available products start at the **Finnish Design Center,** Kasarmikatu 19, which is a design museum of sorts. It sells nothing, just exhibits for Helsinki stores, and is open weekdays 10am-5pm, Sat. 10am-3pm, Sun. noon-4pm.

Evenings

Commercial nightlife is grossly overpriced in Helsinki, so a night on the town should be approached with caution. Relaxation, Finnish-style, can be had in any of the local saunas, which usually run until 9pm. You'll find a complete list of prices and hours of saunas and pools in the pamphlet *Tourist Information,* available at the Tourist Office. You can meet Finnish students in any of the summer cafés; **Ursula,** in Kaivopuisto Park with a view of the harbor and the Suomenlinna fortifications, is popular and a pleasant walk from the Esplanadi. Open until 9:30pm every day in good weather.

Club Ostrobotnia, Museokatu 10 (tel. 446 940), known as On, is another good place to meet young people. Discotheque and occasional live music. Upstairs from the huge dance hall are a "beer-and-rowdy-song" room and a quieter "wine room." Open from about 8pm-1am every day. Admission Fri. and Sat. 10mk, Thurs. and Sun. 5mk, other days free. Tuesday there is traditional Finnish dancing. Next door, under the same management, is the popular, crowded **St. Urho's Pub,** open every day until 1am.

Outside Helsinki

It is possible to visit Leningrad or the Estonian capital, Tallin, for several days on a no-visa cruise. The trick is that you sleep on the boat and thus avoid spending the night on Russian soil. You must book at least two weeks in advance, through BORE/FFOA USSR Department, Etelaranta 8, 00130

Helsinki (tel. 178 2506). All-inclusive rates start at $200 for two full days in Leningrad, $90 for the overnight cruise to Tallin.

Even though it's only a two-hour train ride away, Tampere, a modern industrial city and Finland's second largest, doesn't merit a stopover unless you're heading in that direction anyway.

Turku (Finnish: Turun, Swedish: Åbo)

Geography is destiny. As Finland's closest mainland point to Sweden, Turku evolved from a marketplace settlement seven hundred years ago into the country's primary seaport and capital city in the nineteenth century. Turku is still popular as a port of entry into Finland. After the splendid boat trip from Stockholm, you'll be rewarded by the aura of its ancient **castle** and **Cathedral,** as well as the vigor of the modern city center.

Orient yourself by the natural environment: central Turku is surrounded by seven hills and bisected by the **River Aura.** Maps and lists of sights, hotels, and eateries can be picked up at the **Tourist Kiosks.** There's one at the Silja Line Terminal, and one at the centrally-located marketplace (tel. 15 262); the latter is open weekdays 9am-8pm, Sat. 9am-6pm, Sun. 9am-3pm. From the Ferry Terminal, take bus #1 or 3B to the center. From the Rail Station, walk down Humalistonkatu and turn left on Yliopinstonkatu to get to the market.

Accommodations

Turistikoti Kåren, Hämeenkatu 22 (tel. 20 420), has singles for 60mk, doubles for 74mk, and 3- to 6-bed rooms for 98-180mk, all prices including breakfast. Pleasant sunlit rooms. Located across the river from the market, not far from the Cathedral. Open June 1-September 1.

Kaupungin Retkeilymaja (IYHF), Linnankatu 39 (tel. 16 578) IYHF, although listed and run like a Youth Hostel, caters to travelers of all ages, charging 12mk for dorm-style bed. The place is spotless, the proprietor friendly and English-speaking, but no cooking facilities are available. Midnight curfew. Reception open 1pm-midnight, but try to arrive early. Bus #3B from the Station; get off just before the bridge. Twenty-minute walk up the river from the harbor, or take a bus. Open all year.

The nearest **camping** is on the lovely island of Ruissalo (tel. 306 649), reached by bus #8 from the Market. 20mk for a tent spot (10mk if you're traveling alone).

Food

Satisfy your gastronomic, sightseeing and pennypinching cravings all at once. Go to the **marketplace** when it opens at 8am and observe how the tempo of the bargaining increases by the time you leave (it closes at 2pm). Half a block away, in the old brick building at Eerikinkatu 16, is the **Kaupahalli** (covered market), open weekdays 8am-5pm, Sat. 8am-1pm. Let your nose be your guide: the aromas of sausage, cheese, and fresh-baked goods fill the air. Picnic on the banks of the Aura, a block and a half away; or hike up **Puolatanmäki Hill** (on the same street as the marketplace) to the gardens behind the **Turku Art Gallery.** If you're in a less creative mood, try any one of the small bakery-cafés or the **Restaurant Kåren (kårres-taurangen),** Hameenkatu 22, which is studenty, clean, good, and relatively inexpensive (lunch 10-17mk, dinner 28mk). Their discotheque is open 7pm-midnight.

Sights

At either end of the city stand Turku's most magnificent sights: 700-year-old **Turku Castle,** originally a stronghold for the Swedish Crown, and the equally venerable **Turku Cathedral** (open 9am-7pm daily). The Castle, near the Ferry Terminal at the mouth of the Aura, can be explored for 2mk between 10am and 4pm every day (take bus #1 from Market Square).

The labyrinth of islands guarding the approach to Turku is one of the world's most spectacular. You can take an excellent daytrip through the archipelago to the old village of **Nauvo** or the **Church of Seilli;** the seven-hour trip costs about 25mk. Check with the Tourist Office for departure times.

Turku celebrates a **Music Festival** during the second week of August. On one day there is an all-day rock festival; the rest of the week, there is a wide variety of classical, jazz, and folk music.

Outside Turku

Pori is the location of an **International Jazz Festival** during the second weekend in July, featuring well-known American and European bands. Some 25 musical events are crammed into four days: small evening jam sessions as well as huge open-air concerts. Tickets 10-40mk. The bus from Turku takes about three hours.

Savonlinna

Savonlinna is an enchanting town, the oldest in eastern Finland, located in the heart of the lake district. The center is built on islands amid the lake waters of **Saimaa** so it has both beautiful surroundings and easy access to neighboring towns by boat. Savonlinna grew up around the castle **Olavin-linna** and prospered in the early 1900's when tourists from Russia flocked to the healing waters of Savonlinna's health spa. Today Savonlinna's biggest attraction is the **Opera Festival,** which takes place from July 10 to July 27.

You can reach Savonlinna by train from Helsinki, but if you have time and about 75mk to spare, go by train to Lapeenranta and take the magnificent nine-hour ferry ride. If you come by train, get off downtown, instead of continuing to the Station, about a mile from the center. The **Tourist Office** is only a few steps away at Olavinkatu 35 (tel. 23 492); it's open 7:15am-10pm every day in the summer.

Don't rush through your visit to **Olavinlinna Castle.** Stroll past the wooden houses of **Linnankatu,** the town's oldest street, and through the surrounding park before you cross the moat. You may creep up the winding, steep stairways to visit the defense passages, bedrooms with medieval privies, and munitions room, accessible only through a hole in the ceiling.

The one-hour guided tour (ask for one in English) is obligatory, and is included in your 3mk admission.

The Opera Festival is staged in the courtyard of the Castle. Seat tickets cost 80-90mk and must be ordered the previous winter (beginning in October). Even standing-room tickets (15-29mk) are sold by mail, but you should ask at the Tourist Office or **Festival Office** next door (tel. 22 684) to see if there are any kind of rush-ticket arrangements.

Other places worth visiting are the lively fish and fruit market at the harbor where you can get a good lunch of fruit and vegetables or meat sandwiches from the truck counters. **Riikisaari,** in the old state granary, has changing exhibitions by Finnish artisans and craftsmen (5mk to see the Finnish handiwork). It's located on the other side of the wooden bridge leading to the Castle. The one-and-a-half-hour archipelago cruise (15mk) is a must if you have not skiffed the lakes of east Finland. At the very least, walk around on the two islands just north of the center, **Vääräraari** and **Sulosaari.**

Outside Savonlinna

July is the most exciting time to visit the vicinity of Savonlinna, with motor races, sailing regattas, and **Savonranta's** wild pig feast. This takes place whenever the residents of Savonranta get in the spirit to kill the pig; they celebrate by roasting the pork, singing, and folk dancing. You are invited to feast for free and Savonranta is only a short ride from Savonlinna. Ask the Savonlinna Tourist Office for more details.

Kultakivi (tel. 315 110), a holiday and camping village, offers a convenient, concentrated, and economical way to enjoy Saimaa's waterways. Besides modern, clean **cottages** (two to four persons, lowest 40mk a day) set in a lush pine and birch forest, Kultakivi features smoke saunas, salmon fishing, waterskiing, bicycles, row and paddle boats, horses, and a discotheque. Kultakivi is only 20 kilometers from the barbed wire of the Russian border. If you have friends to split costs, Kultakivi can be paradise. If not, admission for a day is only 5mk—worth it for the free fishing and hiking paths.

Accommodations and Food

The accommodations outlook is not good in Savonlinna. Beware of arriving during the opera season: everything is usually full, including the Hostel. The Tourist Office may be able to book you into a private home for a 10mk fee, but the price is a steep 35mk per person without sheets. The town's only bargain is the **Kisalinna Youth Hostel** (IYHF), Olavinkatu 13 (tel. 22 907)—15mk for a dorm bed, 5mk extra for sheets. Still, this is a bargain only in price: rooms are stuffy and overcrowded, dirty showers cost 2mk extra, no English is spoken, and the 11pm curfew makes it impossible to return from the Opera in time to be admitted. The town's camping site, **Kyrönniemi** (tel. 21 507), is situated across from the Castle, an easy walk from the center. 22mk per tent, 10mk per one person; groups of three can rent a cabin for 50mk per night.

The Finnish folklore characters etched into the second-story windows of **Wanha Veijari,** Olavinkatu 53, beckon you upstairs to this popular and comfortable student café. As in most of the town's lunch spots, which are generally good, the bill is a reasonable 10-15mk. **Majakka,** Satamkatu 11B, facing the harbor, is famous with residents for cheap Finnish dishes. Smorgasbord lunch daily 11am-2pm for 18mk; Sunday buffet (11am-3pm) costs 23mk.

Northern Finland

Consider it, and then think again. Even if you are a Commodore Perry type, heading towards **Lapland,** let's say to **Nordkapp,** from the Finnish side entails at least twenty hours of train, bus, and ferry travel, which cannot be continuous because of unsynchronized scheduling. Not that sleeping over a couple of nights in **Joensu,** a plywood town, **Normes,** also an industrial town, or **Oulu,** a historical port town, is a bad experience. But traveling towards the same destination from around the steep mountains of Norway or through the forests and reindeer-grazing land of northern Sweden is scenically a much more rewarding trip. See the sections on Lapland in the Sweden and Norway chapters.

Still, Finland is cheaper than Norway or Sweden, and you may not want to go both to and from Nordkapp on the Norwegian side. **Rovaniemi,** at the end of the rail line in Finland is, besides Norway's Narvik, the most convenient jumping-off point for trips to Europe's northernmost point. If you do go the Finland route, collect various brochures and youth hostel addresses before you leave Helsinki. For sailing into the midnight sun, contact local tourist offices in Oulo and Rovaniemi. On their way out the Nazis burnt Rovaniemi to the ground, so today's town is quite modern in architecture (and firmly touristic in sentiment!). If you're going farther north, you might want to compare student flights and bus prices. There is often little difference, and flying saves a lot of time. Avoid staying at the youth hostel in **Karasjok** if you cross into Norway. For 15kr, it will give you broken beds, unstable tables, run-down cabins, and no showers.

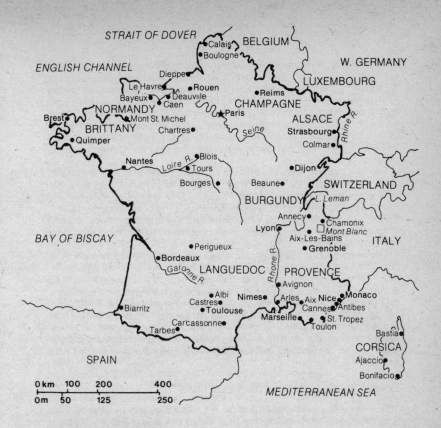

FRANCE

$1U.S.=4.2 francs(F)   **1F=$.24**

France is the first country that most Americans associate with Europe, and we've nurtured some formidable stereotypes of the French: non-stop womanizers, insufferably officious bureaucrats, and the girls of the Folies-Bergère are only a few. But the French have their own legends about themselves. Part of their self-image characterizes France as the eternal cultural capital of Europe, and we have this pride to thank for the renowned French cultural and educational institutions.

Preconceptions aside, the *"Français typique"* is neither our fantasized passionate individualist who exudes *joie de vivre;* nor is he the stiff, rule-conscious conformist who disappoints so many first-time visitors: he is both. French individualism is responsible for the *élan* and sophistication that attract foreigners like moths to a candle. But foreigners will wince at the rigidity of French etiquette, any transgression of which is greeted by a shocked, *"Non, mais . . . c'est impossible!"* The socialization process that binds the French together is strict—the refined manners of French children reflect the training which tempers exuberance with behavior *comme il faut.*

159

So if you want to avoid the rudeness which the French so often show towards tourists, pay close attention to what "they" are doing and act accordingly. The most flagrant *faux pas* is to assume that everyone speaks English (they don't). Brush up on your French, use a phrase book if you have to, but only as a last resort should you inquire, *"Parlez-vous anglais?"* Get used to sprinkling *Monsieur* and *Madame* liberally throughout your conversations with salespeople and your elders. Do not serve yourself at greengrocers. But do make sure that you're standing in the right line before you get to the front of it.

Too many people make the mistake of thinking that if they've seen Paris, they've seen France. Since the French Revolution, Paris has been the country's pulsating heart and calculating mind without ever being its soul—the French spirit has forever remained in the villages and fields of the provinces. France's regional differences mean more than just different shades of wine, and each region will try to convince you that its particular folklore is more authentic than any other.

France occupies a middle ground between the budget-devouring prices of Scandinavia and northern Europe, and the budget-boons of the Mediterranean. Here, as nowhere else, a well-spent budget will reward you with comfortable accommodations and a reasonable sampling of the French gastronomic style. And since the vacation is an integral part of French life, campgrounds, youth hostels, hotels of all sizes and prices, and tourist offices abound. Despite all efforts of government and industry to stagger vacations, August remains the cherished holiday month. Beaches, resorts, and highways become jam-packed and the cities—especially Paris—are left to the tourists.

TRANSPORTATION AND ACCOMMODATIONS

French trains can be crowded to the hilt, but are usually quite good. Seat reservations will prevent standing from Calais to Cannes, and you'll probably find your seatmates more than willing to swap food and wisdom. If the trains don't go where you want, there are always the buses, designed to service the very routes the trains pass up, hitting all the small towns and hamlets.

Those with cars can use the *autoroutes*, but these are both boring and expensive, averaging out to 15 centimes per mile. If you have the time, it is far better to drive the secondary roads *(routes nationales)* and put the savings into food. A chain of truck stops (the name doesn't do them justice, as they are first-rate restaurants and inns) known as the **Relais Routiers** are your best bet on the road. Marked by a red and blue shield with the logo *les Routiers,* they are often family-run places, and all have been selected for their good food and low prices. Often the "regulars" and the truckers make the meal a real experience. Gas stations are easiest to find on the outskirts of towns, but gas is expensive everywhere—roughly $1.75 per gallon.

Hitchhiking in France is difficult and slow—even on the autoroutes. The secondary roads, meanwhile, meander through the countryside, limiting you to slow, short lifts.

Stores in France are closed on Mondays and also from noon to 2 or 2:30pm, with many regional variations and exceptions. For example, the "Monday tradition" seems to be on the wane, especially in the large cities, and particularly for large stores. Most museums are closed on Tuesdays and from noon to 2pm, with some summer variations.

Hotel reservations are advisable in summer in the more-touristed areas. Check on meal requirements *before* you register at a hotel, since some provincial hotels impose required meals on visitors. A little forethought can save you a lot of headaches. You can get all the information you need before leaving Paris at the **Accueil de France,** 127, avenue des Champs-Elysées (open 9am-midnight). Or, for generally cheaper accommodations, check with the local tourist offices (**Syndicats d'Initiative**), who will give you free advice or help you find a room for a small charge. The **S.I.** (as it appears on billboards and maps) is a storehouse of information on restaurants, shopping, touring and camping. Every French town has one and we highly recommend that you take advantage of their facilities.

Campsites are plentiful throughout France. The Michelin Green Guide *Camping and Caravanning in France* details the best sites. For decent camping gear, **La Hutte** is well-known for quality and reasonable prices. It is a large chain, with a store in almost every major French city. The **Club Alpin Français** has branches throughout France and can give you advice on what to buy and where to use it.

FOOD

Everything you've ever heard about French food is true. More care, thought and energy go into the preparation of meals in France than anywhere else in the world.

Few generalizations can be made about exactly what French food is, because the French eat practically everything. Meat dishes include *steak au poivre, boeuf bourguignon, tournedos* (an expensive steak), *cervelles* (brains), *rognons* (kidneys), *tripe,* and *steak tartare* (raw hamburger). Taste *pâté* and you'll never go back to liverwurst. Along the coast you can get fresh *moules* (mussels), *langoustes* (small lobster-type shellfish), *oursins* (sea urchins), as well as all sorts of oysters. For dessert, try *crème de marrons* (a chestnut pâté), *yaourt* (yogurt), or a restaurant's *tarte maison* (its homemade fruit pastry). If something is marked *specialité de la maison* you can bet the chef is proud of it. Wine is the proper accompaniment to almost any meal, regardless of whether it's a tart *vin ordinaire* or a *grand cru* of superior vintage.

You won't get truffled goose for budget prices, but what you will get will be astonishingly tasty and carefully prepared for the price. Look for the *prix fixe menu* or the *plat du jour,* which will be less expensive than ordering à la carte.

Paris

Nobody can be objective about Paris. Even children who visit it for the first time look for a silver Eiffel Tower, and are disappointed to find that it's really rust-red. And the longer you wait to come, the more laden you'll be with dreams and fears: pictures of a shimmering Seine and dusk under the chestnut trees will collide in your mind with tales of stifling August heat and cursing taxi drivers.

The warnings are true, but so are the myths. Steeped in history and allusions right down to its sewers, Paris weaves a spell in stone and sunlight. Palaces and bridges become more than a backdrop: they unite mysteriously with screeching horns and sexy clothes to form a city where nothing feels out of place.

The long boulevards were carved out of the old dark and tangled city of the 1800s in an attempt to foil radicals who could out-maneuver the police in little streets and alleys; merging art with politics, Baron Haussmann made

Paris

1 Palais de Chaillot
2 Tour Eiffel
3 Les Invalides
4 Musee Rodin
5 Grand Palais
6 Petit Palais
7 Elysee Palace
8 Orangerie
9 Musee du Jeu de Paume
10 Madeleine
11 American Express
12 Opera
13 Sacre-Coeur
14 Musee du Louvre
15 Comedie Francaise
16 Post Office
17 Centre National d'Art et Culture
18 National Archives
19 Musee Carnavelet
20 Sainte Chappelle
    and Palais de Justice
21 Notre Dame
22 Musee de Cluny
23 Sorbonne
24 Arenes de Lutece

Paris
Arrondissements

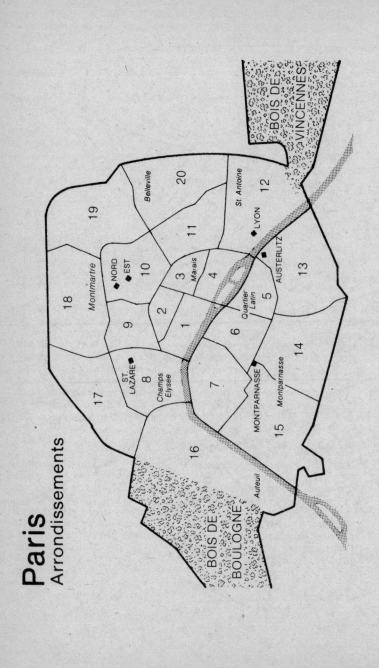

them attractive as well as practical. The French government decided to build a suburb of skyscrapers called *La Défense* in a suburb of Paris, which you can see shooting purposefully up toward the heavens out past the Arc de Triomphe. A ten-minute train ride away, it shows how old-fashioned a city Paris really is.

But what if you're a tourist and you're only staying for four days and you don't like crowds and everyone has told you how nasty the Parisians are, especially to Americans? Paris *is* crowded, and the sociology of its layout makes it seem more so, for the places that French students (and you) will spend most of their time are concentrated in a few areas: the Latin Quarter, Montparnasse, Montmartre. The combination of the crowds and the natural energy of this kinetic city can assault your senses unmercifully, especially if you've set your mind on seeing everything that *matters* in one short week. Try not to spend all your time in the Latin Quarter, and when you feel your senses overloading, do as the Parisians do—head for a park or a *bois*, to a quiet corner of a ritzy St. Germain café, or to the Seine for a shaded promenade.

Orientation

Paris is divided into districts *(arrondissements)*. There are twenty in all, clockwise by number in a rough spiral from the 1st (*Premier,* around the Louvre). If you're planning on staying a while, you might want to pick up a copy of *Plan de Paris,* which at 20F contains all the street details you'll ever require.

Another distinction of sorts is that between the **Right Bank** and the **Left Bank**, a distinction which, in terms of cost and lifestyle, has genuine meaning. Generally, the Left Bank of the Seine refers to the southern area of the city, while the Right Bank refers to the northern half. The streets are numbered with the low numbers closest to the river. The Seine, unfortunately, weaves and turns so profoundly as it cuts through Paris that street directions can be difficult at best. Traditionally, the Left Bank stands for a more Bohemian life-style, more student-oriented activities and lower costs, but there are similar neighborhoods on the Right Bank worth visiting and less touristed (**Le Marais, Pere Lachaise, Belleville**). Most of the hotels listed in this section lie in the 5e, 6e, and 14e *arrondissements* of the Left Bank or the 3e, 4e, 12e of the Right Bank, and these are probably the best areas to base your stay in the city.

Paris has one of the finest subway systems in the world—the **Métro** (stations are abbreviated as "Mo."). If you arrive in Paris by train, remember that every railroad station is also a Métro stop, offering direct access to almost every part of the city. While in Paris, use the Métro often, buying tickets in inexpensive lots rather than individually. A second-class *carnet* of ten tickets costs 11F and is the cheapest and quickest way of getting around. For longer stays, a two-zone *carte orange* gives you one month of unlimited Métro transportation for 48F. You must begin the *carte* at the beginning of the month. The last trains run at 12:45am, but buses prowl selected routes all night. Métro tickets are valid on buses, but most bus fares take two Métro tickets. Still, at least you can see the city from a bus. Ask for a bus map at the larger Métro stations. If money is no object, taxis can be had by phoning 587-67-89, 205-77-77, 354-40-40, or 267-28-30.

Phones can be found in cafés, restaurants, Métro stations, and post offices. It won't take you long to master the technique: buy a *jeton* for 60-80 centimes, put it in the slot, pick up the receiver and dial the number. When the party answers, push the button. If you don't press it, those on the other end can't hear you; if you press it too soon, you'll lose your *jeton*. Many pay phones, especially in places like railway stations, now take three 20-centime coins instead of *jetons*. These phones either have a window where you first deposit the three coins and then dial, or have a slot that accepts coins only after your dialing has produced a beeping noise. To call the suburbs, look for a yellow phone marked *automatique interurbaine*. If you can't reach someone by phone, inquire at the post office about sending a *pneumatique* message (9F), delivered anywhere in Paris within two hours. For long-distance phoning or cabling you have to go to a post office (**PTT**).

Three airports serve Paris, but most international flights land at **Charles de Gaulle/Roissy** (usually called simply "Roissy"), a marvel of modern architecture. The cheapest way to get into town is to take bus #351, which costs 5 Métro tickets and lets you off at Metro stops Nation or Vincennes. The Air France bus goes to Porte Maillot and the Métro is right there. The fastest way to get in is by **Roissy-Rail**, a train-bus combination, leaving from exit 30, building 1. It takes a half hour, costs 12F, and goes to Gare du Nord.

For those arriving at **Orly** Airport, an Air France bus will take you to the Invalides Terminal for 12F. The Métro is across the street. From Orly, bus #215 will take you to the Métro at Denfert-Rochereau for four Métro tickets or 5.10F. **Orly-Rail** is the most convenient for Latin Quarter destinations: straight to St. Michel for 12F.

Le Bourget is only used for charters and not very many charters at that. The Airport is currently being phased out of operation. In case you find yourself here, take bus #350N to Gare de l'Est (3 tickets).

The **Accueil de France** has offices in each airport, where you can pick up maps and hotel information. Their city office at 127 ave. des Champs-Elysées (Métro Etoile; open 9am-10pm daily) is well stocked with information about all of France, and they can find you a hotel room in just about any price range.

GETTING OUT OF PARIS

Those leaving by train should go to the correct railway station: **Gare de l'Est** for eastern France and Germany; **Gare de Lyon** for the Riviera and Marseille; **Gare d'Austerlitz** for central France, the Atlantic coast, and Spain; **Gare Montparnasse** for the suburbs (*banlieues*) such as Chartres, and for Brittany; **Gare Saint Lazare** for Normandy and *banlieues* such as St. Germain en Laye; and the **Gare du Nord** for the north coast, Belgium, Holland, and Great Britain. **Transalpino/BIGE** discount train tickets (20-50% off) are sold to anyone under the age of 26, for destinations inside and outside France. Buy them at **CIEE,** 49 ave. Pierre Charron (Mo. Roosevelt).

Hitching out of town is time-consuming. Use the Métro lines of Paris which run out to main highways leading to all points in France. Go to **Porte de la Chapelle** for the Autoroute du Nord, north to Normandy or England (Beauvais, Amiens, Calais); **Porte Maillot** for Rouen; **Porte de St. Cloud** for Autoroute de l'Ouest to Chartres or Versailles; **Porte d'Orléans** for the Autoroute du Sud 3 to Orléans, Orly Airport, and the south; and **Porte Berny** for Nancy, Strasbourg, and Switzerland. If you foresee bad luck, consult the hitching service (**Provoya**), at 14 rue du Faubourg St. Denis, 10*e* (tel. 246-00-66). They charge 15F a ride and 5F membership fee, so after you pay that and split gas, you may not save much money. Still, it's worth it for long distances, and people with cars should definitely check here for riders.

Addresses and Telephone Numbers

Tourist Office (Accueil de France): 127 ave. des Champs-Elysées, 8e (tel. 723-72-11; Mo. Étoile). Open 9am-10pm seven days a week.

CIEE: 49 ave. Pierre Charron, 8e (tel. 359-23-69; Mo. Roosevelt). An English-speaking student travel office. Intra-European student flights and charters to New York. Transalpino discount train tickets for anyone under 26.

Accueil des Jeunes en France (AJF): 16 rue du Pont Louis Philippe, 4e (tel. 278-04-82; Mo. Hôtel de Ville or Pont Marie). A brand new youth office which finds hostel and hotel accommodations with no service charge, sells university restaurant tickets, and reduced-price theater tickets.

American Express: 11 rue Scribe, 9e (tel. 073-42-90; Mo. Opéra). Intersects with rue Auber. Cheaper to have mail sent here than to *Poste Restante* (1.20F per letter), but you must show at least $10 worth of American Express checks to collect mail for free. Open 9am-5pm Mon.-Fri.; Sat. till noon.

All Night Post Office: 52 rue du Louvre, 1e (tel. 488-84-60; Mo. Louvre). All general delivery *(Post Restante)* mail is held at this office unless otherwise directed. The branch at 71 ave. des Champs Elysées, 8e (Mo. George V) is open until 11pm Mon.-Sat., and until 10pm Sun.

Late Money Exchange: Most banks close at 4:45pm and all day on weekends. Exchange at Orly Airport open until 11:30pm; Charles de Gaulle (Roissy) Airport until 1:30am; Gare du Nord until 10pm; Gard de Lyon until 11pm. Saturdays: American Express 9am-noon; Gare du Montparnasse until 8pm.

Police Headquarters: 9 blvd. du Palais, 4e (tel. 326-44-20; Mo. Cité). Emergency: dial 17.

English-speaking hospitals: Hôpital Américain de Neuilly, 63 blvd. Victor Hugo, Neuilly (tel. 747-53-00; Mo. Pt. de Neuilly); Hôpital Franco-Brittanique de Paris, 48, rue de Villiers, Levallois (tel. 757-24-10).

All-night Pharmacy: Pharmacie Proniewski, 5 Place Blanche, 9e (tel. 874-77-99; Mo. Blanche). Open all night every night except Sun; Pharmacie des Arts, 106 blvd. Montparnasse, 6e. Open daily until 1am.

U.S. Embassy: 2 ave. Gabriel, 8e (tel. 266-09-99; Mo. Concorde).

Canadian Embassy: 35 ave. Montaigne, 8e (tel. 225-99-55).

Lost and Found (for RATP Buses and Métro): 36 rue des Morillons, (tel. 828-97-30; Mo. Convention).

Public Baths: If your hotel charges 7F for a shower, try the Public Baths at 50 rue Lacépède. Hours: Thurs. noon-7pm; Fri. and Sat. 7am-7:30pm; Sun. 8am-12:30pm. Another one is located at 8 rue de Deux Ponts on Ile St. Louis. Similar hours. Shower and rental of towels costs 2.50F.

Laundromats (We cite only a few around the Latin Quarter): 3 rue de la Montagne Ste. Genevivè, 5e; 60 rue Gay Lussac, 5e; 65 rue Mouffetard, 5e;

24 rue Monsieur le Prince, 6e; 72 rue Monge; 113 rue Monge. Figure about 11F to wash and dry one load. Laundromats are no cheaper outside of Paris.

Swimming Pools: Piscine Deligny, on the Seine, opposite 25, quai Anatole France, 7e (tel. 468-72-15; Mo. Bac); Piscine Molitor, 1, ave. de la Porte-Molitor, 16e (tel. 288-91-49; Mo. Michel-Ange-Molitor).

Accommodations

STUDENT HOTELS AND DORMITORIES

Paris itself has no IYHF Youth Hostel, but there are two just outside the city. They are no great deal. You usually have to eat two meals a day there, they are dirty, and this is not the city where you want to go to bed at 10:30. The headquarters of the French Hostel association, **Fédération Unie des Auberges de Jeunesse,** 6 rue Mesnil, 16e (tel. 874-66-78; Mo. Victor Hugo) will give you a list of all the Hostels in France and sell you a Youth hostel card for about 55F. If you can produce an address in France, indicating that you are a resident, you may be able to get the card for as little as 25F.

Centre de Séjour: Choisy-le-Roi. ave. de Villeneuve Saint Georges, 94600 Choisy-le-Roi, (tel. 890-92-30). Train from St. Michel or Gare d'Austerlitz to Choisy-le-Roi and follow the signs to the hostel. 240 places. Bed and half pension 44F. Near Orly Airport.

Auberge de Jeunesse Rueil-Malmaison—intersection of rue des Marguerites and rue Lakanal, 92500 Rueil-Malmaison (tel. 749-43-97). Has 8-bed rooms for 12F a night. Take bus #144 from Pont de Neuilly to Place de la Paix, Cité Jardins-Juresnes.

The student hotels below are not much cheaper than regular hotels, but usually have good facilities and are a good place to meet people.

Hôtel de Jeunes le Fauconnier, 11 rue de Fauconnier, 4e (tel. 277-85-85; Mo. St. Paul or Pont-Marie) has 2-, 4- or 6-bed rooms with private showers. 26F per person, including breakfast. Curfew 1am. English-speaking staff. Recommended.

Hôtel de Jeunes Maubuisson, 12 rue des Barres, 4e (tel. 277-67-53; Mo. Pont-Marie or Hôtel de Ville). Run like le Fauconnier by the same people, but is a little less elegant, 26F per person.

Foyer International d'Accueil de Paris, 30 rue Cabanis, 14e (tel. 589-8915; Mo. Glacière). A modern hotel with good facilities. Dorm beds 25.75F with breakfast; *demi-pension* 40.25F. Singles and doubles also available.

Foyer Franco-Libanais, 15 rue d'Ulm, 5e (tel. 329-47-60; Mo. Cardinal-Lemoine or Luxembourg). Open only in July, August and the first part of September. Singles 21F, doubles 36F, without breakfast. Good location.

Résidence Internationale du Comité d'Accueil, 14 passage de la Bonne-Graine, 11e (tel. 355-62-66; Mo. Ledru-Rollin). 2- and 3-bed rooms for 39F per person, including breakfast. Clean and modern, no curfew. Technically for students only.

Maison des Clubs UNESCO, 43 rue de la Glacière, 13e (tels. 336-00-63 and 707-98-57; Mo. Glacière). Modern, well-maintained *foyer*, with decent prices; 28F per night, breakfast included. Now for the bad news: the door closes at 12:30am, and the maximum stay is five days. During the summer months, UNESCO also runs the *foyer* **Jemmapes**, 152 quai de Jemmapes, 10e (tel. 607-90-76; Mo. Château Landon) near the Gare de l'Est.

HOTELS

You'll have to pay $5-8 a night for a hotel room, a bit less if you're with a few other people. Doubles with one large bed cost less than with two small ones, and triples almost always come with one large and one small bed. In the less expensive hotels practically none of the rooms come with their own shower, though they do have sinks with hot and cold water. Most also have bidets, and the value of these far transcends the mere washing of genitalia—use them for chilling wine, soaking tired feet, washing underwear and socks, and so on. Showers are always available at about 6F. You might want to stop at a drugstore or supermarket and buy your own roll of toilet paper, since the range of paper products French hotel owners provide for that purpose runs from wax paper to strips of yesterday's *Le Monde*.

At many hotels, a 7-8F breakfast consisting of a *croissant* and bad coffee is included in the price of the room. Though most proprietors won't let you out of it, some will, and it's a good idea to try—you can always do better on your own. Complain, cajole, or plead poverty.

Unmarried couples who wish to take a room together will rarely be hassled anymore, especially in the cheaper hotels.

If you arrive in Paris on a summer evening without a room, chances are all the Latin Quarter hotels will be full. The area around **Place de la Bastille** has cheap hotels which are more likely to have rooms. For the more adventurous, the area around the **Place Pigalle,** the red light district of Paris, is chock full of one and two-star hotels, most of which have vacancies throughout the year. And if you don't mind having the people in the next room change on the hour, it can be very entertaining.

The **AJF Information Office**, 16 rue du Pont Louis Philippe, 4e (tel. 278-04-82) has all kinds of student-oriented travel information and will also find you a cheap room. Closed in June.

One further note: the prices quoted here are for the least expensive rooms in the hotel. Frequently a proprietor may need a little prodding to remember that he has those cheap rooms somewhere on the top floor. Understandably, the cheapest rooms go first, so if you arrive late, don't be too surprised if what is left has no showers and is more expensive than *Let's Go* indicates.

Left Bank

Latin Quarter—Sorbonne. Probably the best area to stay in Paris. Even though the streets where scholars once strolled conversing in Latin (hence the name) are now filled with short-order cafés catering to the tastes of foreign tourists, there is still a student air to the *quartier*. This is where the demonstrations of May 1968 took place, and students from all over the world still flock to the Sorbonne. These hotels are especially crowded in the summer, so make reservations in advance if you can, or start looking before noon.

Hôtel du Brésil, 10 rue 1e Goff, 5e (tel. 033-76-11; Mo. Luxembourg, Odéon, or St. Michel). One-star hotel. Near Luxembourg Gardens and the blvd. St. Michel. Singles 33F, doubles 47F, triples 70F, all with breakfast.

Hôtel de la Sorbonne, 6 rue Victor-Cousin, 5e (tel. 033-58-08; Mo. Luxembourg). Across a narrow street from the Sorbonne. Run by a kind, elderly woman. Singles 39F, doubles 47.50F and up, all with breakfast.

Hôtel Cluny-Sorbonne, 8 rue Victor-Cousin, 5e (tel. 033-66-66; Mo. Luxembourg). Not immaculate, but the prices are low: doubles at 44F, triples 66F, breakfast included. Showers 6.50F. A few singles.

Grand Hôtel Saint-Michel, 19 rue Cujas, 5e (tels. 033-47-98 and 633-65-03; Mo. St. Michel or Odéon). Unremarkable, except for a well-furnished salon (including piano). Convenient to the blvd. St. Michel. A good idea to reserve in advance. Singles 28.30F, 33-45F for doubles.

Notre Dame Hôtel, 1 quai St. Michel, 5e (tel. 033-20-43; Mo. St. Michel). Run down, but cheap at 25.50F per night single or double occupancy. No breakfast. The hotel is owned by the same people who own the modern café **Le Notre Dame** underneath the hotel, so inquire there. No reservations.

Hôtel Esmarelda, 4 rue St. Julien le Pauvre, 5e (tel. 033-19-20; Mo. St. Michel). A 300-year-old building with stone walls and wooden beams, this hotel has three tiny, but pretty, single rooms for 26F. Doubles around 79F. Helpful management. A block from Notre Dame. Breakfast 10F.

Hôtel Dacia, 41 blvd. St. Michel, 5e (tel. 033-34-53; Mo. St. Michel). Good, convenient one-star hotel. 35F singles, 55F doubles, 75F triples, breakfast included. Good value, and not usually full.

Université Hôtel, 160 rue St. Jacques, 5e (tel. 033-76-79, Mo. Luxembourg). Opposite the Sorbonne's Law School. Singles 30F, doubles 50-60F. Try to book in advance; if the noise bothers you, avoid the street-side rooms.

Hôtel de l'Avenir, 52 rue Gay-Lussac, 5e (tel. 033-76-60; Mo. Luxembourg). One-star hotel and a good deal. The higher the floor, the lower the price. Singles 22.50-25F, doubles 28-35F, triples 43-45F. Breakfast optional at 7F, showers 5F.

Hôtel le Home Latin, 15-17 rue du Sommerard, 5e (tel. 326-25-21; Mo. Maubert-Mutualité) has singles for 35F, doubles for 60F and up, and triples for 90F and up, breakfast included. Plain. Reservations accepted.

Hôtel de Flandre, 16 rue Cujas, 5e (tel. 033-67-30; Mo. Luxembourg). Tattered furniture, not too clean, but singles and doubles only 34F. Breakfast optional at 7.50F.

Grand Hôtel de la Loire, 20 rue du Sommerard, 5e (tel. 033-47-60; Mo. St. Michel or Maubert-Mutualité). Plain rooms, sagging beds, but clean and the owner is friendly and helpful. No breakfast, but you may eat in your room. Pleasant salon. Near the Cluny Museum. Singles 25F, doubles 30F, triples 45F.

The **Place de la Contrescarpe** area, near rue Descartes and rue Mouffetard, is the least spoiled part of the Latin Quarter, the center for little clubs catering to an artsy clientele, and home to dozens of restaurants offering every imaginable type of cuisine. There are sleazy hotels galore, but you might try:

Hôtel de Nations, 34 rue Monge, 5e (tel. 033-07-04; Mo. Monge or Cardinal-Lemoine). Unexceptional except for the prices: singles 29F, doubles 44F, breakfast included; shower 6.50F. Noisy, but interesting street below. Advisable to reserve in advance; send check for one night's stay.

Résidence de Lufece, 71 rue Monge, 5e (tel. 331-25-64; Mo. Monge or autobus #47). Sign outside says "Hôtel du Globe," which was the hotel's former name. Recently refurbished and pretty good rooms. One-star hotel. Singles 31.50F, doubles 48F, triples 64.50F, all with breakfast. Showers 7F. Reservations taken for long or short stays.

Hôtel Familia, 11 rue des Ecoles, 5e (tel. ODE-55-27; Mo. Cardinal-Lemoine). Nicely furnished. Singles 38F, doubles 45F, breakfast included. A few humbler singles at 31F. Try to reserve in advance.

Hôtel Saint-Christophe, 17 rue Lacépède, 5e (tel. 331-81-54; Mo. Monge or Jussieu). Good for a one-star hotel. Full bar, English spoken. On a quiet street just off rue Monge. Singles 42F, doubles 50-60F, with breakfast.

Grand Hôtel Oriental, 2 rue d'Arras, 5e (tel. 033-38-12; Mo. Jussieu, Cardinal-Lemoine, or Maubert-Mutualité). Very pleasant hotel on a quiet street. 38F singles, 45-66.50F doubles, breakfast included. Good idea to make prepaid reservations.

Hôtel Vendôme, 8 rue d'Arras, 5e (tel. 326-80-98; Mo. Cardinal-Lemoine). Somewhat dusty and dingy, but friendly. Doubles with toilet 47F, breakfast included. A couple of singles.

Café Hôtel at 5 rue Linné, 5e (tels. 535-33-15 and 331-24-02; Mo. Jussieu or Monge). Doubles are only 29.30F; a couple of singles for 26F. No breakfast, shower 5F. Near the Jardin des Plantes.

Hôtel Résidence Monge, 55 rue Monge, 5e (tel. 326-87-90; Mo. Monge or Cardinal-Lemoine). Singles and doubles 32-48F. Optional breakfast 8F.

Odéon—St. Germain-des-Prés.

As you move down the blvd. St. Germain away from St. Michel, the economic level moves up. Odéon, still within the Latin Quarter, has a higher French to foreign ratio, and is full of interesting shops and cheap restaurants. Further down the boulevard the scenery gets lusher: St. Germain-des-Prés is the home territory of the young jet-set and foreign businessmen. Two of Paris' most famous cafés are here: **Aux Deux Magots** (where coffee costs $3) faces the oldest church in Paris, and down the street **Café Flore** commands a similar elegance. The hotels listed in this section are convenient, and have the advantage of being slightly removed from the decaying quality of life around St. Michel.

Le Petit Trianon, 2 rue de l'Ancienne Comédie, 6e (tel. 033-94-64; Mo. Odéon or St. Michel). A small, easily overlooked hotel that is not normally full. Clean, friendly. With breakfast, singles cost 33F, doubles 56F (with shower 71F).

Hôtel Molière, 11 rue de l'Ancienne Comédie, 6e (no phone; Mo. Odéon or St. Michel). Elderly proprietress is not too helpful, but singles are only 27F, without shower or breakfast. Usually full, so come early. Up a dilapidated stairway. Not bad—a good value.

Hôtel St. André-des-Arts, 66 rue St. André-des-Arts, 6e (tel. 326-96-16; Mo. Odéon). You get a lot of comfort for the higher prices. Close to blvd. St. Michel. Singles 42F, room with double bed 50F, 2-bed room 60F, triples 67.90F. 20F extra for rooms with shower. Breakfast included.

Hôtel le Régent, 61 rue Dauphine, 6e (tel. 326-76-45; Mo. Odéon). Mostly doubles for 34F, without breakfast or shower, 67F with shower. Some singles at 27.50F. Several medium-quality, medium-price hotels on the street.

Hôtel du Vieux Paris, 9 rue Git-le-Coeur, 6e (tel. 033-41-66; Mo. St. Michel). Another place where you get your extra money's worth. Friendly, and on a quiet side street. With breakfast, 48F for singles; doubles with bathroom 79F, 86F with a shower, 124F with a bath. To reserve, just call or write. Two stars.

Hôtel Nesle, 7 rue de Nesle, 6e (tel. 033-62-41; Mo. Odéon or St. Michel). The laid-back owners here really enjoy their work. Rooms have purple walls, glitter curtains—you name it. Private garden in back. The management is open and friendly but cleanliness is not their forte. Singles 35F, doubles 40F, triples 60F, including breakfast. Guests either love or hate this place.

Hôtel de la Faculté, 1 rue Racine, 6e (tel. 326-87-13; Mo. Odéon). Good for a splurge. Doubles 52F, with breakfast. More for rooms with showers. English-speaking owner. Call or write at least a week in advance in the summer.

Hôtel des Vosges, 5 passage de la Petite-Boucherie, 6e (tel. 033-79-07; Mo. St. Germain-des-Prés or Odéon). On a quiet street only half a block from the lively blvd. St. Germain. Well-kept by a cheerful, helpful staff. A few singles at 24F, most more, and doubles at 41.80F, triples for 65.50F. Optional breakfast costs 8.50F. Guests are asked to return before 2am.

Ile St. Louis

Hôtel Henri IV, 25 Place Dauphine, 1er (tel. 033-44-53; Mo. Pont Neuf or Cité). One of the best cheap hotels in Paris, located between the Left Bank and the Louvre. Friendly, helpful owner. Singles 30F, doubles 37F, triples about 55F, breakfast included. You must reserve at least two months in advance for the summer; if you do, ask for a room with a balcony.

Right Bank

Louvre—Les Halles—Marais. This is one of the oldest parts of Paris, and it has undergone a renaissance in the past few years, with new restaurants springing up and many Parisians renovating apartments in the area. Les Halles, once Paris' food basket, is now a giant pit a half-mile square that is supposed to eventually be a complex of office buildings, theaters, and parks. For the next few years, though, there will be a lot of construction going on, with all the noise and dust that implies. These hotels are near the rue de

Rivoli, and not far from the Jewish quarter along the rue des Rosiers, where you can get the best *cornichons* (pickles) this side of New York.

Hôtel du IVe Arrondissement, 19 rue de Bourg-Tibourg, 4e (tel. 278-47-39; Mo. Hôtel-de-Ville). Well-situated hotel on a quiet side street off the busy rue de Rivoli. Singles from 23.50F, doubles from 34F. Optional breakfast 7.50F. Try to reserve in advance for the summer.

Select-Hôtel, 20 rue du Temple, 4e (tel. 272-34-28; Mo. Hôtel-de-Ville). Singles for 30F, doubles 45F and up, triples 59F, breakfast included.

Hôtel du Parc Royal, 25 rue de Turenne, 4e (tel. 887-86-77; Mo. St. Paul or Bastille). Right off Place des Vosges. Has beautiful old wooden floors and is impeccably clean. All rooms (one or two people) 34F. Breakfast 7.50F. Highly recommended.

Hôtel de Cambrai, 30 rue de Turenne, 4e (tel. 272-73-47; Mo. St. Paul or Bastille) is right across the street from the Parc Royal but isn't as nice. Singles 31F, some doubles 48F. Breakfast 8F.

Once the *de rigueur* hangout for artists, **Montmartre** is still alive today. Avoid the tourist-ridden **Place du Tertre**—artists assault visitors with five-minute portraits, caricatures and lurid still-lifes painted on velvet. Instead, wander through the steep streets around the rue Mt. Cenis. At best, the cafés echo Pigalle's vivacity without its squalor, St. Germain-des-Prés "avant-gardism" without its pretention.

Although not swarming with nightlife, the **Opéra** district is adjacent to Montmartre and is on a direct Métro line to the Left Bank. Many cheap and surprisingly clean hotels cluster around the Gare St. Lazare.

Hôtel Lamartine, 39 rue Lamartine, 9e (tel. 878-78-58; Mo. Notre-Dame de Lorette or Cadet). A spotless, family-run pension near the Gare St. Lazare. 22.50F for a single or room with a double bed, but breakfast required at 8.50F. Try to reserve a month in advance.

Hôtel du Nord et d'Anvers, 12 rue de Mauberge, 9e (tels. 526-97-71 and 526-97-72; Mo. Notre-Dame de Lorette or Cadet). Very friendly two-star hotel with cheerful rooms. Doubles without shower 60F, optional breakfast 8.50F.

Hôtel de Nantes, 55 rue Saint-Roch, 1er (tel. 261-67-78; Mo. Pyramides, Opéra, or Palais Royal). Friendly, and kept up better than the average one-star hotel. Singles 40F, doubles 50F, with breakfast. Near the Tuileries and the Louvre.

Regyn's, 18 Place des Abbesses, 18e (tel. 254-45-21; Mo. Abbesses). For the price—singles 30F, doubles 35F and up—it is quite good and conveniently located. Breakfast not included.

FOR LONGER STAYS

The **Alliance Française,** 101 blvd. Raspail, 14e (tel. 222-25-28, Mo. Notre Dame des Champs) is the best-known center for foreign students, and rents rooms by the month. They also have language courses, notice boards, job placement, and a restaurant. The **Cité Universitaire,** located on the southern edge of Paris at 19 blvd. Jourdan, 14e (tel. 589-68-52; Mo. Cité

Universitaire) is a huge and handsome complex of apartments, restaurants, and parks for primarily foreign students. They rent rooms by the month for about 600F. To reserve, write them well in advance. Warning: sometimes the Cité Administration will turn you down even though rooms are actually available. It's wise to check with the individual pavilions (called *fondations*).

COPAR, 39 ave. Georges Bernanos (tel. 326-07-49) manages several residential facilities in Paris for stays ranging from a few days to a few weeks. COPAR can also give you a list of the university restaurants open during the summer, and a student card. This is a good place not only for information, but also to meet students.

There are several other organizations that can help you find rooms for a few days or a few months, and give you information on living, studying or simply keeping afloat in Paris. Their services tend to change from year to year, as do their addresses, but try the **Centre d'Information et de Documentation Jeunesse,** 100 Quai Branly, 7e (tel. 566-48-20; Mo. George V); **Accueil des Jeunes en France,** 12 rue des Barres, 4e (tel. 272-72-09 and 277-67-53; Mo. Pont Marie or Hôtel de Ville), and **Fédération Française des Maisons des Jeunes et de la Culture,** 15 rue de la Condamine, 17e (tel. 387-30-04; Mo. Rome).

Food

In Paris, with more than 6000 restaurants and an unchallenged reputation as the gourmet mecca of the West, the search for gustatory nirvana at times appears to overshadow all other secular pursuits. The same care that characterizes French cooking in the provinces is evident in Paris, but the capital's claim to culinary greatness lies equally in the variety of foods it offers.

Thanks to France's colonial past, a broad range of non-French food is available. Chinese and Vietnamese restaurants are all over the Left Bank, and are relatively cheap—about 16-22F for a meal. For an Oriental snack, stop in one of the many Chinese/Vietnamese grocery stores for a *pâté imperial* (egg roll), a package of *ravioli vietnamien* (little rolled noodles with meat inside), or a *ben boa* (a bun of pork, Chinese vegetables and egg), each for about 2.50F. Tunisian and Algerian restaurants, offering various degrees of cleanliness, serve *couscous,* a steamed semolina grain over which sauce, vegetables and meat (usually lamb) are heaped, for about 15F. North African restaurants are all over Paris, but are heavily concentrated on **rue Xavier Privas, rue de la Huchette,** and **rue St. Séverin,** all little streets between blvd. St. Michel and rue St. Jacques. Also along these streets are a number of Tunisian sandwich shops selling tuna-potato-tomato-olive-pepper wonders for about 3F, as well as mysterious rainbow-colored pastries. Sensitive stomachs should stay away from the sandwiches. Greek souvlaki and shish kebab (5F) can be had, day and night, on the rue de la Huchette.

Cafés are an art form and an integral part of French intellectual life, but are not made for cheap eating. They specialize in sandwiches too small for a meal or meals too expensive for tight budgets. A *croque monsieur* (grilled ham and cheese) or *croque madame* (a *croque monsieur* with an egg on top) costs 5-8F, other sandwiches a little less. Omelettes, however, are a good deal. Three eggs for 6F, with cheese or ham for 8-9F, and all the bread you can eat. Cafés offer a dazzling selection of drinks. *Pernod,* an anisette, is the classic French licorice-like aperitif; *cassis* is a black current flavored wine; *eau de vie,* a clear liqueur made from practically any fruit that can be picked. Beer comes either by the bottle or on tap, the standard unit of the latter being *un demi.* Unless you specify otherwise, if you ask for water in a café or restaurant you'll get mineral water—either *Evian* (which is plain) or *Perrier* (which is bubbly), both of which will cost a few francs. Ask for *eau du robinet* (tap water) and you may or may not get it. The cheapest drinks available are wine and *limonade,* a carbonated 7-Uppish soft drink, not to be confused with *citron pressé,* which is lemonade.

The past decade has seen the flowering of self-service restaurants in Paris, and they seem to be something of a success. They are fairly cheap (10-15F per meal), but why eat camouflaged plastic, when for a few francs more you can eat real food? University restaurants are a different story, for they are honestly cheap—9F for a filling meal. Still, institutional food is institutional food even in Paris. Go to the ticket window at any university restaurant and ask for a *passager* ticket. Some places require an international ISIC card, but most don't. If you feel brave and think you look French, buy a ticket from a student for about 4F and don't say anything when you give the collector your ticket. See below for the most central university restaurants, but for a complete list go to **COPAR,** 39 ave. Georges Bernanos, *5e* (tel. 326-07-49).

Parisian street markets are worth a visit just to see the colors, sniff the air, and hear the fruit vendors' come-ons. More than food is sold there, especially on weekends when spice ladies and politicos hawking their tabloids add to the crush. The French style of shopping makes buying food for picnic meals easy, for storeowners are used to people shopping once or twice a day before a meal and buying one piece of ham or enough salad for two.

Unlike the post-Napoleonic government, the French food industry is still decentralized. A *charcuterie* is the French version of the delicatessen, with cooked meat, sausages (try *saucisson sec*), *pâtés* ranging from the plebian *pâté de campagne* to truffled *pâté de foie gras;* salads, and any number of prepared little dainties like sculpted pheasant in aspic. *Crémeries* sell the wonderful dairy products that account for the richness of the French cuisine and the hardness of the average Frenchman's arteries. Your run-of-the-mill street-corner *crémerie* will stock upwards of 100 kinds of cheese, from old favorites like *Camembert, Brie,* and *Emmenthal* (Swiss cheese) to *Chèvre* (goat cheese) and any number of spreadables, like *Boursin* and *Boursault.*

A *boulangerie* sells bread and some pastries, while a *patisserie* sells pastries and some candy, and a *confiserie* sells candy and some ice cream. *Boucheries* are butcher shops, and *boucheries* with a gold horse's head outside sell you-know-what. *Epiceries,* grocery stores, usually have staples, wine, and a little of everything else. *Supermarchés* à la America exist, but in small numbers. Several chain stores fall in between *épiceries* and *supermarchés,* and may be the easiest places to shop if your French isn't that hot. Look for a *Viniprix, Félix Potin, Prisunic* or *Monoprix.* Their prices tend to be lower than smaller stores.

If you are down and out, try wandering around the markets a few minutes before closing time, especially on Sunday noon when the stalls close until Tuesday morning. A few minutes later, after the vendors go home, the gutters will be filled with over-ripe but often only half-bad vegetables and fruit.

STUDENT RESTAURANTS

Most of these are closed in the summer.

La Table d'Hôte. Full meals for 16F. Buy your tickets next door at the youth center, 16 rue du Pont Louis-Philipe, *4e* (Mo. Pont Marie). Open all summer.

Bullier, 39 ave. Georges Bernanos, 5*e* (tel. 329-69-11; Mo. Port Royal).

Albert Chatelet, 10 rue Jean Calvin, 5*e* (Mo. Censier-Daubenton).

Grand Palais, Cours-la-Reine, 8*e* (Mo. Champs-Elysées-Clemenceau).

Alliance Française, 101 blvd. Raspail, 6*e* (Mo. St. Placide). Has a restaurant with better than average student food for 11F. A place to meet students from all over the world.

RESTAURANTS

Right Bank

Au Vieux Paris, 75 rue Vieille du Temple, 4*e* (Mo. Hôtel-de-Ville). A small restaurant frequented by the local business crowd. The cheapest *menu* at 16.50F is well prepared, with drink and *service* included. Open Mon.-Fri. noon-2pm, closed August.

Le Ménéstrel, 51 rue St. Louis-en-Ile, 4*e* (Mo. Sully-Morland), is small with two interesting *menus* at 21F and 33F.

Le Smalah, 9 rue de la Verrerie, 4*e* (Mo. Hôtel-de-Ville). Low lights, low prices. Specialty is *couscous*. Menu at 20F, drink and *service* included. Open every day for lunch and dinner, including the summer.

Chartier, 7 Faubourg Montmartre, 9*e* (Mo. Montmartre) is a turn-of-the-century-style restaurant: the waiters wear tuxedos, and the drawers in the walls are where the regulars used to keep their napkins between meals. Huge variety of high quality food at 17-30F a meal.

Au Pied de Cochon, 6 rue Coquillière, 1*er* (Mo. les Halles). When les Halles was Paris' main food market, it was chic to drop in here in the early morning to have onion soup and watch the food being brought into the market. The market is now in the suburbs, but this restaurant is still open 24 hours and still serves its *soupe à l'oignon gratinée* (13F). Meals are cheaper at the bar than at the tables.

Haynes, 3 rue Clauzel, 9*e* (Mo. St. Georges). Soul food, cooked by a New Orleans expatriate. *Menu* at 30F, drink and *service* included. Open for lunch and 7pm-1am; closed Sundays.

Casa Miguel, 48 rue St. Georges, 9*e* (Mo. St. Georges). Grimy, starvation-budget fare, but no one can beat their 5F price for a full *menu,* drink and *service* included.

Mother Earth's, 66 rue des Lombards, 1*er* (Mo. Châtelet). The classic American restaurant. Cheeseburgers, sandwiches 16-25F. Chili is the specialty at 14.50F. Sunday brunch (25F) features bacon, eggs, pancakes, and bloody mary. Open noon-3:30pm and 8pm-midnight. A good place to meet people.

Pizza San Carlo, 76 rue Rambuteau, 4*e* (Mo. Rambuteau). An excellent Italian restaurant specializing in fish. Eel, squid, also pizzas. *Menus* from 20F. Open for lunch and dinner.

Chez Jacques et Madeleine, 17 rue Oberkampf, 11e (Mo. Oberkampf or République). Moderately priced, nice atmosphere. *Saumon grillée* at 24F is cheaper than elsewhere in Paris. Outdoor seating, too. Open for lunch and evenings from 7pm. Closed in August.

Left Bank

Restaurant des Beaux Arts, 11 rue Bonaparte, 6e (Mo. St. Germain-des-Pres). Crowded for a good reason. Choice of *menus* at 19.50F, drink and *service* included. Fish and homemade pastries especially recommended. Open noon-2:30pm and 7-9:30pm. Open in August.

Lou Pescadou, 16 rue Mabillon, 6e (Mo. Mabillon), is one of the few inexpensive restaurants in Paris to specialize in seafood. Their soups are glorious, and the fish is always fresh and well prepared. Non-seafood dishes available as well, but less exciting. *Menus* 19F and 30F. Closed Sundays.

L'Auberge des Cordeliers, 11 rue de l'Ecole Médecin, 6e (Mo. St. Michel). Decorated like an old inn. Good variety of traditional dishes. *Menus* at 15F and 24.70F, *service* included. *Soupe à l'oignon gratinée* 6.80F. Open noon-2:30pm and 7-9pm.

Le Bon Couscous, 7 rue Xavier Privas, just off rue de la Huchette, 5e (Mo. St. Michel). The best of the *couscous* places on the block. *Couscous* 13F and up, *menus* start at 20F.

Restaurant du Dragon, 14 rue du Dragon, 6e (Mo. St. Germain-des-Près). A down-to-earth restaurant in a neighborhood more pretentious than populist. Hearty French cooking: *steak au poivre,* various *sautés,* good vegetables, fast service. *Menu* 21.80F. Closed weekends and in August.

Macrobiothèque, 17 rue de Savoie, 6e (Mo. Odéon or St. Michel), has vegetarian, macrobiotic food in pleasant surroundings, 15-20F. *Menu* at 19F. They also sell organic groceries. Open noon-2pm and 7-10pm.

Le Procope, 13 rue de l'Ancienne-Comédie, 6e (Mo. Odéon). A large landmark restaurant dating to at least 1686 that still serves good food. Lunch *menu* at 16.50F. Open noon-2am. Closed Mon. and all of July.

Place de la Contrescarpe is also full of cheap restaurants at similar prices to those around the rue de la Harpe. Somewhat less touristy, this area is inhabited by many students, and is an interesting place to poke around. There are a number of Armenian, Israeli, Greek, and Italian restaurants along the rue Mouffetard.

La Droguerie, 1 rue Mouffetard, 5e (Mo. Cardinal Lemoine). Generous *menus* at 20F, 22F, and 35F, drinks and *service* included. Good seafood. Outside seating and large à la carte selection available. Open every day noon-midnight, in August, too.

Le Poêle, 47 rue Descartes, 5e (Mo. Cardinal Lemoine) is a tiny place with the largest portions in Paris. The *menu* at 29.50F will leave you barely able to waddle out. This restaurant has been so successful that the owners started a second one, with the same name, around the corner at 12 rue Thouin. Chicken dishes are original and good.

Restaurant MY-VI, 6 rue des Ecoles, 5e (Mo. Cardinal Lemoine). An excellent, cheap Chinese-Vietnamese restaurant. 16F *menu* includes appetizer, entrée, rice, dessert, and *service*. Polite, English-speaking management.

Le Lotus d'Or, 8 rue Descartes, 5e (Mo. Maubert). Another Chinese-Vietnamese restaurant with low prices: 20F *menu*. Open 11am-1am. Closed Wed. and the last two weeks of July.

Crêperie de la Mouffe, 9 rue Mouffetard, 5e (Mo. Cardinal Lemoine). Good for a meal or snack. Crêpes and *galettes* 4.50-10F. *Menu* at 15F includes drink and *service*. Closed Sun., Mon., and in August. Open noon-2:30pm and 5-8pm.

Le Volcan (chez Bali), rue Thouin and rue Descartes, 5e (Mo. Cardinal Lemoine). A large restaurant, a menu with considerable variety, decent French and Greek food, reasonable prices, fast service, and lots of customers. The *brochettes* are consistently good. Closed Sundays and in August.

Splurges

Unless you're a gourmet of impeccably refined taste, it's probably a waste of money (some 300F) to sample the cuisine of the famous Parisian restaurants (Maxim, La Pérouse, La Tour d'Argent). French waiters can make you feel uncomfortable if you aren't familiar with the array of intricate customs associated with *haute-cuisine*. The restaurants below are relaxed, but the superb food they serve will give you an idea why French cooking is so renowned.

Aux Deux Marches, 15 rue Git-le-Coeur, 6e (Mo. Odéon). A family place. The one cooking at the stove is the grandmother. Meals for 40F, drink and service included.

Le Relais Basque, 71 rue St.-Lazare, 9e (Mo. Notre-Dame de Lorette). Basque cuisine. *Menus* at 37F. *Omelette basquaise* 11F. Closed weekends. Open noon-2:30pm and 5-9:30pm.

Ty-Coz, 35 rue St.-Georges, 9e (Mo. St. Georges). Fish from the Breton coast is brought here daily to prepare the delectable, though costly dishes: *moules marinières* (mussels) or *langouste grillée* (sea crayfish)—about 35F, *service* included. Open 12:15-1:30pm and 7:15-11pm, closed Sun.

Sights

It is of course possible, as it is for any major city, to set down a list of sights that should be seen when visiting Paris. Yet the best sight of all is the city itself. So, while you will certainly want to see the Eiffel Tower or tour the Louvre, the best course of action is to walk the streets of the city, stroll along the Seine, and savor the sights and sounds of the parks and open markets. While we offer a few suggestions for touring, you will certainly find that the best places are those you'll discover yourself; the narrow side street, the shuttered houses on some unimportant square, or the small café on the Left Bank.

Outdoor markets are as much a part of Paris as the Bastille, and though **Les Halles,** the celebrated market of Paris, has been moved to more modern quarters in the suburbs, a number of other markets still flourish. The **Marché aux Puces** is probably the most interesting—a huge flea market near the Métro Porte de Clignancourt, where everything sprawls about in interesting disarray. Open Saturday, Sunday, and Monday, and full of thieves and entertainment. Another interesting flea-market can be found at **Place d'Aligre** (Mo. Ledru-Rollin), every morning except Monday. Come around noon when the stands are closing to get the best deals. The **Bird Market** thrives Sundays at Place Louis Lepine, Ile de la Cité, where there is a **Flower Market** every day except Sunday. The food market at the bottom of **rue Mouffetard** should be visited on a Sunday morning when the hawkers vie with the student pamphleteers to be heard above the market's din. Rue Mouffetard (literally Stink Street) is one of the oldest streets in Paris, and is all at once a slum, an arty hangout, and home to some fairly expensive restaurants.

The **Marais** is a moody quarter near the **Place de la Bastille,** one of the oldest sections in Paris. Within is the beautiful **Place des Vosges,** a regal square built by Henry IV, so he and his Medici queen could have a playhouse. Unfortunately, he died before he could use it, but you can still see the **Pavillon du Roi** which looks across the square at the **Pavillon de la Reine.** The cafés in the square supposedly serve the best *croissants* in Paris. Be sure to see the **Place du Marché St. Catherine,** a beautiful little square in white stone. Two of the finest mansions which have survived the downfall and recent renovation of the Marais are now museums. **Musée Carnavelet,** 23 rue de Sévigné, is dedicated to the social history of Paris since the Renaissance. Fans, miniature guillotines, and last-minute scrawls of Louis XVI are the highlights of its excellent collection of Revolution artifacts. Open 10am-5:40pm, closed Monday and Tuesday. Admission 2.50F. A little farther up the same street is the **Palais Soubise.** A few remnants of the original medieval building remain, but it is mostly an elegant example of early eighteenth-century architecture. It now houses the **National Archives** and the **Musée de l'Histoire de France,** which displays documents dating from Charlemagne to Napoleon I.

The parks of Paris are essential to its splendor, and you'll do well to investigate them. The well-groomed **Jardin du Luxembourg** offers children sailing model boats and old men playing *pétanque,* a French version of bowling. In the huge **Bois de Boulogne,** you can rent a rowboat, ride horses, or go to the races. Wander through the gardens of the **Palais Royal,** the favorite *promenade* of Parisians since the Revolution. If you tire of people, try the zoo in the **Bois de Vincennes.** In the middle of the Latin Quarter you may come across a small Roman arena—the **Arènes de Lutece,** on the rue Monge between rue des Boulangers and rue de Navarre. The ruins are located in a pretty, uncrowded park which makes a fine picnic spot. The ruins of Cluny originally contained a third-century Roman bathhouse and are the oldest walls of Paris. And finally, and most impressive of all, there is the **Tuileries,** a hopeful reminder of what metropolitan parks ought to be.

For somewhat more untraditional sightseeing, you have your choice of the **Catacombs,** where members of the Resistance hid during World War II, or the **Sewers,** which you can tour, by boat, for a mere 2F. The Catacombs are at 2 Place Denfert-Rochereau (July-October, every Saturday at 2pm, and for all other months, every third Saturday of the month at 2pm), while the Sewer line (and it's a long one) descends at the corner of Pont de l'Alma and quai de Branly (open every Monday and Wednesday 2-5pm, and the same hours the last Saturday of the month, 2F admission).

Though the **Bateaux-Mouches,** the excursion boats on the Seine, may be the height of middle-class tourism, they are still the best introduction to

Paris. Trips run frequently starting at the Pont de l'Alma (Métro Alma-Marceau); tickets cost 10F. You might also try the smaller **Vedettes du Pont Neuf,** which are based at the Pont Neuf on the Ile de la Cité (Mo. Cité), close to the Latin Quarter. They cost 10F during the day, 15F at night (because of the illumination of the river).

While on the Ile de la Cité visiting **Notre Dame,** by all means don't overlook the **Sainte Chapelle** in the nearby **Palais de Justice.** Try to go on a sunny day to see this magnificent jewel of stained glass (mostly thirteenth-century), built by St. Louis to house the crown of thorns and other relics he acquired on crusade. Enter from the boulevard du Palais. Also in the Palais de Justice is the **Conciergerie,** built in the fourteenth century when the king lived in this palace. During the Revolution it was a prison, and held Marie Antoinette, Robespierre, and many others on their way to the guillotine. Enter from the quai de l'Horloge. Both the Sainte Chapelle and the Conciergerie are open 10am-noon and 2-6pm, closed Tuesday. Entry 5F, 2.50F Sun. or with student ID.

For seamy Paris, there's the **Pigalle,** rather tatty these days, but still alive and pulsating. Shabby little places and even shabbier prostitutes in these parts, thought a few spots are elaborate and expensive.

And, of course, there is the **Eiffel Tower,** especially at night when the monuments are illuminated and the city is at its most beautiful. Open 10am-6pm, Wednesdays until 9pm. The elevator ride costs 5-15F, depending on how high you go. The esplanade of the **Palais de Chaillot** offers an excellent free view of Paris with the Eiffel Tower in the foreground, and one of the towers of Notre Dame can be climbed for a small charge—you get a close-up look at the gargoyles, as well as of Paris. Less spectacular panoramas can be had, without charge, from the top of the two department stores, **Galeries Lafayette** (Mo. Chausée-d'Antin) and **La Samaritaine** (Mo. Pont Neuf), and, oddly enough, from the terrace of the **Pere Lachaise Cemetery** (Mo. Père Lachaise), where Balzac, Molière, Oscar Wilde, Chopin, Baudelaire, and Edith Piaf rest. Last, the **Basilica of Sacré Coeur** in Montmartre (Mo. Abesses) still boasts one of the most impressive tableaus of Paris; you can take the funicular to the top and sit in the old artists' square or enjoy the view from the steps.

And finally, the museums—for Paris is a home for art and artists of all generations. We list a few below, and remind you that upon presentation of your student ID or university card you will usually be given a discount or *demi-tarif.* Sunday is generally a free or *demi-tarif* day.

Musée du Louvre, at the opposite end of the Tuileries from Place de la Concorde (Métro Louvre). The Colossus of art museums, the Louvre houses the *Mona Lisa,* the *Winged Victory,* the *Venus de Milo,* not to mention *Whistler's Mother.* Limit yourself to the sections you favor most—or prepare to spend a few weeks within its walls. Open 9:45am-8pm. Closed Tuesdays and free Sundays. Otherwise, 5F or half that with a student ID.

Jeu de Paume (Mo. Concorde). The world's finest collection of Impressionist paintings, just across the Tuileries from the Louvre. Open 9:45am-5pm daily except Tuesday. Admission 5F, half price for students and on Sundays. Go early in the morning, since the place is fairly small, often crowded, and stiflingly hot.

Musée Rodin, 77 rue de Varenne, 7e (Mo. Varenne). The best of Rodin's work, displayed in a fine old hotel and garden. Open 10am-6pm. Closed Tuesdays. Entry 5F, 2.50F on Sunday or with student ID.

Petit Palais et Grand Palais, ave. Winston Churchill, 8e (Mo. Champs Elysées-Clemenceau). In addition to the regular collections, they receive many important exhibits. Admission 8F. Check posters in Paris for their agenda. Open 10am-8pm, till 10pm Wed. Closed Tues. Reduced admission on Sat.

Musée de Cluny, 6 Place Paul Painlevé, at the corner of blvd. St. Michel and blvd. St. Germain (Mo. Odéon). A fifteenth-century hotel built next to the Roman baths of Paris. An excellent collection of medieval art, including the famous tapestries of *The Lady and the Unicorn*. A pleasant and peaceful place in the middle of the Latin Quarter. Open daily except Tuesday, 9:45am-12:45pm and 2-5pm. 5F, half price on Sundays.

Musée Marmottan, 2 rue Louis-Boilly, 16e (Mo. Muette). A quiet place in a residential district. Tapestries and furniture of various periods, and the fabulous legacy of Claude Monet's son Michel. Open 10am-6pm except Monday. 5F entry fee.

Centre National d'Art et Culture Georges Pompidou, more familiarly called **Beaubourg,** between the Marais and Les Halles on rue Rambuteau (Mo. Rambuteau or Hôtel de Ville). Conceived as a cultural center where the arts of all kinds would coexist and influence each other, the building itself also plays a role. Much of Paris' collection of modern art has been moved to the **Musée National d'Art Moderne,** now housed in the center. Also in the center are a library, movie theater, numerous rotating exhibitions and plays. A place to spend the day. 10F buys entry into everything for a day, although you can get separate tickets. Free Sunday. Open 10am-10pm except Tuesday.

Pick up a complete list of museums, temporary exhibits, and special tours, published by the minister of Cultural Affairs *(Visites des Musées, Expositions et Monuments de Paris)*, at most museums, at **L'Hôtel de Sully,** 62 rue St. Antoine, 4e (tel. 887-24-14), or at the Tourist Office on the Champs-Elysées.

Outside Paris

The environs of Paris—the **Ile-de-France** region—are rich in monuments, museums, and simple picnic spots. **Versailles,** the magnificent palace of the Sun King, Louis XIV, is impressive, but crowded with tourists. Take the tour, then go out into the spacious green park. Be sure to see the **Trianons** and **Le Hameau,** the fake village where Marie Antoinette and her friends used to play peasant. You can reach Versailles by train from Pont Alma or Invalides for 2.50F, or take the Métro to Pont de Sèvres and transfer to bus #171 (three Métro tickets). Trains also leave for Versailles from Gare Montparnasse. The main palace is open every day 10am-5:30pm, (entry 5F, or 2.50F with student ID). The Trianons are open 2-5:30pm except Mondays—separate tickets are necessary for the interiors. The park is free.

Fontainebleau is older than Versailles, and more appealing in many respects. Much of it dates from Henry IV and Louis XIII, and it lacks the heavy pomposity of Versailles. The principal residence of Napoleon I for much of his reign, the palace was the scene of his dramatic farewells in 1814. The park and forest are exceptionally beautiful, and were beloved by the Impressionists. (Open from 10am-12:30pm and 2-6pm, except Tuesday; admission, 5F, or 2.50F with student ID. Take the train from Gare de Lyon). Many other châteaux around Paris offer enjoyable day trips. All have good grounds for picnics. **St. Germain-en-Laye** has a remarkable view of Paris and a museum of prehistoric, Gallo-Roman and Merovingian artifacts. (Open from 9:45am-noon and 1:30-5:15pm, except Tuesdays; take the RER suburban train at Métro stop Charles de Gaulle and travel past Pont de Neuilly. **Malmaison** is a lovely palace, with the apartments of Napoleon and Josephine. (Take the RER from Etoile to Défense, then Bus #158 to the Daniel-Casanova stop. Open 10am-noon and 1:30-5:30pm; closed Tuesdays). **Chantilly** is a beautiful small château which seems to float in a large pond. The surrounding park and forest are perfect for quiet picnics. Be sure to see the **Hameau** and the ornate eighteenth-century stables. (Open Sundays and holidays only, 10:30am-6pm; entry 7F. Take the train from Gare du Nord.)

The famous Cathedral at **Chartres** is only an hour away by train (20F from Gare Montparnasse). See description in Loire Valley section.

Evenings

Paris is a city that blossoms at night—the monuments glow, lovers stroll along the banks of the Seine, and restaurants stay lively till 1 or 2am. The fountains at **Place Trocadero** cool a hot summer night and the view of the Eiffel Tower is excellent. You can also enjoy the **Place des Vosges,** the beautiful old square where Henry IV lived. Walk through the little park in the center and stop at any of the arcade cafés.

A lovely spot to sit at dusk is the **Place du Vert-Gallant,** on the Seine under the Pont–Neuf. On a warm evening, it's much frequented by guitar players and young lovers. **Place de Furstemberg,** right behind St. Germain des Prés, may be the prettiest square in Paris by night, and watching the back of Notre Dame in the moonlight (from Pont de l'Archevêque or Pont de la Tournelle) could entrance one for hours. Later on in the evening, go to any one of Paris' innumerable cafés for a *demi* of beer.

CINEMA AND THEATER

Paris has the finest *cinémathèque* in the world, showing very good films (often old classics) for 5F: **Cinémathèque Chaillot,** Palais de Chaillot, corner of ave. Albert-de-Mun and President Wilson, 16e (Mo. Trocadero). There is almost always an English or American film playing. When checking cinema listings of non-French films, remember that "v.o." means "*version originale*" (the original language with French subtitles), while "v.f." means "*version française*"—the film is dubbed in French.

Government-subsidized theaters include the **Opéra-Comique** (Mo. Richelieu-Drouot) normally closed in July. The **Comédie Française,** (Mo. Palais Royal; closed in August); and the **Opéra** (closed Tuesday and in late July and August). If you're homesick, go to the **American Center Theater,** at the American Center for Students and Artists, with plays by famous Americans and young playwrights; otherwise, try the **Théâtre de Ville,** Place du Châtelet, with dance, poetry and *spectacles* for 8 to 15F (discount for students at the Saturday matinees) or the **Théâtre de France,** at the Place de l'Odéon, for 10-20F (discount for students, but the season runs only from September to May). Superb performances of Ionesco's *La Cantatrice Chauve* (The Bald Soprano) and *La Leçon* have been playing at the **Théâtre de la Huchette** non-stop for over twenty years. Performances at 8:30pm (tel. 326-38-99). The opera ballet gives outdoor performances of the classics in the **Carée du Louvre** every summer, June through August. Tickets are sold at the Louvre ticket office.

The Paris Metro, an English language biweekly, features comprehensive listings of films, theaters, restaurants, exhibits, etc., and is worth the 5F cost.

Look for signs advertising concerts of troubadour music at old churches, classical guitar at the Conciergerie, or *commedia dell'arte.* The Tourist Office has a list of current street festivals.

CAFÉ-THÉÂTRES

Café-théâtres are the home of the French dramatic creation–*le spectacle.* The term encompasses recitation of texts, singing, dancing, mime, informal theater, and whatever else the performer feels like doing. Many *spectacles* focus on recent political events—your French will have to be pretty up-to-date to understand everything. You pay your way in by buying an expensive drink (10-25F). Performances usually start after 9pm, and reservations are advised.

Théâtre Mouffetard, 76 rue Mouffetard, 5e (Mo. Monge; tels. 331-59-79 and 336-02-84), and **Théâtre Le Troglodyte,** next door at 74 rue Mouffetard. Prices vary with the events, but are about 15-25F.

Chat Qui Pêche, 4 rue de la Huchette, 5e (tel. 325-23-06; Mo. St. Michel). A jazz club in the Latin Quarter. Enjoyable and cheap. Admission 15F; *menu* at 20F in the restaurant upstairs. Closed Mondays.

Les Blancs Manteaux, 15 rue des Blancs Manteaux, 4e (tel. 277-42-51; Mo. Rambuteau) is still called by its old name, Pizza du Marais. Easy going. 20F.

Shakespeare and Company, 37 rue de la Bûcherie, 5e, just across from Notre Dame, is a unique, wonderful Parisian institution. It started out more than 30 years ago as an American expatriate literary book store. Hemingway and Gertrude Stein were the first members of the lending library, and the book store published the first edition of Joyce's *Ulysses.* Under the present owner, George Whitman, Shakespeare's is as literary as ever, with poetry readings during the fall, winter and spring. The library is open to the public. The store sells new and used books. Chess games outside. Open noon-midnight daily.

BARS AND DISCOTHEQUES

Note: outside many clubs in Paris you will see the sign *"club privé."* However, if you are well-dressed and show that you intend to buy a drink, you won't have any trouble getting in. In general, if you are not going to a student club, we suggest that you dress up.

Le Palace, 8 rue Fg. Montmartre, 9e (tel. 246-10-87; Mo. Montmartre), wins the 1978 award for the most popular disco in Paris: multi-leveled dancing and drinking in an Art Deco theatre hollowed out. 50F entrance including one drink. 15F for each drink thereafter. Dancing 11pm-6am. Open Thurs.-Sat.

Caveau de la Montagne, 18 rue Descartes, 5e (tel. 033-82-39; Mo. Maubert-Mutualité). Three floors of jazz, each with different performers. Admission 10-30F.

Bobino, 20 rue de la Gaîté, 14e (tel. 633-30-49; Mo. Edgar Quinet). A famous Parisian music hall where you can hear good French vocalists and occasional foreign stars. Reservations a day or two in advance required for best seats. Tickets 10-45F. Closed Monday and in June.

Caveau de la Huchette, 5 rue de la Huchette, 5e (tel. 326-65-05; Mo. St. Michel). You need a student ID to get into this semi-official student club. Jazz and dancing. Admission 15F, drinks 3-6F. Open 11:30pm-2am.

Katmandou, 21 rue du Vieux-Colombier. A bar for women only, while **Le Sept,** 7 rue Saint Anne, 2e, and its two neighbors, **The Bronx** and **The Colony,** are male gay bars.

As in all major cities, the clubs that are "in" or even "in business" change radically from year to year. In general, the area along the Seine between the rue St. Jacques and the rue Bonaparte (Left Bank) is crowded with jazz and rock clubs of all descriptions, while the rue Descartes and rue Mouffetard (near the place de la Contrescarpe) are lined with smaller and more student-oriented clubs.

If the discos and jazz clubs of Paris change with the seasons, one of the constants of Parisian nightlife is the celebrated cafés of Montparnasse. Most famous, perhaps, is **La Coupole,** at the intersection of blvd. Montparnasse and blvd. Raspail, where after 11pm you can watch Paris go by while savoring some ice cream or perhaps onion soup. **Le Select** and **Le Dôme,** also old cafés, are somewhat less intriguing. Up the blvd. Montparnasse at #171 is **La Closerie des Lias,** a sedate, expensive café once frequented by Joyce and Hemingway. Today, one drink will cost you more than a copy of one of their novels.

Champagne

Champagne is more than just a province with a celebrated name. Lying just to the north and east of Paris, it offers a peaceful respite from tourists and city life, with its tranquil fields, gentle rivers, and quaint villages. Though the fields are for the most part cultivated, isolated little forests of pine and poplar are easily spotted from the road, for sleeping and picnicking. There are organized campgrounds here as well, within a few miles of any clump of houses that presumes to call itself a town. And if you're adventurous and lucky, hitch a ride on one of the many open barges leaving **Reims** or **Troyes,** and see Champagne by water as you coast along the river.

To do Champagne justice, though, you should visit the vineyards and their cellars, subterranean *caves* up to 30 kilometers long, buried deep in the chalk sediment that is the secret of the champagne. The best cellars are in **Épernay,** a short train ride or hitch south from Reims on N51. Visit **Moët Chandon,** avenue de Champagne, for an especially enjoyable tour as well as a free sample of some of the world's best champagne. Many of the *caves* date to Roman times and are decorated with sculptures carved in the soft limestone.

For a tour of the region, go south from Reims to Épernay or to Troyes, the ancient capital of Champagne. Trains connect to most towns in the region, though it is cheaper and more scenic to take the **Relais de Champagne** buses which stop at small villages and hit the one-lane roads in the countryside far from the tourist paths.

Reims

Reims, the center of the Champagne country, can either be a daytrip from Paris or a relaxing stopover (trains out of Paris leave from the Gare de l'Est, take one and a half hours and cost 36F). The **Cathedral** is one of the finest in France, with its magnificent rose window. Don't miss the Chagall windows in the apse. Over the centuries the Cathedral served as the coronation site of the French kings. The small museum next to the Cathedral in the former Episcopal Palace offers a chance to inspect some of the original medieval carvings. Also worth a visit are the **Basilique Saint-Rémi** (near the wine cellars) with its delicate stained-glass windows and the **Place Royale**, restored to look as it did during the reign of Louis XV. The **Salle de Guerre** (12 rue Franklin Roosevelt), where the Germans surrendered to the Allies in May 1945, is open from March to November. It hasn't been touched since the end of the war. The **Musée Saint Denis,** once an ancient abbey, has a superb Corot collection, and portrait sketches by Cranach, elder and younger.

Yet Reims is equally famous for what lies below its surface—the *cité souterraine* of champagne *caves* and cellars. There are about a dozen which can be visited with free guided tours. The **Syndicat d'Initiative,** 3 blvd. de la Paix, will supply the details. Not all of the concerns will let you taste their product. For good quality samples go to **Veuve Clicquot Ponsardin,** 1 Place des Droits-de-l'Homme. **Mumms,** 34 rue du Champ-de-Mars, has one of the better English tours (samples as well). **Piper-Heidsieck,** 51 blvd. Henri-Wasnier, a firm that takes you through its *caves* in a fast, electric train, is good for those whose primary interest is imbibing. Most *caves* are open weekdays 9-11:30am, and 2-5:30pm. Weekend hours vary—check with the *Syndicat d'Initiative.*

For more sober forms of entertainment, the modern **Maison de la Culture** offers contemporary exhibitions and nightly performances by the **Théâtre Populaire** (16F and up admission) as well as a lively cafeteria-restaurant (closed Mondays). In May there is a **Joan of Arc Festival,** and in June, a city fair and exhibition.

For hitching out of Reims, get on N31 via Soissons for Paris (bus #2 direction Tinqueux). For Luxembourg, get on N380 (ave. Jean Jaurès—route to Rethel). Bus B, direction Point de Witry, will take you there.

Accommodations

The **Syndicat d'Initiative,** 3 blvd. de la Paix (tel. 47-25-69), will give you a list of hotels, restaurants, and wine *caves*. There is also a **Bureau d'Accueil** on rue Libergier (near the Cathedral), open Sundays and holidays as well as weekdays.

Centre International de Séjour, Parc Lèo-Lagrange (tel. 40-52-60), is the best place to stay. Small and sparkling dormitories, as well as private rooms. A quiet location near the Maison de la Culture. 17.50F a night in the dormitory (breakfast included), 26.50F in a private room with breakfast, 23.50F without. The price in private rooms goes down 5F after one night. Open July and August; 11pm curfew. Hostel card or student ID usually required.

Hôtel Saint-Maurice, 90 rue Gambetta (tel. 40-04-49), is in a working-class area a short walk from the Basilica of St. Remi. Basic, but clean rooms. Singles 24-30F and doubles from 30F; breakfast included. Take bus K or walk.

Hôtel Beauséjour, 11 rue Camille-Lenoir (tel. 47-47-28), has clean rooms, low prices, and a restaurant downstairs. Singles 18F, doubles 25F, triples and quads 32F; breakfast 6F. Meals at the restaurant are about 20F.

Hôtel Champagne, 1 blvd. Général Leclerc (tel. 47-27-74), near the Station and overlooking the park. Restaurant underneath. Nondescript, but clean. Singles 21-25F, doubles 25-56F; breakfast 7F.

Campground, ave. Hoche (route de Châlons) (tel. 49-94-31). A three-star site, but remote and near the industrial zone.

Food

Unlike the liquid produced in the region, the food in Champagne is not particularly good, at least within our price range, since the local specialities are cooked—of course—in champagne. The **Place Drouet d'Erlon** is lined with expensive as well as inexpensive cafés and *brasseries*. Check the prices, then sit down and enjoy the street scene over espresso and pastry. For full meals try:

Sorbiers, 180 rue de Vesle, is a gathering place for locals and offers a varied menu from *couscous* to the house speciality, *choucroute au champagne*. *Menu* at 23F and 39F; bar attached.

La Boule d'Or, 39 rue Thiers, serves filling meals in a homey French atmosphere, complete with white-linen table cloths. *Menus* at 20F, 30F, and 35F. Try the local *pâté champenois* with its light, flaky crust. Closed Mondays.

The Loire Valley

Poised along the graceful curves of the fertile Loire River are châteaux, cathedrals, and abbeys illustrating seven centuries of architectual evolution in France. They rise above the surrounding countryside, visible for miles, luring the traveler down roads flanked by rows of stately trees.

If you are coming from Paris, stop first at the château of **Fontainebleau** on N5, or in the cathedral town of **Chartres,** farther west on N10, and then continue into the Loire Valley. Despite its splendor and pageantry, the Valley is static—to visit all the châteaux would be expensive, tiring, and boring. Pick a well-located town and plan an itinerary of three or four châteaux. **Tours** is a convenient base, as there are local trains leaving for **Amboise, Langeais,** and **Chinon.** An ideal way to see the Loire châteaux is to rent a mobylette, in Paris (40 rue Gay-Lussac, 5*e*), or in Tours (addresses below) for about 20F a day. Pick up a map of the area from the *Syndicat d'Initiative* and ride along the country roads from château to château, without worrying about train connections. Hitchers will have problems getting out of Tours. Hitching is fairly easy in the region as a whole, though, since tourists visiting one château are likely to be heading toward another and willing to give you a lift. Alternatively, you could make use of the buses that run regularly between the châteaux and the major towns, or of the trains that skirt the valley.

Many hotels in the small towns in the Loire have their own restaurants, and require you to take breakfast (6-8F) or *demi-pension* (breakfast and one other meal). This usually costs 40-50F per person per day, and can make a visit to the château country more expensive than a stay in a capital city. The countryside is loaded with campsites, however. You can pick up a list at any *Syndicat d'Initiative*.

Economize on food by buying the local everything—from wines (*Vouvray*, for example) and cheeses (*Port-Salut* and *Dieux*) to fish (trout and pike). Just remember to stock up on Sundays because most *boulangeries* and food stores close from Sunday noon to Tuesday morning.

Chartres

Rising above the town and the **Beauce** plain, the **Cathedral** of Chartres merits the closest attention. Completed by the thirteenth century, its flying buttresses, slender spires, and world-famous stained-glass windows set the precedent for Gothic architecture. The carved portals and statues illustrate biblical tales, and once served as a lapidary bible for illiterate pilgrims of the Middle Ages. Try to go on one of the in-depth tours given by Malcolm Miller, who has been lecturing about different sections of the building for the last twenty years. His tours, at noon (except Sundays) and 2:45pm (except Tuesdays), are pay as you like. You might want to hear both, since he does not repeat the same lecture.

Though the Cathedral is obviously the city's main attraction, there are other things to see. The **vieux quartier** has many restored houses of the Middle Ages. Any walk through Chartres' winding streets will turn up interesting roofs, carved doors, or awesome views of the Cathedral.

In July and August, Chartres hosts an art exhibition. In addition, there is a summer-long music festival of *Samedis Musicaux*—the events range from Baroque chamber music to gospel songs. Student discounts available. Tickets and information at the *Syndicat d'Initiative*. Sundays at 5pm there is a free organ recital in the Cathedral. In July and August, an audio-visual show on Chartres is given in the **Crypte Eglise St. André,** at 9pm every night.

Addresses and Telephone Numbers

Syndicat d'Initiative: in front of the Cathedral (tel. 21-54-03). Open Mon.-Sat. 9:30am-12:30pm and 2-6:30pm, Sun. 10am-noon and 3-6pm. Provides maps of the town.

Public Baths: Bains de Samaritaine, 25 blvd. Charles (tel. 21-36-75). 1F.

Boat Rentals for a *promenade en bateau* on the river, at La Petite Venise, just off the boulevard de la Courtille.

Hitching: For Paris, try along the rue d'Albis or the rue Jean Mermoz (N10). You might also take bus #9 to the Carrefour shopping center and try from there. For Tours, take the N10 in the opposite direction (rue du Docteur Maunoury).

Accommodations

Auberge de Jeunesse (IYHF), 23 ave. Neigre (tel. 21-27-64), only 2 km from the heart of Chartres. Bed and breakfast 20F. Quite a nice hostel.

Hôtel St. Jean, 6 rue du faubourg Saint-Jean (tel. 21-35-69). Simple but adequate, with singles for 28F, doubles 31-45F. Breakfast 6F.

Hôtel de Paris, Place de la Gare (tel. 21-10-13). Right outside of the Train Station but still a two-star splurge. With breakfast, singles are 37.20F, doubles 43.40F, triples 76.60F, and quads 83.80F. Ask for a room in back to avoid street noise.

The nearest campsite is **Camping Municipal,** Stade des Bas-Bourgs, to the southwest of the city, near the hippodrome and swimming pool. Open June 15 through September 15 7am-9pm. Friendly staff.

Food

The covered market at Place Billard opens early in the morning and closes by 3pm.

A la Petite Sablaise, 18 rue des Ecuyers (tel. 21-21-36). A tiny restaurant with a *sympathique* management. Excellent *menu* at 29F, service included.

Le Minou, 4 rue du Maréchal de-Lattre-de-Tassigny. Both locals and tourists frequent this place, which has led to a large, moderately-priced à la carte range of traditional foods and several *menus:* 23F, 26F, or 30F. Generous servings, too. Open from noon on for lunch and 7-9pm for dinner. Near the Hôtel de Ville, five minutes from the Cathedral.

Bourges

Almost exactly in the middle of France, Bourges shares the attractions of its neighbors, Burgundy and the Loire Valley, but also adds spectacular sights of its own. The elaborate **Cathédrale St. Etienne,** with its unusual five-portal façade and a vivid thirteenth-century carving of the *Last Judgment,* ranks among France's finest.

The **Palais Jacques Coeur,** rue Jacques Coeur, is one of the most sumptuous urban buildings of the late Middle Ages. Built in the mid-fifteenth century by one of the richest merchants of France, it is every bit as extravagant as the châteaux of the Loire—and much more accessible if you don't have a car. Admission is 4F or 2F for students, closed Tuesdays.

The region around Bourges contains a number of interesting châteaux, less renowned but also less crowded than those on the Loire. The **Syndicat d'Initiative** (by the Cathedral) can give you full information. Several of the châteaux, such as **Menetou** and **Gien,** can be reached by the regular bus service (information: **Gare Routière,** tel. 24-36-42).

For hitching to Lyon, the Alps, or the Midi, take rue Jean Baffier (bus#3 for the N153). For Tours and Orléans, try the ave. d'Orléans at the corner of the ave. des Près le Roi (N76). For Paris, try ave. du Général de Gaulle (N140).

Accommodations and Food

Bar-Hôtel-Restaurant Jean Baffier, 57 rue Jean Baffier (tel. 24-23-15). Pleasant one-bedrooms, off the street. 23F for 1 person, 29F for 2; breakfast 7F. A bit far from the Station, but bus #3 goes right by. The restaurant has a *menu* at 18F.

Hôtel de la Nation, 24 Place de la Nation (tel. 24-11-96). Doubles for 26-28F. Very nice and centrally located.

Auberge de Jeunesse (IYHF), 22 rue Henri Sellier (tel. 24-58-09). A modern hostel, much nicer than average. 13F per night. Decent meals for 11F. In a rustic site overlooking a small river.

Camping Municipal, 26 blvd. de l'Industrie (tel. 24-29-31). Close to town, but not terrific.

Au Fin Renard, 60 blvd. Maréchal Foch. A simple working-class restaurant, but you get a veritable feast for about 18F; wine and service included.

Beaugency, Chambord, and Blois

The Beaugency château's exquisitely-vaulted bridge over the Loire has served as a principal crossing point for centuries. Lace caps, redingotes, and children's games are among the most unusual of the château's display. Open 9-11:30am and 2-4pm, closed Tuesdays. The village streets are worth exploring—look at the **moyen-age donjon** and **Tour de l'Horloge.**

The **Syndicat d'Initiative,** 28 Place du Martroi, open daily 6am-10pm except Sundays and Wednesdays, gives help for routing itineraries to Chambord, 21 kilometers south; or to Blois, 31 kilometers west. The cheapest and most picturesque hotel in town is the **Hôtel du Midi** just up the street at 1 Place du Martroi (tel. 44-53-30): 21F for one or two. Try to reserve, since they're usually full. Also has a good restaurant, with *menus* at 23.20F and 38.50F. For 10F a night, the **Auberge de Jeunesse** (IYHF) will put you up in their old schoolhouse, route de Châteaudun (tel. 44-61-31). Meals and kitchen available. The well-equipped municipal **campsite** sprawls over a vast beach on the far side of the bridge. The **market** is one block up from the château and sells the cheapest local *chèvres* (goat cheeses) in town.

To Chambord, the largest Loire château, the route du François I pierces the **Forest of Chambord.** The château, with a hundred spires and domes, exults in its whiteness, its rooftop terrace, and its double-helix staircase. The enthusiastic François I, who built the château, even diverted the Cosson River to run past the length of his creation. Often visited by Louis XIV and Molière, it was ransacked by revolutionaries—its interior has been only partially restored. Now a 13,600 acre National Reserve, the woods surrounding Chambord were once a royal hunting and falconry preserve—a tempting but illegal campground. (Open 9:30am-noon and 2-7pm. Admission 5F, but 2.50F on Sundays and holidays, or with student ID. Closed Tuesday, except in July and August.)

Nearby **Montlivault** has a Youth Hostel (IYHF), **l'Oribus,** off N751, 10 kilometers from Blois on the route de Chambord. Open July 1 through August 31, it offers showers and an adjoining campground. The most pleasant official campsite, **Château de la Genouillère,** with camping in the park of the château, is about 10 kilometers northeast of Blois on N152.

Blois is a *bouillabaisse* of different epochs: grey, hewn thirteenth-century feudal stones coexist with Gothic galleries, Renaissance wings, Italian decorative panels and neoclassical façades. It was here, on the second floor, that Henry III had the Duke of Guise done away with; and it was from the same second floor that stout Marie de Medici lowered herself into the moat one night to escape the imprisonment forced upon her by her son, Louis XIII. Open 9am-noon and 2-6:30pm; 7F, or 2F with student card.

Leave time to stroll around château grounds and towards the **Eglise St. Nicolas** in Blois. **Place Victor Hugo** in front is presided over by an enormous Lebanon cedar and fountain—an oasis in this otherwise industrial city. But sometimes industry can be sweet—write ahead to the famous **Poulain Chocolate Factory** (Service des Relations Extérieures, 6 ave. Gambetta) and take the tour (1F). The **Syndicat d'Initiative,** at 3 ave. Jean Laigret (tel. 74-06-49), will find you lodgings free of charge. You can also try the **Hostellerie du Tournebride** (tel. 78-04-79), or **Au Cheverny** (tel. 78-06-70), each with beds for about 30F. Camping is at **Blois la Bloire,** 1.5 kilometers east by N751 or route de st. Dié-sur-Loure. There is also a **Youth Hostel** (IYHF) 4.5 kilometers from the Station at Les Grouets (tel. 78-27-81), reachable by bus. Simple, remote, and in a beautiful setting; 14F per night. Kitchen available.

Chaumont, Amboise, and Chenonceaux

Chaumont-sur-Loire is a small, perfectly-proportioned feudal castle (built from 1465-1510), complete with rounded turrets, pointed conical roofs and a drawbridge. Open 9-11:45am and 2-6:30pm from April 1 to September 30; earlier closing in winter, and closed on Tuesdays. Admission 5F, or 3F for students and on Sundays and holidays.

The cheapest place to stay near Chaumont is at the riverside camping facility, **La Grosse Grève;** take the road near the bridge. Open April to September. There is a **Youth Hostel** (IYHF) at 11 rue Decrès. Hotel seekers should avoid the expensive **Hostellerie du Château,** and head instead for Blois or Amboise, or for one of the scattered roadhouses in the countryside.

From Chaumont, continue to the small town of Amboise, dominated by the high wall of its sixteenth-century château. Though much of the original building was destroyed in World War II, the **Chapelle St. Hubert,** the **Royal Apartments**, and panoramic terrace give you a good idea of what you're missing. Open 9am-noon and 2-7pm in summer, for 7F admission; 4F with student ID. Leonardo da Vinci died in Amboise, and at the da Vinci Museum **(Le Clos Lucé),** you can marvel over the models and toy machines (open 9am-noon and 2-7pm; 4F with student ID).

Amboise makes a good anchor point for Loire exploration. The **Syndicat d'Initiative,** quai Général de Gaulle (tel. 57-09-28) will find you lodgings at no charge (open continuously in July and August 9am-10pm; otherwise 9am-noon and 3-7pm, Sun. 11am-12:30pm. Hôtel **Chanteclerc** (tel. 57-11-94), route de Tours, rents rooms at 20F and 28F, *menus* at 17.50F and up. The municipal **camping** sprawls over the large island in the Loire, next to the town swimming pool. 2F per site plus 2.50F per person. Hot showers or baths 2F. Some good inexpensive meals can be found in Amboise: **l'Epicerie,** 18 rue Victor Hugo is best for *potage* (6F), omelettes, or crêpes.

A universal favorite, slender Chenonceaux rises over the Cher River, just 15 kilometers south of Amboise through the forest on route D81. Known as "the château of six women," Chenonceaux was home to Diane de Poitiers (mistress of Henri II), and Catherine de Medici, (Henri's long-suffering queen), who delighted in evicting her rival after Henri died. The *Son et Lumière* is a tourist trap, but renting a rowboat there is a refreshing way to explore the château. Open 9am-7pm in summer, with shorter winter hours. 7F, 4F with ID.

Hotel prices have risen drastically in the past few years, but try the bucolic **Hôtel au Punch,** in the woods next to the Chenonceaux-Chisseaux Railroad Station, whose four rooms go for around 35F. Or try the **Hôtel "Clair Cottage"** (tel. 29-90-69), or the **Hôtel du Roy** (tel. 29-90-17), both offering

45-55F *demi-pension*. **Campground l'Arabe,** 100 meters from N76 by the allée du Château, is right on the castle grounds (tel. 29-90-13). After traipsing around a château, no place is more inviting for a meal or tea than **Au Gàteau Breton,** 16 ave. de Dr. Bretonneau. Plentiful *menus* at 17F, 20F, 26F, and 35F.

Tours

All puns on its name aside, Tours makes a very convenient base for day excursions to the Loire châteaux. It offers a number of good, cheap hotels, and a slew of inexpensive restaurants along the rue Nationale. Tours is primarily an industrial city, but if you have the time, a stroll through the **old town** could be of interest. The city was gravely damaged during the war, but the area around the **rue Briçonnet** and the **rue du Change** retains its charm. You might also visit the **Cathédrale Saint Gatien,** which has examples of all periods of the Gothic from the thirteenth to the sixteenth centuries, and the **Musée des Beaux Arts** in the former episcopal palace next door. The **Musée du Compagnonnage,** 8 rue Nationale, is unique in France in its expositions on the pre-industrial artisan. Student entry 1.50F. Open daily 9am-noon and 2-6pm, except Tuesdays. On summer nights the **Musée des Beaux Arts** pipes classical music into their courtyard from 9-11pm. You can sit and listen for free.

The **Syndicat d'Initiative** and the **Accueil de France** run a large information office in the square in front of the Station with information available on tours, hotels, and the whole château region. The **SNCF** (French National Railways) also has an office for booking bus tours of the châteaux (some of them quite reasonable) right in the station. Bikes and mobylettes can be rented from **M. Barat,** 156 rue Girandeau (tel. 61-89-17) and 28 rue Nericault Destoucles (tel. 20-89-17). There are **laundromats** at Place Thiers and 102 rue du Commerce. Open every day 7am-9:30pm. Laundromats are a rarity in the Loire, so come to clean here: about 10F to wash and dry one load.

Accommodations

Auberge de Jeunesse (IYHF; tel. 28-15-87) in the Parc de Grandmont, 5 km from town. 14F per night, meals available. Take bus #5 or 10.

Hotel Grammont, 16 ave. Grammont (tel. 05-55-06) rents mostly doubles with breakfast, 44F and up. Spotless. Rooms with terraces. Highly recommended.

Hotel l'Olympic, 74 rue Bernard-Palissy (tel. 05-10-17). Decent and clean. Singles and doubles 25-46F. Breakfast 7F, but not required. Restaurant downstairs is filling and cheap 9-13F.

Hotel Comte, 51 rue August Comte (tel. 05-53-16). Singles or doubles 30-46F, triples, 59F. They prefer you take breakfast (7.50F). Very nice and clean, just behind the Station.

Camping: 5 km south at Joué-les-Tours, 40 blvd. de Chinon on N751. Plenty of others in the region.

Food

La Renaissance, 62 rue Colbert. Gastronomically rejuvenating *menus* at 19F, 23F, and 36F. The four or so courses include several regional specialties: *poulet aux cocotte* and *plateau des fromages.* The *terrine du chef* is also good. *Service* included. Subdued roses-on-the-table atmosphere. Open in August, closed Mondays. A good place to splurge.

Café Chez Roger et Frère, 94 rue Colbert, is a dingy place, but their prices can't be beat; 15F for a complete *menu*—hors-d'oeuvres, entrée, *fromage, pain, vin, dessert* and *service* included.

Villandry, Langeais, Ussé, Azay-le-Rideau, and Chinon

Though Villandry has lavish three-tiered gardens (the only remaining French examples of sixteenth-century green-thumb formality), the required guided tour (in French) makes this a hard place to spread out your picnic lunch. Open March 15-November 12 9am-7pm, otherwise weekends and holidays only. 6F, 4F for students.

Langeais envelops you in the past. Built from 1465 to 1469, it has remained untouched since. Visit the tower, the drawbridge, and the still-furnished inner rooms, and wander back to the days of Charles VIII and Anne of Brittany. Open 9am-noon and 2-6:30pm in summer, and closed Monday mornings; earlier winter closing: 6F, 3F with student ID. Municipal **camping** is located on the N152 (tel. 55-85-80).

Massive Ussé, with its fairy-tale forest of white spires, turrets, and chimneys, is a fine place to loiter an afternoon away. Open 9am-noon and 2-7pm in summer. 10F entry, 6.50F with student ID.

Azay-le-Rideau meets postcard specifications. The entrance along a tree-lined walk opens onto a turreted castle overlooking the Indre River. Open 9am-noon and 2-6:30pm; 5F, students 2.50F. Hotel prices soar high, so head instead for the campgrounds **Parc du Sabot,** rue de Stade, 500 meters from N751 (tel. 56-30-85), on the banks of the Indre. Or try along the ave. Adélaide Richer, with several hotels with singles from 24F and doubles from 30F.

Chinon rises like a stone wall over the Vienne River. It was here that Jeanne d'Arc began her march on Orléans. Three fortresses stand in a ruined barricade, separated by moats and lawns, overlooking the childhood village of Rabelais. Open 9am-noon and 2-7pm in summer, to 5:30 from mid-October to mid-March. Closed Wednesdays and all of December and January. Admission 5F, students 3F.

Restaurants in the winding streets of the old town offer salmon from the Loire and other regional specialties. **La Panurge** is more of a café than a restaurant, but offers great food at very low prices, in the place de l'Hôtel de Ville. **Le Rendezvous du Commerce** at 18 Place Jeanne d'Arc (tel. 93-06-13), has huge four-course meals, plus drink, for 23F. This brash, bustling place is also a *pension,* where for 50F daily you get a room and three meals. The **Hôtel du Lion d'Or,** down the street at #10, has singles for 26.50-38F and doubles 46-58F. There is a very nice IYHF **Youth Hostel,** with television and pool table, on the rue Descartes; 14F. The **campground** is across the river, on the Ile Augur, 200 meters from N749.

Fontevrault and Saumur

The only Romanesque kitchen left in France and the tombs of the great Plantagenet kings of France encourage a side trip to the **Abbey of Fontevrault.** As elaborate as the tombs and church is the octagonal towered kitchen and the twenty-chimneyed **Evraud Tower.**

Pass by the small château of **Monatsoreau,** whose women once inspired Dumas; and the city of Saumur. There are also free tours of the wineries and champagneries which you'll see along the highways. The **Castle of Saumur** is a good example of the transition between the defensive fort and the pleasure château, and it's worth climbing the hill to see it. Admission 5F, with student discounts; open 9am-7pm and 8:30-11pm in the summer. The **Musée des Arts Decoratifs,** inside the château, is one of the finest in France, exhibiting medieval sculptures and ceramics work, as well as a collection of porcelain. The town itself is quite pretty, with numerous hotels. There is also an **Auberge de Jeunesse** (IYHF, tel. 50-45-00) at the Ile d'Offard in Saumur, with meals and kitchen available. Bed-and-breakfast 16F. There are several cafés and a couple of cheap hotels along the quays, whose beauty is best appreciated during lunch or in the evening, when the highway traffic thins out. The last week of July, Saumur boasts the haughty equestrian **Carrousel,** with demonstrations by the elite riding group, *le Cadre Noir*. The **Syndicat d'Initiative,** 27 rue Beaurepaire (tel. 51-03-06) is very helpful and will provide you with information on festivities and tours of the vineyards nearby.

Normandy

Normandy is a province of historical unity and geographical variety. Since the raiders from the north settled here, the rule of the great dukes has determined its outlines. Within these borders are the **Suisse-Normande,** an "alpine" region (don't expect lofty heights—you can drive right through unawares); fields of pasture and farm land divided by hedge; a rocky coastline at **Dieppe** and along the **Manche** and flat sandy beaches along the **Côte Fleurie.** Sheltered among this diversity are Norman churches, lovely countryside, the pretentious resorts of **Etretat** and **Deauville/Trouville,** and **Mont-St.-Michel.** Once isolated and unique, the tenth-century abbey of Mont-St.-Michel now has a ratio of 100,000 tourists for every monk. Most towns and the cities in Normandy suffered heavily in the war, and restored churches of **Caen** are now surrounded by modern buildings. **Rouen,** though severely damaged, has a restored old quarter and makes an excellent starting point for a trip through Normandy.

Good food in Normandy is more a measure of the fine produce of the region than the culinary skills. The seafood, river trout, and salmon are excellent; the cider and apple desserts are fine; but best of all are the dairy products: *pont l'Evêque* and *camembert* are only two of the local cheeses which have made good. Duck is a traditional dish, often served with the local cherries, *à la Montmorency,* or more simply, *à la Rouennaise*.

Cheap hotels are difficult to find along the coast but readily available just inland or in the cities. There are hostels in all the major cities and along the coast in St. Valéry-en-Caux, Fécamp, Yport, Pennedepie and Isigny-sur-Mer. Campgrounds are plentiful everywhere.

Rouen

Accessible from the Seine, comfortably surrounded by fertile hills, Rouen has known Gallic, Roman, Norman, English, French, and German rule, but is best known and admired as a bastion of Norman art and architecture. The old city is practically free of jarring modern buildings, and is best explored on foot. We suggest starting at the obvious, the **Cathedral,** an impressive combination of the various Gothic styles from 1201 to 1514. From the Cathedral, take rue de la Grosse Horloge, a rather nice pedestrian street (especially active at night). Pass under the arch with the **Grosse Horloge,** a fourteenth–century clock tower and Renaissance gatehouse, entrance free with a student ID. Walk on to the **Place du Vieux Marché,** where Jeanne la Pucelle, a.k.a. Joan of Arc, was roasted by the visionless English in 1431. Go straight on rue Thiers to **St. Quen,** for the second most interesting church—Gothic, with greater height and greater congruity of styles.

From the **Eglise St. Quen,** head down the picturesque rue Daimette to the **Eglise St. Maclou,** a fine example of the fantasy of the last flamboyant period of Gothic architecture. For a different sort of Gothic, go behind the Church to the **Aître St. Maclou,** 184 rue de la Martinville—down the little passage to the courtyard of one of the few surviving charnel houses of the plague years. Note the macabre wood carvings. The Cathedral is a block away via the **rue St. Romain,** which passes between some fine half-timbered houses and the archbishop's palace where Joan of Arc was condemned.

Rouen takes pride in its museums for good reason. The **Musée des Antiquités** (8 Cloître Sainte-Marie) has a fascinating collection of relics from antiquity, the Middle Ages and the Renaissance. Particularly interesting are the Gallic artifacts from the Merovingian period, all excavated in the Rouen area. The **Musée des Beaux Arts** boasts masterpieces by Delacroix, Géricault, Ingres, and the Impressionists, including Monet's rendition of the Rouen Cathedral. Here, also, is the region's finest collection of *faïences* (painted earthenware).

If you're hitching to Paris, try either the quai de Paris for local roads or the left-bank side of the Pont Guillaume-le-Conquérant for the autoroute. For Deauville or Caen, start on ave. de Caen.

Accommodations

If you arrive in Rouen without reservations, check your bags at the Station and walk to the Place de la Cathédrale, where the **Syndicat d'Initiative** at #25 will find you a room at your specified price for a telephone charge of 3F (tel. 71-42-77). They have city maps and a brochure, *Suggested Tours in the Seine-Maritime.* Pick up a copy of *Les Logis de Normandie* for out-of-the-way *auberge rurale*, hotels, and restaurants. Transalpino/BIGE discount train tickets are sold at **Wastels Voyage** office up the street.

Cité Universitaire Mont-St.-Aignan, blvd. Siegfried (tel. 70-51-80), 300 beds at 17F per night, no meals. Book in advance through CROUS, 3 rue d'Herbouville, 76 Rouen. Reach by bus #16 to Terminus Cité Universitaire. Open July 1 to September 30.

Auberge de Jeunesse (IYHF), 17 rue Diderot (tel. 72-06-45). The usual complement of youth hostel advantages and restrictions. 2 km from the Station, so take bus #12 to rue Saint-Julien or #6 to ave. de Caen. Hot showers. 18F per night. Nicer than average. Closed 10am-5pm.

Modern Hotel, 59 rue Saint-Nicolas (tel. 71-14-42) has elegant rooms in a wooden fourteenth-century Norman house. Near the Cathedral. Every room has an opulent double bed at 26-34F. Rooms with two single beds are available at 36F. Breakfast 6F.

Hotel du Carillon, 34 rue Ganterie (tel. 71-67-70). Centrally located on a pedestrian street. Set back on a small courtyard with a small restaurant. Elegant, airy, and large rooms. 26F for rooms with one big and one small bed, 35-38F with shower or bath. 10F supplement for third or fourth person. Breakfast 7F.

Camping: the nearest campground is two-star and about 6 km from the town center. **Déville-les-Rouen,** rue Jules-Ferry (tel. 74-07-59), just past the *Mairie,* is small and extremely clean. Hot showers are included in your bill whether you take them or not (1.50F a person). Conveniently located near a large SUMA for cheap shopping, but bus fare into Rouen is 5F each way.

Food

A produce market fills the streets around Place St. Marc. There are a number of good and inexpensive restaurants in the **Place du Vieux Marché** and in its neighboring streets. Recommended are:

La Mouliére, at the intersection of rue de Florence and rue du Cercle, off the Place du Vieux Marché, has a four-course *menu* for 19F, drink and *service* included. Also a large à la carte menu at very reasonable prices. Friendly service and clientele, and a popular spot with the locals. Closed Sunday evenings and Mondays.

Le Vieux Logis, 5 rue Joyeuse (tel. 71-55-30). A rare eating experience at this price range. You dine in a tiny room with birds in cages, antique chairs, daintily-flowered china, even French flowers in vases. There's one 23F *menu* each day, which includes everything from soup to wine and coffee. The waiter is also the chef, the dishwasher, and the proprietor of the little hotel above. One of the last of a dying breed.

Le Restaurant Chinois, 40 rue St. Nicholas, beats *menu* prices just about anywhere: 11F for entrée, rice, and dessert, lunchtime only, Tues.-Fri. 17.50F *menu* with soup. A little run down. Closed Mondays.

The Normandy Coast

Dieppe is a rather honky-tonk port resort whose main attraction is its accessibility to Rouen and Paris by train. It's not a place with much to offer, but if you're there check out the combination medieval château and museum (10am-noon and 2-6pm, 1F admission) with its eclectic collections including carved Dieppe ivory, Braque prints and mementoes of the composer Saint-Saëns.

Varengville-sur-Mer is Normandy at its purest—coastal and agricultural, with a low-keyed beauty. It's no wonder that Georges Braque spent so much of his life here. He's buried in the cemetery of the **Eglise de Varengville,**

under a mosaic tombstone of his own making. The church has two naves, one Gothic and one Roman, a Braque stained-glass window, and a fine view along the coast out into the English Channel. Not far away are the **Manoir Ango,** a sixteenth-century château (open daily 2:30-6:30pm, 4F admission) and the **Parc Floralies des Moutiers,** a botanical garden that was started in 1900.

All along the coast World War II blockhouses squat silently in memory of the most recent bloody period in Normandy's history (there have been many), and there are several Allied cemeteries along the road to Le Havre. **Veules-les-Roses** is a sleepy stone town on the beach, filled with roses of every hue and scent, and some very narrow streets. **Fécamp,** a down-to-earth fishing village was once the home of Guy de Maupassant. A whole range of styles of ecclesiastical architecture can be found in the **Holy Trinity Church,** as well as an angel's footprint (to the right of the altar). Of dubious value is a visit to the **Musée de la Bénédictine,** 110 rue Alexandre-le-Grand, where they still make, but do not bottle, the liqueur. For 2F you get a tiny taste of the juice, but before they give it to you there is a mandatory tour of their collection of schlock religious relics, with a running commentary (heavy on the PR for their drink). Go to a café instead. The **Syndicat d'Initiative** is at the Place Bettet (tel. 28-20-51).

Nature decided to pull out all the stops when she put together **Etretat.** The sheer cliffs that rise unheralded from the ocean look as though they belong to another world. One, the **Needle Rock,** shoots straight out of the sea for 200 feet. Today, the town is an expensive resort, but—even if you can't afford to spend the night—you can still swim on their beach or walk along the **Falaise d'Aval** for a good view of the cliffs.

Nearby is **Le Havre,** a large modern city without any charm whatsoever. The old town was bombed unmercifully during World War II, so the buildings standing today are all of the post-1945 functional-anonymous school of architecture. Worth a visit is the **Musée des Beaux-Arts,** blvd. J.F. Kennedy (open 10am-noon and 2-6pm, closed Tuesday, 1F admission) with many canvasses by Eugène Boudin, the Norman Impressionist. Hotels are plentiful and cheap in Le Havre—try along the cours de la République across from the Train Station. Or ask at the **Syndicat d'Initiative,** Place de l'Hôtel de Ville (tel. 21-22-88), open Mon.-Sat. 8:30am-8pm; Sun. 10am-12:30pm. There's an **American Express** office at 57 quai Georges V.

Bayeux and Mont-St.-Michel

Bayeux would have charm even without its world-famous **Tapestry,** displayed in the museum directly opposite Bayeux's other attraction, the **Cathedral.** There is a 40% reduction for students and you can, for an extra franc, rent an earphone which narrates the story of the fight between Harold of England and William the Conqueror. But test your Latin: the Tapestry has its own narration stitched into it, like a comic strip, and it is exciting to follow it along the scenes of preparations for the battle, the death of Harold, and the rout of the English. (Open 9am-noon and 2-6:30pm; 9am-7pm from June 1 to September 15.) Cross the street to visit the awesome **Norman Cathedral,** for which the tapestry was originally commissioned in the eleventh century. Outside, the Romanesque towers are topped by Gothic spires, just as on the inside, large Romanesque arches were completed a century before the Gothic stained-glass windows. (Open 8am-noon and 2-7pm.)

The **Tourist Office,** 1 rue des Cuisiniers (tel. 92-16-26) is housed in a worn, sixteenth-century wood building. They will help book reservations for hotels. Information on seacrafts to England. The **Auberge de Jeunesse** (IYHF) is on rue St. Loup 28. Sixty beds, meals, and kitchen available, but 10am-6pm lock-out. A standard-looking hotel, but with cheap rates and an unbeatable location, is the **Hotel Notre-Dame**, 44 rue des Cuisiniers (tel. 92-02-56), a block down from the Tapestry. Rates 28-38F for a double or single.

A trip to Mont-St.-Michel is most likely the culmination of your Norman excursion, but unfortunately, you are not alone. Plan your visit for early on a weekday morning, and never, never on Sunday. Avoid the spring festival of St. Michel (first Sunday in May) and the two large pilgrimages (September 29 and October 16). A train leaves Gare de Montparnasse in Paris every morning—pick up a timetable outside the information booth on the second level to check the exact time. A tour through the Abbey is worthwhile only if you can get inside from the crowds. You can catch a daily 12:15 mass, or a simple, pleasant service at the Eglise Paroissale on the left as you approach the Abbey (8am weekdays, 9am Saturday, hourly 8 to 11am on Sunday). Skip the "Museum." Check the tides (high twice a month for three or four days) if you plan to walk on the sand around the island.

Hotels on Mont-St.-Michel are expensive tourist traps, as are the restaurants. **Hôtel de la Confiance** (tel. 60-14-07), offers a reasonable deal—28-60F for smallish, dark, but clean rooms. Optional breakfast 7.50F. Better to stay in the nearest town, **Pontorson,** or in the **Centre de Rencontres Pax Christi,** 2 kilometers before Mont-St.-Michel, or at one of the two camping spots near the causeway (the bus between Pontorson and the Abbey will stop at them). Unfortunately, the nearest **Youth Hostel** (IYHF) is located at St. Malo in Brittany, 37 ave. du P. Umbricht (tel. (99) 56-15-52). On national route 155, and just a couple of blocks from the sea. Restaurant serving three meals a day there. Open all year.

Brittany (Bretagne)

Brittany, the big western peninsula that juts into the Atlantic, is one of the more ruggedly beautiful and less-expensive areas of France. The infinitely-varied coastline is the province's star attraction, and by far the easiest part to tour by rail. And quite a tour it makes: from the smooth, vast beaches of the **Emerald Coast** in the north to the rocky **Corniche Bretonne** and the striking pink granite of the **Corniche l'Armorique.** Further on you come to the bleak **Presqu'île de Crozon,** the thundering shores of **La Cornouaille,** and the inlets along the southern coast. Brittany used to live off her fish, but today both industry and tourism are economically more important. Even so, the highly emotional response to the 1978 oil spill off the northwestern shore made it clear that many Bretons still feel strong ties to the ocean.

Inland from the coast the dramatic scenery and the crowds disappear; so does most public transportation. Without a car, getting around the interior of Brittany is difficult and time-consuming, but well worth it if you're not rushed. You'll find rolling green countryside (ideal for bicycling) dotted with farms, isolated villages, wayside churches, and prehistoric remains, all hewn from the characteristic gray Breton granite.

The Bretons are Celts, ethnically and linguistically closer to the Welsh, Irish, and Cornish than to the French. It would be interesting to make a combined tour of Celtic Britain and Brittany: the common roots are apparent in the decorative arts and in the music. Breton nationalism has waxed and waned several times since the annexation by France in 1491; one recent manifestation was the successful fight to have *breton*, the national language, revived in the public schools; even more recent was the bombing of Versailles by separatist activists.

While in rural parts of Brittany, look for announcements of local *pardons*, religious festivals celebrated on saint's days. Clergy, laity, and thousands of pilgrims—many in traditional dress with lace hairpieces and garments—gather for the largest *pardons*. **Sainte-Anne-d'Auray,** near Vannes, is the scene of the most well known one, on July 25 and 26, but there are many others throughout the year.

Except for the fresh seafood and the crêpes, Breton cuisine is undistinguished by French standards. If you have the money, feast on *crabe* (crab), *crevettes* (shrimp), *huîtres* (oysters) and *saumon fumé* (smoked salmon), washed down with a bottle of *muscadet*, the superb dry white wine of Brittany. *Cidre* (hard cider) is often drunk in place of beer.

ORIENTATION

For information in Paris, consult the **Maison de la Bretagne** at 3 rue du Départ, on the first floor behind Galeries Lafayette. A ticket from Paris to Brest via the northern or southern coast of Brittany will cost about $20 and you can get off anywhere along the way, and board buses which will take you to the neighboring villages. With the points of interest scattered throughout the province, hitchhiking and driving are the most enjoyable ways to explore Brittany. You will find hitching easiest along the main coast road. The quickest hitching route returning to Paris is via Avranches in the north and Nantes, Angers, Le Mans in the south, rather than the less developed road through Rennes.

Almost everywhere decent hotels pop up for 20-30F. **Syndicats d'Initiative** provide lists of campsites. Brest, Concarneau, Dinan, Fougères, Lannion, Lorient, Morlaix, Pontivy, Quiberon, Quimper, Rennes, St.-Brieuc, St.-Guen, St.-Malo, and Trébeurden all have youth hostels.

TOURING

The circuit outlined below runs east to west along the northern shore, then back again along the southern coast. You might start at **Rennes,** where the **Musée de Bretagne** gives an overview of what you'll be seeing. Open 10am-noon, 2-6pm except Tuesday; admission 1F for students. Should you stay overnight at the IYHF **Youth Hostel** at 40 rue Montaigne (tel. 50-52-67), visit the splendid **Jardin du Thabor.**

Coming from the Loire Valley, you can reverse this itinerary, and start off in the port and general excursion center of **Nantes.** It has a folk museum in the **Château Ducal.** The **Hôtel Renova,** 11 rue Beauregard (tel. 47-57-03) offers the best cheap accommodations in town. The super crêpe called *pavé nantaise* makes a full meal at the **Crêperie,** rue des Echevins.

Climb **Mont Dol,** actually a hill, to discover a superb panorama, not to mention footprints supposedly left from a battle between St. Michael and Satan. **St. Malo,** an old shipping town and pirate stronghold, the star attraction of the Emerald Coast, is remarkable for its tall granite ramparts, with pretty beaches sprinkled at their feet. Scramble about them, and at low tide, walk over to the **National Fort** (admission 2F). Outside the town, on the island of **Grand Bé,** within walking distance at low-tide, visit the tomb of Châteaubriand, native son of St. Malo, who himself requested this wild, lonely grave site. For other sights, inquire at the **Syndicat d'Initiative,** Parc de Plaisance, St. Malo (tel. 40-84-67), 10am-noon and 2-6pm. The rose-covered IYHF **Youth Hostel,** 37 ave. du Père Umbricht (tel. 56-15-52) requires a hostel card and charges 13.50F a night. Dine down the street at **Au Beau Rivage.** Nearby are a campsite and reasonable hotels, such as **Eden,** 1 rue de l'Etang, Parame-St.-Malo (tel. 56-02-99).

Inland down the Rance River, high on a hill, is **Dinan,** a village of traditional cobbled streets and gabled roofs, with encircling ramparts brooded over by an imposing castle. The IYHF **Youth Hostel,** Moulin de Méen̦, Vallée de la Fontaine des Eaux (tel. 39-10-83), is excellent. About 3 kilometers from the Train Station, in the woods. 13.50F a night, optional breakfast. Camping is available at **les Nielles,** blvd. de Rothereuf.

The rocky Corniche Bretonne and the pink granite Corniche de l'Amorique have suffered less from commercial inroads than has the Emerald Coast. In **Trébeurden,** the small but modern IYHF **Auberge de Jeunesse du Toeno** (tel. 35-52-22) has kitchen facilities available. From Trébeurden, you can head north to the dazzling pink coast between **Perros-Guirec** and **Trégastel-Plage,** or inland to the sixteenth-century chapel of **Kerfons** nestled in the trees. The best beaches are **St. Michel-en-Gréve, Plestin,** and **Plage des Curies.** The estuaries called **Les Abers** are picturesque but not accessible by rail.

Continuing through the arid **Monts d'Arée,** skip modern Brest and take in the harsh beauty of the Presqu'île de Crozon. **Morgat** is one of the loveliest resorts in Brittany. A beach of thin white sand stretches before a clear and sparkling bay. Morgat's hotels are expensive. The **Syndicat d'Initiative,** Pavillon de Tourisme, Morgat, (tel. 81-02-92 in season) is open 10am-5pm and will give detailed information about sights and accommodations. After lolling on the beach, go to the **Cap de Chèvre,** 3 kilometers from Morgat for a startling contrast. On the other side, away from the sheltered bay, is a savage coastline where crashing waves attack high cliffs. You can walk down the cliffs to the water and rocks by narrow paths. From the **Pointe des Espagnols,** journey through impressively stark countryside studded with *menhirs,* monoliths set up over 3000 years ago. The spectacular **Pointe de Penhir** and the gorgeous beach of **Veryach** lie off the beaten track.

You should try and head for **Quimper** at the end of July, to take in the **Folklore Festival of Cornouaille.** Don't miss the Cathedral and the old quarter to the west. Skip the museums and tour the pottery works at the **Faïencerie de Quimper, HB-Henriot,** Locmaria, on the route to Concarneau. In Quimper, stay at the IYHF **Youth Hostel,** ave. des Oiseaux, Bois de l'Ancienne Seminaire (tel. 95-34-04), the adjacent campsite, or the **Hôtel St.-Mathieu,** 18 rue St.-Mathieu (tel. 95-03-80), with rooms 23-42F. The **Restaurant des Nouvelles Halles,** 2 rue St.-Marc, is a lively neighborhood restaurant near the old quarter, serving delicious five-course meals for 16F.

Catch the bus from the Quimper Station to the unspoiled coastal villages: **Port-Manech, Brigneau, Doelan,** and **le Pouldu.** At Port-Manech, you can eat some of the tastiest oysters in Brittany or attend the August *pardon,* the religious festival. Doelan is an artists' colony and fishing port. The **Café du Port** is a good place to dine and spend the night.

One of the biggest French tuna markets is the walled port of **Concarneau,** which hosts the **Festival of the Blue Nets** the second to last Sunday in August. Stroll around the harbors, cluttered and lively with sardine boats early in the morning, and stray into the old walled town. **Pont-Aven** was Gauguin's last French residence before he abandoned France permanently for Tahiti. Further to the east is the village of **Quiberon,** a former island now joined to the mainland by salt deposits. A very pretty beach awaits you.

From Quiberon, you can find an hour's boat-ride to **Belle-Ile,** a sizeable island famed for its salt-flavored mutton. Disembarking at **le Palais,** rent a bicycle and spend the day pedaling around this magnificent island, stopping for lunch in **Sauzon,** a little fishing port. Close by is the famous **Grotte de l'Apothicaire,** where cormorants once built nests resembling brown bottles.

Return to the mainland and ramble amongst the prehistoric dolmens, tombs reminiscent of Stonehenge, and vertical *menhirs* which abound near **Carnac.** Nearby at **Sainte-Anne-d'Auray** a well-known *pardon* takes place July 25 and 26. **Vannes** is an old town on the lovely **Gulf of Morbihan,** filled with islets where you can island-hop for next to nothing. We suggest that you not spend the night in Vannes, but in one of the little hotels in the much smaller and more attractive villages of **Port Navalo** and **Loc-mariaquer.**

Alsace

Alsace, in northeastern France, is a large, lightly-touristed province descending from the wooded ranges of the **Vosges** to the **Rhine.** The Rhine has proved less a border than a conduit, and Alsace has frequently been a battleground. The influence of German cuisine and language is heavily felt, yet the Alsatians are passionately, unmistakably French. **Strasbourg,** the capital, is a friendly city with a large student population and a renowned cathedral.

Colmar to the south has become a tourist center, since it is situated at the intersection of the **Route Verte** (a tourist route running from Vittel in the west to Lake Constance) and the **Route du Vin** (a string of wine-producing villages). The town is also noteworthy for its old city, and for Grünewald's great *Isenheim Altarpiece* in the **Unterlinden Museum.**

Alsace offers medieval villages, castles, and plenty of camping opportunities. Contact the Club Vosgien at 4 rue de la Douane, 67000 Strasbourg (tel. 32-57-96) for maps and suggestions.

Strasbourg

Strasbourg is a beautiful, welcoming city, with spacious *places,* wide boulevards, narrow medieval streets, old timbered houses, quays and covered bridges. Start with the **Cathedral,** whose light, open spire rises 470 feet above the historic core of Strasbourg. While waiting for the play of the astronomical clock at noon (admission 1.50F), be sure to look over the **Doomsday Column,** one of the high points of Gothic sculpture, rising from the middle of the south transept. Across from the Cathedral are the **Château des Rohan,** housing porcelain, archaeology, and fine arts museums; and the **Maison de l'Oeuvre Notre-Dame,** a huge collection mostly of Gothic art. All museums are open 10am-noon and 2-6pm, admission 3F (students 2F).

Most students and many restaurateurs are away in the summer, but there are folklore and music programs; and a walk along the quays of **La Petite France** (the old quarter) is best on a warm summer night. In early June, Strasbourg hosts an **international festival of music.**

Addresses and Telephone Numbers

Syndicat d'Initiative: 10 Place Gutenberg (tel. 32-57-07). Open 8:30am-7:30pm in the summer. Maps, programs, and room-finding service.

Post Office: Main office at 5 ave. de la Marseillaise. Pick up *Poste Restante* here. Open weekdays 8am-7pm, Sat. 8am-noon.

Commissionaire de Police: 11 rue de la Nuée Bleue (tel. 32-99-08).

Red Cross: (tel. 61-05-23).

Accommodations

Auberge de Jeunesse (IYHF), 9 rue de l'Auberge de Jeunesse (tel. 30-26-46). A large, modern hostel. Take bus #3, 13, or 23 from the rue du Vieux-Marché-aux-Vins. Stops near the hostel. 13.20F per bed.

Hôtel Patricia, la rue du Puits (tel. 32-14-60), near St. Thomas, is a special treat with singles at 28F, doubles from 32.50F, and breakfast in bed for 6.50F. The house is about 400 years old.

Hôtel Central, 10 Place du Marché aux Cochons de Lait (tel. 32-03-05). An excellent location in the old town, on one of the streets converted into a pedestrian mall. Three *mansardette* singles for 32F. Doubles 46F. Both with breakfast.

Foyer de l'Ingénieur, 54-56 blvd. d'Anvers (tel. 61-59-89). A modern student residence. Mostly singles, but some doubles. 20F per person, free showers. Open July 1 through September 30. A bit out of the way.

Camping: Terrain Municipal, rue du Schonkeloch (tel. 30-25-46), and Strasbourg-Meinau, at Lac du Baggersee, on the route de Colmar (tel. 34-03-40).

Food

Cold cuts and Muenster cheese are Alsatian specialties, as are dishes prepared in the regional white wines. You'll find several German-style beer halls on the Grand-rue.

A la Chaîne d'Or, 134 Grand'rue. Several *menus* with *coq au riesling* and *charchutierie* selections. Meals 19F and up. Open 8am-11pm.

Ancienne Douane Restaurant, 6 rue de la Douane. A good place to go for a picturesque splurge. Be sure to sit out on the terrace. A *menu* at 15F, à la carte very expensive. Try the *jambon braise au riesling* or *tarte à l'oignon.* For dessert, try the *vacherin* (an ice cream and meringue concoction) or the *tarte aux pommes.* Closed Wed. Open 10am-12:30am.

F.E.C., the student restaurant at place St. Etienne, not far east of the Cathedral, has a fine variety of meals. Buy the tickets in the office for 7F, or for less from a local student. Reasonable wine also available in a restaurant atmosphere.

Another student restaurant is **Esplanade,** 32 blvd. de la Victoire, open in summer 11:30am-1pm and 6:30-8pm, meals 7F. Check with the Tourist Office if others are open during your stay.

Burgundy (Bourgogne)

Burgundy is the home of some of the finest dishes of traditional French cuisine and some of the greatest vineyards in the world have flourished on Burgundy's soil. Many peoples and ages have left their mark on this cross-roads province. There are prehistoric sites at **Chassy** and **Solutré**; Gallo-Roman remains at **Aléssa**, where the legions crushed Vercingetorix and Gallic independence: and Carolingian frescoes in many church crypts. Abbeys of the powerful monastic orders of the Middle Ages at **Vézelay, Cluny, Auxerre** and **Fontenay,** were the inspiration for Romanesque art and architecture. Dijon, the capital of Burgundy since the fourteenth century when the Dukes of Burgundy vied with the monarchy for France, is a busy, but beautiful town. The countryside is a well-watered terrain of thick woods giving way to rolling cultivated fields and vineyards dotted with medieval abbeys and Renaissance manors. If you are around during September and want to make some money (in return for some very hard work) ask any local *Syndicat d'Initiative* about joining the *vendanges* (grape harvests).

Burgundy is known for its cooking—many of the classic French dishes such as *escargots, coq au vin,* and *boeuf bourguignon,* among others, got their start here. This might be the place to splurge on a fine French dinner.

Dijon

Dijon wears its past as a retired soldier wears his medals—proudly and boastfully, because that's all he's got. In the fourteenth and fifteenth centuries the Dukes of Burgundy turned this traditional provincial capital into a shimmering center of French bureaucracy and justice. Not a lot has happened in Dijon since then, but no matter. If you come, it's to breathe in the stateliness and pomp of an age when the mayor, magistrate, and marquis one-upped each other with the splendor of their digs. More than fifty mansions *(hôtels)* decorate the town, most of them exquisitely preserved, many true urban châteaux. Get a list of the flashiest ones from the Tourist Office, whose guides lead tourists on walks around town twice daily.

The **Musée des Beaux-Arts,** occupying a part of the imposing **Palais des Ducs de Bourgogne,** contains a splendid array of medieval tombs and paintings by Flemish artists as well as works of more modern times. The **Musée Archéologique** with Roman and medieval artifacts is also worth a visit. Both are open daily 9am-noon and 2-6pm except Tuesday.

Orientation

Tourist Office: Place Darcy (tel. 05-42-12), open 9am-noon and 2-9pm seven days a week. Room-finding service.

Hitching: for Paris—try the ave. Albert 1er. **For the South,** ave. Jean Jaurès (the N74 for Châlon). If you are in a hurry, don't hitch—it could be a long wait.

Bus Station: Place Darcy, a block from the Train Station. Bus service very limited on Sundays. Buses do not operate after 9pm. For tickets, open 6am-8pm. For information, call 41-50-39.

Gare S.N.C.F. at the end of ave. Maréchal Foch. About 2½ hours to Paris. For **discount tickets,** available to those under 26, walk up one block from the Station to 16 ave. Foch to **Agence Wastels** (tel. 43-63-34). Reductions of 25%. Open 9am-6pm weekdays; Sat. till 5pm.

Accommodations

Auberge de Jeunesse (Centre de Rencontres Internationales) (IYHF), 1 blvd. Champollion (tel. 71-32-12). Modern and clean but a long bus ride from the Station. 16F bed and breakfast; 12F for rather blah meals. Take bus #5 or 6 direction Bocage to Epirey for 5 km.

Hôtel Miroir, 7 rue Bossuet (tel. 30-54-81). Singles 32F, doubles 38F. Decent hotel, centrally located but quiet; on a small side street.

Foyer International d'Etudiants, ave. Maréchal Leclerc (tel. 30-41-07). Sleek and shiny. Open July-September, and you must have a student card. 18F without breakfast. Far from the center of town—a half hour by foot—and the bus which takes you out there, #4, stops running at 8:30pm. Dinners and lunch for 10F.

Hôtel du Théâtre, 3 rue des Bons Enfants (tel. 32-54-72), is centrally located but on a quiet side street. The cheapest rooms go for 27F per night; singles and doubles. Optional breakfast 7.50F. Reception in back of courtyard.

Campgrounds: Camping Municipal du Lac, ave. Albert 1er; on a small lake, fairly near the center; and **l'Orée du Bois,** 9 km out of town, 21 route d'Etuales in Darois (tel. 35-40-16).

Food

Dijon is no place for feasting on fancy foods. Unless you want to get rid of money fast, better off saving a Burgundy meal for a smaller town. Market stalls line rue de la Liberté from where it intersects rue Quentin. Go late for the best buys. Open Tuesdays, Fridays, and Saturdays 6am-12:30pm. Local specialties include *pain d'épice,* an overpriced honeycake, and a huge variety of mustards. For fancy gift jars of mustard at very reasonable prices, visit 32 rue de la Liberté, the **Maille** store, which has been making mustards since 1777 and even showcases its collection of antique jars.

Moulin à Vent, 8 Place Françoise-Rude, is in a Renaissance house on a lively plaza. Four-course *menus* at 24F, 28F, and 38F. Very reasonable à la carte.

Diversions

The **Syndicat d'Initiative** (Place Darcy) can give you full information on a very active cultural life, as well as excursions (on your own or on a bus) to the wine country and châteaux of the region. Also escorted tours of the city to the *Monuments Historiques.* For nightlife, try the various establishments around the **Place Darcy,** or **L'Acropole** (boulevard Mansart), which is near the University and popular with students.

Beaune

Known primarily for the fine wines of the **Côte de Beaune,** Beaune is the center of many pleasant excursions into the vineyards and châteaux of the region. A number maintain *caves* right in the city, and most offer free samples. Many of the wineries occupy ancient cellars that are of some architectural interest in themselves. Unfortunately, the proprietors are not very generous with blue-jeaned visitors. Unless you are considering a purchase, go first to the **Maison Calvet,** on boulevard Perpreuil, whose cobwebbed caves are 3 kilometers long. The Calvet guided tour discusses storage and manufacturing processes, and samples are free and plentiful. The oldest is the **Cave du Bourgogne** in the ninth-century crypt of the former **Eglise Saint-Martin.** Probably the most interesting tour is offered by **Maison Patriarche Père et Fils** on the rue du Collège. This is the only house to charge admission (6F, 5F with ID), but it's worth it, as you get a tour of an actual working cellar, not just an exhibition, as well as the chance to taste several wines, and a small bottle to take home. The guide should be tipped 0.50-1F; the admission proceeds go to charity. If you can stay sober enough, visit the fifteenth-century **Hôtel-Dieu** in the center of town, a colorful landmark of typical Burgundy architecture, as bright on the inside as it is somber on the outside. Also worth a visit are the **Musée du Vin** in the **Hôtel des Ducs de Bourgogne** and the **Basilique Collégiale Notre-Dame** with its fifteenth century tapestries and serene cloister.

The surrounding countryside is full of vineyards, whether you head south towards Cluny or north towards Dijon via **Nuits-St.-Georges.** The famous **Pommard** vineyards are just south of Beaune, and we especially recommend a stop at **Clos de Vougeot,** about halfway to Dijon. If you don't have a car, fairly reasonable bus tours are organized by the **Syndicat d'Initiative** of Beaune, Dijon, and Autun.

To hitch to Dijon, try the route de Dijon (N74). For Lyon and other points south, try the Route de Pommard (N73). The *Syndicat d'Initiative* also provides an up-to-date list on all *caves* offering tours.

Accommodations and Food

The **Hôtel Saint Nicholas,** 69 faubourg Saint-Nicholas (tel. 22-18-30) rents singles at 27F per night and doubles from 30F up. Pleasant and only a few minutes' walk from the town center. Charging about the same rates is the **Hôtel du Square des Lions,** 24 boulevard Foch (tel. 22-04-29).

A noteworthy *boulangerie* is at 2 rue Monge. The house specialty is also a regional one: *gougère* (made with gruyère cheese). For a splurge, check out the 40F or 52F *menu* at the **Auberge Bourguignonne,** 4 Place Madeleine (tel. 22-23-53) which proudly serves regional dishes.

Vézelay and Cluny

Vézelay is more spectacular from the distance, perched high atop a hill and competing only with the greenery to dominate the valley. Try camping in the woods, say 5 or 10 kilometers distant or try the **Youth Hostel** (tel. 22-24-51) near Vézelay, on the route de l'Estang-pres-Vézelay. Close to nearby **Avallon,** another medieval center, is the **Maison de Breuil,** a sort of rustic youth hostel—you have to bring your own sleeping bag. It is in part of the **Parc Regional du Morvan,** a popular hiking and camping area.

Farther south, after a glorious drive through weaving farm roads, forests and valleys, you come to **Cluny,** an entire town of churches and abbeys which provided the architectural inspiration for the whole southeast of France. It is a sleepy and dignified relic of the monastic fervor that swept the continent in the eleventh and twelfth centuries. Take one of the excellent free guided tours of the Abbey which argues that the decline of the Abbey's importance was coincident with the increasing control of the king of France over it in the fifteenth century. (Open 9-11:30am and 2-6pm April through September. Other times from 10-11am and 2-4pm. Closed Tuesdays. Sundays and with student card, 2.50F entrance). Visit the **Farinier de Moines** (mill) and the **Bâtiments Claustraux,** stopping perhaps at the outdoor café on the plaza of the Abbey.

The **Syndicat d'Initiative,** 6 rue Mercière (tel. 59-05-34), will find you accommodations and help map out bicycle trips or other excursions. **Hôtel du Commerce,** 8 Place du Commerce (tel. 59-03-09) lets the cheapest rooms in town: 24F for a single and 28-62F for a double. Right on the main street, which is fairly quiet in Cluny. Breakfast 7.50F. **Relaxare,** Place du Champ de Foire 13, is a small but excellent hostel on the outskirts of Cluny. A bargain at 12F (no card required) and cooking facilities are available.

A few kilometers from Cluny is **Taizé,** a modern monastery with Protestant and Catholic sections, and a center of ecumenical meetings and meditation which draws young people from all over the world. The members of the community welcome seriously-interested visitors, and sell pottery to passers-by. The chapel is by Le Corbusier. Also nearby, the little town of **Azé** offers magnificent caves and a good campground.

The Alps

From whichever direction you arrive, suddenly the Alps are there, without warning, without introduction. Gone are the lazy, sunlit farm villages: suddenly you're in a lush mountain enclave, where everything tempts you to hike, boat, and drink in the air.

The cities of the Alps are bright and clean—definitely French, but with a certain twist that reveals the **Savoyards'** kinship to the Swiss. Train service is good only in the valley of **Chamonix** (Eurailpasses valid on the mountain train between **St. Gervais** and **Vallorcine**). Otherwise, the train will only take you to cities such as **Grenoble** and **Bourg-St.-Maurice** which serve as jumping-off points for Alpine excursions. Fortunately, bus service in the mountains is fairly good. If your time is limited, look into the special excursions available in cities like **Geneva,** Grenoble, and Chamonix. Hitching, at least for short hops, is fairly easy, and safer than most places. For sleeping, there are abundant campgrounds and a number of youth hostels. Many towns also have commercial chalet-dormitories, where you can stay for about 18F. In the high country, there are refuges run by the **Club Alpin Français,** which cost 20F for nonmembers. Most of the mountains and fields, of course, are not too diligently patrolled, so unofficial camping isn't difficult with a little discretion.

Grenoble is the region's only big city, a good starting point, and a good place to get information. A *cirque* of snow-peaked mountains provides the backdrop to a fascinating mix of modern architecture and old quarters unchanged since the time of Stendhal, the nineteenth century novelist and native *Grenoblois*. If you have time to spare from the mountains, the city has a number of interesting museums. There is an excellent **IYHF Youth Hostel** just out of town on ave. du Gresivaudan, Echirolles (tel. 09-33-52).

Some of the most renowned Alpine resorts are in the Department of the **Isère**, of which Grenoble is the capital. They include the spectacular **Alpe d'Huez, Chamrousse, les Deux Alpes** and more. **Chamrousse** is the base for tours of the **Isère Valley**, and of the **Belledone** mountain chain. **Alpe d'Huez** and **Bourg d'Oisans** open up the high mountain country of the **Oisans** with its glaciers and extensive winter sport facilities.

North of Grenoble lies **Aix-les-Bains,** with its sedate lake—the largest in France—and **Annecy.** The latter is one of the most enjoyable towns in France, its lake surrounded by the first of the high Alps. The vast nature preserve of the **Vanoise National Park** has numerous huts and shelters for hikers. The park is accessible from **Val d'Isère** or from **Pralognan.**

For beautiful green upland country, head for the area of **Les Dranses.** There are extensive tourist facilities in **Morzine, Les Gets,** and **Abondance.** Another pleasant green resort area is the valley of the **Giffre.** It is dotted with towns like **Samoëns** and **Sixt** that are popular with vacationing French families. Tourist offices in these areas can give you detailed hiking information and direct you to the **Club Alpin Français** for more ambitious projects. An excellent destination for those who want to get away from cablecars and crowds is the **Cirque du Fer à Cheval,** a high mountain valley sparkling with streams and nearly thirty waterfalls (especially in the spring)—but no cars. There's a vigorous but not difficult hike up to the ''Bout du Monde'' (end of the earth), the source of the Giffre, under the suspended glaciers higher up the mountain. Fer à Cheval is easily accessible by bus from Geneva.

While in the Alps, be sure to sample the smoked mountain sausages and the local cheeses (*emmenthal, beaufort, tomme de Savoie, reblochon* and others) as well as the *eaux de vie* which the mountain people distill from every sort of fruit. And, particularly in the high mountain country, you'll want to indulge in at least one warm pot of *fondue. Bourguignonne* is meat; while *savoyarde,* like the Swiss version, is cheese and bread.

Annecy

Annecy lies at the northern tip of the beautiful, clean **Lac d'Annecy,** fed by the clear run-off from the surrounding summits. The lake is the town's major attraction, fronted by a green, inviting park, where you can actually sit on the grass. A number of companies at the **Place aux Bois** offer rides on the lake for about 20F. The upper part of the lake is beautiful, ringed by mountains, its shoreline dotted with châteaux. If you saw the film *Claire's Knee* you have some idea of what it's like. Several establishments on the lakefront rent boats of all types (8.50F per hour for a rowboat, 25F per hour for a sailboat). A number of the towns around the lake have beaches; and in Annecy, you can swim at the **Stade Nautique,** rue des Marquisats, south of the main public garden.

The **old town** is laced with small, fast-running canals and narrow streets shaded with cool, stone arcades. In the middle of the old town is the **Palais d'Isle,** a fantastic little edifice that looks like it belongs in Disneyland but actually used to contain the town dungeons. Towering above the city is a large fifteenth-century **Château,** well worth the climb up the hill for the view it offers over the town and the lake.

Every year in July, there is a **Festival de la Vieille Ville,** a week-long celebration with concerts, folklore, medieval costumes, a free street dance, and fireworks over the lake. The first Sunday in August is the **Fête du Lac** with illuminated *embarcations* and fireworks.

Evenings in Annecy focus on the **Casino,** with its games, theater, cinema, restaurants and dancing. If you don't want to pay to go in, you can usually hear the band just as well on the large lawn between the casino and the lake.

Bicycle Rentals: Cycles des Fins, 24 ave. de Genève (tel. 57-06-89).

Alpinism: Compagnie Annecienne des Guides de Haute-Montagne information at the Maison du Tourisme.

Hitching: For Aix-les-Bains and Grenoble try the ave. de Chambéry. For Geneva and Chamonix, take the ave. de Genève (a sign will come in handy as this road serves many directions).

Accommodations and Food

Cheap rooms are scarce and usually booked up in season, but see what the **Maison du Tourisme** (Place de l'Hôtel de Ville, tel. 45-00-33) can suggest. They also have information on the many nearby campgrounds.

Hôtel du Château, 22 côte Saint-Maurice (tel. 45-27-66). Near the Château in the old town. Singles and doubles 29-58F plus mandatory 6.50F breakfast. Closed in October.

Hôtel au Balcon, 3 rue de la République (tel. 51-09-83). An old rambling building with comfortable, if plain, rooms at 23-35F.

Auberge de Jeunesse (IYHF), route to Semnoz (tel. 45-33-19). A rambling chalet in a wooded glade is the reward for a 45-minute uphill climb. 17.80F for bed-and-breakfast; no curfew.

Annecy is part tourist village and thus cheap restaurants are even scarcer than cheap hotel rooms. There are plenty of restaurants where a splurge, 40-50F, will reward you with a superlative Savoyard meal. If this doesn't suit your budget, the popular **Bar de Faucigny,** 19 rue Filaterie, has a 17F *plat du jour* and a reasonable à la carte menu.

Environs

There are lots of excursions to be taken. For bus trips, inquire at Voyages S.E.A. Crolard, Place de la Gare (tel. 45-00-56). If you take the tour of the lake by boat, you can stop at the **Téléphérique du Montveyrier,** which commands a view over the lake, and Mont Blanc in the distance. (Tour of the lake plus *téléphérique* costs 33F.) A short drive or train ride from Annecy are the **Château de Montrottier** (a fine military edifice) and the **Gorges du Fier,** carved out by a mountain stream (take the N508 to the D14, or the train, direction Aix-les-Bains).

Chamonix

The approach to Chamonix is beautiful. At Saint Gervais, you change from a larger express to a small mountain train, for the trip through the little town of **Servoz,** dwarfed by its awe-inspiring gorges, and finally up to Chamonix and **Mont Blanc.**

In fact, though there is a town of Chamonix, the name usually includes the community of surrounding villages, any of which may be reached by bus for a few francs and all of which are within 5 kilometers of the town. **Les Bossons, Les Pèlerins, Les Bois,** and **Les Praz** have the greatest number of campsites, but there are eighteen camping facilities in the immediate area. Directions and locations of places are all expressed in altitude, by the way, rather than by roads or distance, and at first this is confusing. But if you memorize the altitude of Chamonix (1035 meters) the rest is intuitive, up the mountain or down the mountain.

You really can't appreciate Chamonix without getting up out of the valley. If you're willing and able, there are several hikes (not to mention rock climbs) that will take you high enough to appreciate the Mont Blanc *massif.* Otherwise, there are several *téléphériques* to take you up. The most spectacular is the **Aiguille du Midi.** Unfortunately, it's also the most expensive—44F round trip (25% reduction with coupon available at the Youth Hostel). Even more expensive is the cablecar across into Italy. These are well worth it if you can afford them, but if you're counting your centimes, the best solution is to take the **téléphérique du Brévant.** This costs 20F (13.70F with coupon from Auberge de Jeunesse or hotel) and takes you up a peak across the valley from Mont Blanc, commanding a wide view of the whole range. The cost can be cut if you ride up and walk down. Not too difficult, but you should have good shoes.

Also worth seeing is the **Mer de Glace** glacier. There is a train (20F round trip, 12F one way), but it is a fairly easy hike up and a very easy walk down, and can be done in a couple of hours. One tip about the cablecars: it is best to go up in the morning, as the peaks tend to cloud over in the afternoon. There are a large number of well-marked, easy-to-follow trails in the area. Invest 3F in a trail map at the Tourist Office and you're all set. One pleasant and easy trail is the **Petit Balcon:** take the train or hitch to **Argentières** and walk back to Chamonix. You can also climb up to the Argentière glacier without too much difficulty. If you want to get away from the crowds, take the train to **Vallorcine**—a beautiful little hamlet with an extensive trail system of its own. Get a free map at the tourist information booth on the road near the Station. (By the way, this is the limit of validity for Eurailpasses). For the more ambitious, the **Compagnie des Guides,** Place de l'Eglise (tel. 53-00-88), has a climbing school, guided excursions (including a weekly trip to Zermatt via the high country), and insurance. Upstairs in the same building is the **Office de l'Haute Montagne,** with information, maps, and a retired guide who speaks English.

In addition to the mountains, Chamonix offers golf, tennis, riding, cinemas, nightclubs, and a casino. There are also ice-skating facilities and an excellent swimming pool complex. (Bois du Bouchet, tel. 52-23-70—entry 7F, 4F with coupon from the Youth Hostel.) The **Office du Tourisme,** Place de l'Eglise (tel. 53-00-24), is open daily 8am-8pm and has information on hotels as well as on the forthcoming events, sports, weather forecast, and money exchange. This is where you get your trail map (8F), and find out about summer skiing (usually lousy, but it exists).

Addresses and Telephone Numbers

Club Alpin Français, ave. Michel-Croz (tel. 53-16-03). Open 9:30am-noon and 3-7:30pm daily except Wed. morning and Sun. Information on their mountain refuges. They keep a message board in their window, with notices of mountaineering equipment for sale, rendezvous, etc.

Mountain Rescue: Société Chamoniarde de Secours en Montagne, Place du Mont Blanc (tel. 53-16-89), but somebody'd better be able to pay.

Clinic and Hospital: route du Valais (tels. 53-01-82 and 53-00-59).

Centre Equestre de Chamonix (horse-riding): Les Tines (tel. 53-20-99).

Bicycle Rental: Lucchini, ave. de l'Aiguille du Midi, near center of town.

Accommodations

Auberge de Jeunesse (IYHF), Les Pèlerins (tel. 53-14-52). By bus from the Place de l'Eglise in Chamonix. If you come by train, you can save yourself the bus ride by getting off at the Les Pèlerins Station. Then cross the river and walk straight up the hill. A barracks, in fact, but quite serviceable; 17F per night, hot showers free. Decent meals at 13.50F, breakfast 4.50F. Free discount coupons for cablecars and pool. Closed May, October, and November.

Refuge des Amis de la Montagne, 53 chemin de la Cascade (tel. 53-17-83). Simple but clean dormitory, 18F per night, hot showers 5F, meals 18F. Well located, near the Mer de Glace Railroad Station.

Chalet le Chamoniard, just off the main road near the bois du Bouchet (tel. 53-14-09). A pleasant dormitory. Clean and modern. Free hot showers and use of kitchen. Bed and breakfast 26F, other meals available. This and many other chalets have special three-day rates.

Chalet Ski Station, just below the Téléphérique du Brévant (tel. 53-20-25). Plain dorms but friendly management and good location. 18F per night. Showers 5F. Sheet rental (if you haven't got your own) 3F. English spoken. Offers 35% discount on Brévant téléphérique.

Chalet Refuge Premier de Cordée (take the road to the Brévant téléphérique, turn left, watch for the arrow; tel. 53-08-80). Very nice dorms. Friendly and recommended. A gorgeous view but long hike up the hill. (No problem with a car.) Bed and breakfast 26F; demi-pension 46F. Free showers. 50% discounts on Brévant and Flegère cablecars.

Camping: a complete list of available sites is available at the Office du Tourisme; or try Bel Air, at Les Bosson, on the road to Annecy (tel. 53-17-13), and on the same road Ile des Barrats. In Les Pèlerins, there are two sites near the Auberge de Jeunesse. Be prepared for a rather cool Alpine evening.

Food

Food here is generally pedestrian and over-priced. There are a number of places in the center of town that offer a *plat du jour* or *steak-frites* for 16-20F. The rue Wymper has stands selling crêpes, *frites*, ice cream, and waffles from 3-10F. Or try:

La Boule de Neige, 362 rue Joseph Vallot. Excellent 34F *fondue savoyarde* for two and a *menu* at 16.50F; served in a pretty garden in summer.

Brasserie le Fer à Cheval, rue Wymper. The outside tables front on a dusty vacant lot, but inside there's a very lively atmosphere. *Fondue savoyarde* for 16F, *fondue bourguignonne* 24F.

La Crecelle, rue Wymper. A *crêperie* with polyglot service and *menus*. Crêpes 4.50-15F, *galettes* 8-20F. Odds and ends like spaghetti 15F.

Hôtel Suisse Restaurant, rue Paccard, near the Post Office. A more elegant place. Trout 18-20F, gourmet *menu* 40F, service included.

Côte d'Azur

Even at its most commercial, the Riviera can be beautiful, but to truly enjoy a trip along France's famed Mediterranean Coast, selectivity is required. For while there are some beautiful beaches, especially on the **St. Tropez** peninsula, many others are small, crowded, dirty, rocky, and inundated by fumes from the nearby roads. Some cities on the coast have preserved identity and beauty, but others have fallen prey to the mediocrity of mass commercialism. So to best enjoy what the Mediterranean offers, get away from the throngs; seek out a pleasant inlet or *calanque* (the Riviera's answer to the fjord), along the **Esterel** or **Maures,** or on any of the small peninsulas between St. Tropez and Marseille.

The best way to assure yourself space to worship the sun *au naturel,* without the crowds, the umbrellas, and the noise is to come during the spring or autumn. Not only are the beaches infinitely more pleasant, but hotels have vacancies and prices are generally *at least* 25% lower.

During July and August obtaining a room without a reservation is virtually impossible in all cities except **Nice** and **Marseille.** The youth hostels and *relais* on the Riviera are frequently booked up for the summer by as early as March. If you don't have a room, your only recourse is the local *Syndicat d'Initiative,* or, if you insist on finding one yourself, the many cheap hotels that tend to congregate around the train stations in every major town. We recommend camping: warm weather and little rain will allow you to sleep in the open, and campgrounds are super-abundant, close to beaches, and very safe, as well as being good places to find a ride in your direction. Showers, toilet facilities, and sinks are almost always available. On beach camping: it *is* illegal, but also frequently done. It takes a little subtlety—don't set up your flaming orange mountain tent. The smaller coves are safer than the open beach. The police may or may not tell you to move on, but they don't pose much of a danger beyond that. One word of warning: stay clear of drugs. If the police do come, the one thing they'll be seriously worried about is drugs—and there are few countries worse than France for drug offenders.

The specialties of the Riviera are *bouillabaisse* (fish stew), *salade Niçoise*; and *aioli,* a garlic sauce which is spread over fresh vegetables, fish, and snails.

Unless you have a date or are part of a mixed group, nightclubs and discotheques are not the way to amuse yourself at night; they are usually expensive and not conducive to meeting people. Instead, nurse a drink at a sidewalk café, enjoying the free entertainment at roadside.

Trains and buses run frequently on the Côte d'Azur, and, due to the compactness of the region, are reasonably priced. All of this is doubly fortunate since hitchhiking is so poor. A beautiful road runs along the entire stretch from **Hyères,** near Marseille, to **Monaco** and the Italian border, and buses run regularly along this route. But even the trains provide a good view of the sea. For more exciting transport, rent a mobylette, or motorbike, in Nice at rue des Prés (off 22 boulevard Dubouchage) for 25F a day and 100F deposit. Don't worry about their being too slow, for traffic along the coast is frequently blocked up for 50 kilometers at a stretch. If you are in a group, renting a car might be better. **Mattei** is a reputable firm with offices in Marseille (121 avenue du Prado, tel. 77-66-00), in Cannes (M. Brucker, 8 rue Frères-Pradignac, tel. 39-36-50), and in Nice (5 rue Halévy, tel. 87-14-30). A 500F deposit will be required. In addition, **Solvet** with offices in Antibes, (15 avenue Grand Cavalier, tel. 34-44-79), Cannes (29 boulevard Général Vautrin, tel. 38-50-88), Nice (24 rue de France, tel. 88-63-12), St. Raphael (11 rue de l'Amiral Baux, tel 95-16-71) and Toulon (5 avenue François Curzin, tel. 93-16-71), rents bikes, motorbikes, and cars at average prices. They will waive the deposit (500F for cars) if you have a recognized credit card, such as American Express.

Monaco

Farthest east on the French Riviera, the celebrated principality of Monaco is a closely packed maze of skyscrapers, old Rococo buildings, players and businessmen, bankers, and grand dukes. **Monte Carlo,** within Monaco, is the elegant and international city whose casino has brought the principality its fame. It is separated from **Monaco-Ville** by the harbor district, **La Condamine,** where the cheapest hotels and restaurants may be found.

The **Casino** in Monte Carlo is palatial, glorious, and romantic, almost surpassing the palace itself for its splendor. You don't have to wear black tie to get into the Casino, but you won't get in with jeans or shorts. Anything medium nice will do (e.g., cords, etc.). There is no dress code for playing the slot machines just off the main entry, however. Gambling rooms open at 10am, with a 12F entrance fee. You have to be 21 years old. If you can afford it, enter the "private rooms" (20F admission; open at 4pm but more lively at night) for a taste of the sheikhs and their counterparts at play. Follow this up with a whirlwind visit to the spectacular **Rock of Monaco,** the **Palace** (for the changing of the guard or the nightly concert in the courtyard), the **Oceanographic Museum,** and the **Exotic Gardens.** The **Aquarium** is also interesting, but expensive (admission 16F, 8F with student ID). The **American Express** office is at 35 boulevard Princesse Charlotte (tel. 30-96-52). Open Mon.-Fri. 9am-noon and 2-5:30pm, Sat. 9am-noon.

Accommodations

Cheap hotels cluster around the station in La Condamine, but a more diverse selection can be had around the Casino. The **Tourist Office,** 2 boulevard des Moulins (tel. 30-87-01) will make hotel reservations for you. (They also have an office at the Railroad Station.) Five minutes from Monaco, the cheapest place of all is the **Relais International de Jeunesse,** boulevard de la Mer, Cap d'Ail (tel. 06-81-10), where you can room for 18F a night, breakfast included; IYHF card required. A beautiful location right on the sea. Easy access from the Cap d'Ail Railroad Station (take the Metrazur or Omnibus). Better atmosphere than youth hostels. Midnight curfew. The only drawback is cold showers. Dinner 13F. Other hotels include:

Hôtel Cosmopolite, 4 rue de la Turbie, La Condamine (tel. 30-16-95). Near the Station, with singles at 30F, doubles 31-38F, breakfast 8F.

Hôtel de France, 6 rue de la Turbie (tel. 30-24-64). A shade more expensive than the nearby Cosmopolite, and a shade more attractive. Singles 31F, doubles from 42F, breakfast 8F.

Hôtel de la Poste, 5 rue des Oliviers (tel. 30-70-56). A good location near the Casino and the beach, but often full—write for reservations well ahead of time. Singles 29-32F, doubles 30-35F, breakfast 7F.

There are three campgrounds in **Roquebrune Cap Martin,** on the way to Italy, though the only one on the sea is **Camping de Banastron** (tel. 35-74-58). There is also a Youth Hostel (IYHF) in **Menton** at Plateau St. Michel (tel. 35-93-14), 3 km from the Train Station.

Food

In the narrow little streets of the old city, on the Rock, or in La Condamine, many interesting restaurants offer moderately-priced fare. Equally good are the cafés along the boulevard Moulins. Try:

Bar-restaurant Bacchus, 13 rue de la Turbie, on the 23F *menu* try the *ravioli avec fromage*. Near the Train Station.

Restaurant de la Roya, 21 rue de la Turbie, a bit crowded at times but good *menus* beginning at 22F. Try the *moules farcies* (stuffed mussels).

From Monaco to Nice

It is only 20 kilometers from Monaco to Nice; and the trains, which run every half hour or so, cost just 4F, so it is probably not worth the bother of hitching. If driving you will pass through **Eze** on the N559, with its nice campgrounds. **Azur Camping** (tel. 01-50-43) offers seaside camping. Another nearby campground is **Eze Camping,** on the N7 Grand Corniche at the "Le Pous" bus stop between Nice and Monaco. You will then pass through **Villefranche sur Mer,** a surprisingly untouched fishing town. Nice is the next point on the road, and if you're unwilling to tackle the resort crowds for a few days, head inland instead, about 30 kilometers to the Maritime Alps. The **River Var** cuts through the Alps to Nice and boasts a series of gorges and bluffs which rivals all the glories of the Riviera. **Entrevaux,** 75 kilometers north, forms an array of old houses in the *provençale* style, perched on rocky bluffs.

Nice

Behind the huge hotels lining the waterfront lies a large and surprisingly pleasant city with its own flavor and low prices. The beach, however, is disappointingly small and rocky. Instead, try **Cap Ferrat,** a beautiful beach only ten kilometers from town.

The **Old Town** (Vieille Ville), bounded by the quai des Etats Unis and avenue Jean Jaurès, is a maze of tiny streets, teeming slots between six-story buildings, where prices are half those of tourist Nice and where the impoverished can eat well at low cost. Organize your meanderings to see both the **Marché aux Fleurs** and the **Marché aux Poissons.** At night the concerts and plays in the **Théâtre de Verdure** are fun, outdoors, and informal.

You will find the **Musée Matisse** (Villa des Arènes) in **Cimiez,** the chic residential section on the hills behind the city. The museum is beautifully set among gardens and Roman ruins (open 10am-noon and 2-7pm daily, until 5pm in winter; admission 4F, 2F for students). Take bus #15 from the place Masséna. Also well worth a visit is the **Musée Nationale du Message Biblique de Marc Chagall** (open daily 10am-6pm May-September; 10am-12:30pm and 1:30-5:30pm October-April. Closed Tues. Admission 5F, students 2.50F.

The **American Express** office is at 11 promenade des Anglais (tel. 87-29-82). Open Mon.-Fri. 9am-noon and 2-5:30pm, Sat. 9am-12:30pm. The **U.S. Consulate** is at 3 rue du Docteur Baréty (tel. 88-89-55).

Accommodations

Because Nice does not die in winter, high and low season rates do not vary as much here as in the smaller cities of the Riviera. Most of Nice's hotels lie between the Station and the sea, especially between the ave. Durante and the ave. Jean-Médecin. The **Syndicat d'Initiative** is just outside the Train Station, with a good room-finding service (tel. 87-07-07).

Auberge de Jeunesse (IYHF), route Forestière du Mont Alban (tel. 89-23-64). 4 km. by bus #14 from the Station or the place Masséna. Bed and breakfast 17F, dinner 13F. Lockout 10am-6pm.

Relais International de la Jeunesse, ave. Scuderi, in Cimiez (tel. 81-27-63). Bed and breakfast 18F, optional dinner for 13F. Swimming pool 2F. Take bus #15 or 17 plus a short walk.

Hôtel Les Orangers, 10*bis* ave. Durante (tel. 87-51-41). A small hotel near the Station. Most of its clean, modern rooms have showers and cooking facilities: 32-60F. The kindly proprietors don't mind if 4 or 5 people stay in a room with 2 beds.

Hôtel Ann-Margaret, 1 ave. St.-Joseph (tel. 88-72-23). Just off blvd. Gambetta; clean rooms and very pleasant staff. Singles for 29F and doubles for 36-39F including breakfast on a shaded patio.

Hôtel Auber, 27 ave. Auber (tel. 87-05-67). Lots of compatriots here. 18F per person in doubles, triples, and quads. Breakfast 5F, but the management is resigned to not forcing guests to spend the extra buck.

Hôtel Beausoleil, 2 rue St.-Siagre (tel. 85-19-66). Near the Station. Rooms 22-32F. For the area, rock bottom in price and quality.

Hôtel Mimosas, 26 rue de la Buffa (tel. 88-05-59). Three blocks from the beach on the third floor of a building with hotels on several of the floors. Comfortable singles 24F, doubles 31F, breakfast 7F, shower 4F. Make-shift camping-style cooking equipment is available if you want to prepare your own omelettes, etc.

Food

Chez Suzanne, 16 rue Paganini. French cooking and local specialities; frequented and run by students. Excellent 18F, 24F, and 35F *menus*.

La Trappa, at the end of the rue de la Préfecture in the Vieille Ville. Lots of atmosphere; specializes in local seafood dishes. Try the *friture du pays* (small fried fish). You can eat for just over 15F.

Le Paprika, 9*bis* rue Halévy. A very small restaurant in the pedestrian district, serving good Hungarian/Niçoise specialties from 17-35F.

Festival des Glaces, at the end of the rue Masséna, serves huge and exotic bowls of ice cream concoctions for 12-24F, either in a snazzy mirrored interior or at sidewalk tables. Quite a scene at night.

There is a large open-air market on the **cours Sallya,** and the department stores on the avenue Jean Médecin have supermarkets which are open all day long.

From Nice to Cannes

Art lovers should detour off the coast to **St. Paul de Vence** to visit the **Fondation Maeght,** a beautiful half-park, half-museum with an outstanding collection of modern art, and developing programs in theater, music, and dance. On the same trip, visit the **Matisse Chapel** in nearby Vence.

First stop west on the coast from Nice is **Haut de Cagnes,** which is a suburb of **Antibes,** but was once a haunt of famous French artists, notably Renoir. Antibes itself is 10 kilometers from Nice along the coast. It has little to offer except a lovely Picasso museum, the **Grimaldi.** On the **Cap d'Antibes,** with its imposing lighthouse, is the **Relais International de la Jeunesse,** blvd. de la Garoupe (tel. 61-34-40), where 18F will buy you bed and breakfast. There are a few uncrowded beaches on the Cap and a larger, sandier, and more bustling stretch further along the coast in **Juan-les-Pins.** There are also fifteen or so campgrounds around Antibes and Juan-les-Pins, most of them on N7. Two of the smaller and less expensive ones are **Fontemerle,** chemin de Fontemerle (tel. 34-25-66), and **Lauvert Juan Plage** (tel. 61-26-35). You might also try:

Hôtel-Pension le Brebant, 1 ave. de l'Esterel, Juan-les-Pins. Very plain, but about the cheapest in town.

Hôtel de la Gare, 6 rue du Printemps, Juan-les-Pins (tel. 61-29-96). Singles 25F, doubles 35F.

Hôtel Trianon, 14 ave. de l'Esterel, Juan-les-Pins (tel. 61-18-11). Very nice, with doubles at 50F in season, but reserve far in advance (before May, if possible).

You can rent **bikes** at the baggage office in the stations of both Juan-les-Pins and Antibes.

Tourist Offices are located on place Général de Gaulle, Antibes (tel. 34-55-64), or boulevard Baudoin, Juan-les-Pins (tel. 61-04-98), but they don't make hotel reservations.

Cannes

Cannes is a large city, but its streets are narrow, and it looks less like the perfect tourist resort than you might expect. Stroll the palm-lined **La Croisette,** window-shop at the expensive boutiques, or enjoy a drink at one of the elegant sidewalk cafés. There's a fine view of Cannes, the port, and the **Iles de Lerins** from the **Tour du Mont Chevalier** up in the Old Town.

The public beach is showy, sandy, and crowded. Round-trip voyages to the Iles de Lerins run about every hour. **St. Marguerite** (6.90F round trip) has a splendid eucalyptus forest and the prison of the "Man in the Iron Mask;" **St. Honorat** (8.60F round trip) has a fortified monastery. Every two or three days there is a night trip for 20F, when the islands are lit up with a sound and light spectacle. Boats leave from the Gare Maritime des Iles on the port (tel. 39-11-82).

Accommodations and Food

The **Syndicat d'Initiative** has offices at the Station (tel. 99-19-77) and at the Palais des Festivals on La Croisette (tel. 39-24-53). They will arrange accommodations for you or direct you to nearby campgrounds. You might try:

Hôtel Chanteclair, 12 rue Forville (tel. 39-68-88). Near the Station. Off a courtyard and with a bit of a view. 23F per person, breakfast 6F.

Hôtel National, 8 rue Maréchal Joffre (tel. 39-91-92). Rooms 24F with an optional 6F breakfast. Also near the Station. Closed mid-October to mid-November.

Camping: Bellevue tends to be crowded. You might try Le Grand Saule in La Bocca on the ave. J. Jourdan (tel. 47-07-50).

Les Glycines, 32 blvd. d'Alsace (tel. 38-41-28). Just the other side of the tracks. A 20F *menu* with good and plentiful portions, served in a lovely garden. You can stay here as well: singles 24F, doubles 33F, but you should write ahead for beds and be willing to put up with the trains that pass all night.

Le Réfuge, quai St. Pierre. The best of the waterfront restaurants. Very good food and quite reasonable prices: 25.50F *menu* and extensive à la carte choice.

From Cannes to Saint Tropez

From Cannes, the road passes through the resort towns of **La Napoule** and **La Galere,** both expensive and commercial. **Mougins** is about 8 kilometers from Cannes and offers magnificent panoramas of the whole coastline. **Les Lentisques,** on the D3, route de Valbonne (tel. 90-00-45) is the better of the two campgrounds in the area (open Easter to October). Between Mougins and **Saint-Raphaël** is **Agay,** a sheltered little town built on rugged red rocks above a cove, and a good place for a respite from the crowds. Fifteen kilometers farther along the coast is Saint-Raphaël itself, retreat of Brigitte Bardot and a pleasant historical town combining the flavors of the idle rich and the Mediterranean fishermen. There is a Youth Hostel (IYHF) in nearby

Fréjus on the route de Cannes, 1.5 kilometers from the Station (tel. 40-21-85). Closed mid-December to mid-January, and Saturday nights.

St. Tropez

St. Tropez is the most pretentious place on the Riviera, and for that reason alone is probably worth a visit. Fortunately, there is more than pretention, for the beaches of St. Tropez are good, though a few kilometers out of town. **La Plage de Pampelonne** is one of the most spectacular beaches on the Riviera, while **La Plage de Tahiti** is the haunt of the very rich. And the farther east you walk on **La Plage des Salins,** the fewer the people and the fewer the clothes.

With a little skill, you might even maneuver around the exorbitant cost of living that makes St. Tropez a nice place to visit, but not to stay overnight. Sleep either on the **Plage des Salins** or in a campground. You'll find a good one 5 kilometers west on N98a at **Cogolin Plage,** while east on route des Salins you will find another one after about two kilometers. All hotels are too expensive and booked far in advance. You might stop by the **Syndicat d'Initiative,** on the quai Jean Jaurès and rue Vi Laugier (tel. 97-03-64), and try to have them place you in a private home for 15-30F, but that, too, might be difficult in summer. The *Syndicat* will also provide information on additional camping in the area.

From St. Tropez to Toulon

The main roads tend to drift inland, but detour if you can to **Hyères,** where you can get a boat to the **Iles de Hyères.** These islands are also served by boats from La Tour Fondue and Le Lavandou and, for a bit more money, from Toulon. Fares run about 20-40F round trip, depending on the particular passage you choose. The **Ile du Levant** is the home of one of Europe's most famous nudist colonies—**Heliopolis.** The **Ile de Porquerolles** is the largest and has sandy beaches and shady forests. **Port-Cros** is perhaps the wildest of the Riviera's off-shore islands: much of it is a national park dedicated to the preservation of the original Mediterranean flora.

Toulon is a city of sailors and women, with a music festival from the end of June through mid-July. Rising behind the city, **Mt. Faron** may be approached by car or by cable car and offers a fine view of the coast. There are some small but nice enough beaches in Toulon; take bus #3 to Mourillon from the Station. Toulon is full of tourists, but the hotels are cheap, and if you've been craving a bed on the Riviera, there are worse places.

Hôtel de la Majorité, 16 rue Anatole-France (tel. 93-07-51) is well located near the port. There are a few fourth-floor rooms for 22F, otherwise 29F plus. **Hôtel du Théâtre,** 8 rue de l'Humilité (tel. 92-70-81) is decent and central. Doubles 24F, and with shower 39F. The **Hotel des Trois Dauphins,** Place des Trois Dauphins (tel. 92-65-79) has simple rooms for 23-37F; showers 4F extra. The **Auberge de Jeunesse** (IYHF) at 382 chemin Lombard, Six-Fours-les-Plages (tel. 25-21-43) has closed, but during the summer camping is permitted there; take a green line bus from the Station towards Bandol.

From Toulon to Marseille

Near Toulon, you can explore the beautiful little coves of the **Cap Brun.** West of Toulon, there are good beaches at **Les Sablettes** and **Bandol** (this is somewhat crowded). Farther along is **La Ciotat,** which fairly drowns in campgrounds. **Cassis** has become a minor resort for the middling-beautiful people of Marseille, but you can duck the crowds simply by avoiding the main beach. The **Tourist Kiosk** at Place Baragnon will give you directions to the nearby Youth Hostel; for 3F the bus will drop you off at a level approach overlooking a five-kilometer stretch of herb-covered cliffs, or you can hike straight up the steep trails from Port Miou. The hostel is delightfully isolated from most people, electricity, or plumbing—water is collected in cisterns. But there's a well-equipped communal kitchen, easygoing young management, and a breathtaking wind-whipped view for 16F a night. Several paths descend from here into the sheltered *calanques*. If you'd like a meal in the village, try the fish soup cooked with olive oil at **La Défense,** 3 rue Lamartine—contents of the daily pot are posted on the door; which opens at 8:30pm, as do most other restaurants here.

For hitching to Marseille, try the entry to the autoroute at the carrefour Vieille Ville; for Nice, go to avenue Alphonse Juin (Rond-Point Bir Hakeim).

Marseille is a huge, industrial and maritime city, low on tourist attractions and high on urban specialities such as noise and pickpockets. The **Old Port** does have its own brand of exotic appeal, as well as boat departures for Corsica and just about every international port in the entire Mediterranean. If you do want to explore Marseille, stay at the better of the city's two large IYHF **Youth Hostels: Château de Bois-Luzy,** ave. Bois-Luzy (tel. 49-06-18). Both charge 13.50F a night. Take bus #6 or 8 from the Allée Gambetta.

Corsica (Corse)

In Corsica, the mountains finger their way down to the Mediterranean. Seasons happen simultaneously at different altitudes, and snow remains through the summer on the highest mountains. Poverty and severe underdevelopment have conserved the natural beauty. Tourism is as yet primitive, and the financial opportunists have yet to rear an ugly head. The Corsicans' separate identity, closer to the Sardinian than the French, persists not merely as a quaint holdover but in the form of a growing separatist activism.

You can reach Corsica by air from Paris, Nice, or Marseille. The **Société Nationale Maritime Corse-Méditerranée (SNCM)** operates car ferries from Marseille, Toulon, and Nice, docking at Bastia, Calvi, and Ile-Rousse in northern Corsica, and Ajaccio and Propriano in the west. Second-class one-way fare from Marseille or Toulon is 120F, from Nice 86F. The cheapest way to go is fourth class (on the deck) from Nice: 68F one way. The cost of bringing a car along varies with its size and the season. Low-season rates are 55-69F one way, doubling in high season and tripling for the first weeks in July and August. There is also a boat service between Italy (Genoa and Livorno) and Bastia, and there are three crossings daily of the 14-kilometer passage between Bonifacio on the southern tip of Corsica and Santa-Theresa, Sardinia.

Once on the island, car or motorbike is the most convenient way to travel, and rental is simple in Ajaccio, Calvi, and Bastia. Trains connect Ajaccio and Bastia, the main towns, with Corte in the center and Ile-Rousse and

Calvi on the north coast. Eurailpasses are not valid on the island. Bus service fills the geographical gaps but connections often strain itineraries and patience, e.g., arriving in Bonifacio at the southern tip of the island to find that the next bus leaves two days later. Hitching is impractical but possible—not recommended for anyone in a hurry. Finally, whenever possible, travel clockwise on Corsica. The roads, etched into the mountainside, rattle even the most reckless drivers.

Tourism is super-developed in only a few places. Accommodations, therefore, are relatively scarce, isolated, and expensive. Since there are no youth hostels, camping is probably the best way to survive cheaply. Official sites are abundant enough, but so much of the island is sparsely settled that you can virtually pick your site. Some discretion is advisable, of course. If you're obviously on someone's property, ask permission before setting up.

Corsican cooking draws heavily on the sea, including all varieties of Mediterranean fish and seafood. Local goat's milk cheeses include a *roquefort*-type blue cheese and *brocciu,* a milder white cheese.

Ajaccio

Ajaccio, Corsica's capital and the more pleasant of its two main towns, is a good place to begin a tour. Birthplace of Napoleon, Ajaccio preserves the home where he was born, and a family portrait hangs in the hall of the **Hôtel de Ville.** The **Musée Fesch** has an outstanding collection of Italian primitive and Renaissance paintings. Excursion boats ply the route to the grottoes of the **Iles Sanguinaires,** just off the coast.

The **Syndicat d'Initiative,** Place Foch (tel. 21-40-87) dispenses the necessary brochures, lists of campgrounds, etc. For accommodations, try the **Belvedere Hotel,** 4 rue Henri Dunan (tel. 21-07-26), with singles 25-35F, doubles 45F. If full, they relay customers to other inexpensive places nearby. **Chez Pardi,** upstairs at 60 rue Fesch is a restaurant patronized by a Corsican clientele that delights in non-French foreigners; they serve seafood specialities for 20-30F. **U Foconu,** at the foot of rue Général Campi, specializes in Corsican dishes and has an 18F *menu*. The morning market by the port offers fruit, vegetables and, of course, fresh fish.

Ajaccio is the perfect departure point for the interior or the coast. **Corte,** the historic capital of Corsica, is surrounded by mountains and buttressed against attack. The town embodies the Corsicans' traditionally defensive, isolated, independent attitude. The nearby **Mt. Cinto** and **Mt. D'Oro** offer challenging climbs or less arduous hikes along the forested trails on the slopes. Technically, for camping in the forests you need authorization from **La Compagnie des Eaux et Forêts,** 4 boulevard Marcaggi, Ajaccio. In any event, be extremely careful with cigarettes, etc. on the mountainsides: the *maquis* (Corsican scrub) is unbelievably inflammable. If you decide to sleep inside, try the **Hôtel de la Poste** (tel. 46-01-37), across from the Post Office in Corte.

From Ajaccio to Calvi

From Ajaccio to **Porto** and Calvi, the road sweeps first past beaches and fledgling resorts before climbing steeply wooded gorges and massive mountains. From **Piana** to Porto, the road twists through the tortured **Calanques,** the finest scenery in Corsica. Red-rock cliffs plunge into a deep-blue sea serrated by the mountains into inlets. Piana is more remarkable for its site than its charms as a village. Porto lies deep in a gulf, with many plain hotels offering single and doubles for 35-45F. Try **Le Maquis** (tel. 26-12-19) or **Hôtel Bon Accueil** (tel. 26-12-10). **Girolata,** hidden on the last of a series of bays and isolated by rugged cliffs, is inspiring, but lacks accommodations. A boat (20F round trip) links Girolata to Porto.

The splendidly scenic mountain road between Piana and Calvi would test any driver. The mountains soften somewhat near the desolate valley of the **Fango** before the road resumes its mountain-hugging course. At Calvi, fortifications fuse with the promontory, and dominate a panorama of turquoise water, crescent beaches, pine woods, and rugged mountains. If you plan to stay anywhere for a couple of nights, Calvi is probably the nicest town on the island. Accommodations are expensive, and rooms fill up fast. Try the **Hôtel du Centre,** rue Alsace-Lorraine (tel. 65-02-01) with rooms for 38-43F. Camping sites are plentiful, however. Calvi has cafés along the port, good seafood restaurants, and something of a nightlife.

From Calvi to Bastia

To the northeast of Calvi is the most fertile area in Corsica—**La Balagne.** Its coast is dotted with small but growing beach resorts. Farther on is **St. Florent,** an attractive fishing village turned tourist trap. The road to Bastia now climbs and winds across the mountainous neck of the **Cap Corse** before snaking down to the coast.

Bastia is both an unappealing town and an active port, serving France and Northern Italy. War damage reduced the picturesque **old port** (just south of the current port) to just a few façades over expensive restaurants. Bastia is a good point to start a tour of the Cape, but avoid it otherwise. The Cape is a finger-shaped peninsula with small fishing villages linked by a *corniche* road curling along the mountainside. At **Nonza** stands a medieval fortress astride a high cliff. Buses for the tour of the Cape leave at 8:30am from rue du Nouveau Port 1.

In Bastia, stay at the **Hôtel Riviera,** 1*bis* rue du Nouveau Port (tel. 31-63-04) with singles, doubles, and triples 35-60F; or the **Hôtel de l'Univers,** 1 and 3 ave. Maréchal Sebastiani (tel. 31-03-38) with singles, doubles, and triples 28-64F. Both lie between the Train Station and the dock, about six blocks away. For restaurants, **Jack's,** 18 rue César Campinchi, is small but one of the best on Corsica; 24F seafood *menu*. There is a **Tourist Office** on Place St. Nicholas at the port; and the **Syndicat d'Initiative** is at 33 blvd. Paoli (tel. 31-56-35).

Bastia to Bonifacio

From Bastia, the road leads south to the coast with long, flat, straight stretches. If you like, veer off south of Bastia for Corte and the island peaks described above. Along the coast to **Bonifacio,** the route passes **Solenzara** and **Porte-Vecchio**, beach towns as yet undeveloped. Porte-Vecchio is an old fortified town, set high above a wide bay with good beaches. Accommodations along the way are rare and camping is more readily available.

Bonifacio will turn your head around. Sheer, white cliffs surround a harbor dominated by a medieval citadel. From the ramparts, you can look across to Sardinia only eight miles away across the straits. Stay a bit and wander the narrow streets of the old town and the fishing village below. Hotels and restaurants are down in the port but aren't cheap. Try the **Hôtel**

des Voyageurs (tel. 16) or the **Hotel des Etrangers** (tel. 49) where doubles start at 60-70F. There are several campgrounds within the immediate area. The best is **Campo di Liccia** (tel. 159), on the N198, open June 1 through September 20.

From Bonifacio north to Ajaccio, the road again turns mountainous, offering some splendid seaward vistas. **Sartène** and **Propriano** on the water offer pretty rock coves and sand beaches. Sartène also has an interesting old town and one of Europe's most remarkable Good Friday penitential processions: *"La Catenacciu,"* with a hooded Christ bearing his cross in a complicated dance through the streets.

Provence: The Southern Rhône

The colorful region of Provence, in southern France, is best known for its Roman monuments and its architectural masterpieces of the Middle Ages, but summer brings to Provence the adventure of bullfights, festivals, and spectacles, all staged in the dramatic setting of the monuments themselves. For the hitchhiker, Provence is especially attractive, offering a number of interesting cities and sights within fairly short distances of each other.

Provençale cuisine is a further treat, with its Mediterranean emphasis on garlic and olive oil. Seafood and fish soups are specialties.

Aix-en-Provence

Aix-en Provence may be the perfect place to restore your faith in the myth surrounding southern France, after the prices, crowds and glitter of the Côte d'Azur. The gentle grace and dignity that one associates with life in the unhurried Midi can still be found here. Aix (pronounced "ecks") isn't the place if you're looking for nightlife or excitement—but spend a couple of days here to unwind, to relax at the cafés or under the magnificent electric blue sky of the *provençale* countryside. In the fifteenth century, the city was the home of Roi René, king of Provence and a genial patron of the arts. While the kingdom has disappeared, his statue still surveys the bustling **Cours Mirabeau,** seemingly approving its tempo and its enticements.

In winter, Aix remains a sleepy, smug university town inhabited by students and the *bonne bourgeoisie.* Summer brings hordes of European tourists (especially for the **Mozart Festival** in July), and small groups of artists, who come to sketch in the special sunlight of Cézanne's favorite city. But the crowds are manageable and Aix is a good base for exploring the region. Aix has a number of small museums worth visiting, including the **Musée des Tapisseries** with a fine collection of Beauvais tapestries (open daily 10am-noon and 2-6pm. Closed Mon.).

Accommodations and Food

Accommodation is hard to find at festival time in any price range. The **Syndicat d'Initiative,** Place du Général de Gaulle (tel. 26-02-93) has an accommodation service and information on the festivals and excursions in the area. There is an IYHF **Auberge de Jeunesse,** Quartier du Jas de Bouffan, ave. Marcel Pagnol (tel. 20-15-99), 2 kilometers from the Station, bus #8 from the place de Gaulle. Closer to the center of things is the **Hôtel de**

l'Opéra, 8 rue de l'Opéra (tel. 26-07-16) at the end of the cours Mirabeau, charging 22.50-48F for singles and doubles. Two good campgrounds lie just outside the city on the route de Nice: **L'Arc-en-Ciel** and **Chantecler.**

The center of life in Aix is the **cours Mirabeau,** devoted to the languid ideal of seeing and being seen. The cafés on the *cours* are perfect for watching the promenading crowd and sipping your *pastis* across from some of the best preserved seventeenth-century **hôtels** (manor houses) in France. **Le Mazarin** commands a fine view, and a constant popularity with local students. Off the *cours,* **Le Carillon,** rue Portalis, is a good student-filled restaurant with a 19F *menu.* The **University-Restaurant les Gazelles,** ave. Jules-Ferry, is a bit far away but with a 3.50F ticket (buy it from a local student) you can get a complete and filling meal.

Arles

Arles has been a center of commerce and culture since the age of the Caesars, but it was the paintings of Van Gogh, who came here in 1888, that showed Arles to the world. Today, a visit to the **Place Lamartine** will seem hauntingly familiar.

The center of town is dominated by the **Arena,** the most intact of the many reminders of the time when Arles was the "little Rome of Gaul." During the Middle Ages, the arena doubled as a fortress, and three towers added at that time still stand. Today the amphitheater (as it is also known) has been restored to its original purpose of bloody entertainment—this time with bulls and matadors imported from Spain. Much less intact but more picturesque than the arena is the **Antique Theater**—now used extensively in summer for drama, opera, and ballet. The **Syndicat d'Initiative** at 35 Place de la République (tel. 96-29-35) can advise you of events and prices.

You will also want to visit the Romanesque **Church of St. Trophime** and the **Cloister of St. Trophime,** perhaps the most charming of the town's sights with its fine medieval carvings and cool arcades. The Christian necropolis **Les Alyscamps** is a hauntingly beautiful avenue of the dead, leading to the semi-ruined **Eglise St. Honorat.** Also worth a visit if you have time are the **Thermes Constantin,** (the ruins of the Roman Baths of Arles) and the **Musée Réattu,** which is housed in a former Grand Priory of the Knights of Malta, and now contains some fine drawings by Matisse and Gauguin, and several exhibits of photography. The **Musée d'Art Chrétien** is one of the richest in the world in early Christian sarcophagi. Under it is an extensive underground gallery dating back to Roman times. A ticket for all the monuments and museums costs 14F (10F for students). In summer the Cloister and the outdoor sights are open 8:30am-7pm, while the museums take the customary noon-2pm lunch break.

The area around Arles offers a number of interesting excursions, most of them quite difficult without a car. However, bus excursions are available (inquire at the *Syndicat d'Initiative*). Among the most interesting is **Les Baux,** a mountain-top village and château, once a stronghold of Protestantism, in ruins since the days of Louis XIII. **Aigues-Mortes** is an especially vivid reminder of the Middle Ages. Rising abruptly out of a rather dreary landscape, the fortified ground-plan of Aigues-Mortes still follows the quadrilateral design favored in the twelfth century, with streets intersecting each other at right angles.

Nature lovers will want to see some of **La Camargue,** which forms part of the marshy delta of the Rhône, now mostly nature preserves with flamingoes and semi-wild cattle and horses. Public transportation and accommodations are sparse around La Camargue, with the happy result that a little hitchhiking will bring you into the vicinity of vast and deserted areas along **l'Etang de Vaccarès.** If you plan on swimming here, don't forget to pack food and water.

Accommodations

Hôtel Moderne, 12 Place du Forum (tel. 96-08-21). Comfortable and friendly, with rooms from 25-43F, breakfast 6.50F. 30% more to have an extra bed put in any room.

Hôtel Trident, 9 rue de la Liberté, near Place du Forum (tel. 96-00-60). A rambling old residence, with singles for 27F, doubles 39F and up.

Hôtel-Bar Mistral, 16 rue du Docteur Fanton (tel. 96-12-64). Extremely simple, but acceptable. One large bed 19F, two beds 25F. There are a couple of other cheap hotels you might try on this same street.

Hôtel le Rhône, 11 Place Voltaire (tel. 96-43-70). Near the Station and the Arena. A spotless place, some rooms have balconies overlooking the square. Singles 31F, doubles 35F, breakfast 6.50F.

Auberge de Jeunesse (IYHF), ave. Foch (tel. 96-18-25). A large, modern hostel. 20.50F for bed and breakfast (25.50F if you don't have your own sheets). Often booked up by groups, so come early. (From the Station take the ave. Talbot to the ave. Emile Combes, then follow the arrows at the large intersection at the end of this avenue.) Closed at 11pm (10pm October to May). Also closed 10am Sat. to 5pm Sun. and from late November to late January.

Camping: Free *"camping sauvage"* (freelance camping) at the Plage d'Arles, Salin de Giraud. Inquire at the *Syndicat d'Initiative*. There are also several paying sites in the area. The closest one is Camping City, 67 route de Crau (tel. 96-26-69).

Food

Restaurant le Criquet, 21 rue Porte-de-Laure. A tiny, brash place where the couple who own it serve up a 20F *menu* (with wine) featuring *provençale* specialties. To get in, arrive early for the noon sitting, or reserve a place for the 1:30 sitting.

Le Galoubet, rue du Docteur Fanton, near Place du Forum. Good *menus* for 18 and 22F, wine included. Very simple, and popular with local people.

Le Poisson Banane, rue du Forum, across from Hôtel Trident. A friendly and somewhat eccentric place, with good and filling food. Tunisian dishes and *provençale* specialties on *menus* for 23 and 35F. The leafy patio is a nice place for lunch. Closed Wed.

Avignon

In the fourteenth century, a feud between the King of France and the Vatican brought the Papacy to Avignon for what history knows as the

"Babylonian Captivity." History is history, and the Pope went back to Rome, but Avignon was left with the colossal **Palais des Papes,** an incredible structure whose ransacked interior, apart from a few beautiful murals, unfortunately fails to measure up to its magnificent façade.

Avignon itself is dominated by a huge park and garden set atop a hill—**le Rocher des Doms.** The Palais des Papes is directly adjacent, and from the park you'll also enjoy a fine view of the **Pont St.-Bénézet** (the "pont d'Avignon" of the nursery rhyme), now only a ruin. The well-known Avignon **summer drama festival** unfolds in the courtyard of the Palace while concerts are held in its cloisters. You can reserve seats in advance from the **Syndicat d'Initiative,** 41 cours Jean Jaurès (tel. 82-65-11).

Most inexpensive lodging in Avignon is strictly seasonal; it materializes during July and August to catch the flow of young performers, stage-hands, and aficionados attending the festival. Prices are geared toward extended stays. **Club Léo Lagrange,** 20 ave. Monclar (tel. 86-53-54) offers lodging in simple 4-6 bed dorm rooms for 15F a night and 25F more will buy two meals. You'll find the Club behind and to the right of the Train Station. The Club stages a festival within the festival—improvisational theater, mime, jazz, modern dance, and more. **CEMEA,** 8 rue Frédéric Mistral (tel. 81-69-40) is nicely located in a courtyard near the *Syndicat d'Initiative.* This is a good place to meet students working with the festival, but you're expected to stick around at least four days; reservations are recommended. Open July 15 to August 5, bed and breakfast cost 29F nightly.

Hotels fill quickly at festival time but try the **Hôtel Angleterre,** 29 blvd. Raspail (tel. 86-34-31) with rooms 21-63F; or the **Hôtel Raspail,** 38 blvd. Raspail (tel. 81-33-25), with rooms 35-45F. Two good campgrounds sprawl over the Ile de la Barthelesse. **Camping Bagatelle** (tel. 86-30-39) is the cheaper of the two.

If you can't take the crowds at the Palais des Papes, go across the river to **Villeneuve-les-Avignon.** There is a fine feudal castle, the **Fort St.-André,** semi-ruined and romantic—usually not crowded—and the interesting **Chartreuse du Val de la Bénédiction.** About a half-hour train ride north of Avignon is the sleepy but pleasant little city of **Orange,** which is well worth a stop for those interested in Roman ruins. Orange has the best preserved Roman theater in the world—an impressive sight—and a very fine triumphal arch.

Nîmes

The bustling city of Nîmes offers the tourist some of the finest Roman ruins in France and an exceptionally beautiful park, **le Jardin de la Fontaine.** The **Roman Arena** is the principal sight, similar to that in Arles but better preserved. One ticket, entitling you to enter this and all other city monuments, costs 6F.

Equally impressive is the Roman **Maison Carrée,** (Square House), which is actually a rectangular temple. Dating from Augustus, it illustrates the strong Grecian influence on Roman architecture, with its fine Corinthian colonnade. Louis XIV's finance minister, Colbert, thought the building so magnificent that he wanted to tear it down and reconstruct it at Versailles. Inside, the **Museum of Antiquities** boasts the statue of Venus of Nîmes, a bust of Apollo, and Roman mosaics.

The Jardin de la Fontaine is itself a remarkable creation, an eighteenth-century melange of fountains, pools, and stairways, incorporating the ruins of the Roman **Temple of Diana.** From the summit of the hilltop **Tour Magne,** also Roman, there is an excellent view of Nîmes and the surrounding countryside.

The **Syndicat d'Initiative,** across from the Maison Carrée at 6 rue Au-
guste (tel. 67-29-11), is open 8am-noon and 2-7pm. Several daily excursions
by bus to nearby towns begin here, and the office will fill you in on times and
fares (the average is 30F). Municipal buses in Nîmes grind to a halt at the
inconveniently early hour of 8pm, but the city is not hard to negotiate on
foot.

The **Auberge de Jeunesse** (IYHF) at Chemin de la Cigale (tel. 67-63-53)
is in a wooded hillside glade, quite a trek away from the Station. It provides
breakfast, hot showers, cooking facilities, and a bed for 17F a night, 5F for
sheet rental if you don't have your own. There's a 10pm curfew. If you
arrive too late to catch bus G or H at the Station (bus E on Sun.) follow the
aqueduct until you see the signs on the Arles highway (about a half-hour's
walk from the Station). It's uphill after that, but marked. Also adjoining the
aqueduct, off blvd. Gambetta, is rue de la Corcomaire, where you'll find a
couple of inexpensive hotels. The municipal **campground** is 2 kilometers
from the center of town, on the route de Montpellier (tel. 21-75-16).

The **Arena** is the site of an annual **international jazz festival** in mid-July.
Tickets range from 20 to 100F, and reservations can be obtained from the
Jazz Club, 45 rue Flamannole, 30000 Nîmes.

Le Pont du Gard, a short ride to the northeast of Nîmes, is a Roman
aqueduct, built in 19B.C.and composed of three levels of arches. You'll
have a fine view from either end of the modern bridge adjacent to it. The bus
excursion costs 19F, departures every Tuesday, March to October, also
Sunday in July and August.

Southwestern France

Carcassonne, Albi, and Castres

The **Languedoc** region of southwestern France, near the Pyrenées and the
Mediterranean, offers a maximum of scenery and a minimum of tourists.
The area's distance from Paris and the haunts of the south have saved it from
invasion.

On the banks of the **Aude River,** inland from the sea, is the greatest
medieval fortress city of Europe: Carcassonne. With its double row of ramparts and its winding streets, it is a city not only of present beauty but of
historical fable. It was here in the ninth century, after a five-year siege by the
armies of Charlemagne, that Dame Carcas (after whom the city is named)
saved the starving town by feeding its last remaining grain to a sow in full
view of the besieging forces. Convinced that the city was still well supplied,
Charlemagne withdrew.

Completed in the thirteenth century under Philip the Bold, the city is
restored to look as it did six hundred years ago. Visit the **Château** (somewhat touristy at 5F, 3F with student card), the **Basilique Saint-Nazaire,**
with its famous stained-glass windows, and the open-air theater built to
provide entertainment during the town's long sieges. Nowadays, the amphitheater hosts the excellent and innovative summer series, **les Tréteaux du
Midi.** The program runs the gamut from French pop to tragedy to the
literature spread by tenth-century troubadours in their now defunct dialect,
langue d'oc, from which the region takes its name. Reservations at the
Bureau du Festival, Chapelle Saint François Xavier, 50 rue Barbès (tel.
47 06 33

All but a thousand of Carcassonne's inhabitants live in the **ville basse** (lower city) which is of little particular interest, but you may have to come here to find a room unless there is room in the **Auberge de Jeunesse**(IYHP), on rue du Vicomte Trencavel (tel. 25-23-16) within the walls of the *Cité*. Bed and mandatory breakfast cost 19F. If this is full, the **Syndicat d'Initiative,** blvd. Camille Pelleton (tel. 25-07-04) and in the Porte Narbonnaise in the *Cité,* can help find a room. On your own try the **Hôtel Bonnafoux,** 40 rue de la Liberté (tel. 25-01-45) with rooms for 25-55F, breakfast 6F, or the **Foyer International d'Accueil,** quai Riquet (tel. 25-75-51), on the banks of the Canal du Midi, near the Station, where 17F covers bed, breakfast, and use of the kitchen. Call before coming.

The regional dish is *cassoulet,* a stew of white beans, pork, goose, and sausage, but most menus here are uninspiring, if filling. **L'Ostal des Troubadours,** 5 rue Viollet-le-Duc, is within the walled city. *Menus* start at 18F and there's a large à la carte choice.

North of Carcassonne are the delightful towns of **Albi** and **Castres.** The pleasant drive north cuts through the low, forested hills and valleys of the **Montagne Noire.** The small towns along the way are splendid—better than postcard perfect. In Castres, visit the **Cathedral,** the balconied houses overlooking the river and the **Musée de Goya** (Goya Museum) housing Goya's largest tableau, *La Jointe des Philippines.* The museum is in the Hôtel de Ville (Town Hall) in the Jardin de l'Evêché; closed Mondays.

The Castres **Syndicat d'Initiative,** blvd. Henri Sizaire near the Jardin (tel. 59-22-98), will help you find a room. On your own, try the **Hôtel Splendid,** 17 rue Victor Hugo (tel. 59-30-42). Rooms cost 25F.

Albi, on the **River Tarn,** is a haven for anyone interested in Toulouse-Lautrec. It hosts the largest collection of his work in the world in the **Musée de Toulouse-Lautrec** (in the Palais de la Berbie) along with works by such masters as Dégas, Corot, Matisse and R05ault. Adjacent to the museum is the marvelous **Basilique de Ste. Cécile,** a looming relic of the Albigensian religious wars of the thirteenth century. This massive fortified brick structure dominates the town and conceals an interior filled with Italian frescoes and Burgundian statuary. For accommodations, consult the **Syndicat d'Initiative,** 19 Place Ste.-Cécile (tel. 54-22-30).

From Albi or Castres, make a sidetrip to **Millau,** gateway to one of France's most overwhelming natural wonders, the **Gorges du Tarn.**

Périgord and Auvergne

Auvergne, in the mountainous and strikingly austere **Massif Central,** is one of the least traveled areas in France. Just to the west, the beauties of the lush, old province of Périgord have received more attention, but almost exclusively from French tourists. If you're ready for a break from the international-youth-on-the-march scene, come to the heartland of France, and spend some time exploring the scenery and the art, the history, prehistory, and folklore of the Périgord and Auvergne.

PÉRIGORD

More than a province, Périgord (now the *département* of **Dordogne**) is a well-kept secret tucked away northeast of Bordeaux, with **Périgueux** as its chief city, and the Dordogne River as its major artery. A land of cliffs, rivers, medieval châteaux, and prehistoric remains, it is perfect for camping and hiking. Without a car or bicycle, you're going to have a hard time getting around, since train and bus service between the interesting places is infrequent at best. During July and August, however, the SNCF sponsors special excursion circuits: the train (or bus) makes special all-day loops through clusters of sleepy hamlets (including those areas mentioned below), boasting either prehistoric caves or Roman, ecclesiastic, or feudal sights. These circuits are a good alternative to the itineraries that the Syndicats d'Initiative will map out for you, and a bargain if you take advantage of the *demi-tarif* discount offered to students.

Périgueux is a good home base for a few days in Périgord. Within the town are traces of Roman, medieval, and Renaissance architecture, though the Roman ruins are not as well preserved as those in Provence. The medieval **Cathédrale Saint-Front** is considered one of the most unusual in France, with its Greek cross-shaped construction and domed roof.

Périgueux offers a number of inexpensive and comfortable hotels, particularly along the rue Denis-Papin, which parallels the Railroad Station. For precise information, stop by the **Syndicat d'Initiative** on the avenue d'Aquitaine (tel. 53-10-63). Or you might try **Hôtel Regina**, 14 rue Denis-Papin (tel. 53-48-09), with singles starting at 25F and doubles at 40F, including mandatory breakfast. The **Hôtel Au Bon Coin,** at the corner of rue Denis-Papin and rue Mobiles des Coulmiers, has the cheapest rooms—18F per person. The nearest campground is **Camping Périgueux-Boulazac,** Barnabé Plage (tel. 53-41-45), open all year.

Périgord's gastronomic specialties—*pâté de foie gras, cêpes* (a wild mushroom), *confit d'oie* (goose dishes), and especially truffles—are all readily available in Périgueux. If you want to buy cans of the famous local pâtés and truffles as gifts, try **Couderac,** 11 place St. Silain; or **Champion Foie Gras,** 21 rue Taillefer. For dining, we recommend **Restaurant Marcel,** 37 avenue de Limoges (tel. 53-13-43). This place is a twenty-minute walk from the town center, but worth it. The *menus* start at 17F, and regional specialties are available.

Sarlat is another interesting Périgord town. Built almost entirely of warm yellow stone, Sarlat has a large medieval quarter, one of the best in France. There is a **Youth Hostel** (IYHF) at 15*bis* avenue de Selves, route de Périgueux (tel. 59-14-20). The Hostel rents bicycles for 10F a day. Don't stick around Sarlat for too long: the real Périgord is in the countryside, where every little hamlet has something to call its own, be it a fortified church, a ruined château, or a sweeping view of the river valley. Traces of prehistoric days are all around. **Les Eyzies,** 40 km southeast of Périgueux, is where the Cro-Magnon man was found, and is now home to the **National Prehistoric Museum.** Other impressive sites of more recent vintage are: **Rocamadour** (now the most touristed sight in France after Mont St. Michel), a pilgrimage town carved out of a rocky hillside; and **Beynac,** from whose hilltop castle you can see three others in nearby towns.

AUVERGNE

The *Auvergnat* landscape is more dramatic than Périgord's. Core of the Massif Central, Auvergne's rugged geography of volcanic peaks and long gorges has kept it quite isolated. The traditional way of life held on tenaciously until quite recently, and a large part of the population still works on farms. Aside from the heavily-industrialized pocket of **Clermont-Ferrand,** Auvergne is largely unspoiled and only very sparsely populated, making it a haven for French campers and mountaineers. Of particular interest is the regional **Parc des Volcans d'Auvergne,** safeguarding a large chunk of Auvergne's awesome natural heritage. For information on travel and camping in the area, consult the **Syndicat d'Initiative** in Clermont-Ferrand, at the Place de Jaude (tel. 92-14-11). There is a **Youth Hostel** conveniently located at 55 avenue de l'Union Soviétique (tel. 92-26-39), across the street from the Train Station and about one block to the right.

Bordeaux

Bordeaux, centuries-old center of wine and commerce, is not particularly attractive, though fabled vineyards surround the city. To the south lies the flat, empty, forested **Landes** region. On the coast near Spain, within view of the Pyrenées, you'll find the rejuvenated resort of **Biarritz** and smaller, faster towns like **St. Jean de Luz.**

Bordeaux is the capital of the greatest wine-producing region in France and her fourth largest city. Nevertheless, Bordeaux is often a disappointment, even for the wine lover. Its main attraction, both for its architecture and its performances, is the **Grand Théâtre** in the Place de la Comédie, whose design inspired the Opéra in Paris. You should also visit the **Place de la Bourse** with its eighteenth-century façades and the **Esplanade des Quinconces.**

The **Syndicat d'Initiative,** 12 cours du 30-Juillet (tel. 44-28-41) will provide you with much information on the city and the wine country around it. It conducts daily wine tours, covering a different route each day (40F, but worth it—includes three wine samplings). Also worth visiting is the **wine museum** of Château Mouton Rothschild, north of Bordeaux in the Pauillac area. For information on working on the grape harvest *(vendanges),* contact the **Maison du Paysan,** 13 rue Foy (tel. 44-84-43). You get little more than room and board for a lot of hard work, but it can be great fun.

The **Centre d'Information Jeunesse d'Aquitaine,** 5 rue Dufour-Debergier (tel. 48-55-50) is especially helpful for tips on eating and entertainment in Bordeaux. Open Mon. 2-7pm, Tues.-Fri. 8:30am-7pm. **Mobylette Roques,** 11 allées de Tourny (tel. 44-59-84) rents *mobylettes* (20F per day) and bicycles (15F per day).

To the south, the coastal town of **Arcachon** is a popular excursion from Bordeaux. Try some excellent oysters with a bottle of *Graves.* You can take a boat excursion around the bay and across to **Cap-Ferret,** where there is a Youth Hostel (IYHF tel. 60-64-62), open July-August only.

Accommodations

There are scores of cheap hotels around the Train Station (about 2 km south of downtown) and around the Esplanade des Quinconces.

Hôtel de l'Opéra, 35 rue Esprit des Lois (tel. 48-41-27). Singles 18F, but seldom available. Doubles 29-31F, triples 40F. Not lovely, but clean. Good location, around the corner from the *Syndicat d'Initiative.*

Hôtel de la Poste, 66 rue Porte Dijeau (tel. 48-14-18). Doubles at 28-31F and rooms with two beds at 41F, 47F with shower. Try for one of the larger rooms overlooking the mall.

Auberge de Jeunesse (IYHF), 22 cours Barbey (tel. 91-59-51). Near the station. Follow cours de la Marne to cours Barbey, on the left. 250 beds. 12F a night, breakfast 4F.

Food

As might be expected, the *spécialité de la région* is wine. Look for dishes in *Bordelaise* sauce (made with claret wine, butter, tomato sauce, herbs, and spices).

Le Petit Louvre, 93 rue Porte Dijeaux. A big food factory where vast quantities of good food are dished out to a large local clientele. *Menus* 11-16.50F. Closed Sat.

Rif, 20 place de la Victoire, is a North African restaurant/coffeehouse. The portions are filling and the specialties delicious. Usually filled with students and open late. *Couscous* 16-26F, Tunisian salads 6-7F. Next door, the **Ets. Lamonzie** sells large sandwiches and brochettes (5-7F).

There are two university cafeterias in the downtown area. The **Central,** 42 rue Sauteyron; and the **BEC,** 38 rue de Cursol. Lunch from 11:30am-1pm, dinner 6:30-8pm. Tickets for both locations are 3.50F per meal, and may be purchased only by students at the Central from 11am-1pm. With luck, however, you may wrangle one at the door.

WEST GERMANY

$1U.S.=1.72Deutsch Marks (DM)   **1DM=$0.58**

The next few years will be a fascinating time to visit the Bundesrepublik Deutschland (BRD). The country is going through a phase reminiscent of America's fifties. The economic boom, increasing materialism, and conservative reaction to acts of terrorism (**Bonn** was patrolled with tanks in one instance) have contributed to this. Consequently, political activism has picked up in the universities, and fascist and anti-fascist graffiti covers the stalls in university buildings.

You may find it difficult to divide your time between the cities, university towns, and countryside in West Germany. For landscape, hiking, and camping, the **Black Forest** has always been the country's primary resort, but most of the tourist traffic stays near the roads, leaving the heartland to the hardy hiker. To the north, the **Harz Mountains** by Hanover offer much of the charm of the Black Forest, but none of the traffic. The **Bavarian Woods,** between Nuremberg and Czechoslovakia, are also beautiful.

The oldest university towns in West Germany are **Heidelberg, Tübingen,** and **Göttingen.** Heidelberg's attraction has been diminished, however, by the huge American installation and herds of tourists. **Freiburg** has come to take its place as the most characteristic, vital university community. **Marburg, Celle,** the towns along the **Romantic Road** and those in the **Moselle Valley,** have preserved much of their sixteenth- and seventeenth-century half-timbering; while **Aachen** (Aix-la-Chapelle) maintains the greatest Carolingian cathedral. **Hamburg** is a rousing international port, while **Munich** is Germany's friendliest, most beautiful, and most cultured big city.

Music festivals occur in **Göttingen** in late June, and in Munich and **Bayreuth** during July. The country respectfully closes the doors of its concert halls while **Salzburg** celebrates in August. Actually, the main reason for this is that most Germans go on vacation in August, although businesses are beginning to stagger holidays throughout the summer. **Kiel** holds a week-long regatta in June, while Munich's famous **Oktoberfest** begins in the middle of September. Many cities have special festivals just before Lent.

PRACTICAL INFORMATION

Germany's train system is one of Europe's best—and most expensive. Railpass holders should remember a couple of things. In major cities, the **U-Bahn** (subway), is run by the city, and you must pay. However, the **S-Bahn (Schnell-** or **Stadt-)** is run by the railroad, and your pass is valid on these (everywhere but Berlin). Trains marked "D" are faster than the "E"'s, while the "TEE"'s and "IC"'s are fastest, but you must pay the 10DM supplement *(Zuschlag)* for a *Platzkarte* (reservation).

Germany offers its own railpasses. The **Germanrail Touristkarte** gets you nine days of unlimited second-class travel for $85, or sixteen days for $115. The *Touristkarte* is not sold in West Germany, and does not exempt the holder from the supplements described above. Like the international railpasses, it does not cover the part of the ride to West Berlin through East Germany. It does, however, give free rides on ferries and buses (including the Romantic Road bus), as they do. Those under 23 can buy a **Junior Pass,** which for 98DM entitles you to 50% off the regular fare in first and second class for one year. Anyone with a railpass or ticket can rent a bicycle at the rental shops in the rail stations at half the standard daily rate. If you bring your bike on board a train, you must pay a 5DM storage fee.

It's hard to get around the stiff *Bundesbahn* prices without a railpass. There are a few possibilities. Hitching is legal anywhere except on the *Autobahn* (freeway), where you'll be fined if you're thumbing beyond the entrance ramp. The heavily-traveled secondary roads, federal *Bundesstrassen,* are good for hitching or driving. All major cities have license-plate codes, which greatly facilitates sign-making and enables you to look familiar: M=Munich, HH=Hansestadt Hamburg, F=Frankfurt, etc.

The second alternative is the network of **Mitfahrzentrale,** a chain of offices that brings drivers and riders together. If you seek either a ride or riders, call the *Mitfahr* in your departure or destination city. The rider pays the driver a set fee per kilometer when the two meet at the *Mitfahr* office, most of the sum going to the driver, plus a small commission for Mitfahr, which gives the riders complete insurance coverage and thus protects the driver. Their rates beat the railroad by 50%: Hamburg-Paris 45DM, Paris-Munich 44DM, Munich-Vienna 23DM. Nevertheless, you can never count on getting the transport connections you need with *Mitfahr*, although the Munich office is surprisingly reliable.

The third alternative for those under 26 is to buy **Transalpino** rail tickets, which are 20-50% less than the regular price. The trouble is that most Transalpino offices in Germany do not have their own tickets, and require one to two weeks to book anything. Exceptions include Hamburg, Cologne (Köln), and Munich.

Rooms can always be booked for a small fee through the local tourist offices (*Verkehrsamt, Verkehrsverein,* or *Informationszentrum*), usually located at the main Train Station *(Hauptbahnhof)* in the larger cities or at the marketplace *(Marktplatz)* in the towns. So-called *Hotels* are expensive, while *Gästehäuser, Fremdenzimmer,* and *Pensionen* are more reasonable. Cheapest are private homes advertising rooms *(Zimmer Frei)*, but these are usually unavailable for one-night stays. Be sure to specify length of stay when asking for a price. Unmarried couples will not have problems, except perhaps in rural parts of the South.

Laundromats *(Münzwäschereien* or *Automaten-Waschsalons)* are rare, but a *Schnellreinigung* will give same-day cleaning service at an outrageous price. Drugstores *(Apotheken)* offer all American amenities and, in the large cities, rotate all-night and weekend service.

While drugs are readily available in the cities, discretion is advised; there are several dozen Americans sitting in jail here on drug charges, and the public reaction to marijuana is quite hysterical.

Local phone calls cost 20pf (two ten-pfenning pieces). The procedure for calling is: 1) lift the receiver, 2) insert the coins, 3) wait until you can see them through the plastic window—if you can't, bang on the box, and 4) dial. Short rapid beeps are the busy signal, longer-spaced beeps the ringing.

FOOD

The only unpleasant thing about German food (besides the price) is the cholesterol content. The famous *Wurst* (sausage) comes in hundreds of varieties, including several delicate pâtés and jellies, and is usually served cold on a platter *(Aufschnitt)* for the evening meal. At noontime dinner is served, usually beginning with a light consommé which often contains dumplings *(Klösse* or *Knödel)*. A main course of meat and potatoes follows: either a roast *(Braten)*, a steak, a meatloaf *(Leberkäse)* or a stew *(Goulasch)*, again with dumplings or noodles, such as *Spätzle*, a rough egg noodle from Bavaria. German cooking uses a lot of innards; heart-and-lung stew is a challenge to the brave.

One of the most pleasant alternatives is a picnic lunch; don't be afraid to ask for only one of something at the market or bakery, or only fifty grams at the butcher's *(Metzgerei)*. If you are with someone, you can always do well by sharing a *Hausplatte*. Vegetarians should head for the chain stores called **Reformhaus**. Restaurant meals start around 7DM. Look for three-course menus around lunchtime. *Schnell-Imbisse* offer the cheapest food at stand-up counters. In a restaurant or *Gaststätte*, service and tax *(Bedienung* and *Mehrwertsteuer)* will be included in your bill, but you will be charged separately for anything that you eat, such as the rolls that were sitting on the table.

The word for tap water is *Leitungswasser*—if your waiter/waitress growls at you, say *"aus gesundheitlichen Gründen"* ("for medical reasons"). They like to serve bottled water because it's expensive.

Munich

1 Post Office
2 Justizpalast
3 Alte Pinakothek
4 Michaelskirche
5 American Express
6 Frauenkirche
7 Universitat
8 Residenz
9 National Theater
10 Neues Rathaus
11 Altes Rathaus
12 Viktualienmarkt
13 Neue Pinakothek im Haus der Kunst
14 Bayerisches Nationalmuseum
15 Deutsches Museum

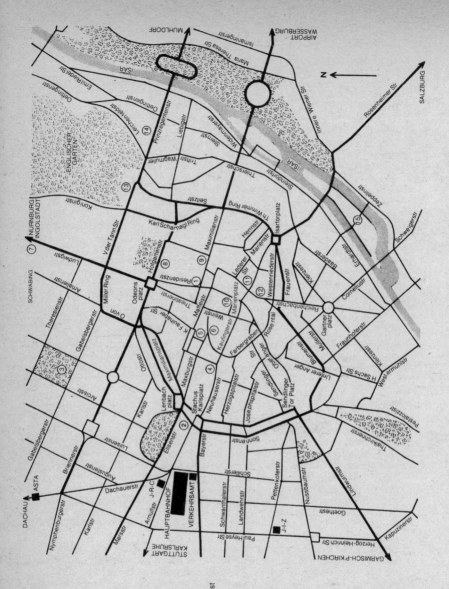

Munich (München)

Munich is West Germany's showpiece. By 1920, the city had inherited tremendous art treasures and brilliant landscaping from seven centuries of Wittelsbach (Bavarian) rule. Today, having covered its war wounds entirely, Munich once again gleams like a polished gem.

Munich leads three lives. There are the guardians of German High Culture—the people who buy the $100 seats during the annual July **Opera Festival.** Then there are 35,000 university students to keep the city going late at night. Lastly come the Bavarians, who occasionally join the Americans in the *Hofbräuhaus*, but usually have a favorite *Kneipe* (pub) for drinking beer, tucked away somewhere in the outskirts of the city.

Aside from the Opera Festival, Munich becomes most lively during *Fasching* (January) and *Oktoberfest* (end of September), the two most famous of Munich's many carnivals. But the city rarely slows down.

Orientation

The **Fremdenverkehrsamt** (Tourist Bureau) is located along the front of the **Hauptbahnhof** (the main Railroad Station)—turn right leaving the main exit. It offers a number of maps and programs for Munich, plus a room-finding service (2DM). From the *Hauptbahnhof*, it is a ten- to fifteen-minute walk straight ahead (east) along Prielmayerstrasse or Schützenstrasse to the middle of the town—marked by the **Mariensäule** (The Virgin's Column) in the center of the Marienplatz. The **Museuminsel,** site of the famous **Deutsches Museum** (Technical Museum), lies just southeast of the old city ring; while the **Residenz,** home of the Bavarian rulers since the seventeenth century, and beyond it, **Schwabing**—Munich's overwhelming answer to Greenwich Village—are on Ludwig/Leopold Strasse to the north.

Munich's transit system is refined to the point of exasperation. (Don't get frustrated—you can often hear Müncheners themselves arguing about how the system works.) We recommend that you buy a **Streifenkarte** (blue or green), with either eight stripes (5DM) or twelve stripes (7.50DM),. and forget about the red **Kurzstreckenkarten,** which are good only for limited rides, the distance determined according to the frighteningly complex transit maps plastered all over the city. To ride legally, fold the bottom two stripes over and cancel the second; for a second ride, cancel stripe #4, and so on. The cancellation of two stripes allows travel with unlimited changes between buses, trams, U-Bahn, and S-Bahn in one direction within the center of the city for up to two hours; the effective cost is 1.25DM. Travel outside the center requires the cancellation of more than two stripes at a time. The cancellation of any stripe cancels all consecutive unmarked stripes below it. Be warned that bus numbers may change in winter. Eurailpasses are good for travel on the S-Bahn, but not the U-Bahn.

To hitchhike north to Nuremberg, take U-6 to Nordfriedhof. To hitch west toward Stuttgart, take tram #17 to the end, and from there take bus #73 or 75 to Blutenburg. To hitch to Salzburg, take any S-Bahn to Ostbahnhof, and from there bus #95, 195, or 416 to the Innsbrucker Ring (only a few stops farther).

Addresses and Telephone Numbers

ASTA: Student Information, Dachauerstrasse 145. Open 8am-12:30pm weekdays. Also at Lothstrasse 52 (tel. 195353).

Jugend-Informations-Zentrum: Paul-Heyse-Strasse 22 (tel. 531655). Open weekdays 11am-7pm, Sat. 11am-5pm.

JRC-Reisen: Arnulfstrasse 6-8 (tel. 592220), across from Sternberger Bahnhof. Student rail and air tickets.

Studiosus-Reisen: Amalienstrasse 73 (tel. 28 07 68). Advance booking for student tickets to all events.

Mitfahrzentrale: Lämmerstrasse 4 (tel. 59 45 61), near the Train Station. Open 8:30am-5:30pm weekdays, Sat. 8:30am-noon. For hitchers seeking drivers and vice-versa. See chapter introduction

American Express: Promenadeplatz 3 (tel. 22 81 66). Open weekdays 9am-12:30pm and 2-5:30pm, Sat. 9am-noon. Bring checks or American Express card, otherwise fee of 2DM to pick up mail.

Cook's Travel: Lenbachplatz 3 (tels. 591167, 591168, and 591169).

Post Office: corner of Maximilianstrasse and Residenzstrasse, two blocks north of Marienplatz.

Police: Central Station, Ettstrasse 2 (emergency tel. 110; otherwise tel. 2141).

Medical Aid: Ambulance (tel. 222666). Emergency Pharmacy (tel. 594475).

American Drugstore: Pharmacie Internationale, corner of Luisenstrasse and Elisenstrasse at station. Open 8am-6:30pm (tel. 595444). Another one is **Bahnhof-Apotheke,** Bahnhofplatz 2 (tel. 59 41 19).

Crash help (drugs): (tel. 2 33 36 and 2 32 36.)

Olympia-Schwimmhalle: At the Olympic Village (tels. 38 63 90 and 38 64 90). Open Tues.-Sun. 7am-8pm, Mon. 1-8pm. Admission 3DM. Take U-3 to Olympiapark.

Showers: Best bet is at the Olympic Village, for 3DM.

Accommodations

The efficient room-finding service in the **Verkehrsamt** at the Train Station will help you find a place to sleep in Munich. Things can be especially tight during the summer and around the festivals. Most *Zimmer Frei* will cost 18DM and up without breakfast.

STUDENT ACCOMMODATIONS

Check with **ASTA,** Dachauerstrasse 145 (tel. 195353) for possible openings at one of the dormitories.

Jugendlager Kapuzinerhölzl, (tel. 1414300). This is "the Tent." 3DM gets you blankets, space on the wood floor of the circus tent, hot showers, tea in the mornings and evenings, and perhaps even an air mattress. Administration and company are enjoyable. No curfew. Take tram #21 or 17 north (left from Station) to the Botanischer Garten, and walk out Franz-Schrank-Strasse.

Jugendherberge (IYHF), Wendl-Dietrichstrasse 20 (tel. 131156), is a large hostel by German standards. The doors are locked between 9am and noon; 11:30pm curfew. Take tram #21 or 4 to Rotkreuz-Platz. Be warned that complaints about this place are interminable, mostly based on its size and authoritarian atmosphere. If these might bother you, look elsewhere first. 6.80DM (breakfast and showers included), plus 1.80DM linen charge.

Jugendgästehaus (IYHF), Miesingstrasse 4 (tels. 7236550 and 7236560), is quite a way out of town. 340 beds and a 1am curfew. Take the U-Bahn to Harras then #16 or 26 to Boschetsriederstrasse. 9DM a night in a dorm room, 15DM for a single room, including breakfast, linen, and shower. Most pleasant of the Munich hostels.

Jugendherberge (IYHF), Burg Schwaneck, Pullach (tel. 7932381). Renovated castle about 20 minutes south of the main station on the outskirts. Take S-Bahn line #10 (direction Wolfratshausen) to Pullach and follow the signs. No lockout during the day. Registration 5-10pm. Curfew 11:30pm. 7.80DM a night, with sheets and mandatory breakfast, showers 0.50DM. Bicycles available at 3DM a day. One of the best hostels to be found.

Haus International, Elizabethstrasse 87 (tels. 185081, 185082 and 185083), 400 beds, from 18DM in a 5-bed room to 25DM for a single, to 45DM for a double, with breakfast, showers, heated swimming pool included. Also a bar, restaurant, and lots of high school groups. Comfortable, but adolescent vibes. Take tram #7 to Nordbad and walk left on Hohenzollernstrasse and on to the gas station.

CVJM (YMCA), Landwehrstrasse 13 (tel. 55941) has clean simple rooms, 19.50-28.70DM, depending on how many in the room, including breakfast and shower. Curfew 12:30am. Not bad, slightly sterile. Between the Station and Sendlinger Tor.

Campingplatz München-Thalkirchen, Zentralländstrasse 49 (tel. 7231707), 2.90DM for a tent site plus 1.50DM per person, open March-October. Hot showers 1DM and a laundromat. Autos 2DM. Bus #57 to Thalkirchen from Sendlinger-Tor-Platz.

PENSIONS

There are lots of pensions clustered around Schellingstrasse and Kaulbachstrasse.

Beck, Thierschstrasse 36 (tels. 22 57 68 and 22 07 08). The pension has 100 beds, distributed in widely ranging patterns. Singles range from 14-28DM, doubles 30-42DM, triples and quadruples (reserve well in advance for these) 15DM and up per person, breakfast available at 4DM. Baths and kitchens available free on every floor. The proprietor is well traveled and interesting to talk with. S-Bahn to Isartor.

Fremdenheim Hirschbeck, Kaulbachstrasse 69 (tel. 396323). Singles 15.50DM, doubles 26DM, no breakfast available. An old house, heat your own water. Good location in the studenty Schwabing district.

Frank, Schellingstrasse 24 (tel. 281451). Singles 15-20DM, doubles 30-40DM, a good breakfast included. Showers 2DM. Lower rates for longer

stays; one-nighters discouraged. Well located in an interesting part of
Schwabing, U-Bhf. Universität. Well kept.

Isabella, Isabellastrasse 35 (tel. 373503), offers modest accommodations at
16-20DM per person and up, with breakfast. Tram #12 from the Station to
Kurfürstenplatz.

Pension Tyroller, Hohenzollernstrasse 152 (tel. 303119). Singles 18.50DM
and up, doubles 35DM and up; breakfast 7DM, showers also extra. From
Station take tram #7. A little posh.

Hotel Pension Erika, Landwehrstrasse 8 (tel. 554327). Singles 20-27DM,
doubles 41-51DM with breakfast); showers 1.50DM. Midway between the
Station and Karlsplatz. An easy walk.

Food

Bavarian cuisine relies heavily on veal, pork, and several sorts of sausage
(Wurst). The most famous is *Weisswurst,* whose color and flavor are derived
from its content of veal and parsley. *Leberkäse,* which despite its name
contains neither liver nor cheese, is a mixed meatloaf, served sliced and
fried. *Schweinshaxen,* a pork roast, is a local favorite with sauerkraut and
beer, and *Leberknödelsuppe* is a delicious clear broth with liver dumplings.
Beer, customarily served with fresh *Pretzele,* is available in diverse species:
Hell designates any light beer, usually weak in alcohol, but *Pils* is strong,
golden, and bitter. *Weissbier* is sour and bubbly, often served with a slice of
lemon or a shot of syrup, and *Alt* is dark, savory, and slightly sweet. Don't
overlook the city's cafés or *Konditoreien,* with their rich, fresh pastries.

In addition to the beer halls (whose back rooms should be explored)
throughout the old town, the **Viktualienmarkt** (open-air food market) is an
old Munich tradition. Nothing is cheap here, but everything is fresh. For
cheap eats at 1.80DM, try the **Mensa** at the Technische Hochschule (Ar-
cisstrasse 17, Mon.-Fri. 11am-2pm), or at Leopoldstrasse 13.

Gaststätte Weinbauer, Fend-Strasse, 5, is a still-robust Schwabing tradition.
Come here for good low-cost food. Meals from 6.50DM. Open 8:30am-1am;
closed Wed.

Zum Bögner, Tel. 72 (near Marienplatz): Front of restaurant serves traditional
Bavarian cuisine stand-up style, but the back rooms serve daily specials at
7DM and up. Central location, good solid Bavarian atmosphere. Favorite of
Müncheners for lunch.

Rolandseck, Viktoriastrasse 23 near Bonner Platz in Schwabing, has a large
selection of German wine by the glass for about 3DM, and an a la carte menu
with traditional and international dishes ranging 5-15DM. Food until midnight,
drinks until 1am; a student favorite.

Isabellahof, Isabellastrasse 4 at corner of Neureutherstrasse in Schwabing, has
a largely Serbian menu at 5-15DM; serving 10am-midnight daily. Lots of
students.

Gaststätte Atzinger, Schellingstrasse 9. Open Mon.-Fri. 8am-1am, Sat.
5pm-1am, Sun. 11am-1am. Complete *menus* at 7-8DM. A student hangout.

If you have a chance to get outside Munich, the numerous country inns all offer feasts for 5.50DM, plus the best Bavarian beer. Try taking any S-Bahn out to the end and looking around.

Sights

The **Marienplatz** is flanked by the **Altes Rathaus** (Old Town Hall) on the east and the impressive mock-Gothic **Neues Rathaus** on the north. Throngs of tourists gather to see the Neues Rathaus' *Glockenspiel*, which features a ring of dancing coopers celebrating the medieval craftsmen of that guild, which kept up the civic morale during The Plague. They play daily at 11am and 5pm. In the second week of July, there is usually a street festival in the pedestrian zone.

A walk southwest from Marienplatz towards **Sendlinger Tor** takes you past Munich's finest Rococo church, the **Asamkirche**. To the west along Neuhauserstrasse is **St. Michael,** an outstanding Renaissance church. The sober **Frauenkirche,** Munich's Cathedral, which houses the tomb of Emperor Ludwig the Bavarian, stands a short distance northwest of the Marienplatz.

The roads on either side of the Neues Rathaus lead north past the **Theatinerkirche** (one of the finest examples of Bavarian Baroque), and the restored **Residenz** (Royal Palace). The **Schatzkammer** (Treasury Museum), in the Residenz, contains a spectacular collection of the riches accumulated by Bavarian royalty (admission 1.50DM). Continuing north past the University, through Schwabing—you'll reach the **Englischer Garten,** a tremendous eighteenth-century park dotted with beer gardens and occasional pavilions. This is the Münchener's favorite weekend spot. They haven't yet exactly figured out what their long-haired guests are taking advantage of, sitting in small circles in the center of large grassy meadows, but the local police certainly have. Be careful! The park is a gathering place for travelers, and many people sleep there at night. The police move in towards 5-6am to make sure none of the sleepers are corpses; but aside from that, there is rarely any trouble.

Tierpark Hellabrunn is the largest zoo in Europe; open daily 8am-6pm, admission 3.50DM; discounts available. Further out from the city is **Schloss Nymphenburg** (Nymphenburg Castle), the Baroque summer residence of the Bavarian rulers. The surrounding park contains four pavilions including **Amalienburg,** the last to be built, which Cuvilliés furnished elegantly as a hunting lodge for Princess Amalia. Admission to all pavilions 2.50DM.

MUSEUMS

Alte Pinakothek (Old Picture Gallery), Barer Strasse 27, Munich's spectacular collection of early German, Italian, and Flemish schools—do not miss Dürer's *The Four Apostles*. Open Tues.-Sun. 9am-4:30pm, Tues. and Thurs. evenings 7-9pm. Admission 2.50DM, free for students, free Sundays.

Some of the most fantastic technological displays in the world can be found at the gigantic **Deutsches Museum,** located on an island in the Isar River by Ludwigsbrückle. Included are a Zeiss Planetarium, a full-sized ship, walk-through models of salt and coal mines, and 297 other rooms filled with working displays demonstrating past and present techniques for doing anything that man has ever done. Like the *Whole Earth Catalog* in 3-D. Spend a whole day here, from 9am to 5pm, for 2DM; admission with student ID 1DM. S-Bahn to Isartorplatz.

Bayerisches Nationalmuseum (National Museum of Bavaria). Prinzregentenstrasse 3, presents collections illustrating the arts and handcrafts of the area from the Middle Ages to the nineteenth century. Open during the summer 9:30am-4:30pm, weekends 10am-4:30pm, closed Monday. Admission for 2DM, free with a student ID; free Sunday. Tram #20 from station to Lerchenfeldstrasse.

In the 1930s Hitler built the **Haus der Kunst,** Prinzregentenstrasse 1 at the Englischer Garten, in order to display the achievements of Nazi art. Now it houses principally those artists that he censored. On the west side, the **Staatsgalerie Moderner Kunst** has a fair collection of French Impressionists. Van Gogh, Picasso, and Braque, and a powerful exhibition of the *Die Brücke* Expressionist group. Admission 2DM, free with student ID, free Sunday; open daily 9am-4:30pm. Tram #20 to Lerchenfeldstrasse.

The **Städtische Galerie,** in the Villa Lenbach, Luisenstrasse 33, contains works by Kandinsky, Klee, and the *Blauer Reiter* (Blue Horseman) School. Open daily 9am-4:30pm, admission 1.50DM, 0.50DM with student ID; free Sunday.

The **Münchener Stadtmuseum,** St. Jakobs Platz 1, on the site of the old arsenal, hides in its basement (get the guard to open it) a series of carved wooden figures called the *Moriskentänzer* (Moorish dancers) by Erasmus Grasser. The third floor of the museum has an incredible marionette museum, featuring some acid social commentaries made during the Weimar Republic. The **Filmmuseum** on the first floor shows old German classics (Fritz Lang, etc.) at 6 and 9pm for 3DM, 2DM with student ID. The museum is open daily 9am-4:30pm; 1.50DM admission, .50DM with an ID. U-Bahn to Marienplatz or Sendlinger Tor.

Antikensammlung and **Glyptothek,** at the Konigsplatz (tram #7 or 12), open Tues.-Sun. 10am-4pm (both museums 3DM), have an amazing collection of Greek and Roman antiques, including one of the best presentations of the art of Greek vase painting you will ever see.

Near Munich

The **Valley of the Isar** is a sure cure for urban claustrophobia. Take tram #25 out Grünwälderstrasse, S-Bahn #12 or 22 to Grosshesselohe, or S-Bahn #10 to Pullach and enjoy the idyllic scenery of the deeply embanked Isar River valley. We suggest a dip for the hardy who can brave the current and the chill. A good place to crash in your sleeping bag, free, with relative privacy.

Dachau concentration camp, 22 kilometers northwest of Munich, unfortunately needs no introduction. Its museum, memorial, and expiatory chapel are open daily 9am-5pm. Take the S-Bahn line #2, direction Petershausen, and then the bus from in front of the station (less than 1DM). A clergyman who survived the camp works in the Protestant Church and is willing to talk of his experiences. Ironically, the area has long been known for its beautiful scenery, and bicycles can be rented at the Dachau Train Station.

Evenings

Munich's concert offerings are enormous—buy a monthly or weekly program, and purchase tickets in advance at one of the dozens of ticket dealers listed. For seats during the **July Opera Festival,** it is recommended that you buy tickets in North America. Contact the Tourist Office.

Student discounts are often granted by many theaters and concert halls on unsold seats shortly before curtain.

The **Bayerisches Nationaltheater,** Max-Joseph-Platz, presents first-class opera in a magnificent opera house, reconstructed in its original style after having been burned out in an air raid in 1943. *Stehplatz* (standing room) tickets from 8DM. Advance sales at Maximilianstrasse 11.

The **Altes Residenztheater,** Residenzstrasse 1, was built by Cuvilliés in 1753 for the Palace. The interior, with four rows of magnificent gilded marble boxes, appears as splendid as ever. Tickets from 8DM for the performances of light plays and opera can be secured in advance from the box office (tel. 221316).

Student life centers around the beer halls, jazz saloons, discotheques, and cabarets. We recommend the following:

Memo Land, Siegesstrasse 19, offers good jazz in a dark 1930s atmosphere. Booths fill the room and prevent both dancing and mixing. Admission usually free, depending on the group, but beer costs 4.50DM. Open 8pm-1am daily.

Schwabinger Nacht Eule, Occamstrasse 7, lets you progress smoothly from café to discotheque to a late-night *Schnitzel* priced at 3.50DM, if you can find a place at one of its tiny but tightly packed tables. Open until 1:30am weekdays. Munich's best disco and a good place to meet people.

Allotria Jazz Saloon, Türkenstrasse 33, provides jazz in a large but always full hall with stand up bars. No cover and beer under 4DM. A warm atmosphere. Open from 7pm.

Muh, Sendlingerstrasse 75 (entrance around the corner), open daily 8:30pm-12:30pm with entrance fee 3-6DM, is a free stage featuring young, relatively unknown artists who sometimes "make it." On Mondays, you can get on stage yourself.

Kekk, Kaiserstrasse 67, the students' cabaret. Show begins at 8pm. Entry fee Thurs. 3DM, Fri. 4DM, Sat. 6DM. Get off at U-Bhf. Münchener Freiheit.

Münchener Lach-u, Schiessgesellschaft (tel. 39 19 97), corner of Haimhauser and Ursula, is a sophisticated political cabaret that requires good German to enjoy. Show begins at 9pm, student tickets 9DM. U-Bhf. Münchener Freiheit.

Romantic Road

From **Würzburg** on the Main River to **Füssen** in the Alps, this picturesque route winds through ancient cities and misty towns with medieval towers, past the vineyard hills of **Franconia,** and rolling Bavarian farmland. While the road itself is pretty but unspectacular, each town on the way has its charms and deserves a visit. Both to preserve a way of life almost extinct in post-War Germany, and to cultivate the tourist dollar, most of the road is protected as a national monument. Not a single change in size, color, or use of buildings can be made without the approval of the Bavarian state government. The Baroque city of Würzburg boasts of an exuberant **Residenz Palace** by Balthasar Neumann, and the stern hilltop **Marienburg Fortress.** Just outside **Creglingen** you will find the **Herrgott Church,** housing Tilman Riemenschneider's *Virgin Mary Altar.* **Rothenburg** and **Dinkelsbühl** are open-air museums of medieval architecture and seventeenth-century lifestyle. A perfectly preserved set of fourteenth-century fortifications including thirteen towers and gates can be explored in **Nördlingen.** Further on, **Harburg Castle,** overlooking the Wörnitz River, contains rich collections of woodcarvings, tapestries, and illuminated manuscripts. The stepson of the Emperor Augustus founded **Augsburg,** a banking and financial center in the fifteenth century; its two richest families, the Fuggers and the Welsers, were said to have shared the world's material wealth between them. The city's **Fuggerei,** built by Fugger the Rich as the world's first social housing project, remains in use. If you are short on time, however, you may wish to skip Augsburg to see Nördlingen and Dinkelsbühl, which are better preserved.

From Augsburg the road rolls through the foothills of the Alps to Füssen, where Bavaria's mad king, Ludwig II, set his romantic visions into stone at the castles of **Neuschwanstein, Linderhof,** and **Herrenchiemsee,** near his father's retreat of **Hohenschwangau.**

The easiest way to get a superficial view of the Road, but perhaps the worst, is the **Europabus** of the Bundesbahn. There are two routes: Füssen to Würzburg, and Munich to Wiesbaden, near Frankfurt—each runs complete with an unintelligible English-speaking guide and uselessly short stops for selected sights on the way. Unfortunately, other bus and train connections are very inconvenient, and the Europabus is free with your Eurailpass. Ordinarily, 53DM one way. You can pick up the bus along the way— Rothenburg to Würzburg, for example, costs 8DM.

Würzburg

Würzburg stands at the edge of Bavaria in **Lower Franconia,** where the rolling hills and country of the south meet the flatter, more industrialized areas of the north and west. It is a pleasant, unspectacular middle-sized German city which makes a good start or finish to a trip on the Romantic Road. Catholic **Freistaat Bayern** makes its religious orientation evident, as you turn from the eleventh-century **Dom,** to the **Neumünster** right next door, and then raise your eyes to a hillside across the Main, in the southwest part of town, where Balthasar Neumann's **Kappele** thrusts its curvaceous spires from a heavy wood. Neumann's work is also visible in the nave of the **Augustinerkirche,** a Dominican church begun in the thirteenth century; and in the **Marienkapelle** you may visit his grave. The Marienkappelle also houses work by Tilman Riemenschneider, sculptor-son and mayor of Würzburg who died here in 1531. Many of Riemenschneider's pieces may be found in the **Mainfränkisches Museum** (open daily 10am-5pm; admission 1.50DM, 0.50DM with student ID) in the Festung Marienburg. The major piece of secular architecture in the city is Balthasar Neumann's **Residenz,** built in 1719-1744, open 9am-5pm (closed Mon.).

A number of **Bürgerhäuser** brighten narrow streets in the city. The **Haus zum Falken,** on the **Marktplatz,** is the most Baroque of the lot. Neumann's **Alter Kranen,** the first machinery used in the port, stands on the quay of a sundrenched Main. Stop in one of the cafés along the river, and enjoy the water traffic and the view of the Marienburg covered by vineyards and crowned by an old fortress.

Perhaps the best time to visit Würzburg is in the second half of June, for the annual **Mozartfest,** or during the last week in November, for the **Würzburger Bachtage.** Most ticket prices are way out of student budget range, but certain concerts do have seats at 5 and 10DM. Check with the *Verkehrsamt,* or with the **Mozartfest Büro** in the Haus zum Falken (tel. 54100). The city is fairly packed during the festivals, so make reservations if you can.

For hitchers, the Frankfurt-Nürnberg Autobahn runs near the city. Take streetcar #3 (direction Heidingsfeld) to Dallenbergbad for all directions.

Orientation, Accommodations, and Food

The **Verkehrsamt im Falken** (Mon.-Thurs. 8am-5pm, Fri. 8am-noon, closed weekends) on the Marktplatz, or the bureau at the Train Station (Mon.-Sat. 8am-9pm) will provide you with a surprisingly thorough coverage of the city: museum times and admission fees, tourist routes, etc. Room prices in Würzburg are fairly uniform at 20DM for singles, and 38DM for doubles. The *Verkehrsamt* will find you a place to stay quickly and easily.

Jugendherberge (IYHF), Burkarderstrasse 44 (tel. 42590) just below the Festung Marienburg. Take streetcar #3 to the Rathaus, cross the river and turn left. 9:45pm curfew, 6:30am reveille, 2-night stays are the maximum. 4.20DM per night, breakfast 2.30DM.

Jugendherberge (IYHF) Frau-Holle-Weg 27, Heidingsfeld (tel. 705913). A little farther out of town than Burkardstrasse, but less crowded and less authoritarian. 3.40DM per night, breakfast 2.30DM. Curfew 9:45pm. Take tram #3 (Heidingsfeld) to Wendelweg, then take #23 to the Hostel.

Camping-Zeltplatz beim Kanu Club, Nergentheimerstrasse 13B (tel. 72536). Take tram #3 to second stop after Ludwigsbrücke, 2.50DM per night. No curfew. Free showers. You must have a tent.

The university has two **Mensen** (open Mon.-Fri. at noon through the summer), one in the *Studentenhaus* (at the corner of Münzstrasse and Jahnstrasse) and one on the University property near the Train Station (take a left on Koellikerstrasse, and another left into the lane bisecting the area). A little hard to find.

Rothenburg-ob-der-Tauber

Rothenburg is a sixteenth-century Disneyland. Having miraculously survived the Thirty Years' War, the local population is now being conquered by armies of foreign tourists.

On **Marktplatz,** the town center, stands the **Rathaus,** half Gothic and half Renaissance. The view from the 197-foot belfry is worth the precarious climb and 0.50DM fee. Open daily 9am-5pm. The figures in the clock of the **Ratstrinkstube** (Town Councilor's Drinking Room) re-enact the *Meistertrunk* daily on the hour from 11am to 3pm and at 9 and 10pm. The legend of the *Meistertrunk* began when Mayor Nusch drank 3¼ liters of rancid wine to win Rothenburg a respite from the Thirty Years' War. Enter at the drive-through on the side of the Rathaus to view the **Historien-Gewölbe** (Historical Vaults) where artifacts of the Thirty Years' War are displayed. Open daily 9am-5pm, 1.50DM admission, 1DM for students. Behind the Marktplatz, upstairs in the Gothic **St. Jakobskirche,** you'll encounter the superbly carved *Heilig-Blut-Altar* by Tilman Riemenschneider. Admission 0.50DM; students 0.20DM. An English tour of the entire town begins daily at 1pm from in front of the Hotel Goldener Hirsch, Schmiedgasse 16; cost from 1 to 3DM depending on the number of people taking the tour.

Rothenburg has set up two unconventional museums. The **Reichsstadtmuseum,** located in a 700-year-old Dominican cloister behind St. Jakobskirche off Klingengasse on Klosterhof, still preserves the original medieval kitchen and the tankard from which the heroic Mayor Nusch supposedly drank; admission 2DM, students 1DM. The **Folterkammer** (Torture Chamber), in the Burggasse in the city wall, has tours in English which

explain the intricacies of medieval legal practice and serve as a guaranteed
cure for a case of tenacious nostalgia; open daily in summer 9am-6pm,
admission 2.50DM, 1.50DM with student ID. Throughout the tourist season
you can enjoy the **Rolf Trexler Puppet Show** near the garden gate on
Herrngasse. German-speaking visitors might take in one of the medieval
Hans Sachs plays presented in the Kaisersaal of the Rathaus on Wednesdays
and Saturdays.

To escape the tourist hordes, bicycle, walk, or take a *Postbus* along the
steep, green Tauber valley, south towards **Dombühl** or towards **Creglingen,**
where Riemenschneider's greatest creation, the **Marienaltar,** resides in the
Herrgotteskirche.

Orientation and Accommodations

The **Verkehrsamt,** on the Marktplatz (tel. 2038) has maps, information,
and a room-finding service (1DM). They also have a free hiking map full of
suggested walks through the beautiful surrounding countryside. Open weekdays 9am-noon, 2-6pm; Saturday 10am-noon, 2-7pm; Sundays (summer
only) 10am-noon. Those arriving by train or the Bahnbus connection from
Dombühl or Würzburg should walk left out of the station, right on
Ansbacherstrasse and straight into the city until reaching Marktplatz.

Accommodations in Rothenburg are sufficient to provide for all comers
except on holidays and weekends. Camping is available only in the nearby
village of Detwang. The site, **Tauberidyll** (tel. 3177) lies 3 kilometers north
along Klingengasse, and charges 3.50DM for a tent site and 2.50DM per
person. About thirty private homes in Rothenburg offer rooms, with prices
starting at 15DM and reductions for long stays available. Check for listings
at the *Verkehrsamt.*

> **Youth Hostel Spitalhof** (IYHF), turn right through arch after church on
> Spitalgasse, (tel. 889). Comfortable hostel in renovated old barn, near south
> wall of city. Free showers, 3.40DM a night, 2.40DM for breakfast. Curfew
> 10pm.

> **Youth Hostel Rossmühle** (IYHF), on Rossmühlgasse past the Plönlein tower
> (tel. 4510). Follow Schmiedgasse out of Marktplatz and proceed down Spital-
> gasse. Set up in an old mill, this hostel is comfortable though not luxurious. No
> hot showers or hot water, 3.70DM a night, 2.30DM for breakfast. Curfew
> 10pm.

Food

There are many small food shops near Marktplatz (market days are Wednesday and Saturday) and the **Kaiser Supermarkt** is one block up Hafen-
gasse. Try one of the many cafés before you leave, for a *Torte* or *Schneeball*
(snowball), a Rothenburg specialty (sort of a large ball of hard pastry, filled
with rich whipped cream). For a splurge, try the opulent **Baumeisterhaus** at
Oberschmiedgasse 3. Old Germany lives on in its back room courtyard.
Gasthof Schmölzer, at Rosengasse 21, is also good, and you can get a quick
beer at **Guckloch** in the Klingengasse.

Dinkelsbühl

Dinkelsbühl survives in full medieval regalia, but is smaller, less touristy,
and less artificial than Rothenburg. Most of the visitors are German, and

clicking cameras are less omnipresent than they are on the Tauber. Inside the gates you can walk along wide cobbled streets flanked by houses cunningly positioned so their owners can peer down the whole length of the roadway. In the middle ages, Dinkelsbühl's location on the important trade routes brought it prosperity; today, however, it has employment problems.

Fifteenth-century citizens, 6000 strong, built themselves the lovely and simple Gothic **St. Georg Kirche** (Church of St. George), with its elaborate fan vaulting, on the **Marktplatz** (Market Square). You can climb the original Romanesque tower for 0.60DM. Another fifteenth-century creation is the ornate, half-timbered **Deutsches Haus** on the Marktplatz, now a hotel. The **Altes Rathaus** (Old Town Hall) lurks behind St. Georg on **Alt-Rathausplatz** (Old Town Hall Square).

Stroll through the town and along the fortifications to the **Chapel of the Magi** (1378), next to the onion-domed **Segringer Tor** (Segringer Gate). The Chapel, legend has it, marks the spot where the bones of the Wise Men were set down briefly on their way from Milan to Cologne. It is today a war memorial. Notice that few of the old houses are perfectly rectilinear. This is because medieval superstition held that houses with 90° angles were homes of demons.

Every mid-July, tourists outnumber Dinkelsbühlers at the week-long **Kinderzeche.** The festival play re-enacts the salvation of the town through its children's pleas during the Thirty Years' War. In summer the town is illuminated from 9-11:30pm. Get a good view from where Am Brühl bridges the Wörnitz River.

Orientation, Accommodations, and Food

The **Städtische Verkehrsamt,** on the Marktplatz (tel. 3013) provides all the usual tourist services, and books rooms for free. (Open weekdays 9am-noon and 2-6pm; Sat. and Sun. 10am-noon, and 2-4 pm.)

Ask about swimming in the excellent **Hallenbad** just outside of town, fishing and swimming in the Wörnitz River, hiking in the nearby countryside, coach trips and riding instruction as well as open-air drama in the **Garten am Wehrgang** (daily at 8pm in the summer, except Monday and Tuesday). In the city itself, hotels and pensions line both sides of Segringer Strasse and Nördlinger Strasse; while further out Siebenbürgerstrasse is the street for families renting rooms to tourists. Check with the *Verkehrsamt*. The IYHF **Youth Hostel,** Koppengasse 10 (tel. 509), is located in an old granary dating from 1378. Comfortable though showerless. 3.70DM per night, breakfast 2.30DM. Walk up Segringerstrasse and turn right just before the city gate. A new campsite is being opened in 1979. Ask for information at the *Verkehrsamt*.

For a splurge, try the **Weisses Ross** at Steingasse 12, just behind the new Town Hall, open 10:30am-2pm and 5pm-midnight every day, except closed Thursdays.

Nördlingen

The streets of the circular town of Nördlingen, girded by a beautifully preserved set of medieval fortifications, converge on the **St.-Georgskirche,** a simple but imposing Gothic structure containing a charming carved altarpiece. Go up the tower of the church, popularly known as the "Daniel" (open from 8am to sunset) for a view of the old town, lying in the center of the bowl-shaped **Ries,** the second largest meteorite crater in the world. Near the Daniel tower, the fourteenth-century **Rathaus,** and the comfortable burghers' houses with their carved Baroque gables, bear witness to the former prosperity of the area. The walk around the top of the walls takes about an hour—the thirteen squat fortified towers are impressive reminders of the defense needed to protect this nucleus of trade and culture in the Dark Ages.

The **Stabenfest** celebrates the arrival of spring in May with parades, costumes, and dancing in the streets. In July, the **Scharlachrennen,** horse races for the traditional prize of a scarlet cloth, crowd the town with visitors and horse fans of all descriptions.

The **Verkehrsamt** in the Marktplatz (tel. 4380) will book rooms for free and answer almost any questions you might have about the surrounding area. Open weekdays 8am-noon, and 1:30-5:30pm; Sun. 10am-1pm, closed Sat. *Zimmer Frei* cost about 15DM and up in Nördlingen, with reductions for stays of more than one night. The **Jugendherberge** (IYHF), Kaiserwiese 1 (tel. 4041), is a modern, comfortable hostel, 3.70DM a night, breakfast 2.30DM. Cross the bridge just outside of the Baldinger Tor and follow the signs to the right of the Würzburgerstrasse. Camping is available on the hostel grounds.

The *Gasthöfe* all serve good, reasonably-priced meals. The **Braunes Ross,** in particular, has a good kitchen, and the **Zum Weissen Ochse,** Deiningerstrasse 17, has a garden for eating outside on summer evenings. Usually closed during most of June.

Black Forest

For two centuries, the Black Forest has been the center of German vacation spas and health resorts, but with the exception of **Baden-Baden,** the one-time favorite of Queen Victoria and Napoleon III, foreigners don't often venture into the area. Stretching from **Karlsruhe** to **Basel,** the forest has been named for the dense spruce forests that cap the steep hillsides above flowering alpine glades. On the west the hills drop abruptly to the broad upper Rhine plateau, the district of the flavorsome Baden wines, and on the east they slope gently down to the fertile plains around **Donaueschingen** (the source of the Danube) and the castle-strewn cliffs of the **Schwäbische Alb** (Swabian Jura). The Black Forest is among the most productive fruit-growing regions of Germany, and features a wide assortment of local brandies: *Kirschwasser* (cherry), *Himbeergeist* (raspberry), and *Zwetschgengeist* or *Slivovitz* (plum).

The Virgin Mary stands over every path crossing in the Black Forest, for the area is heavily Catholic and has preserved many of its folk customs. Women still wear the local dress to church on Sundays, and farmers in traditional kneeboots, knickers, and vests tend the herds of dairy cattle. Holidays, such as *Schwabing* and Christmas, are causes for great celebration and colorful costumes, and the many village churches hold frequent concerts throughout the year.

The highest summits, **Feldberg** and **Belchen,** crown the Upper Black Forest about an hour out of Freiburg; bus connections are available in **Gün-therstal** and **Neustadt** stations, both easily accessible from the Freiburg Train Station. Check at the **Schwarzwald-Reisebüro,** Rotteckring 14 in Freiburg, for schedules and more detailed information. In most of the larger towns you can rent bicycles from the Bundesbahn; ask for the list of these towns in Freiburg. At **Lake Titisee,** a forty-minute ride away through the **Höllental,** rowboats and electric motorboats are available. For inexpensive accommodations look for *Zimmer Frei* signs. If you're not traveling by car or bike, though, you're better off taking advantage of the frequent train and bus connections to make daytrips—hitchhiking here can be pretty tedious, as most motorists in the Forest are tourists.

Freiburg

Although Heidegger no longer occupies the chair of Philosophy, the University at Freiburg continues to be one of Germany's finest. Unlike most university towns, however, Freiburg does not fold up in the summer—the summer schools keep it lively.

Freiburg is also the base for excursions into the **Hochschwarzwald** (Upper Black Forest). For information on the town and the region, walk two blocks straight down Eisenbahnstrasse from the Railroad Station to the **Städtisches Verkehrsamt,** at Rotteckring 14. The **Schwarzwald-Reisebüro** (Black Forest Travel Service), is next door.

Freiburg's **Altstadt** (old city) is nearby, surrounding the Freiburger **Münster,** one of Germany's great cathedrals, and one of the few that stands as it was completed in the Middle Ages. The local sandstone used in its construction glows orange at sunset. Walk all the way around the Münster, and notice the gargoyles depicting the grotesque beasts of pagan lore and the rich Renaissance carvings around the entrance through the southern porch. Don't miss the gargoyle on the south side, giving Freiburg a medieval "moon." The Tower can be climbed for 1DM Tues.-Sat. 9:30am-5pm, Sun. 1-5pm. Also of interest in the Altstadt is the **Augustiner Museum,** an excellent collection of the Gothic art of the Upper Rhine. The museum itself is in a thirteenth-century cloister (open Tues.-Sat. 10am-5pm, Sun. 10am-1pm, admission 1.50DM, 0.75DM for students).

Behind the Augustinerplatz are two remnants of the town's medieval fortifications, the **Schwabentor** and the **Martinstor.** Silver and goldsmiths were the first industries of Freiburg in the thirteenth century; around the Schwabentor craftsmen and antique dealers still display their wares proudly in picturesque shop windows. Saturday is market day on the Münsterplatz. Many of the women behind the stands still wear traditional costume. For those who can time it right, Freiburg celebrates its **Weinfest** with great exuberance during the last week in June.

There are three routes out of Freiburg by road or rail: east through the Höllental into the Black Forest, and north or south along the Rhine Valley towards Frankfurt or Basel. For fast connections to Munich, head north and change at Karlsruhe; otherwise weave your way by train or thumb through the mountains towards Donaueschingen and Ulm, a beautiful but slow route for hitchers. For fast thumbing to Basel or points north, take Bus J from the station in direction Umkirch and get off just past the *Autobahn* entrance.

Accommodations

Hotels in Freiburg are generally expensive and crowded, especially on the weekends. There are only limited student accommodations open to the traveler during the summer.

Youth Hostel Ottilienwiese (IYHF), Kartäuserstrasse 151 (tel. 67656), is located a half hour from town in a beautiful hilly area near the river. IYHF card required. 4.20DM for 24 years or under, 5.90DM for others a night plus 3.20DM mandatory breakfast. Lockout 9am-5pm while the office closes. Curfew 11:30pm. Take tram #3 or 4 from the Train Station, direction Littenweiler, to the Römerhof stop and walk down Fritz-Geigesstrasse across the river and to the right.

Hercynenhaus, Mercystrasse 16 (tel. 75512) is a co-ed Catholic fraternity that lets its rooms out during university vacation and the summer months. 12DM per person. Breakfast 4.50DM; showers free. Take Bus A to Mercystrasse.

Gasthaus Grünhof, corner of Belfortstrasse and Schnewlinstrasse (tel. 31108), across from the railroad tracks (turn right when leaving the Station). Singles 14DM, doubles 28DM, breakfast 4.50DM, showers 1DM. The restaurant downstairs serves as a local meeting place—try the *Jägerschnitzel* for 8DM.

Hotel Margarete, Lehenerstrasse 59-61 (tels. 277563 and 276262) is further out behind the station. Turn left, and left again through the underpass. Singles 18-21DM, doubles 40DM, including breakfast. Showers 1DM. Bare, simple, well run.

Pension Dreisam, Gartenstrasse 30 (tel. 28227), is at the Kronenbrücken on the Dreisam River. 18DM for a single, from 30DM for a double, with breakfast. Showers 3DM extra. Landlady is friendly and relaxed.

Camping: Two areas are located off the same tram lines as the hostel, #3 or 4. For the one at **Kartauserstrasse 99** (tel. 35054), get off at Bleicherstrasse and walk across the river. For **Waldseestrasse 77** (tel. 72938) get off on Möslestrasse and prepare yourself for a long walk. A third area is in **St. Georgen,** south of the station, at Basler Landstrasse 62 (tel. 43183). Take bus C to end and walk north.

As a last resort, there is a Catholic and Protestant **Bahnhofsmission** at the Station, which could probably provide a bed in a pinch.

Food

Thanks to its student life, Freiburg has enough cheap international eateries to satisfy the most avid pizza addict, but the best feature of the many *Stüben* and restaurants is their wide selection of good local wines for about 3DM a glass. The tangy, rich flavor of the Baden white wines is well worth the price; all are available during several Black Forest wine festivals throughout the year. During the harvest celebrations in October, be sure to try the traditional *Zwiebelküche,* an onion pie designed to complement the slightly sweet flavor of the newly-pressed wines. Other Black Forest specialties, such as *Schwarzwälder Schinken* (Black Forest ham) and fresh brook trout can be found both around the Schwabentor and the Ludwigstrasse.

Rauchfang, Nienensstrasse 7, behind the New University, specializes in quick, inexpensive grill items and crêpes. Take-out service as well. Meals 5DM and up. Open daily 10am-midnight, closed Sun.

Mensas at the corner of Werderring and Belfortstrasse and on the Main Campus north of Albertstrasse are open 11:45am-2pm and 5:45-7:30pm weekdays, until noon on Sat. The noon meal costs 1.80DM.

Harmonie-Gaststätte, Grünwälderstrasse 18 (near Augustinerplatz) is a good place to sample traditional local fare. Three-course menus 9-18DM. Open 10am-midnight daily, closed Mon.

Evenings

Theater and musical performances draw large crowds in Freiburg. The local music school is well-known, and various groups perform usually in the

Münster, in the *Festsaal* of the **Kaufhaus,** or outdoors at a number of locations. The ten o'clock mass on Sunday mornings in the Münster is beautiful, and organ concerts are held there throughout the summer at 8:15 on Tuesday evenings. Check with the *Verkehrsamt* for programs.

Student bars are easily found around the Augustinerplatz, but avoid the expensive places on Münsterplatz, including the exorbitant International Student Club. A well-honored student locale is **Sankt Valentin** in the woods near the nearby village of Günterstal, reached by tram #2. From the village, hitch with students or walk up east into the woods.

Le Caveau, Oberlinden 8, through the narrow doorway marked *Zur Insel Gaststätte Feierling.* Downstairs is a candlelit cave conducive to conversation around the small tables and dancing to low-key recorded music. Admission free and only with student ID. Beer 2DM. Open until 2am during the week, 3am Friday to Sunday. Closed in July. **Der Bären,** next door, is the oldest bar in town.

Canapee, Grünwälderstrasse 18, is a student favorite for its lavish art-nouveau interior and low prices. Open 5pm-midnight.

Heidelberg and Tübingen

The Black Forest drains into the Rhine on the west, but the principal flow from these mountains and the Swabian Jura Mountains empties into the **Neckar,** meeting the Rhine at **Mannheim.** In modern times the area has become heavily industrialized—**Stuttgart** is now the center of the German auto industry. But the prominence of the Neckar Valley dates from the rise of the Rhineland-Palatinate before the sixteenth century, and a few towns still preserve this medieval glory. **Rottweil,** known largely for its *Karneval,* and **Bad Wimpfen** are both the sites of impressive fifteenth-century fortifications, while the university towns of **Heidelberg** and **Tübingen** remain the most lively in the area.

Heidelberg remains the most famous university in Germany, at least in foreign eyes, and the atmosphere is one of student life at its most exuberant. Most sights center around **Hauptstrasse** and **Marktplatz** (Wednesday and Saturday are market days) with its **Heilig-Geist-Kirche** and **Haus zum Ritter,** a knight's magnificent Renaissance mansion—the only major building to survive the French raid of 1693. Also interesting is the **Studentenkarzer** (old student jail), Augustinergasse 2, behind the **Old University,** where obstreperous students left artistic memorials of their internment. If you feel energetic, you can cross the Neckar over the old **Karl-Theodor Bridge** and climb via the **Philosopher's Walk** to the top of the 1400-foot **Heiligenberg.** There you will find ruins—the **Felerstätte** (reconstructed Roman ruins), **St. Stephen's Cloister** (twelfth-century ruins)—and a spectacular view of Heidelberg.

Heidelberg's real attraction, however, looms behind the town. The **Schloss,** an imperial castle that the French pillaged in 1689, is a colossal set of ruins with extensive gardens. Inside is the **German Apothecary Museum** (open daily 10am-5pm, admission 2DM, students 1.20DM) with reconstructed seventeenth-century laboratories; highly recommended for biochemists and alchemists.

Rooms in Heidelberg start at about 18DM and can be booked (for a 1.50DM fee) by the **Verkehrsbüro** (open 9am-8pm Mon.-Sat., 2-8pm Sun.; tel. 21881) at the Train Station. To get from the Train Station to the Altstadt, take bus #10 or 11. The IYHF **Youth Hostel** (tel. 42066) is modern but awkwardly located; to reach it from the Station take bus #11 away from town to the Tiergarten.

Tübingen houses a 500-year-old university with the 12,000 students making up 25% of the city's population. In the summer, with most of the students gone, the city is pleasantly quiet and provides an ideal retreat from the hectic pace of Germany's larger tourist areas. The old center, with its winding streets and gabled houses, is unmistakably Swabian in character. The town can be viewed from the balcony of the **Castle Hohentübingen,** though one cannot enter the Castle itself. You can also rent a boat on the quay beneath the bridge on Karlstrasse.

From the Station, the **Verkehrsverein** (tel. 35011) is on the right, just before crossing the main bridge over the Neckar, on the way to the old town. Open weekdays 8am-12:30pm and 1:30-6:30pm, Sat. 8:30am-12:30pm. They will give you pamphlets, programs, and will find rooms for 2DM.

Tübingen, like Heidelberg, is expensive. Eat at the **Mensa** for the cheapest meals. The **Youth Hostel** (IYHF), at Hermann-Kurz-Strasse 4 (tel. 23002), is ten minutes from the Station—cross the Neckarbrücke (also called Eberhardbrücke) and turn right immediately after the bridge. For anyone 25 or under beds are 6.20DM, including breakfast; for others 7.90DM. 10pm curfew.

Frankfurt

Frankfurt presents a depressing picture of the modern metropolis—gray, sprawling and—despite cosmetic potted trees in the carless section of the city center—busily impersonal. It is the commercial center of post-war Germany and is closer to America than almost anything else you will see in Europe. Nearly totally destroyed during the war, the city was rebuilt with the help of American planners and now has many of the problems of U.S. cities—high crime, a decaying core, and urban sprawl. There is no reason to go out of your way to visit Frankfurt. Frankfurt is listed for the many travelers who use its airport, and a stay here need not be a total waste. **Sachsenhausen,** on the south side of the Main River, remains green and alive and more European, and the area around Frankfurt is rich with forests and fine walks.

Connections between the **Airport** and the **Hauptbahnhof** (Train Station) are easy and spelled out in all imaginable languages. Do n⸱ ⸱⸱eglect to buy a ticket for the metro before you get on, since Frankfurt has recently raised the fine for traveling without paying to 40DM. Inside the *Hauptbahnhof* is the **Information Center** (follow the signs for "Tourist Information"—the circled "i"'s are for train information), which will find you a room for 2DM per person, and has brochures and maps. (Open Mon.-Sat. 8am-10pm Sun. 9:30am-8pm, tels. 23 22 18 and 23 11 08). There are also branches at the Airport, in the metro at Hauptwache (tel. 28 74 86, open Mon.-Fri. 9am-6:30pm, Sat. 9am-2pm), and in the center of town (Information Römer, open weekdays 8am-4:30pm, Sat. 8am-noon).

The center of town, including Frankfurt's few surviving relics from the past, lies straight ahead, if you are leaving the Railway Station's main exit. Be warned that the region between the *Hauptbahnhof* and the inner ring is one of the most crime ridden in West Germany. Seemingly innocent by day, this area should be avoided at night, and unaccompanied women might feel uncomfortable at any hour. Fortunately, however, trams to most points of town leave from the *Hauptbahnhof*—the platforms are accessible from the underground passage. Transit tickets must be purchased in advance from one of the automats scattered across town. "Zone 1" tickets (1.10DM, 1.50DM at rush hours) are good for all points within the city proper, plus the Airport, and allow unlimited changes in one direction of travel (no round trips).

Sachsenhausen, just across the river from Frankfurt, is also included in Zone 1.

Hitching out of Frankfurt is complicated. For Munich, take bus #36 from the Dominikaner Platz to Südfriedhof and look for signs for the *Autobahn*. For all other directions, take #16 from the Youth Hostel or the Hauptbahnhof to Wilhem-Hauff-Strasse and then bus #50 (from across the median) to Opel-Rondell; then start walking in the direction of travel of the bus. This is the access road to *Autobahns* north, west, and south—bring a sign.

Addresses and Telephone Numbers

Student Travel (SSJ): Weissfrauenstrasse 2-8, 6000 Frankfurt 16 (tel. 28 23 11). Sells **Transalpino** discount train tickets, but you must book them ten days in advance. Open weekdays 9am-6pm.

Römertelefon: (tels. 2124100 and 2124000). Gives information on all events in Frankfurt. Operates weekdays.

American Express: Steinweg 5 (tel. 2 10 51), open weekdays 8:30am-5:30pm, Sat. 9am-noon.

Post Office: Zeil 110, near the Hauptwache.

U.S. Consulate: Siesmayerstrasse 21.

Mitfahrzentrale: Baselerstrasse 7 (tels. 23 61 27 and 23 10 28), in the middle of Baseler Platz. Open weekdays 8am-5:30pm, Sat. 8am-noon. Hitching service (see chapter introduction).

Accommodations

Haus der Jugend, Deutschherrnufer 12 (tel. 619058). Well run, but impersonal. Leave all valuables at desk. Beds at 8.70DM (6.50DM if you're under 20), including breakfast; obligatory linen charge 1.80DM. Showers 0.50DM for six minutes. 10:45pm curfew. Take tram #16 from the Main Station to Frankensteiner Platz—you will want a tram traveling to the right as seen from the Hauptbahnhof.

Lohmann, Stuttgarterstrasse 31 (tel. 23 25 34), charges 22DM for singles, 38DM for doubles, with breakfast, showers 2.50DM. The hotel's dangerous proximity to the station is outweighed by the 16 clean beds and well-lit entrance. Exit through south wing of station to Baseler Platz.

Hotel Zur Post, Alt Schwannheim 38 (tel. 35 55 17) is in a quiet suburb next to a long wooded park. With breakfast singles cost 25DM, doubles 44DM, with 6DM extra for a private bath. Take tram #19 across Friedensbrücke, change to #21 to the end of line, then walk three blocks to the right.

Bahnhofsmissions: The German Red Cross runs a dormitory at Nidenau 27 (slightly removed from the danger zone) with beds from 8DM, but reserve space at the office at the south entrance of the Station (tel. 23 36 86), open until 11pm.

Camping Maul: Niederräder Ufer (tel. 67 38 46), on the far side of the Main from the Station, 2.20DM per person, 1.50DM per tent. Take tram #19 from the Station to the Heinrich-Hoffmann-Strasse.

Food

Cheap food is difficult to find in Frankfurt outside of the *Schnell-Imbisse*. The **University Mensa** is at the corner of Bockenheimer Landstrasse and Senckenberg Anlage (bus #32, or trams #17, 19, 21, or 22 to Bocken-

heimer Warte), open weekdays 11:30am-1:30pm, with meals around 3DM.
A popular long-bench-and-table restaurant is **Lorbacher Tal** in Sachsen-
hausen, set back from the Grosse Rittergasse at #49, serving Frankfurt's
Äpfelwein (apple wine).

Sights and Evenings

The center of the city, **Römerberg,** is an interesting blend of renovated
antiquity and modern landscape architecture. The **Romer,** a conglomerate of
Renaissance houses, occupies the west side of the square and contains the
ornate **Kaisersaal,** formal feast room for the Holy Roman Emperors (open
Mon.-Sat. 9am-1pm and 1:30-5pm, Sun. 10am-4pm, entry 1DM, 0.25DM
for students). Free concerts abound in the summer—check with the information offices. Frankfurt's most cherished museum is the **Goethe Haus** at
Grosser Hirschgraben 23 (open Mon.-Sat. 9am-6pm, Sun. 10am-1pm, entry
2DM, 1DM for students). The museum divides into three parts: the bottom
floors give a feeling for the Goethes' bourgeois opulence, and include part of
the family library; the exhibits on the display tables on the top floor docu-
ment worldwide critical response to *Faust;* and the portraits on the walls of
the fourth floor trace Goethe's phenomenal love life.

Two other refuges from the large department stores around the central
Hauptwache are the **Palmengarten** in the west, a tropical garden also
hosting summer classical and rock concerts (open 8am-sunset, entrance
2DM, tel. 212 33 82 for concert info; take tram #19 to Palmengarten), and
the **Zoo** in the east, Alfred-Brehm-Platz 16, one of Europe's best, particularly for its collection of unusual reptiles in native habitats—the **Exotarium**
(Zoo open 10am-10pm, entrance 3DM, take tram #10, 13, or 15). Some
out-of-town possibilities are the **Stadtwald** (city forest) to the South,
reached by public transportation from the Station; the ruins of feudal
Königstein and the view from the **Grosser Feldberg,** both a short train ride
northwest into the rolling **Taunus Mountains;** or a day-return boat ride west
down the Main and Rhine past castles and wine country to **Koblenz** (Eurailpasses valid).

Opera, drama, and comedy appear on the stages of the modern **Städtische
Bühne** at Theaterplatz (tel. 21 06-435). Advertising itself as the world's
worst theater, **Die Schmiere,** Im Karmeliterkloster, offers literary-political
cabaret (tel. 28 10 66).

The nicest places to drink some of the local *Äpfelwein* and hear jazz are
Gallery Pub, at the corner of Jordanstrasse and Kiesstrasse near the Univer-
sity; and **Jazz Haus,** with taped music, but in a fantastic old house in the
Kleine Bockenheimerstrasse (parallel to Goethe Strasse).

Sachsenhausen (on the left bank of the Main) offering innumerable
stand-up bars and discotheques, manages to attract a strange mixture of
tourists, seedy locals, and Universität-Frankfurt students. **Dauth-
Schneider,** Neuer Wallstrasse 7, offers a coffeehouse-with-beer atmosphere, plus accordion music. **Alt Prag** (Klappergasse 14), true to its name,
serves fantastic beer. Sachsenhausen's flea market comes to life on Saturdays along the bank of the Main between the bridges Untermainbrücke and
the Alte Mainbrücke.

The Rhine and Moselle Valleys

Since the northward expansion of the Roman Empire, the Rhine Valley
has been one of the world's major trade routes, and here along the central
stretch from **Bingen** to **Bonn** countless fortress walls are the legacy of the

bishops and princes who vied for the lucrative rights to the passage. Unfortunately, the Rhine is still as important as it was in the Middle Ages, so the channels are filled with local barges, and the banks are lined with freight trains and trucks. Boat trips are the most popular way of enjoying the vineyards, cliffs, and castles; the **Köln-Düsseldorfer Lines** run tourist boats from **Frankfurt** to **Düsseldorf** (and on the Moselle from **Koblenz** to **Trier**), with stops at every point of interest along the way. The passage is free with a Eurailpass, except that a Youthpass gets you only a 50% discount on the express boats. InterRail is also valid for 50% on all routes. The right bank is more interesting and less touristed for bicycling or driving, but the castles are deceptive. They were all, with the notable exceptions of **Marksburg** on the Rhine and **Burg Eltz** on the Moselle, destroyed by the French under Louis XIV, and later reconstructed into essentially the same kind of medieval military museum; visit one (especially **Burg Rheinfels** or **Marksburg**) and from there on enjoy the landscape. If you want to interrupt the journey, stay in one of the picturesque towns such as **Bacharach** (good IYHF **Youth Hostel**), **Oberwesel,** or **St. Goar,** but studiously avoid the tourist traps of **Rüdesheim** and **Koblenz.** In the smaller Rhine towns a pension with breakfast will cost about 17DM per person, in Koblenz about 20DM.

Less strewn with castles, but also less commercial than the Rhine is the Moselle, the major tributary that meets it at the **Deutsches Eck** in Koblenz. Wine-growing is still the Moselle's only major industry besides tourism, and in summer ducks and swans nest along the bank, barely bothered by the occasional kayaks, sculls, and barges. From Trier to Koblenz the river stretches some 200 kilometers, but the narrow steep walls that yield some of Germany's most famous vintages lie mostly between **Bernkastel-Kues** and **Cochem,** where the Moselle twists through four hairpin bends in a 75 kilometer stretch. The entire valley makes excellent biking or boating— traffic is light and camping sites can be found about every five miles. *Bundesbahn* bicycles can be rented in **Kell** and **Hermeskeil** in the **Hochwald** above Trier, and in **Traben-Trarbach.**

Every summer weekend is a prolonged celebration in the three to five towns staging *Weinfeste.* Tourists come from all over Germany for the brass bands in period costume and the cheap wine. *Qualitätswein,* a sweet, light white wine, starts at 3.50DM per bottle. Better (and twice as expensive) is the *Spätlese* (late vintage). Best (at 9DM) is the *Auslese* (last vintage of the year).

Trier

Trier advertises itself as Germany's oldest city, and has the Roman baths and amphitheater to back up its claim. Some light industry has recently developed in this one-time capital of the Western Roman Empire, but Trier has always been a spa town at heart—when Constantine arrived in 306 A.D., he added the extensive **Kaiserthermen** (Emperor's Baths) to the **Barbarathermen** (around 150 A.D.), making Trier a city with double baths as well as a double cathedral.

Built in the fourth century as a double basilica, the **Dom** (Cathedral) grew as the city evolved into an Archdiocese, the main church acquiring Romanesque apses and early Gothic vaulting. The southern part eventually collapsed and was replaced by a Gothic cross-church. No one should miss the recently reset fragments of ceiling paintings from the original Helena-Palast, on display in the **Bischöfliches Museum,** Banthusstrasse 6, around the block from the Dom, open daily from 10am-noon and 3-5pm, entry 1DM (students 0.50DM).

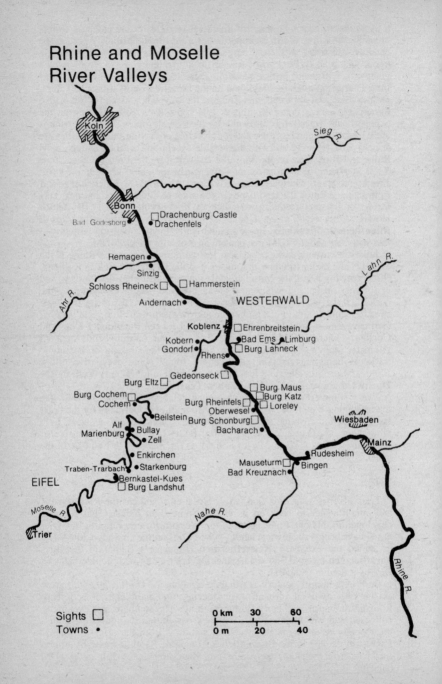

Rhine and Moselle River Valleys

Köln

Sieg R.

Bonn

Bad Godesberg

Drachenburg Castle
Drachenfels

Hemagen

Sinzig

Schloss Rheineck   Hammerstein

Andernach

Ahr R.

Lahn R.

WESTERWALD

Koblenz   Ehrenbreitstein

Kobern   Bad Ems   Limburg
Gondorf   Burg Lahneck
Rhens

Burg Eltz   Gedeonseck

Burg Cochem
Cochem

Burg Maus
Burg Katz
Burg Rheinfels   Loreley
Beilstein   Oberwesel
Burg Schonburg
Alf   Bacharach
Marienburg   Bullay
Zell

Wiesbaden

Mainz

Enkirchen
Traben-Trarbach   Starkenburg
Bernkastel-Kues
Burg Landshut

EIFEL

Moselle R.

Nahe R.

Mauseturm   Rüdesheim
Bad Kreuznach   Bingen

Rhine R.

Trier

Sights ☐
Towns •

0 km   30   60

0 m   20   40

Another of Trier's Roman monuments is the **Porta Nigra.** This massive, arcaded portal was at one time the center of the city's northern fortifications and later a church. Napoleon, however, ripped out the remnants of the House of God in a fit of imperialist fellow-feeling, preserving the remains as a testimony to Rome's former greatness. All the Roman relics, including the baths, the amphitheater, the Porta Nigra, and two sites outside town, are open Tues.-Sun. 9am-1pm and 2-6pm (1DM each, or 3DM for a ticket to everything).

From the Porta Nigra, turn left onto Simeonstrasse to get to the **Hauptmarkt** (main market). Here you will find several half-timbered houses, the **St. Peter's Fountain,** (1595) and the reconstructed early-Baroque **Rotes House** (Old Town Hall) with the inscription: "Trier stood 1300 years before Rome." A Baroque portal leads to the choirless **Marktkirche St. Gangolf.**

If the vestiges of feudalism and nascent capitalism begin to get you down, there is the **Karl-Marx-Haus,** Brückenstrasse 10. His birthplace now houses a museum of Marx's life—including some fascinating documents from Marx's student days and correspondence with Engels (you must understand German, though). Open daily 10am-1pm and 3-6pm, closed Mon. mornings (admission 1DM, students 0.50DM).

Accommodations

Tourist-Information Trier will book rooms for 2DM, as well as provide maps and brochures. Located right next to the Porta Nigra, the Office is open Mon.-Sat. 9am-1pm and 2-6pm, Sun. 10am-1pm (tels. 71 84 48 and 7 54 40). Breakfast is included in the rates at all of the following:

Hotel Alken, Paulinstrasse 13 (tel. 4 07 74). Singles 18DM, doubles from 34DM. Showers 2DM. Enter through a downstairs café. Near Porta Nigra.

Pension Binnefeld, Gervasiusstrasse 10 (tel. 764 45), is ten minutes from the Porta Nigra down Simeonstrasse. This modern 20-bed home is spotless and friendly. Singles 15DM, doubles from 32DM. Showers 1.50DM.

Gasthof Pieper, Thebäerstrasse 39 (tel. 7 34 26), 20-22DM per person; large rooms, large breakfast; five minutes from Train Station. Free shower.

Pension Kaiserthermen, Weberbach 54 (tel. 4 25 09), 15DM per person with breakfast and 1.50DM shower. Downstairs restaurant serves good cheap food and is distinctively local. Near the baths.

Zur Gerichts-Klause, Dietrichstrasse 36 (tel. 7 34 80). 15DM per person, including a good breakfast. Fine location, too.

Youth Hostel (IYHF), Maarstrasse 156 (tel. 4 10 92). 6.60DM with breakfast. Hostel swarms with kids of all ages—up to about 13. Administration very strict about times (9:45pm curfew, 9am lock-out), but does not enforce quiet hours. Located on the right at the end of Maarstrasse, past the underpass, on the bank of the Moselle.

Camping Schloss Monaise, Monaisestrasse (tel. 8 62 10), has taken over the grounds of a rundown eighteenth-century palace. Modern facilities include hot showers, a store, and a washing machine operated by the keeper for 3DM per kilo of laundry. 2DM per person, 3.50DM for auto plus tent, 2DM per tent. Take bus to Flugplatz Stadion, walk ahead 100 meters, turn left towards the Moselle, walk a few minutes, and turn left again for the campsite.

Camping Ruderverein Treviris, Luxemburgerstrasse 81 (tel. 8 69 21), 2DM per tent plus 1.80DM per person, showers 0.75DM. Take the Bahnbus #1 from the Station in direction Westbahnhof and get off at the second stop over the river.

Food

Oen der Beiz, Viehmarktplatz 8, open 10am-1am daily. Wide range of foods and liquors—you can get meals for anywhere from 5DM to 20DM. Menu in the incomprehensible Trierisch dialect. Not a tourist spot.

Mensa, take bus #12 across the bridge to the Universität. Students at this small college are apt to approach you with soft-spoken gentility and tentative curiosity. Consult the *Speisekarte* posted outside for daily *menus* at either 1.80DM or 2.80DM. Open Mon.-Fri. noon-1:30pm. Bring student ID.

Moselle Towns

BERNKASTEL-KUES

Bernkastel may have one of the most picturesque marketplaces along the Moselle, but the town is very touristy and the merchants near the square are often arrogant. Kues, across the river, is more quiet and pleasant, with the **Cusanusstift** monastery, library, and cloister. A narrow road twists out of the Bernkastel market (to the right looking at the Rathaus) past one of the world's narrowest houses, and on up to the ruined summer castle of the Trier archbishops, **Landshut.** Just beyond the fortification is a **Youth Hostel** (IYHF), with spectacular views (3.40DM for people up to 24 years old, 5.10DM for seniors, breakfast 2.40DM, tel. 2395). In Bernkastel, the **Tourist Information Office** is at Gestade 5 (tel. 3588), open Mon.-Fri. 8am-12:30pm and 2-5:30pm. Information for the entire middle Moselle Valley can be obtained at Gestade 18 (tel. 3075). There is **camping** at the upstream end of Kues. **Pension Coen,** Im Viertheil 2 (tel. 8186), has comfortable rooms (16DM per person) and a private vineyard. From Bernkastel, cross the bridge to the Bahnhof, turn left onto Friedrichstrasse, follow it over the tracks and proceed directly uphill on Mariental to the end of the block.

From Bernkastel, there is a lovely path heading north (downstream) out of the town, and over the isthmus to **Traben-Trarbach.** The walk takes about an hour—turn left when you get to civilization for the marketplace. Trarbach, on the right bank of the Moselle, offers a regional museum, paths into the hills, and the exemplary **Pension Bartz,** Wildbadstrasse 161 (tel. 9910). It offers nice rooms for 12DM per person, excellent breakfasts, and a wonderful landlady. **Traben,** on the left bank, is nearest the French ruin **Mont Royal,** and features an interesting marketplace which handles much of the middle Moselle wine trade. The **Information Center** is nearby (Alte Marktstrasse, open weekdays 8am-12:20pm and 3-5pm, Sat. 10am-noon and 3-6pm). The IYHF **Youth Hostel** is also near, at Dam Hirtenpfädchen (tel. 9278). 5.50DM for juniors, 8.50DM if you're over 25.

COCHEM

The center of Cochem, built into the hillside, is a maze of streets, alleys, passageways and stairs that make getting around a lot like playing Chutes and Ladders. There's not much to see in town besides the pink **Rathaus** (Town Hall) on the **Markt,** and **Burg Cochem** (open daily 9am-6pm), the creepy-looking castle on the hill, which was built in the eleventh-century, destroyed in the seventeenth, and restored about a hundred years ago. Tours 3DM or 1.50DM with a student ID; walk up Schlosstrasse or follow the signs.

For a good view of the Moselle Valley, there's a **Sesselbahn** (chairlift) a few minutes out of town on Endertstrasse. For 3DM you can ride up to the top of the hill and back, but if you have some energy it's more fun to walk down through the vineyards. For walkers and medievalists, **Winneburg,** a ruined castle where a jousting tournament is held under every full moon, is about a two-hour march up Endertstrasse.

Accommodations are easy to find in the 15DM range either through the **Informationszentrum** (open weekdays 9am-6pm, Sat. 10am-noon and 2-6pm; tel. 1214), directly underneath the bridge or from the *Zimmer Frei* signs that line the road. The **Youth Hostel** (IYHF) on Klottenerstrasse in **Cond** (tel. 633), is directly across the river from the Train Station, but is a half-hour walk away due to the location of the bridge. Beds are 3.20DM for people under 25 years, 5.10DM for seniors, breakfast 2.40DM, linen 1.80DM. Just below the Hostel is one campsite (on the river); another is on Endertstrasse further out of town. The Hostel serves quite good food; otherwise *gute bürgerliche Küche* can be found at **Onkel Willi** on Endertstrasse 13 or **Zum Fröhlichen Weinberg,** Schlaufstrasse 13. Both are in the 8-11DM range.

BURG ELTZ (ELTZ CASTLE)

Burg Eltz is a steep climb north of Müden or a gentler 45-minute walk from Moselkern. (Open April 1 to October 31, Monday-Saturday 9am-5:30pm, Sunday 10am-5:30pm; entrance 4DM, students 2DM.) Worth the side trip. Still the property of its title family, the Princes zu Elz-von Stromberg, this Castle displays every architectural style from the eleventh to the seventeenth centuries. Because the buildings were never taken or destroyed, the walls are still covered with the original arabesques and religious frescoes; paintings of the Cranach school still hang in rooms with the original sixteenth-century furniture, and the state room is decorated with a vast Gobelin tapestry. The setting, too, is spectacular, with half-timbered towers rising out of a tiny stream valley.

Bonn-Bad Godesberg

Bonn's Train Station has only five tracks. That's one of the best things about Bonn—it does not look like a nation's capital. There are commercial sections, and the market has become a little touristy, but most parts still have the feel of a university town. Add to this the fact that the diplomatic community lives entirely in the suburb Bad Godesberg, and Bonn begins to appear downright provincial.

The **Informations-stelle** (near the Station) is in Cassius-Bastei, Münsterstrasse 20 (tels. 77 34 66 and 77 34 67). Open Mon.-Sat. 8am-9pm, Sun. 9:30am-12:30pm. This office has its act together, and offers innumerable pamphlets plus a room-finding service for 0.30DM. Bad Godesberg also has an **Informations-pavillon** at Moltkestrasse 63 (tels. 83 05 48 and 83 06 62), across from the Station. Open Mon.-Fri. 8am-6pm, Sat. 8am-1pm.

In the city center you will find a **Cathedral** built in the Rhineland transitional style—essentially Romanesque with a slight upward movement. Also interesting architecturally is the Rococo **Rathaus** in the market square, scene of the free musical and theatrical events comprising **Bonner Sommer.** Outside the city center, at the end of Poppelsdorfer Allee, is the **Poppelsdorfer Schloss,** a Baroque Palace and grounds including a botanical garden (all open weekdays 8am-7pm, Sun. 9am-1pm), and a petrological museum for all the Shell lobbyists in Bad Godesberg. The most interesting museum is the **Rheinisches Landesmuseum** at Colmanstrasse 14-16 (open Tues., Thurs., and Fri. 9am-5pm; Wed. 9am-9pm, weekends 10am-6pm, admission 1DM) featuring the best finds from local digs.

Bonn's most precious monuments are the least visited, however. Go see the **Doppelkirche** across the river in Schwarzrheindorf on Dixstrasse, a Romanesque double church with an incredible cycle of frescoes recounting Ezekiel's dream, and the destruction and rebuilding of Jerusalem—an unusual theme for the twelfth century. More intimate is the little Romanesque church of **St. Martin** in **Muffendorf,** on a hill above Bad Godesberg. The village is one of the best preserved along the Rhine, but nothing goes back beyond the Thirty Years War. Across the river, below Oberkassel, you can swim in the **Dornheckensee** or **Blauersee.** For boat trips to Bingen or up the Moselle, call **Köln-Düsseldorfer Lines** at 63 21 34 in Bonn.

A note on transportation in Bonn—to avoid the stiff 1.50DM tariff, buy a white **Streifenkarte,** cancelling two stripes for each ride, or a blue Streifenkarte (2.50DM for four rides) if you have a valid student ID.

Addresses and Telephone Numbers

American Express: Deischmanns Aue, Bad Godesberg (tel. 35 40 28).

Post Office: Bonn—Münsterplatz 17 (tel. 131). Bad Godesberg—Koblenzerstrasse 67 (tel. 801). Open Mon.-Fri. 8am-6pm, Sat. 7am-1pm, Sun. 11amnoon.

Police: For emergency dial 110. In **Bonn:** Friedrich-Ebert-Allee 144 (tel. 151). In **Bad Godesberg:** Zeppelinstrasse 1 (tel. 36 58 64).

U.S. Embassy: Mehlemer Aue, Bonn 2 in Bad Godesberg.

Canadian Embassy: Friedrich-Wilhelm-Strasse 18, Bonn (tel. 23 10 61).

Concert Information: (tels. 77 36 66 and 77 36 67).

Accommodations

Beds, like everything else in Bonn, are viciously overpriced. Some consolation is provided by the youth hostels, which in both Bonn and Bad Godesberg are better than average and close enough to the center of town to be convenient.

Weiland, Breite Strasse 98a (tel. 65 24 24), modern and comfortable; singles 28DM, doubles 49DM. Tram #1, 2, H or S, one stop from Station direction Siegburg or Bad Honnef.

Youth Hostel (IYHF), Haager Weg 42 (Venusberg, tel. 28 12 00). Take bus #20 or 21 from the Bus Terminal left of the Bahnhof. A very nice setting; many footpaths leading through the woods into the city. Hostel closes 9amnoon daily, registration after 5pm. Bed-and-breakfast for juniors (to 24) 6.70DM, seniors 8.40DM, 10pm curfew.

Berners, Yorckstrasse 7, Bad Godesberg (tel. 36 22 52). Singles 25DM, doubles 50DM, with breakfast. The best of Godesberger living—flowers, quiet, sunlight. Private bath, 5DM extra, showers free. Bus #14 from Bad Godesberg center.

Youth Hostel "Landeshauptmann-Horion-Haus" (IYHF), Horionstrasse 60, Bad Godesberg (tel. 36 39 91). Take bus #15 to Venner-Strasse. Closed 9am-noon. Relaxed, beautiful view. 6.20DM with breakfast. For 23 and over 7.90DM.

Food

Im Bären, Acherstrasse 1-3, in the mall. Meals for 6-11DM. A popular student haunt, where you can dine or just drink beer. Closed Sun.

Dalmatien, Berliner Freiheit 2, at the Bonn end of the Kennedy Bridge, open noon-3pm and 5:30pm-midnight. One of the countless restaurants here serving Balkan food—share a *Grillteller* with a friend for 12DM.

Mensa, Nassestrasse 11, walk south from Am Hof (the University Mall), then follow Lennestrasse to Nassestrasse. Tokens are obtainable from the lady in the booth inside the main hall. 1.50DM for a full meal. Open noon-2pm and 6-8pm weekdays. Closed mid-July to mid-August. Student ID required.

Zum Lindenwirten Aennchen, Aennchenplatz, Bad Godesberg. Meals 5-12DM, wine from 2.50DM. Open 4pm-1am.

Tondorf Dolff, Sternstrasse 66, open 6am-midnight. The only hope for good, cheap German food in Bonn.

Der Apfel and **Au Château** are two popular student bars. Der Apfel, on Roon Platz and Argelanderstrasse (near the Botanical Gardens), is one of the better student bars. Au Château, Argelanderstrasse and Königstrasse, is open Tues.-Sun. after 8pm (entrance only with student ID).

Cologne (Köln)

The choir of the **Kölner Dom** is Germany's best-known Gothic monument, but Cologne's real prizes are the eleven great Romanesque cathedrals, any one of which would be the main church in most cities. Also worth a visit is the **Roman-Germanic Museum,** next to the Dom and Train Station (open 10am-7:45pm, entry 1DM, students admission half price).

Cologne's **Verkehrsamt** (Information Center) sits across the square from the main façade of the Dom, and is open Mon.-Sat. 8am-10:30pm, Sun. 9am-10:30pm (tel. 2 11 33 45). Their room-finding service costs 1DM. It's hard to find anything in Cologne for less than 20DM, however, so consider the IYHF **Youth Hostel** across the Hohenzollern Bridge from the Dom at Siegesstrasse 5a (tel. 81 47 11), 6.70DM for travelers up to 25 years of age, 8.40DM for seniors. Walk down the street to the right of the bridge on the far side until you come to a large intersection (Ottoplatz), and there will be a sign for the *Jugendherberge* across the roadway on the right. There's another IYHF **Youth Hostel** at Elsa-Brandströmstrasse (tel. 73 17 20). **Transalpino** has an office at Hohenzollernring 47 (tel. 21 98 03) and **Mitfahrzentrale** (see our chapter introduction) is at Brandenburgerstrasse 13-15 (tels. 12 38 48 and 12 36 48).

North Germany

Hamburg

Hamburg, like Munich, is a diverse, sophisticated city with a distinctive flavor. The bustling port, the famous sex-zone of **St. Pauli,** the sailing lake **Alster** in the middle of town, and the green countryside just outside the city limits strike the note of Hamburg, and it is concordant.

Orientation

For any kind of information, turn to the excellent **Fremdenverkehrszentrale Hamburg** (Information) at Bieberhaus, 100 yards to the left of the Hauptbahnhof from the Kirchenalle exit (tel. 241234), open weekdays 7:30am-6pm, Sat. 7:30am-1pm.

Transportation within the center of the city costs 1DM for tickets which must be bought from an automat before you board. There are also all-day excursion tickets for 4DM. For transportation to and from Hamburg, **Studenten und Schuler-Reisen** has a **Transalpino** franchise that can book tickets on the spot, at Rothenbaumchaussee 61 (tel. 4102081). Open weekdays 9am-6pm, Sat. 9am-noon. **Mitfahrzentrale** (see our chapter introduction) lives at Bundesstrasse 9 (tel. 410 42 28). Open Mon.-Sat. noon-7pm.

You can hitch to Berlin on Bundesstrasse 5; the same road heading nor-

thwest out of town serves as an access road to the Kiel Autobahn. Hitch to
Lübeck from Horn (U-3 to Rauhes Haus and walk north); hitch south from
Billhorner Brückenstrasse (S-2 to Rothenburgsort, and walk west) with a
sign.

Police: (tel. 110).

First Aid: (tel. 112).

American Express: An der Alster 30 (tel. 280 11 01).

Accommodations

The branch of the information service inside the Hauptbahnhof will find
rooms for a fee of 1.50DM per person (but 2.50DM for a single traveler);
open daily 7am-11:30pm. We recommend, however, that you get a copy of
the pamphlet *Hotelführer*, and find yourself a room, since the room-finding
service does not believe in any of Hamburg's numerous cheap pensions
(singles around 18DM, doubles at 30DM) scattered throughout the city's
red-light and commercial districts.

There are two IYHF **Youth Hostels. Auf dem Stintfang,** at Alfred-
Wegener-Weg 5 (tel. 31 34 88). Beds are 4.20DM for juniors up to 24 years
old, 5.90DM for others. Breakfast is 3.40DM, showers free. 11:30pm curfew. The Hostel is in an excellent location over the harbor near St. Pauli.
Take the U-3 to Landungsbrücken from Hauptbahnhof-Sud, or the S-10 from
the Hauptbahnhof. The second Hostel, **Horner Rennbahn,** is at Renn-
bahnstrasse 100 (tel. 651 16 71). Take U-3 to Horner Rennbahn. **Camping
Anders,** Kieler Strasse 650 (tel. 5 70 44 98) is probably your best choice
among the four campsites in the Hamburg vicinity. Closed from 9am-
4:30pm. Take the S-Bahn to Holstenstrasse and then bus #183.

Food, Sights, and Evenings

Getting hungry in Hamburg is not the disaster it is in Bonn and Frankfurt.
Go to the Mensa at Schlüterstrasse 7 (middle of the interesting university
sector). Between 11:30am and 2pm, there's a 2DM meal. For something of a
splurge, try **Fischerhaus** at St. Pauli-Fischmarkt 14, open 10am-10pm, with
fantastic fish dishes from 7.50DM. Several small fish restaurants along the
St. Pauli Quay (Landungsbrücken) are open for lunch.

St. Michaels, in the middle of town, is one of the most original Baroque
churches you are likely to see. Across the street, at Krayenkamp 10, is a
well-preserved complex of seventeenth-century houses originally built by the
merchants' guild for members' widows. But these are the only traditional
sightseers' goals around. Spend your time walking through the **port**—
Germany's largest—on both sides of the Elbe. The **fish market** along the
water in St. Pauli comes alive on Saturdays.

Brahms and Mendelssohn may have been born here, but jazz reigns in
Hamburg today. Look at the free magazine *Hamburgtips* for listings, or try
Onkel Pö's Carnegie Hall at Lehmweg 44 in Eppendorf, or **Winterhuder
Fährhaus** at Hudtwalckerstrasse 5-7.

Celle

Celle belongs along the Romantic Road, but its location just north of
Hannover (lower Saxony's "dead center") protects it from the droves of
Romantic tourists in Bavaria. The **Rathaus** and **Church** along Stechbahn
deserve a visit, as do the **Hoppener-Haus** (corner of Rundestrasse and
Poststrasse), with its dionysian Renaissance façade, and the narrow
Kalandgasse behind the church. But several hours are enough to wander
through every street of the old city, and each one is picturesque. The
Bomann Museum, on the Schlossplatz, houses an ethnographic collection

from the Lüneburg Heath (open Mon.-Sat. 10am-5pm, Sun. 10am-1pm, 1DM), and a wonderful old lady gives inspired tours through the **Palace** across the street, featuring a mirrored room with countless mirror tunnels (tours 1DM every day on the hour from 9am-4pm, with occasional irregularities on weekends). To get to the old city from the Railway Station, walk straight out Bahnhofstrasse a little past Thaer-Platz, then turn left onto Schlossplatz. The first **Palacial Residence** on the left along Bahnhofstrasse (walking to town) is now a prison.

Bicycles can be rented for 5DM per day at Schollmeyer in the Kanzlei-strasse.

Accommodations

Check with the **Verkehrsverein,** Schlossplatz 6a (tel. 2 30 31), open Mon.-Fri. 8am-6pm, Sat. 9am-1pm, for a list of pensions, but expect to pay 18-20DM per person. Room-finding service .50DM.

Youth Hostel (IYHF), Weghausstrasse 2, corner of Dorfstrasse (tel. 5 32 08). Take Bus #3 from the Station to Dorfstrasse. Pleasant and modern, 3.70DM for 24 and under, 5.40DM for others, breakfast 2.40DM.

Camping Silbersee (tel. 3 12 23), north of town on a large lake. Tent site 4DM plus 2.50DM per person; access to swimming facilities 1DM. Take bus #2, 6, 8, or, at night, bus B from the end station at Vorwerk.

Hotel Stech, Haarburger Heerstrasse 3 (tel. 3 36 11), singles 21.50DM, doubles 43DM, with breakfast. Take Bus #6 from Schlossplatz to Haarburger Heerstrasse.

Lübeck

Lübeck is the most interesting of the towns in the unspoiled countryside around Hamburg. Head of the Hanseatic League, Lübeck was the urban center for shipping leaving from **Travemünde.** The delta is a favorite vacation spot for Scandinavians, and they flock to Lübeck as well, to admire the city's brickwork. The town was only slightly damaged during the war, and though the major churches are still being restored, much of Lübeck has remained intact. A stroll through the narrow streets, lined with gabled houses, past the **Buddenbrookhaus,** evokes images of Thomas Mann's nineteenth-century bourgeoisie. Walk through the center of Lübeck from the Romanesque **Dom** in the south, past the striking **Rathaus** (thirteenth century) into the courtyard of the **Burgtor** (mid-fifteenth century) in the north. The inner city is surprisingly small, and every block brings another historic building to light. Continue on to the **Tannenhof,** a heavily-wooded and very beautiful cemetery along the Travemünder Allee, which stretches toward the Baltic.

The Railroad Station is to the west of the city, two blocks from the Holstentor.

Hitchers headed for Hamburg or Travemünde can reach the *Autobahn* uniting the two by hitching out Travemünder Allee in the north or Fackenburger Allee in the west. Those desiring to reach Kiel should remain on the Fackenburger Allee beyond the *Autobahn* connection, or follow Schwartauer Allee north along the railroad tracks.

The **Touristbüro** in the Railway Station operates a room-finding service for 2DM (tel. 72300). It's open Mon.-Sat. 9am-1pm and 3-8pm; Sun. 6-8pm. There is another **Tourist Office** at Markt 1(Lübecker Verkehrsverein). open weekdays 9am-6pm, Sat. 9am-1pm. Rooms start at 22DM for singles and 40DM for doubles. The **Youth Hostel Folke-Bernadotte-Heim** at Am Gertrudenkirchhof 4 (tel. 3 34 33) charges 9.50DM per night. Take bus #1, 3, 6, or 12 from the Station near the Bahnhof.

West Berlin

The trip across East Germany to Berlin may have been foreboding in the past, but the city is now more accessible than ever—and well worth the journey. While the East Germans still don't officially recognize the city as part of West Germany, new agreements do admit that Bonn speaks for West Berlin. It receives massive subsidies from the West German government, but the seeming prosperity is to a large extent an artifical construction. Behind the sparkle of **Kudamm** (short for Kurfürstendamm), West Berlin's main artery, is an aging city that is steadily losing population. The poverty is visible in sections like **Wedding** and **Kreuzberg.** For years considered too close to the wall to be a secure investment, they were little rebuilt, and they now house most of the city's *Gastarbeiter* (immigrant laborers). Berlin's divided nature is unique—half of the city is surrounded by a wall, barbed wire, and mine fields. Yet the feeling of one city remains. (Travel the U-Bahn under the wall for an experience.) Berliners themselves are part of the attraction—independent, unaccommodating, arrogant perhaps, but very much alive. For a sense of what the Cold War has meant to them, walk along the wall. It is chilling.

Orientation

If you arrive at West Berlin's **Tegel Airport,** take bus 9 to **Bahnhof Zoo,** in the heart of the city. There is also bus service from **Schönefeld Airport** in the German Democratic Republic (GDR) to West Berlin. (It ay be worth checking out student air fares to this airport.)

From most major West German cities, there are direct train connections to Berlin, three times a day in the summer. (Rail passes aren't valid after the border of the GDR.) Be sure to get off at Bahnhof Zoo, the main station in West Berlin. Otherwise, most trains go on to the east, and in ten minutes you might find yourself on a platform in East Berlin.

If you are traveling to Berlin by car you will have to pay 10DM for a two-way transit visa through the GDR, 6DM for mandatory car insurance and registration in the GDR, and, depending on your route, a toll of 20-40DM round trip. When you get to the border checkpoint, have ready your vehicle registration, insurance papers, and International Drivers License or one from another European country, and the passports of all persons in the car. Formalities at the border are now usually limited to a passport control.

You can hitch via any of the automobile access highways into West Berlin if you can get a ride before the border. Hitching in the GDR is forbidden; if driving, do not pick up anyone hitching after having crossed the border.

Once you get to the Bahnhof Zoo, orient yourself by going to the **Verkehrsamt Berlin** (Tourist Office) at Hardenbergstrasse 20, across from the station. This office offers a room-finding service for 2DM, which may be worth it since pensions and hostels do fill up (particularly in January, July, and August). While you're at this office, pick up any available maps, including the *Liniennetz* of the transportation system (1DM); the *Berlin Programm*, which lists events and addresses (2DM); and a current listing of hostels and pensions. The maps, unfortunately, tend to be limited in detail, and you may want to buy a better one at the newsstand (5-6DM). The people who run the Verkehrsamt can be extremely friendly and helpful.

The transit system consists of the city railway (**S-Bahn**), the underground (**U-Bahn**), and an extensive network of bus lines. Although the S-Bahn is less expensive than the U-Bahn, it is also less crowded—the East Germans run the S-Bahn, and West Berliners have had a quiet, unofficial boycott underway for years. U-Bahn tickets cost 1.30DM each, or 5.50DM for a

Berlin

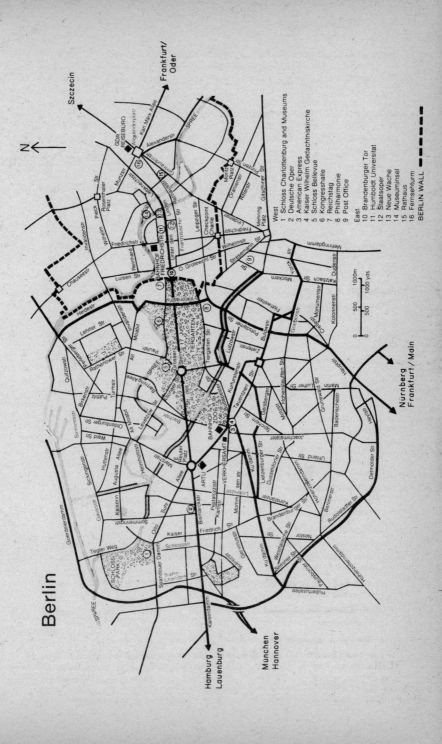

N ←

GDR REISEBÜRO

Szczecin

Frankfurt/ Oder

Alexanderstr

Karl Marx Allee

Ackerplatz

SPREE

Rosenthaler Platz

Pieck Str

Münzstr

Linienstr

Moritz Platz

Prinzen Str

Gitschiner Str

Oranienstr

Ritterstr

Leipziger Str

Wilhelm

Hannah

Friedrichstr

Luisen Str

Chausseestr

Invalidenstr

Checkpoint Charlie

Unter den Linden

Französische Str

Grotewohl Str

Wilhelmstr

Stresemann Str

Mehringdamm

Mehring Platz

BAHNHOF FRIEDRICHSTR

Heidestr

Lehrter Str

TIERGARTEN

Str des 17 Juni

Mockern

Mockernstr

Katzbach Str

Dudenstr

Kolonnenstr

Cheruskerstr

Gneisenaustr

Monumentenstr

Yorckstr

Quitzowstr

Rathenower Str

Birkenstr

Putlitz

Turmstr

Alt Moabit

Pauli

SPREE

Paulstr

Lüneburger Str

Tiergarten Str

Potsdamer Str

Lutzowstr

Zietenstr

Kurfürstenstr

Budapester Str

Flottwellstr

Tauentzien

Nürnberg Frankfurt / Main

Summstr

Waldstr

Helmholtzstr

Alt Moabit

Levetzow Str

Bachstr

Marchstr

Berlichow

Franklinstr

ZOO

BAHNHOF ZOO

VERKEHRSAMT

ARTU

Reuter Platz

Kurfürstendamm

Kantstr

Sochstr

Sochern Str

Goethestr

Joachimstaler

Geisberger

Hohenstauffen Str

Martin Luther Str

Grunewald Str

Badenschestr

Hejdstr

Detmolder Str

Rudolstadter Str

Sickingenstr

Huttenstr

Kaiserin

Augusta

Allee

Otto Suhr Allee

Sommeringstr

Bismarckstr

Pestalozzistr

Kantstr

Momm sen str

Leibnizstr

Kurfürstendamm

Letzenburger Str

Düsseldorfer Str

Konstanzer

Brandenburger Str

Uhland Str

Nestor

Berlinerstr

Detmolder Str

Tegler Weg

Spandauer Damm

Kaiser

Friedrich

Str

Schlossstr

Sophie Charlotten Str

SCHLOSS PARK

Gierdel verdamm

Gausstr

Kaiser Friedrich Str

SPREE

Kaiserdamm

Gervinusstr

Westfalische Str

Seesner Str

Brandenburgischestr

Hohenzollerndamm

Hohenzollerndamm

Hubertusallee

Paulsbornestr

Hamburg Lauenburg

München Hannover

0   500   1000m
0   500   1000 yds

West

1 Schloss Charlottenburg and Museums
2 Deutsche Oper
3 American Express
4 Kaiser Wilhelm Gedachtniskirche
5 Schloss Bellevue
6 Kongresshalle
7 Reichstag
8 Philharmonie
9 Post Office

East

10 Brandenburger Tor
11 Humboldt Universitat
12 Staatsoper
13 Neue Wache
14 Museumsinsel
15 Rathaus
16 Fernsehturm

BERLIN WALL ■ ■ ■ ■ ■ ■

five-ride ticket (**Sammelkarte**). You may wish to buy a two-day (9.50DM) or a four-day (17DM) **Touristenkarte**. U-Bahn tickets allow unlimited changes between underground lines and buses in one direction of travel for two hours from the time they are canceled *(entwertet)*. Hold on to your tickets until you leave the bus or U-Bahn station, since the fine for traveling without tickets or with uncanceled ones is 20DM if you are caught—which is more likely in Berlin than in most German cities. Late nights require taxis—only a few bus routes keep running past 1am, while the U-Bahn shuts down entirely.

Finding addresses in Berlin is a hassle. The city is huge and unfocused; its transportation network is expensive, confusing, but unavoidable; and street names change every few blocks. Numbers run consecutively up one side of a street and down the other. The small numbers under the street signs at intersections indicate the addresses within that block.

To hitch out of West Berlin, go to S-Bahn Station **Eichkamp** and hitch northward along Messedamm (i.e., the side of Messedamm across from Deutschlandhalle). This is the entrance ramp to the *Autobahn* heading south. To hitchhike north—direction Hamburg or Denmark—take bus #94 to the end of Heerstrasse in Staaken.

Addresses and Telephone Numbers

Verkehrsamt Berlin: Hardenbergstrasse 20 (tel. 31 70 94/95). Open daily 7:30am-10:30pm.

ARTU Reisebüro: Hardenbergstrasse 9 (tel. 3 13 40 31), near Bahnhof Zoo, also offices near U-Bahnhof Dahlem-Dorf at Takustrasse 47 (tel. 8 32 49 88) and in Wedding, at Triftstrasse 39, near U-Bahnhof Amrumer Strasse (tel. 4 65 91 35). A student travel bureau offering low-cost trips and aid with travel plans. Also headquarters for two student association hotels. Issues student ID for the socialist countries (IUS). Special discount rail tickets available. All branches keep the following hours: Mon., Wed., Fri. 9:30am-2pm and 3-6pm; Tues. 10:30am-2pm, 3-6pm; Thurs. 9:30am-2pm and 3-7pm. IUS cards available only after noon.

American Express: Kurfürstendamm 11, 1000 Berlin 15 (tel. 881 43 33). On the second floor of the building across the mall from the Gedächtnis-Kirche. Open Mon.-Fri. 8:30am-noon and 2-5:30pm, Sat. 9am-noon.

All-Night Post Office: Bahnhof Zoo, on main floor opposite ticket windows. Pick up general delivery mail *(postlagernde Sendung)* at the central Post Office *(Hauptpostamt)*, Möckernstrasse 138, near U-Bhf. Möckernbrücke.

Ambulance and First Aid: (tel. 3871).

Pharmacy: West Berlin drugstores *(Apotheken)* alternate all-night service. When in need, go to any *Apotheke*, where a sign in the window will give the address of an open one nearby.

Crash Pad and Drug Help: call Release, (tel. 2 62 21 11 or 6 14 60 11) for go-between information.

U.S. Consulate: Clayalee 170 (tel. 819 74 51). Near U-Bahnhof Oskar-Helene-Heim.

Canadian Consulate: Europa Center, 12th floor (tel. 2 61 11 61).

Lost and Found: Office for U-Bahn and Bus, Potsdamerstrasse 184 (tel. 2 16 14 13).

Accommodations

During the peak summer months, Berlin becomes very crowded, so it is best to book in advance. Fortunately, a central office handles reservations for all pensions and most hotels. Write to **Das Verkehrsamt Berlin,** Europa-Center, 1000 Berlin 30 (tel. (030) 21 23-4, telex 0183356). Make sure your rooming request is precise, including how much you are willing to spend, and that it arrives in Berlin at least two weeks before you do. To reserve places in a hostel, write directly to the hostel, but you must have a Youth Hostel card. Berlin hostels usually offer lunch and dinner for under 5DM each.

If you arrive at Bahnhof Zoo at three in the morning, your best bet is to go to the **Bahnhofsmissions** office in the station, where a nurse will give you directions to the dorm at Franklinstrasse 27. Bunks start at 5DM. Not recommended ordinarily; women should stay away. Take bus #90 to Einstein-Ufer.

HOSTELS AND CAMPING

Jugendherberge Ernst Reuter (IYHF), Hermsdorferdamm 48/50, 1000 Berlin 28 (tel. 404 16 10). 9DM under 25, 10.70DM over 25, both including breakfast. Curfew at 11pm. This hostel books only one month at a time. Near the northern tip of the city, it is beautifully situated between the Tegel Forest and the village of Lübars, but far from town. Pleasant atmosphere. Take the U-Bahn direction Osloerstrasse to Leopoldplatz, then U-Bahn #6 to Tegel, and finally bus #15 (direction Frohnau) from Tegel to the door.

Jugendherberge (IYHF), Bayernallee 36, 1000 Berlin 19 (tel. 305 30 55). Same prices as Ernst Reuter. Check-in 5pm-midnight, check-out 7-9am. Ritzy neighborhood. Take the U-Bahn to Neu-Westend, and walk south along Preussenallee.

Jugendgästehaus (IYHF), Kluckstrasse 3, 1000 Berlin 30 (tel. 261 10 97). 11.30DM, including breakfast. Reservation by mail or phone only. Take bus #29 (direction Oranienplatz) from Kurfürstendamm to the door. Central location. Something of a zoo.

Jugendhotel Berlin, Kurfürstenstrasse 132, Berlin 30 (tel. 261 17 87). A bed in a 6-bed room will cost 18DM, breakfast 7DM extra. Registration is from 9am-6pm. Take the U-Bahn to Nollendorfplatz. Geared primarily for group tours.

Camping: Zeltplatz Kohlhasenbrücke, corner of Neue Kreisstrasse and Stubenrauchstrasse, 1 Berlin 39 (tel. 805 17 37). Expect to pay 3DM per person over the base fee of 3.20DM. The Verkehrsamt keeps an updated listing of camping facilities.

HOTELS AND PENSIONS

Pensions cluster around Uhlandstrasse, Fasanenstrasse, and Meinekestrasse. If you prefer not to use the room-finding service at the Verkehrsamt, try these streets first. The following pensions are clean and fairly friendly. Some pensions lower their prices in off-season.

Pension Christine, Uhlandstrasse 142 (tel. 87 30 46) near U-Bhf. Hohenzollernplatz. Singles 22-25DM; doubles 40DM, with reductions for stays over one night, breakfast 5DM. Recommended. Couple running it speaks English readily.

Pension Bamberg, Bamberger Strasse 53 near U-Bhfs. Augsburger Strasse and Wittenbergplatz (tel. 2 11 78 77). Spacious doubles on quiet street 35DM, bath included. Breakfast 4.50-5.00DM.

Hotel Mix, Rütlistrasse 31-36, behind Pflügerstrasse 29-31 (tel. 6 23 58 83). On a quiet, tree-lined street in the old residential neighborhood of Neukölln. 25DM per person including breakfast. U-Bhf to Hermannplatz.

Pension Riga, Rankestrasse 23 (tel. 2 11 12 23), singles 25DM, doubles 38DM, bath included.

Pension Nickel, corner of Fasanenstrasse and Meierottostrasse (tel. 8 81 87 56). Singles 25-30DM, doubles 50-60DM. The landlady serves tea every afternoon, which gives her a chance to tell you the history of Berlin. Recommended for travelers who are tired of stand-offish Berliners.

Food

Real bargains are the **Mensas.** The one at the **Freie Universität** is on Van't-Hoff-Strasse; the **Technische Universität's** is at Hardenbergstrasse 34. Full meals (only at midday during vacation) for 2-3DM.

Across from Bahnhof Zoo on Joachimstaler Strasse is the **Speisewagen am Zoo,** an ancient self-service joint with sludgy pea soup for 2.50DM or *wursts* around 2DM; a cheap way to fill yourself up. Beware the town's many "hamburger" pushers—their proud "original American recipe" is ninety percent soy and oatmeal.

There are two local beer specialties, **Maximator** (or "Maxi"), a potent black brew that tastes like liquid gingerbread, and the famous **Berliner Weisse,** a combination of *Weissbier* and raspberry or mint syrup, that tastes a bit like sweet champagne. *Eisbein* (pickled pig's knuckle) is always served with sauerkraut and *Erbsenpuree,* a solid and tasty split-pea soup. Less expensive are the *Königsberger Klopse,* veal and pork meatballs in a sauce of lemon and capers. In the twenties and thirties, the ladies of high society would meet in the Kudamm cafés for *Kaffee und Kuchen.* The *Konditoreien,* particularly the **Kranzler** at Joachimstaler Strasse, have maintained their prices and tradition, but equally good pastry can be found more cheaply in the side streets. Also worth noting are Berlin's hundreds of *Kneipen* (German-style pubs), each with its private, constant clientele.

Diener Tattersall, Grolmanstrasse 47, near the Kudamm. Good solid food at low prices. The cartoons and pictures lining the walls chronicle the boxing days of the late Franz Diener. The crowd is a bit more interesting after 10pm. 6-10DM. Opens at 8pm. Closed in July.

Tegernseer Tönnchen, Mommsenstrasse 34 near Wilmerdorferstrasse. A thoroughly delightful Bavarian restaurant. For a real mountain of food order the *Grosse Schlachtplatte,* an assortment of Bavarian *wursts* for 12DM. Also features a wide selection of beer. On summer nights you can sit outside on the terrace.

Zum Ambrosius, Einemstrasse 14, corner of Kurfürstenstrasse. Good native cuisine with daily local specials from 4.50DM, fat waitresses and a lively beer garden. Open 9am-1am.

Jeruschalajim, Bleibtreustrasse 7, open after 4pm daily. Meals 4-10DM with an excellent selection of salads. Good for vegetarians.

Savigny-Klause, by S-Bhf. Savignyplatz. Persian specialties from 6DM, and sandwiches for 3.50DM.

Sights

West Berlin has two sorts of monuments—the sobering and the soothing. If the gravelike fields around **Anhalter Bahnhof** and the graffiti on the wall (Western side, that is) don't impress you, try the exhibition, at **Haus am Checkpoint Charlie** (entrance 1DM, open 9am-8pm daily), a pictorial history of the city's partition. The central landmark of **Kudamm,** the **Kaiser-Wilhelm-Gedächtniskirche** (known locally as the "lipstick case and powder box") is a graphic symbol of destruction, but go inside for a dazzling confirmation of the city's faith. Over the wall, at the end of **Strasse des 17. Juni** (named for a suppressed revolt in the Eastern Sector in 1953), the **Brandenburger Tor** can be seen, already the symbol of the German Reich a century ago. Nearby at **Platz der Republik,** the former parliament, the **Reichstag,** has been rebuilt for the second time. A mysterious fire which gutted the building in 1933 allowed Hitler to frame his opposition, but since the reconstruction the Reichstag has housed only a historical museum. The 222-foot **Siegessäule,** a colossal monument to Imperial Prussian conquests, peers ironically onto a more modest thanksgiving plaque to the Soviet liberators of the city.

All of the historical center is housed in a vast and beautiful park called the **Tiergarten,** old hunting grounds of the Prussian Kings, but even better retreats from urban tension lie further west. In the summer the sailboats and sandy beaches of **Wannsee** will clear your head of politics, as will the birch forests of **Grunewald.** Take the boat trip from **Tegel** to **Pfaueninsel** and visit the palace's collection of exotic birds. **Charlottenburg** is the vast rococo palace and garden which Frederick I built for his wife Sophie-Charlotte. Since Sanssouci is in Potsdam, East Germany, Charlottenburg is the most accessible of the great Prussian residences.

Daytrips to Lübars and Spandau are also refreshing. These were the last two villages to be incorporated into Berlin, and have struggled to remain distinctive.

To see it all in one day, take one of the boat trips leaving Kottbusser Brücke (a bridge in Kreuzberg) at 9:10 and 9:30am. The trip costs 6.50DM, and takes you through Kreuzberg, by Charlottenburg, Spandau, Pfaueninsel, and, late in the afternoon, back to Kreuzberg.

MUSEUMS

Berlin's museums tend to cluster around **Dahlem-Dorf** and the Charlottenburg Palace. A free listing of all museums is available at the Tourist Office.

Dahlem Museum, Arnimallee 23-27 (tel. 8 30 11) is actually a complex of seven independent museums, each of which would be worth a separate half-day visit: Ethnography, Indian Art, Far Eastern Art, Islamic Art, Sculpture, Prints and Drawings, and Paintings. The last is the most frequented for its spectacular collection of Italian, German, Dutch, and Flemish old masters. Open Tues.-Sun. 9am-5pm. Take U-Bahn #2 to Dahlem-Dorf.

The **Reichstag Building's** German history exhibit is an interesting, largely photographic exposition of Germany's recent past, good and bad, leading to the formation of the Federal Republic in 1949. If you're planning to head over to East Berlin later, note the different ways this exhibit and the one at the Museum für Deutsche Geschichte on Unter den Linden treat the same events.

Schloss Charlottenburg contains several museums, all open daily 9am-5pm, closed Friday. Exceptions are noted below. The 34-century-old bust of Queen Nefertiti is the star attraction at the **Egyptian Museum,** open Sat.-Thurs. 9am-5pm, closed Friday. The **Antikenabteilung** houses Greek, Etruscan and Roman gold, silver and ceramics; the **Museum für Vor und Frühgeschichte** shows special archaeological exhibits; and the **Museum für Gestaltung** contains the large archives of the Bauhaus movement. Take U-Bahn #1 to Sophie-Charlotte-Platz and walk up Schlossstrasse.

Entertainment

West Berlin has one of the world's best symphony orchestras, the best German dramatic theater, an excellent conservatory, and enough of anything else a culture lover might desire. The annual international **Film Festival** occurs in late June/early July, followed by an intense week of concerts, the **Bachtage** in mid-July, and the **Berliner Jazztage** and **Berliner Festwochen** in September. Throughout the summer the Neue Nationalgalerie sponsors **Jazz in the Garden.** Information on all of these events is given in *Berlin Programm.* For student tickets to most (not all) events, check the **Theater-kasse** of the Technische Universität. Hardenbergstrasse 34, open weekdays 11am-2pm. *Tip Magazine* (2DM) gives biweekly student entertainment listings.

Deutsche Oper Berlin, Bismarckstrasse 34/37, U-Bhf. Deutsche Oper (tel. 3 41 44 49). Box office is open from 10am-2pm daily; and an hour before the performance. Ten minutes before the performance you can get student reductions—up to 50% off depending on the price of the ticket, and prices range from 5DM up.

Philharmonie, Kemper-Platz (tel. 2 61 43 83). Bus #29 from Kudamm to Potsdamerstrasse, and then it's a short walk. The Berliner Philharmonisches Orchester is the best in the world, and the hall is an acoustic wonder. The Philharmonic is usually sold out and when von Karajan is conducting, it is even more difficult to get tickets. Nevertheless, it is definitely worth trying. Check an hour before concert time.

Schiller-Theater, Bismarckstrasse 110 (tel. 3 19 52 36), has a vast repetoire including experimental productions. Even with no knowledge of the language, the drama will be worth it. Box office open 10am-2pm and an hour before curtain; U-Bahn #1 to Ernst-Reuter-Platz.

Stachelschweine, Europa Center (tel. 2 61 47 95), and **Wühlmäuse,** Nürnberger Strasse 33 (tel. 2 13 70 47), are Berlin's sophisticated political cabarets. Unfortunately, your German must be equally sophisticated. Tickets from 10DM, less with student ID. **Go-In,** Bleibtreustrasse 17 (tel. 8 81 72 18), is a literary cabaret specializing largely in international folk songs; entrance varies with performance, 0-5DM, student reductions.

The student district begins around S-Bhf Savingy platz and includes **Bleibtreustrasse, Schlüterstrasse** and **Knesebeckstrasse.** Only a short walk from Bhf. Zoo, this area is the best place to meet people in West Berlin. One of the liveliest beer gardens is **Jahrmarkt.** Bleibtreustrasse 49, along the S-Bahn tracks. Some of the popular wine places are:

E. & M. Leydicke, Mansteinstrasse 4, near S-Bhf. Grossgörschenstrasse and U-Bhf. Yorckstrasse (tel. 2 16 29 73). An inexpensive wine cellar very popular with students. Far out in Schöneberg.

Leierkasten, Zossenerstrasse (U-Bahn line #7 to Gneisenaustrasse, tel 6 91 27 00), is like nothing else—one of the last of the old *Berliner Kneipen.* Even its name comes from the old organ grinders who used to populate Berlin's streets. Because of the great food and excellent jazz, it has become a popular student locale. The section of town, Kreuzberg, is not the best, and women are advised not to go alone through the streets. Cover 2DM Fri. and Sat.

Eirschale Berlin, U-Bhf Podbielskiallee in Dahlem. Food from noon on, jazz from 7pm on. On Sundays, jazz and food are also available from 10:30am-6pm. This area is the hunting ground for Freie Universität students, and is worth exploring.

Loretta's Garden, Lintzenburgerstrasse, at the foot Knesebeckstrasse. Go where the Germans go, but bring extra money. Probably the best place if you're feeling isolated as a tourist.

EAST GERMANY

$1 U.S.= 1.72 marks(M)   **1M=$.58**

A trip through the German Democratic Republic (GDR) will pit you against some of the worst bureaucratic hassles in Eastern Europe, but you may be amply rewarded for your trials. East Germany's contradictions are fascinating. The cities are clean, safe, and free from the physical decay that characterizes Western capitals, and even nearby Prague. Meanwhile, much of the countryside has been spoiled by industrialization. In one of the least liberal of the Soviet bloc countries, East Germans show a spread of political opinions as diverse as is found in America. The GDR strictly controls the importation of printed material (West German calendars are banned because they note June 17 as Unity Day, signifying hope for a reunited Germany), but its Evangelical church is healthy and active, a far cry from Czechoslovakia's struggling underground sects.

The villages skirting **East Berlin** maintain much of their pre-war character. **Dresden**, on the other hand, is cosmopolitan and refined. **Erfurt,**

Eisenach and **Naumburg** have preserved all the medieval glory of Old Germany. The **Thüringer Wald** and the **Harz Mountains** are national tourist resorts with a national character. If you're coming from Scandinavia, cross to **Warnemünde** or **Sassnitz** and visit Germany's oldest trading ports, **Wismar, Greifswald,** and **Stralsund,** or drive through the unspoiled **Mecklenburg Lake District.** If on the way to Poland or Czechoslovakia, visit the spas of the rugged **Erzgebirge** and the **Sächsische Schweiz,** or stop in **Meissen,** where porcelain manufacture was invented and continues today.

PRACTICAL INFORMATION

For details on the easily obtained day-visa for East Berlin, see our section on that city. If you wish to stay longer in the GDR, you must arrange for accommodations before arriving. There are several ways that this can be done.

It is no longer possible for individual travelers to book in advance for youth hostels. (A group of ten or more can do so by writing at least two months in advance to **Jugendtourist,** Haus des Reisens, 1025 East Berlin, Alexanderplatz 5, stating the number of people, the proposed itinerary, and the precise dates desired. The cost is 7-8M per person per night, which is paid upon arrival in East Berlin. It is unlikely that Jugendtourist will give you your itinerary exactly as requested, so it is best to propose alternatives.) We recommend that individuals desiring to stay in hostels apply for camping visas. These enable you to stay in any campground in a given district *(Bezirk)* for the dates specified, but if you find a hostel in the district with room, it is legal to stay there. However, when applying for the visa, you may be asked to prove that you have camping equipment. This proposition may not sound reassuring; but if you have camping equipment, it should work pretty well, allowing you flexibility at a relatively low cost. Try to wrangle a list of hostels in the GDR from Jugendtourist.

Foreigners may reserve space in any of roughly three dozen camping sites. You are required to pay the hard currency equivalent of 20M per person per day in advance (children under 16 excluded), for which you will receive a voucher. When the voucher and reservations are presented at the border, you will be handed cash in the prepaid amount, from which the visa fee of 15M and the camping fees of 3-15M per night will be deducted. Write at least two months in advance to **Reisebüro der DDR** at the same address as Jugendtourist. In West Germany, visit any branch of the **Deutsches Reisebüro (DER)** at least two months beforehand. If you decide to stay in a hostel, expect to pay about 8M; your camping fees, needless to say, will not be refunded. Camping grounds are open only between May 1 and September 30.

The easiest and costliest alternative is to stay at **Interhotels,** a chain expressly for foreigners, costing about $20 per night. Contact Koch Overseas Co., 206-8 East 86th St., New York, NY 10028 (tel. (212) 535-8600) or Krueger's Travel Service, 6507 Bergenline Ave., West New York, NJ 07093 (tel. (201) 868-9623). Note that accommodations must always be paid for in Western currency, even if booked upon arrival in East Berlin. Once you've paid for your Interhotel accommodations, you are not required to change any more currency. The Reisebüro der DDR occasionally has rooms for foreigners at less expensive hotels. You can inquire about this, or any other travel matters, at Window 13 on the second floor of the Haus des Reisens, Alexanderplatz 5 (tel. 2 15 44 02).

If you're traveling through the GDR en route to a neighboring country, you will be issued a one-way transit visa at the border for 5M. An overnight interruption is possible only with a stay in an Interhotel; ask at the border about *Transit Verlängern*. Do not under any circumstances try freelance camping or looking for accommodations in a city for which you have no visa. Driving in the GDR is not restricted. The International Green Card is recognized, but foreigners must also purchase GDR insurance at the border and pay a toll *(Strassenbenutzungsgebühr)* of 5M per 100 km. When you enter, ask for a map of **Intertank** stations, or purchase **Intertank coupons.**

Hitchhiking is forbidden in East Germany.

Neither Eurailpass nor InterRail is valid. Trains are extremely crowded, so try to buy a seat reservation (1M), or a couchette (5.80M) on overnight trains. Note that for any train leaving the GDR you *must* have a reservation.

Whatever your mode of travel in the GDR, do not try to bring any extra East Marks in with you, and stay away from any sort of black market transactions while there. Currency smuggling and illegal exchanges are serious offenses (just for your information, though, one Western mark brings four GDR marks on the black market). You must declare all Western currency you have upon entering the GDR, and totals of receipts and money are occasionally checked when leaving. Finally, travel reading should be limited if at all possible to travel guides and maps. Literature can be brought along only if it is not "harmful to the interests of the GDR," but what this is supposed to mean is left to the discretion of the individual guard controlling you at the border.

East Berlin

Filled with broad, open expanses of concrete and metal, East Germany's "new" capital is certainly impressive and modern, but also a little ridiculous, like Ozymandias' statue in the desert. No matter what your politics are, you may well find East Berlin a little creepy. Drab colors, hushed voices, and stern-looking *"Vopos" (Volkspolizei)* pervade the middle of the city. The problem has something to do with the feeling that everything is on display—both to the numerous Russian visitors and to the Western world. But the story changes as soon as you get into the surrounding *Vororte* (suburbs). Here you can find good food at low prices, attractive streets, and relaxed people. Or, for a closer refuge from the atmosphere downtown, head for one of Berlin's fabulous art museums.

One-Day Visas

The rules for visiting East Berlin on a day-visa have become quite simple. For foreigners there are two entrances, both open 7am-8pm: **Checkpoint Charlie** (officially Friedrichstrasse/Zimmerstrasse) for pedestrians and drivers, and **Bahnhof Friedrichstrasse** (pedestrians only), accessible from the S-Bahn or U-Bahn #6. The Friedrichstrasse Station entrance tends to be more crowded than Checkpoint Charlie, and requires the ability to count in German, since pass-numbers are read over a loudspeaker in the waiting room between the *Passkontrolle* and customs.

Be prepared to present a valid passport and to complete a customs declaration *(Erklärung),* including a list of all currencies and gifts of value which you are carrying into the country. The day-visa, valid until midnight, costs 5DM (Western currency only) and there is a mandatory exchange requirement of an additional 6.50DM—at the official rate of 1 East mark for 1 West mark. If you are carrying much baggage, expect a customs search; printed matter in particular may cause trouble. (The *Vopos* are usually polite, but thorough!)

Your day-visa expires at midnight and requires that you exit at the same crossing where you entered. Officially the visa is valid only for travel within the district of Berlin itself, but elsewhere in the country papers are not checked, so that a daytrip to **Potsdam,** for example, is easy. When you leave, have all papers—passport, customs declaration with completed exit portion, visa *(Anlage zum Pass),* and currency exchange receipts—ready to hand to the successive officials in line. (Don't lose any of these documents before leaving.) If you entered on a day-visa but want to stay longer, you should proceed immediately to the Reisebüro der DDR, Alexanderplatz 5 (tel. 2 15 44 02). Once they have made reservations for you (payable in Western currency), you can obtain a tourist visa for 15M.

Orientation

The two checkpoints (both on Friedrichstrasse) straddle the intersection of Friedrichstrasse and Unter den Linden, the one-time center of the city. East of this intersection are the two new focal points of the city—the **Museumin-sel** (Museum Island), which boasts the new Parliament Building, the *Dom* (Old Cathedral), and the four main Berlin museums; and the **Alexan-derplatz,** the new commercial center. Seven outlying districts surround **Bezirk Mitte** (central district of the city), some of which deserve as much attention as the middle—particularly **Pankow** and **Köpenick.**

The extremely efficient system of public transportation in East Berlin allows you to travel to all parts of the city relatively easily. Travel on the tram, bus or U-Bahn costs only .20M, and five-ride tickets can be purchased at most U-Bahn stations. Payment is on the honor system—you have to have a ticket or change ready to put into the pay-box in the bus or at the entrance to an U-Bahn station. Pull the lever on the pay-box and tear off a ticket. You can transfer within the U-Bahn network on the same ticket, but for transfers from bus to U-Bahn you have to take a new ticket. S-Bahn rates are deter-mined according to distance traveled, ranging from .20M *(Preisstufe 1)* within the downtown area to .50M *(Preisstufe 3)* for longer distances.

Newsstands sell a biweekly booklet *Wohin in Berlin* for .30M, which includes complete schedules of events.

You may be approached in the streets or on the Alexanderplatz by people wanting to change money or by beggars. If you give out any Western currency, it may well be brought to the nearest *Vopo,* and you will be ushered to a police bureau or the border. Also, be sure to get a stamped confirmation *(Bestätigung)* for any Western currency you may pay out for gifts, tickets, etc.

Addresses and Telephone Numbers

Informationszentrum am Fernsehturm (Tourist Information): underneath the TV tower next to Alexanderplatz (open Mon. 1-7pm, Tues.-Sat. 9am-7pm, Sun. 10am-6pm; tel. 2 12 46 75). A second office is across from Bahnhof Friedrichstrasse (tel. 2 07 12 04), and a third is the Reisebüro der DDR.

Reisebüro der DDR: Alexanderplatz 5 (tel. 2 15 44 02). They can answer any question, if you can tolerate the lines. Train tickets and reservations are also available here, but it's faster to buy them at the appropriate station. If you wish to extend your stay in the GDR, the Reisebüro is occasionally able to get you a place at hotels less expensive than the Interhotels. Open Mon., Tues., Fri. 8:30am-5:30pm; Wed. 10am-5:30pm; Thurs. 8:30am-7pm; and Sat. 9am-1pm. Foreigners' Service *(Ausländer-Service)* open daily 7am-10pm at window 13 on the second floor.

Currency Exchange: The Reisebüro, Alexanderplatz; or at Bahnhof Friedrichstrasse; or the Ostbahnhof.

Volkspolizei (Police): (tel. 110). It is highly unlikely that you will need to call the police—they are everywhere.

U.S. Embassy: 108 Schadowstrasse 4, just off Unter den Linden (tel. 2 20 27 41). Stop by and let them know you're here if you're staying in the GDR for a while.

British Embassy: Unter den Linden 32-34 (tel. 2 20 24 31).

Food

Food in Berlin, as in the GDR as a whole, is generally unspectacular, and if you want variety, stay downtown. Note that there is no such thing as a private table—if a place is free, you are expected to take it or let it be taken, and groups larger than two may be split. It is customary to tip by "rounding up" about 10%.

GDR students are frustrated by Berlin's lack of student *Lokale,* but there is some hope that **Zur Letzten Instanz** will reopen soon on Waisenstrasse (at the foot of Parochialstrasse, tucked in behind the Haus der Jungen Talente).

The many **Schnell-Imbisse** offer quick, stand-up service at dirt-cheap prices. Try the new complex on Karl-Liebknecht-Str. across the street from the Fernsehturm. The **Agrar-Spezial** is a good place to buy fresh food, and the **Café Alex Treff** in Alexanderplatz offers inexpensive, if bland, cafeteria-style eating.

Ratskeller, Rathausstrasse, located in the basement of the Rote Rathaus, the old city hall, is a good place to meet young people and eat under 5M. Try the *Käseplatte* (cheese plate). Open 9am-midnight.

Gastmahl des Meeres, Spandauer Strasse 4 at Karl-Liebknecht-Str. is a fish restaurant noted for quick service and meals for 3-6M. Open 11am-9pm.

Hotel Restaurant Sofia, Friedrichstrasse 136, walk about a block north from the S-Bahnhof. Features Bulgarian food for 4-7M. Open 7am-midnight.

Operncafé, Unter den Linden 5, and **Linden-Corso Café,** Unter den Linden 17, are perhaps the two best cafés in Berlin, GDR. Operncafé open 10am-midnight, closed 6:30-7:30pm Wed.-Sun. Linden-Corso Café open 9am-midnight.

Sights

Turn right on Friedrichstrasse when leaving the S- and U-Bahnhof Fried-richstrasse, or walk straight ahead from Checkpoint Charlie to reach **Unter den Linden.** This spacious avenue, with a **triumphal arch** at one end and the Cathedral at the other, was the Champs-Élysées of Brecht's Berlin.

Very little goes on west of Friedrichstrasse. At the now-sealed end of Unter den Linden stands the **Brandenburger Tor.** In an open field to the left of the Tor is **Hitler's bunker.** Facing back towards the middle of town, you see the Soviet Embassy immediately to the right, quiet but imposing.

Proceeding along Unter den Linden east of Friedrichstrasse, you will pass the **Staatsbibliothek** (State Library), and **Humboldt University** (whose alumni include Hegel, Marx, and Einstein). Permission is required to attend classes, but no one will stop you from making friends in the large entrance vestibule. The columned **Deutsche Staatsoper** (Opera House) is to the right; to the left stands the **Monument to the Victims of Fascism and Militarism,** which features guards who goose-step at the half-hour changes.

The bridge connecting Unter Den Linden with its extension, Karl Liebknecht-Strasse, crosses the **Spree,** the river running through Berlin. Bounded on one side by the Spree and facing onto Marx-Engels-Platz is the **Museuminsel,** one of the major attractions in Berlin, GDR. It includes the **Neues Museum,** the **Pergamon Museum,** the **National Galerie,** and the **Altes Museum** (see Museums). The **Dom,** also on the Museuminsel, was built in 1904, a whim of Kaiser Wilhelm II. Its grotesqueness was only heightened by bomb damage during the war. Proceeding along on Karl-Liebknecht-Strasse, you can see on your right the **Rotes Rathaus,** the big red town hall, which has long been famous as a symbol of Berlin. Across the street is the **Marienkirche,** Berlin's oldest church, dating back to the thir-teenth century. Its stark simplicity is striking. In the entrance hall is a fresco, a *Dance of Death,* probably originating from the plague epidemic at the end of the fifteenth century.

Dominating the skyline is the **Fernsehturm,** the huge television and ob-servation tower nicknamed the *Spargel* (asparagus) by the Berliners. For 3M (students 1.50M) you can take an elevator to the top of this symbol of the "new" Germany. The tower is open daily 8am-10:30pm. Permission to take pictures costs a mark extra. Beyond the tower opens the main shopping square of modern Berlin, the **Alexanderplatz.**

The Jewish community maintains two telling monuments to its fate under the Nazis. The once splendid **Synagogue,** Oranienburger Strasse 31, is an empty shell, and the **Jewish Cemetery,** Schönhauser Allee at Senefelder Platz, also remains as Hitler left it, if slightly more overgrown; open Mon.-Thurs. 8am-4pm, Fri. 8am-1pm.

An indication of somewhat more recent national trials is the **Soviet War Memorial** at S-Bahnhof Treptower Park, a mammoth promenade built with marble taken from Hitler's destroyed Chancellery. The Soviets built the site in 1948, dedicated it to the memory of the soldiers of the Red Army who fell in the Second World War, and adorned massive granite slabs along the walk with quotations from Stalin. For a sense of the historical roots of the GDR, the memorial is a must.

Also in Treptower Park are the docks of the **Weisse Flotte,** the ship service which can take you on a pleasant journey around the waterways in the city. For information and reservations, check with the **Verkehrspavillon Treptow,** at the dock (tel. 27120), or with the **Städtischer Nahverkehr-Service,** S-Bahnhof Alexanderplatz, tel. 2 46 22 55.

The most valuable excursion is to **Potsdam,** the old imperial residence, technically not on your day-visa, but then no one will check. Take the S-Bahn (direction **Erkner** or **Friedrichshagen**) to Karlshorst, then change for a double-decker train to Potsdam Hauptbahnhof. Trains leave every hour in either direction; the journey takes about fifty minutes and costs .70M each way.

MUSEUMS

Student reductions are available, but you may be asked to show an IUS card (the ISIC is not recognized in the GDR). Since this happens only rarely, always ask for the student price.

The most important group of museums is on the **Museuminsel.** For only 1.05M, you can buy a three-day pass to all of these museums (buy the ticket at Berolinahaus, Alexanderplatz 1, or at the Reisebüro.) All four are open Wed.-Sun. 9am-6pm. For museum information dial 2 20 03 81. The **Pergamon Museum,** a complex in itself, houses collections of Near Eastern, Islamic, and East Asian art, as well as an extensive collection of Greek and Roman sculpture, including the Pergamon Altar and the Ishtar Gate. Behind the museum is the domed **Bodes Museum.** According to GDR authorities, West Berlin stole the bust of Nefertiti from the Bode. But even without it, the Bode has one of the best Egyptian collections in the world.

In the **Altes Museum,** you will find a collection of social-realist paintings, together with prints by northern Renaissance masters. To see the Albrecht Dürer holdings in the archives, walk around to the building's east entrance (nearest the *Dom*) and present your passport. In the **National Galerie** resides a collection of works by nineteenth- and twentieth-century German artists, covering art from expressionism to the present.

There are three other museums of note. The **Museum für Geschichte** covers German history from 1789 to 1949, from a Marxist, pro-Russian standpoint. Open Mon.-Thurs. 8am-7pm and Sat.-Sun. 9am-4pm. The **Märkisches Museum,** Am Köllnischen Park 5 (open Wed.-Sat. 9am-5pm, Sun. 9am-6pm), details the history of Berlin from prehistoric settlement to socialist capital. The organs and pianos of the automatic instrument collection are demonstrated Wednesday at 11am and Sunday at 4pm. The **Museum Im Schloss Köpenick** presents choice examples of German furniture and jewelry, porcelain, and leatherwork. It's rarely crowded; open Wed.-Sat. 9am-5pm, Sun. 10am-6pm. Take the S-Bahn to Köpenick, then bus #27 or tram #83.

Evenings

In Berlin, students and workers tend not to mix. Most of the bars, which cluster around the theater district across the river from the Bahnhof Friedrichstrasse, are filled with older locals from early hours on. The last two mentioned below attract younger crowds, but you may find more West Berliners than Easterners in them.

Seglerheim, Regattastrasse 117 in Grünau. If you're staying at the Grünau hostel, the best place to eat and drink with the locals. Go *early* if you're hungry—they don't get high priority on food deliveries and run out fast.

Zum Wein ABC, Schiffbauerdamm 8, is lively even though it only serves wine. Open 5pm-1am, closed Sun. and Mon.

Kleine Melodie, Friedrichstrasse 127. Open Mon., Wed., Thurs. 9pm-4am; Fri. and Sat. 8pm-4am; Sun. 9pm-3am. A lively discotheque. Sometimes charges a 2.50M entrance fee.

Theater and music abound and can be of very high quality. In the summer, check the posters and *Wohin in Berlin* for notices of concerts in the courtyard of the old Arsenal, on the Schlossinsel Köpenick, or in the parks. The **Berliner Sinfonie-Orchester** (tel. 2 07 11 70) performs in various halls, notably the Metropol-Theater (tel. 2 07 17 39). Advance tickets for most performances are available at **Zentralbesucherdienst der Berliner Bühnen,** Oranienburger Strasse 50, off Friedrichstrasse (tel. 2 82 45 07). Open Mon. 1-5pm; Tues.-Wed. 10am-1pm and 2-5pm; Thurs. 10am-1pm and 2-7pm; Fri. 10am-1pm and 2-5pm.

Deutsche Staatsoper, Unter den Linden 7 (tel. 2 00 04 91) about a ten-minute walk from Bahnhof Friedrichstrasse. Tickets range from 3-15M. If you join the Russian generals and others attending an evening performance, you can expect a real treat. In addition to opera there is ballet, performances of major sacred works, and orchestra and chamber music. *Kasse* (box office) open noon-6pm weekdays, weekends 4-6pm, again 1½ hours before each performance.

Haus der Jungen Talente, Klosterstrasse 68-70 (tel. 2 10 92 01), is a place where young musicians, groomed for future stardom, offer concerts. Tickets are virtually free for students.

Berliner Ensemble, at Bertolt-Brecht Platz (tel. 2 82 58 71)—turn left out of Bahnhof Friedrichstrasse, tickets 3-12M. This world-famous theater was established by Bertolt Brecht and still specializes in his plays. If your German is up to it, it is definitely worthwhile.

Potsdam

After Frederick the Great selected Potsdam as his permanent residence in 1744, the town grew into one of the greatest imperial seats in Europe. The 600-acre **Sanssouci Park** alone houses four castles and countless pavilions. The **Neues Palais,** the second castle to be built, is the largest, and although less filled with gilded nymphs than cherubs than Sanssouci itself, it is a better place to judge the vagaries of Rococo taste. Check the billboards for oper performances in the Palace Theater; tickets are available one hour beforehand.

Charlottenhof is a prime example of early Romanticism; the unassuming building is designed as part of the landscape and is surrounded by grape arbors. Above the **Sicilian Garden** hovers the **Orangerie.** Built in a pseudo-Italian style, this palace is famous for its **Raffaelsaal** with 67 dubious copies after the Italian master. The best joke on the grounds is the **Chinesisches Teehaus,** a gold-plated opium dream. The Buddha on the roof looks like Neptune with a parasol. All the major buildings are open daily 9am-5pm in summer, and admission varies from .50M to 1.60M, half-price for students (IDs rarely demanded).

Except for the omnipresence of Soviet troops, modern Potsdam hasn't changed much since the war. Many of the old patrician houses around the **Stadttor** (now **Platz der Nationen**) have been restored to their original beauty, but even the rundown back streets have a timeless quality. The **Wochenmarkt** (farmer's market), along Am Bassin near Platz der Einheit, is held Tuesday and Thursday 5am-1pm, Friday noon-5pm and Saturday 5am-noon.

Food

All of the sights have **Schnell-Imbisse** nearby, usually open 10am-6pm, which offer *Bockwurst* and beer. For better food or more atmosphere, we recommend: **Zur Fähre,** Berliner Strasse 149 (take tram #3 from Platz der Einheit). A family operation with strictly local clientele and good filling meals for 3-5M. Open Wed.-Sat. 3-11pm, Sun. 10am-6pm.

The best place to drink with the locals is **Schwarzer Adler,** Gutenbergstrasse 9 (off Friedrich-Ebert-Strasse). Closes at 9pm, but the guests are all drunk by 6:00 and the stories they tell are fantastic.

Dresden

Berlin may be the administrative center of the GDR, but Dresden is its *Kunststadt,* its artistic and architectural gem. Ruins still dot the city center, yet there is enough elegance and grace here to make Dresden worth the two-hour trip from the capital. Famous as the seat of the Elector of Saxony and later of the rulers of the Kingdom of Saxony, Dresden was long known as one of Germany's major cultural centers. The city was all but levelled by British and American bombing raids in the night of February 14, 1945, at a time when the Allied victory was virtually assured. This has become a propaganda point, and the museums abound with placards thanking Soviet liberators for having preserved Dresden's art treasures. It is not clear how Dresdeners take all this—they often seem more polite to English speakers than to Russians. But it is clear that they have not decided to nurse those very deep wounds. They are obviously at ease in their city, with its striking mixture of contemporary architecture, restoration, and ruin.

Orientation

An important first step should be the **Dresden Information Center,** Pragerstrasse 10/11 (tel. 44031, open Mon.-Sat. 9am-8pm, Sun. 9am-2pm) about a five-minute walk from the main Train Station in the pedestrian zone past the Interhotel Newa. Here you can buy a city map as well as a copy of *Dresden-Information,* which includes program listings for theaters and concerts. Information is available here about area excursions to the **Sächsische Schweiz** or **Meissen.** Money can be changed here or at the Hauptbahnhof. Note that most trains to the east leave from a second station, **Bahnhof Neustadt,** across the river. Bus and tram tickets have to be bought in advance and are available at most major intersections; a six-ride *Sammelkarte* costs 1M. Dresden is filled with tourists, mostly Russian, and on weekends the galleries become packed.

Sights

The gorgeous Baroque palace **Zwinger** now contains half of Dresden's museums. (The name "Zwinger" comes from the German slang for "prison"—August the Strong reputedly built the palace as a domicile for his sixty concubines.) The painting collection **Gemäldegalerie Alte Meister** (open daily 9am-6pm, closed Mon.) is one of Europe's oldest and best; its star piece is the *Sixtine Madonna* of Raphael. The **Historisches Museum** is an ornamental weapon collection (open 9am-5pm except Wednesdays), and the **Mathematisch Physikalischer Salon** is for sextant fiends. The **Zinnsammlung** and **Porzellansammlung** trace the decorative history of Dresden's two most famous crafts, pewter and porcelain (both open daily 9am-4pm and 10am-4pm, respectively, except Fridays).

Across the street from Zwinger are the ruins of the old residential **palace of Saxony's electors and kings.** This decrepit complex continues to embrace the Catholic Cathedral (**Katholische Hofkirche),** which allows an interesting comparison with the Protestant church in the Altmarkt. On the wall of the alley leading to the main entrance of the Catholic Cathedral is the *Fürstenzug* (Procession of Kings), pictorially tracing the rule of Saxony (and giving each prince's epithet) from the Middle Ages.

From the other side of the Hofkirche runs a high, fortified embankment, the **Brühl'sche Terrasse.** Behind the terrace once rose Germany's most splendid Protestant church, the **Frauenkirche,** whose ruins have been left as a memorial to the city's destruction. The **Albertinum,** which stands at the terrace's far end, is Dresden's other museum complex. The **Gemäldegalerie Neue Meister** doesn't quite measure up to the old, and the **Skulpturensammlung** consists mostly of Roman copies of Greek works. But the **Grünes Gewölbe,** the Saxon treasury, contains some of Europe's greatest hand work. The **Münzkabinett** is a history of European coinage, and the Albertinum's front rooms hold special exhibitions.

Across the Elbe from the Zwinger is Dresden's **Neustadt,** paradoxically now the oldest part of the city because it escaped the totality of the bombing. The **Goldener Ritter,** a gold-plated statue of August II, usually stands in the Markt, but has been temporarily removed during the building of some prefab housing around it. The streets to the west of the Markt retain much of their nineteenth-century flavor, and make an interesting walk. Readers of Vonnegut can take a tram directly to the slaughterhouses *(Schlachthofring),* which don't look like they have changed since the war. Take tram #10 from the Hauptbahnhof.

Northwest of Dresden, **Meissen,** on the Elbe, was once the seat of Saxon bishops and counts. The town, which can be reached by a steamer ship from Dresden, has retained its Renaissance flavor. 1M by train from the Hauptbahnhof, .50M from the Radebeul hostel. Or if the weather is good and you can spare the two hours, the **Weisse Flotte** boats run twice daily from the Brühl'sche Terrasse for 1.45M. The intricate Gothic **Dom** was built between 1200-1400 on the foundations of an even older cathedral. **Albrechtsburg,** next to the Dom, the castle of Meissen's counts, was built in the fifteenth century. Its rooms have been made into a museum, and particularly impressive is a spiral staircase leading up to a tower in the castle. Meissen is best known for its porcelain, and you can visit the factory, **Staatliche Porzellan-Manufactur,** where guided tours (Tues.-Sun. 8am-4pm) demonstrate how a 250-year-old tradition is preserved.

Dresden's camping grounds are quite far from the city generally, so if you want to visit here, push hard for a bed in the **Radebeul Hostel.** And if you're visiting in the summer, expect long lines wherever you go.

Food

You can eat a full meal relatively inexpensively (2.50-6M) at **Gastmahl des Meeres,** at Pernaisches Tor, the big intersection at the end of Thälmannstrasse, and even more cheaply and quickly at the cafeteria next door. Also inexpensive is the **H.O. Gaststätte** next to the new concert hall. On Thälmannstrasse at Postplatz there is a complex of restaurants called **Am**

Zwinger where you can get everything from *Bockwurst* to *cordon bleu* in the *"Weinrestaurant."* Good for splurges are the **Ungarische Gaststätte Szeged** (Hungarian) on the first floor at Ernst-Thälmannstrasse 6, and **Am Gewandhaus,** on Gewandhausstrasse and in the hotel of the same name. The **Körnergarten in Dresden** (take S-Bahn to Körnerplatz in Loschwitz) and **Bärenzwinger** (on Terrassenufer) are student hangouts.

Weimar

Through the patronage of the Dukes of Sachsen-Weimar, this provincial seat blossomed into the capital of German humanism. Once Wieland and Goethe were appointed top government positions here, Germany's other great poets followed. Weimar's notoriety has continued to the present day; in 1919, Friedrich Ebert chose it as the site to endorse the new Republican Constitution, and in the thirties, Hitler erected a concentration camp in nearby Buchenwald.

Upon arrival in Weimar, first visit the **Weimar Informationszentrum,** Marktstrasse 4 (tel. 2173, open Mon. 10am-5pm, Tues.-Fri. 9am-5pm, Sat. 8:30am-noon) and the **Zentralkasse,** Frauentorstrasse 4 (tel. 2945), open daily 8:30am-12:45pm and 1:30-4:30pm, both off the **Marktplatz.** (To get there, take bus #1 from the Station to Goetheplatz, walk left out Geleitstrasse until you come to the Herder Kirche, then walk right along Dimitroffstrasse for a block to the Markt. Around the corner, to the right, is the Information Center.) The Information Center has a limited, but useful, map for 1M, while the Zentralkasse will sell you a pass to eight literary museums for 3M. Individual museum tickets cost 1.05M (students .50M), and are in most cases also available *only* at the Zentralkasse. All museums are open 9am-5pm; they stagger their lunch breaks and days off (Monday or Tuesday), so that something is open at any given time. The Zentralkasse also handles the cultural events of the city; check here for theater and concert tickets. Bus tickets must be bought here or at the Station in advance. Try to arrive in Weimar during the day—it is a little country town and curls up at sundown.

Sights

The most attractive building on the **Marktplatz** is the Renaissance **Lucas-Cranach-Haus** covered with flowers and mermaids. From here walk over **Burgplatz** to the **Schlossmuseum** (open Tues.-Sun. 9am-1pm and 2-6pm; tickets 1.05M, students .50M at the door). The first floor is devoted to Cranach, his son, and their Thuringian contemporaries. It is one of the best places to experience the passionate character of the German Renaissance. The upper floors contain a large but random collection of later paintings. From the Schloss, Vorwerksgasse leads to the Gothic **Herderkirche** (open daily 10:30-11:30am and 2:30-3:30pm), named for the preacher whom Goethe brought to Weimar in the eighteenth century. Nearby on Jakobstrasse 10, is the **Kirms-Krackow-Haus mit Herder-Museum,** a strange attempt to fit the *Sturm und Drang* literary movement of young noblemen—notably Herder, Goethe and Schiller—into a Marxist mold. At the end of the Rittergasse from the church is the **Wittumspalais mit Wieland-Museum,** a museum devoted to the Enlightenment spokesmen in Duchess Anna Amalia's old residence. A block away is the **Schiller-Museum,** on the street named after the dramatist.

Weimar's main attraction is the **Goethe-National museum,** together with the adjoining **Goethe-Wohnhaus** (closed Tuesdays). The museum gives a chronological account of Goethe's life; note the Marxist treatment of *Faust*. The house is fascinating—the back rooms (set now as Goethe prescribed in his will) reveal the image the poet wished to preserve for posterity, while the six front rooms show how Goethe presented himself to his contemporaries. For a glimpse of a more relaxed Goethe, visit **Goethes Gartenhaus im Park,** a simple cottage decorated with the poet's sketches. In the surrounding **Goethepark** are also the **Römisches Haus,** Carl August's neoclassical summer residence, and the **Liszthaus,** where the composer spent the last years of his life. The conservatory he founded, now the **Hochschule für Musik "Franz Liszt,"** holds an international seminar annually in the last two weeks of July, with daily concerts, a treat for those who can attend.

Outside of town is the Rococo **Schloss Belvedere** (open Wed.-Sun. 9am-1pm and 2-5:30pm), one of the retreats of Anna Amalia, Carl August, and their cultured friends. The Belvedere Express Bus leaves from the Goetheplatz every hour on the half-hour, 12:30-6:30pm; and on weekends, every half hour. In the opposite direction from town lies **Buchenwald,** accessible by bus from the Train Station. The government has turned the camp, among whose victims was Communist leader Ernst Thälmann, into a museum.

Food

Weimar, accustomed to fame and tourists, is equipped with many good restaurants. Be warned, though, that they keep strange hours—many open only at meal times (and each seems to have a different idea of what this should be), and few serve anything after 7pm or on weekends. **Gastmahl des Meeres,** on Herderplatz (open Mon.-Fri. 11am-8pm), is an inexpensive fish restaurant. In the **Elephantkeller,** on the Markt (*not* the expensive hotel restaurant), you can also eat well and relatively inexpensively at 3-5M. **Zum Schwarzen Bären,** also on the Markt, is reasonably priced, as is **Zum Weissen Schwann** on Frauentorstrasse, and if it was good enough for Goethe, well. . . . The **Alt Weimar,** Steubenstrasse 27, is inexpensive and less likely to be filled with tourists. **Zum Goldbroiler** in Theater Kasino stays open until 10pm; and **Zum Stadtpark,** Amalienstrasse 21 near the cemetery, is a strictly local place open until 11pm Tues.-Fri.

For a quick beer and a chance to rub shoulders with locals, try the **Weinsanatorium** at Vorwerksgasse 5, or the **Altweimarische Bierstube** on Frauenplan. Local students recommend **Zum Pilsner** at Friedrichstrasse 18. It is also worth dropping by the **Conservatory Mensa** at the end of Geleitstrasse nearest Goetheplatz. Even if they will not let you eat there, you might still pick up times of free student recitals.

Erfurt

Erfurt is the GDR's city of churches. Famed for the **Dom** and **Severi-Kirche** complex, the city also boasts tens of smaller chapels and cloisters, often Gothic. Nevertheless, a German will probably tell you that Erfurt is the *Blumenstadt* (City of Flowers), because it hosts **Iga,** the immense annual flowers-and-crafts exhibition for nations within the Soviet circle.

The entire Old City is a visual delight, with rows of ancient houses sagging into the streets, and an unusually bright, cheerful pedestrian zone, with some beautiful Baroque façades. Erfurt is a short ride from Weimar (half an hour by train), and is well equipped for tourism. To get to the **Information Center,** walk left from the Station and turn right onto the Bahnhofstrasse—the Center is at #37 (open Mon. 10am-noon and 1-6pm; Tues.-Thurs. 9am-noon and 1-6pm; Fri. 9am-noon and 1-7pm; Sat. 9am-12:30pm). Money can be exchanged across the street at the Staatsbank weekdays from 7:30am-6pm.

GREAT BRITAIN

1 U.S. = .48 pounds (£)   1 £ = $2.07

(Note: There is a map of Scotland in the Scotland section of this chapter.)

At one of Queen Elizabeth's Buckingham Palace garden parties (guest lists totalling 21,000) a journalist noted: ''Beneath two elegant canopies, the bands of the Coldstream Guards and Royal Marines bash out hits from *Oklahoma!* and *South Pacific.''* *Oklahoma!* and *South Pacific?* It takes a while to realize just how foreign a country Britain is when something as glorifiedly British as the Queen gets mixed up with something as mundanely American as Rogers and Hammerstein.

You have to give Britain time. The pace of life is slower. Britons won't rush for you—but they also might just wait for you. You'll find most of them friendly, obliging, and chatty, willing to sit down for a pint of ale or a cup of tea to talk with you. Anglo-American overexposure works both ways. To the soft-spoken Britons, the loud, flat American accent is a source of infinite amusement. But once you have pushed aside all the cultural swaps—the American movies, the British pop songs—once you begin to sense that even our language is only partially shared, then you will start to observe more deeply-rooted differences.

279

When you go looking for differences, look to the countryside. (Even during the worst of the summer travel crunch, the provinces are not over-crowded with American tourists.) The British tend to think of their islands as continents in themselves. Fifty miles will take you from one region to another of sharply contrasting character. **Scotland** and **Wales** are in many ways separate countries, although Scots and Welsh nationalists sometimes overestimate the differences.

The countryside is easily approachable: gracious old cities dominated by Gothic cathedrals bigger than most in Europe; country estates with magnifi-cent grounds, homes, and furnishings; and villages snugly nestled into the bends of unmarked roads. But there are also remote, rugged regions, like the moors and the **Scottish Highlands,** rewarding the hiker with solitude and ever-changing vistas.

And traditions continue. A wayfarer's dole (now a crust of bread and a thimbleful of ale) is given out at **Winchester** and **Rochester** as it was 600 years ago; Oxford University Press begins its 501st year publishing books; Shakespearean plays are produced in Elizabethan pubs.

Britain is not the empire it once was—no amount of pomp and cir-cumstance can change that. And while it still has its problems—inflation and racial tension large among them—there is no longer the sense of imminent doom that pervaded the country a few years ago. So whatever you've heard, cast aside your preconceptions, and discover England, Scotland, Northern Ireland, and Wales as they are.

PRACTICAL INFORMATION

Hospitality, not tourism, is Britain's stock in the visitor trade. Bed-and-Breakfast owners welcome you into their homes—not their businesses. Don't forget the common courtesy of saying goodnight to the publican when you leave his pub. Travel in Britain is a series of small, unexpected pleasures—the odd village, the picture in the National Gallery next to the famous ones, the B&B listed in no guidebook, the tea shop providing shelter from the rain.

Bed-and-breakfast homes are really to be considered among Britain's greatest institutions. It may be hard to find anything under £3.50, but you will be provided with a clean room and a good-sized English breakfast (fruit, cereal, eggs, bacon, tomato, toast, marmalade, and tea). The best B&Bs tend to be the smaller enterprises where proprietors will treat you almost like one of the family. But many other proprietors want to preserve their family's privacy. They will ask you not to return to the house before a certain hour in the evening, except in large cities. Bed-and-breakfast places are supposed to be just that—be careful about confusing them with hotel rooms. Most towns have tourist information centers that will provide you with B&B listings and prices, but if you're hunting on your own, ask the price before you take the room. You may want to pick up a copy of *Let's Go: Britain and Ireland,* which lists B&Bs in many British cities and towns.

The alternatives to B&Bs are camping and hosteling. Hostels are generally a good place to meet young Britons; their main disadvantage is their 10:30 pm curfew. They are priced according to your age and their class; for those 21 and older, simple 90p, standard £1.10, superior £1.35; for those under 21, simple 75p, standard 90p, superior £1.10. Camping is a wet proposition in an English summer, but it also may give you the most freedom. Bring a lot of warm clothes and a reliable portable stove.

Where food is concerned, Britain is hardly a nation of connoisseurs. The French like to linger over their meals, prolonging them with endless cups of coffee. The English eat and run. You'll see why when you try their food. An old Yorkshire toast puts it grimly enough: "God bless us all an' mak' us able/to ate the stuff what's on this table." But what you don't get you don't pay for; if the stuff is bad, it's also cheap, though prices are rising rapidly. Local cheeses are excellent; try Stilton (the only English blue cheese), Cheshire and Wensleydale in England; Caerphilly in Wales; Caithness and Orkney in Scotland.

You'll want to have at least one roast beef and Yorkshire pudding and several teas. Teas are the be all and end all of English tradition: high tea, good tea, low tea, thief tea, tea for two or three or four, and—of course—the cream tea.

For pastries try the cream cakes and scones in England and pancakes in Scotland, filled with fresh whipped cream and jam. Britain is justifiably proud of its beer, which is consistently dark and rich, and is usually drunk warm. In addition to the local "bitter," which most pubs carry on tap, you can usually get bottled "stout" (try Newcastle Brown Ale, a very thick and sweet beer), or hard, fizzy cider. Guinness, a thoroughly unique Irish beer, is no good unless you can get it on tap.

Transportation in Britain should pose few problems except cost. Eurail passes are not valid in Great Britain, but InterRail passes are. The state-run train system is comfortable and efficient, and the bus service is equally good. If you plan to travel extensively, you might want to buy a **Britrail pass** before leaving home, offering seven days of unlimited second-class travel for $75; fourteen days for $105; 21 days for $135; and one month for $165. A first-class Britrail pass is somewhat more expensive, and a **Youth Pass** is available to those under 23 at the following rates: $65 for one week, $95 for fourteen days, $120 for three weeks, and $140 for one month. Britrail and Youth passes can be bought in North America; write to **British Rail International,** 630 Third Ave., New York, NY 10017; 510 W. Sixth St., Los Angeles, CA 90014; or 55 Eglinton Ave. E., Toronto, Ont. M4P 1G8. If you're going to be in one area for a week or two, you might do better with regional passes known as **Railrovers.** Other reduced fares throughout the British Isles include day returns (up to 50% reductions) and weekend returns (up to 35%).

The British bus system also has reduced-rate tickets. If you are a foreign citizen (bring your passport), you can purchase a **Coachmaster Ticket** that is the equivalent of the Britrail pass: £23 for eight days, £40 for fifteen days, £63 for 29 days. The only stipulation is that you cannot use the eight-day pass to go directly to Scotland. The local bus companies associated with National Travel often have some kind of day-return or rover tickets as well. All of these are available at **National Travel,** Victoria Coach Station, Buckingham Palace Road, London (tel. 01-730-0202).

Hitchhiking in Great Britain, whether you're leaving London or Edinburgh or are in the middle of the Welsh countryside, is among the best in Europe. Ride waits are rarely long—single or pairs of women have the best luck, next single males and couples. Two guys (though still not bad hitching) might consider hitching separately and meeting at each destination. Unless you're in a really out-of-the-way place, the hitching should be good enough to get you both there within half an hour of each other. We don't advise women to hitch alone, but you'll probably meet more single women hitching here than anywhere on the continent.

London

London thrives on drama, and not all of it is in the theaters. The city presents itself best under lights; from the footlights that come up on Big Ben and Parliament at full moon, to the beams of (rare) sunshine that bleach townhouses white against a backdrop of (typical) storm clouds. The Empire may have declined, but London still feels like the top of the world. Even the people play their parts to a tee. Twice daily, the yeomen of the guard—all hat and no chin—trombone their way through the streets around Buckingham Palace. The Queen, encased in her Rolls Royce, with nary a bow of the head, offers but a hint of a wave for her subjects' applause.

Many Englishmen are horrified by their capital. They find it flashy, foreign, enormous, and congested. They are partially right, of course. For centuries London grew without supervision, out from the walled city; and now its suburbs stretch throughout the "Home Counties" almost to the limits of the island. And more than a million of its seven million residents come from overseas, making London less and less like Britain's provincial cities.

But the amazing thing about London, to Americans at least, is what a civilized place it is. Most buildings are on a human scale. There are over 5000 acres of park land, not including the gems of green squares and half-hidden gardens that crop up everywhere. Maybe because the pace is slower, maybe because of the sprawl, urban manners here are refined. Don't expect gentlemen in bowlers queuing at every double-decker bus stop, but Londoners keep their politeness amidst the bustle. Taxi drivers may grumble, but horns are hardly ever honked.

London strikes some people as unfocused because, with typical English distaste for planning and rationalization, it has no climax. More than most great capitals, London is the sum of thousands of small parts—St. James Park on a summer morning, the back streets of Chelsea on a summer night, the columns of the British Museum mantled with snow, Lincoln's Inn in the rain.

Freddie Laker may have put London on the map for many Americans in 1978. While the situation this summer should be better than last's, you would be wise to do some planning before arriving. London is not an inexpensive city, but it can be managed. The best it has to offer—museums, galleries, theater, and concerts—are either free or cheap by American standards. While an English countryman would warn you not to judge England by London, nor should you judge England without it. London is too good a show to miss.

Orientation

A main branch of the **London Tourist Board** is located in **Victoria Station,** near Platform 15 (open daily 8am-10:30pm in summer, and until 7pm October through April). They have an accommodation service that handles budget rooms; but if you're interested in student accommodations, you should head directly upstairs to their second office, which has a larger pool of cheap rooms. The staircase is about three doors down from the Platform 15 office. Both services cost 50p per person. Although bookings are adequate, there is no guarantee you are getting the best room for the money. **Victoria Student Travel,** 52 Grosvenor Garden (tel. 730-8112) has a friendly staff that also handles budget-room bookings, but you need 50p per booking and a student ID (open Mon.-Fri. 9:30am-5:30pm). You can pick up reams of leaflets, maps, and pamphlets at the **London Tourist Board** office at 26 Grosvenor Gardens.

Central London is easily accessible from all its airports and train stations. The Piccadilly Underground Line connects **Heathrow Airport** to London. It costs £1 and takes about 45 minutes, but you will have to transfer to a District or Circle Line Tube at Earl's Court if you are heading for the accommodation services at Victoria Station. Both Pan Am and British Airways provide bus service direct to Victoria. These cost £1.20 and take about 45 minutes. British Airways has a second stop at the West London Terminal Building on Cromwell Road (convenient to hotels in the Earl's Court Area). If you arrive at **Gatwick Airport**, you can take the regular British Rail train service straight from the Airport to Victoria Station. All London train terminals serve as stations for two or more Underground lines. Connections between rail and tube are easily made.

Navigating London streets is a different matter altogether. Odd and even numbers follow no rational scheme. One road may change names four times in fewer miles, and a name may designate a street, villa, square, and row in totally different corners of the city. Obviously, a good map is a necessity. Available at any newsstand, the Nicholson series of pocket-sized guidebooks are the best. They're handy and cover in detail the central London area (75p). *Nicholson Street Finder* (75p) or the harder-to-read *London A to Z* (75p) are only necessary if you stay a fairly long time or intend to explore areas in outer London, like Hampstead or Richmond. London has been partitioned into districts, designated by their direction and relative distance from **Trafalgar Square.** The system isn't foolproof, and you'll find it simpler to refer to areas by their traditional names.

In 1965 everything that could conceivably have been considered London within a territory of 610 square miles was brought together under the administration of the Greater London Council (GLC). The oldest part of London, founded by the Romans and enclosed by them with a wall, is still called the **City of London** or simply The City. This is the financial center, which the residents are rapidly abandoning to banks and business. The City has its own traditional government, including its Lord Mayor—the City of London police force, for example, though well integrated with the rest of the metropolitan force, is technically entirely separate.

The only other section of London that ever qualified as a city in its own right is the **City of Westminster.** Although in common usage, the term Westminster denotes only a small area around the Houses of Parliament and government offices in Whitehall, the Royal Borough of Westminster administers a large section of London from **Temple Bar** to **Chelsea.** Once separated from the City of London by miles of meadow and marsh, Westminster grew up as the political, ecclesiastical, and royal capital of England paralleling the City's financial dominance. During the tremendous expansion of London from Tudor times to the present, the area between Westminster and the City became one continuous city. From the visitor's point of view, though, London is Central London, the roughly rectangular piece of land bordered on the south by the meandering **Thames,** on the north by a line drawn tangent to **Regent's Park,** from **Paddington Station** to **Tower Hill**—in fact anything that falls within the **London Transport's Circle Line Underground.**

In general, the Underground system works very simply, if expensively. It opens around 5:30am and stays open till around midnight, the last train leaving from most central London stations around 12:30am. You can pick up a free map at any station's ticket window. The fare is calculated according to distance at 5p intervals. Be sure to *save your ticket* until it is collected when you leave the station that is your final destination—traveling without a ticket is illegal.

Not as interesting or efficient as the Underground, but more scenic, are London's buses, which can be cheaper for some types of journeys. The red double-deckers are the regular city buses; the red single-deck buses are called **Red Arrows** and are expresses on which you pay a standard fare; green buses serve the suburbs. London Transport issues a free bus map for

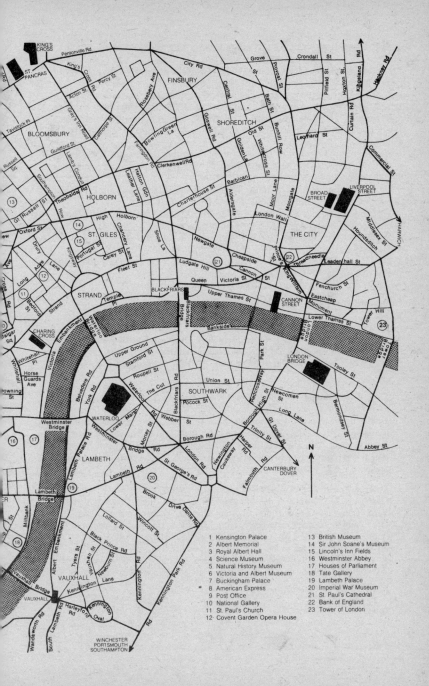

1 Kensington Palace
2 Albert Memorial
3 Royal Albert Hall
4 Science Museum
5 Natural History Museum
6 Victoria and Albert Museum
7 Buckingham Palace
8 American Express
9 Post Office
10 National Gallery
11 St. Paul's Church
12 Covent Garden Opera House
13 British Museum
14 Sir John Soane's Museum
15 Lincoln's Inn Fields
16 Westminster Abbey
17 Houses of Parliament
18 Tate Gallery
19 Lambeth Palace
20 Imperial War Museum
21 St. Paul's Cathedral
22 Bank of England
23 Tower of London

the central area, and bus stops are clearly marked with information about routes. Night Buses run on specifically indicated routes from midnight to 5am.

London Transport offers a range of **Faresavers**, none of which is likely to save you any money unless you're sleeping in an area where you need to make a long trip to the center of the city every morning. **Go-as-You-Please** tourist tickets entitle you to travel on any and all bus and Tube lines for four or seven days (£8.20 or £11.40). Try out the public transport system for a day or two before you invest in one. London, you may find, is a great city for walking.

If you are hitching out of London, remember that drivers are not allowed to stop on **Motorways (M-roads)** and that walking alongside motorways is illegal. Some suggested routes:

To Cambridge: Underground to Turnpike Lane (Piccadilly Line); bus W1 to Great Cambridge Roundabout; then A10.

To Canterbury and Dover: Bus 53 to Blackheath (Shooters Hill Road). Then A2 for Dover; A2 to M2 for Canterbury.

To Edinburgh: Bus 16A to M1. Then M18; finally A7.

To Lake District: Bus 16A to M1. Then M1 to M6.

To Oxford: Underground to Hangar Lane (Central Line); walk along Western Ave. to A40; take A40 to M40.

To Stratford-upon-Avon: As to Oxford; then A34.

Addresses and Telephone Numbers

Tourist Information Offices; British Tourist Authority, 64 St. James St. (information tel. 499-9325; Tube: Piccadilly). **London Tourist Board,** 26 Grosvenor Gardens (tel. 730-0791; 24-hour information tel. 246-8041; Tube: Victoria). **City of London Information,** St. Paul's Churchyard (tel. 606-3030; Tube: St. Paul's).

Tourist Accommodation Bureaus: Budget: **London Tourist Board**, Platform 15, Victoria Station. Open 8am-10:30pm in summer. Student: London Tourist Board, one flight up from Platform 15, Victoria Station. Open same hours; both cost 50p per person. **Victoria Student Travel Service,** 52 Grosvenor Gardens (tel. 730-8112), 50p per booking and student ID required. At least two private firms have accommodation services in other parts of Victoria Station.

Student Youth Travel Agencies: Victoria Student Travel, 52 Grosvenor Gardens (tel. 730-8112; Tube: Victoria). Open Mon.-Fri. 9:30am-5:30pm. **YHA Travel,** 14 Southampton St. (tel. 836-8541; Tube: Covent Garden). Open daily 9:30am-5:30pm, Thurs. until 9pm, Sat. until 4pm. **Transalpino,** 71 Buckingham Palace Rd. (tel. 834-9656; Tube: Victoria); headquarters for discount rail tickets for anyone under 26. Same-day bookings only at Platform 2, Victoria Station 8am-8pm. **National Union of Students,** 202 Pentonville Rd. (tel. 278-3291; Tube: King's Cross); advice to foreigners studying in England.

American Express: 6 Haymarket (tel. 930-4411; Tube: Piccadilly). Open Mon.-Fri. 9am-5pm, Sat. 9am-noon. Money changing till 9pm on Sat. Mail pick-up facilities in the basement—be prepared to show passport or ID and some proof of being an American Express client (otherwise inquiry fee of £1.); leaving messages costs 20p.

Post Office: All mail addressed simply *Poste Restante* (General Delivery), London is delivered to: London Chief Office, King Edward Building, London EC1A 1AA (King Edward St.; tel. 601-9252). More convenient is to have your mail sent to the Trafalgar Square P.O., London WC2N 4DL (St. Martin's Place; tel. 930-9580), which is open 24 hours a day.

Phones: Directory information for London, tel. 142; for the rest of Britain, tel. 192; international operator, tels. 100 and 155. You can make pay calls to the U.S. from the Trafalgar Square P.O.

London Transport: 6 information booths at the following Underground stations: St. James Park, Euston, King's Cross, Oxford Circus, Piccadilly Circus, and Victoria. Telephone inquiries 24 hours daily: 222-1234. Calls answered on rotation eventually—let it keep ringing.

British Rail Travel Centres: Certain inquiries and bookings must be made in person at 12-16 Regent St. (Tube: Piccadilly). This is the only office for Seaspeed, Sealink, and Continental tickets. Other branches at Oxford St. and the Strand; and at main line stations: Victoria, King's Cross, etc. Phone numbers for inquiries about trains to particular destinations are listed in the White Pages of telephone directories under British Rail.

Banks with late hours: Usual banking hours are 9:30am-3:30pm. Extra hours at Heathrow and Gatwick Airports; American Express; Barclays, Marble Arch (open 8am-10pm Mon.-Sat.). Cheque-point (commercial business with two 24-hour branches): 37 Coventry St. and 236 Earl's Court Rd. Trafalgar Square **Post Office** Exchange Bureau: Open 9am-9:30pm Mon.-Sat.

Police: in an emergency, tel. 999.

Medical Services: Middlesex Hospital, Mortimer St. (tel. 636-8333). **Westminster Hospital,** Horseferry Rd. (tel. 828-9811). Dial 999 for ambulance service. **Boots** has an all-night chemist at the south side of Piccadilly Circus (tel. 930-4761). **Bell and Croyden,** 50 Wigmore St. (tel. 935-5555; Tube: Bond St.), open 8:30am-10pm daily for prescriptions. Pregnancy tests and abortions: **Well Women Centre,** Marie Stopes House, 108 Whitfield St. (tel. 388-0662; Tube: Goodge St.)

Down and Out: Release, 1 Elgin Ave. (tel. 289-1123 and 603-8654) for 24-hour emergency aid; legal aid mostly. **Samaritans** (tel. 626-9000), a Britain-wide hotline highly respected for helping with all sorts of problems. **YWCA,** Platform 8, Victoria Station, has a booth manned to help travelers in distress.

U.S. Embassy: Grosvenor Square (tel. 499-9000; Tube: Bond St.).

Canada House: Trafalgar Square (tel. 629-9492).

Bike Rental: Saviles, 97 Battersea Rise (tel. 228-4279; Clapham Junction via British Rail); £5.50 per day, 50p insurance, £10 deposit. **Kensington Rent-a-Bike,** Kensington Student Centre, Kensington Church St. (tel. 937-6089; Tube: Kensington High St.); £1.50 per day, £10 deposit.

Camping Equipment Rental: Eatons of Wimbledon, 100-106 Haydons Rd.,

Wimbledon (tel. 542-1088), rents 2-man tents from 85p per day, sleeping bags from 20p, plus VAT; £10 deposit on either. Sells its used equipment in December.

Accommodations

The housing market in London is extremely tight and expensive for residents and tourists alike. You may be shocked at how much you have to pay for your budget hotel room, but your landlady may tell you that her own rent has risen 250% the past year. With luck, you'll be able to find a decent hostel-style place with bed and (undoubtedly Continental-style) breakfast for around £4. In hotels, expect to pay at least £6 for a single and £8 for a double room. Many London hostels are set up for young people working in the city. These places are generally more drab and less savory than hostels designed for tourists. It never hurts to book in advance. The London Tourist Board will help you do this if you write at least four months before you plan to arrive. A better idea is to contact these places directly—you'll surely find something cheap. If you are staying a month or more, you might consider renting a "bedsitter." There are agencies like **Universal Aunts,** 36 Walpole Street (tel. 730-9834), which will help you find a room for stays as short as a week in a private home for a very reasonable fee. Never pay an agency anything until you actually sign the lease—avoid those that demand a fee just to register with them. You might be able to get a decent (though small and inconvenient) flat for about £20 a week.

YHA HOSTELS

In London YHA Hostels are less of a bargain than elsewhere. They are also likely to be filled months in advance. You do know precisely what you are paying for: they are clean, offer showers and (with only one exception) cooking facilities. Luckily, curfew hours are extended for London Hostels until 11:30pm (except Carter Lane: 11pm). The maximum stay in any Hostel is four nights. Although non-card holders are allowed to stay (at a premium price), card holders have priority at busy times of the year. The YHA London Headquarters is located 14 Southampton Street (tel. 836-8541; Tube: Covent Garden). Senior memberships costs £5.

Holland House (sometimes called King George VI Memorial), Holland Park, Kensington W8 7QU (tel. 937-0748; Tube: Holland Park or High Street Kensington). This Hostel is the best equipped of the four. The reception area is closed only 10-11:30am. 21 and over £2; 16-20 £1.60; 5-16 £1.35.

38 Bolton Gardens, SW5 OAQ (tel. 373-7083; Tube: Earl's Court). A converted townhouse in a busy, transient neighborhood. 21 and over £1.65; 16-20 £1.35; 5-16 £1.10.

36 Carter Lane, EC4V 5AD (tel. 236-4965; Tube: Blackfriars or St. Paul's). The old dorm for St. Paul's Choir School. No cooking facilities and only cafeteria continental breakfast. The city streets near it are deserted after dark. Closing time is 11pm. 21 and over £1.65; 16-20 £1.35; 5-16 £1.10.

84 Highgate West Hill, N6 6LU (tel. 340-1831; Tube: Archway Station). Take bus #210 or 271 from the tube to the Hostel. Poor location: the neighborhood is out of the way and somewhat drab. 21 and over £1.60; 16-20 £1.30; 5-16 £1.05.

HALLS OF RESIDENCE

These places are the living quarters for many young people in London, both students and the employed. While most are not rock-bottom cheap, the university dormitories at least are usually better equipped than similarly-priced hotels. Most only have space during the summer (mid-July through September) and are good places to scout if you want a single room.

Carr-Saunders Hall, 18-24 Fitzroy St. WIP 5AE (tel. 580-6338; Tube: Goodge St.). One of three London School of Economics halls. 120 single rooms, 10 doubles, and 78 flats are available. Bed linen and towels provided. The furnished flats are 2-, 3-, 4-, or 5-bed with private kitchen and bathroom. They range from £60 to £158 per flat per week depending upon the season. Just bed-and-breakfast is £5 per person plus VAT.

International Student House, 229 Great Portland St., W1N 5HD (tel. 636-9471; Tube: Great Portland St. or Regents Park). As much a club as a dormitory, the ISH is located on a busy street literally on the doorstep of Regents Park. Superior temporary accommodations in single (£5), double (£4.25), or triple rooms (£3.50). Breakfast included.

Lee Abbey International Students Club, 26-27 Courtfield Gardens, SW5 OPQ (Tube: Earl's Court or Gloucester Rd.). Besides this main building, the Club has two or three nearby halls under its wing. Only continental breakfast. Longer stays are welcome. Private coin-operated laundry and coffee bar. The residence has a Christian orientation. Prices range from £3.42 to £4.62 in 1-, 2-, 3-, and 4-bed rooms, plus VAT.

William Goodenough House, Mecklenburgh Square (tel. 278-5131; Tube: Russell Square). Quite elegant, designed for postgraduate students of the Commonwealth, U.S., and EEC countries on extended stays—but try in case of cancellations. Women only. Meals not included. For stays under 3 months £2.95-3 a night in study bedroom singles, £2.10 per person in doubles. **London House,** at the same address, has similar accommodations for similarly-qualified men.

YWCA Central Club, 16-22 Great Russell St. WC1B 3LR (tel. 636-7512; Tube: Russell Square). Somewhat dreary but has a swimming pool. £6, £5, £3, or £2.25 in single, double, triple or dorm beds. Includes "light" breakfast. Plus VAT. 20p extra if only one night stay. Women only.

ACCOMMODATIONS UNDER £2

Most of these places are run by church grooups or are located in church halls and run by private concerns. It's generally a good idea to have a sleeping bag. You won't find anything more basic than these digs.

Hinde Street Hostel, Methodist Church, corner of Thayer and Hinde Sts. (no phone; Tube: Bond St.). Although located in the church, the hostel is run by a separate concern. Get here after 6:30pm, but before 1am. 80 beds on the floor of a big hall and smaller adjoining room. Blankets, sheets, baggage facilities, and hot breakfast provided. £1.50 but only open during August.

Torbridge School Clubs Ltd., Cromer St. (tel. 837-4406; Tube: King's Cross). Arrive at 10pm, leave 9am. Men sleep in the basement gymnasium, women in the hall of the best karate club in England. No breakfast; showers. ID required. 70p per night on foam-rubber mattresses.

Pax Christi, Maria Fidelis School, Phoenix Rd. near Chalton St. (tel. 485-7977; Tube: Euston Sq.). Bunk beds in a Catholic School. Continental breakfast included, plus extra cereal or cheese. One of three in London run by a Catholic activist peace group. Open only during August, give or take a few days. £1.80.

Pax Christi, St. Catherine Labore School, Herbal Hill, Clerkenwell Rd. (Tube: Farringdon Rd.). Same deal as the above, also £1.80.

St. Peter's Church, Eaton Square (Tube: Victoria). Closed 9am-9pm. Sleeping bags required, one night only. Open mid-June to end of September. 50p.

St. Anne's Student Shelter, Abbey Orchard St. (tel. 222-5402; Tube: St. James Park). Unisex dorms, continental breakfast included. You must have student or youth hostel card. Cooking facilities, luggage security and showers available. £ 1.60 per night.

HOSTEL-STYLE PLACES

These places range from brand-new, luxurious hostels to budget hotels where you share a cramped and dreary room with three or four strangers. The latter places tend to serve better breakfasts. Hostel-style accommodations are concentrated in the usual areas for inexpensive lodgings: Bloomsbury (best quality but most expensive), Paddington, Bayswater, and Earl's Court. Some, including those listed here, also have singles and doubles.

Astor's Museum Hostel, 27 Montagne St. (tel. 580-5360; Tube: Holborn). Just opened in July '78. Exuberant staff. Informal activities like Bastille Day party and Dylan Concert Bus sometimes planned. They might have an overflow hostel available; ask about it if no vacancies. £9.72 doubles, £3.23 in dorm rooms.

Central University of Iowa Hostel, 7 Bedford Place (tel. 580-1121; Tube: Russell Square). Nice neighborhood near British Museum. Clean, well-kept. Kitchen facilities. £4 singles (there are only 1 or 2), £3.50 per person in doubles, £3 for dorm bed. Continental breakfast plus unlimited corn flakes. Vacancies only during non-term time.

Fieldcourt House, 32 Courtfield Gardens (tel. 373-0152; Tube: Earl's Court). Clean, spacious converted Victorian mansion. New bunk bed, lockers, laundry, and ironing room. Awful continental breakfast. Quiet street. One of the best. £2.50 in dorms, £3.50 per person doubles, £4.60 singles. £10 deposit required for linen and quilt.

Richmond Court, 5 Courtfield Gardens (tel. 373-5322; Tube: Earl's Court). Clean, being remodeled. English breakfast. One of the best values in Earl's Court, if not London. £2.50 in shared accommodations, £4.50 per person in doubles, £7 singles.

Lancaster Student Hotel, 41 Lancaster Gate (tel. 402-6735; Tube: Lancaster Gate). Continental breakfast. Good facilities. Since this hotel is run mostly by students, there are often opportunities for work as cleaners and night porters. £3.23 for sharing an 8-bed bunk room, £4.32 per person in double, £5.40 for a single.

Lancashire, 22-26 Norfolk Sq. (tel. 723-2189; Tube: Paddington). Includes continental breakfast. £6-8 singles, £12-14 doubles, £5-6 per person in sharing situation.

73 Oakley Street, (tel. 352-5599; Tube: Sloane Square or South Kensington and a walk). Pleasant. English breakfast and cooking facilities. Tea always available. £3.25 sharing, £3.50 triples, £3.75 doubles.

St. Simeon's, 38 Harrington Gardens (tel. 370-4708; Tube: Earl's Court). One of seven hotels under the same ownership. At least three are student-geared. English breakfast, large dorms. This is one of the nicest of the seven. £5.50 single, £8.50 double, £2.75 sharing.

Gayfere Hostel, 8 Gayfere St. (tel. 222-6894; Tube: Westminster). On a quiet street near the Houses of Parliament. £2.85 per person in a dorm.

Rena House, 34 Craven Hill Gardens (tel. 732-3225; Tube: Bayswater). Prices depend on what floor you're on. Weekly rates, kitchen, and full breakfast are available. £6 singles, £12 twin, £4.50 for sharing.

ACCOMMODATIONS FOR £5 AND UP

Victoria

Although Victoria Station has spawned quite a few inexpensive hotels, you still have to walk five or ten minutes to get to them. They are not especially convenient to either sights or inexpensive restaurants, or traveler services. It is just as easy to take the Underground out to Earl's Court or Bayswater.

Tino's House, 40 Charlwood St. (tel. 834-8611; Tube: Victoria). Clean; good English breakfast. £5.50 per person in doubles. **Romano's** (tel. 834-3542) shares a kitchen with Tino's. Similar accommodations.

Earl's Court

A seemingly endless bundle of streets, squares, and townhouses going more or less to seed, Earl's Court tends to have less traffic passing through it than Bloomsbury or Victoria. The area is always full of visitors from all parts of the world and the sidewalks are, if anything, more crowded at night than during the day. There are probably more late-night eating places, groceries and news agents in this neighborhood than in the rest of London put together. Prospecting carefully for lodgings is particularly recommended here; you should look cautiously at what you're getting. Every street outside the Underground Station is lined with hotels. The best accommodation in Earl's Court happens to be in the hostel-style places. See that section for more listings. Or try:

Rushmore, 11 Trebovir Rd. (tel. 370-1114; Tube: Earl's Court). Continental breakfast. Rooms are only okay but are scheduled for remodeling during the winter of '78-79. £5 singles, £8 doubles, £10 triples.

Bloomsbury

Bloomsbury is a great location—within walking distance of most of London's theaters, the National Gallery, the British Museum, and the University of London. Good restaurants are nearby in Charlotte and Goodge Streets. Standards are high here, but so are prices and you may find a lot of "no vacancies" signs. Unfortunately, a lot of noisy trucks travel through the area. The best streets to cruise for rooms are Gower, Bedford Place, Cartwright Gardens, and Argyle Square.

St. Margaret Hotel, 25-27 Bedford Place (tel. 636-4277; Tube: Russell Square). A very pretty hotel. Fresh flowers and white linen in the ground-floor breakfast room. Quiet street near British Museum and the gardens of Russell Square. £7.02 singles, £6.48 per person in other rooms.

Cavendish Hotel, 75 Gower St. (tel. 636-9079; Tube: Goodge St.). Clean. Friendly landlady. £6 singles, from £10 for doubles.

St. Athans Hotel, 20 Tavistock Place. (tel. 837-9140; Tube: Russell Square). £7 singles, £12 doubles, £15 triples, £18 family rooms. Clean with good-sized rooms. Prices drop considerably with longer stay; subtract £2 from doubles' tariff.

Avalon, 46-47 Cartwright Gardens (tel. 387-2366; Tube: Russell Square.). Full English breakfast, very clean, lots of paperbacks in the library here. £6.50 singles, £11.50 doubles, £16 triples.

Paddington/Bayswater

The Paddington/Bayswater area has excellent places with high standards. Unfortunately, it has dumps too, and quality can vary drastically from one door to the next. Queensway is the neighborhood's main street, a sprawling bazaar of a place that happens only incidentally to be indoors. The streets with the highest concentrations of guest houses include: Norfolk Square, Sussex Gardens (try odd numbers first), Leinster Square, Talbot Square, and Prince's Square.

Warwick House Hotel, 6-8 Norfolk Square (tel. 723-0810; Tube: Paddington). Clean and comfortable—even chipper. Full breakfast. Associated with three Sussex Gardens hotels: **Park House** (tel. 723-0268), **St. Lawrence** (tel. 723-4284), and **New Commodore** (tel. 723-6223). Doubles £13.50-14.50, family rooms £21.06, triples £18.63. Singles (only on rare occasions) £8.10-9.25.

Talbot Lawn Hotel, 12-14 Talbot Square (tel. 723-5962; Tube: Paddington). Continental breakfast. Nice rooms. Part of a chain of eight other nearby hotels with central reservations (tel. 286-5294). £6-8 singles, £4.50-8 per person in a double, multis £3.50-5 per person.

Transit's London Club, 18 Kensington Gardens Square (tel. 229-4400; Tube: Bayswater). The home base of a company that arranges trips and tours. The rooms are standard but clean. Nice staff. Mainly Australians. £10 per person for singles, £7 in doubles, £5.50 in triples, £4.50 in quads.

St. George, 46 Norfolk Square (tel. 723-3560; Tube: Paddington). English breakfast included. Very clean, quite nice arrangements in spacious rooms. Book in advance. £5.40 per person in doubles.

Camping

The London Tourist Board has information on at least thirty sites within thirty miles of London. Unless otherwise indicated, the following have spaces available for campers and caravans. Prices are per tent and include two people.

Hackney Camping, Milfields Rd., Hackney Marshes, E5 (tel. 985-7656; Tube: Liverpool St. and then bus #22A to Mandeville St.). Hot showers, luggage storage. Tent camping only £1.40.

Edmonton-Picketts Lock, Picketts Lock Lane, N9 (tel. 803-4756). Swimming and tennis. £2.05.

Chingford, Sewardstone Rd. E4 (tel. 529-2600). 50 spaces available for tents at £1.08.

Food and Drink

If the human organism could survive on custard cream cakes and milky tea, the problem of eating inexpensively in London would be solved. Simple, inexpensive, and filling pub grub is the most dependable fare; Shepherd's Pie or Ploughman's Lunch (bread, cheese, and sometimes pickles) are usually good at any pub for 60p and up. "Whole food" restaurants and wine bars can be more expensive, but at least you'll get some edible vegetables. Another alternative is to eat ethnically; but the most popular foreign delicacy in London at the moment is the American hamburger. London's parks are ideal for picnics; the **MacMarket** chain of supermarkets is one of the cheapest places for groceries; or try an outdoor market like Berwick Street in Soho.

The Galleon, 35 Pembridge Villas (tel. 727-9260; Tube: Notting Hill Gate).
Absolutely standard fare but at prices lower than elsewhere. Simple, decent;
formica and tile decor. Entrées around 80p.

Geales, 2-4 Farmer St. (tel. 727-7969; Tube: Notting Hill Gate). The best of
London's fish-and-chips shops, this is really more of a restaurant. Variety of
inexpensive fish from 70p. Open Tues.-Sat. noon-3pm and 6-11pm. Closed
for a two-week summer holiday during July.

The Pot, 5a Hogarth St. (tel. 370-4371; Tube: Earl's Court) has a nicer
atmosphere than the **Hot Pot** around the corner or the **Golden Pot** across the
street. But all 3 serve nearly identical menus of omelettes (60p), *moussaka*
(80p), spaghetti, and more expensive meat dishes. Good, filling, and cheap.
Hot Pot has the best omelettes; Golden Pot the quickest service.

Malaysian Kitchen, 234 Old Brompton Rd. (tel. 270-2421; Tube: Earl's
Court). Very good Malaysian, Indonesian, and Chinese cooking, served in
large helpings amid candlelight and South Pacific decor. **Sar Ho Fun** (a dish
of rice stick noodles, chicken, meat, and prawns) is tangy: £1.35 plus VAT
and *service.* Most dishes are in the £1.10-£1.20 range.

Chelsea Kitchen, 98 Kings Rd. (tel. 589-1330; Tube: Sloane Square). Institutional quality food, pleasant atmosphere, very low prices—most main dishes
(*moussaka,* chicken *chausseur* (sic), etc.) come with chips and vegetables, all
for around 70p. Open seven days, noon-midnight.

Ambrosiana, 194 Fulham Rd. (tel. 351-0070; Tube: South Kensington and
bus #14). A large selection of Italian-style *galettes* and crêpes from 60p to
£1.30. Convenient to a good wine bar, although you can buy wine there. Both
savory and sweet crêpes are excellent.

Cranks, 8 Marshall St. (tel. 437-9431; Tube: Oxford Circus or Piccadilly).
Excellent whole-food restaurant tucked away behind Carnaby St. The food is
tempting and filling, and you could spend a fortune if you didn't restrain
yourself from ordering too many of the salads. Flans, pies, and side dishes 45p
and up. Probably the best of its type. Food is served cafeteria-style. Open
Mon.-Sat. 11:30am-8:30pm.

Glory Kebab House, 57 Goodge St. (tel. 636-9093; Tube: Goodge St.).
Mouth-watering lamb kebabs (£1.30) in a simple, candle-lit place that is open
late. Friendly service. Other Greek dishes are available.

Blooms, 90 Whitechapel High St. (tel. 247-6001; Tube: Aldgate East). This
strictly kosher restaurant is well known and most popular on Sunday mornings
after a trip to Portobello Market, but it is open the rest of the week, too (except
for Fri. nights and all day Sat.). Very good salt beef sandwiches (70p) and
other meat dishes.

Cooke & Son, 41 Kingland High St. (Tube: Liverpool St. and bus #22 or
22A). Eels hot and jellied 45-90p, pie and mash 43p, fruit pie and custard 22p;
that's the menu in this amazing, spotless Edwardian place. Erratic hours:
usually Mon.-Sat. 10am-6pm and 8:30pm-11:30pm. Closed Thurs.

As for **Indian restaurants,** Westbourne Grove between Queensway and Pembridge Villas is lined with more than a half dozen—a few of them among the best in London. **The Standard** at #23 is perhaps the most widely known, but it is also expensive. Try **Khan's** at #19, or **Asia Grill,** 26 Pembridge Villas. Most curries with rice cost about £1.60.

London's **Chinatown** is located between Lisle and Gerrard Streets in Soho, which makes it a convenient location if you'll be going to the theater afterwards. **Chan May Mai** is one of many small and bustling places along Lisle Street. Most dishes in the £1 range.

Greek restaurants are easily found along Charlotte and Goodge Streets. Besides the one listed above, the **Blue Dolphin** and **Greek Prince** are good. Be wary of the very cheap kebab places—as well as inexpensive **Italian restaurant** chains, the exception being the **Pizza Express.** While the pizza won't be what you are used to in the States, the restaurants serve decent fare and the surroundings are trendy but attractive.

London is the kind of city where at least once you might want to have a really good meal. Usually, you should resist the temptation, since you can pay twice as much as what you would at the places listed above and find the quality only marginally different. But if you have something to celebrate, we have a few recommendations. First of all, don't go to **Simpson's-in-the-Strand.** You'll have to wear a tie and jacket if you do, and it's not worth it—the food is now expensive (nearly £3 for roast beef), not very good (the roast beef is sliced thin and not always juicy), and the service is rude, particularly to young people. Whether or not a dinner at **Rules** (another old English restaurant) is worth the splurge is a matter of heated controversy. In general, it's very good. With the decor ornately British, the meat well prepared and the service attentive, it might be worth a night out. And if it seems to be filled with foreigners, that's because Rules is where many Londoners take their out-of-town guests.

If you still aren't satisfied and wish to go the custard cream route, try **Patisserie Valerie,** 44 Old Compton Street in Soho, for fabulous (and not expensive) pastries of all sorts.

Pubs

London pubs tend to have character rather than local characters. You go to have a few pints and check out the decor, rather than mingle in friendly camaraderie with neighborhood types. One of the most unusual is **Blackfriars,** 174 Queen Victoria Street (Tube: Blackfriars), a nearly perfect example of art nouveau. The place is as lushly decadent and claustrophobic as an Edgar Allan Poe nightmare. Many pubs have more direct literary associations. The **Sherlock Holmes,** at the end of Northumberland St. (behind Trafalgar on the Strand side) has a pub, grill, and Holmes memorabilia—including his room, the stuffed head of the Hound of Baskervilles, and assorted letters to and from Arthur Conan Doyle. The **Pindar of Wakefield,** 328 Grays Inn Road, doesn't rest on its laurels as the local pub of Marx and Engels. It sponsors poetry readings on Thursday nights 7:30pm (see *Time Out*), which are recorded for later BBC radio broadcasts.

The English typically visit their favorite country pub during the hour before Sunday dinner. You can simulate the feeling of a country pub crawl within the boundaries of London if you head up to **Highgate** and **Hampstead** around noon on Sundays. Begin at the **Flask Tavern,** 77 West Hill, Highgate and cross the huge and lovely Hampstead Heath to **Spaniards Inn** and **Jack Straws Inn.** All three of these pubs are vaguely historical, but it is the crowds that make them most enjoyable. A few other comfortable (and more central) pubs include: **Annsleigh Arms,** (Onslow Gardens, near Earl's Court); **The Lamb,** (Lamb's Conduit Road, Bloomsbury); and the **Sun in Splendor** (Pembridge Villas, Notting Hill Gate).

Sights

London is bound to disappoint the traveler who searches for grandeur. It has neither a Notre Dame nor a St. Peter's. Its most spectacular buildings are quiet, muffled; you always feel a sense of restraint, even conservatism about London architecture. Four hundred years ago London was a sprawl of a Tudor city, made of wood and plaster buildings. Building speculation was rampant, and "urban blight" had already set in. City planning was a Continental, Renaissance idea, and the Renaissance had yet to spread to England. At this point, in stepped a young, Italian-educated architect named Inigo Jones, appointed by James I as Surveyor to the King's Works. He is London's master planner; and though only four of his buildings remain, London is Jones' city. New construction needed his approval, and he encouraged construction upon existing foundations. The noble, pillared structures designed by Jones stood as harbingers of a strange future in "rustic" London. His work is still visible—the **Queen's Chapel** at St. James's Palace, the **Banqueting House** in Whitehall, **St. Paul's Church** at Covent Garden, and the lovely **Queen's House** outside of London in Greenwich. But his influence is in every building, and every street. On **Lincoln's Inn Fields** (Holborn Tube) are a row of terrace houses he designed (#59-60), which stand as testament to the influence he exerted on the face and character of London.

Jones is little remembered—his work was far too straightforward and simple for anyone to think of immortalizing him. And yet, the measured stance of his descendants (especially Christopher Wren) owes more than a cursory nod to England's greatest Renaissance architect.

Wren is remembered for his churches, in particular **St. Paul's Cathedral** (Ludgate Hill, EC4). Wren seems more at home building smaller, more intimate structures, as the churches that surround St. Paul's will attest: **St. Clement Danes** (Strand); **St. Magnus Martyr** (Lower Thames St.); **St. Mary Aldermary** (Queen Victoria St., EC4); **St. Michael's,** and **St. James** (both in the banking district). Each is unique, and well worth your time.

Of course, there are the monuments that hardly need mentioning: **Westminster Abbey,** the **Houses of Parliament** (where you can sit in on debates), **Buckingham Palace,** and the **Tower of London.** All are worth a visit despite the crowds. Of less renown, but no less interest, are **Lincoln's Inn** and the temple which boasts **Wren's Gatehouse** in Middle Temple Lane; or **Sir Johns Soane's Museum,** 13 Lincoln's Inn Fields—a wonderful, crazy place built by an architect to serve both as his own home and as a museum for his students. It contains an excellent gallery of Hogarth prints. Catch Sir John Summerson's brilliant tours at 2pm on the first Saturday of most months. (Other Saturday tours are given by the museum librarian.)

To get an overview of the London sprawl, take the **London Transport Tour** (from the top of a double-decker bus), a two-hour unconducted tour for £1.50. But London is a town to walk in. Since it is blessed with miles of lovely green parks, you'll never be far from picnic and rest spots. **Regent's Park** contains an open-air theater, the zoo, and the United States Embassy. **Hyde Park** is so enormous that by a trick of perspective, you'll think the people in the distance are strolling off the edge of the world; coincidentally, the soap-box orators at **Speaker's Corner** on Sunday mornings seem to have been there and back. On those mild summer days that Londoners consider a heat wave, the **Serpentine Lido** overflows with swimmers and sun bathers. **Kensington Garden** is a giant games field for neighborhood children, except in the winding **Flower Walks.** Flamingos stretch their wings and peacocks strut in **Holland Park;** but the London pigeon is, as always, in the majority. If you are hiking by **Green Park** or **St.** James between 11am and noon, you might be able to keep step with the changing guards of Buckingham Palace. **Hampstead Heath** and the **Highgate Cemetery** are Sunday places—countryside either somber or lush depending on your mood. (The grave of Marx is here, along with George Eliot and hosts of other luminaries.)

The streets of London are mostly winding roads and alleys, squares and crescents lined with white mansions flourished like wedding cakes. London neighborhoods are reserved and don't reveal their characters at first glance. It will take a while to realize that the women loitering under shop awnings in **Shepherd's Market** are streetwalkers, a specialty in this neighborhood for centuries. You will have to look up above the super-modern airlines offices and tourist board centers on the street level to see that crusty old gentlemen still enjoy the luxurious private clubs on **St. James Square. Brick Lane** is a grim area out beyond Liverpool Street Station. Few of the Bengalis and Pakistanis who live on the outskirts venture into the local Sunday market in this East End Cockney conclave. **Earl's Court** was once a second Australia; now all the newsstands carry Arabic newspapers. But the characters of these residential areas are more clear-cut than elsewhere. It's not unusual for elegant townhouses to be door-to-door with hostels for Chilean refugees.

When you decide to go indoors, you'll find museums and galleries overflowing with treasures. (Nearly all have free admission.) The **British Museum** (Great Russell Street, Bloomsbury) is the repository of everything: the Rosetta Stone, Elgin marbles, diverse manuscripts like *Beowulf* and *Troilus and Cressida,* and the world's oldest mummy. The **Victoria and Albert** (Cromwell Road, South Kensington) has a fine series of period rooms set up as if people still lived in them, plus fine and applied art from all ages and continents. London has its own museum devoted to regalia and history at the **Barbican,** named sensibly **The Museum of London.**

Galleries are even more bountiful than museums. The **National Gallery** (Trafalgar Square) is one of the finest general collections in the world. A visit to the **National Portrait Gallery** (next door) is like a refresher course in English History. The **Tate Gallery** displays British and twentieth-century artists: Turner, Hogarth, Blake, plus modern old favorites like Henry Moore, Picasso, Chagall. Stare long and hard at Naum Gabo's *Head*. The **Courtauld Institute** (Woburn Square, Bloomsbury) is small, but almost every painting is a masterpiece of Impressionism. The **Royal Academy of Arts** (Burlington House, Piccadilly) is run by the Arts Council—so be ready for anything. During the **Summer Exhibition** spectators are allowed to vote for their favorites among the assembled best of that year's British art. Finally, the **Dulwich College Picture Gallery** (College Road, SE21) and **Leighton House** (12 Holland Park Road, W14) are both worth visits. The former houses Rubens and Rembrandts—that should be enough to pique your interest. Leighton House is designed like an Arab building, and houses interesting Victoriana.

Shopping

Window-shopping in London is another form of sightseeing. **Harrods** (Tube: Knightsbridge) seems as encyclopedic as the British Museum. It has proven to be a more enduring monument than the Crystal Palace, another product of the Victorian penchant for the all-inclusive. The store occupies a turreted, terra-cotta block in Knightsbridge. Harrods can do everything from selling you a live rhinoceros to arranging your funeral. The cavernous food hall is perhaps the most interesting—check out the thirty varieties of butter on sale. Londoners consider a visit to Harrods as obligatory for the tourist as a visit to the Tower.

The two most famous London markets are **Portobello Road** (Tube: Notting Hill Gate) and **Petticoat Lane** (Tube: Liverpool Street; look for Middlesex Street on your map). At the first you find yourself in a herd of tourists grazing for antiques, knick-knacks, and junk on Fridays and Saturdays. Going early won't help because the merchants open their booths at their leisure. Petticoat Lane is a London institution on Sunday mornings—street after street of stalls, mostly cheap clothing and appliances. Wander away from the stream of tourists and you'll be in some of the toughest neighborhoods of London: **Brick Lane** and **Club Row.** The people jamming these narrow streets are mostly white East Enders, true Cockneys. There are more cops here than at any other London market. **Ridley Road** on Fridays has mangos, dasheens, reggae music, kosher delis, and plucked chickens (Tube: Liverpool Street and then bus #22). Less well known than Portobello are **Bermondsey Road** (Tube: London Bridge); open Friday mornings only; and **Camden Passage** (Tube: Angel) open on Wednesday and Saturday mornings only; they have antiques and bric-a-brac at somewhat lower prices.

In general, manufactured goods in England are less attractive and more expensive than in the U.S. Woolens are an exception. You can find good quality and relatively low-priced classical styles at **Westaway & Westaway,** 65 Great Russell Street (Tube: Russell Square). **Marks & Spencer** (458 Oxford Street and branches everywhere) has fewer cashmeres and shetlands, but it's a London institution, begun by a button seller and his friend at the turn of the century. You may not find high fashion, but their St. Michael's brand "jumpers" will keep you warm at reasonable prices: good Shetland sweaters currently cost about £8. The main store for the popular, floral-printed **Laura Ashley** dresses is 9 Harriet Street (Tube: Knightsbridge).

Charing Cross Road is still the best place for books. **Foyle's,** the largest, most disorganized and unpleasant book store in London, is there. Try **Zwemmer** (78 Charing Cross Road) for art books and Oxford University Press publications; **Samuel French, Ltd.,** 26 Southampton Street, for theater books; **Edition Peters,** 119 Warden Street, for sheet music; and **Stanfords** (Long Acre, Covent Garden), for maps and travel books.

Everything goes on sale in London during July and January. (All the more reason for avoiding Oxford Street.) You'll probably be two sizes smaller once you've weathered the crunch, but sales definitely worth visiting are at Harrods, and along Regent or Jermyn Street at **Jaeger's, Burberry's,** and **Liberty's.**

Entertainment

The best source of information on entertainment of all kinds is the weekly magazine *Time Out*. Published on Thursdays, it costs 35p and is available at any newsstand. You needn't agree with the judgments of its reviewers to find helpful the lists of upcoming plays, concerts, sporting events, dance performances, movies, and poetry readings.

First and foremost, London is the theater capital of the English-speaking world. Not only are the big-name, big-budget productions usually excellent and cheap, but London has thriving fringe, lunchtime, and open-air theater as well. You would never know that summer is off-season. Curtain time is generally between 7:30 and 8. Seats can cost as little as £1. Avoid service charges by buying tickets at the box offices. Three of the most eminent theaters offer student or standby tickets. Check at the **National Theatre, Aldwych,** and **Old Vic** for details. Many theaters sell inexpensive tickets on the day of the performance. There is generally a line forming for these before the box office opens, and you will probably be limited to the purchase of only one or two tickets. Experimental interpretations and the work of young playwrights are tried out in various locations. The big three theaters all have a "fringe" stage, as does the equally respected **Royal Court Theatre.** But keep an eye out for productions at **The New End, Bush, Hampstead,** and **ICA** theaters. Tickets here can cost as little as 50p. (You can get backstage at the National Theatre if you take one of the excellent conducted tours given four times daily except Sunday, £1.25.)

Only New York City rivals London's musical preeminence. Major festivals of classical music take place at the acoustically brilliant **Royal Festival Hall** and the small, elegant **Wigmore Hall**—not to mention regular performances of opera at Covent Garden and the **London Coliseum.** But the "Proms," held nightly from mid-July to mid-September, are perhaps the most endearing part of the London musical scene. The orchestras and soloists are first-rate. If you are in London in September, try to get a ticket to the final Prom. Crying and singing *Rule Britannia* is probably the most moving experience you can expect to have in stolid Britain.

Ronnie Scott's, 46 Frith Street, is London's most famous jazz club, featuring the best in Continental jazz and stateside jazz. *Time Out* will give you the schedules of some smaller, less expensive clubs. The **Marquee,** 90 Wardour Street, is a rock concert hall where punks promenade nightly. The foyer of the National Theatre on the South Bank always has a varied schedule of free concerts—everything from Irish folk to John Cage. You can order drinks from the theater bar and enjoy a great view of the Thames; you don't even need a theater ticket to get in to the foyer.

London will disappoint the movie buff. 90% of the films currently showing are recent Hollywood exports. **Paris Pullman,** 65 Drayton Gardens; **Electric Cinema Club,** 191 Portobello Road; and **London Film Maker's Co-op Cinema,** 42 Gloucester Avenue, are a few welcome exceptions. Prices are in the £1.40 range.

Horse racing takes place regularly at **Windsor, Sandown,** and **Kempton** Parks. The **football** season begins around August. Teams with names like West Ham United and Tottenham Hotspur battle with only a fraction of the ferocity of some of their fans—none of which hurts the bookmaking business, a sport all its own. Legal gambling goes on in any of the smoky bookie joints that line heavily trafficked streets.

Probably more restful is a day of **cricket.** Don't try to understand it, just enjoy the controlled, almost stupefying pace of the game, and the demeanor of the fans. This wonderful game of men in stately white on the green will tell you a lot about the Empire, and the gentility of a slightly proper, slightly Victorian sensibility. Tests are played at **Lord's** (St. John's Wood Road, NW8) and at the **Oval** (Kennington Oval, Kennington, SE11).

Southeast of London

Dover and Folkestone

If you are coming in by train or boat from Boulogne or Calais, you will probably land in Dover or just below, in Folkestone. There is no need to rush through this area, especially if you are interested in castles. The small seaside resort town of **Deal,** about twenty minutes from Dover Priory by train, boasts two, both open to the public. Dover is a good place to begin exploring Britain's Roman past. On the grounds of **Dover Castle** you can enter the empty **Pharos,** once a lighthouse, the only complete Roman building still standing in England. The English Tourist Board publishes a small guide, *Discover Roman Britain* (25p), which could be helpful for further exploring, as would the *Ordnance Survey Map of Roman Sights* (£2.50), available at any good book shop.

Dover tourist information centers are convenient to the Dover Priory Train Station. There is a **free accommodation service** at the Town Hall, Biggin Street (tel. 206941) for Dover only. The center on Townwall Street (tel. 205108) is a major **Tourist Office** which can book anywhere in England (fee: £1). Open 8am-midnight in the summer. You can change money at the banks along Market Square. The **Folkestone Tourist Office** on Harbour Street (tel. 58594) will also help you find a room. In Dover:

YHA Hostel, Charlton House, 306 London Rd. (tel. 201314). Directly on the A2. A superior grade hostel. £1.10 and £1.35. There is a second hostel at **Hillesden House,** 14 Godwyne Rd. (tel. 201698)—quieter location but standard grade. 90p and £1.10.

YMCA, Godwyne Rd. (tel. 206138). Summer only. Coed. £1.50 without breakfast. Later curfew than hostel across the street.

Mrs. Hayes, 283 London Rd. (tel. 203476). Good choice if nearby hostel is full.

Balgownie, 26 Gilford Rd. in Deal (tel. 5238). Clean and very comfortable. £3.50 per person. One of a couple along this street.

Canterbury

For centuries, the most heavily traveled road in England has been that between London and Canterbury, the pilgrimage route to the shrine of England's favorite native saint, Thomas à Becket. Chaucer's pilgrims never made it here, but David Copperfield and others did.

If you approach **Canterbury Cathedral** at dusk through the grounds of Kings School, you'll have the area nearly to yourself and you'll see the entire 537-foot length of the Cathedral in all its intricate detail. Parts date from 1070 A.D.; this was one of the first Gothic cathedrals to be built in England. Successive archbishops believed that they could improve on their predecessor's building by adding to it, so that now the Cathedral's structure is really that of two attached cathedrals, with yet a third downstairs in the crypt.

Tourist Information and Accommodations Service (35p) is located at 22 St. Peter's Street (tel. 66567). (Open Mon.-Fri. 10am-6pm, Sat. 10am-5pm, and Sun. 10am-4pm, with a one-hour lunch break at 1pm.) If they're closed, call 68307, a room-finding service set up by B&B owners. Trains from London to Canterbury leave Victoria, Charing Cross, and Waterloo Stations at least twice hourly, and the trip takes about an hour and a half.

YHA Youth Hostel, 54 New Dover Rd. (tel. 62911). Superior grade with beds for only 56 people. £1.10 and £1.35. The building is a converted Victorian villa in a shady spot.

Friends Meeting House, Friar Rd. More basic, but cheaper than the Youth Hostel. Mattresses or couches on the floor of a Quaker hall. English breakfast, but no showers. The wardens are exceptionally nice and helpful. £1.50. Ten people only.

Tudor House, 6 Best Lane (tel. 65650). This B&B deserves its name—the house is 300 years old, £4-4.50 per person. Very good breakfast. Friendly.

Mrs. Wainwright, 7 South Canterbury Rd. (tel. 66396). £4 per person. Very friendly proprietor, makes great omelettes.

The Southern Counties

Salisbury and Stonehenge

Salisbury is best known as a base for exploring the undulating plateau surrounding it, **Salisbury Plain.** But the city has enjoyed nearly seven centuries of uneventful prosperity, and is a quiet, pastoral town—the perfect subject for painters like Constable. Cows still graze sleepily on the meadow around the **Cathedral,** which, for the unity and understated audacity of its design, is among the two or three best in England. Its distinguishing feature is its 400-foot spire, the tallest in the country. Inside, the building is less impressive, but there are other things to look at in this peaceful town. Wander around for a while in the **Cathedral Close**—one of the best of the picturesque old houses to go into is the **Mompesson House** (open Wed.-Sat. 11am-6pm, April through September; Wed. and weekends in October, closed November through March; admission 40p).

If you want to see Stonehenge, give yourself at least one night in Salisbury. That will enable you to arrive early in the morning—the best time for viewing. Stonehenge is only ten miles north of Salisbury. The primary road, which you'll take if you go by bus, has the advantage of passing by the site of **Old Sarum,** the original Salisbury. But the alternate route is more pleasant and leads through the small villages of Woodford and Wilsford. You should take this winding road (leaving Salisbury by Castle Street) if you are walking or cycling. After nine miles turn left on A303 or ask in Woodford for directions to a short cut.

Stonehenge strikes most visitors as a disappointment. It is only a circle of stones. You can't even get close enough to touch them because a barrier keeps you fifty yards at bay—but even to get this close you'll have to pay 40p. Stonehenge looks just like its pictures. Standing there, hearing RAF planes drone overhead, looking out over the crowded car park and the hordes of other tourists snapping photos, you begin to wonder if that's all there is to Stonehenge. But a visit here is a humbling experience. Your wonderings seem insignificant. People have been gazing at this incongruous mound for thousands of years. For all our sophisticated gadgetry, Stonehenge is a technological feat. We don't even know exactly how or why it was built. Tradition has it that Stonehenge was built by Merlin, who is said to have brought the stones from Ireland by magic. This story has more than a grain of truth in it, for although some of the stones come from the surrounding countryside, the inner horseshoe of five large trilithons is made of stone quarried in Wales. The stone may have been brought overland or by water, but both feats required more technology than earlier archaeologists thought the Bronze Age builders of Stonehenge capable of.

Accommodations

The **Tourist Information Office** at 10 Endless Street, Salisbury (tel. 4956) offers an accommodations service (open Mon.-Sat. 9am-7pm in summer, 9am-5pm in winter). A list of hotels that will help you find a vacancy in local B&Bs is posted outside when the Office is closed.

YHA Youth Hostel, Milford Hill House, Milford Hill (tel. 27572). About a half mile east of the center. Standard hostel; 90p and £1.10. Closed Tues., except during the first week in June, and closed July 15 through September 2.

Mrs. Helliwell, 33 Castle Rd. (tel. 27520). Four singles. £3.50 per night. Very friendly and helpful owner.

Mrs. Hogg, 51 Salt Lane (tel. 27443). Convenient location in a 200-year old house. Friendly family. £3.50 per person.

Hudsons Field, Castle Rd. (tel. 20713) is open for camping May through September. Tents only.

Food

Burkes Bar and Buttery, 1 New St. (tel. 5665). Very comfortable and pleasant wine bar serving mainly salad plates; ham, chicken, or pâté, 85p and up. Closed Sat.

Haunch of Venison, Minster St. Not a particularly friendly pub, but being nearly 600 years old, it has lots of atmosphere. Story goes that the object in the brightly-lit glass case is a mummified hand severed from its arm during the pub's more notorious days. Real ale.

Isle of Wight

Long before the 1969 rock festival brought the old and new devotees of the Isle of Wight into conflict, this small island, separated from Hampshire by the **Solent,** was one of England's favorite summer vacation spots. In 1850, Queen Victoria bought a large house here called Osborne and set the fashion. Now the island has the artsy combination of rich and not-so-rich that characterizes Martha's Vineyard and Fire Island, essentially summer communities for city-dwellers and not a real piece of countryside.

Practical Information

You can reach the Isle of Wight from Lymington, Portsmouth, or Southampton. The trip by Sealink (British Railpasses are valid) is shorter from the first two ports. Both Lymington to Yarmouth and Portsmouth to Ryde take about half an hour.

Once on the island, hitching is difficult but there is comprehensive bus service. Beware: although two towns may look close on the map, the bus could take a long time getting from one to the other. Alum Bay to Newport is an hour trip. **Island Rover** tickets (which cost £1.70 for a day, £5.50 for a week) are good on all buses and on the railway. Trains run between Ryde, Brading, Sandown, Shanklin, and Ventnor.

The island has no less than seven **tourist information offices,** all with free accommodations services. The main branches are: Newport, 21 High Street (tel. 4343); Sandown, Esplanade (tel. 3886); Shanklin, High Street (tel. 2942); and Ryde, Western Gardens Esplanade (tel. 4214). All open 9:30am-5pm, Mon.-Sat.

Holiday accommodation is a major industry of the Isle, so cheap lodgings are hard to find—especially during the high season from mid-July through mid-August. One solution is hosteling. There are three regular **YHA Hostels** on the Isle: Sandown, The Firs, Fitzroy Street (tel. 2561), 90p and £1.10; Totland Bay, Hurst Hill (tel. Freshwater 2165), in a particularly beautiful setting, £1.10 and £1.35; Whitwell, next to a church in Whitwell village near Ventnor (tel. Niton 730473), 90p and £1.10. There are also a few summer hostels. Those expected to be open in July and August are graded simple and priced 75p and 90p: Shorwell, The Old School House; Newport, St. James Street, Wooten Bridge, New Road; Yarmouth, Station Road, Victoria Road. For camping, it is usually advisable to reserve space in advance. Sandown, Ventnor, and Shanklin each have more than 150 Guest Houses, most of them charging £4 per night and up.

Sights

The best reasons to come to the Isle of Wight are relaxation and walking. It has been said that the island is just like the rest of England—only more so. Newport is dusty and seems like any mainland city. The resorts of Ryde, Shanklin, Sandown, and Ventnor are overcrowded and middle-aged. Set out for the countryside on some of the 148 miles of well-marked footpaths. You can purchase a series of pamphlets describing various hikes (from 5 to 65 miles long) at any tourist office (5p each).

Two of the Isle's best walks are between **Alum Bay** and **Freshwater Bay** via the **Cliffs of Tennyson Down** (part of the Tourist Office's Tennyson Trail Walk); and the 15-mile cliff walk from Freshwater Bay to **St. Catherine's Point.** Alum Bay is an unusual formation of brightly-colored sand. Try to see it either early in the morning or at dusk when the crowds have thinned. From the Bay you can see the eerie white-chalk rock islands, called the **Needles,** that make the solent a tricky place to sail.

Other Turrets and Spires in the South

Train service is excellent to and from the towns between Canterbury and Salisbury. **Chichester** is almost more famous for its **summer theater festival** than for its **Cathedral,** but the latter is worth a visit to see the way it has maintained the ecclesiastical tradition of support for the arts, juxtaposing modern creations with medieval ones. The **Tourist Information Office** is in the Council Offices, North Street (tel. 82226), open 9:30am-5 pm Mon.-Sat. In **Winchester** the Cathedral (which nearly crumbled at the turn of the century because of water swamping its foundations) will be celebrating its 900th anniversary in 1979, with concerts and special events.

Without doubt, the most bizarre residence in the south and southeast of England, perhaps in England itself, is the **Royal Pavilion** at **Brighton.** It is impossible to exaggerate when describing the summer home of the Prince Regent (later King George IV). Sometimes described as ''Indian,'' it might just as well be called Chinese or Moorish, and it contains large dollops of high Gothic, neoclassic, and Early Hot Air Balloon as well. The kitchen holds 600 shining copper-bottomed pots, but all that shine is spartan after the **Banqueting Room,** which is modeled after the royal tent of an oriental potentate. Around the corner from the Royal Pavilion is the **Brighton Museum,** which contains a good exhibit of art nouveau stage sets, furniture, and clothing. (The Pavilion is open daily 10am-5pm; in the summer till 8pm; 50p with student card, 80p without. The Museum, on Church Street, is open Tues.-Sat. 10am-5:45pm, Sundays 2-6pm; admission 20p.)

Brighton itself is either rusting and peeling away or uncomfortably modern. Accommodations are expensive and difficult to come by in the high season. The main **Tourist Office** is located at Marlborough House, 54 Old Steine (tel. 23755), open 9am-6:30pm Mon.-Fri., 9am-12:30pm Sat.

The West Country

Bath

A visit to Bath remains *de rigueur,* even if this elegant Georgian city is now more of a museum than a resort. Immortalized by Jane Austen, Dickens, Fielding, and countless others, Bath was for nearly a century the second social capital of England—where the aristocrats came when they wanted something more calmly posh than *the* metropolis, and a trifle more lively than the country. The aristocratic patronage has left Bath with rows of glorious buildings, a long list of famous residents, literary and historical associations, and many minor artistic treasures. But Bath's popularity can be traced back to the days of Roman Britain, when the city of Aquae Sulis was created on the site that is now central Bath. For over four hundred years, the spot flourished as a spa, taking full advantage of the only natural hot springs in Britain.

Bath seems to swirl down the sides of the encircling hills and collect itself in the valley. The whole area is terraced with curves of "Crescents," "Circuses," and serpentine row houses, a white stucco sculpture in the verdant countryside.

Orientation

Bath is well served by rail routes leading to all parts of Britain. Trains from London's Paddington Station leave approximately every hour and reach Bath Spa in an hour and fifteen minutes (about £6 single). Bristol is less than twenty minutes away on the same line (69p single). Frequent service to and from Oxford (change at Didcot) links Bath with the Midlands and the North.

Long-distance "express" coaches are still nearly twice as slow as the trains, but can be half the fare to the same destination (£3.35 from London). All long-distance coaches leave Bath from the **Manvers Street Station** (tel. 63075), just one hundred yards from the **Rail Station** (tel. 64446). Walking up Manvers Street to Orange Grove and turning left will put you in the historic center of Bath, the **Abbey Churchyard.**

Tourist Information Centre: Abbey Churchyard (tel. 62831 for information; 60521 for accommodation service). Free street plans and leaflets on current activities and entertainment available here. They will find you a room in town for a nominal charge. Open October-May Mon.-Sat. 10am-5pm, June-September Mon.-Sat. 10am-8pm and Sun. 2-8pm.

Off-hour Currency Exchange: Jane's Hotel, Manvers St. (tel. 26511). Open every day 8:30am-10:30pm. Cash and travelers checks exchanged.

Emergency Services and Police: dial 999 (free call).

Accommodations

YHA Youth Hostel, Bathwick Hill (tel. 65674), in the east side of the city. A fine Hostel in a gracious hillside mansion. 100 beds, hostel meals, plus a cafeteria (open 6-8:30pm). Usually full during the summer; if you haven't booked, try to arrive at 5pm and join the queue. Superior-grade charges: £1.10 and £1.35 per night. Take bus #218 (the University bus) from the Bus Station and Grand Parade. Closed daily 10am-5pm and on Mondays (except during school holiday periods); 10:30pm curfew.

Mrs. Lynn Shearn, Prior House, 14 Gordon Rd., off Prior Park Rd. A young couple who really enjoys putting up young people. Eat breakfast and watch TV with the family. A great value at £3 per person. Call 313587 and ask for directions; about a ten-minute walk from the Bus or Rail Station.

Mrs. K.M. Pickering, Holly Villa, 14 Pulteney Gardens (tel. 310331), entrance around the corner. The conscientious management has decorated the six rooms nicely; all have washbasins and are centrally heated. Bed-and-breakfast for £4.50 per person.

Mr. Smith's Guest House, 9 Queen St. (tel. 4328). Above Mr. Smith's restaurant. Mr. Smith really does exist, has a goatee, is friendly, and often sits down for a chat with his guests. TVs and showers. £4 per person.

Melrose Hotel, 20 Bennett St. (tel. 22467). Ideal location, next to the Assembly Rooms. A well-run private hotel with rooms from £4 per person.

Kennet Guest House, 27 Pulteney Gardens (tel. 25925). Clean and convenient, but on the corner of a busy road; can be noisy. £4.25 per person for bed-and-breakfast.

YMCA International House, Broad Street Place (tel. 60471). Far more central than the YHA Hostel. Some dorm accommodations, but also a large number of doubles. Bed-and-breakfast from £4 per person; few restrictions.

If the above are full (they may well be during the high season), try the row of B&Bs along the **Wells Road** (A367). They tend to cater to truck drivers on their way south, and may not be as used to backpacking Americans as the tourist-oriented houses. Expect to pay £3.50-4 for no-frills bed-and-breakfast.

There are no campsites close to Bath that accept tents, and public transport is limited to the rural sites in Wiltshire and northern Somerset.

Food

Fresh fruit and vegetables can be found at the **City of Bath Provisional Market,** between High Street and Grand Parade. Open 7am-6pm and until 1pm on Thursdays (closed Sundays).

The Walrus and the Carpenter, 28 Barton St., near the Theatre Royal. A friendly place, music-filled and intimate. Great burgers in a basket with such toppings as sour cream and crushed garlic (£1.15-1.50). Huge slice of homemade cake for 50p. Open 6:30-11pm every day. There's often a line to get in.

The Abbey Café, 18 York St. Substantial meals for about £1. Sunday lunches are particularly good. The upstairs restaurant is a bit fancier; meals for about £2. Open until 10pm.

The Hole-in-the-Wall, George St., was once considered England's most "gourmet" restaurant. It is still a good place to splurge, but its prices are up and the quality down. The appetizer table—laden with salads, shellfish, and vegetables—is superb; the main dishes—all in the £4.50-6 range—vary from adequate to excellent. Inexpensive wines are available, but with service, VAT, and the urge to order dessert, it is unlikely you will be able to eat here for less than £8-10. Closed Sun.

Sights

Despite the ravaging of Hitler's raids in 1942, the best of Bath's Georgian heritage survives peacefully in the northwest residential part of the city. To get to the heart of this past, walk up Gay Street (a continuation of Barton Street) to **The Circus,** a full circle of Georgian town houses. Number 17 housed the painter Thomas Gainsborough for sixteen years; the late Prime Minister William Pitt had #7 and 8 built for himself. Leave the Circus on Brock Street and you will encounter the renowned **Royal Crescent,** the premier accomplishment of John Wood the Younger.

The **Assembly Rooms** are on the other side of the Circus; these rooms staged *the* social events in the West of England during the last fifty years of the eighteenth century. They now contain the most comprehensive **Museum of Costume** in Britain. (Open Mon.-Sat. 9:30am-6pm; Sun. 10am-6pm; admission 65p, combined tickets for the Assembly Rooms, Costume Museum, and Roman Baths-Pump Room complex are £1.)

Bath's most treasured possession must surely be its **Roman Baths.** Most of the remains, the finest collection of Roman artifacts in Britain, have been cleaned up for display in the Museum. Enter the Museum from the Abbey Churchyard and head for the display; look out for the non-display, a gushing hot spring, very warm and misty. Catch one of the free informative tours of the Baths. In conjunction with the Baths is the **Pump Room,** the room to which the hot spring water was, and still is, pumped for drinking purposes. If you visit in the morning (10am-noon), sit down here and enjoy a cup of coffee to the sounds of the jazzy Pump Room Trio—all for 25p. The Roman Baths-Pump Room complex is open every day 9am-6pm; admission to both is 65p, 10p for the Pump Room only.

Acting as a beacon for disoriented tourists, **Bath Abbey** stands solidly by the Pump Room, looming over the busy Abbey Churchyard. Technological advances during the Gothic period (the structure was finished in 1616) allowed the Abbey to turn its wall into windows; the resulting effect earned the church the name "Lanterns of the West."

The **Parade Gardens** is the setting for afternoon concerts by the Pump Room Trio, starting at 3pm Mon.-Sat. On Sundays, at the same time, the park fills with the sounds of big band brass at Sunday Band Concerts. For only 15p admission, it is an ideal way to break up the afternoon, and if you're really lucky, catch some sunshine. The park grounds are open every day 10am-8pm.

A quick bus ride up Bathwick Hill brings you to **Claverton Manor,** the home of the one-of-a-kind **American Museum in Britain.** Many of the rooms on display here were brought over intact from American houses; others were pieced together from materials shipped across the sea. Come watch the British get a kick out of it (open Tues.-Sun. 2-5pm; admission £1). Take bus #218 (the University bus) and alight at The Avenue (22p single).

Evenings

For a city which has earned its livelihood from affluent rheumatics, Bath entertains the young and impoverished fairly well. The **Entertainer Pub** in the Fernley Hotel, North Parade, features live local talent each evening. The entertainment is free, and hot bar meals are served 6:30-9:30pm. On Walcot Street are two of the more popular young people's pubs. **The Bell** is known for its jazz and blues, live every night except Tuesdays and Sundays. The **Hat and Feather Inn** is where you'll find Bath's freak contingent. Always packed and lively; druggy atmosphere.

The last week of May and first week of June witness Bath's most famous annual event, the **Bath International Festival of Music.** The world's leading musicians perform in the great halls of Bath: the Assembly Rooms and the Guildhall Banqueting Room. The **Tourist Office** (tel. 62831) can provide you with details and even sell you tickets.

The Mendip Country

The northern fringe of low-lying **Somerset County** is brought to an abrupt halt by the heights of the Mendip Hills. While many tourists migrate to the Mendips to view the prehistoric remains in the hills, many others choose to concentrate on the towns that lie just south of them. Within ten miles of each other, **Wells, Cheddar,** and **Glastonbury** create a triangle of attractions as diversified as they are historic.

There is no rail station in the immediate area—the closest is **Weston-super-Mare,** on the shore of the Bristol Channel, but bus service from Bath and Bristol are regular, if expensive. Bus #175 runs between Bath and Wells every hour (£1.15 single). A quick change at Wells puts Cheddar or Glastonbury just minutes away.

Wells has the distinction of being the smallest cathedral city in England (St. David's in South Wales is the littlest in Britain), but the community lacks pretension and presents itself as a quite prosperous market town.

Dominating the otherwise unremarkable architecture of the town, the **Cathedral Church of St. Andrew** is the hub of one of the best surviving examples of a whole Cathedral complex—complete with princely **Bishop's Palace, Vicar's Close,** and **Chapter House.** The Cathedral's striking West Front still carries almost 300 separate pieces of medieval sculpture. Beneath the central crossing under the tower is a huge X-shaped double arch, resembling an hourglass; it was an anonymous medieval architect's solution to the structural problem of the central tower, which threatened to collapse and bring the rest of the building down with it.

Take an afternoon off from the man-made sights and visit the caves at **Wookey Hole,** just a two-mile walk from the center of Wells. Alexander Pope used to plunder the caves for "uncommon petrefactions" which he later used to decorate his Twickenham Grotto. The ravine, caves, and mill were purchased by Madame Tussaud's Wax Museum in 1973, so that the visitor of today is entertained by better than 2000 wax heads, a motley array of profiles if ever there was one. The conducted tour (mandatory) lasts an hour and a half and costs £1.10. Buses (route #172) run every two hours from Wells Bus Station, Priory Road, to Wookey Hole (22p single).

The **Tourist Information Centre** (tel. 72552) in the Town Hall will find you a bed for a 30p service charge. (Open seven days a week in the summer, 10am-5pm) Inexpensive accommodation is hard to come by; expect to pay at least £4 for bed-and-breakfast. **Flagstones,** 26 Chamberlain Street (tel. 72178), has a fourteenth-century fireplace in the lounge and a great chappy for a landlord. He charges £4 per person for bed and an exceptional breakfast. Mrs. M. White's **Bekynton Guest House** at 7 Thomas Street (tel. 72222) is recently redecorated and nicely done up; her six rooms are let for £5 per person; an evening meal is available as well (a plus since Wells is short on good eating places). The closest campsite is the **Homestead Caravan and Camping Park** at Wookey Hole (tel. 73022). Excellently equipped and therefore expensive—by British standards: £2.35 per night for a tent and two people; each additional person is 25p. Take the Wookey Hole bus (#172) and look out for the site, a few hundred yards before the village on the Wells road.

The town of Cheddar itself has little to offer; the attraction here is purely a natural one. Perhaps nowhere else will you see such a blatant example of the Britons' ability to exploit every inch of cave and cliff. But no matter how commercialized and tacky, the **Gorge** remains awe-inspiring. Try to approach Cheddar from the Mendips, via the B3371, so that you can descend dramatically through the Gorge. At the top of the Gorge signs say, "Cyclists are advised to walk. You have been warned." While the craggy walls of the Gorge tower above the motorists or cyclists, the most impressive vantage point is reserved for walkers. The easiest access (if you can call 300 steps easy) to the top is via **Jacob's Ladder** (15p charge). A footpath runs along the cliff edge for about a mile and a half, dropping down to the main road opposite Black Rock Gate.

All of the commotion at the foot of the Gorge is around the **Cheddar Caves.** The complex includes three caves (one with a waterfall), a museum, a "Grotto Bar" and a couple of restaurants. Admission charges vary from 15-40p; you pay for each attraction separately. Open seven days a week 10am-sunset.

Cheddar's **Tourist Information Office** is in the Library on Union Street (tel. 742769). Although they don't offer an accommodation service, the free map of Cheddar is worth stopping in for. (Open Mon.-Fri. 10am-5pm, Sat. 10am-12:30pm, closed for lunch 1-2:30pm.) Just a fifteen-minute walk from the village center is the **YHA Hostel** (tel. 742494). Overnight charges are 90p and £1.10; closed 10am-5pm daily and every Sunday. If they are full or closed, try **Clementine** on Station Road. This is a private hostel with a dorm and one small bedroom, no day lock-out, and plenty of beds. Standards aren't as high as the YHA's, but for £1.25 per night it's a viable alternative. There are two **campsites** within walking distance of Cheddar Village; both are on the Wells Road (A371), just past the Parish Church. **Frogland's**

Farm is the more picturesque of the two, and is quieter as well. Tent camping from £1.50 per night; call 742058 for bookings.

Junk food reigns in Cheddar. And don't bother trying the "Cheddar" cheese; it's all prepackaged, overpriced, and no longer made in the town. For real food drop by the **Edelweiss Restaurant,** midway between the village and the Gorge. A diverse à la carte menu and a substantial three-course lunch will fill you for £1.40-2.

Glastonbury is the original center of Christianity in Britain. The noble ruins of **Glastonbury Abbey,** the oldest abbey on the British Isles (built in 678), still outline where the walls once stood. The Abbey grounds are entered from Market Cross (open daily 9:30am-7:30pm; admission 25p). In 1191 the monks dug up a coffin they claimed contained the remains of King Arthur and Queen Guinevere. And in 1276, in the presence of King Edward I, they were solemnly re-interred in front of the high altar. According to another Arthurian legend, Glastonbury, the mythical island of Avalon, is supposed to be the place where the Messiah will arrive for the second time. Not surprisingly, the place has become a Mecca for all denominations of religious enthusiasts, and droves of worshippers return to Glastonbury for the two pilgrimages: Church of England and Roman Catholic. Others congregate on the slope of **Glastonbury Tor,** the grassy mound that supports what remains of St. Michael's Chapel. From this height of 525 feet you can view the Wiltshire Downs, the Mendips, and on a really clear day, the Bristol Channel. On your way back down, try to make it past the **Chalice Well,** where Arthurian legend places the burial site of the Chalice Cup (or Holy Grail).

In town, stroll down High Street and try to find two of Glastonbury's famous façades: The **Tribunal,** which was the Abbot's Courthouse in the fifteenth century, and the **George and Pilgrims Hotel,** where pilgrims to Glastonbury have been housed since 1475.

Around the corner, past the Market Cross, is Northload Street, where the **Tourist Information Centre** is at #7. For the price of a phone call (10p) they will find you a bed in town; street plans are dispensed free of charge (open Mon.-Sat. 9:30am-5pm, May through September only; tel. 32954). If bed-and-breakfast in a grand Georgian house a few minutes from the town center interests you, drop by **St. John's Vicarage** on Lambrook Street. Actually, it might be a good idea to call first (tel. 32362), as Mrs. Clarkson has many devoted guests and rooms go quickly at £4 per person. A bit farther out of town, along the Shepton Mallet road (A361), is **Tor Down.** Home cooking at its best and a super view justify the per-person charge of £4.50 for bed-and-breakfast. Located on Ashwell Lane, about three-quarters of a mile out of town; call 32287 and ask for Mrs. Parfitt. A few hundred yards along the A361 is **Ashwell Farm House** (tel. 32313), offering tent camping for 90p on the adjacent field. No showers, but hot running water and plenty of space. They also have rooms to let for £4 per person. The closest **YHA Hostel** is a mile and a half south of the village of **Street.** This simple-grade Hostel is small, so it's a good idea to call (tel. Street 42961). The Hostel is closed 10am-5pm daily and every Tuesday. The **Coach House Cafe,** Northload Street, opposite the Tourist Office, serves salads from 70p and steaks from £1.20; good value and reliable food (open Mon.-Sat. 9am-9pm).

To get to the ancient **Isle of Avalon,** hitch along the A39 from Wells (about six miles), or take bus #376, leaving Wells every half hour (39p single). The closest rail station to Glastonbury is Bridgewater, about twelve miles along the A39—very hitchable.

The West Country Moors: Exmoor and Dartmoor

Unlike the coastal resorts of the West Country, the moorlands of Exmoor and Dartmoor have managed to resist commercialization, and the people that farm the land continue to live in peaceful isolation. The moorland ponies—especially the ancient Dartmoor—still roam freely, as rugged as ever. A drive through the parks will introduce you to these hardy beasts, as well as to the native sheep.

As a single expanse of land, Exmoor combines nearly all of the features for which English countryside is so loved. Its cliffs plunge into the sea along the West Somerset coast; the fringe of the park is rolling with lushly covered hills; and subtly colored heath and moorland cover the western side of the park. R.D. Blackmore immortalized Exmoor in his romance, *Lorna Doone*. Man's intrusion here has been well-mannered; the few lanes run over the tops of the heather-clad moors, just to drop dramatically into jungle-like dales. The best way to cover the ground is by foot, but a car would be handy to give you access to the out-of-the-way spots. If you intend to hitch, be prepared for lengthy waits along the inner roadways. Cycling in Exmoor has its ups and downs.

The easiest place from which to enter Exmoor is the coastal resort of **Minehead.** There are daily buses to Minehead from Bath and Bristol, changing at Taunton along the way. The **Tourist Information Centre,** The Parade (tel. 2624), offers a free accommodation service and lots of local information. Open 9:30am-1pm and 2-5pm daily. Upstairs from this office is one of the **Exmoor National Park Information Offices** (open April through September, same hours as TIC; tel. 2984). This is the place to pick up dozens of informative leaflets detailing the activities and attractions of the park itself.

From **Minehead Bus Station,** on the Avenue (tel. 2365), you can catch a bus that follows the coast road to **Lynton,** another good touring center for the park. There is also an occasional service (Tuesdays and Saturdays) south through the moor to **Dulverton.** The main office of the **National Park Information Service** will be found here in Exmoor House (tel. Dulverton 23665). Dulverton is an excellent base for hiking in the moor; the office can provide you with invaluable advice. While a walk across the moors can be exhilarating, it can also be dangerous. Make sure you bring solid footwear, waterproof clothing, map, and compass.

Exford, in the very center of the park, is also a good base. This quiet village has a couple of inns that offer bed-and-breakfast and light meals. Right in the middle of the village, next to the river bridge, is a superior-grade **YHA Hostel.** This is a popular place, so it's best to call (tel. Exford 288) to see if they have a bed for you. (Closed 10am-5pm daily and every Thursday.)

In the wilder Dartmoor, you will escape into a land that is as isolated and desolate as the Scottish Highlands. The land is farmed by the "Commoners" of Dartmoor, who have vigorously preserved their rights to graze animals, collect heather for thatching, and gather stones and sand from the "Common Land."

Dartmoor's reputation as one of the most desolate areas of the British Isles is enhanced by the presence of *the* maximum-security prison of Britain at Princetown. The other evidence of man's presence here is far older; the ruins of the Bronze Age—the largest array to be found in Europe—have been left undisturbed. Burial chambers, ritualistic stone rows, huts, and enclosures can be explored and mulled over without the fences and coach parks of sites like Stonehenge and Avebury.

Certainly the best, and sometimes only, way of seeing the wonders of Dartmoor is on foot. The National Park Authority conducts guided walks. Some tend to specialize on certain topics (bird life, Bronze Age remains, or perhaps wild flowers and plants), but most try to introduce the visitor to a variety of aspects of Dartmoor. Any Dartmoor National Park Information Office can provide you with a leaflet listing the dates and starting times of walks throughout the park. Dartmoor is renowned for its highly changeable weather, so always carry waterproof gear, and an extra sweater. If the mists drop suddenly over the moor tops, you would be really lost without a compass and reliable map (the *Ordnance Survey 2½-inches-to-the-mile* series is one of the best for walking).

Unlike many of Britain's National Parks, Dartmoor can be toured easily by public transportation. A special bus service bisects the park and connects with regular services that skirt the moor. The main route, "the Transmoor Link," cuts right through the park from Plymouth to Moretonhampstead. En route is the village of **Postbridge,** a lush oasis amidst the harsh land that surrounds. The National Park Information Caravan here can advise you on the footpaths in the area and sell you the appropriate maps. One mile south of Postbridge is the **Bellever YHA Hostel** (tel. 88227). This small hiker's Hostel is closed 10am-5pm daily and every Monday; overnight charges are 84p and £1.02. The best towns in the park for bed-and-breakfast accommodation are **Bovey Tracey, Two Bridges,** and **Tavistock** (just west of the park boundary). The greatest concentration of campsites is around **Okehampton,** on the northern edge of the moor. Pick up a leaflet listing all the sites in the area at any **DNP Information Office.** The head office is in the County Hall, Exeter (tel. Exeter 77977, extension 727); caravans are situated at **New Bridge, Bovey Tracey, Postbridge, Tavistock,** and **Dunsford.** All are open from Easter to October, usually 11am-5pm daily (including Sundays).

Devon

Devon, the eastern half of the South West peninsula of England, is a county of wild moors and rugged coast, just three and a half hours from London by train from Paddington Station. The south coast of Devon has always been a popular vacation spot with middle-class British families, and old-age pensioners return to the same hotel year after year. Indeed, the resorts of **Torquay, Torbay,** and **Exmouth** are prototypes for what is now found on every bit of suitable—or even not so suitable—British coast.

Inland, Devon is largely rural, pleasant country, but is also largely inaccessible unless you have a car or moped. In contrast to this soft country are the bleak moors of the huge **Dartmoor National Park.**

The two logical choices for touring centers in Devon are the West Country cities of **Exeter** and **Plymouth,** a large and hectic port city. Exeter is more appealing. The **Cathedral,** Exeter's greatest glory, stands alone on a grassy plain amidst shopping precincts and office buildings. The West Front is covered with intricate carvings and sculptured figures; inside the doors is the longest stretch of Gothic stone vaulting in the world. If you're lucky, you may hear the world's second heaviest ringing peal echoing from the south tower.

The city's **Tourist Information Centre,** Civic Centre, Paris Street (tel. 77888), offers a free accommodation service and can give you a brochure of campsites in the County of Devon. (Open Mon.-Sat. 8:45am-1:15pm and 1:45-5pm.) The **West Country Tourist Board,** Trinity Court, 37 Southernhay East (tel. 76351) produces a series of useful brochures, covering all of the West Country. (Open Mon.-Fri. 9am-5:15pm.)

Exeter's **YHA Hostel** is a superior-grade worthy of the rating, even if it is two miles out from the city center. Located at 47 Countess Wear Road (off Topsham Road); take bus #356 or 357 from Paris Street Station. Closed on Wednesdays except during school-holiday periods. A bit more central is the private hostel known as **L'Abri Cotier** at 17 Mont-le Grand (tel. 52493). There are no restrictions here, but the house is slightly run down. Dorm beds go for £1.25; bed-and-breakfast for £2.50. More comfortable, and far more pleasant is the **Radnor Hotel** (tel. 72004), St, David's Hill, about 200 yards from the Rail Station. The cheerful landlady manages the house well and at £4.50 per person it's worth trying. If you're in town from mid-July to mid-September, the **University of Exeteer** opens up its halls of residence for student travelers with IDs. Modern singles are let for £1.65 per night and bed-and-breakfast costs £3. Take bus C from the city center and ask to be let off at Cornwall House. The nearest **campsite** is the **Cat and Fiddle Leisure Park,** Clyst St. Mary, four miles east of Exeter on the Lyme Regis Road (A3052). They have lots of amenities and plenty of room for tents at £2 per night (tel. Topsham 5008).

The Mint, 154 Fone Street, is an appealing wine bar serving hot and cold meals; everything on the menu is less than £1.50. Open Mon.-Thurs. 10:30am-10:30pm; Fri. and Sat. until 11pm; Sun. noon-2:30pm and 7-10:30pm. Downstairs is a seven-nights-a-week disco that starts rolling at 8:30pm. **The Ship,** in Martin's Lane right by the Cathedral Close, is the place to try "scrumpy," a freshly-made draught cider; Sir Francis Drake used to imbibe here along with his cronies.

Buses to all parts of the West Country depart from Exeter's **Paris Street Station.** For city and country bus route information call 56231; for details of long-distance coach runs call 74103. Trains from London (Waterloo) arrive at St. David's Station, where trains to the West and the Midlands can also be found. All British Rail information is available by dialing 33551.

Cornwall

Cornwall, too, has its moor—**Bodmin Moor,** between Launceston and Bodmin, the setting for Daphne Du Maurier's *Jamaica Inn.* The Inn itself actually exists, on the A30, an old-fashioned and delightful pub. If moor trekking is still in your blood after Devon, the **Information Bureau** in Bodmin, in Priory House (tel. 2216), is your best source of information.

But Cornwall is better seen for its coast, both on the north and south.**St. Austell,** on the south coast, offers heavy seas, sand and pebble beaches, and stark clay cliffs, though the coast is perhaps better seen from the fishing port of **Mevagissey,** where a wide selection of guest houses awaits you in Polkirt Hill, overlooking the sea. Farther down the coast, **Gorran Haven** affords more accommodations, as well as a marvelous bakery called Cakebread's. Try, too, the fresh fish and oysters for which the South West is famous.

The northern coast offers even rougher seas and a good deal of surfing, especially at **Polzeath.** History buffs can explore **Tintagel Castle,** believed by many to be the ancient seat of Camelot (open daily 9:30am-7pm; 30p).

The western end of Cornwall begins at the country town of **Truro,** with its **Regional Information Office** in the Municipal Buildings, Boscawen Street (tel. 4555). To the south, the resort towns of **Falmouth** and **St. Mawes** offer palm trees, shark fishing, and boat trips to islands off the coast. Particularly nice is the boat ride to Truro and back along the coast. West of Falmouth, you'll come to **Lizzard Point,** one of the National Trust's most treasured possessions. You can spend the afternoon hiking around the point at the top of the magnificent cliffs.

On the north coast, **St. Ive's Bay** has water so clear you almost can't see it. You can take a boat ride from here to **Seal Island,** where families of seals bask in the sun; or head out along the coast to the hilly artists' town of **Mousehole** (pronounced "mouzill") or to **St. Michael's Mount,** the English counterpart of Mont-St.-Michel (70p). You have to travel across a long causeway to reach this island fortress, with one eye on the tide. Finally, at the very tip of Cornwall is **Land's End,** with all the tourist paraphernalia that surrounds it.

Hikers will be interested in the **Cornwall Coast Path,** a 268-mile trail that follows the coast virtually continuously from Morsland Mouth in the north to Cremyll in the south. Several youth hostels and plenty of B&Bs are within easy reach of the path. The **Cornwall Tourist Board** in Truro will sell you a brochure called *The Cornwall Coast Path* (15p), containing a map and a list of accommodations.

The Midlands

Oxford

At the base of the Midlands sits Oxford, bridging the gap between the tiny agricultural villages of the **Cotswold Hills** and **Chiltern Downs** and the great industrial centers further north. As you approach, the signs of the twentieth century are plain enough. Coming north on the A34 over the hill that marks the **Ridge Way** (the oldest road in Britain, built during the Bronze Age; it goes all the way to Salisbury Plain—some great walking along it, if you can use a compass), you catch a sweeping view of **Harwell,** Britain's center for atomic energy research. The Cowley works, where they make Morris cars, are in the southeast corner of the city, while bigger and better office complexes rise each year in the west. But you won't be aware of industrial power plants once you are in the heart of Oxford, on the campus of the University. While Cambridge sets magnificent college halls in the midst of huge greens, Oxford is personal. In the narrow cobbled streets between the bell towers and chapels of fifteenth-century residences, you get a sense that actual people lived and learned here. Oxford colleges are part of real-world bustle on crowded streets along with shops and houses. The manicured lawns lining Cambridge's River Cam become the tree-shaded, overgrown paths along the **Cherwell** and **Thames.** Cows graze in Christ Church Meadow, and Magdalen College gets its venison from its own Deer Park, just behind the main quad.

Most of the important University buildings cluster around the streets that meet the High Street between **Carfax** and **Magdalen Bridge.** The famed **Bodleian Library** is next to the Sheldonian on Catte Street, along with the domed **Radcliffe Camera.** Just behind is the fifteenth-century **Divinity School.** Continue up Catte Street to the Broad and you come to **Blackwell's,** the world-famous bookshop.

Follow the Broad to St. Giles Street, where you'll find the **Ashmolean Museum,** on Beaumont Street, with an excellent collection of Italian and English art (open weekdays 10am-4pm, Sundays 2-4pm; free). Of course, you shouldn't miss the colleges—you can visit most of them during the afternoons. Especially worth seeing is sixteenth-century **Christ Church,** on St. Aldate's, begun but left unfinished by Cardinal Wolsey, and endowed with the monastic spoils of Henry VIII; the library here is considered one of the most beautiful rooms in Oxford. Among the other colleges, visit thirteenth-century **Merton,** and its lovely chapel; **Magdalen** (pronounced "Maud-lin"), with its fifteenth-century cloisters; and **New College,** with its famous chapel that contains works by Jacob Epstein and El Greco, in addition to fine stained glass. **Addison's Walk** isn't all that pretty any more—the Dutch elm disease has denuded it.

Punts are for hire at Folly Bridge, Magdalen Bridge, and at the **Cherwell Boat House** (tel. 52746) at the bottom of Bardwell Road. Prices are about £1.20 per hour, but deposits can be as high as £10. Bicycles can be rented at **Denton's,** 39a George Street, and at **Pennyfarthing's,** 27 George Street, for £1.50 a day plus £15 deposit. It's great fun to bicycle around Oxford—but you won't be able to take the bike inside most college gates.

The **New Theatre,** George Street (tel. 44544), shows movies in summer, but during the fall it presents everything from Oscar Peterson to the Royal Ballet. The **Oxford Playhouse** on Beaumont Street (tel. 47133) holds a summer theater festival between June and September. **The Phoenix One and Two,** Walton Street (tel. 54909) shows art films. They run two double feature bills weekly plus an extra 11pm show (£1 for tickets). During June and early July when the University is still in session, keep an eye out for outdoor concerts and college theater.

Orientation and Accommodations

Oxford is about an hour from London by train from Paddington. Departures are frequent—about three an hour. National Express Coach from Buckingham Palace Road to Oxford takes about one hour and forty-five minutes. The city center is an easy, well-marked walk from the Train Station. Be sure to bring cash if you arrive on the weekend. Banks are closed on Saturday and Sunday with the exception of **Lewis Bank,** inside Selfridge Department Store, Westgate, open till 5pm Saturday.

The **Oxford Information Center,** St. Aldate's (tel. 48707), is open Monday-Saturday 9am-5:30pm, Sundays in summer 10:30am-1pm and 1:30-4pm. The accommodations service, open till 5pm weekdays, will help you find a vacant room. When it's closed, call 40236 and Mr. S.J. O'Kane, president of a B&B owners' association, will help you out. The **Student Travel Office** is located one flight up at J. M. Menzies bookshop on High Street.

YHA Hostel, Jack Straw Lane (tel. 62997). Good Hostel with showers, baths, kitchen, and food shop. 90p and £1.10. 10:30pm curfew. Take bus #570 from Queen's Lane.

YWCA, Alexandra Residential Club, 133 Woodstock Road (tel. 52021). For women between 17 and 45; £2 per person for transients. Singles £10.75 per week, doubles £8.50 per week. No meals, but cooking facilities. Very good for the price. Vacancies usually available only during school vacations.

Mr. and Mrs. Beer, 35 Bainton Rd. A bit out of town, but good value for £3.50. Very helpful, talkative proprietors—retired school-teachers with university connections. Take any Woodstock Rd. bus, get off at Frenchay Rd. Turn left and your first right is Bainton.

Like any English town, Oxford has its streets for B&B. Try #11, 131, 137, 192, 238, 244, 281, and 283 on **Iffley Road,** where prices range from £3.50-4. In **Cowley Road,** #255, 322, 331, and 343 offer comparable rooms. **Abingdon Road** to the south has several B&Bs (#90, 106, 180, and 234). The B&Bs in St. John's St. and Walton St. to the north are a bit more expensive but more convenient.

There are two camping sites in the area: **Cassington Mill Caravan Site** (tel. 881490), about five miles northwest of Oxford on A40 and B4449, has hot water showers. Tents £1. Take bus #440, 441, or 442 from the Woolworth's off Cornmarket St. **Temple Farm** (tel. 779359) is about 5 miles south on the A423 to Henley. Tents £1. Take bus #5, 510, 512, or 513 from New Rd. or Queen St.

Food

Brown's Restaurant and Wine Bar, 7/9 Woodstock Rd. (tel. 511995). Where the action is—wood floors, hanging plants, loud music, young crowd. The food is good and surprisingly inexpensive. Large helpings of spaghetti, garlic bread, and one of the best salads in England for £1.20. Grills and salads about £1.45. Cappuccino 25p. Open noon-2:30pm and 6-10:30pm, Fri.-Sat. till 11pm.

Pippin's, 8 Ship St. (tel. 723459). Health food and homemade dishes at prices from 80p up. Crowded and popular with students. Go around 3pm for tea. Closed Sun. and at 6pm weekdays.

Turf Tavern, 4 Bath Place, entrance from Holywell St. A large cold buffet (salads, vegetables, fish, pâté, etc.) at lunch or dinner make this a popular place to eat. Go early for the homemade hot dishes. Expect to spend at least £1-1.50, depending on how much you take. Great for eating outdoors in one of their three small courtyards.

The fish-and-chips shops along Walton St., St. Clements, and Cowly Rd. serve food wrapped in newspapers, piping hot, for around £1.

Pubs

The King's Arms, Holywell St. Not as unusual is the nearby Turf Tavern, but just as popular. As many as three different real ales available. Meals also a good buy.

The Bear, Alfred St. and Bear Lane. The local for Christ Church; a snobbish, dyed-in-the-wool Oxford landmark. It could do without the collection of ties, but some of them have been snipped from England's best, brightest, and most boastful.

The Wheatsheaf, High St. Real ale (according to the definition by the *Good Beer Guide*) is served here. Down an alleyway behind High Street. Good decor.

St. Michael's Tavern. Good for drinking as well as eating. Hook Norton, the Oxford brew, is served.

Stratford-upon-Avon

Exploiting Shakespeare to the hilt, Stratford-upon-Avon is crowded, commercialized, unworthy, and yet inevitable. Even a visit for a performance of the **Royal Shakespeare Theatre** can be a disappointment unless you are prepared for what could be an avant garde or innovative interpretation. If you plan to go, you will need to book ahead (tel. 0789-2271, 24-hour information 0789-69191). Ticket prices range from £1.20 to £7; standing room 80p. Although you can see an afternoon production on a daytrip from London, the ride (nearly three hours) is really too long to take twice in one day comfortably. Stratford is an easy daytrip from Oxford. A day return bus ticket costs £1.65. Buses leave four times a day and take about two hours. You pass Blenheim Palace on the way.

Accommodations in town are high priced and hard to get. The **Tourist Information Center,** Judith Shakespeare House, 1 High Street (tel. 66175 or 3127) will help (open 9am-5:30pm Mon.-Sat., Sun. 1:30-5pm). You can write ahead and make reservations through them. Family farms aren't a great option, since they are scarce and more expensive than B&Bs.

Among the things to do in town there are, however, one or two that are worthwhile. Shakespeare's birthplace would be picturesque if it were empty . . . but the garden in back weathers the crowds much better. Shakespeare, born in Stratford in 1564, retired from playwriting after finishing *The Tempest* and returned to his home town, where his chief interest seems to have been real estate and litigation. Many of the places of interest in Stratford are parcels of land that Shakespeare once owned. Contrary to popular belief, we know more about the bard than about any of his contemporaries with the sole exception of Queen Elizabeth. This is partly the result of the diligent labors of generations of scholars, and partly the result of Shakespeare's incessant litigation, which has preserved his name in court records. Buried beneath a savage couplet, the greatest English poet and playwright lies in **Holy Trinity Church,** a lopsided affair which is about the only place in Stratford where a sort of pilgrimage might make sense.

Accommodations

YHA Youth Hostel, Hemmingford House, Alveston (tel. 2823). Two miles from Stratford on the Wellesbourne Rd. (take bus #518 to the Alveston-Loxley crossroads). £1.10 and £1.35. Late passes for theater 16p. Curfew 10:30pm.

Avon House, 8 Evesham Place (tel. 3328). About £9.60 for a double.

Craig House, 69 Shipston Rd. (tel. 2471). £4 and up per person.

Ravenhurst Private Hotel, 2 Broadwalk (tel. 2515). £9.60 for a double. Small but pleasant and friendly.

Camping is at The Elms, one mile northeast of Stratford in Tiddington (tel. 2312). Tents £1.75. Shower and laundry facilities.

Food

The Horse Shoe, 33-34 Greenhill St. (tel. 2246). Good food and low prices. You can get savories for around 60p and fixed lunches at £1.20 or £1.45 (not including VAT). Open Mon.-Sat.

The Cobweb, 12 Sheep St. (tel. 2554). Good for both tea and meals. Set price for high tea is 90p but items available à la carte.

Kingfisher, 13 Ely St. (tel. 2513). Chips and anything (fish, chicken, eggs). Prices range from 35p to £1.18. Open Tues.-Sat.

East Anglia

Bulging from the east coast of England between the Thames Estuary on the south and The Wash on the north, East Anglia is best described as flat. The **Fens** that cover the northwest quarter of the region are dark marshes, for centuries flooded with sea water until the Romans started their reclamation project soon after conquering Britain. Today most of the drainage is done by diesel and electric pumps, but dozens of windmills still dot the countryside. The **Norfolk Broads,** open expanses of water with navigable approach channels, spread east from Norwich to the English Channel. Rivers, lakes, and streams form a waterway maze; you can rent a craft and try to make sense of the scheme yourself. The sandy coast—sorry, no white cliffs here—is laden with typical English seaside resorts, such as **Great Yarmouth, Lowesfort, Clacton-on-Sea,** and **Southend-on-Sea.** Walking promenades, pleasure piers, and amusement arcades all thrive on East Anglia's coast.

Cambridge and **Norwich** are the best centers for touring the region; both offer extensive rail and bus services, and are easily accessible from London. Hitching about the area is easier than in many parts of Britain; major towns are connected directly by roads with steady flows of commercial traffic. For the trains, the best deal is the **Anglia Ranger** ticket, entitling you to unlimited travel throughout the region, costing only £6 for one week (£2.30 for a daily ticket). For daytrips or a long haul, the **Anywhere** bus ticket at £1.30 is another good way to go; you can buy them on any bus and then travel as far as you wish for the rest of the day.

From Cambridge, **Ely** (the market town known for its immense Cathedral) lies to the north, surrounded by the Fens. While most of the fenland is now drained and prosperously farmed, you can see the undrained version at the **Nature Preserve** at **Wicken Fen.** Further north, you can visit one of the other great East Anglian cathedrals at **Peterborough,** while a detour east from Ely takes you to **Bury St. Edmunds,** so called because King Edmund was buried there in 970, where the fine Norman Abbey still stands.

On the northern fringe of the Fens, at the basin of the Wash, is **King's Lynn,** a town with a legendary mercantile heritage going back to the days of King John. Half-timbered merchants' houses remain, alongside black-and-white checked guild halls on cobbled lanes. Norwich, once the second city for commerce in England, retains some of its medieval charm. It now serves as the shopping center for East Anglia, a sort of honorary capital of the region. With one of the finest urban castles to be found anywhere, and a cathedral that ranks along with Ely and Petersborough, Norwich should not be missed.

Complete your tour of East Anglia by visiting one of the coastal resorts, if only to see what middle-class English holiday-making is all about. Try some of the delectable Colchester oysters, and take a stroll along a seafront promenade. From Ipswich, you can get back to Cambridge (where trains leave for London frequently) in a few hours.

Whatever you do, don't rush through East Anglia. Cyclists and hikers will delight in the fact that East Anglia enjoys the lowest annual rainfall of any region in Britain. A pedal through the tranquil countryside will make you understand how it inspired the paintings of Constable and Gainsborough.

Cambridge

Cambridge adds to the virtues and charm of an old-fashioned market town an architectural and cultural heritage that goes back about seven hundred years to the founding of **Cambridge University.** The bitter scholastic rivalry between Oxford and Cambridge does not extend to their scenery— Cambridge is Britain's university town par excellence. It takes full advantage of its river, the **Cam,** instead of ignoring it as Oxford does the Isis. Less industrialized than its rival, Cambridge is green where Oxford is gray, quaint where Oxford is seedy.

The University is comprised of over twenty autonomous colleges, which in recent years have lost much of their elite character, although a student handbook proclaims, "The colleges still maintain their 2800 servants on rock-bottom wages, tradition is preserved and the cameras keep clicking at the quaintness of it all." The town-gown split is bitter—be sure not to confuse the University with the city when referring to the two.

Orientation

Coaches leave London's Victoria Coach Station every two hours, and take two hours and forty minutes to reach Cambridge (£2.35 one way). Trains run more frequently (from London, Liverpool Street Station), and take only an hour and twenty minutes (£3.25 one way). If you arrive by rail, take the bus to Market Square, which lies between the two main streets. Long-distance coaches and local buses usually terminate their routes at Drummer Street, just two blocks east of the marketplace.

The names of the two main streets change every couple of blocks. One— starting at Magdalene Bridge—is the main shopping street of the town. The other is the academic main drag, with several colleges lying between this road and the River Cam.

Some shops close at midday on Thursdays.

Addresses and Telephone Numbers

Tourist Information Office and Accommodation Service: Wheeler Street (tel. 58977), one block south of the marketplace. They can find you a room for a fee of 35p and give you piles of leaflets and listings for Cambridge and East Anglia. Open Mon.-Fri. 9am-6pm, Sat. 9am-5pm, and Sun. (in summer) 10:30am-3:30pm. At other times, call 53363 for help finding accommodations.

British Rail Information: Cambridge Station (tel. 59711), London Timetable (tel. 59602).

Bus and Coach Information: Drummer Street Station (tel. 53418). Information and booking office open 9am-5:15pm Mon.-Sat.

Emergency Services: for fire, police, or ambulance, dial 999.

Cycle Hire: University Cycle and Electrical, 93-95 King's Street (tel. 311560). £1.50 per day, £3 per week, and £15 deposit.

Swimming: Corner of Mill Road and Gonville Place, not far from the YMCA. A swim costs 33p and a sauna is £1.50.

Accommodations

Youth Hostel, 97 Tenison Road, entrance on Devonshire Road (tel. 54601). Modern and large, but always crowded during the summer. The warden is overworked and can be difficult. Members' kitchen, £1.10 and £1.35 per night. Closed from 10am-5pm daily.

Cambridge YMCA, Queen Anne House, Gonville Place (tel. 56998). A well-equipped student hotel that accepts men and women, ages 15 to 35. The nightly charge, including breakfast, is £4.96 singles (lots of these), £3.88 doubles. The weekly rates include two meals a day: £24 singles, £19.65 doubles.

During the "Long Vac" (early June through the end of September), and the Christmas and Easter vacations, the best accommodations are the "digs" that students usually occupy during the term. These meet minimum standards set by the colleges' Lodging House Syndicate, are accustomed to young people, and tend to be much closer to the center of town than other bed-and-breakfasts. A few (as noted) also take in guests during term time. Try these first:

Mrs. F. Rowe, 29 Malcolm Street off Jesus Lane (tel. 64940). Very friendly, even entertaining, landlady; the beds are comfy. Guests accepted year round. £3.75 per person in singles and doubles.

Mrs. H. Barden, 27 Malcolm Street (tel. 67265). Well kept and convenient. £4 per person in singles and doubles (you may be asked to share a room). Shower or bath is 25p. Guests are accepted throughout the year.

Mrs. J. Willcox, 70 Jesus Lane (tel. 65497). Another well-tended place with six rooms and a bath, as well as TV room and ironing facilities. £4.25 per person.

Mrs. C. Barden, 23 Malcolm Street (tel. 52079). Special diets are accommodated for. £4 per person; baths 25p extra. Open year round.

Ellensleigh Guest House, 37 Tenison Road (tel. 64888). Immaculate, and great breakfast. Open year round with central heating throughout. £4 per person in singles, doubles, and triples.

Mrs. Pilmer, 33 Tenison Road (tel. 55823). The management is young and enjoys the "rucksack set." The breakfasts are satisfying and all of the rooms have washbasins. Highly recommended at £3.50 per person. Rooms available throughout the year.

Meadow Way Camping, in Great Shelford (tel. Trumpington 3185). Three miles south of Cambridge on the A10, then half a mile along the A130. Toilets, running water, and there are shops nearby. Open April-Sept. inclusive.

Food and Pubs

For fresh fruit and vegetables, shop at the outdoor market held in the Market Square (Mon.-Sat. starting at 8am). Close by is a small health-food store at 3 Rose Crescent.

Corner House Restaurant, 9 King's Street. Without dispute, the cheapest meals in town. The menu is varied, the portions large, and the service lightning fast. Chips and a vegetable come with all dishes, most of which are under £1. Sharing the family-sized tables is the habit—a great way to meet Cambridge students. Open 11:30am-3pm and 5-10pm Mon.-Fri.; 11:30am-10pm Sat.

Holy Trinity Church, Market Street. For about 40p on weekdays, you get all the salad, fruit, bread, etc. you can eat. Open only from early July to mid-August.

The Rembrandt, Market Square, is the place to go for a really good meal that won't devastate your budget. Traditional English menu with a sprinkling of continental dishes. Full dinner without wine runs about £3. Open Tues.-Fri. 6:30-10pm, Sat. until midnight.

The Coffee Pot, on Green Street (open 9:30am-5:30pm Mon.-Sat.), is one of the few places in England where the coffee is as good as the tea, and the munchies (quiche and homemade cakes) are excellent as well.

The Baron of Beef, Bridge Street. A lively town pub with a chummy atmosphere. Try the local bitter brew *(Abbot)* and visit the men's room, where you can revitalize your favorite rhyme on the chalk board (bring your own chalk).

The Little Rose, King's Parade. Jammed on weekend nights with all sorts. Try to be there just before closing (11pm), so you can catch one of the greatest sights in England—the herding techniques used by the management to clear out the swaying crowd by ten past.

Sights

The pamphlet, *Cambridge: a Brief Guide for Visitors,* provides you with basic information about the colleges and the various museums, and includes a street plan (available at the Tourist Office for 5p). If you're staying in Cambridge for more than a couple of days, invest 50p in the *Official Guide,* available at the Tourist Office and in book shops. It covers the sights, entertainment, and history of Cambridge, and tells you about places of interest outside the city.

Most of the important buildings are located along the river between Magdalene Bridge and Silver Street. Oldest and most picturesque are those that lie between Trinity Street-King's Parade and the River Cam. On the other side of the river are **the Backs,** gardens and meadows that give Cambridge its pastoral quality. If you only have time for a few colleges, try to see **King's, Trinity, Queens', Christ's,** and perhaps **Jesus.** While wandering through Christ's, visit the gardens (open 2-4pm Mon.-Fri.). The other college known for its sculptured flora is **Clare's** (gardens open from 2:30-4pm Mon.-Fri.). At King's College, visit the impressive **King's Chapel,** the tallest building in the area. Look out for the frequent concerts; or if you prefer, listen to the choir at Evensong or Sunday morning services. Most of the colleges are open all day until around midnight; but during exam periods, the hours may be shortened (people *do* study around here).

Probably the best way to enjoy Cambridge is to rent some form of river transportation (rowboat, canoe, or most characteristic, a punt—a long, flat-bottomed boat propelled by pole). Not hard, but some sense of balance might help. The Cam is least crowded early in the morning and after 4:30pm on weekdays (on weekends the Cam turns into a floating "bumper cars"). **Scudamore's Boatyards** at Magdalene Bridge rents by the hour: £1.60 for punts, £1.40 for rowboats, £1.20 for canoes, all plus a £5 deposit.

Arts and Entertainment

During the term, Cambridge has an active program of theater, music, and film. The **Arts Theatre Club,** founded by John Maynard Keynes, offers 20p off regular seat prices to students. Located at 6 St. Edward's Passage, the box office is open 11am-8pm Mon.-Fri., and 10:30am-8pm Sat. (tel. 52000). You can book seats by telephone or try for the special standby tickets—on most Friday and Saturday evenings, any seats left unsold one hour before show time go for £1.

Foreign films and classics are screened regularly at the **Arts Cinema.** Call the box office, Market Passage (tel. 52001) for schedules. Tickets start at 60p. Founded in 1855, the University's **Amateur Dramatic Club** on Park Street offers lively entertainment throughout the year, put on by various dramatic societies in the Cambridge area. The variety here is almost as great as the enthusiasm, and for 30p to £1 for a seat, you can't go wrong. Call the box office (tel. 52001) to see what's on while you're in town. The **Cambridge Union,** a private debating club, sponsors a program of social activities for the myriad of foreign students that spend their summer in Cambridge. The clubhouse can be found just behind the unmistakable "Round Church," off Sydney Street.

Each summer the **Cambridge Festival** puts on an extensive and varied series of musical concerts and special exhibits during the last two weeks of July, ending in a large folk festival. Tickets are available from the Central Library Box Office in Lion Yard (tel. 57851). Try to buy them early.

North England

There is a certain moderation about the Midlands that is missing in the North. The cities sprawl in the Midlands all right, and have their share of sooty smokestacks—but there is always the bucolic, homey atmosphere of the surrounding farmland to soften the blow. Not so in the North. Here, the people are packed tighter in the cities, spread further apart in the country. Northerners, more than Midlanders, are fiercely loyal to where they come from. In a Midlands pub, you'll never hear a Banburyman arguing with a Coventryman over which city makes better cars; but walk through a **Liverpool** Street wearing a **Manchester** rugby league sweatshirt, and you're likely to be laid out flat. Indeed, many Lancashiremen and Yorkshiremen think that the War of the Roses hasn't ended yet. Even national patriotism is more evident in the North than elsewhere in Britain—if you hitch a lift with a Yorkshire lorry driver, don't be surprised if he asks you, point-blank, "Which do you like better, America or Britain?", and you'd better be sufficiently diplomatic with your answer.

Perhaps at the root of some of these attitudes lies the harshness of the land itself. Unlike the gently rolling Midlands, much of the North is difficult to farm. Sliced down the middle by the north-south spine of the **Pennine Mountains,** with the **North York Moors** to the east and the mountains of **Cumbria** forming the **Lake District** in the west, it is a land full of natural barriers, not conducive to the free and easy exchange of goods and ideas. The provincialism of the North can be seen most clearly in tiny villages like **Dent** in the **Yorkshire Dales,** where many of the older people have never ventured outside their parish. Even in a large, international seaport like **Newcastle-upon-Tyne,** the "Geordies" have maintained their distinct sub-culture and accent far more successfully than the Cockneys of London.

Except for a quick look around **York**—the premier city in any historical account of the North—few people on their way to or from Scotland take time to explore the region. Between the Peak District and the Scottish border you'll find both the grimiest cities and the most untouched, desolate scenery in England. In the no-nonsense towns of **Sheffield** or **Hull,** you can examine the archetypes of Blake's "dark Satanic Mills" at their worst. If you've always wanted to see what a real "local" pub was all about, follow a group of factory workers when they go out for a pint at dinner time (that's lunch time to you).

York

To anyone who comes to York expecting a town wallowing in the memories of its medieval past, the reality of York's burgeoning industry is quite disconcerting. In fact, there are few spots on the three-mile-long **City Walls** from which you can't see a smokestack. The power station, with its monstrous cooling towers, vies for attention with the spires of **York Minster.**

Not that the medieval flavor doesn't remain in some of York's narrow streets. **Stonegate** is lined with the greatest number of preserved medieval houses of any street in England, while the **Shambles** and **Low Petergate** offer other examples of ancient architecture. At the end of the Shambles look out for the "**Whip-whop-ma-gate,**" the old city whipping post.

The thirteenth-century city walls are a rare example of an intact circuit in England (Chester is the other great claimant). The medieval walls include the four chief gates to the city—**Micklegate, Bootham, Monk,** and **Walmgate**—and much Roman, Saxon, and Norman work, all renovated and enclosed during the reign of Henry III (1216-1272).

Well within the walls, and well within the hearts of every resident of York, is York Minster, the largest medieval church in Britain. Its windows are estimated to contain more than half of all the medieval stained-glass windows in England. For an incomparable view of the city, ascend the **Central Tower** (admission 40p). Across the Cathedral Close, the **Minster Library** (open Mon.-Fri. 9am-5pm; admission free) has a collection of antique books and rare manuscripts.

The **Merchant Adventurer's Hall,** in Piccadilly, is the most elaborate surviving example of York's famous guild halls (open Mon.-Sat. 10am-12:30pm and 2-5:30pm; admission 20p).

Lying within the bailey of the ancient **York Castle** is the **Castle Museum,** one of the best folk museums in the country. It was endowed primarily with the vast collection of Dr. Kirk, a nineteenth-century physician who often accepted antiques, relics, and ''bygones'' in lieu of a fee. A complete cobbled street has been recreated underground, lined with shops containing utensils of various crafts. Upstairs is a costume collection and an Edwardian street, complete with pub. (Open Mon.-Sat. 9:30am-6pm, Sun. 10am-6pm; admission 55p.)

Orientation and Accommodations

Fast and frequent trains—the **Inter-City 125** service—will take you from London's Kings Cross Station to York in under two and a half hours, if you catch a limited-stop run (£10.80 single). Coaches from London's Victoria Coach Station will get you there in under six hours.

The **Tourist Information Centre** is located in the De Grey Rooms, Exhibition Square (tel. 21756). The extended summer hours are Mon.-Sat. 9am-8pm, Sun. 2-5pm. The accommodation service (35p per booking) is often necessary during the summer months. When planning your shopping in York, keep in mind that some shops and businesses close at midday on Wednesdays. York has a tremendous selection of all types of accommodation, especially in the medium-priced guest house range. The following are reasonable and well situated:

YHA Youth Hostel, Haverford, Water End, Clifton (tel. York 53147). A YHA superior Hostel, about a mile from the city center; follow the Thirsk road (A19) to Clifton Green and turn left. £1.10 and £1.35 per night; curfew is 10:30pm, but late passes are available for 30p.

Mrs. M. Passmore, 66 Kilburn Road off Fulford Road (tel. 53142). A 15- to 20-minute walk from the center, in a quiet residential area. Basic lived-in-looking rooms—one double, one twin and one single—not done up in typical guest house style. £3.75 per person plus 10p for a bath.

Whitwell House, 62 Scarcroft Road (tel. 24222). From £3.50 per person in doubles or in a family room. Television lounge and private parking space.

Heworth Guest House, 126 East Parade (tel. 26384). A convenient guest house, just outside the city-center to the northeast. Three singles and three doubles, some bedrooms on the ground floor—appropriate for handicapped people. Special diets can also be catered for and there is a television lounge. Bed-and-breakfast from £4 per person.

If these are full, or if you prefer to hunt around on your own, the best place to look for B&Bs are Queen Anne's Road, the side streets off Bootham and Clifton, and the neighborhood around Scarcroft Road.

The closest camping site to the city of York is the **Caravan Club** site on Terry Avenue (off Bishopthorpe Road; tel. 58997). The site is operated from Easter through October and there is only room for about a dozen tents, so you should call before beginning the ten-minute hike along the river. The overnight charge is 84p per person plus VAT; hot showers are free. If you prefer to set up camp outside the city, try **Poplar Farm** in Acaster Malbis (tel. 706548). There are showers and hot and cold running water; space for about twenty tents; open April through October. Take bus #15, running every hour from the Rail Station.

Food

Bibis, 115-119 Micklegate. A large, informal restaurant with the feel of a Mediterranean café. Freshly-made pastas (your choice for £1.10 each), outstanding pizzas from £1.05-1.55. Specialties of the day are good but more expensive. Open Tues.-Sat. noon-2pm and 6-11:30pm, Sun. 6-11:30pm only, closed Mon.

Plunkets, 9 High Petergate. Ideally situated in the old part of the city, around the corner from Exhibition Square. Great *chili con carne* (small 75p, large £1.50) and "real American style" hamburgers with fries and salad from £1.05-£1.40. Try also "Uncle Plunket's Vegetarian Salad," a meal in itself for £1.35. And you can wash it all down with wine or beer. Open seven days a week from 11am-11pm.

Aquarian Wholefoods, 98 Micklegate. A well-stocked health-food shop with a restaurant upstairs. Quiches (with wild ingredients—eggplants!) are 50p each. You can get a huge plateful of organic salad for only 80p. Also try their teas, coffees, and snacks. Open Tues.-Sat. 8:30am-5pm, Wed. until 4:45pm, closed Sun. and Mon.

Yorks's many pubs are noted more for their atmosphere than their food. Many retain their medieval character, offering lenient drinking hours and a devoted student following. The most popular drinking, eating, and socializing spot has to be the **Black Swan Inn** in Peasholme Green, once the home of Martin Bowes, who was twice Lord Mayor of London and goldsmith to Queen Elizabeth I. Be sure not to miss the Delft tile fireplace on the first floor—there aren't many like it in Britain. Free jazz on Tuesday evenings. Dating from at least 1644, the **Olde Starre** in Stonegate is the granddaddy of York public houses. But the interior decoration that you will see there is not that old: it is typical Victoriana. Other cushy, plush Victorian interiors will be found at the **Blue Bell** in Fossgate and at the **Bay Horse** in Blossom Street.

Festivals

Every three years (next in 1980), York performs plays from its medieval collection of **Mystery Plays.** The city has 48 to its credit. The term "mystery" is a corruption of the French *"métier"* (meaning trade, craft, or career), so called because the different craft guilds produced and played different parts of the cycle according to custom. The plays, similar to the renowned once-a-decade "Passion Play" of Oberammergau, tell biblical and gospel stories in popularly understandable form. They were the chief means of religious education in an age when the Bible had not yet been translated into the vernacular. In the original scheme, the plays were performed in twelve separate places in the city in sequence (probably because of the twelve Stations of the Cross). Nowadays they are all produced at **St. Mary's Abbey.** The broken columns and withered nave make a perfect backdrop for the performance. During the Mystery Play season, an **Arts Festival** goes on around the plays, emphasizing orchestral and choral music but including drama as well. Tickets and ticket information are available from the Festival Office, St. Mary's Lodge, Marygate, York YO3 YDD (tel. 27939).

Near York

York lies on a plain, so the surrounding countryside is easily accessible by bicycle, even for the not-too-energetic. Old country estates abound in the area. The beautifully landscaped grounds of many of them are open to the public, perfect for a picnic. **Castle Howard,** one of the more renowned, is located about 15 miles northeast of York. Take bus #43 (the Malton bus) to Welburn Lodge; the Castle is three and a half miles along the lane.

North York Moors, Yorkshire Dales, Pennines

It was on the windswept moors of **North Yorkshire** that Emily Brontë set *Wuthering Heights*. The choice of scenery was apt; in this total desolation, you too may feel the urge to run off raving across the heather, Heathcliffe-style. However, we urge you to resist the temptation and channel your energies into a walk across the Moors. The possibilities are limitless, governed only by your ability to exist without civilization, and by the relative lack of good starting places. However, there are a few roads through the Moors, and each of them is bound to have a few inns along the way. The **Glykwake Walk,** a traditional 40-mile trek across the entire region, is a slog across peat bog and heather. If you can do it in 24 hours, you are entitled to a certificate from the Rambler's Association. There are many guides to this and other walks in North Yorkshire, available in York from the York Minister Bookshop, or from the Yorkshire office of the National Trust, 32 Goodramgate (tel. 29621). If you do walk on the Moors, remember that you are completely exposed, and subject to sudden mists—suitable clothing, maps, and compass are essential.

The **Yorkshire Dales,** in the southwestern part of the country, are far more tame, with sheep grazing on most of the grassy hills. This is limestone country, as you can see from inspecting the dry stone fences that lay a grid in relief across each hill. An area of geological marvels cut out by running water, of dramatic white pinnacles, potholes, gorges (called "scars" here), and waterfalls is yours if you take the trouble to wander beyond the cultivated areas that can be seen from the road. Much of the Dales is poorly known by hikers, even in England; if you really want to explore the less known corners, we recommend a reputable guide, such as Wainwright's, *Walks in Limestone Country*. For the less dedicated, there are several points of interest within easy reach by car. At the southern end of the Dales, near **Settle** (a good base for exploring this part of the Dales), is **Malham,** with the great limestone cliffs of **Malham Cove** nearby. Wainwright recommends a single walk taking in the Cove, **Malham Tarn** (a small lake), and **Gordale Scar.** A road also leads to the mouth of the latter, where you can walk amidst thousands of tourists, and stand at the bottom of Yorkshire's answer to Cheddar Gorge. Near the Scar is a **Youth Hostel,** and **The Buck Inn,** a pub popular with hikers. Another popular part of the Dales lies not far from **Ingleton,** on the western edge. Here, ambitious fell-runners attempt to break the speed record for the **Three Peaks Walk,** which takes in **Whernside, Pen-y-Ghent,** and **Ingleborough** (all about 2300 feet high). The 24-mile "walk" has been done in 2¾ hours. Driving into the middle of the Dales can be exciting, for the roads are among the steepest and narrowest in Britain, with some of the most spectacular views. Some roads go straight over the tops of hills, and the sense of open space is tremendous. Try to work your way over to **Wensleydale,** for a sample of the cheese (here not as much of a ripoff as in Cheddar), or to **Wharfdale,** where the area around **Kettlewell** offers many pleasant spots for a picnic. Continue south through the dale and stop off at the **Dales National Park Information Centre** in Grassington. Located in Clovend on Hebden Road, it is the central information service for the National Park and can provide you with dozens of leaflets on hiking, pony trekking, bird-watching and even details on the geology of the region. During the summer the center is open seven days a week from 11am-5pm (tel. Grassington 75278). Finally, visit **Dent,** on the north side of the Dales, one of the most provincial villages in Yorkshire. In this little wool-spinning hamlet, the "Terrible Witches of Dent" won their name by their super-natural ability to spin seven strands at once.

The **Pennines** begin about 20 miles northeast of **Stoke-on-Trent,** and don't stop until they get to the Scottish border. The southern part of the range, lumped together with the **Peak District,** is popular for daytrips from the northern industrial cities, since it is within shouting distance of **Bradford** and **Leeds,** and practically casts shadows on **Sheffield** and **Manchester.** The range also encompasses parts of the **Yorkshire Dales** and the **Cheviot Hills of Northumberland.** For walking, the thousands of minor paths are over-shadowed by the **Pennine Way,** the Countryside Commission's 400-kilometer path along the central ridge of the watershed. Begin about 25 miles from Manchester, in the village of **Edale,** and quickly take in the massive, boggy plateau on top of **Kinder Scout.** You enter the Dales at Malham, and actually traverse the lip of the Cove before rounding the Tarn and proceeding to Pen-y-Ghent. The rest of the route, which ends at **Kirk Yethorm,** passes through nearly every type of country to be found in the North, and some quaint villages as well. Hostels are spaced within a day's walk of one another, and the whole walk is designed to be accomplished in two weeks. For further details, write the Countryside Commission, John Dower House, Crescent Place, Cheltenham, Glos. GL50 3RA (tel. (0242) 21381); and buy a copy of Wainwright's *Pictorial Guide to the Pennine Way.* But be warned that the Pennine Way can be dangerous; parts of the trail are devoid of markings and mists can descend quickly. Even the best maps aren't enough: a compass is essential. The distances listed on a map are unrealistic; frequent changes in direction and pitch of the path can add as much as 25% over the map reading.

Lake District

The Lake District brings beauty to England's northwest corner in the form of the most expansive National Park, the highest mountains and the largest and most beautiful lakes in all of England. The valley towns around the lakes teem with tourists (especially on weekends), but you can easily avoid them by taking to the hills for hiking and camping, or bed-and-breakfasting in one of the many charming stone cottages whose sign is out for the wayfaring stranger. Look closely at some of these houses. Many are constructed with-out mortar, but the builders have so precisely fitted the stones that they will cohere for centuries.

For information about camping and recreation rules and suggestions on what to see, where to walk, and where to stay, stop by the **Lake District National Park Information Service,** District Bank House, High Street, Windermere (tel. Windermere 2498). For the casual tourist interested in sampling a variety of wildlife, local village life, history, archeology, and sports besides walking (e.g. sailing on the Lakes), the *Lake District Na-tional Park Guide,* published by Her Majesty's Stationery Office, should be sufficient, supplemented by the one-inch Ordnance Survey map of the region. Serious walkers, however, should procure Wainwright's seven-volume *Pictorial Guide to the Lakeland Fells*. As in the Moors and Dales, there are innumerable walks and climbs—the mountains are far more densely packed than in Scotland, and connecting ridges between peak systems more common, so you are more flexible in planning your walks here. If nature trails and historic homes are more to your liking, inquire at the National Trust's North West Regional Office, Broadlands, Borrans Road, Ambleside (tel: Ambleside 3003). For advice on more rugged hiking and mountaineering, contact the Head Warden at the District Bank House, High Street in Windermere. The Lakes have the highest density of Youth Hostels in the world (22 at last count); however, they are all needed, and you may still have to book ahead during the summer. Details on the Hostels in the region, and advice on how to plan a hosteling tour can be provided by the **YHA Regional Office** (tel. Windermere 2301), Elleray, Windermere (across the road from the District Bank House).

We cover only the area around the largest lake in any detail, because it acts as both the transportation and accommodation center for the area. Of course, it is also the most crowded and commercialized, and we hope that you don't spend all of your time around Windermere and Ambleside. Sailors, shoppers, and swimmers will feel at home here, and there is plenty of opportunity for playing around Lake Windermere. But the best, most unspoiled, scenery will be found around the more remote lakes to the west and north. Even villages as small as **Patterdale,** at the southern tip of Ullswater, contain ample accommodations and can be used as bases. **Derwentwater** is perhaps the most beautiful lake; **Wastwater** the most sublime (fitting the Romantic requirements of both beauty and horror); and **Borrowdale** the best-looking valley. Ambitious hikers will probably want to head for **Eskdale** in the west, or Langdale and Borrowdale to the northwest of Ambleside.

LAKE WINDERMERE

A good ferry service on Lake Windermere links up the towns of the north, east, and south shores, but remember that the ferries don't run after about 7pm. If you have a Britrail pass, you may use it on the ferry. The Railway Station which serves the Lake District is in **Windermere,** the largest lakeside town. You can sleep nearby at **Limefit Park's Campsite** on Route A592, open March to November, or in the **Youth Hostel** at High Cross Castle, Troutbeck. This very popular, standard-grade Hostel fills up fast, so call them before walking all the way up the hill (tel. Windermere 3543). The Hostel is reached by hiking up Bridge Lane from the Windermere-Ambleside road (A591); overnight charges are 90p and £1.10. The numerous cafés in Windermere, with or without such elegant come-ons as tablecloths and classical muzak, serve equally bland food, so stick with the grocery store routine. The **Hotel Windermere,** across from the Railway Station, has a very jovial pub, and hosts dances on several nights a week where you're certain to meet some of the English students who roam Lakeland.

Down towards the lake from Windermere is **Bowness.** From here ferries depart every twenty minutes to other parts of the lake. At Park Cliffe Farm Mr. J.D. Brockbank manages a six-acre campsite called "Tower Wood." Inquire about walks or amusements at "The Glebe," where the **Information Centre** people will be glad to help you. Up the hill from the lake, next to the church, you'll find students, excellent draughts and a jukebox at the **Stag's Head.**

Take the ferry from Bowness to **Ambleside** and drop by the **Information Centre** at the Waterhead Car Park as you get off; they'll shower you with free pamphlets about hiking trails, etc. You'll also see the National Trust pamphlets there which describe your walks in meticulous detail and depict the fauna and flora you'll encounter along the way. A ten-minute walk from the car park will bring you to the town of Ambleside. The largest YHA Youth Hostel in Lakeland (it's more like a student hotel, complete with wall-to-wall carpeting, large lounge, and private dock area) stands a mile south of the town at Waterhead. Once a large lake-front hotel, the Hostel is one of the few special-grade YHA Hostels; free hot baths and small rooms, all with washbasins, provide for unheard-of luxury. Overnight charges are £1.30 and £1.60, but it is worth the little extra. Call to see if they have room for you (tel. Ambleside 2304).

Borrowdale, Wasdale, and **Langdale** are generally held to encompass the best of the Lakeland's walking and climbing areas. All three come complete with hostel complexes, campgrounds at the head of the valleys, and friendly climbers' pubs where you can meet other hikers.

In Borrowdale, near Keswick, try the YHA Hostel at **Buttermere** (tel. Buttermere 254) or **Derwentwater** (tel. Borrowdale 246). Both of these are within easy reach of Keswick and you can catch buses there or at Cockermouth for Buttermere. A camping club is at Derwentwater and there are **campgrounds** in Borrowdale itself.

Wales

The tallest mountains south of the Scottish border, 750 miles of coastline, and three National Parks show off a Wales as distinct in appearance as it is in custom. Though Wales shares a boundary and government with England, it has been able to maintain its own rugged, rural traditions in a far less pretentious way than has England. But, to be fair, some of the local crafts and traditions have been revived only recently and given a bit of polish for the sake of the ever-increasing number of tourists that venture into the farming country of Wales. Slate from North Wales is now used to make jewelry and clocks, potteries around the country produce smartly-polished gifts, and even the famous Welsh tapestries are being woven at faster-than-hand speed.

Despite concessions to the burgeoning tourist industry, Wales remains one of those few places where you can feel that you are stepping back in time. Don't bring the expectations you have of travel within England with you when you cross the border (a border so elusive that you won't notice any difference at first). Whole counties of Wales are vacant of the kind of "places of interest" that cluster so richly in England. While a castle can be found at almost every turning, stately homes and manicured gardens have never felt comfortable on Welsh soil. Wales' charm, rather, is in its natural beauty and in the fascinations of a culture apart.

PRACTICAL INFORMATION

Due to the terrain of much of inland Wales and the ability of some areas to avoid the Industrial Revolution, large tracts of the land are untouched by railway lines. In fact, many of the most attractive parts of Wales are well removed from the trunk lines that were built to link manufacturing areas and to join the ports for Ireland with the cities of England. Scenic spots such as

Brecon or Llangollen are only accessible by local buses and infrequent long-distance coaches. It's therefore a good idea to plan your trip, in order to best take advantage of British Rail's bargain offers. The **Freedom of Wales** ticket gives unlimited travel on all of the British Rail lines in Wales, including the English border cities of Chester, Shrewsbury, and Hereford; the one-week pass costs £18 second class. In addition, a variety of less expensive **Ride-about** and **Runabout** tickets are available for seven days of unlimited travel within a limited area (the Wye Valley, for instance). Daytrips can also be surprisingly reasonable on the railways; pick up a pamphlet at any of the larger stations. For rail information on all lines north of Shrewsbury-Aberystwyth, call: Stoke-on-Trent 48261; for the south, call: Cardiff 499811).

Nearly every village and town in Wales that receives even a trickle of tourists supports a tourist information office. Many offer a bed-booking service (40-50p) that covers the local area as well as everywhere else in Wales where there is a bed-booking office. If you prefer to make your own reservations, pick up a copy of *Where to Stay in Wales* for 50p; its 300 pages are filled with every type of accommodation, from farmhouses to luxury hotels to self-catering bungalows. The main office of the **Wales Tourist Board** in Llandaff, Cardiff CFS 2YZ, South Wales will answer queries and provide some invaluable pamphlets.

Youth hostels are the best accommodation bargains in Wales; they can be anything from a refurbished country mansion or a medieval castle to a crofter's cottage. Don't be deceived by their frequency—there are fifty of them—or by their obscure locations: some of the most popular (i.e. always fully booked in the summer) hostels are those accessible only by foot or bridlepath. The hiker's hostels in the Snowdon Mountain range area are particularly crowded. Wherever you are, it's always a good idea to call ahead to a hostel to check if they have room. A copy of the *YHA handbook* is essential for hostelers; most Youth Hostels can sell you a copy for 20p, or write to Trevelyan House, 8 St. Stephen's Hill, St. Albans, Herts AL1 2DY. Hostels are also excellent places to pick up tips on the area; the wardens are often enthusiastic and knowledgeable about their neck of the woods. Hikers should leave their itinerary with a warden or the police since the foggy hills and dales of Wales are easy to get lost in.

Campers can purchase the pamphlet *Touring, Caravan, and Camping Sites* for 15p at tourist offices or by writing to the head office in Llandaff, Cardiff.

South Wales

For detailed regional information, visit or call the **South Wales Tourism Council**, Darkgate, Carmarthen, Dyfed (tel. Carmarthen 7557).

Once the world's largest coal-exporting region, South Wales' reputation as a stripped and scarred land is only partially justified. Lush valleys, a rambling range of hills, and plenty of unspoiled farming country defy the image created by the bleak mining valleys of central South Wales.

One by-product of the industrial development of this region is the best transportation network in Wales. Today, the **Inter-City 125** service can take you from London (Paddington Station) to Cardiff in a brisk hour and forty-five minutes. Bus service is also well developed (for Wales anyway); take advantage of the **Roverbus** ticket which enables you to travel as far as you like on any of the bus routes (express coach runs excepted) throughout South Wales for only £1.50 per day.

Unless you happen to find yourself on a through train from Shrewsbury, your first glimpse of South Wales' better half will be of the **Wye Valley.** Meandering north from the Bristol Channel, the River Wye provides a natural boundary between the English Midlands and the Welsh county of Gwent (formerly Monmouthshire). By crossing the enormous Severn Bridge from Bristol (along the M4 motorway), you can begin a trip through the Wye Valley at Chepstow. With the Wye flowing at its feet, **Chepstow Castle** is a forceful reminder of Norman strength. (Open Mon.-Sat. 9:30am-7pm, Sun. 2-7pm.) Nearby Caldicot Castle turns itself into a medieval banquet hall each weeknight; to find out how you can take part, ask at the **Tourist Information Centre** in the Old Arch Building, High Street, Chepstow (tel. Chepstow 3772).

Just a hitch or quick bus ride along the A466 (the Monmouth road) brings you to the famed **Tintern Abbey,** set amongst the "steep and lofty cliffs" that inspired Wordsworth. The Abbey, with its majestic arches and curved windows, couldn't hope for more peaceful neighbors than the slopes of the Wye Valley. The stone structure is open (9:30am-7pm Mon.-Sat., 2-7pm Sun.; admission 20p). To avoid the inevitable deluge of daytrippers, come to Tintern early in the morning and spend the afternoon exploring the cliffs.

There is a **YHA Youth Hostel** only four miles to the northeast in St. Briavels Castle (tel. St. Briavels 272). You won't find statelier digs anywhere for 90p (£1.10 if you're 21 or over). But keep in mind that the Hostel is closed every Sunday except during school-holiday periods.

Following the Wye Valley north brings you to the ancient market town of **Monmouth.** It was here that Harry of Monmouth was born in 1387; he was to become Henry V. Spanning the **River Monnow** at this spot is **Monnow Bridge** topped with the only fortified bridge gateway in Great Britain. The key to the gateway is available from the seventeenth-century Robin Hood Pub, at the bottom of High Street. Look for the spout that was once used to pour boiling oil on the Welsh separatists.

From Agincourt Square, in the center of Monmouth, you can catch a bus or head southeast along the A40 (a good road for hitching) to the fifteenth-century **Raglan Castle,** a youngster by Welsh castle standards. The most outstanding feature of the castle is its drawbridge:—there are actually two of them: one for show and one for use. What remains of the living apartments and buttery are open Mon.-Sat. 9:30am-7pm, Sun. 2-7pm; admission 15p.

Continuing along the A40 will bring you to another busy market in Abergavenny. Besides being the eastern gateway to the **Brecon Beacons National Park,** Abergavenny maintains the best of Welsh country traditions: livestock and produce are sold each Tuesday in the open-air market and the town hosts the annual **Abergavenny and Border Counties Show,** a day-long event that draws the liveliest people and animals from miles around. If you're around on the last Saturday in July don't miss it.

The **Tourist Information Centre** at 2 Lower Monk Street (tel. 3254) can provide you with dozens of leaflets telling you about activities and trails around the town as well as throughout the Brecon Beacons National Park.

For spectacular views of the **River Usk** carving its way through the park's meadows, direct your energies to **St. Mary's Vale.** There is a well-marked nature trail here, about two miles in length designed to point out the indigenous bracken, bilberry, and alder trees. Ask at the Abergavenny Tourist Office for directions and the leaflet (2p) that describes the walk.

Before venturing west towards the Beacons, consider spanning the **Black Mountains** that rise to the north, sloping down upon the drowsy border town of **Hay-on-Wye.** Bibliophiles will be overwhelmed by what is reputed to be the largest second-hand book shop in the world. The castle of Hay acts as headquarters for the **Booths** book network where you can browse or admire some of the treasures on display.

The best place to base yourself for hiking and pony trekking in the Beacons is Brecon. It has a very helpful **Tourist Information Centre** in the Market Car Park (open in summer, seven days a week 10am-6pm; tel. 2485) and the main Brecon Beacons National Park Centre at 7 Glamorgan Street (open Easter to October, Mon.-Sat. 9:15am-5:15pm; tel. 2763). The latter will provide you with all the information you need to spend weeks in the Park.

Stretching from the southern edge of the National Park to the south coast are the infamous mining valleys. While some of the slopes are scarred and gray, others show signs of new-found growth in the way of green pines and brightly-colored terrace houses. The picture often isn't as bleak as painted. An easy way to see this part of South Wales is via public transport: buses from Brecon to Cardiff pass through the one-time center for iron and steel, **Merthyr Tydfil.** The route takes you past the ill-fated town of **Aberfan,** where a whole generation of school children was wiped out in 1967 by a pit landslide.

Wales' capital city, **Cardiff,** won't win any awards for beautific urban planning (except perhaps for the City Hall area which is meant to impress); but with a University College, theaters, and a couple of first-rate museums, it is the true cultural capital of South Wales. Deserving of its name, the **National Museum** (open Mon.-Sat. 10am-6pm, Sun. 2:30-5pm during the summer; admission free) presents both the natural and industrial sides of Wales. A reconstruction of a mine tunnel, the "Mining Gallery," is properly darkened and reveals life-sized models at work in the pits. The Impressionist gallery upstairs is highlighted by Renoir's *La Parisienne*.

Providing a focus for the bustling city center, **Cardiff Castle** is an urban fortress dating back to the Roman occupation of Wales. But the **Norman Keep** is the high point of the Castle grounds today. Centuries after the Normans had control, the third Marquess of Bute ordered a drastic rebuilding scheme; the lavish living quarters evidence his Victorian sensibilities. The Castle can be visited Mon.-Sat. 10am-12:40pm and 1:40-6:20pm, Sun. 10am-12:30pm and 2-6pm; admission is 60p for the complete tour, 30p for entrance to grounds only. Directly across from the Castle entrance you'll find the **Tourist Information Centre** at 3 Castle Street (open Mon.-Fri. 9am-5pm, Sat. 10am-3pm; tel. 27281). They can find you a room in town for a 40p service charge.

Just a four-mile bus ride from Cardiff center is one of Europe's finest museums of rural life, the **Welsh Folk Museum** at St. Fagans. Nearly twenty buildings were taken, piece by piece, from different parts of Wales and reconstructed. Also displayed are traditional costumes, agricultural implements, and vehicles. **St. Fagan's Castle** (the home of the Earl of Plymouth) is also open to view; and contains some fabulous examples of Welsh wood carving. Surrounding the mansion are manicured gardens and the sheds where a wood turner and cooper can be seen at work. (Open Mon.-Sat. 10am-6pm, Sun. 2:30-6pm; admission 10p.)

Another fascinating afternoon can be spent at the second largest fortress in Europe (Windsor in England is number one) at **Caerphilly.** Size alone doesn't distinguish Caerphilly; rather its system of water defenses and concentric design defied the most persistent Welsh chieftains. Even Cromwell had trouble when he attempted to blow up the Castle: the famous leaning tower of Caerphilly is the result of his only partially effective explosives. The remaining stone-work and the grounds can be explored 9:30am-7pm, Sun. 2-7pm; admission 15p.

No less important, and a good deal more ancient, is the **Roman fortress** at Caerlon near Newport. In fact, the backbone of the Roman imperial army, the Second Augustan Legion, was based here. The grassy amphitheater was once the stage for gladitorial battle; the surface and walls were smoothed to ensure that the hunted beasts couldn't find a decent foothold. (Open Mon.-Sat. 9:30am-7pm, Sun. 2-7pm; nominal admission charge.)

It would be difficult to find coastal scenery anywhere in the British Isles more spectacular than that in the southeast corner of Wales. To preserve the cliffs and beaches, the **Pembrokeshire Coast National Park** was established and a coastal footpath—more than 150 miles in length—was routed along the cliff tops. The scenery is perhaps less "Welsh" than any to be found in South Wales. Moreover, the area has long been a favorite among the retiring English.

Haverfordwest is the market town for the area and is a good place to stop over, gather information and decide which beach to head for. The **Tourist Information Centre** at 40 High Street (open Mon.-Sat. 9am-5:30pm, Sun. 9am-5:30pm in summer) can find you a bed in the area and provide you with details on "walks and talks" that are featured at selected places of interest throughout the National Park. Whatever you do, don't miss **St. David's,** the smallest city in Britain complete with a glorious cathedral and bishop's palace complex. The hidden coves of **Caerfan** are only a mile away by footpath; from here you can see across St. Bride's Bay to **Skomer Island,** world famous for its seabird colonies, especially puffins and guillemots. The boat *Arklow* will sail you from Martin's Haven to the island for £2.05, providing that no more than 100 visitors are already on the island (the National Nature Reserve is doing its job here).

Mid Wales

The coordinating **Tourist Information Centre** for the region is in Machynlleth in the Owain Glyndwr Centre (tel. (0654) 2401).

It's tempting to say that the farmers of mid Wales have resisted modernization, but the truth is that the region has been largely neglected by the forces that be. Indeed, the old county of **Radnorshire** (now incorporated into **Powys**) has long been underpopulated even though it is the most Anglicized area of Wales. Although few people speak Welsh in the eastern border country, sheep are herded and wool woven much as they were centuries ago. Even the dozen or so coastal resorts along the Cardigan Bay have yet to attain the commercialism of the north coast holiday spots, and offer a few more square inches of beach per person.

Aberystwyth, the grandfather of Cardigan Bay resorts, began to prosper because it had the sandiest stretch of beach for miles. Although most of the good sand has been swept away to neighboring **Clarach,** Aberystwyth has retained a loyal following of holiday makers that fill up the guest houses and hotels along **Marine Terrace** and **New Promenade** each summer. In the off-season, the **University College of Wales** keeps up the town's pace. The **National Library,** majestic and flora-lined, contains the bulk of surviving medieval Welsh manuscripts, and frequently hosts art and photographic exhibits (open to the public Monday-Friday 9:30am-6pm, Saturday till 5pm; admission free). A bit further up the hill is the **Aberystwyth Arts Centre,** housing the very active **Theatr Y Werin;** ask at the **Tourist Information Centre,** The Seafront (open daily 10am-6pm; tel. 612125) for their schedule of performances.

Climbing and twisting its way inland from Aberystwyth, the **Vale of**

Rheidol Railway is the sole remaining steam-operated line in the British Rail network. It links the seaside resort with the thrashing waterfalls and gorged slopes at **Devil's Bridge.** For 20p, you descend some amazingly steep steps, gape at the rushing water, and climb up the other side of the gorge (the turnstiles that accept your coins never close).

Turning north to the equally lush **Dovey Valley,** you can visit the market town of **Machynlleth,** at the southern end of **Snowdonia National Park.** The town center is dwarfed by the **clocktower** given to Machynlleth by the Marquess of Londonderry more than one hundred years ago. About three miles north of town, in Pantperthog, you'll find the fascinating and innovative **Centre for Alternative Technology** (open every day 10am-5pm; admission 60p, students 30p).

Continuing north along the coast you will encounter **Barmouth,** a seaside spot that combines brilliant coastal scenery with views of the mountain-ringed **Mawddach Estuary.** Circuits of footpaths take you away from the gay **Promenade** and lead you to magnificent vistas. Drop by the **Tourist Information Centre** on the Promenade (tel. 280787) and ask them to tell you about the walks in the area. If you would prefer to take in the sights the easy way, hop on board the **Fairbourne Railway,** the smallest of the "little trains" of Wales. The four-mile round trip from Fairbourne (across the mouth of the estuary) takes you for a lazy ride along the shingle beach.

By following the estuary inland, you'll come upon the very Welsh market town of **Dolgellau.** The southern gem of the Snowdon Mountain Range, **Cadair Idris,** towers over the town, challenging hikers that base themselves in the village and environs. We advise that you prepare yourself well before tackling the peak; sturdy shoes, a reliable and detailed map, and waterproof gear are essentials.

For exploring the rural heartland of Wales, head east to the sheep-lined hills of **Radnorshire.** Center your ramblings around **Llandrindod Wells,** built in the Edwardian age when spacious accommodations and spas were quite the thing. At its prime, upwards of 80,000 visitors came to Llandrindod each year to take the cure. The gracious hotels and hostelries now cater to touring coach parties and conventioneers. An early-morning stroll around the lake is a good way to re-absorb some of the tranquil grace that has largely been lost. The **Tourist Information Centre** in the Town Hall, Temple Street (tel. 2600) will help you find inexpensive accommodations—which are abundant here.

North Wales

Regional information is provided by the **North West Tourist Council,** Civic Centre, Colwyn Bay, Clwyd (tel. Colwyn Bay 56881).

North Wales, more than any other region in Britain, brings together three of the most sought-after tourist attractions: mountains, sandy coastline, and castles—lots of castles. The holiday resorts of the North Wales coast— **Prestatyn, Rhyl, Colwyn Bay,** and **Llandudno,** just to name the biggies—are favored by families from England's industrial northwest. Innumerable caravan parks along the coastline overflow with Liverpudlians, and Lancashire drawls fill the air. With their funfairs, piers, and promenades, these seaside towns may remind you of Brighton, but on a much smaller scale and with far less pomposity. There is always a sense of the mountains, for it is from the coast that some of the finest views of them are to be enjoyed. The 800-acre **Snowdonia National Park** covers much of the western half of the region and gentler hills spread over the rest, separated by lakes and rushing rivers. The castles along the coast are, for the most part, products of Edward I's scheme to secure Wales under English rule in the thirteenth century.

Frequent bus and train service from Chester and Liverpool, and more accommodations than anywhere else in Wales, make the coastal resort of Llandudno an almost inevitable overnight stop. A few miles further along the coast, the old fishing port of **Conwy** comes into view. In good weather, tourists deluge **Conwy Castle,** making navigation of the spiral staircases an unexpected cheap thrill (open daily 9:30am-7pm; admission 35p). In this walled town, you can also visit what is supposedly the best surviving Elizabethan townhouse in Great Britain, **Plas Mawr** (in the High Street, open daily 10am-5:30pm; admission 25p).

From Conwy you can continue along the coast through **Penmaenmawr** and on to **Bangor.** If you are enjoying the water, however, stay over at the **Penmaenbach Youth Hostel** (YHA), just one mile west of Penmaenmawr village along the beach (tel. (049265) 3476). From here you can take a day's hike to colorful **Sychnant Pass;** ask the Warden for directions. Bangor is a large University town and center for shopping and communications in the northwest corner of Wales. It's a good place to rest and stock up on supplies before beginning a jaunt around the island of Anglesey. Some of the best live theater in Wales is at the nationally renowned **Theatr Gwynedd** on Garth Road. During the summer, films are shown on weekends. Drop by the Box Office (open daily 10am-9pm; tel. 51708) to see what's on while you're in town.

From Bangor, buses and trains leave frequently for **Anglesey** and the port of **Holyhead** where you can pick up a ferry to Dublin (about £8 one-way). **Beaumaris Castle,** one of the best known in Wales, overlooks the entrance to the **Menai Straits.** Another major attraction of Anglesey—other than its untouched, serrated shoreline—is the "Church of Saint Mary in the hollow of white hazel, near to a rapid whirlpool and to Saint Tysilio's church, near to a red cave," known by the natives as **Llanfairpwllgwyngyllgogerychwyrndrobwllllandysiliogogoch.** You can call it Llanfair P.G., if you must.

Back in Bangor, you can head for the hills by taking a bus to **Capel Curig.** Before hitting the Snowdon Mountain Range, spend an afternoon in **Betws-Y-Coed.** This is the most tarted-up and commercially exploited of the North Wales villages, but try to ignore the tartan shops and enjoy the scenery. The heather-ringed **Llyn Elsi Reservoir,** accessible by footpath from the town, affords the best views of the **Glyders,** a cluster of peaks overshadowed by Snowdon.

From Betws-Y-Coed, you can reach the base of Snowdon by going back through Capel Curig and on to **Pen-Y-Pass.** One of the best-equipped YHA Youth Hostels in Britain is located at the doorstep of the massif, and well-trodden footpaths lead off in all directions. Five other youth hostels surround the majestic mountain, giving you an idea of how popular the area is with hikers. **Llanberis** is the center for all sorts of outdoor activities in the area and there are plenty of B&Bs to choose from. The best source of information on hiking and mountaineering in this region is **Merseyside Y.H.A. Ltd.,** 40 Hamilton Square, Birkenhead, L41 5BA (tel. 051-647-7348). If you're not up for the hike, the **Snowdon Mountain Railway** can take you right to the summit from the base station in Llanberis. Those looking to get away from the mainstream of hikers should challenge the Glyders that are approached from the opposite side of the **Llanberis Pass.**

The famous slate quarries of **Blaeneau Ffestiniog** can be reached easily by train from Betws-Y-Coed. The best way to see these wonders of Victorian enterprise is to take a tram ride through the **Llechwedd Slate Caverns.** This tour is so well done that it has won awards. A train takes you through the chilly innards, filled with genuine period equipment and atmosphere. (Open every day 10am-6pm; admission 75p.) If you're still getting a kick out of those "little trains of Wales," the **Vale of Ffestiniog Railway** will chug you through one of the most luscious valleys in Wales, dropping you in **Porthmadog** where you can pick up a British Rail train.

Heading east for **Llangollen** requires more difficult transportation maneuvers (but you can always hitch). "Here they come, to this cup and echo of hills," wrote Dylan Thomas about Llangollen's **International Musical Eisteddfod,** held here every June (the 1979 festival will run July 3-8). Over 100,000 people invade this idyllic country town to hear choirs from more than thirty nations—tickets sell out early.

But Llangollen is worth a visit even when the Eisteddfod isn't taking place. Nearby are the ruins of the **Valle Crucis Abbey,** almost as picturesque as those of Tintern Abbey in South Wales (open every day 9:30am-7pm; admission 15p). Be sure also to visit **Plas Newydd,** a gracious house inhabited by a pair of eccentric eighteenth-century women who eloped together from Ireland and lived here for fifty years. They were truly the talk of the town in those days; today you can see the dazzling wood carvings and paintings that kept them company for all those years. (Open Mon.-Sat. 10:30am-7:30pm; Sun. 11am-4pm; admission 15p.)

Scotland

Scotland is majestic without the self-conscious cultivation of the English lake district or the rugged earthiness of Wales. The mountains soar, the hills rise endlessly, the water stretches past the eye's ken. Walking here also takes on a different character. There are no afternoon jaunts in Scotland; mere walks wind into the evenings' silhouettes and half-lights.

In Scotland's cities, the majesty translates into quiet sophistication—**Edinburgh,** the capital, is self-possessed and dignified. The underbelly of Scotland holds its rough, churning industrial cities, notably **Glasgow.**

If you just have three or four days, we urge you to spend them in the Highlands, even if you get no further than **Loch Lomond** or the Clyde's **Isle of Arran,** both within easy reach of Glasgow. There is nothing (not even Norway's fjords, the usual comparison) that can compare to returning to the crofter's hearth for oatcakes and scones, after a day's trek into the hills.

Edinburgh

Edinburghers are as aloof from one another as Edinburgh is from the rest of Scotland. Prouder than stately Bath, with a collection of Georgian architecture in the New Town that rivals in quantity what the spa boasts in quality, Edinburgh is above all a capital city. Walk down **George Street**—every other townhouse shelters a banker or insurance broker. Most of the parks you see are private, and require a key for entry; those that are public (**Royal Botanic Garden, Holyrood Park,** and **Princes Street Gardens** are the principal ones) tend to be so carefully manicured that you wouldn't dare bring your picnic lunch there. Visit Edinburgh during the festival (last week and a half in August and the first week in September); there is music every day in Princes Street Gardens.

The pride of tourist Edinburgh is the **Royal Mile,** stretching from the **Castle** (30p for Historical Apartments, open 9:30am-6pm, Sundays 11am-6pm). In between the main attractions, the street is lined with bagpipe

SCOTLAND

ATLANTIC OCEAN

SHETLAND IS.

ORKNEY ISLANDS

• Kirkwall

Hoy

Pentland Firth

Thurso •   John O'Groats

• Wick

Care Wrath   □ Durness
     □ Ben More

OUTER HEBRIDES

LEWIS   • Stornoway

HIGHLANDS

• Lochinver

The Minch

Loch Broom

• Tarbert

• Ullapool

HARRIS

TORRIDON

Isle of Skye

Moray Firth

Fraserburgh

• Inverness

Loch Ness

Aberdeen

GRAMPIAN   TAYSIDE

• Ft William

• Dundee

Perth •   *Firth of Tay*

• Oban

Loch Lomond

Firth of Forth

★ Edinburgh

• Glasgow

BORDERS

Arran

Firth of Clyde

• Prestwick/Ayr

NORTH CHANNEL

DUMFRIES

• Dumfries

Solway Firth

ENGLAND

0 km	30	60
0 m	20	40

makers, piping schools, kilt shops, and other purveyors of Scottish esoterica. Along the way, you might also want to stop at **Lady Stair's House** (free), now a museum containing literary relics of Burns, Scott, and R.L. Stevenson; **John Knox's House** (15p), where the religious reformer is believed to have spent his last years; **Huntly House** (free), the main museum of Edinburgh history; and the unique **Museum of Childhood** (5p), on High Street at Hyndford's Close.

There are several art galleries worth visiting. The **National Gallery,** on the Mound, has a collection of Old Masters including the *Bridgewater Madonna* of Raphael. Open daily from 10am-5pm; Sundays 2-5pm. In the middle of the Botanic Gardens lies the **National Gallery of Modern Art.** There are three pieces by Henry Moore, drawings by Picasso and Rouault, and rotating monthly exhibits. Open daily 10am-6pm; Sunday 2-6pm. Admission is free to both museums. For some more works of modern art, go to the **Richard Demarco Gallery,** 61 High Street. (Open Tues.-Sat. 10am-5:30pm; admission free.)

Orientation

For an excellent view of Edinburgh, climb **Arthur's Seat,** an 823-foot (extinct; volcano located in Holyrood Park, or tramp around the lip of **Salisbury Crags,** with some impressive vistas, though less than half as high. To get a more central view, walk to the tip of **Scott Monument** (5p; closed Sundays) in East Princes Street Gardens, a Gothic structure that puts London's Royal Albert Memorial to shame. **Calton Hill,** just past the east end of Princes Street, offers beautiful views of the city at night, as well as a close-up look at "Edinburgh's Disgrace," the row of large pillars that was once intended to grow into a replica of the Parthenon. Money ran out midway through the first row of columns.

The city is divided into the **Old Town,** to the south of Princes Street, including the **University,** the libraries, and most of the historical museums; and the **New Town,** to the north of Princes Street, built on a grid plan of three main avenues, containing most of the large stores and the residential areas. The dividing line between the two sections is formed by Princes and High Streets.

Princes Street is the heart of the shopping district, although many specialty shops are found along the Royal Mile. On Sundays, there are open-air markets in several parts of the city. Several market areas appealing to young people have been developing in recent years. Presently, **Cockburn Street Market,** with its cheap jeans shops and student proprietors, and **Greyfriars Market,** on Forrest Road opposite Better Books, are best-established. The market area around **St. Stephen's Street** is particularly good for antiques and browsing. For complete information on where to find the cheapest food, clothing, and shelter, and for an underground look at the social scene, invest in *Alternative Edinburgh,* available at Better Books, 11 Forrest Road, or at Grayfriars Market across the street.

The **Tourist Information Bureau,** including an accommodation service, is at 5 Waverley Bridge (tel. 226-6591), up the ramp from the Waverley Rail Station. The **Scottish Tourist Board** also has a counter there (tel. 332-2433), and will help map out your itinerary for the rest of the country. Make sure to pick up *What's On In Edinburgh* and *Day and Afternoon Tours.* The trips range from £2.00 to £4.00 and are top-notch, particularly the one through Burns' region. Most bus services operate from St. Andrew's Square.

Addresses and Telephone Numbers

Student Travel Centre: Student Centre House at the University. Bristol St.

(tel. 668-2221). Discounts for anybody under age 26. Open Mon.-Fri. 9:30am-5pm and Sat. 10 am-noon.

British Student Travel Centre: Bristol St. (tel. 226-5700).

U.S. Consulate: 3 Regent Terrace (tel. 556-8315).

Police: East Fettes Ave. (tel. 811-3131).

Doctor: University Health Service, 20 Marshall St., students only (tel. 667-1011). Non-students should go to Community Health Centre, Johnstone Terr. (tel. 225-8474).

American Express: 139 Princes St. (tel. 225-7881). Open 9am-5:30pm Mon.-Fri., 9am-noon Sat.

Cook's: 9 Castle St. (tel. 225-7125).

Emergency: Royal Infirmary (tel. 999—no coin needed).

Accommodations

Though room-finding should not be very difficult except during the Festival, you can always find help at the **Accommodation Bureau,** open till 9pm. If you decide to go it alone, the best hunting grounds for guest houses and B&Bs are centered around **Newington** (on the southeast side of town and **Canonmills** (to the north of the city center). Or try:

YMCA Hostel, 14 South Saint Andrew St. (tel. 556-4303). Open to both men and women, and centrally located. B&B for £2.40. Dorms only.

YHA Youth Hostels are at 17-18 Eglinton Crescent (tel. 337-1120) and 7-8 Bruntsfield Crescent (tel. 447-2994). Eglinton is in a better location, but Bruntsfield will admit you in the morning. Eglinton opens its doors at 2 pm. If these two are full, they can direct you to one of the several temporary hostels.

Pollack Halls of Residence, 18 Holyrood Park Rd. (tel. 667-4331), behind the Royal Commonwealth Pool, offers 1500 large rooms (all singles) in modern college buildings. Bed-and-breakfast £5.50 or £3.25 with student ID; free showers. Generally booked-up by groups during the Festival. Highly recommended. Take bus #14, 21, or 33.

YMCA International Club, 12 Rothesay Place (tel. 225-2134). Singles £4.75, doubles £3.50. June-Sept. only.

Mr. A. Milne, **Arlington Guest House,** 11 Eyre Place (tel. 556-6178). £4.00-4.50 per person in singles, doubles, and family rooms.

Mrs. J. Owens, **Castle Guest House,** 38 Castle St. (tel. 225-1975). £3.50 per person in mostly double rooms. An excellent location on a street with a view straight up to the Castle. Or try the **Ashling Guest House** nearby at #47 (tel. 225-7796) £4.50 per person.

Mrs. F. Winkler, 41 Albany St. (tel. 556-1140). £3.00-£4.00 per person in a couple of singles, four doubles, and one family room. Cozy.

Muirhouse Municipal Caravan Site is the closest for camping, about one and a half miles west of the city center (tel. 225-2424, Ext. 6311). Open April 1 to September 30 and has extensive facilities. 60p-£1.20 for tents. Advance bookings may be sent to the City of Edinburgh District Council, Parks and Recreation Department, 27 York Place, Edinburgh EH1 3HP.

Food

Whether you dare to try *haggis* (made from sheep's bladder), *cock-a-leekie soup,* or other traditional fare, you'll find eating out a real treat in Edinburgh. Even specialty restaurants are moderately priced and there is a spate of health food—salad bar places. The Information Office distributes a free restaurant guide detailing house specialties and opening hours. Here are some recommendations:

Laigh Coffee House, 83 Hanover St., is popular with students and young professionals. A self-service counter serves salads, shortbread, good coffee, and wholemeal bread with lemon spread. Also a selection of "vegetarian-esque" hot dishes for under 90p. Open 10am-7pm, Sat. 10am-2pm.

Edinburgh University Union, Teviot Row House. Three good cafeterias in the 80p range. Three bars and a reading room. Lunches and evening meals available.

The Farmhouse, 121 Princes St., emphasizes fresh farm produce; the results are plain, fresh and excellent. Self-service in the 50p (salad) to 90p (fish 'n' chips) range. Try a Melton Mowbray (pork-and-egg sandwich) for 50p. Come early or late to avoid the queue.

Henderson's Salad Table, 94 Hanover St., doles out good vegetarian food in a cellar atmosphere. Hot plates around 80p, soups 25p. Also 50 types of wine by the glass, (50p). Open 8am-11pm, closed Sun.

For inside information on Edinburgh's 500 pubs, pick up *The Complete Edinburgh Pub Guide* from the Edinburgh University Student Publications people at 1 Buccleuch Place. You might want to make the traditional **Rose Street** pub crawl, from **Abbotsford** to **Scott's Bar,** nineteen pubs in all.

The Edinburgh Festival

The **Edinburgh Festival** transforms the city; thousands of culture-minded Europeans and Americans congregate and the city makes a determined effort to keep them happy. Museum hours are extended and special exhibitions arranged. The Festival itself lasts from the third week in August to the middle of September, and attracts artists of the highest caliber—in the past, participants have included many musicians of international repute; Leonard Bernstein, Mstislav Rostropovich, Claudio Arrau, and André Previn among them. Opera, ballet, symphony and chamber groups are all included in the Festival, along with somewhat less famous and more adventurous theater groups. (Stoppard's modern classic, *Rosencrantz and Guildenstern Are Dead,* was first performed in Edinburgh.) A fringe festival of music and drama supplements the official one; an avant-garde film festival represents the cinema. The **Military Tattoo** is performed at the Castle during the same period as the Festival—massed military bands, pipes, and drums.

Tickets are available by mail—and for the major events, writing in advance is nearly a necessity—from the Festival Box Office, 21 Market Street, Edinburgh, Scotland EH1 1BW, starting the first week in May. During the Festival, the Box Office is open seven days a week. Prices for musical events range from £1 (most are at least £2.50) to galactic concert hall and opera house prices. Prices for the Tattoo start at £1.

Inverness

Shakespeare's Macbeth murdered King Duncan in the old castle of Inverness, originally a prehistoric Pictish settlement. Inverness developed early as a strategic trading point, and today serves as a transport center. Sometimes called "Capital of the Highlands," it is certainly the capital of tourism. Yet Inverness is not as saturated with holiday-makers as Fort William, and can be a welcome town to return to after a ramble through the desolation of the Grampians. You can take several excellent daytrips from Inverness—hop on a bus to nearby **Urquhart Castle** or to **Cawdor Castle.** You'll pass **Culloden Battlefield,** where Bonnie Prince Charlie was defeated. Further north in the same direction lies eighteenth-century **Fort George,** now a splendid museum of silver and medallions. Inverness is five miles away from **Loch Ness,** more of an inland sea than a loch, hide-out for Nessie, the monster so beloved by tourist officials. For a list of full-day or half-day bus excursions from Inverness (there are at least ten different trips from £1.25-4), ask for a brochure at the **Tourist Office,** or the **Bus Station** on Academy Street.

In Inverness itself, you'll find **Dunbar's Hospital** and the **High Kirk,** dating from the seventeenth and eighteenth century respectively; worth a look. Whiskey distilleries, woolen mills, and pottery shops sprinkled throughout the vicinity generally open their doors to visitors. For more information inquire at the **Tourist Information Center,** 23 Church Street (tel. 34353). Their office is open from 9am-8pm weekdays, till 6pm Saturdays and 2-7pm Sundays.

Accommodations

Inverness is packed during the summer, so to assure yourself a bed, arrive as early in the day as possible. The Tourist Office can usually find you a B&B for 30p, or give you an accommodation list for the town and you can try dialing yourself. If you can't arrive early, consider the "Book a Bed Ahead Plan" (see The Highlands section).

YHA Youth Hostel, 1 Old Edinburgh Road. Inverness IV2 3HF (tel. 31771), saddles Castlehill and offers an unbeatable view of the countryside. £1.10 and £1.30. Advance bookings are essential for July and August. Roomy nineteenth-century house, but don't count on the hot water.

Mrs. McEwan, 12 Rangemore Rd. (tel. 33380). £3.75 per person.

Mrs. Cowan, 31 Green Drive (tel. 35615). £3.75 per person.

The best camping is at the **Bught** site, one mile west of the city on A82 (tel. 36920). Tents £1.50. Good facilities; quickly booked. Another site near the town is **Bunchrew** (tel. 37802), three miles out on A9 North.

The Highlands

The Scottish Highlands are worth visiting for the clouds alone. Whether orchestrating a majestic sunset across the **Firth of Lorn** from **Oban,** creating a misty vista of Skye's **Black Cuillin Hills** from **Applecross Pass,** or channeling into spooky **Glen Coe,** the clouds have a quality seldom known in England.

Unlike the Pennines, Alps, and Rockies, which were violently folded and thrust into place, the mountains of Scotland were carved out of a plateau by glaciers, the glens slowly and deliberately gouged. Men finished the job by destroying the forest nearly one thousand years ago, and today every chisel-mark of nature is visible. The accessibility of the peaks, and the steepness with which they rise from sea-loch to summit make them breathtaking, although they are actually very low mountains (the highest barely tops 4400 feet).

Early August through mid-September is heather-time in Scotland, when whole mountains erupt in purple. September has the best weather—if you're lucky, you might get cloudless days and temperatures in the 70s, even in the north. June is especially wet—a good time for misty moors and bogs—while early spring is a good time for exploring the **Hebrides,** before the local folk disappear to make room for the growing number of summer tourists. Winter is the time for ice-climbing, or skiing in the **Cairngorms,** dotted with lots of cozy inns for the long winter nights.

Transportation is not so easy. **Caledonian MacBrayne, Ltd.,** which runs a monopoly on much of the heavy industry in western Scotland, also monopolizes public transport, and offers expensive bus service in the popular Oban-Fort William region. **British Rail** goes up the west coast as far as **Loch Carron,** before it cuts east to **Dingwall** and **Inverness.** Along the east coast, you can go as far as **Thurso,** the northernmost town in Scotland. The rest of the Highlands, including the rugged coast of **Ross** and **Cromarty** and the stark, loch-studded landscapes of western **Sutherland,** are virtually inaccessible by public transport. Exceptions are the busy resorts of **Lochinver** and **Ullapool,** served by regular buses. Most small villages are served by private minibuses, which run to the nearest town with public transport two or three times a week. Very expensive (for example, Durness-Tongue, 30 miles, 75p single), but you may not have a choice. Most of the islands off the coast of Scotland (**Inner and Outer Hebrides** to the west, **Orkneys** and **Shetlands** to the north) can be reached fairly easily by the large number of reliable ferries. About the only islands which may give you trouble are the Shetlands, since the only ferries from the mainland leave from Aberdeen, and are usually booked solid months ahead of time by the oil companies, who need all available transport for men working on the North Sea oil project. However, it may not be too difficult to hitch a ride aboard a fishing vessel or tanker—just ask around the docks of any northern port.

Accessibility is no problem until you hit the west coast north of Skye, where train services end. Bus services here aren't bad; most small towns in this area are serviced regularly Monday through Saturday. **Warning:** whereas Sunday transportation in England is mildly harassing, it simply dies in Scotland. Even hitching is appreciably worse on Sunday. Pick up a copy of the exhaustive *Getting Around the Highlands and Islands* (50p). It is available at most large train stations, tourist offices, and also some newsstands. Hitching on the west coast is definitely not as good as elsewhere. People are very friendly throughout the country—chances are you'll get an offer of a bed or floor along with your lift and even a breakfast of tea and scones.

If you're planning to do a substantial amount of traveling, consider the **Highlands and Island Travelpass.** The ticket allows unlimited travel on most rail, bus, and ship services for eight days (£28 off-peak season or £35 peak) or for twelve days (£34 off-peak, £42 peak). Inquire at **Duncan Duffy Limited,** 25 Queensgate, Inverness (tels. 32134 and 33888). You can also get a Travelpass in the U.S., but this one lasts ten days and cost $76. Contact Britrail Travel International, Inc., 630 Third Ave., New York, NY 10017. Remember that for any of the travelpasses to be worthwhile you have to do *a lot* of traveling. You might also want to look at a copy of *Getting Around the Highlands and Islands,* which gives fares for all the major travel routes, and compute the cost of your planned trip: you may well find it cheaper to buy your tickets one by one.

If you are traveling in the off-season, you will have a magnificent time, no troubles, and you don't have to read any further. During the summer months, however, beds become scarce as tourists of all nations flood into the area. Any tourist office will book you into a B&B or guest house (though not a hostel) in their town for a 30p fee; for £1, they will call ahead to another region and find you a place (the **Book a Bed Ahead Service**), but only on the morning of the day you want your bed. The Youth Hostels in the area are even more jammed in the summer; so unless you've made reservations in advance, plan on staying in B&Bs for about £4 per person or on camping. With all the open spaces in the Highlands, you're never far from a place to pitch a tent, but you should check with the local tourist office (or simply with the locals) to see which farmers mind and which ones don't. The Scottish Tourist Board publishes a guide to camping and caravaning sites in Scotland (about 50p, available at most tourist offices). Just remember that it rains about one out of every two days in the Highlands, so be prepared to be a bit soggy. And speaking of the weather, even when you are not camping, a raincoat and a pair of waterproof pants will come in very handy. It's also smart to waterproof your shoes before you come.

Cycling is a possibility—Scotland offers some of the most exciting cycling country in the world. Bikes can be rented in any of the major cities, and transported to your starting point by train, for half-fare. There are even cycling organizations that will help you plan routes. Make sure to carry reliable rain gear, and all the tools (remember the patchkit!) necessary to repair the bike.

For general information about this region, contact the **Highlands and Islands Development Board,** Bridge House, Bank Street, Inverness 1V1 1QR (tel. Inverness 34171) or the Scottish Tourist Board, 23 Ravelston Terrace, Edinburgh EH4 3EU (tel. 031-332-2433).

Warning: Scottish mountains, moors, and glens are extremely dangerous; you can't rely on cairns or well-marked paths to guide your way, and you can never (even though the day may be cloudless) predict when the mist will come down. Blizzards are frequent even during July, and exposure usually kills several people every weekend. So—*never* go up a mountain without sturdy boots with nailed or Vibram soles, well broken-in; a one-inch or 2½-inch Ordnance Survey map plus a compass you know how to use; adequate waterproof gear and clothing to withstand freezing temperatures; aluminized mylar blanket; and an emergency food supply. Always leave a planned route and timetable at the hostel, croft, or nearest mountain rescue station. For more details on proper equipment for mountaineering in Scotland, consult a reputable guide, such as Poucher's *The Scottish Peaks.* A further danger from mid-August to mid-October is the possibility of being shot accidentally by a deer stalker. During this period, always consult the hostel warden or innkeeper before heading for an area where deer stalkers might be at work.

TOURING

There are so many spots worth visiting in the Highlands that we can only suggest a few. Chances are, if you show our list to your Scottish landlady, she'll rant and rave and say, "That's not the best of the Highlands at all," just as one landlady we spoke to insisted that Strathpeffer (near Dingwall) is the best base for touring the Highlands. Don't hesitate to leave our suggested route whenever the mood seizes you.

Start at **Glasgow,** which can be reached by several excellent roads from England. On the way, you might want to stop and explore the turbulent history of the **Border Country,** pay homage to Robert Burns in **Dumfries,** or enjoy the excellent beaches near **Ayr. Wigtown,** jutting into the Irish Sea to the west of **Kirkcudbright,** has rolling farmland, quiet sandy beaches, and no tourists. The main road from Carlisle to Glasgow, the A74, passes through the **Southern Uplands,** one of the most sparsely populated areas of Scotland, with excellent opportunities for walking in the desolate grassy hills.

At **Tarbet,** you can either turn left for **Inveraray** and **Oban,** or continue up Lomondside towards **Crainlarish, Rannoch Moor,** and **Glen Coe.** Inveraray is an old county town set beautifully on **Loch Fyne.** The Castle is worth a visit; the loch is popular for sailing. On the way from Lomond, you go up Glen Coe, where you should keep an eye out for **Ben Arthur,** "The Cobbler," with its impressive pinnacles.

Once a quaint Victorian seaside resort, Oban still manages to exude some of its pre-World War I charm in spite of throngs of tourists. Its popularity stems mainly from the ease with which you can get to other places in the Highlands and Islands. The **Tourist Office** on Argyll Square (tels. Oban 3122 and 3551; if you're coming from the Railroad Station, turn right) is open Mon.-Fri. 9am-5:15pm and 6:30-9pm, Sat. 9am-5:15pm, Sun. 3-6pm. They will find you a B&B and give you general information on the town and its surroundings. There is a **Youth Hostel** (YHA) on the Esplanade (tel. Oban 2025) which is grade 2, with 130 beds. The regular caveats about hostels in the summertime apply. You can rent bikes from the **Warehouse** on John Street (tel. Oban 3488) for £1.75 a day. The town has its own little theater, the **Dunollie,** on George Street (tel. Oban 3794) where performances of traditional Scots music and dance are held.

Oban has the advantage of making **Mull** close enough to be nearly irresistible. A walker's paradise, Mull is also filled with *bothys* (huts in the mountains for campers' free use). Check with the Oban Tourist Office about the location of the *bothys*—which occasionally change—and help with Mull accommodations. The boat from Oban takes 45 minutes, costs £1.10 each way, and leaves several times a day. The YHA **Youth Hostel** on Mull is located in Tobermory (grade 3, 42 beds), about 20 miles up the coast from Craignure, where most of the Oban boats sail to. Several buses a day make the Craignure-Tobermory run, however. Generally, don't be too hopeful about hitching on the Mull—the people are great but there are very few of them.

Boats also leave Oban for Iona, where St. Columba is said to have brought Christianity to the Scots in 563 A.D.; and for the isle of **Staffa,** whose magnificent offshore grotto, **Fingal's Cave,** inspired Mendelssohn's *Hebridean Overture.* The excursion to Iona takes most of the day (you go to Mull from Oban, across Mull on a bus, then across a channel to Iona on a small launch—if the sea is choppy, you'll get wet). It costs £4.50, or £2 with a Travelpass. The trip to Staffa takes about a day as well, and costs £4-10, depending on the length of the trip, the tour operator, and the mode of transport. Check in Oban for details.

Rannoch Moor: Once a forest, until the advancing English army cut it down in the 1400s, the moor is one of the eeriest places in Scotland. Ancient treestumps still rise out of the treacherous bogs. The hamlet called **Bridge of Orchy,** at the edge of the moor, is named after the little stone bridge behind the hotel. The rail line from the south to Fort William runs through the center of the moor.

Glen Coe: In 1692, Clan Campbell asked Clan MacDonald for shelter for the fierce winter. One night, when the glen was socked in by a blizzard, the guests murdered their hosts in bed. If this hadn't actually happened, there would be some other blood-curdling tale associated with the spooky glen. It's not so bad, though, if the sun is shining. Entering Glen Coe from

Rannoch Moor, note the crags of **Aonach Eagach** on the right, reputed to have the most spectacular knife-edge ridgewalk in Scotland. One way to reach the ridge is by ascending the **Devil's Staircase,** the remains of one of the military roads built by General Wade to improve defenses after the 1745 insurrection led by Bonnie Prince Charlie nearly succeeded. On the left is the **Bidean nam Bian** range, highest in Argyllshire, with impressive spurs known as the **Three Sisters of Glencoe.** Turn off A82 just before the bridge over the **River Coe,** and head for the venerable **Clachaig Inn,** one of the most popular pubs among climbers—it also houses a mountain rescue post. Further down the road is the **Youth Hostel** (YHA; tel. Ballachulish 219; grade 2, 96 beds); still further, in the village of **Glencoe,** is the **Glencoe and North Lorne Folk Museum.**

Coming to the banks of **Loch Leven** under the shadow of the famous **Pap of Glencoe,** you can turn right and go all the way round the loch, through the bauxite-smelting village of **Kinlochlevin;** or head left for **Ballachulish,** three miles away. Here you catch the car ferry which saves you about 20 miles drive around the loch. Be prepared to queue if you have a car, though.

Fort William, at the southern end of the **Caledonian Canal,** is the main tourist center for the Western Highlands, and the base for climbing **Ben Nevis,** the highest peak in Britain. Otherwise it is not a very attractive town, and very difficult to hitch out of. For information, maps, and accommodation lists for the Highlands, visit the **Information Centre** in Cameron Square.

At Fort William, you must choose again, whether to head for the fishing port of **Mallaig,** or continue up the **Loch Lochy** segment of the Great Glen, the fault which runs all the way from Oban, at the mouth of **Loch Linnhe,** to Inverness, and cradles the Caledonian Canal. Since the road ends at Mallaig, the former route is advisable only if you intend to use the car ferry to **Armadale** in Skye. If you choose the latter road, you are on the road to **Inverness.** Turn left at **Invergarry,** and head for **Kyle of Lochalsh.** Along the way, you might want to stop at the excellent YHA **Youth Hostel** near the **Shiel Bridge,** (**Ratagan,** in the Hostel Guide, grade 3, 50 beds), perfectly situated for an exhausting day's traverse of the **Five Sisters of Kintail.** From the top of the highest peak in the chain, you can often see the great massif of Ben Nevis, over 30 miles distant. From Shiel Bridge, head down **Loch Duich** to **Eilean Donan Castle,** so beautifully situated at the **Meeting of the Three Waters** (Lochs **Duich, Long,** and **Alsh**) that it appears on the dust jacket of nearly every book about the Highlands.

Torridon Region

Follow the coast road north to **Loch Carron,** where the road winds through a beautiful pine forest planted in this century by the Forestry Commission. At **Kishorn,** you can turn onto the hair-raising **Bealoch-nam-Bo Pass,** "Pass of the Cattle," leading to the remote coastal village of **Applecross.** Until recently, this hamlet was accessible only by sea or crofter's pass. The road rises steeply to 2054 feet and contains many hairpin turns, so it should be attempted only by skillful drivers, and avoided during winter and in bad weather.

Getting around the Torridon region is difficult if you are carless. This part of Scotland has no train lines, and almost all the buses that serve the area make only one trip a day. Hitching is difficult because so few people venture farther north than Ullapool. Still, if you have the time and want to leave civilization as far behind as is possible in the British Isles, a trip to the Torridon region will reward you with isolation amidst unforgettable scenery.

It is on the way from Loch Carron to **Loch Torridon** that you note how the south highland scenery, with long ridges and densely packed groupings of mountains, begins its transition to the scenery of the far north, with lone peaks and vast stretches of moor and bog. Rounding **Beinn Damh** into **Shieldaig,** the main village of Torridon, you catch your first glimpse of the **Liathach,** considered by many to be the most beautiful mountain in Scotland. At first glance, you may mistake its white quartzite cap for snow. At the foot of the **Liathach** is the Torridon **Youth Hostel** (YHA; grade 1, 80 beds, tel. Torridon 294). For general tourist information on the area, contact the office at Gairloch (tel. Gairloch 2139); open all year. Seasonal information centers open at Ullapool and Lochinver during the summertime.

To the left of the Liathach, looking across Upper Loch Torridon, is **Beinn Alligin,** which can be climbed fairly easily by walking up the inside of the corrie (a circular indentation carved by a glacier; also called a *cirque*). Beinn Alligin is made of Torridon Sandstone, the oldest exposed rock in the world. For landlubbers, there is a nature walk which runs through the valley between Alligin and the Liathach.

Another worthwhile day's walk follows the crofter's path from **Loch Shieldaig** to Applecross. At the highest point, a 1200-foot saddle between two mountains, you get an unbelievable view of the Torridon mountains in back, and the Black Cuillins of Skye rising out of the mists ahead. The village of Applecross has a fine sandy beach, perfect for a picnic. Also, don't miss a sunset from **Diabaig Bay,** reached by a dirt road from the village of **Inver Alligin.** Finally, if you really want to get away from it all, trek up the coast to **Craig Youth Hostel,** one of the few hostels that can be reached only by foot. There the isolation is so complete that wardens are rotated on three-week shifts; at least one warden has written a book on the experience.

The coast road now brings you along the shores of beautiful **Loch Maree,** and finally to **Gairloch.** Then pick up the famed **Road of Desolation,** with great views of rugged **An Teallach,** and some fine scenery along **Loch Broom,** as you come into the busy resort and fishing village of **Ullapool.** From Ullapool it is three hours by boat to Stornaway on the outer Hebridean island of Lewis. Boats leave during the summer Mon.-Sat. 9:30am and 5:15pm. Fare is £4 single; if you have a car, count on a £17 fee to get it across.

The Far North

You are now on the edge of the most remote area in Britain. Traveling north from Ullapool, watch the mountains thin out, each one seeming more majestic than the last because of its increasing isolation. Stretches of peat-bog, dotted with hundreds of tiny lochs, appear. Finally, you glimpse **Suilven,** affectionately known as "The Sugarloaf."

It's a long way from the road to the base of Suilven from any direction, but the usual approach is from the little resort of **Lochinver.** Bear left at **Sklag Bridge.** The peninsula just north of Lochinver has a beautiful coast, and lots of sandy beaches with dunes. There is an excellent hostel located right off the beach at **Achmelvich,** but it may be necessary to book ahead during the summer. A temporary hostel at **Stoer** has been set up to handle the overflow, but it is a good idea to check with the warden at Achmelvich, to make sure it's open. The warden at Stoer encourages an atmosphere of conviviality, and chances are you'll spend the evening drinking with him in the bar at the **Drumbeg Hotel** ("I have to keep an eye on you. After all, I'm the warden.") Continue round the peninsula, with some fine views of precipitous

Quinag, until you come to the car ferry at **Kylestrome** (saving about 100 miles of driving). The ferry costs 6p for passengers, £1 for cars. The narrow road from Kylestrome to Durness has some of the best scenery in the north—it is certainly worth braving on a bicycle, in spite of its one in four gradients. Keep an eye out for Highland cattle roaming onto the road, though.

Durness, a barely noticeable village on the north coast, is an excellent base for visits to Cape Wrath and other points of interest along the coast. One mile from Durness proper is **Balnakeil Craft Village,** set up to encourage Highland artisans to continue practicing their trades. North of Balnakeil is **An Eharaid,** a peninsula with a long, flat, sandy beach backed with dunes. Swimming is possible, and a path leads to the cliffs of **Faraid Head.** Next to the **Durness Youth Hostel** (YHA) about a mile east of the center of Durness, is **Smoo Cave,** a huge system of sea-caves that can be easily entered at low tide. The Hostel deserves a special recommendation for its great warden, who plays records in the common room most evenings, and occasionally throws Scottish folk-dancing parties.

Finally, there's **Cape Wrath,** the northwest corner of Britain, marked by a lonely lighthouse on the tip of a huge, uninhabited peninsula. There is a road leading to the Cape, but you can't take your car on it. In fact, the only way to reach the road is by walking onto the peninsula from further south (no easy stroll) or by taking the tiny motorboat across the **Kyle of Durness** (50p one way). The landingplace of the boat depends on the state of the tide, so make sure you read the notice at the end of the road from Durness. Then, to signal the ferryman (who will probably be having tea across the Kyle), all you have to do is stand in a conspicuous place and wave your hands wildly. Once on the other side, you can get to Cape Wrath by minibus, for £1.25 return. The trip is 11 miles by road each way, so it may be possible to walk to the Cape, though the cliffwalk is much longer than the road. If you like, the bus driver will let you out near **Cleit Dhubb,** and you can walk back to the ferry from the highest cliffs on the British mainland (about 900 feet; Hoy, in the Orkneys, has higher cliffs). In any case you probably shouldn't try to walk both ways, unless you are prepared for camping. Even during the early summer, when it never really gets dark, the ferry stops running at 5:30pm and doesn't start again until after 9am the next morning. Durness has a one-day festival of sorts, the **Durness Highland Gathering** in late July.

There is a single minibus which leaves the **Parkhill Hotel** at 10:40am, three times a week, bound for **Tongue.** At Tongue, a lot of holiday traffic from the south reaches the north coast, and it shouldn't be too difficult to continue hitching east to **Thurso.** Right before Thurso, the bleak Highland scenery abruptly ends, and you find yourself on the fertile plains of **Caithness County.** Dairy is big here, and be sure you don't leave without trying some of the local cheese. The only valid excuse for spending much time in Thurso is to catch the boat to Orkney at nearby **Scrabster.** Just beyond Thurso is **Dunnet Head,** the northernmost point on the British mainland, with some impressive cliffs and the wide stretches of **Dunnet Sands.** It is only about 15 miles further to **John O'Groats,** traditionally the "Land's End" of Scotland, so you probably won't be able to resist the temptation to go. Don't say we didn't warn you, when you get there to find the "Last House in Scotland Souvenir Shop" and a signpost says "Land's End 857 miles," with one blank arrow where they'll put up your home town and photograph you standing next to it for 50p. About the only redeeming features here are the walk to **Duncansby Head,** the true "Land's End" of Scotland, with good cliff scenery and views of the offshore islands; and the cheap boats to Orkney, which leave frequently from John O'Groats pier. (See the Orkney Islands section.)

The Inner Hebrides: The Isle of Skye

Skye is easily the most spectacular island in the Hebrides, highlighted by the **Black Cuillin Hills,** the most jagged and awe-inspiring peaks in Britain. Unless you are an experienced rock-climber, there is not much you can do with them, but try to get as near as you can to sense their grandeur. The best way is to take the small motor launch from **Elgol** into **Loch Coruisk.** As you cross **Loch Scavaig,** the Cuillins loom larger and larger, until you reach a small cove at the head of Coruisk, and stand directly under the main ridge. On the north side of the island, visit **Dunvegan Head,** with the great basalt stacks called **MacLeod's Tables,** after the local clan.

There are several ways of getting to Skye. If you are already in the Hebrides, boats sail to Uig, on the northern part of the island, from either Tarbert, on the Isle of Harris (£2.80 one way, at least one boat a day, different departure times depending on the day of the week), or from Lochmaddy, on North Uist (also £2.80 one way, also at least one boat daily). From the mainland, you can get to Skye from either the Kyle of Lochalsh or from Mallaig, both of which are served by rail lines. From the Kyle of Lochalsh, it is only a five-minute (12p) crossing to Kyleakin on Skye. The ferries run every few minutes from Mallaig (where the train from Fort William arrives); the crossing takes half an hour to Armadale (£1.05 one way). There are five departures daily.

Portree is the largest town on Skye. The Information Center, overlooking the harbor, will book you into a bed-and-breakfast house. (Open 9:30am-8pm, except Sundays; tel. Portree 2137.) Orient yourself by walking around the beachhead to the top of the harbor and then into the moors beyond. Portree's main campsite, **Torvaig,** is just out of town on the Staffin Road. It is well equipped and costs £1 a night (tel. Portree 2209).

Nightlife in Portree is confined to the town's pubs and hotel bars. Food here tends to be expensive, with the exception of the fish (or haggis, or chicken, or sausage, or black pudding) 'n chips served at the **Bayview Fish and Chips Shop,** down the hill from the Post Office.

Many of Skye's visitors use as their base the **Youth Hostel** (YHA) in Broadford (grade 2, tel. Broadford 442). The Hostel is spartan, but quite adequate. A youth hostel (still listed in some guidebooks) at Uig burned down last year, and will be out of commission until further notice. Go to Broadford, in any case. The **Broadford Tourist Office**—open Mon.-Fri. 9:30am-7pm, Sat. 9:30am-1pm and 2:30-5:30pm—provides an accommodation service. Try not to arrive after hours or on a Sunday, as you'll find it difficult getting a space in a B&B on your own. For a walk here, you might try the **Princess Hill,** with an excellent view from the top. It is three hours up to the top, and you don't have to know how to climb.

Glenbrittle is right in the midst of the craggy Black Cuillin Hills. Climbing is unfortunately restricted to the expert. (You really have to know what you're doing to lay a foot on these.) The best way to get near here is to take the small motor launch from Elgol into Loch Coruisk (£1.30 return). Ask the driver to let you miss out on the return and take the next boat back so you'll have more time to wander. If you're coming from Broadford, you can take the post bus here for 30p—it'll take one and a half hours and is an experience in itself.

The Outer Hebrides: Lewis and Harris Island

To get to the Outer Hebrides, you can either leave from Oban or from Ullapool. The Oban crossing takes about seven hours, deposits you in Lochboisdale, on the island of South Uist, and costs £5.90 one way. Making your way up through the Hebrides via post bus is scenic but slow. From Ullapool, the crossing takes six hours, goes to Stornoway, on the Isle of

Lewis, and costs £4 one way. Boats on each run leave at least once a day. Most of the sights lie on the western shore and you can catch a bus that leaves Stornoway at 12:30pm (Mon., Tues., Thurs., Fri., and Sat. only) which runs past many of these places. The **Information Office** at the South Beach Quay in Stornoway (tel. 3088) will give you more details. The old croft house, called **Black House,** in Arnol, has been preserved with its original utensils as a museum. The monument to fishing can best be appreciated at Bragar where an archway fashioned from a whale's jawbone stands. The harpoon that did the dirty work dangles from the arch. Bird sanctuaries and observation points are scattered liberally throughout the islands so take your pick of native puffins, seabirds, fulmars, kittiwakes, and mute swans. Equally fascinating are the various monoliths. To get a feel for early settlement in Britain, run your hands over the **Callanish Standing Stones,** dating back to 2000 B.C.

The southern part of the island is called **Harris,** boasting the west coast's finest beaches. They're hard to reach, however, so contact the **Tourist Office,** Pier Road, in **Tarbert** (tel. 2011). The office will also give you directions to the two small youth hostels in Tarbert which lie off the main road. From Tarbert, a ferry goes south to **Lochmaddy** on North Uist, but only on Tuesdays and Fridays. **North Uist, Benbecula,** and **South Uist** are connected but not by public bus system. You're stuck with being taken as a passenger on a post bus which delivers mail to outlying regions.

The Orkney Islands

For God's sake, don't let **Pentland Firth** scare you. Sure, they say it can be rougher than a gale-swept English Channel, but as often as not, it's perfectly calm. And don't be misled by the black humps of Hoy (the "High Island" to the Norsemen who settled there), rising ominously from the mists across the Firth—they're nothing more than the beacons that guided the Norse sailors into the lush glen of Rackwick.

The *St. Ola* leaves Scrabster for Stromness daily at noon (Sunday service during July and August only); the fare is £4.40 one way, bicycles free, taking a car will run £10-15 one way depending on the make. The trip takes two hours, and the boat passes by the base of St. John's Head.

There is definitely something in the air that makes Orcadian life slow without making it lazy. The work gets done, but without the harassment of the clock. We're not suggesting that you come to Orkney for a snooze, however—for one thing, the weather is usually not good enough for lounging on the beach (although the water can be very warm, thanks to the Gulf Stream). There is plenty to see. The Isles have been inhabited for a lot longer than most of mainland Britain, and are jammed with sites of historical and archaeological significance; the coastal scenery is some of the best found anywhere. If you don't have at least three or four days, you probably shouldn't bother coming. But if you do have the time, settle down in one of the several hostels or dozens of guest houses, get to know the locals, and relax. You'll be amazed at how easy it is to spend days talking to the fishermen at **Kirkwall** pier, or watching the gulls from the cliffs of Black Craig (20 minutes' walk from Stromness) and never even think of going to see **Churchill Barriers** or **Skara Brae.**

Orientation and Accommodations

Unless there's a hurricane brewing, arrive by sea. The most spectacular route goes up the west coast of Hoy.

If you intend to do anything outside of Kirkwall or Stromness, the two towns on the Mainland, invest about 90p in a one-inch Ordnance Survey map

(map #6 for the Mainland, #7 for Hoy, #5 for northern islands). The maps are indispensable for finding places of archæological interest, as well as for walking, since virtually none of the footpaths are marked. Even on the coastal paths, where it's pretty obvious where to walk, the maps are helpful in finding interesting geological formations.

Recently, alternate ways of getting to the Orkneys have appeared. An air service flies to **Kirkwall Airport** from such places as Wick and Aberdeen, for outrageous fares: Aberdeen-Orkney £24; Inverness-Orkney £23; Glasgow-Orkney £38. In any case, you miss half the fun if you don't take a boat to Orkney. A relatively new service, from John O'Groats, seems to be cutting into the business of the *St. Ola*. Three or four operators take several converted PT-boats a day to South Ronaldsay (connected to the mainland by a causeway), where they are met by a bus (30p) to Kirkwall. The trip costs £4 return, but the Travelpass is not valid on this trip, while it is on the Scrabster crossing. One or two boats land on Hoy. Main disadvantages: 1) You miss the Hoy cliffs; 2) You have to put up with the tacky tourism of John O'Groats. One more advantage: PT-boats go so fast (crossing takes about 45 minutes) that you may even be able to put up with a choppy Pentland Firth.

There are also several ways to travel between the islands themselves. **Loganair, Ltd.** (tel. Kirkwall 3025), runs frequent circle flights originating at Kirkwall, and touching down at several of the northern islands. Fare is £4.50 between Kirkwall and any island, and at least £2 between any two islands. **Orkney Islands Shipping Company,** 4 Ayre Road, Kirkwall (tel. Kirkwall 2044), has a few sailings per week between Kirkwall and the northern islands, £2.75 single, £3.80 round trip, and the regular passenger service to **Shapinsay** (50p). Smaller operators also carry passengers to the northern islands; details are available at the Kirkwall or Stromness docks. There are three main services to Hoy (55p) and **Flotta** (66p) all originating in Stromness. **Bremmer & Co.** (tel. Stromness 381), sails the *Watchful* to **Lyness** twice a day (except Saturdays) and stops on Hoy, if you request. Brenner's *Hoy Head* makes similar circuits every day except Sunday. The Travelpass is not good on the boats going around the Orkneys.

Transportation on the islands is easy. The only time you may have difficulty hitching is on a weekend. Cycling is almost as efficient, and you can hire a bicycle from **Mrs. W. Work,** Davaar, 6 Old Scapa Road, Kirkwall (tel. Kirkwall 2006). If you intend to stick to the larger villages and towns, **James D. Peace** runs buses between Kirkwall and Stromness, and other places on the Mainland (and islands connected to the Mainland by causeway). Schedules are posted at the Information Bureau in Kirkwall, and at the pier in Stromness Harbor. No service on Sunday. **Mr. I. Moar,** Post Office, Hoy (tel. Hoy 201), has a car for hire on Hoy. Then, of course, there is walking. Just be sure to wear your waterproof boots, and try to avoid fields containing bulls.

Guest houses and crofts offering B&B are plentiful in Orkney; obtain the list at the offices of the **Orkney Tourist Organisation,** Mounthoolie Lane, Kirkwall (tel. Kirkwall 2856). There are official Youth Hostels in Stromness (grade 2, 42 beds), Kirkwall (grade 2, 100 beds, on Old Scapa Road, tel. Kirkwall 2243), and Hoy (20 beds, grade 3).

Sights

Kirkwall, capital of Orkney County, is situated on the Mainland, 15 miles east of Stromness. While not as picturesque as Stromness, it contains several buildings of historical interest, all located within a few hundred yards of one another. The red sandstone **Cathedral of St. Magnus** was started in 1137, and is done almost entirely in Norman style, although the building was begun by the Norse Earl Rognvald, and finished well into the Gothic period. Also be sure to visit the **Tankerness House Museum,** on Broad Street (free: 10:30am-1pm, and 2-5:30pm), which also houses the Orcadian history museum. Kirkwall is the shopping and cultural center of the Orkneys, with lots of pubs, and dances several times a week. It is also the base for most of the fishing. Drop by the piers about 5pm, just after the day's catch has come in, and you can get fresh crab or haddock for a song. And if the pubs aren't enough for you, arrange to take a tour of the **Highland Park Distillery,** located just south of the town, where they make the local 100 proof whiskey.

   Stromness looks as if it has just slid down the hillside and lost half its houses to the harbor, for its bayfront buildings, with their private piers, literally project into the water. The main street, **Victoria Street,** is narrow and paved with flagstones, and looks more medieval than anything in York or Chester—yet the town dates from the late eighteenth century, when it became a port of call for transatlantic shipping.

   Archaeological sites abound in the Orkneys. Some of the more important ones, open to the public, are: **Skara Brae,** a Stone Age village near the Bay of Skaill; the **Standing Stones of Stenness** and the **Ring of Brodgar,** impressive Bronze Age monuments similar to Stonehenge and Avebury Circle; **Maeshowe Cairn,** a Stone-Age chambered tomb with a fine set of runic inscriptions on the interior walls, left by twelfth-century Norse plunderers; the **Runnibister Earth House,** an Iron Age structure built into the ground, just two miles from Kirkwall on the A965; and the **Dwarfie Stone,** the only rock-cut tomb known in Britain, located a half-mile from the Rackwick road, on Hoy.

   Finally, there is the land itself, best explored by walking. On the Mainland, there are excellent walks throughout the interior; however, the path along the western coast has to be one of the finest cliff-walks in Britain. Start at Stromness, and walk out to **Black Craig,** where you can pick up the path. The trail will awe you with views of magnificent waterfalls, great sea-caves *(geos),* and more birds (Orkney is popular with bird-watchers) and rabbits than you've ever imagined to be ecologically possible. The best part of the trail goes from Black Craig to the **Bay of Skaill,** where you can take in Skara Brae before returning to Stromness. Continuing further north leads to the 300-foot cliffs of **Marwick Head.**

To The Shetlands

   The Shetlands are accessible by boat or plane from **Kirkwall** in the Orkneys. Flying costs £16 for the half-hour flight, though see if you can get a youth fare. The **Orkney Islands Shipping Company's** boat leaves from Kirkwall pier, usually on Saturday. The eight-hour voyage costs about £10, but you should generally reserve a spot, as few passengers are taken. You can always try your luck asking for a lift from the fishing boats at Kirkwall pier. You can also fly or boat from Aberdeen. £30 for the one-hour flight or £15 for the twelve-hour (overnight) cruise. From **Scrabster,** a shipping and passenger service will sail you farther into the midnight sun—to the Faroe Islands, Iceland and Norway. Please note that only seventeen of the hundred islands are inhabited so you probably have to pay extra to visit the Shetland wilds. For further information about the Shetlands contact the **Shetland Tourist Organization,** Information Centre, Larwick, Shetland ZE1 011 (tel. Larwick 3434). For information about the ferries (and for reservations) contact **P&O Ferries,** P.O. Box 5, Aberdeen AB9 8OL Scotland (tel. Aberdeen 572615).

GREECE

$1U.S.=36drachmas (dr)   **1dr=$.028**

Greece may be the most visited and least explored country in Europe. Most tourists head for the islands—with their sun-drenched beaches and easy-going lifestyle—and leave them only for a quick glance at Athens. But the mainland also deserves a visit: village life, especially in the mountains, is still untrampled by tourists; archaeological sites are extensive and well-preserved; and the coastline is often equal or superior to that of the islands.

A composite view of Greece's attractions—its history, lifestyle, and natural beauty—helps to explain the zealous resistance of the Greek people to the frequent foreign occupation of their soil, from the uprising against the Ottomans in 1821, to the fight against Mussolini's troops and the Germans, to the more recent uproar over Turkish muscle in Cyprus and the Aegean.

If at all possible, come to Greece in the off-season. The tourists are gone, accommodations are cheaper and easy to find, and the Greeks themselves are more relaxed, more receptive. You can sightsee all day without having to retreat from the afternoon heat. And you can still get your tan on **Crete,** which offers year-round swimming. For the majority, however, who are only able to make the trip during the summer, take some compensation in the

351

fact that every July and August Greece becomes one of the world's best under-30s social scenes. An incredibly international assortment of hippies, hikers, young package tourists, and yacht-owning sons of tycoons crowd the discotheques, cafés, beaches, and hostels. Interaction is open and constant.

TRANSPORTATION AND ORIENTATION

The most heavily-used boat connection to Greece is the daily car ferry from **Brindisi,** in Southern Italy, to **Patras,** Greece (with a stop at **Corfu.**) Passengers are allowed a free stopover on Corfu for up to one month, but you must declare your intention to do so when booking, or at the latest just prior to embarkation, at the Brindisi office. There is some variation in the fares of the boats that make the crossing. The cheapest boat is the **Oinoussai,** on which students get a deck seat and then a bus from Patras to Athens for between $24 and $27, depending on the season. Their office in Brindisi is at 122 Corso Umberto (tel. 20560). Normally the four-hour bus trip to Athens costs $6.

Holders of Eurailpasses and Eurail Youthpasses can make the boat trip for free on the **Adriatic** or **Hellenic Mediterranean** lines, and then the rail connection to Athens from Patras; they often delay your entry onto the ferry, however, favoring paying passengers, so insist on your rights. Such problems are standard in Brindisi, which is a monument to chaos. Delays and ticket lines can run as much as four hours in the summer; advance reservations are often impossible to make or not honored at the gate. Plus, the trains from northern Italy, ostensibly timed to coincide with boat departures, are often late, causing a mad stampede of luggage-laden tourists through the town. We suggest getting to Brindisi a day before your departure to avoid last minute tangles. Don't forget to save enough Italian currency to pay the port tax (about 4000L). Also, bring food on board with you, since the meals and snacks are exorbitantly priced.

There are less frequent boats to Patras from other Italian cities, as well as from Dubrovnik. It is also possible to sail to Greece from Haifa, Marseille, Barcelona, Istanbul, and Alexandria. A student ID merits a discount on some fares.

Athens is an excellent center for cheap transportation to Europe and other parts of the Mediterranean. Prices of student charter flights are rising, but still a bargain: one way to or from London $90, Paris $115, Rome $78, Tel Aviv $60, Cairo $60. These flights are usually dependable, but leave only on certain dates. If you try to get student rates on regular airlines, make sure you have a certificate from your school testifying to your student status—they may not accept student IDs.

Several student-oriented bus lines offer direct service between Western Europe and Athens at remarkable prices. One-way tickets from London or Munich go for $35-50. Buses to and from Istanbul cost only $23.

Drivers should be informed that despite the high price of gas in Greece (17-20dr per liter, or over $2 per gallon), the Tourist Office has introduced **petrol coupons** enabling foreign tourists to buy gas at just over half the normal price. Coupons can be purchased at tourist offices and at some campsites. A list is available at the Tourist Office in Athens.

Hitching to Greece is unrewarding. To make even passable time, you must thumb on the most direct and least scenic route through Central Yugoslavia. Thumbing from Istanbul through Kavalla to Athens may take single men the better part of a week. Inside Greece, women generally have the best luck, but they should proceed cautiously, for the taker is apt to be male. Outside of the cosmopolitan locales, Greek women rarely strike out unaccompanied, and a female alone is all too often assumed to be flaunting her loose morals until she proves otherwise. The easiest hitching is on the well-traveled road between Athens and Thessaloniki.

Train service in Greece is improving steadily, and Eurailpasses are now valid, as is InterRail. Bus routes are much more extensive and frequent and cost about the same as a second class train ticket. The **Greek State Railway** office is at 31 Venizelou Ave., Athens (tel. 3624-402).

In towns and cities, local buses and trolleys charge around 6dr. You must stand at the stop and flag them down, or the driver will ignore you. Taxis are no bargain.

Though a variety of Olympic flights connect Athens to the islands, the common mode of travel is by boat. Fares are relatively cheap; try to get overnight boats for longer trips. They will save you time and a night's accommodations cost, and will spare you from the scorching sun on deck. An interesting new twist in the boat service is the **Fragpass,** a Eurailpass for inter-island transportation. In 1978, only two lines were included, so the options weren't flexible enough to justify the investment (two weeks $34, one month $40); but if other lines have since joined, it should be worth investigating.

Tourism in Greece is managed by two nationwide organizations: the **National Tourist Organization of Greece (NTOG)** and the **Tourist Police** *(Touristiki As-Tee-No-Mia)*. The former supplies general information about touristic sites and accommodations all over the country, while the Tourist Police deal with more local, immediate problems—where to find a room, a dentist, what the bus schedule is or what to do when you've lost your passport. The Tourist Police keep long hours (some branches are open 24 hours a day), and are especially good at finding you a room in any price category you desire.

One area where the Tourist Police could be less omnipotent is in their fixing of hotel prices. They classify and set the rates for every establishment in the country that has at least five rooms to rent, and determine the level of the price increases each year. In areas that are not full to capacity, many small pensions will offer their rooms (illegally) at below the official price.

There are IYHF **Youth Hostels** in Greece where you'd least expect to find them—and sometimes no hostel where you were depending on one. You can get a list of them from the NTOG offices in Athens. Rates 50-60dr per person. You don't need an IYHF card at most hostels—a passport or student ID will suffice.

Campsites vary from spartan to huge overbuilt quasi-amusement parks. The **NTOG Campgrounds** usually fall into the second category and charge 50-60dr per person, plus 50dr per tent. The humbler facilities maintained by the **Hellenic Touring Club** charge about half the price.

Public telephones can be found at almost every sidewalk kiosk. Local calls cost 2dr. Dial 162 for information abroad from an English-speaking operator.

Those wishing to spend a couple of months or longer in Greece might consider working while there. During the summer many Western youths, especially women, find casual employment in hotels, bars, and restaurants; or as governess/babysitters. Pay is usually enough to get by, rarely more. Check the bulletin board outside of **Host Travel** on Filellinon Street in Athens, or read the classifieds in the English-language *Athens Daily News*. Another option which will help you leave the tourists behind is working as a farm laborer—the Peloponnese and Crete have the most work, especially in the off-season.

Learning a little Greek before coming is of course very helpful, although you'll never be very far from someone who speaks some English. It is highly advisable, however, to at least master the Greek alphabet, since street signs are rarely transliterated.

The most comprehensive guide to Greece in English is *Benn's Blue Guide*, although the price is steep at 520dr. The locally published *Greece: History, Museums, Monuments* (150dr) provides good orientation when you are sightseeing.

FOOD

If there is an "art" in Greek cuisine, it's ingenuity, for the people have managed to do well by the sparse yield of a dry and stony land. A meal without olive oil is unthinkable, and even the pine-forest resin has been put to use in the everyday wines: *retsina* (a light white) and *kokkinelli* (the rosé version).

Dinner in Greece is a leisurely late-evening affair; some restaurants don't even open until 9pm. Cafés and *tavernas* handle the morning and afternoon business. Breakfasts are usually light—coffee or tea and a pastry. The coffee is a vestige of Turkish rule—syrupy sweet and so strong it comes in miniature doses; standard coffee goes by the catch-all name of *Nescafe*. Greek pastries, with their heavy honey base, are delicious. *Baklava* is a honeyed strudel, filled with chopped nuts; *galaktobouriko* is similar, except for the creamy filling; and *kataifi* consists of nuts and cinnamon rolled up in strands of dough.

The siesta hours and early evening are given over to relaxation and light eating. Most people quiet their stomachs with a side dish of *choriatiki*, the "peasant's salad" made up of *feta* cheese, cucumbers, tomatoes, onions, and olives.

In restaurants, don't bother trying to decipher the menu—head for the kitchen and browse—it's accepted (even encouraged) in most places. Start your meal with a salad or *lathera*—any vegetable, usually beans, eggplant, or zucchini steeped in oil, tomato, and oregano. The most common meat entrées are lamb *(arni)*, chicken *(kotopoulo)*, and veal *(moschari)*; For the more adventurous palate, there is *stifado*, a rabbit stew simmered in onions until sweet—rare, but worth looking out for. On the islands, fish and shellfish are fresh, though generally expensive. Squid *(kalamarakia)* and octopus *(htapodi)* are plentiful and fairly cheap.

There are some traditional dishes you'll find everywhere. *Moussaka* is made of baked layers of ground meat and eggplant, smothered in a rich tomato sauce; *pastitsio* substitutes macaroni for eggplant. The small packages of minced meat and rice wrapped in vine leaves are called *dolmades* when served hot with egg and lemon sauce, *dolmadakia* when they come plain as a side dish. Most Greeks finish the meal with some fruit—usually watermelon *(karpouzi)* or yellow melon *(peponi)*. The evening is then put to bed with a few shots of *ouzo*, a licorice-flavored liqueur that can take your head off if you think it's weak stuff.

If you don't feel like eating in a restaurant, fill up on *pita souvlaki* (grilled meat wrapped in coarse bread, about 10-12dr) or cheese or spinach pies (8-12dr each) at the numerous stands in every town.

FESTIVALS

Festivals erupt for all seasons and in the remotest of villages. Two famous religious events are the Easter celebration in the Peloponnesian town of

Tripolis, and the biannual pilgrimages to the island of **Tinos.** Keep especially alert on the islands, with their surfeit of chapels. Traditionally, a villager who credits a particular saint with helping him out of a rough spot will feed and entertain all callers on the saint's birthday, after a liturgy at the church dedicated in the holy figure's name.

The main artistic events in Greece take place at the amphitheater of **Herod Atticus,** below the Acropolis, from May through September, and at the outdoor theater of **Epidaurus** during July and August. The program for the **Athens Festival** features international concerts, opera, and ballet, as well as classical drama. But the ancient plays are more impressive on the circular Epidaurian stage, surrounded by a wooded grove rather than a jagged cityscape. Don't worry about the language barrier, it won't detract from the ominous choreography of the Furies' chorus which, in the time of the ancient tragedian Aeschylus, made "boys die of fright and women have miscarriages." Tickets and programs for both series are available at the **Athens Festival Box Office,** 4 Stadiou St. (inside the arcade, tel. 3221-459); while you're there, ask about the **Dora Stratou Folk Dances.** But stop by several days before a performance and expect a line shortly after the 8:30am opening time.

There are a number of annual local **wine festivals** throughout Greece. The largest of these are at **Daphni, Rhodes,** and **Alexandroupolis;** all run from July to the end of August or early September. Hours are 7pm-1am. The 65dr admission gives you a jar and glass and unlimited "tasting." On Crete, Rethymnon's popular festival runs the last two weeks of July.

MUSEUMS, MONUMENTS, AND SIGHTS

Everyone who visits Greece contemplates the remnants of its past; the most avid sightseers spend a good portion of their budget doing so. Most important sights and museums charge an admission fee of 25-50dr, but all are free on Sundays. Student cards will get you in for 5dr at the 25dr places, 25dr at the 50dr ones. To avoid the crowds, start out early in the morning.

Athens (Athinai)

Take away the Parthenon and what have you got? A noisy, crowded, colorless, modern city full of tourists. Even **Monastiraki** and **Plaka,** two older, more appealing sections of Athens, have of late been smothered by gift shops and discotheques.

At best, the visitor salvages a few moments of respite here and there—a horse-drawn cart lost in the sea of traffic, a glimpse of sophistication in the posh **Kolonaki** district, a crumbling old house or a tiny Byzantine church hiding in the shadows of modern gray apartment blocks, an animated argument between old men in the Monastiraki flea market—and, of course, the **Acropolis,** perched majestically above, and looking down disapprovingly at it all.

Orientation

Get the free map of Athens from any Tourist Office or the Tourist Police. It shows all the monuments and the bus, trolley, and subway routes. The touristic center of Athens is quite small, so after a quick look at a map you should be able to find your way around with little trouble. **Syntagma,** or Constitution Square, is the focal point, where you'll find the Parliament, the

Athens

1 Funicular
2 University
3 Moussion Ethnikon Archeologikon
4 Post Offices
5 American Express
6 Parliament
7 Akropolis
8 Olympion

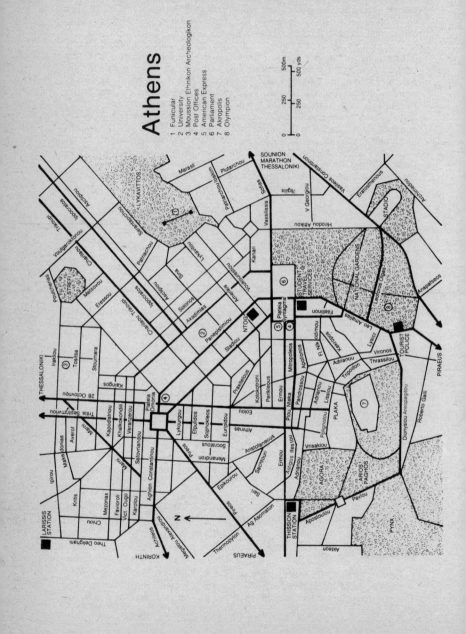

top hotels, the most expensive cafés, the airline offices, the American Express, the most important banks, and the most traffic. For relief, stroll through the lush **National Gardens** behind Parliament—there are drinking faucets near the duck pond. The adjacent **Plaka,** which was the original city of Athens and is today the nightlife center for tourists, is a maze of narrow streets lined with taverns and discotheques. The Plaka and Syntagma collide around Mitropoleos St., which burrows into the heart of the flea market of **Monastiraki.** This is the place for *souvlakia* wrapped in flat bread and shopping for every quaint item imaginable. Merchants usually tag on prices for their own peace of mind and haggling will get you nowhere. About fifteen minutes from Syntagma in another direction is **Omonia Square,** where the scene suddenly shifts from elegance to brazen metropolitan hustle. Its notable asset: prices for all sorts of practical goods plummet. **Piraeus,** the port of Athens, is the last stop on the subway. If you do not find maps satisfying enough, take the funicular to the top of **Lycavitos Hill,** the highest point in Athens; the view is magnificent as well as instructive. (25dr round trip).

All students should browse around the maze of student travel agencies on Filellinon Street. The best of these is **Lotus** (#7, tel 322-1680), offering a good, free *Student Guide to Athens,* a room-finding service, a *Poste Restante* service, and a "left luggage" office; it also sponsors low-priced island tours and arranges for student travel discounts. **ISYTS Travel** Office at 11 Nikes St. is another good place with a large, free left luggage area. Both offices have information about all forms of cheap transportation to the rest of Europe, including a $35 bus to London. Nearby **Host Travel** has a bulletin board for foreign travelers—good for finding travel partners, roommates, even employment, or for buying and selling anything from a used car to a sleeping bag.

Athenian business hours are staggered day by day; in general, stores are open in summer from 8am to 2:30pm on Monday, Wednesday, and Saturday; and from 8am to 1:30pm, then 5-7:30pm on Tuesday, Thursday and Friday. Winter hours differ slightly.

If Athens is not the most enchanting of cities, it is the best place to gather information about the Islands and the rest of the country. Not only are its travel agents and tourist offices the best equipped, but, with a little initiative, the advice you get from other travelers will prove invaluable in planning your itinerary. Athens' student hotels and youth hostels are also good places to pick up travel partners for the next leg of your journey, especially if it is to the Greek Islands.

The Tourist Office discourages it, but many travelers who are short of cash earn 450dr, a snack and a free hot shower by donating blood. Contact the **Blood Research Center** at 32 Ioulianou St. (tel. 8221-575).

When hitching out of town toward **Thessaloniki** and the northeastern parts of Greece, take bus #6 from Omonia Square to Acharnon Street; for **Patras** and the **Peloponnese,** take a bus out to Achilleos Street.

Addresses and Telephone Numbers

National Tourist Organization of Greece (NTOG): Head Office, 2 Amerikis St. (tel. 322-3111). Information desk in Syntagma Square at 2 Karagiorgi Servias St. (tel. 322-2545).

American Express: Syntagma Square, corner Hermes Street (tel. 324-4975).

Central Post Office: 100 Eolou St., near Omonia Square. Also in Syntagma Square. Both open 7:30am-8pm for business, stamps available until 10pm, closed Sun. Parcel Post at 4 Stadiou St.

Emergency Police: (tel. 100).

Tourist Police: (tel. 171) Headquarters at 7 Singrou St., open 24 hours daily. Office at Train Station open 6am-midnight. There is also a Tourist Police Station at the airport with the same hours.

First Aid Center: 21 Tritis Septemvriou (tel. 150) and 119 Alexandrias Ave. (tel. 646-7811).

U.S. Embassy: 91 Vasilissis Sofias (tel. 712-951).

Canadian Embassy: 4 Ioannou Genadiou St. (tel. 739-511).

All-Night Drugstore: (tels. 107 and 102).

Self-Service Laundry: 46 Didotou St. (tel. 36 10 661). Open Mon.-Sat. 8am-9pm. Price is same whether you leave your load or watch it: 50dr for 5 kilos, soap extra; 10dr for dryer; free use of iron.

Accommodations

Athens becomes unbelievably crowded by the end of June, and it stays that way well into September. Many hotels are booked solid through the high season, while most student hotels fill up each day by early afternoon. If a clerk at a cheap hotel tells you that he's full, ask if you can sleep on the roof—many places will let you, if you have a sleeping bag, for 60-75dr. If you're arriving on a late train, you may want to look for a room near the station. Try the **Tourist,** Deligianni and Paleologou Sts.; **Astra,** 46 Deligianni St.; or **Rea,** 50 Deligianni St. All charge about 120dr per person.

If you arrive late at night, check with the **Tourist Police** before heading blindly into Athens. The ones at the Airport are very helpful. If worse comes to worst, wander through the Plaka with your backpack—the room hawkers will find you. For complaints or problems, contact the **Hellenic Chamber of Hotels,** 6 Aristidou St., or 2 Karagiorgi St. in Syntagma Square.

The nearest **campsite** is on the road to Daphni at 190 Athinon Ave., Peristeri (tel. 571-5326); it charges 20dr per tent and 20dr per person. A full listing of all official campsites and Youth Hostels may be picked up at the NTOG Office in Athens.

Hostels and Student-Style Hotels

Youth Hostel #1 IYHF, 57 Kipselis St. (tel. 822-5860), is a large, crowded hostel run by a veteran traveler who speaks good English. Trolley #2 stops right in front of it. The rooms have 6-10 beds, 60dr apiece, with free hot showers. Same price to sleep on the roof. Kitchen facilities are available, and a laundry nearby. 1am curfew and closed 10am-1pm daily. Open year round.

Youth Hostel #4, 3 Hamilton St. (tel. 8220-328), near the Archaeological Museum. This hostel lost its accreditation. It is cramped and the bathrooms are slightly dirty, but the atmosphere is good—the snack bar is packed every night. 1am curfew, but open all day. 60dr, no hot water. Take the #12 trolley.

XEN (YWCA), 11 Amerikis St. (tel. 362-4291). You pay for the Syntagma location here. Singles are 160dr, doubles 155dr each, triples 148dr each, and

127dr per person in a 4- or 5-bed room, breakfast included. An inexpensive cafeteria below is open to both sexes.

XAN (YMCA), 28 Omirou St. (tel. 3626-970). Near the XEN. Popular with Greek students, this place has large dorm rooms for 80-90dr a bed. There are lockers for your valuables and luggage. Both Y's are clean and pleasant.

The most popular places in Athens are the slew of dormitory-style hotels in and around the Plaka. Though they require no student or hostel cards, the clientele is almost exclusively under 30. Their appeal varies considerably—the ones listed below are in order of descending quality:

The Funny Trumpet's Guest House, 30 Mitropoleos St. (tel. 3243048). Though in a noisy location, this is easily the best of the lot, with a helpful staff and pleasant atmosphere. Recently renovated, it has doubles for 200dr, dorm beds 60-80dr. Free hot showers and a café, with breakfasts for 25dr. Open all year.

Ilon House, 48 Nikis St. (tel. 3232664). Conveniently located, it has clean, pleasant rooms. 250dr for a double, 100dr in 4- to 7-bed rooms, and 60dr on either of the two roofs. One has an outstanding view of the Acropolis. Hot showers 20dr extra.

Plaka Inn, 4 Lisikratous St. (tel. 3223351). A bit crowded, but very popular with a good atmosphere. Dorm beds (bunks) are 70dr a head; kitchen facilities and showers are free.

Fotis House, 6 Agelou Geronda St. and Iperidou St. (tel. 3247165). Crowded but acceptable, and right in the middle of the Plaka bustle. Tiny doubles are no deal at 210dr. Better to stay in the 4- or 5-bed rooms (100dr) or dorm (90dr). The roof is 60dr, but crowded. Free hot showers.

International Students House, 46 Nikis St. (tel. 32 29 567). Sterile and cheerless. 12:30am curfew. 90dr per person in the dorm, 200dr for a double. Free hot showers.

HOTELS AND PENSIONS

For those who prefer hotels to the multi-bed rooms of the above establishments, the Plaka and its vicinity still offer the cheapest accommodations. There are also lots of cheap hotels in the Omonia Square area, but the streets are very noisy.

In the Plaka

Clare's House, 16A Frynichou St. (tel. 322-9284). A beautiful old house converted into a hotel, this is one of the finest budget pensions in Athens. Huge rooms and good facilities worth the extra cost: 380dr doubles, 500dr for triples, including large breakfast and hot showers—but worth every cent. The owner and staff are extremely helpful.

Dios Kouros Guest House, 6 Pittakou St. (tel. 32 48 165). A clean, relaxed place across from Hadrian's Arch. Doubles cost 300dr; in a 3- or 4-bed room, it's 120dr per person; and 70dr for a mattress on the roof—all with free hot showers.

Diogenes House, 12 Xerefondos St. (tel. 3224560). the doubles (300dr) are good, but the dorm rooms (120dr) are crowded. 75dr for a mattress on the roof. All prices include hot showers. In the middle of the Plaka. Friendly manager speaks good English.

Outside the Plaka

Carolina Hotel, 55 Kolokotroni (tel. 3220 837). Expensive, but worth it. Run by two brothers from South Carolina, it oozes Southern Hospitality, with services including washing machine and left luggage area for guests. Doubles 385dr; triples 430dr, quads 550dr. In a pinch, you can sleep in their dorm for 150dr, shower included.

Hotel Rodos, 33 Geraniou (tel. 5246532). Off Omonia Square, but in a quiet locale. Bright, cheerful rooms, most with balconies. Singles 185dr, doubles 244dr, triples 350dr. Hot showers are 20dr, cold 10dr.

Hotel Milton, 4 Kotsika St. (tel. 8216806). On a quiet side street near Areos Park area and the Archaeological Museum. Take trolley #12. Fantastic for the price, with clean, cozy doubles for 200dr; triples 260dr, showers extra.

Hostel Tsakalof, 13 Tsakalof St. (tel. 3608458). A small, modest hotel in the fancy Kolonaki district. 130dr per person in a double, showers free.

Food

Athens isn't a good restaurant city—the few good places are hard to find, the mediocre are too easily available. The Plaka is touristy; you'd do better to head for the suburbs or ask Athenians for recommendations. If you do stay in the Plaka, try the outdoor places in the **Metamorphosis** area.

In picking your restaurant, don't go by the menu alone. Head for the kitchen to size it up. Watch out for places advertising *"bouzouki* entertainment''—they'll hit you with a whopping ''music charge.''

Sintrivani, 5 Filellinon St. A large garden restaurant specializing in traditional Greek food—*moshari stifado* (veal in onions in a wine sauce), *moussaka,* and various stews. Most dishes in the 40-60dr range.

Kostayiannis, 37 Zaimi St., near Areos Park. Excellent Greek specialties. Visit the fantastic kitchen before you order. Try the stuffed squid. Simple surroundings, reasonable prices. Entrees 40-80dr. Opens at 8pm. Highly recommended.

Fatsio, 5 Efroniou, in the residential district behind the Hilton. Serves excellent Istanbul Greek dishes. Try the eggplant salad, the potato croquettes, and the brain salad for hors d'oeuvres, and the *yaourtlou kebab* (spiced meat with yogurt) for the main course. *Ekmek kadaif* (sponge cake soaked in honey) is delicious. Moderately expensive. Opens late for dinner.

Restaurant Dioscouri, at the top of Dioscouri St. One of the few good Plaka places, with a nice view above the bustle. Dishes 35-75dr. For a splurge, try the swordfish.

Bretania, in Omonia Square, specializes in dairy products and pastries. A huge slab of yogurt smothered in honey *(meli)* is 25dr. A great place for breakfast or lunch.

Sights

The **Acropolis** is stunning. At its summit, the **Parthenon** is once again free of repairmen's scaffolding. These, unfortunately, have shifted to the **Erechtheum,** whose famous Karyatids may be replaced by copies due to decay. Also impressive are the **Propylaea,** and the **Temple of Athena Niki.** Most days the Acropolis is open from 7:30am to sunset, but on nights with a full moon, it re-opens 9-11:45pm. If you are in Athens on such occasions, by all means go at night. Otherwise plan your visit near opening time, before the heat and crowds (admission 50dr, 25dr with student ID, free Sun.) For the best view of the Acropolis, hike up the **Pnyx Hill,** the old meeting place of Athenian elders; but avoid the evenings, time of the hokey sound-and-light show.

The **National Archaeological Museum,** 1 Patission St., is also a must, with an extensive collection of marble and bronze sculpture, pottery, and jewelry. At the same address you'll find the **Numismatic Collection.** Both are open daily (except Mondays) from 7:30am-7:30pm and Sunday 10am-6pm; admission 50dr; 25dr with student ID.

Also visit the ancient **Agora** and the **Temple of Hephaestos,** and the adjacent museum, which is housed in the restored **Stoa of Attalos.** The temple is reputed to be the best preserved in Greece, and in the Agora you can see the ruins of the administrative center of ancient Athens. Open daily until sunset, 25dr, 5dr with Student ID.

Evenings

The **Plaka** is the top nightspot in Athens, but in the last few years it has become quite honky-tonk, what with the neon lights, the electric *bouzoukis,* and the mushrooming discotheques with their loud bouncers. If you do go into a *taverna* or a discotheque, price everything beforehand to avoid any unpleasant surprises. It may be more fun to sit at a table on the steps and watch the crowds stream by.

Understandably, most Athenians flee the heat and carnival atmosphere of summer evenings in their city. Some head for the **Piraeus** for an evening of promenading, followed by a late dinner in one of the *tavernas* or waterfront restaurants. Others head in the opposite direction, to the eastern suburb of **Kifissia,** the last stop on the subway. Here the streets are tree-lined and shaded, giving a slight respite from the heat; pick your restaurants carefully here—most are expensive.

Before the junta in Greece, the **National Garden** was one of the most popular places to gather in the evening. The dictatorship clamped down on park activities, but since its collapse the park has experienced something of a revival. Every evening the cafés in the **Zappeion** area of the Park present singers, comedians, and acrobats on an outdoor stage. Free if you stand, as most people do, or get a table at one of the expensive cafés.

Athens has a number of English-speaking cinemas. For addresses and timetables, check the *Athens Daily News.*

Near Athens

The **Temple of Poseidon** awaits you on Cape Sounion, some 65 kilometers from Athens. The staggering clifftop view of the Aegean is only appropriate for the setting of the cult of the Sea God. A bus on Mavromateon St. leaves on the hour and costs 65dr one way. Try to make it in the morning, before the tour buses start arriving. You can spend the afternoon at one of the uncrowded beaches nearby. Hotel rooms in the area tend to be expensive, because there are several popular resorts here, but there is a campground (open all year), and plenty of room on the beach to sleep. Also along the Western Coast are a series of beaches frequented by Athenians: **Glyfada** is the most popular. Admission is charged for all of these, varying with each beach. Take the "Glyfada" bus from the Zappeion stand.

Also unforgettable is **Delphi,** 180 kilometers from Athens on the slopes of a steep mountain overlooking the Gulf of Corinth. This is the site of the famed **Delphic Oracle,** where the ancient Greeks believed the earth touched the divine. There are several buses daily from 260 Liossion St. (205dr one way), but they often fill up early. You can stay overnight in the 100-bed IYHF **Youth Hostel** (tel. 82-268) for 60dr (open all year), or camp nearby (tel. 82-363).

Only a few minutes outside Athens, the eleventh-century monastery at **Daphni** displays the awesome Christ Pantocrator, one of the greatest Byzantine mosaics. Every summer evening a wine festival is held across the street. A 65dr admission fee entitles you to a night of unlimited "tasting."

The Peloponnese

A huge peninsula with a forested mountainous interior, the Peloponnese is separated from the main body of Greece by the **Isthmus of Corinth.** Its main attraction is the extensive remnants of 3500 years of Greek, Turkish, Roman, Frank, and Venetian history that litter its soil. Away from these sights and some beaches on its eastern coast, the Peloponnese is untouristed and traditional.

Public transport in the Peloponnese requires time and patience. Trains and buses often run late, and even in the best of times, their connecting schedules often miss each other by a matter of maddening minutes. Buses serving the Peloponnese leave Athens from the station at 100 Kifissou St. (take #62 from Omonia Square). Once you're within the area itself, trains are more comfortable and service more areas. Hitching here is only mediocre, due to the lack of cars on the roads.

New Corinth was completely destroyed by earthquake in 1928; fortunately, the ancient city was spared. The columns (sixth century B.C.) at the **Temple of Apollo** still stand, along with the baths and a theater. The hour-long hike up to the **Akrokorinth,** the large rock that juts over the city, with its ruins of Venetian and Turkish fortresses, is rewarded with a splendid view of both gulfs.

The cheapest hotels are near the water in **New Corinth:** the **Hotel Akti,** 1 Basileus Konstantinou St. (tel. 23337) is near the beach but slightly noisy; the **Emporikon** (or Hotel Commercial) at 3 Dervenakion St. (tel. 22120) is smaller and quieter. Both have doubles for 250dr, triples for 300dr, showers extra.

Mycenae, 131 kilometers from Athens, may be the most interesting archaeological site in Greece. Many of the treasures of this 3500-year-old city are in the Archaeological Museum in Athens, but the **Gate of Lions,** the remarkable **beehive tombs,** and the **tombs of Agamemnon** and **Clytemnestra** make the journey worthwhile. There is a campsite near the ruins (tel. 66247), open from mid-May to mid-October, and a Youth Hostel open all year (tel. 66224).

Further south is the perfectly-preserved fourth-century B.C. amphitheater of **Epidavros,** site of Greece's most popular festival: the presentation of a series of classical dramas (in the original Greek. There are student discounts to all performances as well as a special daytrip deal from Athens. The Athens Festival Box Office offers ticket holders a bus trip to **Nauplion** early in the morning and a return to Athens (225dr round trip) after the performance. You might find Nauplion worth more than a morning, though; in addition to a number of good, nearby beaches, the old section of town is full of cobbled strets and old buildings, all of which are overseen by the huge **Palamidi** fortress.. Another fortress, the isle of **Bourdzi,** guards the other side of the city. Lodgings are good here—a pleasant IYHF **Youth Hostel** (70dr a night) is open all year. There are also three camping areas nearby. Or try the **Hotel Acropole** at 7 Vasilissis Olgas (tel. 28583), where singles go for 175dr, doubles for 225dr, showers extra.

The Western Peloponnese is far less touristed. If you don't have a car, the best way to explore this region is to travel along the coast and venture selectively into the interior. The beaches that line the Patras-Pirgos-Pilos route are easily among the best in Greece.

Cut in at Pirgos to get to **Olympia,** 20 kilometers to the east. The site of the ancient Olympics, it is now a cluster of varied ruins. The fine **museum** houses the pediments of the temples of Zeus and the *Hermes of Praxiteles*. If this isn't enough, Olympia's setting, tucked among richly-wooded mountains, is one of extraordinary beauty. There is a **Youth Hostel** (IYHF) here (tel. 21580) and **camping** (tel. 22745), both open year round.

The coastline south of Pirgos is particularly inviting. In many spots, the pine forests run into the water's edge, providing excellent camping and respite from the sun. Take the train south towards Kiparissia and get off in **Kakovatos,** or at any of the unmarked spots that catch your eye.

The main city in the southern Peloponnese is **Kalamata,** a port with a majestic setting. Travel connections from here are good. Perhaps the most interesting region of the Peloponnese can be seen by heading south into **Mani,** the middle of the three lower peninsulas. This area is rough, stark terrain, strewn with caves, castles, towers, and Byzantine churches. The people here are very traditional—vendettas and elaborate funeral rites are not uncommon. The port of Gythion connects to Crete by a weekly boat.

The unimpressive ruins of ancient Sparta are compensated for by nearby **Mystra,** an intact Byzantine city often termed "the Pompeii of Byzantium." The atmosphere within its thick ramparts, winding streets, frescoed churches, and fourteenth-century palaces is enhanced by Mystra's ban on cars. Athens is five hours away by bus.

Northern Greece

The earthquake that rocked **Thessaloniki,** Greece's second largest city, in June 1978, resulted in the relocation of many of its citizens and the condemning of many of its buildings. Nevertheless, the port city is well on its way to recovery, and should once again provide an enjoyable stopover on the way to or from Turkey or Yugoslavia.

To its southeast is **Halkidiki,** a peninsula with three fingers of land reaching into the Aegean. **Kassandra,** the western finger, is lined with sand beaches and fishing villages; the beach resorts of **Gerakini** and **Paliovrion** are the most popular areas. **Sithonia,** the middle finger of land, is the place to go for forests and rugged inlets. Roads are poor as is public transportation, except for the buses that serve the western beaches. World-famous **Mt. Athos,** the easternmost peninsula, is a self-governing monastic community. Athos' twenty isolated monasteries are treasure troves of Byzantine relics and artwork. But the most unique feature of Athos is the extremely austere lifestyle of its monks. Women have been banned from the peninsula for 900 years. Not even female animals are allowed to set foot on the "Holy Mountain." To visit Mt. Athos or to hike in the rugged mountains of the area, you must apply in advance to the Ministry of Foreign Affairs in Athens. They reject most tourist applications, so cite some academic reason for your visit.

The Islands

In choosing Greek islands to visit, decide first what you're after: sights, solitude, or action. Every island has its share of each, but proportions vary sharply. Do some research; don't simply rely on hearesay. Even the most notorious islands offer plenty of room to be experienced according to one's personal inclinations. Not every beach in Mykonos is wall-to-wall nudist-jet-setter, not every village on Ios is inundated with the remnants of the Woodstock Nation; not every house on Hydra is inhabited by a yacht-owning count and his artist friends.

Almost every island, however, has to a greater or lesser degree its share of tourists, and your visit will be affected by the kind and numbers of people that are there with you. Before leaving the mainland, find out as much as you can about the islands that interest you. Ask every well-tanned person you meet in Athens to confide to you a favorite island or secret beach.

First, the islands are not all the same. Travel brochures be damned, they are not all dramatically barren affairs, replete with isolated, white-sand beaches and quiet, whitewashed villages whose *tavernas* are full of pensive fishermen. It may be better to avoid the handful of islands which once did live up to this fantasy, because most of them have been surrendered to the tourists. Peasant homes have been turned into discotheques and boutiques, and the once pensive fishermen are now rude, overworked waiters. If your dream is to spend weeks on a deserted beach, then try one of the less known islands described below.

A good strategy almost everywhere to escape the crowds is to take a bus from the port to the other side of the island. Before you do so, however, find out where the beaches are, because much of the shoreline on most islands is rocky and windy.

Tourism has stimulated the economy of many islands, but with side effects. The islands are no longer much cheaper than Athens. Also, the government has started clamping down on unauthorized camping and nude bathing. The degree of enforcement varies with each island, so check out the situation when you arrive.

Orienting yourself on most islands is easy. Most have a **Tourist Police Office** *(astinomia)* at the port. For accommodations, rooms to let are usually cheaper and more enjoyable than hotels. Your ferry will most likely be met by women in black dresses who'll offer you rooms in their homes. Bargain with them before you accept. You should never have to pay more than 100dr a night.

There are regular ferries from Piraeus to most islands in the Aegean: these are slow but cheap. Unfortunately, inter-island connections are sporadic and next to impossible to find out about except at the islands themselves; so those who wish to island-hop must either have a lot of time on their hands or double back to Piraeus and take another boat from there. Ferry transportation is available in two cheap classes, second and third (or deck)—a comfort difference to be reckoned with, especially in cooler weather.

The National Tourist Organization publishes a weekly schedule of departures to the islands. The numerous student travel bureaus along Filellinon St., which sell tickets to all island boats, are the most likely to have current information.

The Argo-Saronic Islands

This group of islands, with the exception of Hydra, is largely ignored by the young crowd, but the Greeks have long recognized their charm and have flocked here for vacations. Good beaches, forested interiors, and accessibility make the Argo-Saronic group well worth a visit, especially for those with only a few days for the islands.

AEGINA is a beautiful island only an hour's boat ride from Piraeus. The main town—also named **Aegina**—has a large number of rooms to let and cheap *tavernas*. There is a decent beach right in town, or a better one in **Marathon,** a twenty-minute bus ride to the south. The bay of **Aghia Marina,** on the other side of the island, has Aegina's best beaches and liveliest crowds. Two kilometers up from the bay is the well-preserved **Temple of Aphaia,** a miniature Parthenon with a great view.

POROS is actually two small islands connected by a walkway. The lower island contains the port and island's accommodations, but little else. The upper island—reached by bus or foot—has a pine-laden interior and a number of rocky beaches. One attraction of Poros is its location—separated by only 200 meters from the Peloponnese. A 5dr boat ride will bring you to Galatas, where you can get buses to the interior of the Peloponnese; 8dr will get you to the good beaches of **Aliki** or **Plaka.** Many take this route to the Epidavros festival, rather than the hot, dry, overland route.

HYDRA does have one of the most spectacular ports in Greece: pastel houses cover the steep hills on all three sides of the land-locked harbor. A recently established artists' colony created the necessary atmosphere to attract hordes of tourists, and although the real artists are mostly gone, the tourists keep arriving. Still, once you get resigned to the fact that the only Greeks present are waiters, you will find the island exciting. The **Sophia** and the **Hermes** are the two cheapest hotels. As rooms are hard to get, you should just climb up the hills in search of a private room. The higher you go, the better your chances. The restaurants along the waterfront are reasonable, the cafés expensive. Most people swim off the rocks to the left of the harbor.

The Cyclades

MYKONOS has more tourists per square foot than any other Greek island. Every summer both jet-setters and simpler beach people crowd what was once the prototypical dreamlike Greek island. It is still beautiful, and its beaches are among the best, but unless you plan on making the fast social scene here, or you are coming in the off-season, opt for a quieter, less popular island.

The Youth Hostel near the dock charges 60dr per person. Single bedrooms are scarce in the main town, and doubles cost 250dr and up. If you wish to enjoy the wicked nightlife of the island you should take one of these rooms. Otherwise, you will probably find the beaches more exciting. If you want to stay on the predominantly nudist **Paradise Beach** you must sleep in the tent city set up there (50dr per person). You can take an inexpensive boat to Paradise Beach from where the ferry docks to **Super-Paradise,** a mainly gay nude beach; or to the even more distant beach at **Illia.**

If you are in Mykonos, you should spend one morning on **DELOS,** the nearby island that was once the center of the religious life of the Aegean—the ruins are extensive and spectacular. Three boats leave each morning between 8-9am and return about 12:30pm; the fare is 45dr round trip, and there is an admission charge to the island.

The beauty of **IOS** has made it the second most popular island in the Cyclades, especially among young backpackers of all nationalities. This has created some problems recently with the island's inhabitants encouraging the police to crack down on nudism and camping on the beach. Both are still practiced, but only on more remote parts of the shoreline. **Mylopotas,** the magnificient beach near the town of Ios, is fairly crowded. The predominance of young budget travelers on Ios has made it one of the cheaper islands to stay on.

NAXOS is the largest and the most prosperous of the Cycladic islands, with a mountainous interior full of vineyards, lush valleys, citrus orchards and terraced olive groves. Fortunately too, the Naxiotis have not thrown themselves into the tourist trade as enthusiastically as the inhabitants of poorer islands. The port city, dominated by the remains of the **Temple of Apollo** and the **Venetian Castro,** is still adjusting to its recent "discovery" by tourists, so rooms are often hard to find. The cheapest are near the Castro, in the rooms to let; or try the **Hotel Dionysus** or the non-accredited **Greek Youth Hostel** (80dr). To the south, the beach of **Aghios Georgios** has camping and more expensive rooms to let. A good restaurant in town is the **Apolausis**—their stuffed eggplant is excellent.

For beaches, try the long stretch of sand on the southwest coast of the island. **Aghia Anna,** half an hour by bus from Naxos City, is the most popular (you can camp here), but the best is **Mikri Vigla,** further south.

But the special appeal of Naxos is the interior—mountains surrounding rich valleys full of Byzantine churches, a variety of crops, and dozens of villages. The hiking and camping is great, especially the area of the **Tragea.** From Filoti, a thoroughly untouristy mountain village, you can scale **Mt. Zeus,** the highest peak in the Cyclades, in about six hours, up and down.

Across the channel from Naxos is **PAROS,** a beautiful but crowded island. The main port of **Paroikia** is pretty, but touristed to death. The Tourist Police here are good at finding rooms in high-season. If everything is full, head around the cove to the north, where swarms of backpackers have formed a tent city.

A better way to see Paros is to head to the other coasts. **Naoussa** is a pleasant fishing village on the north shore; from here, head east to **Santa Maria,** an isolated beach, or take a quick boat ride to **Agios Ioannis** for good beaches in remote coves. On the east shore, running between the resort towns of **Logaras** and **Drios,** are a series of crowded (but fantastic), golden beaches. Your best getaway is to **ANTIPAROS,** a less touristed island with good beaches and caves.

Formed by the massive volcanic eruption that destroyed the Minoan culture on Crete and gave rise to the Atlantis legend, **SANTORINI** (or Thira) is the most spectacular island in the Aegean. The island is actually the outer rim of the sunken volcano, its entire western coast a succession of 1000-foot-high cliffs. Perched atop these, with a fantastic view, is **Thira,** the main town, beautiful but usually sickeningly mobbed with tourists. Both **Pelagos** and **Atlantis Travel** offer free room-finding services, or you can set out on your own to the several rooms-to-let that rim the cliff south of town. The IYHF **Youth Hostel** (tel. 21267) here is open year round. If everything else is full, head south to the village of **Messaria,** 3 kilometers from Thira.

With the exception of **Oia,** a traditional village on the north tip of the

island, most of Santorini's attractions are to the south of Thira. Three popular beaches are **Monolithos** (grainy white sand), **Kamari** (small black
stone), and **Perissa** (black sand). Of these, Perissa is easily the best.
Separating Kamari and Perissa is a huge jutting rock, atop which are the
remains of **Archaia** (ancient) **Thira,** with impressive Greek and Roman
ruins and a great view. Even better are the late-Minoan ruins of **Akrotiri,**
buried by the volcano and only recently brought to light. Or for a closer look
at the cause of it all, take a boat trip to the volcanic islet of **Mikra Kameni,**
still smoldering in the bay below you.

SYROS, the capital of the Cyclades, is a stopping point for many boats.
Its port city, **Ermoupolis,** is large but picturesque, dominated by two large
hills dotted with churches. The best beach is at **Galissas**—lots of camping
here, but no hotels and few rooms to let. Further south, **Finix** and **Posidonia**
are good beaches with accommodations; and **Vazi,** on the southern coast, is
a small sand beach. The cheapest rooms are found in Ermoupolis, in the
unofficial hostel up from the port, or in the rooms to let.

ANDROS is a large, quiet island reached by the ferry from Rafina. There
are still isolated beaches and fishing villages to be found here—**Nimboro**
and **Korthion** are among the best. The interior is fertile; two sights worth
visiting are the springs at **Menites** and the theater and stadium remains at
Palaiopolis.

The island of **TINOS,** served by the same line as Andros, is a tame and
pretty island whose wonder-working icon (safely concealed in the Main
Cathedral) attracts large crowds of pilgrims with diseases and inoperative
limbs, twice a year (late March and mid-August). The rest of the time Tinos
is ideal for a quiet escape. So are **SIFNOS, SIKINOS, SERIFOS,** and
MILOS, known collectively as "the dry islands," but possessing good
swimming beaches and that characteristic Cycladic beauty. Sifnos is the
most popular of these, especially in mid-August (festival time). **AMOR-
GOS,** with its high, orange cliffs, is dramatically isolated from the rest of the
world. It is long and thin, so you can see the sea on both sides from the main
town in the center of the island. Conditions are spartan, but the atmosphere is
invigorating.

The Sporades

This group of islands in the northern Aegean has long been a Greek secret
and is only now being discovered by foreign tourists. Reached from the ports
of Aghios Konstantinos, Volos, and Kimi, they are enough off the beaten
path to give you a quiet vacation on some of the best beaches in Greece.

SKIATHOS, the most popular of the islands, has two outstanding
beaches in **Koukounaries** and **Lalaria,** the latter reached only by motorboat. The interior of the island is lush and full of streams. **SKOPELOS** has a
variety of attractions—remains of a Cretan colony, a large number of
churches and monasteries, and excellent beaches. The best of these are
Agnontas, Aghios Konstantinos, and **Chryssi Milia.**

Lying northeast of Skopelos, **ALONISSOS** is still relatively isolated. Its
coast is lined with sand beaches interrupted now and again by sea caves.
Boat is the only effective transportation here. **SKYROS** is famous for its
architecture and crafts—folk crafts live on here.

Islands in the Northeast Aegean

Closer to Turkey than to Greece, these are an excellent alternative to the more crowded southern islands. All of these islands connect by steamer to Piraeus ($10-12 one way), and to one another by smaller launches.

SAMOS' beauty is diverse—the interior is heavily wooded, with a number of clear, fast streams; the coast—though more rock than sand—yields spectacular views and settings, along with some nice beaches. The port village of **Samos** is relaxing; pensions (**Laghos, Grigoriou,** and **Karpathiou** are all good) run about 200dr for a double, shower extra. But most travelers head 10 kilometers west to **Kokarion,** a beautiful, little beach town. To get oriented, go to the **Café Manos**—the friendly proprietor will (free of charge) find you a room. The **Phillipaion** is the most popular restaurant here. Finally, for a getaway, head for **Ormos Moradokampos,** an unspoiled fishing village on the other side of the island.

LESBOS is heavily wooded, but also holds a long string of good beaches. The coastline around **Methymna** is the best, but **Petra** and **Eressos** aren't far behind. In July, the fishing town of **Plomarion** holds a festival where free *bouillabaise* is given to all who come.

THASSOS is a popular island, due mostly to its abundance of good, sandy beaches. The bay of **Prinos** is famous for its beautiful setting. The lush interior of the island contains a wide variety of vegetation.

The Dodecanese

Situated directly off the Turkish coast, **RHODES** is a marvelous contrast to the whitewashed wonders of the Aegean. The town is dominated by the towers and ramparts built by the Knights of St. John, but the Turkish mosques and the innumerable luxury hotels are also very much in evidence. During the summer, Germans and Scandinavians flock to the island en masse, in search of sun and duty-free furs. Don't worry, though—they stay in their hotels and tourist shops—you can have the rest of the island to yourself.

The walled old city of Rhodes is strewn with monuments and relics from its various epochs. At dusk the tiny, winding cobbled alleys, the medieval inns and ramparts, and the mosques make this an enchanting spot.

From the dock, follow the waterfront to the right. After passing the **Old City,** climb up Papagou St. to the **Tourist Police** and **Tourist Office.** They have maps and information about accommodations, buses and boats.

There are regular boats from Rhodes to Crete, Cyprus, Israel, and the nearby Turkish town of Marmaris.

If you're in Rhodes during July or August don't miss the **Rodini Wine Festival,** just outside of town. It's touristy, but the 65dr entrance fee entitles you to all the local ambrosia you can hold.

There are no youth hostels or campsites on the island. Away from the crowded shoreline near the town of Rhodes, sleep on the beaches. In town the cheapest accommodations are in pensions in the old city.

Lindos, a beautiful, though slightly touristy whitewashed village easily reached from the city of Rhodes, is on a protected cove, where you can camp out. The remains of an acropolis at the top of the hill afford a spectacular view of the coast and the turquoise sea.

The southern half of the island is completely untouristy. The beaches tend to be pebbly, but deserted. Several picturesque towns lie inland. **Monolithos** and **Messanagros** are both in the mountains, with Byzantine ruins nearby. Camp out in the open, or ask in the local café—someone will put you up for about 60dr.

KOS is a very green island filled with plants and fruits native to Greece. It is manageable on bicycle. In the very traditional island of **KARPATHOS,**

try to visit the cliff village of **Olympos. PATMOS,** the island where John wrote the Book of Revelations, is a rocky place more attractive to pilgrims than beach-goers. **KALYMNOS** is a bare, mountainous island; most of the men work as sponge divers off the coast of northern Africa during the warm months. When they return at the end of the summer, the town goes wild for a couple of weeks.

Crete

Crete is not just another Greek island. The astounding landscape alone puts Crete into a separate category; its wild, rugged mountain range, the great expanses of olive and citrus trees, the treacherous mountain passes and gorges, the isolated villages along the Libyan Sea, all create a rather forbidding atmosphere. The islanders, who very rightly have the reputation of being proud, independent, and belligerent if provoked, complement the scenery. Travelers spend more time on Crete then on any other Greek island, some not budging for weeks from a cave on a deserted beach, others exploring the incredible array of old cities, ruins, and mountains that make this the most varied of the islands. Lots of tourists come here, but Crete is more than big enough to hold everyone. With a little effort you can find exactly the kind of place you're searching for.

All of Crete's major cities, save one, lie along the more liveable northern coast. The southern coast, steep and wind blown, holds Ierapetra and a multitude of small inlets and fishing villages. Crete is divided into four regions, each one with a north-coast capital. All are pleasant towns, worth visiting in their own rights; and since most bus connections involve returning to these larger cities, you may wish to use them as your bases, leaving the bulk of your luggage in hotels or bus stations, and setting out on one- or two-day trips.

Due to its proximity to the most famous Minoan palace at **Knossos, Heracleion** is very touristy. But apart from some handsome Venetian fortifications, and of course the **Archaeological Museum** (open 8am-6pm daily, Sun. 10am-4pm, Monday to 1pm), which houses most of the finds from Knossos, Crete's largest city has little to offer. But it is a good starting point for several excursions.

The first is, of course, Knossos, the incredible Minoan ruins that lie 6 kilometers to the south (open 8am-sunset every day). Further south, but within an easy day's journey are the twin Minoan sites of **Phaistos** and **Aghia Triada,** and the Roman site of **Gortys.** On the southern coast is **Matalla,** with its excellent sand beach and "hippie caves," made famous by *Life* magazine. Stepping out of the ancient past into a fantasy world, visit the Plain of **Lassithi,** with its hundreds of working windmills. The mountains that loom over the Plain are great for hiking. To the east of Heracleion is **Amnissos,** the ancient port of Knossos (now the area's best beach), and **Mallia,** (a well-preserved Minoan site).

Heracleion's cheap accommodations focus around the waterfront and the marketplace. The best of the waterfront places is **Hotel Rea** on Kalimeraki St. (tel. 223638). Doubles are 290dr, triples 360dr. The location is quiet, and the rooms are large and clean. Around the corner is **Mary's Renta Rooms,** 44 Handakos St. (tel. 281135). Open summers only, it offers spacious doubles (200dr) and triples (270dr). Up the street is the IYHF **Youth Hostel** at #24 (tel. 286281), a large, non-descript affair with crowded conditions and a 12pm curfew. But it's cheap (60dr) and seldom full. Up in the market area, on Evans St., you'll find the Hotels **Ionia** and **Kritikon** (tel.

220211), both cheap but noisy. Prices are 250dr for doubles, 330dr for triples, showers extra. The nearest campsite to Heracleion is in Mallia, 27 kilometers to the east and not worth the commute. Stay in town.

Budget tavernas and restaurants are concentrated on and around two streets: **Fotiou** St., connecting Evans St. and the market; and on nearby **Dedalus** St.

Rethymnon, 81 kilometers west of Heracleion, is a slice of Crete's past. A pleasant harbor town, its Turkish and Venetian history lives on in its old ornate houses, its winding back alleys, and the imposing Venetian fortress that guards the harbor. The **Youth Hostel** at 7 Paulou Vlastou (tel. 22848) is one of the best in Greece. Located just off Arcadiou St., it offers good kitchen facilities, friendly management, and no curfew (closed in January and February). The best of the cheap hotels are the **Achilleion** on the waterfront (tel. 22581), and **Minoa** (tel. 22508) at 62 Arkadiou St. Both have doubles for 250dr, triples for 350dr, showers extra. Two kilometers west of town are a series of good campgrounds. For dinner, head to the waterfront and its row of inexpensive restaurants. Though fish is expensive in Crete, here is the place to splurge. Rethymnon fills up in late July for the **wine festival,** so book in advance if you're coming then.

The fishing village of **Aghia Ghallini,** on the southern coast near Rethymnon, was too picturesque to be safe. It is still very pretty, and by no means ruined; but for some more isolated spots, head away from the town in either direction.

The blend of Ottoman and Venetian architecture continues in **Chania,** the capital of Crete. The charming, old port area, lined with cheap restaurants, is the place for dining and an evening promenade. The **Acta** gives the widest variety at low prices. Downtown, try **Taverna Annitsaki** at 27 Gianari St. This is a cavernous *taverna* with rough, cheap food and twenty enormous wine barrels lining the walls. Its owner calls his *taverna* "the parliament" because it is for serious drinking. There is no music because "it is a church," and water is "strictly forbidden."

Reasonably-priced rooms for rent line the harbor. One block off, with good views of the sea, is the **Hotel Piraeus,** 10 Zambeliou St. (tel. 22754). Doubles go for 228dr, triples for 318dr, showers extra. If the port area is full, try the **Viennos,** on Skalidi St. (tel. 22470) or the **Averof** on Sfakianaki (tel. 23090). Both have large, clean rooms—doubles 240dr, triples 300dr. The IYHF **Youth Hostel,** 33 Drakonianou St. (tel. 53565) is just out of town. Take the bus to Aghios Ioannis, and get off at the fifth stop.

For the best beaches near Chania, head west to **Kastelli**—a port with boats to the Peloponnese—and catch the bus to Platanos. From here, hitch or hike the 5 kilometers to **Falasarna,** a fantastic stretch of coves, excellent sand beaches, and dilapidated ruins. The entire west coast of the island is remote, but the beaches here are real hideaways. Another excursion from Chania is to **Paleohora,** a beautiful fishing village rapidly becoming a tourist draw.

Accessible from both Chania and Rethymnon is the **Samaria Gorge,** a spectacular 18-kilometer trek through granite cliffs and heavy forests. The gorge empties on the south coast, at **Aghia Roumeli,** where you can take a boat to **Hora Sfakion.** Between Hora Sfakion and **Loutron** there are some spectacular, almost empty beaches, including one with fresh-water springs. A boat ride away from Hora Sfakion in the other direction is **Frangokastello,** one of Crete's greatest and gloomiest fortresses. The bus to **Omalos,** the town at the beginning of the gorge, and the trip back to Chania costs 300dr in all.

THE EASTERN COAST

The eastern part of Crete has three potential bases—**Aghios Nikolaos, Sitia,** and **Ierapetra.** All are pleasant ports jammed with young travelers. Of these, Aghios Nikolaos is the most picturesque. With a harbor that connects to a small lake and a beautiful mountain backdrop, it is rapidly developing into a tourist enclave. Hiking in the back hills and valleys is very good, and there are boat tours out to **Spinalongi,** an old fortress island later converted into a leper colony. The best beach is 3 kilometers south of town, along the main road.

Accommodations in Aghios Nikolaos are hard to find. The best deal is **Hotel Lato** (tel. 22319) on the port. Large doubles and triples go for 280dr and 360dr respectively. Or try the cheaper **Egaion,** one block up from the water (tel. 22773). Doubles here are 240dr, no triples.

Ierapetra has little to offer besides a slow pace and mediocre beaches. The IYHF **Youth Hostel** here (tel. 22463) is right on the water. Sitia is the best base for seeing the east coast of the island. Built up from the harbor, it has several cheap rooms to let and a good IYHF **Youth Hostel** (tel. 22693). For hotels, try the **Flisvos** and **Pressos;** both offer doubles for 250dr, 360dr for triples, showers extra. From here, you can bus out to the good eastern beaches. **Vai** is an excellent sand beach, surrounded by the only palm forest in the Aegean, but it is packed. A better trip is to **Zakros;** a hike or short bus ride will take you to **Kato Zakros,** site of a Minoan temple. The beach beyond is a long, smooth crescent of sand.

Boat connections out of Crete vary by the destination and the sea conditions. There are daily boats connecting Piraeus to Heracleion and Chania. There are also boats from Aghios Nikolaos to the Cyclades and Rhodes. There is also a weekly boat connecting the western port of Kastelli to the Peloponnese.

Corfu (Kerkyra) and the Ionian Islands

Corfu fills up every summer with package tourists and transients on their way between Brindisi and Patras, but it is still an island of unique beauty. It is ironic that this is the first island most people see, because it is very atypical of Greece. The main town is more Venetian than Greek, and the luxuriant countryside is more like an English country club than anything else. Even the food reveals a healthy Italian influence.

Because of its size and the fact that only the north of the island is well serviced by buses, cars or motorcycles are the best way to get around Corfu. Two days of hard travel can give you a good overview of the island—from the heavily-forested hills and excellent beaches of the north to the farms and rocky coasts of the south.

The major city is the port of **Kerkyra,** a lively base for seeing the island. Cheap accommodations can be found in the old port area. Zavitsianou St. offers the **Costantinople, Acropole,** and **Anasis,** with the **Hotel New York** around the corner. All attract a student crowd, and offer good rooms for 250dr (doubles) and 360dr (triples)—showers extra. Cheaper but noisier are the hotels **Elpis, Kriti,** and **Eptanissos,** all on Theotakis St. off the town square. There are two IYHF **Hostels**—one in the center of the island at Aghios Ioannis, and the other 6 kilometers north of town at Kondokalion; both charge 60dr a night. Camping spots are spread over the island, the best being at **Paleokastritsas.** There are also rooms to let (inquire at the Tourist Office) as well as houses for longer stays (available through **Exportimpex** in Theotaki Square).

The best, but most expensive, restaurants are along the Esplanade, modeled after the rue de Rivoli in Paris. The **Aegli** offers both good food and reasonable prices. In the port area, try the **Averoff** or **Gystakis.** All of these offer the Corfiot specialties: *sofrito* (meat cooked in a heavy garlic sauce) and *bourdeto* (whitefish cooked in pepper sauce).

Corfu's beaches are excellent. Perhaps the best of these is Paleokastritsas, a spectacular bay and smaller coves among rocky headlands. Climb up to the monastery for the view. Stretching to the south are a number of good beaches—the most isolated of these is **Myrtiotissa;** take the bus to Vatos and walk the 4 kilometers to the beach. Far to the south is the beautiful, remote, sandy beach of **Aghios Georgios.**

For two widely different views of Corfu's elegance, visit **Pelekas,** a popular village with the best panorama of the island and of Albania; then head off to the grotesque **Achilleion Palace**—now a casino—whose murals and statues are a salute to schmaltz and kitsch at their finest.

PAXOS is a tiny, rocky island just to the south of Corfu. Covered with olive groves, it has a rough western coastline, riddled with sea caves. Better beaches are found in the adjacent island of **ANTIPAXOI.** More austere is **LEFKADA,** a barren, mountainous island separated from the mainland by a narrow channel. The island hosts a **prose and art festival** every summer. **CEFALONIA** is the largest and most majestic of the Ionians. The main town of **Argostoli** should be avoided in favor of the exquisite villages of **Assos** and **Fiscardo** to the north. The southeast coast offers a series of good sand beaches. **ITHACA,** the fabled home of Odysseus, is small and rocky, but its beaches are excellent and uncrowded. The small port of **Vathi** has an enchanting setting, almost closed in by two rocky headlands. **ZAKINTHOS** is a green, tame island famous for its food and singers. Its exquisite Venetian town was completely destroyed in an earthquake in 1953, but the newly-built town is graceful and lively.

HUNGARY

$1U.S.=18.9forints(Ft)   **1Ft=$.053**

Although geographical location and political pressure have subjected it to influence from both east and west, Hungary maintains much of its cultural autonomy. The Magyars are, after all, linguistically and ethnically unique in Europe—their closest relatives are the Osztyaks in Siberia.

The capital, **Budapest,** is an amazingly vital city which equals most European capitals for historical, cultural, and culinary interest. See Budapest, and then explore the little-traveled country between Budapest and Vienna. Old-time hospitality still reigns in the peasant villages of the area.

PRACTICAL INFORMATION

If you're not driving into Hungary, you can choose between trains, buses, or the Danube hydrofoil (Vienna-Budapest). Though a bit more expensive, the foil is fast and comfortable. A one-way 2nd class train ticket from Vienna costs about 210 Austrian Schillings, or about 50% less if you buy it at the student travel office at Fürichgasse 10.

Everyone who visits Hungary must have a visa. If you come by train, you must get it in advance. Visas are issued "on the spot" if you are driving or flying, but you'll avoid the possibility of a long hassle at the border if you have your visa already. Visas are issued by the Consulate General of the Hungarian People's Republic, 8 East 75th Street, New York, NY 10021 (tel. (212) 879-4125); or the Hungarian Embassy, Consulate Section, 3910 Shoemaker Street, N.W., Washington D.C. 20008 (tel. (202)362-6730). In Europe, the Vienna, London, and Frankfurt **IBUSZ** (the Hungarian Travel Bureau) branches can also obtain a visa for you, but charge a handling fee. If you're passing through Vienna, the IBUSZ office at Kärntner Strasse 26 (open Mon.-Fri. 8am-5pm, Sat. 8am-noon) is remarkably fast and easy to deal with. If you come by car and decide to get a visa at the border, don't forget to bring two photos or they'll turn you back. What they call a "48-hour" visa at the border is just that. If you're even a few hours late leaving, you can expect trouble on your way out.

Fortunately, there is no longer a minimum enforced daily currency exchange rate. We strongly recommend changing money only as you need it, because it remains difficult to reconvert forints into dollars. On Hungary's black market, U.S. dollars can fetch as much as twice the official rate, but the penalties are extremely stiff. Unlike in the USSR, jeans and other western articles don't bring a high price here.

Upon arriving in Hungary, you *must* register with the local police within 24 hours of the date stamped on your visa. Failure to register is a criminal offense punishable by heavy fines (100-3000Ft). If you stay at a hotel or campground, or if you find a room through a paying guest service *(fizetövendégláto szolgálat),* the registration will be taken care of for you; but if you arrange your accommodations privately, you must fill out the alien registration form (1Ft) obtained from the Post Office, Police Station, or IBUSZ Office, and return it to the local police station. Since no registration is necessary when you leave a town, it is possible to get by without registering on subsequent nights, although you are officially required to do so every night of your stay in Hungary.

Hotel accommodations in Hungary are insufficient to handle the ever-increasing flow of tourists. IBUSZ and the local **Tourist Office** (Budapest Tourist in Budapest, Eger Tourist in Eger, etc.) operate a paying guest service which will place you in a private home for 40-100Ft per night. Turn to them first. Tourist class hotels do exist, but are hopelessly crowded during the summer when the dreaded groups from the east arrive. You can legally accept private offers of accommodation on the street (in small towns, look for the sign *Szoba kiadó)* but be sure to register with the police if you do.

Camping offers a good alternative to staying in hotels and guest houses. There are over seventy campgrounds in Hungary (27 at Lake Balaton alone). Many rent bungalows and virtually all can rent the equipment you forgot to bring along. According to the category of the campground (1-3), the cost per person per day is 6-12Ft. Most sites are open May 2-Sept. 30, and there is a 20% discount at the beginning and end of the season. For information and maps, write to the **Hungarian Camping and Caravanning Club,** 1088 Budapest, Múseum u. 11 (tel. 141-880).

Trains in Hungary are slow, but usually reliable. You will pay almost twice as much for an express train *(gyorsvonat)* as for a local *(személyvonat),* but the slow trains aren't for the impatient. Both international and domestic tickets are available at IBUSZ, or in Budapest at the main **MAV** (Hungarian Railway) booking office at Népköztársaság 35 at Nagymezö u.

If you're headed for another socialist country, remember that an IUS card (the eastern European student ID—see Documents and Formalities section of introduction for details) will get you a reduction of 25%. If you're traveling to the west or Yugoslavia, we recommend that you buy a ticket only to the border and work it out from there. By a delightful twist of the Hungarian bureaucratic mind, if you buy a ticket to the West, you must change *double* the price of the ticket into forints—half for the ticket and half to spend in Hungary. Outside of Budapest, though, they don't seem to have heard of this one, so play it by ear.

The buses are inexpensive but crowded, and will get you to your destination no more than twice as slowly as the train. The main Bus Station at Engels tér. in Budapest has schedules and fares posted. When you're outside a city, just try flagging any bus that is moving in the right direction.

Hitching is not the fastest way of traveling in Hungary. The main roads are unpleasantly crowded, and the rest are almost traffic free. Hitching is not officially forbidden, but few Hungarians do it.

Cafés, restaurants, and an infrequent street corner will have telephones. Most take a 1Ft piece for each three minutes and some older ones take a token *(érme)* which can be bought at **Trafik** shops. You often have to deposit the coin before even lifting the receiver, but even this method hasn't been standardized. Convincing the phone that your cóin or token is genuine may prove frustrating, but do persist.

Hungarian is among the more exotic languages you'll come across. But if you can make yourself understood in German, you should get along well in most everyday situations. Students, and increasingly waiters, display a better knowledge of English than you might think. Making some attempt at Hungarian will definitely be appreciated. Your knowledge might not get past *kérem* for "please" and *kösönöm* for "thank you," but a couple of books will help you translate important signs and menus—you're definitely going to need some help. If you can find it, *How to Say it in Hungarian* is fairly helpful for 14Ft. (Try the **Akademia Könyvesbolt,** 22 Vaci u. in Budapest.) If you're planning a longer stay, or are leaving the capital at all, pick up the *Tourist's English-Hungarian Dictionary.* It costs 33Ft and is extremely helpful—an important investment here.

FOOD

Magyar cuisine is one of the best in Europe, specializing in fantastic combinations of meat, spices, and fresh vegetables. Even after the recent hefty increases in food prices, meals are still relatively cheap. You won't starve in Hungary so long as you know that *vendéglö* (or *étterem*) means restaurant, or you can recognize the paprika smell which pervades spicy Magyar cooking. You might begin your meal with *gulyas,* which in Hungary is usually a beef soup seasoned with paprika. Closer to what we know as goulash is *pörkölt,* a pork or beef stew, again with the ever-present paprika. Stuffed cabbage and stuffed peppers, *töltött káposzta* and *töltött paprika* respectively, are also typical entrées. The most tasty fish, or so the Hungarians claim, are *fogas* and *süllö,* pike-perch found in Balaton, which are grilled in one piece and served up with lemon.

For your main course, don't miss *paprikaś csirke galuskaval,* chicken cooked in a delicious paprika-sour cream sauce and served with dumplings. *Rosztbif,* roast beef, appears in several different forms—try it with sour cream and mushroom sauce. Finally, if you really want to splurge, go with some friends and order a whole roasted wild pig, *vaddisznó.*

Even after such a meal, dessert will be a crowning treat. Fresh fruits and compotes are the lightest dish, but don't pass up a chance to try the superb *rétes*. (The Hungarians claim that the Austrians stole the recipe and called it *strudel*.) Try the addicting *meggyleves* (sour cherry soup). Don't leave Hungary without sampling the sinfully rich pastries. One of the specialties is *dobostorta*, about ten layers of mocha filling topped by a hard caramel coating.

Bottles of rich Hungarian wine go before, during, and even after the meal. A good, dry white wine is *Tokaj szamorodni;* somewhat more full-bodied are the wines of the Balaton Lake district, particularly *Badacsonyer Szürke Barat* and *Somloer Furmint*. *Rizling* tends to be sweeter and enjoys a delicate bouquet. Save the other Tokaj wines, particularly the very sweet *Aszu*, until after dinner. *Egri Bikaver* is justifiably Hungary's best-known dry red wine. Drier and more aromatic are *Szekszard* and *Soproni kekfrankos*, both from the Danube valley.

For more prosaic eating, a *Büte* or a *Bisztro* offers fast and reasonable food at about 10Ft and up, though you'll often have to eat standing up. For pastry and coffee, look for a *Cukrászda*. Coffee, by the way, is invariably excellent, but tea is a rarity here.

Budapest

Splendidly situated between the forested Buda hills and the Transylvanian plain, the ancient capital of the Magyars successfully combines its two-thousand-year history with a socialist present. If somewhat removed from the aristocratic elegance of its nineteenth-century heyday, Budapest is far more than a slightly tattered Vienna, and is less touristy. Its street life and glaring neon make the city unique in Eastern Europe. There is a certain Mediterranean craziness here, a carnival atmosphere along the Danube and the main shopping streets that lasts until the cold sets in during the fall. Budapest is a city of forgotten corners, somber Teutonic palaces, and glowering monuments which seem curiously out of step with the *joie de vivre* of its inhabitants.

Orientation

Three train stations serve Budapest: **Déli pu** (south) handles connections to Balaton and the Southwest. You'll probably arrive either at **Keleti** (east) or **Nyugati** (west). If you're departing, make sure you check which station your train leaves from, since both Keleti and Nyugati have trains in all directions. There is an IBUSZ office at both of these train stations, open 8am-8pm. If you arrive by hydrofoil, the closest IBUSZ office is at Felszabadulás tér 5 (tel. 180-860).

A remarkable network of trams and buses will take you anywhere you want to go in Budapest. All Trafik Shops and an occasional sidewalk vendor sell yellow tram tickets *(villamos jegy)* and blue bus tickets *(autóbusz vonaljegy)* for 1Ft and 1.50Ft respectively. They also sell an excellent map with a street index for 11.60Ft. Many of the trams and buses stop running around midnight, and the time of the last run is posted on the sign bearing the route number at each stop. If you prefer, taxis average 25Ft (forint, not feet) per mile ride. But fares are substantially higher if the trip is uphill! Budapest's new metro adds a new dimension to city transport. The completed portions are huge, elegant, and free of ads. Try it for a forint; a bar pops up in front of you if you forget to pay.

If things are looking down for you and you desperately need someone who speaks English, just head for a good hotel; most desk clerks will be able to help you. Hotels are also the best place to pick up free monthly issues of *Coming Events in Budapest*, a useful guide to cultural events, special exhibitions, and sightseeing. Hotels are also the exclusive source for the *Herald Tribune*, *Time*, and *Newsweek*, but come early in the afternoon as copies disappear rapidly. The U.S. Embassy also has a reading room where you can read recent American newspapers and magazines.

Addresses and Telephone Numbers

IBUSZ: V., Felszabadulás tér 5 (tel. 180-860).

KEOKH (Alien Registration Office): Népköztársaság u. 12. Open 9am-1pm weekdays. Will direct you to the Police Station of the district in which you are residing. Also the place to come for visa extensions.

Budapest Tourist, Paying Guest Service: V Roosevelt tér 5-6 (tel. 173-555). Open every day 9am-5pm; VII, Baross tér 3 (tel. 336-934), open every day 2-8pm; VI, Bajcsy Zsilinszky u. 55 (tel. 314-545), open every day 8am-8pm.

Post Office: *Poste Restante (Postán Maradó)* at Városház u. 18. Open 8am-9pm, closed Sun. 24-hour Post Offices at both East and West Train Stations.

Police: (tel. 07).

Ambulance: (tel. 04).

U.S. Embassy: V Szabadság, tér 12 (tel. 124-224, after hours 329-374). Open weekdays only 8am-1pm and 2-5pm. Holds mail and distributes a general information sheet for U.S. visitors to Hungary.

Canadian Embassy: Budakeszi u. 55/D P/8. (tel. 365-728). Take bus #22 from Moszkva tér.

Foreign Language Bookstores: V Vaci u. 22 (tel. 189-432); off Kossuth L. a couple of blocks from the Erszébet híd.

Laundromat: Rákóczi u. 8.

Accommodations

A paying guest service is also handled through **Express, Cooptourist,** and **Volantourist,** if you can't find what you want at Budapest Tourist or IBUSZ. Ask for the cheapest place; rates are usually 50-60Ft per person. Some rooms have a set price, regardless of how many people, and hover around 100Ft. A few triples are available, but singles are hard to find. Most are not in the center of town, but transportation is excellent. Don't expect much social contact with the family you stay with. Your privacy is more or less recognized, although if you come in later than 11pm you are expected to slip the landlady or doorman a couple of forints. If you stay more than 2-3 days, you can save a little by staying on with your family unbeknownst to IBUSZ. Your family receives only 35Ft per single, and 60Ft per double; the rest of what you pay is service to the middleman, IBUSZ.

The Express office will be able to provide you with a complete listing of student accommodations in Budapest, but will probably assure you that they are all booked up. A good idea would be to call to see if any vacancies for individuals have opened up. Budapest Tourist also handles a lesser number of student accommodations in a more hectic way. If you want to live in a specific area, ask the doormen, hotel receptionists, and other likely people if they know of any free rooms. It shouldn't cost you more than 40-50Ft. If all else fails, you can camp out in a park. Try the one on the Buda side of the Petöfi Bridge. Although the practice is illegal because you need a police registration stamp on your visa, if you are inconspicuous enough, there should be no problem, especially now that many young Eastern Europeans have taken up the practice.

The budget hotel scene in Budapest is not too bright. The government seems to be closing most of the C Hotels to individuals, and upgrading what is left to B prices ($10-15). While they are all booked months in advance, you may have some luck trying for sudden vacancies, or enlisting the services of IBUSZ or Budapest Tourist, which sometimes have space available. You might also try Cooptourist or the **Pannonia Hotel Service,** V, Kigyó u. 4-6 (tel. 389-138).

Hotel Citadella, XI Gellért-hegy (tel. 665-794). Actually a C-class tourist hotel, but virtually a hostel for its clientele and prices. Beautifully located atop Gellért Hill in an old Hapsburg fortress. A bed in a 10-, 13-, or 14-bed room costs only 24Ft. Clean and not without comforts. A demanding climb from the Gellért Hotel or a 15-minute bus ride from Móricz Zsigmond körtér (bus #27 leaves about every 15 minutes).

Hotel Universitas, XI Irinyi Józsefus u. 9 (tel. 453-507). This student dorm often has vacancies. 92Ft per 2-bed room with hot and cold running water. Open July and August. Trams #6 and 12.

Hotel Express, XII Beethoven u. 9 (tel. 155-612). Old, but attractive, a little far in a quiet part of Buda. No singles, doubles 60Ft per person. No curfew, but silence after 10pm.

Lido Szallo, III Nanasi u. 67 (tel. 888-160). Located in Romai Park, this sports hotel offers simple doubles for 150Ft per person, as well as basic wooden bungalows for 60Ft per person. Take the *HEV* or buses #34 or 42 from Polger tér, on the Buda side of Arpad híd; get off when you see the campground, walk past the pool, and continue to Nanasi u. Lido is to your right. A little far.

Food

Eating well in Budapest is not a problem, but a full meal isn't quite the bargain it once was. Almost all Class I and Class II restaurants offer a special, fixed price meal at lunch (1-3pm) and some even have one at dinner. At a Class II restaurant, such a meal will cost between 18Ft and 30Ft for soup, main course, and often dessert. Ask the waiter about what the selection of the day is. Most restaurants have printed menus in German, and a few even in English, but you have to ask to see them.

Czékelky Étterem, Ferenczy István u., right off the Múzeum körút. Delicious Hungarian cooking in a plain neighborhood restaurant. Try the nut-filled *palascinta* (crêpe) doused with chocolate sauce for the richest dessert around. *Menus* at 17Ft and 19Ft for lunch, full dinners for 40Ft.

Kukorica Étterem, Wesselényi u. 43. A quiet little restaurant with curtained windows. Serves delicious simple fare in the 17 and 23Ft lunch *menus*.

Dunakorzo Étterem, Vigadó tér 3, on the Danube. With an outside terrace. Lunch *menus* at 18 and 22Fts, meals for 35 Ft.

Budapest has many Class I restaurants that really aren't very expensive. Two excellent possibilities are **Arany Szarvas,** I, Szarvas tér 1 (tel. 351-305), an old baroque inn that specializes in wild boar, venison, and pheasant. Quite elegant with good gypsy music. Meal from 50Ft. Open every day but Tuesday, 5pm-1am. Call for reservations, or go early or late. **Citadella Etterem,** on Gellért Hill offers indoor or outdoordining with gypsy music at night. Delicious meals from 40Ft (less expensive for lunch). Open noon to midnight.

Budapest abounds in cheap restaurants *(büte, bisztros, grills,* and *self-service)*. At many you have to pay for your meal before you order. Pantomime and tenacity pay off. At self-service restaurants, you can see what you order. The one on the corner of Bajcsy Zsilinsky u. and Marko u. (a few blocks from Nyugati Pu) and the one on the corner of Honved u. and Szt. Istvan Körút (near Margithíd) are two of the best. At both you can get a full meal for 15Ft, and if really down and out, a bowl of hot and filling cabbage or carrot stew for about 8Ft.

WINE CELLARS

If you don't have the time to visit the Wine Museum near Lake Balaton, sample some of the great Hungarian wines in Budapest's traditional wine cellars, most of which also double as restaurants. Three of the most convivial are:

Fortuna, I Fortuna u. 4. A fine restaurant, part of which is located in a home dating from the Middle Ages. Downstairs, a huge brick-and-stone wine cellar is draped with boar skins. The food is fine, but overpriced. The nightclub upstairs opens at 6pm and costs 30Ft extra. A good wine cellar, but you're better off eating beforehand next door at the **Fortunahaz Sörözö** (beer house), where main courses are a more reasonable 20-25Ft.

Borkatakomba, XXII Nagytetenyi u. 63, the state wine cellar. The name means "wine catacombs" and booths are sawed-up wine barrels. Possibly Budapest's best selection of inland wines, served up with great provincial cooking. Needless to say, there's gypsy music, too. Far from the center, so watch bus times carefully.

Badacsoni, Havas u. 7, is a small tavern which serves the white wines of the region of which it bears the name. Serious drinking during the day. Great locals.

Just look for the sign *Börök* and you can't go wrong.

PASTRY SHOPS

Vörösmarty Cukraszda, V, Vörösmarty tér 7 (tel. 181-708). Formerly the meeting place of Budapest's elite literati, this café retains its nineteenth-century parlor-style elegance and its fine Herend china coffee-maker. The best pastry around. There are also two smaller branches on Népköztársaság—one called **Müvész** (artist) across from the Opera at #29; and another called **Különlegességi,** at #70 near the Varosliget Park. Expensive. Closed Sun. Otherwise open 8am-9pm.

Paris Cukrászda, Népköztársaság 38. A *retés* (strudel) specialty shop, with about six or seven kinds, all at 4.50Ft a slice. They bake all day, and it's usually still warm when you buy it. Also serves espresso.

Sights

The castle district of **Buda** and the inner city of **Pest** were settled and developed as separate towns until 1873 when they merged into one municipality. Each has preserved its own character, each is rich in its own monuments and points of interest. Buda, the western bank of the Danube, contains many suburban residential areas on the slopes of its seven hills. Ancient Buda, though, is sharply defined by the castle walls on **Varhegy** (Castle Hill). Enter the old town through Vienna Gate in the north, wander through the quaint **Fortuna utca** lined with baroque townhouses; or along **Táncsics Mihály u.,** in the old Jewish commercial sector. Don't miss the excavated foundations of the **old synagogue** at #26. Continue to the central square in front of the magnificent **Matyas Cathedral,** first built in the thirteenth century, but destroyed and rebuilt innumerable times since. It is a uniquely Hungarian confusion of styles. Compare the splendid gothic exterior to the quiet, oriental interior. The romantic nineteenth-century colonnaded **Fisherman's Bastion** was built to frame the Cathedral as it is seen from the town. Now the new, gleaming bronze Hilton frames them both. The **Royal Castle** is still quite a mess—the **historical museum,** though, is worth the visit, although the labels are in Hungarian only.

Neither the **Statue of Liberty,** atop Gellért Hill, or the **Citadella** (which houses a hostel, restaurant, and dancing) justify the long uphill trek. But the view from the top of **Gellért Hill** is stupendous. It includes Castle Hill, the **Parliament of Hungary** (on the Pest Side),as well as the **Szechenyi Lánchid** (chain bridge), built by the Englishman Adam Clark as the first permanent bridge across the Danube in Budapest.

Sprawling Pest is also visible from the Buda hills. Pest is for window-shoppers and café-hoppers. The heart of Pest is in the **Inner City,** the old section which used to be walled. It centers around the pedestrian zone of Váci utca and the quaint Vörösmarty tér but the popular and crowded boulevards like Lenin körút and Múzeum körút, as well as the avenues radiating outwards (Rákóczi utca and Népköztársaság utca in particular), have also become crowded shopping areas.

To escape from this congestion, head for either one of the two main parks. **Margit-sziget,** an island in the Danube, is free of private cars. Trees shade outside terraces, and ruins of several old monasteries pop up between tennis courts and swimming pools. **Varosliget** (City Park), beyond the Heroes monument at the end of Népköztársaság utca shelters a lake with rowboats for hire—watching the Hungarian landlubbers trying to maneuver a boat is quite a spectacle. This park also features several amusement parks and a handful of museums.

Budapest's museums, on the whole, have little to offer. Two exceptions are the **Museum of Fine Arts** on Heroes Square and the **Aquincum Múzeum** on Szentendrei u. 139. The former houses a fine collection of European drawings which it exhibits on a rotating schedule, as well as one of the best collections of Spanish painting outside of Spain. The latter contains the ruins of a Roman amphitheater and other mementoes of Budapest's earliest conquerors. Museums are a good place to escape from the crowds; free for students, open 10am-6pm and closed Mondays.

If you're not going to get to Turkey, Budapest is the place for your Turkish bath. **Rudás fürdö**, Döbrentei tér 9 (at Erzébet hid) has a bath built by the Ottomans themselves over three hundred years ago. The baths have huge domes and arched rooms with reclining benches, and half a dozen pools with water varying in temperature from warm to boiling. Tickets cost about 30Ft, including a massage.

Evenings

On a warm summer evening, a Danube cruise on the *Sétahajó* (pleasure craft) is a romantic way to enjoy the night splendors of this picturesque city. Boats depart at 5:30pm and 8pm below the Duna Hotel, for a 2-3 hour cruise featuring nostalgic music, dancing, and drinking. Fare is 12Ft and 15Ft on Saturday night, depending on departure time. Along similar lines, the **Express Cocktail Ship** departs at 8:30pm on Tuesday, Thursday, and Saturday from the same dock. Rather more raucous and student-oriented, it offers rock music, drinking, and dancing (16Ft). Pick up tickets as early as possible.

Budapest's students also tend to frequent the **Ifjúsági Park** (Youth Park), near Buda's Royal Castle. Here, for 10Ft you can dance on a large outdoor terrace to the music of local rock bands, or sit and drink at one of the numerous tables. The action is furious on weekends, when the park stays open until midnight. A good choice if you like to dance, or just want to catch some reasonably good live rock music.

Another popular spot is the **Casino** on Margitsziget. A beautiful area day and night, the island is particularly alive from 10pm-1am, when the strains of live rock music drift across the spas and fountains along the Danube.

For more cultural fare, sample Budapest's array of operas, plays, and concerts. Tickets are cheap, and available at the Budapest Tourist Office and IBUSZ offices. In general, theatre starts at 7pm (unfortunately mostly in Hungarian) and concerts at 7:30pm. The *Pesti Mosor* and *Budapest Müsorfüzet* available at most newsstands, have details of monthly programs.

The Danube Bend

For the best excursions from Budapest, take a boat to this area some fifteen miles north of Budapest, where the Danube makes a sweeping turn southward between the Börzsony and the Visegrád mountains. Boats leave early each morning (7 and 7:30am) from the Vigadó tér. dock, and steam up-river to **Esztergom**, stopping along the way. On the weekends a special-service hydrofoil makes the trip in under two hours; but if convenient, come on weekdays to avoid the crowds. For information on boat trips, contact Dunatours at Bajcsy Zs. u. 17 (tel. 314-533). This office will also make hotel, hostel, and camping arrangements for you in this area. The suburban railway **(HEV)** starts from the underground terminal at Batthyány tér and runs as far as **Szentendre,** while buses leaving from Engels tér serve all the towns on both banks.

The first stop on the right bank is the village of Szentendre. This village emanates a peculiar Mediterranean atmosphere. Delightful small museums appear at every street corner, two of which should not be missed: the **Kovacs Margit Múzeum** on Washtag-Gy u. (off Göröng u.) houses a unique collection of exquisitely entertaining ceramic sculptures by the twentieth-century Hungarian artist Kovacs Margit (free for students; 4Ft otherwise). Up the hill, at the foot of the red tower of the Serbian Cathedral is a private collection of Serb and Greek Orthodox ecclesiastical art (admission 2Ft for all). Step into any one of the orthodox churches—try the **Blagoveshenska** Church in the center of the village—for a look at the iconostases. While in the area, try some of the Greek and Serbian dishes served in the local restaurants, such as in the 16.70Ft *menu* at **Görög Kanoco Vendéglö** (on Görög ü. down by the Danube). For bathing in the area, head for the Szentendre island—ferry every fifteen minutes.

Ten miles up-river, by the bend proper, is the village of **Visegrád.** The stone fortress at the top of the hill was constructed to resist the Mongol onslaughts of the thirteenth century. The security afforded by this stronghold convinced the Anjou Kings of Hungary to build a **Royal Palace** just down the hill. Visegrád offers inexpensive dining and sleeping. **Diofá Étterem,** the restaurant at Fö u. 59 is crowded with locals. The fish is excellent; start with the *halászalé* (fish soup). The low à la carte prices (30-50Ft for a meal) make the cheap 16Ft *menu* an unnecessary limitation.

The tourist hotels, with up to six beds in a room, are crowded in the summer, but cheap (25Ft). Get the local Tourist Office to find a place for you, as most of the managers speak no foreign languages. A room in a private house will cost you 70Ft.

The Visegradi-Hegység mountains, part of the Pilis range, make for wonderful walks. Inquire about trails, or follow signs for Pilisszenttászló, a small village within two hours' walk to Dobgókö, the high point of the area (three to four hours' hike from **Visegrád**).

Esztergom, the capital of medieval Hungary, boasts some of the biggest and oldest monuments in the country. On **Varhegy** (Castle Hill), overlooking the Danube, are the remains of a once-magnificent romanesque **Royal Palace.** The **Cathedral**—you can't miss it—is the biggest church in Hungary. Its neoclassic boredom is broken by the high Renaissance red marble Bakocz chapel on the left side of the nave. The Treasure Room contains the coronation cross upon which all the Kings of Hungary, the last one in 1916, swore their oath. The guard will give you a guided tour if you let her know that you are a foreigner (a few forints tip will be well received). The **Christian Museum,** at the foot of the hill, houses an exceptional collection of early Hungarian church art. The country-town atmosphere of this once-capital city can be sensed at an early morning market on Petöfi Sandor u. The **Tourist Office** will find a bed for you.

Addresses and Telephone Numbers

Szentendre: Idegenforgalmi Hivatal (Tourist Office), Somogyi Bascó part. 6 (tel. 91-48), on the Danube embankment. It will locate a bed, and provides a map of the town and a list of museums.

Visegrád: Idegenforgalmi Hivatal, Danube Embankment (tel. 280). Same services as above.

Esztergom: Idegenforgalmi Hivatal, Sechenyi tér. 13.

Eger

Although much of Eastern Hungary is a dusty plain, the Northeast is a haven of rolling hills and vineyards. The town of Eger, the country's red-wine capital, is a three-hour train ride from Budapest. Both the Bus and the Train Stations are within easy walking distance from the most helpful of Tourist Offices, **Eger Tourist** on Bajcsy 25 u. 9 (tel. 17-24). It will provide you with a map, as well as with information on accommodations. Two other offices, **Cooptourist** at Hibay 22 (tel. 13-62) and **Express** at Séchenyi u. 28 (tel. 10-05), will also be able to locate a room for you in a hotel (singles from 180Ft), in a bungalow (50-75Ft), or in a private home (60Ft). Eger is the home of the potent wine *Egri Bikaver,* "the bull's blood of Eger." The southern part of the town (walk through the Nepkert Park and out Uttoro u.) shelters more than 2000 private wine cellars as well as the large **Borkatakomba State Wine Cellar.** Ask for the restaurant **Ködmön** (tel. 10-69), and sample the wine alongside a fine veal dish, the *töltött borjú.* In the center of town, the restaurant **Kazamata** is unbeatable for its wine list, fish dishes, and its setting under the neoclassical Cathedral. Most of Eger's discotheques are open-air affairs in the park (admission 10Ft). Try **Nepkert Park** or inquire at the Park Hotel.

Western Transdanubia

Balaton, the sunny lake southwest of Budapest is Hungary's largest and most vigorously promoted resort area, with high rise (and high-priced) hotels, and camping for 36,000 people. Still, if you're in the area it's worth a short stopover. Despite its 42-mile length, the lake is extremely shallow, rarely more than 10 feet deep. The water is very warm and quite clean, despite its chalky, pale-blue color.

You can reach Balaton quickly and inexpensively by train from Déli pu in Budapest, for 80Ft round trip. **Tihany** on the northeast side has the most to offer. You can take the ferry from here to many spots on the opposite shore. The best beaches are in **Siófok** (directly across from Tihany).

For accommodations all around the lake, check with the local paying guest service. The tourist bureaus at Siófok and **Balantonfüred** will find you a room for about 80Ft per person. If the campgrounds are overcrowded, head for the empty areas on the southern shore and find yourself a nice spot. Restaurants are packed and overpriced, so stick to the local stores. But check carefully—their hours are very irregular.

Between the crowded beaches of Lake Balaton and Vienna lie some quiet little villages well worth the trouble to get to. Most towns of interest will have an *Idegenforgalmi Hivatal* (Tourist Office) that will provide you with a brochure or map, and will also locate a room for you. Plead poverty and they will usually scrape up a private room for 50Ft. Bungalows in camping areas are usually the cheapest alternatives for less than 30Ft, if you don't object to the walk from the town center. Throughout the region, vineyards cover the southern sides of hills. The Badacsony wines are particularly fine.

One especially nice and untouristy town is **Köszeg,** near the Austrian border. Roam through the narrow streets of the old town, admire the churches and the Baroque houses, or carry your picnic to the orchards on the slopes overlooking the village. Just the place to recover from Balaton and Budapest. The Tourist Office is on the main square, Várkör tér 59 (tel. 195). Ask to stay in the Jurisch castle hostel that has beds in dorm rooms right on the castle court for 30Ft.

DENMARK STRAIT

NORWEGIAN SEA

Isafjorthur

Akureyri

L. Myvatn

Breidafjordur

Langjokull

Egilsstather

Faxafloi

Thingvellir

Reykjavik

Keflavik

VESTMANN IS.

Heimaey

0 km   80   160
0 m   50   100

ICELAND

$1U.S.=260 krónur (kr)   10kr=$0.04

Just south of the Arctic Circle and sitting on the mid-Atlantic rift, Iceland
is the land of glacier and volcano, ice and fire. No other habitable land
exhibits such dramatic opposition of natural forces. Steaming geysers spout
away on the fringe of glacial ice caps, snow-locked lunar mountains give
way to moss-carpeted plains, and black lava castles drop into a jagged
seacoast serrated by fjords. Iceland's isolation discourages the conventional
tourist; the few foreigners you'll meet outside **Reykjavík** will be intrepid
hikers and ecstatic geologists, people almost as exotic as the Icelanders
themselves. To enjoy Iceland, you need either bags of money or the heart to
make yourself at home camping in the cold and windswept moors. But
Iceland will prove your mettle and reward you for your pains.

Iceland is geologically young, but it is the world's oldest republic. The
Althing, the famous open-air parliament, was established in 930 A.D.,
shortly after the arrival of the first Norse settlers. You can visit it at
Thingvellír, and stand on the "law rock," from which the leader of the
Althing recited the laws to the people below as his voice echoed off the sheer

rock cliffs. Iceland finally became totally independent in 1944 after 130 years of Danish rule. Sensitive about misconceptions concerning their country's relationship to Denmark, Icelanders are as proud of their independence as they are of their land's natural wonders.

With only one sixth of the island habitable, Iceland's 220,000 people rely on their energy and creativity to sustain a hard life. Most Icelanders insist on building their own homes. Everywhere you look there is construction: new office buildings, power plants, and greenhouses dot the cities as well as the lava fields. Despite the recent growth of industry and the cities, Iceland retains something of a small-town spirit. Don't be surprised when your bus driver waves to half the people in sight; they're probably childhood friends.

But Icelanders are also a sophisticated and highly literate people. Their literature is both world renowned and domestically popular. Currently, more books per capita are published in Iceland than in any other country. If you haven't read one of the sagas—written in the vernacular during the twelfth and thirteenth centuries—pick up a translation of *Njal's Saga*. Despite a strong attachment to their native language, most Icelanders study English in schools, and speak it with wry, tight-lipped humor.

PRACTICAL INFORMATION

The weather is best here in summer. You'll have perpetual daylight (compared to the 19-hour nights of midwinter), and in the far north, you can watch the pale sun sliding around just above the horizon. Sunshine abounds in the summer months, but the air is generally cool, especially in the evenings. The weather is also quite fickle; carry a thick sweater and a poncho, or a sudden drenching may leave you cold and miserable.

While roaming sheep and Icelandic ponies have become adept at subsisting on the stubborn, treeless land, vegetables have been less successful. Most of the local "crops" are to be found in greenhouses in the southern regions. Other vegetables and fruits are imported in tin cans, at extravagant cost.

With food prices sky high and rising, seafood is Iceland's tastiest and most reasonably-priced commodity. Dairy products are also moderate in cost. If you have access to a kitchen or a camping stove, we suggest cooking fresh fish bought at the neighborhood fishmonger. Haddock is cheap (less than $1 a meal) and plentiful, but you should sample some more exotic seafood dishes as well: *humar* or *smahumar* (the small summer lobster of the south coast), *rjupa* (the Icelandic grouse with spiced sauce), and *saltfiskur* (salted cod). *Harthfiskur* (slabs of dried, flaking fish) fried in butter make a delicious snack. *Skyr* (a yogurt-like curdled milk), *hangikjöt* (smoked mutton), *blothmor* (blood sausage), and *hverabrauth* (rye bread baked in natural hot springs), are both exotic and edible, which most foreigners won't say of *hakarl* (shark buried in sand until it ferments) or *thorramatur* (a cold assortment of pickled whale, shark, and seal).

Getting around Iceland can be difficult if you're on a tight budget. Hitching can be counted on only for the major routes between large towns; on the little-traveled roads inland, you could easily be stranded for a day or longer. Public buses run infrequently, usually once a day, even to the most popular attractions. Nevertheless, the new **Omnibus Passport** is probably the cheapest way to see the country. A one-week, unlimited travel ticket costs about $72. Alternatively, the **Full Circle Passport** ($64), allows you to circle the country with no time limit, but you are confined to the main route. The unmatched scenery of the interior is accessible, for the most part, only to those with four-wheel drive vehicles, which are available in Reykjavík for about $35 per day plus mileage for a basic seven-seater. The best alternative is to take an organized cross-country camping tour. Leaving Reykjavík, a six-day tour costs $100, food and equipment excluded. The **Tourist Bureau** will provide details.

For those going out on their own, a tent, gas stove, sturdy boots, and a thick coat are essentials. Camping equipment can be rented in Reykjavík from **Tjaldleigan** at Laufásvegur 74 (tel. 13072). Hikers should deposit their itineraries with the Tourist Bureau.

Camping is definitely the cheapest way to see the country, and is legal almost everywhere. Organized campsites can be found near every sizeable town. They charge about 200kr per tent plus 200kr per person per night. Facilities vary, but some sites have hot running water and electricity. Iceland also has six **youth hostels**, scattered across the island. IYHF card holders pay 800kr per night; nonmembers pay 1100kr. There are also schools and summer hotels where travelers with sleeping bags can stay at reduced charges (they are called *svefnpokaplåss*). Finally, the **Edda** chain of hotels offers a limited number of rooms to travelers with sleeping bags at about $8 per night. The pamphlet, "Hostelling in Iceland," lists hostels, *svefnpokaplåss*, Edda hotels, and some mountain huts. Contact the Tourist Bureau for further details.

Note: Because of the declining value of the krónur, American dollars are widely accepted as payment. Therefore you don't have to change all the money you plan to spend into krónur. Make sure, though, to change any leftover krónur before leaving the country, as it is harder to exchange them at a reasonable rate outside Iceland.

Reykjavík

As the northernmost metropolis in the world, Reykjavík is a tribute to man's triumph over nature. The ingenuity is everywhere evident; Reykjavík is heated almost entirely by boiling water from the hot springs whose steam inspired its name—"Smoky Bay."

The city faces **Faxaflói** (Faxa Bay), viewing the world through its congested harbor. Schools of fishing vessels stream in and out, and the smell of the sea dominates Iceland's capital city. But there is another side to this sprawling, weatherbeaten port. Reykjavík is very much a cosmopolitan city, complete with expensive boutiques, perfumeries (in the *Apóteks*), and no less than six daily newspapers. Reykjavikíngars possess an outlook both worldly and confident—confident that they will not be left behind by their progressive Scandinavian neighbors.

Orientation

All international flights arrive at NATO's **Keflavík Airport**, 50 km southwest of downtown Reykjavík. The bus to the city meets every flight and costs 600kr. You could try to hitch, although traffic is not heavy on this two-lane highway.

The road to Reykjavík winds its way past NATO barracks and through the grey lava heaths of the **Reykjanesstagi Peninsula.** The Loftleider bus ends its route at the expensive Hotel Loftleider. To get to the city center, you can wait for the hourly municipal bus (#10), or walk for 20 minutes on the often muddy Hringbraut to Sóleyjargata, and then past the lake **(Tjörnin)** to the central square. The **Iceland Tourist Bureau** *(Ferthaskrifstofa Rikisins)* is on the way to the center, not far from the entrance road to the municipal airport. This office offers free lists of hostels, restaurants, hotels, transportation schedules, and maps. They can also book hotels and tours for you.

Emerging from the city bus, you'll find everything you need just a step away: shops, groceries, banks, movies, and (expensive) laundry services. The municipal tourist information booth (marked "i") is also right there at the beginning of the pedestrian street (Austurstraeti). Most of the city bus routes stop at this terminal area. Buses run from 7am to midnight weekdays, and until 1am on weekends. The fare is 100kr, covering any distance, and you should ask the driver for a free transfer ticket (valid only for 30 to 60 minutes). The tourist booth can provide you with a comprehensive route map. If you are going to Luxembourg after your stay in Iceland, you may need to get to the Hotel Loftleider in time for the 5:45am bus to Keflavík. Arrange for a taxi the day before, as the city buses aren't running at this hour.

About a dozen firms in Rekjavík have cars for hire. One-way rentals are not available, and you must be 20 years of age and hold an International Driver's License. Daily rates begin at $12.75 plus $0.11 per km. Advance reservations are recommended.

At the outset, forget about hunting for bargains; there aren't any. If you're looking for an Icelandic sweater, one of the finest souvenirs you'll ever find, expect to pay 7500 to 8000kr. The Handknitting Association of Iceland at Skólavördustígur 19 has an excellent selection, as does the duty-free store at Keflavík terminal.

Shops and businesses are open from 9am to 6pm, some closing for lunch. Banking hours are from 9:30am to 3:30 or 4pm. On Saturdays, most shops close at noon, and on Sundays, Reykjavík is a ghost town. If you are arriving on a weekend, bring some food with you, or resign yourself to searching out one of the few cafeterias that remain open.

Addresses and Telephone Numbers

Iceland Tourist Bureau: Reykjanesbraut 6 (tel. 25855), 9:30am-5pm weekdays.

Municipal Tourist Information: Austurstraeti at Laekjartorg (tel. 10044), 9am-6pm weekdays, 10am-2pm Saturdays.

American Express Representative: Ustyn Tourist Agency, Austurstraeti 17 (tel. 20100), 9am-5:30pm weekdays, 10am-noon Saturdays.

Central Post Office (Póststofan): Pósthússtraeti 5 (tel. 26000), 9am-5pm weekdays, 9am-noon Saturdays.

Telegrams and Long Distance (Landssimahusith): Austurvöllur Square, in center of city (tel. 16411).

Long-Distance Coach Terminal (Umferdamidstödin): Hringbraut, near the municipal airport (tel. 22300).

Icelandic Airline Office (Loftleidir): Laekjargata 2 (tel. 22300).

Taxi: B.S.R., Laekjargata 4b (tel. 11720).

Police: (tel. 11166).

Doctor: (tel. 11510 day, 21230 night).

U.S. Embassy: Laufásvegur 21 (tel. 29100).

American Library: Neshaga 16, just west of the University, part of the U.S. Information Service.

Canadian Consulate: Skúlagata 20 (tel. 25355).

Accommodations

Accommodations cost a lot. Full service hotels begin at $21 for a single or $29 for a double room without bath, shower, or breakfast. Guesthouses are only a few dollars less. The **Viking Guest House,** at Ránargata 12 (tel. 19367) is a good choice at $16 single, $22 double.

Bed and breakfast accommodation is also available at several private homes. Although no list of homes taking guests is issued, the prices are standardized. Singles are $18 and double rooms go for $25, including breakfast. A good opportunity to learn about Icelandic lifestyle. The Iceland Tourist Bureau can provide more information and make the arrangements for you.

Camping is the cheapest way of all to spend your nights in Reykjavík. The official campsite, complete with running hot water and electrical outlets, is located at Sundlaugavegur, adjacent to the Swimming Pool (take bus #5). The nightly charge is 200kr per tent plus 200kr per person. No advance reservations are taken, but you can call for details (tel. 86944).

Youth Hostel (Farfuglaheimili), Laufásvegur 41 (tel. 24950), three minutes from the center, up the street from the U.S. Embassy. The cheapest bed in town at 800kr if you have an IYHF card, 1100kr without. Renting a sleeping sheet costs 300kr more per night. The warden is cheerful and pleased to offer advice. He will also change your travelers checks and sell you an Icelandic sweater. The members' kitchen is a big asset and the hot water never stops steaming. Open 8-11am and 5-11pm, other times it's locked.

Salvation Army Hostel (Hjálpraedisherinn), Kirkjustraeti 2 (tel. 13203). The only reasonably-priced rooms in the city, just one block north of the lake. Singles 3000kr, doubles 4000kr, triples 4700kr. A few rooms are less. The steaming, sulfurous showers are free, and the communal dining hall downstairs serves hearty meals, all you can eat. Breakfast (9-10am) 800kr, lunch (noon-1pm) 1100-1200kr, supper (6:30-7:30pm) 1050kr. Well kept, but located on a noisy corner. The friendly management will advise you and store your luggage while you trek around Iceland.

Food

The only moderately-priced prepared meals are found at the several self-service cafeterias in downtown Reykjavík. One minor relief: tipping is not expected in any Icelandic restaurant. A store-bought meal of bread, cheese, lumpfish caviar, and some *skyr* is cheap and filling.

Kirna, Laugavegur and Klapparstigur streets. A typical Icelandic cafeteria, pleasant and clean with appetizing food. Sandwiches are 480kr and up, meat dishes start at 1490kr. Open 8am-9pm weekdays, 8am-2pm Saturdays.

Skrinan, Skólavördustígur and Bergstadestraeti streets. A slightly fancier cafeteria. Fish 1290-1440kr, egg dishes 630-1370kr, and sandwiches start at 530kr. Open on Sundays.

Matstofa NLFR, Laugavegur 20. A bargain-priced vegetarian restaurant, on the second floor above the grocery. Also the best place for afternoon tea—an enormous pot for 120kr. Salads 300-800kr. Open 11:30am-7pm weekdays only.

Hressingarskálinn, Austurstraeti 20. Central, modern-drab, family style. Not cheap, but comprehensive menu. Dinners 1300-2500kr, omelettes for 1150kr, salads 450kr and up. Waitresses speak little English.

Naust, Vesturgata 6. Expensive, but the right place to go for a seafood splurge. Nautical decor, music, and cocktail lounge, and dance floor. Entrees 2000-6000kr.

Sights

Though Icelanders naturally pride themselves on their austere, modern buildings and monuments, the visitor will probably be more interested in the nation's artistic accomplishments. Within walking distance of the city center are the attractive historical and artistic exhibits of the **National Museum** *(Thjódminjasafnid),* next to the **University** *(Haskolinn)* on Hringbraut. It is stuffed with national artifacts, including the chessboard used in the Fisher-Spassky match of 1973. Unfortunately, all descriptions are in Icelandic only (free entrance, open daily 1:30-4pm). In front of the museum stands the **Nordic House** *(Norraena Hsid),* a joint project of the five Scandinavian nations. The smart coffee shop (open 9am-6pm Mon.-Sat.) features 40 Nordic newspapers, and the ultra-modern library is open to the public (2-7pm weekdays, 2-5pm weekends).

On the other side of the lake is the **Listasafn Einars Jónssonar** which houses the works of Iceland's greatest sculptor, the patriotic and mystical Einar Jónsson (1874-1954). With six over-filled rooms, this museum certainly merits a visit at 50kr (open 1:30-4pm daily). While you're in this part of town, go up the **Tower of Hallgrimskirkja** (weather permitting) for the ultimate view of the city and the mountains to the north. At the top of Skólavördustigur, the tower is open daily 2 to 4pm for 100kr.

The **Kjarvalsstadir** Gallery, situated on Flókagata in the eastern part of the city, displays extensive and well-chosen collections culled from artists around the world. Specializing in modern art, this airy glass and concrete forum often features special exhibits and off-beat concerts. Call for specifics (tel. 26131). Bus #1 gets you there from Laekjartorg, and the hours on weekdays (except Mondays) are 4 to 10pm, weekends 2 to 10pm. Admission cost varies from free to 500kr, depending on the exhibit.

Continuing towards Arbaer, at the edge of the city, you reach the outdoor **Arbaer Folk Museum.** This is an engrossing, if small, collection of traditional buildings, including an old turf farm and church dating from 1842. Admission is 300kr; take bus #4 from the city center to Hlemmur Station, and then catch bus #10 to Rofabaer. From June through August, the exhibit is open from 1 to 6pm (except Mondays). After the summer season, call to arrange a visit (tel. 84412).

The Icelanders love to swim—it's a sign of triumph over the climate. Reykjavík itself maintains two outdoor and one indoor pool facilities. **Laugardalur,** the largest and most popular of these, boasts four hot-water pools and a sauna. In the eastern quarter on Sundlaugavegur, the complex is open from 7:20am to 8:30pm weekdays, 7:20am to 5:30pm Saturdays, and 8am to 5:30pm on Sundays. For 350kr you can have a sauna and a swim; access to the pool alone costs 180kr. Take bus #5 from Laekjartorg Square.

Evenings

Reykjavík is not known for its nightlife, but evenings provide a chance to experience a different—and very prevalent—side of Icelandic living. Beer (*pilsner*) is only 2% alcohol here, but drinking is serious business, and it is not unusual to see patrons dead drunk before midnight. There is little to worry about though—Icelanders get rather happy after a few. The best place to meet these characters is in **Óðal,** a bar and disco with a futuristic interior. Located in the heart of the city at Austurvöllur Square, this spot gets jammed by 10:30pm, especially on weekends. Be sure to try some of the local favorite, *brennivin* ("firewater"), at 400kr a shot—sweet and warm. Cover is 350kr.

Remember also that the swimming pools remain open until mid-evening (8:30pm) on weeknights. The Kjarvalsstadir Gallery closes at 10pm every evening (except Monday).

Daytrips

To make your stay in Iceland really worthwhile, leave Reykjavík and tour the countryside. A day's trip from the city lie glaciers, basalt caves, fjords, historical and saga sites, lakes and wildlife. There is a variety of organized tours available, and while you might be inclined to shy away from that sort of thing in general, Iceland may be the one place on your itinerary where they really make sense. Although, like everything else in Iceland, they're not cheap, they're not substantially more expensive than bus fare alone. Moreover, the non-tourist buses don't stop long enough to let you enjoy the sites—you either rush out to snap a few pictures while your driver gulps his coffee, or linger and find yourself stranded. (There is only one bus per day on most routes.) The tour guides are informative and speak perfect English. The best tour to get a real feel for the Icelandic countryside is probably the nine-hour **Golden Circle Tour.** It costs $20 while non-tourist bus fare for the same route would be about $14. Your only alternative is hitching—but be prepared for long waits in lunar landscapes without any sign of a car. A tent and sleeping bag come in handy here.

All tours run by **Reykjavík Excursions,** including the Golden Circle, pick up passengers at the Hotel Loftleidir, a few other hotels in town, and at Laekjargata 3 (in front of the white building labeled **Gimli**). Information and reservations are available at the Tourist Bureau (tel. 25855) and inside Gimli, at the downtown Reykjavík Excursions Office (tel. 28025). Non-tourist buses leave from the long-distance coach terminal daily at 9am.

Gullfoss, one of the most powerful waterfalls in Europe, thunders away only 120 km to the east of Reykjavík. Bring raingear with you on this trip, as the windswept spray is wetter than it looks. With the right conditions, this spray plays host to a dazzling rainbow. The often washed-out road leads from here directly to the steaming plumes around **Geysir.** Although the

"Great Geysir" (the original spout, hence the name) has puffed itself to death, the world's most active geyser, "Strokkur," continues its 100-foot outbursts. An hour's drive to the west brings you to the green plains of historic **Thingvellír,** stretching to the north of the largest lake in Iceland, **Thingvallavatn.** Besides being the site of the ancient **Althing** (National Assembly), Thingvellír is a geologist's wonderland. About 10,000 years ago, the 5 km-wide plain subsided, creating the awesome **Almannagjá** chasm. An icy blue stream runs along the length of the chasm, and is cluttered with coins tossed in by tourists. The Golden Circle covers all of the above sites, as well as mossy lava fields, craters left behind by now-defunct volcanoes, and Icelandic greenhouses. Bring your own lunch, or opt for the all-you-can-eat halibut luncheon (1700kr).

Those with more time and endurance should make their base camp at craggy Thingvellír. From here you can climb extinct volcanoes for great views, row on windy Lake Laugarvatn and visit the **Húsafell Farm** (camping site and cheap accommodations for those with sleeping bags), 70km distant. From Húsafell visit the nearby **Surtshellir Caves** or the more distant **Reykholt,** home of the great thirteenth-century saga-writer and historian Snorri Sturluson. From Reykholt you can either complete a circle, returning to Reykjavík via the large coastal road, or turn north to Isafjörthur or Akureyri.

Shaggy, docile Icelandic ponies afford the most interesting transportation for short day trips. The Icelandic Tourist Bureau runs a three-hour pony trek (twice daily) for $20, including transfer from and back to Reykjavík. In addition, there are a number of pony farms offering guided tours (many suitable for beginners) and accommodations during the summer months. Inquire at the Tourist Bureau.

For the ski bum, Iceland offers some not-so-cheap thrills year round. The ski school at **Kerlingarfjöll** offers week-long packages with all the trimmings, including equipment rentals. Bookings can be made through Úrval Travel Agency at Pósthússtraeti 2.

The Vestmann Islands (Vestmannaeyjar)

Heimaey, "the Pompeii of the North," survives, despite volcanic catastrophes, as the only inhabited Vestmann Island. In 1973 an eruption sent all of its 5300 inhabitants scrambling to the mainland. The flow was finally halted after five months by pumping 5.5 million tons of seawater onto the eastern part of the island. Although several hundred buildings were buried in ashes, recovery has been startling; the villagers are currently devising ways to harness energy from the crusty slopes to heat their homes.

Icelandair runs three flights a day from Reykjavík to Vestmannaeyjar in the summer (5470kr for the 25-minute trip). There is also a bus that leaves the long-distance coach station in Reykjavík daily at 12:30pm (700kr), connecting with the ferry at **Thorlákshöfn.** The three-hour crossing can be deadly when the winds act up, and for 2500kr one way, it hardly pays to suffer.

The entire island of Heimaey can be toured on foot in a day. Wander through the gray mounds of lava rising to the east of the town, and follow one of the footpaths to the top of **Eldfell** ("Fire Mountain") for the awe-inspiring view of the harbor. Continue skirting the village, passing **Helgafell** ("Mount Holy"), a volcano that erupted around 3000 B.C. Each year, in the beginning of August, the villagers gather in the lush **Herjólfsdalur Valley** for a three-day festival.

A **Youth Hostel,** (IYHF) is located at Höfdaveg 25, about 1.5 km up Heidarvagur from the harbor. You can prepare your own meal in the large members' kitchen. Otherwise, there is a cafeteria on the ground floor of the **Hotel Vestmannaeyjar,** corner of Vestmannabraut.

The Western Fjords (Vestfirdir)

Jutting like a huge claw into the Greenland sea, **Vestfirdir** was for years largely isolated. For those wishing to escape the "crowds" of Reykjavík, this stark and rugged land is worth the effort.

Ísafjördur, its main township, is a rapidly industrializing port, run-down and dirty. The cheapest rooms and food are to be found at the **Salvation Army,** Managata 4. There is a well-situated camping site 3 km out of town, at **Tungudalur.**

Transportation can be a problem here, especially in the uninhabited extreme north. Ferries are often the quickest and most reliable way of getting about the peninsula. Spectacular fjords can be seen even in a one-day excursion. The ferry tour of the Ísafjardardjúp inlet, leaving Ísafjördur Harbor early in the morning, passes some of the remotest farms in Iceland. Buses run irregularly throughout the central region of Vestfirdir. During the summer two flights daily connect Reykjavík and Ísafjördur (7630kr one way).

Akureyri and the Mývatn District

Because of its strategic position as capital of the north, **Akureyri** is the second most important city in Iceland. It is breathtakingly set at the head of the great **Eyjafjördur,** nestled between snow-capped basalt mountains in one of the most fertile valleys in all of Iceland. Although 100 miles closer to the Arctic Circle than Reykjavík, Akureyri's climate is generally drier and more pleasant. The city is most easily reached by Icelandair, with 55-minute flights departing Reykjavík Airport six times daily. The one-way fare is 7990kr, not much more than the day-long bus trip (6500kr). Although the regular commerce between Akureyri and Reykjavík makes hitching relatively easy, plan on a full-day trip, and be prepared for variable weather.

Akureyri itself boasts five museums. There is also a **botanical park** complete with every species known to grow in Iceland. You can see the sights in just a few hours, then go for a swim at the **municipal pool** on Thingvallastraeti, and float beneath the snow-capped peaks.

The cheapest place to stay in Akureyri is the **campground** on Thorunnarstraeti, right in the heart of town next to the swimming pool. The IYHF **Youth Hostel,** Stórholt 1 (tel. 23657), is not as well-kept as the one in Reykjavík, but it is less restrictive. Open all day, with small rooms holding two to four people. About 2 km out of the center, but only 800kr per night. The cheapest rooms are available at the **Hotel Edda** on Hrafnagilsstraeti, which has a limited number of sleeping-bag accommodations in singles and doubles for about $8 per person.

If you stay in the hostel, you should buy some fresh fish from the **KEA** market in the main square, **Radhustorg,** and prepare it yourself at the hostel. Alternatively, try the **Matstofa KEA Cafeteria** at Hafnarstraeti and Kaupvangsstraeti: a simple but good place filled with locals at lunchtime.

Akureyri makes a good base to explore the unmatched scenery around **Lake Mývatn.** The first Apollo astronauts trained here because of its similarity to the moon's surface. Strange lava formations known as black castles spring up near intensely active geothermal fields, which are being harnessed to produce electricity. Two hundred minor earthquakes are recorded in this region each day, while major tremors have recently opened large gaps in the earth's surface. In underground caverns you can soak in hot pools; elsewhere boiling, sulfurous pits bubble in the middle of plains. The bus from Akureyri leaves daily at 8:15am from the center of town and returns from Mývatn at 4pm.

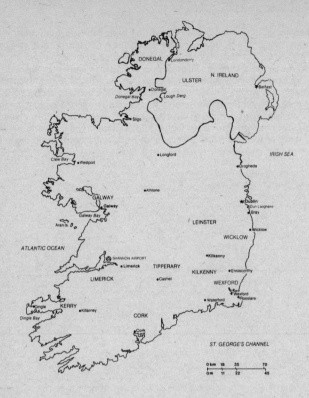

IRELAND

$1U.S.=£.548   **£1=$2.07**

  Ireland was for centuries the mysterious western fringe of the known world. Haven for hermits, rebels, and adventurers, this island, only 64 miles away from Britain across the Irish Sea, remained a land with its own lawless freedom despite the efforts of wave after wave of conquerors. The hills and fields have not yet lost their magic even under the influence of commercialization; Eire seems likely to elude the impositions of tourism as it did those of the English—by refusing to cooperate. The country is still notorious for ruining timetables, itineraries, and pennypinchers.

  Don't fight the gray and green seduction. Allow Ireland to see you on its own terms—the unplanned day in the **Donegal highlands** or on the **Galway coast,** in the near-tropical verdure of the **Ring of Kerry** or in the **Dublin** streets which Leopold Bloom walked (in *Ulysses*) and made famous—those will be the days you will remember.

ORIENTATION

The Republic of Ireland (known as Eire) is divided into some twenty-six counties, whose names are usually taken from their largest town. Ireland is most interesting where its green earth meets the gray sea, so a good plan is to follow the coast. Begin in Dublin, the capital, and head south around the island until you reach Donegal in the northwest. No point in Ireland is more than 70 miles from the sea, so side trips into the rolling midlands or the lake country are easy. If you have only a limited number of days and want to sample Ireland at its gray and rocky peat-smoked bones, go straight to the *Gaeltacht* ("Irish speaking area") west of Galway city where the traditional language, Irish Gaelic, is still the first language of the people, road signs, and shopfronts, and where little has changed in fifty years. The Irish have always been a rural people—in early times they favored small, self-sufficient fortified sites scattered over the land. Most major Irish cities exist today compliments of the Vikings **(Dublin, Waterford, Limerick),** the Normans **(Kilkenny, Galway),** and the English, and the urban scene is characteristically devoid of Continental excitement. Instead, capitalize on the countryside—you'll save money, and meet the Irish in the process.

Before you leave, check out *The Shell Guide to Ireland* by Lord Killanin and Michael V. Duignan. It is crammed with information on everything you would ever want to know about matters archaeological, historical, and cultural, and includes a helpful set of gridded maps. Literary types are urged to comb through the section on Dublin. For all the tumble-down castles you may see, the Irish government maintains an extensive number of historical and archaeological sites. Discreetly signposted, they are easy to overlook unless you have the *Guide to the National Monuments of Ireland* by Peter Harbison, available at tourist offices and book shops for £4.25. He will even tell you if you have to jump over a ditch, cross a field with a cow watching you suspiciously, or ask for a key from the man in the pub.

The **Irish Tourist Board** *(Bord Failte Eireann)* operates a network of 88 tourist information offices throughout the country. They can be extremely helpful in booking accommodations and supplying regional information, town maps, and schedules of weekly attractions and local events. On arrival, find the nearest tourist office and pick up the following: *List of Official Tourist Information Offices and Room Reservation Services,* which gives you addresses, phone numbers, and hours (usually 9:30am-6pm daily in June; until 9pm in July and August) for all tourist offices throughout the country (always identified by a green and white "i"); *Official Guide to Hotels and Guesthouses; Official Guide to Town and Country Homes and Farmhouses,* an invaluable guide for foraging in the countryside; and an annual *Calendar of Events,* lest you inadvertently miss out on a good time at the **Connemara Pony Show,** or **Puck Fair,** or the **Galway Oyster Festival.** *Land of Youth* describes discounts and youth-oriented accommodations and activities. You will also want to pick up a good map—the Tourist Board issues one at 60p.

Ireland's 48 IYHF Youth Hostels range from barracks to converted country houses. They supply beds and bedding, cooking facilities, and charge 70p-£1.15 a night, depending on your age, the hostel, and the season. You'll need an International Youth Hostel Card, which you can buy in Ireland for about £5. Unfortunately, many hostels are out of the way and irritatingly hard to get to, especially if you're hitching. The most convenient plan is to combine hostelling with guesthouses. Usually signaled by a "B&B" sign, these offer bed-and-breakfast for about £3-4. Even better than guesthouses for meeting the Irish and seeing the country are the farmhouse B&Bs, working farms a mile or two off the main road.

GETTING THERE AND GETTING AROUND

Between Ireland and Britain or the Continents a myriad of ferry routes offer the cheapest access. **B&I,** The Irish company, makes daily runs between Liverpool and Dublin, and between Swansea and Cork. Students who purchase tickets through **USIT** (52 Grosvenor Gardens, near Victoria Station, London SW1; tel. 01-730-8111) are entitled to a 25% discount on the $19-22 one-way B&I fare.

British Rail Sealink's one way fares from Wales—Holyhead to Dublin, and Fishguard to Rosslare—are $15-17. The **Irish Continental Line** ship between Le Havre (France) and Rosslare costs $42 for a reclining seat on board.

C.I.E., the Irish Transport System, runs a network of train and bus services to the major cities and towns, as well as tours and cruises on the River Shannon. Rail fares are fairly expensive (e.g. Dublin-Cork, £9.35 one way) so you should look into **Rambler Tickets,** good for 8 days of second-class rail travel, for $33; 8 days or rail and/or bus, $42; 15 days rail, $48; or 15 days rail and road, $60. Students and those aged 15-26 can buy **Youth Rambler Tickets** (valid on trains and buses) for 8 days, $35; 15 days, $50; or 30 days $65. The Youth Rambler tickets must be purchased outside of Ireland. In the U.S. contact **C.I.E. Tours,** 178 Forbes Rd., Braintree, MA 02184. Students with ISIC cards can buy a **C.I.E. Travelsave Stamp** from USIT in London or Dublin for £2; affixed to your ISIC card, it entitles you to a 50% discount on all rail and bus travel in Ireland (except on local buses costing less than £1).

Bicycles are available throughout the country—**Raleigh "Rent-a-Bike"** offers a durable three-speed model for about £1.75 a day (£10 a week) plus a deposit of £10. Of course, you can always ask about renting a bike at the nearest tourist office, or at your guesthouse.

As for hitching, you may never discover a safer place than Ireland. As long as you choose major well-traveled roads, and never presume to go further than twenty miles up the road at a time, you should have no problems.

If you are an incurable romantic, and happen to have three or so friends just like you, the **horse-drawn caravan** is for you. You will see Ireland in slow-motion from a barrel-shaped wagon, equipped with four bunks, utensils, stove, and lamps, and pulled by a stolid, dependable horse (i.e., he can take care of himself). Prices range from £60 a week in low season to £90 a week in peak season (mid-June-September 30) and you may want to reserve ahead. Any tourist office can give you a list of caravan agencies.

The basics of Irish food—wholemeal bread, porridge, potatoes, milk, and fresh fish—are all tasty and filling, though the routine gets tedious. Alternatives are similar to England's: fish-and-chips, Chinese or Indian food, pub grub (safest). The best way to eat cheaply is to do as the Irish do—eat a large breakfast, have a meal at midday, and just have tea in the evening, with sandwiches. Restaurants are usually geared to this schedule, closing around 8pm in all but the largest cities. You can also eat in pubs, at your guesthouse (ask your host) or, cheapest of all, buy food from shops.

Ireland's wonderful pubs embody the Irish ethos of generosity, lively talk, and good spirits. Their only drawback, aside from the fact that they are required to close at 11:30pm (earlier on Sundays) is that women are not welcome to share what is still considered male entertainment. Unless you have a male escort, or are in a student pub in one of the larger cities, women are segregated by unspoken rules in "lounge bars." Don't be surprised at cold stares if you walk into a local hangout (but we encourage you to try it anyway). The standard Irish beer is *Guinness,* a rich, dark brown stout you may not like at first. Try building up to it with a pint of light Harp lager and then follow it, as the Irish do, with a whiskey chaser.

Linger and listen to the lilts of conversation: some of the country's best literature hangs in the smoky air. Seek out a singing pub, where groups of varied talents perform traditional music, folk songs, etc. While most of these are now for the tourists, you can still find some that play Irish music for the natives too. In the larger towns, pubs also host jazz concerts, theater, poetry readings, etc.

MISCELLANEOUS INFORMATION

The weather is traditionally fickle, from the low 50s to the upper 60s even in summer, and can be damp and chilly (which explains all that hot tea drinking). Have a rain poncho or fold-up umbrella in your survival kit and include a warm sweater (or buy a *báinín* sweater, the rich cream-colored Irish fisherman handknit at bargain prices). The green-fronted post office is always labeled in Irish—*Oifig an Phoist.* English money and Irish money are not mutually interchangeable—cash in your Irish pounds when you leave Ireland, since they are not negotiable in England. August 1 is a **bank holiday,** and everything will close up coast to coast; beware also of half-days in the towns, one day during the work week when business ends at lunchtime.

Dublin

Dublin has seen the drama of Irish history played on its streets since ancient times, when it was just a ford on the **River Liffey** along the road to Tara, the ancient religious center. The Irish called it (and still do) *Baile Atha Cliath* ("the town of the hurdle ford"), but such peaceful beginnings were to give way to the tumults of Viking raids and bloody struggles for Irish independence. Today, the eighteenth-century Georgian charm of the city is decaying under the grime of modern life. (Dublin comes from *Dubhlinn,* or "dark pool," and you may find this name accurate.) But don't be discouraged; with a bit of poking into corners, you can still discover James Joyce's beloved "strumpet city in the sunset" on the banks of Anna Livia's (Liffey's) Guinness-brown water.

To enter Dublin from its **Airport,** six miles north of the city, take either the special direct coach to **Busarus,** the **Central Bus Station** just behind the Customs House (80p), or local bus #41A to "An Lár" (Gaelic for "city center"). If you arrive by ferry at **Dún Laoghaire,** nine miles south of the city, take the train from the pier to Connolly Station, Amiens Street, or bus #7, 7A, or 8 to O'Connell Bridge in the center of town. The B & I Ferry from Liverpool arrives at **Dublin Ferryport,** on the eastern fringe of the city on Alexandra Road; several buses run between the city center and this point.

To head out of Dublin into the countryside, you can catch provincial buses at Busarus Station for all points as well as trains from Dublin's three main railway stations: **Connolly Station** in Amiens Street; **Heuston Station,** Kingsbridge; and **Pearse Street Station. Corás Iompar Éireann** (C.I.E.), the national transport company, operates nearly all buses and trains both in Dublin and the rest of Ireland, and can tell you how to get to where from where (tel. 787777). Buses leaving from Aston Quay can take you to the fringes of the city where you can begin hitchhiking.

Most everything of interest in Dublin lies south of the River Liffey. The city center runs from the top of **O'Connell Street** (Dublin's main drag), across **O'Connell Bridge** (*the* center of Dublin), and down to the bottom of **Grafton Street** (the main shopping street) at St. Stephen's Green. Bus fares start at 12p, but the essential city is best—and without much difficulty—seen on foot. For longer stays, students can buy a transit pass for Dublin and environs: two weeks for £6, three weeks for £9, from the **Tourist Office** at 51 Dawson St.

Addresses and Telephone Numbers

Tourist Information Offices: 14 Upper O'Connell St. (tel. 747733). Open in summer 8:30-7:30pm Mon.-Sat., 10am-5pm Sun.; rest of the year 9:15am-5:15pm Mon.-Sat. only. Also at 51 Dawson St. (same phone). Open 9:15am-5:15pm Mon.-Fri.; and at Dublin Airport Arrivals, open daily in summer 8:30am-10pm, rest of the year 9:30am-5:30pm. All three will book accommodations.

USIT (Irish Student Travel Agency): 7 Anglesea St. (tel. 778117). Quite helpful; information on student travel, jobs, events, and accommodations. Next door is the **Union of Students** (tel. 710622).

An Óige (Irish Youth Hostel Association): 39 Mountjoy Square (tel. 745734).

American Express: 116 Grafton St. (tel. 772874). Across from Trinity College. Open Mon.-Fri. 9am-5:15pm, Sat. 9am-noon.

GPO (Post Office): In the center of O'Connell St. Open until 11pm including Sundays.

C.I.E. (National Transport Company): 59 Upper O'Connell St., across the street from the Tourist Office. Call 787777 for information. Open 9am-9pm daily.

Taxis: Tels. 766666, 761111, and 772222.

Thomas Cook Travel: 118 Grafton St.

American Embassy: 42 Elgin Rd., Ballsbridge (tel. 688777).

Canadian Embassy: 65/68 St. Stephen's Green (tel. 781988).

Cycle Hire: McHugh Himself, 38 Talbot St. (tel. 746694) and many more; check with Tourist Office.

Accommodations

The Tourist Office's excellent booking service costs only 30p. Especially during the summer, they will save you time and phone calls by finding you a place in an approved home, guest house, or hotel.

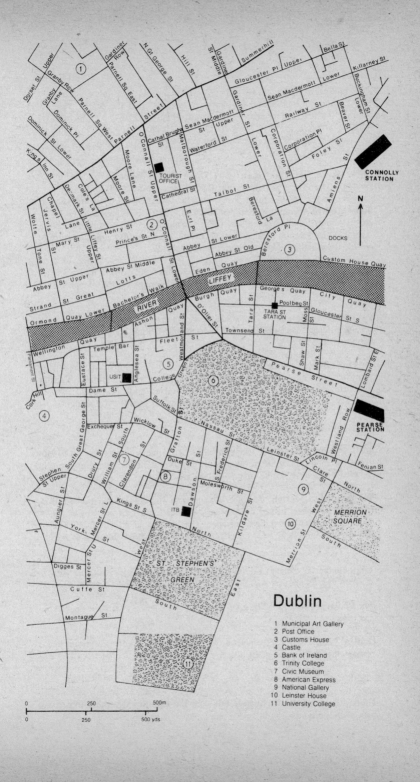

Dublin

1 Municipal Art Gallery
2 Post Office
3 Customs House
4 Castle
5 Bank of Ireland
6 Trinity College
7 Civic Museum
8 American Express
9 National Gallery
10 Leinster House
11 University College

N

CONNOLLY STATION

TARA ST STATION

PEARSE STATION

TOURIST OFFICE

USIT

ITB

LIFFEY

RIVER

DOCKS

Custom House Quay

MERRION SQUARE

ST STEPHEN'S GREEN

0   250   500m

0   250   500 yds

Hostels

Morehampton House (IYHF), 78 Morehampton Rd., Donnybrook (tel. 680325). Large, well-served by buses, 10 minutes from the center. More centrally located and smaller is the **Youth Hostel (IYHF)**, 39 Mountjoy Square South (tel. 745734). These An Óige hostels charge about £1.15 in July and August, 10p less other months; you may have trouble leaving your baggage here during the day.

Liffey House, 5 Beresford Place; and **I.S.A.A.C.,** 2-4 Frenchman's Lane (tel. 744641). The first is a combination B&B/student hostel with bunks in the dorms costing £2.50 per night; just around the corner, the 300-bed **International Student Accommodation/Activity Center** is under reconstruction from ancient warehouse to glorified hostel. £2.50 a night, £2 with your own sleeping bag. Great location, behind Customs House, but very noisy with trains just outside the windows. Not strictly limited to students.

YWCA, 64 Lower Leeson St. (tel. 766273). For men and women. B&B £3 in singles, £2.50 per person in doubles. Special weekly rates. Near St. Stephen's Green.

YWCA, Radcliff Hall, St. John's Road, Sandymount (tel. 694521). £3.50 per person in singles and doubles, bed and breakfast. Some rooms with bath. Service charge 10%.

The **Halls of Residence** at Trinity College offer Bed and Breakfast during the summer, but they are usually booked way in advance. But try **Trinity Hall,** Dartry Road, Rathmines (tel. 971772). Bed-and-breakfast £3.50 in singles, £3 per person sharing doubles and triples. Mainly for students.

Bed-and-Breakfasts

B&B will run at least £3.50, with baths or showers extra. Try not to stay far from the city center; since buses stop running at 11:30, late nights on the town will mean long walks or costly taxi rides.

Burstenshaw's Marian, 21 Upper Gardiner St. (tel. 744129) is the best of four excellent guest houses on the same street, all about £4 per person, all popular, and worth booking in advance. The **Viona** is at #11 (tel. 748384). The **Stella Maris** is at #13 (tel. 740835), and the **Carmel House** is at #16 (tel. 741639).

Eagle Lodge, 12 Clontarf Rd. (tel. 336009). A fine, well-kept old house with many rooms, £4 per person. Take bus #30 or 44A. A few doors down at #8 is

The Boulevard (tel. 339524), small, friendly, and £3.50 per person in doubles and triples.

Golden Vale, 13 Upper Pembroke St. (tel. 766653). £4.50 per person in perhaps the city's nicest guest house.

Hotels

There are a number of cheap hotels near the Bus Station; more expensive

and safer hotels are found near the quays west of O'Connell St. Those listed
below offer good value.

Kelly's Hotel, 36 South Great George's St. (tel. 779277). Big, clean rooms;
singles at £4.50, doubles £8.50, breakfast extra. Meals available in dining
room; cheap lunches. Quite convenient.

Mount Herbert Guesthouse, 7 Herbert Rd. (tel. 684321). £4.85 per person in
singles and doubles, cheaper in winter. Modern, highly popular. 88 rooms, 77
with bath (£1.35 extra).

Hollybrook Hotel, Howth Rd. (tel. 336623). £4.50 per person, with bath £1
extra. Breakfast not included (70p extra). Large, plush place in quiet
neighborhood.

Food

Pubs serve filling, enjoyable lunches. For £1 or less, try **Stag's Head,** 1
Dame Court or the **Lord Edward,** near Christ Church Cathedral. The
cafeterias at **Trinity College** and **University College** have inexpensive self-
service meals, as does **Bewleys** (in Grafton Street, South Great George's
Street, and Westmoreland Street), a chain of traditional coffee and tea shops.
For lunch or dinner try **Gaj's** in Lower Baggot St., a popular student place
with a nice dining room, good menu, and meals from 80p.

Country Shop, 23 St. Stephen's Green North, is run by the Irish Country-
women's Association and serves good country food for low prices.

The Granary, 34-36 East Essex St. (next to Project Arts Center). Cold and hot
buffet, homemade breads. Popular with the local business crowd. Excellent
value; meals £1.50 and up.

The Golden Dawn, 2 Crow St. (off Dame St.). Good and interesting vegetarian meals; quite inexpensive main dishes around £1. Closed Sundays. Another
vegetarian restaurant which is open Sundays is the **Supernatural Tea Rooms,**
53 Harcourt St. (closed Mondays).

The Tandoori Rooms and **The Golden Orient** are two Indian restaurants,
both at 27 Lower Leeson St. (southeast of St. Stephen's Green; tel. 762286).
The first is extremely elegant and highly acclaimed, with main courses around
£7 (call for reservations). The second is good, with curries at around £2.25.

Joyce's "hot reeking public-houses" still exist; **Davy Byrne's** in Duke
Street has become a bit expensive. Inside **The Baily Pub** across the street
you can see the door to #7 Eccles Street, the home of Leopold and Molly
Bloom in *Ulysses*. **Mulligan's** in Poole Beg Street is as crowded as ever.
O'Donoghue's in Merrion Row is something of a Dublin legend and must be
seen; elbow your way through the crowd to hear some of the best traditional
music in the country. Nearby, **Nesbitts,** the **Baggot Inn,** and **Toner's** are all
worth a visit, or try the student pubs like **MacDermotts, O'Dwyers,** and
Hartigans in Lower Leeson Street, or the journalists' pubs like the **Pearl
Bar** and the **Fleet Bar** in Fleet Street near the **Irish Times** offices. The
Brazen Head, in Bridge Street off Usher's Quay, is Dublin's—and perhaps
Ireland's—oldest public-house; its license dates from the beginning of

licensing under Charles II in 1666 and its interior looks every day as old—
some say it's even older.

Sights

If the traffic and neon of O'Connell St. jangle your senses, escape to **St. Stephen's Green** at the bottom of Grafton St. to find 22 acres of lawns, fountains, statues, and bright flowerbeds. You won't meet Joyce's Stephen Dedalus (look around the corner at what was once **University College**), but you can watch the children play, rest your feet, and eat your lunch. At the top of Grafton St. is **College Green** (no greenery here), where you can slip through the gates and into the quiet cobbled yard of **Trinity College;** while you're here head for the Old Library to see the *Book of Kells,* the wondrous, illuminated manuscript of the eighth century. Open Mon.-Fri. 10am-5pm, Sat. 10am-1pm, admission free. Cross College Green to see the **Parliament House** whose bold, pillared façade (now being restored) embodies Dublin's unique approach to Georgian architecture; it is also a symbol of the growth of Irish independence in the eighteenth century. (The building is now The Bank of Ireland, while the legislature meets in **Leinster House** in Kildare St.)

A tour around the classical buildings of Dublin might include: the residences on St. Stephen's Green, **Ely Place,** and **Merrion Square** (the fashionable street which housed Oscar Wilde behind its brass-knobbed, fan-lit doors); Gandon's **Custom House,** and **Four Courts,** north of the river; and the **General Post Office,** which was glorified as a site of fighting during the Easter Rising of 1916.

Christ Church Cathedral, with its ancient crypt, was once used as a stable by Cromwell. Nearby, Jonathan Swift lies buried in **St. Patrick's Cathedral,** where he was dean from 1713 to 1745. From here go on to thirteenth-century **Dublin Castle,** from which British rule once stretched out over Ireland. The more macabre sort might look in at **St. Michan's** where corpses have lain in the vaults for centuries without decomposing, thanks to a special dry atmosphere; or for a different sort of macabre, visit **Kilmainham Jail,** in whose grim corridors countless Irish patriots were held prisoner and often executed. It was in operation until 1924. Jail and museum open Sundays only, 3-5pm.

To see everything from elaborate Celtic gold ornaments to more artifacts of revolutionary Ireland, visit the **National Museum** in Kildare St. Open Tues.-Fri. 10am-5pm, Sun. 2-5pm, closed Mondays. Just opposite is the **National Library,** and around the corner on Merrion Square is the **National Gallery** where you can see paintings by John Butler Yeats (the poet's father) and an excellent collection of Dutch Old Masters in fine surroundings. Free admission, weekdays 10am-6pm, Sun. 2-5pm, Thurs. until 9pm. At the **Municipal Gallery of Modern Art,** Parnell Square, you can pay your respects to portraits of Yeats, J. M. Synge, and Lady Gregory. Open Tues.-Sat. 10am-6pm, Sun. 11am-2pm, closed Mon. Free admission.

For over two hundred years the **Guinness Brewery** at St. James Gate has brewed and bottled *its* stout, and no other stout or porter, and is now the largest exporting brewery in the world. You can see a film of the operation (tours canceled indefinitely) and sample a half-pint or two (or three) of the product for free. Open Mon.-Fri. 10am-3pm; take bus #21 or 78 from the city center.

For wide open spaces, lakes, and a zoo, there's the 1800-acre **Phoenix Park** on the western fringe of the city. The residence of the President of Ireland is on the grounds.

Hop on bus #8 from College Green (with a *Ulysses* map in hand—get one from the Tourist Office) and ride eight miles south to **Sandycove** to visit

Joyce's **Martello Tower** and **Museum** and cool off in the sea breeze. Open 10am-1pm and 2-5pm in summer (15p students; 20p non-students).

If you are lucky enough to be in Dublin on June 16, try to fall in with a crowd celebrating **Bloomsday,** the day on which Joyce's *Ulysses* takes place. Start with kidneys for breakfast (in the tradition of Leopold Bloom), and set off on his marathon day-long odyssey across the city, in and out of pubs, stores, and perhaps even a couple of "houses" in **Nighttown.** The entire walk is likely to take more or less thirty hours (with the appropriate drinking and debauching), but you will fall into bed more than a mere visitor to Joyce's city.

Evenings

One of the most rewarding ways to spend an evening in Dublin is to see a play at the famous **Abbey Theatre** on Lower Abbey St. Downstairs is the more experimental **Peacock** theater. The magazine *In Dublin* or the evening papers can tell you what's playing at the **Gaiety,** South King St., the **Gate** on Parnell Square, the **Olympic** on Dame St., or—for a variety of experimental entertainment—**The Project Arts Centre** in East Essex St.

If you fancy authentic Irish traditional music, go to **O'Donoghue's** in Merrion Row, **Slattery's** in Capel St., or The **Stag's Head** off Dame St.; all three pubs have great music and big crowds, particularly on weekends. Or try **Comhaltas Ceoltoiri Eireann,** the traditional music society of Ireland which runs frequent sessions at its headquarters at 32 Belgrave Square, Monkstown (bus #7A or 8 from O'Connell St.). Give them a call (tel. 800-295) to find out the latest on sessions around town.

The **Dandelion Market** (through the Gaiety Green Arcade on the west side of St. Stephen's Green, open Saturdays and Sundays) is the place to buy "hip" clothing, leather work, jewelry, used books, junk, and drugs. In the evenings, especially on weekends, the scene moves into cinemas, pubs, discos, and clubs. Some discos will ask for a membership fee in addition to the admission, but you should not have to pay more than £1.75 or £2. Highly popular and trendy is **Lord John's Knight Club,** 14 Sackville Place (off O'Connell St.); also try **Sloopy's,** Fleet St., and **Zhivago's,** Baggot St. They're open and licensed from around 10pm to 2:30 or 3am, but the pace picks up only after the pubs close at 11:30.

Near Dublin

Two places near Dublin are particularly worth visiting, the first as a daytrip and the second for a few leisurely days. **Howth** lies on the rocky headland which forms the northern arm around Dublin Bay. Bus #31 will take you from Abbey Street (30p for thirty minutes) to **Howth Castle** and environs, whose lush rhododendron gardens are worth a stroll. High above the old fishing village is the **Hill of Howth,** where cliffs fall to the sea on all sides and a path goes right around the edge—a magnificent walk.

North of Dublin, near Drogheda, the **Boyne Valley** is a region rich in farmland and in remains from all eras of history. Take your time here and walk the peaceful country lanes—you have no choice since there's little in the way of public transport. The **Mellifont Youth Hostel** (IYHF) is actually within the grounds of the ruins of **Mellifont Abbey,** the first Cistercian monastery in Ireland. Early in the morning, stand near the graceful arches of the octagonal lavabo, and in the half-light you can almost see the monks filing silently to prayer. A few miles northeast is **Monasterboice,** an ancient monastic settlement with a round tower and some beautifully carved high crosses. To the south you enter the twilight of the mysterious passage-grave builders of Neolithic times: the chambered tomb at **Newgrange,** with its spiral-carved stones, is one of the most famous prehistoric sites in Europe; similar tombs at **Knowth** and **Dowth** have yet to be fully excavated. Further along the Boyne, near the Bridge of Boyne Hostel, is **Slane Hill,** where St. Patrick kindled his Paschal fire in 433 proclaiming Christianity throughout the land; from the hill one has a sweeping view of the whole region. Also nearby is **Tara Hill,** the ancient religious center of the kings of Ireland.

Southeast

County Wicklow

The road into Wicklow is a hitcher's dream, full of cars and unforgettable scenery. You could spend a day hitching from Dublin and back—to get out of the city, take bus #8 from Eden Quay to Dalkey and the Wexford Road, or for a more inland route, #51, 68, or 69 from Aston Quay to the Cork Road. As you pass through **Dun Laoghaire,** take a look at **Bulloch Castle,** a twelfth-century fort overlooking the harbor (open weekends, 2-5pm; admission 25p). Farther along the Vico Road are the villages of **Dalkey** and **Killiney** (you can get a boat to **Dalkey Island** from Coliemore Harbor for about 30p) and past them, the cliff of **Bray Head.** From the top (there's a chair lift) the view is spectacular.

The Tourist Office on Dublin Road (tel. 867128) can find you a room in **Bray** if you want to explore the surrounding area to the south and west. **Misses Loughlin,** Tig Muire, Meath Road (tel. 863952), run a large B&B (fifteen rooms) where the price is £3.25 per person. **Mrs. P. O'Brien,** Convent Avenue, at the same price, is the least expensive of the B&Bs along the Esplanade.

A few miles to the west of Bray, you can visit the 14,000 acres of the **Powerscourt Desmesne,** whose Italian and Japanese gardens include the tallest waterfall in Ireland. More natural spectacles in the area include the **Glen of the Dargle,** a woody, romantic valley. Wind onwards through desolately beautiful hills into the **Sally Gap,** through **Roundwood,** and finally to **Glendalough,** a dark pine-tree-lined valley cradling two silver lakes and the ruins of a monastic settlement. Here the sixth-century hermit St. Kevin founded a school to which scholars flocked from all over the continent.

There are small, rather basic Youth Hostels at **Glencree** (tel. Dublin 867290) and **Glenmalure** (no telephone); better ones are at **Tiglin** (tel. Wicklow 4259); **Glendalough** (tel. 5143), **Aghavannagh** (tel. 6102), and **Baltyboys,** near Blessington. Alternatively, you can stay in **Wicklow** town, which is a dull but convenient stop. With eight rooms, **Mrs. A. O'Reilly's** B&B on Church Hill (tel. 2718) is the largest in town; £3.25 per person. **Mrs. J. O'Shea,** at 2 Summer Hill (tel. 2418) charges £3.50 per person in double rooms for B&B.

County Wexford

The weather is mild and sunny around Wexford and there are miles of uncrowded beaches, especially along the southern coast near Kilmore Quay. Every afternoon, a boat does a three-mile run to the **Saltee Islands,** Ireland's largest bird sanctuary, where you can picnic and watch the puffins, razor-bills, and kittiwakes. If you're too early for the **Wexford Festival of Opera** in October, Waterford offers a **Festival of Light Opera** in September with amateurs from all Britain competing.

Wexford town is pretty, but it's hard to find a room, especially when a festival is on. The Tourist Office on Crescent Quay (tel. 23111) will help you out. Open daily except Sundays, 9:30am-5pm. **Mrs. A. McKeown's** B&B is a bit noisy, but it's pleasant and the cheapest in town at £2; Hazelmere, St. John's Road (tel. 23637). **Mrs. S. Doyle,** in Cnoc Mhuire, St. John's Avenue (tel. 23097) is in a good B&B hunting ground; she charges £2.25 per person. For a splurge, go to **Whitford House,** a small hotel on New Line Road (tel. 23405), about two miles out of town along Duncannon Road. Summer prices are £4.60 for a single, £9 for a double, but the rooms are large and there's an indoor heated pool. Low season prices are £3.50 and £7 respectively. The **Crown Bar,** also called "The Armory", on Monch St., is the finest pub in town. Check out the excellent collection of ancient weapons in the lounge room.

The **Strawberry Fair** in **Enniscorthy** during the first week in July is an excuse for dancing, drinking and sports. The Tourist Office in Enniscorthy (open summer only) can book you a room. It's located just off the **Abbey Square,** near the Norman castle. On the borders of the Boro River near Enniscorthy are the picturesque ruins of **Wilton Castle** and **Castleboro.**

County Kilkenny and County Tipperary

Skip **Waterford,** with its glass factory, and the **JFK Memorial Park** near New Ross (both full of American tourists spending money and/or searching for memories) and continue along the River Nore. Near the lovely village of **Inistioge** are the ruins of **Jerpoint Abbey** (admission 20p), and the villages farther down the river are quiet and charming.

Kilkenny is ruled over by **Castle Ormond,** in whose converted stables the artisans of the **National Design Centre** have set up a workshop to display and sell pottery, silver and textiles—expensive, but worth a look. In town, the old stone houses and churches scattered through the streets blend centuries together. Stop by **Rothe House,** A Tudor mansion, now a small museum (open 10:30am-12:30pm, and 3-5pm weekdays, Sundays 3-5pm, admission 20p, 15p with Student ID), and **Kyteler's Inn,** home of Dame Alice Kyteler—accused of witchcraft after surviving four husbands, she disappeared from her cell the night before her burning. Unfortunately, the Kilkenny Beer Festival has been discontinued, but the last week in August is the **Kilkenny Arts Week,** with concerts, recitals, and poetry readings.

Located at No. 1 The Parade, the Tourist Office (tel. 21755) supplies information on the area and room-finding assistance. **Miss S. C. Coogan,** 26 James St. (tel. 21954) offers pleasant B&B for £3.25. If you can get there, the nicest place to stay is at **Mrs. McNeary's,** Tara Farmhouse, Troyswood, Freshford Road (tel. 27619), three miles from Kilkenny in the Nore Valley; £4 per person, but with a good breakfast. The Kilkenny IYHF **Youth Hostel** is in Jenkinstown, near Ballyragget (tel. 27674), occupying the sixteenth-century Foulksrath Castle.

Cashel, about thirty miles away in County Tipperary, was the hub of the civil and ecclesiastical life of medieval Munster. The **Rock of Cashel,** a dark limestone outcrop rising some 300 feet above the plain north of town, marks the seat of the southern kings of Ireland. The complex of ruined churches that remain are haunting; **Cormac's Chapel** most of all. You can stay in Cashel town, but **Clonmel,** to the south, has better accommodations.

Southwest

County Cork

Perhaps the gentlest green county of Ireland, **Cork** stretches down the coast through coves, hills and fishing villages. Come over the **Knockmealdown** mountains by the Vee Road, stopping in **Lismore,** with its castle built by Bad King John.

Though the oft-sung "lovely River Lee" is now an open sewer, **Cork** is the exception to the rule about dismal Irish cities. The church-filled town grew up around a monastery founded by St. Finbarr in the 500s—the only churches that now merit attention, however, are the Gothic **Cathedral of St. Finbarr** and **St. Anne's Shandon,** for the view from the tower and the two-hundred-year-old bells—which you can play for 20p.

Cork hosts the well-attended **International Film Festival** in early June—it lasts a week, so get a schedule at the Tourist Office. The smaller **Choral and Folkdance Festival** takes place at the very beginning of May. But there's always lots going on here. Buy the *Evening Echo* to see what's playing at the **Opera House,** where they put on Irish plays in summer. Cork is the place to see hurling matches. Kerry may dominate football, but Cork has been all-Ireland in hurling for years. Matches every Sunday afternoon in summer. Both hurling and Gaelic football are played at **Pairc Ui Chaoimh,** Marina, and **University Grounds,** Mardyke.

Addresses and Telephone Numbers

Irish Tourist Office: 42 Monument Buildings, Grand Parade St. (tel. 23251). One of the nicest in the country. Open Mon.-Fri. 9:15am-5:30pm, Sat. 9:15am-1pm. In July and August, open 9am-9pm.

USIT (Student Travel Office): University College (tel. 23901).

CIE Bus Station: Parnell Place, one block from Patrick's Bridge (tel. 54422). Buses run from Cork to most of the towns along the southern coast which are not reachable by rail. Cork itself has a comprehensive and easy-to-understand bus network which extends out into the suburbs.

CIE Train Station: Kent Station, Lower Glanmire Rd. (tel. 54422).

Cook's: Patrick St.

Bike Rental: Ross and Co., Winthrop St. (tel. 22055), or Harding's 15/17 South Terrace (tel. 23930).

Accommodations and Food

Cork is full of inexpensive B&B's, the greatest concentration being around the University in the Wilton area and along Connaught Avenue, off Donovan's Rd. Take bus #5 or 8. At £2.55 per person, **Mrs. P. Harrington's,** at 69 Wilton Gardens (tel. 41374) is the cheapest B&B around.

Mrs. M. Vaughan, Ouvane House, Connaught Ave. (tel. 21822) has simple, clean rooms for £3.20. The cheap hotels near the Train Station are recommended only as a last resort.

The IYHF **Youth Hostel,** 1-2 Redclyffe, Western Road (tel. 432891) is located near University College; take bus #5 or 8. Very large and quite comfortable, it costs £1.15, £1, and 80p in summer (slightly less in spring and fall).

Arbutus Lodge, Montenotte (at the head of Glanmire Road; tel. 51237), is one of the best restaurants in Ireland, serving rare Irish specialties as well as Continental fare—expect dinner to run at least £7. In an old house overlooking the city. Back down to earth, check out the longshoremen's bars by the docks to find out where Cork got its hard-drinking reputation.

Near Cork

Cork is an ideal base for exploring the south. Avoid **Blarney Castle** unless you've always wanted the gift of gab, and don't mind wrestling with tourists trying to kiss the Blarney Stone (40p). Head for the coast instead.

Kinsale, a fishing town just south of Cork, boasts the twelfth-century church of **St. Multose, Desmond Castle** and **Compass Hill.** Even better views can be had from the **Old Head** of Kinsale, spanned by a castle at its narrowest point. The lighthouse at the end marks the spot where the Lusitania was sunk in 1915. About a mile and a half from Kinsale, at Summer Cove, there is an IYHF **Youth Hostel** (tel. 72309). Or stay farther down the coast in **Clonakilty,** a bright little town which has little to offer but inexpensive accommodations and few tourists. The Tourist Office in Clonakilty is at 7 Ashe St. (Tel. 43226).

Farther along the same beach-filled coast is **Rosscarbery,** a charming village surrounding a tidal inlet. **Mrs. Calnan** (tel. 48149) offers B&B at £3. As you continue southwest the gulf stream begins to warm the beaches—by the time you get to **Skibbereen,** swimming is no longer an arctic adventure. There are daily ferries from nearby Baltimore to **Sherkin Island** and to **Cape Clear Island,** where Gaelic is still spoken and the **Youth Hostel** is described in the hostel book as "the last Youth Hostel in the Old World." The crossings take 45 minutes and cost £1 round trip.

The mountains, lakes, beaches, and ancient ruins of the **Ring of Kerry** is scenically impressive. Queen Victoria loved the area, but so do too many other people these days. To get away from it all, try a trek through the wilds of **Healy Pass,** begun in 1845 as a famine relief project. You may meet only a few workmen trudging the road, sharing with you the mist-hung hill.

Killarney, Ireland's number one tourist city, is situated in the midst of heavenly countryside—but the city is all hassles. Take advantage of the four Youth Hostels in the area: about three miles from Killarney off the Killorglin Road is **Aghadoe House** (tel. 31240), a really comfortable hostel—reservations essential. Farther out in the country are the **Black Valley Hostel,** no tel. (12 miles); **Corrán Tuathail Hostel** (4 miles from Beaufort, 12 miles from Killarney; tel. Beaufort 87); and the **Loo Bridge Hostel** (tel. Clonken 2) at Loo Bridge, 15 miles from Killarney off the main road to Cork. The area is one painter's vista after another—the **Gap of Dunloe** and the **Upper Lake,** in particular, shouldn't be missed.

Dingle is different. The peninsula is one of the surviving Gaeltachts—you'll hear Munster Irish still spoken by the people. In contrast to the crowded green hills of the rest of County Kerry, Dingle's sandy beaches are deserted. The ocean rolls in beneath the walls of clustered stone beehive huts, built without mortar by early hermit monks who enjoyed the solitude. Just offshore are the **Blasket Islands,** inhabited until the mid-fifties and a focus for scholars of the ancient language and storytelling of Ireland. You could start in **Dingle** town and bicycle around the coast—the further west you get, the better it gets.

Northwest of Limerick, in County Clare, is the **Burren,** an eerie, lunar-like landscape of limestone which boasts rare botanical, geological and prehistoric curiosities that have inspired local legend. The **Cliffs of Moher** on the coast fall in a sheer drop hundreds of feet to the Atlantic.

Near **Gort** is **Thoor Ballylee,** the sixteenth-century tower W. B. Yeats restored for his wife in the 20s. The best guide to the area and its ghosts is the poetry he wrote there: *The Tower* and *The Winding Stair* are famous and appropriate. Open 10am-7pm (admission 20p), the tower is indeed, as an old man said, "a poet's place." A few miles away is **Coole House** or, at least, the foundations of Lady Gregory's home, torn down in the '40s. You can still see the long **Yew Walk, Coole Lake,** and the famous **Autograph Tree,** initiated by notables of the Irish Literary Renaissance.

Galway

Galway, gateway to the strange and barren west, is a different color than the rest of Ireland. Grey and green change to purple and pink and silver in the sky and sea, making Galway perhaps the most romantic town in the country. Some of its narrow streets—**Shop St., Middle St., Abbeygate St.,** and **St. Augustine St.**—preserve tantalizing remnants of the exotic days when trade with Spain prospered and wine was brought in on huge merchant ships.

Galway is well worth a leisurely stroll—a Norman port, it was eventually ruled by the "Tribes of Galway," rich Anglo-Norman families who isolated themselves from the natives. Thus a 1518 by-law resolves "that neither O nor Mac shall strutte ne swagger thro' the streets of Galway." As a result of all that English banking and trading, the city enjoyed an educational renais-sance throughout the sixteenth century, boasting the most renowned classical school in the country. Decline followed soon afterwards with the loss of the wine trade. The city now meanders between river and sea, full of old mer-chant houses, odd leaded windows tucked above stone arched doorways, and bits of stone walls.

Addresses and Telephone Numbers

Irish Tourist Office: off Eyre Sq. one block east of the station; and in Salthill, the Promenade (May-Sept). (tel. 63081 for either office.).

USIT (Irish Student Travel Office): University College Galway, in the New Science Building (tel. 7611).

Post Office: Eglinton St. Open Mon.-Sat. 9am-6pm.

CIE Bus and Train Station: Eyre Square. 3 hours to Dublin.

Early closing: 1pm Monday; some shops closed all day Monday.

Accommodations

Many moderately priced B&B's operate in the **Renmore** area on the eastern edge of the city, and in **Salthill,** the summer resort suburb with its panoramic ocean boardwalk. Another good area to try is **Prospect Hill,** full of seedier but more centrally-located B&Bs. The city is usually jammed during 1) **Race Week** at the end of July or beginning of August, 2) the **Galway Oyster Festival** in September, and 3) **Orange Day,** a Protestant celebration in Northern Ireland in mid-July, when Catholics head for the south en masse. Try to reserve in advance for these periods.

> **Mrs. S. O'Kelly,** Grianan, 12 Glenard Ave. (tel. 63387). Cheap, only £2.75. A bit out of the way and the rooms are cramped, however. Exactly the same accommodations and prices can be found down the street at #24 (tel. 63869) and #15 (tel. 64821).

> **Helly's,** St. Joseph's, 17 Devon Pk. (tel. 62880) is good value at £3 in an area that is good B&B hunting grounds.

> **Mrs. B. Barrett,** St. Declan's, 7 St. Mary's Avenue (tel. 64806). An old standby; only £3 for the five small rooms.

> **Mrs. N. O'Donnell,** Mount Carmel, 41 Fr. Griffin Rd. (tel. 64619). At the end of a street lined with B&Bs, this is one of the nicer ones. Clean rooms for £3.50.

Food

There are plenty of chippies around town, but the pub food is better: try **Richardson's** or **The Tavern,** both more or less in Eyre Square. The latter has good soups for 17p, cheddar with brown bread 55p, etc., in a dark tavern interior. For a little more, the **Corrib House,** upstairs at the corner of Eglinton and William Streets is a good value. A nice place, good grills, full meals from start to finish around £3.

Sights

The center of town is **Eyre Square** where the **Spanish Arch** stands, the only surviving gateway of the old trading town. A walk down the main drag, **Shop Street,** will lead to **Lynch's Castle,** an elegant stone building dating from the mid-fourteenth century—now home of the Allied Irish Bank. Cross the river and wander along the docks. The nearby **Long Walk** was a popular promenade for Spanish gentlemen and their ladies; a museum has recently been opened in an adjacent house. As you wander along the lovely banks of the Corrib river up towards **Salmon Weir Bridge,** a spawning ground for the fish, try to avoid glimpses of the deceptively medieval **Cathedral**—built in the 1950s. In the evening, there is the **Taibhdhearc na Gaillimhe** (pronounced "tive-yark"), Galway's Irish-speaking theater, tucked away on Middle St., where actress Siobhàn McKenna, and Galway's own writer, Walter Macken, trained. During July and August (Mon., Wed., Fri. at 8:30pm; box office open 2-6pm, student discounts available) local, but by no means amateur talent, presents **Seoda,** a program of traditional music, song, and dance which brings down the house. For aficionados of traditional music, **Larry Cullen's Bar** on Forster St. (near the railway station) is a classic. Music is best Tuesday and Thursday nights, especially after 10.

Consider a three-hour boat ride to the **Aran Islands,** thirty miles from Galway and among the last outposts of Irish folk life and culture. On these rugged rocks live the fishermen and their families whom Synge immortalized in *Riders to the Sea* and his Aran journals. Two steamers dock at **Kilronan,** on **Inishmore,** the largest of the three islands, leaving in the morning and returning in the afternoon—but after you've paid the £7.70 fare, you might want to stay a few days and explore at your own pace. The **Tourist Office** in Kilronan, on the Pier (tel. Kilronan 29), will book rooms for you. Old circular forts and ruined churches dot the isles—don't miss **Dunn Aengus,** a prehistoric fort perched precariously on a cliff 300 feet above the ocean at "the edge of the world," and the ruined monastic cells built by the same monks who sought solitude and sanctity on the Dingle Peninsula.

Connemara, stretching northwest from Galway, is dominated by a rocky purple mountain range, the **Twelve Bens.** This is a land of large barren bog areas where turf is cut for fuel (or for sale to the turf-powered electricity stations), and of stone-mottled fields edged with gray stone walls. A Connemara man will insist that there is no more beautiful place in Eire—and, seeing the changing colors of the landscape, or catching a glimpse of a herd of wild Connemara ponies with the silver sea behind them, you might agree.

Two main roads lead out from Galway—one west through **Inverin** and **Spiddal** (site of a hospital once kept by monks from Aran), **Carna** and **Roundstone;** the other northwest to **Oughterard** on **Lough Corrib,** and **Clifden** (take in the **Connemara Pony Show** there in August, when the rugged native ponies share the stage with traditional arts and crafts). Either route is perfect for a day trip—hitching, or by bike—or you can use the tourist board *Farmhouse Guide* to find accommodations with a family. Plan to get lost a few times—you'll always end up at **Recess** or **Leenane,** and the scenery is best experienced and discovered as you go. **Rosmuc** on an isolated peninsula near **Screeb,** is where 1916 patriot Patrick Pearse spent his summers writing and learning Irish; his white-washed cottage bears witness to his spartan dedication.

The area between **Spiddal** and **Oughterard,** and **Clifden,** is almost uninhabited—farmers let their cows and goats roam freely, since there's nobody to steal them. About the only place to stay is the **Youth Hostel** a few kilometers west of Recess. Once at Clifden, accommodations are easy to find, though rather expensive. Linger over a pint at **An Crúiscín Lán** or **An Droighneain Donn** in Spiddal. Both feature sing-songs nightly. Or try the pubs in **Carraroe** where the talk and the entertainment are all in Irish.

Northwest

Relatively bare of the comforts that tourism and a warmer climate bring to the South, the counties of **Mayo, Sligo** and **Donegal** represent the bones of Ireland—piety, patriotism, and poetry. The land is sprinkled with the remnants of the past: Stone Age ruins, beehive settlements founded by early Irish saints, medieval keeps, and memorials to the rebellions against the British. The towns, for the most part, are depressing collections of cement and stone; the more prosperous, the uglier. Pass through to catch the train or bus, or use the towns as a base to explore the surrounding countryside by bicycle and foot. Tents, or a horse-drawn caravan, give you that extra degree of freedom.

Westport, on Clew Bay, was designed by the Georgian architect James Wyatt, whose idea of town life is best preserved in **Westport House,** home of the Marquess of Sligo. Check out the incongruous Zoo Park in the grounds, or come here in early June for the Westport Horse Show. The **Westport Tourist Office** (tel. Westport 269), the Post Office, and just about any other office can be found in the Mall, along the Carrowbeg River. **Distillery** and **Castlebar Roads** are good places for B&Bs, try Mrs. B. Cox, St. Martins (tel. 5), £3 a night.

Pilgrims flock to Westport the last Sunday in July to climb **Croagh Patrick,** the Holy Mountain, where St. Patrick supposedly fasted and prayed. The summit is often mist-shrouded, but from the slopes you can see out over Clew Bay's expanse. Devotees of fishing also throng the town for the almost continual summer angling championships, the biggest of which is the four-day festival held in June. **Ballintubber Abbey** is a few miles southeast of the town; founded by the King of Connaught in the thirteenth century on the site of one of St. Patrick's churches, it has been restored recently. Mass has been said continuously here for 750 years.

Northwest of Westport lies **Achill Island,** connected to the mainland by a bridge. The coast fronts the grey Atlantic with spectacular beaches and cliffs. Walk around **Slievemore Mountain** on the island to see the giants' graves, or go out to the cliffs of **Achill Head** at the tip. Near the southern tip of the island is the castle of **Kildarnet,** stronghold of Grainne Ur Mhaille, warrior sea-queen of the 16th century. Stay in **Dooagh** for about £3 B&B; try Mrs. C. McHugh, Ailblin (tel. Keel 38). In **Achill Sound,** a larger town with more amenities and less charm, try Mrs. F. Masterson, Rockmont, St. Fionan's Road, B&B £3. There are Tourist Offices in **Keel** (tel. 27, open in July and August) and **Achill Sound** (tel. 51, open mid-May through mid-September). There is an IYHF **Youth Hostel** at **Currane.**

Castlebar, inland on the road between Westport and Sligo, is an administrative center surrounded by small fascinations. Villages like **Turlough, Straide** or **Balla** have ruined churches and old crosses; three well-preserved castles stand near the town of **Ballyglass;** Bronze Age tumuli lie near **Carrowjames.** The **Castlebar Four Days Walk,** held annually at the end of June, is the most sporting way to see the countryside, but you can do it non-competitively on your own. Get information at the Tourist Office (tel. Castlebar 21207) on the walks, and on the **International Castlebar Song Contest,** held in October.

South of Castlebar, the area around **Lough Mask** and **Lough Corrib,** between Mayo and Galway, is filled with castles, churches and crosses. **Cong,** situated on the neck of land between the two lakes, is a good place to stop, though accommodations are sparse. The **Rising of the Waters Inn** (tel. Cong 8) has singles for £3 B&B, doubles for £5. **Mrs. M. McTigue,** three miles out of town at Dowagh Cross (tel. Cross 116) has B&B for £3. In Cong, stop by the twelfth-century abbey, and **Ashford Castle** (now a luxury hotel). The **Dry Canal** runs by the village—the canal was cut during the Great Famine to connect Loughs Corrib and Mask, but when it was opened with due ceremony, the water seeped away into the earth. Detour to **Rath Croghan,** the legendary home of strong-minded Maeve of Connacht, the amazon queen who, as the traditional story tells it, led the men of Ireland against Ulster's warrior hero, CuChulainn, to win a brown bull.

Sligo is unquestionably W. B. Yeats country—the poet spent his childhood summers here, and landscaped his poetry with the countryside. But it was already an area rich in mythic tales and the remains of early warfare between the men of Connacht and the men of Ulster—cairns, dolmens, passage graves, ring forts. The roads from the center of Sligo out to **Rosses Point** to the north and **Strandhill** to the south are lined with inexpensive guesthouses. In town, look for B&Bs on Wolfe Tone St. near the bus station. **Mrs. Elliot,** Avilreagh, at #3 has nice, large rooms for £3.30 per person. There are two farmhouse B&B's just outside Sligo that are worth noting. **Mrs. Henry,** The Farmhouse, Cregg (tel. 77189) overlooks Sligo Bay, near the beach at Rosses Point; £3.75. Take the Rosses Point Bus. **Mrs. Alvey,** Urlar House (tel. 73110), off the main Sligo-Bundoran road, a mile north of Drumcliffe Bridge, charges £3.85. Of course, the **Tourist Office** on Stephen Street (tel. 2436) knows the lot and will get you a room.

Ben bulben and **Knocknarea** mountains tower ominously over Sligo town. Not much goes on in town, except the **Yeats Summer School** in August, which attracts a large and devoted coterie to lectures, productions of Yeats' plays, harp recitals, poetry readings, and concerts of Irish music.

Some of the wildest, most beautiful, and least crowded country in Ireland, with heather-covered hills, deep lakes, and glens, lies virtually unnoticed by tourists in Donegal, from **Donegal** town all the way to **Malin Head,** the most northerly point in the Republic.

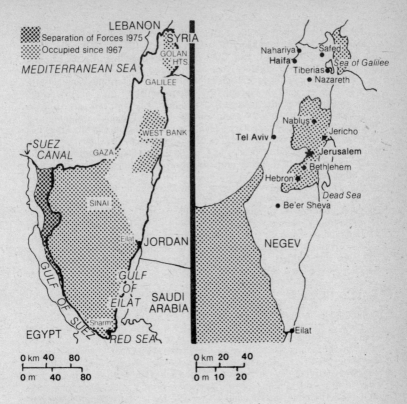

Separation of Forces 1975
Occupied since 1967

LEBANON
SYRIA
GOLAN HTS.
MEDITERRANEAN SEA
GALILEE
WEST BANK
SUEZ CANAL
GAZA
SINAI
Eilat
JORDAN
GULF OF EILAT
SAUDI ARABIA
GULF OF SUEZ
EGYPT
Sharm
RED SEA

Nahariya
Haifa
Safed
Sea of Galilee
Tiberias
Nazareth
Nablus
Tel Aviv
Jericho
Jerusalem
Bethlehem
Hebron
Dead Sea
Be'er Sheva
NEGEV
Eilat

0 km 40 80
0 m 40 80

0 km 20 40
0 m 10 20

ISRAEL

$1U.S.=18.2 pounds, or lira (IL)   **1IL=$.055**

   Israel is a phoenix—a modern nation risen from the religious and political ashes of her past. The Holy Land—to Jew, Christian, and Muslim
alike—is now "the Jewish state," a nation which cites the past as her claim
to the present.
   Armed with socialist visions of collective farming, the Zionist pioneers of
the late nineteenth and early twentieth centuries pulled fertile soil back from
desert and swamp. In the process they too were transformed: today's Israeli
is hardly the stereotyped *shtetl* Jew made humble and fearful by pogroms and
persecution; rather, the native-born Israeli is nicknamed *sabra*—a cactus
fruit—tough and prickly on the outside, tender and sweet within.
   Sharing this land are 500,000 Palestinian Arabs who see themselves as a
disenfranchised people. The Palestinian question—what is owed to these
Arabs under Israeli hegemony and to the exiled thousands who feel they
were evicted from their homeland—has contributed to the outbreak of four
wars and to countless acts of terrorism in between.

413

But Israel has endured the conflict, along with growing pains and the strains of integrating into its midst Jewish refugees from Nazi Europe, Muslim Asia, and the Soviet Union. But the price has been high. Before entering the university, every eighteen-year-old male serves in the army for three years; every female for two. Their fathers' lives are interrupted annually for reserve training until the age of fifty. Paying 50% of their income to the government in taxes, the average Israeli family, it is said, can only afford to live comfortably if the wife works and the husband juggles a minimum of two jobs. Hence national nervous habits: quick eating, heavy smoking, fast driving. For in almost three decades of independence, Israel has not known ten consecutive years of peace, and national arms expenditures are at the point where Israel now spends proportionately more money on weapons than any other nation.

But whatever your political or religious viewpoint, you will find Israel worth a modern-day pilgrimage. For a small nation, it offers an almost unbelievable amount of ethnic, geographical, and historical diversity. Patriarchal tombs, Roman forts, the birthplaces of the Holy Family, Crusader castles, and mosques all stand within miles of modern factories and universities. Visiting these sights will take you to the deserts of the **Negev,** fertile fields of the **Galilee,** ancient cities and modern metropoli, sun-flooded beaches, and even a snow-capped mountain.

GETTING THERE

Unless you're in Jordan, you have only two ways of getting to Israel: boat or plane. Between Southern Europe and Tel Aviv, the prices on student flights are: Rome $112, Athens $60, Istanbul $71.

Even cheaper is the passage by boat from Venice or Greece to Haifa. **Hellenic Mediterranean Lines,** 200 Park Ave., New York, NY 10017, runs a regular five-day trip between Venice and Haifa from April to October. With a 40% student reduction you pay, to or from Venice, $186 for a berth in a six-berth cabin, meals included, or $91 for a "fully reclining aircraft-type seat," meals excluded. The fare for the two-day trip to or from Athens costs $108 for the former, $50 for the latter. If you can get a cheap flight, the long boat trips don't justify the modest amount you'll save over the corresponding plane fare, unless you plan to take advantage of the possibility of breaking the journey for free stops along the way: Athens, Rhodes, and Limassol (Cyprus) are the ports of call.

You may be able to cross into Israel via the Allenby Bridge from Jordan. Right now, Jordanian officials are letting tourists cross over, and then come back again. A change in the political winds, or in the whims of the Jordanian administration or border officials could change all this, and it is hard to elicit an official policy from anyone. If the situation in the Middle East stays calm, you will probably be able to cross; but you are always taking a chance. Before arriving at the border, go to the **Ministry of Foreign Affairs** in Amman and tell them you want to visit the West Bank. (See, the catch is that when you cross the Allenby Bridge, you are not entering Israel, but the occupied West Bank.) They will give you an official letter which you present to the border officials. The only way of crossing is in buses (if you come by car, you must leave it behind). Expect total chaos compounded by deliberate harassment on the Jordanian side, so make your presence both known and felt. When you finally get across, have the Israeli Customs officials stamp your entry on a detachable visa—if you want to cross back or enter any other Arab country, the pages of your passport must be free of the Israeli stamp. Israeli officials are very cooperative and will wave you in and out of the country.

TRANSPORTATION

Distances are short within Israel (except for journeys into the occupied Sinai Desert), and fairly inexpensive buses go everywhere. Except for the **Dan** Company in Tel Aviv, **Egged** has a monopoly of the country's buses. You'll see their stops everywhere—in the cities, in front of a kibbutz, in the middle of a desert. Try to avoid the pre- and post-Sabbath packs, remembering that from mid-Friday afternoon to Saturday sundown, no buses operate, except those within Haifa. If you're in a mob, don't be afraid to use an aggressive elbow, muttering *slikha* (excuse me) all the way. Otherwise, you will be left behind.

For longer trips, as to Eilat, reserve seats at least one day (preferably two) before departure. Make sure the ticket seller has affixed a sticker with the date and seat number on the back of the ticket. Students get 10% off all fares. Unlimited travel passes good everywhere except in the Sinai are available, but you'll have to be zooming from place to place to save any money with them: two weeks, $30; three weeks, $35; four weeks, $40.

There is limited train service in Israel. The prices are comparable to the buses and there's a 10% discount for students. The best service is on the express trains between Haifa and Tel Aviv, where the journey takes less time than the bus trip, especially when there's traffic. Otherwise the trains are slower than buses.

The fastest way of getting around is in a communal taxi or *sherut*. Between the large cities, or between a city and its suburbs, these leave as soon as they fill up. To Eilat, however, there's a fixed schedule and you must buy a ticket two days in advance. The locations of the main *sherut* stations in Jerusalem and Tel Aviv are listed below. A *sherut* costs about 25% more than the same trip on a bus. Make sure that the car you get into is a *sherut* and not a regular taxi, which charges a good deal more. *Sheruts* operate on Saturdays and late at night when buses are not running, but watch that the price isn't inflated. Also, if you want to get from the airport to Jerusalem ask the fare first and make sure it's within orbit of the price of the bus—this route is often a price-gouger's free-for-all.

Hitchhiking in Israel is widespread and accepted, but is only mediocre for women and lousy for men. Remember that soldiers get first priority. If you hitchhike in the Sinai—and we advise against it—make sure your ride is going all the way to your destination.

A car of your own, of course, is great, but rental rates and gas prices are astronomical. Also, driving in Israel is an aggressive, dangerous art.

ACCOMMODATIONS

Because of the high prices of hotels in Israel, we list very few, preferring to stick to the extensive network of IYHF Youth Hostels. When you go to Jerusalem, stop in at the office of the **Israel Youth Hostels Association** at 3 Rehov Dorat Ha-Rishonim for a list of hostels to make reservations or buy an IYHF card. The price of accommodations at the hostels is fixed, with breakfast usually included: under 18, 44IL for IYHF cardholders, 54IL for "visitors"; 56IL for card holders over 18, 66IL for those without. In a few cities hostels aren't the best deal; check our listings for alternatives. If a hotel is what you want, the local tourist office will be happy to assist.

There are several campgrounds with full facilities, but these are relatively expensive, as far as camping goes, starting at $1.50-$2 per person, with your own equipment. You may prefer to pick your own site. In the north and east, though, think before you hammer in your stakes—don't just plop down near the border or in the occupied territory.

FOOD

In the tug of war between Occident and Orient, Israelis lean gastronomically toward their Middle Eastern neighbors. Dishes are generally light and there is a healthy emphasis on fresh produce. For the Israeli on the street, the combination of heat and hurry usually means lots of light snacks rather than a heavy meal in a restaurant. The three most popular fast foods are *felafel* (pita stuffed with balls of ground chickpeas fried in oil, plus salad, topped with *tehina* sauce), *humus* (pita stuffed with mashed chickpeas) and *shawarme* (chunks of roast lamb and salad wrapped in pita). The Israeli typically goes home for lunch, the big meal of the day, and eats a light, late supper.

If you wish to eat out, Israel has an impressive variety of restaurants. There are daily newspapers published in eleven languages in Israel, and the number of cuisines represented by its restaurants is even greater. Just be aware that most establishments serve exclusively meat or dairy dishes (dairy includes fish), so check first. To avoid single-handedly subsidizing the Israeli soft drink industry, always carry a canteen with you.

PRACTICAL INFORMATION

The first thing you must know is how completely things close down between Friday afternoon and Saturday afternoon, the Jewish Sabbath. All administrative offices and stores are shut, buses stop running, and you may have to walk a good way to find an open restaurant. Sundays, however, are just another weekday, with business as usual. General business hours are 8am-1pm and 4-6pm, with no afternoon hours on Friday and one other weekday, usually Tuesday or Wednesday.

The second thing you must know is that while the prices given herein were correct as of summer 1978, the combination of 35% annual inflation, frequent devaluations of the Israeli pound, and the constant reorganization of the tax structure will shortly make them seem prehistoric. To get a better idea of how much things will cost, remember that the Israeli pound was worth 5½¢ when this book was being written, and figure the prices in dollars—these prices are more stable. Many hotels and hostels now even use dollars rather than pounds in citing their prices.

The changes in the economy have made the exchange rates in Israel's Black Market, centered in the old city of Jerusalem, lower than those in the Israeli banks. But change is constant, so wait until you compare the rates before changing large sums of money. Just make sure you see what you're getting before you hand over your dollars to a black marketeer and remember that if you wish to support the State of Israel, exchange your much-needed hard currency through legal channels. Lastly, change back all leftover currency before leaving the country since you're likely to get a poor rate elsewhere.

About drugs: Israel is a young country with half the population under 25. Israelis generally abhor drugs as a threat to their youth and act accordingly—violators are fined and expelled from the country.

You should have no language problems in Israel, as most Israelis speak at least a little English and those that don't often speak German or French. There is an English language paper, the *Jerusalem Post,* and English news on *Kol Israel* at 7am, 2pm, 6pm, 8pm, and 10pm.

The Tourist Information offices will give you free maps, help you find a place to stay, and supply you with any information you're likely to need. The offices of the **Israel Student Tourist Association** (ISSTA) will help you with student flights to and from Israel and travel within the country. They offer a package which includes a two-week bus pass plus bed and breakfast at campgrounds. For slightly more, the Israel Youth Hostels Association offers a similar package with accommodations in its hostels.

A unique organization that every young tourist should know about is the **Society for the Protection of Nature,** or the *Hevrat Hagganat ha Teva*. This active, non-profit organization sponsors all kinds of outings and trips, from walking tours of a city to week-long tours of the Sinai. The guides are extremely knowledgeable, and the atmosphere of the group is always friendly. An outing of a few days is even a good thing to do when you first arrive in Israel, for in addition to getting a feeling for an area, you are sure to meet Israelis and travelers who share your interests to some degree. It isn't hard to come out of a tour with friends and places to stay all over the country. Visit or write the organization at 4 Hashfela St., Tel Aviv (tel. 35063).

If you plan to visit many archaeological sites, the comprehensive *Vilnay's Guide to Israel* leaves no stone unturned.

KIBBUTZIM

Many people point to Israel's *kibbutzim* (collective farms) as the only model of socialism yet created that really works. Participation is voluntary, bureaucracy is minimal, cooperation and efficiency are maximized, and all members share in relatively high levels of culture and material wealth. Although only a small number of Israelis live on *kibbutzim,* their influence on the country has been profound. A visit to a *kibbutz* is a must while you're in Israel.

Many *kibbutzim* offer bed and breakfast accommodations in their guest houses, but your stay is sure to be expensive ($8 and up per night) and superficial. It is better to get invited by a kibbutznik or a volunteer to be his personal guest.

But the only way to get a real feeling for *kibbutz* life is to work on one yourself. This involves a commitment of at least one month of hard work and early hours. In exchange, the volunteer receives room, board, work clothes, sundries, pocket money, and occasional tours of the region. The most memorable thing about volunteering is not always your contact with *kibbutz* life (which depends on your initiative), but the acquaintances you make with the other volunteers, who are usually the most geographically diverse group of people one could put together. The off-season months are the best time to work on a *kibbutz,* because your fellow volunteers are likely to be more serious and long-term than the highly evanescent wayfarers and Jewish youth groups that keep changing all summer long, and the kibbutzniks are more likely to invest time in trying to get to know you. If you have no choice but the summer months, apply well in advance (addresses below) or contact a **Kibbutz Aliya** representative at the Jewish Agency in any major American city. If you are in Israel during the summer and you decide on the spur of the moment that you want to work on a *kibbutz,* your best chance is to contact ISSTA. They have a package for $35 that includes registration, bed and breakfast the night before the *kibbutz* stay, transportation, and mandatory insurance. Although this program is always fully booked, spaces occasionally open up.

In more normal circumstances, however, you should apply directly to the office of the Kibbutz Association in Tel Aviv (each *kibbutz* is aligned along political/ideological lines, and cooperates economically and administratively with other *kibbutzim* in its group): **Kibbutz Haartzi,** 13 Leonardo da Vinci St.; **Ichud Hakibbutzim,** 14 Dubnov St.; **Kibbutz Hameuchad,** 27 Sutine St.; or **Kibbutz Hadati** (religious), 7 Dubnov St.

You must be between 18 and 35 and have a medical certificate stating that you are in good health and capable of doing agricultural work in a hot climate.

Before you commit yourself, do some advance intelligence work. *Kibbutzim* have varied physical facilities: there are many suburban-type *kibbutzim* featuring swimming pools, theaters and factories, while some newer *kibbutzim*, housed in pre-fab huts, are probably more like the pioneer settlements you've read about in books. Most importantly, different *kibbutzim* accord different treatment to their volunteers: some will make a real effort to introduce you to *kibbutz* life, while others will treat you as a free source of manual labor; so choose carefully.

ARCHAEOLOGICAL DIGS

Working on a dig is another popular way to earn your keep, learn something completely new, and meet people. It is not for everyone, however. The work is hard and often monotonous. Digging pits and shoveling shards are only occasionally interrupted by an exciting moment. Your individual experience depends on your interest in archaeology, the quality of the findings, and how much the leaders of the dig care whether you have an idea of what's developing. The Ministry of Industry, Trade, and Tourism publishes a brochure with information on the excavations that are currently accepting volunteers. The cost ranges from $3-25 a day, room and board included. This program is only offered in the summer. Reserve far ahead.

Jerusalem

Jerusalem is Israel's queen, the most important and beloved city in the land. Jews, Muslims, and Christians alike hold it in reverence, and have fought for it—and each religion has left its mark on the history and face of the city.

The evidence of Jerusalem's importance—both political and religious—is everywhere, from the religious monuments of the **Old City** to the concrete trenches of the Six-Day War. And if the physical sights aren't enough, you can feel the importance through the people, whether it be the pilgrim at prayer or the noisy politicos in the Arab coffee-houses.

Despite the myriad of political questions that surround her current status, Jerusalem is above all a holy city. On Friday the Muslim merchants of the Old City close their shops and move in waves through the labyrinth of alleys towards their mosques; on Saturday the ultra-religious Hasidic Jews of the **Mea She'arim** sector barricade their streets to guard the sanctity of Shabbat; and on Sundays the inhabitants of the Armenian quarter put down their tools to attend churches along the **Via Dolorosa,** the traditional road on which Jesus carried the cross to Calvary.

Orientation

Jerusalem is divided into three main parts: **East Jerusalem,** the walled **Old City,** and **West Jerusalem.** Until 1967, the first two were in Jordanian hands; East Jerusalem is all Arab, the Old City is predominantly so. The more modern West Jerusalem, part of Israel since the foundation of the state, is the center of commercial and administrative activity. The triangle formed by King George, Jaffa, and Ben Yehuda streets is the heart of the downtown area. The **Israel Government Tourist Office,** at 24 King George Street, is the obvious place to load up with maps and brochures. Continue down King George Street, turn right on Jaffa, and walk until you reach the **Israel Student Travel Agency** (ISSTA), where you will be showered with more material. Along the way, on your right, you will have passed a branch of **Steimatzky's,** a high-quality chain store of English and foreign language books; if you plan to stay in Jerusalem more than a few days, you should pick up a copy of *Footloose in Jerusalem,* a knowledgeable, detailed, and offbeat guide for walking tours—this is not your typical dry commentary.

Continuing down Jaffa Rd. will bring you to **Jaffa Gate,** one of the eight gates to the Old City. Most of Jerusalem's historic sites are crammed inside its formidable walls. Outside of **Herod's Gate,** you'll find the downtown area of East Jerusalem, spreading out from Saladin Street.

Addresses and Telephone Numbers

Israel Government Tourist Information Office: 24 King George St., West Jerusalem (tel. 241281/2). Branch office inside Jaffa Gate, in the Old City (tel. 282295/6).

Municipal Information Office: 34 Jaffa Rd. (tel. 228844).

ISSTA: 5 Eliashar St. Turn up at the corner of Café Alaska, 40 Jaffa Rd.—one block on left (tel. 231418).

American Express (Meditrad, Ltd.): 27 King George St. (tel. 222211).

Central Post Office: 23 Jaffa Rd. Open Sun.-Thurs. 7:30am-7pm, Fri. 7:30am-3pm.

Central Bus Station: Jaffa St. (tel. 521121). Buses #6, 6/1, 6/2, 12, 18, and 20 stop in front of it. There's also an **Arab Bus Station** on Derekh Shekhem in East Jerusalem. Frequent buses to Hebron, Ramallah, Nablus, Bethlehem, and other cities on the West Bank. Egged Buses #12 and 27 stop at the Arab Bus Station.

Railway Station: HaRakevet St. (tel. 717764).

Sheruts: Off Ben Yehuda St.

Police: Russian Compound off Jaffa St. (tel. 100).

First Aid (Magen David Adom): near Central Bus Station (tel. 523133).

U.S. Consul: 18 Agron St. (tel. 226312); another on Nablus Rd. (tel. 272681).

Swimming Pools: To avoid the expensive hotel facilities, pick up the long list of swimming pools, available at the Tourist Office.

Accommodations

The cheapest accommodations are in the Old City and East Jerusalem, but unescorted women will feel uncomfortable on the streets at night. The various Christian hospices are among the best—they're open to everyone, too.

For information on reservations at any of them, contact the **Christian In-formation Center** just inside Jaffa Gate (tel. 287647). For those who prefer the less intense atmosphere of the New City, we list below several cheap pensions in the downtown area. Stay away from the **YMCAs,** however, which in Jerusalem are essentially two-star, middle-class hotels. Be warned that most places calling themselves hostels, student hostels, or youth hostels are really private hotels using the word hostel to lure the innocent. Their quality varies greatly. IYHF hostels are listed as such below.

IN THE OLD CITY

Evangelical Lutheran Hostel, St. Mark's Road (P.O. Box 14051, tel. 282120). The place to try first. Immaculate, newly renovated, friendly man-agement, free use of kitchen facilities, excellent view from the roof. Only 25IL for a dormitory bed. You must be 32 or under to stay in the dorms; otherwise you can stay in the annex: $7.50-8.50 for bed and breakfast. Try to make reservations, or come early in the morning. Highly recommended. 10pm cur-few, however.

Jewish Federation Hostel (IYHF). A new hostel, around the corner from above. Quiet location, good facilities, but booked solid during July and Au-gust.

Armenian Catholic Patriarchate, 3rd Station, Via Dolorosa, down the street from Damascus Gate (tel. 284262). 100 beds in rooms for five or six; usually some space here. Appealing, but 10pm curfew. 50IL per dorm bed.

"Ecce Homo" Convent, alias **The Sisters of Zion** (Catholic), 41 Via Dolorosa, near the above. Another appealing hospice, but for women only. 35IL per night, free use of kitchen facilities. Check-in starts at 5pm, the doors lock at 10pm.

Danish Tea House, near Jaffa Gate. 20IL for a quiet, clean, but spartan place run by a friendly management.

Al Ahram Hotel, opposite Via Dolorosa, 3rd Station (tel. 280926). 40-50IL in acceptable 4-bed rooms, but you have to bargain over price.

Casa Nova, St. Francis St. (tel. 282791). For a moderate splurge, we recom-mend this marbled-interior home of the Franciscan Fathers. $9 per person includes all meals and choice of single or double room. If you ask the night before, they'll pack a lunch for you. 10pm curfew.

EAST JERUSALEM

Outside Damascus Gate two roads, Nablus Road and Hanevi'im Street, converge. Each has a number of student hotels and hostels. Shop around. Some choices:

Jerusalem Student House, 20 Hanevi'im St. (tel. 283733). A fairly clean hostel. 30IL for bed in 3- or 4-bed rooms. 50IL for bed in a double.

Nav Raghadan Youth Hostel, 10 Hanevi'im St. (tel. 282725). Not the cleanest place, but pleasant management, lounge with TV and music, and coffeehouse. 30IL for dormitory, 50IL for double, 25IL to sleep on roof. 11pm curfew.

Hotel Columbia, near Damascus Gate (tel. 283342). Slightly shabby, but acceptable. 10:30pm curfew. 35IL in a multi-bedded room, 60IL for a double. Nice view from the terrace.

WEST JERUSALEM

In addition to the two internationally-affiliated Youth Hostels listed below, there are three more within 25 km of the city (an easy bus trip away) that are less used. The Tourist Office has a list of student-oriented hotels in West Jerusalem.

Bernstein Youth Hostel (IYHF, formerly **Beit Atid**), corner of Karen Hayesod St. and Agron St. (tel. 228286). A clean hostel with a perfect location: 10-minute walk to both downtown and the Old City. Pleasant young staff offers free tours and talks to orient the traveler. Unfortunately the hostel is usually booked solid every summer by American groups. Try anyway.

Louise Waterman Wise Hostel (IYHF), Bayit Vagan, Pisgah Rd. (tel. 528990). Big (250 beds) and fairly new. Very clean, though not centrally located. Buses #6/2, 12, 18, 20, and 24 to Mt. Herzl.

Hotel Klein, 10 King George St. (tel. 228988). Run by an elderly religious woman, so no mixed groups in the same room. 55IL for bed in 3-bed room. Doubles for 60IL each. Singles for 80IL. Clean but noisy.

Hotel Noga, 4 Bezalel St, one block up from King George St. (tel. 224590). A quiet, very attractive place. It's really the owner's large apartment. Each tenant has his own key to the front door, and may come and go as he wishes, with free use of kitchen. 3 in a room. 60IL each.

Food

Wherever you go, check whether the restaurant gives student discounts. Many places, without advertising it, will give you ten percent off or waive the service charge. The cheapest places are in or near the Old City (especially inside Herod's Gate), but watch the cleanliness.

The **Umayyah,** across from Herod's Gate in East Jerusalem, offers a good oriental meal in a clean, appealing restaurant. Specialties: *mansaf,* a dish of lamb in a curry sauce with stuffed rice, or stuffed pigeon. Most dishes 30-40IL plus 10% service charge. Wine served.

Uncle Moustache, down the street from Herod's Gate. This is the cheapest decent meal in town. 10IL for omelette, salad, and chips; 20IL for meat dishes. Often jammed with young tourists.

To fill up for even less, try this: enter the Old City through Damascus Gate. At the fork in the road, turn left onto Aqabat esh-Sheikh Rihan St., and at #5 on your left, you'll find a dark, cavernous store where a **Mr. Muhammad Ali** bakes *pita* bread for the whole neighborhood in a huge oven. If you ask him, he'll make you a pizza out of pita, eggs, tomatoes, and cheese for 7IL.

The restaurants below are all in West Jerusalem:

Abu Shaul, a small inexpensive place near the Mahane Yehuda Market, reputed to have the best *shawarme* in Jerusalem. Anyone on the street will tell you how to get there.

The Barn (or **The Pizza Barn**) on Hillel St. just off King George St. A restaurant and porch café with a pleasant atmosphere. Good Italian food for 30-40IL, also *fondue* for a little more. Often quiet entertainment in evenings.

The Jerusalem Restaurant, 52 Jaffa Rd., is a large, impersonal, pay-before-you-eat restaurant serving full meals of soup, salad, entrée, vegetables, and dessert for 30-40IL.

The Hebrew University cafeterias (student union building, administration building, library and dormitory complex at **Givat Ram;** science and education building, which has an amazing view, at **Mount Scopus**) serve good food year round at low prices. Buses #9 and 28 go to both campuses.

Sights

Face it: it will take you weeks to see all that's worth seeing in Jerusalem. The Old City, where it all began, and where the best continues, may be less than a square mile in size, but it hides worlds within its maze-like alleyways. Here are some strategies to help you at least get a feel for Jerusalem's richness: to repeat, buy *Footloose in Jerusalem,* and take some of its self-guided walking tours. Go to the office of the **Protection of Nature Society,** 13 Heleni haMalca St. (tel. 222357) and find out about their walking tours, which are often free. A good way to start on your own is to get a free street map from the Tourist Office, enter the **Damascus Gate,** climb to the walkway on the top of the walls, and follow it east. As you walk, you will have a changing view of the Old City and of East Jerusalem. Just after you pass **Herod's Gate** you will see the **Rockefeller Archaeological Museum** across the street (Open Sun.-Thurs. 10am-6pm, Fri.-Sat. 10am-2pm). The huge Golden Dome you see in the Old City is the **Dome of the Rock.** After Mecca and Medina, it is the most holy shrine to Muslims, who believe that the Prophet Muhammad rose from here to heaven one night. Don't content yourself with this distant perspective. This is the most spectacular example of Islamic architecture in all of Israel; its exterior walls and the inside of the dome are not to be missed. The same ticket of admission entitles you to inspect the adjacent **el-Aksa Mosque,** with its silver dome, the largest mosque in Israel (open 8-11am, noon-3pm, 4-5:30pm, except Fridays and Muslim holidays).

Continuing on the walls, the next gate you reach after Herod's is **St. Stephen's Gate.** If you descend here and enter the Old City you will be near the first station of **Via Dolorosa.** Each successive station marks another incident on the path Jesus took on the day of his crucifixion. The last five stations are located in the **Church of the Holy Sepulchre,** the site of Jesus' entombment and resurrection. Every Friday afternoon at 3pm, priests lead a procession for pilgrims along Via Dolorosa, starting at St. Stephen's Gate. If you are still on the Walls above the gate, you may wish to descend into the valley on the other side to visit the four churches there. The most striking is the onion-domed **Russian Church of Mary Magdalene.** To the south of these churches, on the slopes of the **Mount of Olives,** you'll find the **Tomb**

of Absalom, traditionally believed to contain the body of David's son, but probably dating only from the Hellenistic period. Nevertheless, the hill on which the tomb stands has been a Jewish burial site for millennia and tombs from various epochs are still visible. Continue further south, following from outside the walls until you reach the valley of Kidron—this will put you face to face with the **Dung Gate**—where one of Israel's most unique ar-chaeological sites is to be found, or rather, experienced: the **Pool of Shiloah.** In the eighth century B.C. King Hezekiah built a network of tunnels to divert water to the city in the event of a siege. You can wade through the subterra-nean passage, which is about half a mile long. The water is thigh high. Wear shorts and sneakers, and bring a flashlight to see the way, and to read the occasional inscriptions on the wall.

You will probably need little prodding to explore the Old City on your own; for most, it is love at first sight. But don't always start your expeditions from the same place. There are eight gates to the Old City, and each opens up into a setting of remarkably different atmosphere. During your stay, you should plunge in from each gate. The **Jaffa Gate** is nearest to the crafts and fruit markets. It is by far the most touristy area. Now go try the other seven.

The Old City's market (*shuk* in Hebrew, say *suq* in Arabic) offers every-thing from archaeological artifacts to Bedouin dresses to hashish. The key to reasonable spending and a good time is haggling. Never accept a first offer—cut it in half, at least. And don't be afraid to walk out of a shop; if your offer was good enough, they'll call you back. As for drugs, exercise extreme caution, as dealer and informer are often the same person.

The **Wailing Wall,** or **Western Wall** (the name preferred by the tough Israelis), the last remnant of the Second Temple, is the holiest of Jewish sites. Religious Jews sway back and forth in prayer before it, often cram-ming hand-scrawled entreaties to God into the cracks of the Wall. To get a better feel for the Jewish religious life of Jerusalem we suggest the following itinerary: modestly dressed (no shorts, preferably no jeans; women, cover your arms), spend Friday morning walking through the most Orthodox neighborhood in Jerusalem, **Mea She'arim,** as its residents hurry through the streets preparing for the Sabbath. Many of them will be found in the nearby **Mahane Yehuda** market, a colorful outdoor market whose mer-chants and shoppers are Jews from all over the world. When you return in the afternoon to Mea She'arim, a quarter reminiscent of an Eastern European *shtetl,* the profane bustling of the morning will have been superceded by the sacred spirit of the Sabbath—this is, after all, the most important holiday of the Jewish calendar after Yom Kippur, the day of atonement. Follow the families of Hasidim as they go singing, chanting, and dancing to welcome the Sabbath at the Wailing Wall. Later, wander through the **Jewish Quarter** of the Old City. The Quarter boasts a number of centuries-old synagogues, many of which are only now being cleared of the rubbish that accumulated in them during the years of Jordanian rule.

The **Israel Museum,** with its **Shrine of the Book** housing the Dead Sea Scrolls, is Israel's largest and most varied (open 10am-4pm Mon., Wed.-Fri.; Tues. 4-10pm; Sat. 10am-2pm). One of Israel's most-prized treasures is the set of stained-glass windows Marc Chagall made for the **Hadassah Medical Center.** To reach the hospital, take bus #9 or 27.

To understand the source of Israeli determination, visit **Yad Vashem,** the Martyrs' and Heroes' Memorial to the six million victims of Nazi terror. Among the most gripping memorials anywhere, Yad Vashem contains both a shrine, where services are held daily, and a permanent exhibition, *Warning and Witness,* which documents the horror of the holocaust. (Open Sun.-

Thurs. 9am-4pm, Fri. 9am-1pm. Buses #6/1, 6/2, 12, 18, 20, 24, and 27).
Entrance free.

For a pleasant half-day excursion, take the Arab bus towards Jericho and
get off in the town of **Bethany** 3 km outside Jerusalem. There you can visit a
first-century tomb reputed to be the one from which Jesus raised Lazarus
from the dead. Then, ascending from the dirt road road outside the tomb,
you'll reach the Mount of Olives, with its unmatched view of Jerusalem.

Evenings

Café/bars are very popular, ranging from the bright Israeli café to the
subdued coffeehouse. **Tzavta,** at 38 King George St. (tel. 4330), offers a
variety of entertainers and evening moods, from bluegrass to religious
folk-rock. Moderate admission charge; get there early to beat the crowds.
The Tourist Office has the weekly list of performers. The downtown triangle
area offers a number of bright, loud bars, most with a predominantly Israeli
clientele. For a slightly different atmosphere, try Rivlin Street (off Jaffa
Road). In quick succession are: **Rasputin's,** an easy-going bar; **Chocolate
Soup,** a coffeehouse with delicious drinks and crêpes; and **The Tavern,** a
bar catering to Americans and Englishmen living in Jerusalem. Further out,
on Bezalel Street, is the **32 Club,** with a quiet piano bar; and **Pargod** (at
#94), which offers movies and jazz. Check hours before hiking down there.

There is Israeli **folk dancing** *(rikudei am)* on Wednesdays at the Givat
Ram campus of Hebrew University, Thursdays on the Mt. Scopus campus,
and Saturdays at the YMCA and ICCY Hall (12 Emek Refaim). Or try the
disco at the Student Club, Mt. Scopus campus. Open only on Friday nights,
so you'll have to hike. And finally, try walking the walls of the Old City,
particularly the South Wall, with its beautiful view of the illuminated Wailing Wall.

Jerusalem is a good city for film buffs, so good in fact that one revival
house, the **Jerusalem Cinema,** shows a movie every Friday afternoon,
while another, the **Khan,** covers Friday evenings. To get the addresses and
programs of these cinemas and a third revival house called the
Cinematheque ask at the Tourist Office or look in the *Jerusalem Post.* Also
check the activities at Hebrew U. The office also has a schedule of (mostly)
classical concerts at the **Jerusalem Theatre** on Chopin Street. Reduced-
price tickets are available at the Hebrew University Student Union Box
Office.

The West Bank

The West Bank refers to the land to the west of the Jordan River which
was administered by Jordan from 1948 until it was captured by Israel in
1967. It is an area rich in biblical sites. Both its city dwellers and its peasants
are, in general, more traditional than the Arabs living in Israel proper.
Before you travel on the West Bank, inquire about security problems there,
and remember that even if living conditions here have improved since 1967,
the West Bank Arabs are generally unhappy with the continued occupation
of their land. **Bethlehem** is one of the few places on the West Bank that is
visited by hordes of tourists. The **Church of the Nativity,** built on the site of
Jesus' birth, is the main attraction—there are stairs leading down to a cave
which marks the exact spot. This large church was built by the Emperor
Justinian in 325 A.D. and restored during the Crusades. About twenty miles
south of Bethlehem is the larger city of **Hebron** (buses leave frequently from

Jerusalem and Bethlehem). This is an ancient city, and its citizens are proud, religious, and renowned for their artisanry (especially ceramics and glassworks). Of all the cities on the West Bank, Hebron has the most individual character. The main sight in town is the **Tomb of the Patriarchs** mentioned in Genesis, the burial site of Abraham, Sarah, Isaac, and Jacob. There is a Roman fortress built around the tombstones and, inside it, a later mosque. Both Jews and Muslims come to worship here (visitors are not allowed on Fridays). Head for the market—Hebron is a good place for buying gifts.

The area of the West Bank to the north of Jerusalem is completely untouristy. The capture of this area has cut the travel time between Jerusalem and **Tiberias** to a mere two and a half hours, but you'd get more out of the area by taking an entire day to make the trip. The first town you reach when you leave Jerusalem is **Ramallah,** the richest town on the West Bank. Cooled by its location in the hills, Ramallah was the summer resort of wealthy Jordanians. There is a tourist office here and a restaurant, **Na'oum's,** famous among Arabs around the world. From Ramallah there are frequent buses and shared taxis to **Nablus,** the largest city on the West Bank. Just before you reach the city you'll pass on your right a large refugee camp called **Balata,** built to house those who fled Israel in 1948. Nablus is the biblical **Shechem,** and just above town on **Mount Gerizim,** according to the Samaritans, Abraham offered to sacrifice his son Isaac. A few kilometers on the road north of Nablus is the small village of **Samaria/Sabastia,** namesake of two famous ancient cities. The ruins—from the Israelite, Hellenistic, and Roman periods—will mainly interest archaeology buffs, but the walk through the beautiful Arab village that surrounds it makes the detour worthwhile for anyone. The road continues to **Jenin,** a large town with a colorful market, and then to **Afula** in Israel proper, a town of mostly Sephardic Jewish immigrants.

Tel Aviv

Tel Aviv is Israel's latter-day boom town. Founded in 1909 as a Jewish suburb of the ancient city of **Jaffa,** Tel Aviv grew rapidly, uncontrollably, and without any kind of planning. Now the center of a metropolitan area of half a million people, Tel Aviv is hot, humid, crowded, noisy, polluted—just like New York, right? Well, the truth of the matter is, if you like the Big Apple, you'll also go for Tel Aviv. Because, with all the problems that make people swear off urban life forever, Tel Aviv also happens to be the liveliest, most sophisticated metropolis in Israel. Visit the galleries, take in a concert, and above all sit at one of the cafés on **Dizengoff St.,** but come late and stay late, because Tel Aviv does not roll up its sidewalks at 9pm. Just don't expect the warmth of Israel's older cities.

Addresses and Telephone Numbers

Israel Government Tourist Office: 7 Rehov Mendele, off Ben Yehuda St. (tel. 223266). Open 8am-6pm, Fridays 8am-3pm.

ISSTA: 109 Ben Yehuda St. (tel. 247164/5).

American Express: 16 Ben Yehuda St. (tel. 294654).

Central Post Office: 132 Allenby Road (tel. 623613). Open 8am-8pm, Fridays to 3pm. *Poste Restante.*

Central Bus Station: at end of Allenby Rd. (Information, tel. 31132). If they haven't yet finished building the new station, watch out! This is the 9th circle. Bus #4, 5, or 89.

Railroad Station: to Haifa and Netanya, Arlozoroff St. (tel. 253548). Hitch on Derech Haifa to go to Haifa. To Jerusalem and Beersheva, Tel Aviv South Station. Hitch in front of this Station for Jerusalem and Ben Gurion Airport. For Central Train Information call 254271.

Sheruts: Allenby Rd. near Yehuda Halevi St. Sheruts to suburbs leave from near the Bus Station.

Police Emergency: (tel. 100).

U.S. Embassy: 71 Hayarkon St. (tel. 54348).

Canadian Embassy: 220 Hayarkon St. (tel. 228122).

Accommodations

Most of Tel Aviv's cheaper hotels are located within two or three blocks of the beach, on or near Allenby Road, Ben Yehuda, and Hayarkon Streets. If you're sensitive to noise, be especially choosy about where you sleep, and even in a relatively quiet hotel, ask for a room off the street.

The Hostel, at 60 Ben Yehuda St. (tel. 287088) is not an official hostel, but is popular due to its central location and friendly atmosphere. 55IL for a dorm bed (50IL for students), 75IL for a bed in a double room. Midnight curfew. Bus #4.

Youth Hostel (IYHF), 32 Bnei Dan St. (tel. 455042), is a good hostel near Yarkon Park, but not very central. 10 minutes by bus #5 or 25. Try to reserve an air-conditioned room.

Beach Hotel, 6 Allenby St. (tel. 57465), is the cheapest of a row of cheap hotels on Allenby, all within a block of the beach. Drab accommodations, but 40IL for a dorm bed, 60IL for a bed in a double. In a mild red light district.

Nes Ziona, 10 Nes Ziona St. (tel. 56587), is close to Ben Yehuda St. and the sea. Friendly, helpful staff. $6-7 in a single or double without breakfast.

Hotel Tamar, 8 Gnessing St. (tel. 286997). A quiet, small set of rooms. $6 for a single room.

Food

Tel Aviv offers few restaurants that are both cheap and good. If the former is your main objective, try the inexpensive self-service restaurants on Ben Yehuda.

The **Mensa** at Tel Aviv University will tempt you with the cheapest conventional meal. And once you've schlepped (buses #25, 26, or 27) to the campus, located in suburban Ramat Aviv, it's worth your while to spend some time in nearby **Museum Ha'aretz.** A complex of specialized smaller museums—including the Glass, Ethnography, and the Tel Quasile Excavations—is free on Saturday (open 10am-2pm; Sun.-Thurs. 9am-4pm, and Fri. 9am-1pm).

You can rival the Mensa's prices by buying your own food at the crowded

Carmel Food Market. Picnicking on the beach or in the seaside Clore or Ha'atzmaut Parks or the more rolling Hayarkon National Park helps you escape the city.

For good oriental food, try the Yemenite Quarter between the Carmel Market and the beach. There are a few very cheap workers' restaurants on Peduim St., as well as the spruced-up **Zion Restaurant,** at number 28, the place outsiders go when they want a Yemenite meal.

Sights and Nightlife

Because of its relative youth, Tel Aviv has none of the historical attraction of Jerusalem or the West Bank—in fact, outside of its museums there are very few sights worth seeing by day. Most travelers bake on the beaches and wait for the evening, when Tel Aviv comes alive.

Tel Aviv's number one evening attraction is **Dizengoff St.** where strolling on the café-lined boulevard has become so much a way of life that Hebrew even has a verb describing it: to *dizengoff.* If you are successful in negotiating the crowds that throng the neon-lit Dizengoff Circle, turn up Gordon St., and walk six blocks up to the towering City Hall—right next to it is Malchei Yisrael Square, where you can step into Israeli rhythms every summer Saturday night with community folkdancing from 8-10pm.

A quieter, more relaxed evening can be had in **Old Jaffa,** an ancient port city now reconstructed into a quarter of art galleries, cafés, restaurants, and silver shops. The prices and atmosphere are touristy, but there's a lot going on there in the evenings, the view of Tel Aviv is magnificent, and if you do a little exploring, you can find a few unspoiled alleyways. If you want to eat, walk down the hill to the restaurants near the illuminated clock tower—prices are lower there. The Jaffa flea market **(Shuk Hapishpishim),** which features everything in antique and contemporary junk, is open every day a block from the tower. From Ben Yehuda St., take the #10 bus; from the Youth Hostel, take the #25.

Evenings in **Kikar Atarim,** near the marina in Tel Aviv, are crowded and exciting, especially on Saturdays. Challenge one of the *sheshbesh* (backgammon) or chess players, or join in the weekly Wednesday happenings of music and song at 6pm. Bus #4 or 7.

In the daytime visit some of Tel Aviv's fine museums (free on Saturdays). The new, highly-praised **Museum of the Diaspora** at Ramat Aviv (buses #24, 25, and 27) provides a good introduction to Judaism in Israel and abroad. Open Sun.-Tues. and Thurs. 10am-5pm; Wed. 3-10pm; closed Fridays. The **Tel Aviv Museum,** whose split-level galleries are as intriguing as the fine Israeli and international art displayed, stays open 7-11pm on Saturday nights. Tuesday is another late night (until 10pm), but, like every other weekday, will cost you 41L with a student ID. Take bus #18, 19, or 70 to 27 Shaul Hamelech St. The admission ticket you've bought at the Tel Aviv Museum will also entitle you entrance to the nearby **Helena Rubenstein Art Pavilion,** 6 Rehov Tarsat (bus #5, 11, or 63). Open Sun.-Thurs. 10am-5pm; except Tues. 10am-1pm and 4-7pm; Fri. 10am-2pm, Sat. 7-11pm. Next to Helena Rubenstein you'll spot **Mann Auditorium,** the country's main concert hall and home of the Israeli Philharmonic and the Habimah, Israel's National Theater.

Ignore all of the luring advertisements for **The Shalom Tower Observatory.** Although 35 stories make it the tallest building in the Middle East, the dull Tel Aviv skyline is hardly worth 20IL. The Shalom Tower might be a good place to do some shopping, particularly in the Maskit store, with its fine and expensive merchandise.

The beachfront is beautiful in Tel Aviv, but intermittently polluted. Most of the popular beaches are those adjacent to the Sheraton, Hilton, and Gordon Hotels. Gordon Beach also boasts a swimming pool and boat rental.

Mediterranean Coast Toward Haifa

Excellent beaches lie both to the north and south of Tel Aviv. On the way south to the Gaza Strip are the cities of **Ashdod** and **Ashkelon.** Stretching north are the expensive resort towns of Netanya and Herzliyah, where you'll have to pay about 20IL to get onto the beach.

About halfway to Haifa is **Caesarea,** with its partially-restored Crusader castles and Roman ruins (the famous amphitheater is the scene of summer concerts). To the north of Caesarea, you'll find relatively isolated beaches, good for swimming and camping.

Haifa

Haifa is a new, clean, pleasant city with plenty of scenic views. It is much loved by its inhabitants, but when pressed, they will admit that compared to Tel Aviv or Jerusalem, Haifa is a dull place. There is no old city, and little nightlife. Perhaps the most worthwhile thing to do in Haifa is to try to meet some Israeli students. **Haifa University** and the **Technion** are located here, and the students are very receptive to their peers from abroad.

Haifa is built on three levels. The lowest is the port area, a raucous neighborhood where the bus and train terminals are located. Then comes the **Hadar** area, where you'll find most of the city's businesses, hotels, and restaurants. And finally, a residential area, **Carmel,** reigns. Take a ride on Israel's only subway, the **Carmelit,** which connects the three tiers. Haifa's municipal buses run all day Saturday.

Addresses and Telephone Numbers

Israel Government Tourist Office: 18 Herzl St. (tel. 666521). Open Sun.-Thurs. 8am-6pm, Fri. 8am-3pm. There is a Municipal Information Office in the bus station.

ISSTA: 16-20 Herzl St., Room 245 (tel. 669139). Open Sun.-Thurs. 9am-1pm and 3-6pm, Fri. 9am-1pm.

American Express (Meditrad, Ltd.): Khayat Square (tel. 665069).

Central Post Office: 219 Sderot Hameginim. Open Sun.-Thurs. 7am-6pm, Fri. 7am-3pm.

Central Bus Station: Derech Yafo (tel. 641761).

Railway Station: next to Bus Station, on Derech Yafo (also tel. 641761).

U.S. Consul: 37 Derekh Ha-atzmaut (tel. 663145).

Swimming: Take bus #44 or 45 to the free Carmel Beach; although 15IL is not much to pay for the more convenient Hof Shaket Beach. The Bat Galim beach near the bus station has a swimming pool. In Central Carmel, near the last stop on the Carmelit, is the Maccabee Pool. Both charge 15IL admission.

Accommodations

Haifa is short on the budget hotels and pseudo-hostels that flourish in Jerusalem. Its Youth Hostels and camping sites, while not centrally located, are in beautiful spots.

Bethel Hostel, 40 Geffen St. (tel. 521110). Take bus #41 from central bus station. Pleasant hostel with Christian emphasis, but all are welcome. Large, clean dormitory rooms for 40IL. Quiet location with large yard and recreation area. Regular hostel hours; also 10pm curfew.

Hotel Eden, 8 Rehov Shmaryahu Levin (tel. 664816). Convenient, but noisy location, facilities so-so. 40IL for bed in 4-bed room, double for 75IL each.

The Carmel Youth Hostel (IYHF), Hof Hacarmel (tel. 531944), is new, fits 400 beds, and commands a splendid view. It's a great deal except for the 20 minute walk from the bus stop after the 20-minute bus ride out of the Hadar. Bus #43, 44, or 45.

Kiryat Tivon (IYHF), 12 Rehov Alexander Zaid, Kiryat Tivon (tel. 9311482), is reached by a moderate ride on bus #74 and 75. Near Beit She'arim, site of an ancient synagogue and vast catacombs.

Newe Yam Campground on the beach 25 km south of Haifa. Full facilities; run by kibbutz of the same name.

Food

Haifa's best inexpensive restaurant is probably the **Betteinu** on 29 Jerusalem Street near the Haifa Theatre. **Farm Foods** at 30 Herzl Street is a popular and cheap dairy restaurant. For a fine meat or dairy meal at semi-expensive prices, take a look at the **Balfour Cellar's** menu at 3 Balfour Street. Haifa's cheapest meals are to be had at the **Haifa University** cafeterias, where a full meal goes for 18IL, but these are a good way from the center of town. The Rumanian **Restaurant Karol** on the corner of Haneviim and Hazeitim streets grills more organs than you knew existed at 30-50IL. The **Iskander,** on Allenby Road near UNO Boulevard, is a well-known Arab restaurant. Haifa is a good *felafel* city, and Haneviim Street is *felafel* row. Cheaper yet is a picnic in Gan Ha'em Park.

Sights

There is a free walking tour of the city at 10am every Saturday, which meets at the Sha'ar Levanon Panorama.

The "must" in Haifa is a visit to the golden domed **Baha'i Temple** in Hadar, center of the rapidly growing Baha'i religion. The building is impressive, set in elaborate Persian gardens overlooking the harbor, and housing the remains of El Bab, Baha'i's holy figure. Reached by buses #22, 23, or 25, the Temple is open from 9am to noon. The gardens are open in the afternoon. Entrance free. **Elijah's Cave,** where the prophet hid in his flight from Ahab, is interesting more for the Oriental Jews who come to worship there than for the shrine itself. It is at the foot of Cape Carmel, about 1 km east of the bus station. Always open and free. Haifa also offers a number of good museums—archaeology, maritime, illegal immigration, and agriculture—with admission free on Saturdays.

The Baha'is are not the only interesting minority in the Haifa area. There are several Druze villages, and two **Daliyat Isfiya** (21 km) and **Daliyat el-Carmel** (25 km) are within easy reach. In the thirteenth century the Druze split off from a sect of a sect of Islam, and today their religion, which they are very secretive about, is different from Islam. While the Druze speak Arabic and have always lived near Arab Muslims and Christians, they have preserved their identity, and even look different. Indicative of their separateness is the Israeli Druze's strong support of Israel. The community insisted that its sons serve in the Israeli army so that they would enjoy the same rights as Jews. Just before you reach Daliyat el-Carmel, you'll see a building with the sign. ''The Druze Zionist Club.'' In town there is a tourist bazaar. The Druze are known for their hospitality, and both Daliyat el-Carmel and Isfiya are nice to walk around in. In the afternoons bus #92 from the Central Bus Station goes to both villages. There are always *sheruts* (14-17IL) on Rehov Eliyahu, near the Zim building.

Evenings

Asked once about the city's sparse entertainment, Haifa's first socialist mayor is reputed to have pointed to the around-the-clock factories of the city, saying: ''There is our nightlife.'' Your most memorable evening activity in Haifa may be to hike up to the **Carmel,** and view the panorama of lights of Haifa Bay. There are several outdoor cafés in the area.

Folklore evenings and film showings take place frequently at **Beit Rothschild,** 104 Hanassi Ave., right next to the last stop on the Carmelit. **The Club 120,** at 120 Panorama Rd., is a nice, civilized discotheque. Once again, check out what's doing at the Technion or Haifa University: dances, coffeehouses, and movies are frequent, especially during the school year.

Beit Hageffen, at 2 Geffen Street (tel. 525251), is a club run jointly by Jews and Arabs to foster cooperation, and sponsors lectures and discussions. Visitors are always welcome. The complex also includes **Exotica,** a fairly posh nightclub/restaurant. Beit Hageffen is next to **Chagall House,** a gallery of modern Israeli painters, but no Chagall.

Galilee, the North, and the Golan

Twenty kilometers north of Haifa is the ancient port city of **Acre** (the Arabic name is **Akko**), scene of a major siege during the Crusades and of an incredible prison-break by the Israeli underground in 1947. The escape scene in *Exodus* was in fact filmed in Akko. The old city, with its medieval ramparts, winding alleys, and colorful markets, is being renovated to make it more attractive to tourists, so visit it now before it's too late. The **Municipal Museum** (5IL for students) includes the well-preserved fortress complex of the knights. The Turkish eighteenth-century **Mosque** was once the largest in what is today Israel, but it pales in comparison with the Dome of the Rock. The **Museum of Heroism** (5IL for students), housed in the **Citadel** that was used by the British as a prison in the 1930s and 1940s, has an interesting exhibit documenting the incarceration of Jewish activists and terrorists, and their escape. There is a good view of the city from the roof. The **Akko Youth Hostel** (IYHF; tel. 911982) with its clean, spacious rooms in a newly-renovated 200-year-old building, is one of the nicest urban hostels in Israel.

Further north along the coast, past a Roman aqueduct and a Holocaust Museum is **Nahariya**, a favorite Israeli resort, with crowded cafés and a fine beach. Rooms in private houses go for about 80IL per person, but we recommend that you head five kilometers north to the **Yad le Yad Youth Hostel** (IYHF; tel. 921343) or nearby **Campground** (tel. 921792) in **Achziv.** The beach here is less crowded, and is one of the nicest on Israel's Mediterranean coast. At the campground you can bring your tent or rent one, or rent a bungalow (reserve in advance; one with two beds costs 70IL per person). The prices at the store/restaurant are very reasonable.

A few kilometers further north brings you to the Lebanese border, and the white cliffs and grottoes of **Rosh Hanikra.** Unfortunately, the only way you can descend to the caves is to pay 12IL for the cable car, but they are too beautiful to be missed.

The road between **Ma'alot** and **Rama** passes through some of the most beautiful countryside in Israel. This is the undisturbed Galilee, off the beaten track, with green mountains, Arab villages, and goatherds. Be sure to stop in **Peqa'in**, a village that has been inhabited by Jews uninterruptedly throughout the centuries. Today one lone Jewish family remains. They live next door to the Synagogue, and will be happy to show it to you. The rest of Peqa'in's residents are Druze, Christian, and Muslim Arabs. The **Restaurant** in the Gas Station in Rama is happily nothing like an American roadside Hot Shoppe. It is, rather, a quality Arab restaurant with excellent salads and *kebabs* at reasonable prices.

About twenty kilometers from Rama, **Safed** was once the center of the Cabbalists, a sect of Jewish mystics, and it remains today one of Israel's most religious towns. The old quarter is best appreciated on a Friday evening, when its narrow streets are closed to traffic, and all is silent except for the chanting that emanates from its numerous synagogues. The mild summers make this a popular vacation spot, so cheap accommodations are scarce in the high season. But the modern **Beit Benyamin Youth Hostel** (tel. 31086), on the outskirts of town, is rarely full. The town is very quiet on Saturdays (the first bus out is at 3pm), but the swimming pool, just beyond the Bus Station, is open.

The trip from Safed to the **Sea of Galilee** is a beautiful one, but the descent of 3,400 feet to the sea brings an unwelcome increase in the heat and humidity. Get off before Tiberias at the **Karei Deshe Youth Hostel** (IYHF; tel. 20607), one of the nicest anywhere. The hostel, with its luxurious accommodations, private beach, and personal peacocks, is deservedly popular, so make reservations. If they're full though, you can camp outside for 35IL per person. From Karei Deshe it is only a short hike to the mosaic-floored **Church of the Multiplication of Loaves and Fishes,** the **Capernaum** excavations, and the **Mount of Beatitudes,** a beautiful spot where Jesus delivered the Sermon on the Mount.

If you enjoy the bustle of hordes of vacationers, both Israeli and foreign, stay in **Tiberias,** the major town of the area and a crowded winter resort. The IYHF **Youth Hostel** (tel. 21775) here is modern, appealing, and large, but in the summer it fills up early every day. The **New Hostel** (tel. 21175) is not an official hostel, but a dormitory-style student hotel on the waterfront. It is less appealing than the Youth Hostel, but with the 40IL rate you can use the kitchen facilities for free. On the main street of town, Rehov HaGalil, not far from the Bus Station, **Hotel Adler** is a large, old hotel, past its prime if it ever had one, where beds go for 50IL per person. If you take the road out of Tiberias a kilometer or two to the north, you can camp for free by the side of the road, near the water. There is also an organized campground two kilometers west of the city. Most beaches in the town of Tiberias are privately maintained and charge admission. Try the misnamed **Quiet Beach** or the adjacent **Blue Beach.** Both offer discos and Israeli folk dancing in the evening.

Nazareth, the home of Jesus, is a disappointment to many tourists. The largest Arab town in Israel, it offers little in the way of sights, although the open market and narrow, winding streets provide a nice atmosphere. The major sight is the **Basilica of the Annunciation,** a modern church with interesting representations of the Holy Family from all over the world—an oriental Jesus, a black Jesus and Madonna, etc. There are several other churches in Nazareth as well as a couple of handsome mosques. Dress ''modestly'' for all of these. To stay the night in Nazareth, try the **Dames de Nazareth hospice** (tel. 54304), 35IL for a dorm bed, or the **Ukrainian Ecumenical Guest House** (tel. 71407), for the same price.

East of Nazareth, the **Jezreel Valley** offers many of Israel's oldest, nicest and richest *kibbutzim.* One evening a week (usually Sundays) the kibbutzniks and townspeople from **Beit She'an** gather at **Gan Hashelosha** (or Sakhne) Park for folk-dancing. The park itself, one of the most beautiful and popular in Israel, features a waterfall and three natural swimming pools. Not far away is the mosaic-floored **Beit Alpha** synegogue, built in the sixth century, and **Kochav Hayarden** (or Belvoir), a Crusader fortress commanding a majestical view of the entire area. Also of archaeological interest is **Megiddo,** one of the most important sites in the Mid-East. The *tel* (hill) is well labeled and has a small museum at its base to help the visitor through the roughly two dozen civilizations that have settled at Megiddo.

Northeast of the Sea of Galilee a e the **Golan Heights,** captured from Syria in 1967 and occupied since the 1967 war. This area can only be reached by private car or organized tour, but if you get the chance, you should see it. Besides the remains os the war—fire-gutted tanks, bombed deserted villages—the fertile Golan offers some beautiful natural sights. Among them: **Mt. Hermon,** with views in all directions as well as winter skiing; **Birkat Ram,** a jewel-like crater lake; and the **Banias,** an archaeological site and nature reserve.

Negev Desert

After Jerusalem, the desert is considered by many to be the most fascinating place in Israel. Contrary to Hollywood-fed expectations, the desert is not an endless plain of sand, scorched mercilessly by the sun. The Negev is rugged and mountainous, mostly barren, and dotted with Bedouin camps and ruins. It is even cool here at night. When in the desert, drink at least a gallon of liquid daily, wear a hat, get an early start, trying to avoid physical exertion between noon and 3pm, and avoid hitchhiking. Buses to the Negev, especially to the Dead Sea and Beersheva, leave frequently from Jerusalem.

Jericho is a magnificent oasis city and one of the hottest in the world. If you have the stamina, visit the excavated city north of town. There's not much to see, but these 7,000-year-old ruins are the basis of Jericho's claim to being the oldest city in the world. Near Jericho, too, is the **Mount of Temptation,** where asatan reportedly visited the fasting Christ; it's a steep and rough climb past a monastery to the summit. Yet another trek for the adventurous is the hike to **Wadi Kelt,** an oasis with small waterfalls and refreshing pools, set in a spectacular narrow gorge. To reach Wadi Kelt, you must leave the main road from Jerusalem to Jericho, trek for an hour by foot, and follow the channeled brook to the water pools.

South of Jericho is the **Dead Sea,** the lowest point on earth. Because of the high salt content, swimming is quite an experience, as you actually have to struggle to keep your feet down. But save your swimming for the **Ein Feshha Nature Reserve,** where a number of sweet springs provide relief after the oily water of the Dead Sea. On Fridays Ein Feshha fills with Muslims, on Saturdays it's packed with Jews. There are buses to Ein Feshha from Jerusalem; on Saturdays there are *sheruts*. On the way to Ein Feshha you'll pass the **Caves of Qumran,** where excavations reveal the site of the discovery of the Dead Sea Scrolls. The scrolls are now in the Israel Museum, and the site is likely to be of interest only to those familiar with Biblical scholarship.

No one should miss **Ein Gedi,** however, about 30 kilometers to the south. Here you'll find a stream, waterfall, and natural pools, surrounded by the lushest vegetation in the entire Negev. This is where David hid from King Saul in the second book of Samuel, but the biblical reference that first comes to mind is the Garden of Eden, especially for someone who is plunging into the sweet-water pools after baking in the barren desert. The IYHF **Youth Hostel** has a good ambiance (everyone's so elated after setting eyes on the springs) and 200 beds. If it's full you can sleep on the grass outside.

Twenty kilometers south of Ein Gedi is **Massada,** one of the best known archaeological sites in Israel, and especially meaningful to Jews. The huge fortress-palace built by Kind Herod on the top of a plateau-topped mountain was the scene of the last holdout of the Jews against the Romans. When defeat was imminent, the defenders all committed suicide together rather than submit. There are two trails to the top of Massada and a new cable car. The easiest trail starts on the west side of the mountain, on the Arad road. The path you see from the Dead Sea side is the more difficult ''snake path.'' Whichever path you choose, start early, even at the crack of dawn, and bring a canteen. There is a **Youth Hostel** and a moderately priced hotel, run by the National Parks Authority, at the base of the mountain on the Dead Sea side.

About sixty kilometers due west of Massada is **Beersheva,** once a frontier town on the edge of the Negev, now a city of 100,000. Most of the city is new, and there's little to see. One big exception: every Thursday morning, hundreds of Bedouins, both semi-settled ones from around Beersheva, and the real thing from deep in the desert, gather in the area of Hebron St. to sell camels, clothes, cloth, jewelry, and whatever comes into their hands. The market lasts from 6 to 9am. If you buy, bargain vigorously, or bring some jeans and offer to swap. So if you are going to or from Eilat on a Wednesday, break up your journey in Beersheva, stay for the market, and then continue your trip—Beersheva has plenty of buses in both directions.

Eilat

Until 1948, Eilat was little more than a modest police outpost. Until 1956, it was a small, unremarkable town far from everything else in Israel. It began to grow when the 1956 war opened the Red Sea to Israeli shipping, and mushroomed when the capture of the Sinai gave the city enough elbow room to become Israel's major resort. In the past ten years, dozens of luxury hotels, restaurants, and tourist shops have sprouted along the beach, which boasts year-round swimming. Eilat has become a crowded, expensive and touristy resort, and most young travelers with a couple of days on their hands head south to the less commercialized beaches of **Nuweiba, Dahab,** or **Sharm el-Sheikh** on the Sinai Coast, south of Eilat.

Orientation

Using the sea as your reference point, it's easiest to divide Eilat into three major sections: the town itself, on the sloping hills above the sea; below, to the east, **Lagoon Beach,** lined with luxury hotels but also including a public beach area; and to the south, the ancient and modern ports and **Coral Beach.**

Leaving the bus terminal, you have only to cross the main road, called **Atmarim Boulevard,** to find yourself in the newly-built Commercial Center, where the Post Office is situated. Half a block down toward the waterfront is an arcade housing the very helpful Government Tourist Office (tel. 2268) and a couple of travel agencies offering tours of the Sinai. Further down Atmarim and to the right is another Tourist Office (tel. 6737), a series of eating places, and three of our recommendations for lodging.

If you plan to take the bus to Dahab or Sharm el-Sheikh, buy your ticket one to two days in advance; get a seat number attached to the ticket. To Jerusalem or Tel Aviv, do the same; and advance ticket or not, be aggressive in line and in claiming your seat—otherwise you may stand for five sweaty hours.

Caution: Before you hit the beach or head south, equip yourself with covering for your head, and a canteen or two. The dry heat here can dehydrate you quickly.

Accommodations

The IYHF **Youth Hostel** in Eilat (tel. 2358), across from the Red Rock Hotel, is clean and air-conditioned. 61 and 71IL. Next door is the cheaper, more appealing **Nophit Hostel** (tel. 2207), which charges 50IL for a bed in a 4-bed, air-conditioned room, or 100IL each for a two-person bungalow. No meals, but you can cook your own and use the refrigerator. The manager is very friendly and will store your luggage for you while you tour the Sinai.

For **camping,** there are two possibilities. There is, of course, the beach. Though obviously the cheapest bed in town, it has its problems. First, there are thieves—try not to sleep alone; women should join up with a reliable party. Secondly, rats are now on the beach near the major hotels, drawn by the garbage areas. To lessen both problems, go instead towards the Jordan border or south of the Red Rock Hotel. Alternatively, **Sun Bay** (tel. 2362), an enclosed area of bungalows near the border, charges campers 35IL, but they must have their own tents.

Food and Evenings

There are dozens of restaurants in Eilat but none are both memorable and cheap. The self-service restaurant in the bus station and the dairy café in **Hotel Etzion** best satisfy the latter condition. If you're in the Youth Hostel, eat in their restaurant; if not, try to eat there anyway. The cheapest place to buy unprepared food is the supermarket on Atmarim St., four blocks up from the beach road. There is one cinema in Eilat, but the program changes nightly. Discotheques here are noisy and a bit sleazy, but often the best opportunities to meet travel partners or buy hashish (still, caution). Beers in these places and in bars cost 10-15IL.

Sights

Eilat's number one sight is underwater. Not only will all the superhotels be out of view, but you'll find yourself in an incredibly colorful world of corals, shellfish, and exotic fish. Scuba-diving equipment and lessons are available, but a mask, snorkel, and fins are almost as good. There are coral reefs along Coral Beach, but the best ones in the Eilat area are off the Southern coast of **Coral Island,** 14 km south of Eilat (take bus #5). From the nearby shore you can take a boat to this island, on which the remnants of a crusader castle still stand. A kiosk on the shore facing the island rents skin-diving equipment for 45IL a day.

Since there are occasional sharks in the water, take the following precautions: don't swim out far from shore or with an open wound, and don't wear anything that glitters. Don't worry, the risk is very small, and the reefs are usually in very shallow water. If for some reason you don't go diving, don't miss the **Coral World Underwater Observatory and Aquarium.** A chamber fifteen feet below the surface allows you to examine coral reefs from up close. The complex might also be of interest to divers, since the aquarium tanks contain and identify specimens of many of the animals you will see in your underwater explorations. Open 8am-sunset, admission is 40IL (less with student ID). Five km south of Coral Islands is the **Fjord:** steep rugged hills plunging down into turquoise inlets. For information on day hikes and tours into the Sinai on jeep, bus, and even camel, inquire at the **Tourist Office** on Atmarim Blvd. or at **Johnny's Desert Tours** next door.

Sinai Desert

South and west of Eilat stretches the Sinai, a vast and barren desert that is greater in size than Israel itself. Under Israeli administration since the Six-Day War, the Sinai is now open to tourism, and the visit is an exciting one. Unfortunately, the only part of the Sinai that is easily toured without a four-wheel-drive vehicle is the Gulf of Eilat coast from Eilat to **Sharm el-Sheikh.** The rest of the desert hides an unexpected variety of treasures in its rugged mountains, but you have no choice but to join an organized tour to see them.

Warning: In the desert, drink more fluids than you think you need, since the dry heat dehydrates you quickly and imperceptibly. Wear a hat and don't exert yourself excessively. Ask the Tourist Office about other health precautions.

Because of the quality of the roads and the beaches, the oases on the Gulf of Eilat are fast becoming popular resorts. **Nuweiba,** 75 km south of Eilat, sports a holiday village and miles of fine, white sand beaches. There is a snack bar, a skin- and scuba-diving rental shop (40IL for snorkel, mask, and fins), and showers. To get to the nudist beach, walk south from the snack bar for about twenty minutes, or until you see people with no clothes on, whichever comes first.

The afternoon bus from Eilat continues on to **Dahab,** a less crowded, more scenic alternative to Nuweiba. A special attraction here: Bedouins will transport you from where the bus stops (**Di Zahav,** an Israeli cooperative settlement) to their Dahab, where they have built small shacks on the beach (10IL a night) for travelers. No food or water, so bring your own. The bus from Dahab continues to Sharm el-Sheikh, near the southern tip of the Sinai. Here you have two choices for lodging. The first is the air-conditioned youth hostel in Ophira—a town with facilities but little in the way of charm. The rates at the hostels are 25% higher than normal. The other option is to get off at **Na'ama Bay,** 6 km north of Ophira. There are two cafés here, plus shade pavilions under which everyone camps for free. Also located here is the **Red Sea Divers Center,** which offers good deals in scuba equipment and transport to choice diving spots. Their best deal is an all-day trip to **Ras Muhammad** plus equipment and two dives—all for only $25. Whether you go with them or make it alone, Ras Muhammad should be seen. At the tip of the Sinai, it offers rugged scenery and perhaps the best diving in the world. To appreciate your underwater exploration, purchase *The Red Sea Divers Guide,* a thorough treatment of the area.

The main stopping point on any trip inland is the **Santa Katerina Monastery** at the foot of Mt. Sinai, by tradition the mountain on which Moses received the Ten Commandments. This was one of the most isolated monasteries in the world until the Israelis built an airport next to it. Possessors of one of the world's oldest extant libraries, the Greek Orthodox monks here are also curators of some of the finest icons and mosaics in the Byzantine tradition, masterpieces that survived when almost all other contemporary work was destroyed by iconoclasts in the eighth and ninth centuries. Also of interest is the Skull Room, containing the bones of the 1500 monks who have died in the monastery. There is a wide path leading up to the peak of Mt. Sinai. The moderate climb takes four hours. To get to Santa Katerina, there are one- and two-day tours by Egged and other agencies out of Eilat and Nuweiba—costs are $33 and up. But a cheaper, more interesting trek is offered by the Bedouins in Nuweiba and Dahab—a two-day tour to Santa Katerina, including lodging and the climb, all for 250-300IL.

As long as you're spending that kind of money, it's worth it to invest a little more and really see the desert with a **Nature Protection Society** tour. They last six or seven days, and cost $140-160, food supplied. Some are for more experienced hikers, but most tours can be handled by anyone who is reasonably fit. In addition to Santa Katerina and isolated beaches along the coast, you will see lush oases, Bedouin camps, breathtaking passes and valleys, and **Serrabit el-Khadem,** the ruins of an ancient Egyptian temple. Tours leave every week during the year, but reservations far in advance are necessary for the summer. The tours offered by **Haron Ltd.** (34 Assaf St., Ramat Gan) cater to backpacking hikers. You walk several miles a day, so you have to be a good hiker, but mountaineering experience is not necessary. The extremely knowledgeable guides take you well off what little beaten track there is in the desert, to spectacular mountains, and meals with Bedouins. Rates are $200 for seven days, $270 for ten days, and $410 for a fourteen-day trip, camping gear and food included. Both agencies' tours are highly recommended.

ITALY

$1 U.S. = 800 Lire(L)   100L = $.25

The rhythms of Italian existence—mellow, capricious, and above all civilized—make up Italy's chief attraction. Except for the traffic, there is very little wild about the country; the pressures of business and pleasure have been tamed without any loss of spontaneity or vigor. Surrender yourself to the gentlest lifestyle in Europe—eat, drink, lie in the sun, and look at the world's greatest art in a place where men have been able to divide and conquer time.

Italians have domesticated history—the first century has been encased at **Pompeii** and even better at **Herculaneum;** parts of **Ravenna** are straight out of the sixth century and **San Gimignano** is maintained in its fourteenth-century entirety. Thus wrapped and packaged and left unchanged for hundreds of years, Italian cities have been preserved and not destroyed by time. In extreme cases the opposite method had to be used—at **Rome,** for example, where each century built on the ruins of the last and juxtaposed millennia in a way possible nowhere else.

The Italian view of history, of course, is not so sanguine. Controlled by petty tyrants until the 1500s and foreign overlords after that, Italy has failed to develop any sense of national unity even during Garibaldi's campaign and the *Risorgimento* movement. For Italy, the only strong government in the last century has been fascist—and some Italians today wonder if strong government in their country will ever be possible without it.

But more often they talk of local affairs and regional problems. **Milan** and **Turin** keep pace with contemporary Europe, with their long flashy boulevards and dark slums. **Venice** keeps to itself and cares about itself, as it always has: The hill towns of **Tuscany** ane **Umbria** preserve local art and customs which once influenced the world. **Emilia-Romagna** turns Communist as it prospers from farm produce and industry.

But all these areas have one thing in common—they're not the South. The problem of the **Mezzogiorno**—its poverty, its grime, and its inability to develop—is rooted in history and inclination: the North has never contributed to the South's economic development, and doesn't really want to start now as its own unemployment rolls increase. This makes a difference for the tourist—the South courts you less deftly, perhaps, but more genuinely and with more authentic "old customs" such as women in sober black dresses and food proffered on long train rides. This is even more true for **Sicily** and **Sardinia,** although not for **Naples** where petty theft is dismayingly common.

TRANSPORTATION AND ORIENTATION

Depending on where you're going, getting around inside Italy can be quick and pleasant, or fairly difficult. The *Autostrade* are fast, deserted, but very expensive; and Italian driving habits will probably make them a harrowing experience for all but the most confident. Gasoline is about $2 a gallon, though you can halve this by buying coupons at the border where you enter the country. These may be impossible to get elsewhere, so plan ahead, and buy enough coupons to cover your entire stay. Hitching is not easy, but possible; it is not recommended for women traveling alone, and is strictly prohibited on the *autostrade*—you have to wait on the approaches. As long as the dollar has a favorable exchange rate vis-à-vis the lira, Italy remains a moderately-priced country for the American tourist—but given an inflation rate of over 20%, even foreign currency buys less each month.

The major centers—Milan, Florence, Venice, Rome, and Naples—are connected by frequent, fast, and inexpensive trains. But to get from one middle-sized city to another requires some research at the train station and careful route planning. Italian trains come in several categories. The slowest *locale* stops everywhere; and the *diretto* is not much faster. The *espresso* is pretty quick, and the *rapido* is a fine express, but you need a first-class ticket or Eurailpass and have to pay about 1000L for a seat reservation. Of course, a Eurailpass is valid in Italy, and the Italians sell national railpasses (see below), but second-class fares are cheap anyway—about $5 from Rome to Florence. At the **Centro Turistico Studentesco** offices in Rome, Milan, Florence, Bologna, Naples, Turin, Padua, and Perugia you can get big reductions on long journeys inside or outside Italy as well as on student charter flights. There's really no reason to travel first class most of the time; if you get terribly uncomfortable, just move into that section of the carriage (there are always empty seats); the most the conductor can do is kick you out. The **Italian State Railways,** 500 Fifth Ave., New York, NY 10036, can sell you an Italian **Go-Anywhere** pass or Eurailpass: the former lasts 8, 15, 21, or 30 days, but is probably not worth it except for convenience's sake.

One of the extra benefits of traveling by train is the convenience of the *bagaglia a mano* booths in the station where you can leave your bags while you forage for rooms. Even if you have a reservation, it's sometimes a good idea to come back and pick up your stuff after a few hours' rest. Train stations in major cities maintain an *albergo diurno*, usually fairly clean if unenticing places where you can find toilets and showers. Like the baggage deposit service, this costs 200-500L. Your ISIC or hostel card gives you free entry to the washrooms in any national museum. All bars have bathrooms which they'll let you use, and will usually give you a *bicchiere* of water if you ask.

In general, women traveling without men will receive a lot of attention from Italian men, which may become annoying, but is rarely dangerous. The best way to get rid of someone who is really annoying you is to behave as though he weren't there—after a while even the most persistent will give up the game. Unmarried couples will have no problems getting a double room, even when specifying a *letto matrimoniale* (double bed). Where *pensioni* have multi-bed rooms, though, men and women will invariably be segregated.

The drug scene is fairly dangerous. The police are indiscriminately efficient and vindictive; the courts are merely slow, and you can wind up in jail for a year without trial, where the authorities can or will do nothing to help you.

The Italian telephone system works in the following way: you buy a *gettone* (token) for 50L at a bar, and hold it in the slot of the phone while you dial your number. When a voice at the other end says *"Pronto"* you push the coin into the slot and begin to talk. In the more modern phones, you drop the token in first.

Finding a street address can be tough. Evens are on one side of the street and odds on the other, but 81 and 82, for example, might be blocks apart. In Florence, it's even more confusing—shops are numbered with a separate sequence of red numbers, as in Via delle Terme 53/r. The back of the Yellow Pages *(Pagine Gialle)* in many Italian cities has a good street map with cross-indices; often the Tourist Office will too.

Italian bars are more like social clubs than drinking holes, serving more *gelati* (ice cream) than anything else. If you drink, you order what you want from the cashier, pay for it, then take the receipt to the counter and get the goods. This is true for *tavole calde* and many small stores also. Tips—even if minute—are a necessary courtesy in Italy; you'd be surprised how many more things a museum guard will show you for 500L. Bus tickets and *gettoni* are acceptable tips for bathroom attendants.

Most buses are equipped with ticket machines that require change of 100L or 150L; but if you don't have change, just sit down (although there are ridiculously few seats, because the buses are so narrow). Conductors rarely check for receipts except on longer, extra-urban journeys, but if they do, you can almost always plead foreigner's ignorance.

For information on study in Italy (either during the summer or during the year), write to **Istituto Italiano di Cultura,** 686 Park Ave., New York, NY 10021.

ENIT, 630 Fifth Ave., New York, NY 10020 has an invaluable list of hostels and campsites in Italy and a general information booklet.

Getting the change required for survival in Italy may prove difficult. One of the most noticeable symptoms of the country's myriad economic problems, for the tourist, is the drastic shortage of *spiccioli*—coin. Rumor has it that the officials of the Italian mint are selling the metal to Japan to make cheap watches—in any case, no Italian seems to have any. Cities have responded to the problem by printing their own paper currency—you may get a 100L note stamped *"Banca di Credito di Genova,"* for example. These bills are no longer illegal, but may not always be accepted outside the area where they were issued. Pawn them off in tips or when making a minor purchase. Other common forms of changes are bus tickets, *gettoni,* stamps, and candy (10L).

Hotel prices are posted, but be sure you know the total before you take a room. Most of the places to stay listed for the various cities are *pensioni;* most Italian cities also have cheap hotels near the railroad station whose prices are comparable. These, though, are usually bleak, sordid, and depressing; but even with *pensioni,* it is a good idea to break the railroad-station-accommodation syndrome even at the cost of a few hundred lire—you'll probably like the city a lot better and see more of it.

Finally, Italy in the summer is hot. Not as hot as Greece, North Africa, or Spain, but the heat is something to contend with. You'll get used to it after a week or so, and the public swimming pools may help, but remember the weather when deciding what to take with you and how to allot your time. More and more lodgings are trying to keep room costs down by charging 500-1000L for showers, so you might as well hit a pool for the same price, and shower there.

FOOD

Italian breakfasts are light. *Cappuccino* or *cafè latte*—espresso with milk—is the staple, and a roll will complete your *prima colazione.* Lunch is the big meal in Italy; everything closes down from 1-4pm, so you might as well enjoy it. *Tavole calde* and *rosticcerie* (grill) are two forms of inexpensive eateries. *Trattorie, osterie,* and *ristoranti* are, in roughly ascending order, fancier and more expensive places. Many cheaper restaurants don't have menus—if they do, don't expect them to have everything on it. Always check the bread and cover charge *(pane e coperto).* Also, bills are often wrong in the restaurant's favor—check them too.

Italian meals consist of a *primo piatto,* pasta or soup; and a *secondo piatto,* meat or fish—usually followed by salad, cheese, or fruit. If you don't want both courses, say so firmly.

Pasta is the national specialty of Italy, and it comes in all shapes and under all sauces. After tomato, the most common kind of sauce in the north is called *panna* and is made out of cream. Milan and Bologna lean heavily on the meat-and-tomato sauce called *bolognese,* and in Rome the favorites are *amatriciana* (tomato and bacon) and *carbonara* (bacon, eggs, and cheese). Try some sort of pasta *al pesto*—a green sauce made with basil and garlic—and *algorgonzola* (in the north), perhaps the best of all. Italy's cheeses—notably gorgonzola and parmesan—are excellent. In bars try *acqua minerale,* (which tastes like club soda), or *spuma* (apple soda). Whiskey is within range—800-1000L—but be sure to try some Italian alcoholic beverages. Among them are: *grappa,* a liqueur native to the Dolomites and flavored with different fruits; *sambuca,* a sweet Roman specialty with coffee beans floating in it; and *Campari,* a bitter-sweet concoction which comes in alcoholic and non-alcoholic versions.

The only way to avoid art in Italy is to travel through the country with your eyes closed. If you follow the rest of the tourists, though, and trudge through miles of dull museums, you will leave feeling bored and cheated. To get off the beaten track and enjoy it, however, takes preparation, legwork, and patience. In the first place, pick up a reference guide—the *Michelin Green, Benn's Blue,* or Fodor's *Companion* series are all reliable if uninspired. You might want to skim an introduction to the subject like L. and P. Murray's *Architecture of the Renaissance* ($3.95) or Berenson's *Italian Painters of the Renaissance* ($5.95).

One aspect of museum-craft especially important in Italy is the practice of closing works of art for restoration, or, in the Italian phrase that will become dismayingly familiar—*chiuso per restauro*. This can mean that honest, important work is going on that shouldn't be interrupted—a collapsing building may need to be shored up, or a lost fresco may have been uncovered; but just as often it means that the Italian art bureaucracy is taking its time about reopening a site. The best way to get into these places is straightforward—ring the bell and tell whoever answers it that you want to go in. If he tells you it's closed, there are more devious lines of attack open. You can make believe you don't understand him and hope he'll let you in to avoid the trouble of standing there explaining; or you can offer him a modest sum for his help.

Northern Italy

You can tell you're in the North when tourism gets more packaged, plumbing gets better, and Germans predominate as fellow travelers—but beyond its more Western attitude, Northern Italy defies any generalizations. **Emilia-Romagna** is Italy's breadbasket; **Bologna** and **Parma** deserve visits because of their food alone, although they both have fine artistic traditions as well; **Lombardy** is dominated by **Milan,** a cosmopolitan and increasingly grimy city; to the west, **Genoa** and **Turin** are gateways to the Italian Riviera and France; to the north and northeast is the **Dolomite Range,** one of the world's premier hiking areas. Along the center strip between Romagna and the Dolomites is the province of **Veneto:** travel from Milan through this necklace of jeweled towns, from **Verona** to **Mantua, Vicenza, Padua,** and finally the capital city, **Venice** itself. South of Venice is good, but not great, coastline; the best is around **Ravenna** with its Byzantine mosaics.

Although prices are higher in the North (Venetian accommodations are roughly 33% higher than the rest of the country's), there are youth hostels and religious-run dormitories in most major cities, as well as campsites everywhere. Hitching is the best in Italy; train fares seem high though they're still reasonable.

Milan (Milano)

For every church in Rome, it is said, there is a bank in Milan. Rome is the ceremonial capital, but the power lies here. The city has been maligned for so long for being over-industrialized and crowded that most people don't bother to leave the Train Station when passing through; for its size, Milan is surprisingly untouristed. If you don't already know about them, you'll be amazed by the scattered treasures that make Milan trail only Florence, Rome, and maybe Venice as an art city. And if you're tired of the living-in-the-past atmosphere of most Italian cities, Milan has more than enough contemporary energy.

Orientation

Milan's inhabitants have grumbled over its expansion for centuries, and today only a small part of the oldest Roman section remains. Two monuments dominate the old medieval city, whose walls were torn down for wide nineteenth-century boulevards: The **Castello Sforzesco** in the northwest and the fairy-tale **Gothic Duomo** (Cathedral) in the center. Like most Milanese, you probably can't afford lodgings in this area, but the best subway and train system in Italy makes it no more than fifteen minutes and 200L away. Once there, you'll find most of Milan's art, opera, theater, fine architecture, and good stores. Six train stations penetrate the middle rings of Milan; the chief one is the **Stazione Centrale** in the northeast. Be sure to go to the right station for your departure train. The Centrale and the **Stazione Garibaldi** are the most convenient, since Metro line #2 goes to them. The city is huge and walks are long except in the old city.

Addresses and Telephone Numbers

Ente Turismo (Tourist Office): Via Marconi 1 (tel. 87 00 16), off the Piazza Duomo. Also at the Stazione Centrale and the airports. Open 8:30am-12:30pm and 2:30-6:30pm. Closed Sundays. Extremely professional information services.

American Express: Via Vittore Pisani 19 (tel. 66 97 21), near the Main Station. Open Mon.-Fri. 9am-6pm, Sat. 9am-noon.

Post Office: Stazione Centrale or Via Cordusio 4 (tel. 80 75 95).

Vacanze (Student Travel): Via Rastrelli 2 (tel. 87 84 91).

CIT (Railroad Office): In the Galleria (tel. 86 66 61).

Police and First Aid: (tel. 113).

U.S. Consulate: Piazza della Repubblica 32 (tel. 65 28 41).

Canadian Consulate: Via Vittore Pisani 19 (tel. 65 26 00).

Pool: Via Ponzio 35 (tel. 29 22 24). Admission 500L; closed Wednesdays.

Accommodations

Milan is full of lodgings, with over sixty *pensioni* in the 5000-7000L per double range. You can usually find a room west and north of the Stazione Centrale; try **Piazza Aspromonte** on **Via Lulli, Via Lippi, Via Vallazze,** or **Via Ricordi.** There are a few places in the old city, but try to reserve ahead of time or call before trudging to the center. The **Catholic Youth Association** has a room-finding service at the Stazione Centrale and the Tourist Office has a cross-indexed map of hotels. The first three *pensioni* listed are near the Stazione Centrale (a fifteen-minute walk).

Albergo San Luca, Via Porpora 48 (tel. 236 53 71). Typical cheap lodgings at 4000L for singles, 6000L for doubles. Showers extra.

Pensione Cuba, Via Ricordi 14 (tel. 271 64 70). Drab rooms but cheap prices and friendly management. Singles 3500L, doubles 5500L. Instead of taking a shower for 500L, go to the pool on Via Poncio.

Pensione Lippi, Via Lippi 48 (tel. 236 12 05). On a street filled with *pensioni,* it's the cheapest of them all. Doubles a steal at 4000L, but not too convenient.

Albergo Castello, Via Rovello 9 (tel. 80 78 35), is a good place in a terrific location, but is usually full, so call early. Doubles 8000L with board, 6000L without; singles 4000L.

Pensione Moscova, Via Moscova 27 (tel. 66 55 23). Not inside the old city, but near the Castello and a subway stop. Doubles 5500L, singles 3800L, but showers cost.

Youth Hostel Piero Rotta (IYHF), Viale Salmoiraghi 1 (tel. 36 70 95). Places for 200 men and 200 women at 2200L per night. Take Metro 1 or bus #90 to San Siro and walk the length of the racetrack. Then turn left onto Viale Salmoiraghi. 11pm curfew.

Food

There are inexpensive *rosticcerie* and *trattorie* scattered throughout the city, especially in the Piazzale Loreto area. **Trattoria da Mino,** on Viale Abruzzi 11, is typical; try the cold soups, *lasagne al forno,* and *insalata mista.* Nearby on Viale Abruzzi 86, **Salumeria Barchiana** has the lowest prices for provisions in the city—if you haven't had parmesan cheese yet, get it here. Around the corner on Via Pecchio, **La Zingarella** serves unbelievable portions of *gelati*—a *vaschetta* for 600L will stuff two people with or without a meal. Via Gran Sasso is lined with *trattorie.* For a 4000L fixed price, you can get a truly sumptuous meal at **Mamma's,** Via Tommaso 6. **Trattoria da Silvano,** on Corso Garibaldi 11 (around the corner from the Biblioteca Ambrosiana), has good food at moderate prices. The **University Mensa,** Via Festa del Perdono 7, serves meals for 1000L and up.

Sights

Start with the **Duomo** (open 7am-7pm), a 600-year-old tribute to Milanese talent and money. Stylistically, it's a mixture of flamboyant French and stolid Italian Gothic; but the individual gables, pinnacles, and belfries could keep you and your camera occupied for hours. Walk around it first; then after a look at the stained-glass and rose windows inside, ascend to the roof (stairs closed; elevator 500L, closed Mondays) and stroll among the 135 pinnacles and 200 statues. The **Galleria Vittorio Emanuele** on the left (a *galleria* is a Victorian iron and glass enclosure of a city block, and Milan is full of them) has some of Italy's finest shops. Go through it to **La Scala,** the world's most famous opera house. The opera season is over by May, but there are evening concerts in the summer. Balcony seats cost 1000L and should be bought early at the box office (tel. 80 70 41).

Up Via Verdi is Via Brera and the **Pinacoteca di Brera,** one of Italy's finest museums (open Tues.-Sat. 9am-2pm, Sun. 9am-1pm; 500L without ISIC card, Sun. free). There are 38 rooms filled with an incredible collection of Italian masters, but due to a lack of funds at least 25 of them are closed. Look for Raphael's *Marriage of the Virgin,* Mantegna's foreshortened *Dead Christ,* and Caravaggio's *Supper At Emmaus.* The **Museo Poldi-Pezzuoli** (open 9:30am-12:30pm and 2:30-5:30pm; also 9-11pm on Thurs. except in August; closed Mon.; admission 500L), is a beautiful product of the nineteenth-century mania for collecting art in one's *palazzo.* The gallery's trademark is the *Portrait of a Woman*, but it is strong in Persian carpets, bronzes, and other *objets d'art*. The **Castello Sforzesco** (open 9:30am-noon and 2:30-5:30pm; admission free), has walls twelve feet thick, and its interior has been redone in super-modern style to provide an excellent setting for sculpture, including Michelangelo's second-best *Pietà*. The grounds in back of the Castle are perfect for a pick-up soccer game or picnic in an anything-goes atmosphere.

The High Renaissance began with Leonardo da Vinci's *Last Supper*, made for the dining room wall of **Santa Maria delle Grazie** (open Tues.-Sat. 10am-5pm, admission 200L; Sun. 9am-1pm, free). The fresco is not nearly as ruined as some say, though it is rumored that restoration has been so extensive that not a single piece of Leonardo's paint remains. Nearby, the **Biblioteca Ambrosiana** in Piazza Pio XI (open 9:30am-5pm, closed Sat.; admission 500L), houses his *Codice Atlantico*, along with Petrarch's copy of Virgil with his annotations, and several thousand other fascinating manuscripts. The da Vinci and the Virgil, however, are so fragile that you will only be allowed to see reproductions. Upstairs, the **Pinacoteca Ambrosiana** possesses a portrait by Leonardo and Raphael's cartoon for the School of Athens fresco in the Vatican. The da Vinci devotee can also hunt down the master in various churches in Milan, such as the **Chiesa de'Affori,** which holds a serene Madonna—there is more Leonardo in Milan than anywhere else in Italy.

Verona

Despite its thoroughly professional treatment of tourists, Verona is undeniably charming—a melange of Roman ruins, pink *piazze,* and fanciful sepulchres. The town is the setting of the original *Romeo and Juliet* which a local movie house has been running assiduously for the last fifteen years. Moreover, Verona has been a trade crossroad for millennia, and remains the gateway to the Dolomites, the Veneto, and Lake Garda all at once. Come during late July or August when the annual summer festival climaxes with nightly opera in the 22,000-seat Roman arena. It's a five-hour extravaganza; tickets are fairly expensive at 3500L (usually available the day of the performance), but staging and productions are imaginative and the traditional candle-lighting during the overture is unforgettable. Bring a cushion, though.

Verona is easy to get to, but it's expensive to stay in. Accommodations should be booked way in advance if you don't fancy a hardy hike after the opera. Try the **Rosa,** Vicolo Raggiri 9 (off Via Rosa) with doubles at 6000L or the **Marina,** Via Ponte Nuovo 5 (tel. 25968) for 8100L. The **Casa della Giovane,** Rigaste San Zeno 3 (tel. 24968) houses women for the unbeatable price of 2500L a night. They run a reception office at the Station in the afternoon, but if it's closed just take bus #2 to Castelvecchio and walk back along the river; the entrance is in a warehouse courtyard. The male equivalent is **Istituto Don Bosco,** Via Provolo 16. Take the same bus to the same stop. It's 500L cheaper but has an unfortunate 10:30pm curfew. If you don't find a room, try **Camping Romeo e Giulietta** on Via Bresciana 54 (tel. 56 49 12) for bunk-bed hovels at 5000L. Buses run hourly from the Train Station (450L). Better still, stay at one of the many campsites on Lake Garda. The **Tourist Office** at Piazza Bra 10 (tel. 30086) has a list.

The University quarter, across the river, has some cheap lodgings and restaurants, but for local specialties hit the *tavola calda,* at **Via Regina d'Ungheria 5,** off the Piazza dell' Erbe in the old quarter. The real specialty of Verona, though, is its wine—the *Soave* and *Valpolicella* grown nearby. You can sample the different varieties for 200L a glass at Via Arche Scaligeri 4, right opposite the tombs; the *bottega vini* at Scudo di Francia 3, off the Via Mazzini is slightly more expensive, but in a pleasant setting, and sells salads, cold meat, and so on.

From the Rail Station take the bus (150L) or walk to the **Piazza Bra,** still dominated by the almost perfectly preserved **Roman Arena** where the acoustics are still uncannily good. Walk up Via Mazzini to the **Piazza dell'Erbe** where hokey modern trinkets are sold beside merchant palaces and symbols of Venetian hegemony. Around the corner are the **Piazza dei Signori** and **Tombs of the Scaligers** (open 9am-12:30pm and 3-6pm), the peculiar Gothic remnants of Verona's medieval tyrants, the della Scala. Their effigies are perched so high that it is difficult to judge their personality, but you can take note of the fact that it was a family tradition to name male della Scalas after dogs. Thus, *Cangrande,* the name of the clan's most prominent representative, means "big dog," *Mastino* "mastiff," and *Cansignorio* simply "chief dog." The stronghold of these enigmatic men was the **Castelvecchio,** completely destroyed in the last war and rebuilt soon after. Inside is an unexciting, modern museum. The **Duomo,** a mixture of Gothic and Romanesque architecture, stands on the supposed site of the Temple of Minerva. Note the typical Lombard doorway.

If it is there, see Mantegna's altarpiece in **San Zeno Church,** which is a very slippery painting. Napoleon took it to Paris and parts of it are still scattered through France. In 1973, it was stolen, but it is now on view, a bit the worse for wear. Don't hesitate to pay 100L to have it lit up if you have to. San Zeno itself is the most beautiful church of Verona, full of twelfth-century carvings and frescoes.

Mantua (Mantova)

Between the Bologna-Milan and Milan-Verona-Venice train routes, lovely and remarkably untouristed Mantua is rich in Renaissance art and architecture. If you plan on seeing Verona during the day, take the forty-minute train ride (700L) down here for the night; prices are much more reasonable, and a morning of sightseeing should cover the town pretty well.

From the **Rail Station** along Lago Superiore, Corso Vittorio Emanuele (which changes to Umberto later on) leads into **Piazza Duomo,** one of the only Romanesque remainders of a town which boasts about Virgil, Mantegna, and Giulio Romano. The last's work is evident in the **Palazzo Ducale,** built for the Gonzaga family; the highlight of the Palace complex, however, is Mantegna's *Marriage Chamber,* now the center of a museum that includes Raphael tapestries and classical sculpture. (Open Tues.-Sat. 9am-2pm, admission 150L; Sun. 9am-1pm, free). A lengthwise stroll through the town brings you past Mantegna's and Romano's houses to the **Palazzo del Te,** designed and decorated by Romano for a horse-loving Gonzaga (open Tues.-Sat. 9am-12:30pm and 3-6pm, Sun. 9am-1pm; admission 300L). Don't miss (you can't miss) the *Room of the Giants,* a neurotic apocalypse of *trompe d'oeil*. Cool off with a visit to the pool next door (500L).

The nearby hamlet of **Lunetta San Giorgio** has the IYHF **Youth Hostel** (tel. 22415) and Campsite **Sparafucile,** both open March 15-October 15 and extremely comfortable. Buses go from the Piazza Duomo to the renovated citadel. Mantua itself has a bevy of *locande* (hotels) in the 3500L single, 5000L double range: the **Palazzina** on Piazzale Don Leoni, the **Gambarara** on Via Gambarara, and **La Bruscetta** on Via Cremona. The **Arduini** on Via

Giulio Romano is especially cheap and convenient. The same is true of eating spots—nothing spectacular, but everything's nice; with *pane e coperto* charges rarely above 300L.

Padua (Padova)

Padua has been a student city for more than six hundred years and profited handsomely from it. The city is small but cosmopolitan, and is a good stopover on the way to Venice, or a place to re-adjust to the mainland afterwards.

Like all Continental universities, Padua has no campus in the American sense, but penetrates the whole city. Look for the satiric posters on the walls of the **Palazzo Bo'**, which commemorate the academic and sexual careers of graduating seniors. The Palazzo Bo', which can be loosely translated as "Cow Palace," is the University's headquarters and contains a famous anatomical theater, which you may be allowed to see if no classes are being held. The **Cafe Pedrocchi** across the street was the focal point of the University in the 1800s; once the haunt of the liberal intelligentsia, it is now rather stodgy and expensive.

Padua's greatest treasure is the **Cappella Scrovegni,** located in the gardens along the Corso Garibaldi. (Open 9am-12:30pm and 2:30-5:30pm, entry 500L.) Giotto designed the chapel and decorated it with a magnificent cycle of frescoes, depicting the life of Christ. Mantegna's frescoes in the **Chiesa degli Eremitani** next door were severely damaged in World War II, but the remaining fragments are brilliant. Keep following the Corso Garibaldi (which turns into Via VIII Febbraio), and you'll come upon the Piazzas delle Erbe and delle Frutta, which surround Padua's famous food market, the **Salone.** Take a look at the **Sala della Ragione** upstairs and its wooden horse. It's not worth the entrance fee unless there's an exhibit on—just peek in the door. Take the Via Antenore, then turn left down Via del Santo to get to **Il Santo,** an amazing church dedicated to the patron saint of Padua, St. Anthony—the saint of lost objects. The architecture mixes half a dozen major styles. Don't miss Donatello's **Gattamelata,** an imposing statue in the courtyard. The **Oratorio di San Giorgio** just outside shows where Giotto's students studied his art, and the **Scuola di Sant'Antonio** contains the sixteenth century's tribute to the saint in frescoes, among which are four early Titians.

Padua has lots of good, cheap rooms. Cheapest is the IYHF **Youth Hostel** (tel. 81076) in the reconstructed medieval Castle of Alberi at Porta Legnano in nearby Montagnana. It houses men and women in dorm rooms for 1500L a night. Take the bus for Montagnana from Via Trieste 42 (every thirty minutes from 7am to 10:30pm); the trip takes an hour. If you prefer to spend your time in the city, the **Mazzini,** on Via Giotto 36 (tel. 39302), has fair but showerless lodgings at 2000L per head. The **Moderno,** Via Manin 35 (tel. 24432) is still a good buy at 3500L for a single and 6500L for a double. Also try **Locanda Lidia,** Via Foscolo 2 for 3000L and 5000L respectively.

The best place to eat is the Salone Market, but there are a few inexpensive *trattorie* along the Via del Santo; and the **Mensa Universitaria,** Via San Francesco 122, is well located and serves meals for 800L (open 11:30am-1:30pm and 7-8:30pm, closed in August). Also try the **Mensa Ampi,** Via Padovanino; or the **Mensa Leopardi,** Via Leopardi; both have meals around 1000L. **Mappa,** a self-service in the basement of a modern office complex (Piazza Matteotti) across from the Scrovegni Chapel, has excellent cheap food. **Pe Pen** is a restaurant/*trattoria* near the Piazza Cavour; try the minestrone or rice first courses.

Addresses and Telephone Numbers

Tourist Office: Rail Station and Riviera Mugnai (tel. 651856).

University Offices: *(Ufficio Informazione)*, Via San Francesco 122, open 9-11:30am weekdays.

Police: Via Santa Chiara (tel. 113).

First Aid: Ospedale Civile (tel. 661011).

Pool: Strada Canal Morto 3 (tel. 68 14 40).

Venice (Venezia)

Venice, the floating city, balances delicately over a hundred islands. It is not her art, history, or scenery that attracts hordes of tourists here, but her peculiar mode of existence. The myth of Venice—mystery, romance, and deception—makes her one of the most intriguing cities in Europe. Sure, there will be some disillusionment. Visconti caught the cackling of the tourists and the private sneering of the Venetians just right in his film version of *Death in Venice* (a movie you'll never see in this city). But this is still the *Serenissima*—the most serene republic, and the amusement-park atmosphere can't destroy its sinuous strength and beauty.

Venice rose to power, and kept it, by guile and subtle exploitation. The great bronze horses on **San Marco** come from the sack of Constantinople in 1204, a sack the Venetians carried out in repayment for shipping Crusaders to the East. One triumph followed another. Venice grew strong enough to monopolize Adriatic trade routes, to outfit one galley in a day at the State Arsenal, and to take on the rest of Europe in 1508 and fight to a draw. But with the advent of national monarchies and huge standing armies, Venice fell by the wayside; she remained a peculiarly stable oligarchy only because no one bothered to push her over until Napoleon.

Now, Venice is still masking and exploiting; the powers that be fix its hotel rates at one-third higher than anywhere else in Italy. You'll also find the finest con artists in the country here.

But the city itself is being threatened—by the sea that covers the lower steps of all the *palazzi* on the Grand Canal. Venice is using up the fresh-water cushion that keeps it afloat, and no one has found a solution to its sinkage of an inch per decade. Whether her ending is clean and spectacular or slow and sordid, the city is not going to be around forever and you should make up your mind about her while you can.

Orientation

You won't see any cars in Venice. Banning them was one of the smartest things the city could do: the river-traffic is hard enough to cope with. The rewards of this absence are many—Venetian buildings have not been turned black by exhaust fumes, the city is very quiet for an Italian town, and, for the first few days or hours, Venice is an endlessly surprising labyrinth of water, stone, and flowers.

If you drive to Venice, you'll have to leave your car in the **Piazzale Roma**, where you'll have to pay; or park on the long causeway approaching it, if you can find a spot. Once inside the city, use the *vaporetto* which runs up the **Grand Canal** (lines 1 and 3 (200L) are locals; lines 2 and 4 (400L) express). They're slow and crowded, but foot traffic is even more so. You can usually get away with flashing the same ticket over and over since transport costs add up—the guards are too harassed to check. Motorboat taxis are 2000L and the gondolas a whopping 20,000L. If you want to hear the traditional *barcarolle* of the gondoliers, lean over the bridge at night on any of the larger canals.

Telling you to "get lost" in a beautiful city is one of the easiest things a guidebook can do, but in the case of Venice, getting lost can't be avoided, even if you have a map and even if you are the greatest navigator since Marco Polo. But since there is no direct way of getting anywhere, you're not much worse off than the local populace. On top of this, you probably won't be able to make yourself understood when you ask directions, even if you know some Italian. Venetians have their own dialect and tend to do things like call San Giovanni e Paolo "San Zanipolo." The best thing to do is to follow the signs to the main destinations—San Marco, rail station, etc.—and move on from there.

Since Venice became the main stop of the eighteenth–century Grand Tour, the literature about her has grown tremendously. The best of the current crop is Hugh Honour's *Companion Guide to Venice* (Fodor), a fine scholar's enthusiastic description of the city's art.

Addresses and Telephone Numbers

Tourist Office: Piazza San Marco, Ascensione 71/C (tel. 26356), in the corner of the square farthest from the church. Also at the Rail Station (tel. 715016).

Youth Tourist Organization: Ca' Foscari, Dorsoduro 3246 (tel. 38969). San Toma stop.

American Express: San Marco, Bocca di Piazza 1261 (tel. 700 844). Near the Piazza on a side street past the Post Office. Totally inefficient and almost sure to misfile your mail.

Cook's Travel: Piazzetta dei Leoncini 289.

CIT: San Marco 48.

Albergo Diurno: at the far end of Piazza San Marco, near American Express.

Police: Fondamenta San Lorenzo (tel. 20406).

First Aid: (tel. 30000).

Accommodations

Ironically, the cheapest lodgings in Venice are at places which don't have to register with the city, such as private homes and religious- or charity-run dormitories. Try to look for these; the **San Pantalon** area is good for this. Avoid the **Lista di Spagna,** even if you arrive late, because prices run about 5500L a head, and the quality is awful. Also, watch out for closet-like rooms and hefty surcharges tacked on for showers. A final note: Venice has big, beastly mosquitoes; and if you're sensitive, head for the upper floors of buildings, where their numbers diminish. The Train Station EPT has a list of hotel rooms and is well meaning if fairly ineffectual.

STUDENT ACCOMMODATIONS

Domus Cavanis Accademia, Rio Terra Foscarini 912A (tel. 87374), behind and to the left of the museum. Modern, clean, and well located, but expensive for student accommodations—singles 4000L, doubles 7000L. Open mid-June through September; midnight curfew but friendly management.

Casa della Studentessa "Domus Cívica," San Rocco 3082 (tel. 24332). Unadorned but OK, singles 4000L with bath; doubles 7000L. Breakfast is 400L and lunch and dinner about 1500L each. Open July-September, women only; 11:30pm curfew.

Casa dello Studente, "Ca'Foscari," Dorsoduro 3863 (tel. 35809). Decent rooms in a modernized building. Open July and August, men only, and a 1am curfew. Singles 3500L, doubles and triples 3000L per person; free showers.

Ostello della Gioventù (IYHF) Giudecca, Fondamenta Zitelle 86 (tel. 38211). 2500L per night in 12-15 bed rooms. On La Giudecca, the large island off the main part of the city—take the *vaporetto* for "le Zitelle" from the Riva degli Schiavoni near San Marco. 11pm curfew; in the summer, get there before 5pm registration or you won't get in.

Camping: There is no longer any camping on the Lido di Venezia, but the whole area of **Litorale del Cavallino** is one long row of camping sites on the beach. Take the *vaporetto* from San Marco for **Punta Sabbioni** (#14 or 15). The two largest sites are: **Marina,** Punta Sabbioni (tel. 966 146), and **Union,** Via Fausta (tel. 968 081), but some of the smaller ones are nicer.

HOTELS AND PENSIONI

Hotel Falier, Calle de Ca'Falier 1266, off the Salizzada San Pantalon (tel. 28 882). Not cheap but an excellent buy in Venice—a new building with clean, modern rooms. Doubles are 11,400L and triples around 13,000L.

Alloggi Stefania, Fondamenta Tolentini 181A, near the Piazzale Roma and the Church of the Tolentini. Another excellent choice, especially for larger groups—pleasant place with new bathrooms, showers at no extra cost in many rooms, some rooms with frescoed ceilings, others overlooking a canal or a garden. Double 9600L, triples and quads 3000L per person. Walk to the Railroad Station and take the *vaporetto* from there. No singles, but if it's not full, you might get a room to yourself.

Casa da Pino, Salizzada da San Pantalon 3942 (tel. 23646). Clean with free showers in a noisy but untouristed area. Singles 3800L, doubles 9600L.

Casa Peron, down the street and across a bridge, at #85 (tel. 86038) has even better rooms and showers, but watch the mosquitoes. Singles 3800L, doubles 8500L; one of the city's best buys.

Locanda della Mora, San Croce 42 (tel. 35703). Clean and friendly. Singles 6000L, doubles 10,000L without breakfast.

Locanda Ca'Foscari, Calle della Frescada 3888 (tel. 25817). Near the Fores-

teria Universitaria, fairly clean, and pleasant. Singles 6000L, doubles 9500L,
triples 10,800L.

Locanda Riva, Ponte dell'Angelo (or Anzolo) 5310 (tel. 27034). Just a block
or two from San Marco, a very pleasant place with doubles for 10,800L, triples
for 4500L per person, including hot showers.

Pensione Bernàrdi Semenzato, Calle Bembo 4363 (tel. 27257). Quiet, but
rooms are not very large. Nice doubles for 9400L, triples around 12,000L.

Locanda Sturion, Rialto 679 or Calle Sturion 6 (tel. 36243). Some rooms
with excellent views. Singles 5000L, doubles 7000L.

Locanda Greggio, 100 meters from the Ponte Zaccaria on Campo SS. Filippo
e Giacomo, quite near San Marco (tel. 31315). Clean, huge rooms of faded
elegance. 4000L for a single, 7200L for a double. Bath 400L.

Food

Venice's exotic specialties—squid, octopus, and crayfish—are complemented by more mundane seafood like *zuppa di pesce* (fish soup), *risotto*
(rice with various fish sauces) and *fritto misto di mare* (mixed seafood).
Watch out, though— Venetian seafood is ridiculously expensive. One way to
beat the system is to eat as the Venetians do—at tiny *osterie* or *tavole calde*
where you can sample a little of many dishes. Another is to buy seafood by
the *etto* (100 grams) at these places, then go to a *trattoria* and have a proper
primo. The **Dorsoduro** near the Rialto is great in this respect. If you don't
like seafood or find it too expensive, *fegato alla Veneziana* (liver cooked like
steak) is well worth trying.

Trattoria Antica Torre, Campo Beccerie Rialto 833, near the bridge. Good,
reasonably-priced food, even the meat dishes.

Taverna Livio, Calle San Pantaleo, Dorsoduro 3757. As cheap as you'll find
in the city and quite tasty; the *risotto con pesce* is delicious.

Gatto che Ride, Bacino Orseolo. The cheapest *tavola calda* near San Marco,
with stuffed peppers and pasta dishes for 1000-1200L.

Trattoria Città di Brindisi, Campo San Margherita. In a cheap eating area;
good food for 3000L although selection is limited. Drinks not included so
watch it. Closed Fridays.

Mensa Universitaria, Calle de la Fìscada, off the Salizzada San Pantalon.
The absolute cheapest meal you can get—450L for pasta, a main course,
vegetable, fruit, bread, and wine. Lunch noon-2pm, dinner 7-8:45pm; technically you're ineligible but look woebegone.

Sights

If you can, approach the **Piazza San Marco** by water or at the far end—
the blues and golds of San Marco, the pinks and whites of the **Doge's
Palace,** and the red and gray of the **Campanile** are electric. San Marco is
more crowded with tourists than any other place you've ever seen, so climb
the **Galleria Basilica** (open 9am-5:30pm, admission 200L) to see even more
in the square outside, as well as the bronze Moors that strike the clock hours.

Don't miss the **Pala D'Oro,** an unbelievably rich reliquary (300L) or the Byzantine mosaics in the narthex. The rich collection of paintings in the Doges' Palace is displayed well, and the 1000L admission price was recently reduced to 300L for ISIC card holders.

Some Venetian art is still scattered in local churches—**Santa Maria dei Frari** (open 9:30am-1pm and 2:30-6pm, admission 75L for students) has some superb Titians, and both this church and **San Zaccaria** have Giovanni Bellinis—but the cream of Venetian painting is in the **Accademia** (9am-2pm, closed Mondays). The works of Giorgione and Giovanni Bellini are the highlights here, and works of different generations of the Venetian dynasties—Vivarini, Palma, and Bellini—are interesting to see in one place. The Venetians preferred Tintoretto, though, and his career is distilled in one place—the **Scuola di San Rocco** (9am-1pm and 3:30-6:30pm, admission 1000L). The *scuole* were peculiarly Venetian institutions devoted to religious purposes, and Tintoretto was commissioned to decorate this one with a series of 56 paintings.

The **Ca'd'Oro,** if it ever re-opens after its restoration, is the best example of a Venetian Gothic *palazzo* in the grand style, and has a good picture gallery. The **Museo Correr** (open 10am-4pm, Sun. 9:30am-12:30pm, closed Tues.; admission 500L), at the far end of the Piazza San Marco, has a collection of Venetial memorabilia—Doges' hats, etc.—that will interest you if you want to know about the city's customs and ceremonies. The place to see modern art in Venice is the **Peggy Guggenheim Foundation,** near the Accademia at San Gregorio 701 (open Mon., Wed., and Fri., 3-5pm). The collection is strong in Picasso, Léger, and Chagall, and is well displayed in an informal setting. Admission is free, but the paintings are unlabeled, and the catalogue costs 5000L. Venetian museums are particularly troubled by lack of staff. This can result in free entrance, a closed museum, or new hours. Check with the *Ente Turismo* for exact times and dates.

There are many trips you can make through the Lagoon, all using the *vaporetto* and leaving from San Marco. **Torcello,** an island which has been in steady decline since the eighth century and has some interesting Byzantine remains, is perhaps the best of these; **Murano** is a typical fishing-village-for-tourists. The **Lido** is a grand old resort fallen to seed, but the beach is an excellent place to soak up the Venetian sun. The water's pretty unhealthy these days, though. Take bus B from the left side of the *vaporetto* stop.

Evenings

Evenings in Venice are the best time for sightseeing. As twilight edges into darkness, board the slow *vaporetto* at either end (San Marco or the Train Station) and take it the whole length of the Grand Canal. The palaces go by, gnarled and Gothic; stately, domestic, and Baroque, for more than an hour.

Informal nightlife can be found near the Rialto, San Marco, and Lista di Spagna. Most of the squares offer a café or two. The **Bar alla Salute** on the Giudecca Canal (get off the *vaporetto* at "Salute" and cross the island) is very peaceful and has a wide-ranging view of the harbor and the stars. You can find all-night bars along the Lista di Spagna if the mosquitoes keep you awake.

Festivals

Every even-numbered year, Venice holds the **Biennale,** a large art exhibition whose program is posted all over town. Music centers on the **Teatro La Fenice** (tel. 25191) with a fine program of guest artists in the summer, and there are also concerts in San Marco, the Chiesa dei Frari, the courtyard of

the Doge's Palace and the Campo del Ghetto Nuovo. Tickets begin at
1500L.

In the third week of August, the feast of the **Redentore** awakens the
sleepy islet of **Giudecca.** The evening *Veglia* commences with banqueting,
singing and a great fireworks display and concludes at the Lido, watching the
sun rise over the sea. On the first Sunday in September, Venetians stage the
classic **Regata,** a pell-mell gondola race down the Grand Canal, preceded by
a procession of decorated gondolas.

Dolomites (Dolomiti)

Between Bolzano and the Yugoslavian border lie the Dolomites, a series
of stunning limestone spires rising from lush, billowing fields of grass and
pine forests. About half of the Dolomites region belonged to Austria until
1919, and much of the local populace still speaks German. The German-
speaking towns sport dual Italian and German names such as Dobbiaco and
Toblach, Moso and Moos, and have Tyrolean whitewashed walls, flower-
pots, and carved porches. The Italian villages, like Tolmezzo, are pastel,
with laundry hanging out windows. Austrian banners wave rebelliously in
some towns, and a tiny separatist movement occasionally dynamites government property.

The visitor can traverse the Dolomites in several ways. The conventional
route south from Innsbruck through Bolzano to Verona lies right on the
major rail line but skirts the Dolomites. To plunge into the mountains, get off
the train at Bolzano, and walk two blocks to the central Bus Station, **Societa
Automobilistica Dolomiti, (SAD)** at Via Garibaldi 36. From here, an ar-
mada of buses departs regularly for **Canazei** (two hours), **Ortisei** (one hour),
Cortina d'Ampezzo (three and a half hours), and a host of smaller settlements along the Strada delle Dolomiti. Hitchers will have better luck between Bolzano and Cortina than elsewhere in the Dolomites.

The slightly more adventurous will prefer to take the train from Innsbruck
south to **Fortezza.** Minor rail lines and a narrow road head east to Dobbiaco
and ultimately **Klagenfurt.** The train is local, full of friendly housewives,
gruff old men, and an occasional tourist. This route also skirts the Dolomites, but it is convenient and attractive to stop in Dobbiaco and turn south
to Cortina. Even so, car owners, rugged cyclists, and patient hitchhikers
might want to reject the more well-worn routes and penetrate the Dolomites
region by the **Timmelsjoch Pass.** From Imst, Austria (about 80 kilometers
due west of Innsbruck), it comes up the **Oxtal Valley** through Sölden to
Moso, Italy. The barren rocks, snow drifts, and wilderness justify the $3 toll
levied by the Austrians (less for motorcyclists). Car owners should acquire
discount gasoline coupons at the border.

Accommodations pose little problem. Campers with adequate discretion
have unlimited possibilities. Those seeking indoor lodgings will be con-
fronted by countless *Zimmer frei* signs.

The largest city is Bolzano. It is of little interest but can be a convenient
base for daytrips into the mountains. **Merano,** the only other real city, is an
Austro-Hungarian resort spa in the old style, complete with promenades and
big airy hotels. Unless a need for culinary variety and Austro-Italian nightlife
monopolizes your tastes, the smaller towns will be adequate for hiking and
viewing, and much better for informal camping.

CORTINA D'AMPEZZO AND CANAZEI

Despite its glitter, Cortina is the star attraction of the Dolomites, with superb surrounding crags and extensive (but unobtrusive) lift services. Cortina is Italy's largest ski resort; some snowfields high on the mountains last throughout the year and are accessible by cablecar. Running down the bobsled run, with its fantastic banked sides, is recommended for those who want to get into the athletic spirit of things. Wear good shoes. Or perhaps just walk around the slopes. Get a map of the town in the main Tourist Office in the town hall, **Azienda Autonoma di Soggiorno e Turismo,** or at the branch office next to the Church, Piazzetta San Francesco 8 (tel. 3231).

For lodging try one of the numerous private homes with *Zimmer/Camere* signs posted. They generally cost around 5500L per person, with rates as much as 50% more in high season (July 15 to August 25). A discount plan is available for certain weeks during both summer and winter which allows for full room and board at comfortable hotels for as little as $120 weekly ($180 with ski pass in the winter). Check with the Tourist Office for details and reservations.

The spectacular cliffs and spires that brood over **Canazei** attract many tourists, but Canazei bears her visitors gracefully and is friendlier than her neighbor, **Ortisei.** Check in at the helpful central Tourist Office, which shares a building with the local cinema, for the usual maps and tourist information. Skiers should write ahead for reservations to **Azienda di Soggiorno e Turismo,** 38052 Canazei. Private rooms run about 4500L per night, without breakfast. **Hotel Stella Alpina,** near the Pecol/Belvedere cablecar, charges 12,500L with full board. The **Villa Soreghina** is located right in the village and has a good board plan at 12,000L a day.

The Sierra Club publishes a detailed book describing hiking possibilities in the Dolomites. Check with the tourist office in the region you want to hike for maps and information.

Latium

Rome (Roma)

Rome is a city built to rule the world. The Caesars and the popes continued to build until there was a church on every block and an obelisk in every piazza, and the result is the most extensive collection of monuments on the face of the earth.

But Romans have never been inhibited by the magnificence around them—they used the portico of the **Pantheon** as a fish market for almost a thousand years—and you shouldn't be inhibited either. Past and present in Rome seem to pass each other without meeting—the stateliness of the **Palazzo Farnese** is unaffected by the raunchy neighborhood beneath it, which ignores it in return. You should wander a lot, if you have the legs for it—Rome is one of the world's greatest theaters. If **St. Peter's Square** doesn't convince you, a pre-dinner stroll around **Piazza Navona** (a former Roman race-course) or the morning market at **Campo dei Fiori** will.

Orientation

The Seven Hills which defined ancient Rome are now hardly recognizable. Rather, the old city is best approached in terms of its fourteen *rioni* (districts), each containing important sights, and usually connected by well-established routes. You'll probably want to plan your days around one or two of the central *piazze* of these districts—you can't see everything anyway, and this way, you'll get a sense for the Roman tradition of adding on monuments and churches to classical and medieval bases.

Virtually all trains from north and south stop at the **Termini Station.** If you're arriving on a regular flight, you'll land at **Fiumicino Airport**—an Acotral bus leaves about every hour for Termini for 500L. There's also a Fiumicino-Termini airport bus for 800L. Most charters land at Ciampino Airport, which has subway and bus connections to Termini for 400L.

Once you're there, your first stop should be to the **EPT (Regional Tourist Office)** in the Station. They have an invaluable street map and room-finding service; the back of the map has useful addresses and museum hours as well. For 500L, you can get a map of bus routes at the **ATAC** booth in the Piazza del Cinquecento, right in front of the Station. It's worth it, if only to know what number goes where—the front of the Yellow Pages also has this infor-· mation, though.

The bus service is cheap (100L), and relatively efficient. Routes you'll probably use are #64 (from the Piazza del Cinquecento to St. Peter's) and #78 (to the Piazza di Spagna, home of American Express and the **Spanish Steps**). But the best way to get anywhere in the old city during the day is to walk, because Rome is one slow-moving traffic snarl (where traffic is permitted). Work on the subway has proceeded since the turn of the century, but the tunneling unearths so much of archaeological value that it can only proceed at the rate of inches per year. The stations already completed serve mainly suburbs; a round trip to the **Ostia-Lido** beach, 30 kilometers away, costs 1000L.

When it comes to schedules, Rome is mystifying and frustrating. Some generalizations are possible: most shops and offices are open 9am-1pm and 4:30-7pm on weekdays. Churches follow a 9am-1pm and 4-6pm schedule if they are used for Mass. Museums are almost all closed on Mondays, and shut down at one or two in the afternoons. (There's one exception—the Campidoglio museums are open late Tuesday afternoons and Saturday nights.) The city really rolls up the sidewalks on weekends; in particular, don't forget to change money on Friday mornings, because only the Station's *cambio* is open on Saturday mornings and the lines are long. Above all, try to avoid going to Rome in mid-August, because most Romans are on holiday and it's much harder to find anything, even a restaurant, open.

Addresses and Telephone Numbers

EPT (Regional Tourist Office): in Termini Station.

CTS (Youth Travel Service): Via Genova 16 (tel. 465023). The most efficient office in Rome. *The* place to go for flight, ferry, and train discounts (they'll even accept travelers checks at prime rate), ID cards, and a room-finding service (open 9:30am-1pm and 4-7pm).

Student Help Office: Relazioni Universitarie, Via Palestro 11 (tel. 4755265). Can recommend and give small discounts on nearby *pensioni* and restaurants. English spoken. Open 9am-6pm weekdays, 9am-noon Sat.

American Express: Piazza di Spagna 38 (tel. 688751). Open 9am-5pm weekdays, and one of the branches in Italy where you can cash a personal check with an American Express card.

Main Post Office: Piazza San Silvestro. Open 24 hours a day.

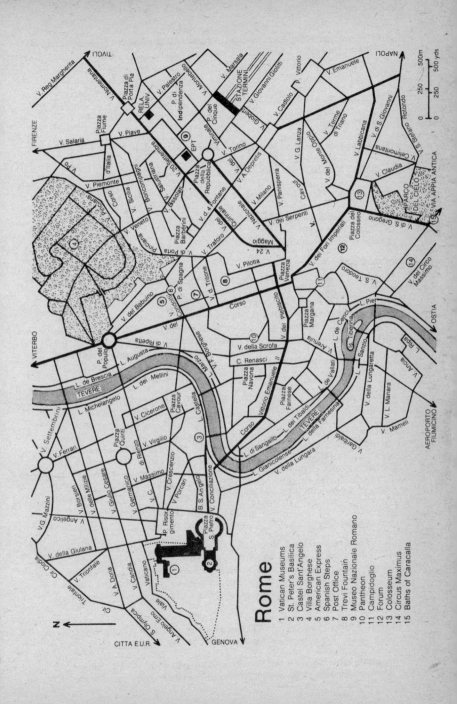

Rome

1 Vatican Museums
2 St. Peter's Basilica
3 Castel Sant'Angelo
4 Villa Borghese
5 American Express
6 Spanish Steps
7 Post Office
8 Trevi Fountain
9 Museo Nazionale Romano
10 Pantheon
11 Campidoglio
12 Forum
13 Colosseum
14 Circus Maximus
15 Baths of Caracalla

CIT (Compagnia Italiana Turismo): Piazza della Repubblica 64 (tel. 4759041). They sell "Tourist Tickets" for trains, etc.

Taxi: (tel. 3576).

Police (Questura di Roma): Via San Vitale 15 (tel. 113).

Red Cross: (tel. 555666).

U.S. Embassy: Via Vittorio Veneto 119a (tel. 4674).

Canadian Embassy: Via Zara 30 (tels. 854825 and 865004).

Laundromat (Lavanderia Automatica): Via Montebello 11.

Moped and Bike Rental: Motonoleggio, Via Cavour 302 (tel. 6780206).

Camping Equipment: Deluca, Via Cavour 88.

Accommodations

Rome is crowded in July and August, but the city overflows with *alloggi, pensioni, locande,* and other incarnations of inexpensive lodgings. Thus Rome is one of Europe's few heavily touristed cities where advance reservations are not imperative during the summer months. If, however, you show up in the late afternoon, you may have to settle for less than the ideal. The Student Help Office will find you a cheap place near the Station, and you get a small discount. CTS is even better, with more convenient and less grubby lodgings. The **Tourist Offices** at the Station (tel. 465461) and at Via Parigi 5 (tel. 4955228) also have services, but they're out to spend your money, not save it.

Housing costs have shot up all over Rome, even in the traditionally cheap areas around Termini. Expect to pay 3500L for a single, 6000L for a double—but the quality of places for these prices varies tremendously, so use part of your first morning in Rome to locate a place you like. The blocks to the left of the Station (Via Amendola, Via Principe Amadeo, and down to Santa Maria Maggiore) are preferable to those on the right (Via Palestro, Via San Martino della Battaglia, Via Castelfidardo)—they're closer to the city and in a real Roman neighborhood. The area between the Spanish Steps and the Piazza del Popolo (Via del Babuino) has some higher-priced, but still inexpensive, *pensioni,* and the location is extremely convenient.

NEAR THE STATION

Pensione Asmara, Via Castelfidardo 31 (tel. 482894). The prices here—4000L for a single—are typical for the nondormitory accommodations in this area, but the Asmara is of superior quality. Very clean and quiet, with a conscientious management and a super-modern bathroom. The **Pensione Blanda** (tel. 464756), downstairs, has the same quality, similar prices, and is less likely to be full.

Pensione Mina, Via Villafranca 10 (tel. 4951355). 3500L for a single, 6000L for a double. Hot showers are free, but rooms are tiny and depressing.

Pensione Vittoriana, Via San Martino della Battaglia 4 (tel. 478330). One of the most interesting places to stay. Each room bears the marks of the lords who once lived here. Frescoes, intricately carved wooden ceilings, and gilded walls abound. 4-6 bed rooms 3000L, doubles 6200L, no singles. Often filled with groups, so book in advance.

Pensione Katty, Via Palestro 35 (tel. 4751385). Somewhat makeshift multibedded rooms cost 3500L. Doubles also available. Very helpful owner. A friendly, student atmosphere.

Pensione Dolomiti, Via San Martino della Battaglia 11 (tel. 491058). 4000L for a single, 3000L per person in a double. Free hot showers, but extremely noisy and indifferent mangement.

Pensione Lachea, downstairs from the Dolomiti (tel. 4957264). Clean, but most rooms on street side. Doubles for 7000L.

Pensione Pezzotti, Via Principe Amadeo 79a (tel. 734633). Very clean and comfortable rooms, with free hot but dribbly showers. 4000L singles, doubles at 6000L, and quiet courtyard views.

Locanda Lucia, Via Amendola 77 (tel. 487722). No hot water in the sinks, but the price is great—singles at 3000L, doubles at 5000L.

ELSEWHERE IN ROME

Albergo Pantheon, Via dei Pastini 131 (tel. 6795305). Very close to the Pantheon in an old elegant building. No singles, doubles 8700L. An ideal location.

Pensione Navona, Via dei Sediari 8 (tel. 6564203). A block away from the Piazza Navona in a noisy neighborhood. Singles for 4500L and doubles for 7700L.

Suore Oblate dell'Assunzione, Via Doria 42 (tel. 3599540). This is a convent, but it is clean, quiet (with a nice courtyard) and 3000L per person in doubles and singles. Near the Vatican.

Albergo Palermo, Via del Gambero 21 (tel. 6791825). Just off the Corso, a bit noisy, but very convenient. 4700L per person.

Istituto Madre Pie, Via Alcide de Gasperi (tel. 631967). Run by nuns, bare, clean, and cheap at 1750L singles, 2650L doubles, including breakfast.

Albergo Provincia Romana, Largo del Pallano 8 (tel. 6541038). Very inexpensive for the area: singles 3000L, doubles 5200L. Rooms are a bit tacky.

STUDENT ACCOMMODATIONS

Centro dei Giovani, Via degli Apuli 41 (tel. 490558), is maintained by a charitable organization which keeps the rates low. Clean and large. Singles only for 3300L. Located in a working class district behind the Train Station. Open to men only. Reduction for longer stays. Next door at #39 (tel. 4957803) is the women's equivalent, for 1400L per night and 250L for showers. Doors close at 10pm.

Casa del Conservatorio, Via del Conservatorio 62 (tel. 659612), is clean and homey, with modern rooms in the heart of Renaissance Rome near the Ponte Sisto. Doubles only for 4500L, with showers and cooking facilities.

NBBS Student Hotel, Via dei Bichi 17. A long bus ride (40 minutes) on bus #98 from the Ponte Vittorio Emanuele, but recommended and friendly. 2200L for a single, dorm space for less.

Foresteria del Pellegrino, Piazza della Trinità dei Pellegrini 36. Offering singles from 2000L, it's very near the center of Rome. Clean and fairly pleasant.

Hotel Vanny, Via Forlì 31 (tel. 859354) is near the Basilica of San Lorenzo. 2800L singles and 4000L doubles. Cold showers are free, hot for 500L.

Centro d'Accoglienza "Pax Christi," Piazza Adriana 21 (tel. 6568140). Dorm accommodations (20- to 30-bed rooms) in a clean and airy building for 2000L per night, showers included. Open July and August only.

Ostello per la Gioventù del Foro Italico (IYHF), Viale delle Olimpiadi 61 (tel. 3964709). In a somewhat inconvenient location and quite run down, but the price, 2400L, may tempt you anyway. Take bus #64 until it crosses the river. Then walk 4 blocks or change to bus #32.

The least distant camping is the **Roma Camping** (tel. 6223018) on the Via Aurelia at Trastevere, charging 800L and requiring a Hostel card. Further out is **Tiber Camping** on Via Tiberina (tel. 6912314); take bus #67 or 99 to the Piazzale Flaminia, then the subway to Prima Porta. **Turistico Internazionale di Castelfusano,** Via Litoranea de Ostia (tel. 6023304) is in nearby Ostia, right on the beach. Open April through October.

Food

So long as it doesn't get too expensive, the ritual of a Roman evening—Vermouth or Campari at a sidewalk café, followed by dinner, and coffee at another café—is one of Rome's great contributions to civilization. This should last from about 6pm till midnight, and tends to obscure the eating itself. Any neighborhood in Rome is full of inexpensive *trattorie* and *rosticcerie*. Rome's cuisine is not as individual as that of the provinces, though it is more expensive.

The area near Termini is full of places selling *pizza rustica* and other snacks, like *calzoni* and *suppli* in the 600-800L range (the cheapest in Italy). Even these, however, close their doors at 10 or 11pm, and even earlier in less-frequented parts of the city. Bars stay open somewhat later, so your *gelato* addiction can be satisfied easily—**Orsetto,** a *tavola calda* and bar at Piazza del Cinquecento 64, stays open especially late. Meat dishes, in particular, are expensive and often poorly roasted. Fresh *gnocchi* is made on Thursdays, and bread every morning around three—if you're up, knock on a window and ask for some.

There is virtually no reason to walk halfway across Rome to get to a particular *trattoria*. The standard price for a *menu touristico* is now 3000L and up, and even the cheapest *trattorie* are now in the 4000L range for a full meal. There are no great bargains to search for, though there is a cluster of *trattorie* near the Railway Station where the fixed price is around 3000L: **dell'Ippica** (Via Cernaia 41); **Benedetto** (Via Vicenza 56); and the *rosticceria* nearby at Via Vicenza 53. Among Rome's better *trattorie*—and you will discover your own—are:

Il Giardino, Via Zucchelli 29, off the Via Sistina and the Via del Tritone, midway between the Spanish Steps and the Piazza Barberini, is centrally located and worth finding. The food is excellent and reasonably priced; best of all, there's a secluded garden in back that offers a cool, relaxing respite from Roman heat and noise. Expect to spend 3500-4000L for a full meal.

Trattoria Al Moro, Vicolo delle Bollette near the Trevi Fountain. Serves outstanding food in an elegant atmosphere of heavy silver and white tablecloths. A place for a splurge: 5000L. Try the *spaghetti al Moro,* or ask the waiter for suggestions.

Mensa Universitaria, Via Cesare de Lollis. Any student with ISIC card can eat for 700-1000L, excluding beverage—don't expect gastronomic delight.

Alemagna, Via del Corso 150. A high-class *tavola calda* for lunch, and one of the best sweets and pastry selection in Rome.

Sights

Rome is a Baroque city—cluttered, emotional, incredible. The Baroque artist did not work primarily with stone or paint, but with space itself, and Rome's treasures are not buildings or paintings but great squares, streets, and areas—the **Piazza Navona, Campidoglio, Piazza San Pietro, Via Giulia, the Forum.**

But Rome is also a city of interiors, and one of the best combinations of the two is the **Vatican**—visit the museums and then the **Church of St. Peter's** (open until 8pm). The entrance to the Vatican Museum is off the Viale Vaticano, a ten-minute walk from the end of bus #64 in Piazza San Pietro. The museums are only open 9am-1:30pm, are closed Sundays, and are the most expensive in Italy (500L with ISIC card, 1500L without)—but they're worth it. Follow routes C and D—they go through the picture gallery, a great Egyptian art collection, miles of corridors, and finally the **Raphael Rooms,** containing his fresco masterpieces, and Michelangelo's **Sistine Chapel.** You'll have to skip a lot even to reach the latter, but be sure to see Raphael's *Transfiguration,* and classical sculptures like the *Laocoön* and the *Apollo Belvedere*—try to ignore the fig leaves. Be sure to take a long look at the dome of St. Peter's along the way, for it's far better rising above the mist of the tropical Vatican gardens than from the front. You can stay in the Sistine Chapel until 2pm, but the guards won't let you lie down to see the ceiling. While you're in the Vatican, consider using the Post Office there—it's days faster than Italian mail.

Walk back to Bernini's **Piazza San Pietro,** a huge forest of columns, and see St. Peter's, with its awesome façade. The cavernous interior, of course, contains Michelangelo's Pietà, now behind bullet-proof glass since the attack on it with a hammer several years ago. The elevator to the roof and climb to the cupola is well worth the 800L.

The only thing in Rome not dwarfed by St. Peter's and the Vatican is the **Forum** and the complex of ruins around it, including **Trajan's Forum,** the **Colosseum,** and the **Palatine Hill.** Start with the Colosseum, open 9am-7:30pm and closed Sundays. Both the Roman Forum—which contains the Arch of Titus, the Farnese Gardens, and Augustus' ruined palace—and the Imperial Forum with Trajan's Forum and Markets, can be entered from the Via dei Fori Imperiali (open 9am-1pm and 3-6pm; admission 200L). The glory that was Rome survives intact in at least one place—the open-dome **Pantheon,** closer to the Tiber. If you can, arrange your visit to coincide with one of the city's thundershowers—the experience is one of the most power-ful Rome has to offer. Finish the day strolling around **Piazza Rotonda** and the **Piazza Navona.**

For a different kind of power—the calm of perfection—visit the **Piazza del Campidoglio.** Only at night does Michelangelo's design appear to its full effect. The long ramp up provides an awe-inspiring approach to the great bronze of Marcus Aurelius and the three elegant buildings that surround it. Walk around a bit, then stroll through Rome's only two nocturnal museums (Tuesdays and Thursdays 5-8pm and Saturday 9-11pm; 500L for both, no ISIC reduction). In the courtyard of the **Museo dei Conservatori** are the huge fragments (toes, thighs, head, and hand) of a gigantic statute of Con-stantine. And behind the third building in the square (Rome's City Hall) is the best view of the Forum.

Aside from the Campidoglio, Renaissance Rome at its best is the enigma-tic area called **Vecchia Roma,** near the **Campo dei Fiori** and the **Via Giulia,** which combines the working-class ambiance of **Trastevere**—women sitting in the doorways, boys playing ball in the street—with a second world of embassies and palaces. A peek through an old archway is equally likely to reveal a decrepit old yard full of laundry, or a garden, Mercedes-Benz, and liveried footman warning you away.

Baroque Rome begins with the **Church of the Gesù** on Via del Corso, which sent out streams of Jesuit priests and carbon-copy basilicas. **Santa Maria della Vittoria,** near the Rail Station, houses Bernini's *Ecstasy of St. Teresa* while **San Pietro in Vincoli** near the Colosseum contains Michelangelo's *Moses*. Try to attend a Mass, either at one of the scores of neighborhood churches scattered throughout the city, or at the huge basilicas of **Santa Maria Maggiore** or **San Giovanni in Laterano.**

Many Baroque *palazzi* (mansions), built for papal "nephews" and rela-tives, today serve as galleries—hours and admission prices are idiosyncratic and change every few months, though. Also, some galleries number their collection to try to force you to buy the accompanying decoding catalogue—ask if you can borrow one. The **Galleria Borghese,** set in Rome's largest public park, has Bernini's greatest early sculpture and a superb collection of Titians and Caravaggios (Tues.-Sat. 8am-2pm and 150L; Sun. 9am-1pm, admission free). The **Palazzo Barberini** is on the way to the **Spanish Steps** (Rome's legacy of the Counter-Reformation and a great place to people-watch). The Palazzo is open Tues.-Sat. 9am-2pm, and Sun. 9am-1pm, admission 150L. Of the other galleries, the **Farnese** (now the French Embassy, and only open 11am-noon Sundays) and **Colonna** (Sat. 9am-noon, 1000L with ISIC card) are superior to the **Spada** (9am-1pm and 4-6pm) and **Doria** (Tues., Fri., and weekends 10am-1pm, admission 500L; enter at the Piazza del Collegio Romano 1A). The **Museo Nazionale Romano,** near the Train Station, is free with ISIC card and has the best classical sculpture and bronzes in Rome.

Medieval and early Christian Rome is far flung and consists mostly of mosaics and catacombs. The best of the latter are those of **San Callixtus,** and the best mosaics are in the great basilicas *fuori le mura* (outside the walls) of **San Lorenzo** and **San Paolo.** Hadrian's Tomb, better known as the **Castel Sant'Angelo,** is a Roman landmark rich in historical association (the Pope hurried down the raised corridor from the Vatican in times of danger) with a nice lawn for picnics.

Daytrips

The **Villa d'Este** at Tivoli is the best example of the Renaissance ideal of ordered nature. Ice-cold, undrinkable water pours down the mountain-side through 500 fountains, spouts, and pools, and descends into the valley, creating some of the world's most sublime fountains on its way. Bus RT leaves for Tivoli from Via Gaeta near the Train Station at frequent intervals, but the ride is slow and hot (3000L round trip). The fountains are best seen during the day, when a student card will get you in free and the coolness of the garden is especially endearing. The Villa is also open at night, when it is spectacularly illuminated, but there are more tour groups then and admission is 800L. **Hadrian's Villa** nearby consists of the ruins of a fascinating idea—the reconstruction on one estate of all the most beautiful spots Hadrian had seen in his travels as Emperor. It is served by the same bus as Tivoli.

Mussolini's "new Rome," called **E.U.R.** (the subway goes here), has an amusement park (**Luna Park**), and a museum (**Civiltà Romana**) which is a very thorough reconstruction of ancient Rome. Further out on another subway line, you can visit **Ostia Antica**, Rome's former port with its ancient tenement blocks and underground piping. Even further out (925L round trip from Termini) is the beach of **Ostia-Lido**, which has huge waves and crowds. Trams leave twice an hour.

Evenings

Evening is virtually the only time of day when Rome seems fully alive. There are three great squares where you can taste the flavor of a city, where people pay to sit down and watch others who have done the same. All of the cafés in the Piazza Navona, Piazza del Popolo, and Piazza Santa Maria in Trastevere are expensive—you should consider having your drink in a side street and sitting in the center of the square, becoming part of the act instead of the audience. The three Bernini fountains of the Piazza Navona make it the most beautiful setting for outdoor nightlife; it is also one of the most stylish, a fine place for intrigues of any kind. The **Trevi** fountain area is also filled with kids at night. A walk along the **Via Condotti** will take you past some of the world's most fashionable shops, though the Spanish Steps at the end are not quite the student hangout they once were. The nearby **Via Veneto** has lost its charm since *La Dolce Vita*—go if you're homesick for Midwestern accents and have a wad to spend.

Among the great spectacles of the Roman summer is the outdoor opera at the **Terme di Caracalla**, beginning in July. The setting in vast ruins of Roman baths—and the price—2000L and up—make it something to try. American movies are more familiar, and the only theater in town that doesn't dub out the English is the **Cinema Pasquino**, in the Vicolo del Piede in Trastevere. Also in Trastevere, for the last two weeks of July, is the festival called *Noantri "Ours"*), when the streets become the scene of carousing reminiscent of the ancient Roman *saturnalia*.

Umbria

Umbria is the underappreciated area of Italy above Rome, getting lost in the Venice-Rome-Florence triangle, even for Italian tourists. It shouldn't—its gentle hills, medieval hill towns, and cool breezes give it a sense of peace and restfulness unmatched by any other region. The railway stations are usually at the base of the town, and buses stop around 10pm. Also, motor vehicles are banned from many areas of each town, and streets turn into steep stairways with dismaying regularity. The entire area is a detour from the national railways, so getting around by train may be difficult unless you plan an itinerary beforehand—a counterclockwise route from Orvieto to Spoleto, Assisi, Perugia, and on to Tuscany, for example. But once you're here, relax—the age of the fierce medieval factions is long gone, and only the spirit of mystics such as St. Francis remains. Umbria seduces your senses with country vistas, and the twittering of swallows above silent streets.

Perugia

Perugia, the capital of Umbria, pretends to be cosmopolitan along its main street (Corso Vannucci) and in the university area. But its inaccessibility, strong local flavor, and steep streets reveal its hill-town origin. The agreeable blend of old and new is evident in the attention lavished upon its two famous namesakes: **Perugino** (Pietro Vannucci), the Renaissance master whose work is all over town; and **Perugina,** the chocolate firm whose nut-filled *Baci* (kisses) are one of Italy's most popular candies. The **Tourist Office,** Corso Vannucci 96 (tel. 23327, open 8:30am-1pm and 4-7pm) has information on the city and the region.

Perugia has two universities—a regular Italian one and a national university for foreigners—so cheap housing is hard to find, even in summer. The bulletin boards at the latter (Palazzo Gallenga, Piazza Fortebraccio 4, tel. 64344) often advertise rooms; or ask one of the many American students for suggestions. There is a **Youth Travel Center** at Via del Roscello 21 (tel. 61695), which can find you a room—they'll probably direct you to the **Centro Internazionale Accoglienza per Giovani,** Via Bontempi (tel. 22880), which has multibed rooms for 2000L a night with sheets provided. Doors open at 4pm and close at 11:30pm. Conventional lodgings are overpriced—try **Albergo Centrale,** Via Balbo 4 (tel. 61431), right off the Corso Vannucci, with nice rooms—singles for 4500L, doubles for 8000L.

Places to eat, in contrast, are plentiful and cheap. Perugia has terrific bread and cheese, and the combination of the two in a pastry-like *pane al formaggio* is a local specialty. The city is also packed with *pizzerie, trattorie,* and *rosticcerie.* Two of the best are **Osteria da Vianzo,** Piazza Dante 16; and **La Botte,** Via Volte della Pace 31, both of which cater to student appetites and budgets.

Sights

Perugia's center is one of Italy's most solid squares, rough, grim, but well proportioned. The pulpit in the **Palazzo dei Priori,** where medieval politicians harangued the crowds, and the colored marbles on the side of the **Cathedral** add a bit of grace, but the harmony of the **Fonte Maggiore** is the focal point. All this work dates from the period of Perugia's independence, before it became a papal stronghold in the sixteenth century.

Around the corner from the Cathedral is the Palazzo dei Priori, which even today houses the city administration—go in by the frescoed **Sala dei Notari,** and continue upstairs to the **National Gallery of Umbria** (open 9am-1pm and 2-5pm Tues.-Sat., Sun. 9am-1pm; admission 150L but free with ISIC card) for a look at some of Perugino's and Pinturicchio's best work. Next door, the Perugino frescoes for the **Collegio del Cambio** (moneychanger's guild) show what a very good painter could do with a very mundane commission—the figures have a delicacy and gentleness transmitted to his pupil, Raphael. The **National Archaeological Museum** at San Domenico (open 9am-1pm) emphasizes the Etruscan origins of the town. On the way down the hill to the two universities, off the **Via delle Prome,** stands the

Arch of Augustus. This includes the largest piece of Etruscan stonework still in existence.

Spoleto

Spoleto has kept the bits of its past separated more than most Umbrian towns—Roman polis, Lombard duchy, free commune, Papal fief. The piazza in front of the twelfth-century **Cathedral** is one of the most striking public spaces in Italy. Spoleto is another sleepy hill town—except during the **Festival of Two Worlds** in late June and July, which features some of America's and Europe's best musicians, with up to nine performances daily.

Spoleto is on a small train line between Foligno and Rome, and buses circle between the station in the new part of town and the **Piazza Libertà,** where the **Tourist Office** (tel. 23190, open 8am-2pm and 3-9pm) can supply you with information. Buses connect the town with Perugia, Ancona, and Florence. There is a **camping** area near the church of San Pietro on the road to Monteluco; Circolare A takes you most of the way (tel. 28158, open May through September). Within the town, try **Pensione dell'Angelo,** Via Arco di Druso 25 (tel. 32185), for charming and friendly rooms and service (singles 4000L, doubles 7000L); or the cheaper **Locanda Aura,** Via Focardi 3 (no phone) for 3000L per person, doubles only.

Forget about staying within the city walls during the Festivals if you haven't made reservations months in advance. The Youth Hostel, despite signs, is closed.

Aside from the **Cathedral,** with its sophisticated fresco cycle by Filippo Lippi and a Pinturicchio **Chapel,** there isn't that much to see in Spoleto. Note the Cathedral's bell tower—it was built with stones stolen from Roman ruins, and you can still see the ancient bas-reliefs. If you're coming for the Festival of Two Worlds, there are always tickets at 2000L for the noontime chamber concerts, but opera and concert tickets should be reserved ahead. Contact the Italian Government Travel Office in New York, or write **Messaggiere Musicale,** Via del Corso 123, Rome (tel. 6786768).

Assisi

The medieval factional feuds that left squat, honey-colored palaces have passed; and the legacy of **Assisi**'s most famous children, St. Francis and St. Clare, has dominated for centuries. Take the bus from the Station (every thirty minutes) up to the **Basilica of St. Francis,** actually one church on top of another, with lawns and cloisters attached. After looking at the finest assembly of Italian thirteenth- and fourteenth-century frescoes in existence, amble down Via San Francesco to **Piazza del Comune** and on to the **Basilica of St. Clare.**

Assisi is filled with wide-eyed pilgrims and art lovers, so it's an expensive place to stay if you're not daytripping from Rome to Perugia. You might try the **Youth Hostel** (IYHF) in Foligno (**Ostello Fulginum**, Piazza San Giacomo, #11 tel. 50493), a nearby stop on the frequent local train to Rome. Up the road toward the Eremo delle Carceri, in Fontemaggio, there's a **Youth Hotel** connected with Camping Fontemaggio (tel. 812317). Within the town, try the **Locanda Anfiteatro Romano,** on the street of the same name (tel. 813025), singles 4800L and doubles 6800L; or the nicer **Albergo la Rocca,** Via Porta Perlici 27 (tel. 812284), 300L more per person with shower.

If you can get near Assisi in April, try to attend either the secular **Festa di Calendimaggio** or the **Holy Week Ceremonies;** both have dramatic activities, processions, and competition between neighborhoods. If you can't, there are various musical and festive celebrations throughout the summer.

Tuscany

Tuscany, more than any other place on earth, is the Renaissance. With little of the industry of the north and the squalor of the south, it has enough art, history, and landscape for a whole country. Florence, of course, has been the hub of the region since the Medici dukes, but that doesn't mean it's the only place worth visiting. The towns of Tuscany—**Siena, Pisa, San Gimignano, Pistoia, Lucca, Arezzo, Pienza**—are as close as they are distinct, and you should try to plan on at least five days in the region, either daytripping from Florence or touring.

Camping areas dot the region, and there are IYHF youth hostels at Florence, Lucca, Tavernelle, Val di Pesa, and Arezzo. Tuscany's coastal resorts are mostly north of Pisa—Viareggio and Marina di Massa have campsites.

Arezzo is a natural transition point from Umbria to Tuscany—the art is Florentine, but the architecture is ungracefully Romanesque. The main structure, the barnlike Franciscan **Church of San Francesco,** houses what most tourists come to see, the *Legend of the Cross* fresco cycle by Piero della Francesca.

The IYHF **Youth Hostel Piero della Francesca,** Via Borg'Unto 6, offers cheapest accommodations in town at 1500L per night, with a midnight curfew and 200L for hot showers. The **Locanda San Remo,** Piazza San Michele 2 (tel. 28347) and **Locanda Cannoncino,** Via Garibaldi 221 (tel. 29796) offer convenient housing for about 3500L for a single, 6000L for a double. The town's *trattorie* and *osterie* specialize in the local mountain cheese, sausage, and game.

Florence (Firenze)

Carved on Florence's City Hall are the words "Jesus Christ, King of the Florentine People." The Florentines meant it as a compliment.

What Florence is proud of is its success in making the city itself a form of art. From 1300 to 1500, Florence dispensed art and enlightenment to the rest of Europe, but kept the lion's share for herself. The "Italian Renaissance" was born and matured in Florence, though it died in Rome. The art the city loves best is youthful and down-to-earth—the kind that makes a thing of beauty out of a stairway as well as a goddess. The strain of pragmatism is strong—Florentines were the first to practice bookkeeping and they invented most of the techniques of modern banking.

The **Medici** were the natural rulers of this fusion of the practical and the artistic. In some ways, they still rule, because Florence is careful about its past. It has to be—the city has a sort of natural enemy in the river Arno. A stagnant pool from May to September, the Arno takes a stab at destroying Florence every century or so. It came too close for comfort in 1967, when a panicky bureaucrat opened the floodgates too early and buried the city beneath four feet of sludge. Hunt up some old *Life* magazines to get an idea of what the painted watermarks on many buildings represent in terms of mud.

Some of the city's wounds were self-inflicted. Florence has no ancient poor quarter such as Rome's Vecchia Roma because the city government tore it down in 1860. The mayor replaced it with what is perhaps the ugliest part of Florence, the Piazza della Repubblica.

For all its pride, Florence is pretty unpretentious about itself. The whole city is something of a museum, in the best sense of the word. Within it are forty smaller museums, a dozen great churches, and countless buildings of historical, artistic, or gustatory interest. This embarrassment of riches has one great advantage—you never have to plan to see anything in particular. Just start walking and step into the first *palazzo* that catches your eye.

Addresses and Telephone Numbers

Tourist Office: Piazza Rucellai (tel. 298906). Information and accommodations service.

Centro Turistico Giovanile Studentesco: Via delle Terme 53/R (tel. 292150). Student travel, accommodations, and information.

American Express: c/o Ventana, Via dei Banchi 25 (tel. 283825).

Post Office: Via Pietrapiana 33/35 (tel. 270586).

Bus Office: Piazza del Duomo 58r (tel. 212301). SITA, Via Santa Caterina da Siena 15r (tel. 294647), goes to most Tuscan towns.

Taxi: tel. 4798.

Police: Via Zara (tel. 477901).

Arciconfraternita della Misericordia (first aid): Piazza del Duomo 20 (tel. 212222).

Hospital: Piazza Santa Maria Nuova 1 (tel. 27741).

U.S. Consulate: Lungarno Vespucci 38 (tel. 298276).

Swimming Pools: Bellariva (tel. 677521), Lungarno Colombo (bus #14 from the Duomo) 500L admission; popular with Florentines. **Campo di Marte** (tel. 675744) is also 500L. The **Piscina la Pavoniere** (tel. 367506) is much less crowded and in a beautiful setting, but costs 1500L. Bus A from the station.

Accommodations

Between the Railroad Station and the university, near Piazza San Marco, there are many inexpensive *pensioni*. Via Nazionale, Via Faenza, Via Ventisette Aprile, and Via San Gallo are the most likely streets, but the area is decaying and not very central. Florence is tremendously crowded with summer tourists; if you're not up to an afternoon of room-finding, pay the slight booking fee for the accommodations service at the Station.

STUDENT AND CHARITY-RUN ACCOMMODATIONS

Ostello della Gioventù (IYHF), Viale Augusto Righi (tel. 601451). In a beautiful old building reached by bus #17A or 17B. About 30 minutes from the Station. Hostel card required. 2400L per night.

Casa Famiglia, Via dell'Oriuolo 11 (tel. 23779). Airy, comfortably-furnished rooms for 3000L per night, showers 500L, breakfast 200L. 11pm curfew (which for some reason is stretched to midnight on Thursdays). Women only. Open July-September.

Casa di Ospitalità, Viale dei Mille 11 (tel. 576298). Near the Church of the Sette Santi, can be reached by bus #17. Plain rooms, religious auspices, and a rather inconvenient location, but OK for 3000L. Open July-September.

Pensione Universitaria S. Zita, Via Nazionale 8 (tel. 298202). Rooms are huge and a good buy; 6000L per room per night with breakfast, no matter how many people are in it. Run by nuns. Free showers, a beautiful terrace and a 12:30am curfew. Open mid-July to September.

Centro di Ospitalità Santa Monica, Via Santa Monica 6 (tel. 296704). Near the Carmine church in the Oltr'arno, this is a moderately rigorous, but moderately comfortable hostel. 2500L per night, and you must pay 200L every four days for bedding. 6- to 20-bed rooms, midnight curfew, and 9:30am eviction. Free hot showers. Reception opens 3pm.

HOTELS AND PENSIONI

Near the Station and the University

Via Faenza 56 contains six *pensioni* which are among the best in Florence. Reservations here are a good idea for June, July and August:

Pensione Marini (tel. 284824) on the third floor, offers quiet, pleasant rooms (you can write for a balcony or terrace) and an outstandingly helpful management. Single, including breakfast and all taxes, 4000L; doubles 7000L, and larger rooms 3000L per person. **Pensionata Famiglia Azzi** (tel. 23806) downstairs, is superbly furnished and has excellent rooms and a gracious management. Singles 4500L, doubles 7000L, without breakfast. Showers are 100L, and there is a large terrace. **Locanda Armonia** (tel. 211146) offers the same sort of accommodation for women only: singles 4000L, doubles 7000L, without showers or breakfast. Friendly manager. The **Anna** (tel. 298322; 3500L single, 6000L double), **Paola** (tel. 23682; 4000L single, 7000L double), and **Merlini** (tel. 212848; 4000L singles, 7000L doubles) all offer comparable rooms—clean and quiet—in the same building.

Locanda Nella, Via Faenza 69 (tel. 284256) has clean rooms and friendly management at 3500L singles, 6000L doubles.

Soggiorno Caterina, Via Barbano 8 (tel. 483705). Run with a passion for cleanliness and real pride. Singles are 5800L, doubles with shower 8500L, including tax. Breakfast1500L. Free use of a refrigerator, but up four flights of stairs.

Auberge Petrarcha, Via Fiume 20 (tel. 260858). Nicely furnished, quiet, and clean. Singles 5500L, doubles 8300L; both include breakfast. Without food, 5000L and 7000L.

Locanda Parisi, Via San Gallo 31 (tel. 483519). Quiet and unassuming; singles 3000L, doubles for 5000L. Showers 550L and breakfast 400L. If the street door is locked, ring the bell.

Locanda Daniel, Via Nazionale 22 (tel. 260267). Simple rooms, but cheap at 1500L for singles, 2800L for doubles.

Locanda Fabio, Via dei Ginori 24 (tel. 260775) has more ample rooms. Singles 4000L and doubles 6000L. Showers extra.

Locanda Sampaoli, Via San Gallo 39 (tel. 493614) is on the top floor of a rather run-down building, but pleasant inside. Singles 3800L, doubles 5000L.

Elsewhere

Locanda Aily Home, Piazza Santo Stefano 1 (tel. 296505). Clean, pleasant, and quiet rooms in a superb location—a small square right off the Ponte Vecchio, very close to the Uffizi. Singles are 5450L, doubles 8750L, breakfast 800L, showers 350L. Reservations advisable for the summer.

Locanda Orchidea, Borgo degli Albizi 11 (tel. 296646), between the Bargello and Santa Croce. Gloomy and formal, but exquisitely furnished, and in a quiet location. Singles 5000L, doubles 8000L. The bathroom could be cleaner; no breakfast. Baths are 300L. Ask for a room on the courtyard.

Locanda Scoti, Via Tornabuoni 7 (tel. 292128). Quiet, dark, and old-fashioned place marked only by the plaque ''P. Scoti'' on the Via Tornabuoni, Florence's most fashionable shopping street. Singles are 3800L, doubles 6000L. Friendly and lots of real antiques around.

Locanda Amalfi, Via dell'Oriuolo 23 (tel. 260614) is also near the Duomo. Quiet and pleasant rooms at good prices: singles 4000L, doubles 7000L, triples 9000L. Breakfast 800L, showers 500L.

Pensione San Egidio, Via S. Egidio 6 (tel. 282280), small but extremely clean and well run, and between the Duomo and Santa Croce. A good value at 4200L singles, 7000L doubles, but showers are high at 1000L.

Camping: Viale Michelangelo 80 (tel. 663938). Overlooking Florence from near Piazzale Michelangelo, this is reputed to be one of the best campsites in Europe. 500 tent spaces, open April through October. There's also year-round camping at Camping Camerata (tel. 610300), next to the Youth Hostel.

Food

Florentine food is among the best in Italy, but often sounds more exotic than it is. Rabbit *(coniglio)* and quail *(quaglia)* are on many menus and are fairly interesting. *Bistecca alla fiorentina* (steak)—sold by weight and usually the most expensive thing on the menu—is the city's prime specialty. Cheaper and tastier specialties are *lasagne verdi al forno* (baked lasagna made with green noodles), *mozzarella in carrozza* (fried cheese and bread), *ossobuco* (roast leg of veal in an herb sauce) and *cannelloni* (finely chopped meat enveloped in pasta, sauce, and cheese)

Unfortunately, there is no notable concentration of inexpensive *trattorie* in Florence. There are a few with tourist menus in the 2000-3000L range on the Via Faenza, but the best general area for cheap eating is the **Santo Spirito—San Frediano** quarter, in the vicinity of the Via dei Serragli. Incidentally, the Piazza Santo Spirito is also the drug center of Florence, but the police are well aware of the situation and keep close tabs on illegal-looking activity.

Near the Pitti Palace, the **Trattoria da Nello,** Borgo Tegolaio 21, and the **Trattoria Carrai,** around the corner at Via Michelozzi 9r, serve huge help-ings for unbelievably low prices—cover and service 200L, pasta 300-400L, main dishes 1100L, and terrific food in the bargain. On the other side of Santo Spirito, try the **Trattoria Drago Verde,** at Via Leone 50r or **Trat-toria Sant'Agostino** on Via Sant'Agostino 24 for more expensive, but even better fare—a complete meal will run 3500L.

Across the river, the **Casa San Francesco** Piazza Sant'Annunziata 2, is run by Franciscans for students and the poor, and serves large meals noon-2pm for 1900L. There are two student **mensas,** which serve from noon-2pm and 7-9pm—one at Via dei Servi 68 is 1200L, and has slightly better food than the other at Via San GAllo 25r, the cheapest place in town at 1000L. Nearer the sights, **Mario,** just off the Mercato Centrale, has Florentine dishes from 2000L up.

Other possibilities for inexpensive meals are the *tavola calda* of two big restaurants, **da Piero,** Via dei Lamberti 5r and **Giannino,** Borgo San Lorenzo 37r. The first is very good all around, the second notable for its hot fried snacks like *bomboloni* (doughnuts), and *zeppole* (fried dough).

No one doubts that Florence has the best ice cream in Italy—but the debate over Florence's best parlor never ends. **Vivoli,** Via dell' Isola delle Stinche 7, between the **Bargello** and **Santa Croce,** has the lead, but prices are getting outrageous. Across the river, an unassuming *gelateria* at **Piazza Santo Spirito** has larger servings and similar quality.

Sights

Almost the only places you can't walk to easily in Florence are the **Forte Belvedere** and the **Piazzale Michelangelo** (bus #13 from the Station), the best places to get a view of the city. If you go during the day (the Forte Belvedere is also particularly good for a night-time view), the first thing you will notice is that every roof is the same color—red. Now enforced by law, for centuries it was Florentine pride that unified the city with its famous tile. Another thing to look for is the rough triangle of **Santa Croce, San Marco,** and the **Santa Maria Novella Railroad Station**—inside it lies virtually all of Florence worth seeing.

The aimlessness we recommend for enjoying Florence should not provide an excuse to miss the **Uffizi** (open Tues.-Sat. 9am-7pm; Sun. 9-1pm, free with ISIC card, 250L without). The collection—most of it originally the Medicis'—is one of the best in the world, including Botticellis, Filippo Lippis and Titians, plus a few awesome Da Vincis and Rembrandts. Satur-day is the best day to avoid the crowds here, though any lunch hour will provide a respite from tour groups. Like most of Florence, the survival of the Uffizi was a matter of chance. Hitler moved most of its treasures to a salt mine in Linz, Austria. In early 1945, he ordered them destroyed; only the classical education of the Prussian commander in charge saved the day.

The dome of the **Cathedral (Duomo)** was the architectural wonder of the 15th century, but its façade is only a late 19th-century reproduction. Brunel-leschi's dome costs 500L to climb; it and the **Baptistery** are open 7am-noon and 2:30-7pm. Don't miss Michelangelo's *Pietà* in the Cathedral, the Byzantine-influenced frescoes, and the great doors by Pisano and Ghiberti in the Baptistery.

Stroll down Via del Proconsolo to the **Bargello,** the best place to get an idea of the Florentine spirit (open Tues.-Sat. 9am-2pm for 150L, Sun. 9am-1pm free). The setting—the medieval palace of the chiefs of police—is cool and often deserted; in the summer, plays and concerts are held there. The interior houses an unbelievable collection of Florentine sculpture—Donatello, della Robbia, Verrocchio, Michelangelo, Cellini, Ammanati, and others.

Around the corner is the **Piazza della Signoria,** dominated by the sober **Palazzo Vecchio,** still the city hall (open Mon.-Fri. 9am-7pm for 250L, Sun. 9am-1pm, free). Look for the place where Savonarola was burned at the stake in 1498, then go inside to see the Room of the Five Hundred, designed for republican deliberations after the Medici had been expelled, but decorated by Vasari in the 1560s to commemorate their return. The suites above are even more overtly Medicean, and are decorated with hallmarks of Mannerist art. Don't miss the statuary in the **Loggia dei Lanzi,** especially Giambologna's *Rape of the Sabines,* as you turn the corner into the **Piazzale degli Uffizi,** an esplanade designed by Vasari.

Down river one block is the **Ponte Vecchio,** with its assortment of expensive jewelers, souvenir stands, and international flotsam. Notice that the Medici, in their Grand Ducal days, had a private colonnade across the bridge to their residence at the **Pitti Palace,** now a fine museum (open Tues.-Sat. 9am-2pm, Sun. 9am-1pm; free with ISIC card, 200L without). Then go behind the building to the **Boboli Gardens** (open 9am-6:30pm, admission free)—the grotesque grottoes amazed Montaigne, and there's plenty of space for a solitary nap.

Lorenzo the Magnificent, the great patron of art and political boss, is buried in **San Lorenzo,** which also contains Michelangelo's **Medici Chapel** (open Tues.-Sat. 9am-7pm, Sun. 9am-1pm; admission is 250L). Michelangelo's *David* is in the **Galleria dell'Accademia** (9am-2pm Tues.-Sat., 9am-1pm Sun., 150L without ISIC card). Get there early or late to avoid the crush. Go also to **San Marco,** where the monks' cells were painted by Fra Angelico, who was nearly canonized for his unique shade of blue. Florence's best frescoes are probably the Masaccios in the Brancacci Chapel of **Sta. Maria del Carmine,** but the newly-restored Pontormos in **Sta. Felicita,** near the Pitti, run a close second. Both churches are poorly lit—try to go on a sunny day. They are in the least touristed part of Florence.

Shopping

Florentine shops are difficult to resist, and the goods are usually among the best in Italy. The traditions of Florentine craftsmanship survive beneath the touristy veneer of the city's two largest open markets, **San Lorenzo** and the **Mercato Nuovo.** Leatherwork of all kinds is available in all price ranges. Gloves of all varieties are well-made and inexpensive; **Martelli** on the Por San Maria is one good place to buy them. And **Giannini,** at Piazza Pitti 47r, is a magnificent paper store, though not too strong on bargains. If you want reproductions of works of art, **Alinari,** Lungarno Vespucci 82 and Via Strozzi 19, has the world's largest selection, which they'll let you browse through in peace. If you're tired of tramping around, the **BM Bookstore,** Via Borgognissanti 4r has the largest selection of English books. Stationery stores *(cartolerie)* all over the city have fine leather-bound goods.

When shopping, keep in mind that stores often give better rates on travelers checks. One last note—Florentine merchants are increasingly annoyed by the common mistake that all their prices are meant to be haggled over. Bargaining is only a good idea at the most touristy shops and stalls, but you'll have to judge the situation for yourself.

Evenings

June 24, the feast of the city's patron saint, San Giovanni, is marked by fireworks on the Piazzale Michelangelo, best seen from the Forte Belvedere. In the afternoon the *calcio in costume* is played in the Piazza Sta. Croce. This violent version of soccer is fun to watch by itself, but the main attraction is the long parade in sixteenth-century costume which precedes it. Tickets are available only at the CIT office in the Piazza dell'Unità Italiana, near the station, and run from two to ten dollars. Stay around after the game for the inevitable fights between spectators and police.

There are concerts of classical music two nights a week during July and August in the courtyard of the Pitti Palace. Moreover, student discounts are available on all seats, which lowers the price range to 800-1200L. Opera is performed in the **Teatro Comunale,** 12 Corso Italia (tel. 263041); and **Maggio Musicale Fiorentino,** a world-famous music festival, takes place mostly in May and spills over into June. **Fiesole** (about half an hour by bus #7 from Piazza San Marco or the Railroad Station), is a sleepy old town. In June, July and August the **Fiesole Summer Festival** brings the Roman amphitheater to life with concerts, ballet, theater and movies. Check with the Tourist Office for a schedule. Most tickets cost 1500L with an ISIC card. If your mood is otherwise, the best discotheques in town are the **Space Electronic,** Via Palazzuolo 37 (tel. 293082) and the **Red Garter,** Via de Benci 33r (tel. 263004).

Street nightlife thrives on the steps of the Duomo, the Piazzale Michelangelo, and especially the Ponte Vecchio, where Florentine hippies mingle with elegantly dressed tourists. For something more original, take the bus from Piazza San Marco to Fiesole to enjoy some country air. Fiesole's convent and Roman arena are both worth seeing. Try a liter or two of the local *Chianti.*

Siena and San Gimignano

Other towns funded more significant cathedrals or displayed grander *palazzi,* but nowhere else is the town itself a work of art in quite the same way as in **Siena.** Enclosed by high walls, Siena is given spaciousness by its carefully planned public squares and buildings. Even twentieth-century Sienese feel themselves a breed apart: they vigorously preserve the medieval division of the city into seventeen *contrade* (districts), and speak the purest Italian in the country.

Typically, Siena is somewhat off the main transport routes (the old city bans daytime traffic as well). It's about an hour south of Florence, through Empoli (1600L). From Rome and the south, change to a local at Chiusi.

The bus from the Train Station deposits you at **Piazza Matteotti.** From here, stroll down **Banchi di Sopra** to the **Campo,** and get a city map from the **Tourist Office** at Piazza del Campo 55 (tel. 280551). They also have an accommodations service invaluable at **Palio** time—this medieval horserace around the dirt-packed Campo involves ten of the *contrade,* chosen by lot, every July 2 and August 16. On these days, the city erupts with colorful processions, costumes, and ceremonies.

There are dismayingly few accommodations in Siena, and most are fairly expensive. The **Locanda Garibaldi,** Via G. Duprè 18 (tel. 284204) has the cheapest rooms in town, and is right off the Campo. Doubles cost 6000L, singles 3500L, and showers 400L extra.

At **Taverna di Bacco,** Via Beccheria 9, you can get a good meal for 3000L; the *antipasto* is especially fine. The **Mensa Universitaria** on Via Sant Agata has institutional meals for 1000L; the **Mensa** run by the Cloister of San Domenico is better, but more expensive.

Sights

Siena is crammed with art of its fourteenth-century school which emphasizes priestly poses and pink-cheeked, melancholy virgins. Start at the **Piazza del Campo,** and enter the **Palazzo Pubblico.** Admission to the **Civic Museum,** and the chance (which you shouldn't pass up if you have the strength for it) to climb the **Tower,** is 300L with ISIC card, 500L without (open 9am-noon and 2:30-6:30pm in summer). The nearby **Duomo** took so long to build that it started as Romanesque but finished as Gothic. The **Cathedral Museum** across the *piazza,* has some fine Pisano sculptures, as well as the *Maestà* by Duccio, the pinnacle of Sienese painting (open 9-11am and 3-7pm Tues.-Sat., 9am-1pm and 3-6pm Sun.; admission 500L). If you want to see more of this school, the **Pinacoteca** is the place; free with ISIC card. It's open 8:45am-1:45pm Tues.-Sat., 9am-1pm Sun. If you go for the *Palio,* try to get there a day early to see some of the test races, find a room, and choose a *contrada* to root for. And don't miss the torchlight procession of the winning *contrada* through the city the night of the Palio.

Halfway between Siena and Florence, **San Gimignano** is the museum town of Tuscan feudalism and factionalism. As tensions escalated in the twelfth century, so did the towers each noble family built to control its neighborhood and survey its enemies.

San Gimignano makes a good afternoon excursion from either Siena or Florence. Take a bus or train to Poggibonsi, then a SITA bus to St. John's Gate (about 800L and an hour one way). Walk down **Via San Giovanni** to the **Piazza del Cisterna,** surrounded by towers, then around the corner to the **Piazza del Duomo.** The Duomo combines Romanesque architecture and fourteenth-century Sienese painting. The nearby **Torre Civica** is the only tower you can ascend (200L); a long hike, but worth it.

Pisa

Pisa is quiet and peaceful—it's a serious university town (Galileo was born and taught here). Back in the twelfth and thirteenth centuries, though, Pisa was a busy Crusader and commercial port, and developed its own brand of wedding-cake Romanesque. The **Prato dei Miracoli**—with its impossibly white complex of **Cathedral, Baptistery** (both open 8am-1pm and 3-7:30pm), and the **Campanile** (the **Leaning Tower,** open 8am-8pm in the summer; 1000L)—is set on one of the only urban lawns in Italy big enough to play frisbee on. The adjoining **Camposanto** (Christian Cemetery, open 8am-7:30pm, admission 500L) has some famous frescoes. The **Jewish Cemetery,** masked behind the wall (go outside the Prato, turn the corner, and ring for the caretaker) is equally moving. Pisa's 1300-year-old Jewish community is served by the **Synagogue,** one of Europe's finest, on Via Palestro.

Food and lodgings are cheap and student oriented. The clean **Locanda Galileo** at Via Santa Maria 12 (tel. 40621) has frescoed ceilings; singles 3500L, doubles 5500L, and triples 7450L, but towels 500L extra. Via San Lorenzo has several cheap, though slightly run-down, places—the **Bertini** at #19 (no phone) has doubles for 2500L, and the **Giglio** (tel. 23304) and **Spanò** (no phone) at #23 are about 1200L per person. There's also camping at **Camping Pisa,** right outside the Prato Gate at Viale delle Cascine 86 (tel. 501512). The cheapest food in town is 1200L at the **Mensa Universitaria,** on Via Bonanno; Via d'Arancia, off the University at Piazza Dante, has several places with 2800L fixed meals.

Emilia-Romagna
Bologna

Jacob Burckhardt, the nineteenth-century historian of the Renaissance, called Bologna the most beautiful town in Italy; it isn't any more, but Emilia-Romagna's capital still has a lot going for it. Foremost is the food— at last count, Bologna had 432 restaurants (not to mention *alimentari*), and hardly a bad one among them. Second comes the porticoes—since medieval times, every house on major streets has been required to have a portico of uniform height and width, enough for a horse and rider to pass underneath. The result is a city of lovely, shady arcades, which, like its city plan, recall Roman days and seem incongruous with Bologna's role as Italy's leading communist hotbed.

Bologna is easy to reach—it has major connections with Florence, Milan, and Venice; and minor connections with Pisa and Ravenna, among others. The **Railway Station** is at the northern edge of town, on Piazza Medaglio d'Oro (tel. 372126). The **Tourist Office,** at Via Leopardi 1/e (tel. 236602, open 9am-12:30pm and 3:30-5:30pm) has a helpful and well-organized staff giving information and accommodations service. The **Student Travel Office** at Via delle Belle Arti 6/b, near the University (the oldest in Europe) and close to the **Pinacoteca** (Picture Gallery), have similar services (tel. 264862).

From the Train Station, walk or bus down Via dell'Independenza to the main east-west street, Via Ugo Bassi. Straight ahead is the **Piazza Maggiore,** where students and citizens mingle under the Corinthian columns of the **Palazzo della Podestà** (Governor's Palace). In the afternoon the crowd shifts (with the shade) to the steps of **San Petronio,** a huge unfinished Gothic structure which was going to be even bigger, but money ran short before the nave was finished. Fortunately the city had already purchased the doorway by Jacopo della Quercia. The **Two Towers,** to the west on Via Rizzoli, are considered symbols of the city, and the **Loggia dei Mercanti,** in the *piazza* next to them, are the bizarre remains of Bologna's activity as a trading center.

The piece of architecture which makes Bologna really worth a visit, however, is down the Via Santo Stefano, where the triangular piazza of the same name opens onto a complex of Romanesque churches unrivalled for their simple beauty. The most spectacular of the four small churches that make up the **Basilica Santo Stefano** is the round **Santo Sepolcro** in which San Petronio, patron of Bologna, is buried under a spiralling carved pulpit. In the courtyard behind is the **Basin of Pilate** in which that judge is supposed to have absolved himself of responsibility—it's big enough to take a bath in. Don't miss the cloisters behind the **Church of the Crucifixion** next to the San Sepolcro, or the arches of **San Vitale,** the oldest church in the group. The **Church of San Domenico,** a few blocks away, contains the body of the saint under a marble monument with statuettes by Michelangelo and Niccolo da Bari (known ever after as "dell'Arco" for the ornate arch he designed for the top of this); also four softly modeled reliefs by Niccolo Pisano.

Accommodations and Food

Because the **University** attracts thousands of European students, it's fairly hard to find inexpensive lodgings. The **Hostel Città di Bologna,** Via Ca' Branca 32 (tel. 384417) charges 2400L per night, including showers and breakfast, but there's an 11pm curfew and it's fairly inconvenient. Take bus #21 from the Station and switch to #13 for Noce at Piazza Maggiore. **Camping** is next to the hostel. Inside the old city, try the **Locanda Anna,** Vicolo dell'Orte 3 (tel. 224518), with nice doubles for 5500L; or **Locanda Neva** near the Station at Via Serra 7 with even nicer doubles for 7500L. The **Locanda Villa Azzura,** Via Felsina 49 (tel. 544068) has singles for 3500L and doubles for 6000L.

The food situation is, happily, different—Bologna didn't get the nickname of *La Grassa* (the Fat) for nothing. Try *tortellini* (mini-ravioli), *lasagna,* and any sausage at all. **Da Franco,** Via Mentana 10, is always crowded and for good reason—it's near the Piazza San Martino and serves a complete meal for 1600L. **Da Mano,** Via Brocchindosso 71, is more expensive but also jammed with students. The **University Mensa,** Piazza Verdi 2, has filling meals for 800L (closed Sun.). If you're buying your own, **Ditta Tamburini,** Via Caprarie 1 (7:30am-1pm and 5-7pm) has an awesome assortment of provisions.

Ravenna

It may not look like much now, but in the sixth century, Ravenna was the western capital of the Byzantine Empire, and the base of Justinian and Theodora's campaign to recapture Italy from the barbarians. They didn't succeed, but the artistic legacy remains. The undisputed highlights are the mosaics at **San Vitale, Sant'Apollinare Nuovo, and Sant'Apollinare in Classe,** all well preserved and stunningly fresh.

By train, Ravenna is one hundred minutes from Bologna, an hour from Ferrara, and four hours from Florence. Buses run along the coast to the beaches at **Marina di Ravenna, Lido Adriano,** and others. The **Train Station** is at the east end of town, two blocks from Sant'Apollinare Nuovo and six from the **Tourist Office** at Piazza San Francesco 7 (tel. 36129, open 9am-1pm), which has maps of the city.

Ravenna, like its resort satellites on the coast, is swamped with German tourists in the summer, and accommodations are extremely tight. The new IYHF **Youth Hostel** has partially helped the situation—**Ostello Dante,** Via Aurelio Nicolodi 10 (tel. 420405) charges 2400L, hot showers free. There's a midnight curfew, though, and it's only open March through August; take bus #1 from the Station. There are several campsites at Marina di Ravenna, a 300L bus ride away—**Piomboni** (tel. 420230), **Rivaverde** (tel. 430491), and **Villaggio dei Pini** (tel. 437115). A **Casa Famiglia,** Via Cavour 111 (tel. 36514), charges 2500L for women only in doubles and up, with a 500L "offering" for the shower. The male equivalent, the **Sant'Andrea** at Via Oberdan 6 (tel. 22970), charges 1500L for singles, 1000L for triples and up. Curfews are 10:30pm for both. The **Albergo Bella Venezia,** Via Novembre IV 16 (Tel. 22746) has nice singles for 4000L and doubles for 5500L; while the **Mocadoro,** Via Baiona 18 (tel. 26003) charges 3500L and 6000L respectively.

Via Novembre IV has quite a few *tavole calde,* and there is a **Casa dello Studente** at Via Mariani 5 that serves lunch all summer for about 1000L. Another **Mensa** at Via Oberdan 8, near the center of town, serves large helpings noon-2pm and 7-9pm for 1000L, but it's closed in August. **Da Alfro,** on Via Garatoni 6, has meals for 3000L and up; try the *cappellati,* a meat-stuffed pasta. *Romagna* wines can be sampled for free at the **Ca'de Ven,** Via Corrado Ricci 24.

You can cover the sights in and around Ravenna in a brisk morning, if mosaics are your objective. Walk crosstown from the Station to San Vitale, with its grand murals of Justinian and Theodora performing a brighter-than-natural Mass in a superb octagonal church. Then stroll through the cloister courtyard to the tiny **Tomb of Galla Placidia.** It's dimly lit through translucent alabaster windows; as you get accustomed to the light, the mosaic subjects sparkle in the order of their creation. The grounds of the **Church of San Francesco,** near the central **Piazza del Popolo,** contain **Dante's Tomb** though not much else; continue back to the Station, detouring on Via Roma for Sant'Apollinare Nuovo's basilica-length procession of virgins. The freshest and lightest mosaics of all, however, are in Sant'Apollinare in Classe, 5 kilometers out of town; take bus #4 (round trip 100L every forty minutes) from the Station, and enjoy both the real and the artistic gardens and birds.

Ferrara

Ferrara can be seen as a daytrip from Bologna or Ravenna, and is a beautiful example of Renaissance town planning. The d'Este family castle dominates the center of the town much as the d'Estes themselves dominated the artistic and literary life of Ferrara. Today the melancholy, long streets of their grandiose schemes are lined with deserted Renaissance *palazzi* and gardens, while the medieval center still hums busily. Any look at Ferrara starts with the **Castello Estense** (open Tues.-Sat. 9am-noon and 3:30-6:30pm, Sun. 9am-12:30pm). From there, proceed to the **Cathedral,** begun in days when the Po River was alive and gushing. Like everything else in town, the Cathedral has work by the local master Garofalo, but the medieval allegorical months are more entertaining.

Food and lodging here are cheap. The IYHF **Youth Hostel Estensa,** Via Garofalo 5 (tel. 21098) is cheapest; take bus #1, 2, or 9 from the Station at the west end of town to Corso Porta Po, for multibed rooms at 1500L per person. The **Albergo Stazione,** Via San Romano 41 (tel. 33790) is in a very central location, but a bit noisy; singles 3000L, doubles 6000L. **Mensas** are at Via del Gambero 4, Via Lucchesi 5, and Via Aldighieri 40. All are open noon-2pm and 7:30-9:30pm.

Southern Italy
Naples (Napoli)

Famous for its traffic jams, dirt, and pizza, Naples seems to be a human anthill—quite a change from the orderliness of the northern cities. Once you look beyond the chaos, though, Naples becomes a living opera set. The foreigner runs the risk of having all his Italian stereotypes reinforced here. In addition to the mental caution you should use before succumbing too easily to the preformed image, a certain amount of physical caution is necessary in Naples. Purse-snatching, robbery and car-stealing are prevalent, and single women will be hassled on the street at night. The behavior of American sailors on shore leave from the Sixth Fleet has created a rather unfortunate anti-American attitude among some of the population, as well. But if you accept the biases of the Neapolitan—or at least learn to cope with them—the city can be quite rewarding.

Try to avoid both the port area and the neighborhoods near the Railway Stations; lodgings are sleazy, restaurants are few, and crime is lamentably prevalent. Free maps of the city are available at the Tourist Office at the Station, but try to use buses; being a pedestrian is time-consuming and hopeless.

Addresses and Telephone Numbers

Tourist Office: Stazione Centrale (tel. 268779), open 8am-8pm. Also at Via Partenope 10/A (tel. 403909).

Youth Hostels: Piazza Lorenzo 5, Agerola (tel. 791025, take the SITA bus to Agerola), Ostello Posillipo (tel. 691531, take bus #106 or 140 to Viale Costa), Ostello Mergellina (tel. 685346, take bus #150 to Salita della Grotta 23 in Mergellina).

American Express: c/o Ventana, Via Vittorio Emanuele 49/50 (tel. 322738).

American Consulate: Piazza della Repubblica (tel. 660966).

Accommodations and Food

All of the Youth Hostels (see above) cost 2000L, but are inconvenient, especially if you use Naples as a base for excursions around Campania. There is **camping** on Viale Giochi del Mediterraneo 75 (tel. 7605169); take bus #152. Better, however, is one of the cheap *pensioni* near Piazza Dante on Via Roma, situated between the harbor and the museums. Despite a grubby courtyard, the **Soggiorno Messina** (tel. 347652; from Via F.S. Corr-era off Via Roma, find 7 Vicolo Luperano) has clean rooms for 2500L single, 4000L double—hot water is 500L more. The **Rinascimento,** 323 Via Roma (tel. 407893), is less comfortable but cheaper—singles are 2200L, doubles 3650L.

Naples is not a place where you dine; rather, grab the local specialties from sidewalk vendors, or dive into the endless varieties of pizza, Naples' own invention. Make sure your pizza is baked *forno a legno*—in a wood-burning stove. A *margherita* pizza has extra cheese, and runs 800-900L; a *marinara* has extra tomato sauce; and a *quattro stagioni* (four seasons) has something of everything at 1500L. If you want to splurge, eat in the seafood restaurants on the waterfront known as Santa Lucia (**La Cantinella** is good). In the evening the view of the bay and the **Castel dell'Ovo** (Egg Castle) overpowers the industry visible in the distance.

Sights

Begin with the museums, which provide a respite from the noise. The
Museo Nazionale contains all the statues, furnishings, jewelery, etc., excavated from the Roman towns of Pompeii, Herculaneum, and Cuma. The
museum also houses the Borgia collection of Etruscan art. On the highest hill
overlooking the city stands the **Museo di Capodimonte** on the edge of a
large park (take bus #24). The museum is divided between the National
Gallery, which houses paintings ranging from Simone Martini to Masaccio
to Titian, and the Nineteenth Century Gallery with its collection of Neapolitan painters of the era (open 9:30-3pm, closed Mon.). The **San Martino
Museum** in a Carthusian monastery on the hill of San Elmo (take bus #49 or
the funicular) contains all sorts of odds and ends that give a complete picture
of the city when, as the center of the French kingdom, it was a cultural
mecca. The ornate rooms of the **Palazzo Reale** illustrate the life style of this
"Kingdom of the Two Sicilies." All the above museums except the
Capodimonte are open 9am-2pm, 9am-1pm Sundays and holidays, and are
closed Mondays.

The churches of Naples are like its desserts—sweet, chubby, and condu-
cive to overconsumption. If cherubs and gilt are your taste, **San Gregorio
Armeno** and **San Gennaro Cathedral** are stuffed with them; the latter has
catacombs as well, with guided tours at 9:30am and noon. **San Domenico
Maggiore** contains some interesting paintings from the Caravaggiesque
Neapolitan School, as well as a good example of a Neapolitan crèche.

Excursions

The Bay of Naples has been inhabited since pre-Roman times. The Greeks
colonized the area first—and the conquering Romans copied their art, their
life style and their beliefs. The peninsula just north of Naples, the **Phlegrean
Fields,** was considered the entrance to the Underworld, and looking at the
dark volcanic lakes of **Lago d'Averno** and **Lago Misano** (thought to be the
river Styx, across which the souls of the dead were ferried) it is not hard to
see why both Homer and Virgil began their heroes' descents to hell from this
point. The recently excavated Roman baths at **Baia** show what other use the
volcanic springs (hot and cold) were put to. Perhaps the most impressive site
of all, however, is **Cuma,** one of the oldest Greek colonies (dating from the
eighth century B.C.).

The beaches and countryside of the area are beautiful; try camping (unofficially) near the sea or one of the many volcanic lakes. There are also
several camping sites with facilities in the area; if there are only two or three
of you, this might be a safer proposition. The **Automobile Club d'Italia,**
Piazzale Tecchio 49/D, has information on camping.

The area south of Naples has even more spectacular offerings—Roman
ruins, islands in the Bay of Naples, and the Amalfi coast. The 79 A.D.
eruption of **Mount Vesuvius** covered **Herculaneum** in lava and **Pompeii** in
ashes. Herculaneum, the smaller and less crowded of the two, is open from
9am to one hour before sunset, but you can't get in after 5pm. The ruins are
accessible by train (the Circumvesuviana line, 700L round trip from Naples),
or better yet, by bus (#255, every ten minutes from Piazza Municipio in
Naples). Further down the bay, the ruins of Pompeii offer a complete vision
of Roman life in the first century. Among them, the Forum, the House of the
Vetii, the Villa of the Mysteries, and the Lupanare (brothel) are the most

entertaining. Ask the guides in the black caps to unlock whatever you want to investigate. Take the Circumvesuviana from the Stazione Vesuviana (near the Central Station) to the *Villa dei Misteri* stop; round trip is 700L. A few kilometers further out are well-preserved Greek temples at **Paestum,** best reached from Salerno.

Boats leave from the Molo Beverello, at the end of the Piazza Municipio, for the green-and-white islands of **Ischia** and **Capri.** Ischia, the closer of the two (round trip 1800L) has a nice camping ground, **Pineta Villari** (tel. 991449), and some inexpensive *pensioni*. The **Tourist Office** on the Scalo Porto Salvo (tel. 991146) can find you a room for about 3000L per person. The public beach is free, but crowded and littered. Further away from the boat dock the beaches become calmer. Chair rental 1000L. Boats leave Naples at 9:15am and 1pm.

The boat to Capri costs 2100L round trip, and departures are hourly, except at noon. The trip is eighty minutes, so plan your day around it; or don't plan, because you may not want to leave. Capri is not only for the Beautiful People; there is unofficial **camping** by the **Arco Naturale** (the arch of rock on the eastern cliffs of the island). Inexpensive *pensioni* include the **Faraglioni** (tel. 8370230, Via Camerelle) at 1650L single, 2850L double, and the **Metropole** (tel. 8370267, Via Grande Marina) at 3150L and 6600L.

From the dock at Marina Grande, take the funicular (150L) to the town of Capri, then follow the steep Via Tiberio to **Villa Jovis,** the Emperor Tiberius' ruined but still magnificent Xanadu. Then descend to the **Marina Piccola** to swim in the uncannily blue water for 500L.

South of Naples

Italy south of Rome is a lot more than just Naples. In fact, if coping with Naples doesn't appeal to you, consider staying at Capri or Sorrento, daytripping to Naples, and then working your way down the boot along either coast. Even in late summer, **Apulia, Campania,** and **Calabria** (the three coastal provinces of the south) have miles of deserted beaches, rich vineyards and cropland, and a relaxed atmosphere you just won't find up north. And despite the massive sums poured into the south for economic development, there's not much evidence of it trickling into villages and towns; the Apulia you'll see, for example, will be that of Hohenstaufen castles, cathedrals, and fields. However, travel is slow, and if individual sights are what you're after, aim for Sicily or Naples.

The western Tyrrhenian coast below the Amalfi coast has the instinct for hospitality, if not the means. Campers can sleep at several camping grounds, along the shore, or ask to sleep on a farmer's land (and often get a free meal in the bargain). One of the most picturesque spots is **Scilla,** a ten-minute and 400L round-trip train ride from Villa San Giovanni. The **Youth Hostel** is a fifteenth-century castle that overlooks a sand-and-pebble beach and the Straits of Messina. Lodgings, with an IYHF card, are 1500L per night, and management and fellow hostelers are invariably congenial. The **Tourist Office** in Reggio di Calabria (at the center of the "toe") is located at Via C. Colombo (tel. 98496) and has information on itineraries and camping.

The eastern Adriatic coast has more beaches, but they're harder to reach except for those near **Bari** and **Brindisi,** old Roman cities now ports for ferries to Corfu and Patras, Greece. The inland region near Bari is rich in medieval architecture, and **Castel del Monte** is the finest fortress in Italy.

Bari's **Tourist Office** (tel. 369228) at 33A Piazza Roma can recommend lodgings, and there is a IYHF **Youth Hostel** 8 km away at Palese (tel. 320282). Take bus #1 from Bari; the address is 33 Via Nicola Massaro.

Sicily (Sicilia)

On the edge of one continent and on the verge of another, Sicily is far removed from the Italy most travelers visit: **Palermo** is as close to Tunis as it is to Naples. For more than 2500 years, Sicily has suffered almost every Mediterranean invasion—Greeks, Romans, Arabs, Byzantines, and Normans. Today poor and underdeveloped, Sicily still holds to her ways. But there have been changes, such as the yearly migration north of the men to Italian and Western European factories. Sicily itself has an expanding economy, and a circular train-hopping route around the island (the best way to tour Sicily) will reveal factories next to miles of sun-scorched crops and burnished beaches.

Getting There and Getting Around

Except for late July and August (the vacation period for Italians, when Sicily is also clogged with European tourists), getting to Sicily is not difficult. The fourteen-hour overnight trip on the Cagliari-Palermo ferry from Sardinia costs 11,300L second class. Boats leave Fridays and Saturdays. The **Tirrenia** line has daily service from Naples to Palermo (21,600L), and from Naples to Reggio Calabria and Syracuse (18,000L). They also sail to Tunis, the capital of Tunisia, from Trapani (18,600L) and from Palermo (31,300L). Each trip runs twice a week. An IYHF or ISIC card gives you a 30% reduction on most of these. Reservations should be booked for the peak season, well in advance. You can do this in Italy or at **Extra Value Travel,** 5 World Trade Center, New York, NY 10048.

The cheapest way to get to Sicily is the train from Calabria (Villa San Giovanni), which crosses to Messina on a state railways ferry. The fare to Catania is 1700L; the trip takes longer during the holiday period, when reservations should be made if you want a seat. You can do so in major Italian cities by using the telephone booking system. The free train schedule booklets for each city, have the pertinent information.

If you are under 22, flying can be economical—Rome-Palermo 26,000L—and reservations are not a big problem. Still, don't try to buy your ticket the day you want to leave.

Once in Sicily, take your time—you'll have to—so plan on the unplanned and be prepared for slow, inefficient transport. Many of the major sights can only be reached by local trains; and a trip may include a two-hour "snack" which a Sicilian family will insist on sharing with you. For more independence, a car or motorcycle, with a tent, beats hitching hands down, since there just are not enough cars on major roads.

Sicilian food is highly spiced and its wine strong. Palermo is heavy on pasta-seafood combinations and pizza, while Trapani has many borrowings from nearby North Africa (such as *couscous*). The varieties of bread and cheese are endless—experiment.

Palermo

Much of Palermo is a bad imitation of an American city—teenagers in jeans and T-shirts with unlikely logos; disco music blaring from shops and cars; and unrelenting noise, grime, and traffic. After the initial shock, however, Palermo's Norman past will win you over.

From the Railway Station or docks, follow Via Roma up to Corso Vittorio Emanuele; then stroll up to the **Palace of the Normans**, admiring the several planned *piazze* and the **Cathedral** along the way. **The Palatine Chapel** in the Palace (open daily 9am-1pm and 3-5pm, except Sun.) reflects Norman and Arab styles, and has wonderful mosaics; the guard will turn on the lights if you ask. **San Giovanni degli Eremiti,** around the corner, is now semi-ruined, but its pink domes shield an exotic cloister garden.

But the area's chief mosaics and cloisters lie 8 km up the Corso Calatafimi in **Monreale** (take bus #9 from the Palace, or from the Piazza 13 Vittime near the harbor—100L each way). The **Cathedral** combines Norman architecture with Sicilian and Arabian motifs, and features a breathtaking mosaic depiction of the Old and New Testaments. The **Benedictine Cloister** next door frames a refined garden with the most imaginative medieval columns and capitals you'll ever see. Back in Palermo, the **Museo Nazionale** (off Via Roma at Piazza Olivella) has a collection of Punic and Phoenician artifacts (open 9am-2pm, except Mon.; admission 150L; free with ISIC card).

In the mornings, an open-air fish market operates at the Porticello gate, and gardens like the **Garibaldi** on Via Libertà provide atmosphere for a lunch of bread and cheese (*Pecorino* is recommended). Palermo, with 600,000 people and the regional government, has an active nightlife; try to catch one of the 9pm puppet shows which play throughout the city (such as **Cuticchio,** off Piazza Quattro Canti).

The **Albergo Firenza,** Via Candelai 68, (tel. 215869) has large rooms and a friendly English-speaking manager. Doubles 7500L, singles 4000L. As in many Italian cities, the grid near the harbor has many cheap (but less than spectacular) lodgings. Try the **Albergo Quattro Canti,** Vicolo Paternò 4 (singles 3000L, doubles 5000L), or the **Pensione Castlenuovo,** 50 Piazza Castelnuovo, for airy rooms at 4500L and 7500L. The **Tourist Office** is cater-corner at 34 Piazza Castelnuovo, and has complete listings of lodgings, material on Sicily, and free city and regional maps.

The **Fico d'India** restaurant, at 68 Via E. Amari, has an incredible array of antipasto—squid, sardines, pickled onions, eggplant, etc.—for 1700L. **Giannettino,** at 11 Piazza Ruggiero Settimo, is a *tavola calda* specializing in Sicilian dishes.

BEACHES ON THE NORTHERN COAST

Mondello, twenty minutes by bus #14, 15 or C from Via Roma, has excellent beaches, one of which is reserved for guests in Palermo hotels. Get a ticket from your hotel. The private beaches are less crowded, especially at lunch time, and as long as you don't try to change in the bathroom no one will bother you. The beaches east of Palermo are not as pretty, but much less crowded. Take the Agrigento train a couple of stops and walk along the shore.

Ustica, 60 km off the coast, is a volcanic island famous for underwater fishing and caves. The **Pensione Clelia** (tel. 841039) has singles for 4000L, doubles 7500L, and its own beach. You can also find accommodations in private homes. Boats for Ustica leave from the Palermo Maritime Station four times a week; but once again, reserve in advance for July and August.

Other possibilities for beaching it are the **Camping lo Scoglio,** an excellent campground at **Castel di Tusa,** halfway between Palermo and Messina, or at cheap hotels like the **Pensione Guttila** (tel. 631 960) in **Santa Flavia-Olivella** (doubles 7500L, private beach). There are youth hostels in **Castroreale** (Ostello delle Aquile, Salita Federico II d'Argona—open only

June-September, no telephone), and on the island of **Lipari** (Via Castello 17, tel 911 540), where a guide will take you up onto the volcano which formed the island. Ask for information at the hostel.

AGRIGENTO

Among Sicily's classical remains, the ensemble of temples at Agrigento shares top honors with Selinunte and Syracuse. Although early Christians damaged most of the sites and turned the **Temple of Concord** into a basilica, enough remains to give you a feeling for the Greek viewpoint: sea, sky, and the work of man in harmonious equilibrium. The helpful **Tourist Office** is on Piazza Vittorio Emanuele (tel. 20391). From the adjacent Piazza Roma, buses marked "S. Leone" or "Porto Empedocle" leave and return every thirty minutes. Hitchhiking is easy. Halfway to the temples, the **Museo Archeologico Nazionale** has a fine Greek vase collection (open daily 9am-2pm).

You can't sleep amidst the ruins, although they're lit nightly from 9:30-11:30pm May to September. The **Albergo Atenea,** 1 Vicolo Pancucci (just off the Via Atenea, tel. 23723) has doubles for 3500L and singles for 2100L, but not much else. The **Gorizia,** Via Boccerie 39, runs 3000L single and 5000L double without hot water. For a great place to soak and sleep after a day's clambering, try the centrally-located **Hotel Belvedere,** 20 Via S. Vito (tel. 20051) at 4900L single, 8400L double. Campers and beach lovers are welcome at **San Leone** (tel. 44912) in the town of the same name, Agrigento's coastal outpost. To get there, take the S. Leone bus beyond the Valley of the Temples to the end of its route, and walk along the dunes on the left. Good, cheap Sicilian food is served at the **Trattoria Atenea,** off the Via Atenea.

SYRACUSE

Once a victorious rival of Athens and the scene of Plato's efforts to shape his philosopher-king, Syracuse is now a bustling town and the setting for some extraordinary buildings. Go to **Ortygia,** the site of the earliest settlement (and originally an island), for the **Temples of Apollo** and **Athena;** the latter has become the Cathedral. Across the street, the **Museo Archeologico Nazionale** (open 9am-2pm daily, 9am-1pm Sun., free for students) has terrific Greek vases and a famous Venus Andiomene. Papyrus is still made at **Istituto del Papiro,** 66 Viale Teocrito. Here you'll get to see real scribes in action.Free bicycles for touring Ortygia are available through the **Tourist Office** (33 Via Maestranza).

But for the big sights, travel crosstown to **Neapolis** in the northwest (open 9am to just before sunset). Here, for the most part cut out of the living rock, are the **Greek Theater,** on the site of which Aeschylus' *The Persians* was first performed; the **Latomie,** or quarries, now shady parks, where thousands of prisoners of war were incarcerated and died; the **Roman Amphitheater** and an enormous **Altar to Zeus the Liberator,** where hundreds of bulls were sacrificed at the annual celebration of the end of tyranny.

The **Youth Hostel** at 45 Via Epipoli (tel. 711118) has single rooms for 2500L, but is beyond Neapolis; the **Stazione** at the Railway Station (tel. 67897) has rooms for 2520L and 4480L; the **Milano,** 8 Corso Umberto (the road connecting the Station to Ortygia) for 3100L and 5200L. *Trattorie* abound in Ortygia, and one of the best is the **Ortygia,** 37 V. XX Settembre.

Sardinia (Sardegna)

Sardinia is farther from the rest of Italy than the 200-odd kilometers that separate it from the mainland. Mountainous, barren and wild, Sardinia has never been completely civilized or conquered. Today it proudly proclaims its status as an "autonomous region" and flies its own flag from municipal buildings.

Sardinia's history is largely non-Italian; it reflects a highly-developed native culture and waves of foreign domination. The 7000-plus circular stone huts *(nuraghi)* still standing in Sardinia are relics of a highly-developed civilization, rivaled during the Bronze Age (1500B.C.) only by the Minoans in Crete. Many of them are grouped in planned towns around a central *nuraghe* fort. The ruins of **Nuraxi** near Barumini are perhaps the best preserved.

The art of these *nuraghi*, surprisingly, resembles the work of Modigliani, the twentieth-century painter, more than any classical art; the same is true of the votive images produced under Punic and Phoenician hegemony. Sardinia was passed to Rome, Byzantium, Catalonia, and finally the House of Savoy, and each major town shows traces of them all.

But the land itself is what most people come to see. The west is hilly and occasionally lush; the east is mountainous and wild. The coast alternates between granite cliffs and long, sandy beaches, where camping is crowded in late July and August, but otherwise is a solitary affair.

Tourism has come to this island with a vengeance. Stick to the older towns, where traditional hospitality, regional customs and food, and Sardinians survive in a less exploited form.

GETTING THERE AND GETTING AROUND

From the mainland of Italy, there are daily ferries to Sardinia's major port cities: **Cagliari** (the capital of the island), **Olbia** (on the east coast), **Porto Torres** (at the northern tip) and the smaller port of **Golfo Aranci** (on the Costa Smeralda). From France, boats ply between Toulon and Porto Torres, and from Bonifacio on Corsica to Santa Teresa di Gallura.

The **Tirrenia** line is the biggest, and operates a convenient overnight ferry from **Civitavecchia** (a port one hour north of Rome) to Olbia; the Railway Station at Civitavecchia is across the street from the dock. In Olbia, buses and trains are lined up to greet the ship. On the ferry, a second-class reclining seat *(poltrona)* costs 10,100L, while deck space for the hardy is 6400L. In summer, reservations are advisable; the Tirrenia company has offices in Rome at Via Bissolati 41 (tel. 481753) and at Civitavecchia in the harbor.

A cheaper alternative is the national railways ferry from Civitavecchia to Golfo Aranci; a *poltrona* costs only 3500L, and the train fare from Golfo Aranci to Olbia is minimal. Tirrenia also operates a fourteen-hour ferry from Palermo to Cagliari on Fridays and Saturdays (Cagliari to Palermo on Thursdays and Fridays); *poltrone* cost 10,300L one way. Cagliari is also connected by ferry to Tunis, Trapani, and Naples. Contact Tirrenia's Rome office for information.

On Sardinia the major rail and auto routes connect the northern and western coasts, and not much else. Rail transport is cheap but inconvenient, and hitchhiking is slow, especially along the lightly-traveled stretches. Buses are best, but don't often go to archaeological sites. If you want to see a lot of

Sardinia in a limited period, rent a car or motorcyle in one of the larger towns.

ACCOMMODATIONS AND FOOD

Cheap *pensioni* and hotels in this relatively undeveloped island are not always easy to come by, though the **Ente del Turismo** in any larger town will help you out. In most good-sized towns, there are a few pleasant *pensioni* which have clean if shabby rooms for about 2500-3500L per person, and the mountain villages have lodging for about half that price—but you'll find even that expensive for what you get. The seven or so youth hostels, situated for the most part in the north, are an excellent alternative; they are all on the beach and have airy, though crowded, rooms. Best of all, they cost 2000L a night. But by far the best way to see Sardinia is to camp; the island is full of official and semi-official camping sites, many of which are accessible by public transport. Of course if you have a car, you can camp just about anywhere you please. Unlike the rest of Italy's countryside, Sardinia has no poisonous snakes. And you will never find more deserted, or more beautiful, hills and coves.

The "gastronomic specialties" of Sardinia are eccentric. In the mountains, suckling pork, lamb and goat are cooked in medieval ways—one delicacy is pig cooked in sheep's stomach. On the coast, fish and shellfish are fresh and cheap (if you cook them yourself). *Vernaccia* wine is something different and rather strong—try it out. And flat shepherd's bread, fresh goat and sheep cheese, and fruit are delicious staples. Unfortunately, it is almost always expensive to order a sit-down meal; restaurants exist for tourists alone. Eat at *pizzerie, rosticcerie* or *tavole calde,* or cook (most youth hostels have facilities). One delicacy of the island which the energetic and unsqueamish can sample free is the sea urchin. Pull them carefully off the rock (if you crush them they sting) and scoop out the inside. They taste like cheap caviar.

THE EASTERN COAST

The ferry from Civitavecchia deposits you at **Olbia,** an old town with little but villas, shops, and foreign tourists. Walk up the Corso Umberto from the waterfront to find the helpful **Azienda di Turismo** on the Via Catello Piro. If you stay, try the **Terranova** (tel. 22394), 3500L single, 6500L double; or the **Locanda Deiana** (tel. 23002) 2500 single, 5000L double. Both are on the Corso, as are several *cambi* (exchanges). Short excursions from Olbia include trips to *nuraghi* at S'Abe on the road to Castello Pedrese (a ruined Spanish fort) and the "giants' tombs" of Su Monte; buses leave from the AkST Bus Station on the Corso.

South of Olbia lies the most mountainous, unspoiled area of Sardinia; women still wear native costumes and (except in late July and August) beaches are deserted for miles. Nuoro and Arbatax are particularly famous for their archaeological treasures, traditional ways, and physical beauty. But no trains run there from Olbia, although they do (infrequently) from Macomer and Cagliari. Buses leave daily from the Olbia quay. Hitchhiking is slow but dependable. For beaches, try the coast around Santa Maria Navarrese.

To the north, Olbia is the gateway to the **Costa Smeralda,** a mountainous, bay-filled coastline. Previously a series of poor fishing villages, the area is now filled with luxury hotel settlements, and the jet-set fly in to gamble, eat, hobnob, and bathe in the clear green water. Join in on the swimming, which you can do for free. A good beach-hunting strategy, in fact, is to look for a luxury hotel that advertises a "private beach." Often they have picked the best spots, but nearby there is always some public access to the edges of a sandy cove.

Trains run frequently to Golfo Aranci on the Costa, and a round trip ticket to Marinella, two stops before, costs 400L. But you can reach more spectacular coastline by a 400L bus ride to **Arzachena** further north, a sleepy town of pastel stucco, wrought iron, and swallow nests. At the terminus, retrace the last two turns of the bus to reach the main drag, the Viale Costa Smeralda, for accommodations at the **Pensione Innocenti** (tel. 82056), 3500L single, 6400L double; or the **Albergo "4 Mori"** (tel. 82214), 3600L per person. To get to the beach, wait at the Bar Smeralda for buses to Cannigione, Baia Sardinia, Palau, or Porto Cervo—all perfect for swimming, sailing, and snorkeling.

Cannigione, 8 km from Arzachena, has a 70-bed **Youth Hostel** near the beach (1200L in rooms of four and over, 200L for hot water). You can also camp at the **Insuledda** (tel. 82372) or the much smaller **Golfo di Arzachena** (tel. 828089).

From **Palau,** buses and boats go to **Santa Teresa di Gallura,** a smaller port at Sardinia's northern tip, in sight of Corsica. Trips to Bonifacio (Corsica) run twice daily from Palau and cost 8500L. Palau's **Azienda di Turismo** in Piazza Vittorio Emanuele (tel. 74127) has a room-finding service; **camping** is at **Cala Sambuco** (open June-September).

THE WESTERN COAST

The twentieth century has affected **Sassari**'s romanesque core only superficially; eat at a pizzeria like **Al Corso** (tel. 234210) on the Corso Vittorio Emanuele, where pizzas are baked in brick ovens with wood fires; and wander through the ageless alleys and discover a parish church or two. The best inexpensive lodgings are at **Pensione Famiglia** (tel. 230543), 65 Viale Umberto, with singles for 2850L, and doubles for 4800L, all with showers. Or try the **Paradiso** at 55 Via Cavour (3000L singles, 5000L doubles). Accommodations fill up for the Feast of the Candles (August 14th).

Southwest of Sassari is the coastline of the **Riviera del Corallo.** One hour and 500L can get you a train to Sardinia's prettiest town, **Alghero.** For most of its formative years, Alghero was a Catalan outpost; and the architecture, dress, battlements, and dialect remain more Spanish than Italian. The churches are worth exploring; from **San Michele**'s brightly-colored majolica dome to the **Duomo**'s doorway, and **San Francesco**'s arches and carvings. In the cloisters of San Francesco, concerts of classical music are given every evening in July and August—tickets at the door cost 800L.

A short boat trip away (or a walk from Capo Caccia along the coast) is the **Grotta di Nettuno,** a huge underwater cavern that puts Capri to shame. Boats leave from Alghero at 9am, 10am, 3pm, and 4pm. The excursion lasts three hours and costs a total of 3500L. On the way back, try the beach at **Le Bombarde.**

CAGLIARI

The capital city of Cagliari, a dizzying spiral of alleys and towers on the southern coast, manifests a number of foreign occupations. The **Cathedral** is thirteenth-century romanesque with a colorful mosaic façade; the **Basilica di San Saturnino** is early Byzantine. The towers of **Elefanti** and **San Pancrazio** were built around 1300 for Pisan overlords, who started the **City Hall** on Via Roma overlooking the harbor. The **Museo Archeologico Nazionale,** however, is undoubtedly the most impressive of Cagliari's sights: Sardinia's prehistoric, Phoenician, Punic, and Roman periods are represented by remarkably complex bronzes, statutes, coins, and pottery. The **Roman Amphitheatre** down the street is open only for Sunday strolls.

Inexpensive lodgings in Cagliari are easy to find in the grid between Via Roma and the Corso Vittorio Emanuele, but don't expect the Ritz. Try the **Hotel Centrale,** 4 Via Sardegna (tel. 654783), 4000L single, 5500L double; or the **Locanda Palmas,** down the street (tel. 651679). Singles for 3000L; doubles for 5000L. If you want comfort, the **Hotel Italia** on 31 Via Sardegna (tel. 656888) is 5500L single, 9500L double. Don't leave without eating some seafood—**Trattoria La Damigiana** at 116 Corso Vittorio Emanuele has delicious shrimp and eels.

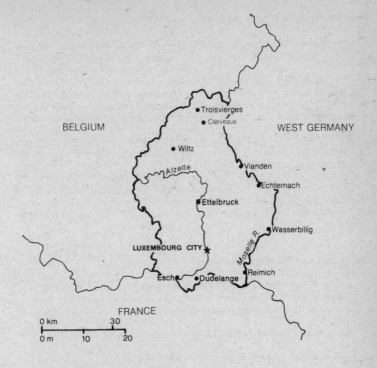

BELGIUM

WEST GERMANY

- Troisvierges
- Clerveaux
- Wiltz
- Vianden
- Echternach
- Ettelbruck
- Wasserbillig
- **LUXEMBOURG CITY** ★
- Esch
- Dudelange
- Reimich

Alzette

Moselle R.

FRANCE

0 km		30	
0 m	10		20

LUXEMBOURG

$1U.S.=30 francs (F)   **1F=$.033**

Luxembourg has been pushed around for centuries. This is not hard to understand of a nation 999 miles square which takes two hours to traverse by car. But there is a strong sense of independence here, and a resolve to remain as a roaring mouse amidst towering neighbors. The Luxembourg motto, "We wish to remain what we are," is taken seriously. This can be seen in the adherence to *Letzeburgesch,* the national language.

Even if your only reason for coming here is that you flew to Europe on Icelandic Airlines, don't despair. Luxembourg offers good camping, boating, hunting, fishing, and horseback riding. Youth hostels dot the nation (**Hollenfels** has one in a castle), there is no restriction on camping, and cycling and hiking trails crisscross the open land.

The everyday language is *Letzeburgesch,* actually a German dialect. French, however, is the official language, but German will serve you well. Some people speak English. The Luxembourg franc is tied to the Belgian franc and the two are interchangeable.

Luxembourg City

Set in ravines and sliced by the Pétrusse and Alzette Rivers, Luxembourg City is a friendly town with medieval charm. The **Tourist Office** (tel. 481-199), in the Air Terminus Building to the right of the Train Station, will supply you with a walking guide to the city which will take you through the **Casemates** (underground passages of a fortress hewn from solid rock) to the **State Museum** and the **Grand Ducal Palace.** But take time to enjoy the city on your own, following the winding paths into the park in the ravine of **La Pétrusse.**

Bus #9 runs between the Station, the Hostel, and the Airport (14F, and another 14F for luggage or backpack). It is much cheaper than the Luxair bus which runs the same route.

Crisscrossing the Grand Duchy is hardly a grandiose proposition. For 100F, Luxembourg City's Railroad Station issues a pass good for a day of unlimited second-class train and bus hopping *(Billet Réseau).* Longer stints of five days and one consecutive month of travel cost 300F and 800F respectively.

Addresses and Telephone Numbers

Grand Duchy National Tourist Office: Air Terminus building at Place de la Gare (tel. 481199), open from 8:30am-8:30pm, closed for lunch. Free information for the entire country and hotel reservations.

Luxembourg Student Travel (TEJ): 15 rue Louvigny (tel. 9146514).

U.S. Embassy: 22 blvd. Emanuel Servais (tel. 40123).

Main Post Office: 8 ave. Monterey (tel. 47651); also a branch across the street and to the left of the Train Station at 38 ave. de la Gare. Open 8am-noon, 1:45-7pm.

Accommodations

Rooms in Luxembourg City are expensive, and owing to its small size, reservations are usually imperative, though the Tourist Office will assist you in finding a room. Most of the affordable hotels are near the Station on Place de la Gare. The older part of town across the ravine is more scenic, but you will pay for the view. There are several hotels along the rue Joseph Junck, where you can go if you get stuck. The area, however, is rather seedy.

Baezel, 30 rue de Fort Niepperg (tel. 487255) has 15 bright and spacious rooms, with a kitchen if you plan on staying a while. Singles 240F, doubles 380F, shower 25F, breakfast 50F. A good buy.

Des Ardennes, 59 ave. de la Liberté (tel. 488582), singles 250F, doubles 400F, breakfast 50F. Often full, so come early in the morning.

De l'Avenue, 43 ave. de la Liberté (tel. 488865), singles 270F, doubles 400F, breakfast 60F, dinner available at bar downstairs. The place is aging, but clean.

Feipel, 11 rue de Strasbourg (tel. 485829) has singles for 450F, doubles from 500-600F. Expensive, but the rooms are large and cheerful. Breakfast 75F.

Zurich, 36 rue Joseph Junck (tel. 491350), singles 450F, doubles 600F, breakfast 65F. The rooms are clean; one of the best places on the street.

Youth Hostel (IYHF), 2 rue Fort Olisy (tel. 26889). One of the most modern and comfortable hostels in Europe—actually more like a hotel, with a laundry room and disco. Bed and breakfast 130F a night, 40F to rent sheets if you don't have them. The warden's reputation for being difficult is justified, but if you don't hassle him, you'll have no problems. He is strict about the 10pm curfew. You must check in daily during busy weeks. Take bus #9 from the Train Station, or walk, following the well-placed signs (about a half-hour by foot). The hostel is often full with groups of adolescents.

Camping: Bonnevoie Plage, Itziger Ste (tel. 482498). Operated by a jovial *chef de camp;* pitch a tent for 50F or rent a room equipped with cot, minus blankets, sheets, and sink for 175F; hot showers 20F, swimming pool free. Bus #6A from rue Origen **Plage Grünewald,** rue Echternacht (tel. 432731), bus #10. Both a good half hour bus ride, plus a 15-minute walk.

Food and Evenings

EMS, 30 Place de la Gare, across from the Train Station. Good food, always crowded with locals. A complete meal will run 130-200F. Daily specials.

Café Oennert de Steiler, 2 rue de la Loge, near the Musée de l'Etat and the Hostel. Prices are reasonable. Enjoy lunch or dinner, or just relax on the terrace with a drink. After eating, wander through the stone-lined streets and shops nearby. Be sure to sample the *Mousel* beer, Luxembourg's specialty.

The **Place d'Armes** is *the* place to go at night. It is the scene of frequent free concerts by visiting orchestras, operas, ballets, and theater companies. A drink or a bite to eat at one of the outdoor cafés lining the square will cost very little and come with lighter entertainment in the form of banter and a stray burst of song from a bevy of local philanderers out to enjoy the night air. Several discos are listed in a pamphlet called *La Semaine à Luxembourg,* available at the Tourist Office. Try **Blow up,** 14 ave. de la Faïencerie; or **Pole Nord,** 2 Place de Bruxelles.

The Countryside

The real beauty of Luxembourg is its countryside. Most of the villages can be seen on daytrips from the capital, but you may want to stay longer. No problem, as youth hostels abound.

Remich, on the Moselle River, is famous for its sparkling white wine. Sample some at the **Caves of Saint Martin,** open April 1 through October 31, daily 8:30-11:30am and 2-5:30pm. For 30F you will be taken on a guided tour which displays the wine-making process. Afterwards, walk or fish along the banks of the Moselle, or take one of the boat excursions down the river. To get to Remich, take bus #A200 from Luxembourg Station, 95F.

Troisvierges, in the northernmost reaches of the Ardennes, forms a verdant hub for hiking trails, and wayfarers can see the seventeenth-century
Franciscan monastery and the sixteenth-century hermitage chapel at
Hachinisille, a few kilometers away. From here, explore the **Clerve Valley,**
with its cluster of frescoed churches. Clervaux is the prime attraction. Illuminated at night, it really does have a fairy-tale allure. Its castle contains
native son Edward Steichen's photographic exhibition, the *Family of Man*
(25F; open Mon.-Sat. 10am-5pm, Sun. 1-5pm). Clervaux has an IYHF
Hostel at 7 Route de Marnach (tel. 91024). It is a little dismal, but only 120F
for bed and breakfast. While you're in the area, ask a grocer for some of the
pock-marked and nicely flavored local cheese called *Trapiste.*

Vianden, on the eastern border, is an almost vertical town, with a majestic, ninth-century **castle.** In the summer, the landscape can be viewed from a
chairlift that goes to a height of almost 1500 feet. Stay at the newly-
renovated IYHF **Hostel. Echternach,** just to the south, offers gorges, a
dazzling Benedictine Abbey, and a **summer festival** of music, dance, and
art, which runs continuously from June 16 through July 16. The place is
filled with tourists and prices run high, but there is an IYHF **Hostel** at 9, rue
André Duchscher (tel. 72158). Also, don't forget the **Basilica,** the most
important religious building in the country.

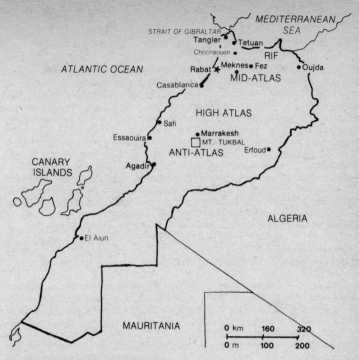

MOROCCO

$1U.S.=4.1 dirhams (dh)   **1dh=$.244**

If there is anything left of North Africa's fantastic traditions, it is to be found in Morocco. You can't just sightsee here; your senses are barraged with every step you take: the crowds, the animals, the bazaars, the hot desert sun, and, a few steps away, the cool, shaded silence of a fountain in a fabulous sixteenth-century mosque. As soon as you cross over from Spain—only ninety minutes by boat—you know you're in a different world. The people: Arabs, Berbers, Oriental Jews, Blacks, the nomadic Blue-men; the food, the architecture, the pace, and the customs—all are instantly exotic, here in the sole remaining monarchy in North Africa.

But Morocco is a lot more than a collection of similarly colorful towns and cities, each with its boys on donkeys, veiled women, and ancient minarets. For in the richness and tenacity of its traditions, each of Morocco's cities and regions remains closely in touch with its own unique past. **Fez,** always the religious and artistic capital, is a huge labyrinthine city full of tiny shops where craftsmen work away on the artifacts that grace the scores of glorious mosques and monuments all around them. **Meknes** is a Berber city; **Marrakesh** is the meeting place of the desert, mountain, and coastal peoples. Fez is gray, Marrakesh is pink, **Chechaouen,** a mountain village, is blue, and **Rabat,** the modern capital, is neon. Morocco's landscape is just as varied: the fertile **Rif** mountains in the far north, the **High-, Middle-,** and **Anti-Atlas** mountains in central Morocco, dotted with Berber villages, and the desert of the deep south descending into the Sahara.

489

Morocco, for better and for worse, is being tamed. The government is doing its best to herd in tourists of all classes, and parts of the Mediterranean and Atlantic Coasts are overrun with crowded little campgrounds and bungalow villages. The cities inland are less affected, but you'll really have to go out of the way to get where the natives don't know what's in your wallet. On the other hand, visiting Morocco no longer means being constantly surrounded by hostile, distrusting faces with only your wits to see you through. Moroccans are now more used to tourists, and are better able to help and accommodate them.

Note: the far south has been the scene of endemic conflict between Morocco and Mauritania on the one hand, and Algeria on the other. Cuban troops are rumored to be helping the Algerians, and although the Moroccan Tourist Office has nothing to say about the situation, the area way south of Agadir is not secure, and the roads at Tan-Tan are closed.

GETTING THERE AND GETTING AROUND

There are several boat lines connecting Algeciras and Málaga to **Tangier** and **Ceuta** (Arabic: Sebta). Most people take the boat from Algeciras, which is the cheapest and shortest trip. Tickets may be bought at the port or from travel agencies at uniform prices. Boats leave for Ceuta very frequently, the ride takes ninety minutes or so, and costs 200 Spanish pesetas for Tourist "B" class. The trip to Tangier is supposed to take three and a half hours, but is more often delayed. There are three or four daily boats each way between Algeciras and Tangier. Tourist "B" costs 600ptas (or 37dh). In the summer, there is also one daily ferry between Málaga and Tangier, which takes about five and a half hours. Tourist "B" costs 825ptas (or 60dh). There are also ferries between Tangier and Marseille, the Canary Islands, and Gibraltar. A catch with the cheaper Ceuta trip is that the customs officials there have of late been making themselves more difficult than their colleagues at Tangier. If you are hassled at the border, don't go back to Spain. Hang around for a few hours and check to see if the official has been replaced. Two measures you can take to help make the customs officer happy: look respectable (men, that means comb back or hide long hair and have plenty of money to wave around to show that you're not a vagrant. If they see an Israeli stamp on your passport, you may be refused entry, although they don't always look for it.

Trains are cheaper than buses in Morocco (InterRail passes are valid), while buses are more frequent, and go more places. **CTM** is the national bus line, but there are also dozens of smaller lines. All of these are usually located near each other, and you'll have to inquire at each of their ticket windows to piece together a complete schedule. The price of the same trip varies considerably depending on the bus you take, but even the first-class buses are cheap by American standards. A word about the cheaper buses—the seats can be cramped, the ventilation poor, and the bus may stop in every hamlet for a quarter of an hour. Otherwise, the buses are full of color, with beggars and water carriers passing through at every stop, blaring radios, and staring faces. Note: If you get off at small towns between large cities, you may find yourself stranded for a day or more, as buses are infrequent and often arrive and leave full. If that worries you, invest in two reserved seats, one from big city A to little town, and one from big city A to big city B on a later departure.

Hitching is erratic, even on well-traveled roads. Don't take short hops that will get you stranded. Truck drivers often request more than buses traveling the same route. Women should *never* thumb it alone.

Within the cities buses never cost more than 0.60dh. **Petits taxis** are very cheap—fares usually run between 1.50 and 3dh. There is a 50% surcharge late at night. Remember as you look for addresses that many streets (especially those with foreign names) are being renamed, and the houses renumbered. Almost everywhere, *zanqat* is being substituted for *rue* or *calle*.

ACCOMMODATIONS AND BASICS

It is not difficult to get by cheaply in Morocco. You can make do on next to nothing, depending on how rugged you and your stomach are.

The cheapest digs, other than sleeping at someone's house (a likely prospect, especially for hitchhikers), are the campgrounds, and next, the youth hostels. In every city, though, you can find a decent hotel room for 10dh or less, 20dh for a double. Many such hotels are to be found around the main entrances to the old city. It's OK to accept the offer of a cheap room from a boy on the street. Just fix the price before accepting, and don't pay until you've seen the place. Showers, when available, cost 1 or 2dh extra, and toilets are—well, practice your deep knee-bends before coming. If there is no shower, don't be afraid to use a nearby public bath. Also, have toilet paper with you at all times in Morocco, preferably brought from abroad.

There are laundries in the large cities, but often the maid in your hotel will wash your clothes for a few dirhams. Ask her, and fix the price beforehand.

Exchange money in banks—rates are uniform and no commission is charged. Keep the receipts if you want to get rid of your dirhams at the border—you won't be able to change them anywhere else. Black market transactions are often perilous—the hustlers have a full bag of tricks for ripping you off, including forgeries.

FOOD

Unfortunately, the triumphs of Moroccan cuisine, such as *pastilla* (or *bisteeya*)—a sweet pigeon pie—and a fancy *couscous* (a semolina grain covered with chicken, fish, or lamb, and onions, beans, fruit, and nuts), are served only in the expensive restaurants. Cheaper places serve good but unspectacular food. You will find everywhere chicken and lamb, served plain or in a *tajine* (fruit and vegetable stew). You will occasionally find simpler couscous dishes, but Moroccans eat so much of it at home that they rarely order it in restaurants. Probably the most common dishes are *brochettes* (kebab) of grilled chunks of lamb or beef and *kefta* (skewers of ground meat). It is never hard to find a full meal for under 10dh. In the old cities, there are greasy one-table-holes-in-the-wall where you can fill up for under 5dh. They are sometimes good, but check cleanliness, and ask for things well-cooked.

SIGHTSEEING, HASSLES, ETC.

You are going to see a lot of outstretched palms in Morocco and the amount you successfully withhold depends on your nerve and stubbornness.

The man who handles your luggage on the buses may demand a dirham—but half a dirham is enough. You don't owe the guardian of a monument anything, unless he gives you a tour—he's paid by the state.

At every tourist spot you visit you will be approached by local boys telling you that you need a guide. They are illegal and often incompetent, but if you hire one that's half-way intelligent, you can get him to show you places you would never have found. If someone approaches you and says he's not a guide, just a student who wants to practice his English, caution! This is the oldest line in the book. Even the most legit-looking of Moroccan ''friends'' have a way of turning into hustlers after a day around town: the stories of shake-downs and extortion will make your hair stand on end. This doesn't mean every local is out to get you—the instances of hospitality are just as extreme—but be wary of all strangers who approach you without your asking. If one offers you something which you don't want, make this absolutely clear from the start. This will take some getting used to for polite Westerners, but it will soon come all too naturally.

Bargaining is the rule in all handicraft shops and anywhere else where you suspect the price has been inflated just for you, including some places that display a *prix fixe* sign. Don't rely on any formula such as offering a third or half the merchant's asking price. You must know 1) what the product is worth, and 2) how easily you can find it elsewhere; and then offer even less than its value. And never let a figure pass your lips, no matter how apparently ridiculous, unless you're ready to pay it. If you've hired a guide, don't let him take you shopping—he gets a large commission on everything you buy.

All Moroccan cities are divided into a New City and an Old City (the *medina*). Most of the markets *(souks)* are in the Old City. Each *souk* specializes in one type of product—thus the carpet *souk,* the perfumers' *souk,* the fabric *souk,* etc. *Kasbah* refers to the old fortress, and in many cities it is now just another quarter. The old Jewish quarter in each city is still referred to as the *Mellah,* while a *medersa* is an old theological school and dormitory. The new downtown areas are best enjoyed from late afternoon until about 8pm, when everyone comes out and crowds the streets and cafés.

Many towns have both a **Tourist Office** and a **Syndicat d'Initiative.** The *Syndicats* are better for specific information on local monuments, history, markets, etc. The regular tourist office will have something on every town you'll want to go to. It will also help you locate food and lodgings in town. Offices of both kind are generally helpful and reliable. Some offices will changge money for you when banks are closed, as will large hotels.

As we all know, hashish *(kif)* is bountiful in this wonderful country. Contrary to appearances, however, drugs are illegal, and, especially in the north, there are road checks. Confine your smoking to campsites and secluded areas, and deal whenever possible with foreigners. Many Moroccan dealers double as narcotics agents—caution is the key word.

To best enjoy Morocco, we have one final word of wisdom, and that word is ''patience.'' One thing Moroccans know how to do better than anyone else is relax. If your bus leaves half an hour late, and then stops for a half-hour rest just before its destination; if your Moroccan friend wanders in innocehtly twenty minutes late to a rendezvous at a café; if the man you ask for directions on the street pauses to consider all the possibilities and then asks passersby for their opinions; if the rug merchant you need is taking a nap on his carpets—don't get excited. Moroccans must have fewer ulcers than any other people—efficient use of time is not the national priority. So take your time. don't cram too much into your schedule, and sit back, sip your mint tea, and never set your mind so fixedly on your plans that you forget to attach to them that ever-calming clause: *"In Sha' Allah"* (if Allah wills).

Tangier (Tanger)

If you are going to see more of Morocco than its large coastal cities, there is little that will impress you in Tangier. On the other hand, if your stay in Morocco is limited, or if you don't feel like plunging immediately into the thick of the country, you will find that Tangier does have its charm. It has both cosmopolitan appeal and local color, especially on market days (Thursday and Sunday). Many of its streets are lined with houses with lovely balconies and elaborate grillwork.

Warning: many tourists will join Mark Twain in cursing "that African perdition they call Tangier." The city lives up to its reputation as a seedy port, full of tourist traps, and you will get good practice here fending off hustlers and freeloaders. Also, if you're alone, watch where you walk after dark.

Walk up from the port, where the Boat, Bus and Train Stations are located, to the **Grand Socco,** a bustling plaza connecting the modern downtown and the *medina.* The **Hotel Grand Socco** (tel. 319-46) is a decent hotel overlooking the square. 10dh for a single, 18dh for a double, 2dh for a shower. Nearby, at 12 Alexandre Dumas in the Old City, the **Pension Istanbul** (tel. 394-76) is popular among backpackers; singles for 10dh, doubles 20dh, cold showers free.

If you're up for some sightseeing, start with the **Mendoubia Gardens.** Just inside the gate on the north side of the Grand Socco is a monstrous 800-year-old "dragon tree." A stroll through the gardens brings you to a lookout with 27 old Portuguese and Spanish cannons. The **Kasbah** offers the best view of the port and city. Nearby is the **Museum of Moroccan Art,** housed in **Dar el Makhzen,** an eighteenth-century sultan's palace. The architecture is lavish, and there is an especially fine collection of ceramics.

From the Grand Socco, the **ave. de la Liberté** takes you up to the **Blvd. Pasteur,** the main artery of the new city. In the evenings it is jammed with strollers and loafers. The **Tourist Office** is at #29 (open 8am-6pm every day except Sundays). The **American Consulate** (tels. 359-04 and 359-06) is on the Chemin des Amoureux.

Tetuan

As in Tangier, Spanish gets considerable mileage in this former administrative center of the Spaniards. But Tetuan, only an hour and a half by bus from Tangier and Ceuta, is instantly more Moroccan, more traditional. Come here for an unhurried, subdued introduction to Moroccan cities—it is a cheap and untouristy town. Its *medina,* climbing the side of a hill above the new city, is small, and extremely picturesque, especially on Wednesdays and Sundays—market days—when peasants from the surrounding Rif mountains overrun the city.

Orientation

Chances are you'll arrive by bus or car—Tetuan has no train station. To get to the **Tourist Office (O.N.M.T.)** from the Bus Station, walk up two blocks to the Boulevard Sidi Madri then to the Avenue Mohammed V. Turn left and walk another two blocks. The Tourist Office is on your right just before the circular Place Moulay el Mehdi. A free map and a list of hotels are offered, as is a 15dh "official" guided tour of the city. Five blocks from the Place in the other direction on Ave. Mohammed V is the Place Hassan II, a bustling square offering three entrances to the *medina*.

Addresses and Telephone Numbers

Tourist Office: 30 ave. Mohammed V (tel. 44-07). Summer hours: 8am-noon and 4-7pm Mon.-Thurs.; 8-11:30am and 4-7pm Fri.; 8am-noon Sat., closed Sun. When the banks are closed, the Tourist Office exchanges money for tourists.

Post Office: Place Moulay el Mehdi. Open 8:30am-noon and 2:30-6pm, Mon.-Thurs., 8:30-11:30am and 3-6pm Fri; Sat. afternoon and Sun. closed.

Bus Station: blvd. Ouadi Al Makhazine CTM Lines (tel. 65-23); AMA Lines (tel. 38-59). The ticket offices, baggage check, and arrival-departure schedule are all upstairs.

Accommodations and Food

There are hotels and pensions in Tetuan at all prices. The **Pension Iberia,** at Place Moulay el Mehdi (tel. 36-79) is clean and pleasant. Singles are 8.50dh; double bed for two, 15dh; room with two beds 17dh. There are several cheaper pensions around Place Hassan II. One of the nicest, in an alley off Place Hassan II, is the **Pension Africa,** 17 rue Kaid Ahmed (singles 8dh, doubles 14dh, including hot shower). Tiles everywhere, and an airy roof with a view. The cheapest are deep in the *medina*. **Hotel Restaurante Chababi,** at 5 Zanqa Mocadim, next to a mosque, may be hard to find, but it's clean and cheap: 5dh per person.

The cheapest places to eat are in the *medina*, and you'll probably survive the grime. The restaurant at 5 Zanqa Mocadim is pretty clean, and the old man speaks Spanish and is very friendly. 2.50dh for a vegetarian meal, 3dh with meat. Two fried sardines for 0.50dh. Near Pension Africa, on the first little alley to your left as you go down Mohammed V towards Place Moulay el Mehdi, is **Restaurant Madani,** rue Zaouian. Morocco's delicious *harira* soup served everywhere should be sampled at the nameless place at 4 Place Hassan II—0.60dh; better than the best *"restaurant typique."* If you're into hygiene, try **Restaurant Moderne,** rue Mohammed Torres, 1 Passaje Achaach; you have to go through the arcades to your left as you leave Place Hassan II in the direction of Place Moulay el Mehdi. Twelve *brochettes* for 6dh; *paella* 8dh. The adjoining **Café la Union** is a good place to kill time. Buy a drink and ask for a parcheesi, checkers, or domino set. You can sit all day.

Sights

As in most other Moroccan cities, the place to go in Tetuan is the *medina*. If the *medina* in Fez is dominated by artisans, Tetuan's is very peasanty—

full of farmers from the local countryside coming to town. The main access is at **Place Hassan II,** but if you go through **Bab (Gate) an-Nawadir** near Moulay el Mehdi, you'll find yourself in the teeming market area. A climb up the winding alleys will reward you with a splendid view of the white-washed city and the surrounding mountains.

In the evenings the downtown area is full of strollers. Place Hassan II is especially lively. There is a delightful little café upstairs looking out on the square, just across from the Pension Africa, that turns into a hashish den in the evenings.

The **Royal Palace** is, unfortunately, off limits. After restoration, it was put back into royal use. But you can walk around the outside—it's a splendid example of seventeenth-century Arab-Andalusian architecture. Tetuan also boasts an **Archaeological Museum** and a small **Folklore Museum.**

The only buses from Tetuan to Meknes and Fez leave early in the morning. The trip is a six- to nine-hour roller coaster ride on a narrow winding road through the mountains. If you wish to break up the trip, **Chechaouen** is an extremely picturesque town perched on a mountain two hours from Tetuan. There are five buses per day from Tetuan (4.20dh).

Many houses in Chechaouen's *medina* are painted light blue "against the flies," villagers explain. The town constantly teems with peasants in their hooded capes, especially on Monday (market day).

Access to the uncomplicated *medina* is through a small gate at the end of ave. Hassan II, a couple of blocks up from the Bus Station. As you enter, the **Hotel Rashidi** on your right is a good, clean place to stay with singles at 6dh, doubles 12dh, cold showers free. 200 yards down the first alley to your left is **Hotel ibn Batouta,** basically the same, but you can sleep on the roof (no beds) for 3dh. A short climb uphill brings you to Place uta el Hammam, a charming square in front of the fragile-looking *kasbah*. Here you'll find several cheap restaurants.

The CTM **Bus Station** is at Place Mohammed V, at the far end of ave. Hassan II, where a bus to Fez and Meknes stops early each morning.

Meknes

Meknes may be less of a knockout than its neighbor Fez, but it is less touristed and has wonders and a pace all its own. Its *medina* is cleaner and more peaceful. Narrow alleys are covered with vines, and in the evening an old man may invite you into his tiny shop to listen while he plays the *oud*.

Half of Meknes is strewn with ancient walls and historic sites. Most of them are from the reign of **Moulay Ismail,** a seventeenth-century sultan who rebuilt and revived Meknes as an imperial city. The result is the most varied collection of architectural splendors of any Moroccan city—including the only Moslem sanctuary in the country that non-Muslims are allowed to enter: **The Tomb of Moulay Ismail.**

Orientation

The Old Town, with the adjoining monuments of the imperial city, is separated from the modern center by a long valley, about half a mile wide. It's a forty-minute walk, or a 0.50dh bus ride from the middle of the New City—around the **CTM Bus Terminal** at the junction of Hassan II and Ave.

Mohammed V—to the dusty **Place el Hédime** in the Old City. There is a smaller CTM Station among the other bus terminals on rue Dar Smen just north of El Hédime. Most CTM buses depart from this terminal one half-hour before the scheduled New City departure. The **Train Station** is a few blocks to the east of the center of town, on ave. de la Gare, parallel to ave. des Forces Armées Royales (rue de Fès).

The main **Tourist Office** is in the New City, on Place Administrative, off rue de Tetuan (tel. 212-86). Hours are 8:30am-2:30pm Mon.-Thurs. and Sat., 8am-1:30pm Fri., closed Sun. They only speak French and Arabic, but are very helpful.

Accommodations and Food

There are several relatively cheap hotels on **rue Dar Smen,** a noisy street which starts at Place el Hédime and skirts the *medina*. For quieter surroundings, turn right at the bottom of rue Dar Smen onto ave. de Rouamzine. A couple of blocks down, on the left, is **Hôtel de Paris,** with singles at 6dh and doubles for 9dh. A little further down in Derb Benbrahim, an alleyway on the right, **Hôtel Maroc** has singles for 10dh and doubles for 15dh. Both are clean but have no showers at all. For a beautiful hot shower, try the **Bains et Douches Ismailia** by the café at the end of Rouamzine. 1.50dh, and you can soak for an hour or two without being hassled. Towels are 0.50dh, soap and shampoo 0.45dh.

> **Camping,** way out of town in the Beni-Mhamid area, just beyond King Hassan's Royal Palace. Plenty of signs to show you the way. You can take a bus to the modern mosque in Beni-Mhamid, but it's still a fifteen-minute walk. 1dh per night; 1.50-2dh per tent, but you can sleep without one. Grassy, pretty area, with lots of trees. Free cold showers.

> **Youth Hostel (IYHF),** Cercle Meknes Banlieu. Follow the signs to Hotel Transatlantique. 5dh, stuffy, far, not too clean. Dismal.

For dining, rue Dar Smen and ave. de Rouamzine have lots of el-cheapos. A good restaurant in the **Kissariat** section of the *medina* is the **Café du Souk (chez Louali);** it's got the low tables that Moroccans eat from in their own homes.

Sights and Entertainment

From the tourist's point of view, Meknes can be divided into three parts: the New City, the Old City, and the Imperial City. Enter the Old City from rue Dar Smen. **Medersa Bou Inania** is reached after a five-minute walk through the carpet and crafts souks. This fourteenth-century *medersa* is in better condition than any other in Morocco. Its elaborately-ornamented and calligraphy-covered wood and stone pillars, walls, and ceilings should not be missed. The *medina* here is lively, but not frenzied. Like Fez, it is dominated by artisans.

To tour Moulay Ismail's Imperial City, start at **Bab Mansour** in front of Place el Hédime. This multi-colored portal is the most extravagant of the many exquisite gates in Meknes. Follow the road straight past the buses, past the intersection, and you'll see on your left the mosque with the **Mausoleum of Moulay Ismail.** Entry is free, but some pushy kid will rush you through and demand a few dirhams—highly optional. A few-minutes' walk to the southeast will take you to the ruins of the old **Royal Palace** and the **Greniers de Moulay Ismail,** the king's huge warehouses and stables. From the roof you can see much of the wall which encircles and divides the city.

Dar Jamai is a good museum of Moroccan art on the Place el Hédime, housed in a mansion whose splendor rivals that of any mosque. Especially impressive are the ambassadorial reception rooms upstairs and the carpet exhibit downstairs. Entrance is free, but the guides will want tips.

In the evening, find out when the cabaret at **Roi de la Biere,** on ave. Mohammed V (tel. 214-21), is having one of the local electric Berber rock ensembles; admission 12dh, including one drink. Fat young ladies on five-inch platform shoes and polyester dudes. No one dances, but the overstuffed chairs are comfortable. Open 9pm-3am every night, closed Mon.

An indispensable daytrip: **Volubilis,** the Roman metropolis (2dh admission). It has an impressive bordello and well-preserved mosaics, including a large bestiary and a floor with representations of the twelve labors of Hercules. To get there, get a bus for **Moulay Idriss,** 26 kilometers north of Meknes. The buses, 2.50dh each way, leave from the area inside Bab Mansour hourly, starting at 7:30am. The hamlet of Moulay Idriss derives its importance from the presence of the tomb of the founder of the Idrissid dynasty (eighth century). Non-Muslims are not permitted to spend the night in this holy town. There are festivals and large pilgrimages to his tomb in August and September.

Fez (Fes)

Fez is sorcery. This is a city that reaches out for the intruder and toys with his mind; it is a hallucination. Even before you stumble fried from the bus, the voices and hands of the hustlers will rush you through the windows. Inside the **Bab Boujeloud** (the main entrance to the old city), the *medina* is a cauldron of activity. The sounds of hammers ringing on the copper and of harsh voices in perpetual skirmish; the laments of chickens bandied about upside down by their legs; the sweet, mingled scents of mint and cedar shavings, donkey droppings, whiffs of hash; the hisses of *brochettes* on open grills swirl thickly around you. Here is the *medina* of *medinas*. Within its walls you can forget your bearings, get lost, and drift happily for hours—and emerge certain that you've barely skimmed the surface.

This medieval, pearl-gray city, four hours by clattering bus from Tangier, was one of the holy cities of Morocco, and traditionally the most intellectual. It is also the northernmost of the very African cities. The flies, the dirt, the exhausting summer sun will take their toll, so come prepared to spend a few days, and let the city get a hold on you.

Orientation

The old and new cities are a bus or taxi ride apart. The bus will cost you 50 francs, the taxi about 2-4dh. If you're at Bab Boujeloud, take a right just before entering the gate and after a five-minute walk you'll get to Place Batha, wherebus #9 or 108 will take you to the **Tourist Office** on **Ave. Hassan II,** the main artery of the new city. If you arrive by CTM bus, notice the map by the departure-arrival schedule at the exit of the blvd. Mohammed V Station.

Addresses and Telephone Numbers

Tourist Office: Ave. Hassan II at Place de la Résistance (tel. 234-60). Summer hours Mon.-Fri. 8am-2:30pm and 4-7pm, Sat. 8am-2:30pm, closed Sun. No map, no English, but helpful in French.

Syndicat d'Initiative: Place Mohammed V (tel. 247-69). No map, no English spoken. Hardly worth the bother.

Post Office: Three post offices on Hassan II. If you're in the Old City, nearest one is at Place Batha. With Bab Boujeloud and the *medina* at your back, make your first left and walk for five minutes. It'll be on your left. Open 8-11:30am and 3:45-6pm; closed Sat. afternoon and Sun.

Train and Bus Stations: The express buses of the CTM are on the upper Blvd. Mohammed V; other companies operate out of garages on or around the Bab Boujeloud. The Train Station is on Ave. des Almohades.

Swimming Pools: The municipal pool is located on the ave. des Sports, near the stadium, in the New City. 2dh admission. Open June 20-September 15. Most hotels have pools open to the public, though they are much more expensive, running up to 15dh.

Accommodations

If you want to be near the Old City, there are several hotels around **Bab Boujeloud,** but you probably won't find singles under 10dh or doubles for less than 25dh. Popular among young travelers are:

The **Hotel Kaskade** and the **Hotel Mauritanie,** located next to each other, just inside the Bab Boujeloud, charge similar prices: 12dh for a single (if there's one available), a double bed for 15dh, a double bed and a single bed (two or three people) for 20dh. **Hotel du Jardin Publique** is about 150 yards down the road leading out from the Bab, and to the left (tel. 330-86). Neat and roomy, the best of these three hotels. 15dh for one person in a double bed, 17dh for two in a double bed, 18dh for a room with two beds.

Hotel Volubilis, 42 Blvd. Chefchaoueni, near the Tourist Office. Clean, but gloomy. Singles 13dh, doubles 20dh.

Youth Hostel (IYHF Auberge des Jeunes Morocains), 18 rue Campardon (tel. 240-85), parallel to Blvd. Chefchauoeni in the New City. 5dh per night, IYHF card required, no meals. Supposedly closed 10am-6pm, but not really. Cold showers available all day long. Good place, near the *Syndicat d'Initiative.*

Camping Moulay Slimane (tel. 415-37). Probably your best bargain in Fez. The camping grounds have three swimming pools (which may or may not be filled) shade, cold showers, bathrooms, and a restaurant (beware!). 2dh per person per night plus 1dh per tent per night (if you have one). To get to the camp, take #9 bus to the Place Mohammed V and then follow the arrows for five minutes. Slightly remote and toilets are OK. Avoid their grocery store.

Food

The cheapest places are in the *medina* and in **Fez Djedid.** You can get vegetable soup *(harira)* or *brochettes* almost anywhere for about 0.50dh each. Pigeon pie, called *bisteeya,* is the local specialty, but you're not likely to find it anywhere but in the expensive restaurants. It costs 20dh at both the **Dar Sa'adi** and **Palais des Merinides** in the old city. A worthwhile splurge. Order the day before.

Restaurant Bouyad, just inside the Bab Boujeloud. A good quick-and-dirty in the old city.

Cremerie Sandwich Belkhiat, 41 Blvd. Mohammed V, actually just off the boulevard (New City). A variety of salads and cheap dishes, a cut above the quick-and-dirty. 5dh should cover three or four dishes plus bread.

The restaurant with the blue decor at Rue du Commandant Melier, parallel to Blvd. Chefchaoueni (New City), doesn't have a name, but in the neighborhood, try asking for **Idris Sabaa'i's** restaurant. Two blocks from the Hostel, 4dh for a huge meal. Highly recommended. At the nearby *épicerie*, 58-59 Bernes Combo, you can buy liquor and wine. Beer is 1.50dh.

La Crêperie, 23 Rue Mohammed es Slaoui (tel. 223-77). If you're up for a real change, go pseudo-French for a night. Decent crêpes at 3-9dh.

Sights

The *medina* allows no spectators. Interaction is the name of the game, as the advance of a carted horse leaves pedestrians clinging to the walls, as you push and get pushed by children darting through the crowds, as the aromas of the perfume *souk* seduce you, and the stench of the tannery makes you queasy. It is both exhilarating and exhausting. Actually navigation is not difficult. If you're coming through **Bab Boujeloud,** take your first left and then a right, and you are on the main street. After aa couple of minutes the **Medersa bou Inania** will be on your right. This fourteenth-century Merinid edifice is only one of several ancient religious schools in the *medina* covered with elaborate ornamentation in stone, wood, and ceramic. Deeper into the *medina* is the **Attarine Medersa,** from the same period, considered to be the most beautiful in Fez. It is near the **Karouiyne Mosque,** whose minaret dates from the tenth century. It is a feast for the eye, even for non-Muslims who must look from the doors.

Fez has a long tradition as Morocco's artistic capital, and its *medina* has more *souks* of individual trades than any other city. You will never forget a visit to the **tannery,** but brace your stomach. The nauseating stench of fresh hides soaking in vats of a solution of pigeon waste and water, and then dyes, cannot possibly leave you indifferent. Buy a sprig of mint before entering the tannery, and keep it in your nose.

Fez has the most secretive *medina* in Morocco, and you can explore it for days and still miss a lot. If you hire a guide once in Morocco, it should be in Fez, but make him take you everywhere and not just on the regular tourist run. Most shops close on Friday afternoons. For your feet's sake, don't wear sandals in the *medina*.

The couple of thousand Jews that remain in the city are now scattered throughout town, but the old **Jewish Quarter** still deserves a visit. The streets are lined with large, handsome wooden balconies, and the atmosphere is much like the old city, minus the tourists and consequent hassle. The large Jewish cemetery, with its gravestones from this and the last century, provides a moving chronicle of a once-thriving community of tens of thousands that has only so recently departed.

Walk up to the **Tombs of the Merinids** on a hill overlooking Fez for a breathtaking view of the entire city.

South from Fez and Meknes: Azrou

Azrou, a little town about 75 kilometers south from both Fez and Meknes, is a good place to look for Middle-Atlas handicrafts. Rugs are cheaper in this sheep-grazing area than almost anywhere else in Morocco, if you stay away from the Cooperative, and bargain.

For accommodations, the best bet is the **Hôtel Cedres,** with single 13dh and doubles 17dh and up. If you're busing south to Marrakesh, can be tough to get out of. Buses are few and usually arrive full; don't even think about hitching out. It might be a good idea to reserve places on a Fez-Marrakesh bus before you go to Azrou.

Marrakesh

Marrakesh has become relatively commercialized, but still has its glories. It is a pink, open, languorous town with nothing of the grey congestions of Fez. Unfortunately, a good deal of the old *medina* went up in flames not too far back, and the rebuilt parts won't wow you any. If Fez is ingrown, always preoccupied with sorcery and the past, Marrakesh, essentially a caravan city for many centuries, is accustomed to strangers and still a haven for the traveler. The city's trump card is unquestionably the **Djemaa el Fna.** This Times Square of North Africa, a huge plaza in the *medina,* is an eternal circus of snake charmers, desert musicians, dancers, acrobats, folk-medicine shows, and Koran classes. As in Times Square, hold tight to your wallet. The Djemaa el Fna is full of thieves, tricksters, and hustlers.

The midsummer heat in Marrakesh is enough to prostrate most tourists: 110°F in the shade is common enough, and you *expect* 100-105°F every day. If you can afford to have a bath in your room, you'll probably spend a good part of the afternoon soaking in it. Best time to see Marrakesh is the winter.

Orientation

All the useful addresses are located either along the ave. Mohammed V or in the Djemaa el Fna. If you arrive by train you are just a stone's throw-and-a-half away from the former, and if you arrive by bus you're right smack in the middle of the latter. Taxis are cheap but may refuse to run their meters. The normal charge should be 2 or 3 dirhams, not more. Buses cost 60dh. Several routes relay between the Djemaa el Fna and the New City (called **Guéliz**)—the #1 goes along the ave. Mohammed V. The **Banque de Commerce Extérieur** at 114 ave. Mohammmed V (tel. 319-48) is the only bank open on Saturdays and Sundays, 9am-noon. Most of the large hotels in the New City will also change money for you on weekends.

Addresses and Telephone Numbers

Tourist Office: Ave. Mohammed V at Place Abdel Moumen ben Ali (tel. 302-58). English is not spoken, but there is an excellent map for 3.50dh. Open daily 8:30am-7pm.

American Express: Voyages Schwartz, on rue Mauritania (tel. 331-21). A tough one to find. Rue Mauritania meets Mohammed V across from the *Syndicat d'Initiative;* the building, at the end of the second block from Mohammed V, is across from #21. Office is on second floor. Open 9am-noon and 3-7pm Mon.-Fri., closed Sat. afternoon and Sun.

Bus Station: All lines are in the Djemaa el Fna.

Train Station: Ave. Hassan II, two blocks away from the Place Haile Selassie.

Accommodations

Marrakesh is touristy and commercial. There are a lot of hotels but finding one under 10 dirhams a night can be quite a problem. The best place to look for such accommodations is in the immediate environs of the Djemaa el Fna. You might let a small boy take you to one, but be sure to check the room and the shower and toilet facilities before you agree to stay. Otherwise, the following might be helpful:

Hôtel de France, 197 Riad Zitoun Kédim (tel. 230-67), charges 15dh a room with double bed, 18dh for two beds. Cleaner than average rooms but no hot showers. With the CTM terminal at your back, walk to your right, enter the *medina* and keep going for about 100 yards. The hotel is on the left. Further on, you run into a whole cluster of little hotels. **Hôtel Mus** charges 10dh for one or two in a double bed; **Essaouira** charges 8dh for one, 10-12dh for two. Even further down, you'll see a sign pointing to **Hôtel Chellah,** a little gem in the middle of nowhere (14 Derb Sekia, tel. 229-77). Chellah offers singles for 15dh, doubles for 20dh; hot baths cost 2dh, breakfast 4dh, and gourmet meals in their verdant, tiled patio will run you 20dh—but you have to order in advance.

Youth Hostel (IYHF), on rue el Jahid off rue Mohammed al Hansali, near the Train Station, 5dh a night. It is run by a pleasant, earthy manager and is clean and comfortable for a Moroccan hostel. Card required. Closes officially at 10pm, but hours are flexible, and it is not locked during the day in the summer. A ten-minute walk to the bus stop.

Camping Caravaning: A hard, rocky campground with no shade. Toilets OK, but no hot showers. Watch the price at the grocery. 1.50dh per person, 1dh per tent. A 15-minute walk from downtown or take bus #3 or 8 to the Djemaa (last buses around 10pm).

Food

For cheap-to-moderate food, eat in the Djemaa el Fna. There are a lot of restaurants here, but the population of eating places goes up threefold in the evenings as food vendors set up their stalls. Check prices before you eat.

Snack Hippies, not much variety, but the price is right: beefsteak or *kefta* with rice, salad, and yogurt, costs 5dh; omelette, salad, and yogurt, 4dh. Facing the CTM, take the street to your left. It's a small place on the left, half a block after the arch.

The Café-Restaurant Oriental, 33 rue Bab Agnaou (off Djemaa el Fna), serves food more hygienically, at higher prices. Ask for the complete meal for 8.50dh (including service)—not mentioned on the menu. Facing the CTM, it's 100 yards down the first street on your right.

Sights

First and foremost: **The Djemaa el Fna,** especially at its busiest, between 6 and 8pm. **Warning:** you may be bothered here more often, more persistently, and by more different types of people than anywhere else in Morocco. If you don't want what you are offered, or you want someone to leave you alone, make it 100% clear from the start.

In the *medina,* visit the **dyers' souk,** with its brilliantly colored skeins of wool hanging overhead. The fourteenth-century **Medersa ben Youssef** resembles the *medersas* of Fez and Meknes in its elaborate and colorful ornamentation, but this is the country's largest.

The twelfth-century minaret of the **Koutoubia Mosque,** a wide pink tower rising two hundred feet near the Djemaa el Fna, deserves a close look. The lavish **Saadi tombs** (sixteenth century) can be reached by following the signs from the Koutoubia. This multi-chambered mausoleum is open 8am-1pm and 2:30-6pm; free, but tip the guide. If it's finally been reopened, don't miss the **Bahia Palace,** built three centuries after the Saadi tombs by one of the King's viziers.

The carving and painting of the cedar wood on the walls and ceilings are especially impressive (open 9:30am-1pm and 4-7pm). The nearby **Dar Si Saïd Museum,** housed in a former palace, has a good collection of Moroccan art and artifacts, especially rugs and guns. Open 9am-1pm and 4-7pm. Small fee for a guided tour.

Excursions

If you're in decent shape physically, you may be interested in scaling **Jbel Toubkal,** at 4167 meters, the highest peak in North Africa. The first step is to **Asni,** 47 kilometers south of Marrakesh. Buses leave the Djemaa every hour (4dh). Asni has a nice IYHF **Youth Hostel,** for 4dh per night on route, Midelt, alongside Toubkal Hotel.

From Asni you can hitch or share a taxi for the seventeen miles of switchbacks to **Imlil.** Imlil, at 1750 meters altitude is scarcely a village; you can get an omelette (3dh) but not much more at **Café Soleil,** so if you're planning to stay a while, bring food. The valleys around Imlil are breathtaking—extensive irrigation has made this a sort of Shangri-La of the Atlas. The beautiful costumes worn by the women in the fields are not for the tourists' benefit—in fact, they *don't* want their pictures taken.

If you're going to tackle Toubkal, plan on two days, and bring food and a good pair of hiking boots. The walk is generally made in two stages: first to the Alpine refuge at 3200 meters, then the assault on the peak. The walk to the refuge can be made in four and a half hours, but take your time, enjoy swimming in the mountain streams, and *stop when you get tired.* There is a real danger of fatal altitude sickness if you push yourself. At the first signs (headache, dizziness), stop. If the symptoms persist, or if you begin to feel mucous accumulating in your lungs, *go back down.* This is just a warning, and most people don't have any trouble. Drink and urinate as much as possible.

The refuge is well equipped, but there is no food for sale. Beds are 8dh per night, use of cooking facilities costs a little extra. The final stretch (three to five hours) should under no circumstances, be undertaken without a guide. Fix the price beforehand—20-30dh. The air is thin, so don't push yourself.

The view from the top beggars any description: Imlil, 8 kilometers away, is a collection of fly-specks squeezed between half a dozen other major peaks.

Essaouira

A small Berber town on the Southern coast, Essaouira's fishing and wood-working industries enable the town to avoid occupying itself excessively with the relatively small number of tourists who visit it. Essaouira is much less resorty than Agadir, to the south, and more traditional. Almost every woman is tightly veiled, and many of the young men are not yet ashamed to wear the traditional capes. This calm and picturesque town, with its lovely uncrowded beach (where you can camp out for free), is a great place to relax for a few days.

In the mornings, and after three in the afternoon, the docks are always busy. Men are unloading, cleaning, and auctioning fish, building boats, and mending nets. The **Skala,** an eighteenth-century Moorish fort lined with cannons, offers scenic views of the town and the sea. To get there take the narrow alley (rue de la Skala) across the street to the left of the CTM Station. Along this alley you'll pass many shops in which inlaid wooden furniture, boxes, and chess sets are made, a craft in which Essaouira specializes.

Orientation

There is no train station here. The Bus Stations are at opposite ends of the *medina.* The smaller lines are just outside Bab Doukala; the main **CTM** garage is outside the Porte Portugaise. The **avenue de l'Istiqlal,** the main shopping street of the *medina,* runs from one gate to the other. The **Tourist Office** is across the square from the large CTM Station. Facing the Tourist Office, the beach is to your left. On weekends, the Hôtel des Iles will change money for you. The **Post Office** is one block from the hotel on avenue al Muqawama.

Accommodations and Food

Hotel du Sud, rue l'Attarine 9. Singles 7dh, doubles 10dh, triples 15dh. No showers. Take the wide street to the left of the CTM station. Turn right after one block and then left. Rue l'Attarine is 100 yards up on your right.

Hotel du Tourisme, rue Mohammed Ben Messaoud. Singles 8dh, doubles 15dh. Hot showers 2dh extra. Clean, with inner courtyard. Recommended. Standing in front of the Tourist Office, follow the city walls around to the right for 150 yards.

Camping, a 15-minute walk from the city, on rue Mohammed V, across from the beach. Clean, but you must have a tent. Cold showers. 2dh per person, 1dh per tent. You can also camp out on the beach.

The cheapest meals are at the **Bab Doukala** end of the *medina* in those one-table joints. During the day you can have a plate of grilled sardines on the dock for 2-3dh. For a more varied selection of the local catch, you'll have to eat at one of the more expensive tourist restaurants. The most reasonable, although not the best, is the **Café Restaurant Horloge,** where a full meal costs 12dh. Go through the Porte Portugaise, and the restaurant will be just through an arch close to the second gate.

Rabat

Clean, orderly, and dignified, Rabat is just what you'd expect of a modern capital—and a total anomaly in the context of the nation it represents. There is, of course, a *medina,* but it is straightforward, and almost rectilinear in layout. Ave. Mohammed V, the city's main thoroughfare, slices boldly right through the *medina* towards the **Kasbah,** and you sense that the Old City has been overpowered by the new. Unlike Fez or Marrakesh, Rabat has no traditional atmosphere, despite the fact that it is almost as old, founded near the ruins of an ancient Roman city, **Sala Colonia.** Yet, with its cafés with their pinball machines and Stevie Wonder on the radio, sports cars, art galleries, and all the embassies, Rabat is worth visiting for precisely what it is—modernity Moroccan style. More interesting than either Casablanca or Tangier, Rabat resembles a mini-Madrid in the nocturnal pilgrimage of its citizens to the numerous local bars, restaurants, and avenues. What it lacks in tradition, it makes up in convenience—good food, nightlife and fine beaches.

Orientation

Most of the important facilities—banks, Post Office, and Train Station—are on the ave. Mohammed V. The ave. Hassan II runs perpendicular to it, separating the New and Old cities. Note that Rabat is in the process of renumbering many of its streets, so ask around if the addresses we give don't lead you to the right doorstep.

Addresses and Telephone Numbers

Tourist Office: 22 ave. d'Alger (tels. 21252, 21253, and 21254). English spoken and they have a good map. Open 8am-2pm in summer; 8am-noon and 2:30-6pm in winter. Closed Sat. afternoon and Sun. Far from ave. Mohammed V. Take a taxi for 1.50dh.

American Express: Rabat Hilton (outside of city; tel. 721-51). Take the Agdal Bus.

Post Office (PTT): ave. Mohammed V, two blocks north of the Train Station. Open 8am-2:30pm Mon.-Sat.

Train Station: ave. Mohammed V.

Bus Station (CTM): ave. Hassan II, near ave. Mohammed V. The other lines and the *Grand Taxis* are near Bab el Had, a couple of blocks away.

U.S. Embassy: far end of the ave. de Marrakesh (tel. 303-61).

Canadian Embassy: 13 Zanqat Joafar Essadik, Agdal (tel. 713-75).

Accommodations

Nouvel Hotel, 8 rue Hamame Chourafaa (Old City). New, clean, with firm double beds. No showers. Rooms with one large bed (for one or two people) 15dh; with two beds 25dh. The fifth street on the right off ave. Mohammed V in the *medina.*

Hotel Regina, 24 rue Sebbahi (Old City) (tel. 307-57). No showers, small rooms, but acceptable. Singles 10dh, doubles 15dh. The third street on the right off ave. Mohammed V in the *medina.*

Hotel Central, Zenkat Al Bassra (New City) (tel. 229-31). Across the street and two blocks north of the Train Station. Singles 12dh and up, doubles 16dh and up. Showers 3dh, bath 3.50dh. Rooms are large and clean, and have sinks, good toilets.

Hotel Splendid, 8 Zanqat Ghazzah (New City) (tel. 232-38). Off ave. Mohammed V, two blocks north of the Post Office. Singles 17dh, without shower; doubles 22dh without shower, 27dh with shower; use of hall shower 2dh.

Auberge de Jeunesse (IYHF), (New City) 66 rue de la Résistance. Hot and stuffy and not worth the price. 5dh. Hot showers extra.

Now that Camping Sun Dance Village in Salé has gone out of business, the nearest grounds are 12 km away, in **Temara.**

Food

As you enter the *medina,* there are plenty of stands where you can eat fillingly for under 3dh. For a more comfortable meal, try:

Restaurant Café de la Jeunesse, 305 ave. Mohammed V, may be the best budget restaurant in town. Generous *menu* at 5dh. Just inside the *medina,* with a large, clean upstairs dining room.

Restaurant Milk-Bar, 291 ave. Mohammed V, diagonally across from the Train Station, (to the south). *Menu* for 10dh, plus tax and service; entrées 3.50-9dh.

Sights

Try to coordinate your sightseeing so that you arrive at either the **Chellah** or at the **Oudaias Kasba** at sunset. The settings and the views from each are quite impressive.

During the day you may wish to visit Rabat's museums. The **Antiquities Museum** houses the findings from excavations all over Morocco. The collection covers many epochs, but the Roman bronzes are especially interesting. (Open 9am-noon; 2:30-6pm, closed Tues.) The museum is near the **Sounna Mosque,** an eighteenth-century mosque at the top of the ave. Mohammed V.

To get to the Chellah, walk around the Sounna Mosque, and follow the ave. **Yacoub al Mansour** to its end. The Chellah is the site of the ancient Roman city **Sala Colonia,** and it was near its ruins that the Merinid sultans in the thirteenth and fourteenth centuries chose to bury and glorify their dead. The lush vegetation that surrounds the ruins provides for a romantic, peaceful setting, ideal for picnics. (Open from 8:30am to 7pm.) Free, and no guides to rush you along.

The **Hassan Tower** and the **Mausoleum of Mohammed V** are a mile away from the Chellah, but the walk is through Rabat's poshest neighborhood, that of the ministers and ambassadors. The Hassan Tower is the huge, uncompleted minaret of what was, in the twelfth century, the largest mosque in the west. All that remains of this Almohad mosque is a grid of columns, but the present king tried to make up for this by erecting an edifice almost as grandiose adjacent to it, the mausoleum of his father, Mohammed V.

A walk through Rabat's *medina* will bring you to the Oudaias Kasba, a fortress overlooking the ocean on one side, and the entire city on the other. There is a lovely garden and outdoor tea-house up here, and a **Museum of Moroccan Arts,** which has a good exhibit of musical instruments, carpets, furniture and Berber artifacts. (Open 8am-noon, 2-6pm; Sat. 8am-noon. Closed Tues.)

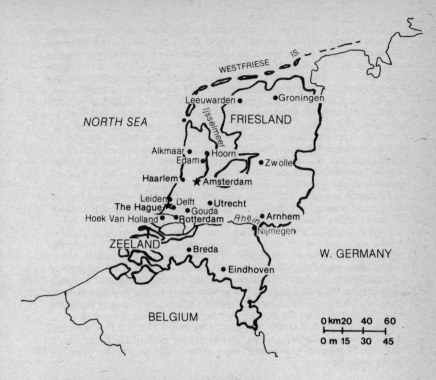

NETHERLANDS

1U.S.=1.96 guilders (f)   **1f=$.51**

If a word could convey the character of the Dutch, their adjective *gezellig* comes very close. Translated into English, it connotes a sense of quiet intimacy as well as outgoing sociability. What is immediately striking about the Dutch is their warmth, best seen in the commonplace, in the little accoutrements of everyday life. Home interiors have not radically changed from the time when Dutch masters portrayed them on canvas. The windows display fine, handmade lace curtains (almost never drawn), delicate pottery, and arrays of plants that not only decorate but virtually fill the windows. Even the bars and cafés are cozy, often looking more like living rooms, with dark wood panelling, antique clocks and candelabra, old paintings and prints lining the walls. The countryside has a soothing warmth of its own. Seen from train or bicycle, it gives the impression of patchwork—plowed green fields interlaced with blue canals; dots of grazing cows, sheep, and horses, neat rectangles of gardens, and an occasional windmill.

Despite its well-preserved charm, Holland is not quaint. The people and the atmosphere are too modern to be quaint. From the cobblestone streets—with their gabled houses and steep stairways—you will hear American disco music, and see the latest European fashions, even in the more remote regions. **Amsterdam** is one of most youth-oriented cities in Europe. To the south, **The Hague** (the seat of the Dutch government) is graceful and elegant, but caters less to students. The cheese town of **Alkmaar** and the fishing village **Monnickendam** lie to the north of Amsterdam. **Haarlem,** to the west, offers small cobbled lanes between rows of gabled houses and churches. **Utrecht,** in the midsection of Holland, is a wonderful old university town with deep-sunken canals which escaped damage during the war. **Rotterdam** has become Europe's largest port, but offers little of tourist interest. **Groningen,** in the north, is a relatively unspoiled city, a regional center with many university students.

Friesland, a region with a language and identity of its own, is a land of lakes interconnected by canals, a haven for sailing and camping. Off its coast lie the beautiful **Westfriese Islands.**

VVV (Tourist Information Offices) are run by each town individually. VVVs are found even in the most obscure villages. Look for the triangular signs with blue letters. The **NBBS,** Holland's outstanding student travel organization, operates student hotels both in and out of Holland, as well as offering charter flights. They have nineteen offices throughout Holland, including the main offices in Leiden at Rapenburg 6, and in Amsterdam at Dam 17. Check the Railway Information Offices about special programs which allow you to see the country by train and by bicycle at reduced rates.

One final word of caution: don't try to impress a Dutch person with the story of the little boy who saved the country by sticking his finger into a dike. The Dutch do not have such a story in their folklore, and they think it's stupid when they hear it.

Food

Dutch food is hearty and high in carbohydrates: plenty of bread, potatoes, cheese, vegetables, and milk. Specialties include herring (at its prime in June), smoked eel, pancakes, and liqueurs. Dutch breakfasts usually consist of cheese, meat, assorted breads, and tea (sometimes chocolate sprinkles for the toast). Lunch means *broodjes*—small, buttered rolls filled with tomatoes, cheese *(kaas),* fish or meat.

For a filling and cheap meal, try an *uitsmijter*—ham, cheese, or beef with a fried egg on top. French fries *(frites),* served with mayonnaise, are sold from sidewalk vendors. Vegetarians will have no problem, as the cheese, milk, and yogurt are among the finest in Europe. Shop at the numerous outdoor markets to save money. After dinner, sample the *genever,* the excellent Dutch gin, served straight with no ice in tiny, fluted glasses. Ask for the *jong* (young) or the *oud* (old), which is heavier and more perfumed, but more potent as well.

Amsterdam

You may find the green canals a bit dirty (though they do support ducks and occasional fishermen), but their quiet, tree-shaded elegance and night-lit beauty make Amsterdam one of the loveliest cities in Europe. Bordered by tall and gabled houses, the **Keizersgracht** (Emperor's Canal), **Herengracht** (Gentlemen's Canal), and **Prinsengracht** (Prince's Canal) contrast with the eerie atmosphere of the Red Light District and the trendy **Leidseplein.**

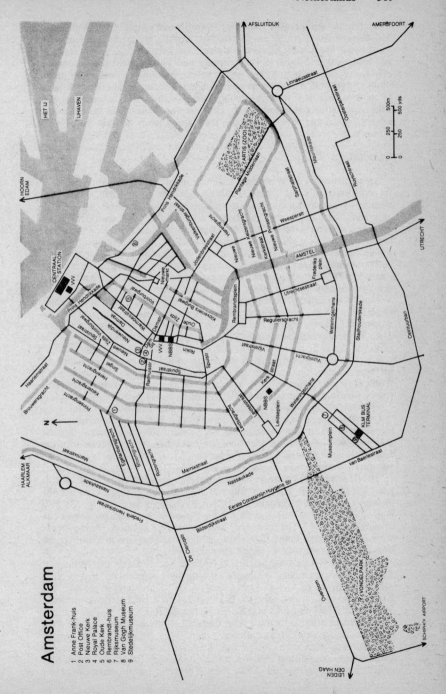

Amsterdam

1 Anne Frank-huis
2 Post Office
3 Nieuwe Kerk
4 Royal Palace
5 Oude Kerk
6 Rembrandt-huis
7 Rijksmuseum
8 Van Gogh Museum
9 Stedelijkmuseum

And in its fabulous **Rijksmuseum, Rembrandt's House,** and **Van Gogh Museum,** Amsterdam boasts some of the world's great art treasures.

Although the hordes of flower children no longer exist, the diversity of Amsterdam is still found in **Dam Square** and **Vondelpark,** former counter culture havens. Young people gather to exchange ideas, and more often, drugs. Street vendors will approach you and whisper, "Hassshh." A word of caution: dope is still illegal (though you wouldn't know it), and the stuff sold on the streets is usually trash. One Amsterdammer told us, "You can send it back home to your mother—there's absolutely nothing in it."

Orientation

Amsterdam's **Central Station,** although usually mobbed, contains a useful conglomeration of tourist facilities, including late-night money exchange, clean washrooms, luggage storage, and bicycle rental. Most streetcars and buses begin and end here. Damrak, the main thoroughfare, is crammed with restaurants and hotels, but student hostels are located mainly in the outlying areas. Nightlife focuses around the Leidseplein and the more sedate Rembrandtsplein. The city streets, though marked, are tangled; and numbers on one side of the street do not always correspond with those on the opposite side. The side streets, full of pubs and shops, are the most fascinating, so you may want to invest in a detailed map.

The **VVV** tourist office can arrange for you to meet a Dutch family (apply in person, two days in advance), smother you with pamphlets, find accommodations, change money, plan excursions, and sell you theater tickets. Their kiosk opposite the Central Station is open daily 9am to midnight. The office at Rokin 5, near the Dam, is open 9am-5:30pm Mon.-Sat.

The city publishes *Use It,* a paper for young tourists. Multilingual, it includes a map, information on accommodations, restaurant listings, a problem-solving index to youth agencies, and news about Amsterdam. This can be obtained free from the VVV. For up-to-the-minute listings including cinema and theater, pick up a copy of *Amsterdam this Week* (f.50).

Unless you need to cross the entire town in a hurry, Amsterdam is most pleasantly seen on foot. A metro service is still under construction, but the tram system is outstanding. Pick up a free route map at the **GVB** Information kiosk in front of Central Station. Amsterdam has a "stage-fare" system, and you pay by distance: a one-stage ticket costs f1, a two-stage ticket costs f1.20. Both are valid for one hour. A three-stage ticket costs f1.30, and is good for two hours. The best way to determine the distance is to ask the driver. A day ticket *(dagkaart)* can be purchased from the driver for f3.75. It is good on trams and buses and valid for 24 hours. A set of four tickets can be purchased for f3. The trams are "self-service." The fine for being caught without a validated ticket (one stamped in the self-service machine on the tram) is f15. Tram routes change after midnight.

Bike riding is a national pastime in Holland, and certainly one of the best ways to see Amsterdam. Watch the cars though, Amsterdam drivers are a menace! You can rent a bike from a slew of dealers for about f6 per day. Try **Koender's,** Utrechtsedwarsstraat 105 (tel. 234657); **HEJA,** Bestevaerstraat 39 (tel. 129211); and **Fikkert,** Rokin 71 (tel. 247608).

Amsterdam is home-base for several so-called "freak-buses," which are a cheap means of long-distance transportation. They are becoming more reliable than they used to be. **Magic Bus,** Damrak 87 (tel. 223242) promises to get you from Amsterdam to London for f60, Munich f65, Copenhagen f70, Athens f150, Istanbul f200, Delhi f395. They also handle cheap flights.

Addresses and Telephone Numbers

VVV: Rokin 5 (tel. 266444). Open 9am-5:30pm. Closed Sun. Also at Central Station (tel. 221016).

NBBS: Dam 17 (tel. 237686) is the Dutch student travel organization. Student flights and trains. Open Mon.-Fri. 9:30am-5pm, Sat. 10am-2pm.

Transalpino: Rokin 44 (tel. 239922). Reduced train fares on international journeys for students.

American Express: Damrak 66 (tel. 262042). Open 9am-5pm, Sat. 9am-noon.

Main Post Office: Nieuwezijds Voorburgwal 182. Behind the Dam Palace. Open daily 8:30am-6pm, Sat. 9-noon. Closed Sun.

GVB Tram and Bus Information: tel. 160022.

Police: Elandsgracht 117 (emergency tel. 222222, otherwise 75911).

Medical Aid: *Doctors:* tel. 425277/425278 (day and night). First aid free in every hospital. *VD clinic:* Groenburgwal 44. Free.

U.S. Consulate: Museumplein 19 (tel. 790321). Open 9am-noon and 2-4pm.

Laundromats: Look for a *Wasserette* sign, or try: Banstraat 16; Haarlemerdijk 157; Ferdinand Bolstraat 9; or Herenstraat 24.

Public Bath: (Bath f.75, shower f.25) Da Costakade 200: Marnixplein 5-9, and Zocherstraat 52.

Swimming: *Outdoor:* Brediusbad, Spaarndammerdijk; Van Galenbad, Jan van Galenstraat 315; Floraparkbad, Sneeuwbalweg 50. *Indoor:* Sportfondsenbad, Fronemanstraat 3; Marnixbad, Marnixplein 5-9.

Legal Aid: Droogbak la (tel. 242757).

Accommodations

If you arrive without reservations, try calling either the hostels or the hotels from the Station. If you arrive early in the morning, you should be able to locate a place without much trouble, especially if you seek student accommodations. If you get stuck, stop in at the VVV, which charges f2.50 to book rooms.

The famed Dutch breakfast, with all the ham and eggs you can eat, is nearly extinct. If you have your heart set on this, better try a restaurant. Most hotels serve a breakfast that includes bread, cheese, jam, and coffee. With luck, an egg, juice, or a slice of meat may be included. Even the more expensive hotels rarely offer more.

Student Accommodations

Before you put your money down at any of these, inspect the living quarters carefully. A few are quite dirty; we've received complaints of insects, and even rats. Also look out for hostels that cater to groups, lest you find yourself surrounded by hordes of young brats. And watch your valuables, as things get stolen. Many hostels have safes with locks, which require a small deposit. All told, hostels are still the cheapest places to stay, and with some careful choosing, very pleasant. Many offer discounts on bike rentals and canal trips. And due to new fire regulations, most hostels are being forced to rebuild. Although this shows in prices, it also shows in the improving safety and quality of the rooms.

H88, Herengracht 88 (tel. 24446). This hostel is subsidized by the University of Amsterdam, so it can offer dorm rooms for f11, including breakfast, shower, and sheets. Linen f2.50 deposit. Open from June to September. Student meals at f4.20. A bar as well.

International Student Center: Keizersgracht Hotel, Keizersgracht 15 (tel. 251364/247012). Open all year. Prices range from f8-18 for a room with two to six beds. There is a big dormitory as well. Free showers. f3 gives you one of the largest breakfasts around. The bar is open until 4am. Situated on one of the prettiest canals.

Christian Youth Hostel Eben Haezer, Bloemstraat 179 (tel. 244717), allows stays up to seven nights. 12am curfew. Dorm beds at f6.50, f7.50 if you need sheets. f3.50 for key deposit. Breakfast (continental) f2.25 and f2.75 (hot). Other meals are available at low prices. In a run-down area. No drinking or smoking in rooms.

Stadsdoelen (IYHF), Kloveniersburgwal 97 (tel. 256832). f12 with breakfast. Linen f3.50. Curfew at midnight, 1am on Sat. Locker f5 deposit. A pleasant atmosphere, and a cheap grocery store nearby.

Hans Brinker Stutel, Kerkstraat 136 (tel. 220687). An NBBS hostel and former monastery. Discount of f2.50 with student ID. f14-18 for a dorm bed, f24.50 each in triples, f27.50 for singles. No curfew, bar open until 4am. Sheets and breakfast included, and a great little coffeehouse across the street. A small garden, too.

Adolesce, Nieuwe Keizersgracht 26 (tel. 263959), is one of the oldest hostels and one of the most peaceful. Located within walking distance of the museums. Take bus #5 or 55, or tram #9. f15.50 in a small dorm, f21 in a double, f25 singles. Continental breakfast included. Curfew 1:30am.

Adam and Eva, Sarphatistraat 105 (tel. 246206). Take tram #6 or 10, bus #5 or 55. f12.50. Showers, sheets, and breakfast included. No curfew. Lunch and dinner available.

Vondelpark Youth Hostel, Zanpad 5 (tel. 831744 or 185220). Recently remodeled and overlooking the park, the hostel has small clean rooms. f12 if you have sheets, f15.50 without. Curfew 12pm. A restaurant, lounge area, and gardens with rabbits and chickens.

Cok, Koninginne Weg 30 (tel. 796653). Out of the way, but rooms are very modern, almost plastic. Many have private showers. Prices range from f17 in a dorm to f30 for a single. No curfew. Patio and self-service restaurant. Take tram #2.

Red Light District

Student hotels here range from clean to filthy. But you should not fear them just because of their location. Women alone should be careful, especially at night (you will get hassled during the day, too).

Parima, Warmoesstraat 91 (tel. 241406) is seedy, bordering on filthy, but cheap, f10 in a multi-bed room. Breakfast f2.50. A last resort.

Kabul, Warmoesstraat 38-42 (tel. 237158). A bad neighborhood, but a friendly and clean hostel. Prices range from f13 (dorm) to f20 for a double. Breakfast f2.75. f15 for key deposit. Request a room with a view.

Christian Youth Hostel: The Shelter, Barndesteeg 21 (tel. 253230). A rather unlikely neighborhood. No drinking or smoking in rooms, but prices are cheap. f6.50 if you have sheets, f7.50 without. Curfew 12pm. Breakfast f2.50. A lovely courtyard with a fountain and small garden.

Fat City, Oudezijds Voorburgwal 157 (tel. 226705). A raunchy place, but the price is only f9.50. Restaurant on the second floor, with very low prices. Curfew 2am, 3am on weekends. Disco and bar on ground floor.

Hotels

We recommend advance bookings (with international reply coupons). Otherwise, try to arrive early in the day and call from the station. Most hotels have an assortment of rooms with beds for one to four persons. Singles are usually costly.

Hotel Van Onna, Bloemgracht 102/108 (tel. 265801). A beautiful canal house charging around f21 per person. Generous breakfast included. Fresh flowers in the rooms, and a charming owner.

Hotel Schirmann, Prins Hendrikkade 22 (tel. 241942), is right next to the Train Station. Recently remodeled rooms at f17.50 and up. Shower included. No breakfast, though restaurants abound on the street below.

Hotel My Home, Haarlemmerstraat 82 (tel. 242320). Simple but clean, and near the Station. f17.50 with breakfast and shower. No singles.

Hotel Brian, Singel 69 (tel. 244661). A friendly atmosphere and an American breakfast. Two-night minimum. f19.

Westertoren, Raadhuisstraat 35b (tel. 244639), has large rooms with Old Dutch warmth. Clean and quiet, with wonderful owners. Doubles f45 with a good breakfast.

Galerij, Raadhuisstraat 43 (tel. 248851). A charming house run by a friendly, bustling woman. f50 for doubles, f27.50 singles. Shower and breakfast included. There are other hotels on the same street. Try **Hotel "Ronnie"** at 41b for singles. f25 with breakfast.

Keizershof, Keizersgracht 630 (tel. 222855). Singles f24, doubles f48. Includes breakfast and shower. Friendly management, and a lovely garden with rosebushes.

Hotel Prinshof, Prinsengracht 810 (tel. 231772). One of the nicest places in the entire city. Large rooms, beautifully decorated. Not cheap, but great when you have had it with hostels. Room service and oriental rugs, plus a large breakfast. f30 single, f50 double. Take tram #4.

Hotel Albert, Sarphatipark 58 (tel. 734083). Take tram #24 or 25. Small hotel on a park, f22 per person. Breakfast and showers included. Pleasant rooms with good view.

Hotel Van Ostade, Van Ostadestraat 123 (tel. 793452), located in a working-class area. Take tram #25 from the Station. Rooms are sparse, but clean. f15 with breakfast and lunch. The woman who runs it is motherly and helpful. A good buy.

Hotel Acro, Jan Luykenstraat 42/44 (tel. 720526, 725538, 732609). Prices run from f17 for one of the cleanest dorms around to f30 for a single. Breakfast included. A good location near the museums. There are other hotels on the same street; try #15 or 22.

Down and Out

Amsterdam's **Sleep-Ins** are highly rated by some, and they are certainly not the worst of facilities. They are open only during various times of the summer, and their continuation is precarious from year to year, so check *Use It* before you go. The Sleep-Ins each contain several hundred beds. Pretty much anything goes in them—they are coed to the hilt and every evening someone will come around selling hashish. An experience in themselves. Check your belongings at the office. **Sleep-In I,** Looiersgracht 35 (tel. 229402), is brand new and clean. It has a lounge area and a small cafeteria. **Sleep-In 2,** Rozengracht 180 (tel. 235871), is filthy, but here as in other Sleep-Ins you pay only f6. No breakfast, and you get a thin mattress on a dorm bunk. A bar serves drinks and sandwiches. The Sleep-Ins are open only during various times of the summer and have about 550 beds.

Sleeping near Dam Square and in Vondelpark is no longer permitted. Vondelpark is closely watched and if you do get caught sleeping there, you'll most likely lose your sleeping bag.

Camping, Foreigners need only a passport. **Zeeburg,** Ijdijk (Amsterdam-Oost, tel. 946688) f3.25, including shower; and **Vliegenbos,** Meeuwenlaan 138 (Amsterdam Noord, tel. 368855) f2.75 excluding shower. Check *Use It*.

Food

There are many restaurants near the Dam, but these rate high in atmosphere, prices, and numbers of Americans.

Good Indonesian restaurants are found throughout the city. Don't miss an Indonesian *rijstafel*, or rice table. Get really hungry, then fill up on rice surrounded by perhaps two dozen small dishes of raisins, peanuts, coconut, hot pickles, vegetables and meats in curry sauces, and "ape hair" (fried coconut and peanuts). The same filling meal usually costs less at lunchtime, and many restaurants let two people split one order. There's an art to eating *rijstafel* properly; you eat it mostly with a spoon, aided by a fork in the left hand. Put a little rice in the plate and surround it with dishes, but don't mix the dishes with the rice or each other. Just eat each individually with a little rice. Beware of those little dishes of sauce: they're amazingly hot. It is best to drink cold beer with this dish; tea and soft drinks don't mix well with the hot flavors. For good values on Indonesian food try **Shanghai,** Kerkstraat 47, and restaurants in the **Binnen Bantammerstraat,** off the Geldersekade near the Central Station. If you wish to splurge on a superb *rijstafel,* try **Sama Sebo** (see below).

If you go away from the center of town, you'll find that the prices are cheaper, and there are fewer tourists. Or, buy food at the local streetmarkets. The one on **Albert Cuypstraat,** near the Heineken Brewery, is open every day but Sunday. Stop in the local bakeries as well. **De Olde Backereye** on 80 Rosengracht has some of the best bread in town.

There is a student **Mensa** at Damstraat 3. The price is f4.20 for a complete meal. The food is institutional slop at times, but well balanced. Check the menu first. Open noon-2pm, 5-7pm.

De Keuken van 1870, Spuistraat 4, is open noon-7pm. This is a municipal kitchen with basic meals between f4 and f5. The clientele is mostly the Salvation Army down-and-out type, but it's cheap.

The Pancake Bakery, Prinsengracht 191, offers soups, huge omelettes, and a wide variety of pancakes for f4.25-7.50. Try the pancake *Grand Marnier* (f6.25). Open noon-9pm. Closed Sun.

Cantharel, Kerkstraat 377. A cozy place with candlelight and dried flowers. A complete meal averages f13.75. A la carte from f6.75. Open 5-9pm, closed Sun.

De Pijpenla, Westermarkt 23. One of the best places around, with complete dinner for f10-19. Try the pork steak with paprika sauce.

Smackzeyl, Brouwersgracht 101. A café/restaurant with a good atmosphere and better food. Lunch noon-2:30pm, dinner 6-10pm. Prices from f5-15.

Beit-Hamazon, Anjeliersstraat 57, is a kosher/vegetarian restaurant with Israeli specialties. Prices from f5. Worth the climb up the steep stairs. Open 5-9pm Sun.-Thurs., closed Fri.-Sat.

Sama Sebo, P.C. Hoofstraat 27. The restaurant has one of the city's best *rijstafels* at f25. If you don't want to splurge, try the *bami goreng* (noodles with meat) f12.50, or the *nasi goreng* (rice with meat) f13.50.

Sights

By day or night, the canals of Amsterdam present a setting for long and pleasant walks. Stroll along Prinsengracht, with its lone fishermen, ducks, and canal boats.

Be sure to explore the **Jordaan,** roughly bounded by Prinsengracht, Brouwersgracht, Marnixstraat, and Elandsgracht. This is in some sense the real Amsterdam, a mixed working-class and bohemian quarter, full of little cafés and quiet streets.

The city is rich in museums—over forty of them, in fact. The

Rijksmuseum, Museumplein at Stadhouderskade 42, is one of the world's greatest. Its collection includes Rembrandt's *Night Watch,* works by Vermeer and Hals, and a wing of Delft pottery and Dresden China. (Open weekdays 10am-5pm, Sun. and holidays 1-5pm. Admission f3, no student reduction).

In 1973 the city opened a brand new **Van Gogh Museum** at Paulus Potterstraat 7. It is an airy modern building, containing Van Gogh's first masterpiece, the *Potato Eaters;* and the *Sunflowers,* a common fixture on college dormitory walls. The original *Sunflowers,* however, has a luminosity that no reproduction can capture. Museum entry f2.50. There's even an *atelier* where you can paint for f1 (watercolors included). Open Mon.-Sat. 10am-5pm, Sun. 1-5pm. Next door, the **Stedelijk Museum** has one of the world's great collections of modern art, including Chagalls and Calder mobiles. Admission f2.

A visit to the **Anne Frank House,** Prinsengracht 263, is profoundly moving. The concealing bookcase and rooms of hiding are preserved, as are Anne's photo collection of her favorite movie stars. Go early in the morning, before the hordes of schoolchildren descend. Admission f2.50. Open 9am-6pm, Sun. 10am-4pm. **Rembrandt's House,** Jodenbreestraat 2-6 (open 10am-5pm daily, 1-5pm Sun.) is the building where the master lived, worked, and taught, until it was taken away by the city for taxes. It contains a vast collection of his etchings and drypoints, and you can see many in various stages of process. His tools and plates are also on display. Admission f1.50.

Off most tourists' itineraries, the **Jewish Portuguese Synagogue** at Visserplein Centrum is a wonderful building, with elegant gold candelabra, dark wooden benches, and enormous arched windows. Open 10am-5pm daily, Sun. 10am-2pm; admission free. An oasis of tranquility is the **Beginhof,** a beautifully preserved grassy courtyard surrounded by eighteenth-century buildings. To find it, walk down Kalverstraat and turn into a small side street, the Begijnensteeg, between Kalverstraat 130 and 132.

Not to be missed is the famous tour of the **Heineken Brewery,** which includes all the beer you can drink and a free mug if it's your birthday. Tours are at 9 and 11am, and cost f1. The profits go to charity. Get in line early though, as it is very popular.

Cafés

The Amsterdammer's favorite place is a cozy café. Day and night, they flock to their favorite little pubs for beer, comfort, and conversation. The nicest cafés of the city are the old "brown cafés" of the Jordaan, each with its stove and dark wood panelling. Most of these cafés resemble living rooms; there are old prints and paintings, sometimes oriental carpets instead of table cloths. **Papeneiland,** Prinsengracht 2, is among the most charming. It has old Delft tiles on the walls and a wooden candelabrum. **Café de Prins,** Prinsengracht 124 is very popular with students, and **Café de Eland,** on the corner of Prinsengracht and Elandsgracht, has a lively crowd and a super bartender.

Het Amsterdamsch Litterair Café, Kloveniersburgwal 59, draws an intellectual crowd. This combination beer house and bookstore holds frequent poetry readings and jazz sessions. For folk music try the **Folk Fairport,** Prinsengracht 282; and for folk dancing and entertainment, try **Jerusalem of Gold** (Israeli), Amstel 102. These are only a few suggestions; you'll undoubtedly find your own favorite spots.

Evenings

Amsterdam boasts a broad spectrum of nightlife. Most nightclubs charge a membership fee in addition to entrance, so they can be expensive for a one-shot affair. Few places get lively before 11pm, so stroll along one of the illuminated canals after dinner and have a beer *(pils)* in a quiet café. Most of the youth activity centers around Leidseplein, while more traditional entertainment is to be found on the Rembrandtsplein.

The **Red Light District** around Zeedijk and the Central Station end of Oudezijds Achterburgwal has sailors' bars, "sex shops," and real red lights. It is enough to enrage the most reluctant feminist, though even the most virulent one may find herself strangely fascinated. Women should not go alone. The atmosphere is otherworldly, like that of a bizarre carnival, and should be visited no matter what your sexual politics.

One of the best ways to party is to head for one of the city's youth havens; **Melkweg, Paradiso**, and **Kosmos.** These, however, are no longer bastions of the counterculture. Here, as elsewhere, you can find anything you're looking for. Check *Use·It* for current prices and locations.

Melkweg (Milky Way), Lijnbaansgracht 234a, is the most popular of the clubs. It is housed in an old factory off Leidseplein. Open Wed.-Sat. 7:30-2am. Entrance fee f4 weekdays, f5 weekends. Membership f5. Music, theater, dance, mime, cinema, teahouse, and restaurant.

Paradiso, off Leidseplein at Weteringschans 6 (tel. 264521), is alive with films, pop groups, and light shows. Entrance fee varies. Membership f2.50. Open Wed.-Sat. 8pm-2am.

De Kosmos, Prins Hendrikkade 142 (tel. 267477). Features meditation, a vegetarian restaurant, and classes in yoga and zen. Entrance fee f6. Membership f2. Also a sauna.

Sociëteit 't Okshoofd, Herengracht 114, is a *club* (not disco), so popular that it never advertises. Open every day at 10pm, but don't come in till midnight or 1, when it starts to fill up. The place to go when all else closes. Student cards may be asked for. Membership f5.

Daytrips

Holland's small size and efficient rail and bus network enable you to radiate from Amsterdam into the surrounding urban areas, as well as to the picturesque windmill and dike country. The density of Americans, the number of English-speaking Dutchmen, and to a lesser degree, prices, all drop outside of Amsterdam. This is especially true in the smaller towns.

The best way to tour Holland is by car or bicycle; rentals are fairly cheap, and a few of the local firms may give student discounts. If you want to see the country, **Ena's Bike Tour** leaves from Utrechsedwarsstraat 105 every day at 10am for the countryside where you'll visit a cheese farm, working windmill and take a rowboat ride. The trip including bike and rowboat costs f21. Return to Amsterdam is at 6pm. Call 015-143797 anytime for information. The railways offer several discount tickets, including a one-day unlimited mileage pass for f32; a **2-Plus Card** that gives unlimited mileage for two persons for f49; a f68 eight-day card for second-class travel; and an f30 card for those under 19, which offers four days of unlimited travel in June, July, and August.

Hitching is fairly good, except at the exits of Amsterdam, where competition is rough. For ideas on suggested tours, pick up a copy of *Out and About Holland* (f4) from the VVV.

North of Amsterdam

Red-bricked **Monnickendam** is a small and peaceful fishing village, where traditional costume can still be seen. Another fishing town, **Volendam,** caters to the more affluent tourist. It is usually mobbed and can be skipped. **Edam** is a small village with clean canals and abundant ducks. It is the place after which the famous Dutch cheese is named. All can be reached by the **NZH** bus service, leaving Amsterdam every half hour from near the St. Nicholas Church, opposite the Central Station. Cost is around f3 round trip. **Marken,** formerly an island, now a touristy peninsula, can be reached by ferry from Monnickendam for f4.75. Go early in the morning on weekdays to avoid the crowds.

Alkmaar, in the north of Holland, is one of two remaining "cheese towns" that still hold the traditional open-air cheese markets. The other, **Gouda,** lies to the south of Amsterdam and holds its market on Thursday mornings (VVV at Markt 36, tel. 072-14284). Alkmaar's market with its elaborate weighing-in ceremony is held Fridays beginning at 10am, May through mid-September. A direct train leaves Amsterdam twice an hour and costs f9.25, but you may want to think twice about the trip. The journey is made by hordes of tourists.

A more enjoyable destination is **Hoorn,** a seventeenth-century port town, less visited than most. Every Wednesday from mid-June to mid-August, Hoorn offers the **Oud Hollandse Markt,** a colorful traditional market, Punch and Judy shows, and stunt men. You may want to visit the town's **Westfries Museum,** which contains relics from the town's medieval heritage (open daily 10am-5pm, Sun. noon-5pm; admission f1.50). The train ride from Amsterdam takes forty minutes and costs f10.

If you get fed up with the urban frenzy of Amsterdam, there's at least one trip within the city limits that will get you away from tourists and traffic and noise, and into small-town Holland. This is **Waterland,** a large rural lowland area behind the harbor. To get there, take bus #32 from Central Station to Vollendamerweg in **Nieuwendam,** one of Amsterdam's modern suburbs, and change there for bus #30 (direction Holysloot), a mini-bus designed for the narrow and winding rural roads. The bus goes through several villages, including **Durgendam,** a hamlet built on a dike; a picturesque little yacht harbor, **Ransdorp;** and finally **Holysloot,** a tiny place surrounded on three sides by water. From here you can take a pleasant walk across the polder fields through the *Vogelreservaat* (bird sanctuary), across tiny bridges and past sedate cows to the dike of the **Ijsselmeer,** formerly the Zuider Zee. Bring a picnic and sketch pad on a nice day, and pass an hour or so watching the sailboats and the diving birds. For this trip, invest in a day card *(dagkaart)* for f3.75. It will save you some money.

Southwest of Amsterdam

Haarlem, a quaint riverside town, lies just to the west of Amsterdam and is readily accessible by bus or rail. The **VVV** is at Stationsplein 1 (tel. 319059) and can provide information, suggest sights in town and throughout the area, and find accommodations for a f2.50 fee. Hotels start high (f25), but there are two IYHF hostels in the area, with beds at f10. **Jan Gijzen,** Jan Gijzenpad 3 (tel. 373793), open 7-11pm; and **De Zanderij** at Korte Zijlweg 9, Overveen (tel. 326599). The VVV can give you information as to beaches and camping in the vicinity, in such areas as **Bloemendaal** and **Zandvoort.**

The **Frans Hals Museum,** Groot Heiligland 62, is an old seventeenth-century mansion with a formal garden in the courtyard. It displays works of

Haarlem artists since 1500, as well as furniture, silver, and pottery; but most important is the work of Hals himself. Be sure to see *The Regents of the Old Men's Home,* a masterpiece done when Hals was in his eighties. The portraits, bordering on caricatures, are devastating. (open daily 10am-5pm, Sat. nights, Sun. 1-5pm). Admission f1.75. In July, Haarlem's churches host an international organ recital month. The VVV has schedules, and prices range from f4-10. Free recitals all through the summer, Tuesday evenings and Thursday afternoons.

Going south along the coast, you come to the heart of Holland's flower region. The magnificent **Keukenhof** displays over 5 million bulbs during April and May (admission f5). The gardens may be reached by bus #50 from Haarlem's Central Station. For those unable to visit Holland at this time, an international flower auction is located in the town of **Aalsmeer,** not far south of Amsterdam's Schiphol Airport; open Monday through Saturday, 8am to noon.

. Between Haarlem and The Hague lies Leiden, the Netherlands' premier university town. It's a handsome, gracious city, well worth an afternoon, and it's not far from the beach at Katwijk Aan Zee. Pick up a walking tour brochure from the VVV at Stationsplein 3 (tel. 146846). The main thing to see in Leiden is the town itself. It is compact and picturesque in a real and livable way. There are, however, no fewer than ten museums to see. The **Botanical Museum Garden,** Rapenburg 73, is one of the oldest such museums in Europe. It houses lush ferns and exquisite orchids, admission f.25. If you want to see a fine old Dutch windmill, try the **Molenmuseum "De Valk,"** 2 de Binnenvestgracht #1 (open daily 10am-5pm, Sun. 1-5pm. Admission f1). The windmill was built in 1743, and used until 1945. If you come on a breezy day, when the sails are put up, the miller might take you up to see the impressive wooden gear system.

There is a **Mensa** at the new student center on Kaiserstraat 25, off Rapenburg Canal. Complete meals run around f4 (open noon-2pm and 5-7pm). A good place to have a beer and meet local students is **Bodega Barrera** at 56 Rapenburg, across from the main university hall. For some fantastic *ijs* (ice cream), visit **Ijssalon La Venezia,** Steenstraat 11. Prices range from f.35-.75.

The Hague (Den Haag)

Green parks, wide tree-lined avenues, and old aristocratic mansions make The Hague one of the most refined cities in Europe. If Amsterdam is your vision of perfection, you will find The Hague stuffy and bourgeois; but if Amsterdam's frenzied pace fazes you, you will welcome the quiet elegance here. Pick up from the VVV the walking tour called *The Hague, Antique Town* (f1), which will lead you through the most beautiful streets, antique shops, old-print dealers, and book stores.

The Hague is the seat of Holland's parliament and the International Court of Justice. These two sites of political interest attract tourists to The Hague: the **Binnenhof,** the governmental complex begun in the thirteenth century (open Mon.-Sat. 10am-4pm, admission f3), and the **Peace Palace** at Carnegieplein 2, home of the World Court. It can only be visited on tour. English tours are at 11am and 2:30pm, weekends 2:30pm. Admission f1.50 (no student reduction).

The Hague boasts two excellent museums and several minor ones. **Mauritshuis,** Plein 29, is open Mon.-Sat. 10am-5pm, Sunday in season 11am-5pm, and holidays 11am-5pm. Entry f3. This is one of the most important museums for the Dutch school, with fine paintings by Rembrandt,

Vermeer, Rubens, Frans Hals, and others. The guards can be gruff, and some rooms close from noon-2pm, but the collection is worth the inconveniences. **Haags Gemeentemuseum,** at Stadhourderslaan 41, concentrates on modern art. It has the world's largest collection of the Dutch master Piet Mondrian. Don't miss the series of "Trees" and the progression from representational to abstract, geometrical form. Open Mon.-Sat. 10am-5pm, Sun. 1-5pm, Wed. 8-10pm. Admission free. When you leave, be sure to see the pond of water lilies—a perfect place to rest or munch a sandwich.

But **Madurodam,** Haringkade 175, is the real pride of The Hague's tourist industry. Here miniatures of buildings and industry from all over Holland comprise a scale model of a Dutch town. Open April through June, 9:30am-10pm daily, July and August to 10:30pm, September to 9pm. Admission f4.50 at the gate. Tram #9. Not for everyone.

Scheveningen is an international beach resort that has seen better times. Parts are being revitalized, and a new casino is being built. In its mild deterioration it has acquired an atmosphere that could only be called "camp." Try to stay here—the prices are lower and you have the best of both worlds, beach and museums. Take trolley #7 or 8 (f1.15).

Addresses and Telephone Numbers

American Express: Plaats 14 (tel. 469515).

American Embassy: Lange Voorhout 102 (tel. 624911).

Canadian Embassy: 7 Sophialaan (tel. 614111).

MedicalAid: For information on doctors, telepnone 321780 during the day or 643838 after 5pm. For emergencies and ambulance, tel. 222111.

Police: Emergency tel. 222222. Headquarters: Alexanderplein 19 (tel. 614141).

Main Post Office: Nobelstraat.

Release: Zieken 187 (tel. 881187), near the H.S. train station, for help with any problem. Open Wed. and Sat. 3-6pm, Tues.-Fri. 8-11pm.

Laundromat: Frederik Hendriklaan 220. In Scheveningen, Renbaanstraat 100.

Public transport: You can buy a ticket good for an unlimited number of bus and tram trips for one day *(Dagkaart)* for f3.80 at the VVV office in Scheveningen or the HTM bus company. Highly recommended, since The Hague is very spread out. A booklet of 8 trips costs f6 with free transfers, or f5.50 without transfers.

Accommodations

You will arrive at either the **H.S. Station** or **Central Station.** If you find yourself at the former, take tram #12 (f1.15) to Central, where the **VVV** is located. At Kon. Julianaplein 8 (tel. 546200), open Mon.-Sat. 8:30am-8pm, Sun. 10am-5pm. The VVV will provide you with maps and a list of hotels. For a f2.50 booking fee, they will place you in a private home or a hotel. Prices run from f20-25, or try one of the following:

Marie-Louise, Hoefkade 2 (tel. 883014), has the lowest prices in town. Singles f15, doubles f30, breakfast included. Nothing fancy, but good for the price. Near the H.S. Station.

HotelNeuf, Rijswijkseweg 119 (tel. 900748), also near the H.S. Station, has rooms from f22, breakfast included.

There are a few pensions in The Hague's residential areas (worth a stroll even if you're not staying there). The nicest are **Minnema,** Dedelstraat 25 (tel. 463542), f25 with an outstanding breakfast; **Huize Massy,** Willem de Zwijgerlaan 58 (tel. 556224), f25; and **Mem,** Anna Poulownastraat 8 (tel. 637571), doubles only, from f35. Closed in winter.

> **Youth Hostel Ockenburgh** (IYHF), Monsterweg 4, Kijkduin (tel. 250600) costs f12.50 per night. Bus #51 or 53 from Central Station.

> **Camping: Ockenburgh,** Wijndaelerweg 25 Kijkduin (tel. 252364) is close to a beach. Bus #51 or 53 from Central Station. **Duinrell,** Duinrell 1, Wassenaar (tel. 19212), is near a beach and sand dunes, yet close enough to the town center. Both f6 per person.

Food

Food is not cheap here. **Oud Scheveningen** Keizerstraat 14, has entrées from f7. Try the goulash soup, almost a meal at f3.50. Your best bet is to fill up on the cheap food stands which line the boulevard along the beach at Scheveningen. The herring sandwiches are fresh and delicious.

Delft

The air of serenity in Vermeer's painting of the streets of Delft has been replaced by the beat of disco music, but the houses and cobblestoned lanes in the old core remain virtually untouched by the twentieth century. Delft is a charming town, but it caters to the tourists who come to buy the famous white and blue china. Even if you intended to bring some home, the plethora of identical pieces in all the shop windows will make you think twice. If not, the prices will. **Royal Delftware** "de Porceleyne Fles" at Rotterdamscheweg 196 is the best place to buy China if you remain undeterred. Open Mon.-Sat. 9am-5:30pm, Sun. 1-5:30pm. Delft has two fine museums, **Het Prinsenhof Museum,** off Agathaplein; and **Museum Huis Lambert Van Meerten,** Oude Delft 199. Both display paintings, tapestries, and Delft China. Open Mon.-Sat. 10am-5pm. Entrance fee of f1.75 will admit you to both museums and the **New Church** on the market, burial place of the Dutch sovereigns.

Try to make your trip to Delft in either the morning or early evening. This way you will avoid most of the shopping crowd and still catch a glimpse of the town's beauty. Delft makes an easy daytrip from The Hague. If you wish to stay overnight, the VVV at 85 Markt will help you.

Utrecht

When you arrive in Utrecht you may feel that you never left home, if home means suburban America. At **Central Station,** you will find yourself ensconced in a vast, climate-controlled shopping mall, complete with muzak and fast-food outlets. There are two **VVVs,** one in the mall and one to the left of the Station—choose the latter.

But you should forgive Utrecht and head for the core of the old town, which has huge, sunken canals, book stores, and fine antique stores. Explore the side streets along the sunken canal of **Oudegracht;** and at night visit the clubs, bars, and cabarets with their "caves" opening on brick walls at the waterlevel. On busy days, an old Dutch barrel-organ or two will probably be operating, giving the whole district a carnival air. These organs—supported by contributions gathered in tin cups—are a Dutch tradition commemorated in Utrecht at the **Van Speeldoos tot Pierement Museum** ("music boxes to barrel organs") behind the Cathedral. Admission free. Open all year. The Cathedral's **(Domkerk)** only claim to fame is that a hurricane separated it from its tower in the late seventeenth century. It is open in summer 10:30am-5pm daily. Winter hours vary. There are free concerts during the week and on Saturday afternoons. The Tower **(Domtoren),** which has 465 stairs, offers a fantastic view. It can only be seen with a guide, though. In summer, tours run daily 10:30am-5pm. Admission f1.50. Be sure not to miss the **Gothic Cloister,** next to the Cathedral (free). It contains a beautiful formal garden and various herbs, each with its own allegorical significance.

If you have the time, take the bus to **Kockengin** to reach **De Haar Castle-Museum** at Haarzuilens near Vleuten; cost about f2.50 for the bus and f3.50 for admission. The castle was rebuilt in the nineteenth century and is surrounded by a park and a partial moat; open February 15-August 15 and October 15-November 15, 9am-noon and 1:30-5pm; Sundays 1:30-5pm; closed when the owners are in residence (ask at the VVV about this and other castles). Also nearby lies the little town of **Amersfoort,** which offers some fine old Dutch architecture and a double ring of moats built in the Middle Ages. The VVV is at Stationsplein 8a (tel. 033-12747). There is an IYHF **Hostel** at De Genestetlaan 9 (tel. 033-14271).

Addresses and Telephone Numbers

VVV: Smakkelaarsveld 3 (tel. 314132). Open during the summer Mon.-Sat. 9am-8pm, Sun. 10am-6pm. In winter open to 6pm. Closed Sun.

JAC: Oudegracht 371 (tel. 313824). A youth organization with free help and advice. Open Mon.-Sat. 3-8pm.

ICU (Information Center Utrecht): 5 Lange Janstraat (tel. 315415). Open Mon. 1:30-4:30pm, Tues. 9am-4:40pm, Thurs. 9am-7pm.

Post Office: Neude (tel. 328611).

Police: Paardeveld (tel. 321321, in emergencies 333333).

Laundromat: De Groot, Korte Smeestraat 15.

Bike Rentals: at the station (tel. 311159) or V. Bijinkeshoeklaan 413 (tel. 936368) April-October. f5 per day, or f16.75 per week. There are several others in the city. Check with VVV.

Canal boat rides: Oudegracht at Lange Viestraat, f4.

Accommodations and Food

The **VVV** will find rooms for you in private homes, at f20 per person, including breakfast. There is a f2.50 booking fee. VVV reports that it can always find rooms, even at the height of the summer season. Inexpensive hotels are easier to find in the smaller towns outside of Utrecht. The VVV can provide the listings and information.

IYHF Hostel in Bunnick, right outside the city (tel. 03405-1277, f10.50). Set in verdant country with canals and a nearby park, it serves one of the best breakfasts around. Take bus #60 from the Station (f1) and walk down Rhij-nauwenselaan. Highly recommended.

Camping: For f3 per person per tent at **De Berekuil,** Ariënslaan 5-7 (on the far side of town from the train station, tel. 713870).

De Neude, Neude 29, in the center of town. The best place in town for low-budget eating. Full of students and friendly town folk who may offer to show you around. Dinner f5 with meat, f4 without. Try the asparagus soup, a meal in itself for only f.50. Open Mon.-Fri. noon-1:30pm and 4:30-7pm (6:30 on Fri.).

Boerderij Mereveld, Mereveldseweg 2, is an old Dutch inn on the road to the Hostel. Take bus #60 and walk down the dirt road. The restaurant has dark wood panelling and stained glass windows, serves authentic and delicious Dutch food. Pancakes from f5, complete meals begin at f10.50. The portions are enormous.

In town, there are numerous canal-side cafés, but you pay for the atmosphere. Try **Huifkar,** at Oudegracht 136, or **Bloem** down the street. **Graaf Floris,** Vismarkt 12 is a student favorite. There are also two fantastic bakeries on the same street.

'THoogt, 'tHoogt 4, (tel. 314751) is an artists' café. Good meals for f7-15 and the building houses a movie theater, art exhibitions and an antique grocery store that still operates. The company is friendly to students, and, at night you might want to check out the movie, often in English. Opens 7pm. Closed Mon.

Arnhem and the Zuid-Veluwe

Arnhem itself is a dreary modern city, but this part of east-central Holland, with its extensive forests and gentle hills, is an oasis of wilderness in the Netherlands, one of the most densely populated countries in the world. The most enticing section is **De Hoog Veluwe National Park,** a 13,000-acre preserve of woods, heath, drifting sands, and small ponds. The park boasts a large population of deer, foxes, and other wildlife, but they are quite shy. There are numerous hiking and bike trails, offering rare wildflowers and jewel-like ponds. Get a good map from the VVV in **Otterlo** (f2), a nearby village.

By far the highlight of the park is the **Kröller-Müller State Museum.** This is one of the great modern art museums in Europe, offering a superb collection of Van Goghs, Mondrians, and Picassos. The art of the museum and the greenery of the park meet in a large and attractive sculpture garden, which is almost worth the trip in itself and contains fine pieces by many modern sculptors, including Lipschitz and Rodin. The museum lies deep inside the park—a 35-minute walk from the nearest entrance. Admission fee to the park (f4.50 per person, f4 per car) entitles you to visit the museum. Take bus #7 from Arnhem (Direction Harderwijk) for f3.50, and get off in Otterlo. From here walk, hitch, or rent a bike at one of the many stands along the way. Between June 18 and August 31, you can take the special bus #12 from the Station for f7.65. It makes three stops within the park, including the museum.

For a trip to a natural preserve free of tourists, visit **Veluwezoom National Park,** a far-spreading park of trees and heather where wild pigs are more common than De Hooge's deer residents. The park can be reached by the bus to Rheden leaving from the Station.

Orientation and Accommodations

The **VVV,** as usual, will supply you with all information on the sights of the area, and on numerous boat trips available in the region. Located at Stationsplein 45 (tel. 085/452921). Open in season Mon.-Sat. 9am-8pm, Sunday 10am-3pm. Accommodations include several reasonably-priced pensions in Arnhem, as well as in other towns in the area. Prices run about f19-27. For the lowest prices, try **Pension Warnsborn,** Schelmseweg 1 (tel. 425994) f19, or **Pension Buiten,** Karel v. Gelderstraat (tel. 420608), where you may get a room for as low as f16. There is also a **Sleep-In,** during July and August, Thomas à Kempislaan 15 (tel. 422106), f6 per person, without breakfast. The IYHF **Youth Hostel,** clean and modern, is located at Diepenbroclaan 27 (tel. 420114); f12.50 a night in a rural setting. Take the #3 trolley (f.95) and walk up the hill. **Camping** at De Hoog Veluwe, Koningsweg 14 (tel. 432272) costs f3.50 per person and you need a camping carnet.

Friesland and the Westfriese Islands

Across the **Ijsselmeer** lies the province of **Friesland,** a distinctive region with its own language. It is best to approach Friesland by car or bicycle over the eighteen-mile-long **Afsluitdijk,** which has turned the old Zuider Zee into an enormous fresh water lake. It's a long day's ride from Amsterdam, but a bicycle enthusiast will be rewarded by the scenery and the ride across the dike. The train goes the long way around by land. While **Leeuwarden** is the capital of Friesland, less industrialized **Sneek** is a better destination. Sneek has an excellent **Youth Hostel** (IYHF) at Oppenhuizerweg 79 (tel. 05150-12132). From here you can explore some of the well-preserved villages of the region. A trip to **Makkum** with its pottery plant and then down to **Hindeloopen,** a charming village protected on three sides by seawalls, will give you a good taste of the countryside.

The Westfriese Islands, which buffer the coast of Holland from the North Sea offer some of the country's most exquisite scenery. **Texel,** reached by ferry from Den Helder is the largest and most populous of the islands. It has two IYHF Youth Hostels, while the other islands (with the exception of Vlieland) each have one. Don't miss **Terschelling,** reached by ferry from Harlinger (f18.50). Terschelling, a wildlife sanctuary with grass-covered dunes, attracts many young people. Nicknamed the "Love Island," it has the highest divorce rate in Holland. Sample locally-produced cranberry wine and brandy at **Braskoer,** Torenstraat 32. This is a good place for a light lunch or dinner as well. Stay at the **Youth Hostel** overlooking the sea at Burg, Van Heusdenweg 39 (tel. 05620-2338), f10.50. You can walk to some of the islands from the mainland at low tide across the mudflats—but you need a guide. Check with the VVV.

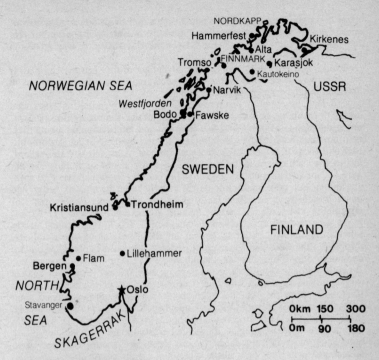

NORDKAPP
Hammerfest
Kirkenes
Alta
Tromso
FINNMARK
Karasjok
Kautokeino
USSR

NORWEGIAN SEA

Narvik
Westfjorden
Bodo
Fawske

SWEDEN

FINLAND

Kristiansund
Trondheim

Bergen
Flam
Lillehammer

NORTH
Oslo
Stavanger

SEA
SKAGERRAK

0km 150 300
0m 90 180

NORWAY

$1U.S.=4.9kroner(kr)   **1kr=$.20**

(Note: There is a map of Northern Scandinavia in the Sweden chapter.)
Cottages reduced to doll houses, ships to toyboats—all human construc-
tions are miniaturized by the gargantuan mountains of Norway. Her steep,
rough-hewn slopes inspire awe not only in their size, but in their spectacular
variety as well. Fjords open jaggedly on the west coast, while ragged
plateaus and bleak tundra end at the continent's northernmost point,
Nordkapp. In the south you can hike through woodlands of pine and spruce,
while the more rugged may venture further north to the Midnight Sun and the
icy-blue **Jostedalsbre,** the largest glacier in Europe. Norway has huge tracts
of some of the most unspoiled natural beauty in Europe. With only four
million people, its population density is the lowest in Europe. The most
spectacular fjord country extends south from **Åndalsnes** to just beyond
Bergen. Medieval **Stavanger,** a bit further south, is now the major center of
Norway's North Sea oil operations. If you want to see **Lapland,** you'll have
to invest substantial time and money, but shorter trips to the scenic mountain

areas are a good substitute: the **Oslo-Bergen rail line** stops at a number of small villages above the timber line. Climb the mountains if you can, or visit the pastoral farming villages in the **Gudbrandsdal Valley,** or take in the sun on the beaches of **Kristiansand** in the south.

Besides being the best way to take advantage of the scenery, camping is the only way to beat the high cost of accommodations. In Norway, as in Sweden, you have the right to camp where you like for one night, except on fenced land or close to private homes. If you're planning any extended hiking or camping, be sure to contact **Den Norske Turistforening,** at Stortingsgata 28 in Oslo (tel. 33-42-90) for maps and information on hiking trails and mountain huts. Many campgrounds are run by the **Norges Automobilforbund (NAF);** at these and other sites the overnight charge varies according to the facilities, but is usually 12-18kr for a tent spot, plus 3kr per person. Norwegian youth hostels *(ungdomsherberger),* which serve all ages, are among Europe's finest. Rooms are usually small (two to six beds), and many hostels have excellent facilities. Their outrageous prices (22kr, or where breakfast is required 40kr; 7kr more if you don't have an IYHF card) are a great bargain by Norwegian standards. You'll find hostels nearly everywhere that you want to go—in all the cities, along the rail lines, throughout the fjord district, even in remote villages in Lapland. Many are open only during the summer, though.

Getting around Norway's tortuous geography is easy, especially with a railpass. Pick up a train schedule *(lomme ruter)* at any station. Domestic train reservations are free, and often absolutely necessary if you don't want to stand. On trains leaving Oslo for Copenhagen, seat reservations should be made at least 36 hours in advance (48 hours for weekend travel). There are no couchettes on Norwegian trains, but second-class sleeping berths are quite nice and relatively cheap (35kr); these also should be reserved in advance (two to three days ahead when leaving the country).

Buses go everywhere in Norway, even to the most isolated hamlets. If you're hitching, carry a bus schedule just in case; although if you're a woman you don't have to worry much—hitching is very easy and safe. It can be pretty difficult for men, though—traveling Swedes, Germans, and Englishmen are better bets than Norwegians, so look for foreign license plates.

Norwegians compound the problem of the high cost of food by eating four meals a day—at 8am, noon, 4pm, and 8pm. The best way to beat the system is to try the ubiquitous cafeterias where you can get substantial, often surprisingly good meals for 20-30kr. Atmosphere is usually lacking, though, and you'll get fresher, better food around noon than in the late afternoon or evening. Fish in Norway is excellent and relatively inexpensive. Sample the local specialties, or try *sild* (herring), *laks* (salmon), and *torsk* (cod), found fresh everywhere. On the famous flatbread crackers *(flatbro* or *frokostbro),* try some national cheeses *(ost): jarlsberg,* and a peanut butter-colored goat's cheese, *geitost.* An authentic Norwegian breakfast rivals its English counterpart: an assortment of cold cuts, herrings, eggs, cheeses, breads, crackers, jams, and milks.

Oslo

Oslo will delight the eclectic but disturb the purist. The city has artistic treasures both raw and refined—from Munch's *Scream* and Vigeland's *Howling Infant* to varnished Viking ships and polished king's palaces. There are natural treasures, too: the official city area is three-fourths farm and forest, and a short distance from the center are lakes good for swimming and a world-famous ski jump. If Oslo seems to lack a unifying style or distinctive spirit, it is nonetheless a pleasing anomaly, a little bit out of place in its own grand land.

Orientation

The axis of Oslo's compact center is busy **Karl Johansgate,** which runs straight from the **East Station** to the park-surrounded **Royal Palace.** To explore this area you won't need to use the comprehensive but confusing transit system; many of Oslo's chief sights, however, are some distance outside the center. All public transportation costs 3kr; your ticket is valid for one transfer (to any mode of transport) within an hour. Buses and trams are the most convenient, but outlying areas are also served by subways, ferries, and local trains (the latter are free with a railpass). Pick up a free transit map at the Tourist Office or the Rail Station.

You will probably arrive at the East Station, the terminus for trains from Trondheim and Bergen, and for all international trains (**West Station** trains run to Kristiansand, Stavanger, and Drammen). Here an **exchange office** is open every day in summer 7am-11pm; the rate is the same as a bank's. The Information Office has schedules of the bus and ferry connections in the fjord district that are synchronized with trains on the Oslo-Bergen line. **Innkvartering,** the room-finding agency, is also located in the East Station (see Accommodations). Finally, the restaurant in the Station (above the mediocre cafeteria) serves a delicious, hearty smorgasbord breakfast for 24kr: it is guaranteed to revive you after a sleepless night on a train, or fortify you for a day's journey.

The **Oslo Travel Association Tourist Information Center,** despite its forbidding name, has a very helpful and friendly staff; pick up a city map, a transit map, and the *Oslo Guide,* which lists current hours and prices of sights and has much useful practical information. You should also get a copy of *Oslo This Week* for details on free concerts and other goings-on. The office is a fifteen-minute walk up Karl Johans gate from the East Station, near the **National Theater,** at Munkedamsveien 15 (tel. 42-71-70); it's open in summer 9am-7pm weekdays, to 4pm Sat. and to noon Sun. This office has information on Oslo only.

Oslo Airport (**Fornebu**) is reached by bus #31 "Snaroya" from the National Theater. **Gardermoen,** the Airport for charter flights, is about an hour north of Oslo on E6.

Addresses and Telephone Numbers

Den Norske Turistforening (The Norwegian Mountain Touring Association), near the National Theater at Stortingsgata 28 (tel. 33-42-90), maintains mountain huts along many hiking trails. Contacting DNT is a must if you are planning any extended hiking or camping. They sell a very useful little book called *Mountain Touring Holidays in Norway* for 15kr. You can get free sketch maps and buy detailed topographical maps here. Membership in DNT (75kr; under 21: 50kr) gets you a 10kr discount on lodging at mountain huts and a 5kr discount on meals. Open weekdays 8:30am-4pm, Sat. until noon.

Student Travel Bureau: University Center, Blindern (tel. 46-68-80). Low-cost trains and planes.

American Express: c/o Winge Travel, Karl Johans gate 33 (tel. 20-50-50). Open 8:30am-4pm Mon.-Fri., Sat. 8:30am-1pm.

Main Post Office: Dronningens gate 15. Open Mon.-Sat. 8am-8pm, Sun. 5-8pm.

Telephone-Telegraph: Kongensgate 21 (tel. 013 for telegrams). Open 24 hours.

Police: Mollergata 19 (tel. 33-12-90).

Medical Help (Oslo Municipal Policlinic): Storgata 40 (tel. 20-10-90).

24 Hour Pharmacy: Jernbanetorvets Apotek. In front of East Railway Station. Open 24 hours.

U.S. Embassy: Drammensveien 18 (tel. 56-68-80).

Canadian Embassy: Oscarsgate 20 (tel. 46-69-55).

Laundromat: Vibesgate 15 (tram #1 or 11, direction Majorstua). Open Mon.-Fri. 9am-8pm, Sat. 9am-4pm.

Women's Center (Kvinnehuset): Radhusgata 2, (tel 41-28-64), three blocks from the East Station, above Guldfisken Jazz Club. Snacks and conversation; open Mon.-Fri. 5-10pm

Accommodations

Finding a cheap hotel in Oslo is a nearly impossible feat. The *pensjonats* have the only relatively inexpensive rooms, but they are usually unappealing and do not serve breakfast. Neither of the IYHF Youth Hostels are in the *centrum*. If you are staying at least two nights, Innkvartering, in the East Station will find you a room in a private home for 43kr for a single, 66kr for a double, plus a 7kr per person fee. They can also book you into an inexpensive *pensjonat* for the same fee, and they have current information on youth hostels. The office is open daily in summer 8am-midnight, Sun. 8:30am-noon and 6pm-midnight.

Bjerke Studentheim (IYHF), Trondheimsveien 271, a university dorm in winter; has modern and immaculate 2- and 3-bed rooms. 22kr with a Hostel card, 29kr without. Fills up fast. Reception open 5-11 pm, but you can call in the morning between 8 and 10 and leave your name. 11pm curfew. Take bus #30 or 31 to Bjerkebanen; the Hostel is in the tall building back towards the center about 100 meters from the bus stop. Different telephone number each year; call Haraldsheim Hostel or ask Innkvartering for the current number. Open June 20-August 20.

Haroldsheim (IYHF), Haraldsheimveien 4 (tel. 21-83-59), Oslo's largest hostel, has 6-bed rooms and good facilities (washing machine, clothes-drying room, lounge, kitchen). Pleasant terrace with a view over the Oslo Fjord and the city. 39kr with Hostel card includes the required breakfast. Closed 10am-4pm, midnight curfew. Crowded during the high season. Tram #1 or 7, direction Sinsen, to the end of the line; then walk up the hill to the Hostel. Open all year.

Baptistenes Folkhøgskole, Micheletsvei 55 (tel. 53-38-53), a "Folk High School" during the year, offers pleasant summer accommodations in a quiet area west of Oslo. Sleep in a 10-bed classroom for 32kr the first night, 30kr thereafter, including towels and bed linen. You might get a 5kr reduction if you have your own sheets. Also an inexpensive hotel: singles 70kr, doubles 95kr, triples 105kr, quads 130kr. Rooms are nice, if antiseptic. Reception open 7:30am until 1am when the doors are locked. Breakfast served for 15kr. More likely to have room than the two IYHF hotels. The hostel is somewhat hard to find. From the Stabbek Station (ten minutes by local train from Oslo's West Station), follow Kveldsroveien (the road south of the tracks) west and then south, crossing the main road by bridge. Turn left at Micheletsveien and continue half a block. Also reached by bus #32, 36, or 37 from downtown to Kveldsroveien stop. Open approximately June 1-August 31.

Drammen Youth Hostel (IYHF), Korsveien 62 (tel 03/82-21-89), is located on a beautiful hillside 40 km west of Oslo. A student residence in winter, it is modern and very clean, and has at most three to a room. 20kr per night with Hostel card. The Hostel is never full, and the friendly manager lets people in long after the 11pm closing time. Nice kitchens; good breakfast for 16kr. The only drawback is the long commute (1-1½ hours). Train to Drammen from Oslo West Station, then catch the Liejordet bus just outside the Station. There are good train connections from Drammen to the Oslo-Bergen railway at Hønefoss. Open June 26-August 10.

Oslo Sjømannshjemmet (Seamen's Hotel), on Fred Olsengate between Tollbugata and Radhusgata (tel. 41-20-05), is frequented by seamen, families, and tourists. Singles 80kr, doubles 110kr; men who are willing to share a room can get a bed in a double for just 45kr. Some rooms have fine views of the harbor. Reception open 24 hours. Buffet-style meals are served at reasonable prices in the dining room. Comfortable, quiet, and convenient: Just 3 minutes, walk from the East Station.

Viktoria Hospits, Niels Juelsgate 29 (entrance on Frognerveien, tel. 44-52-56), has three singles for 55kr and doubles for 75-95kr; all prices 5kr per person less after the first night. Extra bed costs 30kr. The building is old, but the rooms are large, clean, and nicely furnished. Tram #2, direction Majors-tua, from the East Station or the National Theater.

Cochs Pensjonat, Parkveien 25 (entrance on Hegdehausvein, tel. 60-48-36) has acceptable singles for 54kr, doubles 78kr, triples 108kr, and quads 136kr, all with running water, in a rather unattractive building. A bargain by Oslo standards; try to arrive in the morning. Nice location just north of the park surrounding the Royal Palace.

Campsites: There are two good ones near to the city which charge 17.50kr for a tent spot plus 3kr per person. Ekeberg Camping, Ekebergsletta (tel. 19-85-68) is 3 km southeast of the center, next to a park with various recreation facilities. Open June 1-September 1. Bogstad Camping, near Bogstad Lake (tel. 24-76-19), is about 9 km northwest of Oslo and very pleasant. Swimming, fishing, and laundromat. Open all year.

Food

Carnivores will have to invest hefty sums to appease their stomachs in Oslo. Good fresh fish dishes, however, are relatively inexpensive (20-25kr in cafeterias).

Casino Restaurant, Stortingsgata 18, across the street from the National Theater, serves large, good portions for 22-30kr in a pleasant atmosphere. The fish is excellent. Don't be scared away by the fancy entrance. Open 11am-11pm; closed Sun.

The reliable **Kaffistova** cafeteria chain serves surprisingly good food, including many Norwegian specialities, for 18-22kr. Two centrally-located branches are Karl Johans gate 13, open weekdays 8am-8pm, Sat. 9am-3pm, Sun. 11:30am-6pm. Also at Kristian Augustgate 14, open weekdays 7:30am-7pm, Sat. 10am-4pm, closed Sun.

Norrøna Cafeteria, Grensen 19, in the Norrøna Hotel, has the cheapest lunches around. A *smorbrod* and dessert costs only 8-12kr, hot dishes 12-15kr.

Friskporten, Grensen 18, is a vegetarian restaurant featuring a delicious three-course lunch for 21.50kr which includes soup, a main course garnished with all sorts of vegetables, and an ordinary dessert. For a few kroner more you can splurge on a sumptuous fresh fruit and whipped cream dessert. Large portions of main dishes alone cost 13-17kr. Students pay about 10% less. Casual setting; frequented by young people.

Sights

Oslo's imposing **Rådhuset** (City Hall), located by the harbor and West Station, was completed in 1950 yet is still avant-garde architecture. It is richly decorated by major Norwegian artists. Visiting hours in summer are 10am-2pm weekdays (also 6-8pm Mon. and Wed.) and noon-3pm Sunday. Admission free.

From behind the Rådhuset, facing the harbor, you see on the bluff to your left, **Akershus Castle,** built in 1300 and transformed into a Renaissance palace by Christian IV. The grounds, open from sunrise to sunset, are ideal for a stroll or picnic; there is a fine view of Oslo's harbor from the bluff. The entire castle, with its underground passages, banquet halls, dungeons, and courtyards, is open for exploration weekdays 10am-4pm, Sunday 12:30-4pm (admission 3kr). Akershus houses the **Resistance Museum** (admission 3kr), an unforgettable display recounting the Nazi occupation and the Norwegian resistance.

A fifteen-minute ferry ride from Rådhuset brings you across the harbor to **Bygdøy** and Oslo's finest attractions, her three **Viking ships,** dating from 800-900 A.D. The museum is open every day in summer 10am-6pm, admission 3.50kr. Next door is the **Folk Museum** (admission 7kr) featuring **Ibsen's Study** and a **Stave Church.** A ten-minute walk brings you to Thor Heyerdahl's **Kon-Tiki** and **RA II** (admission 4kr) and to the polar ship **Fram** (admission 3kr) used by both Nansen and Amundsen in their polar expeditions. Fram went further north and south than any other ship in its time. If the Viking ships inspire you, and you wish to learn more about Norway's daring West Vikings, we suggest a visit to Oslo's **Historisk Museum** on Frederiksgate 2.

Norway has produced two outstanding modern artists, Edvard Munch and Gustav Vigeland. The beautifully arranged **Munch Museum** contains an outstanding collection of the artist's expressionist paintings, woodcuts, and lithographs. Tuesday evenings at 7:30pm there are recitals, often featuring Grieg's piano music. The museum, at Toyengata 53 (bus #29, direction

Hasle), is open daily 10am-8pm, Sun. noon-8pm; admission is 5kr or free after 6pm. The **National Gallery,** Universitetsgata 13, devotes several rooms to Munch's work and also features other nineteenth- and twentieth-century Norwegian artists (open weekdays 10 am-4pm, Sat. until 3pm, and Sun. noon-3pm; admission free). Gustav Vigeland worked over thirty years on the impressive statues of iron, stone, and bronze that decorate **Frogner Park.** The famous obelisk of squirming human bodies is one of Oslo's landmarks. **Vigeland's Studio,** now a museum, goes a long way toward explaining what Vigeland thought he was doing. Open every day 1-7 pm, except Monday; admission free. Park and museum can be reached by tram #2, or bus #72 or 73.

The **Henie-Onstads Art Center** at Hovikodden, Baerum, 10 kilometers from the center of Oslo, is a new cultural center combining a museum and live experimental work in the arts. Open every day 11am-10pm, admission 10kr. Bus #32, 35, 36, or 37.

For a great view of the Oslo Fjord and the city, take the train from the National Theater underground station to Frognerseteren and walk fifteen minutes to the radio tower **(Tryvannst årnet).** You can pick wild blueberries along the way. From the top of the tower (open every day in summer, 9:30am-10pm; admission 4kr) you can see as far as the Swedish border. From the tower, it is a twenty-minute walk down to **Holmenkollen,** Oslo's world-famous ski jump. There is an inexpensive cafeteria about halfway up the jump with a fine view of Oslo. You can get back to town on the subway, a five-minute walk from the jump. A good daytime visit and worthwhile for the sunset as well.

Evenings

Oslo has some of the best jazz entertainment in Europe. Small clubs abound, and the music and the atmosphere are well worth the cover charges, usually about 20kr. Two small pubs with a lot of character and good traditional jazz are: **Guldfisken,** near the East Station at Radhusgata 2 (tel. 41-14-89), with music Friday and Saturday 8pm-midnight; and **Bergum Café,** Ploensgata 4 (tel. 33-72-35), with music Thursday evenings 8-11:30pm.

Club 7, Munkedamsveien 15 (tel. 33-37-32), is a terrific jazz club that has evolved from humble beginnings to become Oslo's most popular entertainment spot for young people. Occasional rock, folk, and blues music as well as jazz; on some evenings there are two live bands playing in different rooms. There's dancing, a bar, a restaurant serving Norwegian specialities for 15-20kr, a quiet "blue room" for talking, a foyer for television and chess, even a library. All for 25kr Fri. and Sat., 15kr during the week, except when big-name bands are playing. Open every day 8pm-1am except Mon. Music starts at 9pm.

Chateau Neuf, Slemdalsveien 7, is a good place to meet students. Discotheque on weekends, occasional live music, pub, and restaurant. Tram #1, 2, or 11 to Majorstua. Call 69-37-94 between 9am and 4pm for information on hours and goings-on.

Oslo-Bergen Railway and the Sognefjord

You can't look from side to side fast enough. Fjords, mountains, glaciers, and tundra—the Oslo-Bergen run is one of the most thrilling rides in Europe.

The main line passes pristine lakes which mirror the surrounding hills. Then climbing above the tree line, it crosses savage plateaus strewn with boulders and gouged by glacial lakes. But it is the sidetrips off the main line that are the most rewarding. If you have very little time, at least stop and hike around for a few hours at **Finse**, the highest point on the line, or **Geilo**. Make sure you have a train schedule, and be prepared for cold weather, even in summer.

From **Myrdal**, on the main line, the spectacular side branch of the railway runs down to **Flåm**, plummeting nearly 3000 feet in just twelve miles. The hike down takes about six hours and is even more spectacular, for your view is unobstructed. Flåm is a good place to spend the night. If you are willing to share a room, you can get a bed in a triple at the **Solhammer Pension**, two minutes from the Train Station, for 25kr, 20kr with your own bed linen. Free use of kitchen. The **Tourist Office** by the Train Station has information on ferry and bus connections in the area and will help you find a room.

Flåm is at the head of the **Aurlandsfjord**, a branch of the **Sognefjord** (Norway's longest); it is an excellent departure point for tours of the fjord district. If your time is limited, there is an express steamer all the way to Bergen for 160kr.

A better alternative if you are continuing to Bergen is to take the ferry from Flåm to **Gundvangen**, at the head of the long, narrow **Nerøyfjord**, another branch of the Sognefjord. The unforgettable two-hour ferry ride is an extraordinary bargain for 17kr. The bus from Gundvangen to **Voss**, back on the main Oslo-Bergen rail line, costs 21kr. You can continue directly to Bergen from Voss, but the **Voss Youth Hostel** (IYHF) (tel. 12017) is a superb place to spend the night; it's located right on a beautiful mountain-cradled lake, a fifteen-minute walk west from the Train Station. Open all year, but used primarily as a ski lodge in winter. It has forty 5-bed rooms, each with private shower and toilet. Free saunas and a good breakfast are included in the 41kr charge; you can rent a rowboat for 10kr an hour.

Bus and train schedules are synchronized so that you can leave Oslo on the early morning train and arrive in Voss around dinnertime or in Bergen at about 9pm. The trip can also be done in the reverse direction, beginning in Bergen and arriving in Oslo about 10pm. Pick up a sheet detailing the train, bus, and ferry connections on this route at the Oslo East Station.

From Flåm you can also cruise by express ferry (41kr, every day) or local ferry (26kr, but only twice a week) to **Balestrand**, where there is a good IYHF **Youth Hostel**. Balestrand is a good base for ferry trips up another branch of the Sognefjord to **Fjaerland**, at the base of the great glacier **Jostedalsbre**. Still another possibility if you're heading to northern Norway is to take the very short ferry ride from Balestrand to Hella, then continue by bus along the edge of the fjord to **Sogndal** (23kr). You can stay in the IYHF **Youth Hostel** here, then cross the high mountains by bus to **Ota** (79kr), on the main rail line between Oslo and Trondheim.

Bergen

Groves of orange- and red-roofed houses peek out from the pines and spruces covering the mountains of Bergen, overlooking colorful boats in the harbor. Although it's Norway's second largest city, Bergen has not swapped local charm for tourist dollars. It is still noted for its biggest business, shipping, dating back almost 900 years.

Bergen's focal point is **Torget,** at the head of the harbor, where your nose tells you what's being sold. The market also sells flowers, produce, and crafts, and is open 8:30am-3pm (closed Sundays). You can choose your fish live in open tanks and watch the fishermen net, weigh, and clean them.

From Torget, on one side of the harbor, you will see the pointed gables of medieval buildings. This is **Bryggen,** lined with wooden warehouses that date from Bergen's years as the northernmost city in the Hanseatic league (an association of merchants of German cities). Close to Torget is an excellent **Hanseatic Museum** (open 10am-4pm daily in summer; 1.50kr with student ID) with sixteenth-century furnishings. The museum has been open for around 100 years, with a casualness that allows 250-year-old books just lying around to be leafed through. A bit further out, behind the old wooden façades, painters, weavers, and craftsmen have workshops. Here also is the **Bryggen Tracteursted,** a restaurant literally nestled in history at the end of an alley; it's open 10:30am-11pm except Sundays, and is often full of students drinking beer. In the same area, but reached from Ovregaten, are the old assembly rooms or **Schotstuene** (open daily 10am-4pm; admission 3kr).

Unless you are a resolute sightseer, don't bother visiting thirteenth-century **Haakonshallen** (King Haakon's Hall) or the sixteenth-century **Rosenkrantz Tower,** just beyond the row of wooden buildings. Instead, starting from Bryggen or Torget, explore the jumble of houses on the slopes of **Mt. Fløien.** If you climb high enough through the narrow streets and passageways, you'll get a series of views of the city and fjord. The **Mt. Fløien Funicular** (the station is a two-minute walk up Vetrlidsalmenningen from Torget), will lift you or take you down for 3.50kr each way, but you should try to walk one way.

Bordering the large park **Lille Lungengardsvatnet** is Bergen's most interesting museum. **Rasmus Meyer's Collection** (free, open Mon.-Sat. 10am-3pm, Sun.noon-3pm) gives a good cross-section of Norwegian naturalists, impressionists, and expressionists. Start on the second floor with the excellent selection of works by Edvard Munch. Every day at 3pm there is an hour-long piano recital of works by Edvard Grieg (20kr, half price for students).

Two interesting sights lie a short distance out from the center. The **Fantoft Stave Church,** an example of the oriental-looking wooden churches peculiar to Norway, was built in the early twelfth century in the Sognefjord area and was later moved to Bergen. Reached by the bus to Paradis from the Bus Station and then a short walk; open 3-6pm in summer, also 10am-1pm in July, admission is 2.50kr. Also a quick bus trip away is **Gamle Bergen** (Old Bergen), a collection of characteristic wooden buildings from the last century, recreated as a village. Bus #1 from Vagsalmenning. Open 10am-6pm every day; admission with guided tour 5kr.

Each summer, in late May and early June, for two weeks, the **Bergen International Festival** presents music, drama, ballet, folklore, arts, and other entertainment. Tickets available at Festival Office, Grieg Hall (tel. 23-00-10).

Bergen is a good point of departure for fjord trips ranging from hours to days. The express steamer from Bergen to Flåm and back by train costs 210kr (steamer alone 160kr). Hydrofoil and Westmaran boats to Stavanger run three times a day and cost 146kr (25% discount for students). Inquire at the Tourist Office about the much slower, much less expensive local ferries and steamers. If you have time, why rush the fjords?

Addresses and Telephone Numbers

Tourist Information: is located in the pavilion on Torgalmenning, a ten-minute walk up Kaigaten from the Train Station. Open in the summer Mon.-Sat. 8:30am-11pm, Sun. 9:30am-11pm (tels. 21-14-87 and 21-90-26). Pick up *The Bergen Guide*, which has current information on hours and prices of sights. Change your money here when the banks are closed. They sell a 48-hour bus pass, good on city buses only, (i.e. not on buses leaving from the Bus Station). Regular bus fare is 3.50kr.

Student Travel Service: Parkveien 1 (tel. 23-31-90). Open weekdays until about 3pm in summer. At the same address are the club and office of the **Studentsamskipnaden** (student association, tel. 21-11-60). Open September-June. The **Youth Hostel Association** office is at Strandgaten 4 (tel. 21-68-82).

American Express: Winge Travel Bureau, Strandgate 5 (tel. 21-10-80).

Main Post Office: in the tall green building on Smastrandgate. Open weekdays 8am-5pm, Thursdays to 7pm, Saturdays 9am-1pm.

Bergen Touring Club: Sundtsgate 3 (tel. 21-46-46), designs walking routes and provides complete information on mountain lodges in the vicinity.

Police: tel. 002.

Accommodations

The **Tourist Pavilion** is the main placement agency for rooms; the finding fee runs from 7kr for one person to 10kr for four or more. Rooms in private homes cost 45kr for a single, 70kr for a double. Ask if a new hostel has been built to replace the Fløien Hostel, which burned down two years ago.

Bibelskolen Sommerhotel, C. Sundtsgate 22 (tel. 21-25-31), has only two 11-bed dorms in addition to its high-priced singles and doubles, but it is not well known as a hostel and often has room. Very friendly management; no curfew. 30kr per night including sheets. If the dorms are full, you may be able to spread your sleeping bag on a cot for a bit less. All-you-can-eat breakfast available for 15kr. May be Bergen's best bargain, especially since the central location saves 7kr bus fare.

Montana Hostel (IYHF), Ravneberget (tel. 22-29-00), is set halfway up Mt. Ulriken and has a great view of the city, but tends to be overrun by large touring groups. 39kr for bed and breakfast; 5-bed rooms all have hot and cold running water. Call first, it's often full. Reach by bus #4. Open May 20-September 30.

Hotel Alrek, 25 Aarstadveien (tel. 29-18-00), is a modern student dormitory with singles at 60kr and doubles at 80kr; all rooms with hot and cold running water. It's a self-service hotel: linen provided, but you make your own bed. With 325 beds, the Alrek usually has room. Cafeteria. About a 5-minute bus ride (#2) from near the Train Station. Open July 1 (possibly earlier) to about August 17.

Camping in the Bergen area is beautiful and serene. The closest site is **Midttun, 11** kilometers from town (tel. 10-10-95). **Lone,** Bergen's major camping site, has a service shop, hostel, and all conveniences, and is 20 kilometers from downtown (tel. 24-08-20). Both are just off the main drag E-68 and are accessible via buses from platform #1 or 2 at the Bus Station. Tent spot 16kr, and 3kr per person.

Food

Bergen offers a wide assortment of medium-priced, dull cafeterias. Unfortunately, if you're not picnicking, these are the only options for reasonably-priced meals.

Bergens Indremisjons Kafe, C. Sundtsgate 22, has the best lunch deal in town, though it's hardly cheap: a generous portion of the daily special together with soup or dessert and coffee for 28kr. Main dishes 21-23kr. Open Mon.-Fri. 7am-6pm, Sat. 9am-3:30pm, Sun. noon-5pm.

Torgstuen, on Torget, has a good view of the harbor and Bryggen from its second-floor location. Almost has a touch of atmosphere. Main dishes 20-25kr. Open until 10pm weekdays, until 7pm Sun.

More expensive, but with pleasant old-style decor and frequented by students, are **Hollbergstuen,** Torgalmenning 6, and **Wessel Stuen,** Engen 14.

Evenings

Unless you wrangle an invitation from a sailor to help "set the nets," evening activities in Bergen don't have an especially Norwegian flavor. **Hulen,** in an old air-raid shelter beneath Nygaardsparken, is an inexpensive club run by Bergen University students. Discotheque or live jazz on Friday and Saturday nights. The Tourist Office has their program, which has a map showing how to find the place.

Trondheim

A stop at Trondheim, Norway's medieval capital, can cure any claustrophobia brought on by the interminable trip from Oslo to Narvik. From the Train Station, where you can pick up a map and English guide to the city, cross the bridge and walk to your right several blocks to the indoor fishmarket **(Ravinkloa Fiskhall)** in a squat, green building. Then follow Munkegata south: you'll pass on your left **Stiftsgården** (Scandinavia's largest timber building, now a royal residence) just before reaching **Torget,** the open-air marketplace. Here the Viking King Olav, who founded Trondheim in 997 A.D., sternly stands guard, while the **Tourist Office,** Kongensgate 7 (tel. 25890), sells a brochure (6kr) outlining in detail two walking tours of his city. The Office is open in summer on weekdays 9am-9pm, Sat. 9am-6pm, and Sun. 1-6pm.

South of Torget is Scandinavia's largest medieval structure, the **Nidaros Cathedral,** open 10am-6pm weekdays, 10am-2pm Sat., and 1:30-4pm Sun. Admission 2kr. The nearby **Erkebispegården** (Archbishop's Palace) dates from the twelfth century; 2kr admission includes a guided tour, conducted every hour, weekdays 10am-3pm, Sat.-Sun. 10am-2pm. You can get an excellent view of the old warehouses built on pilings right over the river, from the **Bybrua** (the Old Bridge), east of the Cathedral. Trondheim's one fascinating museum, in a seventeenth-century manor, is the **Ringve Museum of Musical History.** You must take a guided tour (about an hour and a half, 8kr); the English tour is given every day at 9:30am (May-September only). Take tram #2 to Lade or bus #30 from the Bus Station to Attføringsinstituttet.

Across the bridge from the Archbishop's Palace, at Elgesetergate 1, is the **Studentersamfundet** (Student Union) with a popular restaurant and pub (open at 5pm in summer) and a discotheque (open at 8pm). Less expensive is the cafeteria at the **Gildevangen Hotel,** Søndregate 22, a short walk from the Train Station. A splendid smorgasbord breakfast is served here between 7:15 and 10am every day for 25kr. In fine weather, picnic on **Munkholmen,** an island with a small swimming beach. The boat from the fish market at the northern end of Munkegata runs every half hour and costs 9kr round trip.

The IYHF **Youth Hostel** is at Weidemannsvei 41 (tel. 30490); take bus #63 from Munkegata just north of Torget. The Hostel has 200 beds and is open all year; 39kr for members including breakfast, 46kr for nonmembers. Trondheim's hotels don't go below 150kr for a double, but the Tourist Office has rooms in private homes for 40kr for a single, 70kr for a double, plus a 10kr fee.

Bodø

A trip to Bodø will reward you with the most extraordinary ''sunset'' in Western Europe. Unlike Narvik, Bodø enjoys a truly unobstructed view of the Midnight Sun—which remains above the horizon until about July 12. However, for the best view, you must walk up a mountain road (not very difficult) and have good weather (a rarity). To enjoy a most stunning view of the setting sun, walk up the road to the top of **Mt. Ronvik,** 1 kilometer from the **Ronvik Hostel** (IYHF) or 3 kilometers from the center of town.

At the end of the road, you will be able to see 75-125 kilometers in nearly any direction. You will find a parking lot at the top, and an expensive restaurant. But don't stop here. Climb the hill to your right (away from the restaurant) which will take you away from the crowd that assembles on a clear night. From the top of this hill, you can watch the sun sink behind the Lofoten Island peaks—at least 100 of them outlined in the distance. To your back, another range of snow-capped nearby mountains will glow in the pink of the sun. To the left is the ocean, below you the fjords. Sunrise (after July 15) is about 45 minutes after sunset—the sun actually still glows behind the Lofotens. Ask at the Tourist Office or watch for signs in the trains to find out when the last night of Midnight Sun is in Bodø.

The **Salstraumen Current** is one of the most exciting events in this area. It occurs every six hours as millions of gallons of water are squeezed through a thin channel between two fjords. Ask for tide and bus timetables at the Tourist Office or the Train Station. (The ride takes one hour and is 26kr round trip, but you can hitch fairly well.)

If the weather is bad, you should consider staying overnight in **Fauske,** since the main reason to go to Bodø is the sunset. This is also a good option if you are in a hurry to get north or south, since the town is about 50 kilometers before Bodø on the train route south and 50 kilometers after it on the bus route north, and all buses and trains stop in Fauske. You'll save an hour's transportation time each way and about 20kr bus fare by skipping Bodø. Fauske's **Youth Hostel** (IYHF), 1 kilometer from the Station (tel. 43822), is brand new and comfortable (23kr per night). If you don't wish to stay overnight in the area, however, synchronized train-bus connections allow you to go straight through between Oslo and Narvik via Trondheim and Fauske in just over 24 hours.

Accommodations and Food

The **Tourist Office,** at Dronningensgata 1A (tel. 21240), open in summer 9am-9pm daily and 4-9pm Sun., has rooms in private homes for 30-45kr per person (5kr each for shower, use of kitchen, and bed linen).

Ronvik Youth Hostel (IYHF), Årnesvagen 7 (tel. 081/21570), 2km from the town center, offers splendid accommodations in mobile units for just 20kr per night (27kr without Hostel card). Each unit has several 1- to 3-bed rooms and a living room, full kitchen, and showers. Reception closed 1-5pm and after 11pm, but you get a key to the building and your room, so you can stay out as long as you like to see the sun. Just a half-hour walk to the top of Mt. Ronvik. The Hostel usually has room; if you call ahead, you can arrange to pick up a key if you'll be arriving after 11pm. From the center, take bus #14 or 17 from Dronningensgate and Havnegata, and get off at Årnesvagen. If you are arriving by bus from Fauske, ask the driver to let you off at Snippen, then walk down Ronvikveien (about 20 minutes—there are signs indicating the way). Open June 20-August 20.

Domnikus-Senteret Hostel (IYHF), Hernesveien 22 (tel. 21783), is run by friendly nuns and costs only 15kr (though when it's crowded you just get a mattress on the floor). The drawback is a long walk (about an hour) to Mt. Ronvik for a view of the Midnight Sun. Open until 1am when the midnight sun is visible. From the Train Station, walk past the harbor and follow the main road uphill. Open June 15-August 15.

Camping: The closest camping is at Bodøsjøen (tel. 22902), 3 km from the center of town. Reached by bus #12; 9.50kr for a tent site, plus 3kr per person. Geitvagen (tel. 11642) is 11 km from the center, but has a beach and chalets.

University students hang out in **Jarnaes Tesalong,** Storgata 34, not far from the Train Station. 22kr will buy you a full dinner and dessert.

Getting From Bodø to Narvik

The Norwegian rail line ends at Bodø; you have three options (besides hitching) for going north to **Narvik.** The bus runs twice every day; the scenery is spectacular, the cost 115kr (92kr from Fauske). Direct boats to Narvik (95kr) run only twice a week. Every day, however, there is a boat to Narvik via **Stamsund** and **Svolvaer** in the **Lofoten Islands** (127kr). If you take this route, you should definitely stop for a day or so in Stamsund or Svolvaer, both of which have IYHF Youth Hostels. The steep mountains of those remote islands, rising straight out of the sea, should not be missed.

Narvik

Mountains pierce clouds, rising like enormous waves from shimmering valleys. Traveling to and from Narvik is more memorable than the town itself. The train through Kiruna (Sweden), the bus north to Alta or south to Bodø, the coastal steamer north or south: all offer Norwegian scenery at its wildest.

As one of the world's leading iron ore exporters, Narvik attracted hostile planes during World War II; the town was leveled and has since been rebuilt. But Narvik now attracts tourists with its snow-capped peaks, crowned round the clock by the glowing sun from May 31 to July 14. Even later in the summer, there is no need for streetlamps at midnight. A 25kr chairlift (13kr one way) hoists you part way up a mountainside for a good view of sun and nearby fjords. If you would rather expend energy than kroner, walk up to the **Teknisk Skole** (Technical School), where you'll find tables and chairs thoughtfully set up. Or, beginning at the **Malmen Sommerhotell,** just above the Technical School, you can hike up the mountain to or even beyond where the chairlift takes you.

If you tire of all the mountain scenery, head underground: Mon.-Fri at 1:30pm there are guided tours of **LKAB's iron ore installations** for 4kr. The Kiruna-Narvik rail connection wasn't built for tourists; every working day nearly 100,000 tons of ore, mined in Kiruna, are unloaded at Narvik.

From Narvik, the trains run only to Sweden (several times a day, including local trains which stop at mountain villages that are ideal bases for day hikes).

Accommodations and Food

Narvik is jammed during the summer, but since most visitors only stay a day or two, rooms open up often. Try to arrive before the Tourist Office closes or you may be in for a cramped night in the Railroad Station or a chilly one on a park bench. Regular hotels are quite expensive, but the **Tourist Office,** at Kongensgate 66 (tel. 43309), open daily from 9am-9pm, Sun. 5-8pm, will book you into a private home for a 10kr fee; prices are 50kr for a single and 90kr for a double.

Narvik Youth Hostel (IYHF), Havnegata 3 (tel. 42598), is beautifully located on the water, a 15-minute walk down the hill from the Bus or Rail Station. Although the place is spotless, has hot showers and a kitchen, it may be dominated by busloads of elderly tour groups. Closed 11am-4pm; 11pm lock-out enforced except when the sun is visible (then it's 1:30am). 4-bed rooms

39kr for members, 46kr for nonmembers, including breakfast. Expensive by hostel standards but by far the cheapest place in Narvik, so reserve in advance or get there early.

Narvik's campground was closed down two years ago when a plant for manufacturing parts for military equipment was built on the site. Check with the Tourist Office to see if a new one has opened. The next closest campsite is at **Hersletta,** 20 kilometers north of the city.

Most restaurants in Narvik are expensive and noisy. The **Nordstjernen Cafeteria,** Kongensgate 26, has hot dishes for about 15kr and an interesting view of the harbor and LKAB plant (open until 5pm every day). The popular **Kafé** in the Havnens Hus (just beyond the Youth Hostel) is the cheapest place in town, but it's closed in July.

Finnmark

Even further north than Narvik is the city of **Tromso** and the Lapp country, Finnmark. They are accessible by road, boat, and plane. The **Nord Norge** bus line will put you in Tromso for about 85kr from Narvik. For hitching, Tromso is located on highway E78, which branches off E6 at Nordkjosbotn. There is an IYHF **Youth Hostel** in Tromso, but you must apply at the Tourist Office. Tromso is being deliberately developed by the Norwegian government; the world's northernmost university has recently been established there. The **Tromso Museum,** on Mellomvegen, includes exhibits on Lapland. **Tromso Cathedral** (Ishaus Katedraler) is a beautiful old wooden building.

East and north of Tromso, Finnmark begins. There are only 20,000 Lapps in the entire area; few speak English. After you see a few sets of reindeer antlers strapped to car roofs, Lapland may seem like souvenir land.

Canoe trips on the **Tana River** on the Finnish border are relatively inexpensive once you are there. Hiking is probably better in Swedish Lapland, where mountains break the monotony of the highlands (see Sweden). From mid-June until September, mosquitoes will make you miserable unless you learn to tolerate them or to tolerate heavy coats of repellent. A local product, **3x6,** *djungel olja,* seems to be effective. Coverall rainjackets also make good shields.

The best time to visit Lapland for hiking may be late May, although August is the hiking season. In late May there will be fewer mosquitoes and people, because it will be colder. The Lapp fairs and markets are held in February and March. In December, it can be −50°C in Kautokeino. In June and early July the sun never sets, and in December it never rises. Summer can be quite hot, although it will cool toward 2 or 3am, when the sun is low on the horizon. Reindeer meat, although expensive, is good, tasting a little like a cross between liver and steak. *Mult* (cloudberry preserves) is a specialty. Winter skiing is better organized in Finnish and Swedish Lapland. For any kind of travel, it is valuable to get information in Oslo at one of the information offices (see listing under Oslo). See the map of Lapland in the Sweden chapter.

Getting Around Norweigian Lapland

Visiting Norwegian Lapland takes a good deal of time and money. There are bus connections from two points only: Narvik, and Rovaniemi, at the end of the rail line in Finland. From Narvik you can go by the Nord Norge bus route to Tromso, **Alta, Russenes,** and **Nordkapp,** continental Europe's northernmost point, even all the way to **Kirkenes** on the Russian border. From Rovaniemi, you reach Nordkapp via Karasjok and Russenes or via Kautokeino, Alta, and Russenes. Getting to Nordkapp by bus will cost about $40 from Rovaniemi (via Karasjok) or about $55 from Narvik. Although the trip is cheaper from the Finnish side, the scenery is duller. A circular tour from Narvik through Nordkapp to Rovaniemi, traveling fairly fast, takes about five days, longer if hitching.

You need not, however, go all the way to Nordkapp; the landscape is rather barren, and Nordkapp itself is something of a tourist trap. Still, you may feel (not without justification) that once you've come this far, you might as well continue to the "top of the Continent." If you do go, you can stay in **Honningsvag** at the IYHF Youth Hostel (tel. 75113), or at the **Betania Hospits** (tel. 72501) where you can spread your sleeping bag in the cellar for 15kr.

A good alternative itinerary leads from Narvik to Alta, Kautokeino, and Kiruna. This trip includes the savage coast and the highlands, and gives you the opportunity to take the spectacular train ride between Narvik and Kiruna. The bus ride from Narvik to Alta has fantastic scenery and costs 210kr; for just 240kr, though, you can fly from **Bardufoss,** just north of Narvik, to Alta. Apply at the **Alta Tourist Office** for the IYHF Youth Hostel. The bus from Alta to Kautokeino costs 47kr; there is a Youth Hostel here too. From Kautokeino there is a bus to **Enontekio** in Finland; there may be a bus from here to **Karesuando** in northern Sweden, or you may have to hitch. Karesuando is linked by bus to Kiruna, where you meet up with the railroad again.

A final possibility is to sail to the midnight sun—to go north via the many local boats or by the coastal steamer from Narvik or Tromso. Cabins require advance booking, but you can spread your sleeping bag in the lounge. Any boat trip in Norway will provide spectacular panoramas of snowy mountains, even in July.

POLAND

$1U.S.=32.5zloty(zl)   **1zl=$.03**

Probably no European country has had its character and culture shaped
so profoundly by its geography as has Poland. Generally flat and without
natural defensible boundaries, Poland has known invasion after invasion,
conquest after conquest. The understandable result is a people fiercely loyal
to the idea of a sovereign and free Poland. Put this together with a strange
interweaving of Marxism and fervent Catholicism, and you have some idea
of the Polish character. Remember too, that for most Poles, war and conquest are not matters of abstract history, but of living memory. No country
lost as high a percentage of its population in World War II as did Poland.

Planning Your Trip

Although relatively straightforward, the process of obtaining a Polish visa
from the United States will require at least four weeks. You first have to buy
vouchers for currency exchange or prepaid accommodations from **ORBIS**,
the Polish National Tourist Office. The minimum is $5 per day if you are

under 26, or if you are visiting relatives; otherwise the minimum is $12 per day. Send a certified check for the appropriate amount (with a cover letter if you are applying for the $5-per-day rate) to ORBIS, Polish National Tourist Office, 500 Fifth Avenue, New York, NY 10036 (tel. (212) 354-1487). This office can also help make reservations in hotels and hostels. While waiting for the voucher, write to the Polish diplomatic mission nearest you for a visa application: Embassy of the Polish People's Republic, 2224 Wyoming Avenue N.W., Washington, D.C. 20008; Polish Consulate General, 233 Madison Avenue, New York, NY 10016; or Polish Consulate General, 1530 North Lake Shore Drive, Chicago, IL 60610. The fees vary according to the nature of the visa: a regular visa, for a stay of up to 90 days in Poland, to be used within six months of the date issued, costs $10 single entry, $31 for two to four entries; a transit visa, for travel through Poland within 48 hours, costs $5.50 for single entry, $8.50 for double entry. Once ORBIS has returned the voucher, send the completed application with two attached photographs, a certified check, and the carbon copy of the voucher back to the appropriate consulate. If you prefer, it is usually easy to arrange the visa in Western Europe, where with a currency voucher, the visa may be issued within 24 hours.

Inside Poland you can lengthen your stay by presenting additional exchange receipts and paying the necessary fee at the police office in any provincial capital; check with **IT** (*Informacja Turystyczna,* the local travel information office) or ORBIS for further information.

Be warned that ORBIS will tell you that any zloty you have left **over the minimum exchange** when leaving Poland can be changed back to dollars at the border. In practice though, most customs people seize the zloty and give you a receipt—you can spend them next time you're in Poland. Unless you want to fight with customs, spend all of the zloty you have.

Practical Information

No matter what task you have at hand, in Poland you will have to wait in lines, fill out forms, obtain stamps, and pay fees before reaching your goal. The Polish bureaucracies will test your patience at every turn, but the only way to get what you want is to be patient and persevere. The one reward is that usually the ticket, the forms, and the stamps are inexpensive. Plan on things taking at least twice as long as you expect, and if you have limited time, try to limit your itinerary. It will reduce the frustrations drastically.

The biggest problem in Poland is accommodations. Advance reservations through ORBIS in New York is the only way to ensure a place to stay, especially in the cities. ORBIS now provides prepaid reservations, not only for its own expensive hotels, but also for the sixteen International Student Hotels open during July and August, run by **ALMATUR,** the Polish Student Travel Office. The basic Student Hotel cost is 100zl per night, with a miscellany of 1 and 3zl supplements. In any case, you should not have to pay more than 110zl per night. Most ISH are quite comfortable, with two-, three-, and four-bed rooms, snack bars, dining rooms, and student clubs.

Besides ALMATUR and ORBIS, there are four other travel organizations you may have to deal with. **PTTK** runs a number of inexpensive city hotels called **Domy Turysty,** and many fine alpine huts *(schroniska)* in the Zakopane region. PTTK also issues the **Autostop card,** a hitchhiking pass. **PTSM** is the Polish Youth Hostel Federation, which recognizes—sometimes requires—the IYHF card. There are over 1000 hostels *(schroniska mlodziezowe)* open in the summer, and 100 year round. A list is available at the PTSM Office in Warsaw. Although mostly filled by and sometimes reserved for Polish youths, these hostels will usually find a place or two for you. For 20-50zl per night, these hostels are the cheapest, although shoddiest, alternative. IT is not a single organization, but the local bureau in every town, and it is usually the most knowledgeable, friendly, and reliable source of information, although some of its branches may present a linguistic problem. **Biuro Zakwaterowania** is an office that specializes in arranging private rooms for tourists, but be careful—they are unlikely to offer foreigners anything under 250zl per person. **Camping** exists all over Poland in the summer. In addition to tent sites, beds in bungalows are often available. These may cost as little as 70zl, or as much as 280zl, so check first. Each of these organizations is completely independent of the others—with resulting confusion. It's a good idea to recheck any important information (i.e. schedules, prices, fares, police formalities) with at least a couple of other sources. Most of these open by 8am and shut by 5pm.

Travel around Poland is appallingly slow and confusing, but cheap. Each of the three classes of trains *(osobowy, pospieszny,* and *ekspresowy)* requires a different class of ticket, and express trains and trains leaving the country require a seat reservation *(miejscówka).* These are advisable anyway if you want to sit down. The ORBIS offices abroad offer a **Polrailpass** for various lengths of time, but the savings are not substantial unless you travel across the country several times, and it does not spare you from the ordeal of standing in line for seat or couchette reservations. Most advance tickets and international tickets have to be bought at ORBIS, and an IUS card (available to students from ALMATUR in Warsaw) entitles you to a 25% discount on trains to other socialist countries. Also most cities have a network of commuter trains *(pociągi elektryczne).*

Buses are a great way to see the towns. Look for "Dworzec PKS." In the country, the PKS markers along the road indicate the bus stops. Travel by bus is slow and crowded, but inexpensive, and the network is extensive, as most villages have a bus stop.

Hitching in Poland is the cheapest and most interesting way to get around. The rider is expected to pay from 5-50zl, depending on the length of the ride (about 10zl for every 50 km). The Autostop cards, sold by PTTK, are mostly ignored. On the main roads (indicated with green markers E81, E16, etc.) the flow of traffic is considerable, and if you wait just beyond the PKS bus stop, you should get a ride within half an hour. Wave—do not thumb— everything that moves, especially the unloaded trucks; and try to get an early start, as most Poles are on the road by 6am. Practically all Poles hitch, and single women should not run into any trouble.

Although Poland is one of the cheapest countries in Europe, you *must* change the minimum $5 or $12 per day and show the slips for this when leaving Poland. Spending even this much may be a problem, but if you do need more zloty—to sample some of the best food—ask a Polish friend to change money for you, as he can get 60zl to the dollar in the bank. The black market can make life in Poland luxurious and cheap. Be careful and inconspicuous, and don't settle for less than 150zl to the dollar. For the black market, you must remember to "forget" to declare some dollars at the border when you enter, or you may have trouble when leaving the country. You should also carry cash—either U.S. dollars or German marks. A lot of bureaucratic stuff having anything to do with travel, like further visas, air freight, and some vouchers has to be paid for in Western cash. And remember, black marketeers don't take travelers checks. It's also a good idea to have a few dollars as "gifts" for friends, or for stays in private homes.

Receiving mail in Poland can be difficult and unreliable; but ALMATUR, as well as the U.S. and Canadian embassies, holds mail for two weeks. Telephone calls to Europe and to North America can be arranged at the main Post Office in Warsaw. The charges cannot be reversed, and the connections are terrible. If you're sending a telegram, have a Polish friend do it for you—he pays only half as much.

Language may be something of a problem, particularly in smaller cities. Some older people speak German, students know a little English, and if you look interesting or helpless enough, most people will speak and understand Russian although they hate to admit it. Russian will also help you in deciphering signs. ORBIS may help, but surprisingly few people connected with the tourist industry speak any English at all. Practice your sign language. There is a phrasebook available for 20zl called *How to Say it in Polish*, but both this and Polish-English dictionaries are hard to find. If you know some French, there are lots of language guides available.

For photographers, note that in Poland you can take pictures of everything except military and border installations, ports, trains and stations, and "state institutions." Since there are an awful lot of these around, be careful—it's up to the discretion of authorities. You won't have any trouble in big cities, but particularly in small towns, where you're conspicuous anyway, look around before you snap.

An emergency of any nature should be addressed to the well-informed staff of your embassy in Warsaw. They answer calls around the clock.

Food

By western standards, dining out in Poland is inexpensive, so treat yourself at least once to some of the fancier Polish specialties, such as roast duck *(kaczka)*, with plums and apples and rabbit-and-game stew *(bigos)*. The mountain trout is also delicious, as is the lake carp in jelly *(karp w galarecie)*. When in Gdańsk, try the eel, prepared in any number of ways.

For the more budget-minded, the self-service bars provide a fine cutlet in bread crumbs for 15zl. Lately, *hamburgery* and *hot-dogy* have come into style. For a lighter meal, get a portion of *naleśniki*, the Polish version of crêpes, served with a cheese filling, and a bottle of *kefir*, a butter-milk-yogurt drink, together costing less than 15zl. *Żywiec* is by far the best beer available. All of which brings us to vodka, which is drunk in Poland before, during, and after virtually every meal. Try *Wyborowa*, which puts American vodka to shame, or the flavored, but not weaker, vodkas—*Jarzębiak, Zubrówka* and *Soplica*.

If you're preparing your own meals, Polish sausage *(kielbaca)*, bread, and *kefir* make a cheap (5-10zl) and substantial picnic. In the country, most private farmers will sell all they produce: from milk, butter, and eggs to a chicken or goose.

If you're looking more for a place to relax or hang out than eat, drop into one of the numerous *winiarnie* (wine shops) or *kiniarnie* (coffee shops) in the city.

Warsaw (Warszawa)

Warsaw is a symbol of Polish determination. Razed to the ground in 1944, Warsaw has been completely rebuilt according to the original plans of the nineteenth century. The result is almost a perfect restoration, and though construction activities are still taking place almost everywhere in the city, the Warsawer seems prepared to accept the inconvenience in order to see his city reborn.

Orientation

The city has three major railroad stations—**Gdańska, Wschodnia** (east) and the new downtown **Centralna.** Most trains go through Centralna—try to get off here. Wschodnia is really in the middle of nowhere. Both trams and buses run frequently. The trams stop running at 1am, but most buses run all night. You buy tickets for both (bus 1.5zl and tram 1zl) at kiosks marked *Ruch.* Ask for *bilety autobusowe* or *tramwajowe* and then punch the tickets yourself as you board the cars. Note that the buses marked with letters (not numbers) are the express ones. They require punching in 3zl worth of tickets, for which purpose you may use three tram tickets or two regular bus tickets. This is the same system used all over Poland—just look for the *Ruch.*

Taxis are cheap in Warsaw, and often private car owners will moonlight as cab drivers, expecting you to set the price. Hitching, however, is not allowed in the city, and is therefore ill-advised. If you're hitching to Kraków, take bus #124, 129, 134, 206, 207, H or H*bis* out ul. Grojecka and al. Krakowska to highway E7. If you're heading for Poznań you want E8, from bus #105, 106, 129, 149, 163 or F. For Gdańsk or other points north, pick up E81 from ul. Pulkowa—bus #181, 201, or E; or tram 15, 17, 27 or 28.

The official **Warsaw Information Office** is at 28 Aleje Jerozolimskie and 13 Krakowskie Przedmieście (tel. 27 00 00). Open daily 8am-8pm, Sun. 9am-1pm), but in fact any place marked **IT** offers tourist information, and you might find the people friendlier at ORBIS offices in hotels—perhaps because they hope you will join one of their tours. Comprehensive travel information and money exchange services are available at ORBIS in the **Hotel Europejski** (13 Krakowskie Przedmieście) and the **Hotel Metropol** (9a Marszalkowska). Check IT or ORBIS for maps, though the best one can be purchased at any *Ruch* kiosk or bookstore for 10zl. The U.S. Embassy provides U.S. citizens with an orientation booklet full of helpful addresses and a city plan.

Addresses and Telephone Numbers

ORBIS: Main office, al. Jerozolimskie 28 (tel. 27 00 00).

ALMATUR: Welcome Service at Krakowskie Przedmeście 24 (tels. 26 03 04 and 26 80 11); administrative offices and mailing address at 00-364 Warszawa, Ordynacka 9 (tel. 26 53 81).

PTTK: Head office at ul. Marszalkowska 124 (tel. 26 60 25), but Autostop card and information also available at the PTTK Gallery (Wystawa), Rynek Starego Miasta 23 (tel. 31 93 06).

PTSM (Polish Youth Hostel Federation): ul. Chocimska 28 (tels 49 81 28 and 49 83 54). Pick up the list of Polish youth hostels here.

Post Office: Main one is at Świętokrzyska and Jasna, open 8am-8pm. You need your passport to send packages to the U.S. or Canada.

PEKAO Bank: al. Jerozolimskie 89 (tel. 29 60 51).

Emergency First Aid and Ambulance: Hoza 56 (tel. 999).

American Embassy: al. Ujazdowskie 29/31 (tel. 28 30 41).

Canadian Embassy: ul. Matejki 1/5. (tel. 29 80 51).

Express Cleaners: Pralnia "Alba", Rutskowskiego 26 and Nowy Swiat 26, open from 8am-7pm. Express, by the way, can mean a week. A friendly smile and a small bribe works wonders. Anywhere in Poland, look for the unpronounceable *czyścienieodziezy* for cleaners.

Accommodations

Warsaw in the summer is crowded; tour groups from other socialist countries flood the hotels. Your best bet is to stop first at **ALMATUR Welcome Service,** Krakowskie Przedmieście 24, near the University, (tel. 26 80 83 or 26 08 11), or at the ALMATUR administrative office—Ordynacka 9 (off Nowy Swiat, tel. 26 43 87). They run one or two **International Student Hotels** every summer, but since the addresses change yearly and since they might be full, check here first and ask about other possibilities. Usually there is one ISH at ul. Zwirki i Wigury 95/99 (tel. 22 74 08), on bus lines #128, 136, and 175 towards the airport. Certain years there are also places at ul. Akademicka 5 (tel. 22 30 11; tram #7, 9, or 25), or at **Riwiera,** ul. Warynskiego 12 (tel. 25 49 70). If you've made advance reservations (see chapter introduction), you're all set; otherwise you will be given space, at 80zl per night plus 20zl registration fee. That is, if the hordes of socialist tour groups haven't already descended.

If you have an IYHF card you can try the two **PTSM Hostels,** a notch down in price (20-40zl), but a leap down in quality. The hostel most centrally located is at Smolna 30, right off Nowy Swiat (tel. 26 53 88), but it is dingy, without hot water, and cursed with an 11pm curfew. Use only as a last resort. The other hostel, at Karolkowa 53a, is a more modern one but lies farther out of the center of town. Take tram #10 or bus #105 or 109. Alternatively, you might try camping, which in Poland can either mean the tenting variety or living in a bungalow on a regular campsite. By far the cheapest campground is **Gromada,** on ul. Zwirki i Wigury at ul. Rokitnicka (tel. 46 21 84), where a bungalow bed costs 70zl in a triple, 90zl for a single; tentsites cost 9-18zl and parking spaces 18zl. Registration fees are 11zl per person. Modern facilities (including hot water) and a cafeteria on the grounds. Take bus #128, 136, or 175 towards the airport and watch for the signs on the left.

If it's not the ALMATUR or the camping season, or if everything is full, then there are several inexpensive hotels to try: **Dom Turysty,** Krakowskie Przedmieście 4/6 (tel. 26 30 11) is run by the PTTK and charges 72zl for a dormitory bed and 350zl for a single. **Hotel Druch,** ul. Niemcewicza 17 (tel. 22 48 63) has dormitory beds for 100zl, singles for 280 zl. **Dom Chlopa,** Pl. Powslańców Warszawy 2 (tel. 27 92 51) has singles for 270zl and doubles for 400 zl. If you can convince any receptionist that you are Polish, or if you can get a Polish friend to take the room out for you, the price will drop by 50%.

Another possibility is to approach group leaders and ask if they have extra beds. Usually reservations at hotels are made before the tour sets out and a couple extras are saved. Or try hanging around the hotels at 8 or 9pm, when reservations which have not been confirmed are canceled—if someone has not shown up, you will be able to get a room.

There are also two offices that specialize in locating rooms in hotels or private apartments: **Syrena,** ul. Krucza 16 (tel. 25 72 01), and a smaller bureau in the **Hotel Polonia,** around the corner from the main reception on ul. Poznańska. They'll locate a room for you, but undoubtedly at a price far

higher than a Pole would have to pay; and while they will assure you that
70zl-per-night hotels do exist in Warsaw, they will also assure you that all
such hotels are already filled by the natives. So expect to pay at least 200zl
for a single, and somewhat more than that for a double. Rooms in private
homes are a final resort at about 270zl for a single and 450zl for a double.
The home may be in the suburbs, but if you are interested in living with a
family, the price and inconvenience may be worth it.

One more possibility, if all else fails, is to approach waiters in restaurants
and ask if they know of a place to stay. Sometimes you'll get an offer of a
room if the price is right. And if you have American dollars to pay with, it
will probably be possible to make a good deal, maybe less than $2 per night.

If all this sounds so confusing that you've decided to sleep in the park,
don't. Such activity is strictly taboo in Warsaw these days, and you are better
off pretending to wait for someone in the lobby of one of the best hotels—
they have running water and comfortable armchairs.

Food

A word on inexpensive dining: besides the *kawiarnie* and street vendors,
there are self-service milk bars called **Bar Mleczny,** where you can expect
good dairy and egg dishes at minimal cost. They pop up all over Poland, but
one good branch in Warsaw is at Krakowskie Przedmieście 19, the Univer-
sytecki, open from 7am-9pm, 9am-5pm on Sundays. They are great for
breakfast, and where most Poles go when they have a bite. Self-service
restaurants *(bar, sam bar,* or *samoobsluga)* tend to be very inexpensive, but
you'll often have to eat while standing.

Zodiak and **Smak,** both across the street from the Palac Kultury in the giant
Centrum complex. For 35-40zl you can get a filling meal and the *prasztecik*
(ground meat fried in batter) has become a favorite Warsaw specialty.

Klub Rzemiosla, Restauracja Honoratka at Midowa 14. Through an
impressive, unmarked entryway, steps down to the left lead you into a vaulted
cellar where Polish specialties are served starting at 30zl.

Staropolska, Krakowskie Przedmieście 8. Polite waiters and hearty portions
of well-prepared Polish food for about 25zl. Specialties 65-80zl. Packed at
lunch with hungry Warsawers. Turn left inside the building marked *Kawiarnia.*

Kamienne Schodki, Rynek Starego Miasta. The name means "stone stairs"
and you will find the restaurant tucked away at the corner of the old market
where stone stairs go down to the river. Only one dish, *kaczka* (roast-duck, at
75zl), is served, which solves the problem of what to order. A rich decor of
dark wood, candlelight and stone walls. Not inexpensive, but worth it.

Zlota Rybka, Nowy Świat 7, has moderately-priced fish specialties.

The best deal in town is *lody* (ice cream), sold on nearly every street for 5 zl.
One line worth waiting in is the one outside of **Blikle** on Nowy Świat 35. Here,
a Swiss family has baked the best doughnuts in Warsaw for the last 110 years.

Sights

There is no real city center. Two major boulevards run parallel to the

Vistula River. The more important is Krakowskie Przedmieście, beginning in the **Stare Miasto,** or Old Town. In the north, the **Nowe Miasto,** or New Town, used to be the oldest district in the capital. Destroyed during the 1944 insurrection, it was rebuilt in the eighteenth- and nineteenth-century style. Stop in at the milk bar in the rococo building behind the barbican and admire the painted timber ceiling. The **Rynek** (market place), the **Krasiuskich Palace,** and all of this area's eight churches are well worth visiting. Further south, the Stare Miasto combines monuments like the restored **Royal Palace** and the **Warsaw Historical Museum,** with the special charm of stone stair-cases and vaulted archways. Here nestle antique shops and coffee and wine shops *(kawiarnie* and *winiarnie).* Nearby is the **Plac Teatralny,** where the imposing new opera house stands next to the monument to the heroes of Warsaw. Further along the aleje Ujazdowskie, you come to the **Park Lazienkowski.** The park is hilly and wooded, and shelters several interest-ing eighteenth-century buildings, including a theater in period style and guest house **(Bialy Dom)** where concerts are frequently held. The **Chopin Monument** is the setting for noontime Sunday performances by Poland's greatest artists. The graceful **Palac Lazienkowski,** the focus of the gardens, was the home of the last king of Poland, and is now open to the public daily, 10am-4pm, free Thursdays. Near the palace, at the **Gallery of Sculptures** in the Pomarańczarnia, you can listen to excellent daily concerts of classical music. Tickets are available at the palace ticket window until 4pm, and thereafter at the door.

A thirty-minute bus (#180) or express bus B from Marszalkowska, **Palac Wilanów** offers a less-crowded alternative with fine gardens, an interesting baroque facade, a museum of posters (open daily 10am-4pm, except Mon-days), and a stylish café. You can tour the palace any day 10am-4pm except Tuesday and Wednesday (on Wednesdays the entrance is free and the hours are noon-6pm). Tickets for Sunday tours may be bought in advance at **Syrena,** the Tourist Bureau, Krucza 16. Of particular interest in Wilanów is **Muzeum Plakatu,** the largest poster museum in Europe (open daily 10am-4pm, except Mondays). If you want to buy some of the dynamic Polish designs, try the PTTK office at Rynek 23 (tel. 31 93 06), open 9am-6pm. Poster freaks though, should definitely visit the small shop at the *back* of the **Teatr Wielky,** facing the square. The shop is open from 11am-7pm (6pm on Saturdays) and sells many award-winning designs for the ridiculous price of 20zl. If you're in Warsaw during an International Poster Biennial (the next is 1980), head for the **Zacheta Museum** on pl. Malachowskiego, where you can see the best around for 2zl, 1zl for students.

Although the Jewish community was decimated (only one per cent of the number of Jews who were inhabitants of Poland in 1939 remain), there is still enough support to maintain the **Jewish Historical Institute,** al. Swierczewskiego 79 (in the only old building left on pl. Dzierzynskiego, tel. 27 18 43), which houses an infrequently visited museum on the twentieth-century history of Judaism in Poland. The museum is now hidden behind a new skyscraper on the northeast corner of the square, so you may have to hunt a little.

Evenings

Warsaw's social life is dominated by its *winiarnie* and *kawiarnie*, though other choices do exist. Two of the better *winiarnie* are **Fukier,** in Rynek

Starego Miasta, and **U Hopfera,** Krakowskie Przedmieście 53, beside the Aeroclub. Fukier, 300 years old, is Poland's premier wine cellar, and definitely worth a visit. Ask for *miód pitny* (mead) while you're there; this rich honey wine served either hot or cold is a delicious specialty. Order by the glass (20 zl) or by the bottle. Closes at 9pm, and closed Sunday. As for *kawiarnie,* you are unlikely to have any trouble at all finding a good one. Warsaw is full of them. Most close around midnight. We suggest:

Nowy Świat, corner of Switokrzyska and Nowy Świat. Elegant and interesting, with good pastries. Four rooms on three floors, with a cabaret (occasionally) on the main floor.

Gong, aleje Jerozolimskie 42, has the best *herbata* (tea) in town—about 20 kinds, all made the old slow way. Right behind the LOT office.

Antyczna, pl. Trzech Krzyzy 18. Tucked away in the corner of this busy square. A little noisy, but the terrace is nice. OK if you're in the area.

Gwiazdeczka, Piwna 40, a favorite meeting place of students in the Old Town.

Of course, if wine cellars and cafés are too sedate for your tastes, there are always the student clubs. The best one is new **Stodola,** near the Polytechnik in Mokotów—ul. Stefana Batorego, east of al. Niepodleglości (take almost any bus south). It has good live music in addition to discotheque, *kawiarnia,* bar, and game room. Open till midnight on weekdays, till 3am on Saturdays. Be sure to have some kind of student/youth ID card, preferably the ISIC, but others will do. 15zl with the student ID, 25zl without. There are two seasonal possibilities which unfortunately shut down in July and August— **Dziekanka,** on Krakowskie Przedmieście in the orange building behind the Mickiewicz statue, and **Sigma,** Krakowski Przedmieście 24 in the University, which features a string of gothic wine cellars for drinking and dancing. One of the livelier student discos, open year round, is **Remont,** ul. Waryńskiego 12, in the **Riwiera,** and there is a good jazz club, **Aquarium,** on ul. Emilii Plater opposite the Palac Kultury.

Of Warsaw's fifty cinemas, most show foreign films in the original version with Polish subtitles. Check the cinema listings with daily newspapers or get *WIK,* a monthly guide to Warsaw culture. One movie theater, **Bajka,** at Marszalkowska 136/138, specializes in showing the best Polish films with English or French subtitles. Cinema is extremely cheap, about 12-16zl. It's advisable to buy tickets early in the day for evening shows—cinemas sell out fast.

For those more classically inclined, Warsaw boasts a fine opera company which performs eleven months each year, and an operetta company which fills in during their July vacation. Billboards throughout Warsaw also advertise numerous concert performances, many of them at the Philharmonia. Warsaw also prides itself on its avant-garde theater, and you may well come across a student production in French, German, or even English. The central ticket office for all the city's cultural events is **Syrena,** ul. Krucza 16 (tel. 25 72 01).

Gdańsk (Danzig)

Already in the Middle Ages, Gdańsk was a battleground between the

Polish Kings and the Knights of the Teutonic Order. In 1919, the Treaty of Versailles designated it a "free city." Poland's refusal to cede it to Hitler in 1939 was his pretext for launching World War II, and the story of **Westerplatte** now counts as one of the great tales of Polish heroism. Practically all traces of its Germanic past have been scrubbed from Gdańsk since 1945, and together with its sister cities of **Gdynia** and **Sopot,** it is one of Poland's great national showplaces.

Gdańsk, like Warsaw, was razed to the ground during World War II and rebuilt according to its medieval model. Sopot is a large, tourist-oriented beach resort, and Gdynia is the main center of the port—rather ugly and not worth your time. Boat freaks might like it though—but remember, pictures of ports are illegal. A visit to the Three Cities should probably be divided between sightseeing in Gdańsk and swimming in Sopot. If you can, take some daytrips into the surrounding lake district or along the fishing villages of the coast.

Orientation

The major buildings in Gdańsk are all in the **Stare Miasto** (Old Town) and the **Główne Miasto** (Town Center)—but the actual old quarter and everything of interest is to be found in the latter. The **Kościol Mariacki (Church of the Virgin Mary),** a Gothic fourteenth-century cathedral, dominates the skyline. To reach the church from the city's residential areas, you'll pass through the **Dlugi Targ,** the main square of the restored area, where kings of Poland were greeted by their subjects in medieval times. In the Dlugi Targ is the **Neptune Fountain** where the God of the Oceans surveys this Baltic port. At the bottom of Dlugi Targ, the nineteenth-century Gdańsk Port is now used only by the passenger ships to the sister cities. It's an hour's ride costing 12zl to **Westerplatte,** where the first shots of World War II were fired. Even if you can't take another war memorial, it's an enjoyable trip through the old port.

In Stare Miasto, actually the oldest part of Gdańsk, there's a picturesque fourteenth-century **Millhouse,** and a baroque **Ratusz** (town hall) with a large painting collection inside.

Chances are you'll be able to see the major points of interest in Gdańsk fairly quickly, and if you're visiting in the summer, you'll want to head for the beach in Sopot; the electric train from any station in Gdańsk will take you into the center of town in about twenty minutes (get off at the stop marked Sopot, the middle one of three in the city). Stop on the way at **Oliwa** and have a look at the medieval cathedral just west of the station. From the train station in Sopot, a left turn down the tree-lined street right in front of you, a few blocks walk, and a right at the large church will put you on **ul. Monte Cassino,** a long street, restricted to pedestrians, leading to the beach. You won't have any trouble finding anything in Sopot; just follow the multitudes. Entry to the beach is 3zl (1zl with student ID if you enter by the *molo* (pier))—it's free if you walk five minutes to the right of the pier entrance.

ORBIS: pl. Gorkiego 1 (tel. 31 49 44). Open 9:30am-4pm; another at Sopot, ul. Monte Cassino 33 (tel. 51 10 39), open 10am-5pm.

PTTK: ul. Dluga 45 (tel. 31 47 51), open 8am-4pm.

ALMATUR: ul. Waly Jagiellońskie 1 (tels. 31 24 24 and 31 29 31). The ZAK student club is also in this building.

Accommodations

The number of tourists in Gdańsk in the summer months defies reckoning, and inexpensive lodging may be hard to come by. Check first with **AL-MATUR**. They regularly run one **International Student Hotel** in Wrzeszcz at Wyspanskiego 5a—take the electric train to Gdańsk Polytechnikum and walk north or take tram #8 or 13 from the station. Certain summers they also operate a second hotel at ul. Leningradska 2a or in Wrzeszcz at ul. Pulanki 63/65. The cost is 80zl per night plus 20zl registration. There is one inexpensive hotel called **Jantar** on Długi Targ 19 (tel. 31 62 41) where singles cost 270zl.

There are seven youth hostels in the tri-city area, of varying quality, but mostly bearable. The two most central are both in Wrzeszcz and can be reached by tram #8—ul. Smoluchowskiego 13 (tel. 32 32 16) and ul. Dzierzynskiego 11 (tel. 41 41 08). If none of these work out, try one of the several camp grounds in the area. **Gdańsk-Jelitkowo** on ul. Jelitkowska 23 is somewhat primitive, but large and likely to have a place. The **Sopot-Kamienny Potok**, ul. Sępia 51 (Sopot, tel. 51 00 14), is considerably nicer, but usually overcrowded. Also nice and near the ocean is **Gdańsk-Tourist**, on ul. Karola Marksa in Brzeźno. You pay at the campsite, and though prices vary, they are generally reasonable (campsites are open June-September).

Avoid the IT office on ul. Piwna, which only has places beyond your price range. The **Biuro Zakwaterowań** opposite the Sopot train station arranges private rooms, but also tries to rip foreigners off, so see what ALMATUR can suggest.

Food and Evenings

Gdańsk has a number of good restaurants in the Old Town area. Piwna and Mariacka streets are particularly crowded with inexpensive sit-down places like **Pod Wieżą** at ul. Piwna 51. There is also an excellent specialities restaurant well worth the extra zlotys called **Pod Lososiem**, at ul. Szeroka 54 (tel. 31 76 52). Try their eel. For a good summer meal, we recommend that you sample any of the outdoor places on ul. Monte Cassino in Sopot. Roast pork, done over an open grill, served with french fries is a popular and tasty dish here. For dessert, head over to the cotton candy stands or pastry shops.

The three-town area also boasts several fine discos. In Gdańsk, head for **Kameralna** on Olugo 57 to meet other foreigners. If you're more in the mood for Polish companionship, try the art students at **Flisak** on Chlebnicka Ul. In Gdynia, **Kaprys** is the place to go for fine music, while Sopot's best is all in the warm evening atmosphere at **Alga.**

Daytrips

The coast and lake districts offer lots of possibilities for interesting side trips. **Władysławowo,** 30 km north of Gdynia, is a fine old Baltic fishing village. You can continue across the Mierzeja Helska peninsula and spend the afternoon in **Hel,** a resort town, which can also be reached twice a day by boat from any of the Three Cities. The Baltic's best beach is 50 km to the west at another fishing village, **Leba.** Now in a nature reserve, the Leba beaches are separated from the 20 km-long **Lebsko Lake** by a thin strip of pine-covered sand dunes, including the ruins of a Gothic church and German fortifications. There's a **PTTK Dom** at ul. Pierwszego Maja 6, a PTTK **campground**, with bungalows at ul. Turystyczna 1, and two ALMATUR student homes, **Jantar** and **Gorczyn.**

To the southeast, the fine Teutonic stronghold of **Malbork** (Marienbourg) merits a visit for its fort, which houses amber and ancient arms collections. Further east, 17 km from the Soviet border, is **Frombork,** the quiet village where Copernicus chose to spend the last twenty years of his life. A tour of the walls, cathedral and **Copernicus Museum** should be followed by a trip to the unspoilt coast 1 km to the north.

Lublin

The city of Lublin has lost its sixteenth-century splendor. Half-hearted reconstruction efforts in the **Old Town** leave old Lublin a dusty mess, and the provincial city is grey and has little to offer except a lively student life during the school year. Lublin is, however, more Eastern European in feeling than cosmopolitan Warsaw or Austrian-influenced Kraków.

The sights are few. Enter the Old Town through the **Brama Krakowska** (Kraków Gate), and wander the streets surrounding the ul. Bramova and the ul. Grozna. Much is unfortunately closed for renovation, but in the narrow streets along the main square old Lublin still lives—quiet, shadowy, inward-looking. Past the sixteenth-century monastery, just outside the walls, is the restored **Royal Castle**—unfortunately one of the most botched restoration jobs you're ever likely to see, but still of interest. Lublin's setting on half a dozen hills makes for lots of interesting walks.

The city was also the sight of the **Majdanek Concentration Camp.** Take bus #53 out of town, and get off after about twenty minutes when you see an enormous 4-million-zloty sculptural disaster made of concrete, which commemorates the site of the concentration camp. Now hay is grown between the dark shacks, but the crematorium effectively brings back the gruesome past.

ALMATUR has a hotel in Lublin with the standard services, at ul. Czwartaków 13 (tel. 32044). There is also a **Youth Hostel** in the summer at the Skola Podstowowa, ul. Zuchow (trolley 50/53). Friendly managers, and it seems to be usually empty. The local ORBIS office is at 25/29 Krakowskie Przedmieście (tel. 2 81 53).

Eating shouldn't be a problem—the main street is full of restaurants and cafés. Try **Promién** on J. Dąbrowskiego 3 (tel. 2 58 48) or **Polonia** on Krakowskie Przedmieście for inexpensive (40-50zl) Polish cuisine.

Near Lublin

Although a little touristy, the beautiful Polish renaissance town of **Kazimierz,** on the Vistula River, is worth the visit. The **PTTK** office on the market square will find accommodations for you in bungalows (70 zl) or in hotel doubles (250zl).

A little south of Lublin is **Sandomierz,** another renaissance town set on seven hills. Enter the old town through the **Brama Opatowska.** On the main square is the **Town Hall** (fifteenth century), and further along the east side is the fourteenth-century **Cathedral,** with its baroque façade overlooking the valley of the Vistula. Ask someone for directions to the baroque **Synagogue,** built in 1758. The Synagogue is in danger of being renovated into oblivion (like much of Sandomierz, unfortunately), but should be there in some form or another. Accommodations here present something of a problem. The **Youth Hostel,** W. Flisaków 26 (tel. 563), is usually full in the summer, as is the **Camping** along the Vistula. Check at the **PTTK** office at Rynek 26, or on ul. Krakowska, where they have listings of private rooms for 60-70zl. Leaving from ul. Olesniskiejo is a thirty-minute guided tour of an extensive network of underground passageways through the hill on which Sandomierz is built (15zl). The tour winds up in the *winiarna* (wine cellar) of the town hall. Also inexpensive is the best restaurant in town (50zl), located at Rynek 27, on the first floor of hotel **Cizemka.**

The region between Sandomierz and **Kielce** is known as the **Swiętokrzyskie** (Holy Cross). The towns here aren't particularly interesting, but for campers and hikers the area is ideal. Most towns here have rarely, if ever, seen a Westerner, and don't be surprised if the stares you get from the rag collector or the man with the coal-cart are more suspicious than curious. The mountains themselves (rolling hills, really) are interlaced with well-marked trails and adequate campsites. Buy a map of the area for 10zl in any major Polish city. In the town of **Nowa Slupia,** near the **Jadlowa National Forest,** you can see the remnants of ancient iron mines. A thirty-minute walk uphill will bring you to the fabled **Lysa Góra** (Bald Mountain), supposedly witch-infested. Near the summit stands a twelfth-century abbey—try to go on a cloudy day. Tremendous atmosphere, even with the garbage put on occasionally for the tourists. The abbey has *already* been renovated, so breathe easy. Walk back down the other side to the bus stop at **Huta Szlana** or **Trzcianka,** two wonderful peasant villages. Comfortable haystacks are prepared in late June and late September. This is a great area for a relaxing few days away from Polish bureaucracy and crowds—you may have trouble spending your currency quota, though.

Kraków

Kraków is beautiful! The former capital of Poland was miraculously spared the ravages of both war and renovation, and remains the heart of historical and cultural Poland. The center of Kraków is the **Rynek Glówny** (Market Square), where the **Sukiennice** (Cloth Hall) still stands, a relic of Poland's medieval guilds and today a busy arcade. Flower stands decorate the large plaza around the statue of the poet Mickiewicz, while off to one corner of the square is **Kósciol Mariacki** (St. Mary's Church), boasting two uneven steeples, as well as a fine carved altar inside. From the church's taller steeple there sounds hourly an unfinished trumpet call, the *Hejnal Mariacki,* commemorating the trumpeter of Kraków whose throat was split by a Tartar arrow as he warned the town of a thirteenth-century attack. Also on the Market Square is the **Old Town Hall Tower,** whose summit offers a fine view of the city and whose winding stairs descend to an impressive rathskeller.

The square is encircled by shops and cafés, and Gothic buildings line the surrounding cobblestone streets. One of the most important of these is **Florianska,** leading to an ancient tower-fortress called the **Barbakan,** and to the small but superb collection of paintings at **Zbiory Czartoryskich** ul. Pijarska 8 (tel. 535 16). Open Mon., Tues., Fri., Sat. 10am-3:45pm; Thurs.

noon-5:45pm; Sun. 9am-2:45pm, closed Wed. To the west of the Rynek is
the **Collegium Maius** of the University, whose rooms served the student
Copernicus, and which now houses a reconstruction of an alchemist's labora-
tory and the University Treasury. Open Mon.-Sat. noon-2pm.

The **Wawel,** Kraków's razed fortress, was largely rebuilt in the Renaissance, although parts remain from the tenth century. The **Castle Museum**
(open daily 10am-3pm except Mon., Fri.-Sun. also 4-6pm) also includes
among other riches the world's largest collection of pictorial tapestries. Past
the Wawel are the remains of a Jewish ghetto, **Kazimierz.** Show up at the
450-year-old **Remuh-Synagoga** and you will be given a private tour of the
cemetery in Yiddish and told the miracle of its salvation from the Nazis—
don't forget your hat. Nearby, the **Stara Synagoga,** Poland's oldest, has
been rebuilt from ruins, but little of the fifteenth-century glory remains.
(There are no hours—ring the bell and ask.)

If you can take it, the most moving trip is to the dirty industrial town of
Oświęcim, remembered in history as **Auschwitz.** The concentration camp
has been rebuilt as a national memorial. Open daily from May to September
from 8am-6pm, otherwise until 4pm. If you have time, take the ten-minute
walk which few tourists make, to the main camp Birkenau. It has been left
much as it was when liberated, and there are few more numbing experiences
than standing among hundreds of decaying barracks in the knee-high grass.
You can make the pilgrimage yourself by bus; IT also offers excursions.
There is now a hotel just outside the gates.

Accommodations and Orientation

The **Central Tourist Office** on ul. Pawia 6 (tel. 204 71) provides a free
booklet *Co, Gdzie, Kiedy* ("What, Where, When") which includes a
monthly calendar, all tourist information and a list of hotels by category.
Given the popularity of Kraków in the summer, it may be hard to find a place
by yourself if the International Student Hotel is out of space. The **Central
Accommodation Service "Wawel"** at ul. Pawia 8 (tel. 219 21) will set you
up in a hotel or private lodging for 250-300zl, but try to insist on cheaper
tourist hotels. The **ORBIS** office in the Hotel Cracovia, al. Puszkina 1 (tel.
213 43) will also look for hotel rooms, but it's better to deal with the
individuals on the street at ul. Pawia who offer private arrangements—
cheaper and perfectly legal. If pushed, they will always settle for half the
price initially quoted.

International Student Hotel, an ALMATUR operation, 23 ul. Nawojki (tel.
713 33, 720 22 or 312 31), Bus #118, 126, or 218 from pl. Sawickiej, or
minibus M3 (5zl) from the train station. The hotel has a restaurant, snack bar,
pinball machines, and interesting people. 80zl for students, otherwise around
200zl, plus 20zl registration.

Dom Noclegowy ZNP, ul. Szujskiego 5 (tel. 219 45), is regularly a teachers'
hotel, but during the off-season often has single rooms for around 100 zl. Just
say you've been sent from ALMATUR. A short ride on tram #4 or 12.

Dom Turysty Wésterplatte 15-16 (tel. 238 60). 111zl for a bed in a room of
eight to 250zl for a double room.

Youth Hostels: There are two. The better one is at ul. Oleandry 4 (tel. 388-22 or 389-20) on tram #17 from the station. The second is on ul. T. Kościuszki 88 (tel. 219-51) on tram #2. There are seven **Campingi** with bungalows—check the Wawel booklet and ask them to call for you.

Food

Local specialties sold by street vendors include tasty lumps of *bryndza* (sheep cheese) and *obwarzanki,* somewhat like New York pretzels. For a fuller meal, try the inexpensive *obiad firmowy* (suggested menu—around 25zl) in any of the restaurants favored by students. The most centrally located are: **Stare Mury,** 23 Pijarska; **Pod Krzyzkiem,** Rynek Gl. 39; **Ermitage,** ul. Karmelicka 3; **Pod Temida,** ul. Grodzka 43; **Zywieć,** ul. Florianska 19. All those named are open at least from 9am-10pm. Kraków's best known *kawiarnia* is the **Jama Michalika,** Florianska 45—the room is lined with political caricatures (ask a Pole to explain) and becomes a cabaret in the evenings.

Evenings

Although Kraków slows down a little in the summer, it is still the liveliest town in Poland. The *kawiarnie* and *winiarnie* of Florianska ul. (Jama Michalika #45) are pleasant. For dancing, try **Rotunda** at Oleandry 3, across from the Cracovia or **Jaszczuny** on Rynek 9. If this is not enough, bus #103 will take you out to the student town, where **Pod Przewązka** is open until 2am.

Kraków is also full of first-rate theater, music, and cinema, so check the listings in *What, Where, When,* and head for the **Central Box Office,** ul. Sw. Marka 26.

The Southeast

Southeastern Poland was an Austrian province after 1772, with a Polish Catholic population in the larger towns and an Ukrainian Orthodox and Uniate culture in the villages. The Ukrainians were forcibly transplanted to the Soviet Union after World War II, but the land's architectural and agricultural character has not changed much. The icon-filled wooden Orthodox churches have, for the most part, been preserved; and everywhere the squared-log farmhouses stand with their broad, steep roofs and finely-carved shutters.

Directly south of Kraków, the terrain changes abruptly, as the **Tatry Mountains** rise to 8000-foot peaks, rugged enough for any alpinist. The Tatry, which constitute Poland's share of the Carpathian chain, are the setting for many wonderful mountain walks and climbs. The central mountain town is **Zakopane,** expensive and crowded, but a necessary stop for information and maps at **Tatry Center** on ul. Chramcówki 33 (tel. 43 43). Only a mile or two from town, however, are mountains and trails for all. The least crowded trails are the most distant, and walks up **Dolina** (valley) **Kościeliska** and **Dolina Chocholowska** both lead to hostels which are fine bases for further excursions.

To the East, **Nowy Sącz** is the provincial capital, but its streets have preserved their quaint, baroque character. The museum in the fifteenth-century **Gotycki Dom** is a good place to compare the region's two religions. Here are rooms of seventeenth-century icons next to galleries of Catholic sculpture from the same period. Take bus #8, 10 or 21 to **Stary Sącz,** an older settlement upstream whose streets look much as they did two centuries ago, lined with one story burgher houses. The town's *raison d'être* is the **Klasztor PP. Klarysek,** a convent founded by the virgin Queen Kinga after the Tartars ravaged her country. Around the convent the romanesque fortifications can still be seen, but be careful not to step on the roosters in the courtyard.

Near the Slovak border is the vacation town **Krynica,** which was the pearl of Galician spas ninety years ago. Polish labor unions have taken over the white elephants, but the architecture is well preserved and it's an excellent place to see a Victorian resort. The four-mile hike to **Powroźnik** is rewarded by a thoroughly restored Orthodox church from 1643, with one of the best iconostases left west of the Soviet border. The icons in the churches at **Jastrzębik** and **Berest** aren't quite as old, but are also worth a detour.

Accommodations

PTTK runs eight alpine huts *(schroniska)* in the mountains above Zakopane, and several above Krynica, as well as a **Dom Turysty** in Zakopane. Accessible only on foot, these huts are ideal for the hiker and climber. Check with PTTK in Kraków, ul. Westerplatte 5 (tel. 220 94, 565 64 or 238 60) or in Zakopane, ul. Krupowski 37 (tel. 4707). The Kraków **ALMATUR** office, Rynek Główny 7/8 (tel. 267 08, 259 42) runs the **ZSP Bazy** (student accommodations) every summer; four are conveniently at **Polana Miśkówka, Cyrhla, Czorsztyn** and **Lubań.** The Tatry Center also sells a booklet called *Informator Turystyczny–Zakopane* for 12zl. It lists *all* accommodations in the Zakopane area.

Camping can be found along the roads in the lower cities, and there are hostels in **Zakopane,** ul. Nowotarska 45 (tel. 42 03) and ul. Daszyńskiego 3 (tel. 35 57); **Krynica,** ul. Kraszewskiego 158 (tel. 442); **Nowy Sącz,** ul. Bartego 72/74 (tel. 82 18); **Stary Sącz,** ul. Kazimierza Wielkiego 14 (tel. 59); and **Tarnów,** ul. Konarskiego 6 (tel. 39 20).

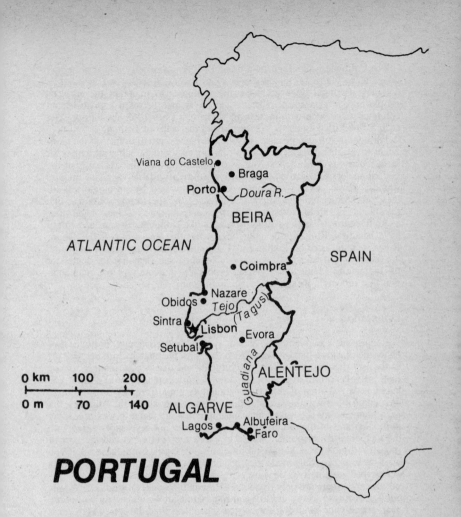

Viana do Castelo

Braga

Porto

Doura R.

BEIRA

ATLANTIC OCEAN

SPAIN

Coimbra

Obidos Nazare
Tejo (Tagus)

Sintra

Lisbon

Evora

Setubal

0 km 100 200

0 m 70 140

Guadiana

ALENTEJO

ALGARVE

Albufeira

Lagos Faro

PORTUGAL

$1U.S. =43escudos(45$50)   1$00=$.023

Community activity retains its meaning in Portugal. The festival—whether a celebration of a saint, child, historic event, or season—is a mainstay of life here. In almost every fishing village, the rowing in of the catch at dusk and the auction afterwards are rituals and semi-festivals that draw a crowd. From the arid, sparser region of the north to the resort areas of the south, the tourist encounters music, impromptu theater, blessings, saints' days, local dances, and bullfights where the "fight" becomes merely an art, and younger "matadors" jump on the horns of the bull rather than try to kill him. And of course, there is always the fair—be it artisan, book, or cattle—and the amusement park, perpetually crowded and noisy. Portugal cooks at least till midnight almost everywhere.

Clearly, the revolution of 1974, which overthrew right-wing Premier-for-life Marcelo Caetano, has not catapulted Portugal into the company of industrial Western Europe. Only **Lisbon, Porto,** and **Coimbra** are real cities.

557

The Portuguese like their own brand of time—a sweetly inefficient crawl which many blame for the current economic woes. It seems that, without its colonies, Portugal does not have the resources to maintain the services people expect of a socialist state, and the debate between capitalists and communists goes on with increasing vigor. Not since 1968 has Europe seen such a flood of political posters as covers the walls of Lisbon.

Portugal is still inexpensive, despite the highest inflation rate on the Continent (over 30% annually). Aside from prices, Portugal's big attraction for most tourists is the beaches. Waves of vacationers are discovering that the 900 kilometers of coastline offer Europe's most affordable vacation. Endless strands, gentle bays, wandering creeks surmounted by promontories: all these are best around the **Algarve.** And since the spectacular cliffs that line the shores are full of caves and hollows, camping out is a cinch; legal, too.

Architecture is best in the north; places like Coimbra, **Braga,** and **Porto** have beautiful Romanesque churches, while the area north of the Douro River contains assorted Roman and Visigothic ruins. In the center and south are massive fortresses testifying to Arab occupation. Lisbon is the center for the indigenous Manueline Style, an exuberant, intricate type of ornamentation that reflects a wealth and vigor long gone.

Orientation

Rooms are clean and convenient, and characteristically Portuguese—either the tiles or a hand-woven bedspread, or a linen table cloth tips you off to the fact that you are indeed in Portugal, and that beauty matters. If you look actively forlorn in pensions and hotels, prices tend to drop. And if you bargain, they'll often plummet. Location does not affect price directly; there are certain cities with higher rates than others (especially in the Algarve), but each municipality sets maximum and minimum allowable prices according to the facilities of the establishment. As you may not necessarily agree with the municipal evaluation, it is best to check the conditions and the cost of showers. Couples should have no problems—when the Portuguese ask if you want a *casal* (marriage bed) they're simply asking if you want one bed (a double bed) for the two of you.

Currently, there are only thirteen IYHF youth hostels *(Pousadas de Juventude)* in Portugal. Those in **Faro** and **Esposende** are only open for part of the year: check your handbook for current schedules. In all hostels, IYHF cards are required. Prices are 50$ per night, 60$ for those over 30, and a 10$ "police tax" is charged the first night only. Linen is furnished on demand without extra charge. The hostel at Rua Andrade Corvo 46, Lisbon, is the only one that charges 80$ per night, 90$ for those over 30. Meals at hostels cost 20$ for breakfast, 70$ for lunch or dinner, but not all hostels provide them.

Portugal has an excellent network of trains connecting most places you'll want to see. Buses aren't much cheaper and may take hours. People assume if you're traveling a long distance you'll take a train, so buses tend to be local with a capital L. In the cities, buses are cheap and go pretty much everywhere; prices correspond to distance. Taxis start at 7$ and usually run about 30$.

The ubiquitous tourist offices (**Turismo**) are extremely helpful, and can usually find you a room. Brave those restaurants which seem never to have seen the hide of a tourist. People are friendly and won't give you a hard time; you will probably be offered help in finding a place to stay. Portuguese currency works officially in escudos and centavos, but the Portuguese often count in 10-centavo units which they call *shtoyns*. Save receipts for each exchange transaction you make, and don't change more than you need; on leaving, you will be allowed to change back only a certain percentage of the amount for which you have receipts; it may be hard to exchange your escudos after leaving Portugal.

As far as language goes, Spanish is a shoe-in both for understanding and being understood. Otherwise, when English seems to fail, French—as the second language of the majority of the educated Portuguese—is always a good second bet. For 45$, you can buy, in any large stationery or book shop, a little *Guide to Conversation: English-Portuguese with Phonetic Spelling*.

Shops in Portugal are usually open from 9am-1pm and then from 3-7pm Mon.-Fri., with only morning hours on Saturdays.

Food

Eating in Portugal is extremely cheap. Fairs (5$ admission) tend to make good places to eat. Look for cleaner stands and then gorge on steak sandwiches *(prego)* or sausage *(chouriço)*, about 30$ each. The specialties of any given stall are sure to be good. Open-air markets are also a good idea—every place you'll visit is sure to have one once a week, most twice. Prices here can be amazingly cheap—especially if you bargain. Get the peculiarly Portuguese potato-derived bread *(broa)* for as little as 12$ per loaf. Try it with *quejo de Alcobaça*, a mild goat cheese; you can get a sizable round for 30$. But Portuguese restaurant prices certainly won't drive you to fairs and markets. A good meal anywhere goes for about 125$ and in small towns and student restaurants complete meals cost about 70$. Fish is always good. Try some *peixe espada grelhado* (grilled swordfish), or *linguado delicia* (sole with bananas—ask for it—pretty much any place with an extensive menu will make it for you). If you're set on meat, stick to pork *(carne de porco à alentejana* is a favorite, made with clams in a coriander sauce) or chicken roasted on a spit *(frango assado)*.

Lisbon (Lisboa)

The *cozido à Portuguesa* of Portugal, Lisbon is a stew comprised of all the Portuguese specialties. The city, settled comfortably in the hills on the right bank of the river **Tagus,** is an exhibition of the various regions, cultures, and histories of Portugal. From port (**Praça do Comercio** district), to medieval ant hill (Old Lisbon—the **Alfama**), to gracious and bending manorial estate (**Praça Marques de Pombal),** Lisbon has charm. Numerous, spectacular churches and museums of this city which has called itself Roman, Moorish, and finally—in 1147, thanks to Dom Alfonso Henriques—Portuguese.

The nearby towns of **Cascais, Estoril, Sintra,** and **Queluz** (among others) combine with Lisbon to provide an even larger range of things to do and see, bits of Portugal to understand.

Orientation

Your first stop should be at the centrally-located **Portuguese National Tourist Office,** at Palácio Foz, Praça dos Restauradores (tel. 36 35 43; open 9am-8pm Mon.-Sat., 10am-6pm Sun.). Ask to see their listing of current prices for all registered hotels and pensions.

If you arrive at **Santa Apolonia Station** (there's a smaller Turismo here you may want to consult), take bus #9 or 9a to the Praça dos Restauradores.

From **Cais do Sodré** station, walk or taxi. If you get in at the **Rossio,** you're there. The information agency at the Rossio itself is helpful for train information. If you come in by air there's another small tourist office at the airport. Open 24 hours. Otherwise, take bus #44 or 45 (the bus stop's a block away) into the center of town. Late arrivals will find that the **Banco Borges & Irmão** at Avenida da Liberdade 9a (tel. 32 10 68) will change money till 11pm. If they're closed, the large hotel down the street (towards Turismo) will also change—as usual—at a lower rate. Normal banking hours are 9am-noon, 2-3:30pm. All banks (including American Express) close down on weekends. So does pretty much everything else on Mondays.

Buses are fairly complicated but will get you anywhere you want to go. The conductor, here as elsewhere, will find you and ask you where you're going (prices vary from 4$ to 11$ according to destination). Use the double-deckers to get to know the city—stairs are at the front of the bus. For **Bus Information,** call 32 79 44. Subways (7$50 a ride) are clean, easy to use, and fast.

As far as daytripping or getting out altogether goes, the trains are probably best. Pick your station according to your direction. Rossio Station handles the Sintra and western lines; Santa Apolonia, all international services as well as the northern and eastern lines; Cais do Sodré is for Estoril and Cascais; and Barreiro, for the southeast and south (the Baixo Alentejo and Algarve). For Barreiro you have to ferry across the Rio Tejo (boats leave from the Praça do Comercio—walk, bus, or taxi)—your ticket will cover the price of the ferry. It's usually a good idea to double-check on schedules. The Rossio is probably the most reliable (tel. 32 62 26), but if you're leaving out of another station you should probably compare schedules with them. Rail-passes work on trains leaving from all stations except the Cais do Sodré, where you have to pay half fare.

Hitching out of Lisbon can be very difficult: tourists, hippies, and the national guard all offer a lot of competition. To travel south, towards the Algarve, take the ferry to **Cacilhas** from the Praça do Comercio, and then start on the Setubal road. For Porto and the North, take bus #1, 2, 41, or 45 to the Rotunda da Aeroporto, and get in line.

The waters around Lisbon have been given over to shipping; the nearest beaches, at **Cascais** and **Estoril,** are 15-20 km away. **Turismo:** Arcadas de Parque 3. Estoril, (tel. 26 01 13). Take the train for about 18$ from the Cais do Sodré. These once-charming fishing villages are now the prime jet-set spots along the Costa do Sol. Beautiful people and their beautiful hotels predominate, but you can still join in the fish action every morning in Cascais. The beach at **Guincho,** not far off, is magnificent in spite of its undertow. For somewhat less crowded swimming, take the ferry to Cacilhas from the Praça do Comercio, and then the bus to the **Costa da Caparica.**

Addresses and Telephone Numbers

Tourist Offices: Portuguese National Tourist Office, Palácio Foz, Praça dos Restauradores (tel. 36 35 43), open 9am-8pm Mon.-Sat., 10am-6pm Sun. **Municipal Tourist Office,** Rua Jardim do Regedor, across Dezembro from the National Tourist Office (tel. 36 79 26). **National Tourist Office Headquarters** (Direcção-Geral do Turismo), Avenida Augusto de Aguiar 86 (tel. 57 50 15), open 9am-6pm Mon.-Fri, 9:30am-1pm Sat., closed Sun.).

Student Travel Organizations: Tagus, Rua Eça de Queiroz 20A; **Europeia,** Rua Rosa Araújo 19 (tel. 56 11 61).

American Express: Star Travel Service, Avenida Sidonio Pais 4-A (tels. 53 98 71 and 56 30 23). Open 9:15am-12:30pm and 2-6pm Mon.-Sat. Smaller office at Praça dos Restauradores 14 (tel. 36 25 01).

Police: Tourist Services, Avenida Antonio Augusto de Aguiar 18 (tel. 55 40 47, emergency number: 115).

U.S. Embassy: Avenida Duque de Loulé 39 (tel. 57 01 02).

Canadian Embassy: Rua Rosa Araújo 2: 6 (tel. 56 25 47).

Swimming Pools: Olympic-sized at Olivais, near Airport. Piscina do Arceiro on the Avenida de Roma is smaller.

Laundromats: At least half a dozen around town. Try Lavimpa, Avenida Paris 22A, near Arceiro (tel. 89 03 88); or at Avenida Estados Unidos da América 105, near Alvalade.

Accommodations

You should have no trouble getting a single for less than 200$ or a double for less than 275$ in a pension or hotel with decent bathroom facilities. Most places will tell you right off that they have only rooms with double beds, but if you take such a room by yourself for more than 70% of the listed price, you're paying too much. The number of different rooms one Portuguese hotel or pension can house is startling, so check two or three in any place that looks okay. Also, for bargaining, the old do-you-have-anything-cheaper ploy often gets you an identical room at a lower price. Disinterest is also always an asset. Rooms are scrupulously clean (true of the following unless otherwise noted) and security and noise aren't a problem. Tall people who are mildly particular should ask for a double bed (*um casal*). And don't let them charge any more for it.

Your best bet is not to concentrate on the area right around the train stations and main avenues. Since prices are officially standardized, only proprietors with many vacancies will be inclined to bargain. Look around Rua da Alegria, which leads from Avenida da Liberdade to Praça da Alegria, for some rather pleasant places often overlooked by the crowds. Rua dos Correiros, between Rua da Assuncão and Rua da Betsga, Rua das Douradores, and some of the other streets around Praça da Figuera, have lots of cheap hotels, some on the grungier side, but all the more likely to have vacancies in high season.

Pensão Imperial, Praça dos Restauradores 78 (tel. 32 01 66). This one's not listed with Turismo. Pretends to have only doubles 180-250$; there's a closet for 130$. Not a bad place, and the location is dead central.

Pensão Restauradores, Praça dos Restauradores 13 (tel. 32 25 24). Currently asking 230$ for singles without shower, 300$ with; 250$ for doubles without shower, 415$ with shower/bath. The old guy loves to haggle; show him this write-up and ask about his one "special room."

Pensão Santa Cruz, Avenida da Liberdade 11 (tel. 32 50 10). Single or double with one bed, 250$. All rooms with private bath.

Pensão do Sul, Avenida da Liberdade 53 (tels. 36 56 47 and 36 54 35).
Singles 210$, doubles 240$, breakfast 25$, shower supplement 15$. Spacious
and light: some of the rooms are huge. Has four annexes. Plenty of beds.

There are three **pensões** at Avenida da Liberdade 141. **Pensão Morais** is a
little squalid, but the prices are good: singles 180$, doubles 220$. The best is
the apparently nameless **Residencial** (actually "Industria Hosteleira Mazarda
Residencial") on the fifth floor. Only doubles with private bath, 300$. If full,
try the sleazy but large **Liberdade** downstairs: singles 260$ and up, doubles
300$ and up.

IYHF Youth Hostel (Pousada de Juventude), Rua Andrade Corvo 46, is
convenient and centrally located, a few blocks from the American Express on
Sidonio Pais. Picoas subway stop is a couple of blocks on Avenida Fontes
Pereira de Melo, or take bus #1, 21, 36, 38, 44, 45, or 49. Not the homiest of
hostels. 80$ per night, 90$ for those over 30, plus 10$ "police tax" on the first
night.

Pousada de Juventude de São Bruno (IYHF), Estrada Marginal, Caxias (tel.
243 50 99). 50$ per night, breakfast 20$. Alleged 10pm curfew, but you
should be able to talk your way around it. In a suburb 15 minutes away by
train.

Camping: Lisbon's municipal campground is called **Parque Nacional de
Turismo e Campismo.** Take the bus to the Parque Florestal Monsanto (tel. 70
44 13). 10$ per person, 10$ per tent, 10$ per car, 4$ for water, 12-25$ for
caravans. Swimming pool. Reasonably-priced supermarket. Otherwise, you
might try the camping at the **Costa da Caporica:** 5km out of Lisbon. Direct
bus from Praça de Espanha (fifteen minutes). Beautiful beaches and plenty of
shade. 15$ per person, tents 15-21$. Bungalows also available. For information on most campsites throughout Portugal call **Orbitur,** Avenida Almirante
Gago Coutinho 25-D (tels. 89 29 38 and 21 23 41), Lisbon.

Beach aficionados might seriously want to consider making **Estoril** their
base; this serene and primarily residential resort town is only twenty to thirty
minutes away from Lisbon and an easy twenty minutes hitching. It should be
easy to find something near the water. **Turismo,** on Arcadas do Parque at the
corner of Rua Melo e Sousa, is very helpful (tel. 26 01 13; open 9am-8pm).
Try the **Pensões Casa de São Mamede,** Estrada Marginal (tel. 26 03 18);
Continental, Rua Joaquim dos Santos 2 (tel. 26 00 50), and Lar de São
Cristovão, Estrada Marginal (tel. 26 09 13).

Food

Unlike hotels and pensions, the prices of restaurants in Lisbon vary tremendously according to location. It is worth your while to walk the extra
block or two away from the Liberdade and Baixa areas.
Also, go with the crowd. If an out-of-the-way place is empty, sacrifice the
quiet for the more crowded one next door. For cheap eating check out the
Mercado Ribeira (open-air market) which runs till 2pm daily except Sundays, outside the Cais do Sodré, (take bus #46 or walk) or the larger market
in Cascais held Wednesdays and Saturdays (a ten-minute walk from the
Railroad Station—ask around). Or try any fair which happens to be around
(check Evenings section). There should always be a restaurant in the area
which will serve you a heaping plate of tuna fish *(atum),* with french fries

and salad, for under 75$. Remember, the price of bread and quality of wine almost inevitably go up with the price of the meal. Bottled wines are cheap, and worth it if you like a good wine with your meal; try some green-white (*mendes* is good) and some *Dao* (white, red or green).

Here are a few real cheapies:

Restaurante Gloria, Rua de Gloria 39A. Main dishes 36-40$, soup 4$. Clean and friendly, with good food.

Rua da Conceição 38 (one of the many nameless establishments). Main dishes 26-45$. Good food, a little less couth than the Gloria, but still hard to beat.

Doce Molotole, Rua de São Jose 59. Try the octopus and potatoes at 40$. Soup 7$.

On the other side of town, mixed in with the restaurant district off the Praça da Figueira, are several other inexpensive restaurants. Directly off the Praça are several good restaurant-cafés on the Rua da Palma and on the Rua da Madaléina.

A Baleal, Rua da Madaléina 277. A big barn of a place with papers instead of straw strewn about. But the fish (particularly shellfish) and the prices (all of them) are good. 65-75$ for a main course. **A Lampreia,** a few doors down at #271, has main dishes at 50-70$.

Restaurante Central, Rua da Madaléina, next to #8, on the corner with Rua de Alfandega. Main courses 40-85$. Better than average *caldo verde* (potato and cabbage soup).

Gambrinus, Rua Portas de Santa Antão. Expensive but the place to splurge for a typical Portuguese meal. Average prices about 225$ for fish and 250$ for meat. 30$ cover charge.

By far the best restaurant area runs parallel to Liberdade, centering on Rua das Portas de Santo Antão and including São Jose and Santa Marta. **Odeon,** at the corner of Rua dos Condes and Portas de Santo Antão, offers a fish filet with rice for 65$ and other dishes for 55-80$. One of the nicest is the moderately-priced **Verde Mar** at Santo Antão 142, where the specialty is the shellfish rice. **Solar dos Presuntos** at #150 is a typical working-class restaurant—meals 100-150$.

Sights

The most interesting area of town, the area of which Lisbon is most proud, is **Alfama.** Originally a Visigothic settlement, this district became during the period of Saracen rule the fashionable, cultured quarter. Its elegance continued under the Arabs, who filled it with costly mansions. After the Christians took it over it became noisy and popular, a favorite residence of fishermen and sailors, and has remained so ever since. The town planners of the eighteenth century didn't dare try to sort out this turbulent brew of balconies, archways, terraces, and courtyards. It would be absurd to suggest an itinerary for Alfama, since you'll get lost no matter what you do. But if you happen to pass by them, look into **San Miguel,** probably the finest of the many churches here; **22 Largo do Salvador,** a nobleman's sixteenth-century mansion; and the busy **Rua de São Pedro.**

Bordering on Alfama is a graceful green square, **Maradouro de Santa Luzia,** which offers a splendid view of Alfama and the harbor below. Further along are the magnificent ruins of **Castelo São Jorge,** the fortress that has dominated the city for almost fifteen hundred years. The ancient walls—really an endless series of stone terraces—enclose lovely gardens, white peacocks, and running water. The views of the city are the best in town. From the center of town, take bus #37 ("Castelo") or trolley #28 ("Graça").

Near the center of town is the **Se,** the Cathedral, worth a visit mainly for its ambulatory and the tombs there, and its elegantly painted Baroque chancel. The **Praça do Comercio,** lined with classical buildings in the best Pombal style, is entered from the north through a massive Baroque arch. A walk straight up from the Praça leads past the old Rossio to the main drag, the **Avenida da Liberdade.** This in turn leads to the big formal **Parque Eduardo VII,** a good place to picnic.

In the quaint old quarter of the **Bairro Alto** are a number of buildings worth seeing. The **Largo do Carmo** is a nice old square surrounded by interesting Baroque buildings, among them the **Archaeology Museum,** inside the beautiful ruins of the late-fourteenth-century **Igreja do Carmo,** destroyed by the earthquake in 1755. Walk along the right side of the church and onto the ramp for a great view of the Baixa. Take the elevator down for 2$50 and you're back in the middle of town. Nearby is the **Igreja São Roque;** the impressive Baroque interior is notable mainly for its rich Italianate chapel of St. John the Baptist, exuberantly decorated with amethyst, porphyry, and lapus lazuli. You might want to enter the **Basilica da Estrela** and admire its fine cupola; otherwise, visit the nearby **Jardin da Estrela,** a pretty, rambling park with a military band that performs late in the afternoon, at the bandstand near the Rua Estrela.

Lisbon's best architecture is on the outskirts of the city. **The Hieronymite Monastery** (Mosteiro dos Jeronimos) is the finest example anywhere of the Manueline style. The intricately carved cloisters are a knockout. From the center of town, take tram #19 and get off at the **Museu Nacional dos Coches,** the Coach Museum. Not far off is the **Torre de Belem,** an elegant and imposing fortress, Gothic inside, Renaissance outside, that lies right at the edge of the water. Both these places look most beautiful towards sunset, when the stone takes on a rich glow the color of white wine.

There are two outstanding museums in Lisbon. The **Museu Nacional de Arte Antigua,** Rua das Janelas Verdes, specializes in the Portuguese Primitives, but also has paintings by Bosch, Dürer, and Holbein the Elder. Like all municipal museums, open 10am-5pm; closed Mondays and holidays. The **Gulbenkian Museum,** Avenida de Berna, has paintings by French Impressionists and contemporary Portuguese artists and some good sculpture, in addition to ancient art. Hours same as above. The **Folk Art Museum,** Avenida Marginal, Belem, has a fairly interesting collection of Portuguese art.

Evenings

The Portuguese are night-owls and Lisbon more than anywhere else makes this absolutely obvious. Café life centers around the *fado*, the Portuguese equivalent of *flamenco* minus the dancing: hauntingly moving, these songs alternately lull their listeners into silence and rouse them into slightly drunken chorusing. Call before you go; there is no fixed night off for *fado*—something's always bound to be open. The **Alfama** is usually the place to hit: bus up (#37 or trolley #28) and then follow the music—there's a lot of it. More *fado* can be found in the **Bairro Alto.**

Parreirnha d'Alfama, Beco do Espirito Santo (tel. 86 82 09). Come for dinner to beat the minimum of 150$. Still, this will buy you a lot and the *fado* is good, the place lively. *Fados* start around 11pm.

O Forçado, Rua de Rosa (tel. 36 85 79). Minimum of 150$ which should buy you quite a bit. Nice cozy atmosphere. Starts earlier than most, at 9:30pm. Still going at 1am. Looks more touristy than it is.

A Lareira, Praça das Aquas Libres 8/10 (tel. 68 96 27). Has the *fado* atmosphere, if not the singers themselves. Mostly records. Minimum 100$, dinner for 250$ if you're careful (Main dishes 180$ and up).

O Caruncho, Rua Alexandre Ferreira 2-2a (tel. 71 08 78). A nice place if you're really out to discover what it means to be a Lisbonite. Action starts around 1am in this dimly-lit music-filled spot. Records only. A 60$ minimum should cover two beers.

The Lisbon Amusement Park (Popular Fair): Filled with Portuguese of all ages, this throwback to the '50s cooks every night till 1am May through September. Take the metro to Entre Campos. Subway and fair shut down at 1am. Rides 5$, bigger ones 20$. And there's a currency exchange here, also open till 1am.

Fairs: *May and June.* There's a three-week book fair in Praça dos Restauradores, open till near midnight. *July and August.* The Cascais fair: Despite touristy appearances, the prices here are as right as you're prepared to make them. Bargaining's the name of the game—otherwise just looking is fun and the food is cheap. Don't miss (here or at any fair you may hit in Portugal) *fretaras,* the Portuguese doughnut—light and just cooked; or the freshly-baked bread from the ten-foot square Portuguese oven.

There is a **casino** in Estoril seemingly made for students. Entrance 40$ or 35$ depending on what you want to do. Incredibly low minimum bids. And very few tourists. Be prepared to prove you're over 21.

Discotheques: Rumor has it that the best dancing spots are **Stone's** and **Ad Lib.** The latter is on Rua Rosa Araújo, but both are publicity-shy, eschew signs, and cultivate a word-of-mouth clientele. High minimums (250$ at Ad Lib, 500$ at Stone's) are waived at the manager's whim. Ask any taxi driver to take you to either.

Concerts: Every night in June, and somewhat less often the rest of the summer, there are folk concerts and dance performances in Cascais, either off the fishing beach or in the bull ring near by. Also, classical and jazz concerts are given throughout the summer by the Gulbenkian Foundation. (Again, Turismo can help you with all this).

Daytrips

About 45 minutes away from Lisbon, **Queluz** is a pleasant place to spend an afternoon. Take the train (Sintra line) or subway and then bus. A pink puff, Portugal's Versailles, this eighteenth-century palace encloses a beautiful Moorish garden and endless rooms richly furnished in the unmistakable Portuguese style. Catch the ceilings and walls which look three-dimensional but aren't—a favorite Portuguese trick. (Entrance 5$, open 10am-5pm except Tuesdays). If you feel expansive, there's an excellent restaurant in the palace which will run you at least 170$. If your pocket is up to it, it's worth it.

Take a bus ride to **Cabo da Roca,** and be awarded (for 15$) a certificate written in medieval script which will attest that you have now set foot on the westernmost point in Europe. The view from the lighthouse here is magnificent as are all the views on the bus ride up. Climb down to one of the surrounding and secluded beaches. Keep hunting till you find one for yourself.

Sintra is the palatial paradise of Portugal. Palace upon palace upon palace. Make an effort to catch the market (fruit, cheese and flea—one of the biggest in Portugal) the second and fourth Sundays of each month. And bargain. Prices can go down as much as 50% here, as elsewhere in Portugal. (Take the bus to the **Feira São Pedro**—7$50). If you feel like treating yourself, stroll up (around half an hour) to the government-run restaurant at the palace of **Seteais** (eighteenth century) for a four-course Portuguese gourmet meal. 250$. Don't miss the hors d'oeuvres.

Taxi or hitch (this may be hard) up to **Pena,** an incredibly massive yet delicate grey palace, built in the mid-nineteenth century. Then take your time and walk down through the adjoining park. (This or the **Parc de Monserrate** next door makes a good place to picnic.) Also visit the **Palácio Real,** built during the late fourteenth and early fifteenth centuries, and the **Moorish Castle.** For information, check with **Turismo** at Largo Rainha do Amelia 3-A and 3-B, across the street from the Palacio Real (tel. 98 11 52). A taxi for the morning which will take you to the palaces and back will cost, if you bargain first, no more than 380$. Definitely try for less.

Northern and Central Portugal

Apart from Lisbon and the Algarve, Portugal is still virgin territory for vacationing students. The climate in the north, mild all year round, is not hot enough until late July to attract the beach crowd. The towns are also shabbier than those further south—**Porto,** for instance, is as ugly an urban mess as you'll find anywhere in Europe. The roads and hitching are the worst in the country. But the rewards are many: a lion's share of the country's historic monuments, the most colorful of *romarias* (popular pilgrimages) and folk festivals, and the best wine—including your old wine-and-cheese party favorite *Mateus*.

Viana do Castelo

You won't know why Viana is known as the garden city of Portugal until you climb **Monte de Santa Luzia.** There's a convenient little funicular most of the way up (**Elevador de Sta. Luzia,** Avenida 25 do Abril; open 9am-8pm, 4$ each way). If you have the time, walk the 4 kilometers of gently rising, twisting road, surrounded by flowers and shrubbery. It leads to a perfect little **basilica** with oversized rose windows. After the walk, you deserve lunch, or at least a swim (20$) at the four-star Santa Luzia Hotel just above and behind the church.

Besides gardens, Viana is known for its colorful folklore traditions. A good time to see these is during the famous **Romaria de Nossa Senhora da Agonia,** a non-stop celebration with bullfights, fireworks, fairs, costumed processions, and dancing late into the night (third week in August). For a close look at local handicrafts, visit **Somartis,** half a kilometer north of the city center on Rua de Monserrate. Viana's **Municipal Museum** (5$ entrance) housed in the Palace of the Barbosa Marcieis, has an especially good collection of Portuguese 16th-19th century ceramics.

Orientation

The **Train Station** *(estaçaõ)* lies to the north of the town center. Across the Avenida da Carreira, on the corner to your right, is the **Post Office** *(correio;* open Mon.-Fri. 9am-7pm). Walk a block to your left, turn right on Candido dos Reis. There, inside the Palacio dos Tavernas, you'll find the **Turismo** (tel. 22620; open 9:30am-12:30pm and 2:30-6pm, closed Sun. afternoons).

Accommodations and Food

Finding a room should be no problem except during the festival in the third week in August. Cheap restaurants are also abundant.

Pensão Viana Mar, Av. dos Combatentes 215 (tel. 23054). Nice place. Singles 195$, doubles 315$, 425$ with shower in room. All prices include breakfast.

Pensão Residencial Laranjeira, Rua General Luiz do Rego 47 (tel. 22261). Singles 195$, doubles 315$. Prices include breakfast. Get a room with a terrace.

Hotel Santa Luzia, Monte Sta. Luzia (tel. 22193). Really not so expensive for one of the most beautifully located four-stars in Portugal. Singles 812$50, doubles 875$.

Campground at Cabedelo Beach (tel. 23243), where the swimming is very good. There's another inexpensive camping ground further away at **Orbitur** (tel. 22135).

Restaurant Regional Alambique, Rua. Mauel Espregueira 82. Here's the splurge you've been promising yourself at prices you can actually afford. Elegant dining, a choice of regional specialties, and it shouldn't add up to more than 225$.

Café Sport, Rua dos Manjoxos 2-10 (tel. 22177). Try the *Lulas à Bordalesa* (baby squid in wine sauce, with rice); the *sopa da peixe,* a spicy fish soup, is delicious and only 12$50.

The Costa de Prata

Here's the "kaleidoscope" all brochures have been promising you. From the cliffs of **Nazaré** to the dunes of **Peniche,** you'll find some of the prettiest landscape, finest beaches, and best-preserved fortresses anywhere.

São Martinho do Porto is a freshly-painted village on a perfect cove. This town is jammed in July and August; but go in June, and you'll be the only tourist in town. **Turismo** is at the northern end of the street running along the beach. There is no fixed address, the director ruefully explained, since the name of the street keeps changing. She called it "Avenida Marginal," but the freshly painted sign said "Avenida 25 de Abril." (Hours 9:30am-12:30pm and 2:30-6:30pm daily. July through September 9:30am-11pm).

One of the most beautiful IYHF **hostels** anywhere is only 4 or 5 km away. Up on a hill above the neighboring **Alfeizerão,** the **Pousada de Juventude** (tel. 98106) is clean and rustic with polished wood floors, acres of garden, and exceedingly friendly managers. Breakfast with eggs(!) costs 20$, lunch or dinner 70$. Accessible from São Martinho by direct bus, or get a bus to Alfeizerão and walk up the path (about 25 minutes). **Self-Service Samar,** centrally located on Largo Vitorino Froes in São Martinho, offers large portions, low prices, and you can see what you're getting.

After dinner, climb up the steps behind the last house on the wharf for a view of the tranquil cove and sparkling beaches inside the bar, and the waves flinging themselves at the iron-red bluffs outside.

Peniche, a walled town, hard-pressed by encroaching sand dunes, is set amidst rolling hills, poppy fields, and windmills. There is a **Youth Hostel** (IYHF) on the offshore island, **Isla Berlenga.** The boat makes only three or four round trips per day, and none when the seas are rough. The journey takes you by islands, reefs, and marine caves. Tickets are sold at a tiny cabin on the dock, by the Largo Ribeira. **Turismo,** Rua Alexandre Herculano, is hidden in a park near a Sacol gas station.

Obidos, 10 kilometers inland, is a flower-hung medieval village, with perfectly preserved ramparts, a castle, and two old churches. **Turismo** is located near the Church of Sta. Maria, on Rua Direita (open 9:30am-12:30pm and 2-7pm; closed Sat.).

Except for the Hieronymite Monastery in Lisbon, the Gothic-Manueline monastery at **Batalha** is the most magnificent in Portugal. The austere and lofty simplicity of the lines somehow works well with the Flamboyant ornamentation, particularly in the largest of the **Royal Cloisters.** The hamlet itself has nothing to recommend it, so plan to visit only for a few hours. Frequent buses come here from Leiria (sixteen minutes, 18$), and from Lisbon (three hours, 130$). **Turismo** is on the shopping mall at the exit from the highway (tel. 96180). Hours 9:30am-12:30pm and 2:30-7pm every day except Sun., when it closes at 6pm.

Coimbra

Surrounded by the rice fields and pinewood forests of the **Beira Litoral** province, Coimbra is a beautiful town of steep streets built in tiers above the **Mondego River.** No city in Portugal, with the exception of Lisbon, can compare with this university town in cultural and historical importance.

The University offers courses for foreigners during the school year. For information, write to the Secretariado do Curso de Lingua e Cultura Portuguesa para Estrangeiros, Faculdade de Letras, Coimbra.

Turismo: Largo da Portagem (tels. 23 79 9 and 23 88 6). Open 9:30am-8pm Mon.-Sat., 10am-12:30pm and 2-5:30pm Sun. and holidays.

Post Office: Rua Nicolau Rui Fernandes. Open 9am-7pm Mon.-Fri. 9am-noon Sat.

Late Currency Exchange: Edificio Chiado, Rua Ferreira Borges 87. Mon.-Fri. 3:30-7pm; Sat. 9:30am-1pm and 2:30-7pm; and Sun. 10am-12:30pm.

Accommodations

High season is rough. Turismo will help out, if necessary. The cheapest of all are the places that say simply *Dormidas*. If you get in late, knock loudly and wake them up.

Pensão Universal, Avenida Emidio Navarro 47 (tel. 22444). Singles 195$, doubles 315$. With toilet and shower 230$ singles, 370$ doubles. No breakfast.

Residencial Balada do Mondego, Avenida Fernão de Magalhães 446. Singles 150$, doubles 200$, no extra charge for shower/bath. High above the street, on fourth floor, with full-wall window balconies, but you still get the noise of traffic and stray dogs below.

Food

Rua Direita has a dozen miniature *Almoço-Jantares;* these are exclusively local spots. At cafés, try a *galão* (the Portuguese *café au lait*), and a *quejada,* a delectable cheesy pastry.

Zé Manel, Beco do Forno 12 (tel. 23790). In a tiny alley off Rua da Sota; Largo da Portagem. A troglodyte's delight. Walls covered with trash—old weapons, broken guitars, game trophies, including a duck's head with blue eye-liner, and a boar's head with a sign *Beiza me na boca* ("kiss me on the mouth"). Good food, cheap, generous portions, and the owner's a stand-up comedian. Open noon-3pm and 5-10pm daily, closed Mon.

O Alfredo, Avenida João des Regras 32 (tels. 25800 and 23288). Just across the river from the center of town, an orange-sided building under a huge "Sonap Motor Oil" sign. Specialty is *cozido à Portuguesa,* and good *paella* at 200$. Expensive, but highly recommended.

Sights

The first thing to see in Coimbra is the **University.** The view from the balcony of the Old University is the best in town. If you like Baroque ornamentation, the nearby **old library** *(biblioteca)* will blow your mind. Hours are 10am-12:30pm and 2-5pm; you have to press the button to get in, and tip the guide on your way out—5$ seems about right. When you visit the University, stop by the **student bar** on the second floor of the main building for a drink.

The **Machado Museum,** nearby on Rua Sta. Miranda, has, among other collections, the best sculpture in Portugal. The *azulejos* (glazed tile) friezes all around the arcaded gallery, depicting scenes of court life, exploration, and hunting, are best viewed from the windows on the second floor. As you pass by the balcony, notice the variety of flora growing out of the old red tile roofs below: yellow, purple, green, and gray mosses and lichens, and thousands of delicate white flowers. Open 10am-1pm and 2:30-5pm. Closed Mon.; entrance 5$, free to students.

Evora

Evora is surrounded by miles and miles of arid land dotted with tough little cork and carob trees. It is a diminutive city with a glorious history of being coveted by a succession of empires. The inner walls, the aqueduct, and graceful temple to Diana recall an early Roman fortified town. The walls were reinforced by the Visigoths, and then by the fourteenth-century Burgundian Dynasty; after liberating Evora from the Spanish in the seventeenth century, the Portuguese further strengthened the walls, especially the part which now borders the public gardens. The long tenancy of the Moors, from the eighth to the twelfth century, is suggested by the ornamental arches connecting white-washed houses across narrow, cobbled streets, and by balconies and grillwork hung with potted plants and caged canaries.

One of Evora's little surprises is the **Capela de Ossos** (Chapel of Bones) in the **Igreja de São Francisco** (entrance 2$50). Above the door, an inscription reads: "*Nos ossos que aqui estamos/ Pelos vossos esperamos*" ("We bones who are here await yours."). As you enter, the empty sockets of the hundreds and hundreds of skulls are trained on you; every inch of wall space is paneled, every arch and flourish, every column and capital built with human bones.

Ten days of festivities celebrate the arrival of summer in Evora, with the **Feira de São João** (June 23 through July 2). The climax, with bullfight, fireworks, and dancing all night, is the feast of São Pedro (June 29).

Orientation

If you arrive by train, you'll have to walk almost a kilometer to the center of town. Go up Rua de Dr. Barohona, which turns into Rua da Republica and leads to the central square, Praça do Giraldo. Here you'll find **Turismo**.

Turismo: Praça do Giraldo 76 (tel. 22671). Open 9am-1pm and 2-7pm daily; in the winter open on Sun. only, from 10am-2pm.

Post Office *(Correio):* Praça do Sertorio. Open Mon.-Fri. 9am-7pm, Sat. 9am-12:30pm. Closed Sun. Telegraph: (tel. 07910).

Bus Station (Rodoviaria Nacional): Rua da Republica (near Igreja de São Francisco), (tel. 2080029). There are five buses daily to and from Lisbon; the express leaves Evora at 9:50am and arrives in Lisbon at 12:40pm. The express from Lisbon leaves at 2:10pm and arrives at Evora at 5pm. 144$ each way.

Accommodations and Food

Pousada de Juventude (IYHF), Rua da Corredoura 32 (tel. 22959). Breakfast 20$; lunch and dinner 70$ each; special macrobiotic meals available for 30-40$. Non-residents may eat here if residents have ordered meal. Manager speaks English.

Pensão-Restaurante "Os Manueis," Rua do Raymundo 35 (tel. 22861). Singles 165$ and up, doubles 250$ and up. The restaurant below serves good meals, with main dishes 65-85$.

Cooperativo, Rua d'Aviz 87. An experimental co-op run by young student types, where you can get a good stuffing for 65$. Only 80 yards from the Hostel, going away from the center of town.

The Algarve

It's been a while since the beaches of the Algarve were anyone's well-kept secret. The skyline at Praia da Rocha has come to resemble Miami Beach; and toy villages for the rich, like Eurotel, just west of Faro, are harbingers of more to come. The rich also have brought their prices—in a country plagued by a 30% rate of inflation overall, this region sets the pace.

The Algarve remains a land of attractions unrivalled in Iberia: more sun than the Riviera, Costa Brava, or California; a steady breeze to keep temperatures bearable; 200 kilometers of perfect beaches; with long, open stretches in the east, rocky coves and red cliffs to the west, and fine gold sand and crystalline water everywhere; and folk festivals celebrated with a gusto that might just reflect a determination to preserve a traditional identity despite the cosmopolitan trends. Nor has it all been sold: to the west, especially, you still stand a chance of finding your own little beach, and there are villages between the towns where not a word of English is spoken.

It is not too hard to get around the Algarve. Hitching here is the best in Portugal—which is not saying a whole lot. **Rodoviaria Nacional** has local buses everywhere, with convenient schedules and low prices. From Ayamonte on the Spanish border to Lagos, there are two daily expresses (200$). The bus from Lisbon to Albufeira takes four hours and costs 350$. Trains are cheaper but much less convenient: Ayamonte to Lagos costs only 136$; Lisbon to Albufeira takes five hours and costs 227$. You can fly from Lisbon to Faro for 840$, no student discounts. Faro is a few kilometers away. There are no buses to the town but the taxis charge a flat 60$ and you can split it. Faro Beach is about 3 kilometers away, in the opposite direction; it's one of the most crowded beaches in the Algarve.

Once arrived, you'll have an easy time of it. A growing colony of Englishmen who have forsaken their rainy homeland has established English as a second language. And the tourist offices, although not up to the standards of their Spanish counterparts, will provide you with enthusiastic pamphlets. The food, especially fish, is generally very good. Beyond the ubiquitous grilled sardines, specialties include *caldeirada,* a chowder of different varieties of fish and shellfish, potatoes, and tomatoes, all flavored with onion and garlic; *cataplana,* a combination of clams, ham, and sausage, flavored with onions and paprika and all cooked in a double pan; squid, often cooked in its own ink; cod, cooked literally hundreds of different way; and *carne de porco à Alentejana,* pork marinated in wine and cooked with clams in a coriander sauce. The local wines, especially white, are full-bodied and robust; *Cartaxo* is a cheap dependable brand.

If you're staying for a month or more, you might look into renting an apartment. Rates have skyrocketed, and it's more frequent to pay 30,000$ for a 4½-room apartment than 15,000$. But with a little leg work, you should come upon something that—split three or four ways—will be a lot cheaper and more comfortable than a hotel; and you'll save quite a bit cooking your own meals.

A good thing to pick up is the **Freedom of Algarve Card,** free at Turismos in the larger towns. This nifty card will give you discounts on a number of restaurants, free entry to several discos, and a sense of identity.

Faro, the province's largest town, is not worth visiting unless you fly into the airport. The dockfront garden park, **Jardim Manuel Bivar,** is the most pleasant spot in town. At the end, near the Arco da Vila (note the stork's nest atop the gate) is **Turismo,** on Rua da Misericórdia 8-12 (tel. 25404, open daily 9am-8pm). If you're staying overnight, you might treat yourself to the **Casa Lumena,** Praça Alexandre Herculano 27 (tel. 22028). Formerly a town mansion owned by a sardine magnate and currently run by a friendly Englishman, Ray Tomison, it's a bit high priced for a shoestring budget, but still reasonable: singles around 450$, doubles 825$, including breakfast and dinner. All rooms have private baths. Even if you don't stay here, stop at their **English pub** or the trellised **Grapevine** for a drink. You might also try the **Pensão Algarve,** Rua de Francisco Gomes 4 (tel. 23346). All rooms, whether occupied by one or two, are 265$; ask to see a few, some are much nicer than others. Showers 30$. Lastly, there is a **Youth Hostel (IYHF)** at Rua Professor Norberto da Silva 30, open from July 1 to December 30.

Faro has two good discotheques. **Scheherazade,** in the Eva Hotel on Avenida da Republica, the more conservative one, occasionally has *fado* nights (120$ minimum). Hotel Faro's **Kontiki,** on Rua da Marinha, is a bit heavier, rumors of drug use and so on. 200$ admission.

Sagres, on the extreme southwestern cape, is as yet unspoiled by the sort of traffic you'll find in the east. The sea seems to have taken great chomps out of the land, as precipitous cliffs rise all around the jagged inlets. Sagres has two beaches, jewels. Other beaches are found up and down the coast. The approach to the **Fortaleza** (Fortress), built by Prince Henry the Navigator out on the promontory, is awesome. Leaving behind the gardens and brightly painted houses at the edge of the village, you pass through fields of windblown cactus and desert flowers. Once the home of a school for navigation where Vasco de Gama, Magellan, Dias, and Cabral studied, the fortress is now a **Youth Hostel (IYHF),** Promontório (tel. 64129), run by a temperamental curmudgeon who calls himself "the warden." If you have the energy, get together with some people at the Hostel, and use the (rather inadequate) facilities there to prepare a feast of *paella,* with mussels, crabs, and limpets collected off the rocks, and a fish or octopus bought at the daily Sagres **fish auction** (9-10am and 3:30-7pm).

Frequent buses connect Sagres with **Lagos,** 32 kilometers east (40$). Aside from the very center of town, which has been developed by a resident English enclave, the streets are not pleasant. Follow the arrows to **Turismo,** on Largo Marquez de Pombal (tel. 63031). The center is fresh, cheerful, and crowded in high season, but the prices aren't too bad. **Pensão Caravela,** Rua 25 de Abril 16 (tel. 62949), has singles for 165$, doubles for 260$, 300$ with shower; breakfast included. Two **campgrounds:** the one at Praia dona Ana, Park Turismo (tel. 62035) is better than Campo de Trindade (tel. 62931). Despite generally high restaurant prices, you can get by for about 100$. Rua 25 de Abril has several possibilities.

In Lagos, you must see the **Igreja de Santo António,** and the adjoining **Regional Museum.** The church's modest exterior belies an eye-shattering interior. Every appalling inch of its walls is gilt with gold paint. The ceiling is done in the usual false perspective. See if you can spot the cow and the dog in the upper balcony. The museum (3$ entrance) has a surprising variety of little collections. Aside from the usual costumes, weapons, and handicrafts, there is the best collection of weird animal fetuses in the Algarve.

The beaches at Lagos are typically excellent, but crowded. You may as well see **Praia dona Ana;** its sculpted cliffs and grottoes are featured on half the postcards of the Algarve. The place is crawling with little kids and sweater vendors. You can get a 45-minute motorboat cruise along the shore for 200$. See if you can get the boat man to find you a secluded spot and pick you up in a few hours. Watch out for the rising tides, though.

Budget travelers will probably want to skip the over-developed **Praia da Rocha.** If you're traveling to **Albufeira** by train, you'll have to get off at Ferreiras, 8 km inland, and grab a local bus. The last hold-out of the Moors in southern Portugal, Albufeira has preserved and cultivated a heritage of graceful Moorish architecture. It is very popular with students, and its fine beaches are the last of the rocky coves as you go east.

The center, despite crowds and construction, is delightful. Local artisans spread their crafts for sale on the walls of the tropical park in **Engenheiro Duarte-Pacheco Square.** Off to the side, there is an open-air fruit-and-vegetable market. The Avenida 5 de Outubro, a block away, is the main drag, and everything essential is clustered together near the tunnel blasted through the rocks to the beaches. **Turismo,** Avenida 5 de Outubro 5 (tel. 52144) is open every day from 9am-8pm. The **Post Office** is next door. A sign indicates **Pensão Silva,** with doubles at 250$. Another cheap place is **Pensão Residencial Albufierense,** Rua da Liberdade 18-20 (tel. 52079) with singles at 250$ and doubles at 400$, including breakfast. Above the tunnel is the discotheque **O Pescador Boite,** belonging to the Hotel Sol e Mar. This place hops from midnight to two (closed on Mondays), good rock, and fancy strobe. Admission is 250$ and includes two free drinks. Or stop by **Sir Harry's Bar,** Largo Engenheiro Duarte-Pacheco 38A. A blackboard posts news headlines in English, including the latest cricket scores. **Club 7½ Disco,** on Largo Cais Herculano near the eastern ''Fisherman's Beach,'' is free to Freedom of Algarve Card holders, except on Saturdays (admission normally 300$).

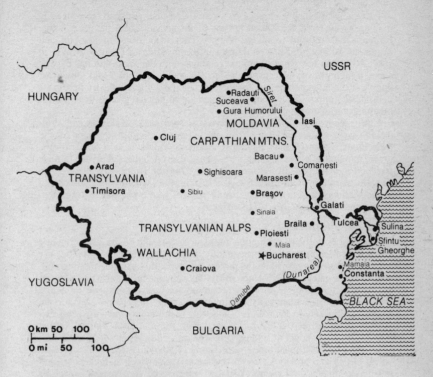

ROMANIA

$1 U.S. = 12 lei   1 lei = $.083

The massive squares and towers of the socialist state and the strong emphasis on industry are as visible in Romania as in her Balkan neighbors, but they have done little to spoil the serenity and lush alpine beauty of the countryside. The fortified towns of **Transylvania** still look like woodcuts of medieval Germany, and the monasteries of **Moldavia** rest amid green hills practically untainted by smokestacks. In the larger towns, modern apartment and factory districts ring the old quarters, but usually the center has been left its gingerbread government buildings.

As her name suggests, Romania has Roman antecedents. In the first and second centuries, Romans and Dacians intermarried and their offspring, the Romanians, retained their identity despite continuous migrations into Romania from Asia and the other Balkan states. Modern Romania began in the mid-nineteenth century when Moldavia, **Wallachia,** and part of Transylvania were united under a Romanian king. Following the Hungarian debacles in World War I, Romania took control of all of Transylvania and assumed roughly her present shape.

Politically, Romania pursues a "neutral" course and has been steadily moving away from the Soviet sphere of influence. Since the late 1950s, Romania has refused to allow Warsaw Pact maneuvers on her soil and Romanian soldiers did not participate in the invasion of Czechoslovakia in 1968. Romania has good economic relations with the West and has experienced a high growth rate during the last ten years. It is often said, however, that the Romanian people pay for their foreign policy and industrial progress in domestic repression and poverty, which are somewhat greater than in most other Eastern European countries.

Until recent times, the purely Romanian provinces, Moldavia and Wallachia, were more backward than the Transylvanian settlements of the meticulous Saxons and Hungarians. Northern Moldavia is a land of soft, green mountains enclosing both delicately carved houses and the famous frescoed monasteries. In the southeast, the **Danube Delta** in Wallachia is a peaceful paradise of willowy forest, river branches where water birds stand in the shallows, and fascinating fishing villages where you can be taken into the depths of the marshes by fishermen.

Practical Information

Romania is actively promoting tourism as a result of the government's craving for hard currency. Consequently, the regulations and formalities are becoming more liberal, while the prices and the facilities are developing with considerable speed. So, while the thirty-day visa is a mere formality (free of charge and no photo required, whether obtained at a consulate or at the border), there is a mandatory minimum exchange of $10 per day for the length of your stay in Romania. It is getting distressingly easy to spend that amount or more, especially if you deal with the **National Tourist Office (ONT),** which is adept at finding supplements and taxes to add to your bill. ONT has offices in most towns and resorts of Romania (local branches are called **OTT**) and provides a room-finding service as well as local tours and ticket sales for cultural events. Usually, some of the staff speaks French or English, but if you insist on the cheapest, they rarely understand you. Unfortunately, the **Youth Tourist Bureau (BTT)** officially handles only tour groups of ten or more. They are nevertheless friendly toward individual travelers, and will provide what advice and help they can. The BTT season is from May 25 to September 15, depending on the weather and university schedules. Accommodations are least crowded at the beginning and end of the season, so if you're in Romania at these times, BTT may just find you a place to stay.

As in all Eastern Bloc countries, hotel prices are regulated and jacked up for Westerners by the government. The cheapest alternative during July and August is the hostel *(caminul de studenti)*. These exist in all university towns—some are run by BTT, some by ONT, but the location changes yearly. So inquire (persistently) at BTT and ONT offices, or ask students near the university. Then arrive at the hostel as early in the day as possible. A bed should cost no more than 25 lei.

Category I hotels are expensive, while category III hotels are extinct, which leaves you with the generally clean and straightforward category II hotels. Singles cost around 130 lei and doubles around 220 lei, with breakfast but without shower.

If you are traveling by road, you will see motels in many scenic spots, as well as at some busy crossroads. Motels are usually inexpensive, running 30-50 lei per person in bungalows, or in modern dorm-like buildings. Don't hesitate to stop and ask if there is room.

It is no longer legal to stay in the home of a Romanian unless he or she is a "first-degree" relative. The fines if you are caught are stiff, both for you and your host—but parties have been known to last all night.

Camping is probably your least expensive option in Romania. If you have your own equipment, you can, with some discretion, pick your spot and pay nothing; or stay in one of Romania's 150 campgrounds, many of which are open year round. A lot of them also rent bungalows for 30-70 lei per person per night.

The train system in Romania centers on Bucharest, and you often have to change once or twice to get on a main line from Bucharest when you are traveling between two of the minor towns. *Rapid* trains are the fastest, *accelerat* trains the next best, and for both of these you pay a small supplement. *Personal* trains stop *everywhere* and go at a snail's pace; avoid them at all costs. They are usually filthy, always packed, and offer little in the way of local color. Whenever you travel by train in Romania you can often save quite a bit of money by doing the following: get on the train with no ticket and sit in a first-class compartment. When the conductor comes for your ticket, tell him you have none. He will ask you out into the corridor where you will discreetly hand him half the price of a second-class ticket, which he pockets. Romanian students all do this and it is so widespread that it is virtually fool-proof. If you don't speak Romanian, the whole scenario can be successfully carried out in sign language. Don't ever buy an international ticket. Travel only to the border and buy a new ticket on the other side. Romania charges a huge fare if you buy a ticket to another country.

Bus service is almost entirely local, and only good for seeing specific areas like the monastery district in Northern Moldavia or the Black Sea Coast. Look for the *autogara* (bus station) in each town.

The national airline, **Tarom,** is an inexpensive alternative for longer trips. From Bucharest, one way to Constanţa is 142 lei; to Suceava 226 lei; and to Tulcea 147 lei. The **Airport** is only ten minutes from Bucharest center. Note that luggage must not weight more than 22 pounds on domestic flights.

Although domestic trains, planes and buses are cheap, Romanians themselves frequently hitchhike. Drivers expect riders to pay the drivers the equivalent of public transportation costs, but foreigners are occasionally allowed to forego this courtesy. Indicating that you are a foreigner will increase your hitchhiking speed considerably, but don't expect to make long distances easily. Women should not hitch alone.

The Romanian language is a godsend to Westerners since it resembles Italian and French. If you know either language, you can decipher public signs and make yourself understood. In Transylvania, German and Hungarian are widely spoken, and in Wallachia and Moldavia Romanians tend to learn French as a second language. Certainly any effort to learn the basics—*mulţumesc* (thank you) and *vǎrog* (please)—will be appreciated.

One of the surest ways to expedite most transactions is to offer an American cigarette, preferably a Kent Long Gold. A carton of them is a must for any traveler in Romania.

One last warning: the black market in Romania is a real racket. The chances are that you'll either get ripped off or turned in to the police—or both. For the fool-hardy, cash dollars should fetch 25-30 lei, but count the lei twice before even showing the bucks. Whatever you do, hang on to the exchange voucher you get at the border—if you don't have it when you leave the country, you will run into problems.

Food

Romanian food is generally quite good and inexpensive, if you remember to double-check the bill afterwards—watch out for excessively friendly waiters. Restaurants generally serve regional specialties. Try the fish dishes in the Danube Delta and on the Black Sea Coast. Moldavian dishes include: *carp roskal* (poached carp), *Nisetru la gratar* (grilled sturgeon), *sarmale* (stuffed cabbage), and *ardei unplati* (peppers). Wherever you go, you'll find the filling, peasant dish of *mamaliga* (a heavy maize porridge), and *brinza* (a rich, creamy cottage cheese). The soups *(ciorba)* are invariably rich and filling. Try the sour meatball soup *(ciorba de perişoave),* which is found most everywhere. The *mititei—mici* for short—are spicy, skinless sausages braised over an open fire.

The workers' stand-up restaurants, often (but not always) labeled *Bufe Expres,* offer the most inexpensive hot meals around, but are quite crowded at meal times. Finally, if you are feeling a little overcome by a large meal, try the strong national spirit called *tvica,* distilled from plums.

Bucharest (Bucureşti)

Although poor, the Bucharester has managed to build a proud, modern capital with busy boulevards; large, well-groomed parks; an important university; and a rich cultural life. Bucharest is the economic, industrial, and administrative center of Romania, and looks it. From 7am to 8pm, every Bucharester seems to be on the street on the wide, old **Calea Victoria;** or in the dustier, poorer alleys further from the center. You will be surprised by the poverty in some areas; in others, you will be overwhelmed by the crowds and the noise.

Orientation

The **Gara de Nord** is the main Train Station of Bucharest, and is not far from the center of town. You can get a map from any hotel lobby or the **ONT Office** at the Station (open 7am-10pm). These maps provide general orientation, but are useless for precise navigation. You may wish to invest in a street plan at a *libraria* (there is one on Calea Grivitei near the Train Station). ONT offices will also provide brochures on the city, sell tickets to cultural events—the folk-dancing is excellent—and try to shuttle you onto guided tours.

Travel in the city is provided by a network of buses, trolley buses, and trams. Buy tickets at the kiosks for the first two, but pay for the tram as you board. Taxis start at 3 lei, and add another 3 lei for every kilometer, but the driver is out to make a profit, so beware. Telephones take 25 bani, and are everywhere.

Addresses and Telephone Numbers

ONT (National Tourist Office): Central Office at Blvd. Magheru 7 (tel. 14-51-60). Branch in the Gara de Nord. All branches change money.

BTT (Youth Tourist Bureau): Strada Onesti 4-6 (tel. 14-06-55). Open May 25 through September 15, for ages 14-30. Usually deals only with groups, but worth a try for room-hunting.

CFR (Rail Ticket Agency): Str. Brezoianu 10 (information tel. 052).

Tarom Airlines: Str. Brezoianu 10 (tel. 16-33-46).

Navrom (Danube Boats): Blvd. Dinicu Goleseu 58 (tel. 18-02-90). Near the Train Station.

Police: (tel. 055).

Emergency: (tel. 061).

U.S. Embassy: Tudor Arghezi 7-9 (tel. 12-40-40). Take a left through the gray door for the consular section which is open weekday mornings 9am-noon.

Canadian Embassy: Nicolae Iorga 36, 71118, P.O. 22, Box 2966 (tel. 50-62-90).

Accommodations

Unless you are really short of money, the most convenient choice of accommodations in Bucharest is one of the centrally-located category II hotels. ONT will provide you with a list of them, and if you like, will book you in one. If ONT says that they are all full, go to the hotels on your own and speak to the receptionists—most of them really like Kent cigarettes. Prices run 110-140 lei, breakfast included. If you can talk them out of breakfast, you'll save 20 lei. You can generally use hall showers for 10 lei extra.

If, however, you are looking for a student hostel, ask BTT or ONT about the *caminul de studenti*. Their addresses change yearly, and are usually open only in July and August, and are filled mostly by organized groups. Even so, we recommend going to the student dorm and asking for a bed, not a room, unless you're accompanied. If they tell you they have nothing just start asking students in the area. African and Arab students usually speak English and will often let you stay in their rooms.

Hotel Cerna, Blvd. D. Golescu 29 (tel. 49-32-50), near the Train Station. Clean, large, and likely to have a room.

Hotel Universal, Str. Gabroveni 12 (tel. 14-60-38). Excellent location, clean and simple rooms.

Hotel Rahova, Str. Rahovei 2 (tel. 15-26-17). Central location, but nice and quiet.

Hotel Veneția, Piața Kogălniceanu (tel. 13-60-69).

Hotel Bucegi, Str. Witing 2 (tel. 49-51-20). Small, far from luxurious, but rarely full.

The only convenient campground is a twenty-minute bus ride from the center of town. **Camping Băneasa** (tel. 33-62-67), in the Băneasa Forest, offers bungalow beds from 40 lei. The airports are nearby, though, so you'll be hearing jets taking off and landing. Call first, since it's often full.

Food

The inexpensive way to eat in Bucharest is to join the crowds in the self-service stand-up **Bufe Expres.** They are generally open 7am-11pm, and offer a wide selection of dishes. If you see a plate with yellow pudding to one side, and white slush on the other, it is the Romanian staple *mamaliga cu brinza,* guaranteed to fill you for 5 lei. The **Bufe Express** on Blvd. 1848, just above Str. Lipscavi, even has some tables where you can sit while you eat.

In spite of the unappetizing name, the **Lacto Vegetarian** chain offers fine pastries and dairy products.

Hotel Intercontinental, at University Square (go down the stairs on the outside of the hotel). Fine, self-service meal for under 25 lei. **Hotel Dorobanti,** just off Piaţa Romana, has the same idea as the Intercontinental.

The pension lunches at **Universitatii,** Blvd. Republicii 6, and **Gradinita,** Blvd. Magheru 24, consist of three-course meals for 30-40 lei. They serve 12:30-4:30pm, and are always crowded.

Carul cu Bere, Stavropoleos 3-5, housed in the 1879 Slatari Inn, features *Crenwurst* (sausages with horse-radish), Oltenian sausages, fresh bread, and the best *mititei* in town.

Kosher restaurant, unmarked entrance on Str. Popa Soarea 18. Meals 30 lei. Bring your passport, but visitors are extremely welcome.

Pescǎrus, in Herǎstrau Park (tel. 17-09-83). Beautiful setting on a lake, Romanian specialties, and fine Continental cooking. For a splurge only. Meals start at 50 lei.

Sights

Bucharest is a city of parks. Wander through the well-groomed, central **Cişmigiu Park,** or the huge **Herǎstrau Park** to the north. Herǎstrau houses the single most interesting exhibit in Bucharest, the Village Museum, a collection of peasant dwellings from all regions of Romania. (Open 10am-7pm, closed Mon.; admission 2 lei.) Bucharest has more than forty museums—from the massive **History Museum** of the Socialist Republic of Romania (of interest only to the patient specialist) to the delightful **George Enescu Museum,** at Calea Victoria 141 (open mornings), dedicated to the famous Romanian composer.

The main synagogue, **Tempul Coral** on Str. Sfintul Viner 7-9 is the center of a dwindling community of Romanian Jews. Nearby is the **Museum of the History of the Romanian Jews** (Str. Manulari 3, open Wed. evenings and Sun. mornings).

In the southern part of town, you will come upon many Byzantine churches. Try to go to a 10am service on Sunday to see the Romanian Orthodox rite. The finest churches are the 1722 **Cretulescu Church** and the tiny **Stavropoleos Church** behind the Romanian History Museum. Bucharest's best sight of all, however, may be the crowd of shoppers and strollers in the old town, particularly on Str. Lipscani.

Evenings

Bucharest is by no stretch of the imagination a swinging city. For information about what is going on, check at ONT, or pick up the weekly magazine *Saptamîina,* available at any newsstand for 1 lei. **The Bucharest Circus,** Aleea Circului 2, entertains all summer. Bucharest cinemas run plenty of old

American and English films, and they are almost never dubbed, so you can go for as little as 5 lei (never more than 12) and just ignore the subtitles. You might also enjoy going to the **Student Club of Bucharest University** at Calea Plevnei 61 (behind the Opera) where you can mix with Romanian students—many of whom speak English. Bucharest also has the only **Jewish State Theater** in Europe. It is located on Str. Iuliu Barasch 15 and performs throughout the summer. The shows are in Yiddish, with simultaneous headphone translations into Romanian—take your pick.

A good place for an American to meet Romanians is, strangely enough, the **American Embassy Library Film Series.** Films are shown at the library, Str. Alexander Sahia 9-11 several evenings each week, and Romanians flock to the library to buy tickets. If you are feeling homesick and are badly in need of imperialist encouragement, head for a ginger ale or cold beer at the friendly **U.S. Marine House** (tel. 33-10-56). Free movies on Tuesday nights, party on Saturdays. Check with the marine on duty at the Embassy for directions and schedule.

Bucharest is surrounded by an arc of lakes, most of which are in parks and recreation areas. All are within an easy bus or trolley ride. A little further out is the **Băneasa Forest,** with a zoo and shaded walks. Further yet are three **monasteries,** each in a pleasant park—Snagov, Căldărusani, and Tigănesti. All three make wonderful escapes on a hot day.

Transylvania

For centuries the rich Transylvanian plateaus have been fought over by Hungarians, Romanians, Russians, and Turks. These conflicts are still in evidence—villages are built around fortified churches, towns encircle castles, and on nearly every other hill stand the ruins of a citadel. Small villages often go by more than one name, the Romanian official name and the traditional German or Hungarian name. Local costume is still worn (particularly on Sundays), and gypsies still camp between the towns. Many farmers speak more German or Hungarian than Romanian, and Romanian Orthodox churches often share the skyline with Lutheran steeples. The whole area is a fascinating ethnic puzzle, rich in folklore for the tourist, problematic for the Romanian Government.

A word about Count Dracula: his reputation as a vicious feudal landlord persists, but he is far more renowned as a vampire in America than in Transylvania. The Romanian Government is even trying to propagate a revisionist view of him, glorifying his role in driving out the Germans from Romania.

Braşov

Braşov, 171 kilometers north of Bucharest, is on the edge of the Carpathian Mountains and of Transylvania proper, and makes a good base for excursions into both. The nearby **Castle of Bran,** often mistaken for Count Dracula's, is overrated (open 9am-4pm, closed Mon. tickets 3 lei, 1.50 lei for students). Considerably more scenic and totally untouristed is the **peasant citadella** overlooking Risnov (between Braşov and Bran). A couple kilometers north of Braşov, the villages of **Harman** and **Prejmer** boast two of the finest fortified Lutheran churches in Transylvania.

Braşov itself has a few monuments of its Germanic mercantile past that are worth visiting. The main **ONT Office** is in the Hotel Carpaţi on Post Office Square. **Hotel Sport,** Str. Mayakovsky 3 (tel. 42840) is a centrally-located Category II hotel. To find out where the **Student Hostel** is located this year, ask at BTT, Str. Armata Rosi 3 (tel. 44009), on a back street not far from Post Office Square. They can also tell you of the locations of BTT bases in the mountains.

Sighisoara

Of all the medieval towns in Transylvania, Sighisoara is perhaps the least spoiled and the most enchanting. Crowning a green hill on the railroad line between Cluj and Brasov, the guild towers, old clock tower, steeples, and irregular tile roofs of the town are almost entirely unobstructed by any modern buildings. The old walled town is preserved as a museum, and visitors can wander here and in the surrounding hilly, green farmland. Sighisoara is also an excellent way to break up the long train ride from Bucharest to Budapest.

The main attraction in the old town is the **Clock Tower** at Piata Maior Isacov I, above the main gate. The fourteenth-century tower houses the **Town Museum** (open Tues., Thurs. and Sat., 9am-1pm; Wed., Fri. and Sun. 9am-1pm and 5-8pm; closed Mon.) At the top a wooden gallery provides the best view of the city, and a close look at the woodcarved figures on the clock which represent the days of the week (they change at midnight).

Following the fifteenth-century walls of the **Citadel,** you pass nine **Guild Towers** (Tailors' Tower, Clockmakers' Tower, and so on), and at the highest part of the walls reach the **Covered Stairway,** which leads to the **Church on the Hill** *(Bergkirche).* Begun in the fourteenth century and built in various architectural styles, it contains a Sighisoaran version of the legend of St. George on an interior fresco.

Following the winding streets back to **Petoffy Square** (the main market square) where you will see the **House of the Stag** (the oldest in town) and the **Minthouse,** where Dracula's father, who ruled Transylvania, coined money. Next to the Clock Tower off the square is the thirteenth-century **Monastery Church,** the oldest building in town, with a Knorpel Baroque altar.

Orientation and Accommodations

From the Railroad Station (on a hill opposite the town), cross the river and go left past the park and across a square to reach Str. Gheorghe Gheorghiu-Dej, the main street. Directly across the street is the **ONT** Office (tel. 11-072), open 8am-1pm and 5-7pm (Sun. 8am-noon). They have maps of the area and other tourist information but are no help with rooms. The **BTT** Office on Str. Muzeula, open 10am-noon and 1:30-4pm, may be able to find a place for you in their dorm.

Hotel Steaua, Strada Gheorghe Gheorghiu-Dej (next to ONT; (tel. 11-594). All foreigners are supposed to stay here. First class and very comfortable, in a lovely old Transylvanian building with a mosaic tile roof. Rather expensive: doubles 199 lei. Both with breakfast, but without shower (tel. 11-052).

Campground Hula Danes, 4km from Sighisoara on the road to Vhedias. Two-person bungalows for 90 lei. A fine restaurant right next door.

Food and Evenings

Gradina de Vara, on Stra. Gheorghe Gheorghiu-Dej, a few doors up the hill from ONT. An excellent outdoor restaurant with reasonable prices. Grilled meat, bread, and salad for about 20 lei.

Restaurant Steaua, in the Hotel Steaua. Reasonably priced and good, with a varied menu at lunchtime—soups, fish, *mamaliga*, grilled meat, and Romanian specialties. Main dishes about 20-30 lei.

Evenings here can be quite fun. The **Gradina de Vara** is a great place to drink local wine, listen to a terrible rock band, and watch the locals strut their stuff. The whole town comes on weekend evenings and if you're alone you won't be for long. A little further up the street at **34 Piata Lenin** is a fine beer hall. Soon after you arrive you'll be drinking and toasting with the natives. If you're looking for more peaceful entertainment, walk up to the old town at dusk, climb among the towers, then wander back down to the square below and have coffee at one of the outdoor cafés.

Moldavia

The rolling, forested hills of Northern Moldavia were once the center of the Moldavian kingdom, around the fortressed capital of Suceava. Within thirty miles are a dozen monasteries, rivalling one another for beauty of location and artistic riches. The best way to see this remarkable region still rich in traditional, wooden villages is to hike, hitch, and camp. There is rarely more than one day's scenic walk from one monastery to the next, and since many tourists cover the circuit by car, hitching works remarkably well.

It is difficult to recommend one monastery over the next although **Voronet Monastery** is perhaps the most famous. The deep-blue background of its exterior frescoes, still vivid despite four-hundred years of storm and wars, has become known as the ''Voronet Blue.'' The exquisite *Last Judgment* scene on the open porch, the *Tree of Jesse,* and the portraits of Greek philosophers are absolutely unique frescoes. The typical peaked-hat roof spreads its broad eaves over walls three-feet thick, as forested hills loom in the background. From the nearby village of **Humor,** a twenty-mile hike on an untraveled dirt road and forest path *(drum forestier)* takes you through small mountain settlements, where the native all-white dress is still worn, to the **Sucevita Monastery,** which ranks with Voronet as the loveliest of the painted monasteries. Built and fortified in 1584, its central church is covered inside and out with frescoes of which the most impressive is the *Ladder of Virtues,* in which the souls of the dead pass numerous customs check-points en route to heaven or hell. Right near the Sucevita monastery is a very good camping facility, where a comfortable bed in a clean two-bed bungalow costs 36 lei. Continuing west to **Vatra Moldovitei,** you take a side road to reach **Moldovita,** a fortified monastery with a church whose frescoes depict the *Hymn to the Virgin, Tree of Jesse,* and *Siege of Constantinople.*

To the north, the country town of **Radauţi,** which unfortunately has no hotels or hostels, is the market town for the area. Markets are held on weekdays, and farmers come from afar in their horse-drawn carts to sell homemade wooden rakes and pitchforks, and embroidered sheepskin vests. The **old synagogue** in Radauţi is still standing, and the oldest stone church of Moldavia, the squat **St. Nickolas of Bogdana,** shelters the tomb of old Moldavian Voevodes.

Suceava

Although there is a campground and a motel near almost every monastery, due to connections you will probably have to spend a night in Suceava before heading for the monasteries. Take bus #16 or 26 from the Gara de Suceava, or bus #1 or 11 from Suceava Nord to the center of town for the **ONT Office** at Nikolai Balcescu 2 (tel. 1-73-39) which will find you a place to stay if there is room in one of the category II hotels—**Hotel Park** and **Hotel Suceava**—and will provide you with information and bus schedules for visiting the monasteries. The **BTT** Office on Str. I.C. Frimu 18 (tel. 1-52-35) will direct you to the student hostels where you should find a bed for 30 lei or less, as compared to 110 lei in the hotels. While in Suceava, visit the fourteenth-century **Princely residence** and the fine old churches: **St. Dumitra, St. Gheorghe,** and **Miranţi.**

Danube Delta and the Black Sea Coast

About 150 kilometers from the sea, the Danube River splits into three arms to create a rich, canal-laced marshland covering 4,340 square kilometers. The two more southerly arms reach the sea at **Sulina** and **Sfintu Gheorghe,** while the northernmost arm, the longest, separates Romania and Russia and reaches the sea beyond the town of **Periprava.** The starting point for expeditions into the Delta is the town of **Tulcea.** River boats *(nave clasice)* and infrequent hydrofoils *(nave rapide)* will take you down the Sfintu Gheorghe and the Sulina arms. A six-hour ride down to Sfintu Gheorghe on a *nave clasice* costs 80 lei, round trip. This gives you a chance to sit in the prow all afternoon, absorbing the sun and wind and watching storks and egrets flying over the water or standing silently in the shadows of willows along the shore. At times the trees give way to thatched fishing villages, with elaborately-carved wooden houses and the narrow black canoes used for everything from mail service to transporting huge loads of marsh reeds.

In Sfintu Gheorghe, you can arrange to be taken out by a fisherman to see more of the Delta, provided you rise at dawn when he is ready to set out. Sfintu Gheorghe has the additional attraction of being on the sea—the beach is a 2-kilometer wide stretch of snowy sand, and to reach it you walk down the main road out of town and continue along the crest of a dune through a salt marsh. An alternative to going all the way to Sfintu Gheorghe is to take the bus to **Murighiol,** where there is a campground. One of the Danube's famous pelican colonies is in the reeds of the lake here, and fishermen will take tourists to watch the birds feed at early morning and dusk. Also buses go from Mirighiol to Tulcea and to the **Caraorman Forest** and sand bank, another area rich in wildlife.

Unfortunately, the Delta is not equipped to handle tourists, so accommodations are a problem. It is now illegal to stay with fishermen, and fines are stiff if you are caught, but you can camp in many places in the Delta—remember to bring adequate protection against the vicious mosquitoes. In Sfintu Gheorghe, **ONT** has a barge with small double-bunk cabins and space for forty people at 20 lei per night. Check with the Office in Tulcea before you head out. Tulcea is the place to give **BTT** a try. If you're interested, speak to the main office in Bucharest to see if you can join an excursion. BTT has a fifty-bunk boat which makes two-, three-, and five-day excursions into the back canals of the Delta. The ONT excursions, which cost $24 and go down the Sulina arm, are both overpriced and worthless.

South of the Delta proper is the third largest fresh-water lake in Europe, **Lacul Razelm.** Its desolate, placid waters can be crossed several times daily for 9 lei, starting from the village **Jurilovca** (one hour's bus ride from Tulcea) to the **Camping Partita,** which is located on a strip of sand and marsh, half a mile wide, between the lake and the sea. Westerners are infrequent visitors to say the least, as this is a hangout for poor fishermen who speak a Romanian dialect, and seasonal Romanian campers. Bungalows for two cost 72 lei per night. The bar is very busy and the restaurant serves excellent fish.

The Socialist jet-set seems to summer at **Mamaia** on the Black Sea, where the beach is crowded and the prices are high. You may prefer the wonderful student camp at **Costineşti,** 25 kilometers to the south. A summer village of over 4000 young people organizes all daily activities, from meals to movies to folk music festivals. If you can, reserve ahead from the BTT Office in Bucharest. The experience of an international regimented summer paradise is a shock to the Western mind. If you can't find a bed there, you can at the least eat three meals a day for 26 lei, and join the crowds on the sports fields.

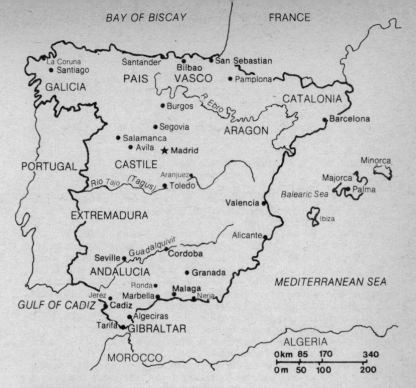

SPAIN

$1U.S.=71pesetas (ptas)   **1pta=$.014**

On November 30, 1978 a sacristan visiting Franco's crypt near Madrid discovers that, on the third anniversary of his death, the Generalísimo has risen to lead his wayward countrymen back into the fold of fascism. Within hours, Santiago Carrillo, Secretary General of the Spanish Communist Party, has slipped on his old wig and is on his way out of the country incognito, while Premier Adolfo Suárez González is trying to make himself believe that "Franco always was a democrat—in his own way." This scenario from satirist Fernando Vizcaíno Casas' bestseller *In the Third Year He Rose Again* has caused ripples of nervous laughter throughout Spain, but he was not the first to see the shades of political revenants. Despite the unexpectedly sensitive stewardship of King Juan Carlos, the transition to democracy has been difficult. Two weeks after riots in the Basque town of Pamplona in July 1978, the machine-gunning of Brigadier General Juan Sánchez Ramos seemed clearly designed to destabilize the political situation by inviting army retaliation. The regime survived that crisis, and succeeded in passing a new liberalized constitution, but it remains to be seen whether the Basques will let the anniversary of the Pamplona riots go unobserved.

Much, in fact, has changed in Spain, and mostly for the better. The tri-cornered pot-hats of the *guardia civil* are less in evidence, and the garrison mentality in the "occupied provinces" has relaxed to the point where Catalán is spoken in the classrooms of the University of Barcelona. Unfortunately, the new freedom of the press is exploited more energetically in the piles of porn at the newsstands than in political debate, and there is a general feeling of disillusion and indirection which, more than anything else, might indicate that Spain has entered the 1970s.

Yet Spain, more than other Western European countries, has resisted change. Centuries after the unification of the old kingdoms into a single state, regional loyalties still outweigh national sentiment. **Galicia, Cataluña,** and the **País Vasco** (Basque country) all have vital and distinct languages and active separatist movements. Local populations have remained so stable that today even the casual visitor will be able to spot traces of ancient invasions: red hair and blue Celtic eyes in **La Coruña,** curly hair and dark Moorish eyes in **Andalucía.** All around the country, especially in **Castilla** and in the area north of **Alicante,** there are hill-top fortresses to remind the world that these differences were once worth fighting over.

Provided King Juan Carlos manages to keep his government on a steady course, there will be few better places to spend your vacation than Spain. The heterogeneity which threatens at times to pull the country apart is fascinating to the traveler, who can enjoy an improbable variety of scenery, cuisine, and cultural distractions. From the alpine forests of the **Pyrenees** through the arid heartland of **La Mancha** to the Moorish palaces and sunny coasts of Andalucía is scarcely a two-day drive—or a 24-hour crawl by train. If you're only going for a short vacation, don't make the mistake of trying to "do" every cathedral and museum in every town. While you're in La Coruña, try to see a wild horse round-up; go to a *pelota* (jai alai) match in **San Sebastián;** if you're anywhere in range, the three-week International Festival of Music and Dances in **Santander** is worth the detour, especially if the restoration work at the nearby **Altamira Caves** is completed. Spend a week picking sherry grapes at **Jerez de la Frontera,** and, when you've burnt yourself out in the sun and schlock of the **Costa del Sol,** drop into the surreal grottoes of **Nerja.** If you are not morally offended or squeamish, you might attend one bullfight, just to see what it is all about. From March to October the ritual of blood is played out in the *plaza de toros.* Try to get *sombra* (shade-side, or preferred) seats for a top-bill *corrida.* Cheaper fights with novice *toreros* are less classical to be sure, but more rock-em-sock-em. If you're really crazy, there are places called *capeas* where for 500-800ptas you can play with a baby bull (there are quite a few of these places around **Salamanca**.

Exchanging Money

Exchange rates are not the same in all banks, and they are often quite disadvantageous at travel agencies, frontiers, and so on. Everywhere, a 1% commission, plus a small tax, is taken off the top. Travelers checks bring higher rates than cash.

Transportation

When Dr. Johnson told Boswell, "There is a good deal of Spain that has not been perambulated, I would have you go thither," he did not take into account Spain's confused transportation system. **RENFE,** the national railroad system is the butt of countless jokes. While they're improving rapidly, the pace of travel can still be excruciatingly slow. Until such time as the trains do run smoothly, we hope the following tips will help see you through. No matter what the hour, be prepared to change trains at the Spanish border because of the different track sizes. The *Talgo* and the *Ter* are the newest and fastest trains in Spain, and require a supplement. The rest are, in descending order of desirability, the *expresso* (middling to bad), *rápido* (anything but what its name promises) and the *tranvía,* which should only be taken by masochists. Eighteen hours for a three-hundred-mile trip is the very least you can expect from the chimerical and somnolent *correo.* Eurailpass holders must, for absolutely no apparent reason, reserve seats in advance. Those who contemplate much (upwards of 1500 kilometers) rail travel in Spain, can save about 30% by buying a **Kilométrico** book at a RENFE office.

Chances are you will become acquainted with the Spanish bus system. It's economical, but beyond that it will try your patience. Better for short excursions than long trips, the buses stop at every place anyone could conceivably want to get on or off.

While always a help, a car is especially nice to have in Spain, both because the public transportation is mediocre and because interesting places tend to be scattered about. Expect to average only 50-60 kilometers per hour on all but the best roads. There are good roads in many areas besides Madrid—in the Basque country, near Barcelona, and on the Costa del Sol, but the bad roads are really bad. If you are traveling with companions, you should check out car rental rates, which average 10-40% less than those in other European countries—the Spanish government imposes no tax on this service.

Spain is not a great country for hitchhiking. Spaniards are simply reluctant to stop for thumbers. And then there's the Spanish sun—it's no treat to spend hours baking on the highway watching the tail ends of occasional cars shimmer off into the distance. Women, especially blondes, can count on frequent rides, but are likely to face more than the usual hassles. Men with long hair are in for some long waits.

Accommodations

Low-cost accommodations are an important factor in Spain's recent tourist boom. The government has kept a tight lid on prices and established a detailed schedule of prices according to categories which are generally reliable guides to the sorts of facilities available. The most common categories, in roughly descending order of luxury and prices, are: *hotel, hostal, hostal-residencia, pensión, casa de huéspedes,* and *fonda.* Further distinctions in the first two categories are indicated with stars, five being the maximum applied to a few rare hotels. All legally-registered establishments must display a small blue plaque identifying their category: H, Hs, HsR, P, CH, and F, respectively.

Ask to be shown a room before you hand over your passport. Not only will you get better accommodations, but you can be absolutely sure of the price, as innkeepers are required by law to post it prominently in every room, as well as by the main entrance. Minimum and maximum prices are fixed for every room according to facilities, but don't expect these to correspond exactly to low and high season. They are applied at the discretion of the manager, and can be undercut, but not legally exceeded. There are also a number of subtleties which can affect the price of lodging. Breakfast is obligatory in some places, and you must pay for it even if you don't eat it. If the place serves food and you don't eat at least one meal, you will be charged an extra 20%. Showers usually cost extra. Thus a "cheap" double for 250ptas can cost as much as 540ptas: 50ptas for no meals, 50ptas each for breakfast, and 70ptas each for a shower. These factors make it difficult to generalize about the relation of cost and category, but if you are on a budget of less than 1000ptas per day, you'll have to avoid hotels and multi-starred *hostales*. A double room in a two-star hostal usually costs from 350-700ptas, and from 300-400ptas in a one-star *hostal* (without private bath). You can usually find a small but clean double for 250ptas and a single for 160ptas in a *fonda, casa de huéspedes,* or *pensión*—but you might have to walk up several flights of stairs, and you certainly should not expect air-conditioning.

If for some reason you have trouble when it comes time to pay the bill (a very rare occurrence), ask for the complaint book, which the ever-vigilant government requires be produced on demand. The argument will usually end right there, as all complaints must be forwarded to the authorities within 24 hours, and a hotel-keep will be shafted if he is caught overcharging a tourist.

In choosing a room your biggest problem will be to steer clear of noise and heat, the Scylla and Charybdis of Spanish city lodgings in the summer. To get around this problem, look for places on the side streets or take a room as high up as possible.

At last count there were more than 65 official youth hostels in the **Red Española de Albergues Juveniles** (Spanish Network of Youth Hostels). Conditions vary considerably, but many of them are very comfortable, and the prices can't be beat: 100ptas per night; breakfast, which may be mandatory, costs 35ptas, lunch 160ptas, supper 130ptas. IYHF cards are invariably required, but other regulations are enforced with varying degrees of rigidity; sheets are not generally required.

Do not confuse the *albergue juvenil* with the ritzy *albergue nacional;* the latter is a high category government-run establishment located in out-of-the-way places for the convenience of motorists. The Spanish government has also set up a chain of *paradores nacionales,* luxury hotels installed in well-restored historical monuments. Very reasonable rates (usually less than 1300ptas for a double room) make these converted castles and convents among the best splurges in Europe. If you are interested, request a list of *paradores nacionales* from any tourist office and make reservations well in advance. The most popular *paradores* often run out of rooms for the summer season by March.

Campgrounds in Spain are also controlled by the government. There is little difference in price between categories, but the facilities are usually substantially better at Class 1 sites than at lower-ranked grounds.

Unregistered rooms in private homes *(casas particulares)* are an excellent last resort—particularly in the popular tourist cities in the summer. Ask around at local bars or check with the tourist offices.

Food

Unlike the French, the Spanish never developed an *haute cuisine.* Delicate spicing and light textures are not to be expected on the peninsula, and the Spanish *pan* (bread) bears more resemblance to the bombshell than the *baguette.* The food is not spicy-hot like Mexican food, but your stomach may want to adjust slowly to the excessive amounts of olive oil and garlic used in almost every dish. Once your stomach settles, you'll probably find yourself pigging out on the fantastic variety of hearty peasant dishes. The *pescado* (fish) and *mariscos* (shellfish) are absolutely fresh everywhere, even inland. Restaurant windows full of "fruits of the sea" are tourist attractions in themselves. In San Sebastián you'll see windows full of grotesque *nécoras* (spider crabs) dangling by invisible threads. Everything is alive: *gambas* (shrimp), *almejas* (clams), *mejillones* (mussels), *cangrejos* (flat-backed crabs), *langostinos* (large sea crayfish). If you've never eaten the creepy-crawlies, don't miss your chance now: *calamares* (squid), cut up and fried in chewy rings, are a good introduction. Then on to *pulpo* (octopus), delicious in marinated tomato and onion salads, and for the final test: *chipirones en su tinta* (cuttlefish in their own ink).

With so many distinct sub-cultures, it is not surprising that Spain should have an endless repertoire of dishes. Unfortunately, less expensive menus rarely venture far afield of the well-known standards: *merluza a la romana* (broiled hake), *pollo asado* (roast chicken), and *paella valenciana* (shellfish and saffron rice). Do try to find some of the arcane specialties, like *perdiz con chocolate* (partridge with chocolate) in Navarra, and, in Majorca, *lenguas de cerdo con salsa de granada* (pig tongues with granada sauce).

To start your meal, choose between soups or a wide variety of appetizers. *Gazpacho andaluz,* the famous liquid salad native to Andalucía, is a good choice, as is *sopa de pescado* (fish soup). For dessert, fruit, ice cream *(helado),* or *flan* (custard with caramel sauce) are usually served.

Perhaps the biggest pleasure of Spanish dining is the price tag. You can usually find a meal for around 150ptas, and 350ptas buys a meal fit for *el Rey.* Dinner *(cena),* like everything else in Spain, is late—usually around 10pm. The main meal *(comida)* is generally eaten around 2pm when the stores shut down. Restaurants are generally open 1-4pm and again 8pm-midnight.

If this schedule seems cruel and unusual, there is an institution that provides relief from pre-prandial starvation: *tapas.* These are light snacks served at bars everywhere. After work Spaniards make for the local bars and *mesones* or *tascas,* to meet friends and to munch on these delightful tidbits. Larger portions are available as *raciones* (rations), which make an excellent cheap, light meal. *Tapas* are always washed down with a glass of wine *(tinto* or *blanco)* or beer, which is ordered by the size of the glass. *Caña* is the standard small glass (9-12ptas). *Tanque* (literally tank) is a larger version. In San Sebastián you can even get a smaller version of a *caña* (about two gulps), called a *torrito* (little bull), for about 6ptas.

Almost every restaurant in Spain offers a *menú del día* (menu of the day), sometimes known as a *menú turístico* (MT). By law, it consists of soup or appetizer, one or two main courses, bread, dessert, and wine or mineral water. The price ranges from 130ptas in a cheap bar/restaurant to 360ptas in a four-fork restaurant (restaurants are rated by forks) and is sometimes as much as 600ptas in a *Parador* or equivalent. The average price is about 200ptas. In addition, many restaurants offer cheap, fixed-price *cubiertos* (set meals) or *platos combinados* (combination plates: main course and side dishes on a single plate, plus bread and sometimes beverage).

One last note: the *cafetería* in Spain is not what you'd expect from the English. The word means the same as *"café"* in French, and in fact, often designates a restaurant. If you want a place where you get up and pick your food look for a "self-service."

Pais Vasco

The Basque provinces are totally different from the rest of Spain. The tourist rediscovers that the rain in Spain does *not* fall mainly on the plain; the rugged hills and mountains, and, unfortunately, the sandy beaches as well, get more than their share of precipitation. The countryside is green and forested, and for the most part unspoiled, despite the heaviest industrialization on the peninsula.

Culturally, the Basque are a people apart. Linguists still disagree on the origin of the *Euskara* language, which, far from a dialect of Spanish or French, seems more closely related to inner Asian languages. This cultural division has caused problems between the Spanish government and the Basques. The men smile with satisfaction if questioned about the 1973 assassination of Prime Minister Carrero-Blanco, when a bomb planted by the ETA (Basque Liberation Front) blasted his car over a six-story church. Things have settled down recently, but only to a degree: fresh accounts of fascist harassment of ETA demonstrators circulate daily.

Two areas of more peaceful divergence from the Spanish mainstream are cooking and sports. *Pelota*, or jai-alai, was born here; to the Basques, this lightning-fast sport is a passion that rivals the *corrida*. Other less sophisticated sports have not spread beyond the region, such as boulder hefting, dead-weight drags by ox teams, and between-the-legs log chopping.

Basque cooking has influenced Spanish cuisine; *Bacalao a la Vizcaína* (salted cod in a tomato sauce) and *chipirones en su tinta* (cuttlefish in their ink) have spread all through the peninsula. And few places can match the energy and gusto which the Basques bring to the table; the streets between restaurants and bars are scenes of frenzy in the evening.

Traveling through the Basque country is a pleasure. The roads are good and the countryside is untrammeled and still. There are beautiful beaches all along the coast, but there are tourists also. So, if cool, lush mountains calm your soul, stay on the inland roads.

San Sebastián

For years one of the tourist capitals of Europe, San Sebastián has not quite held its own against the southern resorts. Still drawing crowds of Spaniards, and, increasingly, Germans, San Sebastián is popular enough to make it difficult to find a place to stay during the *temporada* (July—mid-September), with its frequent fiestas.

The city has a year-round gastronomical obsession. When the crowds aren't on the beach, they're circulating in droves among the bars and restaurants of the old quarter. Tourists are likely to forget the **San Telmo Museum,** with its beautiful cloisters and paintings of ethnic scenes by José Sert; and the **Church of Santa María,** with its towering gilt altars—these are somehow cast into the shadows of **La Viña, La Cepa,** and dozens of other little bars around them.

Orientation

San Sebastián is a convenient stopover on the way to or from France. The Paris-Madrid trains pass through the city. The **Train Station** is on the east side of the river, **Río Urumea,** between the Santa Catalina and María Cristina bridges. The **Tourist Office** is on the west bank, right off Kursaal, the third bridge. San Sebastián was destroyed by fire in 1813, so even the old quarter beneath Urgull is comparatively recent. The "new city," around the broad and elegant **Avenida de España,** faces the scallop-shaped **Bahía** on the west, with two beautiful beaches, **La Concha** and **Ondarreta.**

Addresses and Telephone Numbers

Tourist Offices: Calle Reina Regente, ground floor of the Victoria Eugenia Theater (tels. 41 34 46 and 42 10 02). Central Office is very helpful. Branch at Andia 13 (tel. 41 04 73).

American Express: Viajes Melia, S.A., Avenida de España 39 (tel. 41 79 46). Open Mon.-Fri. 9am-1:30pm and 4-7:30pm, Sat. 9am-1pm.

Post Office: Calle Urdaneta 9 (tel. 41 23 11); Telegraph Office (tel. 41 91 09). Open 9am-2pm and 4-10pm.

Long Distance Telephone: Avenida de España 26.

RENFE: Information: Camino 1 (tel. 41 67 02). Station: Avenida de Francia (tel. 27 27 71).

First Aid: Victor Pradera 39 (tels. 46 40 19 and 46 46 09).

Accommodations

The **Mount Igueldo** campsite is a beauty. It's very hard to get a hotel room in July and August; if you're coming without reservations, good luck. Prices are skyrocketing: don't expect these to last long.

There is a **Youth Hostel** on the outskirts of town, in the **Ciudad Deportiva Anoeta,** a little sports development (with the famous **Frontón,** where the best *pelota* is played). Frequent buses—take the Anoeta line. Although inmates at the Hostel get a reduction at the municipal pool (75 instead of 150ptas), there is not much else to be said for the place: run with a heavy authoritarian hand, it offers lots of dirty old beds and a few unbelievably squeaky new ones. Bathrooms are a mess, and cold showers are available only at a few odd hours; skip the meals. 150ptas, and you need a card; sheets cost 30ptas if you have no sleeping bag.

Hostal-Residencia Gran Bahía, Calle de Embeltran 16 (tel. 42 38 38). Doubles for 330ptas, triples for 445ptas. Breakfast 42ptas, 30ptas supplement for shower. Acceptable rooms, but only 11 of them.

Itxas Gain, Plaza de Miraconcha 19 (tel. 46 52 90). Singles for 310ptas, doubles 510-770ptas.

Hostal Alameda, Alameda Calvo Sotelo 23 (tel. 42 16 87). Singles 290ptas, doubles 440-585 ptas.

Hotel Parma, Calle de General Jaureguí (tel. 42 88 93). Singles with shower 435ptas, single room with two occupants 545ptas, doubles up to 1065ptas (with full bath). Plush, with Muzak in the lobby.

Food

Before dinner (7:30-9:30pm), follow the mobs to the old part of town between the harbor and the mouth of the river. Walk up **Calle Fermín Calbertón** and stop into any bar for *tapas*. **Bartole** at Fermín Calbertón 38 may be the best choice. The *tapas* here are referred to as *banderillas* (the colorful wooden pegs that are placed in the bull in the *corrida*) because of the toothpicks that hold them together. Most restaurants have *menús* for 190ptas, but you might want to order à la carte, since the main dish is usually chicken or some sort of prosaically prepared cutlet. Shellfish is big here, but costs a fortune. Specialties include *nécoras* (spider crabs), *merluza* (hake) *a la*

Basca, and *callos* (tripe). There are also lots of small places in the harbor that serve excellent sardines and cider.

If you're at the Anoeta Youth Hostel, try the restaurant around the other side of the sports loop: **Xanti: Trabena-Jatetxa** (tels. 45 74 36 and 45 01 29). Large portions. Closed Fridays.

> **Bar Iguerategui,** Idiazabal 20. In the town of Urnieta, outside San Sebastián. (Buses are available.) Although this restaurant is a little hard to get to, it is really worth the effort. In the basement of a bar, furnished with long wooden tables and huge barrels of cider. The steaks are cooked in front of you, and although the room gets a little smoky, the flavor's great. Cheap, too.

Sights and Entertainment

There is more to San Sebastián than Pamplona (see below). Rent a boat and splash out to the **Isla de Santa Clara** (motor boats are also available; information at port entrance). See a *pelota* match at Anoeta (the newspaper, **La Voz de España,** carries all the listings). In July, August, and September, there are numerous festivals: **The International Jazz Festival** (in the third week of July), the **International Horse Jumping Competition,** the **International Pigeon and Trap Shooting Competition,** the **Fiestas Euskaras** (Basque folklore), and the **International Film Festival** (in September).

For such a conservative region, San Sebastián has quite a few night spots. The hottest is the **Ku,** about 100 meters from the camp grounds. On Miraconcha, there are several late-night spots, mostly gay. The **Drugstore** (Fuenterrabía 20) usually has good *ambiente* (female to male ratio).

Pamplona

Since there are no accommodations available in Pamplona itself during the **Running of the Bulls** (July 6-14), San Sebastián, about 85 km away, makes a good base for commuting to the Festival if you have a car. This festival, **San Fermín,** is Spain's most celebrated, and was immortalized by Hemingway. Young men in white costumes with red sashes dart in front of the bulls along the streets leading to the bullring. They run each morning at 8am, and a bullfight takes place the same evening. The contests last a full week and are the best in Spain. Drinking and dancing in the streets go on 24 hours a day. If you're lucky, the Tourist Office can place you in a private home during the fiesta, but don't get your hopes up. Be prepared for the park. In 1978, the Festival was canceled because of riots.

Santander

Commanding a central position on Spain's northern coast, Santander is the only Castilian port and one of Spain's most important resorts. Yet the majority of tourists are Spaniards; Santander is not ideally located for the "grand tour" itinerary. The city is modern and beautifully situated, with breathtaking beaches and an international summer university in the suburb of **Sardinero.** Every August, Santander plays host to the three-week long **International Festival of Music and Dance.** The surrounding province of Santander offers as varied an assortment of attractions as you'll find anywhere in Spain. The coastline is dotted with beaches and beautiful ancient villages. Inland lie the snow-capped **Picos de Europa,** ideal for hunting, fishing, and hiking. Only 30 km away are the **Altamira Caves,** in which you'll find some of the world's best-preserved prehistoric art. Visiting hours are 10am-1pm,

3-6pm. To get there, take the train to Torrelavega, and the bus to Altamira. Near the caves are the quaint villages of **Santillana del Mar** and **Castro Urdiales,** which hosts the **Coso Blanco Fiesta** (check Tourist Office for dates). Some of the best beaches are at **Saunces, Noja** and **Comillas.** On the road south to Burgos is the small town of **Puente-Viesgo,** high above which, in the underground caves of **El Castillo,** you'll find more prehistoric cave art from a period even earlier than Altamira.

Addresses and Telephone Numbers

Oficina Municipal de Turismo: Jardines de Pereda (tel. 21 61 20). Hours are 9:30am-1pm and 4-7pm. Neither informative nor gracious, but they do have a little map.

Viajeseu: Camilio Alonso Vega 14 (tel. 23 32 20). Student travel service.

American Express Representative: Viajes Melia, S.A., Paseo Pereda 23 (tel. 21 51 58). Mon.-Fri. 9am-1pm and 4-7pm, closed Sat. afternoon and Sun.

Post Office: Alfonso XIII (post office tel. 21 26 74; telegraph tel. 22 97 41). Open Mon.-Fri. 9am-1pm and 5-7pm, closed Sat. afternoon and Sun. Xerox and ID photo machine in front of building.

Long Distance Telephone: Marcelino S. Sautola 8, Cisneros 76, or Paseo del General Dávila 22 (tel. information: 003).

RENFE: Paseo Pereda 25 (tel. 21 02 11). **Train Station,** Calle Rodríguez. Information window open Mon.-Fri. 9am-2pm and 4-7pm, Sat. 9am-1pm.

Accommodations

There are dozens of little *hostales* and inexpensive hotels around the center of town; we'll leave you to make your own choice of a uniformly unappealing lot. Singles are usually in the 300-450ptas range, doubles 400-600ptas, but almost everything is filled in the summer. Your best bet is **El Sardinero,** a more pleasant exurb—a short bus ride away (#1 or 8). A **campsite** is to the west, off Avenida de la Reina Victoria.

Hostal Liebana, Nicolas Salmeron 9 (tel. 22 32 50). Off to the bay side of the train station, midway between the Jardines de Pereda and the Barrio Pesquero. Ugly neighborhood, but convenient. Singles 297ptas, 460ptas with shower; doubles cost 540ptas with shower. Breakfast 65ptas. Two-star comfort.

Hostal Reigadas, Calle de Ysabel la Católica 1. 300ptas for two. Scruffy.

In El Sardinero

Hostal Luisito, Avenida de los Castros 13 (tel. 27 19 71). 200ptas per bed; shower 30ptas. Reasonably attractive and clean; nice garden. Next door are two others, **Hostal Margarita** and **Hostal Soledad.**

Hotel-Residencia Roma, Avenida de los Hoteles 5 (tel. 27 27 00). Singles 602ptas, doubles 1149ptas, including shower or bath, and breakfast. Looks more elegant than it is.

Hostal Esmeralde, Glorieta de Dr. Fleming 7 (tel. 27 03 93). 185ptas per bed.

Food

Uninspiring, in general. The **Barrio Pesquero** (fishing quarter), although overrated, is an alternative to center-city fare (take bus #5). Situated in the middle of the port warehouses, the Barrio is a shabby cluster of restaurants and bars with beautiful displays of "fruits of the sea" and men barbecuing sardines and shrimp on sidewalk grills. The best and most expensive of the Barrio restaurants is **El Vivero,** with a *menú* (usually not fish) at 245ptas. Ordering à la carte, you'll spend at least 400ptas, and double that if you're not careful. **Los Peñucas** has a *menú* at 190ptas, usually featuring sardines; try the *paella* at 160ptas.

> **Jauja,** Calle Medio #1-3. The place to go for a drink and a seafood snack. In the afternoon the bar is covered with marinated squid *(calamares),* huge shrimp *(gambas),* crabs *(cangrejos)* and fried hake *(merluza).* Try the healthy portion of small snails *(caracolillos),* which are eaten with a pin. A great lunch for under 100ptas. *Menú* for 190ptas.

> **Chupi,** Av. de los Castros 14, Sardinero (tel. 27 50 24). A convenient place to eat near the beach and the university. *Chipirones rellenos en su tinta* (cuttlefish stuffed and stewed in their ink) for 140ptas and *callos* (tripe, a northern Spanish specialty) for 105ptas. *Menú* 130ptas.

Galicia

Traveling through Galicia it is hard to believe that, of all regions in Spain, this westernmost province exports the greatest number of factory workers to Germany, Switzerland, and Sweden. The land is bursting with life, and the northern roads weave through strands of forests and the plunging valleys with their diminutive towns and lush farmsteads.

Galicia is ideal for camping and fishing. *Jabalí* (wild boar) and mustang run free in the hills; every year, horses are rounded up in colorful rodeo festivals called *curros.* The *curros* of Torrona (in early June) and **La Valga** (in the middle of May) are easily accessible by bus from **Vigo.**

Of the large cities, two are of particular interest—**La Coruña** and **Santiago de Compostela. El Ferrol del Caudillo,** despite its claim to fame as Franco's birthplace, is worth missing. If you are touring the fjord-like **Rías Altas,** aim for the little towns outside **Cedeira** and **Ortigueira; Vicedo,** on the **Playa de Area Longa,** is one of the prettiest.

Santiago de Compostela

With the discovery more than 1100 years ago of the remains of Apostle St. James (Santiago, or St. Jacques), this city became the focal point of a pilgrimage which ranked in prestige with the *romerías* to Rome and Jerusalem. In 1130 an enterprising monk even wrote a sort of *Let's Go: Santiago,* a guidebook which detailed the least dangerous routes, the best accommodations, and the safest drinking water along the way. Modern pilgrims no longer wear the uniform of cape and cockled hat, but the religious fervor here has hardly diminished. Tears glisten as the pious fit their hand in the impression worn deep in the marble of the Cathedral's central pillar by centuries of pious pilgrims; as they touch their forehead to the self-portrait of Master Mateo, who sculpted the extraordinary façade; and as they kiss the scallop shell on the back of the silver statue of the Saint, behind the altar.

The Romanesque Cathedral is not the only monument of interest in the city. In fact, the entire inner city is a designated national monument, and hardly a door or square is undeserving of comment. You might invest 250ptas in the guided visits of the city that the Tourist Office runs (daily 10am and 4pm, except afternoons of holidays). This is particularly worthwhile, as the price includes admission to several museums.

Orientation

It is all too easy to get lost in the old town, so get the map at the **Tourist Office.** Follow the signs to the Cathedral, on the vast **Plaza del Obradoiro.** The old city is ringed and separated from the newer districts by a wide avenue, which changes identity each time you've finally oriented yourself.

Hitch to La Coruña on Avenida de San Juan; to Portugal on Avenida de Martínez Anido.

Addresses and Telephone Numbers

Tourist Office: Rúa del Villar 43 (tel. 58 11 32). Open Mon.-Fri. 10am-2pm and 2:30-7:30pm, closed Sat. afternoon and Sun.

American Express Representative: Viajes Amado, Avenida Figueroa 6 (tel. 59 36 41). Mon.-Fri. 9:30am-1:30pm and 4-7:30pm, closed Sat. afternoon and Sun.

Post Office: Travesía de Fonseca (post office: tel. 58 12 52, telegraph office: tel. 58 17 92). Mon.-Fri. 9am-2pm and 4-10pm, closed Sat. afternoon and Sun.

Telephone: Calle del Franco 4, same building as Post Office. (tel. of urban information 004). Open daily 9am-2pm and 4-10pm.

RENFE: Montero Ríos 17 (tel. 59 22 45).

Train Station: General Franco (tel. 59 19 08).

Accommodations

There is no shortage of *hostales* in this pilgrimage city, and except during religious festivals you should have no trouble finding a place to stay. The rock bottom are the *fondas*, which are usually above bars, marked with a large "F" in their windows. They are listed at the Tourist Office with their price, as are all *hostales*.

Hostal-Residencia Suso, Rúa del Villar 65 (tel. 59 36 62). A few paces from the Tourist Office. Singles start at 300ptas with breakfast, doubles with breakfast run 610ptas. Very friendly owner. The bar downstairs is a clean, popular place.

Hostal-Residencia Cacharela, Rúa del Villar 77 (tel. 59 87 70). Bright doubles with sink for 365ptas, singles 290ptas. A very small place with only seven rooms, but try anyway.

Casa Enrique, Franco 28. Singles 215ptas, doubles 400ptas, shower supplement 70ptas.

Camping: 5 km on the road to La Coruña (tel. 2 La Sionilla).

Food

A number of restaurants are concentrated in the old part of town adjacent to the Cathedral, most noticeably along the Calle del Franco and the Calle Raiña. You'll find many restaurants offering *menús* at 190ptas, a number at 130ptas, and a few at 95ptas.

The bars serve a wide variety of shellfish *(mariscos)*, the Galician cheese *(queso gallego)* that is shaped like a giant chocolate kiss, and octopus *(pulpo)*. Unlike the other regions of northern Spain, the white wine *(blanco)* is more popular than the red *(tinto)*. Galician specialties include *caldo gallego,* a delicious broth served before the meal, *merluza a la gallega* (hake), ham cooked with green vegetables, and *bistek de ternera* (veal steak).

Asesino, Plaza de la Universidad 16. A rare find. A small place run by three elderly sisters who bicker with each other constantly, but their cooking is great. Always full of students who know the sisters by name. An excellent meal under 200ptas. Dinner starts at 10pm.

O Papa Upa, Restaurant Mahou, Raiña 20. This breezy place is frequented by student types, and offers about seven *menús* at 190ptas.

La Cueva, Travesía del Franco 1. Prices at this small dining room behind a bar have skyrocketed with its reputation *(menú* 500ptas), but try the generous *paella valenciana* at 175ptas.

Monroy Cafetería, at Raiña and Plazuela de Fonseca. Serves up a frugal dinner for 95ptas.

Villanueva, Franco 48. A small quick-food place. The hot dogs and sandwiches (23-60ptas) make a good, cheap, light meal.

La Coruña

For all its commerce, tourists will find La Coruña a manageable city. Everything of beauty is out on the peninsula, and the outlying newer areas (however significant to the Spanish economy) are tastelessly industrial. Although the city does have a medieval presence in some areas and some monuments, do not come expecting the sort of anachronism which you will sense in Santiago, for example. More reflective of the city's spirit is the little bar, **la metáfora** (Juan Canalejo 27), where young people gather nightly to smoke and groove on American jazz and rock rhythms.

Addresses and Telephone Numbers

Tourist Office: Darsena de la Marina (tel. 22 18 22). Open 9am-1:30pm and 4-7pm.

RENFE: Fontán 3 (tel. 22 19 48). Open daily 9am-1pm and 4-6pm, 9-11:30am on Sundays and holidays.

Train Station: Estación de San Cristóbal, Avenida de Marques de Figueroa 47. Information (tel. 23 03 09). 7am-2:20pm and 3-10:20pm.

Post Office: Avenida de la Marina. Open Mon.-Fri. 9am-2pm and 4-8pm, Sat. 9am-2pm. Telegram window open 24 hours.

Long Distance Telephone: San Andrés 101. 9am-2pm and 4-10pm.

Accommodations and Food

One-star hotels abound in the area enclosed by Calle de Juana de Vega, Calle de San Andrés, and the Cuartel de Infantería. Singles in a *hostal-residencia* should run 250-350ptas, doubles 350-475ptas. Try the **Hostal Provincial,** Rúa Nueva, and ask for a room with a balcony *(habitación con balcón)*. If you're arriving late at the train station and can't get into town, the **Café Bar Curtis,** across the street at Avenida Marques de Figueroa 47, has doubles for 300ptas. A block over, at the intersection, **Hospedaje Café Bar Kensington** is slightly more expensive.

At dinner time, crowds wander from bar to bar along the streets parallel to San Andrés: Calle de la Galera, Calle de la Estrella, and Calle de los Olmos. Most restaurants offer *menús* at 190ptas; at Olmos 20, **Somozas** has low prices and generous portions. If you're already nostalgic for the *tapas* of San Sebastián, drop by **Pavi Caserio Vasco,** a little Basque bar on Alcalde Canuto Berca, off Galera at the Cine Coruña.

Sights and Entertainment

The old city has a number of interesting historical sights lost in the medieval tangle of its streets. The name **María Pita,** which crops up everywhere, commemorates La Coruña's heroine, who rallied the defense against the English attack in 1589; there is a plaque on her house at Calle de las Herrerías 24. On the **Plaza de María Pita** is the **Palacio Municipal,** with a curious collection of old watches, among other minor holdings. From the Castillo de San Antón, designed in the sixteenth century as a quarantine for sufferers from the gangrenous contagion called St. Anthony's Fire, you have a good view of the city. The best view is from the **Torre de Hércules** (Tower of Hercules), a slightly modified Roman lighthouse on the other side of the peninsula (free admission, open officially 9:30am-2pm and 4-8pm Mon.-Fri., other times at the caretaker's whim).

Central Spain (Castile)

Madrid

A country with cities as different as Barcelona and Seville and regions as diverse as Andalusia and Galicia is hard put to find an appropriate capital. But Madrid's central location made it a natural choice. Prior to the sixteenth century, Madrid was little more than a rural market town. Growth came slowly at first but boomed in the nineteenth century, when the city became one of the great modern capitals of Europe, complete with wide boulevards, grandiose fountains, and elegant parks. Very little of the personality of the city is indigenous: the food, flamenco, and the films are all as foreign as San Sebastián, Seville, and San Francisco. In fact, the nicest people you'll meet are not going to be native to Madrid either: *Madrileños* are a surly bunch. But the city has a pace all its own, a zinging rush to live it up as soon as the sun begins to set. In no other Spanish city will you find so many bars, strip-tease joints, gay hangouts, and exotic restaurants (even a Burger King).

Madrid

1 Universidad
2 Palacio Nacional
3 American Express
4 Museo del Prado
5 Post
6 Plaza de Toros
7 Museo de Sorolla

The city is growing now at a rate unparalleled in Europe, but the grace of the older sections around **Plaza Mayor** remains undiminished. So what if the traffic is so hectic that Ben Hur would turn in his hub caps? The city is clean as a whistle—it's hosed down every morning—and the **Prado Museum** alone is worth the trip over the barren Castilian Plains.

Orientation

The free map, available at the **Tourist Office** or **American Express** (Plaza de las Cortes 2) should be a sufficient pathfinder, but better maps are available at the kiosks. Also, scattered throughout the center of town are *Columnas Informativas,* little structures which look like telephone booths and have rolling indexed maps of the city.

You can travel fastest by the **Metro** (8ptas, 11ptas round trip if bought before 9am: Sundays 11ptas, no round trip). Be sure to check the map at the entrance, as it is often the only one available, or ask for a Metro map when you get the city map. The Metro lines form wheel spokes running from the city's center. Buses are cheap (12ptas, 15ptas after 9pm and on Sundays; round trip 21ptas). More comfortable micro-buses are also available at 19ptas. For route information check the **E.M.T. Office** by the kiosks at Plaza de la Cibeles. Yellow buses run between the Airport and the center of town **(Plaza de Colón)** every fifteen minutes or so between 6am-3am; the trip takes thirty minutes and costs 35ptas.

The student area, **Argüelles,** is the cheapest, most youth-oriented part of the city. It starts at the intersection of Calle de la Princesa, Alberto Aguilera, and Marques de Urquijo and can be reached by Metro stops Argüelles or Moncloa and bus #1, 12, 61, or Circular. There are quite a number of inexpensive places to eat and drink in this area, and from September through June while the University is in session, the area is crawling with students. Calle Princesa has lots of bars, and is pleasantly crowded between 12 and 2:30pm and between 8 and 11pm. Nearby, the **Parque del Oeste** is a perfect place to relax and sip *horchata de chufa,* a milky drink available at the kiosks in the park for about 35ptas a glass. There is excellent transportation available to all points of the city from the Argüelles area. The downtown area is not as student oriented. The **Cortes Inglés** and **Galerías Preciadas** are two department stores where one can purchase gear and necessities at a reasonable price.

While in Madrid, take advantage of the *serenos,* a resource that you will find nowhere else in the world. Unfortunately, they're a dying breed. Clap your hands at night and a *sereno* will appear. When he hears you clap, he pounds his wooden stick on the ground to tell you he's coming. You can tell him what you want to pay for a place to stay and he will find it for you. They are only on duty at night, and almost never speak English, so good luck. To open a door at night, (his primary function), the *sereno* expects 10ptas. If he finds you a place to stay, tip at least 15ptas. *Serenos* help keep the streets safe and if you are ever in trouble at night, just clap.

There are three train stations, **Chamartín, Norte (Principe Pio),** and **Atocha.** Chamartín is the main station, but for trains south, go to Atocha.

Addresses and Telephone Numbers

Tourist Offices: Princesa 1, Plaza de España (tel. 241 23 25). Open 9am-2pm, 3-8pm every day except Sat. afternoons and Sun. Branches at Duque de Medinaceli 2, Barajas Airport, Torre de Madrid, and Madrid-Chamartín Station.

Municipal Information Office: Plaza Mayor 3 (tel. 266 48 74). Open 10am-1pm and 4-7pm, closed Sat. afternoons and Sun.

American Express: Plaza de las Cortes 2 (tel. 222 11 80). Open 9am-5:30pm Mon.-Fri., 9am-noon Sat.

Main Post Office and **Telegraph Office:** Palacio de Comunicaciones, Plaza de la Cibeles (tel. 221 40 04). Information open 9am-2pm and 4-9pm. Same phone for 24-hour telephone service.

RENFE: Alcalá 44 (tels. 247 74 00 and 247 84 00). 24-hour service.

Student Travel Office, VIAJESEU/TIVE: Central Office is at Calle Fernando el Católico 88 (tel. 243 00 08). Branch office at José Ortega y Gasset 71 (tel. 401 95 01).

Cook's Travel: Calle de Alcalá (tel. 231 49 67).

Police: Puerta del Sol (tel. 221 65 16). In emergency dial 091.

British-American Hospital: Calle Isaac Peral y Po Juan XXIII 1 (Parque Metropolitano; tel. 234 67 00). Take bus C.

First Aid: Don Ramón de la Cruz 93 (tel. 734 55 00).

U.S. Embassy: Serrano 75 (tel. 276 34 00).

Canadian Embassy: Núñez de Balboa 35 (tel. 225 91 19).

Laundromats: Lavomatique, Calle del Humilladero 14. Take Metro to La Latina. Another one is **Cervantes,** at Cervantes 1. Metro to Antón Martín. There are several others—check with the Tourist Office.

Accommodations

BRUJULA, a private room-finding service, has booths in the railroad stations, airports, and on major highways leading into Madrid. Their commission is supposed to be paid by the hotel. Tourist Offices will give you information, but will not arrange your accommodations. Don't worry, though—there are more than enough rooms for everybody.

Student Accommodations

From early July to the end of September many of the University boarding houses are open to tourists, especially those with reservations. Minimum stay is usually five days—but eyes glistening with tears can sometimes change that. There doesn't seem to be an official directorate for this activity—the **Pavilión de Gobierno, Universidad Complutense,** tucked away in the green at Plaza de la Victoria (right at Metro Moncloa) has a map of the various *colegios mayores,* and someone there can point out which are renting. If you speak Spanish, just open the telephone book to *colegio mayor* and start dialing. One such place is the **Colegio Mayor José Antonio,** Avenida Séneca 2 (tel. 243 26 00). Bed, full board (marginal meals), and laundry cost 700ptas in a single room or 650ptas in a double. Take Metro to Moncloa or bus #12. Nearby, set back from the Avenida, is the **Colegio Mayor San Agustín** (tel. 244 34 04). Singles only, 700ptas.

Youth Hostel Richard Schirrman (IYHF), Casa de Campo (tels. 263 56 99 and 463 56 99). Located in the park close to the lake and municipal swimming pool, a great place to relax. Take Metro to El Lago. 100ptas per bed. Hostel meals are well worth the money: breakfast 35ptas, lunch 160ptas, dinner 130ptas.

Hotels and Pensions

The **Gran Vía** (Avenida José Antonio) is loaded with accommodations, especially between #140 and 65. Many of the buildings on this street have one or two *hostales* per floor with similar prices, so if one is full, just knock on another. Start high up—they tend to be cheaper and quieter. The prices run about 250ptas per person and up.

The best streets for down-and-out spots are **Calle del Principe,** which runs off the Plaza de Canalejas, and the **Calle de Echegaray,** one block away. You should never have to pay more than 200ptas (singles) here, but don't expect hot water. A little farther away on **Calle Magdalena** you should not have to pay more than 175ptas (singles).

You'll find a stack of hostales at José Antonio 44. **Alibel,** 8th floor, (tel. 221 00 51), has doubles for 600ptas, 800ptas with full bath, including breakfast; hot showers 100ptas. **Josefina,** 7th floor (tel. 221 81 41), has singles for 250ptas, 1-bed doubles for 350ptas, 2-bed doubles 400ptas; free showers. **Valencia,** 5th floor (tel. 222 11 15). A 3-star place: singles 495ptas with private shower, 560ptas with full bath; doubles 780ptas with shower, 940ptas with full bath; breakfast 77ptas. **Continental,** 3rd floor (tel. 221 46 40), charges 478ptas for a single (free shower) and 938ptas for a double with private shower; prices include breakfast. **Hispana,** 2nd floor (tel. 221 51 66), charges 640ptas and up for doubles, 60ptas for hot showers; no single rooms.

José Antonio 15. A house of 2-star *hostales*—a little more expensive. **La Selecta,** 6th floor (tel. 231 01 58), charges 415ptas and up for singles, 650ptas and up for doubles, both including breakfast and shower. **Galaico,** 5th floor (tel. 221 46 68), charges 420ptas for singles, 690ptas and up for doubles; prices include breakfast; 70ptas for use of common shower. **Felipe V** (tel. 222 51 43), has doubles for 855ptas, including complete bath and breakfast.

Alcázar Regis, José Antonio 61 (tel. 247 93 17). A grand old place with woodwork, crystal chandeliers, stained-glass sliding doors and antiques—a real find and very reasonable. 465ptas for a double room, same for single occupancy; breakfast obligatory at 48ptas; showers 40ptas. Half pension 576ptas per person, 700ptas per person for full pension. The place downstairs on the 2nd floor is almost as good and cheaper: 295ptas for singles, 435ptas for doubles; 5 or 10ptas for showers at **Buenos Aires** (tel. 247 88 00).

Hostal Don José, José Antonio 38, 7th floor (tel. 232 13 85). A small *hostal* with 6 delightful doubles. A bargain at 600ptas for a double with full bath. There are three other more expensive hotels in the same building.

Hostal Gago, Calle de la Estrella 5, two blocks north of José Antonio, (tel. 221 22 75). Clean and comfortable. Singles 220ptas, doubles 365ptas, 450 with bath; hot showers 70ptas, cold 35ptas. If it's full, try **Hostal Romero** on the 3rd floor (tel. 222 19 36). Singles 240ptas, doubles 365ptas, 450 with full bath; hot showers 70ptas, cold 40.

Hostal de Castro, Desengaño 11 (tel. 221 15 83) is located on a quiet side street just a block and a half north of the Gran Vía. Doubles 600ptas including shower and breakfast, triples 800ptas with breakfast and private shower. (Negotiable). **Pensión Cazorla,** a *casa de huéspedes* on the 4th floor, is an even better deal: singles are 135ptas, doubles 250ptas, both with sinks in the rooms; 50ptas for showers. And on the 1st floor, one of the best of the cheapest: **Fonda Pereda** (tel. 221 81 58), at 80-120ptas per person, 20ptas for a shower.

There is yet another house of hostales across the side street from the American Express at Plaza de las Cortes 3. **Aguadulce** (tel. 232 21 11), on the top floor, has doubles at 540ptas, singles 366ptas, both with showers included. You can find showerless singles for less in the building's other *hostales*.

Hostal Coruña, Paseo del Prado 12 (tel. 239 14 34). Right across the street from the Prado. Singles 260ptas, doubles 400ptas, showers 55ptas. Upstairs is **Hostal Sud-Americana** (tel. 239 16 34), with almost the same prices: singles 255ptas, doubles 465ptas, showers 70ptas.

Hostal Sabina, Calle Duque de Rivas 2, 2nd floor (tel. 265 30 84), two blocks south of Plaza Mayor, has good rooms with small balconies. 200ptas for singles, 350ptas for doubles, 425ptas for doubles with private shower, 30ptas for breakfast, 70ptas for showers. Good value.

Hostal Arrate, Gaztambide 61, 6th floor (tel. 244 30 63). Very clean. Singles 379ptas, 415ptas with full bath; doubles 600-700ptas; prices include breakfast. Showers 40ptas. Next door, same floor, is a *fonda* with beds for 150ptas, and another on the 4th floor charges the same. **Hostal Horche,** on the 2nd floor, is more expensive. Singles 410ptas, doubles 670ptas including breakfast. Full pension is 700ptas, or 1300ptas per person in a double.

Hostal Oxford, Guzmán el Bueno 57, 1st floor (tel. 244 13 01). Doubles 500ptas, including breakfast.

Camping: There are twelve sites within 50 km of Madrid, and two in the city area. Camping Osuna, 15.5 km from center city on Carretera de Ajalvir-Vicálvaro (tel. 741 05 10), is rated first class. Bus P-5. Open all year; 60ptas per person, 35-60ptas per tent, 60ptas per car.

Food

One of the best budget restaurant streets in Madrid is **Ventura de la Vega.** Walk uphill two blocks on Calle del Prado or San Jerónimo from the Plaza de las Cortes. Another good budget street is **Calle del Barco,** off José Antonio. Note that many restaurants in Madrid are closed in August.

The best places for *tapas* are the *tascas* in Old Madrid, south of the Plaza Mayor. **Calle de Cuchilleros** is lined with them. **Café Bar Same,** on Calle de las Maldonadas 9 (next to the Metro Latina) is a regular *tapas* circus. Take care to avoid the *mesones* immediately to the left of the Cuchilleros Arch of the Plaza Mayor—they are geared to the white shoes-double knit tourist set and will startle you when your order of *tapas* totals 400ptas.

The Valencia, José Antonio 44 (tel. 232 01 50), has excellent *paella* for 190ptas, *menú turístico* for 290ptas.

La Estrella, Estrella 5-6, just off the Gran Vía at the Capitol Cinema. Good, moderately-priced food. The *Pollo al ajo* (chicken with garlic) is especially good. *Menú turístico* 175ptas. Closed for part of the summer.

La Trucha, Manuel Fernández y González 3, (tel. 231 90 32). Just northeast of Plaza de Santa Ana. Delicious trout served several ways for 200-220ptas. Solid meals. *Menú turístico* is 190ptas. Closed in August.

El Criollo, Barbieri 21, south of Chueca. A three-course meal costs an incredible 80ptas. A la carte is equally cheap. The food leaves much to be desired, but at these prices . . . Nearby at Barbieri 4 is **Tasca Vasca Onci Etorri,** a clean little hole with fresh seafood *tapas*.

Tienda de Vinos, Augusto Figueroa 35, around the corner and across the street from El Criollo. Meal of the day varies, usually less than 150ptas. A great place to eat.

Casa Poli, Calle de las Infantas 28 (tel. 221 17 67), in the angle between José Antonio and Barquillo. A good cheapie: *menú turístico* 130ptas, *platos combinados* 100-190ptas.

Casa Sobrino de Botín, Calle de Cuchilleros 17 (tel. 266 42 17). Southeast of Plaza Mayor. A good splurge. Its speciality, at 595ptas a serving, is roast suckling pig from an eighteenth-century oven. One of Hemingway's favorite restaurants.

Sights

The **Prado Museum,** one of the world's greatest and oldest art museums, contains over 3000 paintings from all over the Continent, many of them collected by various Spanish kings between the sixteenth and eighteenth centuries. You might want to concentrate on the works of the Spanish masters: Goya, Velázquez, and El Greco—although there are works by Bosch, Rubens, and Italian Renaissance and pre-Renaissance masters that you won't want to miss. You'll burn yourself out if you try to see it all in one day; try to make several visits. Free with student ID, 50ptas otherwise. (Open May-October 10am-6pm Mon.-Sat., 10am-2pm Sun. and holidays; rest of the year closes at 5pm.) The colossal eighteenth-century building is located on the broad Paseo del Prado (tel. 239 00 97).

The **Palacio Real** (Royal Palace) is Madrid's only other real sight. (Open, except during royal visits, from 10am-12:45pm and 4-6:15pm in the summer; 10am-12:45pm and 3-4:45pm in winter. Sundays 10am-1:30pm.) There's a lot to see: the required guided tour will show you an endless collection of porcelain, tapestries, furniture, armor, and paintings. 185ptas for the comprehensive ticket, or you can break it down several ways. Don't miss the exquisite gadgetry of medieval combat and torture in the Armería (Bus #4, 15, 25, 33, or 39; Metro: Opera).

The **Plaza Mayor,** a large seventeenth-century square built by Philip III for celebrations and competitions, houses shops, markets, restaurants and occasional summer festivities. Located in the zestiest part of town, the Plaza Mayor also attracts visiting philatelists to its Sunday morning stamp market. Just off the south side of the Plaza you will be lured to the **Rastro,** or "flea market" where antiques and second-hand goods abound. (Sunday only

9am-2pm). You should practice your bargaining skills even if you don't speak the language.

The **Retiro Park** is 325 acres of green in the heart of the city, with elegant gardens, forests, fountains, botanical collections, and even a lake where you can rent a rowboat (Metro: Retiro). **Casa de Campo Park,** to the northwest, has woods, shaded lanes, municipal pool, and the new zoo. More than ten times the size of Retiro, this park gives you the impression that the city is only a development on the outskirts of forests (two Metro stops: Lago and Batán, or take bus #33).

The little-known **Sorolla Museum,** General Martínez Campos 37, Chamberí (tel. 410 15 84), was the home and studio of the celebrated nineteenth-century Spanish painter. It's a quiet, pleasant place to escape the crowds. (Open 10am-2pm, closed Mondays; 50ptas, free to students. Metro: Iglesia or Rubén Darío.)

Bullfights

The **Plaza de Toros de las Ventas** is the world's most famous bullfighting ring and boasts a bullfight every Sunday. The best matadors are featured in May, during the **fiesta of San Isidro.** Aficionados can purchase tickets in the center of town at Victoria 9 on Sat. 10am-1pm and 5-9pm; on Sundays 10am-2pm. Go early to get good seats. Ticket prices vary wildly, as low as 15ptas for the *novilladas* (messy amateur bloodbaths—they should pay you!), to well above 2000ptas for good seats on a big fiesta. In the summer get a seat in the shade *(sombra);* if you sit in the *sol,* you may expire before the bull.

Evenings

Madrid's nightlife is one of the liveliest anywhere. Every evening of the week it seems *Madrileños* are out in search of amusement. Because of the late dinner, the streets begin to fill around 9:30pm with people on their way to the movies, shows, theater, or simply taking an after-dinner stroll. Late night entertainment usually means nightclubs *(salones de fiesta),* a favorite local bar, or discos—which have become very popular, and much more liberal since Franco's death. For a cheap evening, head for the Plaza Mayor. It is full of life until about 2am.

Discotheques, Nightclubs, and Bars

Aurrera, between Calle de Gaztambide and Calle de Andrés Mellado at Calle Fernando el Católico, in the Argüelles area. This is actually a mall with almost 100 small bars of every sort imaginable. A great place to hang out. Everything from English-style pubs to Hare Krishna.

Drugstores: There are two of them—one at intersection of Velázquez and Goya and one near Bilbao. Open all night. Mixed crowd including gays.

Cerebro: There are three of these popular discos, two near Metro Plaza de España at Princesa 5, and one at Magallanes 1 (Metro Quevedo). Open 7-10pm and 11:30pm-3am. Entrance 300-400ptas.

Flamenco

If you're heading to Andalucía, don't waste your time and money looking for authentic flamenco in Madrid. If Madrid's your only chance, though, the

one half-decent place is the **Corral de la Morrería,** at Calle de la Morrería
17. 600ptas, music 11pm-3am. All seats are good. *Menú turístico* 1300ptas
including music charge.

Daytrips

The most popular short excursions from Madrid are to the northwest. The
Valle de los Caídos (Valley of the Fallen), with General Franco's 500-foot
cross commemorating the Civil War dead of both sides, thousands of whom
are buried there, is open 9:30am-8pm; get there by 7pm. The cross ex-
emplifies the Fascist aesthetic that big is beautiful; the view from the base, at
least, is beautiful. Walk or take the funicular. On the way to the Valley from
Madrid, you may wish to stop in **El Escorial,** the country palace of Spain's
greatest king, Philip II. A massive affair, more like a prison than a palace, it
contains a superb art collection. The tour takes about three hours (open
10am-1pm and 3-7pm; admission 50ptas). **Herranz** runs a few daily buses
from Madrid to both monuments from Isaac Peral 10 (Metro: Moncloa). The
trip to El Escorial takes one hour and costs 66ptas one way. To the Valley,
17 kilometers beyond, the round trip from Madrid costs 190ptas.

The most beautiful area in Central Spain is the **Sierra Guadarrama,**
especially around the pass of **Puerto de Navacerrada.** The road is a coil of
switchbacks through pine forests up to heights of 1800 meters. There's a ski
resort there, as well as an IYHF **Youth Hostel** with all the fixings. In the
summer climb to the top of the ski jump for the dizzying view. The descent
towards Segovia, via the **Granja de San Ildefonso,** is even more beautiful
than the southeast slope.

Avila, just west of Segovia, is a near-perfect, eleventh-century walled city
and a national monument. From Madrid, take the train from Atocha Station.

Aranjuez, 47 kilometers south of Madrid, has often been compared to
Versailles, but the royal splendor of the Spanish palace is as unlike the
French as the Baroque fanfares of *Son et Lumière* are unlike the wrenching
nostalgia of Rodrigo's *Aranjuez Concerto.* The Spanish soul seems to re-
spond to this oasis the way the arid soil yearns for water. The major attractions are the **Palacio Real** and the **Casa del Labrador,** a second palace.

Bus service to and from Madrid is cheap (95ptas each way) and frequent.
The Station in Madrid is at Paseo de las Delicias 18 (tels. 227 12 94 and 230
46 07). There is also a Train Station a few minutes walk west of town.

Aranjuez has one of the most delightful campgrounds in Spain, **Soto del
Castillo** (tel. 294 13 95). Open May through September, all facilities, in-
cluding pool; 70ptas per person, 70-80ptas per tent. Across from the Casa de
Marinos.

Salamanca

For centuries the hand of Salamanca, the brass knocker traditionally found
on the doors of this city, has welcomed students, scholars, rogues, princes,
and saints. The old city is built almost entirely of golden sandstone, and
although almost every architectural style from Romanesque to Baroque is
represented, there is a harmonious quality to this university town that is
found in few other cities. Salamanca's **Plaza Mayor,** at the center of the
city, was built by Philip V in the eighteenth century, and is generally considered the most beautiful main square in Spain. The University is the oldest
in Spain. In the sixteenth century it carried on an interchange of ideas with
Oxford and Bologna. Kings based their defiance of the Pope on the powerful

Salamanca theology. But by the late eighteenth and early nineteenth centuries, the University had sunk so low that it was little more than a fancy
finishing school. Today it thrives again, although the real ambitious types
more often head for Madrid or Barcelona.

There are two big fiestas in Salamanca: June 12 (patron saint San Juan de
Sahagún) and for two weeks, September 8-21.

Three hours from Madrid by train, Salamanca is just a little too far for a
day-trip—but the evenings are half the fun anyway, so bring your pack and
stay for a few days. Trains leave from Madrid's Chamartín Station. The
Salamanca Station is a twenty-minute walk from the center of town. The
Plaza Mayor is the physical as well as the spiritual center of things. The **Rúa
Mayor** connects the Plaza with the University and Cathedral area. The **Gran
Vía (Calle de España),** where the Tourist Office is located, runs parallel to
Mayor. Salamanca is small, and you can easily get around the center on foot.

Those interested in studying in Spain will want to consider the University
and its well-organized summer courses for foreigners. It doesn't have the
beaches of Santander or the big city bustle of Madrid, but Salamanca beats
them both hands down for atmosphere and student life. Students in the
summer course are housed in one of three *colegios* at the University. At
Colegio Mayor Fray Luis de León, at Plaza Fray Luis de Léon 13 (tel. 21 57
00), full room and board costs about 12,000-13,000ptas per month. You can
just show up and sign in usually—even if you're not taking a course. Tuition
costs 5000ptas per month. For information, write to Secretaría de los Cursos
de Verano, Universidad de Salamanca, Patio de Escuelas Menores (tel. 21
66 81).

Addresses and Telephone Numbers

Tourist Office: Gran Vía 11 (tel. 21 37 30). Open 9:30am-2pm and 4:30-
7:30pm, closed Sat. afternoons and all day Sun. Excellent polyglot service.
Also a booth on the **Plaza Mayor** (tel. 21 83 42), open 10am-1:30pm and
4:30-7:30pm in summer; 10am-1:30pm and 5-7pm in winter.

Post Office: Gran Vía (tels. 21 30 21, 21 79 08, and 21 21 92 for telegrams).

RENFE: Plaza de Onésimo Redondo 10 (tel. 21 24 54; Station information tel.
22 03 95).

Bus Station: Héroes de Brunete 31, northwest of the Plaza Mayor. Information: (tel. 23 67 17).

Accommodations

Hotels and pensions are plentiful in Salamanca, so you shouldn't have
much trouble. Rock bottom are the *fondas,* which are everywhere. There are
plenty of *fondas* around the Plaza Mayor, or in the Calle Meléndez just
below it. Beds here run about 150ptas, but don't expect more than the
minimum in comfort and cleanliness. Better than most is the **Fonda Lisboa**
at Meléndez 1 (tel. 21 43 33). 235ptas for a single and 388ptas for a double
(20% less if you eat here). A little further down, at #13, **Hospedaje
Zacharías** has good rooms at 200ptas for singles, 300ptas for doubles, but
the shower is miserable. For *hostales* try:

Colón, Plaza de Onésimo Redondo, just north of Plaza Mayor (tel. 21 99 10).
A fairly cheap place on a pretty plaza; rooms are adequate at 260ptas for a

single and 456ptas for a double, both with breakfast. Showers 75ptas. If full you might try the **Esperanza** around the corner at Concejo 4 (tel. 21 35 33). Doubles only 380-480ptas; breakfast obligatory 46ptas; showers 70ptas.

Pensión Albacete, Caleros 1 (tel. 21 84 80). A small, very clean, and friendly place with 5 cheap rooms (9 beds in all). Singles 228ptas, doubles 388ptas, both with breakfast. Showers depend on how long you stay—usually 50ptas. For full pension, add 385ptas per person and subtract 20% off the room.

Tormes, Rúa Mayor 20 (tel. 21 96 83). Doubles 370ptas with sink, 436ptas with shower; meals are 260ptas, breakfast 42ptas. Showers 60ptas. 20% more on rooms if you eat no meals.

Hotel Conde David, Av. de Italia (tel. 22 63 62). Comparatively luxurious rooms for low prices. Singles 321ptas with shower, doubles 632ptas with full bath. Breakfast included. Unfortunately, a 15-minute walk from the center of things; due north of the Plaza Mayor. Fray Luis de Granada runs right up to it at an intersection just beyond the edge of the *Turismo* maps.

Food

Bar Restaurante Felix, Pozo Amarillo 8, is a simple place with good food and large portions at reasonable prices. Four good *menús* at 240ptas and a tourist *menú* for 160ptas.

Mesón de Cervantes, Plaza Mayor 12, first floor. A bust of Cervantes presides over the bar and the pinball machine. The dining room has wooden benches and looks out over the Plaza. Run by young people and full of students. Combination plates 130-200ptas.

El Candil, Ruiz Aguilera 10 (tels. 21 72 39 and 21 50 58). A cozy dining room lies off a crowded *tapas* bar. *Menú del día* 190ptas. On the same street at #8 is **Roma.** Here the *platos combinados* ranges from 80-195ptas and the *menú turístico* is 115ptas. **Snack Auto Servicio** at #3 is a cheap self-service cafeteria.

Sights

Salamanca has two cathedrals. The **Old Cathedral** is a twelfth-century Romanesque edifice that has an altarpiece painted by Nicholas of Florence in 1495, and an eighteenth-century cloister that replaced the earlier Romanesque one (admission 25ptas). The larger **New Cathedral** stands next door. Begun in 1513, it is one of the last Gothic structures in Spain. (Free admission). Both cathedrals are open 9:30am-1:30pm and 3:30-6pm in winter, and 9:30am-2pm and 3:30-8pm from May through September 30.

The University is entered from **Patio de las Escuelas,** off the bookstore street **(Calle Libreros).** The entryway is one of the best examples of Spanish Plateresque, a style named after the silversmith's art because of the intricate carvings. Visiting hours 9:30am-1:30pm and 4-7pm; admission 50ptas, 25ptas for foreign students.

The **Casa de las Conchas** (House of Shells) is Salamanca's most famous landmark. The otherwise typical fifteenth-century Salamanca house of golden sandstone is decorated with row after row of scallop shells. The house also has beautiful Isabeline windows and wrought iron grills. Inside is the **Provincial Museum.**

The Plaza Mayor, mentioned above, is a fine place to sit for hours and admire the architecture as well as the passers-by. Between the arches are carved medallions of famous Spaniards from Columbus to El Generalísimo.

Evenings

Discotheques are the rage in this student city. But an evening sipping expresso in the Plaza Mayor is a pleasant alternative to the quadrophonic hi-fi and strobe lights. Everyone hangs out in the Plaza—groups of students build human pyramids or sit in circles with guitars and sing folk songs. The bars near the University are also full of life. **La Latina** at Calle de la Latina 5 is a very popular place with a modern bar downstairs and a patio upstairs. **Skorpius**, Generalísimo Franco 44, with its ultramodern dance floor, is one of the hottest discos in town, but **Tartana** on Elvira Zapata, **Aleko's** at Rua Mayor 12, **Hindagala** on Plaza de la Reina, and especially **Titos** in Iscar Peyra, are all popular.

Segovia

Segovia is busily preparing for an inevitable influx of tourists, who thus far have avoided the town. But, at least for the moment, the city is still dominated by the past—a 728-meter-long Roman aqueduct which still carries water to the parched russet countryside; and the **Alcázar** (fortress) which looks as *alcázares* should look and rarely do. Clustered in the city are more than forty churches which compete with Moorish and Visigothic ruins to make up Segovia's diverse architectural heritage.

Finding accommodations in Segovia is not a major problem yet. The **Tourist Office** at Plaza del Franco 8 (tel. 41 42 87), will provide you with help and encouragement. If they're closed, you can check out their list of all accommodations (except *casas particulares*), including prices, posted outside the door. There are five places listed at 175ptas for singles and 280ptas for doubles.

Toledo

If you let yourself be talked out of going to Toledo because it's the most touristy city in Spain, you might as well burn your Eurailpass and take the next charter home. Sure it's mobbed, but Toledo is *the* best museum of Spanish history and culture. If you compare the map *Turismo* gives you to the one held by El Greco's son in the famous oil, *View and Map of Toledo,* you'll discover that nothing has changed in four hundred years. With no room to space themselves out on the naturally-moated promontory, the city's monuments have squashed themselves on top of each other in a dizzying anarchy of periods and styles, held together in a medieval matrix of leaning houses. Emblematic of the cultural confusion are the **Mezquita del Cristo de la Luz** (Mosque of the Christ of the Light) and the **Sinagoga de Santa María la Blanca** (Synagogue of Saint Mary the White). The **Cathedral** (open 10:30am-1pm and 3:30-7pm; closes an hour earlier in winter; admission 50ptas), is a noble hodge-podge of every important architectural style of the Middle Ages. The **Alcázar,** which dominates the skyline, was entirely rebuilt after the 1936 Civil War and is hardly worth the 45ptas admission.

Domenico Theotocópuli, alias **El Greco,** is in large part responsible for mythifying Toledo's image. People who spend days in the city and never see a cloud except on his tempestuous canvases write home about Toledo's "magical sky." The so-called **House of El Greco** is actually only close to where the painter lived. (Open 10am-2pm and 3:30-7pm in summer; 10am-2pm and 3:30-6pm in winter. Closed Sunday afternoons and all day Mondays; admission 25ptas.) **The Museo de Santa Cruz** (open 10am-6pm; admission 50ptas) houses no less than 22 of the master's works as well as important works by other artists. The **Hospital de Tavera** (open 10am-1:30pm and 3:30-6pm; admission 50ptas) is a private museum on the outskirts of town that has five El Grecos as well as works by Titian and Ribera. Among the many treasures of the Cathedral are El Greco's famed *Twelve Apostles* and the *Spoliation of Christ*. Finally, a modest *Mudéjar* church called **Santo Tomé** houses El Greco's masterpiece, *El Entierro del Conde de Orgaz* (The Burial of Count Orgaz). Open every day 10am-2pm and 3:30-7pm in summer; 10am-2pm and 3:30-6pm in winter, closed Sun. afternoon and all day Mon. Admission 15ptas.

Toledo is famous for its swords and knives, and damascene—an ancient and dying craft of inlaid gold on a black steel background, used to decorate everything from swords to ashtrays. You will find tourist shops by the hundreds stocking these items. Check around extensively and get a feel for the market before you buy.

Orientation

Toledo's very helpful **Turismo** (tel. 22 08 43) is located on the north side of town, just outside the Puerta de Bisagra. Open 9:30am-2pm and 3:30-5pm; closed Saturday afternoons and all day Sunday. The **Bus Station** (tel. 22 73 60) is just south of the Alcázar on Explanada de San Miguel. There are five daily departures to and from Madrid. The **Train Station** is on the eastern Paseo de la Rosa, below and beyond the Youth Hostel. The best view of the city is from the balcony of the **Parador Nacional Conde de Orgaz** on the south hill.

Accommodations

Don't panic. Turismo can help out; there are *casas particulares* and there's a great **IYHF Youth Hostel** with a swimming pool at the Castillo de San Servando.

Casa del Maestro, Calle de Santa Leocadia (tel. 22 39 95). Good for the money. Singles 190ptas, doubles 325ptas, triples 459ptas; free shower. Breakfast 38ptas, meals 236ptas each. 15 rooms.

Fonda Las Armas, Armas 7 (tel. 22 16 68). Friendly people run this, and the upstairs turns into a mosque maze. Singles 200ptas, doubles 335ptas, showers 60ptas. 20 rooms.

Fonda Segovia, Recaletos 4 (no phone). Simple and cheap; doubles 290ptas, triples 450ptas, breakfast 40ptas, meals 205ptas, showers 70ptas. 20% more on rooms if no meals are taken.

Fonda Lumbreras, Calle Juan Labrador 7 (tel. 22 15 71). Singles 160ptas, doubles 274ptas, meals 204ptas, cold shower free, hot 70ptas; 20% more on rooms if no meals are taken. Great rooms; highly recommended.

Camping: El Greco, Carretera Toledo-Talavera, March-Oct.; **Toledo,** Carretera de Madrid, April-Sept.; **Circo Romano,** Circo Romano 21, May-Sept.

Food

Food in Toledo is tough on the budget. One of the best restaurants is **La Contrária,** Paseo de la Rosa (tel. 22 30 69), directly across from the Train Station. Set meals are 130ptas, but everything is cheap and tasty here. In town there are a few cheap places with capricious schedules. **Bar Moderno Restaurante** at Hombre de Palo 7 (tel. 22 20 73), and **El Nido** at Plaza de la Magdalena 5 (tel. 22 40 40) are mediocre but won't cost you over 200ptas. Lots of locals go to **Casa Rufo** at Granada 6 for lunch.

Andalucia

Seville (Sevilla)

If you're convinced that there are no romantic cities—only romantic tourists—Seville will change your mind. Wait until dark when your retinas recover from the solar whiteout, and street lamps restore the corners and shadows on the golden stone of the cathedrals and palaces. Wait until midnight and you won't believe your ears: people are singing in the streets, clapping, and playing the guitar.

By day Seville is a real-life city, with traffic, ugly areas, and a withering summer heat. But it also has dozens of beautiful parks and monuments: great garden parks like **María Luisa,** elegant promenades like the **Paseo de Catalina de Ribera** along Menéndez y Pelayo, vest-pocket gems like the **Plaza de Pilatos** at the juncture of Aguilas and San Esteban. In front of the **Córdoba Train Station,** in the middle of the most intolerable traffic are the banks of the **Guadalquivir,** a garden oasis where you can rent rowboats for 150ptas an hour or paddleboats *(patines)* for 125ptas an hour.

Seville's **Semana Santa** (Holy Week) festival, beginning on Palm Sunday, is internationally famous for the processions of penitents in spooky, hooded gowns and the fabulous floats—including one which carries the patron of Seville, the *Virgen de la Macarena.* After the religious solemnities, the city explodes in its **Feria de Abril** (April Fair) with circuses, folklore displays, bullfights, and flamenco (day and night).

Orientation

The **River Guadalquivir** runs approximately north-south through Seville. Most of the city is on the east bank, while the **Barrio Triana**—a rather seedy quarter inhabited by a large gypsy population—lies on the west bank. Right in the bend of the river on the east bank is the **Córdoba Station,** also called Plaza de Armas. Across town to the southeast is the **Cádiz Station,** which handles traffic to the south. Between the two, running north-south, is the main street, **Avenida Queipo de Llano** with the monstrous **Cathedral** and **Giralda Tower.** The **Tourist Office** is a block down at Queipo de Llano 9-B; across the street is the **Post Office.** Due north of the Cathedral is Calle Hernando Colón where the **American Express** Office is. Across the **Plaza de la Falange Española,** Hernando Colón runs into Sierpes, the center of a pedestrian shopping district. The **Barrio Santa Cruz,** a beautiful old quarter, lies behind the Cathedral.

Taxis are relatively cheap; the meter starts at 25ptas, then adds 9ptas per kilometer. Buses are 12ptas and minibuses 18ptas, but most attractions are an easy walk from the center. Parking is not difficult, but in most places the little men in uniform *(guardacoches)* will want 10ptas for protecting your car all day—a bargain, but hardly necessary given the low rate of car theft here.

Seville is hot—a midday siesta here is no luxury; it's a necessity. See the Tourist Office for a list of public swimming pools.

Addresses and Telephone Numbers

Tourist Office: Av. Queipo de Llano 9-B (tel. 20 14 04). 9am-2pm and

4:30-7pm daily.

VIAJESEU: Av. Reina Mercedes 53 (tel. 61 31 88). Student travel service.

American Express: Ultramar Express SA, Hernando Colón 1 (tel. 21 38 46). Open Mon.-Fri. 9:30am-1:30pm and 4:30-8pm; closed Sat. afternoons and all day Sun.

Post Office: Av. Queipo de Llano 20 (tel. 22 88 80).

RENFE: Calle de Zaragoza 29 (tels. 23 19 14, 23 19 15, and 23 19 18).

Train Stations: Estación de Cádiz, San Bernardo (tel. 23 22 56) and Estación de Córdoba, Plaza de Armas (tel. 22 88 17).

Bus Stations (Estación de Autobuses): José María Osborne (tel. 23 22 10). All lines, except Huelva, which is at Segura 18 (tel. 22 22 72) and Badajoz at Arenal 3 (tel. 22 58 20).

Police: Plaza de la Gavidia (tel. 22 88 40). Emergency, dial 091.

First Aid (Casa de Socorro): Menéndez Pelayo 2 (tel. 23 46 67).

U.S. Consulate: P.E.U. Paseo de las Delicias 7 (tel. 21 18 85).

Accommodations

Seville has no youth hostel, and the nearest camping is 6 kilometers away, but don't despair; the city has lots of cheap hotels for sometimes unbelievably low prices—as little as 120-180ptas for a bed *(cama)* in a one-star *hostal*, a *fonda* (designated by a white F on a blue sign) or a *casa de huéspedes* ("guest house" designated by CH). The two primary locations are the old **Santa Cruz quarter** and along the **Calle de San Eloy** and adjacent streets. Check especially around the **Calle de Santa María la Blanca.** In the summer and during the *Feria* in April, many places will be full; but keep looking. The possibilities are endless.

Hostal Pérez Montilla, Archeros 14A (tel. 36 17 40). Off the Calle Santa María la Blanca. A terrific deal; the people who run it are wonderful. Singles 285ptas, doubles 500ptas, both with breakfast; hot showers 60ptas. On the same street at #19 is the **Casa de Huéspedes Orellana** (tel. 36 22 29). Singles 160ptas, doubles 275ptas, both without breakfast. Or try the **Casa de Huéspedes Mateo** at #7 (tel. 36 78 95). One of the nicer cheapies at 150ptas per person.

Hostal Atenas, Caballerizas 1 (tels. 21 80 47 and 21 80 48). Not the cheapest you can find, but worth it—a beautiful place. Only one single at 450ptas with breakfast, 710ptas with breakfast and one meal; doubles 670ptas with breakfast, 1180ptas with the meal also.

Hostal-Residencia Monreal, Rodrigo Caro 8 (tel. 21 54 14). Quiet. Singles with hot shower/bath 328ptas, doubles 660ptas; breakfast included.

Hostal Doña Pepa, Santa Teresa 3 (tel. 22 95 98). Airy rooms with showers; singles 400ptas, doubles 600ptas and up.

West of Campana

There are several possibilities along San Eloy.

Zahira, at #43 (tel. 22 10 61), has singles for 275ptas, 350ptas with shower; doubles 445ptas, 625ptas with a bathroom; breakfast 65ptas.

Hostal Los Angeles, at #41 (tel. 22 80 49) has singles for 201ptas, doubles 343ptas; breakfast 45ptas, lunch or dinner 220ptas. 20% more on rooms if you don't eat a full meal.

A fonda at #45 has singles for 180ptas, doubles for 275ptas, showers 40ptas. 20% extra if you don't take meals.

Hostal La Española, at #17 (tel. 22 11 09) has singles for 218ptas, doubles 347ptas; breakfast 45ptas, lunch or dinner 226ptas, three meals 423ptas. 20% extra on rooms if you eat no meals.

Los Naranjos, San Roque 11 (tel. 22 58 40). A good, clean place to stay. Singles with bath 200ptas, doubles 395ptas. No breakfast.

Campgrounds: Sevilla (tel. 25 63 20). 6 km out, on Carretera de Córdoba. Wilson (tel. 72 08 28). 12 km out, on Carretera de Cádiz, Dos Hermanas.

Food

Food here is generally expensive by Spanish standards, but you can find enjoyable and cheap meals. Some of the best budget eating can be done in the **Barrio Triana** across the river along the Calle Castilla. There are also some inexpensive places near the Plaza de Armas Station on the Calle del Marques de Paradas, where you can eat well for about 130ptas.

Andalusian cooking relies heavily on olive oil. The excellent Andalusian stew *(cocido andaluz)* is often served as a first course. Seville is also famous for its *tapas* and *raciones* that are washed down with wine or a glass of beer. The bars in the Barrio Triana are the best place for *tapas*. There is no need to order any fancy wines here, as the wines of the house *(vino de casa),* usually decanted from large barrels, are almost always good. And don't forget to sample the sherry that is made just south of Seville in **Jerez.**

El Mesón, Dos de Mayo 26 (tel. 21 30 76). The specialty here is bull, and it doesn't have far to come—the Plaza de Toros is a couple of blocks down. James Michener went crazy over this place, and to judge by the memorabilia, the feelings were mutual. The menu still carries a dessert called "el combinado Michenier," which is quince jam *(membrillo)* and *manchego* cheese (90ptas at table, 75ptas at the bar). Michener wasn't the only one to fall in love with El Mesón—the photo gallery is a *Who's Who in Spain.* Fame hasn't hurt the quality of the food much: the *gazpacho* may be the best around. Several *menús,* including one at 190ptas. Food is 15% cheaper if you stand at the bar.

Los Gallegos, Carpio 3 (an alley off Campana). One of the best budget restaurants in Seville. The food is plentiful and delicious. Try the asparagus in mayonnaise *(esparagos con mahonesa),* the fried squid *(calamares),* or the shrimp in garlic *(gambas al ajillo);* each 90ptas. Main dishes 85-200ptas; *plato del día* at 40-50ptas. Closed Wednesdays. Try the bar next door for *tapas*.

Casa Manolo, San Jorge 16 (tel. 33 47 92), in the Barrio Triana. Always crowded with locals, and on fiestas it's a madhouse. The waiters try to out-scream each other. Food is excellent, main dishes in the 150-225ptas range.

Casa Diego, Comidas Económicas, Plaza Curtidores 7, off Av. de Menéndez

Pelayo (tel. 36 33 02). Cheap: a full meal with wine can cost 120ptas, and the *menu* of the day is 130ptas. Try the *piccadillo,* an Andalusian broth with eggs and bread (45ptas). Lots of students here.

Los Alcázares, Miguel Mañara 10 off Queipo de Llano (tel. 21 31 03). An attractively-furnished restaurant (sit in the small upstairs dining room). *Menú del día* with good choice of dishes 190ptas. Otherwise slightly expensive, in the 200-450ptas range for meat or fish.

On Calle de San Eloy 5, there's a nameless **wine bar** where you can sample the local brews at 10-14ptas per *copa,* or purchase them by the liter (bring your own bottle). Decor is strictly functional—a stand-up bar, seven barrels of wine, and a urinal in the corner.

If you want to eat with the bullfighters, go to **El Burladero** (literally, the nook in the bullring where the matador can hide from the bull), in the Hotel Colón, Calle Canalejas 1 (tel. 22 29 00). But be prepared for the big splurge—the *menú* is 650ptas, and most main dishes run 330-520ptas.

Sights

In 1401 the Catholics razed the greatest of the Almohad mosques in Seville. Perhaps to divert history's attention from this insanity, they followed it with another. "Let us build a church," they supposedly declared, "so great that those who come after us will take us for madmen." From the outside, the **Cathedral** is not lovely. Pinched in front by an avenue which does not allow a full view of the sprawling building, the exterior does not reveal the scope of the madness. You absolutely must go inside (35ptas; open 10:30am-1pm and 4-6pm in summer; 10:30am-1pm and 3:30-5:30pm in winter) to get a sense of the dimensions of this Cathedral. Monstrous pillars seem too fragile to support the vaulted roof half a football field above. The wealth of the treasure is fabulous beyond belief. To see the reliquaries containing bones and other scraps of saints and apostles is alone worth the entrance fee. The walls are hung with relatively minor works by the major artists: Murillo, Goya, Luis de Vargas and others.

The **Giralda** (15ptas, same hours as the Cathedral) was the minaret of the Almohad mosque. The Christians made only modest alterations to it; a belfry was added, as was a weather vane whose gyrations inspired the tower's name (*girar* means to rotate). The austerity of the Almohad sect of Islam is apparent in the clean lines and simplicity of ornamentation. From the top, there's a good view of the city, and a better view of the barbed spires and buttresses of the Cathedral roof.

The **Casa de Pilatos** (summers 9am-1pm and 3-7pm; closes one hour earlier in the winter; entrance 50ptas) was the palace of the Duke of Medinaceli. It is a fine example of *Mudejar* architecture (combination of Arabic, Gothic, and Plateresque styles). The **Alcázar** (summers 9am-12:45pm and 4-6:30pm; closes one hour earlier in the winter, entrance 80ptas) is a magnificent fourteenth-century Mudejar Palace, combining both Gothic and Moorish features.

The **Museo Provincial de Bellas Artes** (10am-2pm; closed Sundays and holiday afternoons, also all day Mon., Plaza del Museo), in the former Convento de la Merced, houses the most complete collection of Murillo and Valdés Leal, plus a few works by Velázquez, Zurbarán, and others. More Murillo and Valdés Leal to be seen in the church **Hospital de la Caridad,** on Calle Temprado, parallel to the Paseo de Colón. Open 9am-1pm and 4-7pm; admission 25ptas.

At the **Plaza de España** are tile monuments of each region of Spain, rowboats for rent, and (on Sundays) flamenco.

If you don't suffer from acrophobia, you might enjoy a side trip to **Arcos de la Frontera,** a little town about an hour's drive (somewhat more by bus) to the south. The road snakes through hills covered with great fields of sunflowers, all tilting their broad faces into the sun. Arcos is built on an improbable spike, undercut by the green Guadalete River. The heights are picturesque, with two old churches (**Santa María** and **San Pedro**) and the old castle walls.

Evenings

In Seville you have one single, ineluctable duty as a tourist: if you can't make it up the Giralda, if you don't bother going inside the Cathedral, even if you spend all day in a hotel room writing postcards—for god's sake see the flamenco. That's all. Just do it. A good place is **Los Gallos,** Plaza Santa Cruz 11 (tel. 21 31 98), 350ptas to get in, 250ptas for drinks, but it's perfectly okay not to order one. The room is small, very comfortable, and you can sit there from 10pm to dawn. **La Trocha,** Ronda de Capuchinos 23, is more informal, with a sort of variety show including flamenco, other regional dances, comedy routines, and sexist audience participation: women from the audience are allowed to join the male dancers, but men can't get up to accompany the female performers, although they may get it up at their seats. Admission 300ptas, two shows nightly 11pm-12:30am, and 1-2:30am. No shows Sunday.

Cafetería la Reja, on Santa María de Gracia 15, right off Campana (tel. 21 21 01), is a good place to have coffee after dinner, and there's a discotheque upstairs with a sane male-female ratio. Admission, including the first drink, is 150ptas on weekdays, 200ptas on weekends and holidays; open 7pm-1am, until 2am on Saturdays.

Costa de la Luz

Spain's southern Atlantic coast, from **Ayamonte** to **Tarifa,** can't compete with Costa del Sol and the Portuguese Algarve. There are some long beaches, but those which are easily accessible are marred by rather heavy industrialization and even heavier winds.

Cádiz has been compared (unfairly) to Marseille. Much is made of Cádiz' red light district, yet when all is said and done, the area is relatively tame. Of the city's glorious past, little remains to be seen.

Jerez de la Frontera, about 35 kilometers to the north, is to sherry what Épernay, France, is to champagne. Most of the important sherry *bodegas* (wine vaults) are at the edge of town—the two largest, **Byass** and **Pedro Domecq,** are right next to each other, but the latter attracts by far the largest crowd of visitors. To get there, follow the signs from the central Plaza Reyes Católicos towards Cádiz, and then toward the *bodegas.* Domecq's reception is located on Calle San Ildefonso 3. Guided tours are free, and rather dull, except for the warehouse containing barrels of sherry sampled and signed by the glorious: kings, queens, matadors, Franco, and Charlton Heston. The high point is sampling—more than enough sherry to loosen your eyeballs. The town itself is not too interesting, except in early fall, when many students come to Jerez to work in the harvest *(vendimia),* and take part in the wild **Harvest Festival** afterwards. Wages are about 1000ptas per day, and don't include room or board. Write before September to any of the big houses. Street addresses are not necessary.

Cordoba

Córdoba owes its fame to the brilliance of the various civilizations that it fostered, two of which made it their capital. Córdoba was the Roman capital of the province of Baética (today Spain and Portugal), and it was here that the philosopher and teacher Seneca was born. When the Moors invaded Spain in the eighth century, they made Córdoba the cultural capital of the world. Maimonides, the Jewish philosopher and theologian, ranks among its greatest scholars. When the city was conquered by the Christians in 1236, the Moors retreated to Granada. Fortunately, enough of the past remains to make Córdoba one of the most enchanting cities in Spain.

Orientation

The main street of Cordoba is the tree-lined **Avenida del Gran Capitán.** Perpendicular to it, north of center city, is Avenida de América, with the **Train Station.** To the south, is the **Judería,** the old Jewish quarter around the **Mezquita** (Mosque) and the **Alcázar** on the banks of the **Guadalquivir.**

Addresses and Telephone Numbers

Tourist Office: Av. del Gran Capitán 15 (tel. 22 12 05). Open 9:30am-2pm and 5-7pm, closed Sat. afternoons and all day Sun.

Post Office: Cruz Conde 21 (tel. 22 18 13). Open 9am-2pm and 5-7pm, except Sun.

Telephones (long distance): Plaza de José Antonio 7. For information dial 003; for out-of-town 009; for operator assistance 008.

RENFE: Av. del Generalísimo (tel. 22 58 89). Open 9am-1pm and 4-7pm, except Sat. afternoons and all day Sun.

Train Station: Av. de América (north side of town).

Cook's Travel: Cruz Conde 28. Summer hours: 9am-1pm and 5-8pm, closed Sat. afternoons and all day Sun.

Laundromat: Lavanderías Cordobesas, Angel de Saavedra 2 (tel. 22 85 57); just south of Plaza de José Antonio.

Accommodations

It's harder to find a room in a place with stars than in a dive. Remember that if you let a hotel refer you to one of the latter, they'll be taking 50ptas off the top. Have patience and ask the locals; there are more *casas particulares* with beds than you'd believe. Start with **Rey Heredia** to the northeast of the *Mezquita*. At #12 is **La Milagrosa** with doubles for 275ptas, showers free. They prefer long-termers whom they often treat like family, and will negotiate on rates. Right across the street they have a *casa* with beds for 150ptas; and they can almost certainly find you something somewhere if those are full. **La Purísima,** at #7, also charges 150ptas per bed with free cold showers; at #25, **Andrea** asks 300ptas for doubles and charges 50ptas for hot showers, 30ptas for cold. There is also a very cheap *hostal* one and a half blocks west of the Train Station: **Perales,** Av. de los Mozárabes 17 (tel. 23 21 12), has singles for 145ptas, doubles 240ptas, showers 55ptas. If you

want a room in one of the places listed below, you had best arrive before
noon, just after people check out.

> **Hostal-Residencia Séneca,** Conde y Luque 7 (tel. 22 32 34). One of the best
> budget places to stay in Córdoba. On a typical Cordoban street, this *hostal* is in
> a good location near the Mosque and has a beautiful patio. Singles 260ptas,
> doubles 400ptas, triples 521ptas, all with breakfast; showers 55ptas extra.
> Landlady speaks French.
>
> **Hostal-Residencia "El León,"** Céspedes 6 (tel. 22 30 21). Also in the old
> city, with a beautiful courtyard. Singles 275ptas, doubles 480ptas, including
> breakfast and hot shower.
>
> **Hotel-Residencia Marisa,** Cardenal Herrero 6 (tel. 22 63 19). A good place to
> splurge. Across the street from the Mosque and rated 2 stars, this hotel has
> very attractive rooms. Singles 545ptas, doubles 990ptas. Both with breakfast
> and shower.
>
> **Hostal Las Tendillas,** Jesus Maria 1 (tel. 22 30 29). Just off the central Plaza
> de José Antonio. Doubles for 400ptas, hot showers 40ptas.
>
> **Camping:** Campamento Municipal de Turismo, Carretera Cordoba-Villa-
> viciosa km 2 (tel. 27 50 48).

If worse *really* comes to worst, try the **Fonda Agostina** at Zapatería Vieja
5, off Cardenal González. They have a few beds at 125ptas per night; very
unlikely that they'll all be booked.

Food

Food in Córdoba is good, but it's getting hard to find a cheap meal, even
in the old quarter. As usual, there are a few places with *platos combinados*.
One of the best, with *platos* ranging from 75-95ptas and a great variety of
tapas at 25ptas a *ración,* is **Bar Restaurante Carmona;** this inauspicious-
looking place is located in the newer part of town, on Menéndez Pelayo, a
couple of hundred meters from the Banco de Vizcaya. Just inside the old
quarter, on Plaza Blanco Belmontez, is **El Extremeño,** with the *plato combinado Urtaín* featuring veal or hake, potato salad with hard-boiled eggs,
and Russian dressing all for 135ptas. Finally, two places for full sit-down
meals: several blocks east of the *Mezquita,* off Paseo de la Ribera at San
Fernando 3, is **Restaurant La La La,** with a *menú turístico* at 175ptas; they
also have beds at 250ptas. And right nearby—ta da!—**Taberno El Potro,** on
Coronel Cascajo 2. There's a *menú del día* at 190ptas, but everything is
cheap. The *gazpacho* is beautiful with six kinds of *garnición* you can mix the
way you want. *Gazpacho,* a big plate of chick-pea *cozido,* a stack of fried
calamares, bread, and wine add up to 200ptas.

The Jewish quarter around the *Mezquita* is great for noshing—dozens of
bars with *tapas.* The local wines, *Montilla* and *Moriles,* are excellent, and a
bottle costs about 40ptas. A trip to **Bodegas Campos,** on Coronel Cascajo to
taste wine and read the famous signatures on the barrels is highly recommended.

Sights

Begun in 785, the **Mezquita** was intended to surpass all other mosques in
grandeur. An airy forest of 850 marble, alabaster, and stone pillars supports
425 red-and-white-striped double arches, many of which were taken from
the Visigothic cathedral which formerly occupied the site. (Open 10am-

1:30pm and 4-8pm; October-March open 10am-1:30pm and 3:30-6pm. Admission 25ptas.) The Tower costs 5ptas to climb—it's a good idea to go up there first just to see what's been done to the Mosque. Like a fat cuckoo fledgling squatting in its hijacked nest, the Cathedral rises out of the low Moorish structure. Go inside to see how this Baroque intruder disrupts the cool harmony of the orchard of double-arched candy canes. Off to one side is the **Mihrab,** El Hakam II's psychedelic fantasy, with the richest mosaics in Spanish Islamic art.

The **Alcázar** (open 9:30am-1:30pm and 5-8pm in summer; 9:30am-1:30pm and 4-7pm in winter; admission 25ptas) is more than just an important military monument. There are several excellent Roman mosaics and narcotic Generalife-style gardens with terraced goldfish ponds. Best time to see the gardens is at night when the heat's off and the lights are on, from 10pm-1am.

Other sights include the run-down **Synagogue** and the nearby **Museo Municipal de Arte Cordobés y Taurino** (open 9:30am-1:30pm and 5-8pm; admission 20ptas). Located on the Plazuela de Maimonides, this museum is an important index of the Spanish mentality: one little room for leatherwork, ceramics, and other mundane arts; the rest for *la corrida,* galeries full of the heads of bulls who got their man and others less fortunate, in various states of decrepitation. A copy of Manolete's tomb is exhibited beneath the stretched skin of his nemesis, Islero. If you walk through the Plaza del Potro, take note of the **Posada** where Cervantes wrote part of **Don Quijote.**

Córdoba is famous for silver filigree work *(orfebrería)* and tooled leatherwork, both of which can be found in the tourist shops around the Mosque. But be careful; prices vary unbelievably, so shop around and bargain.

Granada

"Dale limosna mujer, que no hay en la vida nada como la pena de ser ciego en Granada."

"Give him alms, woman, for there is in life nothing like the pain of being blind in Granada."

The words of the poet F.A. de Icaza appear with such Kilroy-like frequency in this city that at times it seems there might be solace for the blind in at least not being able to see them. In fact, you'll find the central city is not so beautiful. You have to lift your eyes to the hills where the stolid red walls of the **Alhambra** nestle between the jostling white houses of the old city and the flashing teeth of the Sierra Nevada peaks beneath the azure Andalusian sky.

Orientation

Granada can be covered on foot quite easily. Pick up a couple of maps at the Tourist Office and walk around. If you're hitching into Granada from the Carretera de Madrid take bus #1 into town; from the Station take #4, 5, 9, or 11 to the center. Don't take a bus from the center of town to the Alhambra. The walk is beautiful and shouldn't be missed.

Across the **River Darro** from the Alhambra and center of town are two hills. On one is the ancient Arab quarter of **Albaicín,** the best preserved in Spain and the only part of the Muslim city that escaped destruction by the Christians. A whitewashed maze of narrow, winding streets and Moorish architecture, the quarter is well worth a leisurely walk. The other hill is **Sacromonte,** the gypsy quarter, with its famous cave dwellings, which can be reached by taking bus #7 to the Puerta Real.

Addresses and Telephone Numbers

Tourist Office: Casa de los Tiros, Calle de Pavaneras 19 (tel. 22 10 22). Open 9am-2pm and 5-7pm, except Sat. afternoons and all day Sun.

American Express: Viajes Bonal, Av. Calvo Sotelo 19 (tel. 27 63 12). Open 9:30am-1:30pm and 5-8:30pm, closed Sat. afternoons and all day Sun.

Post Office and Telegraph: Puerta Real (tel. 22 48 35). Closed Saturday afternoons and all day Sunday.

RENFE: Calle de los Reyes Católicos, next door to #45. **Train Station:** Av. Andaluces, off Calvo Sotelo (tel. 23 34 08).

Bus Station: Estación Camino Ronda. Alsina is the largest bus company. For information, tel. 25 13 58.

Accommodations

There are plenty of rooms to be had in Granada, but most of the *hostales* are expensive enough to tie a shoestring budget up in knots. If you stick to *fondas* or *casas de huéspedes,* you should have no trouble finding a place for under 200ptas per person. But don't overlook the **IYHF Youth Hostel,** one of Spain's finest; it's just outside the center of town in the Colegio Emperador Carlos, Camino de Ronda, (now officially Avenida Carrero-Blanco, tel. 23 16 00). The Hostel is not marked, and locals refer to the place as the "Frente Juvenil," if you're asking directions. 135ptas per night, breakfast included. Swimming pool 75ptas, tennis (9am-8pm) 100ptas per hour for the court; both open to the general public. Very friendly, the only problem being the perpetually swamped bathroom.

There are several cheap, seedy places right near the Train Station on Avenida Andaluces. The cheapest is the *"camas"* just behind Bar Mehincho; 200ptas for two, including cold shower. Moving in towards the center of town, quite a few cheapies can be found between Calle San Juan de Dios and Gran Vía de Colón. On Cardenal Mendoza: **Casa de Huéspedes San Carlo** at #27 (tel. 23 24 82) charges 125ptas per person, 40ptas for hot showers; reasonably comfortable. At #15, **Pensión Mario** (tel. 23 26 81) charges 150ptas for one, 280ptas for two beds, 50ptas for hot showers, 25ptas for cold. Decent rooms. **Hostal Brasil,** at #5 (tels. 27 10 61 and 23 43 73) has 74 beds and is a lot more comfortable. It has two stars and higher prices: singles are 250ptas, doubles start at 410ptas, both including shower; doubles with full bath 545ptas. In the same general area, around the University, three more pretty good places: on Rector Lopez Argueta, **Fonda San Juan de Dios,** with singles 125ptas and up, doubles 225ptas and up, triples at 300ptas. At Mano de Hierro 14 there's **Hostal-Residencia San Joaquín** (tel. 28 28 79): 300ptas for single rooms, 200ptas per bed in multiple-occupancy rooms, shower included. One of the nicest is **Casa de Huéspedes Romero,** at Sillería de Mesones 1 (near Plaza de la Trinidad), with singles for 150ptas, doubles for 250ptas, hot showers for 50ptas.

On Cuesta de Gomérez, the road leading up to the Alhambra, you'll find two gems and a few others that'll do. The **Casa de Huéspedes Gomérez,** at

#2 (tel. 22 63 98) is clean, pleasant, and *simpático*, not to mention cheap: 130ptas per person, hot showers 30ptas. Bravo! If Gomérez is full, try a *hostal*. An excellent choice is the **Hostal California,** at #37 (tel. 22 40 56), which has singles for 200ptas, 375ptas with shower in the room, and doubles with shower for 400ptas. Good meals too.

A list of campgrounds in the province of Granada is available at the Tourist Office. The nicest one near the city is **Sierra Nevada,** Carretera de Madrid (tel. 23 25 04); 65ptas per person, 55ptas per tent. **María Eugenia** on the Carretera Málaga (tel. 23 18 81) is cheaper.

Food

Granada has a large number of places that serve combination plates *(platos combinados),* which usually consist of a first course of *paella,* macaroni, or soup; a second course of meats, fish, or vegetables; dessert, bread, and even wine. Not necessarily the best meals around, but they are at least convenient and cheap. There are four of this type of restaurant at the corner of Cetti Meriem and Elvira, which runs off the Plaza Nueva: **Mesón Andaluz** has meals for 190-250ptas and is air-conditioned; **Restaurante La Florida** charges 120ptas and up; **La Nueva Bodega** charges the same; and at **Riviera,** Cetti Meriem 5, you can eat for 160ptas and up. Other cheap options:

La Gamba de Oro, set back from the street at the corner of Cetti Meriem and Elvira; great for beer and shellfish (about 40ptas a round). No tourists here so far.

Mesón la Chuleta, at Duquesa 4 (just off Plaza de la Trinidad) has great moderately-priced meals: *gazpacho,* hake *alla Portuguesa,* pork chop and potatoes, ice cream, bread and wine, all for 195ptas.

Los Girasoles, San Juan de Dios 24 (we've been saving the best for last). A full sit-down meal, great food, friendly service in a large clean dining room for 120ptas (without wine).

For dessert, the best *blanco y negro* (ice coffee and *nata* ice cream) we've found in Andalucía costs 30ptas (small) and 40ptas (large) at **Heladería La Perla,** Plaza Nueva 16. Save it for the end of a long, hot afternoon at the Alhambra. Good *horchatas,* too.

Sights

The **Alhambra,** open 9am-7pm every day, is an Arab monument of universal fame, built on a hill covered with splendid woods and gardens. A comprehensive ticket costs 120ptas, or 50ptas for students with an ID. The numerous courtyards and rooms inside the palaces which make up the **Casa Real** are among the finest examples of Muslim art and architecture anywhere in the world. A haunting combination of tenderness and strength, beauty and blood, the Alhambra has conjured up tales of romance and intrigue for centuries. Among the most impressive features of the palace are the three-dimensional ceilings, the mosaics and the intricate wall designs and inscriptions. Don't miss the spooky baths down below. Your ticket also enables you to roam the extensive gardens and visit the **Generalife,** the summer retreat of the sultans and the setting today of the **International Festival of Music and Dance.**

The **Cathedral** (open every day 11am-1pm and 4-7pm in the summer;

11am-1pm and 3:30-6pm in the winter) is the only purely Renaissance cathedral in Spain. Begun thirty years after the Christian liberation of the city, the ornate Church, which was intended to outshine the Alhambra, does not rise out of its shadow. Go early to see the oil paintings: the lighting is so poor that by late afternoon they are nearly indistinguishable. Admission is 25ptas, free during hours of mass (9:30-10:30am). The **Royal Chapel,** reached by a separate entrance (for another 25ptas) contains the tombs of Ferdinand and Isabella.

We suggest the following walking tour of the old Arab quarter, **Albaicín.** Take city bus #7 from beside the Cathedral and get off at Calle de Pages on top of the hill. From here walk down Calle Agua and through the **Puerta Arabe,** an old gate to the city at the Plaza Larga. Proceed to the terrace adjacent to the church of **San Nicolás.** This affords the best view of the Alhambra in all Granada—try to come at sunset or in winter when the Sierra Nevada has more snow. The nearby **Church of San Salvador,** built on the site of the Albaicín's most important Mosque, still preserves a *Patio Arabe.* From here, wander through the Albaicín and head towards the hill of Sacromonte, the gypsy quarter. Enter through the Cuesta del Chapiz. You'll find the first part lined with caves of show-biz gypsies playing up to the tourists; be wary, especially of the aggressive youngsters after your money and your belongings!

Granada is also famous for its **Corpus Christi** celebrations which include festivities, processions, and bullfights in early May. Another good time to visit Granada is during the **International Festival,** held at the end of June and beginning of July, and featuring classical ballet and open-air performances in the gardens of the Generalife. Concerts are also held in the Renaissance palace built on the Cerro del Sol by Charles V. There are inexpensive student prices for most performances; write in advance to the Comisaria del Festival, Carrera del Darro 29, Granada (tel. 22 52 01).

Daytrips

Glistening above the Alhambra is the tallest range in Iberia: the peaks of **Mulhacén** (3481 meters) and **Veleta** (3470 meters) are snow covered most of the year. During the summer you can drive right up to the top of Veleta: at first a tranquil *camino* through the arid countryside, the road abruptly begins a long climb up the face of the Sierra wall. When the snow has melted, you can drive or walk right over the peak to **Capileira** in the southern valley of the **Alpujarras.** The walk is an easy 25 kilometers among rock-strewn meadows with only the wild goats and a few birds for company. Even in the summer temperatures drop considerably at night and the wind is severe, so plan to get over in one day. Several good hiking maps are available. Capileira has a *fonda* (110ptas per person) just at the fork as you enter, but the village itself is interesting only as a base for walks up into the hills.

Public transportation to both regions varies from season to season and from year to year. As of summer 1978, Alsina was running one daily bus to Capileira, leaving the Camino de Ronda Bus Station at 1:30pm and departing from Capileira at 8:30am; tickets cost 145ptas each way. **Viajes Bonal,** Calvo Sotelo 19, also had a full-day excursion through the Alpujarras (500ptas) including *aperitivos,* and lunch at Capileira. **Bonal** was also running the only service to the northern Veleta area.

Evenings

The scene is not great. Sacromonte, with its so-called "real gypsy flamenco" is the biggest rip-off in Spain—not a smidgen of talent anywhere on the hill except among the hustlers. The discotheques are overpriced and no one goes there much; it's best not to go alone. The big places are even worse. There may be some talent at **La Reina Mora** (400ptas), but acoustics are so bad and crowds so big you won't know for sure. If the 600ptas *entrada* at **Jardines de Neptuno** on Camino de Ronda doesn't ruin your evening, you might enjoy the slick show (tel. 25 20 50 to reserve seats).

Costa del Sol

A dike of poured-concrete hotels and apartments is rapidly sealing off the whitewashed villages from the shoreline of the Costa del Sol. The beaches are so packed with the carefully bronzed that a fisherman would be hard put to land his trawler, even if his heavy schedule as an ice-cream man permitted. Still, the wayfarer weary from long hours in the museums and cathedrals of Europe may be revived by the sun and surf at the Costa's glamorous, social, and un-Spanish beaches.

The best beaches of the Sun Coast are in the province of **Málaga.** Here also is the most intense *"urbanización."* **Torremolinos** and **Marbella** are the two big names, and the former is too crowded and expensive to be worth the visit. Marbella will be that way very shortly—already developed several steps beyond chic, the town is pouring concrete all over itself (and out into the water). Still, this basically bourgeois resort can cheaply accommodate the thousands of backpackers for whom the name "Marbella" has the same galvanizing effect as "Fort Lauderdale."

There is no train station in Marbella. The **Bus Station** is on Avenida Ricardo Sorano. Walk east into the center of the new town. **Turismo** is on Avenida Miguel Cano (tel. 77 14 42), a block south of Sorano (open 9:30am-1pm and 4:30-7:30pm, closed Sat. afternoon and Sun.), and offers an excellent map and friendly service. For the real low-down, walk into **The English Pub,** or **The Tavern,** which are face to face on Calle Peral. Ask anybody for directions.

The picturesque old town, stacked up behind the central Avenida Ramon y Cajal, is loaded with little *hostales* and *fondas* which fill up quickly. There are several cheap guest houses on Germán Porras and its continuation, San Francisco. There are even more on Aduar, parallel and two blocks west. **Hostal Internacional,** Alderete 7 (tel. 77 02 95), has singles for 170ptas, doubles for 300ptas, cold showers are free and hot showers cost 60ptas. **La Posada,** San Juan de Dios, Dios 4, has singles for 200ptas, doubles 400ptas, and cold showers for 25ptas. Two places likely to have rooms are **El Mero,** Castillo 14 (tel. 77 00 60) and **Los Postigos,** Calle Los Postigos 21. El Mero is one of the better deals and it's a nice place—225ptas for singles, 350ptas for doubles, both including breakfast. Los Postigos charges 200ptas per person, hot showers 50ptas, cold showers 25ptas. In addition, Marbella boasts an excellent Youth Hostel (IYHF) with swimming pool, **Albergue Juvenil Africa** (tel. 77 14 91), located on Trapiche, just above San Francisco. It costs 100ptas—if they have room. It's worth making reservations. Breakfast costs 35ptas, lunch 160ptas, supper 130ptas. If you're stuck for a room, go into a bar and ask if they know anyone who can put you in a *casa particular.*

Eating cheaply is tougher than finding a place to crash, unless you make your own meals. **Sol y Sombra** on Tetuan is popular, but it will cost you at least 200ptas for a full meal. The best of the very few places offering *menus* at 130ptas is **Restaurant Casa Eladio,** at Virgen de los Dolores 4. The most westerly beach, where every woman seems to be working on those last pale areas, focuses on **Frank's Beach Bar.** Here, Neil Young's "Southern Man" and old bubble-gum rock on the cassette recorder sets a very young tone. Big pig-outs on Saturday *(paella)* and Wednesday (barbecue) nights—all you can eat plus all the sangria you can hold down for 600ptas and 500ptas, respectively.

Málaga, like its sweet, syrupy wine, has known greater popularity in other times. These days, most young tourists find that **Paseo del Parque** (the beautiful garden boulevard) and the lofty oasis of the **Gibralfaro** ramparts don't quite compensate for the miserable beaches and the hectic pace downtown. The reconstructed **Alcazaba,** palace of the Moorish kings, is worth visiting; try to avoid thinking of it as a second-rate Alhambra.

Heading east from Málaga, the beaches deteriorate to narrow, rocky strips, exposed to the roar of traffic on the highway just above. The scenery improves as the coastal highway begins to climb, and if you can clamber down the rocks to the sea below, the swimming is great. **Nerja** is not without charm, despite the painfully hasty expansion. From the projecting *mirador* called **Balcón de Europa,** you have a view of the beautiful beaches sculpted from the cliff below, and of the waterfront overhung with vines, shrubs, and palms. The beaches, with their coarse, gray sand and pebbles, are clean and not too crowded. If you get as far as Nerja, don't miss the tremendous cathedral-like cave 5 kilometers east (75ptas admission). Frequent buses (10ptas) will take you to the little speck called **Maro,** an easy walk from the caves.

Maro itself is a genuinely uncorrupted little village, where you might want to spend a couple of days—there's not even a *casa de huéspedes,* but there *are* rooms in *casas particulares.* A one-mile trek down the dirt road will bring you to a great little beach.

If you're traveling south on the coast from Málaga, a detour inland via **Ronda** is not too out of the way, and you'll get to see one of the most picturesque and serene towns of Southern Spain. It is perched atop a 600-foot gorge. The amputated eastern lobe of town is the lovely old city, with Roman, Moorish, and medieval Christian monuments jumbled together. As you cross the **Puente Nuevo** (New Bridge), you emerge from a colonnaded walkway to see the **House of the Moorish King** on your left. Facing it is the Renaissance **House of the Marquesa de Salvatierra;** the *marquesa* had the façade decorated with two Inca couples in amusingly modest posture, in commemoration of her extensive travels. Just below, as you descend the winding stone steps, you'll see the **Roman Bridge,** the **Arab Bridge,** and the **Arab Baths.**

Back across the Puente Nuevo, you run into the **Plaza de España,** the main square of the new town. Here you'll find **Turismo,** which organizes guided tours of the city. Opposite the Post Office is the miniature **Plaza de Toros;** an old lady will want 10ptas to let you in to see this delicately arcaded ring, one of the oldest (1785) in Spain.

Budget accommodations, though not abundant, are usually no problem, as this town has not yet been discovered in the way its coastal neighbors have. Right on the Plaza de Europa is a *casa de huéspedes;* and there is a *fonda* **La Española,** at José Aparicio 3 (just east of the Plaza). Both places have rooms for less than 150ptas per person. **Hostal Aguilar,** on Calle Naranja 28 (tel. 87 19 94) charges 165ptas for singles, 265ptas for doubles, 50ptas for hot showers. **Nuesta Señora de Lourdes,** Calle Sevilla 16, has singles for 125ptas, doubles for 250ptas, with tasty meals at 80-90ptas.

Ronda has both bus and train stations, but connections with most places are not frequent. There are no direct runs to **Algeciras** or Marbella, but there are departures for Málaga (three hours away) at 6:30am (176ptas) and 4pm (178ptas). Buses leave Málaga for Ronda at 7am and 6pm. There is one train daily for Málaga at 7:20am, and 7am for Madrid.

The main attraction in Algeciras is Africa, 13 kilometers away, across the Straits of Gibraltar. The Rock is also visible, just around the bay, but the road remains closed and the only way in is by plane, or by ferry from Tangier. 200ptas is the current asking price for the cheapest accommodations, but that is not always a firm price, so bargain. Try **Hostal Rif,** a *casa de huéspedes* at Rafael de Muro 7, just up from the Plaza de la Palma, where the market is held. In addition to the few overpriced rooms, there are beds on the covered terrace, considerably more comfortable in the summer heat, and a good deal at 100ptas. Showers are a rip-off at 75ptas (hot) and 45ptas (cold), but that's par for Algeciras.

The Mediterranean Coast

Barcelona

Barcelona has come out of the closet. After years of masquerading as just another modern European city, Barcelona has emphatically reasserted its Catalán identity. The language you hear on the streets, suppressed during the long years of the Franco regime, is closer to the medieval *Langue d'Oc* than to Castilian Spanish. It remains to be seen just how far the king will allow this resurgence of separatism to move the province away from central control towards local autonomy.

Meanwhile Barcelona retains its lead among Spanish cities in the headlong rush into the twentieth century. The hand-holding on the streets is no longer tentative—couples on park benches neck unabashedly, and in the grocery stores you hear mothers discussing—with composure—the growing frequency of co-habitation, drug use, and even atheism.

Barcelona is really two cities in one. The **Ensanche,** or newer part of the city, is a showplace of fountains, parks, and tree-lined boulevards, while the **barrio gótico** (gothic quarter) is a fine cross-hatching of small shop-lined streets, and old townhouses. These days the *barrio* is dirty, smelly, and afflicted with a serious crime rate unusual in Spain (minimal by American standards), but it is still the most fascinating part of town, and the center of a hot and often seamy nightlife.

Orientation

Once within the city limits, getting from place to place is relatively simple. The **Tourist Office,** at Avenida José Antonio 658 (tels. 317 22 46 and 301 74 47; open 9am-1:30pm and 4-7pm, except Sat. afternoons and all day Sun.) will give you a map, an urban transport guide, a listing of budget accommodations, and extensive information on Barcelona and surrounding cities. In the **Termino Train Station** you will find another branch of this office, as well as good baggage storage facilities. The **Metro** is bright, clean, and dirt cheap (6ptas), but not as extensive as Madrid's. The bus system is quite comprehensive. A ride anywhere is 10ptas, and public transportation generally runs until 11pm on weekdays and 1am on Sundays and holidays.

Barcelona has several train stations, but most trains stop at either **Termino** or **Paseo de Gracia.** Be sure to check this when you get train schedules. **Las**

Ramblas, the central boulevard, runs from the port to the **Plaza de Cataluña,** the center of the city. To the right of Las Ramblas facing away from the port is the *barrio gótico,* which centers around the **Cathedral,** and where you'll find many cheap *hostales* and restaurants. The new city lies beyond the Plaza de Cataluña.

The city is flanked by the hill of **Montjuich** to the south, with its dramatic fortress and amusement park, and to the north by the fortressed promontory of **Tibidabo.** North of Barcelona are the beautiful but crowded beaches of the **Costa Brava.** To the south is the **Costa Dorada.** The resort towns of Castelldefels and Sitges are good places to escape to the beach and can be reached easily by train from Termino Station.

Addresses and Telephone Numbers

Tourist Office: Av. José Antonio 658 (tels. 317 22 46 and 301 74 47). Open 9am-1:30pm and 4-7pm, except Sat. afternoons and all day Sun.

American Express (Ultramar Express, S.A.): Ramblas 109 (tel. 301 12 12). Open 9am-1pm and 4-7pm, except Sat. afternoons and all day Sun.

Post Office: Plaza de Antonio López (tel. 318 38 31; telegrams 322 20 00).

Telefónica: Fontanella 4, at the eastern corner of Plaza de Cataluña. Open 9am-2pm and 4-10pm every day. For operator assistance on U.S. calls, dial 005.

RENFE: Paseo de Gracia 13 (tels. 319 56 50, 319 56 00, 319 55 00, and 317 64 82). Tickets can be bought or reserved at the various stations 9am-1pm and 4-8pm.

Student Travel Offices: VIAJESEU, Rambla Santa Mónica 8 (tel. 302 06 82).

Interurban Bus Station: Most lines run from Estación Norte, Av. Vilanova.

U.S. Consulate: Vía Layetana 33 (tel. 319 95 50). Open 8:30am-1pm and 2-4:30pm Mon.-Fri.

Laundromat: several in town. Near the Train Station: Lavandería Maxim, Calle de Detrás Palacio 7. Wash and dry, including soap 200ptas for 5 kilos. Open 8am-8pm except Sun.

Accommodations

As in other university towns, some *colegios mayores* offer rooms in the summer. Since these are not centrally located, it's best to find out where the rooms are before you start running all over town. **Colegio Mayor Universitario San Jorge,** Calle del Maestro Nicolau 13 (tel. 250 14 19) takes men and women. 375ptas with breakfast, 425ptas with half pension, 500ptas with full pension. It's west of Plaza Calvo Sotelo: buses #7, 14, 15, and 41 (among others) will bring you within range.

The nearest **campground** is 10 kilometers out of town (catch bus U.C.); the Youth Hostel formerly on Virgen de Montserrat has been shut down.

Along the Ramblas, in the heart of the Gothic Quarter, are a number of places of varying quality; these are close to the center of things, and if one is full, there is always another next door.

Hotel Rialto, Fernando 42 (tel. 318 52 12). More expensive, but a good place to splurge. Very clean, comfortable, and centrally located. Singles 552ptas with sink, 758ptas with shower, 926ptas with full bath; doubles 918ptas with sink, 1020ptas with shower, 1230ptas with full bath; triples 1376ptas, 1530ptas, and 1844ptas respectively. Prices include breakfast; hot shower 70ptas.

Casa de Huéspedes Mari-Luz, Palau 4 (tel. 317 34 63). Walking from Ramblas, take a right off Fernando at Hotel Rialto; Calle de la Enseñanza runs into Palau after 300 yards. No sign downstairs—go in the oversized portal, up 87 dirty steps. Relatively cheap: 200ptas for singles, 400ptas for doubles, 50ptas for hot showers; negotiable for extended stay. Exceptionally friendly management will let you use refrigerator, laundry room, even the stove. Not at all as shabby inside as outside.

Noya, Ramblas 133 (tel. 301 48 31). A small, clean pension just off Plaza de Cataluña in the heart of the city. Great deal at 215ptas for a single and 355ptas for a double; hot showers 70ptas, cold 40ptas. Upstairs (3rd floor), at **Pensión Canaletes** (tel. 319 91 24), 8 doubles 310ptas, hot showers 70ptas, cold 50ptas, no breakfast.

Hostal Roma, Plaza Real 11 (tel. 302 03 66). It's very run down for a 2-star *hostal,* but adequate, and the rooms overlook the Plaza. Singles 374ptas without shower, doubles 613ptas without shower (708ptas with). Prices include breakfast; hot showers 70ptas.

Hostal-Residencia Nilo, Calle de José Anselmo Clavé 17 (tel. 302 41 00). Northeast of Puerta de la Paz. Singles 250ptas, doubles 450ptas, both with shower included. All rooms have at least a sink.

Hostal Universidad, Ronda de la Universidad 10 (tel. 317 13 41), west of Plaza de Cataluña. A big place. Singles 410ptas, doubles 690ptas, including breakfast and the 20% surcharge if you don't take the meals there. Showers 70ptas.

Hostal Residencia La Hipica, General Castaños 2 (tel. 319 45 00), East of the Gobierno Civil, off Plaza del Palacio, not far from the Train Station. Singles 270ptas, 300ptas with shower, 555ptas with full bath. Hot shower 70ptas, cold 40ptas.

Food

Pick up your picnic nicknacks at the **Mercado** (market) **de San José** just off the Rambla San José.

A nameless *económico,* at **Calle del Pino 11** has unbeatable prices: *gazpacho* 30ptas, chicken and fries 75ptas, *paella* 85ptas (or special *paella* for 175ptas). Nothing spectacular, but the food is served reasonably hot, and the atmosphere is far more pleasant than at the famous cheapo, **Casa José,** Plaza San José Oriol 10.

Restaurante Arundel, Calle de Pino 10. One of your classier cheapos. *Menús* at 145ptas and 170ptas.

El Sol, Tallers 75, east off Ramblas (tel. 231 61 89). A popular restaurant filled with locals. *Cubiertos* 100ptas and 150ptas; *menú del día* 190ptas.

Grill Room, Escudillers 8. Very good food for the money. *Menú turístico* 195ptas, *paella* 250ptas. **La Taverna,** at #10, has *combinados* for 130-230ptas and good *tapas*. A hole in the wall at #5 will prepare custom-made sandwiches for you. The chickens turning on their spits out on the sidewalk belong to **Los Caracoles** (#14), whose reputation and prices are beginning to escape reality. Still a good place to eat and a better one to be seen in. Specialties are half a roasted chicken (225ptas), *zarzuela* (shellfish casserole, 375ptas), fancy *paella* (395ptas), and roast suckling pig (550ptas).

La Poste, Calle de Gignas 20 (behind and southwest of the Post Office) is a clean, basic sort of restaurant where many students eat. 130-160ptas buys a meal.

Sights

The **Ramblas** is a three-ring circus. During the day, at least a dozen pet dealers set up shop on the upper end. Come evening, hundreds of people pay 5ptas for a folding chair just to sit on the sidelines and watch—they get their money's worth from the street musicians, eccentric haranguers and sexy sashayers.

Barcelona is custodian to the greatest architecture of the Catalán fantasist Antonio Gaudí. Most astonishing is the **Templo Expiatorio de la Sagrada Familia,** described by Anthony Burgess as a "metaphysical conceit humanized with crockets and pompoms." Begun in 1882 by Villar and continued after 1891 by Gaudí, this ultraneo-Gothic Cathedral was aborted when a trolley car ran over the architect. An inveterate improviser, Gaudi left no masterplan for the eventual completion of his work, and no one since has dared to attempt one. What there is is located on Calles Mallorca-Provenza and Marina-Cerdeña. (9:30am-2pm and 3-5:30pm in winter; 9am-2pm and 3-8:30pm in summer; admission 15ptas. Take bus #15, 19, 45, 47, 50, or 54; Metro: Sagrada Familia.) Other works include a half dozen houses and the **Parque Güell,** with the **Museo de Gaudí.** The park is open all day, free of charge; Museum hours are 10am-2pm and 4-7pm, Sundays only.

Staid and conservative beside Gaudí, the works of that other modernist, Pablo Picasso, are still worth a look-see. You don't have to look far: the design on the façade of the **College of Architects** is typical (if uninspired) Picasso. The **Museo Picasso** on Moncada 15 (tel. 319 60 92) houses some of his better works. (Open 9:30am-1:30pm and 4·30-8:30pm, holidays open only in the morning; admission 15ptas. Take bus #16, 17, 22, 45, or 122.)

Also worth a visit is the **Montjuich,** which hosts a vast collection of buildings from the 1929 International Exhibition. Of these the most interesting are to be found in the **Pueblo Español,** a model town made up of characteristic architecture from every region of Spain. Just avoid the "bargains" on sale. You can reach the Montjuich by funicular until 3am, for a fine view of the city and the port.

Another spectacular mountain view can be had from the town of **Montserrat,** 50 kilometers above and outside Barcelona; here you will also find an early Gothic basilica and monastery. The best transportation is from the Plaza de Cataluña via Catalán Railways.

Evenings

Barcelona boasts a number of discotheques and nightclubs, but they are expensive and not worth it. You'll do better to indulge in the local custom of conversing late into the night over *café con cognac,* either in one of the many cafés along the Ramblas or at the top of the Montjuich. Or you might try **Bar Pasaje Sanlucar,** Rambla Santa Monica 26. A little grungy, but lots of atmosphere. A great place to go on Sunday night after the bullfight, when the bar fills up with aficionados. Or you can always join the circus on the Ramblas.

Balearic Islands

We have good news and we have bad. The good news: the Balearic Islands are beautiful; the bad: they're booked solid all summer. Unless you're planning on camping out, which may mean dodging the *guardia civiles,* don't go without reservations. More than likely you won't be able to make reservations either, unless you start writing in February. Most hotels and even little **pensiones** have contracts with travel agencies and won't bother answering your letters much less sympathizing when you show up. If you're betting on catching that one vacant spot or lucking into a place just as someone cancels out, remember: so are literally thousands of others.

If you go before mid-June or after mid-October, however, you should have your pick of rooms and rates anywhere in the archipelago. Autumn and spring are the best time to go anyway—summers tend to be on the humid side, and winters are not warm. Don't bother with the major cities and towns: except for Palma, they are just cul-de-sacs for the hordes. The countryside is beautiful and for the most part unspoiled. You'll hardly notice the irreversible havoc the tourist industry has brought on the agricultural economy and traditional culture as you pass through. Countless car, motorcycle, and bicycle rental agencies will facilitate your excursions.

You may find the Balearic people less outgoing than other Spanish provincials you've dealt with; in general, they are conservative, contemptuous of the *peninsulares,* and suspicious of outsiders. (Don't look for rooms in *casas particulares* here!) The islanders pride themselves on the relative purity of their own dialect of Catalán as compared with the bastardized version spoken in Barcelona where the Castilian influence is stronger. It is mainly this stubborn spirit (and also wariness about European recession) which is responsible for the slow down in touristic *urbanización* and the consequent shortage of rooms during the summer.

Getting There and Getting Around

Barcelona, Valencia, and Alicante are the three major peninsular ports for ferries to the Baleares. There are also daily boats between Ibiza and Majorca, as well as other less frequent inter-island routes. Prices vary by season and by boat. The lowest categories of ticket (deck seats and ''B'' chairs) are often sold out by reservation in the high season, so if possible book your ticket in advance. **Trasmediterránea Lines** has offices in major cities and at the points of embarkation. Here is a partial list:

Madrid: Alcalá 63 (tel. 225 51 10).

Alcudia (Island of Majorca): Lazareto 1 (tel. 54 53 42).

Algeciras: Recinto del Puerto (tel. 66 52 00).

Alicante: Explanada España 2 (tel. 20 60 11).

Barcelona: Vía Layetana 2 (tel. 319 82 12).

Valencia 3: Avenida Manuel Soto Ing. 5 (tel. 367 65 12).

A one-way ticket between Palma and Valencia, Alicante, or Barcelona costs around 310ptas for a deck seat and 480ptas for a "B" chair.

Flying is not as expensive as you might expect. Last summer's prices: Barcelona to Palma 1476ptas; Valencia to Palma 1765ptas; Madrid to Palma 3158ptas. Look around for better deals in the various travel agencies and ask about hotel reservations; there are good package deals to be had if you book well enough in advance.

Majorca, Ibiza, and Minorca have cheap and pretty extensive bus systems. Majorca has a narrow-gauge train, **FEVE,** incompatible with Eurailpass. Only a few major routes, but service is cheap and relatively quick.

Majorca (Mallorca)

The largest of the islands, with the only serious city in the group, Majorca absorbs most of the tourist blitz every summer. **Palma,** the capital, handles almost all of the island traffic; and, unlike many smaller towns, still maintains the pace of a city that would be, and has been, important even without the tourists. A crust of hotels and high-rises has formed along the shoreline, especially east towards **Arenal,** but the central avenues and old quarter show signs of an older wealth. The **Portella Quarter** (or *barrio gótico*) around the **Cathedral** and **Palace** is a maze of tight streets, half covered by the overhanging carved wooden eaves of elegant townhouses still occupied by island aristocracy. At the same time, there are quarters which rock with the pace of the transient good-timers. The neon-lit **Calle de Apuntadores** orchestrates outdoor parrots, bars, 1960s jukebox rock, eateries, and signs assuring "This is the place you're looking for." The place you are more probably looking for is **Cabala,** at the top of Calle de Ribera.

Addresses and Telephone Numbers

Tourist Office: Av. Jaime III 10 (tel. 21 22 16). Maps, bus routes, all the information you need. Also in the Airport (tel. 26 08 03).

American Express: Viajes Iberia, Paseo Generalísimo Franco 48 (tel. 23 37 42). Open 9am-1pm and 4-7:30pm, closed Sat. afternoons and all day Sun.

Post Office and Telegraph: Av. José Antonio 6 (tel. 22 10 95).

RENFE: Plaza Pio XII 1 (tel. 22 41 63).

Bus Station (Servicio de Carreteras): Plaza de España (tel. 25 22 24). **Train Station** (FEVE: Ferrocariles de Vía Estrecha), Plaza de España (no tel.). Schedules and prices for both train and bus posted at both locations.

Aucona (ferry ticket sales): Muelle Viejo 5. Open 8am-1pm Mon.-Fri. and 8am-noon Sat. Tickets are sold at the ferry dock (Muelle de Paraires) until one hour before sailing time and may be available at the gangplank after that—with a 25% surcharge.

U.S. Consulate: Av. Jaime III 26 (tel. 22 26 60). Open Mon.-Fri. 3:30-7pm; closed Sat. and Sun.

Accommodations and Food

Once again, reserve far in advance for the summer. The **Youth Hostel** (IYHF), Costa Brava 16, El Arenal, is booked by groups all summer. The **Hostal Isabel II,** Calle de la Portella 8, is a nice place where singles cost 180-230ptas with bath, doubles 270ptas, 360ptas with bath, plus 20% if you don't eat in (279ptas for three meals).

If you get a reserved room, chances are you'll be required to eat meals at the hotel. Otherwise, there are plenty of cheap places to eat, and even a few interesting ones.

Yate Rizz, Paseo Generalísimo Franco 2. *Menú turístico* 140ptas, is better than you might expect and offers several choices in both column A and column B. Service is fast and friendly.

Texas Jack's San Felio 26, just off the Paseo. Walls scribbled with graffiti, country-western music, studied western decor. Not particularly cheap, but if you get homesick, try their 250ptas "Menu #3 for meat eaters: Bar-B-Q house special Texas-size rib plate with hot garlic bread."

Bar Pica-Pica, Calle de Pelaires 21 (north of the Post Office). Great place for *tapas;* mix and match informality; make up a big plate and see if it doesn't come to less than 120ptas, including beer.

Sights and Entertainment

The tourist invasion is only the latest in a long series of forcible cultural infusions, and the influence of each is to a lesser extent still palpable. In particular, the Moorish presence is recalled by the mode of agriculture, terraced and irrigated; linguistically, in place names; and also in a number of important structures, including the **Almudaina Palace.**

The **Cathedral** (Open 10am-12:30pm and 3:30-6pm every day; admission 25ptas) is interesting, but not beautiful. With its unadorned steeples it looks like a huge rack of spears and pikes. The ambitious design took more than three centuries to complete from the time the first stone was laid in 1230 (a year after James I of Aragon kicked out the Moors). The rose window, 47 feet in diameter, is the second largest in the world (after Notre Dame), but the new geometric designs just don't make it. Inside, don't miss the brilliant jeweled reliquary containing a fragment of the *Vera Cruz del Redentor* (True Cross of the Redeemer). The small, Romanesque cloister with its banana tree is a welcome relief from the pretentious scale of the rest of the Cathedral. Also, for welcome relief: off to one side of the cloisters are a pair of nice, clean bathrooms.

At night there are the usual *tapas* and nightclub circuits. Of the many discotheques you might try **Cabala,** at the Hotel Almodaina at Ribera 11, where it intersects Jaime III (tel. 22 73 40). The decor is hardly original, but the music is satisfyingly loud, and the crowds are hopping. Moreover, it's cheap: between 11pm and 5am admission is 250ptas including a drink; in the "afternoon" (i.e. before 11pm) men pay 125ptas and women 50ptas, including one hard drink and one soft drink respectively.

Excursions on Majorca

While **Palma** has no beaches worth the sand in your shoes, the rest of the island has miles of sandy coves and rocky cliffs perfect for sunning and splashing or skin-diving. To the northwest, there is a ripsaw of modest mountains displaying an incredible virtuosity of variation in form and vegetation; there are splendid caves, pearl factories, mountain sanctuaries, and also what remains of the agricultural way of life indigenous to the islands.

The first step is to equip yourself with the priceless (100ptas, actually) Firestone map of the Baleares and Palma. Then check out the comprehensive bus schedule given away at *Turismo*. Even if you haven't made reservations (which should be done months in advance), you might call one of the following monasteries to see if you can be put up for a few nights: **Monasterio de Nuestra Señora de Lluch** (or Lluc), near the northwest coast (tel. 51 70 25); **Sanctuario de Nuestra Señora de San Salvador,** near Felanitz, about 45 kilometers due east of Palma (tel. 58 06 56); **Sanctuario de Nuestra Señora de Cura,** near Randa, about 30 kilometers east of Palma (tel. 66 09 94). As you will see on your map, there are other convents and monasteries but these are the most beautiful of those that will put people up. Rooms cost from 200ptas per day. Car or motorbike is the best way to reach them; otherwise take public transportation until you are within hiking or taxi range.

If you have a car or motorcycle at your disposal, we strongly recommend the northwest coastal excursion. Head first for **Valldemossa,** at the southern breach in the mountain chain. A picturesque cluster of dung-colored houses, presided over by the terraced tower of the **Cartuja Real Monastery,** Valldemossa's only fault is that too much is made of the brief stay there by George Sand and Chopin—especially considering how miserably the folks treated the unconventional couple. As long as you're there, you may as well visit their cells in the Monastery (open 9:30am-1:30pm and 3-7pm every day except Sun.) It all looks very prim and chaste, and except for the "officially authenticated Mallorquin piano" used by the composer, will probably not strike a responsive chord.

Lluch is one kilometer off the C-710 and worth the detour. For all its renown, the sanctuary has preserved an atmosphere of spiritual serenity. Here is the statue of the Brown Virgin, *La Moreneta,* patron of all the Baleares; the cell you stay in here was for years reserved for the pilgrims who came to adore her.

Puerto de Pollensa, at the far end of the island, might just be a town to find a hotel room—again, if you're lucky. There are three little places on the beachfront boulevard that don't contract their rooms to agencies or make reservations; you just have to be there at the right time. At Paseo Coronel Llorent (Carretera de Alcudia) 84 is **Torre;** at #48, **Seguí;** at #12, **Rivoli.** All three charge around 200-250ptas for singles, 350-400ptas for doubles. It so happens that there is also, around the corner from Rivoli, a little restaurant worthy of note: **Bodega Ferrá**, Calle San Pedro 3 (tel. 53 10 06) is a little family-run place specializing in *Mallorquin* dishes and seafood in general. Give them a day to whip up a *paella* that will years hence bring tears of nostalgia to your stomach's eyes (190ptas).

Just beyond the beautiful cove of Puerto de Pollensa is the forked devil's tail of the island, **Cape Formentor.** On the road, the *miradores* overlook spectacular fjords. Before the final twisting kilometers to the lighthouse, the road drops down to the **Formentor Beach** where a canopy of evergreens runs almost down to the edge of the water.

Ibiza and Minorca (Menorca)

If you hit Ibiza during the summer, you'll find no one has any use for you. If anything, Ibiza is tougher for rooms than Mallorca. Grab a map at **Turísmo,** on the central Paseo Vara de Rey 13 (tel. 30 19 00), open 9am-1pm and 4:30-7:30pm, except Sat. afternoons and all day Sun. Rent a set of wheels at **Ribas** on Vicente Cuervo 3 for cheap: bicycles 125ptas per day, mopeds 300ptas per day, cars 900ptas per day; less for more than three days (tel. 30 18 11); and start looking. If you slow down to enjoy the beautiful scenery everywhere, you'll never get anything, not even a campsite. There are several campgrounds, including three around San Antonio Abad. **Europark,** on the Carretera Ibiza-San Antonio kilometer 9, has bungalows and a swimming pool and takes no reservations, but you still have to get there at 7am to have a chance at a spot. The nicest campsite, and the largest, is beyond **Santa Eulalia,** between Playa Es Canar and Punta Arabí. Pine canopied, right on the beach—who cares if the toilets are always flooded. Of course, there are no campgrounds at all in the most beautiful area, including **Cala Xarraca** and the coves west of it in the northwest corner of the island. Of all the towns—Ibiza, Santa Eulalia, and San Antonio Abad, and such big-name resorts as Cala Portinatx—the less said the better.

Bus Station: Av. Isidoro Macabich. During the summer, buses run to San Antonio and Santa Eulalia every half hour.

Aucona: (Trasmediterránea), Bartolomé Vincente Ramón 2 (tel. 30 16 50). Ferries.

The tourist jet stream has somehow missed Minorca, which remains a quiet, unspectacular island with many good beaches. **Mahon,** the capital, is the natural sea or air approach to Minorca, though several boats weekly go from Alcudia and Palma to **Ciudadela,** at the other end of the island. The better place to stay on Minorca is probably Ciudadela—a picturesque port with easier access to isolated beaches. As always, bicycles, motorbikes or cars can be rented for the beach safari; otherwise, taxis can be hired inexpensively for the day. Occasional megalithic monuments punctuate an uneventful arid countryside.

SWEDEN

$1U.S. = 4.08kroner(kr)   1kr = $.245

Sweden is the success story of twentieth-century Europe. Her development unhindered by the ravages of two world wars, thanks to a policy of strict neutrality, Sweden has become the affluent society *par excellence*. Yet it is an intelligent, not a blind, affluence: Sweden has created the Western World's most effective social welfare system, and has taken care to preserve the natural beauty of her land, over half of which is forest and lakes.

But Sweden is not all blond hair and blue eyes. In recent years, attention has shifted to the country's shriveling job market, prohibitively high taxes, and emerging racial and ethnic tensions. And for the traveler, the high national income only translates into some of the most expensive supermarket shelves and services in Europe.

If you come to Sweden, don't settle just for **Stockholm.** Prices are lower and people warmer in the countryside. Explore the south, a land of wheat fields and small red farmhouses. Or **Lapland,** the forbidding northern region forested with dwarf birches, foraged by caribou, and lit day and night by the midnight sun in the summer. Or **Gotland,** the Baltic island that was once a center of Viking power and that today boasts a rich inheritance of churches and art, orchids and sunny beaches. Or the **Karlso Islands,** much closer to the coast and famed for their birdlife and scenery. **Ostergotland** is a region on the way from Denmark to Stockholm, known for its sleepy towns, beautiful lakes and valleys, and strong traditional influences.

Swedish youth hostels, called *vandrarhem*, usually cost 15-17kr per night outside of Stockholm, and 5kr more if you don't have an IYHF card. Most are open only during the summer. Get a complete list from **STF (Svenska Turistforeningen)**, at Birger Jarlsgatan 18 in Stockholm. Campgrounds in urban areas, with excellent facilities, usually charge 20kr or more for a tent spot; the mandatory camping pass costs 5kr. Swedish law, however, permits camping for one night anywhere except on fenced land (though it's customary to stay at least 100 meters from private homes, and to ask the owner, if apparent, for permission). Contact the STF if you're planning extended hiking or camping: you can get maps, advice on equipment, and information on the cabins and mountain huts they maintain along many hiking trails.

Banks charge 7-10kr for cashing a travelers check of any amount and for changing currency worth over 50kr. If you have checks in small denominations, it pays to cash more than one at a time (the fee is the same).

Midsummer (around June 21) is Sweden's happiest festival. Wherever you are, but particularly in the north, you can join in an evening (that often lasts a couple of days) of drinking, dancing, and general euphoria.

Transportation

You can set your watch by Swedish trains, which crisscross the southern part of the country and run north all the way to Narvik in Norway. Get the free schedule *(snabbtåg)* of inter-city trains; there is also a good network of slower local trains. A seat reservation (7kr) is required on trains with numbers beginning with "X," marked in schedules by an "R" with a box around it. Hitching is feasible in Sweden, but not easy: be prepared to wait, and remember that distances between towns are great in the north.

At **SFS-Resor** offices in Stockholm, Uppsala, Goteborg, and Lund, you can get youth fares on trains (if you're under 26) and tickets for inexpensive student flights. Last year, from mid-May to the end of August, people under 26 were able to fly on a standby basis anywhere in Sweden for just 100kr, an extraordinary bargain; check with a **Scandinavian Airlines** (SAS) office or travel agent to see if this offer is still available.

Food

Swedish specialties you might want to indulge in are *Janzon's Frestelse* (temptation), made from potatoes, cream, and anchovies; or *Pytt i panna* (like Shepherd's pie). You can easily prepare one of the hundreds of types of herring in the traditional way with dill, boiled potato, and onions. Buying your own food is a pleasure in Sweden's incomparably well-stocked supermarkets, open-air markets, and indoor markets. Make sandwiches with round ruffly crackers called *knäckerbrod*, paper-thin *flatbrod*, or dark, dense, delicious *fullkornsbröd;* try the cheeses: *riddarost, greve,* and *wasterbotten*.

The high cost of restaurant meals can be held down somewhat if you order the specialty of the day *(dagens rätt),* usually offered weekdays only between 11am and 3pm. Beer comes in three grades (and at three price levels): *lattöl* has hardly any alcohol; unpopular *falköl* is the government's new middle-strength beer; and *starköl* is strong and expensive.

Lund

Located on the major rail line between Malmö (across from Copenhagen) and Stockholm or Oslo, Lund will introduce you gently to Sweden: it is atypical in this predominately modern and expensive country. Well-preserved old houses and a Romanesque **Cathedral** give Lund the cobblestone charm of a continental town; and the presence of 17,000 students keeps prices relatively low. The Cathedral is worth a visit for its twelfth-century crypt, but is most unusual attraction is a fourteenth-century astronomical clock: at noon and 3pm (Sundays at 1pm and 3pm) knights clash, trumpeters blow, and clockwork figures emerge to greet the Virgin and Child.

Although Lund is quiet, it is by no means inert in the summer, since the **University,** founded in the seventeenth century, runs a summer school. You can meet students and get inexpensive sandwiches and coffee at the **Bok-cafèt,** a Marxist book shop across from the Tourist Office. Open weekdays from 10am-6pm and Sat. 10am-1pm. There's a Student Center at Sandgatan 2; here you'll find **Chrougen,** an inexpensive cafeteria (daily special 14kr, including milk), open weekdays 11am-6pm. The disco here is open Friday and Saturday evenings from 10pm-2am.

The **Tourist Office** is located near the Rail Station, at St. Petri Kyrkogata 4 (tel. 12 45 90; summer hours: weekdays 9am-6pm; Sat. 9am-1pm). Money can be changed in the **Post Office** across from the Rail Station until 6pm weekdays and 8:30am-1pm Saturdays.

Accommodations and Food

Some of the cheapest and most pleasant places to stay in Sweden are in Lund. From June through August you can get a modern, well-furnished single or double room, with access to a kitchen, in a dorm with Swedish students. Get a current list of student houses with rooms available from the Tourist Office (the list is posted outside at night), or try the two listed below. If you wish, the Tourist Office will find you a room in a private home for 35kr per person, plus a 5kr fee.

Göteborgs Nation, Gullrengnsvägen 1 (tel. 12 50 00). 30kr for a single and 40kr for a double, without sheets.

Smålands Nation, Kastanjegatan 7 (tel. 12 52 20). Officially 35kr for a single and 45kr for a double, without sheets, but if you are really low on funds, you may get a room for much less. One catch: reception is usually open only Mon.-Fri. 8am-4pm.

Youth Hostel, at the **Hotell Sparta,** Tunavägen 39 (tel. 12 40 80). This new hostel is almost too luxurious to deserve the name. 25kr (with a student or IYHF card) for 3-bed room with private shower; free use of the gym, sauna, kitchen. Reception is open 24 hours; take bus #1 from the Rail Station. Open June through August.

The hungry should try **Clemens Matsalar,** down the street from the Tourist Office, at St. Petri Kyrkogata 8. 13kr buys the *Lilla Lunchen* (means "little lunch," but you get all of the main course, milk, bread, and salad you can eat); the 17kr *Stora Lunchen* includes dessert and appetizer. Open Mon.-Fri. 11am-6pm. All pizzas go for 12kr (including coffee) at **Pizzeria**

O'Vesuvio, at 15 Ostra Mårtensgatan, 11am-4pm Mon.-Fri. Picnickers just arriving in the country can be introduced to Sweden's wonderful supermarkets at **Fokus,** on the corner of Bangatan and St. Petri Kyrkogata, open until 8pm weekdays and until 5pm Saturdays.

Stockholm

Stockholm is the focus of the Swedish success story, a model of creative and quality-oriented affluence. Concern for the environment has led to the cleaning up of Stockholm's waters; you can now swim and fish downtown. Bold architectural design and intelligent planning for parks and public spaces have resulted in aesthetic as well as economic successes; here the twentieth century has enhanced, not destroyed, the beauty of the city.

But there is a high price to pay for this cosmopolitan paradise. The cheapest hostel costs 20kr, while a single room in a hotel starts at 55kr. Not only tourists feel the squeeze: central Stockholm is slowly pricing out the lower income groups.

July is Stockholm's vacation month and many restaurants and other businesses are closed. It's better to come in June—the weather is good and the Swedes are still in town. To join in on a Midsummer Night's Eve festival, contact the **SSRS** (see below) for information on outings to the lakes and islands.

Orientation

If you arrive by train, you can pick up a city map and a list of hostels or hotels at **Hotellcentralen,** the main room-finding agency in the Central Station. Otherwise, you can get all the orientation material you need at the **Sverigehuset** (Sweden House), Hamngatan 27, on the northwest corner of Kungsträdgården, the city's most popular park and promenade. The **Tourist Reception Desk** downstairs is open in summer from 9am-9pm every day (tel. 22 32 80); pick up a copy of *This Week in Stockholm* for information on free outdoor concerts and other goings-on. You'll get more personal attention on the first floor from the **Stockholm Student Reception Service (SSRS),** open June through August only, from 10am-6pm daily (tel. 11 64 91); ask about discount tours and daytrips for students. Also on the first floor, through the program **Sweden at Home** (tel. 10 03 26), you can arrange to spend an evening with a Swedish family at no cost. In the same building is the library of the Swedish Institute where you can get "fact sheets" on nearly every aspect of Swedish society free of charge; it's open Mon.-Thurs. 8:30am-4pm, Friday 8:30am-3pm.

Stockholm's excellent subway and bus system operates on a zone fare system. A single ride within a zone costs 3kr; the ticket entitles you to unlimited transfers within an hour in the same zone. The central zone encompasses all of downtown Stockholm. You'll probably want to buy a three-day **transit pass** for 28kr, though it sounds expensive. It's valid on buses and subways for 72 hours beginning when you first use it, within the central zone and the two surrounding zones which extend quite a distance out from the center. The pass is also good for free admission to Skansen, Gröna Lund, and the Kaknäs Tower, and for the ferry to Djurgården from Slussen or Nybroplan (see Sights section). You can also buy a 24-hour pass for 10kr (central zone only) or 15kr (including the two surrounding zones); the

Stockholm

1 Stadshuset
2 Universitet
3 Konserthuset
4 Post
5 Parliament
6 Royal Palace
7 Operan
8 American Express
9 Nationalmuseum
10 Moderna Museet
11 Historiska Museet
12 Nordiska Museet
13 Biologiska Museet
14 Liljevachs Konsthall
15 Wasavarvet

0   250   500m
0   250   500 yds

N ←

ENKÖBING
UPSALA

DROTTNINGHOLM

SOLDERTÄLJE

MÄLAREN

SALTSJÖN

SKANSEN

SKEPPSHOLMEN

GAMLA STAN

RIDDARHOLMEN

CENTRAL STATIONEN

VASAPARKEN

HUMLEGÅRDEN

KRONOBERGS PARKEN

Tegnér lunden

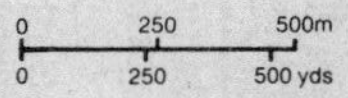

single-day passes don't include admission to any sights. Passes are sold at the Tourist Office and at most subway newsstands.

To get to the **Silja Line** terminal for ferries to Finland, take the subway to Ropsten, then bus #60E direct to the terminal (or walk one mile). Buses to the airports, **Arlanda** (international) and **Bromma** (domestic), leave from Vasagatan 6-14, opposite the Central Station.

Addresses and Telephone Numbers

SFS-Resor: Drottninggatan 89 (tel. 34 01 80), open Mon. 9am-7pm, Tues.-Fri. 9am-5pm. Student flights and youth fares on trains.

Svenska Turistforeningen (STF): Birger Jarlsgatan 18 (tel. 22 72 00), open Mon.-Fri. 9am-5pm, Sat. 9am-1pm. Your best source of information if you're planning extended hiking or camping. STF runs Sweden's Youth Hostels, maintains stations and cabins along hiking trails in the north country, and offers guided hiking expeditions. Go early in the morning to avoid the crowds.

International Youth Center: Tunnelgatan 27 (tel. 21 43 67). Free use of cooking facilities; newspapers; information about long-term accommodations. Open in summer Mon.-Sat. noon-8pm.

American Express: LB Resebyrå, Sturegatan 8 (tel. 22 88 60). Open Mon.-Fri. 9am-5pm. Subway to Östermalmstarg. This branch does not cash travelers checks.

Post Office: main office at Vasagatan 28-34; open weekdays 8am-9pm, Sat. 8am-4pm, Sun. 11am-1pm.

Police: Kungsholmsgatan 37 (tel. 90000).

Medical Emergency: tel. 90000.

Pharmacy: Apoteke C.W. Scheele, Klarabergsgatan 64 (tel. 24 82 80). Open 24 hours.

U.S. Embassy: Strandvagen 101 (tel. 63 05 20).

Canadian Embassy: Tegelbacken 4, 7th floor (tel. 23 79 20).

Women's Center: Birger Jarlsgatan 22 (tel. 10 52 90).

Accommodations

Budget hotels are scarce in Stockholm and are often full in July and August. Rooms in private homes aren't much less expensive: through the **Hotelltjänst,** Vasagatan 38B (tel. 10 44 67), you'll pay 45kr for a single, 65kr for a double (minimum two nights). Fortunately, there is a wide range of hostels and hostel-type hotels to choose from, though the more popular of these are also usually full in the high season. **Hotellcentralen,** in the Central Station, can help in a pinch; they're open until 7pm Saturday and until 11pm every other day; they charge 8kr for finding a hotel bed, 3kr for a bed in a youth hostel. **SSRS,** in the Sweden House (see Orientation section) will book you into the **Frescati Hostel** for free, or into another youth hostel for 3kr. For longer stays, contact SSRS or **All Rum,** Drottninggatan 77 (tel. 21 37 89).

Hostels

Each year brings changes in the hostel scene. Except for old standbys like the **Af Chapman,** it is a good idea to call ahead and see if a hostel is still in operation.

Af Chapman (IYHF) is a fully-rigged nineteenth-century sailing ship, majestically moored off the island of Skeppsholmen, across from Gamla Stan, just a five-minute walk from downtown (tel. 20 57 05). 4- to 8-bed cabins; 21kr with IYHF card, 26kr without. Rooms closed 10am-5pm; midnight curfew. Open March 15 to October 31. Make reservations in advance or arrive close to 7:30am.

Mälaren, beautifully situated on Söder Mälarstrand across the water from the City Hall and Gamla Stan (tel. 44 43 85), is a squat red boat which rivals Af Chapman in setting and price, but hardly in style. 20kr with IYHF or student card, otherwise 25kr for a bed in a small, dingy double room. Café open 8am-midnight. Mälaren fills up fast; arrive shortly after 11am to get a bed. Walk across the bridge from Gamla Stan and turn right to the waterfront or take the subway to Slussen. Open all year.

Columbus Hostel, Tjärhovsgatan 11 (tel. 44 17 17), in an unglamorous part of town, houses men in dorms (20kr) and women in 4-bed rooms (23kr). 24-hour reception; kitchen facilities available. Also a cheap hotel: prices from 60kr for a single to 120kr for 4 beds. Good bicycles available for 15kr per day. Subway to Medborgarplatsen. Open all year.

Frescati Hostel (IYHF), part of the Hotel Frescati, Professorsslingan 13-15 (tel. 15 79 96), has the best deal in town. Double room with a private shower and toilet for 50kr (sheets not included), or one bed in a double for 25kr. Only 46kr for a double, and 23kr for one bed if you show your Hostel Card (they won't ask for it). Reception open 24 hours. If you're discreet, you can use the kitchen (on every floor) and the inexpensive laundry (off the passageway under Professorsslingan), though technically these are only for Swedish students. Subway to Universitet, then take bus #151 to the hotel or walk ten minutes. After midnight take bus #691 from Odenplan. Open June through August.

Zinken Hostel, Pipmakargränd 2 (tel. 68 57 86), has a relaxed, friendly management and good facilities despite its barrack-like appearance. Single and double rooms cost 33kr per person without sheets. Closed noon-4pm, but reception is open all night and you get a key to your room. Free use of laundry facilities and kitchen. Open May-September and sometimes in winter. From the Hornstull subway station follow Horngatan east; turn right at the Teleskolan building (#103) and go down two sets of stairs behind the building.

KFUM Hostel, Mariagrand 3 (tel. 42 68 60), has a rather grim location behind the Slussen subway stop. 42kr in a large 4-bed room, including sheets and breakfast. Open all year; 24-hour reception.

Hotels

Pensionat Oden, Odengatan 38 (tel. 30 63 49), is small but pleasant. 55-65kr for a single, 80-85kr for a double; 38kr per person for larger groups. Free use of kitchen. Subway to Odenplan.

Smiths Hotellpensionat, Linnégatan 9-11 (tel. 61 11 08). Friendly management. Singles 55kr, doubles 98kr, but extra beds (even in a single) are only 25kr. Well-located two blocks from the indoor and outdoor markets (and subway) at Östermalmstorg.

Hotell Callmar, Barnhusgatan 4 (tel. 21 21 75), is old and elegant with high-ceilinged, spacious rooms, most with ceramic fireplaces. Singles 50-60kr, doubles 80-90kr, extra beds 25kr. 10-minute walk from Central Station, or 5 minutes from Hötorget subway stop.

Hotell Gamla Stan, Lilla Nygatan 25 (tel. 24 44 50), has a great location but is for ascetics only (it's run by the Salvation Army). Small singles 56-62kr, 84kr with extra bed. Doubles 106kr, triples 135kr, quads 164kr; 3kr for a shower. English-Swedish bible in every room.

Camping

There are now four government-run campsites within the city boundaries of Stockholm (although this can mean 15-25 kilometers from the center).

Sätra Camping is brand new, only 10km from the center, and near the coast (tel. 97 70 71). Take subway #13 or 15 to Bredäng station, and walk 5-10 minutes. 29kr for tent site. Includes hot running water, washing machines, sauna, café. Open May 1-Oct. 15.

Ängby Camping is on Lake Mälaren, about 10 km west of Stockholm center (tel. 37 04 20). Take subway #17 or 18 to Ängbyplan, then walk 10 minutes. Tent spot 26kr/night. May 1-Sept. 30. Good facilities, and lake swimming.

Farstanäset Camping is 25 km south of the center, right on Lake Magelungen (tel. 94 14 45). Take subway #18 to Farsta, then take bus #833 or walk 25 minutes. Tent spot 7kr/night. Open May 15-Sept. 15.

Flaten Camping, on Lake Flaten, is 20 km southeast of the city center (tel. 77 30 100). Bus #811 or 817 from Olandsgatan, and 401 from Slussen. Tent spot 7kr/night. Open May 1-Sept. 30.

Food

Eating out on a tight budget in Stockholm is next to impossible; to make matters worse, many of the less expensive restaurants are closed in July. At Stockholm's two splendid indoor markets, watching is as much fun as buying: **Ostermalms Saluhall** at Ostermalmstorg and **Hötorgshallen** at Hötorget. Both are open until 6pm weekdays and until 1pm Saturdays, and at both locations you'll also find lively outdoor markets in the morning. Åhlens, a mammoth department store on Klarabergsgatan near Sergels Torg, devotes its entire basement to food—the selection is fantastic. The food section is open every day until 10pm.

Other options for budget meals include the small self-service restaurants called *"Bars,"* where you can get a snack, or a filling meal for 15-20kr, and department store cafeterias, which offer palatable but not particularly cheap meals.

Annorlunda, Malmskillnadsgatan 50, is a good, primarily vegetarian restaurant where you can get a complete meal for about 25kr. Good homemade bread and freshly-pressed juice. Open weekdays 11am-7pm, Saturdays until 6pm. In July, open weekdays only 11am-3pm.

Pirogeri, in Gamla Stan at Stora Nygatan 28, is a comfortable pub where you can get *piroger* for 7kr or pizza for 11kr. Open everyday 11am-11pm.

Swedes prepare *smörgåsbord* only on special occasions, and almost never in summer. A few restaurants offer elegent *smörgåsbord* in summer—the famous **Operakällaren,** for one—but to indulge will cost you over 100kr. For a more modest exercise in gluttony, try the **Centralens Restaurang** in the Central Station. Sample the *Stora Frukost* (an all-you-can-eat breakfast) for 14kr; served daily from 6:30-10am. The buffet lunch, offered Mon.-Fri. from 10:30am-2pm, costs 21.50kr; and the surprisingly fancy dinner (again, an all-you-can-eat affair) costs 25kr. Incidentally, the proper sequence for eating at a *smörgåsbord* (or any well-laden Scandinavian buffet table) is: herring, meats and salads, hot dishes, and finally fruit and cheeses (if you get this far).

Sights

Note: Many sights are free with the three-day transit pass—see Orientation section.

Stockholm's modern, affluent flavor is especially pronounced in the area of "mini-skyscrapers," in the gleaming commercial center between Sergels Törg and Hötorget. To its south, you'll find by way of contrast an interesting working-class neighborhood, **Söder,** usually overlooked by tourists. Many of the city's chief attractions lie on three islands just south of the centrum: **Gamla Stan, Skeppsholmen,** and **Djurgården.** The gaunt, cobbled streets of Gamla Stan, Stockholm's Old Town, are linked to the center by several bridges and by subway. You'll discover fascinating remnants of the original Stockholm (established here because the narrow passage to the Baltic could be easily controlled), especially if you get off the touristy main streets that run lengthwise, and walk through the tiny passages which connect these streets. On the northern edge of the island are the eighteenth-century **Royal Palace** and the seventeenth-century **Riddarhuset** (House of the Nobility).

Visit Skeppsholmen, east of Gamla Stan, to see Stockholm's two finest art museums. The **National Museum,** just before the bridge to the island, has fascinating collections of Swedish and European paintings as well as exhibits of practical arts; it's open daily from 11am-5pm, Tuesdays until 9pm. **The**

Museum of Modern Art, in the center of Skeppsholmen, has an excellent collection of American and European pop art; it was one of the first European museums to show the work of Oldenburg, Dine, Rauschenberg, and Rosenquist. Open every day from 11am-9pm. Admission at each museum is 5kr, or 3kr with a student ID.

Djurgården, east of Skeppsholmen, is Stockholm's pleasure island, reached by bus #47 from the center, by foot from attractive harborside Strandvägen, or by ferry from Nybroplan or Slussen (free with three-day transit pass). You can spend the whole day just walking in the greenery or visiting the many museums (see *This Week in Stockholm* for current exhibits and hours).

The **Wasa,** a seventeenth-century warship dug up in 1961, is an exhibit in a super-humidified shell. Obviously not a "product of superb Swedish engineering," the ship traveled only about ten minutes on her maiden voyage before a wave swept into open portholes and sunk her. Swedes, themselves, come to Djurgården either for **Skansen** or **Gröna Lund.** Skansen, "Sweden in Miniature," is an open-air display of old Swedish buildings and handicrafts. It has an interesting zoo, lots of tours, and much entertainment, all for 7kr. Gröna Lund is Stockholm's Tivoli—though not as good. 12kr between 6 and 8:30pm and 7kr at other times; the big scene, however, features the international stars who visit Stockholm, and is free once you're in. You may have to pay to dance; avoid Jump In (twelve-year-olds) and Dans Ut (aging fox-trotting cavaliers) and head for Dans In.

Crossing the bridge to **Strandvägen,** you will be very close to one of the best prehistoric and Viking museums of the North, **Historiska Museet,** on the corner of Linnegatan and Narvavägen close to Karlaplan. Here you can see Viking treasure, runic stones, and swords bent in curlicues and buried with their owners so that no one else could ever use them.

For a fine overview of the city and the spectacular Baltic archipelago of 24,000 islands, visit the **Kaknäs Tower,** Scandinavia's tallest building, located east of downtown (bus #69 from Normalmstorg); it's open daily from 9am-midnight and is free with a three-day transit pass. There are also good views from the tower of the **City Hall,** an imposing modern masterpiece, located just west of the center on Kungsholmen (3kr).

Kulturhuset, at Sergels Torg, is Stockholm's very popular cultural center. In the crowded Läsesalongen (reading room), open in summer from 9am-10:30pm Mon.-Thurs., and until 6pm all other days (shorter hours in July), you can find newspapers and books in English and listen to records on headphones. There are also areas where you can work with clay, wood, or leather, as well as various historical and artistic exhibits. Everything in this modern pleasure palace is free.

The Swedish sauna experience—a bracing melange of scorching air or steam, cold showers, even massages—can be sampled in style at **Sturebadet,** Sturegatan 4. 9kr buys a swim and steam bath, 20kr for full sauna treatment. For an additional 30kr, hedonists can have a sunlamp treatment and massage as well. The Tourist Office has a list of the less expensive public saunas and pools. (Sturebadet is privately-owned.) It's also possible, thanks to the city's clean-up effort, to swim downtown in Lake Mälaren with a view of Gamla Stan: Smedsuddsbadet, on the south side of Kungsholmen near the Västerbron Bridge is reached by subway to Fridhemsplan.

For a glimpse of Swedish welfare society, take the three-hour tour called

The Swedish Way of Life; with a knowledgeable guide you'll visit a modern suburban center, a school, and a pensioner's apartment. SSRS can sell you a student ticket for 27kr. If you would rather investigate on your own, visit **Skarholmen, Vallingby,** or **Husby,** all accessible by subway, for a look at a planned suburban community.

Near Stockholm

Some of Stockholm's finest sights are a short distance out of town. The sculptures of Carl Milles are exhibited in the beautiful, terraced **Millesgarden** at the edge of a cliff in Lindingo. Take the subway to Ropsten; from here you can catch bus #203 direct to Millesgarden (once an hour), or you can walk across the old bridge (¼ mile long) and up the hill, to the right, about 300 yards. Open 11am-5pm every day and 7-9pm Tuesdays and Fridays; admission 7kr.

At the **Drottingholm Palace,** 12 km west of the center on an island in Lake Mälaren, eighteenth-century operas are presented in an eighteenth-century theater with the original sets and stage machinery. The performances are excellent, but tickets are hard to get: try calling 23 60 00.

SSRS sells tickets to students in the summer for a variety of tours and daytrips at one-third less than their regular price. A trip through Stockholm's archipelago is a must, especially if you're not going by boat to Finland. Take an all-day trip to **Sandham,** three hours by ferry through the archipelago from Stockholm for 45kr (students 30kr). Sandham is the sight of yachting competitions as well as August Strindberg's former summer home. There are no automobiles on the island, which can be explored easily by foot in the three hours between arrival and departure of the ferry. Get to the boat at least half an hour before departure to get a seat in the sun. Don't forget a bathing suit, sweater, and raincoat—the weather changes very rapidly. If you can't spare an entire day, take the three-hour tour to the islands of **Vaxholm** and **Rindö** for 25kr (students 17kr).

Evenings

Evenings in Stockholm, like the Swedes themselves, appear quiet and reserved, but are actually great fun. In summer there are free concerts nearly every night in different city parks: details in *This Week in Stockholm* or from the Tourist Office. On Djurgarden you'll always find concerts and dancing at Skansen and Gröna Lund.

The Student Café Forum, Körsbärsvägen 4B (subway to Tekniska Högskolan, tel. 15 33 50), features television, chess, and inexpensive food every evening from 8pm-1am. Next door the **Mocambo Pub,** which is open daily from 9pm-1am, offers a discotheque on weekends (admission 20kr) and occasional live music (tel. 15 98 55).

Stampen, in Gamla Stan at the corner of Stora Nygatan and Stora Gramunkegränd, has great traditional jazz in a small, cozy setting. Open every day 7pm-midnight; admission 10-20kr. Music starts about 9pm. **Fasching,** Kungsgatan 63, is a jazz club formed by younger musicians who felt Stampen was too traditional. Admission about 15kr. **Bullerbyn,** Kungsgatan 67, featuring Swedish rock bands, is a good place to meet young people; admission about 15kr. There is a discotheque in the basement.

Mosebacke Etablissement, on lovely, quiet Mosebacke Torg (subway to Medborgarplatsen), is a pub with a beautiful terrace overlooking the city from the bluffs of Söder. On summer evenings there is often live music and dancing outdoors. At times there is an admission charge of 10kr.

Uppsala

Uppsala is dominated by the twin spires of Sweden's finest cathedral and the 20,000 students of Scandinavia's oldest university. Most of the students, however, are away in the summer, making the town a quiet refuge from Stockholm.

Uppsala is divided by the **River Fyrisan.** To the west, close to the river, are the University and the well-preserved older area; to the east, along Kungs Angsgatan, is the modern shopping district. The **Tourist Office,** at Kungsgatan 42 (tel. 11 75 00), to the right as you leave the Train Station, will supply you with maps and touring suggestions for the surrounding countryside. Summer hours 9am-8pm weekdays, 9am-6pm Sat., and 1-6pm Sun. They also rent good, new bicycles for just 10kr per day (75kr deposit).

Visit the free **Upplands Museum,** located on the river at St. Erikstorg 10. (Open every day from 11am-4pm, Sunday to 5pm.) The cultural history of the city and province is illustrated in attractively arranged exhibits of handicrafts, examples of architecture, and photographs. The **Cathedral,** right next door, was begun in the thirteenth century. When the stately spires collapsed after an eighteenth-century fire, they were replaced by Baroque hoods; only late in the nineteenth century was this corrected in a major restoration. Surrounding the Cathedral are old university and ecclesiastical buildings, some containing remnants of the medieval town wall. **Carolina Rediviva,** the university library, has a famous silver Bible from about 550A.D. From the library, walk up the hill to **Uppsala Castle,** for a view over the city (and a full view of the Cathedral). **Gamla Uppsala,** the royal burial mounds located a few miles north of the center, is something of a tourist trap.

Carl Linnaeus worked and lived for many years in Uppsala. Botanists will find inspiration in the **Linnaeus Garden,** open daily 9am-9pm. Linnaeus' house, now a museum, can be visited 11am-6pm daily for 4kr. House and garden are located on Linnégatan (off Kungsgatan several blocks west of the Tourist Office).

There are two IYHF **Youth Hostels** in Uppsala. The old Hostel, one of the finest in the country, is at **Sunnerstavägen 24,** 8 kilometers south of the city (tel. 32 42 20). For 17kr (nonmembers 22kr) you are housed two or three to a room. Take bus #20 from Ostra Agatan (which borders the river on the east) just south of Drottningsgatan. The new Hostel at **Norbyvägen 46** (tel. 10 80 60) charges only 13kr per night and is open June through August. Reached by bus #7 or by a twenty-minute walk from behind Uppsala Castle. The **Hotel Sankt Erik** (tel. 13 03 84), near the Train Station at Bangårdsgatan 10 had beds last summer without linen for just 25kr; check to see if the offer is being repeated. The **Hotel Elit,** Bredgrand 10 (tel. 13 03 45) has singles for 55kr, doubles 88kr, breakfast 6kr. You can get a room in a private home through the Tourist Office for 30-35kr per person. There is **camping** at

Graneberg (tel. 32 41 33), just beyond the old Youth Hostel for about 15kr; reached by bus #20.

Gothenburg (Göteborg)

Poseidon rules this city: Carl Milles' gigantic bronze sea god bares his muscle in the middle of **Götaplatsen,** Gothenburg's art center, but his domain extends far beyond. Fishermen auction their catch weekday mornings at 7am (7:30am Friday) at the **Fiskhamnen** (tram #3 or 4 to Stigbergstorget); get there an hour or so earlier to see the boats come in. For an interesting view of the busy, colorful harbor (Scandinavia's largest), take the excursion to Elfsborg, a seventeenth-century island fortress, for 13kr; boats leave from Lilla Bommen. There's even a "fish church" (in Gothenburg dialect, the *feskekârka*), by the canal on Rosenlundsgatan.

Gothenburg is a city of almost half a million, but it can be restful and pleasant if you get out of the modern center. Walk through **Haga,** Sweden's oldest suburb, now a working-class district with interesting wooden houses (tram #3 or 4 to Jarntorget). The city is full of parks. **Slottskogen** (tram #1 to Linneplatsen) has lakes, birds, and a children's zoo; just beyond are the famous **Botanical Gardens.** Among the city's many museums, one of the more interesting is the **Industrial Museum** at the Götaplatsen, open every day from 11am-4pm (free); it features historical exhibits of tools and machines used in Sweden's glassblowing, paper, and textile industries.

Although Gothenburg is a university city, nightlife is not cheap. The pub at the **Puboteque** in the student union, at the end of Götabergsgatan near the Götaplatsen, offers beer and the chance to meet local students, but the disco there costs 15kr. The **Volrat Tham,** Eklandagatan 51, has jazz once a week and disco dancing most other nights after 9pm; open Wed.-Sun., admission about 20kr. If you'll be here a while, membership in the **Student Reception Service** (30kr), giving you free admission to most activities, will save you money. Check their brochure in the Tourist Office.

Orientation, Accommodations, and Food

The **Tourist Office,** at Kungsportsplatsen 2 (tel. 13 60 28) open daily in summer from 9am-8pm, will suggest daytrips and find you a room for the night. The city has an excellent bus and tram system; you should probably buy a 24-hour pass for 8kr since a single ride costs 4kr. **SFS-Resor,** for student flights and youth fares on trains, is located at Götabergsgatan 17 (tel. 16 65 95), and is open Mon.-Thurs. from 10am-5pm. You can listen to records and read English-language papers at the **library** on Götaplatsen, open until 10pm weekdays and until 6pm weekends.

The Tourist Office will find you a room in a private home for 35kr per person or in a hotel for about 45kr for a single, 65kr for a double, plus a 5kr fee. Some good hotels have bargain rates in the summer if you're willing to sleep five or six in a large room; the Tourist Office has details. The **Hotel Oden,** Olskroksgatan 23 (tel. 15 99 60), has a sauna and lounge: singles are 40kr, doubles 72kr. About all that can be said for the dreary IYHF **Youth Hostel,** in a school building at Olof Rudbecksgatan 4 (tel. 20 42 12), is that it costs only 15kr. (Open June 10 to August 10; take bus #40 from Brunnsparken to Spaldingsgatan). The most convenient **camping site,** at

Kärralund (tel. 25 27 61), fills up fast and costs 20kr per night; take tram #5 (direction Torp) to Töpelgatan.

Bistro Chez Amis, Parkgatan 17, open daily until 11:30pm, is a small almost elegant restaurant, featuring delicious seafood dishes. Inexpensive if you stick to the daily special (13kr), served from 11:30am-3pm Mon.-Fri. At **La Gondola,** Kungsportsavenyn 4, you can sit outside and enjoy lunch for 17kr including all the salad you want.

Swedish Lapland

Swedish Lapland, the most accessible part of Lapland, has two major appeals for travelers. It includes the last large area of unspoiled wilderness in Europe, ideal for hiking, fishing, and camping. And it is the home of 10,000 Lapps, some 2,000 of whom still tend reindeer.

The larger towns in Swedish Lapland are accessible by train. The spectacular main line to Narvik, Norway, passes through **Gällivare** and **Kiruna.** The inland line runs north from Östersund, through Arvidsjaur and Jokkmokk to Gällivare. Rather expensive mail buses connect most of the smaller towns. You can find out about them locally at any tourist information office or train station, or from **Postverkets Diligenstrafik,** Fack S-921 00 Lycksele (tel. 0950 129 00).

July and August are the most popular months for hiking and camping. There will be many mosquitoes (especially in July) and vacationing Swedes. Late August or early September may be the ideal time: the weather is good, most of the mosquitoes will be gone, and you'll have the mountains more to yourself. Earlier and later, many of the mountain stations and huts will be closed. Swedish law permits camping anywhere except on fenced land. Since most of Lapland, and particularly the highland region, is wilderness, you can camp where you want.

The only way to get up into the mountains is on foot. You must bring your own food and other supplies. A good part of the terrain is rather rugged, and in the higher mountains you can have snow in July. Good equipment is essential for extended trips. Still, you don't need special equipment (or even any camping equipment) to enjoy the mountains. From the towns described below it is easy to reach mountain tourist stations which make great bases for day hikes. If you plan to hike or camp, contact the **Svenska Turistforeningen** (the Swedish Touring Club), Fack S-103 80, Stockholm 7, before you go, or visit them in Stockholm at Birger Jarlsgatan 18 (tel. 22 72 00). STF has maps and advice; they maintain mountain huts and stations, and 2300 kilometers of trails. They also sponsor guided walking tours that typically last a week or so and cost about 900kr. They will also help you to plan your own hiking tour and can supply you with entrance tickets for the huts. In July and August the huts are very crowded: advance arrangements are essential.

Lapps are difficult to find. Take the inland railroad from Gällivare to Jokkmokk and Arvidsjaur to see reindeer. The train (usually only one car) stops every once in a while to wait for the reindeer to get off the tracks, as they run wild over the entire area during the summer. The Lapps themselves work in mines, on the railroad, or farm and fish during the summer, herding and branding reindeer in the spring and fall. Most have settled down permanently in the towns and villages. They do sponsor fairs in late winter.

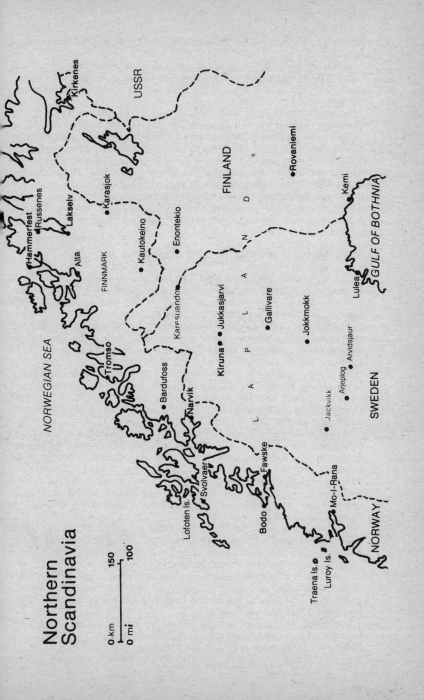

Northern Scandinavia

0 km
0 mi
150
100

NORWEGIAN SEA

Kirkenes

USSR

Russenes

Hammerfest

Lakselv

Alta

Karasjok

FINLAND

Rovaniemi

FINNMARK

Kautokeino

Enontekio

Kemi

GULF OF BOTHNIA

Tromso

Karesuando

L A P L A N D

Jukkasjarvi

Gallivare

Lulea

Bardufoss

Kiruna

Jokkmokk

Narvik

Arvidsjaur

Jackvikk

Arjeplog

SWEDEN

Fawske

Svolvaer

Bodo

Lofoten Is.

Mo-I-Rana

Traena Is.

Luroy Is.

NORWAY

Jokkmokk, for example, is the site of a large fair during the first week of February.

The larger towns are generally parish centers—Sweden "conquered" the Lapps through missionaries. **Karesuando** is one of the larger Lapp centers, reached by bus from Kiruna. It probably has the strongest "Lapp atmosphere."

In general, in order to avoid finding Swedish Lapland to be a series of charmless towns in a barren wasteland, you must plan for extended hiking or camping, for patience in trying to find and talk to Lapps, or at least for day excursions out of the towns and into the lakes and mountains. Particularly good for camping are the National Parks in Lapland. **Sarek** requires advanced mountaineering experience and complete equipment; **Padjelanta** and **Stora Sjöfallet** are more accessible, yet still wild enough for most. The tourist offices in the towns described below are often staffed by people with extensive knowledge of the mountain areas. They also sell topographical maps and arrange for accommodations at mountain huts.

Arvidsjaur, Jokkmokk, and Gällivare

The night train from Stockholm will take you all the way to Narvik in Norway in 21 hours; but the same train, if you change in Jörn, will leave you in **Arvidsjaur** in the morning, a bit off the beaten path. In the town itself there is an interesting Lapp Village—about thirty huts built in the early nineteenth century by Lapps for housing during religious festivals and still used today for this purpose. There are no youth hostels in the area, but the **Tourist Office,** Storgatan 10 (tel. 104 10), open 9am-8pm every day in the summer, will find you a room in a private home for just 20kr per person (25kr if you need sheets), plus 5kr commission. The **Centralhotellet** at Jarnvagsgatan 63 (tel. 100 98), across from the Rail Station, has the cheapest hotel rates, from 48kr for a single to 120kr for four people. **Arvidsjaurs Campingplats** at Storgatan 26 on Tvattjorn Lake (tel. 101 39), has huts for two people at 25kr.

Now that the scenic Silver Highway through to Bodö (Norway) has been completed, it's not too hard to hitch into the mountains from Arvidsjaur. Along the way, **Arjeplog, Jäckvik,** and **Sädvaluspen** are all excellent bases for day hikes, and they all lie along this highway. A mail bus serves this route as well; round-trip fare to Arjeplog from Arvidsjaur is 61kr. Unless you're camping, though, you'll find accommodations hard to get in the summer; be sure to make arrangements for overnight stays with the Arvidsjaur Tourist Office before you leave.

Jokkmokk, between Arvidsjaur and Gällivare on the inland railway, is another good base for trips to the mountains. The excellent **Jokkmokks Museum,** with exhibits of *Sahme* (Lapp) culture, is definitely worth a visit (3kr). The same building houses the **Tourist Office** (tel. 113 47); both open daily in the summer 10am-9pm, Sundays noon-9pm. The IYHF **Youth Hostel,** open from mid-June until mid-August, is at Solgatan 45 (tel. 106 90) and costs 17kr per night. **Notuddens Camping** is 3 kilometers out of town; tent space 15kr, four-bed hut 65kr.

Kvikkjok, an excellent base for hiking trips in the mountains, is reached by the mail bus (74kr round trip) or hitching from Jokkmokk. Stay in the **Pellevas Vandrarhem** (tel. 210 16) for about 20kr. Kvikkjok is on the *Kungsleden* hiking trail, very close to **Sarek,** Sweden's wildest national park. Just 30 kilometers from Jokkmokk is **Muddus National Park,** a good area for hiking if you can't spare the time to get up to Kvikkjok. You'll have to hitch (via Ligga, north of Jokkmokk), but this isn't too difficult.

An old parochial church town and center for Laplanders, **Gällivare** is the site of the Lapland Fair at the end of March, and of Sweden's foremost alpine competition, the Lapland Cup, also in March; it is located at the junction of the main rail line to Narvik and the inland line to Jokkmokk and Arvidsjaur. The town itself has little to offer in summer, but it is a good base for any day excursions in the surrounding mountains and for longer trips to the higher mountains near **Stora Sjöfallet National Park.** You should, however, try calling the **mine** (tel. 210 00) to see if tours are being offered. Here, unlike Kiruna, you visit a mine that is actually being used, but, due to the recent economic downturn, closed in the summer.

The **Tourist Office,** near the Rail Station, at Lasarettsgatan 8 (tel. 136 30), is open in the summer 8am-9pm daily, noon-4pm and 5-9pm Sundays. Ask about the IYHF **Youth Hostel,** which has been in a different place each year. A single room in a private home costs as little as 25kr, plus 10% commission. **Camping** at Kvarnforsen, by the Wassara River, costs 6kr a night; there are also some stark chalets for 20kr.

Kiruna

Kiruna is a mining city, the northernmost large town in Sweden. Tours of a mine (one that is no longer in use) are offered two or more times a day in summer for 15kr. Get the exact times at the **Tourist Office,** Mangigatan 12 (tel. 103 00). Open daily 9am-8pm, Sundays 3-8pm. The office will find you a room in a private house for 40kr for a single, 60kr for a double. The IYHF **Youth Hostel,** Strandstigen, half a kilometer from the Rail Station (tel. 171 95), charges 20kr per night, 25kr for nonmembers.

A short bus ride from Kiruna (45kr round trip) is **Nikkaluokta,** the best base for hiking expeditions to **Kebnekaise,** Sweden's highest mountain. In Nikkaluokta there are four-bed cottages for 85kr; details at the Kiruna Tourist Office. A day's hike from Nikkaluokta is the STF **Kebnekaise Fjäll-station** (tel. 181 44); lodging here will cost about 40kr. If you are short on time and heading through to Narvik, stop at **Abisko Turiststation,** on long Lake Torneträsk, and hike through **Abisko National Park.** As all the Kiruna-Narvik trains stop here, you can get another one in a few hours. You can also get a bus from Kiruna to **Karesuando,** a Lapp center near the Finnish border. Karesuando has an IYHF **Youth Hostel** at the Grapes Hotell (tel. 200 22) where you can stay for 15kr per night.

SWITZERLAND

$1U.S. =1.52Francs(F)   **1F=$.66**

Switzerland has perfected the tourist industry; the people who brought you numbered bank accounts, waterproof watches, and cautious neutrality are ready to greet you with superhuman cleanliness, idyllic mountain scenery, and metal handholds up the sides of the **Matterhorn.** Yet this world of manicured farms, prismatic mountains, and sunlit lakes justifiably rates the most lavish guidebook raves. The Swiss, as you would expect, have meticulously preserved their vision of natural harmony in the face of industrial onslaught, and fully intend to harvest the fruits of their farsightedness.

Switzerland doesn't let you look for free, however. Both large cities and tourist resorts have Europe's shallowest "rock bottom," and it gets shallower every year. Skip the cities altogether if you're on a tight budget—they're gracious, but grace is cheaper in France. Fairy-tale resorts like **Zermatt, Wengen,** and **Grindelwald,** are expensive tacky tourist towns, but the miles of well-managed and isolated trails will make you forget the towns themselves. If the Alps seduce you into a longer stay, choose a smaller and more isolated village.

Campers and youth hostelers can survive. Once you've beaten Swiss hotel prices, the battle is half over. Food is expensive, but the omnipresent **Migros** markets and cafeterias make eating manageable. Hiking and Alpine scenery cost nothing, and clean campgrounds abound. In Switzerland, play by the rules: penalties for littering, illegal camping, and riding trams without tickets are savage.

The major cities are in the German section, which extends east from an approximate north-south line between **Biel** and **Saanen. Bern,** federal seat and university town, has a relatively unspoiled city center, while the outskirts are becoming industrialized. Adjacent to the triangular meeting of the Swiss, French, and German borders is the German-speaking city of **Basel,** which contains a university and vast chemical industry plants. **Zürich** is a bustling and efficient commercial center. Set on a huge lake, the French-speaking sector centers around **Geneva,** an international city proud of her cosmopolitan air. The Italian region of **Ticino** may be the most surprising—palm trees and Mediterranean lakes with tropical vegetation are set against the snow-capped Alpine peaks.

Separated by the Rhone and Rhine, two huge mountain chains slash the southern part of the country, and since Hannibal, have been formidable obstacles to anyone traveling from Italy. In the northern group, the **Bernese Oberland** area, centering on **Interlaken,** challenges the climbers and skiers who attempt the **Eiger** with its infamous north face, the imperious **Jungfrau,** and the vast **Aletsch** glacier. The crescent-shaped southern range spills over onto France's soil, leaving **Mont Blanc,** Europe's highest mountain, in French hands. Within Switzerland are the legendary Matterhorn, towering over Zermatt, and further east a series of renowned resorts including **Davos** and **St. Moritz.**

An ultra-efficient transport system gives access to virtually every corner of the country. Yellow postal buses (with musical horns) and the federal and private railroads are never late. Those planning an extensive tour of Switzerland should invest in a **Schweizer Ferien Karte** (Swiss holiday pass; 11OF for eight days, 155F for fifteen days, 215F for one month), available at railway stations, although it may be cheaper to buy it in the States. Eurailpass is not valid on some of the private lines (to Grindelwald and Zermatt, for example).

Switzerland is the home of *fondue*. Try cheese *fondue,* though the more expensive beef *fondue* is more fun: you dunk pieces of beef fillet into a pot of boiling oil until they are done, and then into any one of the five or six sauces displayed on your tray. Very simple, very good, but more of a game than a feast. Also try *raclette* (melted cheese served with pickled onion and boiled, new potatoes), and *rosti* (the almost-hash-browned potato with onions). For lunch, you can pick up *bratwurst* (made from veal) at outdoor stands, or buy cheese and meats at supermarkets. The **Bahnhof Buffets** (at every train station) feature very good and reasonably-priced food (in contrast to other countries). If you eat in second-class sections, you'll pay less.

Efficient tourist offices, located in most cities near a *Bahnhof* or *Gare* (train station), provide room-finding services and distribute maps and advice. Advance hotel reservations are often necessary in popular tourist areas, so you should write to individual hotels a number of weeks before your intended arrival. Prices always include bed and breakfast; full board is available at most establishments and can be extremely economical. All prices in hotels and restaurants must include a 15% service charge. Be sure to ask at the place where you stay about a **visitor's card** entitling you to discounts and special privileges in town. The **Swiss Student Travel Office (SSR)** maintains offices in most university cities and will aid with travel plans. Be sure and pick up their *Student Guide to Switzerland, The Cheap Way,* 9F.

Stores do business weekdays 8am-6:30pm, often with a two-hour lunch break. Dialing 111 on the telephone connects you with an English-speaking information operator, while dialing 117 anywhere in the country will connect you with the police in an emergency.

August 1 is Independence Day, a national holiday with fireworks and bonfires on top of mountains; banks and most stores are closed.

Zürich

While the streets of Zürich are not paved with gold, its mark is everywhere. There is an abundance of gold under the pavement in the vaults of the banks along Bahnhofstrasse, as well as above it. Fancy boutiques and cars, thriving banks, exclusive hotels and restaurants, as well as stylishly dressed citizens are the more visible signs. But don't let the parade of wealth overwhelm you. Zürich—with the bright-blue water of the **Zürich See** and the handsome façades of the guildhouses along the banks of the **Limmat River**—is a strikingly beautiful and friendly city.

A walk through the cobbled and hilly streets of the **Old Town** will reveal Zürich as it has been for hundreds of years. Begin by following the Limmat River toward the lake on the side nearest the Train Station, then take one of the narrow stairways into the Old Town as you follow the shore.

At Münsterhof you'll find the **Fraumünster Church,** with a frescoed cloister on the outside, and Chagall stained-glass windows within. If you're around on Sundays, come at 10am to hear the organ. Descend by way of **Pfalz-Gasse,** a small park with a view of the river. Locals play chess here on a hopscotch-sized board.

On the other side of the river, the **Grossmünster Cathedral** is a striking example of Romanesque architecture. It dominates Zürich's hippest neighborhood, **Niederdorf,** with its boutiques and antique shops. Come by day to see the vibrant colors of the Giacometti windows, and return at night to listen to outdoor musicians wooing the crowds. The **Kunsthaus,** on Heimplatz, is a museum especially strong in modern art. The building itself is a masterpiece of museum planning—almost exclusively natural light illumines the paintings, with virtually no glare (Open Mon. 2-5pm, Tues.-Fri. 10am-9pm, weekends 10am-5pm; 2F, 1F with student ID). The **Schweizerisches Landesmuseum** (Swiss National Museum), Museumstrasse 2, near the Station, gives a fascinating presentation of Swiss life, with displays of armor and early Christian art (closed Mon. morning and daily between noon and 2pm).

Orientation

The **Verkehrsbüro,** Bahnhofplatz 15 (tel. 25 67 00), is at the main Train Station. Open 8am-10pm every day, May through October until midnight. Hotel bookings, special tickets, and free information are available. **The Swiss Student and Youth Reception Service,** Leonhardstrasse 10 (tel. 47 30 00), provides valuable student-oriented information for all of Switzerland. With student ID you can get reduced train tickets (generally for international trips only), and they also hold mail. Open Mon. 1-6:30pm, Tues.-Fri. 9am-5pm, Sat. 10am-noon.

Exceptionally efficient public trams serve all parts of the city (.60F or .80F, depending on distance). A special shuttle bus runs between the Train Station and the airport for 5F, but bus #68 (board next to the Train Station) makes the same trip for 1.60F. An exchange office is open at the Train

Station until 11pm. Bicycles are for rent at the baggage counter.

Hitching to Basel, Bonn, Geneva, or Paris, take tram #4 from the Station to the end (Wendhölzli); to Lucerne or Italy, take tram #13 from the Station to Allmendstrasse; for Austria, take tram #7 to the end (Wallishofen) and continue to a bridge which leads to Highway 3.

Addresses and Telephone Numbers

American Express: Bahnhofstrasse 20 (tel. 211 29 30).

Main Post Office: Sihlpost on Kasernenstrasse near the Bahnhof. Also a branch (near the Youth Hostel) at Albisstrasse/Rengersstrasse 57.

Railway Information: (tel. 211 50 10).

Money Exchange at Station: open until 9pm.

Emergency Medical Aid: (tel. 47 4700).

Drug problems Drop In: Dufourstrasse 181 (tel. 5553 11).

La Main Tendue: Hotline for any kind of problem (tel. 143).

U.S. Consulate: Zollikerstrasse 141 (tel. 55 25 66).

Accommodations

The hotel situation is gloomy: 22F is rock bottom for a single. Dormitory lodgings cost as much as hotels in southern countries, but you can count on the Swiss to keep even the most crowded dorms spotless. If you want assistance, the **Verkehrsbüro** (tel. 211 40 00) right outside the Train Station will get you a room for a charge of 2F for one person, 3F for two, and 4F for three or more. Open 8am-10pm daily, and until midnight May through October.

Schaefli, Badergasse 6 (tel. 32 41 44) is the cheapest hotel in town. The rooms leave something to be desired, but they are clean. Rooms run from 22F, breakfast 3.60F. The street is hard to find—it is an alleyway off Limmatquai, not far from the Station.

Limmathaus Tourist Hotel, Limmatstrasse 118, second floor (tel. 42 38 00) calls itself a "hostel for adults," and is not to be confused with the Limmathaus Hotel in the same building. Open May through September 10, 10F in dorm rooms. No curfew. But not much nicer than the hostel, and they, too, evict you between 9am and 4pm.

Jugendherberge Zürich (IYHF), Mutschellenstrasse 114 (tel. 45 35 44) is a modern structure with over 400 dormitory beds. It is clean and well equipped, with hot showers, cooking facilities (1F), and free hairdryers in the bathrooms. Unfortunately, muzak is piped in to wake you up at 6:30am, and will grate on your nerves during the rest of the day. 7F with IYHF card, 12F without. Breakfast 2.50F, lunch or dinner 5F. 10pm curfew, but for 1F you can stay out until 1am. Open 7-9am and 2-10pm. Take tram #7 (direction Wollishofen) and walk five minutes.

Foyer Hottingen, Hottingerstrasse 31 (tel. 479315). For women and married couples only. Staffed by friendly, helpful, multilingual nuns. Free kitchen facilities, midnight curfew. Singles 20F, doubles 36-40F, quads 60F, dorm beds 11F, breakfast included. Showers 1F, bath 1.50F. Tram #3 to Heimplatz.

Martahaus, Zähringerstrasse 36 (tel. 32 45 50) only accepts women. Good location, clean but undistinguished rooms. 30F for a single, 38F double. Dorm beds 17F, breakfast and shower included. The desk and door are always open, and there is no curfew. Look for the YWCA sign.

Glockenhof, Sihlstrasse 33 (tel. 221 36 73) is the local YMCA, with a limited number of rooms for men only. The rooms are your basic "Y" variety, but cheap. 18F for a single, 30F for a double. A café next to the main lobby has passable menus from 5F. Not to be confused with the more expensive Hotel Glockenhof next door.

Camping, Campingplatz Seebucht: Seestrasse 557 (tel. 45 16 12), maintains fully equipped sites on the shores of the Zürcher See for 2.60F per person per night. Unfortunately quite far from the central city. Take bus #61 or 65 to Grenzsteig, or the train to Wollishofen, and walk 15 minutes. Open May through September.

Food

There are numerous student and city- and temperance-run restaurants. For the automat connoisseur, there is a 24-hour, dial-your-order **automat** in the Shopville Plaza under the Bahnhofplatz and the Train Station, by the "Central" exit. A small crowd often gathers to watch the machine operate.

The Mensa, in the university building at Ramistrasse 71, is run by a Zürich women's association, and offers good meals for as little as 4.80F with student ID. A cafeteria and an automat are on a marvelously airy and skylit indoor terrace, while the main dining room downstairs has access to a multi-leveled park where you can take your food. Open 7:30am-7:30pm. Lunch 11:15am-1:30pm. Dinner 5:15-7:15pm.

Migros Markt is a supermarket chain which operates bargain cafeterias that are a godsend to the budget traveler (the groceries are inexpensive as well). *Teller service* (luncheon plate) 4-7F, breakfast from 2F, and excellent pastries from 0.60F. Branches are at Limmatplatz, Sihlbrücke, Kreuzplatz Folkenstrasse, Löwenstrasse, and Mutschellenstrasse (near the Youth Hostel). Closed every Sat. evening and Sun.

Walliser Kanne, Lintheschergasse 21, (near the Station) at the corner of Schützengasse, is a good place for *fondue* with a touch of wine and kirsch. The plain *fondue* is 10.50F, but it is large enough to split two ways, making it a good budget meal. Pleasant wooden decor and friendly waiters. Good desserts as well.

Olivenbaum, Stadelhoferstrasse 10, is the best of a number of sedate establishments run by Frauenverein (the city's women's temperance union). The food is good, the pastries are even better, and there are meatless meals for vegetarians. Prices run around 5F for a complete meal. Closed Sat. Others are **Platzli,** Pelikanplatz; **Fronsinn,** Gemeindestrasse 48; **Restaurant Seidenhof,** Sihlstrasse 7.

Jemoli's restaurant, on the third floor of Jemoli Department Store, Bahn-hofstrasse. Offers from 8 to 11am a huge, all-you-can-eat breakfast buffet (cheese, eggs, fruit, meat) for only 8F. Bring along a "doggie bag" for the leftovers. If you are down and out, walk around the ground floor, where free food samples are offered—from champagne to cheese, bread, and candy. However, they like you to buy what you have tried. If you get yelled at, shrug your shoulders, say you don't understand German, and walk to the next booth.

Rheinfelder Bierhaus, Marktgasse 19, in the heart of the old city, is a working-class pub with hearty, German food. A woman alone may feel un-comfortable, but the portions are generous and tasty. The chicken with *spatzli,* (a chunky, homemade egg noodle) is 6.30F. There is another branch at Niederdorfstrasse 72.

Stadtküche, Schipfe 16a, is a city-run restaurant in the center of town, near the river. Prices are unbeatable—soup 0.60F, complete meals from 3.40F. Open Mon.-Fri. 11:30am-12:30pm only. Other branches at Centralstrasse 34 and Luggwegstrasse 27.

The Silberkugel chain serves some of the best hamburgers outside of America at shining counter restaurants all over the city. Their *Beefies* may remind you of home. Open 9am-10pm, closed Sun. Locations at Bahnhofplatz 14, Badenerstrasse 120, Löwenstrasse 7 and Bleicherweg 33, and the underground Shopville.

Evenings

Most of Zürich's nightlife centers around the **Niederdorfstrasse** (off the Limmat) with its cluster of bars, clubs, and street-corner musicians. Much of the city locks up at midnight, if not earlier. Before then, try:

Casa Bar, Münstergasse 30, a small crowded pub with good, live jazz. Come early, though, or you may end up standing in the doorway.

Oliver Twist, Rindermarkt 6, is an English-style pub with an international clientele. A pleasant patio in back. Good for meeting other Americans.

For dancing, there's the **International Student Club,** Augustinerhof 1, between Augustinergasse and Bahnhofstrasse (keep looking, it's more of an alleyway than a street). Open on Wed., Fri., and Sat. nights—you need a student ID to get in. The place has the atmosphere of a 1950s college fraternity without the booze.

Excursions

Innumerable outings are possible on the **Zürcher See** and to the nearby mountains. There are many boat trips available on the Sea (Lake Zürich), ranging from a short trip (one and a half hours) which stops at little villages along the way (6F) to a "grand tour" lasting four hours. Eurailpasses are valid on both. Boats leave from Bürkliplatz every half hour. The boat trip through Zürich, going down the river Limmat, is the best way to see the elegant, frescoed façades of the guildhouses. Eurailpasses are valid (4.60F otherwise). Boats leave from Limmat Quai.

Trains leave Station Selnau every half hour for various mountain villages. Go to Adliswill (1.80F, Eurail not valid) where you can take the funicular to **Felsenegg** (4.60F, half price with Eurailpass). From here there are dozens of hiking paths, all clearly marked, and each leading to a different village. The paths stretch through miles of forests, pine groves, and flowered meadows. From here, hike to **Uetliberg** (one and a half hours) or return to Station Selnau to take the steep train ride there (6F round trip) which yields a panoramic view of the lake, the city, and the nearby Alps. Eurail is not valid, and tickets are checked.

Stein am Rhein is a beautiful little town straddling the river, but a tourist attraction as well. The town's center is made up of old half-timbered houses, many of them painted with colorful frescoes. You can get to Stein am Rhein by train or even by foot (four and a half hours from Schaffhausen), but probably the best way to go is by river boat (only four a day, though). Either walk to the quai, or take bus #4 from Schaffhausen Station. Railpasses are valid, and the boat continues to Reichenau and Konstanz. There is a **Youth Hostel** (IYHF) by the river at the Schifflande (tel. 85255) a short walk along the Rhein. There is camping as well.

Lucerne (Luzern)

Lucerne is Switzerland's picturebook city, but the pages are tainted by mass commercialism. Its popularity among tourists is understandable, though. Situated on the shore of the majestic **Vierwaldstättersee** (Lake Lucerne) at the foot of the Alps, Lucerne embodies all that is traditionally Swiss: antique covered footbridges, an **International Music Festival,** daring cable car ascents to Alpine peaks, flower-decked fountains and squares.

The old city is delightful, even amid the crowds. Walk by the **Altes Rathaus** (Old Town Hall) on Kornmarkt; the **old city wall** with its nine fortified towers; the **Hofkirche**, rebuilt in Italian Renaissance style after a fire destroyed the original structure; and the **Kapelbrücke** and the **Spreuerbrücke,** carved wooden bridges adorned with flowers and seventeenth-century panel paintings. Be sure to visit the **Lion Monument,** a war memorial that is the symbol of Lucerne. It is especially dramatic when illumined at night, when it is the site of concerts.

For music lovers, there is the **Richard Wagner Museum** with Wagner memorabilia—portraits, letters, music sheets, pictures—set in a beautiful home with crystal chandeliers and fine Oriental rugs. Upstairs there is an old music room, with hand-carved lutes and harps. All this is set to the accompaniment of Wagner's operas (open 9am-noon, 2-6pm, 3F). Take bus #6 or 7 to Wartegg, but the boat which leaves hourly from in front of the Station is much nicer—railpasses valid.

Orientation

The **Verkehrsbüro** at Pilatusstrasse 14 (tel. 23 52 22) is close to the Train Station, and provides city maps and guides (open daily 8am-6pm). A **Lucerne Season Ticket** is a bargain at 15F for those planning an extended stay; it entitles you to admission to various monuments, the city beach, and three return trips on assorted cable railways and lake steamers. Bicycles are available for rent at the Station (baggage counter), 8F per day. If you stay in a hotel, ask for a visitor's card which will get you reduced admission for museums, swimming, and tennis. Most of Lucerne can be seen on foot, but there is an extensive tram system. Purchase tickets from the automatic machines—0.60F, 0.80F, 1.20F.

Hitching for Zurich: bus #1 to terminal Ebikron; for Interlaken, bus #1 direction Kriens, get off in the Eichof neighborhood.

Addresses and Telephone Numbers

Swiss Student Travel Office (SSR): Burgenstrasse 5 (tel. 22 02 77).

American Express: Schweizerhofquai 4 (tel. 24 11 77). Open 8am-noon, 2-6pm.

Post Office: Bahnhofstrasse, near the Station.

Travel Information: (tel. 28 21 33).

Money Exchange: at Station, 7:30am-9pm daily, Sat.-Sun. 7:30am-7:30pm.

Police: Obergrundstrasse 1 (tel. 23 51 51; emergencies, tel. 117).

Medical, Dental Emergency Service: (tel. 111 for information).

Laundromat: Mythenstrasse 9, near Bundesplatz.

Accommodations

Lucerne has virtually no student-priced lodgings. Hotel prices are steep, though good locations near the old city and immaculate rooms partially compensate for the expense. If you have transportation, you may find it most practical to look for *Zimmer Frei* (rooms to let in private homes) in small towns elsewhere on the lake.

Hotel Bären, Pfistergasse 8 (tel. 22 10 63). A nice place in the heart of the old city, near the water. Singles 21-26F, doubles 38-46F, breakfast included; 4F less without breakfast. Ask for rooms on the top floor, which run only 19F per person. Good showers 2F. The building itself is impressive, and is over 450 years old.

Pension Wirth, Bruchstrasse 68 and 70 (tel. 22 05 62), 17F for singles, 28-32F for doubles. Breakfast from 3.50F, depending on whether you want Continental or American style. Rooms are large and simple, but pleasant. Check in at the Café Wirth next door.

Haus Pro Filia, Zähringerstrasse 24, at corner of Pilatusstrasse (tel. 22 42 80). A Catholic foyer just for women. Modern, college-dorm type rooms, 22F per person, breakfast and shower included. 20F without breakfast. The price goes down to 18F after one night. Free hairdryers, as well as a lounge. No curfew, but get a key if you plan to return after 10pm.

Hotel Ilge, Pfistergasse 17 (tel. 22 09 18) is one of the best deals in town. Clean dormitory rooms at 15F, breakfast included. Use of swimming pool as well. A good location in the old town.

Youth Hostel am Rotsee (IYHF), Sedelstrasse 24 (tel. 36 88 00). A large hostel, with over 260 beds, 6.50F with IYHF card, 11.50F without. Dorm beds are in two huge rooms, but they are kept spotless. Take tram #1 from the Station to Schlossberg stop and then follow the signs. About a ten-minute walk from the bus stop. Closed 10am-6pm.

Camp Lucerne Lido, Lidostrasse (tel. 31 21 46) has an incredible location right on the lake next to a beach, with tennis and other sports facilities nearby. Well-equipped: steaming hot water, car wash, laundromat, and a supermarket. They hold mail as well. 3F per person; no reception after 10pm. Bus #2 to Verkehrshaus.

Food

Hertensteinstrasse offers a wide selection of restaurants and *stuben* (taverns). For late-night drinking, try the **Braukeller,** at #24, open until 2:30am. **Migros Markt** is at #46. Its cafeteria serves half a roast chicken with a mountain of french fries for 5F (Open 7am-6:30pm on weekdays. Closes 5pm Sat. and all day Sun.).

Vegetarisches Restaurant, Pilatusplatz. A great cheap place to eat, especially for veggies. A wide variety of dishes are served. Try the meatless *schnitzel* or the *glarner hörnli* (a Swiss specialty of melted cheese and noodles). Prices range from 5-8F for a complete meal. In good weather you can eat on the balcony overlooking Pilatusplatz. Closed Sunday.

Evenings

In no way does Lucerne's nightlife violate Swiss propriety. Even the theater closes for the summer, though visitors can catch the **International Festival of Music,** held annually from the middle of August through the first week in September. Tickets start at 10F per evening. Some concerts have student tickets at 5F. (tel. 2 28 12 for details or write to Internationale Musikfestwochen, 6002 Luzern.)

Near Lucerne

Lucerne is a starting point for Alpine excursions. **Mount Pilatus** (7000 feet) is the main attraction, and the focal point of much folklore and mythology. Legend has it that the body of Pontius Pilate was finally buried here, but only after it had caused widespread destruction in other parts of the world. The best way to get to Pilatus is to go up from Alpenachstad (take the boat from Lucerne, Eurailpasses valid) via the steepest cog railway in the world (a 48° gradient) and return by cable car to Kriens, where trolley #1 takes you back to Lucerne. On Pilatus you can climb or hike along the well-marked trails, but come early to avoid the tourists. If you walk away from the populated areas, you can see mountain goats, ibex, and grazing cows with bells around their necks. But don't bother investing the 35F for the round-trip transportation if it's a cloudy day.

For a different sort of excursion, visit the little town of **Einsiedeln,** about an hour's journey from Lucerne. Situated in hilly, pine-forested country, Einsiedeln has been the most important pilgrimage destination in Switzerland and southern Germany since the tenth century. It boasts a huge **Cathedral,** with colorful frescoes and arches, and an ornate altarpiece with a black madonna. The **Fürstensaal,** a large eighteenth-century hall, has changing exhibits of monastic art. The **Engelweihe** (consecration of the angels) is observed on September 14 with a festival and candlelight procession. Einsiedeln is accessible by private railway, on which Eurailpasses are valid. From Lucerne, take the train to Arth-Goldau, switch trains to Biberbrügg, and then change again to Einsiedeln. (Not as complicated as it sounds—14.80F round trip if you don't have Eurail.)

For another excursion with Alpine scenery, take bus #14 to Klinik St. Anna and hike ten minutes on a well-groomed path through fields to **Trachtenmuseum** (Swiss Costume Museum). From the lush grounds surrounding this old-country-mansion-turned-museum you can look down on Lucerne and out at Mt. Pilatus. The museum contains authentic traditional costumes from each canton. (Open 9am-noon and 2-5:30pm; admission 2F.) Catch the bus back, or hike to **Dietschiberg** (35 minutes) where a funicular will take you back to Lucerne.

Bern (Berne)

Bern is Switzerland's very sparkling capital. Surrounded by mountains and tucked into a bend of the Aare River, its medieval city center is characterized by sandstone buildings, long arcades, and flower-bedecked fountains. To tour the old city, begin at the **Church of the Holy Ghost** across from the Train Station and proceed down Spitalgasse through the old city gate, **Prison Tower,** to the **Clock Tower.** The clock, completed in 1530, is still accurate to within ten to thirty seconds a day (if the weather remains stable). About five minutes before the hour, the gilded bears dance and the wooden figure strikes the hours with his golden arms. From here, continue straight to the **Gothic Rathaus** (Town Hall) and **Christkatholische Kirche,** which are on the left of the juncture of Kramgasse and Kreuzgasse. Visit the late-Gothic **Cathedral,** with its spire of "stone lace," and impressive stained-glass windows (open daily 10am-noon and 2-5pm, Sunday from 11am).

The steep descent from the old city to the Aare can be made at many places along winding staircases and wooded paths, but the quickest way up or down is the **Drahtseilbahn Marzili.** This shortest of Swiss railways travels the steep grade beside the Parliament Buildings for 0.50F fare until 9pm.

Bern has a number of unusual fountains in the city center, most notably the **Child-Eater,** which depicts a monster biting off the head of a child.

Bern offers many good museums. Don't miss the **Kunstmuseum,** at Hodlerstrasse 12, which has the world's largest Paul Klée collection as well as some fine Picassos, Renoirs, Monets, and Gauguins. (Open 10am-noon and 2-5pm, closed Monday mornings. Open Thurs. also 8-10pm. Admission 2.50F with student card, 5F without.) The **Bernese Historical Museum,** Helvetiaplatz 5, (9am-noon and 2-5pm; Sunday from 10am) is theoretically dedicated to the history of Bern but digresses into such delightful exhibits as Mongol tents and artifacts, European period costumes, medieval armor and Flemish tapestries. The **Swiss Alpine Museum,** Helvetiaplatz 4 (9am-noon and 2-5pm; Sundays from 10am), offers exactly what its name suggests—a lot of climbing gear, and photographs of mountains. All these museums are closed Monday mornings.

Bern hosts an annual **International Jazz Festival** in April and a **Folk Festival** during the first weekend in July.

Orientation

The main **Tourist Office** is upstairs in the new station complex and open daily 8am-6:30pm, 10am-5pm on Sundays (tel. 22 76 76). When the Office is closed, you can use the automats and information boards on the Office walls to get maps or find a room.

The old city is easily and ideally walked, but a bus-tram network exists for longer distances. Tickets are purchased from automatic vendors at the stops, and cost 0.60F, 0.80F, and 1F depending on the distance to be traveled. The colored maps on the machines explain how much you have to pay. Bicycles can be rented from the little hut by the east side of the station, off Bahnhofplatz. 10F for 24 hours, open 6am-11:45pm. For hitching to Geneva take bus #12 to the terminus: to Zúrich take bus #20 to the Guisanplatz terminus.

Addresses and Telephone Numbers

Swiss Student Travel Office (SSR): Hallerstrasse 4 (tel. 24 03 12), behind the University. Take bus #12 to Universität. Open Mon.-Fri. 9am-5pm, Sat. 10am-noon.

American Express: Spitalgasse 33 (tel. 22 94 01).

Money Exchange: at Station, open 6am-10pm daily.

U.S. Embassy: Jubiläumsstrasse 93-95 (tel. 43 00 11).

Canadian Embassy: Kirchenfeldstrasse 88 (tel. 44 63 81).

Laundromat: Militärstrasse 50.Open Mon.-Fri. 7am-7pm, Sat. 7am-noon.

Swimming: outdoor pools by the river on Marzilistrasse, admission free.

Accommodations

Goldener Schlüssel, Rathausgasse 72 (tel. 22 02 16) is probably your best bet for a hotel. Spacious rooms with sinks, in a good location in the old city. Singles 28F, doubles 50F, breakfast included. Free showers. There are two restaurants attached; the *stube* serves good food at reasonable prices.

National, Hirschengraben 24 (tel. 25 19 88). A charming old-fashioned place which looks more expensive than it is. Singles 20-30F, doubles 34-60F, breakfast included. Shower 2F extra. Only 5 minutes from the Station. Dancing on Thursday and Saturday nights.

Hotel Kreuz, Zeughausgasse 41 (tel. 22 11 62) is huge and often crowded. Not far from the Train Station in the old town. Beds 25-33F per person, breakfast included. 2F for showers. Reduced rates for doubles and triples. A reasonably-priced restaurant is attached.

Marthahaus, Wyttenbachstrasse 22a (tel. 42 41 35) is an attractive 'Y' for women only. 30 beds, 24F per person with breakfast. Free bath or shower.

Office open weekdays 8am-10pm, weekends 6-10pm. Bus #20.

Youth Hostel (IYHF), Weihergasse 4 (tel. 22 63 16) has one of the best locations in Bern, right near the Aare. The bunk beds are cramped and rusty, and the management strictly adheres to the hostel rules, but the place has excellent facilities and filling meals for around 5F. 6.50F with Hostel card, 11.50F without (sheets included). Closed 10am-5pm.

Camping Eichholz: (tel. 54 26 02). A fine location by the river, close to the city, and with swimming nearby. Take tram #9 to Eichholz and walk along Eichholzstrasse.

Food

In the mornings, produce stalls crowd Bärenplatz, especially on market days (Tuesday and Friday). Several department stores have stand-up cafeterias including **Migros Markt,** entrance at Zeughausgasse 31, **Migros Zed Restaurant,** Marktgasse 46, and **Loeb,** Schauplatzgasse 28. *Teller service* around 5F. The **EPA** department store, Marktgasse 24, has meals for 4-8F.

Bärenplatz is full of sidewalk restaurants and cafés, some open late into the night. **Spatz am Bärenplatz** has quick service *wursts* and *pommes frites* as well as full meals for 5-10F, while **Gfeller** has a second-floor self-service line with meals 5-11F. Other places to try are:

Vegetaris, Neuengasse 15, serves good salads and meatless meals. Open Mon.-Fri. 9am-11am and 2-4:30pm, closed Sat.-Sun. Located on the first floor, inside the arcade.

Pinocchio, Aarbergergasse 6, near Bärenplatz, specializes in crusty pizzas 6-10F. The other dishes are also good, but more expensive.

The Universität Mensa, Gesellschaftsstrasse 2, serves institutional quality meals for 3-5F, from 8am-7:30pm. Closed mid-July to mid-October. Take the elevator in the Railroad Station to the top floor, and then walk through the green park and University buildings, or take bus #12 to Universität if you're not near the Station.

Evenings

Nightlife in Bern is either very sedate, very middle-aged, or very expensive. A couple of exceptions:

Kornhauskeller, Kornhausplatz 18, is too steep for a meal, but a great place for an evening beer. It was once the city's grain vaults, and has been transformed into a huge beer cellar with a seating capacity of hundreds. Definitely worth the visit and the 1.50F beer. Open 10am-11:30pm; music after 8pm (but there's often a charge for this).

Pyrenées, Kornhausplatz, is a local bar with a friendly and young drinking crowd. A good evening hangout, with food at reasonable prices as well.

Excursions

Schwarzsee (Black Lake) is a beautiful mountain lake not far from Bern. The *see* looks "black" because of the volcanic rock below the surface. There is a postal bus to the lake, which runs once a day, 18F round trip (free with Swiss holiday pass). Reservations advised. On weekends the Swiss all come here with their dogs, children, and grandmothers.

Another worthwhile excursion is the trip to **Murten,** a medieval town with arcades and a massive stone castle, surrounded by walls. In summer, there are boat trips around the **Murtensee.** Take the direct bus to Murten, or go to Kerzers and change (10.60F round trip, Eurail valid).

Interlaken

Wedged between the **Thunersee** and **Brienzersee,** at the foot of the imperious **Jungfrau,** lies Interlaken. This bustling tourist town, gateway to the **Bernese Oberland,** the heart of Alpine Switzerland, is mainly of interest as a starting point for innumerable excursions in the Alps and around the lakes.

A good way to see the area is by motorbike or moped. **A. Balmer,** 27 Rosengasse (tel. 22 42 88) rents motorbikes, mopeds, and bicycles for full or half days. Prices run 6-20F. The **Westbahnhof** also rents bicycles for 8F a day.

In July and August, Interlaken puts on an elaborate, open-air **William Tell Pageant.** Performances are on Thursday and Saturday nights at 8pm, with prices starting at 8F. The show is in German, but you can buy an English synopsis of the famous Schiller play for 2F. The play has been performed for over 150 years, and incorporates horses and cows which are paraded through the streets before the production begins. Contact **Tellbüro,** Bahnhofstrasse 5 (tel. 22 37 23) for tickets, or purchase them at the Tourist Bureau.

Accommodations and Food

The **BLS Office,** next to the West Bahnhof, will provide you with information on hotels and a map of excursions. The main **Tourist Office** is down the street on Höhweg (tel. 22 21 21). Open 7:30am-noon and 2-7pm; Sun. until 6:30pm. Private rooms are often available for stays of two to three nights.

Balmer's Hostel, Hauptstrasse 23, Matten (tel. 22 19 61) is one of the friendliest and most helpful around. No curfew or ID requirements. Kitchen facilities, laundromat, and assistance with travel arrangements. They also give special discount tickets and will cash travelers checks. A young and knowledgeable staff. Dorm beds are 10F, doubles 36F. Breakfast, with all the bread and hot chocolate you want, is included. Walk, or take bus #5.

Chalet Swiss, Seestrasse 22 (tel. 22 78 22). Not far from the West Bahnhof. Rooms 28-40F, and some attic rooms at reduced prices. A real chalet with a pleasant manager.

Villa Rio, on the Kanal Promenade (tel. 22 31 62). Old but pleasant rooms. Singles 20-28F, doubles 40-52F, breakfast included. A small garden cottage has 2 singles, 15F without breakfast. A good location, near the ship dock and West Bahnhof.

Youth Hostel (IYHF), Aareweg am See in Bönigen (tel. 22 43 53). A nice location, but the woman in charge calls herself ''The Warden'' and will fine you for sloppy beds or littering. Strict about 10pm curfew. 8F, IYHF card required. Extra for sheets and breakfast. Walk from the East Station (25 minutes) or take bus #1.

Camping: There are extensive camping facilities in the area. Among them: **Camp Jungfraublick** (tel. 22 41 14) has sites for 3F and a swimming pool. Just outside of town on the Grindelwald road. Or try **Alpenblick,** 125 Seestrasse (tel. 22 77 57), or **Camping Hobby** 16 Lehnweg, Unterseen.

Bödeli-Beiz, near the Post Office on Marktgasse, serves some of the best food around. A warm atmosphere with wooden beams and a young crowd. Student specials as well. Prices start at 6F. Especially good beer.

Migros Cafeteria, to the right of the West Bahnhof, open Mon.-Fri. 7:30am-8:30pm, Sat. 7:30am-5pm, Sun. 8am-6pm. *Teller Service* 4-7F.

Near Interlaken

Giessbach Falls makes a good afternoon trip. Take the boat from the East Station toward Brienz and get off at Giessbach See. The ride takes about an hour (Eurailpass valid). From here you can climb up for hours alongside the Falls in search of its origin. From Giessbach you can walk to **Iseltwald** and catch the boat back to Interlaken, or continue on to **Brienz,** where there is the only wood-carving school left in Europe—a good rainy-day trip. There is a small shop as well, where carvings by students and masters can be purchased quite reasonably. If you decide to stay in Brienz there is an (IYHF) Hostel on **Axalpstrasse** (tel. 51 11 52).

For climbers, a good excursion for a clear day is the trip to the **Niederhorn.** From the West Station take the postal bus to **Beatenberg** (8.40F), and walk from there. On a perfect day you can see Mt. Blanc, and even on a less-than-perfect day there is a remarkable panorama of the Bernese Oberland. Many animals are visible from the granite pillars and cliffs along the ridge of the Niederhorn.

Grindelwald and Lauterbrunnen

Although Grindelwald's only (and nameless) street is packed with hotels, restaurants, and tourist shops, this hardly detracts from the allure of the surrounding mountains. The town is dwarfed by a trio of famous peaks: the **Jungfrau,** the **Mönch,** and the **Eiger,** with its treacherous north face.

The town of Lauterbrunnen is a valley of cascading waterfalls at the foot of the Jungfrau. Tourism here is less rampant than in Interlaken and Grindelwald, yet the snowy peaks rising above the pine-forested valley are almost as spectacular.

Trains set out from Interlaken's Ostbahnhof (East Station) for Lauterbrunnen (6.40F round trip) and Grindelwald (5F one way). Eurailpasses are not valid on either train, and hitching is difficult (if not hopeless), especially to Grindelwald. 75% of the cars are jammed with families going to the country for the day.

We couldn't begin to list all the hiking possibilities from Grindelwald—hundreds are available, of all degrees of difficulty. You might consider the trip to **First,** which is also serviced by cablecar (21F round trip). You can split the fare any way that you please. Ascend to First, then hike down to **Bort,** where you can picnic by the small lake and Alpine flowers. Or from **Egg,** hike to the **Bachalpsee,** where you can swim.

The vista from **Kleine Scheidegg** is spectacular. You can walk up (four hours) or take the train (13.80F one way, 22.20F round trip). There is an especially fine view of the north face of the Eiger from the restaurant on the hill behind the Train Station—good soup as well. From here, the affluent can continue up to the Jungfrau (11,333 feet) for 56F more. The view is unbelievable, but the cost is much too high. For those who are determined to make the trek, there is a discount on the first two trains in the morning (7am and 8am): 64.20F total from Grindelwald, a savings of 14F. The train trip goes through the famous granite tunnel (built in 1906) with a brief stop to let you look out the "window" that was carved in the Eiger.

On the main street there is a **Bergsteigerschule** (mountain-climbing school) with the standard services. A few guided excursions are available for about 30F (tel. 53 12 13). Mountain rest huts cost 10F per night.

Accommodations

Grindelwald's hotels are fairly expensive and often booked, but there are a number of dormitory-style accommodations. The **Verkehrsbüro** (open 8am-noon and 2-6pm, closed Sundays; tel. 53 12 12) can find you a room in a private home for stays of a week or more. There is a climbing office here as well. The building is on the main street, a five-minute walk up from the Station. There is an automatic hotel-information machine that can assist you if they are closed. If you stay for more than one day, be sure to ask for a visitor's card which will entitle you to discounts for activities (concerts, swimming, tennis) within the town.

Restaurant Glacier, down the hill from the Station (tel. 53 10 04). Hotel rooms for 25-30F per person, breakfast 5F. A large, barrack-like co-ed dorm, with beds at 10F per night. Hot showers 1F.

Naturfreundehaus, Terrasseweg (tel. 53 13 33). A youth hostel-like set-up, but less rigid. It's a club, and you should write in advance for information and reservations, but often they will put you up if you get stuck. 9F for nonmembers, 7F if you are under 20. Write to TVN, Postfach 137, 3000 Bern 22.

Jugendherberge "die Weid" (IYHF) (tel. 53 10 09). A remodeled building with a fireplace and a superb view. But strictly run, with a rigid 10pm bedtime. The Hostel is often full, so come early and write your name on the list to reserve a place. The Hostel opens at 4:30pm, but you can sign up at any time during the day. A twenty-minute uphill walk from the Station.

Camping: There are five campgrounds: **Aspen** (tel. 53 11 24). **Eigernordwand** (tel. 53 12 42), 2.60F per night with carnet. **Zum Gletscherdorf** (tel. 53 14 29) and **Sand Grund** (tel. 53 17 34) are reached by Itramen bus from the Station; get off at Restaurant Glacier. Or get off at Lehn for the **Weisse Spinne** (tel. 53 14 44), 2.40F per person with carnet, open summer only.

Around Lauterbrunnen

Take the gentle (one and a half hours) walk to **Stechelberg** (a cross-country ski trail in winter), which winds by a mountain stream. From here the ambitious can make the trek up to the **Schilthorn** (2970 meters), which is a full day's climb. (The Schilthorn was featured in the James Bond film *On Her Majesty's Secret Service*.) There is a rather fancy rotating restaurant—**Piz/Gloria,** at the top of the mountain. The climb is less arduous if you begin at **Mürren,** accessible by train from Lauterbrunnen or cablecar from

Stechelberg. Those who seek the panoramic view without any exertion can take the cablecar (32F). Other excursions might include the hike to the glacier near Gimmelwald (a one-and-a-half-hour walk from Gimmelwald). For accommodations, try the **Matratzenlager Stocki** in Lauterbrunnen, or the **Naturfreundehaus** in Stechelberg, both around 5F per night. There's also an IYHF **Hostel** in Gimmelwald (tel. 55 17 04).

Zermatt and Saas Fee

"In the beginning was the **Matterhorn,**" writes one Swiss author. Every morning hundreds of hikers march out to test the fantastic peaks that encircle the resort of Zermatt. Join those mesmerized by the proud, jagged mountain of mountains and forgive the Swiss for the prefab chalets and the countless red-and-white pennants. A twenty-minute walk will bring you to Switzerland at its uncommercial best.

If you visit Zermatt, you will not do so by car; only emergency vehicles are permitted. Instead you will find horse-drawn buggies and battery-operated contraptions, which transport people and luggage. The train to Zermatt is on a private railway (Eurailpass is not valid, 50% reduction with InterRail, free with Swiss Holiday Pass). Take the train from Brig (32F) or Visp (31F). To cut costs, hitch (fairly easy except on weekends, when cars are full of families); or drive to Tasch, and board the train there (7.20F round trip to Zermatt).

Accommodations and Food

The **Verkehrsbüro,** open Mon.-Sat. 8:30am-noon and 2:30-7pm, Sun. 4-7pm (write to 3920 Zermatt, Switzerland, for more information on hotels and prices; tel. 77855), to the right of the Train Station, has numerous maps of walks, climbs, and ski runs. Once you get there, Zermatt's prices are surprisingly reasonable. It is, however, a popular resort town, and reservations are suggested. There are private accommodations for longer stays (12F and up), which the *Verkehrsbüro* will arrange for you.

Salzgeber Haus is one of the most beautiful places to stay in Switzerland. It is an old chalet, built in 1607, and far from luxurious—plank beds (if you can call them beds) in crowded rooms, no showers. The view of the Matterhorn, however, is one of the best around. 6F per night, with cooking facilities, and no curfew. A good hike from the center of town, above the Trockener Stegg/Schwarzsee Cablecar Station in Winkelmatten.

Hotel Bahnhof, directly across from the Station (tel. 67 24 60) provides clean, budget rooms without breakfast. Kitchens available. Doubles 36-50F, dormitory rooms 12F with free hot showers.

Youth Hostel (IYHF) (tel. 67 23 20). Located at the edge of town, on a hill, with a good view of the Matterhorn. A comfortable, almost luxurious Hostel set in a wooden chalet, complete with kitchen, hairdryers, and some of the best showers in Switzerland. Come early and sign your name on the list to reserve a place. 6.10F in summer, 7.60F in winter. Breakfast 2.50F, dinner 5.50F. Strict about the 10pm curfew. You can rent hiking boots here as well.

Migros, as always, is the cheapest place to eat or buy food. Turn left onto Hofmattstrasse—it is on the right.

Whymperstube, named after the first man to reach the Matterhorn's summit, is a cozy wooden tavern with Swiss specialties. The *fondue* (9.50F) can easily be split two ways. The *raclette* (3F) is also worth sampling. On the right-hand side of the main street, near the Platzhof.

For a more American cuisine and clientele, try the **Brown Cow** or the **Spaghetti Factory,** both on the main street, near the center of town.

Excursions

The list is endless, and many trips can be done by cablecar for those who don't want to hike all the way. For the most spectacular scenery, walk up to Schwarzsee (two and a half hours) or take the cablecar (16F round trip, 11F up). From here hike to **Hörnli Hütte** (two hours) at the base of the Matterhorn. This is a gathering spot for people about to climb the Matterhorn, those who have just climbed it, and those anxiously waiting for friends to return. A great place for conversations. If you want to stay, rooms at the **Hotel** are 10F per night.

You can ski in Zermatt all year. Three distinct ski areas—**Schwarzsee, Gornergrat,** and **Blauherd**—are serviced by thirty assorted skilifts. A day-ticket for all summer lifts costs 38F. Information is available at the ski and guide office on the main street. The guide office also organizes excursions for both experienced and inexperienced climbers (open only in July and August). In town you may want to visit the **cemetery** dedicated to those who did not make it to the summit.

Saas Fee (one valley east of Zermatt) lacks the spectacular view of the Matterhorn, but brings you much closer to the stark beauty of the 4000-meter peaks, and away from the crowds of tourists. The town occupies a high *cul-de-sac* valley overhung by the immense **Feegletscher.** While there are a number of paths and cablecars for the ordinary tourist, the town is most notably a center of Alpinism, the end point of the "high route" running all the way from Chamonix, France. But even for the less ambitious, the great *cirque* (corrie) of Saas Fee offers a magnificent Alpine experience. To reach Saas Fee from Zermatt, take the train to Stalden, and then the postal bus (12F round trip). You can also reach Saas Fee by postal bus from Visp or Brig (17.50F round trip). Hitching is viable, but be prepared to wait. If you drive, you have to leave your car at the gates of the village.

Accommodations are cheaper in Zermatt, but **Feehof Garni** (tel. 57 23 08) has some rooms for 18F (breakfast included); and **Mascotte** (tel. 57 27 23) and **Rendez-vous** (tel. 57 20 40) have rooms for 20-29F, with breakfast. Maps and hotel lists are available from the **Tourist Office** in the center of town (tel. 4 8158).

Excursions, again, are numerous, but the best vistas are atop **Längfluh;** climb or cablecar (18F round trip); and at **Felskinn,** which offers an ice grotto as well (18F round trip).

Geneva (Genève)

Geneva has been entertaining foreigners for centuries. In medieval days Europeans came from far and wide to barter at Geneva's fairs. Today they barter at the **Palais des Nations.** Real Genevois are a minority among the sea of students, diplomats, tourists, and office workers, which international companies stationed in Geneva draw from all over the world.

Geneva

1 Musee et Institut Voltaire
2 Palais des Nations
3 Post
4 American Express
5 Universite et Musee
   Historique de la Reformation
6 Hotel de Ville
7 Cathedrale St Pierre
8 Musee d'Art et d'Histoire

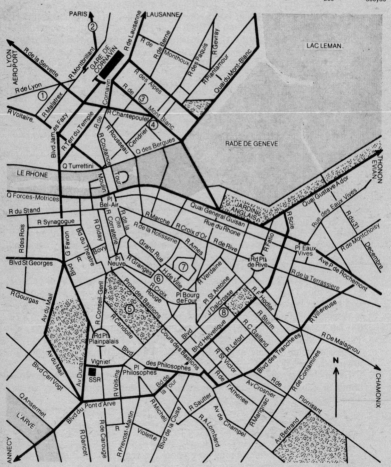
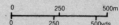

The city's most picturesque area is the **Vieille Ville** (Old Town), with its narrow cobblestone streets, and mansions clustered around the **Cathédrale St. Pierre,** where Calvin preached four hundred years ago. The Cathedral crowns the hill on which the Old Town was built, and dominates the city. One of the towers can be climbed for 2F, for a magnificent view of the city and the lake. Recent archaeological excavations have unearthed the remains of a pagan temple underneath the Cathedral. If the excavation is still in progress, you can look at the findings. The **Hôtel de Ville,** on the corner of the rue Hôtel-de-Ville and rue de Puits St. Pierre, is a sixteenth-century building with a peaceful courtyard, where plays and concerts are given in the summer. For information and schedules, ask at the Tourist Office. Wander around the Old Town and window-shop at the excellent (and expensive) antique shops and galleries of the Grand'Rue, and don't miss **Place du Bourg de Four,** the most picturesque square in the Old Town.

You may want to visit the Palais des Nations, now the European headquarters of the United Nations, but the tour is a bit dull. Inquire at the guard house about tickets to get into the actual session instead. Open 9:30am-4:30pm weekdays during the summer, 10:30-11:30am and 2:30-4:30pm on weekends and holidays, and reachable by bus F or O from the Station. Student entry 2.50F.

There is a vast array of museums to choose from. The **Musée d'Art et Histoire,** rue Charles-Galland, features Greek vases, Egyptian antiquities, relics of prehistoric Geneva, as well as works by Corot and the Impressionists. Free admission. The **Musée du Petit Palais,** 2 Terrasse Saint Victor, has an interesting collection of Impressionists and post-Impressionists. Same hours as above. Admission 5F, 3.50F for students. The city was a center of the Reformation and **Musée Historique de la Réformation,** in the Bibliothéque Publique at the University (founded by Calvin in the sixteenth century). Promenade des Bastions (open Mon.-Fri. 2-6pm, Sat. 9am-noon; free), has a myriad of documents, first editions, and exhibits on the subject. The **Institut et Musée Voltaire,** 25 rue des Délices (tel. 447133), open Mon.-Fri. 2-5pm, is free house the philosopher occupied during the decade he spent in exile here. Free admission. Geneva has a small museum dedicated to the legendary Swiss watches. The **Watchmaking and Enameling Museum,** 15 route de Malagnou, features watches and clocks from the sixteenth to nineteenth centuries. Open Tues.-Sun., 10am-noon and 2-6pm. Take bus #5.

There are gardens and fountain-filled parks all along the lakefront that invite leisurely strolling and picnicking. You can swim in the lake at the **Bains des Pâquis** (0.50F), quai du Mont Blanc; and **Genève Plage,** Port Noir. There is an excellent pool if the lake looks too cold, at the **Piscine de Carouge** on the route de Veyrier. The country around the lake offers many fine daytrips. Among them, we would suggest a steamboat ride to **Nyon,** a beautiful and quiet little town with a fine medieval castle, or to **Coppet,** a picturesque little hamlet with arcade sidewalks and the eighteenth-century château of Madame de Staël. On the opposite side of the lake, in France, is the charming village of **Yvoire.** There are many lake excursions as well. Wildlife lovers will enjoy the Rhône trip to **Verbois Dam,** which leaves from quai Turrettini (opposite Hôtel du Rhône). The trip takes two and a half hours, passing by nature preserves and rare species of birds. Boats leave twice a day on Thursdays, Saturdays, and Sundays, just in the afternoon on other days (12F).

The Genevois know how to party, unlike, some may argue, most of their compatriots. Try to be in town for the **Fête de Genève,** a huge three-day festival in the middle of August with fireworks, parades, and continuous merriment. On the fourth of July, the city cooks up the biggest celebration of the holiday in Europe.

Orientation

On arriving in Geneva at the **Gare Cornavin,** the CFF (Railroad) Office can give you a small map of the city as well as train information, and the telegraph-telephone service is right next door. The **Geneva Tourist Office,** open 8:15am-12:30pm and 2-6pm, is at 2 rue des Moulins (tel. 28 72 33). Walk straight out of the Train Station, down rue Mont Blanc (you'll pass American Express) towards the lake. Turn right and walk along the quai until you get to rue des Moulins. The Tourist Office operates an information and hotel reservation booth at the Station during peak season. The **Swiss Student Travel Office (SSR),** 3 rue Vignier, supplies more student-oriented information as well as cheap travel arrangements. During the summer there is a **Youth Welcome Office,** with accommodation and orientation service, located on the first floor of the **Maison des Jeunes,** 5 rue du Temple (tel. 31 62 39). Run by a friendly and informative American woman, this is a good place to visit upon arrival.

A Swissair shuttle bus runs between the Airport and the main Train Station every fifteen minutes between 9am and 6:45pm; 3.50F. Bus #33 offers an almost identical ride for 1F from beside the main terminal and the Train Station. The public transportation system is clean and efficient. Rides of four stops or less cost 0.60F; for 1F you get a ticket valid throughout the system for one hour. Buy the tickets from the machines on the sidewalk, or get a *carnet* of nine tickets for 7F at the main Station. They have an honor system in Geneva, but it's a good idea to be honorable, as the *controleurs* who check tickets appear frequently and unexpectedly.

Hitchers should note the following: for Paris take bus F from the Train Station to Grand Saconnex; for Chamonix take tram #12 to the French border at Moillesulaz and walk across; for the South of France take tram #12 in the other direction to Rondeau de Carouge. For Lausanne and most of Switzerland, take bus F to Grand Saconnex and then the *autoroute* (for the lakeside route take bus #5 to Bureau International du Travail and route du Lac).

Addresses and Telephone Numbers

Swiss Student Travel Office (SSR): 3 rue Vignier (tel. 29 97 33). Open Mon.-Fri. 9am-5pm; weekends 10am-noon. Cheap travel arrangements.

American Express: 7 rue du Mont Blanc (tel. 32 65 80).

Post Office: Poste Gare Cornavin, 11 rue de Lausanne, 6am-11:45pm; Poste du Mont Blanc, 7:30am-5pm; Poste du Strand, open 24 hours.

Late Money Exchange: Gare Cornavin. Open 5:30am-10:30pm weekdays, until 8:30pm weekends.

Doctors: (tel. 20 25 11), 24-hour clinic at 2 Place Longemalle.

La Main Tendue: (tel. 143). Hotline for any kind of trouble. English spoken.

Welcome and get-together for English-speaking people (tels. 21 83 11 and 28 72 33) on Wednesday evenings.

Laundromats: 61 blvd. St. Georges, open until 6:15pm; 4 rue Montbrillant, behind main Station; and 4 rue Vignier open 7am-noon and 1-7pm every day.

Bike Rentals: At the Cornavin Station (ask at the baggage check)—8F per day. For motorbikes try Hermann Schutz, 6 rue de la Muse.

Women's Center: 6 blvd. St. Georges (tel. 29 22 98). Fri. night open house.

Accommodations

The housing situation in Geneva is usually very tight, so come early if you do not have reservations. When the universities go on vacation (July-August), university residences look for tourists to fill up the vacancies. They prefer stays of at least a week, but a few will take you in overnight. Contact the office at 4 rue de Candolle (tel. 25 70 58).

Hôtel de l'Etoile, 17 rue des Vieux Grenadiers (tel. 28 78 08). Airy, remodeled rooms, with plants and wicker furniture in the larger rooms. Friendly young management. Singles 20-26F, doubles 28-32F, without bathroom. Free showers. Prices go down in the off-season.

Hôtel le Clos Voltaire, 45 rue de Lyon (tel. 44 70 14). Charming old ivy-covered house. Singles 18-30F, doubles 36-50F, quads 68-72F. Hot showers and breakfast included. A fifteen-minute walk from the Station or take bus #6. The hotel is on a hill behind a gas station.

Foyer Henry Dunant, 8 rue Vignier (tel. 20 93 55), is an attractive modern dorm for women only. 14F in 6-bed rooms, breakfast included. Singles 20F, doubles 18F per person, free showers. Closes at 10pm, but you can get a key.

Maison des Jeunes, 5 rue du Temple, becomes the summer annex of the Youth Hostel. In the winter, it is a center for theater, jazz, and craft courses. More relaxed than the Youth Hostel (11pm final curfew), smaller, and cheaper (7F with or without card, sheets included). Opens 5pm.

Home St. Pierre, Cour St. Pierre (tel. 28 37 07) has a good location in the old city near the Cathedral, as well as superb prices. Rooms for 13F per person; dormitory 6F. Small and often crowded, but a good value for the price.

Cité Universitaire, 26 ave. de Miremont (tel. 46 33 55) is far from the center of town (twenty minutes by bus #33 to rue Albert Gos) but is worth the trip. Dorms 8F, singles 18-36F, doubles 28F, without breakfast. 400 beds. Open June 15 through November 1. The cafeteria serves good meals from 4F. Special rates for families, and tennis-court privileges.

Auberge de Jeunesse (IYHF), rue des Plantaporrêts (tel. 29 06 19), off the blvd. de St. Georges, is the official Youth Hostel. Take bus #11 from the Station to Georges Favon, transfer to bus #2 (the stop is on the quai de la Poste, about half a block from the #11 stop), and get off at Pont-Sous-Terre. 7F with Hostel card, 12F without. An old building on the outside, but a clean and modern interior. Hot showers, but often overcrowded. Curfew 10pm. Open 6:30-10am and 2-10pm in summer, 8-10am and 6-10pm in winter.

Crac, 7 blvd. Carl-Vogt (tel. 29 13 43). An old apartment building, with singles, doubles, and dorm rooms. A little on the seedy side, but don't be put off, the prices are low—dorm 8F, single 15F, double 12F each. Kitchen facilities as well as a restaurant with daily *menu* (7F). Continuance is tenuous, so call before walking over.

Camping—The most accessible campsite is **Sylvabelle,** 10 chemin de Conches (tel. 42 06 03). Take bus #8 or 88 to Rond Point de Rive, 2F. They also have 4-person bungalows for 38F. **Camping Pointe a la Bise,** in Vésenaz has some sites for 3F. (tel. 55 12 96). Bus #9 or 99 to Rond-Point de Rive. **Camping d'Hermance,** Chemin des Glerrets (tel. 51 21 98) is near the beach, 4F. Bus #9 to Rond-Point de Rive.

Food

Les Armures, 1 rue du Puits-Saint Pierre, is in the *Vieille Ville* near the Cathedral. Claims to be the oldest restaurant in Geneva. A wide variety of quality cuisine and good prices as well. A cosmopolitan clientele. Come casual or dressy. Cheese *fondue* 10F, pizza 7F and up. Open 8am-1am. Closed Sun. and Mon. till 5 pm.

La Moisson, 25 rue Voltaire, is a fine vegetarian restaurant with friendly and amiable owners. Fresh salad bar, as well as vegetarian specialties with rice and other grains. 6-12F.

Zofage, 6 rue des Voisins, is popular with students for its location near the University and its prices—the *menu* is 6F. Breakfast 3.50F. A glass of nearly anything is 1F.

Migros, the old Swiss standby, has locations throughout the city. The prime locations are at 2 ave. du Mail and 41 rue des Pâques. Open daily, 8am-6:45pm. Meals run 4-10F.

Restaurant sans Alcool, 17 Place Montbrillant, near the Train Station, serves cheap but good food. Most expensive *menu* is 8F. Open for breakfast, lunch, and dinner.

For late-night munchies, there is a **bakery** at 19 rue du Mont-Blanc which is open until 2am.

Evenings

Nightlife in Switzerland is generally meager, but not here. The **Grand Théâtre,** on Place Neuve, offers quite good opera, but the most lively nightlife is to be found in or near the Vieille Ville. Many students go dancing or beer drinking. **Place Molard,** below the Vieille Ville, attracts a continual crowd to its outdoor cafés.

Popcorn Club, 13, rue de la Fontaine, is rather expensive, but attracts some of the finest jazz musicians in the world. Check the schedule first to make sure the evening's program is to your liking.

Le Clemence, 20 Place du Bourg-du-Four, is a small pub with old-town ambiance equal to its popularity. Open until midnight.

Brasserie Landolt, corner of rue de la Candolle and rue du Conseil-General, is an attractive bar with a student clientele. The outdoor terrace is a good spot to people-watch. Food is expensive, but drinks are OK.

Mr. Pickwick Pub, 80 rue Lausanne, adjacent to the U.S. Mission to the U.N., is a meeting place for English-speaking people in Geneva. Sandwiches and meals from about 7F. Beer 2F or 3.50F; drinks are expensive. Open 11am-2pm, 5pm-12:30am. Bus #5 to ave. de France.

Lausanne-Ouchy

Legend has it that Hercules founded Lausanne on one of his journeys, but more reliable sources say it was the bishop of Avenches fleeing the unhealthy lowlands who was responsible.

If you come by steamer you can disembark either at **Vidy,** near the campground, or at **Ouchy,** the lakeside resort. The park and sprawling outdoor cafés are superb places to laze away an afternoon. The main part of Lausanne is almost vertical. In fact, the hill is so steep that the temperature is often several degrees lower at the top.

The city's old quarter is perhaps the best preserved in Switzerland. The sixteenth-century buildings clustered around the cathedral now house part of the university, antique stores, and old-clothes shops. Be sure to explore **Cité Devant** and **Cité Derrière,** to get a real feel for the medieval town Lausanne once was. The **Cathedral** is Switzerland's oldest and finest example of Gothic architecture, and there are free organ concerts every Friday during July and August. From the square you get an excellent view of the town and lake below. The bishop didn't have far to come to work in the fourteenth and fifteenth centuries; **Château Sainte Maire,** the official bishop's residence, is at the other end of Cité Devant and is now the seat of the cantonal government. (Open Mon.-Fri. 9-11am and 2-5pm; closed Wed. and Fri. mornings.)

Lausanne has several unusually intriguing museums. **Le Palais de Rumine,** now a university building, houses a collection of science museums (archaeology, geology, zoology, etc.) and **Le Musée des Beaux Arts** puts on the biennial tapestry exhibition (next in the summer of 1979). The most famous weavers from Europe and North America display their sometimes bizarre and often gigantic creations. (Open 10am-noon and 2-6pm; closed Mon. morning.) **The Musée des Arts Decoratifs,** 4 ave. de Villamont, has itinerant exhibitions ranging from Bauhaus course-work to Latin American photography. (Open 10am-noon and 2-6pm every day, also 8-10pm on Tues.) Probably the most unusual museum in Lausanne is the **Collection de l'Art Brut,** Château de Beaulieu, 11 ave. Bergières. This museum displays art by recluses, eccentrics, and inmates of prisons and mental institutions. Accompanying each work is a biography of the artist. Open Tues.-Sun. 2-6pm, Thurs. till 10pm; admission 2.50F.

Orientation

The **Tourist Office** at 60 ave. d'Ouchy (open 8am-7pm daily) and the annex in the Train Station (open 2-10pm daily) can provide you with a map and reserve you a room (2F). Most rides cost 1F and a *carnet* of ten tickets costs 9F. Nearly all buses pass through **Place St. François,** and you can ask the driver where he goes as you get on. The mini metro right across the street from the Station whisks you up or down the hill for 0.50-0.70F. The **SSR** at 8 rue de la Barre sells student-priced train tickets and has student-oriented information on Lausanne.

For hitching towards Bern and Zurich take bus M5 or 6 to La Sallay; for Geneva bus M4 to La Maladière rotary; for Paris and Neuchâtel take bus M9 to Prilly.

Addresses and Telephone Numbers

Swiss Student and Youth Reception Service (SSR): 8 rue de la Barre.

American Express: 14 rue Mon Repos.

Post Office: ave. de la Gare. Open Mon.-Fri. until 10pm, 8pm weekends. To your right as you leave the Station.

Medical Emergencies: (tel. 32 99 32).

Accommodations

Logements des Prés de Vidy, 36 Chemin du Bois-de-Vaux (tel. 24 24 79) offers 100 double rooms with showers. Very simple, almost austere rooms, but clean and inexpensive, 12F per person. There is a self-service restaurant as well. Breakfast 3F. Open 8-11am and 5-7:30pm July through September.

Hotel Select, 10 rue des Terreaux (tel. 22 33 16) has an appealing frayed elegance, which is unfortunately disappearing in renovations. Ask for an un-renovated room at 19F. New rooms 22-25F. Includes shower and kitchen. The manager will do your laundry for 3.50F. Very friendly.

Le Foyer la Croisée, 15 ave. Marc Dufour (tel. 20 42 31). Run by a Christian evangelist mission, it is a modern complex near the Station with a good view of the lake. Dormitories 11F, doubles 17-19F. Breakfast included. Proselytizing minimal.

Auberge de Jeunesse, Chemin du Muguet (tel. 26 57 82). Near the lake, about a half-hour walk from the Station, or take bus #1 to Reposoir. 6.55F with IYHF card, 12F without. American breakfast with bacon and eggs, 3.50F. Continental 2.80F.

Camping Lausanne Vidy, just past bus stop Le Maladière. A lakeside campground with good facilities. Open all year round.

Food

Like most university towns, Lausanne has an abundance of moderately-priced restaurants. Wednesday and Saturday are the big days at the food markets in the Old Town.

Pinte Besson, 1 rue Neuve, has turned out *fondue* since its grand opening in 1730 and aside from a few sandwiches, it's the only thing they serve. 8.50F.

Au Couscous, 1 Saint-Pierre (on first floor). Tunisian, vegetarian, and mac-robiotic specialties. Live music in the evenings. Virtually unknown to tourists, and open till 1am.

Vieil Ouchy, right on the lake, to the left of ave. d'Ouchy. An atmospheric little bistro, with an outdoor café. Good food, low prices, friendly and young clientele. Meals around 7F.

Restaurant du Vieux Lausanne, 6 rue Pierre Viret, is tucked under Les Escaliers du Marché. Luncheon plate 7F, but arrive early—it goes fast. There is an antique Swiss-style bowling lane next to the bar, where the regulars compete enthusiastically.

Migros on Place de la Riponne, has the usual cheap groceries and restaurant. Mon. 1:30-7pm, Tues.-Fri. 8am-2pm, Sat. 8am-5pm.

Excursions

Steamer-boats serve nearly every village on the lake, and are a good way to see the area. Eurailpasses are valid, but the boats are much slower than the train. On a rock outcrop at the far end of the lake sits the **Château de Chillon,** a stunningly well-preserved thirteenth-century castle built as a prison and tax collectors' depot, guarding the narrow road between the mountains and the sea. (Open 9am-6:30pm daily in the summer. Student entry 2F.)

Vevey, a pretty, wine-growing village, is the home of Charlie Chaplin, Nestlé's chocolate, and the best in finishing schools. You can see the chocolate making in action in the nearby **Broc.** The tour times vary, but you can count on several on Tuesday and Thursday afternoons, the last tour at about 3pm. Right next to the Broc is **Gruyère,** where you can tour the cheese factory.

Montreux throws a colossal **Jazz Festival** during the first three weeks of July. Performances are Friday to Sunday nights, and every night during the second week. Weeks are divided by genre (hard core jazz, country, blues, etc.). Tickets start at 25F. For information write Festival de Jazz, Case 97, CH-1820 Montreux. IYHF Hostel "Haut Lac" is on the lake, 8 Passage de l'Auberge (tel. 620884).

St. Moritz and the Engadin

The **Grisons** (Graubünden) is the largest but least populous of the Swiss cantons. The most remote part of this rugged mountain region is the Engadin, the high country at the source of the Inn River. It has some of the most beautiful scenery in Europe, ranging from deep gorges with romantic, ruined castles to wide Alpine meadows to vast glaciers high above the timberline. Despite tourism and modern communications, the people are trying to keep their culture alive. The native language is Romansch, a Romance tongue found exclusively in this area and spoken by less than 2% of Switzerland's people.

The Grisons and the Engadin are well-served by narrow-gauge train (Eurailpass valid) and postal bus, and you can get almost anywhere without much trouble. You will probably come into the area from Chur; the Chur-St. Moritz railway offers some of the most spectacular scenery in Switzerland.

St. Moritz is the tourist capital of the Engadin. Don't let its reputation turn you off—it is not nearly as expensive or snobby as one might expect. The high-rise hotels may come as a shock, but the town has a beautiful setting, cradled by the mountains and straddling a deep-blue lake. While you probably won't "take the cure," you may want to sample the mineral baths and other assorted luxuries at the **Heilbad** or make use of the new sports center. There are also hundreds of kilometers of well-marked trails in the immediate environs, and several cablecars to take you up higher. There are two interesting museums as well. The **Engadin Museum** displays a fine exposition of local culture and crafts (9:30am-noon and 2-5pm; Sun. 10am-noon, entrance 2F, students 1F; closed in October), and the **Segantini Museum** is dedicated to the works of this modern artist (open Tues.-Sat. 9am-12:30pm and 2:30-5pm, Sun. 10:30am-12:30pm and 2:30-4:30pm; admission 2F).

For all information on St. Moritz and the entire region, get in touch with the **Kur-und-Verkehrsverein,** in the middle of St. Moritz-dorf (tel. 082-33147), open 9am-noon and 2-6pm, closed Sunday. If you're interested in serious climbing, contact the **Bergsteigerzentrum** in Pontresina (tel. 66444 or 66644). There is also summer skiing at **Diavolezza,** above Pontresina (information tel. 66419).

Jugendherberge "Stille" (IYHF, tel. 33969). A "Ritz" among Youth Hostels. Modern and immaculate, with 4 beds to each room, 7.50F per night with card, sheets included. Breakfast 2.50F, a kitchen and laundry room as well. 10pm curfew. From the Station, walk by the lake into St. Moritz—Bad, then follow the signs (25-minute walk) or take the blue-and-white bus which runs every half hour.

Primula (tel. 3 36 96) is a bit out of the way (about half-an-hour's walk from St. Moritz-Bad). In Champfer, but has dormitory accommodations (15F) without curfew. Regular rooms 23-35F, breakfast included.

Excursions

In the valley above St. Moritz is a chain of lakes—all great for swimming—and of course, numerous trails. Cablecars ascend to **Corvatsch** (21F, take the postal bus to the lift) and **Piznair** (18F, leaves from St. Moritz-dorf), both offering spectacular panoramas. At **Sils Maria,** you can visit a house once occupied by Nietzsche, an early tourist in the Engadin.

Perhaps the most spectacular scenery in the area is southeast of St. Moritz. Drive or take the train on the Passo del Bernina route in the direction of Tirano (Italy). This is harsh and rugged country well above timberline, and one of the finest high country rail routes in the world. Get off the train at **Morteratsch** and hike through a pine-scented valley to the **Chunetta** lookout. The uphill footpath of rocks and gnarled tree roots winds by a glacier stream (half an hour). From here you can see **Piz Bernina** and several other peaks ranged around the glacial *cirque* of Morteratsch. Continue on the train to **Diavolezza,** where a cablecar (14F round trip, 10F up) takes you up to one of Europe's most famous glacial panoramas. If the scenery seduces you into spending the night, stay at the **Diavolezza Hütte** (17F with breakfast). Continue on the train, across the Bernina Pass to **Alp Grüm,** for a third outstanding view. You may want to get off at **Ospizio,** and lunch by **Lago Bianco.** Further along the line is **Poschiavo,** in the Italian area, with its stucco houses and rose gardens. Visit **San Vittore,** with its hand-carved wooden doors.

Müstair is one of the more remote towns in Switzerland, a charming, romantic place to visit. Take the train to Zernez, and then the postal bus to Müstair. It commands the **Val Müstair,** and has a church and convent that, according to legend, were built by Charlemagne. The frescoes are especially fine. If you stay here, try the **Münsterhof,** where rooms start at 15F (20F with breakfast) and the English-speaking owner will help you make the most of the area. There is also an IYHF **Youth Hostel** (tel. 85377) in Sainta Maria, a small village on the bus route to Müstair.

Ticino

Palm trees in Switzerland? For those who think of the country in terms of snow, chocolate, and cheese, Ticino in southern Switzerland comes as a shock. South of the Gottard Pass, the climate alters drastically. The vegetation here is subtropical, with pink hibiscus and palm trees everywhere. There is more sunshine than in any other canton. Italian is the official language of the region, although most people speak German, French, or English. There are surprisingly few Americans in Ticino, though there are plenty of European tourists. **Lugano, Locarno,** and **Ascona** are resort towns offering swimming, sunbathing, and numerous boat trips around **Lago di Lugano, Lago Maggiore,** and into Italy.

Lugano

Lugano seems more Italian than Swiss, with its rust-orange roofs, bronze church domes, and narrow stone-lined streets. The pace of Lugano is slow. Start your wanderings through town at **San Lorenzo,** between the Railway Station and the lake. High on a hill, it offers a fine view of the city, as well as a masterful Renaissance façade. **Santa Maria** has some celebrated frescoes by Bernardino Luini. From here, walk to the **Thyssen-Bornemisza Picture Gallery** in the Villa Favorita, Castagnola. This is one of the most important private galleries in Europe, with Jan Van Eyck's *Annunciation,* as well as works by Dürer, Tintoretto, Rubens, and Rembrandt. Open only on Fri. and Sat. 10am-noon, 2-5pm, and Sun. 2-5pm. Admission 7F.

Gandria, a relatively unspoiled fishing village at the foot of **Monte Brè,** is accessible by boat or an hour's walk along a lakeside path.

Orientation and Accommodations

The **Tourist Office,** Riva Albertolli 5 (tel. 21 46 64), by the Lake provides information and hotel reservations as well as maps of the surrounding area. Boats leave from either Lugano Centrale or Lugano-Giardino.

> **Casa Caprino** is a small Italian-style house, run by SSR, located on the lake in Caprino. It can be reached only by boat from Lugano (4.60F round trip). Swimming on the lake; fireplace and free showers. 23F includes dinner on the evening of arrival, bed, and breakfast.

> There is a **Youth Hostel** in Crocifisso-Lugano (tel. 56 27 28), a short ride on bus M5 (end stop) or a twenty-minute walk from the Station. A nice place, complete with swimming pool, but often booked. Write in advance to assure a bed. 6.50F.

Locarno

Locarno shares the warm, Mediterranean climate and vegetation of Lugano, but lacks the hordes of tourists. The charm of Locarno lies not in the town itself, but in the surrounding countryside, valleys, and villages scattered around **Lago Maggiore.** It can be reached by train from Bellinzona.

Accommodations run high, and there are no youth hostels or similarly-priced accommodations. If you decide to stay, try **Pestalozzi** (tel. 31 43 08), near the lake, with rooms for 19-20F including breakfast; or **Gottardo** (tel. 33 44 54), above the Station, with rooms for 16-26F, including breakfast.

In Locarno, visit the **Museo d'Arte Moderna,** in the Castello Visconti. A surprisingly good collection of modern art, featuring Hans Arp and the Dadaists. The town's landmark and symbol is the **Madonna del Sasso** (Madonna of the Rock), which can be reached by funicular. (Pilgrim types can climb.)

Perhaps the most striking section of the region is the **Valle Maggia,** a sparsely-populated valley with forests and pastures. Visit tranquil **Bosco Gurin,** a rustic village with waterfalls and old wooden houses. Bosco Gurin is the only place in the Ticino where German is spoken. (Take bus from Cevio.) If you are in the area, be sure to try the *formaggini* (goat cheese), served with pepper, sausage, and wine.

Back at *"see"* level, don't miss the boat trip to the **Brissago Island,** a vast botanical garden filled with fragrant subtropical plants and palms (admission 2F). There is a small Roman bath where you can swim or just sunbathe. A wonderful excursion.

TURKEY

$1U.S. = 25 lira (TL)   **1TL = $.04**

Turkey's personality mirrors its geography—a large chunk of the Mideast with a touch of Europe. The vast majority of the people maintain their Middle Eastern way of life, as reflected in their pious Islamism, their music and food, and the rigid masculine ethos that governs their social customs. But the evidence of Western influence is there, both in historical sites and in current policy and custom. Ancient Greek civilizations established powerful city-states on its western shores; the political and religious attention of the Christianized Roman Empire focused on Constantinople (modern Istanbul); even the Ottomans were influenced by the peoples they conquered in Southern and Eastern Europe.

Little wonder then, that for French-educated **Kemal Atatürk,** who almost single-handedly carved out the Turkish state after the final collapse of the Ottoman Empire in World War I, modernization was equated with rapid Westernization. He changed the alphabet from Arabic to Roman, and did his best to weaken the grip of Islam on the lives of the people. Turkey, after all,

681

is a member of NATO, and is one of the few democracies in the Middle East, a source of great pride to its people. But today, even though devotion to the memory of Atatürk may seem absolute, the battle still rages between the westernizing trend he began and the still potent forces of Islamic traditionalism.

The Turkish people are usually friendly to foreigners, especially away from the big cities and the resorts. Tourists are still rare enough so that they make a big deal over you.

Women should remember that this is a Muslim country, so behave with modesty, and be prepared for the usual hassles. If you're going to more conservative eastern Turkey, you should be especially careful.

Transportation

Transportation routes, rates, and discounts to and within Turkey are currently in a state of flux. For up-to-date information, write to the **Turkish Tourist and Information Office,** 821 United Nations Plaza, New York, NY 10017. They'll send you boat, train, and plane schedules. **Turkish Airlines (THY)** has regular service to Turkey from European and Middle Eastern cities, and offers student discounts from most of these for International Student ID Card holders under 27 years of age.

Turkish Maritime Lines (TML) has regular services to Izmir and Istanbul from Barcelona ($117), Marseilles ($101), Naples ($89), Venice ($113), and Piraeus ($33). All fares are lower in the off-season. The student discount is 15% one way and 25% round trip in all classes.

If you are in Greece you can get a boat from Rhodes or Samos ($15-18 one way) to nearby towns on the Turkish coast. There are also direct buses from Athens for $23 and up. Avoid the train, which sits and bakes at the border for hours, and then takes up to twelve hours to reach Istanbul. If you are hitching into Turkey, make sure that the driver's car is not stamped into your passport as your own. If it is, the owner can make a mountain of money selling his car illegally in Turkey, and you'll be buried in an avalanche of red tape trying to leave the country without it.

Getting around Turkey is a budget traveler's dream. There are frequent direct buses between all sizeable cities—all are Mercedes Benzes and incredibly cheap. They are run by private companies, so don't be muscled into paying for a ticket until you have gone from booth to booth and pieced together a complete schedule. For long trips, there are always overnight buses. For these you should request a window seat in the middle of the bus, away from the driver's radio. For a frequent run like Istanbul-Ankara you'll have to buy a seat an hour in advance; for a less frequent trip you should buy the ticket a day before. You can reserve a seat by phone, but you'll have to claim it two hours before the time of departure.

Even with their 40% student discount, Turkey's trains are far from being a bargain. In fact, except for the express trains between Istanbul and Ankara (70TL for students), which take seven to ten hours, you should avoid trains altogether. Buses are as cheap and go everywhere. Between small towns there are extensive shared taxi services *(dolmuş)*. They follow fixed routes, leave as soon as they fill up, and are unbelievably cheap. They are often salvation for the weary hitchhiker, because you can get on and off anywhere you like.

Hitching is good in Turkey, when there's traffic. In eastern Turkey, you may be expected to pay for the ride. Offer about half of what the trip would cost by bus.

Look into boat routes as soon as you arrive in Turkey. They are relatively cheap and go to places difficult to reach by road. Prices aren't what they were, now that TML has reduced student discounts to only ten percent; but remember that you can save the cost of a hotel room by taking an overnight boat trip. The TML **Mail Boat,** an excellent way to tour the Aegean and Mediterranean coasts, leaves Istanbul once every other week in the summer, docking at Izmir, Datça, Fethiye, Antalya, Mersin, and Iskenderun. You have the day to explore each area of the coast; then climb on board for the night. The trips cost roughly $35 one way.

There is also a **Black Sea** express route which runs from Istanbul to Hopa, near the Russian border. Though not as leisurely as the Mail Boat, it does offer a chance to explore the rugged, untouristed coast. If you wish, you can debark along the way, and take a bus to Ankara or other interior destinations—the city of Samsun has the most daily buses. If you're staying on the boat, visit **Trabzon,** a picturesque town not far from the Soviet border. Here you can explore the monasteries and forests, and then either continue east or double back through Turkey's interior. Deck space is no longer offered on the Black Sea run; a third-class ticket for the two-day trip to Trabzon will cost you 300TL with a student ID. In the summer, book your seats in advance.

General Travel Tips

Note: Since the devaluation of the Turkish lira to the official rate of 25 to the U.S. dollar, inflation in Turkey has soared to an annual rate of 50%. Allow for large increases in the prices listed in this chapter.

Some people speak English in the big cities, but they are few and far between in the provinces. German and pantomime are often more helpful. Buy a phrase book, and have a pen and pad ready for addresses, phrases, or numbers. Keep in mind that when a Turk raises his chin and shuts his eyes he means "no." But don't think there's any hostility or irritation in this gesture.

Avoid drugs in Turkey. The horror stories of lengthy prison sentences and of dealers-informers are all true; and the embassies are generally helpless in such cases. Turkish law also provides for "guilt by association," making subject to prosecution those in the company of the person caught.

Also to be avoided is the black market. The money changers here are fast-fingered and often stick you with obsolete currency. Also, the government has cracked down on the black market; you need your bank receipts to change back your Turkish money at the border and sometimes to buy boat or train tickets. The ticket price will be doubled if you cannot produce a receipt when they check. Some banks charge a commission for changing travelers checks; the ubiquitous **Yapi ve Kredi Bankasi** does not. Have enough money for the weekends, as banks are closed. If you're coming from Greece, spend your drachmas before arriving. Not all banks exchange drachmas, and those that do invariably give an unfair rate.

There is a slew of student travel agencies in Istanbul's **Sultanahmet** district. Here you can find out about cheap buses both east to India and west to most major European cities and tours within Turkey. If you have an ISIC card, don't waste your money on a Turkish Student Card, despite what the agencies urge you—the international card works everywhere.

Museums, sites, and monuments in Turkey are generally open from 9am-5pm, while many are closed on Mondays or Tuesdays. None charge more than 10TL, most less. Wednesdays and weekends are half-price days at most places. Cameras cost you another admission ticket to bring in, unless you are able to smuggle them by the ticket taker.

Finally, don't be caught *anywhere* without toilet paper. And remember that there are washing facilities at every mosque.

Eastern Turkey and Going Overland

Many young Europeans you meet in Istanbul are either coming from or going to India, and Istanbul is the best place to meet up with travel partners for this trip. There are always caravans of VW buses heading to India, some looking for another traveler or two. The Sultanahmet district—especially the Pudding Shop—is the best place to latch on to one of these.

You might wish to skip these in favor of exploring eastern Turkey. This part of the country is much more backward, traditional, and untouristy than the western half. Travelers have experienced everything from extreme hospitality to outright hostility here—the country is less tame, and your behavior is more conspicuous. A quieter way to get east is to take the Black Sea ship to Trabzon, 400 km on good roads from the Iranian border.

Food

Turkey is one of the few places left in this book where eating cheaply still entitles you to sample a great variety of dishes, carefully prepared. Walk through any city neighborhood, and you'll see how serious Turks are about good eating: no supermarkets, only a cheese store, a bakery, a yogurt store, a *baklava* salon, a restaurant serving only stews; no art too small for specialization. It will be hard to walk from one part of town to another without filling up, but you should abstain at least once, in order to indulge in a full-scale classical Turkish meal:

Though the variety changes from place to place, you'll find dishes such as grape leaves stuffed with rice, nuts, and currants, *beyaz peynir* (white goat cheese), *zeytinyagli* (cold vegetables in olive oil), *pilaki* (Turkish beans), and *midye dolma* (mussels stuffed with rice).

The main course is usually a lamb or fish dish. Near the Bosphorus, *barbunya* (red mullet) is excellent. Lamb is usually prepared as *şiş kebab*, or the equally popular *doner kebab*—slices of lamb packed on a slowly revolving spit. Other specialties include *dolma* (stuffed peppers), and *imam bayildi* (eggplant stuffed with ground meat and tomatoes). For those on a tight budget, there is *fasuliye* (a bean soup) or rice *(pilav)* mixed with house vegetables.

For dessert—pastries. *Baklava* (a flaky pastry jammed with nuts and soaked in honey) or *kadaif* (a shredded wheat dough filled with nuts and sugar) are the popular choices; but there are more exotic variations, such as *hanim göbegi* (literally translated "the lady's navel"). If you're full, finish off with *sutlaç* (a rice pudding) or a piece of fresh fruit.

Most Turks draw these evening meals out interminably, and then linger over a glass of tea *(çay)* or sweet Turkish coffee (*kahve;* known as Greek coffee across the border). The stronger of stomach then throw down a *raki* or two and head home.

Istanbul

Istanbul, like Turkey itself, unites Europe and Asia, in a literal sense. In fact, it is the only city in the world to bridge two continents. Its first period of glory began with the retreat eastward of the seat of the Roman Empire; its second pinnacle came with the Ottomans sweeping in from the Anatolian steppes.

The charm of the city today lies in its blend of the exotic and the civilized. You can lose yourself in the crowded, narrow, cobbled streets of the Old City for an afternoon, and then emerge to watch the sun set as you sail from town to town along the Bosphorus. With the moving of the capital to Ankara, Istanbul has been left to its own course, and has been able to maintain a delightful balance of occident and orient.

Orientation

Waterways divide Istanbul into three parts. The European half of the city is split in two by a narrow river called the **Golden Horn,** and these are separated from the Asian part of the city by the **Bosphorus Strait.** Most of your time will be spent in the European city. Almost all the historical sites, the markets, and the older quarters are located on the southern bank of the Golden Horn. The other, more modern half of the European city contains *Istiklal Cad.,* the main downtown shopping street, and *Cumhuriyet Cad.,* Turkey's own Fifth Avenue, with all the airline offices and expensive hotels.

The entire city is divided into small quarters, and it always pays to know the name of the quarter that the place you are looking for is in. It's about all you need when you're using public transportation or are asking directions. Istanbul's public transportation is one of the best and the cheapest around. Try to avoid taxis; you have to bargain with the driver over the price, and they are still expensive. A *dolmuş,* or communal taxi, is the quickest alternative. Find a *dolmuş* stop—they're always near the bus stops—and when one of the huge old jalopies comes lumbering by, shout out the quarter you want to go to. Minibuses are privately run, but they work just like the larger municipal buses: both are cheap and their fixed routes are posted on their windows. A description of the routes of the municipal buses can be obtained at any Tourist Office. A useful bus route is the #84, which runs between the **Topkapi Bus Terminal** and the Train Station and **Eminönü Boat Terminal,** passing **Sultanahmet** and the **Grand Bazaar** along the way. Municipal buses stop at 1am, at which time *dolmuşes* are few and far between.

Istanbul is an easy city to get lost in. The Hallwag Map (55TL) lists every street by name.

To find out about cheap accommodations and travel, contact one of the Turkish student organizations listed below. **TMGT** is the largest, and the only Turkish member of the **International Student Travel Conference (ISTC),** but the other two are also helpful and more conveniently located.

If you are hitching to Ankara, Izmir, or anywhere in Asian Turkey, take the ferry from Eminönü to **Harem,** in the Asian city. The highway is only a few blocks away. If you're going to be in Istanbul for a while, invest in *Strolling Through Istanbul* ($4), a comprehensive series of walking tours through the city's sectors.

Addresses and Telephone Numbers

Tourist Information Office: Headquarters are at 57 Meşrutiyet Cad., Galatasary (tel. 448619). Branches at entrance of Hilton Hotel, Cumhuriyet Cad. (tel. 406300) and on Divan Yolu Cad. in Sultanahmet. 8:30am-5:30pm weekdays, 9am-6:30pm weekends.

TMGT (National Organization of Turkish Youth): Istiklal Cad. 47 ½, Tünel (tel. 430008); **MTTB** (National Student Union of Turkey) 37 Babiali

Cad., Sultanahmet (tel. 266924); **OGTT** (Tourist Organization of Students and Youth), 15 Piyerloti Cad., Çemberlitaş (tel. 229165).

American Express: Entrance of Hilton Hotel, P.O. Box 70 (tel. 405640). Mail pickup is in a branch office at the Intercontinental Hotel in Taksim Square.

Post Office: 25 Yeni Postahane Sokak, (two blocks northeast of the Sirkeçi Train Station). Open 8am-9pm every day. Collect *Poste Restante* here, 9am-6pm.

Tourist Police: Hilaliahmer Cad. (across from Cisterne Basilique), Sultanahmet (tel. 285369). Open 9am-8pm. The Tourist Police Station at the landing dock in Karaköy is open 24 hours.

Bus Stations: the largest is in Topkapi. There is another one in Harem, on the Asian side.

Money Exchange: Denizcilik Bankasi, Yolcu Salonu, Karaköy (tel. 443876). Open for exchange on Sundays and Turkish holidays. There are also Tourist Bank Services in the Tourist Offices at the airport, in the harbor, and in Sultanahmet.

The two best hospitals are: the **German Hospital,** Siraselviler Cad., Taksim (tel. 454070), and the **American Hospital,** Nişantaş, Güzelbahçe Sokak (tel. 486030).

American Consulate: 106 Meşrutiyet Cad.,Tepebasi(tel. 436200).

Accommodations

Finding cheap accommodations in Istanbul is no problem; finding cheap, decent accommodations complicates the matter a little. But every part of Istanbul offers a huge number of hotels, and with some shopping around you can find a place that fits both your budget and standards.

Your first decision is picking a district. We recommend Sultanahmet, since the best sights and the cheapest accommodations are here. If you find the area too seedy or overrun with other travelers, try the more pleasant **Laleli** district. The **Sirkeci** district is near the Train Station and wharf, but is crowded and noisy. Cheap places are also available across the Golden Horn in the **Beyoglu** district, but the atmosphere leaves something to be desired. Avoid **Taksim,** the most expensive sector of the city. Student and Youth Hostels are your best bet; cheap hotels often attract local low-life (and sometimes the police). If you're low on funds, ask if you can sack out on the roof. For 15TL (shower usually included) it may be quieter and cleaner than the rooms beneath you.

The following places are safe and legitimate.

In Sultanahmet

Hotel Güngör, Divan Yolu Cad. (tel. 262319). Best bet in this area. 30TL for dorm bed, doubles for 50TL each, singles 60TL. Sleep on the roof for 15TL. Hot showers 5TL. 1am curfew. Noisy but cheap. Open all year round.

Yücel Tourist Hostel, Caferiye Sokak 6 (tel. 224790). Large place with a variety of accommodations. Dirty toilets, but good rooms. Still the best of the hostels. Cheap café out back where everyone hangs out. 40TL for dorm bed in 8-bed rooms; 50TL in a 3- or 4-bed room; and 60TL each for a double. Hot water in mornings only, but you can do laundry here. Open to all, families included. Across from Aya Sofya gardens. Open year round.

Hotel Yörük, Incjliçavuş Sok #35. (tel. 276476). Around the corner from Hotel Güngör, this is a beautiful new hotel. Terrace view is the best in Istanbul. Expensive, though: 120TL for singles, 90TL per person in a double or triple. Good place for a splurge.

Hotel Büyük Aya Sofya, Caferiye Sokak 5 (tel. 224293). Prices the same as Yörük, but rooms are a bit smaller. Basement is now converted into dorm rooms, 8 to a room for 50TL. Next to the Yücel Hostel.

Other Districts

ÖGTT Youth Hostel, Piyerloti Cad. 15, Çemberlitaş (tel. 229165). Open June 1-October 15; a university dormitory the rest of the year. Pleasant, but shower and sink water is sporadic, and bathrooms not the best. Friendly students run the place and a student travel agency in the reception office. 35TL per person in doubles and in dorms. No card needed.

Istanbul Youth Hostel, Cerrahpaşa Cad. 63, Aksaray (tel. 212455). Open July 1-Sept. 30; a university dormitory the rest of the year. Facilities are great: hot showers, stoves, irons, closets with locks, cheap restaurant, and roof with a great view. Far from everything though. 35TL in a 4- to 6-bed room with student ID or IYHF card; 40TL without. Take the #35, 84, 95 or 97 bus to Aksaray.

Otel Erciyes, Pehlivan Sok. 3, Beyazit (tel. 272458). Near the Grand Bazaar. Clean; mostly Turkish guests. Singles 75TL, doubles 65TL each, 55TL per person in a 3- or 4-bed room.

Toros Palace Oteli, Vezir Cami Sokak 4, Sirkeci (tel. 227518). One block behind the Railroad Station. Clean but noisy. Few Western tourists and no English spoken. Singles 60TL, doubles 90TL, triples 100TL, but no splitting rooms with another party.

Yeni Konak Pension, Nane Sokak 3, Beyoglu (tel. 446083). Downtown, on a street parallel to Istiklal Cad. Small and clean, but in a red light area. Singles 80TL, doubles for 110TL.

Camping Bebek (tel. 636733). Located on the Bosphorus in the wealthy suburb of Bebek, this is the nearest campground to Istanbul. Clean, uncrowded, on a hill with a good view of the water. Hot showers, when they work, are free. 15TL per person, 15TL per tent. Open June-Sept. Take boat to Bebek or bus M40 from Taksim.

Food

Gastronomically, Istanbul is one of the best cities in the world. From the sandwich stands in the streets to the elegant seafood restaurants on the

Bosphorus, the variety is great, the quality high and the prices reasonable. Everyone should have at least one meal with *meze* on the Bosphorus. It is best to go with several people, because, as in a Chinese restaurant, the trick is to order lots of little dishes and share everything.

In Istanbul there are two havens for seafood lovers on a budget. One is an alleyway running off **Istiklal Cad.** in Galatasaray that is lined with cheap restaurants serving shrimp, crab, stuffed mussels, octopus, and fried fish. A full meal costs 80TL and is well worth it. **Galata Bridge** and its environs has on its underside an interrupted succession of tiny seafood restaurants. Your best bet here is **Amatör Deniz Avcilari Kulübü,** an establishment with excellent meals and reasonable prices. Another option is to wander up the Bosphorus, buy a fish from one of the docked boats, and ask a nearby restaurant to cook it.

For all the above meals, expect a ten percent service charge as well as a 10% luxury tax in all restaurants serving liquor.

The Pudding Shop Lâle, Divan Yolu Cad., Sultanahmet. Everyone comes here, but not for the food. This is the number one hangout for young western-ers. Cafeteria setup. Uninteresting meat dishes at 20-30TL, puddings 8TL, beer 10TL. There is a message board and the menu has been translated into English. The Lâle is a good place to meet up with people heading to India.

Yener, Şeftali Sokak 18. A very famous "hippy" hangout run by the re-nowned Sitki, a friendly and generous soul. The interior is ragged Haight-Ashbury, but the humble meals are cheap (15-20TL). Adorn Sitki's collection of scrapbooks with your own creations.

Vitamin Kebab Salonu, Tiyatro Cad. 4, near the Grand Bazaar. An elegant but inexpensive restaurant serving a variety of *kebab* for 22-35TL. Also salad, soup, chicken, and breads. Friendly management. Highly recommended.

Beograd Restaurant, Laleli Cad., Aksaray. Run by two Yugoslavs, this is a carnivore's delight, serving nothing but simply grilled meats. Most entrees 25-40TL, mixed grill 45TL. Plush room upstairs.

Haci Salih, Sakizagaci Cad. 19, off Istiklal Cad. A good selection of foods for 15-30TL. Large place with predominantly Turkish clientele.

Abdul Vahid's, Ögüt Sokak, around the corner from the Haci Salih. Shabby interior, but good grilled meats. Wine served. Entrees are 15-30TL.

Rejans, Oliviye Pasaji. Close to Galatasaray, which is about 15 minutes away from Taksim, Rejans is run by several old White Russian ladies. They serve excellent Russian food, and make their own lemon Vodka, which you are meant to drink straight. Their *Chicken Kievsky,* their *Lamb Karsky,* and their stroganoff are exceptional. Also try their *piroshky* before the main course. A meal with vodka will cost 80-100TL. As the atmosphere is rather refined, don't wear jeans. Rejans is hard to find, but don't give up. From Taksim Square, walk down Istiklal Cad. until you pass Yeniçarşi Cad., the main intersection in Galatasary. Soon after, you'll see a Greek Church on your left. On the other side of the street, the first alley behind you is the one in which Rejans is located.

Selvi Kafeterya, Siraselviler 38/40, Taksim. A self-service cafeteria with surprisingly good food at unbeatable prices. Full meals 25TL.

Hacibozanogullari Baklavaci, *Ordu Cad. 214, Aksaray.* Excellent pastries, especially their honey concoctions. Stock up here for the next day's breakfast.

Sights

Istanbul's mosques, churches, and museums are endless. The ones listed below are the most important. About half the museums and sites charging admission close on Mondays, the other half on Tuesdays.

Aya Sofya, originally Aghia Sophia, the Church of the Divine Wisdom, was completed by Justinian the Great in the year 537. Aghia Sophia was the center of religious life of the Byzantine Empire up until the Turkish Conquest, when it was converted into a mosque by Sultan Mehmet II. Thereafter it served as an imperial mosque until the time of its conversion into a museum by Atatürk in 1935. It is one of the truly great buildings in the world, housing Byzantine mosaics dating from the ninth to the thirteenth centuries, uncovered and restored in recent years. Open 9am-5:30pm, closed Mon. 10TL, except Wed., Sat. and Sun. 5TL. An extra 5TL to get into the gallery and worth it.

Topkapi Saray is the great palace of the Ottoman Sultans. The museum is justly famous for its unrivaled collections of jewelry, armor, china, imperial Ottoman costumes and, above all, its Turkish miniatures. Part of the famous Harem has recently been restored and is now open to the public; do not fail to see it. Open 9:30am-5:30pm, closed Tues. 15TL except Wed., Sun., and Sat., when it's 7.50TL. The Harem costs an extra 11TL (or 6TL Wed. and weekends.)

Sultanahmet Camii, the Blue Mosque, is one of the most impressive monuments in the city. It was completed by Sultan Ahmet I in 1616, at a time when the great period of classical Ottoman architecture was drawing to a close.

The Hippodrome once occupied the site of the park which now stands before the Blue Mosque. This was once the center of the turbulent public life of Constantinople, the scene of chariot races, circuses, public spectacles, and violent riots. Now there are left only the three columns which once stood in the center of the arena: the **Egyptian Obelisk,** the **Serpentine Column,** and the **Colossus,** at the end of the park. At the Aya Sofya end of the Hippodrome is a small stone building, the entrance to the **Yerebatan Saray** (underground palace), a huge cistern built by the Byzantines to store water in case of siege. Worth the 1IL admission.

Archaeological Museums are located in the garden west of Topkapi Saray. The first building you come to is the oriental museum, with works of the Hittites, Egyptians, etc. in modern attractive exhibit halls. Entry 10TL except Wed., Sat., Sun., 2.50TL. The main museum is a large Ottoman-Classical building through the sculpture garden. It houses a fantastic collection of Greek, Hellenistic, and Roman marbles and bronzes. Among the exhibits is the supposed sarcophagus of Alexander the Great. 10TL, except Wed., Sat., Sun., 5TL. Closed Monday. Across the court is the **Chinili Kiosk,** one of the first buildings of the Ottomans in Istanbul. 1TL admission.

Galata Tower, built under Justinian in 528 and rebuilt by the Genoese in the fourteenth century as part of the defense of the European quarter and a means of spying on the Turkish city, has been restored. An excellent panorama of the city. 5TL admission. Closed Tues.

The Süleymaniye is the most majestic of the imperial mosques in Istanbul. It was commissioned by Süleyman the Magnificent and built by his chief architect, the great Sinan, who completed construction in the year 1557.

Shopping

The **Kapaliçarşi,** or **Grand Bazaar,** is a vast labyrinth of junk and riches, where both Turks and tourists prowl through streets filled with shops. The summer invasion of tourists keeps the prices higher than they are the rest of the year. Bargaining is the name of the game here, and since most of the merchants are pros, you'll have to look hard, and then work hard, to get a good deal. Don't try to buy unless you know the value of the goods. Your strategy then is to keep the merchant from sensing how eager you are to buy. The Bazaar is closed Sundays.

If you're wondering whether you can get the same goods for less elsewhere in Turkey, the answer is a qualified "yes." Istanbul offers the best selection of quality merchandise. Things are somewhat cheaper away from Istanbul, although you'll be very lucky to make a real steal. Turkey is particularly good for rugs and leather goods. If possible, buy these late in your stay to avoid carting them around with you.

Daytrips

On the Bosphorus

The suburbs of Istanbul are one of the greatest pleasures the city has to offer. One of the most popular evening activities of Istanbul is to come out to one of the Bosphorus suburbs, buy a bag of nuts and walk along the water-front. The ferry boats which leave from the Galata Bridge and the immediate vicinity connect the city with its maritime suburbs. There are services up the Golden Horn, to the towns on the Marmara shore and the islands in the Marmara, and to the seaside villages on both sides of the Bosphorus. Service is frequent and very cheap; schedules are posted near the ticket offices.

The Golden Horn ferries leave from the inner side of the Galata Bridge. The boat goes back and forth to both sides of the Golden Horn as far as **Eyüp,** about a mile beyond the land walls. Eyüp is the most famous Islamic shrine in Istanbul, housing the tomb of Eyüp, Companion of the Prophet. The mosque courtyard, the mausoleums, and the cemetery are very pictur-esque.

The ferries to the **Princes' Isles** leave from the Eminönü end of the Galata Bridge. The ferry stops at four of the nine islands of this little suburban archipelago. Come here for a relaxing afternoon. The scenery is beautiful, the towns are not too built up, and best of all, there are no cars on the islands, only horse-drawn carriages. **Büyükada** is the largest of the isles and the most scenic, although some prefer the quieter atmosphere of **Burgaz** and **Heybeliada.**

The towns along the Bosphorus are all modern suburbs of Istanbul, except for the distant **Rumeli Kavagi** and **Anodolu Kavagi,** which are picturesque, but somewhat touristy fishing villages. Ferries leave frequently but follow different routes, some sticking mostly to the European shore, some to the Asian, while some flit back and forth between the two continents. With a boat schedule you can spend the day hopping from one town to the next. The farther you get from Istanbul, the less built-up the towns are.

Bebek is only a forty-minute boat ride from Eminönü, and it is very easy to get back by bus or *dolmuş.* The nicely restored fortress at the nearby **Rumeli Hisari** and the good restaurants along the water make this one of the closest towns for a pleasant evening. Near the fortress, the Karaca Restaurant serves first rate *meze* and fish, although a full meal comes to 100TL.

Highly recommended for a splurge. Further up the European coast is the lovely town of **Sariyer.** The Sahil Lokantasi is a simple little tavern in a romantic setting on the quay of the old fishing port. In **Sariyer** or in **Rumeli Kavagi,** the last stop on the European shore, you can rent a boat to explore the upper Bosphorus, where there are several beautiful sandy coves ideal for swimming. Also, from Sariyer you can get a *dolmuş* to the Black Sea resort town of **Kilyos,** where a magnificent beach stretches for miles. The following are the villages along the Asian shore of the Bosphorus where one might be tempted to stop: **Anadolu Kavagi** (buy a fish in the local market and have it cooked in any of the little restaurants around the ferry landing), **Beykoz** (*dolmuş* service to the extraordinary village of **Polonezköy,** settled in the mid-nineteenth century by Polish refugees; here you can spend the night in a farmhouse and dine superbly at your host's kitchen table), **Kanlica** (famous for its excellent yogurt, served at little cafés near the ferry landing), **Anadolu Hisari** (try Kale Lokantasi, in the shadow of a fourteenth century castle built by Sultan Beyazit I), **Çengelköy** (two fine restaurants in the square beside the ferry landing), **Beylerbey** (several raffish cafés by the port from which one has a superb view down the Bosphorus of the Istanbul skyline, now framed by the new Bosphorus Bridge).

Bursa and Troy

In addition to the above day and half-day excursions on the Bosphorus, there are a number of slightly longer trips you can make, keeping Istanbul as your base. Among the most popular are a visit to Troy, the site of Homer's *Iliad,* and to Bursa, a popular resort town for Turks. Both are better seen in two-day trips, though Bursa can be done in one.

To reach Troy, you have two options—boat or bus. The boat leaves every Wednesday and Saturday morning at 8am (100TL). The twelve-hour ride to Çanakkale stops at a number of islands. The bus from Istanbul to Çanakkale takes only six hours (120TL), but is less interesting. From Çanakkale, take a bus to Hisarlik, the closest village to Troy. Here we suggest hiring a guide, for the ruins are unimpressive unless your own knowledge or imagination can make them come alive.

For the trip to Bursa, take a boat from the Kabataş dock to Yalova, and from there, connect by bus to Bursa. This popular resort has a good number of imperial sights, mosques, and tombs, but is most famous for its mineral and sulphur baths. Self-service baths at these facilities start at 15TL. **Uludag,** the large mountain that lords over Bursa offers magnificent views, and in the winter, skiing. There are a number of accommodations at its top, some moderately priced.

Evenings

Istanbul's formal nightlife is tempered by Muslim conservatism. Much of what exists has been created by and for Westerners; the few discotheques are all within a block of the Hilton. Real Turkish "nightlife" involves eating a large meal late in the evening and lingering afterwards over *çay* or *kahve*. Also, a stroll along **Istiklal Caddesi** or **Meşrutiyet Cad.** will take you to friendly, inexpensive spots where you can enjoy lively music. Try the **Taksim Belediye** in Taksim Square. In the same areas are numerous cinemas, many in English or with English subtitles. Before leaving Istanbul, cross over to the Asian side and view the city's otherworldly skyline at sunset.

Istanbul is a good city for classical music. The symphony season dominates the winter calendar, while summer brings the Istanbul Festival (mid-June to mid-July) with nightly performances of opera, symphony, and dance in splendid settings—Mozart in the Topkapi, a harp recital in St. Irene's.

The "exotic arts" are in decline in Istanbul, but for a glimpse of their remnants, try Çiçek Pasaji, formerly the belly-dancing center of Istanbul; or head to the Sulukele district for gypsy music. Another popular evening activity is a visit to a Turkish bath *(hamam)*. Cagaloglu Hamami, Yerebatan Cad., Cagaloglu (tel. 222424) serves men and women. A complete massage and bath costs 100TL; self-administered bath for 35TL. Any of the student travel organizations will help you find a *hamam*.

Central Anatolia: Ankara, Kayseri, Cappadocia, and Konya

Ankara, the capital, is not a major tourist attraction. Most people come here because they can connect by bus or train to all of Turkey. But once you're in Ankara, there are a couple of things worth seeing. The Archaeological Museum, with its outstanding Neolithic and Hittite collections, is one of the finest in the world. The exhibits are well marked and displayed with great sensitivity; the setting is unique—a restored *caravanserai* (a market and travelers' inn complex), its halls populated by canaries. Open 9am-5pm, entry 6TL (3TL Sat. and Sun.), closed Mon. To get there, take a taxi or bus to the Ulus section of town, and head up the hill, bearing always to the right. Above you stands the ruined Kale, or Citadel. Though the ruins are nothing, the view is excellent. The museum lies at the south foot of the Kale. If you get lost, ask directions in the local Ulus bazaar; your path takes you right through it.

Ankara's other major sight is the Anit Kabir, the tomb of Atatürk. Be sure to visit this monument; its sheer size and the museum of Atatürk's personal effects (admission 2TL) will give you a sense of Turkey's immense reverence for its national hero.

Inexpensive accommodations in Ankara aren't abundant. Try Pension Cebeci, Cebeci, Dumlupinar Cad. 43 (tel. 194538). 50TL for a single, 30TL in doubles or triples. Otel Murat offers clean rooms for 40-50TL; no English spoken. Take Meşrutiyet Cad. to Hatay, Sokak 5 (tel 255019). The Yenişehir Saglik and other hostels are open primarily in off-season; they notify the Tourist Offices when they have openings, so check there first. The cheaper restaurants are found around Ulus and Kizilay. The best moderately-priced Turkish meals can be found on Bayindir Cad., particularly at the Körfez restaurant; the street is two blocks east of Kizilay square. A full formal meal with wine will run you 100TL here. For a varied menu, a filling meal, and a great view, try Kafeteriye Set, atop the Post Office Building.

The ancient town of Kayseri, formerly the Roman Caesarea, is definitely worth a stop on the way either to or from Cappadocia, or if you're heading east. The town centers around an old Byzantine citadel. Next to it is the Hunad Camii (great Mosque), whose simplicity perhaps captures the essence of Islam better than the splendorous mosques of Istanbul. As would be expected in this rug-weaving center, the floors of the Mosque are covered with some of the most beautiful carpets in Turkey. If you walk through the old part of town you can see women weaving similar carpets on their shaded porches. The locals make a big deal over you in Kayseri, and most likely you will be invited in for tea and to observe the carpet-making process. Tucked way back in the dusty old part of town is a nineteenth-century Armenian church still used by the handful of Armenian families that remain. It's hard to find, but ask passersby for the *Kilise* (church) and they'll point out the way.

Food and accommodations are cheap here. For 25TL you can stay in the dormitory of the centrally located **Kayseri Lisesi,** a local high school (summers only). **Hotel Hunat,** behind the Hunad Mosque has singles for 30TL, doubles for 50TL and triples for 60TL, 5TL extra for a hot shower. The balcony on the top floor has an excellent view.

The ancient province of **Cappadocia** is the most interesting part of the central plateau. The area is characterized by beautifully eroded volcanic formations which, in the Göreme valley, were carved out to create churches and monasteries between the fourth and thirteenth centuries. Many of these "rock churches" contain important tenth- and eleventh-century Byzantine paintings. Similar cave churches are found in the nearby **Belisirrama Valley.** If you have time, try also to visit the troglodyte community at **Avcilar.**

South of the Göreme area by about 50 km are the underground cities of **Kaymakli** and **Derinkuyu.** Recently discovered by archaeologists, these cities were carved into solid rock down to depths of 120 feet—seven to twelve levels—and were once home to 50,000 people. Though the most famous and numerous inhabitants were Christians fleeing Islamic persecution, there is evidence that the original cities date back to the Hittite period. A strong flashlight for these and the rock churches of Göreme is recommended.

Though Cappadocia is rapidly becoming a hearty tourist draw, transportation here is still difficult. To get to most of the above sites, you'll have to combine buses and taxis, or *dolmuş* services and hitching. *Ürgüp,* a village tucked within a huge rock shelf, makes the best base. Geared towards a young clientele, the town offers discos and three good cheap hotels: the **Kayseri Otel** (30TL per bed), the **Pinar** (40TL), and the **Sefa** (50TL). There is camping on the road to Nevşehir at Paris Otel, but it costs 35TL.

Konya, a four-hour bus ride south of Ankara, was the capital of the Seljuk sultans, and is still the religious center of Turkey. The most important sight is the **Tekke,** or monastery, of the whirling dervishes, officially the **Mevlana Museum.** The order's founder, who died in 1273, is buried here, as are other saints. The dervishes were regarded with suspicion by Istanbul for being semiheretical, but it was Atatürk who smashed the orders, and turned the mosque into a museum. Be that as it may, most of your fellow "tourists" will be peasants come to pay their respects to the saint Mevlana, who is a popular figure in Turkey's reviving religiosity. To see the whirling dervishes in action, attend the Konya Festival (December 9-17) each year.

Konya is a city of mosques and museums, most of them in the center of the city. Obtain a map from the Tourist Office to orient yourself; after visiting the Tekke, move up Hükümet Cad. to **Alaeddin Tepesi.** Here are located the other main sights of Konya: the **Alaeddin Mosque,** Konya's oldest; **the Karatöy Museum of Ceramics** (9am-noon and 1:30-4:45pm), with its splendid blue-tiled dome; and **Ince Minare Museum,** a showcase of Konya's old marble and wood workings (open same hours as Karatöy).

Most of Konya's cheap hotels are in the center of town, near the major sights. **Otel Selimiye,** Mevlana Cad. 17 (tel. 20014) is the best of these. One block from the Tekke, it has clean, large rooms (singles 60TL, doubles 55TL each, triples 50TL each) and good facilities. Slightly noisy though.

As for food, Konya's specialties date back to the old Selçuk cuisine, such as the famous (and filling) *etliekmek,* a thick bread rolled around ground meat and vegetables. Try one for lunch; the best "Selçuk" restaurant here is, appropriately, **Lokanta Selçuk,** Kayalipark Karşisi 3.

The basis of Turkey's claim to being one of the birthplaces of civilization lies 50 km south of Konya at the site of **Çatal Höyük.** An advanced Neolithic community that competes with Jericho as "the world's oldest city," the site is best seen with the help of a guide. Take a *dolmuş* from Konya.

Mediterranean Coast

The **Turquoise Coast,** named for the color of the water, is one of Turkey's fastest growing regions, but the name brochures give to its most built-up strip (between **Antalya** and **Alanya**), the Turkish Riviera, is at this stage only hopeful exaggeration. A series of sand beaches and coves divided by thickly vegetated ravines, the popularity of this area is limited to vacationing middle-class Turks from Ankara and other cities, and there is nothing of the prices, crowds, and superhotels that plague beach resorts elsewhere.

Antalya is a large, dull city with two mediocre beaches, although **Lara Plaj** (12 km away) is superior to the nearer **Konyati Beach.** Both are accessible by *dolmuş* from downtown. The cheapest places to stay in Antalya are near the bus station. The **Armagan,** just fifty yards to its left, is in a new building and is clean: 40TL single, 50TL double, or 30TL per person in a 4-bed room.

West of Antalya are some spectacular mountains and forests which meet the water in lush coves. The best of these is **Kemer,** a favorite Turkish camping spot out on a peninsula. The road to Kemer is decent, but deteriorates quickly thereafter. If you plan to wind around to the Aegean from here, give yourself lots of time. And stop in **Kaş,** a lovely fishing port with a well-preserved theater. Also of interest is **Demre,** where the martyrdom of St. Nicholas is commemorated in a Byzantine church with well-preserved mosaic floors.

East of Antalya stretches the ancient province of **Pamphylia,** where important ruins remain only partially excavated in wild, beautiful countryside. At **Perge** an important theater and stadium remain, as do the *agora* (market), baths, and a romantic colonnaded street.

Farther down the road, near the village of Serik, **Aspendos** has a monumental theater dating from the second century. It is one of the best preserved in the world, and is still used for folk dancing, concerts, etc. during the **Antalya Festival** in early June.

Side is on a point where the beaches and the ruins are right next to each other. A climb to the bleachers of the ancient theater will give you a view of the acres of ruins, the beautiful, uncrowded beach to the left of town, and the town of Side itself. During the summer it's almost impossible to find a room here, although your best chance is to look in town, away from the beach. There are also several campgrounds, but if you walk through the ancient temple, you'll reach the ideal spot on the beach to sack out on. Side is a uniquely beautiful place, even if it is completely given over to tourism.

To reach Perge, Side, or Aspendos, take a *dolmuş* from Antalya on the Alanya road. Yellow signs mark the turnoffs. Perge is 1 km from the main road, Aspendos 4 km, and Side 3 km—you can thumb them. There are also tours out of Antalya, but they run about 200TL for a full day of sightseeing.

Like Side, **Alanya** is full of tourists, and yet retains a unique beauty. The town is dominated by a massive Selçuk fortress with over 12 km of walls. There are large beaches on either side of town—the one to the west is less crowded and less rocky. Rooms in Alanya are less scarce than in smaller coastal resort towns. We recommend the **Hotel Plaj,** on Gazi Paşa Caddesi, on the waterfront. Most rooms have balconies; try to get one overlooking the sea. Singles 60TL without bath, doubles 100TL without bath. Otherwise try the **Yali Palas Oteli,** Iskele Cad. 48. Bathless, stark, but clean rooms, 30TL per bed. Those with cars may prefer the **BP Mocamp,** 22 km west of town on a fine beach. For meals, the **Yönet Kebab Salonu** on Gazi Paşa Caddesi has inexpensive meat dishes and seafood at reasonable prices.

East of Alanya, the terrain toughens, and the road becomes more precipitous. Sites and cities are farther apart, so your options for camping and exploration are enhanced. **Mersin** is a large, modern port which offers little to the tourist except some Neolithic ruins to its north and three weekly boats to Cyprus. Caution: in leaving for Cyprus, make sure any business or connections you want to make are available on the Turkish part of the islands. Hostilities make transfer to the Greek side impossible.

Aegean Coast

Like the Mediterranean coast to the south, Turkey's western coast offers a succession of fine beaches, archaeological sites, and small towns. But several factors make it a more appealing region to explore. First, the ruins are more spectacular—this area was one of the centers of Hellenistic civilization. Also, the heat here is not as oppressive as it is further south. Getting around is easy: besides the direct bus connections from Izmir to all towns on the coast, you can hop from one point to the next with *dolmuşes*—a perfect way to explore the coast and points inland. Despite these assets, the Turkish Aegean coast is far less touristed than the nearby Greek islands.

Izmir is a large, dull, port city that has been rebuilt almost completely since a fire nearly destroyed it in 1922. You can get a boat from here to the Greek island of Chios. **Kuşadasi,** two hours to the south, is one of the biggest resorts in Turkey—the pirate fortress now houses a discotheque. Accommodations are scarce in summer, but try the **Hotel Atlantik,** Tayyare Cad. 17 (tel. 1039), which offers doubles and triples for 50TL per person. Camp to the north of town or on the beach. There are daily boats from Kuşadasi to the Greek island of Samos.

About 15 km north of Kuşadasi lie the most exciting ruins in all of Turkey. At **Ephesus,** the remains of one of the greatest cities in the Hellenistic, and later, Roman Empire—temples, a library, theater, market, brothel, and graffiti-marked avenues—are scattered over 2000 acres. Guided tours are expensive, but since the awesome ruins are poorly labeled, you should at least invest in one of the guidebooks (40TL) to the site available at the entrance (open daily until 6pm, admission 10TL, 5TL on Wednesdays, Saturdays, and Sundays).

Didum, about two hours south of Kuşadasi is a small resort popular with middle-class Turks. This is a pleasant, unspoiled resort with a Hellenistic temple and miles of spectacular deserted shoreline on either side of the main beach. If you come in the summer, plan to camp out here, because rooms are scarce.

Continuing south along the coast, **Bodrum,** the ancient Halicarnassus, is a beautiful whitewashed fishing village clustering around an imposing castle built by the knights of St. John in the Middle Ages. **Marmaris,** a small port town set in lush scenery, has been getting a lot of tourists lately, but is still worth a visit. To really escape the crowds, take a boat to **Turanç** (an hour's trip to the south), a good beach inaccessible by roads. Camping is, of course, ideal, but there are also a few pensions here—but no electricity.

Fethiye in itself is a quiet port with little to offer, but here you can catch a *dolmuş* to **Olu Deniz,** a fantastic lagoon with a number of campgrounds and guest cottages. Another great place to escape for a day or a week.

Western USSR

USSR

1U.S. = .68 roubles   **1 rouble = $1.46**

It is impossible to approach the Soviet Union objectively. More than a country, it is a way of life, neither an egalitarian workers' utopia nor a vast 1984-like controlled society, but, unsurprisingly, some place in between. The only way to comprehend the Soviet Union is to go and see it for yourself. Since the first English merchants visited the court of Ivan the Terrible in the sixteenth century, foreign travelers have been fascinated and bewildered by Russia. Today, you will be overwhelmed by Russia's cultural heritage, and baffled and irritated by the inexplicable maze of "Catch-22" regulations.

The contradictions are all-embracing. Soviet scientific and technical achievements are world famous, yet clerks in understocked department stores still compute bills on abacuses. Russian ballet companies are the envy of major troupes in New York and Paris, yet modern dance is only now beginning to pick up where Isadora Duncan left off. Pre-revolutionary buildings, unequalled in beauty and taste, stand uncomfortably next to massive sterile "Stalinist-Gothic" architecture. Russia's museums have some of the finest collections in the world (thanks to avaricious tsars and commissars), yet it is impossible for the student of modern art to find a Kandinsky or a Malevich (their works lie in storage vaults). The anonymous Russian on the street may appear cold and rude; yet behind the closed doors of his home, foreign guests are treated like royalty. The ambiguities of Soviet life are perhaps the only certainty in a country Winston Churchill described as "a riddle wrapped in a mystery inside an enigma."

Even a short visit here is guaranteed to be a mind-boggling experience. This is partly the result of sheer physical size. In the largest country in the world, spanning eleven time zones, the tendency to think big is almost a reflex, from the world's biggest bell (Moscow's Tsar-Bell), longest railroad (the Trans-Siberian) to the monster hydroelectric dams of Siberia or the massive political rallies in front of the Kremlim. But beyond this larger-than-life aspect of Russia (Americans are at least used to bigness) there is great variety and richness.

Traveling around the USSR, you may have to give up some of the comforts you enjoyed back home, but presumably these weren't what you came for anyway. Remember that you are visiting a country that has been virtually destroyed twice in the last seventy years. Leave your preconceptions behind, and concentrate on observing contemporary Soviet society as it is. Begin with the Russian people themselves, from swaddled infants to kerchiefed grandmothers *(babushkas)*. Public places (parks, baths, racetracks) are often the best way to get a good feeling for the Russians as a people—whose capacity for work and self-denial is extraordinary.

Regardless of how short your stay in the Soviet Union is, try to visit at least one of the non-Russian republics. Over half of the Soviet population is non-Russian, and the country contains a variety of exotic cities and cultures vastly different from the Russian. The Baltic region (Latvia, Estonia, and Lithuania) is the most modern and westernized part of the Soviet Union (it became part of the USSR only in 1945). The native population here feels superior to the Russians and speaks Russian only as a last resort. The Central Asian Republics, with their 30 million Turkic peoples, evoke the spirit of another time and place. The cities of Tashkent and Samarkand were thriving cultural centers when Moscow was still a frontier outpost. Here you enter an Arabian Nights setting, complete with turquoise mosques, old *medersas* (religious schools) and bazaars where one can find hand-woven tapestries and rugs. A visit to any one of these non-Russian republics can be easily arranged for your itinerary.

Lastly, perhaps more than for any other country in this book, you should do some preparation for your trip, beyond the mechanics of visas and reservations. Your experiences will be much more meaningful if you go with some knowledge of the historical roots of what you'll see. If you have time, read something about contemporary Soviet society, such as Hedrick Smith's *The Russians*. It will give you an understanding of the daily life which the individual traveler here rarely meets.

Getting There

A visit to the Soviet Union requires quite a bit of planning, and you must be prepared to sacrifice the spontaneity that may have characterized your travel through Western Europe. You simply cannot enter the Soviet Union alone or as a member of a group unless you hold the required visa and passport, and have confirmed in advance a day-by-day itinerary with one of the two official Soviet travel organizations, **Intourist** and **Sputnik.** Give some thought as to when and where you want to travel in the Soviet Union, and begin to make your plans *three to four months in advance.* Take note that while any travel agent can in theory make your arrangements, you'd be wise to deal exclusively with Intourist-approved travel agents, who will be more familar with the complexities of travel in the Soviet Union.

There are three touring options for an American in the Soviet Union. First, you can go on a **pre-arranged group tour,** sponsored by a travel agency or educational institution, in cooperation with Intourist. Intourist also offers a number of specialty tours, such as bear hunts in Siberia and health spas in the Crimea. The more independent can travel individually, staying at hotels or on a **camping/driving trip,** both methods subject to Intourist approval beforehand. (Or, if you prefer, you can sign up for one of the group tours and just skip the scheduled sight-seeing on some or all days.) Finally, those who haven't planned ahead can make a short visit on a **Finnish steamer,** with no advance visa.

While the idea of a group tour may conjure up images of "If It's Tuesday, this Must be Belgium," it is nonetheless the cheapest and most common form of travel within the Soviet Union. Group tours vary in character, duration, price, and point of origin. If you are planning a full summer in Europe and desire only a brief visit to the USSR, your best bet is a fixed date tour which both begins and ends inside the USSR.

Of the two separate Soviet travel companies, Intourist and Sputnik, the former is by far the largest and has a virtual monopoly over all Western travel to the USSR, while the latter is primarily a youth travel organization. Sputnik does, however, offer a limited selection of inexpensive group tours for Western students in cooperation with the **Scandinavian Student Travel Service** (SSTS) with which they are connected through the **International Student Travel Conference** (ISTC).

You may book on the SSTS-operated tours through any member agency of the ISTC, but to ensure a place you should make reservations in North America. Connections can be made in Europe, however, through the SSTS and the Student Air Travel Association (Student ID required). As there is no Sputnik office outside of Moscow, for information and application students should write in the United States to the **Council on International Educational Exchange (CIEE),** 777 United Nations Plaza, New York, NY 10017, and in Canada to **Canadian Universities Travel Service Ltd.,** 44 St. George St., Toronto, Ont., M5S 2E4. When writing to CIEE, also ask, if you're interested, for information on "semester break" and summer school tours offered by various American universities.

The SSTS-Sputnik tours are coordinated with the arrival of these student flights to Leningrad and Moscow—the usual first stops in the one- or two-week Soviet itineraries. If you suddenly decide to go to the USSR on such a group tour when you're in Europe, it is possible to obtain a visa and flight reservation in Copenhagen. Allow *at least* 48 hours for completion of arrangements. The SSTS-Sputnik tours can also be joined at the starting points (Leningrad to Moscow) by those wishing to travel into the USSR by rail or water. Before hopping on the Paris-Moscow Express, however, make sure that you have a valid visa for entry into the Soviet Union, with a stamped entry date coinciding with the date on which you arrive at the border (you won't get in if it doesn't).

A typical one-week tour from Leningrad to Moscow including full sight-seeing programs, full board, accommodation in two- to three-bed rooms, tourist-class rail travel, and the services of a local English-speaking guide, costs around $175 per person; a two-week itinerary including Moscow, Leningrad, Tbilisi (the capital of Georgia), and the Central Asian cities of Tashkent, Bukhara, and Samarkand costs about $500 per person, including domestic air fare. Write CIEE for the brochure, *SSTS Student Soviet Union-Poland Tours*, which contains details and prices of the various tours, and an application form.

If the dates for the few tours offered by SSTS-Sputnik are not convenient for you, check the fixed starting date tours offered by Intourist. These are considerably more expensive for the short itineraries, but comparable in cost for the two-week trips. Intourist offers group tours to over 90 Soviet cities, from Moscow, Leningrad, and Kiev in European Russia to Irkutsk in Siberia and Samarkand in Central Asia. Usual duration is 8 to 21 days depending on the trip; and price, of course, depends upon the length of the tour and the distance traveled. Intourist really is a good cut above the youth-oriented Sputnik, and its operation seems much smoother.

Intourist's American office is at 630 Fifth Ave., New York, NY 10017, and you should write them for their booklet *Visiting the USSR*, containing all pertinent general information about travel to the USSR as well as a list of the accredited U.S. travel agents who can put you on to one of the fixed-date itineraries. The Intourist office itself is only an information bureau and does not make reservations, so you must select an approved travel agent.

If you really are an uncompromising free spirit and don't think you can handle the collective effort of group travel, you might consider a driving and camping trip through the Soviet Union in your own car or minibus following one of the many planned motor itineraries supplied by Intourist. This is really the only individual travel available at less than prohibitive prices. Independent travel following itineraries similar to group travel costs upwards of $40 a day not including transportation, while rented cars cost more than $10 a day and $.10 a kilometer. If you have your own vehicle, though, you pay only for campsite privileges, food, and gasoline; also, there are no Intourist guides coming between you and the natives. The campsites are located in attractive green zones near the main cities, often along river and lake shores, with food, stores, cafés, and gas stations nearby. The cost of a parking site ($3 per person per day), includes the use of kitchen facilities, water supply, showers, and one sight-seeing tour of the nearby city. Campsites in the southern parts of the Soviet Union open about May 15. Around Moscow and Leningrad, they open on June 1. All campsites close for the season on September 1. As with group tours however, all motor itineraries must be previously confirmed with Intourist through a Western travel agency and cannot later be changed without great hassle. Write ahead of time—allow at least six weeks for this kind of individual travel—to confirm your itinerary. Ask Intourist for a copy of their brochure, *Motor Tours of the Soviet Union*. This brochure gives detailed maps of motor routes through the Soviet Union including all entry and exit points by land from Finland, Poland, Czechoslovakia, Hungary, and Romania.

For information about sailing schedules and shipping costs for automobiles in both the Baltic and Black Seas contact the **March Shipping Passenger Services,** Room 5257, One World Trade Center, New York, NY 10048 or 400 St. Antoine St. W., Montreal, Que. H2Y 1K1. They explain the myriad of possibilities for shipping existing between London, Le Havre, and Leningrad as well as connections between the Mediterranean and Odessa, Yalta, or Sochi. If you put some careful thought into this kind of travel, you could plan out a terrific trip starting in Finland, traveling through Leningrad, Moscow, Kiev, and Odessa, and ending by boat to Istanbul or Athens with your minibus still in tow.

It is possible to visit Leningrad and certain other Soviet port cities by steamer *without* a visa, provided that you sleep on the boat, and disembark only as a member of an organized Intourist tour. **Silja Line,** the Finnish steamship company, offers four-day trips from Helsinki to Leningrad, and to Tallinn, the capital of Estonia. You must sleep on the boat and can disembark only as a member of an organized Intourist tour. For information, contact **Bergen Line Inc.,** 505 Fifth Ave., New York, NY 10017. Again, plan far ahead, as the full price of the ticket is due two months before departure. Students with an ID card can book from Helsinki at least two weeks in advance as **BORE/FFOA USSR Department,** Etelaranta 8, 00130 Helsinki (tel. 178-2506). Prices start at $200 for a four-day excursion that includes accommodations, meals, sauna facilities, and two full days in Leningrad.

To repeat, it is extremely difficult to alter your itinerary once it has been confirmed by Intourist. Traveling individually it is possible, with a great deal of Intourist negotiations, to extend your stay a couple of days at the end of your tour, particularly if you are in Moscow or Leningrad. But you'll end up very frustrated if you attempt to alter the order of any itinerary in progress. If you are slated to go to Kiev from Leningrad, you cannot cancel this in favor of a trip to Tashkent or to spend more time in Leningrad. Intourist runs a tight ship and more often than not they will tell you everything is booked.

It is also difficult to change the activities slated for any given day. While daytrips and certain evening activities are bookable on the spot at the **Service Bureau** located in every Intourist Hotel, many of the most popular excursions must be reserved in advance. In dealing with your Western travel agent you should press him to find out exactly what your daily itinerary includes. It is virtually impossible during the high season in the main cities to procure even a single ticket for any opera, ballet, circus, or puppet show. However, if you're persistent, you can sometimes get a ticket by showing up an hour before curtain time outside the theater.

General Information

If you're going to be in the Soviet Union for any length of time and don't know Russian, try to at least learn the Cyrillic alphabet and pick up a good phrase book. The Penguin *Russian Phrase Book* covers a wide variety of situations. If you have studied Russian, by all means use it. Russians will warm up to even the most feeble effort to speak their language. In case of problems with Soviet authorities, however, *always* use English—it usually helps to get you off the hook. If it's something major, demand that an embassy representative be present. The American Embassy encourages travelers to give them a copy of their itinerary. Call them if you're at all hassled.

You may bring as much foreign money as you wish into the Soviet Union but all of it must be declared upon entry. If you are caught taking roubles into the USSR, the roubles will be confiscated and you may not be allowed entry into the country. Money can be changed at all Intourist Hotels. Be sure to hold on to your receipts—customs officers have been known to meticulously check tourists laden with gifts and other Soviet goods, especially when such tourists are taking out almost as much foreign currency as they brought in.

Foreigners are required to stay within a 25 kilometer limit of major Soviet cities, unless they are members of an escorted group. Although the Soviet authorities don't often actively enforce this law, foreigners have been deported for its violation. So stay within the limit, or make yourself *very* inconspicuous if you venture farther.

As U.S.-Soviet relations go, so go Soviet customs searches of American tourists. Chances are that you will be carefully checked. When planning your visit, remember the following: no Soviet-banned literary or political writings allowed; no more than three pairs of jeans and four or five rock records (the jackets should be slit if the records are new), and of course, no drugs.

One of the purposes of Soviet customs searches and currency regulations is to prevent foreigners from dealing in the black market. Although an integral part of Soviet life, Soviet officials deny it exists. Unofficially, it is tolerated and even encouraged. Western students are a prime target for Russian *fartsovshchiki* (black marketeers), and you are quite likely to be approached with lucrative offers for buying U.S. dollars, records, or blue jeans. *Be extremely careful*. The Soviets are tightening up, especially on Americans. If caught, you face a stiff punishment, and your trip will be ruined. If you do sell anything, deal only with Soviet students that you have gotten to know, and make your trades in private (your friend's friend could be an informer). If you are caught, play dumb, speak only English, and demand to see someone from the embassy.

Mail into the USSR is still none too reliable, but if you are expecting important mail, have it addressed to: *Poste Restante,* at either K-600, Gorky Street 1, Moscow, USSR or C-400, Nevsky Prospekt 6, Leningrad, USSR. To mail items out, take them unwrapped to the Central Post or Telegraph office; there they will be wrapped and mailed while you wait.

Your picture-taking in the USSR is unrestricted, except for the following: no photographs from airplanes or of military installations or personnel, railroad stations, airports (there is sometimes a problem with the Metro, too), and no factories without permission. Also, ask permission before photographing people at close range. At all times use discretion. Soviets are proud people and will get angry if they think you are taking pictures which show only the negative aspects of their society.

When shopping in the Soviet Union, get receipts for every item you purchase. Icons, old samovars, books published before 1945, and some other items may prove difficult to get out of the country (you need a permit from the Ministry of Culture), and in any case there is a 100% duty charge. In general, the best places to shop are the *beriozka* shops. Purchases in these shops must be made with hard currency (roubles not accepted). There you can purchase a wide variety of high-quality goods not available in regular Soviet stores.

The USSR urban transportation system is one of the best and the cheapest in the world. It is basically the same in all major cities. The heart of the system is the super-fast and efficient *Metro,* which runs from 6am-1am and has stations marked by a large illuminated M. A public address system announces the stops, but stay alert—often a station will have only a couple of signs identifying it. The buses, trolley buses, and trams also run 6am-1am, except trams start and end a half hour earlier and later in the suburbs. These three systems operate on an "honor system" without ticket collectors.

The passenger drops the exact fare into a fare box (5 kopeks for buses, 4 for trolleys, 3 for trams) and pulls off a ticket; a "controller" may also sometimes suddenly appear to see everyone's ticket, just to keep the honor system honorable.

In general, Western-style "nightlife" does not exist in the Soviet Union. The Soviet economy apparently requires rested workers, so Russian restaurants, bars, and other public places close no later than 11:30pm, leaving foreign currency bars in the big Intourist hotels as the only late-night spots for travelers. Unless you have been invited to a private home for an evening gathering, or would prefer to wander about the city at night (Soviet cities are quite safe), we suggest you get a good night's sleep.

The Public Baths

A visit to a Russian public bath (*banya*) offers a glimpse of the self-indulgence of pre-revolutionary Russia, and provides an opportunity to meet and chat casually with Soviet citizens from all walks of life. Virtually every Soviet town has a public bath. They range from one-room wooden huts in the villages to three-story palaces in the major cities. The grandest of all are the nineteenth-century **Sundonovski Bathy** in Moscow (one block from Kuznetski Bridge).

The *banya* are the one great class-leveler in Soviet society. Only in the baths will you find party *apparachiki* and factory workers relaxing, gossiping, and enjoying each other's company. Smoking and drinking are forbidden, but everybody smokes, and for a small tip, the bath attendant will run out to fetch a liter of vodka. In the cities, the baths usually consist of three rooms: one for changing clothes and receiving a sheet (to wear) and a pillow case (to sit on). The next room may contain showers or elaborate marble-enclosed pools with hot and cold water (depending on the age and style of the *banya*). Some older, more luxurious baths even contain marble slabs arranged like beds in a hospital where an attendant gives massages for 30 kopeks. The third room is usually a sauna with bleacher-style benches—if you wish to win some general admiration, sit at the top and endure the heat for a while. When things get slow, flog yourself (or your neighbor) with birch branches to open the pores and promote circulation. Those with weak hearts are advised to stay away from the *banya*. Fees for the *banya* range from 50 kopeks to 1.50 roubles.

Upon leaving, do what the regulars do. Stop at a sidewalk stand and have a couple of mugs of draft beer (much better than bottled beer). Since a visit to a *banya* is not normally a part of an Intourist itinerary, you'll have to ask a passerby or friend for directions. Saturday is the most popular day to go.

Food

While all meals are included on most tours, it is well worth it to get away at least once for a meal on your own in a restaurant or café. Stop for a snack in one of the pastry cafés or cafeterias (*stolovaia*). Be sure to sample the famous Russian ice cream sold year round by ubiquitous sidewalk vendors. Also worth visiting are the specialty restaurants such as *shashlychnaias* (for shish kebab) or *blinaias* (for Russian crêpes). *Ponchiki* (or *pyshki*) are greasy Russian doughnuts, served hot from the fryer and sprinkled with powdered sugar—delicious, especially in mid-winter with a cup of hot coffee.

To begin with the staples: Russian *khleb* (bread) holds an honored place in culinary lore—especially black bread. *Bulki* are sweet buns and *vatrushki* are like cheese Danish. *Pirozhki* (literally, little pies) are made of flaky pastry filled with meat, cabbage, or chopped egg and rice. *Blini* are thin pancakes, often eaten with sour cream and jam; *blinchiki* are what we call blintzes, with meat and cheese fillings and fried crisp. For yogurt freaks, there are variety of sourmilk products: *prostakvasha*—the closest to American yogurt; *kefir*—like liquid sour cream, generally served in a glass at breakfast and good with a spoonful of sugar or jam; and *riazhinka*—similar to *prostakvasha* but with a different flavor. *Kasha* is a standard porridge, often resembling our cream of wheat.

Chai (tea) is, of course, the universal drink and panacea. It is served in glasses with metal holders, often with lemon, sugar, or a spoonful of jam mixed in *Kafe* is improving, but often comes pre-mixed with milk and sugar, so you may prefer to order *expres* if you know the coffee is bad—bad Russian coffee is devastating. *Mineralnaya voda* (mineral water) is refreshing, as is *limonad* (soda); both can be drunk from sidewalk vending machines for a few kopeks. Summer sidewalk stands and wagons also sell *pivo* (beer) and *kvas* (a pungent and thirst-quenching brown drink made from fermented rye bread) from communal mugs.

In the tenth century, St. Vladimir wrote, "It is Russia's joy to drink. We cannot do without it." Little has changed since then, and Soviet per capita consumption of hard liquor is the highest in the world. Vodka is central to almost every Russian celebration. It is sold in half-liter bottles (about 4 roubles each). The tops of the bottles are made of a heavy metal foil, so once the top is off, it can't be put back on—the bottle must be finished. *Stolichnaia* is the most popular brand. If you feel adventurous, try one of the stronger-tasting brownish vodkas like *Starka* or *Okhotnichnaia*. Be warned: Russian vodka goes down smoothly, especially when chased with a hunk of dark bread or a slice of cucumber. You'll feel fine one minute and be flat on your face the next, with a vodka hangover to last for days.

Recently, wine has gained in popularity in the Soviet Union. Georgian wines are probably the best in the Soviet Union. *Tsinandali* and *Gurdzhaani* (dry whites) are famous, as is *Mukuzani* (comparable to a good Beaujolais). Some of the sweet wines from the Crimea such as the *Massandras* are also very fine. Georgian and Armenian cognacs are excellent, and there are two liqueurs from the Baltic republics: *Starii Tallin* and *Chornii Balsam* which are usually drunk with coffee.

The best Russian wines, vodkas, and liqueurs are usually available only in *beriozkas* (or other foreign currency stores). Soviet champagne, which is delicious and relatively inexpensive, can be purchased in both *beriozkas* and regular liquor stores. Another good *beriozka* bargain is chocolate—available to foreigners at half the price Russians pay.

The Trans-Siberian Railway

The Trans-Siberian Express is one of the world's last great railway adventures. The trip from Moscow to Khabarovsk near the Pacific Coast takes about seven to ten days, depending on where you decide to stop off. Many Soviet cities along the Trans-Siberian are closed to foreigners. Still, you may stop off in Novisibursk, a village only fifty years ago, but now a bustling city of one million and a major science center; or in Irkutsk, where you can visit Lake Baikal, the world's deepest. From Khabarovsk, you'll take the boat-train to Naklodka where you can catch a boat for Tokyo. One-way fare in tourist class costs $140-190, depending on your itinerary. Meals are included. Intourist can arrange your railway trip in other ways. You can fly from Moscow to Irkutsk and take the Trans-Siberian back to the capitol. Those with less time can ride the Trans-Siberian as part of a Western tour group. Consult the booklet *Visiting the USSR* or a travel agent.

The 1980 Olympics in Moscow

If you'd like to be in Moscow during the 1980 Summer Olympics, it is not too early to begin planning now. All hotel reservations and tickets for the Games will be handled by Intourist through approved travel agents. Space is going to be tight, and the cost all but prohibitive for budget-minded travelers. The Russian Travel Bureau Inc., 20 East 46th St., New York, NY 10017, is publishing an *Olympic 1980 Newsletter* with up-to-date information. The prices for their tours begin at about $50 a day. CIEE also plans package tours to the Soviet Union with tickets to the Games included. If you know the Russian language and culture well, you may (with luck) be able to get hired as a guide for an Olympic tour. Check Intourist-approved travel agents for possibilities.

Moscow

Moscow humbles even the mightiest. There is no other city in the world which places such a high premium on sheer monumentality, and Soviet are incredibly proud of their capital. The bustle of the seven million Moscovites is scarcely noticed amidst the ten-lane avenues, giant posters of Lenin, and the huge "Stalinist-Gothic" hotels and apartment buildings. Moscow is undisputably the USSR's leading city, the nerve center for the entire country.

While Moscow is mentioned in the Russian chronicles as early as 1147, the city didn't flourish until the latter part of the fifteenth century, when Ivan III made Moscow the center of his United Kingdom. In 1711, Peter the Great moved the court to St. Petersburg (Leningrad) and Moscow declined in importance. The city regained its status in 1918 when the Bolsheviks made Moscow the capital again. During the industrialization of the 1930s, the population of the city soared. In the 1960s an extensive program of urban renewal and large-scale building was undertaken which has already led to the alteration of whole avenues beyond recognition (**Gorky Street** and **Kalinin Prospekt** being the most striking examples). "Moscow builds" has become the watchword of the day.

There has been a price to pay, as some Soviets would admit. Much of the city's old Russian charm has been sacrificed to make way for the new—an entire neighborhood of narrow winding streets, arcades, and pre-revolutionary structures was demolished to make room for the giant Rossiia Hotel, dubbed the "Moscow Hilton" by tourists and Soviet alike. What remains is a curious mixture of old churches and monasteries; pastel-colored baroque town houses; grandiose railway stations; gloomy and imposing apartment complexes and hotels constructed in post-war Stalin Gothic; all interspersed with the newest modern architecture. Moscow lacks Leningrad's harmony, but taken individually many of its buildings are fascinating, and nowhere else in the Soviet Union will you find a comparably inclusive expression of Russian and Soviet history in a city.

Note: Try to get a street map of Moscow before you go, since they are hard to come by there.

Food

Moscow is unquestionably the best city in the USSR for eating, whether your interest is traditional Russian cuisine or the more exotic fare of the different national republics. However, restaurants are few for such a large city, and their quality is uneven. Yet despite their inevitable crowds and slow service, the ambience at Moscow's restaurants will make your wait worthwhile.

Dining out for Russians is a festive occasion. They make an evening of it, with frequent breaks from eating to propose toasts, dance, and flirt. As tables are usually shared by different parties, you will often be invited to join in the festivities by those at your table. You may even be invited home, where the celebration usually continues into the wee hours.

A good meal will run $6-8 if you carefully watch your liquor consumption. To avoid crowds, eat early, even in mid-afternoon. A note at the end of the menu will tell you if the customary 5% service charge is included; if not, tip to that amount. For snacking, try the more modest establishments such as the cafeteria for *pirozhki* on Kuznetskii Most 7/9, behind the Bolshoi Theater or the self-service *blinnaia* at Ulitsa Kirova 14/2. There are also some very well-stocked *gastronoms* on the first few blocks of Ulitsa Gorkogo.

The best cuisine in Moscow is served in the second-floor dining rooms of the **National Hotel.** The specialty is delicious *Chicken Kiev* (boned chicken breasts filled with butter and herbs) which goes well with a bottle of *Tsinandali.*

Slavianskii Bazarr, Ulitsa Dvadtsat Piatogo Oktiabria 17. An old Moscow landmark, used to be a favorite restaurant of wealthy Moscow merchants and the intelligentsia. Stanislavskii and Nemirovich-Danchenko held a famous all-night conversation here which led to the formation of the Moscow Art Theater. Start off with a shot of vodka, *osetrina* (sturgeon), or *ikra* (caviar) and *bliny; Bifshteks* or chicken and *shampanskoe* (champagne).

Valdai, Prospekt Kalinina 19. Bottom floor, a cafeteria-style *pirozhkovaia,* second floor a pleasant bar and *shashlychnaia,* in large, modern premises across the street from Dom Knigi book store.

For more exotic fare from the national republics, try one of the following:

Aragvi, Ultisa Gorkogo 6, Georgian cuisine. Became famous during the reign of Stalin, Georgia's favorite son. Specialties include *satsivi* (cold chicken in a walnut sauce), *suluguni* (fried cheese), and *shashlyk* (shish kebab). Have a bottle of *Mukuzani* or *Tsinandali* with your meal.

Uzbekistan, Ulitsa Neglinnaia 29. A hangout for homesick Uzbeks, Kazakhs, and Tadjiks. Noisy and always crowded. Try *tkhumdulma* (boiled egg with a fried meat patty) or one of the soups, followed by *shashlyk* Uzbek style. Be sure to try the specially prepared Uzbek bread, baked on the premises. End your meal with native dessert wines (best are *Aleatiko* or *Uzbekistan*).

Ararat, Ulitsa Neglinnaia 4; Armenian cuisine. Offers a variety of tasty specialties, among them *solianka* Armenian style, broiled trout, *shashlyk* Ararat or *Liulia-kebab* (ground lamb), and excellent cognacs (best are *Yubileiny, Armenia, Yerevan,* and *Dvin*).

Sights

According to Alexsandr Hertzen (the nineteenth-century populist), the two most famous sights in Moscow were a bell that has never rung and a cannon that has never fired (both are the largest in the world—a piece that once chipped off the bell weighs eleven tons). These have been replaced in the twentieth century by the **Lenin Mausoleum** (in Red Square, in the Kremlin Wall). This imposing red granite structure contains the embalmed body of the founder of the Soviet State. You should not miss the opportunity to visit this shrine—Russians wait in line for hours for a glimpse, but there is a faster-moving line for foreigners (closed Monday and Friday, other days 10am-2pm, Sundays 10am-6pm). Behind the Mausoleum are the graves of Communist notables, among them Josef Stalin. In the Kremlin Wall itself are the ashes of Krupskaya, Lenin's wife, the writer Gorky, Leningrad party boss Kirov (whose assassination triggered the 1930s purges), America's John Reed (the eyewitness author of *Ten Days That Shook The World*), and the cosmonaut Yuri Gagarin.

If Moscow is Russia's heart, the **Kremlin** is Moscow's. This ancient fortress (*kreml* means "citadel") was built in 1156 by Yuri Dolgoruky, the city's founder; and its red brick walls, which date back to the late fifteenth-century, contain buildings, monuments, and treasures of unique cultural and historical importance for Russia. Outside the northeast wall lies **Krasnaia Ploshchad (Red Square)**, marked off at one end by the Historical Museum and at the other by the ten multi-colored, fairy tale domes of sixteenth-century **St. Basil's Cathedral.** (Ivan the Terrible supposedly lived up to his reputation by having the architect blinded to make sure he never designed a lovelier building.)

Within the walls of the Kremlin proper are a series of outstanding Orthodox churches, most notably: the **Annunciation Cathedral,** the tsar's own cathedral, with an iconostasis by the great icon painters Andrei Rublev and Theophanes the Greek; the **Assumption Cathedral,** where the tsars were crowned; and the **Archangel Cathedral,** where Ivan the Terrible and all other tsars before Peter the Great are buried. Also here is the **Armory Museum** (open 9:30am-6:30pm, closed Friday), including the Crown Jewels Exhibition and a priceless collection of royal regalia and riches covering eight centuries. The Kremlin also has one modern building—the huge **Palace of Congresses,** constructed in 1961 to house Party meetings and opera and ballet performances. Inside the **Alexandrovsky Gardens** the eternal flame burns atop the Tomb of the Unknown Soldier—a required visit for all foreign dignitaries.

From the Kremlin you can get almost anywhere in the city with relative ease—and getting there is often half the fun. Try a boat ride on the Moskva river (used for both sight-seeing and transportation) starting from the Kiev Station pier, and definitely use the **Metro,** itself one of the city's attractions. Begun in the early Five-Year Plans of the 1930s, the subway has stations of different designs and materials (marble, stainless steel, mosaics) and is kept spotlessly clean by hordes of broom-wielding *babushki*. Some of the more interesting stations are **Maiakovskaia, Kievskaia, Novaslobodskaia,** and the huge **Komsomolskaia.** Ride the subway out to the **Lenin Hills,** go up two escalators and go right till you come to the viewing area. Below you is the giant **Luzhniki Sports Complex,** including Lenin Stadium, the site of the 1980 Olympics; behind you stands **Moscow University.** On the way back, stop off at **Kropotkinskaia Ploshchad** (another interesting subway stop). Nearby is the **Moscow Swimming Pool,** an outdoor heated pool, open year-round. Walk from Kropotkinskaia Ulitsa for a stroll among some of

Moscow's oldest nineteenth-century homes of the aristocracy and intelligentsia. (A number are now museums.)

Moscow is a city of museums. The greatest is the **Tretiakov State Gallery** (10am-7pm, closed Mondays), which houses under its traditional peaked roofs the best collection of Russian and Soviet art. Look for the icons of Andrei Rublev (fifteenth century); and Theophanes the Greek (late fourteenth century); the magnificent historical paintings and portraits of the underrated Ilia Repin; the lush madness of Vrubel; the works of Ivanov, Serov, Surikov, and Levitan; and a slew of modern ''socialist-realist'' works. The **Pushkin Museum** (11am-5pm), has a good collection of Western art, French in particular, and if you want still more icons, they are in the **Rublev Museum of Early Art** (11am-6pm, closed Wednesdays), though few, unfortunately, are by Rublev himself. The **Museum of Serf Art** at Ostankino Palace (11am-5pm, closed Tuesdays and Wednesdays) was designed, built, and decorated by serfs.

The **Historical Museum** on Red Square (10:30am-5:30pm, Monday, Thursday, Sunday; noon-7pm Wednesday, Friday, and Saturday) is the country's greatest museum for Russian history. Nearby is the **Central Lenin Museum,** (11am-7pm, closed Mondays), which holds many personal belongings and curious memorabilia from Lenin's life.

Even if you don't make it to all the museums of Moscow's luminaries, you should visit the **Novodevichi Convent** where many of them are buried. In the placid setting of this beautiful old convent—the Uspensky Church is still used for Orthodox services—are the graves of Gogol, Chekhov, Stanislavski, Maiakovsky, and many others; there are also graves of political figures, most notably Khrushchev.

Another such institution is **Zagorsk Monastery,** located about two hours outside of Moscow by bus, and well worth the trip. Zagorsk has a museum, several beautiful cathedrals (including one with turquoise domes studded with golden stars), which in some cases contain their original iconostases (icon screens) by Rublev and his followers. Besides its architectural attractions—the main courtyard is a varied melange of styles from various centuries—Zagorsk is also one of the few functioning monasteries in the Soviet Union, and has its own theological seminary. The Orthodox services, with their ritual, choral singing, and flickering candles, are an impressive ceremony—but be modestly dressed and unobtrusive, or you may get a scolding.

Intourist can also arrange a trip from Moscow to **Yasnaia Poliana,** the museum estate of Leo Tolstoy. This beautiful area influenced Tolstoy tremendously and plays a major role in many of his works.

Shopping

The best deals for shopping are certainly at the hard currency *berioska* shops. Good buys on furs (rabbit and wolf) from Siberia, amber necklaces from the Baltic Coast, and hand-painted boxes from the villages of Palekh, Kholui, and Mstere.

Take a stroll down Kalinin Prospekt (Moscow's Fifth Avenue). **Dom Knigi** at #26, the large book store, sells the colorful propaganda posters. At the **Melodiia** Record Store (#40), you can get excellent bargains on classical albums, and watch Soviet teenagers fight for the few rock albums available.

Moscow abounds in second-hand stores where you can buy valuable family heirlooms or junk. The best is located near the French Embassy at 54-58

Dimitrav U.L. It has good bargains on samovars, paintings, and antiques. Be sure to get a certificate allowing you to take your purchase out of the country.

Evenings

Moscow can be a bargain paradise for the theater and ballet buff, who need pay only a few dollars to see world-famous companies. At the top of the list are the **Bolshoi Ballet** and the **Moscow Art Theater,** with a new theater on Tverskoi Boulevard and an old tradition going back to the turn of the century and the days of Stanislavskii, Chekhov and the young Gorky. Today Moscow youth prefer the more experimental and avant-garde **Sovremennik** and **Taganka** companies.

You will miss the above if you're in Moscow during the slack summer season, but don't despair completely. Puppetry here is a real treat, so if Moscow's famed **Obraztoov Puppet Theater** is in town, don't miss it; and the **Circus,** performing throughout the summer at Prospekt Vernadskogo 7 is an equal delight. Also check out the unique **Gypsy Theater** in the Hotel Sovietskaia and the program at the **Tchaikovsky Concert Hall.** Most of these events start at 7 or 7:30 and also finish early. Tickets and information about shows are available at sidewalk kiosks and in Intourist hotel service bureaus; if a performance is sold out, you can sometimes get a ticket—for no more than the original price—from a ticket holder in front of the theater before curtain time.

Moscow has a profusion of movie theaters; the two biggest are the handsome new theaters **Oktiabr** (prospekt Kalinina) and **Rossiia** (Pushkin Square). Films and times are listed for all theaters on special billboards, and in *Kinonedelia* (Filmweek).

In the absence of any real public nightlife, the best way to meet young people is in parks, cafés, or just on the street. Pushkin Square on Gorky Street, with its monument to Russia's greatest poet, is a gathering place for everybody, including students; flanking the monument is the Izvestiia building, a famous example of Soviet architecture of the 1920s which is still in use. The small park containing the monument to Karl Marx, across from the Bolshoi Theater, is another good place to meet young Russians. In the evenings, students, and young people congregate and stroll up and down the first few blocks of Gorky Street. If you feel like sitting down, check out:

Café Lira, ulitsa Gorkogo 19, entrance across from Pushkin Square. This is a popular youth-oriented café with food, drinks, and dancing to a vocalist and band on the bottom floor; drinks are expensive (2.20 roubles per cocktail).

Siniaia Ptitsa, ulitsa Chekhova 23 (near the Sadovoe Koltso). Moscow's closest approximation of a student discotheque.

Leningrad

In 1703, Tsar Peter the Great began to build a capital that would be more modern and accessible to Western Europe than was Moscow. So "over the bones of a hundred thousand serfs" was built St. Petersburg, the "window to the West" and the "Paris of the North." The city became Russia's major port and the gate to the trends, ideas, and fashions that entered Russia from the West, including Marxism in the 1870s. It became the center of the revolutionary movement, and in November 1917, the scene of the Bolshevik victory. Its name, changed to the more Russian-sounding **Petrograd** by Tsar Nicholas II in 1914, was changed again to Leningrad in 1924 to honor the founder of the Soviet state.

The grand Baroque and neoclassical buildings built by Peter's French, Italian, and Russian architects still stand today. From the ornate splendor of the **Winter Palace** to the simple Greek-revival style of the **Stock Exchange** and the **Smolnyi Institute,** Leningrad still exudes the grace and elegance of pre-revolutionary days. The historical center of the city is the **Peter and Paul Fortress.** Today, the major boulevards emanate in a pinwheel from the **Admiralty Building,** which once served as a major shipbuilding and naval center. **Nevsky Prospekt,** the Fifth Avenue of St. Petersburg, is the most famous of the broad *prospekty,* and usually teems with shoppers. The architectural harmony of the city is also reflected in its general layout—broad avenues meeting at right angles, arching bridges crossing canals, massive granite blocks forming graceful embankments. The central, pre-revolutionary part of the city has been well preserved by the Soviets, and the harmony and order Peter desired for his capital are still evident today. Many of the narrow back streets are also unchanged, and a twilight stroll through them may turn up hints of Dostoevsky's Raskolnikov and Gogol's Akaky Akakievich.

Maps of the city transport system can be purchased (48 kopeks) at any kiosk, but guidebooks of the city are much harder to find (especially in English), so we suggest purchasing one in the West.

Addresses and Telephone Numbers

Central Post Office: Ulitsa Soiuza Sviazi 9.

Central Telephone Exchange: Ulitsa Gertsena 3/5.

Money Changing: Exchange Office in Hotel Europeiskaia, Ulitsa Brodskogo 1/7 (one-half block off Nevsky Prospekt) is the most centrally located.

U.S. Consulate: Ulitsa Petralavrova 15 (tel. 725217).

Food

Leningrad may not have quite the array of top-rated restaurants that Moscow does, but there are still excellent ones here plus a variety of other kinds of places to choose from. On or near Nevsky are:

Sadko, corner of Nevsky and Ulitsa Brodskogo. Traditional Russian cuisine. Takes its reputation as Leningrad's "best" rather seriously—you'll probably need reservations and expect to have to pay 8 roubles apiece. You can do better in Moscow, but if this is your one chance for a fancy traditional dinner, go ahead.

Kavkazky, Nevsky Prospekt 25. Caucasian cuisine. Try the *kharcho* soup (a Georgian gazpacho); entrées of *shashlyk, chakhombili* of chicken (chicken in a spicy sauce); the *cherbureki* cakes of mutton, rice and parsley are good; also try the pickled red cabbage.

Baku, Ulitsa Sadovaia 12 (between Nevskii and Ulitsa Rakova). Azerbaidjan cuisine. Bottom floor more informal than the top. Recommended are: Cold appetizer of *satsivi* chicken in a heavy spicy sauce with red onions, *basturma* (a kind of shish kebab) and cold coffee with ice cream in it.

Metropol (directly across from the south side of Gostinyi Dvor). Traditional Russian cuisine. Not quite as full of foreign tourists as Sadko—a better place to meet Russians. Delicious *Chicken Kiev,* rumored to be the best in Leningrad.

Also on Nevsky (#24, across from the Kavkazky) is the **Ogonek,** probably Leningrad's nicest ice-cream parlor. Be sure you get into the larger room on the left side—potted plants and pleasant, quiet atmosphere in which to indulge yourself on ice cream, champagne, wine, candy, fruit, etc. Another specialty café is the **Russkie Samovary,** ulitsa Sadovaia 49 (near Ploshchad Mira), where you can drink tea from samovars and eat excellent *bliny* and pastries in a semi-rustic atmosphere of wooden furniture and peasant crockery.

For pastry, try the **Sever** pastry shop downstairs at Nevsky 44/46. If you're in the University area, drop in for breakfast, brunch, or just a cup of expresso coffee at the **stolovaia** on Tamozhenny lane (turn right off University Embankment at the Museum of Anthropology; the second entrance on the right side is the cafeteria's). This and any of the other university *stolovye* are excellent places to meet students—M8 supposedly serves the best food. It can be reached by walking parallel along the main (and original) University of Leningrad building away from the Neva, and then turning directly left. There will be a small sign with an "8" on it near the door. The **Café Moskva** on Nevsky a few blocks to the south of Gostinyi Dvor was unofficially known as **Café Saigon** during the Vietnam War, and usually boasts a variety of undesirable, but sometimes interesting types—black-market dealers, university dropouts, etc. A small, inexpensive, relatively unknown restaurant is **Demiania Ukha** on Gorky Prospekt across from the Lenin Park—the fish soup served here rivals the best of New England. An inexpensive café frequented by students is the **Fregat,** Bolshoi Prospekt 39/14 on Vasilievsky Island.

If you want just to buy food, there are *gastronoms* everywhere. The most resplendent is at Nevsky 56, a prerevolutionary structure with a high ceiling, stained-glass windows and an illuminated liquor section that looks like a Cecil B. de Mille Shrine to Food and Drink (it does, in fact, carry a good selection of both).

Sights

For a splendid overview of the city, climb up to the dome of **St. Isaac's Cathedral,** a massive example of nineteenth-century civic-religious architecture (open 11am-6pm; Tuesdays 11am-4pm; closed Wednesday). Nearby, on Decembrists' Square overlooking the Neva is Falconet's **Monument to Peter the Great,** the first and most famous memorial sculpture in Russia, and the inspiration for Pushkin's equally famous poem *The Bronze Horseman.*

The major axis of activity in Leningrad is the three-mile stretch of **Nevsky Prospekt.** This thoroughfare was recommended by no less an authority than Gogol, and you should get acquainted with it via a trolley-bus trip or, better yet by walking down one side and up the other. **Dom Knigi** (House of Books) at the intersection of the Griboedov Canal and Nevsky is the Singer

Sewing Machine Building of pre-revolutionary days. Across the street and down a few blocks is **Gostinyi Dvor,** Leningrad's immense department store. Nevsky also links up a number of important squares; **Palace Square** behind the **Winter Palace;** the **Square of the Arts,** with its Pushkin statue; **Ostrovsky Square** and the **Pushkin Theater;** and finally, at the terminus of the avenue, **Nevsky Square.** Off this square stands the **Aleksandr Nevsky Monastery,** containing several cathedrals (services are held in the largest) and two cemeteries where Dostoevsky and Tchaikovsky are buried, along with many other eighteenth and nineteenth-century luminaries. (To get inside the cemeteries you'll have to buy a ticket to the museum.)

For a good view of the Neva from its broadest point, make your way to the **Kirov Bridge.** On the right is the **Peter and Paul Fortress,** dating from the founding of the city itself. Worth a visit to see the beautiful little Baltic-style church (Peter the Great and subsequent stars buried inside), the prison for political offenders, or just to sun yourself on the strip of beach under the walls, as many Leningraders do on summer days. Another pleasant place for relaxing is the nearby **Strelka** (point) of Vasilievsky Island, with its nineteenth-century **Stock Exchange** (now Naval Museum) disguised as a Greek temple and framed by the two great **Rostral Columns**—originally ship beacons, they're now lit at night on holidays. Behind this area lie the eighteenth-century buildings of Leningrad State University.

Superimposed on the contours of classical Petersburg, however, are the features of modern Leningrad, *Gorod-geroi,* the "hero-city" of revolution and war. Leningrad's revolutionary heritage is memorialized in many places; the **Finland Station,** where Lenin arrived in 1917 to take command of the Bolshevik forces (Engine 293, which brought him, is preserved here in a glass case); the **Smolnyi,** Bolshevik headquarters (special permits needed to see the inside); the **Marsovo Pole** (Field of Mars), where an eternal flame and funeral music from loudspeakers commemorate the Bolsheviks who fell in the revolution; and the battleship **Aurora,** which fired the shot signalling the storming of the Winter Palace and is now a floating museum (Monday-Thursday, 11am-4:30pm, Friday, 11am-2:30pm, Sunday 11am-5:30pm) anchored across from the swank new Leningrad Hotel. The vast **Museum of the Great October Revolution** (open Mon. and Fri. noon-8pm; Tues., Wed., and weekends 11am-7pm; closed Thurs.) is worth a quick visit even if you're not devoted to the subject.

The **Hermitage,** Russia's largest and greatest museum, is so vast that several short visits is the only way to approach it. Pick up a museum guide at the entrance (24 kopeks)—it will help even if you don't read Russian. Russian art is represented from early icons to the nineteenth-century *Peredvizhniki* (Wanderers). For classicists, there is an incredible collection of art from the Cimmerian Bosphorus from the fifth and fourth century B.C. In Spanish works, it is surpassed only by the Museo del Prado in Madrid; the French School is better presented only in the Louvre, while in Dutch paintings (especially in Rembrandts), it ranks first (open 11am-7pm daily; Fri. 11am-9pm; closed Mon.).

The **Russian Museum** specializes in the art of the Soviet period; among the literary museums are the beautifully preserved **Pushkin apartment,** where he died of his dueling wounds (Moika embankment 12; open 11am-5:30pm; Mondays 11am-4pm, closed Tuesdays) and the recently opened **Dostoevsky Museum** in the writer's last apartment. (Kuznechnyi lane 5/2; open 10am-6:30pm; closed Mondays. Feature films of Dostoevsky's works are shown here on weekends.)

Reminders of the blockade of Leningrad during World War II are everywhere, from the street sign still kept on Nevsky warning about enemy shelling to the **Piskarevskoe Memorial Cemetery,** where the half million victims of the blockade are buried under the inscription ". . . No one is forgotten, and nothing is forgotten." These are critical to understanding the country today.

Leningrad, once you're off the bustle of Nevsky Prospekt, is a city made for leisurely walking. Savor its beauties with an evening promenade (preferable during the White Nights) along one of the main embankments or, more intimately, along the smaller waterways: the Moika River, the Griboedov Canal, or the Fontanka River. A stroll along the **Palace Embankment** of the Neva toward the **Summer Gardens** will take you past many former embassies, and beautiful examples of nineteenth-century classic revival architecture. Also stop to contemplate some of the interesting cathedrals: the Slavic-revival gingerbread of the **Church of the Bleeding Savior** which is a copy of St. Basil's, in Moscow; the monumental **Holy Virgin of Kazan Cathedral,** now converted into a **Museum of the History of Religion and Atheism** (both these churches are along the Griboedov Canal); and the Baroque grace of the **Nikolskii Cathedral,** near the intersection of the Griboedov and Kriukov canals. Another pleasant way to cover much the same ground (or rather, water) is by a cruise on Leningrad's canals (60 kopeks, leaving from the pier in front of the Hermitage).

Daytrips

Leningrad is surrounded by a string of sumptuous eighteenth-century summer palaces and estates which, while badly damaged during the war, are being restored to their former beauty. All are accessible by bus, electric train, or better yet, a hydrofoil ride on the Bay of Finland (check with your guide or hotel Service Bureau for details). Don't miss at least one of these: **Petrodvorets,** the Versailles-style palace estate of golden fountains, and waterfalls, begun by Peter the Great; you can skip the palace interior but follow the sound of shrieks and giggles to the "joke fountains" which, activated by one mis-step, suddenly drench their unwitting victims. The town of **Pushkin,** formerly Tsarskoe Selo, has a huge parks system, the lyceum where Pushkin studied, and the country's most important Pushkin exhibit. **Pavlovsk,** built by Catherine the Great down the road from Pushkin, has recently had its entire interior restored to a jewel-like brilliance and has some attractive parks as well. And if you're interested in what the country *dacha* of a leading nineteenth-century painter looks like, take the trip out to the **Penates** of Ilia Repin.

It is also possible to make a daytrip to **Tallinn,** the capital of the Baltic province of Estonia only a few hours from Leningrad by train. Arrangements must be made through Intourist.

Evenings

The **White Nights Festival** prolongs Leningrad's theater and entertainment season through the end of July. The major company is the **Kirov Opera and Ballet,** housed in Theater Square in the former **Marjinsky Theater,** which witnessed the classic performances of Pavlova and

Chaliapin and where all the famous Russian operas were premiered. Nowadays, however, the ballet is probably better here than the opera; try to see one of the Tschaikovsky standards. For these and other events, check the large schedules posted inside Service Bureaus or on the outdoor notice boards or ticket kiosks. The nightlife here is, as in Moscow, pretty bleak. One of the better spots is the bar at the **Hotel Oktiabrskaia** on Nevsky near the Moscow Railway Station (a relatively risqué area after nightfall). Two roubles will get you admission and drinks up to that amount in the smoke-filled room populated largely by young Leningraders and Finns; recorded rock (dancing and generally livelier tempo after around ten), but here as elsewhere they pull the plug at 11:30pm sharp. For later diversion, you'll have to resort to a foreign currency bar: the most centrally located is in the Sadko restaurant on Nevsky, which tries to emulate a cosmopolitan atmosphere with dim lighting and some old Beatles and Credence records, though even here they may not stay open till their advertised closing time of 3am. You can also hear your favorites played in the ''American Bar'' down in the basement of the Hotel Leningrad.

YUGOSLAVIA

$1U.S.=18Dinars (ND)   **1ND=$.055**

Historically torn between East and West, Yugoslavia has been the anomaly of Eastern Europe. Preaching and practicing the theory of "different roads to socialism," she has managed to preserve her freedom from Moscow while gradually opening her borders to Western influence, trade, and tourism.

The diplomats at Versailles created Yugoslavia in 1919, and it is less one country than a federation of several tiny ones. Seven distinct peoples in six republics speak five languages, have three religions (Catholic, Orthodox, and Muslim), two alphabets (Latin and Cyrillic), and one boss (Tito). Thanks to his single-mindedness and incredible popularity, Tito has managed to hold off the German invasion in World War II, build a country out of the hatred of a civil war, stand up to Stalin and a decade of almost total isolation, and develop Yugoslavia's unique combination of socialism and capitalism that has given her people the highest standard of living in Eastern Europe.

The division of Yugoslavia between conflicting cultures began even before the arrival of the Slavs (who migrated from Poland in the fifth century). In the fourth century, the Roman Emperor Theodosius divided the empire in two—the Latin-speaking, western half ruled from Rome, and the Greek eastern half controlled by Constantinople. The dividing line ran right down the middle of present-day Yugoslavia. The dichotomy between Roman and Byzantine influences was the first strong divisive force in Yugoslav history, and domination by Venetians, Turks, Hungarians, Austrians, and Bulgars continued the process of fragmentation, creating regions with strikingly different national heritages.

More recently, Yugoslavia has managed to spurn Soviet patronage while bowing to a subtler outside influence—Western-style consumerism. Smuggling household appliances via Trieste has developed into a kind of game. More people wear blue jeans in Zagreb than in San Francisco, and the new sign of success is owning a color TV. On the other hand, the Tito regime's political independence seems positively reflected in the man-on-the-street's outspokenness and the availability of Western, non-communist press.

Yugoslavia's six republics still claim strong, even primary, allegiance from their inhabitants. **Slovenia** in the northwest is full of Alpine villages, hikers, and Austrian ways, and is the most prosperous and industrialized section of the country. **Croatia** extends almost all the way down the Adriatic Coast, Yugoslavia's most delightful, beautiful (and touristed) area, and north into the rich plains near Hungary. **Serbia,** long controlled by Turks, is even more fertile, the granary for the country and the home of some Byzantine frescoed churches and monasteries. The rugged mountains near the coast sweep into the lower half of Yugoslavia—**Bosnia-Hercegovina** remains over 50% Muslim, and every village has its little bazaar and Turkish minarets. The twentieth century gets lost in the hills of **Montenegro** and **Macedonia** where oxcarts outnumber cars; and family feuds and local songs and dances are the main entertainments.

Transportation and Orientation

Transportation is part of the adventure. If you're driving or hitching, remember that Yugoslavia has one of the world's highest accident rates. Except for the coastal route, the roads are hair-raising, and Yugoslavs tear along the dotted line like there's no tomorrow.

Trains tend to be slow and late, and the railway system has notable gaps—the entire coast south of **Split,** for example. There are no student discounts for long trips inside the country, and it's cheaper to buy regular fares at or to the border even when you're entering or leaving Yugoslavia—because you avoid surcharges tacked on for international paperwork. This doesn't apply, though, for through tickets like Venice-Istanbul. **Yugotours,** 350 Fifth Ave., New York, NY 10001, sells a 22-day **Yugo-Rail** pass for $69, but it's not worth it.

Buses, which pick up the slack with varying degrees of success, are cheaper, more direct, and offer a chance to meet the locals. Try to control a window, though; Yugoslavs believe drafts cause colds and keep them shut even in blistering heat. Along the coast, opt for ferries whenever possible—travel by water is always more pleasant and often more direct. The national airline, with service to all provincial capitals as well as **Split** and **Dubrovnik,** has about the cheapest domestic rates on the Continent. Hitching goes well along the coast and on the main Zagreb-Belgrade-Skopje road, but be prepared for long waits elsewhere.

Women may not want to travel alone away from the coast. Even if nothing serious happens, the petty hassles and pawings you will be subjected to will take away from your enjoyment of the country. Take a hint from the natives—Yugoslav women rarely travel alone, and they are considered fair game if they do.

When you arrive at the border, you'll be granted a visa valid for ninety days. Even if the controller waves you through without stamping your passport, insist on it, or you'll have a tough time convincing hotels and banks that you haven't sneaked in to blow up military installations. When you check your bags at a *garderoba,* don't be alarmed when they ask for your passport—they need to copy your name, for no apparent reason. When you hit a town, look around the station for a tourist information service—one will invariably be nearby, with an accommodation service as well. If you want to buy train tickets in advance (a very good idea) or change money, the streets are loaded with tourist agencies. **Atlas** (which serves as American Express), **Kompas, Putnik,** and **Generalturist** are the biggest.

There are quite a few student hostels *(ferijalni dom)* and public hotels, and they're clean and inexpensive at around 60ND a night maximum. If you can, write them for reservations. Also reserve at the sparkling **International Youth Centers** at Rovinj, Dubrovnik, and Budva, all run by **Naromtravel,** Moše Pijade #12, 11000 Belgrade. They have a list of IYHF Youth Hostels also. Hotels are almost totally out of student range. Beware of any places that advertise prices in American dollars. Campsites, on the other hand, are thick as flies, especially along the coast, and cost about 45ND a head. You can get a list from **Yugoslav National Tourist Office,** 630 Fifth Ave., New York, NY 10020—they have maps also. People will hang around the bus and train stations and offer you *sobe* (private accommodations). This sounds sleazy, but it isn't—in a country without many phones, and in which official tourist housing is rigidly fixed at exorbitant rates, this is usually the only way a respectable *pensione* can get the word out. You can save money and occasionally meet some wonderful people this way—just be sure that the place isn't 20 kilometers out of town.

Along the coast and in the major cities you'll have no problem finding people who speak English. Away from the tourist areas few people speak any foreign language, although you can often get by with a little German. If you are staying in Yugoslavia for any length of time, or are planning to head into more remote areas, you will be better prepared to cope with basics if you invest in a good phrase book. And if you're going to the eastern half of the country, be prepared to learn the Cyrillic alphabet if you want to read the street signs.

As the only Eastern European currency not tied to the rouble, the Yugoslav dinar fluctuates according to changes in the world monetary markets. The tourist should, however, take advantage of the provision allowing one to bring in up to 1500ND in notes not exceeding 100ND denominations; the exchange rate in the West is more favorable than in Yugoslavia itself. Since the 1966 currency reform, practically all prices are quoted in ND (new dinars). Old customs die hard, however, and many people still talk in old dinars. So don't be alarmed if the woman you buy an apple from asks for 200 dinars instead of 2. Don't bother running around trying to find a good exchange rate—it's the same everywhere, although banks will never rake off a handling commission, while tourist bureaus sometimes will.

One final note—Yugoslavs rise and retire early, and don't switch to summer hours. So if you're coming from Italy or Germany, sunrise is one hour earlier. But even if you're a late sleeper, stores are usually open 8am-8pm, and banks until 7pm.

Food

The Middle East meets Europe again in Yugoslav cuisine. *Strudel* and *baklava* find common ground, the delicate European veal is skewered like shishkebab, coffee is Turkish. The cuisine varies locally, influenced always by the nearest neighbor. Thus, Slovene food is practically Austrian, Croatian has Hungarian overtones, Bosnian and Montenegran are essentially Turkish. National dishes include *cevapčiči* (chunks of ground beef) and *raznjiči* (lamb chunks roasted on a skewer). *Teleće pečenje* (roast veal) is a popular Croatian dish, often eaten with *ajvar,* a delicious cold sauce made from eggplant and paprika. Paprikas are also used in *sataraš* (with pork and tomato), in fish dishes, and are served stuffed with meat. Along the coast, be sure to try *lignje* (baby squid) and also *pršut* (smoked Dalmatian ham) usually eaten with *paski sir,* the sheep cheese from the Island of Pag.

Try putting together a picnic lunch at a local grocery or village market. With your fruit eat a Serbian cheese such as *kackavalj,* made from sheep's milk, snow white and firm. In the north, try *kransjka kolbasa,* an Austrian-style sausage. Top off your meal with a local wine, either dry and white (*žilavka*) or sweet and red (*dingač*).

Šljivovica (plum brandy) is the national liquor: strong, harsh, and dirt cheap, and guaranteed to make you gasp; close your eyes and pretend it's cod liver oil. *Vinjak,* a Yugoslav cognac, is just as strong but much tastier.

Slovenia

The traveler will find Slovenia a gentle introduction to Yugoslavia. There's more Westernization and more comfort than in any other region except the coastal resorts to the south—hitchhiking is dependable, and festivals and cultural events are frequent. But most of Slovenia is still quiet and rural. Hikers in corduroy knickers, heading for **Bohinj** or **Bled,** tramp the streets of **Ljubljana,** the regional capital. The beaches at **Koper** and **Piran** are remarkably untouristed, although the government is pushing yachting ports at **Bernardin** and **Portorož.** The region is small, and you can go from sea to mountains in about four hours. Trains don't go everywhere, but buses do; a trip from Ljubljana to **Maribor** takes about three hours and costs 50ND.

Ljubljana

Ljubljana, the industrial capital of Slovenia, brings to mind a Léger painting—square and gray. But the small **Old Town,** the predictably severe **Castle** on the hill overlooking the town, and the river which winds through the town, all retain a provincial charm that makes a day or two worthwhile. Ljubljana has Yugoslavia's best university—the only one accredited by other European countries—and there's a wealth of cultural activity and nightlife beneath the stolid exterior.

Addresses and Telephone Numbers

Tourist Office: Kompas at Titova Cesta 12 (tel. 20-032) and **Generalturist,** Gosposvetska 7 (tel. 21-908) are both open 7am-7pm, will provide tourist information, and help find rooms free of charge.

Information Center: Titova Cesta 11 (tel. 23-212) is open 7am-8pm and has an English-speaking staff and an accommodation service.

Student Tourist Office (Mladiturist): Celovška 49 (tel. 312-185). They also help find rooms and have excellent information on travel in the mountains, as well as a list of IYHF Youth Hostels. During July and August, open 9am-2pm.

American Express (Atlas): Titova Cesta 25 (tel. 320-852).

Post Office and **Phones:** beside the Railway Station.

Alpine Club: Dvorzakova 9 (tel. 312-553). Maps and information about trails in the Mount Triglav area.

Laundromat: Pralnica Likalnica on Vratace. Open Mon.-Sat. 8am-noon and 2-6pm. They are rare in Yugoslavia, so take advantage of it while you're here.

Accommodations

The various tourist agencies will gladly find a room for you faster than you can, but may not understand that you are on a limited budget. However, it's easy to find alternative lodgings for students, especially during the summer when most dorm rooms are vacant.

Studentski Domovi, Vecna pot 31 (tel. 23-735). A university dorm; depending on the room sizes, lodgings cost 30-50ND per night. Open only in July and August, and closed on the weekends. Take bus #14 from Titova Cesta, the main drag. Official registration closes at 2pm, but if you get there later someone will help you out.

Dom Fakultete za Sociologijo, Titova 102 (tel. 341-461). Take bus #6 for similar dorm rooms at similar prices; a single room costs 70ND.

Dom Studentov, Ilirska 2 (tel. 314-542). English-speaking; again, open only in summer. Call to make sure it's open.

Gostilne Zibert on Trata 9 is a lovely restaurant that rents out rooms for about 75ND for a single with bath. Bus #8 from center.

Autocamp Yežica, Titova 260a (tel. 341-113). About 8km away, it offers tent space and three free pools for about 40ND. Take bus #6 from the Station.

Sights

From the Train Station, walk four blocks to the right onto Titova Cesta, the main street, and get a city map from one of the hotels and tourist agencies that line it. Continue walking south, to the medieval **Old Town,** built beside the old Roman military camp. Cross the river (where public offenders used to be caged and dunked) to the **Market** near the **Town Hall,** and wander around the unchanged streets. If you have the legs for it, the path to the **Castle** has a terrific panorama of Slovenia. Once you're back down, check out the **Cathedral** and Franciscan Church for lovely interpretations of German Baroque and indigenous rural art.

During the summer, Ljubljana has a major cultural festival, with events nearly every night. There is also an opera house, concert hall, and several theaters. The Information Office has schedules and programs.

Near Ljubljana

Bled is probably the most accessible resort town from Ljubljana, about a seventy-minute bus ride (50ND round trip) to the north. There's also a

Railway Station at **Lesce-Bled,** 3 kilometers away; take a local from Ljubl-jana or Belgrade. A glacier scooped out a tiny lake at the foot of the **Julian Alps,** leaving an even tinier island in the middle (20ND round trip), upon which early Christians built a pilgrimage church. At one end, smart hotels house wealthy European tourists, but along the other shores (especially the far end, near the boathouse) there's free swimming and fishing. A **castle**—owned by the Bishop of Brixen since 1004 and loaned out to various feudal nobles until Austrian hegemony—dominates the scene from a huge bluff (admission 10ND).

For accommodations, there are various *sobe* in Bled which cost 80-100ND per night (showers extra). Your best bet may be the IYHF **Youth Hostel Bledec,** Grajska 17 (tel. 312-185), about halfway up the road to the castle. There are fifty beds for 45ND with an IYHF card, 60ND without. **Camping Sobet,** on its own lake and quite plush, has camping sites and bungalows two kilometers away in Lesce: it's open May through September (tel. 77-500).

Kranjska Gora, like Bled, is a small picturesque town by an alpine lake. This is what Austria was like twenty years ago: a hiker's paradise during summer, and a fine inexpensive ski area during winter. The **Tourist Bureau** in the town (tel. 88-437) can get you a private room, but expect to pay 90ND during July and August, and 70ND the rest of the year.

Serbia (Srbija)

Serbia takes up most of the eastern half of Yugoslavia, and varies im-

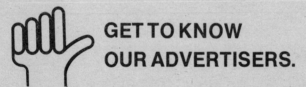
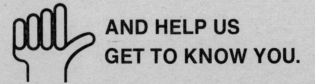

Get to know our advertisers.

Circle the names of the companies from which you'd like to receive FREE information:

Auto Europe (p. 38)   Irish Tourist Board (p. 49)

CIEE Student Travel Services (p. 19)   Kemwel Auto Group (p. 39)

Eurailpass (Inside Front Cover)   Wembly Auto International (p. 40)

Europe-by-Car (p. 34)

Eurorent (p. 46)

Fiat (p. 29)

IBUSZ Hungarian Travel Bureau (p. 54)

Help us get to know you.

In order to suit your travel needs better with each new edition, it helps us to know a little about you:

1. Occupation: Student Non-Student
2. Age: 15-18 19-22 23-26 27-30 31-40 over
3. Are you traveling: Alone With one friend With two or more friends With family
4. Length of stay in Europe: 2 wks. or less 2-6 wks. 6 wks.-3 mos. 3-6 mos. over 6 mos.
5. Primary reason for travel: Study Work Pleasure
6. Plan to spend in Europe (exclusive of transatlantic travel): $200-600 600-1000 1000-1400 1400-1800 1800-2500 over
7. Mode of transportation to Europe: Commercial Flight Charter Flight Commercial Ship Standby or Budget Flight
8. Mode of transportation within Europe: Rented Car Purchased Car Hitch Train Caravan Air Travel
9. Primary mode of accommodation: Camping Hotels Hostels University Friends Other
10. Did you carry: a backpack a suitcase
11. How many times have you been to Europe before: 0 1 2 3 4 or more
12. How did you hear about **Let's Go?** Friend Bookstore Ad Article Travel Service
13. Please circle the countries you plan to visit:
    Austria Belgium Bulgaria Czechoslovakia Denmark Finland France Germany-West Germany-East Great Britain Greece Hungary Iceland Ireland Israel Italy Luxembourg Morocco Netherlands Norway Poland Portugal Romania Spain Sweden Switzerland Turkey USSR Yugoslavia

Name

Address

City   State   Zip

HSA distributes other great guidebooks.
Order now for your next trip:

I enclose check _____ money order _____ in the amount of
_____. (Mass. residents add 5% sales tax)

Let's Go: The Budget Guide to Europe 1979-80	$7.45*
Let's Go: The Budget Guide to Britain & Ireland 1979-80	$6.45
Let's Go: The Budget Guide to France 1979-80	$5.45
Let's Go: The Budget Guide to Italy 1979-80	$5.45
CIEE Whole World Handbook 1978-79	$5.45
Where to Stay USA 1978-79	$5.45
The Budget Traveler's Latin America 1979-80	$6.45
The Budget Traveler's Asia 1979-80	$6.45

The above prices include $1.50 for postage and handling.
For air delivery outside the U.S. and Canada add $4.00.

**(Don't forget to fill in your name and
address on the other side!)**

----------------- FOLD HERE AND FASTEN -----------------

Name _____

Address _____

_____

FIRST CLASS
PERMIT NO. 34979
BOSTON, MASS.

Business Reply Mail
No postage stamp necessary if mailed in the United States

Postage will be paid by:

Let's Go Travel Guides

Harvard Student Agencies, Inc.

Thayer Hall B

Harvard University

Cambridge, MA 02138

Getting there is half the fun.
HSA Travel shows you how.

☐Charters to Europe
☐International Student ID Cards
☐Eurail & Britrail Passes
☐European, Inter-Asian, African Student Charters
☐International Youth Hostel Cards
☐Travel Insurance
☐Rent-a-car in Paris
☐Tours to Europe and the USSR
☐All Let's Go publications, including Europe,
☐France, Italy, and Britain & Ireland

(Just Ask)

name_____

address_____

Harvard Student Agencies Travel.

Comments? suggestions...

Name ______________________

Address ______________________

____

FIRST CLASS
PERMIT NO. 34979
BOSTON, MASS.

Business Reply Mail

No postage stamp necessary if mailed in the United States

Postage will be paid by:

Harvard Student Agencies Travel
Thayer Hall B
Harvard University
Cambridge, MA 02138

Name ______________________

Address ______________________

____

FIRST CLASS
PERMIT NO. 34979
BOSTON, MASS.

Business Reply Mail

No postage stamp necessary if mailed in the United States

Postage will be paid by:

Let's Go Travel Guides

Harvard Student Agencies, Inc.

Thayer Hall B

Harvard University

Cambridge, MA 02138

mensely, from the northern grain fields of **Vojvodina** to forested hills and vineyards near **Belgrade.** Further south are the mountainous sheeplands of the primitive **Kosovo** region. At various times, Serbia was an independent state; and during the thirteenth and fourteenth centuries, splendid, richly-frescoed monasteries sprang up along the Ibar River at **Žica** near **Kraljevo,** **Sopoćani** near **Novi Pazar,** and **Lazarica.** There's a famous fifteenth-century fortress at **Smederevo,** 60 kilometers from Belgrade. But this is not an especially touristed area of Yugoslavia (although an attractive one), with good reason—the north is accessible but looks like Kansas, while the south requires a patient disposition and good health if you're planning to leave the beaten path.

Belgrade (Beograd)

The capital of both Serbia and Yugoslavia, Belgrade is a surprisingly cosmopolitan city, and lacks the modern sterility associated with socialist capitals. Belgrade centers on a jutting point of land at the meeting of the **Danube** and **Sava** Rivers. Cardboard Communist-modern architecture alternates with nineteenth-century palaces, a few narrow Turkish-style streets, and a lone mosque (on Godspodar Jevremova). There is good reason for the heterogeneity of the city, for Belgrade has been destroyed and rebuilt countless times since its founding in the third century B.C.

The diversity of its cultural heritage lends Belgrade an atmosphere all its own. The tree-lined streets and crowded sidewalk cafés around Trg Republike are reminiscent of Vienna or Budapest; and the shopping opportunities, especially for leather goods, equal those anywhere in Europe. Visit the

Turkish fortress at **Kalemegdan Park** when the sun is setting over the two rivers, lose yourself in the narrow streets of the **old quarter** behind Studentski Trg, or linger in the cafés on fashionable **Terazije**—it won't take you long to sense Belgrade's atmosphere.

Orientation

It's tough to orient yourself in Belgrade because street signs and directions are in Cyrillic. The people at the **Tourist Information Offices** (look for big "i" signs at Terazije, Trg Republike, and Trg Bratsva i Jedinstva by the Railway and Bus Stations) are the most reliable and efficient sources of information. Someone there will speak English. The main information center is in the pedestrian underpass by the Albanija building at the beginning of Terazije, open 8am-8pm. **Inex Tourist,** on Trg Republike, around the corner from the underpass, supplies good free maps of Belgrade (save your dinars). At least two book shops in town carry English-language and West European paperbacks; try the **Antikvarijat** at Knez Mihajlova 35 or **Jugoslovenska Knjica,** Knez, Mihajlova 2, in the Albanija building. Both book stores are open 8am-8pm. Any of the above places will give you a free copy of *Beogradskope* (the monthly schedule of events). Bus and tram services are frequent and excellent: 3ND within the city, 6ND to suburbs.

Addresses and Telephone Numbers

Main Information Center: At underpass by Albanija building (tel. 629-522).

Student Cultural Center: Maršala Tita 48. Has student information and an English library.

Yus (Naromtravel): Moše Pijade 12 (tel. 331-610 and 339-898). For 25% student reductions on Yugoslav trains (international lines only), and reservations in their student centers on the Adriatic coast. Open daily except Sundays 8am-4pm. Work opportunities for a few Americans exist in the International Youth Centers—write for details. **Karavan Student Travel Agency,** Takovska 12 (tel. 337-853), open weekdays 7am-8pm, Sat. 8am-1pm. Bookings on student charter flights.

American Express (Atlas): Moše Pijade 11, 11000 Belgrade.

Post and **Telephone:** Post Office No. 1, Takovska 2.

Bus Station: Turist Biro (tel. 23-465).

Bank: Beogradska Banka, opposite the Albanija building on Kolarčeva, open 24 hours a day.

Police: (tel. 92).

Medical Emergency: (tel. 94).

U.S. Embassy: Kneza Milosa 50 (tel. 645-655), office hours in summer 7am-4:30pm. The USIS maintains a reading room at Cika Ljubina 19 (tel. 626-778), open 10am-7pm Mon.-Fri.

Canadian Embassy: Proleterskih Brigada 69 (tel. 434-524, 434-505/7).

Accommodations

Student hotels and the IYHF Youth Hostel are the best choices for cheap lodging. The former are spartan, but generally clean and friendly. At present only three are open to individual travelers (and only between July 10 and September 30). Except in the larger hotels, few people speak English and it

is difficult to get information by phone. Before you set out for one of the
student houses, phone to make certain someone is there, and in whatever
language you can, find out if you can be accommodated. You may avoid
making the trip for nothing.

Studentski Grad, II block Tosin Bunar 145, Novi Beograd (tel. 604-566).
Located across the river from the center; singles, doubles, and triples go for
55ND, 90ND, and 12$ND respectively. Open July through September. Call
ahead. Take bus #36 from Zeleni Venac Bus Station, which is 200 meters
down the hill from Hotel Moskva on Terazije.

Mika Mitrović, Kralja Vladimira 33 (tel. 26-968). Far out, take tram #9 or
10. About 60ND for a single room, 100ND for a double, 140ND for a triple.
Call ahead.

Mladost, Bulevar Jugoslavenske Narodne Armije (JNA) 56a (tel. 463-846), is
clean, modern, and near a park and swimming pool. Take tram #9 or 10 to
Kapetan Zarisica, then ask. About a five-minute walk from the tram stop.
70-100ND per person, depending on number of beds in the room. Less with
Hostel card. Open year round. If full, there is a **workers hotel** across the street
from where you get off the tram. Officially only for Yugoslavs, but it sometimes admits foreigners (a small bribe helps). A dump, but very cheap at
40-50ND. No sign, so you have to search a bit.

If you are stuck, the **Putnik** and **Lasta** offices, Trg Bratsva i Jedinstva 1,
opposite the Train Station (tel. 641-259 and 641-251, respectively), should
be able to find you a room in a private apartment, most of which are centrally
located. One or the other of them is open Mon.-Sat. 7am-8pm, Sun. 10am-
3pm. Although private rooms are supposed to be divided by category, these
agencies do not seem to tell you about any costing less than 80ND for a
single or 140ND for a double. If you want to try your luck by hanging around
the Train Station in the evening, you may be approached. Don't hesitate to
haggle—it is expected.

If you arrive after they are closed, you might have to seek out a hotel,
most of which are quite expensive in summer.

Hotel Balkoni, Prizrenska ul. 2 (tel. 325-042). Located in the center. Most
rooms are expensive, but it does have a few singles for 90ND and a few
doubles for 150ND. Ask nicely and insist you are broke.

Hotel Astorija, Milovana Milovanavića ul. (tel. 645-422). Very close to Train
Station if you arrive late. Again, it does have a few cheap rooms. Don't
hesitate to try to bargain with the desk clerk. Singles 85ND and doubles from
140ND.

Several camping sites are available, but they're far from the city and the
mosquitoes are fierce. **Kosutnjak,** Kneza Viseslava 17 (tel. 555-127) is set
in some woods not far from a swimming pool. Take a bus heading for
Barnovo Brdo—#23, 31, 33, 37, or 58. There are bungalows from 50ND
per person, and camping is 25ND. **Nacional,** Bezanijska kosa (tel. 602-
024), in Novi Beograd, near the Autoput. Camping 24ND per person, bungalows from 85ND per person.

Food

At self-service restaurants a substantial meal can be found for as little as
30ND. If you know little about Serbian food and less about Serbian names,
these places let you point to what looks good. **Zagreb,** Obilicev Venac 29, is

good and very convenient, at the corner of Knež Mihajlova, one block from
the National Museum—the *pljeskavica,* a sort of spicy hamburger, is worth
trying. **Studentski Park,** Bul. Revolucije 106, is filled with local students
who speak English. Other good self-services are **Kasina** on Terazije 25,
Atina across the street, and **Luksor** on Balkanska 7. Turkish sweet shops are
everywhere—gorge on the excellent pastries and candies.

Except at larger restaurants, menus are only in Serbian. But if you want
cheap seafood and beer, plunge into **Polet** at Maršala Tita 31—they have
great *lignje* (squid), *ošliče* (sardines), *skuša* (smelt), soups, and salads;
meals under 40ND. Many cafés *(kafana)* have good food in the 30-40ND
range—to be on the safe side, order a drink first, then ask for a menu and
assistance in interpreting it. If the prices are too high or the menu is lost in
Cyrillic, you can gracefully depart after finishing your beer. There are loads
of open-air markets, but the largest is between Narodnog Fronta and
Terazije. And stuff yourself one evening from the stalls along **Skardarska**
with beer, sandwiches filled with *kajmak* (a curd spread), *sardele* (a paper
cone filled with sardines fried in batter), or *pljeskavica* (spicy ground meat).
If you're in the mood for a splurge, eat at **Tri Sesira** or **Skadarlija** here. Or
try **Dom Lovaca,** Prote Mateje 7, which has excellent wild game specialties
in a lovely setting.

Sights

Wander down Terazije toward Trg Republike; this area may look only like
a shopping district to you, but it's the best quality and most extensive one
you'll see for a long time if you're heading east, so stock up accordingly.
Clothes and sneakers are good buys even if you're returning home. At the
corner of Trg Republike stands the **National Museum,** a mammoth collection of prehistoric artifacts, icons, frescoes, Serbian paintings from the
seventeenth, eighteenth, and nineteenth centuries, and some paintings from
the European schools. There is also a good display by Yugoslavia's best
known sculptor, Meštrović (open Tues., Wed., Sat. 10am-5pm; Thurs.
9am-7pm, Sun. 9am-1pm; closed Mon. Admission 5ND). The area behind
Studentski Trg is full of little cafés and narrow streets, with an occasional
building that survived the April 1941 bombing which leveled the city. Linger
anywhere with an open map and puzzled face—someone is sure to offer to
help you.

Head for **Kalemegdan Park,** the former Roman-Serbian-Turkish-
Austrian fortress that controlled the confluence of the Sava and Danube
Rivers. It is huge, and filled with amusement parks, lovers, and Albanian
and Gypsy indigents (Belgrade is developing its own racial tensions); but the
major attractions are the view, the **Serbian Orthodox chapel,** and an outstanding military museum. Near Kalemegdan is the **Fresco Museum** at Tsar
Urosh 20, which houses originals or faithful copies of the vivid and dramatic
medieval Serbian frescoes (same hours as museum). Head back down to the
modern city, to the **National Capitol** and the Serbian Orthodox **St. Mark's**
on Takovska. This immense building is not as old as it looks, but it's a good
example of Serbian churches—the tower over the main portal, the Romanesque windows and Byzantine roundness, the immense candelabra and innumerable candles set in sand. For an overview of the city, go to the top of
Beograd Palace on Maršala Tita; it's worth the 7ND.

Evenings

Ulica Skadarska, a nineteenth-century haunt of artists and bohemes near
the theater district, has now had its original cobblestones and flavor restored.

Here you'll find lively cafés, real Serbian music, and, at the **Golden Mug,** *lepinja* (crusty bread with cheese). There is a program of street music in **Skadarlija** on various evenings during summer. Check with the information offices for schedules, or just ask in the restaurants along the street. Or get the students you meet at Studentski Trg to take you to their favorite cafés. Belgrade lives in cafés all day and all night. Check with the Tourist Information people about *kolo* (national folk dance) performances and open-air theater. Check at the **National Theater** on Trg Republike for ballet or opera. At the theater **Atelje 212** at Lole Ribara 21 (tel. 347-342), you can see some of the best avant-garde drama in Eastern Europe.

Discotheques *(Disko-Klubs)* play last summer's American music, old and some new English records, and Serbian "rock" which sounds at least five years dated. Cinemas are predominantly Serbian sex flicks and old American westerns.

Near Belgrade

Right across the river, the **Museum of Contemporary Art** looks like a lampshade but houses some impressive Yugoslav art—it's within walking distance, or take a bus for Novi Beograd. Open 10am-7pm, closed Tuesdays. The mountain resort of **Avala** is about 20 kilometers away; buses leave several times a day, costing about 30ND round trip. On your way, stop at **Jaince** and see the monument to the 80,000 Yugoslavs killed here by the Germans during World War II. Few people realize the extent of the atrocities here—at Jaince you can see the remains of one of the largest concentration camps in Europe.

Down the Danube and east lies **Smederevo,** a huge fifteenth-century fortress on an even larger lake. In the **Fruska Gora** hills, game preserves and monasteries predominate.

Bosnia-Hercegovina

Bosnia-Hercegovina is a republic located almost entirely in the central mountains, an impenetrable fortress stretching north south between the coast and the fertile eastern farmlands of northern Croatia and Serbia. Turkish influence is stronger than anywhere else in Yugoslavia, visible and palpable in the mosques, the dress of the people, and the food. The land is tough, and the people are far poorer than the Croatians or Dalmatians, but folk traditions are kept proudly alive and visitors are enthusiastically welcomed.

Worth an overnight stop is **Sarajevo,** with its old Turkish quarter and fine Bosnian food. But you should venture through just for the mountain scenery, which rivals that anywhere else in Yugoslavia. Coming south through Bosnia to Sarajevo, you pass through the old Turkish town of **Banja Luka** and the waterfall at **Jajce.** Jajce is one of the oldest medieval Bosnian towns, and was its capital in the fifteenth century. Beyond Sarajevo on the way to the sea, the mountains become dry again, and startling lakes like **Jablanica** and **Boracko** look too blue to be real. Still further toward the coast is the Turkish town of **Mostar** with its famous bridge, and the striking medieval town of **Počitelj,** whose towers and minarets seem carved out of the cliff on which it sits.

Hitching throughout this area is difficult, because the main roads lie to the east and west of the mountains, and traffic in between is sparse. Trains exist, but buses are cheaper and you see more—besides, they are direct, while the train trips often require changes, and you may find yourself stuck in an intermediate station with the train you were counting on canceled. Buses, however, are rickety and infrequent, so plan your departure times when you arrive. Rooms in private homes are not generally available, and your choices for accommodations are limited to hostels, hotels, or camping.

Sarajevo

Nestled in a green bowl in the mountains of Bosnia, Sarajevo is a fascinating mixture of needle-sharp minarets, gingerbread buildings, red-roofed houses and the inevitable dash of grim modern architecture. The Turkish side of Yugoslavian history emerges here as nowhere else—Sarajevo was ruled by the Turks for five hundred years, and their influence remains in its 85 mosques, in its street market where you bargain with men wearing bright, baggy pantaloons, and in the spicy grilled meats and stuffed vegetables you find in the restaurants.

Addresses and Telephone Numbers

Tourist Bureau: Jugoslovenske Narodne Armije 50 (tel. 25-151). Free city maps, information about Bosnia-Hercegovina, and an accommodation service. Open 8am-8pm Mon.-Sat.

Student Tourist Agency: Radićeva 4a (tel. 22-454).

American Express (Atlas): Jugoslovenske Narodne Armije 81 (tel. 26-271).

Post and Telephone: Obala Vojvode Stepe 8 (tel. 27-100), along the Miljacka River.

Police: (tel. 22-145).

First Aid: (tel. 22-525).

American Center: Omladinska 1. Reading room with most recent major magazines and English library.

Orientation and Accommodations

Kompas, Maršala Tita 8 (tel. 35-955) will sell you a good map of the city with tram and bus routes for 6ND. Closed Sundays, open Saturdays until 2:30pm.

As usual, if you're not into student housing or campsites, the best alternative is to dicker with the women around the train stations. Tourist agencies will find you rooms also; the set rate begins at 90ND per person, though.

Youth Hostel (IYHF), Zadrugina 17 (tel. 36-163) is modern and clean; a bed in a 6- to 8-bed room costs 61ND with IYHF card. It's a short but steep walk from the Train Station, in the hills immediately to the left. From Tešanjska, take a left onto Kalemova and follow the signs. 11pm curfew.

Studentski Dom "Mladenstojanovic," also called **Pansion Index,** Ulica Radiceva 4a (tel. 22-454). For women only, but close to the center, friendly, and cheap. Also serves as the booking center for other student hotels.

Studentski Dom "Bratsvo i Jedinstvo," Nedjerici 1 (tel. 612-186). In the new section of town—take tram #3 or 6.

Hotel Beograd, Slobodana Principa 11 (tel. 23-120). Gloomy, dark, and expensive, but the cheapest official hotel. 180ND per double, breakfast included.

Camping "Student", Dare Dakovica (tel. 39-448) is open from May 1. Up the hill just outside of the town; take bus #22. A bed in a bungalow costs about 50ND.

Food

Stuff yourself on the Turkish specialties in Baščaršija—*halvah* (a grainy, chocolate and honey confection), and *cevapčiči* or *raznjiči* in *somum* or *lepinja* breads. An **Aščinica** on Abadziluk 55, opposite the back of the Brusa Bezistan warehouse, is a great lunch stop. **Cevabožinica,** Gazhusrefbegova 44, is another, higher-grade place.

The place for a typical Bosnian meal is **Daire** at Hulaci 5, just off the market square in Baščaršija. The restaurant is tucked into the old courtyard and warehouse that used to belong to the merchants from Dubrovnik. Turkish grilled meat dishes served with stuffed vine leaves, potato, and special vegetables cost 30-35ND. The best ice cream in Sarajevo is at **Egiptat,** on Vase Miskima next to the Cathedral—they sell only one flavor, a caramel, and it's great.

Sights

Maršala Tita leads east to Baščaršija, the Turkish quarter. The tombstones in the cemeteries have turbans, craftsmen vie with each other to sell you pointed leather slippers or two-foot pipes, and minarets soar from almost every block. If you've never seen the interior of a mosque, the **Gazi-husrefbegova Džamija** (or **Bey's Mosque**) is Yugoslavia's finest out of 2,000, and well worth the 7ND. At some of the smaller ones in the neighborhood, 10ND and taking off your shoes can get you inside. Across the street, the **Serbian Orthodox Church** at Vase Miskina 87 reeks of incense; give yourself ten minutes to get used to the darkness and fantastic icons. Don't miss the **Kazandžijska Čaršija** (Coppersmith's market)—a tiny street totally glinting with metal smith work. If you buy anything, bargain strenuously. Then, circle around to the river, passing the **Market** and the bridge where the student Gavrilo Princip shot Archduke Franz Ferdinand, triggering World War I.

Croatia (Hrvatska)

Extending south and east from Slovenia, Croatia was forged out of the areas that repelled the Turkish invasions five centuries ago. The upper part is more Slavic, with many traces of Austrian hegemony—and the regional capital, **Zagreb,** is the center for its art and produce. The **Istrian** and **Dalmatian Coast** is another story—evidences of Roman and Venetian outposts dot **Rijeka, Pula, Split,** and **Dubrovnik.** If any place in Yugoslavia can be called heavily touristed, this coast is it. The rock cliffs and pebble beaches that define the shores of over a thousand islands and innumerable bays and inlets are simply spectacular—next to the Greek islands, perhaps the clearest water in the Mediterranean. If you can't find an uncrowded beach, you aren't trying—although last year saw unprecedented crowds and resort development, an ominous trend.

You won't be able to cover Croatia in one piece if you're coming from the north; if you visit Zagreb on the Venice-Ljubljana-Belgrade line and then take an overnight train to Split or **Zadar,** you'll miss the northern Istrian Coast and islands. Transportation is a frustrating nightmare of trains, buses, and ferries along the coast, so plan ahead and limit your visions of island-hopping if you can. They're not all that different anyway. A reasonable itinerary would include Zagreb, Split, the island of **Hvar** or **Korčula,** and

Dubrovnik in seven or eight days minimum.

Accommodations for travelers on the cheap are excellent. There are several Youth Hostels. Campsites are even more common and cheaper, running about 35ND per person with tent.

Zagreb

Croatians are a proud and independent people, and Zagreb is the symbol of their independence. Though occupied on countless occasions through the centuries, Zagreb has always managed to assert herself, and foreign domination has never succeeded in crushing the city's spirit. While the cultural capital of Socialist Yugoslavia, Zagreb still clings to its Austro-Hungarian traditions, and retains a small-town atmosphere.

You'll probably want to concentrate on Zagreb north of the Rail Station; to the south, industry and grim housing projects line the Sava River. Zrinjevac St. borders a series of parks that lead up to **Trg Republike** (Republican Square), the city's main plaza; two blocks to the east of the Station, Petrinjska St. runs north to the IYHF Youth Hostel and tourist center. To the north of Trg Republike and the city grid, the Old Town shares a plateau with more parks that afford the best view of the city. The Old Town, with its narrow, cobbled streets and elegant cafés, evokes a nineteenth-century romanticism.

Addresses and Telephone Numbers

Tourist Information: Zrinjevac 14 (tel. 411-833). Open 8am-9pm weekdays, 9am-10pm weekends.

Youth Tourist Center: Petrinjska 73 (tel. 441-738). Next to the Youth Hostel. Open 7:30am-7:30pm weekdays (August 8am-4pm) and Sat. 7am-2pm (August 8am-noon). Books very inexpensive excursions within Yugoslavia and student charter flights. You can also rent any camping gear you need here at quite reasonable prices (6ND per day for a two-person tent). If you're hard up, ask Stella to help you find a room.

American Express (Atlas): Zrinjevac 17 (tel. 440-654). Along with **Generalturist** next door at #18, they have city maps and accommodation services.

Post and Telephones: Branimirova 4 (next to Train Station). Open Mon.-Sat. 7am-9am, Sun. 2-9pm.

Police: (tel. 92).

Medical Emergency: Dordičeva 6 (tel. 94).

U.S. Consulate: Brače Kavurića 2 (tel. 444-800). Open Mon.-Fri. 8am-12:30pm and 1:30-5pm. The **USIS Library,** located on the ground floor of the same building but entered at Zrinjevac 13, is open weekdays 1:30-5pm.

Accommodations

As in the rest of Yugoslavia, if you hang around the Train Station someone will offer to rent you a room. This is easily the cheapest way to find a place to sleep (about 70ND), but you could end up fairly far from the center of town.

A number of agencies offer private rooms beginning at 100ND for a single, 150ND for a double. The most conveniently located are the ones in the Train Station (tel. 38-183), and at the Bus Station (tel. 514-145).

Studentski Centar Turist Buro, Savska 25 (tel. 35-954), open 7am-3pm at the Zagreb Student Union, will get you a room in a student dormitory from

July 1 to September 30 at 100ND for a single, 70ND for a double, and 50ND for a three-bed room. Walk west for seven blocks from the Train Station, then onto Savska, or take tram #10, 12, or 15 (tram #4, 5, 9, or 14 from Trg Republike). If you arrive after 3pm, go directly to one of their three establishments: **Centrotel Sava,** Horvaćanski Zavoj bb (tel. 517-636). Go south on Savska until it hits the river, and turn right. To **Centrotel Moše Pijade,** Trg Zrtava Fasizma 4 (tel. 410-983), take tram #4 from the Turist Buro heading north. To **Centrotel Nina,** Dugandžića (tel. 562-914), take tram #14 from Trg Republike.

Omladinski Youth Hostel (IYHF), Petrinjska 77 (tel. 441-405) has 240 beds in two- to twelve-person rooms, but it's not particularly pleasant, although the management is helpful. 1am curfew, and 53ND for a bed with an IYHF card (77ND without).

Camping remains the cheapest alternative to spending the night on the train to Belgrade or Vienna. If you didn't bring any gear, rent whatever you need from the Youth Tourist Center and head for either **Mladost,** Horvaćanski zavoj bb, near the Student Hotel Sava (tel. 518-198) or **Zagreb,** Dubrovacka aleja bb (tel. 513-255), across the river straight south of the Train Station, then take a left on Avenija Holjevca and follow the signs. Even if you rent, the cost per person won't exceed 20ND.

Food

Zagreb's restaurants offer the widest variety of specialties in Yugoslavia, and its marketplaces overflow with fresh fruits and vegetables. Go to the market behind Trg Republike. Try the honey, yogurt, and Croatia's famous sheep's cheese *kajmak,* and eat a picnic lunch in one of Zagreb's many parks.

Splendid operates a few self-service restaurants of good quality; if you don't mind standing, you can fill up for 30-35ND. Try the main branch at 15 Trg Republike (terrific strudel here), next to the Atlas tourist agency; or **Pam Pam** at 4 Frankopanska. **Sljeme** is another chain; try the *grah,* a thick bean-based soup with whatever happens to be around thrown in, at Jurišićeva 18 or Petrinjska 79. For a splurge, try **Lovački Rog,** Ilica 14; it has a twenty-page menu including hare, partridge, and roast boar. You can eat like royalty for only 110-130ND. Don't leave Zagreb without trying *burek,* made with layers of thin dough filled with *jabuka* (apples), *sira* (cheese), or *mesa* (meat). The best *burek* in Zagreb is right around the corner from the Youth Hostel.

Sights

The upper **Old Town,** with its narrow cobblestoned streets, centers around **St. Mark's Church** and its tile shields on the roof. Wandering around, you'll pass the fourteenth-century **pharmacy** at Kamenita 9 and round stone towers (cannons are shot from them every noon), the remnants of medieval fortifications. Much of the **Lower Town** is a junior Vienna, but there are some interesting museums. The **Historical Museum of Croatia,** Matoševa 9, is just that (open Mon., Tues., Thurs., and Fri. 10am-5pm; Wed. 8am-5pm; Sat. 8am-3pm; Sun. 10am-1pm), but the **Archaeological Museum** is even better and has some real oddities (open 8:30am-1:30pm, Sun. 10am-1pm, closed Saturdays). The **Meštrović Gallery,** Mletačka 8 (open 10am-1pm and 5-7pm, Sun. 10am-1pm, closed Mondays) displays drawings and sculptures of Yugoslavia's best-known artist, Ivan Meštrović. Zagreb is the place to get a look at Yugoslav primitive and naive art—the **Gallery** at Ćirilometodska 3 (open 11am-1pm and 5-8pm) has a fascinating exhibit.

Evenings

Try to be in Zagreb for the **International Folklore Festival,** held the last week in July—it's *the* assembly of European folk dances and songs; over eighty groups perform during the week, with others from Asia and South America as well. Performances are free at **Trg Katerina** (Old Town) at 5pm and **Trg Republike** at 8:30pm; the 6pm indoor concerts, in which Yugoslavs predominate, cost only 5ND.

Zagreb is full of music, from opera to jazz, and there's usually a concert every summer night, often on open-air stages. Every odd year in May, it hosts the **International Festival of Contemporary Music,** and every third June the **World Animated Film Festival.** Check with the Tourist Office for details and schedules.

Discos are generally not terrific, but you might try **Corso 2,** Gunduliceva, or **Western Saloon** on Tuškanac. For homesick insomniacs, **Tomislavon,** 8 May 1945 (that's a street), is open until 3am and plays old American music on the jukebox.

Zagrebacins take to the streets at night. Mill among the crowds on Trg Republike, then head for a café. **Gradska Kavana** (right on the Square) and **Aleksinac** on Kaptol, feature hot, spicy meats *(cevapčiči* and *raznjiči)* and huge mugs of cold beer. Shortly before closing, regular customers often begin singing Croatian folk songs. Within minutes there isn't a dry eye in the place.

Near Zagreb

To get to **Sljeme,** a lovely mountain close to the city, take tram #14 from Trg Republike to the end (ask for a transfer), then #21. From here you can ride to the top by cablecar and hike down. Just when you're starting to tire you'll stumble onto an inn that serves rich dark Tomislav beer (one of the best in Europe). If you're driving up to Sljeme, the road is dotted with excellent restaurants with homemade specialties.

Twenty kilometers from Zagreb lies the lovely village of **Samobor,** known for its mineral waters and sixteenth-century ruins. Take the bus from the main Train Station.

Tito's birthplace, 45 kilometers from Zagreb at **Kumrovec** has been turned into a museum, and has recently become a mecca for young Yugoslavs. Well worth the trip (open 8am-6pm). A bit farther from Zagreb are the **Plitvice Lakes,** sixteen lakes connected by rapids and waterfalls. They form a spectacular (if somewhat touristed) national park.

Croatian Coast: Istria and Dalmatia

The recently-completed coastal road and a flock of new hotels have exposed this Adriatic shorefront to rapidly increasing numbers of foreigners. They concentrate, however, on the large tourist towns or modern resort complexes, leaving the villages in between unspoiled except for the exhaust of passing automobiles. From Rijeka to the extreme south, even the smallest fishing towns have a fortress or a medieval church to enhance their postcard prettiness. Seek them out, sample the islands, stay in private homes, or camp on the beaches.

The scenery and towns along the coast vary greatly. North of Zadar the shore is dry and barren, but the beaches are good and the towns predominantly Venetian. Southwards from Zadar, however, grass and trees reappear. Between Split and Dubrovnik, the **Makarskan Riviera,** with rock-strewn **Mt. Biokovo** falling into the sea, attracts special attention. South of Dubrovnik the coast changes again, becoming increasingly irregular and climaxing in the unique **Boka Kotorska.**

Getting There and Getting Around

There is a major road that runs the length of the coast, so you can drive or hitch along it until you see a spot you like. Public transport is another matter. In the nineteenth century, foreign powers blocked railway investment along the southern coast of Yugoslavia, and even today trains link central Yugoslavia with only a few seaside towns. **Trieste** and Rijeka are connected with **Zadar, Šibenik,** and **Split** via **Knin,** but there's no coastal train south of Split. **Ploce** has a route to Sarajevo (90ND and three hours), and Bar to Titograd (70ND) are on the route to Belgrade. Buses on the mainland and islands take up the slack, but are invariably late, infrequent, not synchronized with train schedules, and packed beyond belief. If you want a seat, buy a departure ticket when you arrive—if you can withstand an hour or more of jostling and occasional shoving at the ticket windows. The Ploce-Dubrovnik journey (74ND) is a particularly horrid recreation of the sardine-canning process.

The best and easiest alternatives, then, are the coastal steamers of the **Jadrolinija** line, both for domestic and inter-European trips. You should write them at Obala Jugoslavenske mornarice 16, Rijeka, for a complete schedule, because some ferries run infrequently and at odd hours (tel. 22-356 for information, 25-203 for reservations). If you're coming from or going to Greece, there's a weekly ferry from Igoumenitsa and Corfu, which stops at Bar ($41 for deck passage), Dubrovnik ($45), Split, and Rijeka ($69). Take deck passage, since a cabin and meals cost double, and you can get equal comfort by bringing food and a sleeping bag aboard. There are numerous and cheaper Adriatic connections with Italy: Rimini-Rovinj, Rimini-Pula-Zadar, Ancona-Zadar ($12.50), Pescara-Split, Ancona-Dubrovnik, Bari-Dubrovnik ($14), and Bari-Bar ($5.20).

Along the coast, you are allowed to get off any boat for up to three days in any of the way stations, if you have the ticket stamped before you disembark. Even if you choose not to stop at the major ports and islands, frequent ferries (10-40ND) link most islands with Rijeka, Split, Zadar, or Dubrovnik. Split to Hvar, for example, runs several times a day and costs 40ND (although hydrofoils can get you there twice as fast, they're twice as expensive). The most adventurous and cheapest method is to haggle with the fishermen along the docks. That way, you can go wherever you want, coast or island.

The Coast North from Split

Rocks and sea—that's the Istrian coast. **Rovinj,** a town with a lively Mediterranean air, has an International Youth Center: **Obala Mladik,** with 200 three-bed chalets and full board for 160ND per person. Reservations must be booked in advance through **Naromtravel,** Moše Pijade 12, 11000 Belgrade. **Rijeka,** Yugoslavia's biggest seaport, looks like a grayer version of Trieste, but you may be forced to stay a night because of transport schedules. Avoid the hotels in town and head for **Dom Crvenog Križa,** Rijeka's IYHF Youth Hostel (J. Polic Kamova 32, bus #2 from the Train Station). Friendly and clean (with a lovely beach); a bed will run 70ND. The only alternatives for cheap housing are the numerous *sobe* which are along the road out of town (again bus #2). Check with tourist information for listings. **Zadar,** down the coast, is a busy if unspectacular market city, known for Maraschino cherries and as the base of excursions to the **Kornati Archipelago** (see The Islands section). **Šibenik** has some beautiful Renaissance buildings, a **Youth Hostel** (IYHF, tel. 26-410, 32ND per night without pension), and great seafood.

Split

Split was originally a prodigious palace which the emperor Diocletian built for his retirement. After the Roman empire fell, a medieval city developed among the Roman palace walls. Through the works of the architect Robert Adam, who made a detailed study of Split in 1757, the singular blend of styles that exists in this city had a profound impact on Georgian architecture. The rectangular wall of the old Roman town still exists. The palace halls have become streets, and the palace rooms are now houses. The conversion process is fascinating; you may turn the corner of a narrow alley and be faced with an old Roman sculpture, now just a stone in a twentieth-century house wall.

Split has terrific connections, for Yugoslavia—an overnight train from Zagreb (about 150ND), steamers from Italy and Rijeka, and local ferries to the major islands: **Brač, Hvar, Vis, Korčula,** and **Šolta,** among others. From the **Rail, Ferry,** or **Bus Stations** on Obala Bratstva Jedinstva, turn right and walk over to Titova Obala, the boulevard between the sea and the **Palace.** The four palace gates, flanked by octagonal towers, can be used as points of orientation. The Copper Gate faces the south and the sea; the Iron Gate (west), the Golden Gate (north), and the Silver Gate (east) have lost their original materials and vistas of the surrounding area. Diocletian's **Mausoleum,** later part of a Romanesque **Cathedral,** is unusual octagonal Roman architecture in the Palace center—forget the flesh and concentrate on the bones of the **Peristyle** and **Cryptoporticus** flanking it. The **bazaar** nearby has a lot of schlock, but some nice native rugs and embroidery. Bargaining is expected—offer half (or less) of what they ask, and look skeptical.

The **Archaeological Museum,** to the northwest of the palace at Zrinjsko-Frankopanska 13, houses much of the reclaimed Roman detritus. It's open 9am-1pm and 4-6pm Tues.-Sat., 10am-noon Sun., closed Mon., and admission is 5ND. If you like the huge bronze prophet facing the northern wall, visit the **Galeria Meštrović,** which has a large exhibition of Ivan Mestrović's work on the grounds of his former country house and studio. It is at Šetalište Moše Pijade 44, 2 kilometers along the western coast road; open 10am-7pm.

In September 1979, Split will host a Youth Olympics with 15 Mediterranean countries and 23 events; contact the Tourist Office for schedules.

Addresses and Telephone Numbers

Tourist Office: Titova Obala 12 (tel. 33-22). Avoid this one—it's convenient, but they'll make you pay 20ND for a map or 30ND for a guide to the city. They do have an accommodation service, but it starts around 120ND a night, less for a stay of six days or longer. Open 7:30am-8pm, Sun. 7:30-noon.

Tourist Agencies: Dalmacijaturist on Titova Obala 5 (tel. 44-666) and **Putnik** on Obala Lazareta 3, that small island of offices between the Titova Obala and the sea (tel. 44-333). Both have free city maps and information; the latter rents cars as well.

American Express (Atlas): Trg Prepotoda 7 (tel. 45-387). Along the southern wall.

Police: (tel. 92).

First Aid: Next to Firule Hospital, Spinčićeva (tel. 94).

Accommodations and Food

You'll have to stick to campsites or student housing if you want inexpensive lodgings in Split; a better idea is to spend the afternoon here and leave. If you do stay, try:

Studenski Centar, Sibenskih Zrtava 6 (tel. 48-644). In the old city, this bureau will get you a bed in a student dorm from July 15 through September 1, for about 60ND per person. Four or five persons per room.

Hotel Srebrena Vista, Kralja Poljana Kraljice Jelene 3 is located on your left immediately after you enter the Bronze Gate (tel. 46869). Old comfortable hotel built right into the Roman wall and overlooking Tomislav Square—still paved with Roman stone. With breakfast, 120ND per person. The best inexpensive lodging. There is also a restaurant with fine food and service for 30-50ND.

Hotel Ljubljana, Graboucena 1 (tel. 44530). Near the western gate. Pleasant accommodations and a good restaurant. Singles 120ND, doubles 180ND.

Hotel Slavija, Buvinova 2, just inside the west wall (tel. 47053). Small, ancient hotel, shower on the first floor. Singles 100-120ND, doubles 180-200ND.

Camping Trstenik, Put Trstenik (tel. 521-971). About 3 km to the east of town; follow the signs to Hotel Split nearby. Tent sites 25ND per person.

One good restaurant is **Jelovnik,** Tvrdojeva Ulica 3, near the west gate; it serves dinners with salad, vegetables, and bread for about 35ND, and à la carte fish dishes for 10-20ND. There is a **market** at Trg Nardnoy Ustanka, near the palace's southeast corner.

Dubrovnik

"The pearl of the Adriatic, a paradise on earth," George Bernard Shaw called Dubrovnik. Its striking architectural unity, achieved with the help of a delicately bone-tinted stone used for both buildings and pavements, its sheltering unifying wall, and its striking setting will take your breath away. Of course it's touristed—it's the pride of the Yugoslav coast and the most cosmopolitan place in the country. But it's an exciting, brilliant fairy-tale town, and no tour of the coast would be complete without it.

Orientation

Since 1976, when the state dismantled a narrow-gauge track from Ploče, Dubrovnik has lacked a railway. With unprecedented numbers of foreign visitors, bus connections from Ploče (70ND) and Bar (58ND) are terribly strained—abandon all thoughts of personal comfort and safety, and don't let the bus conductor shut the door until you've pleaded or shoved your way aboard. Ferries arrive from Split, Bari, Hvar, Korčula, and others.

The Bus and Ferry Stations are both on Gruška Obala, 3 kilometers to the west of the walled city. Take buses #1 or 2 (4.50ND) to **Pile,** the town gate. #1 runs between the Bus Station and Pile; #2 goes from Pile, stops at the Bus Station, continues along the harbor (Gruz) to the beach at **Lapad,** then returns. From Pile, pass through the ramparts to **Placa,** the main street. Dubrovnik is tiny; a stroll of three minutes and you're at the other end. Beyond the eastern wall, a wharf receives the ferry to **Lokrum** (20ND round trip), a nearby beach island.

Addresses and Telephone Numbers

Tourist Information: Poljana Paska Milicevita 20 (tel. 26-354). Just inside the west gate, they have excellent free maps and information, sell concert tickets to the summer festival, and arrange accommodations. Open 7:30am-8pm Mon.-Sat.

American Express (Atlas): Pile 1 (tel. 27-333). This tourist agency has a hammerlock on Dubrovnik tourism—arrange all excursions, train tickets, etc. through them.

Police: Maršala Tita 75 (tel. 92). About 2 km out of the old town.

First Aid: Maršala Tita 61 (tel. 94).

Accommodations

Hotels are expensive; if there is no room at the youth center (see below), ask the Information Office for a *sobe* (90-120ND) or go to the Bus Station in Gruž and someone will approach you. The Bus Station is much better; bargain with the people there. Expect to pay less than at the information center. The rates quoted for hotels are for high season. Don't try sleeping on the beaches near Dubrovnik. The police will bother you all night, and if pushed, they'll issue steep fines.

International Youth and Student Center "Dvorac Rasica," Lapad. Take bus #2 or 4 (a three-minute walk from the beach at Lapad; tel. 238-41). Rows of small, two-person cabins in the former gardens of a fifteenth-century patrician mansion; cabins are 100ND per person. Midnight curfew. The gates are also opened once each at 1am, 2am, and 3am. An excellent, well-managed hostel, and the best place to meet other students. Extremely popular; for July and August, you must book ahead through the Travel Department of Yugoslav Youth and Students, Moše Pijade 12/1, Post Office Box 374, Belgrade.

Ferijalni Dom (IYHF), Oktobarske Revolucije 25 (tel. 23-241). From the Train Station, bus or walk up Maršala Tita toward town until you hit a little triangular park; (or backtrack from the second bus stop). Oktobarske Revolucije is the next parallel street up the hill (Montovjerna)—take a right, walk up the street, and look for the sign. During the Festival (July-August), the curfew is extended from midnight to 1am. Rooms closed 9am-1pm. 45ND per night, with hot showers and clotheslines included.

Hotel Gruž, 68 Gruška Obala (tel. 24-777). From the Bus Station, walk down to the harbor and turn right on the road that runs along the water. The hotel is up the hill opposite the office of Jadrolinja at the boat pier; take the stairway beside #68. An old hotel in a garden with moderate-sized rooms; singles for 150ND, doubles 250ND, triples 300ND, without breakfast or bath. All other hotels are even more overpriced.

Camping Rudine, off Bulevar Lenjijna (tel. 50-234) around the harbor from the Train Station. From Gruška Obala, take a right onto N. Tesla, continue onto Od. Batale, then follow the signs. 25ND per person, 6ND per tent, and quite pleasant.

Food

International Student and Youth Center, Lapad, serves food cafeteria-style, dinner (at noon) 30ND, supper 20ND.

Express, Ulica C. Zuzoric, one block from St. Blaise church. Good cheap self-service meals for 30-40ND.

Burek Grill, Ulica Žudioska, serves meat, fruit, and cheese pies for 10ND— two will leave you stuffed.

Ragusa Kucak, Ulica Zamanjina—a steep little alley left of the main gate. Wine is expensive here, but there's a 60ND *menu fixe* served on charming wooden tables in a candlelight atmosphere. Good place for a splurge.

Sights

If art is your game, there are slim pickings in Dubrovnik, although the **Dominican Cloister and Museum** (open 9am-noon and 3-6pm, closed Sunday, admission 7ND) houses a Titian polyptych. Sit on the steps of **St. Blaise,** catty-corner from the **Bell-Tower**—bronze men strike the hours above **Onofrio's Large Fountain.** The small one's at the western end of the Placa, along with the beautiful **Franciscan Church.** More Mediterranean influence adorns the **Rector's Palace** (open 9am-12:30pm, closed Sunday, admission 10ND) and the unmarked **Synagogue** on the left side of Ulice Žudioska. Dubrovnik had 5000 Ladino (Spanish) Jews before 1941, and the Synagogue is crammed with rich, intricate carvings and bronzes (open 7-11am; Friday night services at 7pm).

Near sunset, don't miss a stroll atop the **City Walls** (open 8:30am-7pm, admission 10ND, entrances near the western and eastern gates) for a panorama of the old town, the harbors, and the beaches; surely one of the world's prettiest perambulations. But Dubrovnik has warm, crystalline water, so don't just admire it from a distance. The hotel beaches on either side of the old town are crowded and cost 5ND; if you're adventurous, dive and sunbathe along the rocks below the park along Maršala Tita. Or take the ferry to forested **Lokrum** for nearly deserted sea coast to the right of the dock, and nude bathing to the left. If you really want to get away, go to some of the picturesque villages nearby—**Zaton** and the island of **Koločep** to the north, **Kupari** and **Srebreno** to the south.

Evenings

From mid-June to mid-September, Dubrovnik has ballet, opera, symphonic and chamber concerts, plays, and folk dances. Concerts are performed in Renaissance courtyards, the orchestra playing at the base of a richly-carved staircase. Plays take place in an ancient fortress, with entrances and exits made through the walls. Tickets for performances range from 60-200ND. Check at **Atlas** for concert tickets, and at the **Dubrovnik Festival Office** for festival tickets and programs.

Roulette wheels and strippers rotate in the hotels, but in the early evening everyone walks the streets and you should too, perhaps stopping for ice cream or coffee. Try the city café (**Gradska Kafana**) at the eastern end of town, facing the old harbor; a huge empty place with schmaltzy music, straight out of a Graham Greene novel.

The Islands

The more than 1000 Adriatic islands are baby Edens in spring and fall. July and August bring swarms of tourists, and rooms are in extremely short supply. Even the campgrounds are tent to tent. As in the rest of Yugoslavia, private rooms are the best deal. Despite the hassle, the islands are worth it. Try not to leave Yugoslavia without sampling at least a few.

To the north off the coast of Istria lie the numerous islands of the **Rovinj Archipelago.** Many are uninhabited, and part of one, **Crveni Otok,** is now a nudist colony. Close to Rijeka are the large, flat islands of **Krk** and **Cres.** Kurk has been occupied by the Romans, Byzantines, Venetians, Croats, and Austrians, and each culture has left its mark. A bit further south and accessible from the mainland by a causeway is **Pag,** the home of the famous (but expensive) sheep cheese.

The most famous and most crowded islands lie between Split and Dubrovnik. The largest, **Brač,** markets a unique wine from the St. Vid Mountains. Its major towns, **Bol** and **Supetar,** are jammed with tourists all summer long. Camping Supetar, a ten-minute walk south of town, is typical, with cold showers, cooking facilities, a private pebble beach, and prices of 30ND per person, 10ND per tent, and 10ND per vehicle. **Postire,** however, a smaller town on Brač, is another story. Perhaps the best-kept secret in the Islands, Postire is lovely and even in July and August the only tourists are Yugoslavs. The people are friendly, lodging is cheap (if you're desperate, just knock on any door) and the food is excellent. Stroll with the natives along the quays in the evening, stop for a drink at one of the cafés, and then head for the local dance held each night behind the Hotel Park. The town is a charming place to visit, and a difficult place to leave.

Next to Brač are the major tourist islands of **Hvar** and **Korčula.** Hvar has such good weather that some of its hotels claim they will charge you half price if it rains, and nothing if it ever snows. Tastefully decayed Korčula, the purported birthplace of Marco Polo, stages the **Moreska** every July 27, a militaristic pageant where soldiers gaudily dressed in red fight and eventually defeat equally gaudy soldiers garbed in black for the honor of local princes. Korčula has a **Youth Hostel** (IYHF, tel. 81-195) with 120 beds at 30ND per night and a private beach. **Mljet,** a national park, has a twelfth-century monastery, now a hotel, in the middle of a beautiful salt lake. Further out in the Adriatic, the less expensive islands of **Vis** and **Lastovo** have comparable beaches and weather, but attract far fewer tourists. When you arrive on Lastovo, take the bus immediately to the other end of the island. You'll find a lovely village built into a hill, with vineyards on one side and the sea on the other. There is no hotel here; you can camp or rent a room. Picnic on the beach, drink homemade wine with the peasants, and sample a life that has changed little through the centuries.

Those who really want to get away from it all should seclude themselves on one of the hundreds of uninhabited islands in the **Kornati Archipelago.** Bring a sleeping bag and some food, and play Robinson Crusoe. To get there, take the daily ferry from Split or Sibenik to **Sali** on the island of **Dugi Otok,** and haggle with one of the fishermen in the harbor. Make sure you make specific and definite arrangements to be picked up, however, or you may find yourself marooned.

Montenegro and Macedonia

The Coast South of Dubrovnik—The Montenegran Riviera

Within the last two years, development has skyrocketed here in response to cheaper prices and warm temperatures. It's still less expensive than the northern coast, though, and you can still find sleepy villages nestled between towering mountains and the sea. The bus to Titograd takes you along the length of the startling **Boka Kotorska** (or Kotor Fjord) which looks almost like a blue sea conjured by magic amid mountains of the moon. The boat to Corfu ($26) leaves at 6pm Wednesday evenings from Dubrovnik and arrives the following day, or you can take the bus on to Titograd, where you are forced by the schedules to stay a night before crossing the Macedonian mountains to **Skopje.** (You *can* do this on an overnight trip, but you miss the harrowing pass.) Hitching is at its worst on this stretch.

The main towns along the coast are **Hercegnovi, Kotor, Budva, Petrovac** and **Bar.** Budva has an old walled city and ruins dating from the fourth century B.C. left by the Phoenicians, Greeks and Romans. During a July fair, you can pick up Indian cotton goods at moderate prices. Just outside of town is a large modern IYHF **Youth Hostel** (tel. 82-357) where you can meet young people from all over Europe. Petrovac, in a rugged mountain setting, offers a sandy beach and two frescoed monasteries. Bar, a Turkish town with a larger beach, holds market day on Fridays, a good chance to see the regional peasant costumes. There is now a direct train connection from Bar to Belgrade. Ultramodern and inexpensive—it's the pride of Montenegro. It's worth paying the first-class fare of 227ND (80ND surcharge on InterRail). The train passes marshy **Lake Skadar,** and after Titograd meanders along the spectacular **Morača Canyon**—take your pictures on the sly, because soldiers will confiscate your film if they catch you. If you stop along the way, there are no youth hostels, but private tourist agencies will get you a room for 70-80ND.

The flower-filled old settlement of Hercegnovi, guarded by three ruined fortresses, meanders down the hillside from the Dalmatian highway to the blue waters of the Boka Kotorska. The beaches in town are small and pebbly, but the water is clear and the pace much slower than in the big tourist resorts. A large sandy beach lies about 3 kilometers south of town, or you can hire boats to cross the fjord and find yourself an empty spot. You can also catch the bus into the mountains to **Cetinje,** the old capital of Montenegro, or visit the ancient monastery of **Savina** outside of town. The **Information Center** at the Bus Station will arrange a private room for about 60-70ND, or you can stay at **Hotel Topoia** on the harbor (tel. 87-048), up a stairway behind the Boat Station. Single rooms start at about 70ND. (Don't confuse it with the expensive Hotel Topla.)

Inland

Going east from the Montenegran Riviera, the road winds upward into the abrupt coastal mountains. Only tough evergreens and yellow Scotch broom can cling to the rocks. The old Montenegran capital, **Cetinje,** has the same inaccessibility. Abandoned as a capital because it had no room to expand, Cetinje sleeps on a mountaintop, and its inhabitants wear the same costume they have worn for centuries. There is a hotel in Cetinje, but if you ask around the bus station, you'll find a room. Cetinje was the home of the priest-prince Peter Njegos. Visit the lovely museum built in his honor.

The new capital, **Titograd,** is symbolic of the path the government hopes this most backward area of Yugoslavia will follow. The road to Titograd leaves the mountains behind, crosses the eerie marshes by Lake Skadar, and enters a flat, hot valley full of wheat and smokestacks. The town is uninviting—pretentious skyscrapers of pasteboard already looking like tenements, the atmosphere nonexistent, the people apathetic. Titograd is unequipped for visitors, but travelers crossing the mountains to Skopje may have to spend the night there anyway, because of the infrequency of buses. The **Hotel Crna Gora** (from the Bus Station, take bus #2 and ask the conductor; tel. 45-777) charges 180ND for a double without bath, 192ND with. **Autocamp Zlatica** (tel. 22-103) is more reasonable at 130ND per double in a bungalow. If you can't find a room at the Bus Station, don't hesitate to sleep in any one of Titograd's many parks. If the police bother you, say you're waiting for an early bus.

From Titograd you climb still higher into the steepest mountains in Yugoslavia. Farms are carved out of forest so high on the slopes that you wonder whether the people who live on them ever come down. Hitching is bad the moment you leave the coast, but it becomes nearly impossible at this point, and there is no alternative to taking a bus to Skopje (about 110ND). The road cuts across the southern tip of Serbia, passing through the monastery towns of **Peć, Priština,** and **Decani**—the latter contains the biggest of the medieval Serbian monasteries. Peć has a **Youth Hostel** (IYHF) at Ivo Lole Ribara 76, but it's rather unsavory.

Once you come down into **Macedonia,** the change is abrupt. The air is stagnant, dust lies thick on the trees, and horse-drawn carts rumble along Europe's most antique roads. Blood feuds are still common in small villages, newborn babies still kiss the muzzle of a gun, and fighting ability is the test of a man.

A word of caution—this part of Yugoslavia is quite primitive. The trip from Titograd to Skopje is long, exhausting and dirty. The population (mainly Albanian) lives the same way it has for centuries, and Tito's socialism has not come to this part of the country. Women should *never* travel without a male.

Southern Macedonia offers more of the country's wealth of mountain scenery. Blue Lake Ohrid edges the impassive mountain wall of Albania, and the ancient town of Ohrid, whose painted houses and winding alleys border the lake, is a treasure of medieval Byzantine frescoed churches.

When you leave the coast behind, you leave most of the private lodgings as well. People are poorer, houses are too primitive to suit most tourists, and the national agencies have done little to develop the area. Campgrounds are available, but you have to play it by ear when camping in the wilder places. Hotels are spartan and sometimes overpriced. They can also be dirty and disreputable, so you should check them out carefully before you accept a room, and fix the price in advance. The same is true of other things—taxis in Skopje, for example, have no meters, and you bargain with the driver *before* you get in. When bargaining, listen for the word *banki*—a *banka* is a 10-dinar note, and it is a favorite term for getting foreigners to promise more money than they think they are paying.

Trains do not exist in the mountainous area between Skopje and Titograd. Buses are the only real answer, and provide good glimpses of the towns and the local people. Hitching is nearly impossible except on the Belgrade-Skopje road; hitching across the Greek border in either direction is very difficult. Knowledge of German is extremely handy here because many men work in Austria and Germany during the year to support their families, and return home in July and August.

Skopje

Skopje, the hot, dusty capital of Macedonia, is a dingy and thoroughly uninviting place, but you have to go through it on the train route south (150ND from Belgrade), and unless you're heading for Lake Ohrid or Lâke Prespa, it's your last look at the twentieth century in Macedonia. The familiar cardboard apartment houses alternate here with buildings still in ruins from earthquakes. The stares of the natives contain less curiosity and more suspicion; and gypsies and vagabonds haunt the markets and the stations. The city has always been important strategically, and has been ruled in various periods by Greeks, Romans, Byzantines, Bulgarians, Serbs and Turks, but little is left to remind you of the conquerors.

The **Tourist Information Bureau** is almost opposite the Bus Station, at Kei Dmitr Vlakov #1 (tel. 233-843) and stays open from 6am-8pm weekdays, 7am-7pm Sat. and Sun. Both the Bureau and the Bus Station are on the same side of the river as the fascinating old Turkish part of town, in the shadow of the **Kale Fortress**—the **bazaar** begins just behind them. A walking bridge connects them with **Ploshtad Marshal Tito,** the center of the city on the opposite side of the river. From the enormous square, Boulevard Marshal Tito leads straight to the Railway Station. At the Station is the other **Information Center** (tel. 25-713), open 6:30am-8pm, Sun. 7-11am. Trams cost 3ND, as elsewhere.

Skopje has an IYHF Youth Hostel, **Dom Blagov Lošovčev,** Ulica 700, br. 25 Prolet (tel. 33-866). Rooms begin at 70ND per person including breakfast. There are also showers (sometimes hot). A good place to meet people heading for Greece. **Studentski Dom,** Bulevar Ivo Ribar Lola (tel. 35-351), is a huge modern dormitory where rooms are available to foreign students between July 1 and September 15. 50ND per person will get you a bed in a double room, and you'll have plenty of chances to meet Yugoslav students. The director urges visitors to write in advance for reservations but if you decide to come unannounced, be sure to show up between about 9am and 3pm on a weekday, or there will be no one around with the authority to give you a room. If you hang around the Train Station you will be approached about a room. Find out where it is first, or you may end up in a village 20 kilometers from Skopje. Hotels are expensive. The cheapest is the **Hotel Makedonija,** Ploshtad Marshal Tito (tel. 220-619), in the middle of the Square. Small but comfortable rooms beginning at 110ND for a single, 210ND for a double. Showers 10ND extra.

Two self-service restaurants are right in the center of town. One, the **Metropol Express,** is on Tito Square; the other, the **Samo-Isvana,** is nearby on Boulevard Marshal Tito. The restaurant attached to **Studentski Centar,** Bulevar Ivo Ribar Lola, is the best place to meet students and get the cheapest meal in Skopje.

If you turn left before you enter the bazaar and go up the steps to the main road past the fortress, you come to the two prime sights of Skopje at the top of the hills. The **Church of the Holy Savior** (*Tserkva Svyati Spas*) is a tiny wooden building which houses a fantastically-carved wooden iconostasis (altar gate), chipped out over a twenty-year period by three nineteenth-century Macedonians. Look for Salome dressed as a Greek dancer. Admission 7ND, postcard included; open 8am-noon and 3-6pm, 9am-noon Sunday; closed Monday.

Just beyond the church is **Mustapha Pasha's Mosque,** built in 1492 and beautifully carved and painted, with a good view of the city (admission 7ND). Fittingly isolated as the highest point of the rise, **The Museum of Contemporary Art** is an anomalous, graceful glass and concrete structure folding around one of the finest multi-media exhibits in Yugoslavia (open daily 10am-5pm, closed Mon.).

Ten kilometers from Skopje in the village of **Nerezi** is the beautiful Monastery of **St. Panteleimon.** The twelfth-century Byzantine Church has amazing frescoes. There's absolutely no public transport there, but if you're a fresco freak it may be worth the 80ND taxi fare.

Lake Ohrid

In the extreme southwest corner of Yugoslavia along the Albanian border lies the hauntingly beautiful Lake Ohrid. Ohrid is an antiquarian's delight; its clear waters contain species of fish extinct everywhere but here and in the Soviet Union's Lake Baikal; the markets and streets are filled with ageless gap-toothed peasants; and along the shores of the lake you can still see the remains of over forty Byzantine churches. But the lake region is moving into the twentieth century, with tourist housing and restaurants that specialize in the delectable fresh-water trout.

It takes about five hours to reach the town of Ohrid from Skopje. You can do it by trains to Kicevo (46ND) or Bitola (55ND), taking buses from either one (25ND). Or take a bus directly to Ohrid; there are over a dozen a day, and they cost about 60ND, traveling over surprisingly good roads. Or you can fly; the plane costs only about 190ND one way.

The **Tourist Bureau,** on Partisanska (tel. 22-494) next door to the Bus Station, will give you a good town map and has an accommodation service, with singles from 69ND. The **Youth Hostel Mladost** (IYHF; tel. 21-626) is cheap at 40ND, and not worth a dinar more; unless you've written ahead for reservations in the building, you'll share a mini-camper unit with up to three others, luggage, and a light bulb—if there's any room left. Private beach. No curfew, but it's abuzz by 7:30am. To get there, backtrack on Partisanska, take a right onto Boris Kidric, then a left onto Goce Delčev, the main street into Ohrid, and follow until the IYHF sign about 2 kilometers away. Or take the bus to Struga and ask the conductor to let you off. There is a slew of camping sites on the coast road to Struga, and all have their own beaches.

Ohrid was the center of early medieval Slavic Christianity and literature, and has some lovely churches from this period. From Boris Kidric, walk toward the lake and up the hill to the west, entering the old town through the **Old Gate.** The **Cathedral of St. Sophia** (open 9am-noon and 3-6pm) has magnificent eleventh-century frescoes and a summer concert series. Near the top of the hill, **St. Jovan Bogoslav** (open 9am-noon and 3-5pm) broods over the lake, but is outclassed by the higher **St. Pantaleimon,** once a great Macedonian university, and **St. Clement's** frescoes, icons, and carvings (open 9am-noon and 3-7pm, except Mondays; admission 6ND, 3ND with student card).

Ohrid rolls up the sidewalks at 10pm on the dot. Before ten the big social scene is on **Moše Pijade,** the main shopping street—all the guys link arms on the curb and watch the girls parade by, like everywhere else in Macedonia. The Youth Hostel has nightly dancing, alternating disco and traditional *bouzouki.*

Monday is market day in Ohrid. Peasants in regional costumes jostle each other and buy and sell in a noisy carnival spirit. This is perhaps the best spot in Yugoslavia to buy hand-made blouses and scarves. Or try a Saturday excursion to less touristed **Struga** (ten minutes and 7ND by bus), and stay the afternoon on the fine beach and in the unbelievably cheap pastry shops along Bulevar Marshal Tito.

INDEX

AUSTRIA

Altmunster 87
Attersee 86
Attnang Puchheim 86
Baden 78
Bad Ischl 87
Bodensee 90
Bregenz 90
Burgenland 79
Carinthia (see Kärnten) 78
Certus 80
Lake Constance (see
  Bodensee)
Dornbirn 90
Ebensee 87
Eisenstadt 79
Feldkirch 90
Fulpmes 90
Gaisbergspitz Mtn. 85
Gmunden 86-87
Graz 79-81
Hafelekar 87
Hallstatt 87
Igls 89
Innsbruck 87-90
Kärnten (Carinthia) 78
Klagenfurt 78
Naturpark Kreuzbergl 78
Linz 78
Mariazell 78
Lake Neusiedl 79
Obertraun 87
Partenen 90
Passau 77
Piber 81
Rust 79
St. Gallenkirch 90
Salzburg 81-86
Salzkammergut 86-87
Schöckel 81
Schwarzenberg 90
Steiermark (Styria) 78
Stübing 81
Styria (see Steiermark)
Traunkirchen 87
Traunsee 86
Tyrolean Alps 87
Valluga 90
Vienna 67
Vienna Woods (see
  Wienerwald)
Villach 78
Vorarlberg 90
Wachau 86
Wienerwald (Vienna
  Woods) 77
Wörthersee 78

BELGIUM

Antwerp 97-101
Ardennes Mtns. 92
Brugge (Bruges) 103-105
Brussels (Bruxelles) 93-97
Dinant 106
Ghent 101-103
Givet 106
Han-sur-Lesse 106
Lesse R. 106
Liège 91
Namur 105-106
Nieuwpoort 92
Oostdwinkerke 92
Oostende 92
Westende 92
Zeebrugge 92

BULGARIA

Black Sea Riviera 107
Buzludza 112
Maljovica 113
Nesebār 116
Pamporov 112
Pirin 113
Pirin Mtns. 113
Plovdiv 113-114
Primorsko 116
Rhodopi Mtns. 112
Rila Mtns. 113
Rusalka 116
Shipka 112
Slancev-Brjag 116
Sofia 109-112
Stara Planina 112
Varna 116
Veliko Turnovo 114-115
Mt. Vihren 113
Vitosha Mtns. National
  Park 111-112

CZECHOSLOVAKIA

Austerlitz (see Slakov)
Bohemia 126
Bratislava 128
Brno (Brünn) 127
Carpathian Mountains 127
České Budějovice 126
Český Krumlov 126
Hornad Valley 128
Karst 127
Košice 128
Levoča 128
Moravia 127
Olomouc 127
Poprad 127
Prague 120-126
Prešov 128
Slakov (Austerlitz) 127
Slovenský Raj 127-128
Spiš 127
Spišská Nová Ves 128
Strbské Pleso 128
Tábor 126
Tatranská Lomnica 128
Velká Fatra 127
Vysoké Tatry 127

DENMARK

Aarhus 142-144
Aero 145
Aeroskobing 145
Boeslum 143
Christiania 140
Christianshavn 140
Copenhagen 132-142
Draby 143
Ebeltoft 143
Faaborg 145
Falster 145
Fyn (Funen) 144-145
Helsingor 141
Hornbaek 141
Horsens 144
Humlebaek 140
Jutland 144
Langeland 145
Liselund 146
Lolland 145-146
Lyo 145
Maribo 146
Marielyst 145
Marstal 145
Mindsten/Bangs Have 146
Mon 145-146
Moregaard 143
Odense 144
Ristinge 145
Roskilde 140
Rudkobing 145
Silkeborg 143
Soby 145
Southern Islands 145-146
South Funen Archipelago
  144
Stege 146
Svendborg 144
Sygehusvejen 145
Tassinge 145
Vordingborg 146
Zealand 145

FINLAND

Helsinki 149-155
Karelia 148
Kaustinen 148
Kultakivi 157
Kuopio 148
Lapland 158
Nauvo 156
Pihlajasaari 153
Pori 156
Rovaniemi 158
Savonlinna 156-157
Savonranta 157
Suomenlinna 153
Tampere 154
Turku (Turun) 155-156

FRANCE

Abondance 206
Agay 215
Aigues-Mortes 221
Aix-en-Provence 220-221
Aix-les-Bains 206
Ajaccio 218
Albi 224-225
Aléssa 202

Alpe d'Huez 206
Alps 205-210
Alsace 200-201
Amboise 190-191
Angers 198
Annecy 206-207
Antibes 214
Arcachon 227
Argentières 208
Arles 221-222
Auvergne 226-227
Auxerre 202
Avignon 222-223
Azay-le-Rideau 192
Azé 205
La Balagne 219
Bandol 217
Bastia 219
Les Baux 221
Bayeux 196-197
Beaugency 189-190
Beaune 204
Belledonne Mtns. 206
Belle-Ile 199
Beynac 226
Biarritz 227
Blois 189-190
Les Bois 208
Bonifacio 219-220
Bordeaux 227-228
Les Bossons 208
Bourg d'Oisans 206
Bourges 188-189
Bourg-St.-Maurice 205
Brest 199
Brigneau 199
Brittany (Bretagne) 197-200
Burgundy (Bourgogne)
    202-205
Caen 193
Calvi 218
La Camargue 221
Cannes 215-216
Cap Brun 217
Cap Corse 219
Cap d'Antibes 214
Cap de Chèvre 199
Cap Ferrat 212
Cap Ferret 227
Carcassonne 224-225
Carnac 200
Cassis 217
Castres 224-225
Chambord 189-190
Chamonix 207-210
Champagne 184-186
Chamrousse 206
Chantilly 182
Chartres 187-188
Chassy 202
Chaumont-sur-Loire 190-191
Chenonceaux 190-191
Chinon 192
Ciotat 217
Clermont-Ferrand 226
Cluny 204-205
Cogolin Plage 216
Colmar 200
Concarneau 199

La Condamine 211
Corniche Bretonne 197
Corniche de l'Amorique 197
Corsica (Corse) 217-220
Corte 218
Côte d'Azur (Riviera)
    210-217
Côte Fleurie 193
Deauville/Trouville 193
Les Deux Alpes 206
Dieppe 193
Dijon 202-203
Dinan 199
Doelan 199
Dordogne 225
Les Dranses 206
Entrevaux 212
Épernay 184
Esterel 210
Etretat 193
Les Eyzies 226
Eze 212
Fango 219
Fécamp 196
Fontainebleau 181
Fontenay 202
Fontevrault 193
Fougères 198
Frejus 216
La Galere 215
Les Gets 206
Giffre 206
Girolata 219
Grande Bé 198
Grenoble 205
Le Havre 196
Heliopolis 216
Hyères 210
Ile-de-France 181
Iles de Hyères 216
Iles de Lerins 215
Ile du Levant 216
Ile de Porquerolles 216
Ile Rousse 217
Isère 206
Isigny-sur-Mer 193
Juan-les-Pins 214
Landes 227
Langeais 192
Languedoc 224
Lannion 198
Locmariaquer 200
The Loire Valley 186-193
Lorient 198
Lyon 188
Malmaison 182
Le Mans 198
Marseille 217
Massif Central 225
Maures 210
Menton 212
Mer de Glace 208
Millau 225
Monaco 211-212
Mt. Blanc 207
Mt. Cinto 218
Mt. Dol 198
Mt. D'Oro 218
Mte. Carlo 211
Mont-St.-Michel 196-197

Morgat 199
Morlaix 198
Morzine 206
Mougins 215
Nancy 166
Nantes 198
La Napoule 215
Nice 212-214
Nîmes 223-224
Nonza 219
Normandy 192-197
Oisans 206
Orange 223
Orléans 166
Parc des Volcans 227
Paris 161-184
Pauillac 227
Les Pelerins 208
Pennedepie 193
Périgord 225-226
Périgueux 225
Plage des Curies 199
Plage de Pampelonne 215
Plage de Salins 216
Plage de Tahiti 216
Plestin 199
Pointe des Espagnols 199
Pointe de Penhir 199
Pont-Aven 199
Pontivy 198
Port Cros 216
Port-Manech 199
Port Navalo 200
Porto 218
Le Pouldu 199
Les Praz 208
Presqu'ile de Crozon 199
Propriano 220
Provence 220-224
Pyrenées 224
Quiberon 199
Quimper 199
Reims 185-186
Rennes 198
Rocamadour 226
Roquebrune Cap Martin 212
Rouen 194
Les Sablettes 217
St. Brieuc 198
Sainte-Anne-d'Auray 200
St. Florent 219
St. Germain-en-Laye 182
St. Gervais 205
St. Guen 198
St. Honorat 215
St. Jean de Luz 227
St. Malo 198
St. Marguerite 215
St. Michel-en-Greve 199
St. Raphael 215
St. Tropez 216-217
St. Valéry-en-Caux 193
Samoëns 206
Sarlat 226
Sartène 220
Saumur 193
Sauzon 199
Servoz 207
Sixt 206
Solutré 202

Strasbourg 200-201
Suisse-Normande 193
Toulon 216
Tours 191-192
Trébeurden 199
Troyes 184
Ussé 192
Vallée de l'Isère 206
Vallorcine 208
Vannes 200
Vanoise National Park 206
Varengville-sur-Mer 195
Veryach 199
Versailles 181
Veules-Les-Roses 196
Vézelay 204-205
Villandry 192
Villefranche-sur-Mer 212
Villeneuve-lès-Avignon 223
Vosges Mtns. 200
Yport 193

WEST GERMANY

Aachen (Aix-la-
    Chapelle) 230
Augsburg 240
Bacharach 251
Baden-Baden 244
Bad Godesberg 255-257
Bad Wimpfen 247
Bayreuth 230
Belchen 244
Bernkastel 254
Bingen 250
Black Forest 244-245
Bonn 255-257
Burg Eltz 255
Celle 258-259
Cochem 254-255
Cologne (Köln) 257
Creglingen 242
Dachau 238
Dinkelsbühl 242-243
Dombühl 242
Düsseldorf 251
Feldberg 244
Franconia 239
Frankfurt 248-250
Freiburg 245-247
Füssen 239
Göttingen 230
Grosser Feldberg 250
Hamburg 257-258
Harz Mtns. 229
Heidelberg 247-248
Hermeskeil 251
Hochwald 251
Höllental 244
Karlsruhe 244
Kell 251
Koblenz 251
Königstein 250
Kues 254
Lübeck 259
Marburg 251
Moselle Valley 250-257
Muffendorf 256
Munich (München) 233-239

Nördlingen 243-244
Nuremberg (Nürnberg) 233
Oberwesel 251
Rhine Valley 250-257
Romantic Road 239-248
Rothenburg-Ob-der-Tauber
    241-242
Rottweil 247
Rüdesheim 251
St. Goar 251
Stuttgart 247
Tauber Valley 242
Lake Titisee 244
Traben 254
Trarbach 254
Travemünde 259
Trier 251-254
Tübingen 247
Valley of the Isar 238
West Berlin 260-266
Würzburg 240-241

EAST GERMANY

Buchenwald 278
Dresden 275-277
East Berlin 269-274
Eisenach 268
Erfurt 278
Erzgebirge 268
Greifswald 268
Harz Mtns. 268
Meissen 276
Naumburg 268
Potsdam 274-275
Sächsische Schweiz 275
Sassnitz 268
Stralsund 268
Thüringer Wald 268
Warnemünde 268
Weimar 277-278
Wismar 268

GREAT BRITAIN

Aberdeen 350
Aberfan 331
Abergavenny 330
Aberystwyth 332
Achmelvich 345
Ambleside 327
An Eharaid 346
Anglesey 334
Aonach Eagach 344
Applecross 344
Argyllshire 344
Armadale 344
Ayr 342
Ballachulish 344
Bangor 334
Barmouth 333
Bath 304-307
Ben Nevius 344
Betws-y-Coed 334
Black Mountains 330
Blaenau Ffestiniog 334
Borrowdale 328
Bovey Tracy 311
Bowness 327

Brading 303
Bragar 348
Brecon 329
Brecon Beacons National
    Park 330
Brighton 303-304
Bristol 304
Broadford 347
Bury St. Edmunds 317
Buttermere 328
Caerphilly 331
Cairngorms 341
Caithness County 346
Caledonian Canal 344
Cambridge 318-321
Canterbury 300-301
Capel Curig 334
Cape Wrath 346
Cardiff 331
Cheddar 307
Chepstow 330
Chester 350
Chichester 303
Chiltern 313
Clarach 332
Cleit Dhubh 346
Cockermouth 328
Colchester 318
Colwyn Bay 333
Conwy 334
Cornwall 312-313
The Cotswolds 313
Craignure 343
Crainlarish 343
Cremyll 313
Cromarty 341
Cumbria 322
Dartmoor National Park
    310-311
Deal 300
Dent 326
Derwentwater 327
Devon 311-312
Dingwall 340
Dolgellau 333
Dover 300
Dovey Valley 333
Dulverton 310
Dumfries 342
Duncansby Head 346
Dunnet Head 346
Dunsford 311
Dunvegan Head 347
Durness 346
East Anglia 317-321
Edale 326
Edinburgh 335-339
Elgol 347
Ely 317
Eskdale 327
Exeter 311
Exford 310
Exmoor National Park
    310-311
Exmouth 311
Falmouth 312
The Fens 317
Firth of Lorn 340
Flotta 349

Folkestone 300
Fort William 344
Glasgow 335
Glastonbury 309
Glenbrittle 347
Glencoe 343
The Glyders 334
Gorran Haven 312
Grassington 326
Great Yarmouth 317
Gwent 330
Haverfordwest 332
Hay-on-Wye 330
Hebrides 347-348
Hereford 329
Highlands 340-344
Holyhead 334
Hoy 348
Hull 322
Ingleborough 325
Ingleton 325
Inver Alligin 345
Inveraray 343
Inverness 340
Iona 343
Ipswich 318
Isle of Arran 335
Isle of Harris 347-348
Isle of Lewis 347-348
Isle of Wight 302
Keswick 328
Kettlewell 326
King's Lynn 317
Kinlochleven 344
Kirkcudbright 343
Kirkwall 348
Kirk Yethorm 326
Kishorn 344
Kyleakin 347
Kyle of Lochalsh 344
Kylestrome 346
Lake District 326-328
Land's End 313
Langdale 327
Lizard Point 312
Llanberis 334
Llandrindod Wells 333
Llandudno 335
Llangollen 335
Loch Benbecula 348
Loch Carron 344
Loch Fyne 343
Lochinver 341-345
Loch Linnhe 344
Loch Lomond 335
London 281-299
Lowesfort 317
Lymington 302
Lyness 349
Lynton 310
Machynlleth 333
Mallaig 344
Malham 325
Manchester 326
The Mendip Hills 307-309
Merthyr Tydfil 331
Mevagissey 312
The Midlands 313-317
Mid Wales 332-333

Minehead 310
Monmouth 330
Morsland 313
Mousehole 313
Mull 343
Needles 303
New Bridge 311
Newport 332
The Norfolk Broads 317
North Uist 348
North York Moors 325-
326
Norwich 317
Oban 343
Okehampton 311
Orkney Islands 348-350
Oxford 313-316
Patterdale 327
The Peak District 326
Pembrokeshire Coast
National Park 332
Pennmaenmawr 334
Pennine Mountains 325-326
Pentland Firth 348
Pen-y-Ghent 325
Pen-y-Pass 334
Peterborough 317
Plymouth 311
Polzeath 312
Portree 347
Portsmouth 302
Postbridge 311
Powys 332
Rackwick 348
Radnorshire 332
Rannoch Moor 343
Ross 341
Ryde 302
St. Austell 312
St. Fagens 331
St. Ive's Bay 313
St. Mawes 312
Sandown 299
Scrabster 346
Scotland 335-350
Seal Island 313
Settle 325
Shanklin 303
Shapinsay 349
Shetlands 341
Shieldaig 345
Shorwell 303
Shrewsbury 329
Skomer Is. 332
Skye 347
Snowdonia National
Park 333
Snowdon Mountain
Range 333
Somerset 307
Southampton 302
Southern Uplands 343
South Uist 347
Staffa 343
Stoer 345
Stoke-on-Trent 326
Stonehenge 301-302
Stornaway 345
Stratford-upon-Avon

316- 317
Stromness 350
Sutherland 341
Sychnant Pass 334
Tarbert 348
Tarbet 343
Tavistock 311
Thurso 341
Tobermory 343
Tongue 346
Torbay 311
Torguay 311
Torridon 344
Totland Bay 303
Troutbeck 327
Truro 312
Two Bridges 311
Uig 347
Ullapool 345
Ventnor 303
Wales 328-335
Wasdale 328
Wastwater 327
Wells 307
Wensleydale 325
Wharfdale 326
Whernside 325
Whitwell 303
Wick 349
Wicken Fen 317
Wigtown 342
Wilsford 301
Windermere 327
Lake Windermere 327
Woodford 301
Wooten Bridge 303
The Wye Valley 330
York 322-325
Yorkshire 325-326

GREECE

Aegina 365
Aghia Anna 366
Aghia Ghallini 370
Aghia Roumeli 370
Aghia Triada 369
Aghios Georgios 372
Aghios Ioannis 366
Aghios Konstantinos 367
Aghios Nikolaos 370
Agnontas 367
Akrotiri 367
Alexandroupolis 355
Aliki 365
Alonissos 367
Amnissa 369
Amorgos 367
Andros 367
Antiparos 366
Antipaxos 372
Argo-Saronic Islands 365
Argostoli 372
Assos 372
Athens (Athenai) 355
Bourdzi 363
Cape Sounion 361-362

Cefalonia 372
Chania 370
Chryssi 367
Corfu (Kerkyra) 371-372
Corinth 362
Crete 369-371
Cyclades 365-367
Daphni 362
Delos 365-366
Delphi 362
Dodecanese 368
Drios 366
Eressos 368
Ermoupolis 367
Falasarna 370
Filoti 366
Fiscardo 372
Galissas 367
Gerakini 363
Gortys 369
Glyfada 362
Halkidiki 363
Heracleion 369-370
Hora Sfakion 370
Hydra 365
Ierapetra 371
Illia 365
Ios 366
Ithaca 372
Kakovatos 363
Kalamata 363
Kamari 367
Kassandra 363
Kastelli 370
Kato Zakros 371
Kavalla 352
Kerkyra (see Corfu)
Kimi 367
Knossos 369
Kokarion 368
Kondokalion 371
Korthion 367
Lalaria 367
Lefkada 372
Lesbos 368
Lindos 368
Logaras 366
Loutron 370
Mallia 369
Mani 363
Marathon 365
Matalla 369
Menites 367
Messanagros 368
Messaria 366
Methymna 368
Mikra Kameni 367
Mikri Vigla 366
Milos 367
Monolithos 368
Mt. Athos 363-364
Mt. Zeus 366
Mykonos 365
Mylopotas 366
Myrtiotissa 372
Mystra 363
Naoussa 366
Nauplion 363
Naxos 366

Nimboro 367
Oia 366
Olympia 363
Omalos 370
Ormos Moradokampos 368
Palaiopolis 367
Paleohora 370
Paleokastritsas 372
Paliovrion 363
Paroikia 366
Paros 366
Patras 352
Paxos 372
Pelekas 372
Peloponnese 362-363
Perissa 367
Petra 368
Phaistos 369
Pilos 363
Piraeus 361
Pirgos 363
Plomarion 368
Poros 365
Prinos 368
Rethymnon 370
Rhodes 368
Samaria Gorge 370
Samos 368
Santa Maria 366
Santorini (Thira) 366-367
Serifos 367
Sifnos 367
Sikinos 367
Sithonia 363
Sitia 371
Skiathos 367
Skopelos 367
Skyros 367
Spinalongi 371
Sporades 367
Syros 367
Thassos 368
Thessaloniki 363
Thira (see Santorini)
Tinos 367
Tragea 366
Tripolis 355
Vai 371
Vathi 372
Volos 367
Zakinthos 372
Zakros 371

HUNGARY

Balatonfüred 383
Lake Balaton 383
Börzsony Mountains 381
Buda Hills 376
Budapest 376-381
The Danube Bend 381-382
Eger 382-383
Esztergom 382
Köszeg 383
Margit-sziget 380
Pilisszenttászló 382
Siófok 383
Szentendre 381
Tihany 383

Visegrád 382
Visegradi-Hegység
  Mountains 382

ICELAND

Akureyri 392-393
Eldfell 391
Eyjafjördur-
  Gullfoss 392
Helgafell 391
Heimaey 391
Herjólfsdalur Valley 392
Isafjördur 392
Kerlingarfjöll 391
Lake Mývatn 393
Reykjavk 386-391
Thingvallavatn 391
Thingvellr 391
Vestfirdir (Western
  Fords) 392
Vestmannaeyjar 391-392
  (Vestmann Islands)
Western Fjords (see
  Vestfirdir) 392

IRELAND

Achill Island 411
Achill Sound 411
Aghavannagh 404
Aran Islands 410
Ashford 411
Balla 411
Ballyglass 411
Baltimore 407
Baltyboys 404
Blasket Islands 408
Blessington 404
Cape Clear Island 407
Carna 410
Carraroe 410
Carrowjames 411
Cashel 405
Castlebar 411
Clare 408
Clifden 410
Clonakilty 407
Clonmel 405
Cong 411
Connemara 410
Cork 406-408
Croagh Patrick 411
Dalkey 404
Dalkey Island 404
Dingle 407-408
Donegal 410-412
Dooagh 411
Dublin 397-404
Dun Laoghaire 404
Enniscorthy 405
Galway 408-410
Glencree 404
Glendalough 404
Glenmalure 404
Glen of Dargle 404
Gort 408
Healy Pass 407
Inishmore 410

Inistioge 405
Inverin 410
Keel 411
Kilkenny 405
Killarney 407
Killiney 404
Kilronan 410
Kinsale 407
Knockmealdown 406
Leenane 410
Limerick 408
Lismore 406
Lough Corrib 410
Lough Mask 411
Malin Head 412
Marina 406
Mardyke 406
Mayo 410-412
Oughterard 410
Rath Croghan 411
Recess 410
Ring of Kerry 407
Rosmuc 410
Rosscarbery 407
Rosses Point 412
Rosslare 396
Roundstone 410
Roundwood 404
Sally Gap 404
Saltee Islands 404
Screeb 410
Sherkin Island 407
Skibbereen 407
Sligo 410-412
Spiddal 410
Straide 411
Strandhill 412
Tipperary 405
Turlough 411
Twelve Bens 410
Waterford 405
Westport 411
Wexford 404-405
Wicklow 404

ISRAEL

Achziv 431
Acre 430
Afula 425
Ashdod 428
Ashkelon 428
Banias 432
Balata 425
Beersheva 433
Beit She'an 432
Bethany 424
Bethlehem 424
Birkat Ram 432
Caesarea 428
Coral Island 435
Dahab 433
Daliyat el-Carmel 430
Dead Sea 433
Eilat 433-435
Ein Feshha 433
Ein Gedi 433
Galilee 430-432
Gaza Strip 428

Golan Heights 430-432
Haifa 428-430
Hebron 424
Herzliyah 428
Jenin 425
Jericho 432
Jerusalem 418-424
Jezreel Valley 432
Karei Deshe 431
Kidron Valley 423
Massada 433
Megiddo 432
Mt. Gerizim 425
Mt. Hermon 432
Mt. of Olives 424
Mt. of Temptation 432
Mt. Sinai 436
Na'ama Bay 435
Nablus 425
Nahariya 431
Nazareth 432
Negev 432-433
Netanya 428
Nuweiba 433
Ophira 435
Peqa'in 431
Qumran Caves 433
Rama 431
Ramallah 425
Rosh Hanikra 431
Safed 431
Samaria/Sabastia 425
Santa Katerina 436
Sea of Galilee 431
Sharm el-Sheikh 435
Shechem 425
Sinai 435-436
Tel Aviv 425-428
Tiberias 431
Wadi Kelt 432
The West Bank 424-425

ITALY

Agrigento 480
Ancona 463
Alghero 483
Apulia 477
Arbatax 482
Arezzo 464
Arzachena 483
Assisi 463
Baia 476
Baia Sardinia 483
Bari 477-478
Barumini 481
Bologna 472-473
Bolzano 452
Le Bombarde 483
Cagliari 483-484
Calabria 477
Campania 477
Canazei 453
Cannigione 483
Capo Caccia 483
Capri 477
Castroreale 479
Catania 478
Civitavecchia 481

Cortina d'Ampezzo 452-453
Costa Smeralda 482-483
Cuma 476
Dolomite Mtns. 452-453
Emilia-Romagna 472-474
Ferrara 474
Florence 464-470
Foligno 463
Fortezza 452
Lake Garda 444
Genoa 441
Giudecca 452
Golfo Aranchi 483
Herculaneum 476
Ischia 477
Lago d'Averno 476
Lago Misano 476
Lido Adriano 473
Lipari 480
Lombardy 441
Lucca 464
Macomer 482
Mantua (Mantova) 445-446
Marina di Massa 464
Marina di Ravenna 473
Marinella 483
Merano 452
Messina 477
Milan 441-444
Mondello 479
Monreale 479
Moso (Moos) 452
Mt. Vesuvius 476
Murano 451
Naples 474-477
Nuoro 482
Olbia 482
Ortisei 453
Orvieto 462
Ostia 461
Oxtal Valley 452
Padua 446
Paestum 477
Palau 483
Palermo 478-479
Parma 441
Perugia 462-463
Phlegrean Fields 476
Pienza 464
Pisa 471-472
Pistoia 464
Pompeii 476
Porto Cervo 483
Porto Torres 481
Ravenna 473-474
Riviera del Corallo 483
Romagna 472
Rome 453-461
San Gimignano 470
Santa Flavia-Olivella 479
Santa Maria Navarresa 482
Santa Teresa di Gallura 483
Sardinia 481
Sassari 483
Scilla 477
Selinunte 480
Sicily 478
Siena 470-471
Sorrento 477

Spoleto 463
Syracuse 480
Tavernelle 464
Timmelsjoch Pass 452
Tivoli 461
Tolmezzo 452
Torcello 451
Trapani 478
Turin 441
Tuscany 464
Umbria 461-463
Ustica 479
Val di Pesa 464
Veneto 441
Venice (Venezia) 447-452
Verona 444-445
Viareggio 464
Vicenza 441
Villa Jovis 477

LUXEMBOURG

Ardennes 488
Clerve Valley 488
Echternach 488
Luxembourg City 486-487
Remich 487
Troisvierges 488
Vianden 488

MOROCCO

Asni 502
Azrou 499
Chechaouen 495
Essaouira 503-504
Fez (Fès) 497-500
Imlil 502
Marrakesh 500-503
Meknes 495-497
Moulay Idriss 497
Mt. Toubkal 502
Rabat 504-505
Rif Mtns. 489
Tangier 493
Tetuan 493-495
Volubilis 497

NETHERLANDS

Aalsmeer 519
Alkmaar 518
Amersfoor 522
Amsterdam 508-519
Arnhem 523-524
Bloemendaal 518
Delft 521
Durgendam 518
Edam 518
Friesland 524
Gouda 518
Groningen 508
Haarlem 518-519
The Hague (Den Haag)
  519-521
Hindeloopen 524
Holysloot 518
Hoorn 518
De Hoog Veluwe National
  Park 523

Ijsselmeer 518
Katwijk Aan Zee 519
Kockengin 522
Leeuwarden 524
Leiden 519
Makkum 524
Marken 518
Monnickendam 518
Ransdorp 518
Rotterdam 508
Scheveningen 520
Sneek 524
Terschelling 524
Texel 524
Utrecht 521-523
Volendam 518
Waterland 518
Westfriese Islands 524
Zandvoort 518
Zuid-Veluwe 523-524

NORWAY

Alta 540
Åndalsnes 525
Balestrand 532
Bardufoss 540
Bergen 532-535
Bodø 536-537
Fauske 536
Finnmark 539
Finse 532
Flåm 532
Mt. Fløien 533
Geilo 532
Gudbrandsdal Valley 526
Gundvangen 532
Jostedalsbre 532
Kristiansand 526
Lapland 539-540
Lofoten Islands 537
Myrdal 532
Narvik 537-539
Nordkapp 539-540
Oslo 526-531
Mt. Ronvik 536
Sogndal 532
Sognefjord 532
Stamsund 531
Stavanger 525
Svolvaer 537
Tana River 539
Tromso 539
Trondheim 535-536
Voss 532

POLAND

Auschwitz (See Oświęcim)
Bald Mtn. (see Lysa Góra)
Berest 556
Frombork 552
Gdańsk 549
Gdynia 550
Hel 551
Huta Szlana 553
Jastrzębik 556

Kazimierz 552
Kielce 553
Kraków 553-555
Krynica 556
Leba 551-552
Lebsko Lake 551
Lublin 552
Lysa Góra (Bald Mtn.) 553
Malbork (Marienbourg) 552
Nowa Slupia 553
Nowy Sącz 556
Oświęcim (Auschwitz) 554
Powroźnik 556
Poznán 545
Sandomierz 552-553
Sopot 550
Stary Sącz 556
Swiętokrzyskie 553
Tatry Mtns. 555
Trzcianka 553
Warsaw 544-549
Wladyslawowo 551
Zakopane 555

PORTUGAL

Albuferia 573
Alfeizerão 568
The Algarve 571-573
Ayamonte 571
Barreiro 560
Batalha 568
Beira Litoral 568
Braga 558
Cabo da Roca 556
Cacilhas 560
Cascais 560
Coimbra 568-569
Costa da Caparica 560
Costa de Prata 567
Costa do Sol 560
Esposende 558
Estoril 560
Eurotel 571
Evora 570-571
Faro 572
Guincho 560
Lagos 572-573
Lisbon 559-566
Monte de Sta. Luzia 566
Nazaré 567
Obidos 568
Peniche 568
Praia da Rocha 573
Praia dona Ana 572
Porto 566
Queluz 565
Sagres 572
São Martinho do Porto 567
Sintra 565
Viana do Castelo 566-567

ROMANIA

Black Sea Coast 584
Bran 581
Braşov 581-582
Bucharest 578-581
Constanţa 577

Costineşti 585
Danube Delta 584-585
Harman 581
Humor 583
Jurilovca 585
Mamaia 585
Moldavia 583-584
Murighiol 584
Periprava 584
Radauţi 584
Risnov 581
Sfintu Gheorghe 584
Sighisoara 582-582
Suceava 584
Sulina 584
Transylvania 581-583
Tulcea 584
Wallachia 575

SPAIN
Alcudia 633
Algeciras 625
Alicante 629
Alpujarras 622
Altamira Caves 594
Andalucía 612-625
Aranjuez 607
Arcos de la Frontera 616
Avila 607
Ayamonte 616
Balearic Islands 629-633
Barcelona 625-629
Cádiz 616
Cala Xarraca 633
Capileira 622
Castile (Central Spain) 599-612
El Castillo Caves 595
Castro Urdiales 621 634 597
Cataluña 625
Cedeira 595
Ciudadela 633
Cala Portinatx 633
Comillas 595
Córdoba 617-619
La Coruña 598-599
Costa Brava 626
Costa Dorada 626
Costa de la Luz 616
Costa del Sol 623-625
El Escorial 607
El Ferrol 596
Cape Formentor 633
Galicia 596-599
Granada 619-623
Ibiza 633
Isla de Santa Clara 594
Jerez le la Frontera 616
Lluch 632
Madrid 599-607
Mahon 633
Majorca (Mallorca) 630-632
Málaga 623
La Mancha 588
Marbella 623
Maro 624
Minorca (Menorca) 633
Montserrat 628
Mulhacen 622
Nerja 624
Noja 595

Ortigueira 596
País Vasco 591-596
Palma 630
Pamplona 594
Picos de Europa 594
Puerte-Viesgo 595
Puerto de Navacerrada 607
Puerto de Pollensa 632
Pyrenees 588
Ronda 624
Salamanca 607-610
San Antonio Abad 633
San Sebastián 592-594
Santa Eulalia 633
Santander 594-596
Santiago de Compostela 596-598
Santillana del Mar 595
Sardinero 594
Saunces 595
Segovia 610
Seville 612-616
Sierra Guadarrama 607
Tarifa 616
Toledo 610-612
Torremolinos 623
Rió Urumea 592
Valencia 629
Valldemosa 632
Valle de los Caídos 607
Veleta 622
Vicedo 596
Vigo 596

SWEDEN
Arjeplog 650
Arvidsjaur 650
Gällivare 651
Gothenburg (Göteborg) 647-648
Gotland 635
Jäckvik 650
Jokkmokk 650
Karesuando 650
Karlso Islands 635
Kebnekaise 651
Kiruna 651
Kvikkjok 650-651
Lapland 648-651
Lindingo 645
Lund 637-638
Muddus National Park 651
Nikkaluokta 651
Ostergotland 635
Ostersund 648
Padjelanta National Park 650
Rindö 645
Sädvaluspen 650
Sandham 645
Sarek National Park 650
Stockholm 638-646
Stora Sjöfallet National Park 650
Swedish Lapland 648-651
Uppsala 646-647
Vaxholm 645

SWITZERLAND
Aletsch 654
Alp Grün 678
Ascona 679

Bachalpsee 666
Basel 654
Beatenberg 666
Bern (Berne) 662-665
Bernese-Oberland 665
Biel 654
Blauherd 669
Bort 666
Brienz 666
Brienzersee 685
Brissago Island 680
Broc 667
Chunetta 678
Chur 677
Coppet 671
Corvatsch 678
Davos 654
Diavolezza 678
Dietschiberg 662
Egg 666
Eiger 666
Einsiedeln 661
Engadin 677-678
Feegletscher 669
Felskinn 669
First 666
Gandria 679
Geneva 669-677
Gimmelwald 668-669
Gornergrat 669
Grindelwald 666
Grisons (Graubunden) 677
Gruyère 677
Hörnli Hütte 669
Interlaken 665-666
Iseltwald 666
Jungfrau 666
Kleine Scheidegg 666
Lago Bianco 678
Lago di Lugano 679
Lago Maggiore 679
Langfluh 669
Lausanne 675
Lauterbrunnen 666-668
Limmat River 658
Locarno 679-680
Lucerne (Luzern) 659-662
Lucerne Lake (see Vierwaldstattersee)
Lugano 679
Matterhorn 653
Mönch 666
Mt. Pilatus 661
Monte Brè 679
Montreux 677
Morteratsch 678
Mürren 667
Murten 665
Murtensee 665
Müstair 678
Niederhorn 666
Nyon 671
Ospizio 678
Ouchy 675
Piz Bernina 678
Piznair 678
Poschiavo 678
Saanen 654
Saas Fee 668-669
Sainta Maria 679

St. Moritz 677-678
San Vittore 678
Schilthorn 667
Schwarzsee (Black
  Lake) 664
Sils Maria 678
Stechelberg 667
Stein am Rhein 659
Thunersee 665
Ticino 679-680
Uetliberg 659
Val Müstair 678
Vevey 677
Vidy 675
Vierwaldstattersee (Lake
  Lucerne) 659
Wengen 653
Zermatt 668-669
Zürich 6 55-659
Zürich - (see Lake Zurich) 658

TURKEY

Alanya 694-95
Anadolu Hisari 691
Anadolu Kavagi 690
Ankara 692
Antalya 694
Aspendos 694
Avcilar 693
Bebek 690
Belisirrama Valley 693
Beylerbey 691
Bodrum 695
Bosphorus Strait 685
Burgaz 690
Bursa 691
Büyükada 690
Çanakkale 691
Cappadocia 693
Çengelköy 691
Datça 683
Demre 694
Derinkuyu 693
Didum 695
Ephesus 695
Fethiye 695
Golden Horn 685
Heybeliada 690
Hisarlik 691
Hopa 683
Iskenderun 683
Istanbul 684-92
Izmir 695
Kanlica 691
Kaş 694
Kaymakli 693
Kayseri 692
Kemer 694
Kilyos 691
Konya 693-94
Kuşadasi 695
Lara Plaj 694
Marmaris 695
Mersin 695
Pamphylia 694
Perge 694
Polonezköy 691
Princes' Isles 690
Rumeli Hisari 690

Rumeli Kavagi 690
Samsun 683
Sariyer 691
Side 694
Trabzon 683
Turanç 695
Uludag 691
Ürgüp 693
Yalova 691

USSR

Lake Baikal 704
Bukhara 700
Crimea 704
Estonia 713
Georgia 700
Irkutsk 704
Khabarovsk 706
Kiev 701
Latvia 698
Leningrad 709-14
Lithuania 698
Moscow 705-09
Naklodka 705
Novisibursk 704
Odessa 701
Pavlovsk 713
Penates 713
Pushkin (Tsarskoe Selo) 713
Samarkand 700
Siberia 704
Sochi 701
Tallinn 713
Tashkent 700
Tbilisi 700
Yalta 701

YUGOSLAVIA

Avala 725
Banja Luka 725
Bar 740
Belgrade 721-25
Bernardin 718
Mt. Biokovo 731
Bitola 740
Bled 719-20
Bohinj 718
Bol 736
Boracko 725
Bosnia-Hercegovina 725-27
Brač 736
Budva 737
Cetinje 737
Cres 736
Croatia (Hrvatska) 727-36
Crveni Otok 736
Dalmatia 730-31
Decani 738
Dubrovnik 733
Dugi Otok 736
Fruska Gora 725
Hercegnovi 737
Hvar 736
Ibar River 721
Istria 730-31
Jablanica 725
Jaince 725
Jajce 725
Julian Alps 720
Kicevo 740
Knin 731

Kolocép 735
Koper 718
Korčula 736
Kornati Archipelago 736
Kosovo 721
Kotor 737
Kraljevo 721
Kranjska Gora 720
Krk 736
Kumrovec 730
Kupari 735
Lapad 734
Lastovo 736
Lazarica 721
Lesce-Bled 720
Ljubljana 718-20
Lokrum 735
Macedonia 737-740
Makarskan Riviera 731
Maribor 718
Mljet 736
Montenegro 737-38
Montenegran Riviera 737
Morača Canyon 737
Mostar 725
Nerezi 740
Novi Pazar 721
Ohrid 740
Lake Ohrid 740
Pag Island 736
Peč 738
Petrovac 737
Piran 718
Plitviče Lakes 730
Ploče 731
Počitelj 725
Portorož 718
Postire 736
Lake Prespa 739
Pristina 738
Pula 721
Rijeka 731
Rovinj 731
Rovinj Archipelago 736
St. Vid Mtns. 736
Sali 736
Samobor 730
Sarajevo 726
Sava River 721
Serbia 720-25
Lake Skadan 737
Skopje 739
Sljeme Mtn. 730
Slovenia 718-720
Smerderevo 725
Šolta 732
Sopoćani 721
Split 732-33
Srebreno 735
Struga 740
Supetar 736
Titograd 738
Vis 736
Vojvodina 721
Zadar 732
Zagreb 728-30
Zatan 735
Zica 721